Psychology: Concepts and Connections

PSY 2012

Spencer A. Rathus

Australia • Brazil • Japan • Korea • Mexico • Singapore • Spain • United Kingdom • United States

Psychology: Concepts and Connections
PSY 2012

Spencer A. Rathus

Executive Editors:
Michele Baird

Maureen Staudt

Michael Stranz

Project Development Manager:
Linda deStefano

Senior Marketing Coordinators:
Sara Mercurio

Lindsay Shapiro

Senior Production / Manufacturing Manager:
Donna M. Brown

PreMedia Services Supervisor:
Rebecca A. Walker

Rights & Permissions Specialist:
Kalina Hintz

Cover Image:
Getty Images*

* Unless otherwise noted, all cover images used by Custom Solutions, a part of Cengage Learning, have been supplied courtesy of Getty Images with the exception of the Earthview cover image, which has been supplied by the National Aeronautics and Space Administration (NASA).

For product information and technology assistance, contact us at
Cengage Learning Customer & Sales Support, 1-800-354-9706

For permission to use material from this text or product, submit all requests online at **cengage.com/permissions**
Further permissions questions can be emailed to
permissionrequest@cengage.com

ISBN-13: 978-0-495-43518-1

ISBN-10: 0-495-43518-X

Cengage Learning
5191 Natorp Boulevard
Mason, Ohio 45040
USA

Cengage Learning is a leading provider of customized learning solutions with office locations around the globe, including Singapore, the United Kingdom, Australia, Mexico, Brazil, and Japan. Locate your local office at:
international.cengage.com/region

Cengage Learning products are represented in Canada by Nelson Education, Ltd.

For your lifelong learning solutions, visit **custom.cengage.com**

Visit our corporate website at **cengage.com**

Printed in the United States of America

To Lois

brief contents

contents

2 Biology and Psychology   36

■ **preview** 37 ■

THE NERVOUS SYSTEM: ON BEING WIRED   39

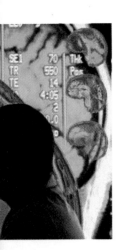

THE BRAIN: WIDER THAN THE SKY   51

THE ENDOCRINE SYSTEM: CHEMICALS IN THE BLOODSTREAM   64

3   The Voyage Through the Life Span   82

4 Sensation and Perception   124

■ **preview   125** ■

5 Consciousness   170

6 Learning 206

7   Memory: Remembrance of Things Past—and Future   240

8 Thinking, Language, and Intelligence   278

9 Motivation and Emotion 320

10 Stress, Health, and Adjustment   362

12 Psychological Disorders   430

13 Methods of Therapy   470

14 Social Psychology   504

preface

The world we live in changes every day. Ten years ago there were no MP3 players. Now many students would not be caught without one, especially one that's lime-green with white earplugs. Ten years ago, couples argued about who should look for directions when they got lost. Now they often argue that the driver should keep his or her eyes on the road and not on the car's navigational system. Ten years ago it seemed that humans had in many ways conquered nature. Since then millions have lost their lives to tsunamis, hurricanes, and microscopic disease agents. Ten years ago college students did most of their learning among stacks of books. Now we "Google" our research desires.

How do we begin to understand the ways in which these developments and thousands of others have changed us? How do we begin to determine what is "good" for us and what poses a threat? How do we begin to sort out the differences between human intelligence and artificial intelligence? How do we distinguish between virtual reality and, well, real reality?

The science of psychology, it happens, provides an ideal interface between these events and us humans. Psychology studies the ways in which we sense and perceive the environments around us and within us. Psychology studies the events that take place in our nervous systems when we surf the Internet or text the message "U R a QT." Psychology explores the anxieties we may experience when we explore our new worlds, and psychology also explores the ways in which we can meet these anxieties with rational thoughts and effective behaviors.

Does the new world bring joy? Does it bring happiness? Psychology studies the emotions of joy and happiness and how we can enhance them. Does the new world bring fear? Psychology studies fear and how we can cope with it.

WHAT'S NEW IN THIS EDITION

The new edition underscores the connections between psychology and the key events of contemporary times. For example, Chapter 5, on "Consciousness," addresses the Terri Schiavo case and the ways in which our activities on the Internet suggest a new altered state of consciousness. Chapter 6, on "Learning," lays out the ways in which a number of mass killers had been drawn into "playing" violent video games. Chapter 8 shows how texting has changed our very language. Chapter 10 portrays human responses—some devastating, some heroic—to Katrina and other natural disasters. Chapter 14 does not flinch from portraying psychology's perspectives on suicide terrorists from Ground Zero to London to Madrid to Iraq and Israel.

This book is about psychology's fascinating history and about its connections to life as we live it today. It is more than a revision; it is a very new book.

Let us first list some improvements we find throughout the book. Then we will focus on chapter-by-chapter enhancements.

New in All Chapters

- A new feature, **Video Connections**, is found in every chapter. These features "connect" with videos that accompany the text and offer audiovisual material to aid students' understanding or supplement the text. Each Video Connection includes learning objectives, applied lessons, and questions for critical thinking. Sample topics include:
  - CHAPTER 3: Piaget's cognitive developmental perspective
  - CHAPTER 6: "Little Albert"
  - CHAPTER 7: Memory as reconstructive
  - CHAPTER 13: Virtual reality therapy
  - CHAPTER 14: Stereotype threat
- Every chapter has a new chapter opening vignette—one that connects with the events of the day. Chapter 1's vignette, for example, addresses reports of abductions by aliens from outer space and how we can use critical thinking to examine these reports. Chapter 4 begins with a discussion of *The Matrix* film series and the issues that confront us in delving into virtual reality. Chapter 11 deals with all the personality tests we find online, and how we can sort out useful tests from entertaining but useless attempts to pick our pockets.
- New feature: **"Truth or Fiction?"** features open every chapter, challenging preconceived notions about psychology. "Truth or Fiction Revisited" items pick up the topics presented in the chapter opening feature and discuss them in detail.
- New **"Learning Connections"** sections contain multiple-choice questions and a critical thinking item. These interim learning checks facilitate use of the book from a modular approach.
- New **"CONCEPT REVIEWS"** help students make additional "learning connections" to the subject matter. Many Concept Reviews have powerful visual elements that will make the material more accessible to visual learners.

Chapter by Chapter

Let us explore the changes in greater depth. Every chapter is quite new.

NEW IN CHAPTER 1: WHAT IS PSYCHOLOGY?

- New chapter opening vignette on abduction by aliens from outer space
- New coverage of Mary Salter Ainsworth, Elizabeth Loftus, Susan Nolen-Hoeksema, Mamie Phipps Clark, Nancy Boyd-Franklin, Tony Strickland, Lillian Comas-Diaz, and Richard Suinn in the section "Gender, Ethnicity, and Psychology: Real People in the Real World."
- New Self-Assessment: "Dare You Say What You Think? The Social-Desirability Scale"
- New Concept Review: "Historic Schools of Psychology"

NEW IN CHAPTER 2: BIOLOGY AND PSYCHOLOGY

- New chapter opening vignette on Phineas Gage
- Expansion of coverage of heredity to include the latest information on the human genome and the relationship of that genome to the genomes of nonhumans, discussion of molecular genetics, genetics and psychological traits, genotypes and phenotypes, twin studies and adoptee studies, and selective breeding
- New Life Connections feature on "On Spiderman, Dr. Octopus, and Brain–Machine Interfaces (BMIs)."
- New Self-Assessment: "Symptoms of PMS"
- New examples of the laborious speech connected with Broca's aphasia
- New Concept Reviews on neurotransmitters and on the endocrine system.

NEW IN CHAPTER 3: THE VOYAGE THROUGH THE LIFE SPAN

- New chapter opening vignette on "Kathy's" effort to conceive a girl
- New coverage of the views of the views of the Russian psychologist Lev Semenovich Vygotsky in the area of cognitive development
- New Self-Assessment: "How Long Will You Live? The Life-Expectancy Scale"
- New Concept Reviews: "Piaget's Stages of Cognitive Development," "Kohlberg's Levels and Stages of Moral Development," and "Erikson's Stages of Psychosocial Development"

NEW IN CHAPTER 4: SENSATION AND PERCEPTION

- New chapter opening vignette on *The Matrix* film series, which carries through the chapter to illustrate various concepts.
- New A Closer Look feature, "How Did the Animals Know the Tsunami Was Coming?" on the tsunami of December 2004
- New coverage of the classic case study of the African pygmy Kenge by anthropologist Colin Turnbull as an illustration of the roles of experience and culture in size constancy
- Update on the number of primary taste qualities
- New mini-experiments that help students determine the sensitivity of their sense of touch and the use of kinesthesis
- New Concept Reviews on "Monocular Cues for Depth Perception" and "The Senses"

NEW IN CHAPTER 5: CONSCIOUSNESS

- New chapter opening vignette on the Internet and the sense of self
- New coverage of the Terri Schiavo case in the context of states of consciousness
- New coverage of mindfulness meditation
- New section on "Altering Consciousness by Connecting with the Internet"
- New coverage of Internet addiction
- New feature on "Rophies—The Date Rape Drug"
- New feature on MDMA ("Ecstasy")

NEW IN CHAPTER 6: LEARNING

- New chapter opening vignette on violence by players of violent video games
- New A Closer Look feature: "RoboRats? Using Operant Conditioning to Teach Rats How to Search for Survivors of Disasters"

NEW IN CHAPTER 7: MEMORY—REMEMBRANCE OF THINGS PAST AND FUTURE

- New chapter opening vignette on "Jeff's" loss of his cellphone phone book
- New reference to the movie *Eternal Sunshine of the Spotless Mind* to help students relate to the biology of memory
- New research on the déjà vu experience
- New research on cognitive explanations for infantile amnesia
- New illustrations: Figure 7.9 illustrates the hippocampus. Figure 7.11 illustrates a way in which dendrites sprout new branches, enhancing long-term potentiation.

NEW IN CHAPTER 8: THINKING, LANGUAGE, AND INTELLIGENCE

- New chapter opening vignette on artificial intelligence
- New anatomical illustrations of apparent rudimentary language structures in the brains of apes
- New A Closer Look feature on language: "'U R a QT' and Other Internet Lingo"

NEW IN CHAPTER 9: MOTIVATION AND EMOTION

- New chapter opening vignette on e-mail, motivation, and the expression of emotions through "emoticons"
- Inclusion of 2005 food pyramid (www.mypyramid.gov)
- New research on sexual orientation and response to pheromones reported in the A Closer Look feature: "Pheromones and Sexual Orientation"

NEW IN CHAPTER 10: STRESS, HEALTH, AND ADJUSTMENT

- New chapter opening vignette on response to Hurricane Katrina
- New reference to the biopsychosocial perspective on health and illness
- Four Life Connections features
- New illustrations
- New Concept Review on "Biopsychosocial Factors in Heart Disease and Cancer"
- General updating, e.g., year 2005 references to the American Cancer Association and American Heart Association

NEW IN CHAPTER 11: PERSONALITY: THEORY AND MEASUREMENT

- New chapter opening vignette on personality tests online
- New coverage of positive psychology in the A Closer Look feature, "Virtuous Traits: Positive Psychology and Trait Theory"
- Updated A Closer Look feature: "Who's Really 'Number One'? On the 'Persistent American Itch to Create Heroes.'"
- New coverage of validity, reliability, and standardization of psychological tests.

NEW IN CHAPTER 12: PSYCHOLOGICAL DISORDERS

- New chapter opening vignette about "Etta," a person diagnosed with schizophrenia and shown on the video accompanying the text
- New discussion of the reliability and validity of the DSM
- New section on "Explaining Psychological Disorders"
- New references to the biopsychosocial perspective
- New section on "Prevalence of Psychological Disorders"
- New focus on positive and negative symptoms of schizophrenia and their implications
- New figure on MRI of the brains of schizophrenic adolescents versus normal adolescents
- New A Closer Look feature on the "reality TV" show *Fear Factor* and how it connects with the evolutionary perspective in psychology
- New section on body dysmorphic disorder
- New research on biological factors in psychological disorders

NEW IN CHAPTER 13: METHODS OF THERAPY

- New chapter opening vignette on virtual reality therapy
- New discussion of interpersonal psychotherapy (ITP)
- New discussion of the meaning of cognitive-behavioral therapy (CBT) and its effectiveness
- New A Closer Look feature on eye movement desensitization and reprocessing (EMDR), and a critical evaluation of the method

NEW IN CHAPTER 14: SOCIAL PSYCHOLOGY

- New chapter opening vignette on suicide terrorism
- New reference to the situationist perspective
- New "Reflect and Relate" features that refer to suicide terrorism
- New coverage of the evolutionary perspective on sexual desire and romantic love

■ New A Closer Look feature that connects social psychology with the question: "Who Are the Suicide Terrorists? A Case of a Fundamental Attribution Error?"

FEATURES

Psychology: Concepts and Connections includes a number of features that are intended to motivate students, enhance learning, and foster critical thinking. These include Video Connections, "A Closer Look" features, Self-Assessments, and "Concept Reviews."

Video Connections

Video Connections features "connect" readers with the free series of videos that accompanies this book. They are integrated into every chapter. Each video is discussed in the text in an interactive format that provides learning objective, prompts to encourage students to apply what they have learned to their own lives, and questions that stimulate critical thinking. The format makes the video more meaningful and encourages higher-order thinking.

"A Closer Look" Features

"A Closer Look" features highlight certain topics, allowing students to pursue them in greater depth. These features can be grouped according to certain themes. Some, for example, highlight case studies or research studies. In Chapter 9 we find the case of Rachel ("Anorexia Nervosa—The Case of Rachel") and an important study on "Pheromones and Sexual Orientation."

A number of "A Closer Look" features underscore the indispensability of human diversity within the field of psychology. For example, Chapter 3's "Aging, Gender, and Ethnicity: Different Patterns of Aging" discusses why women tend to outlive men, and why people from certain ethnic groups tend to outlive people from other ethnic groups. Chapter 10's "Gender Differences in Response to Stress" shows that whereas the "fight-or-flight" response to a threat may apply to men, women, instead, may have a tendency to "tend and befriend."

Other "A Closer Look" features stimulate critical thinking. For example, Chapter 2's "Are You a Human or a Mouse (or a Chimp or a Carrot)? Some Fascinating Facts About Genes" shows that we may be related to other forms of life more closely than we think.

Self-Assessments

Self-Assessment features are another way in which the text connects with students. One of the more fascinating features consists of the psychological tests and measurements that help psychologists and individuals learn about their personality, behavior, and mental processes. The Self-Assessments stimulate student interest by helping them satisfy their curiosity about themselves and enhance the relevance of the text to their lives. Following is a sampling of the Self-Assessments found in the text:

■ Chapter 1: "Dare You Say What You Think? The Social Desirability Scale"
■ Chapter 2: "Symptoms of PMS"
■ Chapter 5: "Sleep Quiz—Are You Getting Your Z's?"
■ Chapter 11: "Do You Strive to Be All That You Can Be?" (A self-test of whether or not one is a self-actualizer)
■ Chapter 13: "Do You Speak Your Mind or Do You Wimp Out? The Assertiveness Schedule"

Students can also access interactive versions of the Self Assessments through their student companion website.

Concept Reviews

Concept Reviews are summaries of the material presented "at a glance." Most of them provide a combination of text and illustrations that tie concepts together in a format that is quick to understand. Here is a sampling of the text's Concept Reviews:

- Chapter 1: "Historic Schools of Psychology"
- Chapter 4: "Monocular Cues for Depth Perception" and "The Senses"
- Chapter 6: "Kinds of Learning"
- Chapter 7: "Memory Systems"
- Chapter 11: "Perspectives on Personality"
- Chapter 12: "Psychological Disorders Listed in the DSM-IV-TR"
- Chapter 13: "Methods of Therapy"

Life Connections

Life Connections help students apply the science of psychology to their own lives. One or more Life Connections is found in every chapter, as in the following examples:

- Chapter 1: "Critical Thinking and Astrology" helps students critically examine a popular but unscientific method of describing personality and predicting the future
- Chapter 3: "Day Care—Blessing, Headache, or Both?" makes students aware of the pluses and minuses of a way of caring for children that has become a necessity for millions of couples
- Chapter 4: "Pain, Pain, Go Away—Don't Come Again Another Day" helps students apply psychological knowledge to cope with pain
- Chapter 5: "Handling Addiction to the Internet" helps students understand the connections between this and other addictions and offers advice on how to regain control of one's behavior
- Chapter 9: "The Skinny on Weight Control" helps students apply psychological knowledge to control their weight, and "'Come On! Get Happy!' A Possible or Impossible Dream?" helps students apply principles of positive psychology to enhance their emotional lives
- Chapter 10: Four Life Connections features in this chapter help students cope with stress and prevent such health problems as headaches, heart disease, and cancer.

Emphasis on the Evolutionary Perspective

The importance of various schools of psychology has changed over the generations. In Chapter 1 we see that we can trace psychology's roots to the Golden Age of Greece and beyond. In the early part of the twentieth century, there were multiple school and emphases, including behaviorism (brought to prominence by John B. Watson and others), psychoanalysis (based mainly on the theory of Sigmund Freud), Gestalt psychology (which focused on perception and cognitive processes). In the second half of the twentieth century, learning theory broadened to include behaviorism and cognitive views, cognitive-developmental theory (as propounded by theorists such as Jean Piaget and Lawrence Kohlberg) gained importance, humanistic psychology developed (to some degree, as an answer to feelings of alienation following the horrors of World War II), work in cognitive psychology mushroomed in the laboratory and the clinic, and the overlaps of biology and psychology exploded in the forms of neuroscience (the study of the nervous system) and endocrinology (the study of hormones).

By now you will not be surprised to learn that few psychologists would agree as to the relative importance of these various perspectives. But perhaps most would agree that there is a current surge of interest in evolutionary psychology. Psychology today explores the influence of evolution not only on physical traits, but also on behavior and mental processes. As humans and their ancestors evolved over millions of years, their fitness for survival gained prominence in terms of intelligence and the ability to acquire various skills, as well as in terms of traits such as sharpness of eye, fleetness of foot, and brawn.

The theme index located nearby shows the scope of coverage of evolutionary psychology in the text:

Emphasis on Human Diversity

Although the profession of psychology focuses mainly on the individual's behavior and mental processes, we cannot understand people's behavior and mental processes without reference to their diversity—diversity in terms of ethnic background, gender, socioeconomic status, age, and other factors. When we consider perspectives other than our own, it's important that we understand the role of a culture's beliefs, values, and attitudes in behavior and mental processes. Our knowledge of the science of psychology is enriched by acknowledging and studying why people from diverse cultures behave and think in different ways.

You will find reference to human diversity integrated within the main body of the text. For example, a study in Chapter 2, "Biology and Psychology," discusses the relationship between perception of people of different races and activity in the limbic system of the brain. A section of Chapter 12, "Psychological Disorders," discusses possible reasons for the greater incidence of depression among women than men. The following theme index shows the scope of diversity coverage in this text.

THEME INDEX

OVERVIEW OF COVERAGE OF EVOLUTIONARY PSYCHOLOGY

- William James as influenced by Darwin's theory (p. 8)
- The evolutionary and biological perspectives (pp. 13–14)
- Introduction to Darwin and the theory of evolution (p. 9)
- Evolutionary psychology as a field in psychology (pp. 13-14)
- Evolutionary forces as favoring people who are curious (p. 21)
- "Older" and "newer" parts of the brain and their functions (pp. 54–61)
- The limbic system and evolution (pp. 56–57)
- Evolution and heredity (pp. 69–77)
- The subject matter of evolutionary psychology (pp. 70–71)
- Evolutionary psychology and depth perception (p. 146)
- The evolution of taste (p. 157)
- Pain as an evolutionary adaptation (p. 159)
- Evolutionary reasons for differences in sleep necessity (p. 177)
- Evolution of taste aversion (p. 213)
- Spontaneous recovery as adaptive (p. 214)
- Generalization and discrimination as adaptive (p. 215)
- Evolution and kinds of learning (p. 218)
- Nature and nurture in language development (p. 299)

- Genetic influences on intelligence (p. 312–313)
- The evolutionary perspective on motivation (p. 324)
- Universal expression of emotions (p. 349)
- Evolutionary perspectives on the flight-or-fight reaction (pp. 337–338)
- Evolutionary perspectives on male and female responses to stress (pp. 378–379)
- Evolutionary perspectives on the tendency to identify with sports teams and heroes (p. 403)
- Nature in the development of gender-typing (p. 404)
- Evolutionary psychology and the popularity of the TV show "Fear Factor" (p. 451)
- Evolutionary perspective on psychological disorders (p. 452)
- The role of anxiety in natural selection (p. 455)
- Evolutionary perspective on gender differences in selection of a romantic partner (pp. 515–516)
- Evolutionary perspectives on romantic love and sexual desire (p. 517)
- Evolutionary perspective on altruism (p. 535)

OVERVIEW OF COVERAGE OF HUMAN DIVERSITY

- The sociocultural perspective in psychology (pp. 15–17)
- Ethnicity in psychology (pp. 15–16)
- Gender in psychology (pp. 16–17)
- Generalization of results of psychological research to groups other than those sampled (p. 22)
- Brain size, number of synapses, and gender (p. 51)
- The amygdala and racially-oriented responses (p. 57)
- Differences and similarities of effects of hormones on males and females (pp. 64–66)

- Premenstrual syndrome (pp. 68, 69)
- Preferences of newborns for their mothers' voices (p. 89)
- Puerto Rican study explains scaffolding as a part of cognitive development (p. 97)
- Stages of attachment in different societies (p. 101)
- Gender differences in moral development (p. 110)
- Gender differences in athletic ability in young adulthood (p. 112)
- Menopause (p. 113)
- Aging, sex, and ethnicity (p. 113)

- Midlife transition for women (p. 118)
- A woman's renewed sense of self (p. 119)
- Cultural differences in size constancy (p. 145)
- Pitch of the voice in men and women (p. 149)
- Female response to male body odor (p. 154)
- Race and hypertension (p. 188)
- Gender differences in alcohol consumption (p. 196)
- Gender, level of education, and smoking (pp. 200–201)
- Gender differences in response to aggression in the media (p. 235)
- Age-related decline in memory (p. 246)
- Memory as it extends to bilingualism (p. 263)
- Sex hormones and memory (p. 273)
- Language and culture (p. 295)
- The linguistic-relativity hypothesis (p. 295)
- Socioeconomic and ethnic differences in intelligence test scores (p. 309)
- Cultural differences in intelligence testing (p. 310)
- Adoptee studies and intelligence (p. 314)
- Racial differences in obesity (p. 330)
- Ethnicity and socioeconomic status amongst women with anorexia (p. 333)
- Racial and gender differences in proneness to eating disorders (p. 333, 336)
- Ethnicity and socioeconomic status amongst women with bulimia (p. 336)

- Ethnic and gender differences in sexual behavior (pp. 338, 340)
- Sex hormones and sex drive (p. 338)
- Sexual orientation (pp. 340–343)
- Gender differences in aggression (pp. 344–345)
- Universality of recognition of facial expressions (pp. 349, 356)
- Differences that lead to levels of happiness (pp. 350,351)
- Ethnic and socioeconomic differences in happiness (p. 351)
- Gender differences in responses to stress (pp. 378–379)
- Ethnic and gender differences in vulnerability to heart disease and cancer (pp. 389, 390)
- Ethnic and gender differences in access to health care (p. 390)
- The sociocultural perspective in personality (pp. 419–421)
- Individualism versus collectivism (p.420)
- Acculturation and adjustment among immigrants (p. 420–421)
- Gender differences in depression and anxiety (pp. 445, 446)
- Ethnic and gender differences in suicide (p. 448)
- Psychotherapy and ethnicity (pp. 494–495)
- Prejudice and discrimination (pp. 511–514)
- Stereotypes (p. 511)
- Depictions of European American and African American men and women in the media (p. 512)
- Gender differences in partner selection (pp. 515–516)
- Matching hypothesis in preferences for a romantic partner (p. 516)
- Gender differences in attributions for friendly behavior (p. 520)
- Fundamental attribution error in different cultures (pp. 521, 536)

OVERVIEW OF COVERAGE OF APPLICATIONS

- Critical Thinking and Astrology (p. 19)
- Dare You Say What You Think? The Social-Desirability Scale (p. 26)
- Steroids, Behavior, and Mental Processes (p. 67)
- Symptoms of PMS (p. 68)
- Day Care—Blessing, Headache, or Both? (p. 103)
- How Long Will You Live? The Life-Expectancy Scale (p. 116)
- Pain, Pain, Go Away—Don't Come Again Another Day (p. 156)
- Getting to Sleep Without Drugs (p. 182)
- Sleep Quiz—Are You Getting Your Z's? (p. 184)
- Are You "Addicted" to the Internet? (p. 192)
- Handling Addiction to the Internet (p. 193)
- Is a Drink a Day Good for You? (p. 197)
- Applications of Classical Conditioning (p. 216)
- What Are the Effects of Punishment? (p. 224)
- Applications of Operant Conditioning (p. 228)
- Teaching Children *Not* to Imitate Violence in the Media (p. 236)
- Five Challenges to Your Memory (p. 243)
- Using the Psychology of Memory to Enhance Your Memory (p. 268)

- Puzzles, Problems, and Just Plain Fun (p. 284)
- The Remote Associates Test (p. 305)
- The Sensation-Seeking Scale (p. 326)
- The Skinny on Weight Control (p. 331)
- "Come On! Get Happy!" A Possible or Impossible Dream? (p. 351)
- Are You Type A or Type B? (p. 372)
- The Locus of Control Scale (p. 375)
- Coping with Stress (p. 382)
- Preventing and Coping with Headaches (p. 387)
- Reducing the Risk of CHD Through Behavior Modification (p. 389)
- Preventing and Coping with Cancer (p. 391)
- Do You Strive to Be All That You Can Be? (p. 417)
- Preventing Suicide (p. 449)
- Do You Demand Your Rights or Do You Wimp Out? The Assertiveness Schedule (p. 485)
- Tackling Depression with Rational Thinking (p. 489)
- Combating Prejudice (p. 513)
- The Love Scale (p. 518)

A COMPLETE PEDAGOGICAL PACKAGE

Psychology: Concepts and Connections' emphasis on making connections is also reflected in the book's pedagogical package. Psychology is a robust science with a lengthy research tradition; therefore, there is a good deal of subject matter in *Psychology: Concepts and Connections.* The book's pedagogy is designed to help students understand the concepts presented so they *take away* more of that knowledge from the book. *Psychology: Concepts and Connec-*

tions fully integrates the PQ4R method in a most stimulating embodiment to help students learn and retain the subject matter.

PQ4R

PQ4R discourages students from believing that they are sponges who will automatically soak up the subject matter in the same way that sponges soak up water. The PQ4R method encourages students to *actively* engage the subject matter, becoming *proactive* rather than *reactive.*

PQ4R is the acronym for Preview, Question, Read, Reflect, Review, and Recite, a method that is related to the work of educational psychologist Francis P. Robinson. PQ4R is more than the standard built-in study guide. It goes well beyond a few pages of questions and exercises that are found at the ends of the chapters of many textbooks. It is an integral part of every chapter. It flows throughout every chapter. It begins and ends every chapter, and it accompanies the student page by page.

PREVIEW

Previewing the material helps shape students' expectations. It enables them to create mental templates or "advance organizers" into which they categorize the subject matter. Each chapter of *Psychology: Concepts and Connections* previews the subject matter with a **Truth or Fiction?** section and a chapter **Preview.** The *Truth or Fiction?* items stimulate students to delve into the subject matter by challenging folklore and common sense (which is often common *nonsense*). Then the *Preview* outlines the material in the chapter, creating mental categories that guide students' reading.

Following is a sampling of challenging **Truth or Fiction?** items from various chapters:

T	F	
T	F	A brain cell can send out hundreds of messages each second—and manage to catch some rest in between.
T	F	Your genetic code overlaps 25% with that of a carrot.
T	F	If we could see waves of light with slightly longer wavelengths, warm-blooded animals would glow in the dark.
T	F	Many people experience pain "in" limbs that have been amputated.
T	F	You can teach a rat to raise or lower its heart rate.
T	F	Some people visit cyberspace with virtual bodies.
T	F	A drink a day is good for you.
T	F	A woman who could not remember who she was automatically dialed her mother's number when the police gave her a telephone.

QUESTION

Devising questions about the subject matter, before reading it in detail, is another feature of the PQ4R method. Writing questions gives students goals: They attend class or read the text *to answer the questions.* Questions are placed in all primary sections of the text to help students use the PQ4R method most effectively. They are printed in *purple.* When students see a question, they can read the following material in order to answer that question. If they wish, they can also write the questions and answers in their notebooks, as recommended by Robinson.

READ

Reading is the first R in the PQ4R method. Although students will have to read for themselves, they are not alone. The text helps them by providing:

- **Previews** that help them organize the material
- **Truth or Fiction?** sections that stimulate students by challenging common knowledge and folklore,
- Presentation of the subject matter in clear, stimulating prose,
- A **running glossary** that defines key terms in the margin of the text, near where the terms appear in the text, and
- Development of **concepts** in an orderly fashion so that new concepts build on previously presented concepts.
- **Concept reviews** that enable students, at a glance, to review the material they have read.

I have chosen a writing style that is "personal." My goal is to speak directly to students and use humor and personal anecdotes to make psychology come alive.

REFLECT & RELATE

Students learn more effectively when they *reflect* on, or *relate* to, what they are learning. Psychologists who study learning and memory refer to reflection on subject matter as *elaborative rehearsal*. One way of reflecting on a subject is to *relate* it to things they already know about, whether it be academic material or events in their own lives. Reflecting on, or relating to, the material makes it meaningful and easier to remember. It also makes it more likely that students will be able to *apply* the information to their own lives. Through effective reflection, students can embed material firmly in their memory so that rote repetition is unnecessary.

Because reflecting on the material is intertwined with relating to it, ***Reflect & Relate*** items are found throughout the text. Here is a sampling of ***Reflect & Relate*** items from two chapters that students frequently find to be most challenging:

From Chapter 2, "Biology and Psychology":

- Would you consider yourself to be more "left-brained" or "right-brained"? Explain.
- Have you heard that adolescents are "hormonal" or affected by "glands"? If so, which glands would they be?
- Which family members seem to be like you physically or psychologically? Which seem to be very different? How do you explain the similarities and differences?

From Chapter 4: "Sensation and Perception":

- Think of times when you have been so involved in something that you didn't notice the heat or the cold. Think of times you have grown so used to sounds, such as those made by crickets or trains at night, that you fall asleep without hearing them. How do these experiences relate to signal-detection theory?
- Have you had the experience of being in a train and not knowing whether your train or one on the next track was moving? How do you explain your confusion? How did you figure out which one was really moving?
- Can you touch your nose when your eyes are closed? How do you manage this feat?

REVIEW

Each *Learning Connections* section contains multiple-choice review items that enable students to judge how well they are learning the subject matter. Learning Connections are found at the conclusion of each major section and help divide each chapter into more manageable "chunks" that some educators label "modules." Each Learning Connections feature provides a review in the form of multiple-choice questions, and a critical thinking question intended to encourage students to think more deeply about the subject matter.

Examples of critical thinking items include:

- Chapter 1, "What Is Psychology?": Do you believe that the richness and complexity of human behavior can be explained as the summation of so many instances of learning? Explain.
- Chapter 2, "Biology and Psychology": What ethical, social, and political issues would be involved in attempting to selectively breed humans for desired traits?
- Chapter 12, "Psychological Disorders": Sick people may be excused from school or work. If some criminals are "sick" in the sense of being diagnosed with antisocial personality disorder, does the disorder relieve them of responsibility for criminal behavior? Explain.
- Chapter 14, "Social Psychology": Critical thinkers do not overgeneralize. Most people would probably agree that it is good for children to be obedient. But is it always good for children—and for adults—to be obedient? As an individual, how can you determine whether or not it is good for *you* to be obedient? How do we define the limits?

RECITE

The PQ4R method recommends that students recite the answers to the questions aloud. Reciting answers aloud helps students remember them by means of repetition, by stimulating students to produce concepts and ideas they have learned, and by associating them with spoken words and gestures (Dodson & Schacter, 2001).[1]

Recite sections are found at the end of each chapter. They help students summarize the material, but they are active, not passive, summaries. For this reason, the sections are termed *Recite—An Active Summary*®. They are written in question-and-answer format. To provide a sense of closure, the active summaries repeat the questions found within the chapters. The answers are concise but include most of the key terms found in the text.

The *Recite—An Active Summary*® sections are designed in two columns so that students can cover the second column (the answers) as they read the questions. Students can recite the answers as they remember or reconstruct them, and then check what they have recited against the answers they had covered. Students should not feel that they are incorrect if they have not exactly produced the answer written in the second column; their individual approach might be slightly different, even more inclusive. The answers provided in the second column are intended to be a guide, to provide a check on students' learning. They are not carved in stone.

ANCILLARIES

Psychology: Concepts and Connections, Brief Version is accompanied by a wide array of supplements prepared for both the instructor and student. Many are available free to professors or students. Others can be packaged with this text at a discount. For more information on any of the listed resources please speak to your Thomson Learning sales representative or go online to www.wadsworth.com.

For the Instructor

INSTRUCTOR'S RESOURCE MANUAL

This easy-to-use, comprehensive three-ring binder with tabbed sections—organized by content area—includes a resource integration guide to assist instructors with integration of the entire ancillary package. The manual contains teaching tips, a sample syllabus, suggested "day-one" activities, learning objectives, an annotated list of suggested readings, thorough lecture outlines, ready-made handouts, and ideas for term projects—many of which are designed to help instructors fully utilize this title's integrated technology resources.

---

[1] Dodson, C. S., & Schacter, D. L. (2001). "If I had said it I would have remembered it": Reducing false memories with a distinctiveness heuristic. *Psychonomic Bulletin & Review, 8*(1), 155–161.

TEST BANK

With more than 3,000 text-specific questions, instructors can draw from this impressive selection of test items, to easily create tests that target the course objectives. The *Test Bank* includes multiple-choice fill-in, true/false, and essay questions for each chapter.

EXAMVIEW®

This computerized testing program has online capabilities and is available for Windows and Macintosh. It contains all Test Bank questions electronically and helps instructors create and customize tests. Instructors can easily edit and import their own questions and graphics, edit and maneuver existing questions, and change test layouts. Tests appear on screen just as they will when printed. ExamView® offers flexible delivery and the ability to test and grade online.

Classroom Presentation Tools for the Instructor

MULTIMEDIA MANAGER WITH INSTRUCTOR RESOURCES

The Multimedia Manager helps instructors enhance PowerPoint® lectures with art from this textbook, videos, animations. Instructors can also integrate their own materials. The Multimedia Manager also provides text-specific lecture outlines, a full *Instructor's Resource Manual, Test Bank,* and other resources.

JOININ™ ON TURNINGPOINT®

JoinIn™ on TurningPoint® includes book-specific content from this text created especially for use with personal response systems. Combined with a choice of several leading keypad systems, JoinIn turns an ordinary PowerPoint application into powerful audience response software. With just a click on a hand-held device, students can respond to multiple-choice questions, short polls, interactive exercises and peer review questions. Instructors can take attendance, collect student demographics to better assess student needs, and even administer quizzes without collecting paper or grading.

THE WADSWORTH PSYCHOLOGY FILM AND VIDEO LIBRARY

This collection of thought provoking films and videos is being continually updated to provide the most current material available. Included are:

- **Psychology Digital Video Library 3.0 CD-ROM with Handbook**—A diversified selection of approximately 100 classic and contemporary clips, this CD-ROM included footage of prominent psychologists, as well as demonstrations and simulations of important experiments.
- **APA Career Video: Introduction to Psychology, Fourth Edition**—This dynamic 13-minute video gives students an overview of emerging growth opportunities in the field.

For the Student

Our lives are rushed and things change—quickly. We are using contemporary methods to help students learn the material as they go from one activity to another and to keep in touch with their author as new research studies are published and current events take new directions: podcasting and blogging.

PODCASTING

I know students are as busy as authors are, and therefore we have created a downloadable audio version of the Recite—An Active Summary sections. Students can download the files from their students' web site to their MP3 players and review them on the go.

BLOGGING

Join the author at his online diary; where he will be positing a personal chronological log of his thoughts on the news items and psychological developments of the day. You will find the author's Web log at http://psychology.wadsworth.com/rathus_brief8e.

THOMSONNOW™ DIAGNOSTIC SELF-ASSESSMENTS
AND PERSONALIZED STUDY PLANS!

After reading a text chapter, students take an online *Pre-Test* to get an initial assessment of what they've learned. ThomsonNow then provides a *Personalized Study Plan* based on the automatically graded *Pre-Test,* which lets them know where they need to focus their efforts. After working through their *Personalized Study Plan*—which includes ThomsonNow's *Integrated Learning Modules,* text pages, weblinks, videos, and animations—students complete a follow-up *Post-Test* (pre and post tests written by Jori Reijonen) to assess their mastery of the material. There is also an instructor grade book built right into ThomsonNow so it is easier than ever to track grades and monitor student progress.

THE BOOK COMPANION WEBSITE

http://psychology.wadsworth.com/rathus_brief8e/

Partnering with ThomsonNow and this book, the website offers students many opportunities for active engagement. Text-specific materials on the website include:

- Video Connections
- PowerVisuals
- Downloadable audio files to help review chapter material
- Interactive multiple-choice quizzing
- Web-based research activities
- Audio flashcards
- InfoTrac College Edition exercises
- Glossary
- Critical thinking guidelines (adapted from *Thinking and Writing About Psychology,* by Spencer A. Rathus)
- Access to NewsEdge—an authoritative, online news feed that instructors can customize
- Author blog

STUDY GUIDE

This invaluable student resource opens with a *Preview* section that encourages students to note initial impressions of chapter material—what surprised them, what they're curious about, and specific queries they have. The *Question* section poses the learning objectives in an outline format and serves as the foundation for the next sections, *Reading for Understanding* and *Reflection Breaks.* These sections include cross-relational activities such as matching and critical thinking exercises, which build on material just covered. *Expand* sections pulls all the material together in applied exercises such as research, writing and Web activities that expand on the themes of the text. The final review provides multiple-choice and essay practice questions.

CONNECTIONS STUDENT NOTEBOOK

Designed to help students take better notes in class and study for tests, the handy *Lecture Outlines* booklet contains a detailed outline of each text chapter with room for notes as well as print outs of PowerVisual art pieces from the text.

vMENTOR™—*LIVE, ONE-ON-ONE TUTORING FROM A SUBJECT EXPERT*

vMentor™ gives students access to virtual office hours with one-on-one, online tutoring help. In vMentor's virtual classroom, students interact with the tutor and other students using two-way audio, an interactive whiteboard for illustrating the problem, and instant messaging.

LIFE CONNECTIONS INFOTRAC® COLLEGE EDITION READER
Correlated with the "Life Connections" features in this textbook, the reader contains an article of interest from the InfoTrac® College Edition library, accompanied by critical thinking questions. Many of these articles are linked to a *Life Connections* box in the main text.

Internet-Based Supplements and Resources

WEBTUTOR™ ADVANTAGE

This program on Web CT or Blackboard helps instructors easily create an engaging online learning environment.

- **Log on and go—or customize in any way you choose**—This versatile, completely flexible online tool is filled with preloaded content from the text, including power visuals, video connection clips, additional video clips, practice quizzes, and more—all organized by text chapter.
- **Great course management tools**—with WebTutor™ Advantage instructors can provide virtual office hours, post syllabi, set up threaded discussions, track student progress with quizzing material, and much more.
- **Robust communication tools**—WebTutor Advantage provides a course calendar, asynchronous discussion, real-time chat, a whiteboard, and an integrated email system.

THOMSON INSITE FOR WRITING AND RESEARCH™—*WITH* TURNITIN®
ORIGINALITY CHECKER
InSite features a full suite of writing, peer review, online grading, and e-portfolio applications. It is an all-in-one tool that helps instructors manage the flow of papers electronically and allows students to submit papers and peer reviews online. Also included in the suite is Turnitin, an "originality checker" that offers a simple solution for instructors who want a strong deterrent against plagiarism, as well encouragement for students to employ proper research techniques.

INFOTRAC COLLEGE EDITION WITH INFOMARKS™
Includes millions of current topic-related articles! This fully searchable database contains more than 20 years' worth of full-text articles (not abstracts) from almost 5,000 diverse sources, such as top academic journals, newsletters, and up-to-the-minute periodicals. The database also includes access to InfoMarks—stable URLs that can be linked to articles and searches.

OPPOSING VIEWPOINTS RESOURCE CENTER
Available for a nominal fee when packaged with this book, the Opposing Viewpoints Resource Center exposes students to various sides of today's most compelling issues.

ACKNOWLEDGMENTS

Writers of novels and poems may secrete themselves in their studies and complete their work in solitude. Not so the textbook author. Writing a textbook is a partnership—a partnership between the author and peers who review the manuscript at every step of the way to make sure that it is accurate and covers the topics it should be covering. My partners for the current edition of *Psychology: Concepts and Connections* include: Carrie Canales, Los Angeles City College; Judy Coleman, Dabney S. Lancaster Community College; Mary Ellen Dello Stritto, Ball State University; June S. Fessenden, Glendale Community College; Maria Fitzpatrick, Chaffey College; Krista Forrest, University of Nebraska–Kearney; Rebecca Fraser-Thill, Bates College; Daniel Houlihan, Minnesota State University–Mankato; Mark D. Kelland, Lansing Community College; Christopher Mruk, Bowling Green State University Firelands College; Katherine Neidhardt, Cuesta College; Ralph G. Pifer, Sauk Valley Community College; Patrick W. Prindle, New Mexico Junior College; Sadie Oates, Pitt Community College; Don Smith, Everett Community College; Gary Springer, Texas State University

In addition to the reviewers for the current edition, I would like to extend my continued gratitude to the reviewers of previous editions who have helped shape my book over the years: Christian D. Amundsen, North Lake College; Beth Arrigo, Central Piedmont Community College; Jeffrey Bartel, Kansas State University; David E. Baskind, Delta College; Julia A. Bishop, Maple Woods Community College; Susan R. Burns, Kansas State University; Saundra K. Ciccarelli, Gulf Coast Community College; Mary Webber Coplen, Hutchinson Community College; Joseph Culkin, Queensborough Community College–The City University of New York; Teddi S. Deka, Missouri Western State College; Susan R. Edwards, Mott Community College; B. J. Hart, Glendale Community College; Mark Kelland, Lansing Community College; Gloria J. Lawrence, Wayne State College; Vicki Lucey, Las Positas College; Laura Madson, New Mexico State University; Joseph Manganello, Gloucester County College; Horace Marchant, Westfield State College; Marnie Moist, St. Francis University; Alinde J. Moore, Ashland University; Russell Ohta, Phoenix College; Brian J. Oppy, California State University–Chico; Debra Parish, Tomball College–North Harris Montgomery Community College District; Michelle L. Pilati, Rio Hondo College; Laura Reichel, Front Range Community College; Theresa Rufrano-Ruffner, Indiana University of Pennsylvania; H. R. Schiffman, Rutgers University; Debra Schwiesow, Creighton University; Carolyn E. Tasa, Erie Community College; Sheralee Tershner, Western New England College; Rhonda G. Trollinger, Guilford Technical Community College; Karen M. Wolford, State University of New York College at Oswego.

The book you hold in your hands would not be what it is without the fine editorial and production team at Wadsworth and assembled by Wadsworth. The book would not exist without Kate Barnes and Michele Sordi. They are essential pleasures and tough taskmasters. Thanks to Eve Howard, Editor-in-Chief, and dinner companion once upon a time in a border town; Michele Sordi, Senior Acquisitions Editor, a friend; Kate Barnes, developmental editor par excellence; Gretchen Otto, one of my favorite perfectionists, of G & S Book Services; Mary Noel, Production Editor; Dan Moneypenny, Assistant Editor; Adrian Paz, Technology Project Manager; Dory Schaeffer, Marketing Manager; Jessica Kim, editorial assistant and Vernon Boes, Senior Art Director.

I would also like to thank the many able-bodied people who worked on the wonderful supplements for this book: Cameron John, Utah Valley State College, for the Instructor's Resource Manual; Mary Ellen Dello Stritto, Western Oregon University, and Kimberly Klein Dechman, George Mason University, for the Test Bank; Rebecca Fraser-Thill, Bates College, for the Study Guide; Robin Musselman, Lehigh Carbon Community College, for the Multimedia Manager; Jori Reijonen for the ThomsonNow Pre- and Post-Tests; and Debra Schwiesow, Creighton University, for the Current Perspectives Infotrac Reader. I would also like to thank Maria C. Fitzpatrick, Chaffee College, for her work writing the Video Connections boxes. Thanks!

Finally, I acknowledge the loving assistance of my family. Lois Fichner-Rathus continues in her role as author's widow, although, with her own books gaining prominence, I am in danger of becoming an author's widower. I thank my children for being sources of delight and pride. I thank Phoebe, the family poodle, for her patience and acceptance. I thank the family Chihuahuas, Audrey and Nadine, for considering becoming housebroken, all of which makes it easier to concentrate on writing.

CHAPTER 1

What Is Psychology?

truth or fiction?

T	F	More than 2,000 years ago, Aristotle wrote a book on psychology, with contents similar to the book you are now holding.
T	F	The ancient Greek philosopher Socrates suggested a research method that is still used in psychology.
T	F	As psychologist Wilhelm Wundt lay on his deathbed, his main concern was to analyze the experience of dying.
T	F	Men receive the majority of doctoral degrees in psychology.
T	F	Even though she had worked to complete all the degree requirements, the first female president of the American Psychological Association turned down the doctoral degree that was offered to her.
T	F	A psychologist could write a believable personality report about you without interviewing you, testing you, or even knowing who you are.
T	F	You could survey millions of voters and still fail to predict the outcome of a presidential election.
T	F	In many experiments, neither the subjects nor the researchers know who is receiving the real treatment and who is not.

Go to www

http://psychology.wadsworth.com/rathus_brief8e/
for an interactive version of this Truth or Fiction feature

preview

My favorite place: the checkout counter of the supermarket. After being buffeted about by the crowds in the aisles and trying to convince myself that I really will survive until the people in line ahead of me are checked out, I am rewarded by the display of all the supermarket tabloids.

The headlines cry out. Each week, there are 10 new sightings of Elvis and 10 new encounters with extraterrestrials. There are 10 new "absolutely proven effective" ways to take off weight and 10 new ways to beat stress and depression. There are 10 new ways to tell if your partner has been cheating and, of course, 10 new predictions by astrologers and psychics.

One of the strange things about the extraterrestrials is that they regularly kidnap us earthlings but never send ransom notes. Although they have the technology to fly between the stars, they apparently still need to prod and poke us to figure out how we work—or don't work. They're also not all that stylish. If you can believe the photos and drawings in the tabloids, aliens have been hopping around in the same flying saucers for half a century. According to a TV interview with a man who claimed to be a kidnap victim, these vehicles tend to be your "classic saucer-shaped silver metallic disk, with a hump on top." Meanwhile, we inferior humans have progressed. We have evolved our modes of transportation from sleek cars with tail fins to boxy Scions and Elements. We continuously update our iPods with the latest music and download the newest ringtones into our camera cell phones. But the aliens keep flying the same model flying saucers. They're nothing to text home about.

Although we can find some humor in these tales of abduction by aliens, psychologists and other scientists are very interested in the questions these tales raise about human nature and the distinction between sensationalism and science. What do we know about people who claim to have been abducted by aliens? What standards or rules should we apply when we are trying to sort out truth from fiction and decide whether we will believe the "kidnap victims"?

Many psychologists have studied the reported alien kidnappings, and one of their conclusions is that the kidnappings never occurred. However, the people making the claims are not necessarily mental ill, nor are they even lying (Newman & Baumeister, 1998). These are by and large people who have "remembered" their "experiences" while undergoing therapy, and often under hypnosis. Tales of alien abduction are widely known throughout our culture, so it is not at all surprising that the "memories" of "kidnap victims" would tend to coincide (Lynn & Kirsch, 1996; Patry & Pelletier, 2001).

"Abductees" generally claim that they are awakened in their sleep by the aliens and unable to move. Psychologists know that many of our voluntary muscles—the ones involved in movement—are "paralyzed" when we sleep, which is why we usually don't thrash about when we dream (McNally & Clancy, 2005). *Hallucinations*—that is, seeing and hearing things that are not really there—are quite common as we are waking from a sleep-paralyzed state, and it seems that the reported experiences of "abductees" fit the pattern.

Psychologists also know that people are quite open to suggestion, especially when undergoing hypnosis (Clark & Loftus, 2004). Memories are not perfect snapshots. When trial witnesses are asked leading questions—that is, questions that might encourage the witnesses to recall events in a certain way—the opposing attorney will usually object ("Leading the witness, your Honor"). Sometimes the person interviewing the supposed kidnap victim asks leading questions, looking for experiences with aliens.

All in all, "UFO memories may be constructed from bits and pieces of sleep-related hallucinations, nightmares, and media attention and fixed solidly into place with the suggestion of hypnosis and the validation of support groups" (Clark & Loftus, 1996). Newman and Baumeister (1998) add that abductees may also be trying to escape, temporarily, from their humdrum lives—just as buyers of the supermarket tabloids might be doing.

Psychologists have thus worked to "explain" how it can be that many people report being abducted by aliens and being subjected to tests by them. But what of the evidence? Is there or is there not evidence that people have been abducted by aliens?

In sum, when we subject the stories in the supermarket tabloids to scientific analysis, we usually find that they fall short of any reasonable requirements of evidence.

This book will take you on a journey. It's not a journey into outer space. (No aliens are hovering about waiting to abduct us.) It's a journey into the inner space of thinking critically about the world around you, about stories and arguments made by other people, about human behavior and mental processes. In our overview of reported alien abductions, we touched on people's memories, the state of consciousness known as sleep, hallucinations, hypnosis, the search for stimulating events, social influences on witnesses, and the effects of social support and the media. All these, and much, much more, lie within the science of psychology. We will see who psychologists are, what they do, what they have learned, and perhaps most importantly, how they sort out truth from fiction.

Let us begin by asking, *What is psychology?*

Courtesy of John Velez Courtesy of John Velez

■ **A Flying Saucer and Aliens as Drawn by John Velez Who Claimed to Be Abducted by Aliens**
Do these photos depict an actual alien abduction or was this man's experience reflect other factors? Some believe stories of alien abductions can be attributed to suggestibility of the person during hypnosis. Others explain alien abduction as a form of hallucination during sleep paralysis while others feel stories like these are simply a means to escape humdrum life. What do you think?

PSYCHOLOGY AS A SCIENCE

Psychology is the scientific study of behavior and mental processes. Topics of interest to psychologists include the nervous system, sensation and perception, learning and memory, intelligence, language, thought, growth and development, personality, stress and health, psychological disorders, ways of treating those disorders, sexual behavior, and the behavior of people in social settings such as groups and organizations.

Sciences have certain goals. Psychology, like other sciences, seeks to describe, explain, predict, and control the events it studies. Psychology thus seeks to describe, explain, predict, and control behavior and mental processes. "Controlling" behavior and mental processes doesn't mean to psychologists what it may sound like to most people. Psychologists are committed to a belief in the dignity of human beings, and human dignity requires that people be free to make their own decisions and choose their own behavior. Psychologists study the influences on human behavior, but they use this knowledge only on request and to help people meet their own goals. For example, a psychologist would wish to help someone who is suffering from anxiety who asks for help.

When possible, descriptive terms such as *a threat* and concepts such as *anxiety* are interwoven into **theories.** Theories propose reasons for relationships among events, as in perception of *a threat* can arouse feelings of *anxiety*. They allow us to derive explanations and predictions, as in Dwayne will feel *anxious* if he perceives *a threat*. A theory of hunger should allow us to predict when people will or will not eat. Many psychological theories combine statements about behavior (such as *evading a threat*), mental processes (such as *thinking that the threat may be harmful*), and biological processes (*rapid heart and respiration rates*). If our observations are not adequately explained by or predicted from a theory, we should consider revising or replacing it.

The remainder of this chapter presents an overview of psychology as a science. You will see that psychologists have diverse interests and fields of specialization. We discuss the history of psychology and the perspectives from which today's psychologists view behavior and mental processes. Finally, we consider the research methods used by psychologists.

reflect & relate

How would you have defined psychology before you began this course? Does the scientific nature of psychology differ from your expectations?

Psychology The science that studies behavior and mental processes.

Theory A formulation of relationships underlying observed events.

⟲ Learning Connections

◀◀   *Psychology as a Science*   ▶▶

REVIEW:

1 Psychology is defined as the study of _____ and mental processes.
   (a) people,
   (b) animals,
   (c) behavior,
   (d) the mind.

2 Behavior is explained through psychological _____, which are sets of statements that involve assumptions about behavior.
   (a) deductions,
   (b) theories,
   (c) principles,
   (d) arguments.

CRITICAL THINKING:
What is the difference between the way that scientists view the world and the way that laypeople view the world?

Go to

http://academic.cengage.com/psychology/rathus
for an interactive version of this review.

WHAT PSYCHOLOGISTS DO— SOMETHING FOR EVERYONE?

Psychologists share a keen interest in behavior; but, in other ways, they may differ markedly. *Just what do psychologists do?* Psychologists engage in research, practice, and teaching. Some researchers engage primarily in basic, or pure, research. **Pure research** has no immediate application to personal or social problems and therefore has been characterized as research for its own sake. Others engage in **applied research,** which is designed to find solutions to specific personal or social problems. Although pure research is sparked by curiosity and the desire to know and understand, today's pure research frequently enhances tomorrow's way of life. For example, pure research on learning and motivation in pigeons, rats, and monkeys done early in the 20th century has found applications in school systems. The research has shown, for example, that learning often takes time and repetition and profits from "booster shots" (that is, repetition even after the learning goal has been reached). And pure research into the workings of the nervous system has enhanced knowledge of disorders such as epilepsy, Parkinson's disease, and Alzheimer's disease.

Many psychologists do not conduct research. Instead, they *practice* psychology by applying psychological knowledge to help individuals change their behavior so that they can meet their own goals more effectively. Still other psychologists engage primarily in teaching. They share psychological knowledge in classrooms, seminars, and workshops. Some psychologists engage in all three: research, practice, and teaching.

Fields of Psychology: From the Clinic to the Courtroom

Psychologists are found in a number of different specialties. Although some psychologists wear more than one hat, most of them carry out their functions in the following fields.

Clinical psychologists help people with psychological disorders adjust to the demands of life. Clinical psychologists evaluate problems such as anxiety and depression through interviews and psychological tests. They help clients resolve problems and change self-defeating behavior. For example, they may help clients face "threats," such as public speaking, by exposing the clients gradually to situations in which they make presentations to actual or virtual groups (see *virtual therapy* in Chapter 13). Clinical psychologists are the largest subgroup of psychologists (Kyle & Williams, 2000; see Figure 1.1). *Counseling psychologists,* like clinical psychologists, use interviews and tests to define their clients' problems. Their clients typically have adjustment problems but not serious psychological disorders. For example, clients may have trouble making academic or vocational decisions or making friends in college.

School psychologists help school systems identify and assist students who have problems that interfere with learning. They help schools make decisions about the placement of students in special classes. *Educational psychologists* research theoretical issues related to learning, measurement, and child development. For example, they study how learning is affected by psychological factors such as motivation and intelligence, sociocultural factors such as poverty and acculturation, and teacher behavior. Some educational psychologists prepare standardized tests such as the SATs.

Developmental psychologists study the changes—physical, cognitive, social, and personality—that occur throughout the life span. They attempt to sort out the influences of heredity and the environment on development.

Personality psychologists identify and measure human traits and determine influences on human thought processes, feelings, and behavior. They are particularly concerned with issues such as anxiety, aggression, and gender roles. *Social psychologists* are concerned with the nature and causes of individuals' thoughts, feelings, and behavior in social situations. Whereas personality psychologists tend to look within the person for explanations of behavior, social psychologists tend to focus on social influences.

Pure research Research conducted without concern for immediate applications.

Applied research Research conducted in an effort to find solutions to particular problems.

Figure 1.1
Students Enrolled in Doctoral Programs in Fields of Psychology
Nearly half (47%) of the doctoral students who enrolled in doctoral programs in psychology in 1998–1999 enrolled in clinical programs. The next most popular field was counseling psychology. The figure combines students enrolled in public and private institutions.
Source: Tables 13A and 13B from *Results of the 1998–1999 APA Survey of Graduate Departments of Psychology*, by T. M. Kyle and S. Williams, May 2000, APA Research Office, Washington, DC: American Psychological Association.

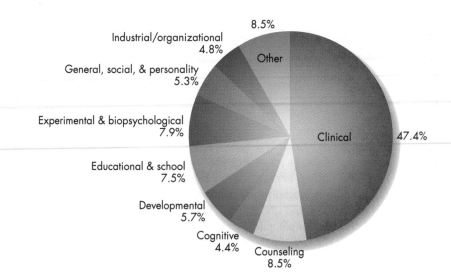

reflect & relate

Think of a friend who either has experienced a problem or is experiencing one now. Would you advise him or her to see a psychologist? Why or why not? If so, what kind of psychologist?

■ **Environmental Psychologists Study the Environment We Live In**
This humanmade environment creates stress for those who are involved in taking the subway every day. Environmental psychologists seek ways to make environments like this easier for people to handle in their daily lives.

Environmental psychologists study the ways in which people and the environment—the natural environment and the humanmade environment—influence one another. For example, we know that extremes of temperature and loud noises interfere with learning in school. Environmental psychologists also study ways to encourage people to recycle and to preserve bastions of wilderness.

Experimental psychologists specialize in basic processes such as the nervous system, sensation and perception, learning and memory, thought, motivation, and emotion. For example, experimental psychologists study which areas of the brain are involved in solving math problems or listening to music. They use people or animals such as pigeons and rats to study learning.

Industrial psychologists focus on the relationships between people and work. *Organizational psychologists* study the behavior of people in organizations such as businesses. *Human factors psychologists* make technical systems such as automobile dashboards and computer keyboards more user-friendly. *Consumer psychologists* study the behavior of shoppers in an effort to predict and influence their behavior. They advise store managers how to lay out the aisles of a supermarket in ways that boost impulse buying, how to arrange window displays to attract customers, and how to make newspaper ads and TV commercials more persuasive.

Health psychologists examine the ways in which behavior and attitudes are related to physical health. They study the effects of stress on health problems such as headaches, cardiovascular disease, and cancer. Health psychologists also guide clients toward healthier behavior patterns, such as exercising and quitting smoking.

Sport psychologists help people improve their performance in sports. They help athletes concentrate on their performance and not on the crowd, use cognitive strategies such as positive visualization (imagining themselves making the right moves) to enhance performance, and avoid choking under pressure.

Forensic psychologists apply principles of psychology to the criminal justice system. They deal with legal matters such as whether a defendant was sane when he or she committed a crime. Forensic psychologists may also treat psychologically ill offenders, consult with attorneys on matters such as picking a jury, and analyze criminals' behavior and mental processes. Forensic psychologists, like other psychologists, may choose to conduct research on matters ranging from evaluation of eyewitness testimony to interrogation methods.

( ) Learning Connections

 What Psychologists Do — Something for Everyone?

REVIEW:

3 _____ research seeks solutions to specific problems.
(a) Basic,
(b) Applied,
(c) Psychological,
(d) Scientific.

4 _____ psychologists assist students with problems that interfere with learning.
(a) Clinical,
(b) Personality,
(c) School,
(d) Educational.

CRITICAL THINKING:
What unites the various fields of psychology?

Go to www
http://academic.cengage.com/psychology/rathus
for an interactive version of this review.

WHERE PSYCHOLOGY COMES FROM: A HISTORY

Have you heard the expression "Know thyself"? It was suggested by the ancient Greek philosopher, Socrates, more than 2,000 years ago. Psychology, which is in large part the endeavor to know ourselves, is as old as history and as modern as today. Knowledge of the history of psychology allows us to appreciate its theoretical conflicts, its place among the sciences, the evolution of its methods, and its social and political roles.

Who were some of the ancient contributors to psychology? One of them is the ancient Greek philosopher Aristotle (384–322 BCE). ◆ **Truth or Fiction Revisited:** More than 2,000 years ago, Aristotle wrote a book on psychology, *Peri Psyches,* with contents similar to the book you are now holding. Like this book, *Peri Psyches* begins with a history of psychological thought and historical views of the mind and behavior. Aristotle argued that human behavior, like the movements of the stars and the seas, is subject to rules and laws. Then he delved into his subject matter topic by topic: personality, sensation and perception, thought, intelligence, needs and motives, feelings and emotion, and memory. This book presents these topics in a different order, but each is here.

Other ancient Greek philosophers also contributed to psychology. Around 400 BCE, Democritus suggested that we could think of behavior in terms of a body and a mind. (Contemporary psychologists still talk about the interaction of biological and mental processes.) He pointed out that our behavior is influenced by external stimulation. Democritus was one of the first to raise the question of whether there is free will or choice. Putting the question another way, where do the influences of others end and "our own selves" begin?

Plato (c. 427–347 BCE) was a follower of Socrates. ◆ **Truth or Fiction Revisited:** Socrates suggested a research method that is still used in psychology—**introspection,** which is based on Socrates' advice to "know thyself," which has remained a motto of psychology ever since. Socrates suggested that we should rely on rational thought and introspection—careful examination of one's own thoughts and emotions—to achieve self-knowledge. He also pointed out that people are social creatures who influence one another.

Had we room enough and time, we could trace psychology's roots to thinkers even farther back in time than the ancient Greeks, and we could trace its development through the

Brown Brothers

■ **Aristotle**
How do we number Aristotle's contributions to psychology? He argued that science could rationally treat only information gathered by the senses. He numbered the so-called five senses of vision, hearing, smell, taste, and touch. He explored the nature of cause and effect. He pointed out that people differ from other living things in their capacity for rational thought. He outlined laws of *associationism* that have lain at the heart of learning theory for more than 2,000 years. He also declared that people are motivated to seek pleasure and avoid pain—a view that remains as current today as it was in ancient Greece.

■ Wilhelm Wundt
Wundt devoted himself to analyzing the "structure" of human experience, even as he lay on his deathbed.

■ William James
In his youth, 19th-century "glitterati" like Ralph Waldo Emerson and Nathaniel Hawthorne visited the James family home. James received an MD but never practiced medicine. Instead he joined the faculty at Harvard University and founded the school of functionalism.

Introspection Deliberate looking into one's own cognitive processes to examine one's thoughts and feelings.

Structuralism The school of psychology that argues that the mind consists of three basic elements—sensations, feelings, and images—that combine to form experience.

Functionalism The school of psychology that emphasizes the uses or functions of the mind rather than the elements of experience.

great thinkers of the Renaissance. As it is, we must move on to the development of psychology as a laboratory science during the second half of the 19th century. Some historians set the marker date at 1860. It was then that Gustav Theodor Fechner (1801–1887) published his landmark book *Elements of Psychophysics,* which showed how physical events (such as lights and sounds) are related to psychological sensation and perception. Fechner also showed how we can scientifically measure the effect of these events. Most historians set the debut of modern psychology as a laboratory science in the year 1879, when Wilhelm Wundt established the first psychological laboratory in Leipzig, Germany.

■ Structuralism: The Elements of Experience

The German psychologist Wilhelm Wundt (1832–1920) looked as if he were going to be a problem child. He did poorly in elementary school—his mind would wander—and he had to repeat a grade. Eventually he attended medical school because he wanted to earn a good living. He did not like working with patients, however, and dedicated himself to philosophy and psychology. ◆ **Truth or Fiction Revisited:** During a serious illness, Wundt's main preoccupation lay in analyzing the experience of dying. He recovered, however, and went on to live a long life.

Wundt also analyzed the experience of living. Like Aristotle, Wundt saw the mind as a natural event that could be studied scientifically, like light, heat, and the flow of blood. Wundt used introspection to try to discover the basic elements of experience. When presented with various sights and sounds, he and his colleagues tried to look inward as objectively as possible to describe their sensations and feelings.

Wundt and his students founded the school of psychology called **structuralism.** *What is structuralism?* Structuralism attempted to break conscious experience down into *objective* sensations, such as sight or taste, and *subjective* feelings, such as emotional responses, will, and mental images like memories or dreams. Structuralists believed that the mind functions by combining objective and subjective elements of experience.

■ Functionalism: Making Psychology a Habit

> *I wished, by treating Psychology like a natural science, to help her become one.*
> —WILLIAM JAMES

Toward the end of the 19th century, William James became a major figure in the development of psychology in the United States. He focused on the relation between conscious experience and behavior. He argued, for example, that the stream of consciousness is fluid and continuous. Introspection convinced him that experience cannot be broken down into objective sensations and subjective feelings as the structuralists maintained.

James was a founder of the school of **functionalism.** *What is functionalism?* The school of functionalism focused on behavior in addition to the mind or consciousness. Functionalists looked at how our experience helps us function more adaptively in our environments—for example, how habits help us cope with common situations. (When eating with a spoon, we do not create an individual plan to bring each morsel of food to our mouths.) They also turned to the laboratory for direct observations as a way to supplement introspection. The structuralists tended to ask, "What are the pieces that make up thinking and experience?" In contrast, the functionalists tended to ask, "How do behavior and mental processes help people adapt to the requirements of their lives?"

James was also influenced by Charles Darwin's (1809–1882) theory of evolution. Earlier in the 19th century, the British naturalist Darwin had argued that organisms with adaptive features—that is, the "fittest"—survive and reproduce. Functionalists adapted Darwin's theory and proposed that adaptive behavior patterns are learned and maintained. Maladaptive behavior patterns tend to drop out; only the "fittest" behavior survives. Adaptive behaviors tend to be repeated and become habits. James wrote that "habit is the enormous flywheel of society." Habit keeps the engine of civilization running.

Habits include such deceptively simple acts as how we lift a spoon to our mouth or turn a doorknob. At first, these acts require our full attention. If you are in doubt, stand by with paper towels and watch a baby's first efforts at eating oatmeal by himself. Through repetition, the movements that make up self-feeding become automatic, or habitual. The multiple acts involved in learning to drive a car also become routine through repetition, so we can focus on other matters such as telling a joke to our passenger, changing the CD, or talking on the phone. (Many state legislatures have concluded, however, that it is too dangerous for drivers to use hand-held phones.) This idea of learning by repetition is also basic to the behavioral tradition in psychology.

———■— Behaviorism: Practicing Psychology in Public

Imagine you have placed a hungry rat in a maze. It meanders down a pathway that ends in a T. It can turn left or right. If you consistently reward the rat with food for turning right, it will learn to turn right when it arrives there, at least when it is hungry. But what does the rat *think* when it is learning to turn right? "Hmm, last time I was in this situation and turned to the right, I was given some Purina rat chow. Think I'll try that again."?

Does it seem absurd to try to place yourself in the "mind" of a rat? So it seemed to John Broadus Watson (1878–1958), the founder of American behaviorism. Watson was asked to consider the contents of a rat's "mind" as one of the requirements for his doctoral degree, which he received from the University of Chicago in 1903. Functionalism was the dominant view of psychology at the University of Chicago, and functionalists were concerned with the stream of consciousness as well as observable behavior. But Watson (1913) believed that if psychology was to be a natural science, like physics or chemistry, it must limit itself to observable, measurable events—that is, to behavior alone—hence, the term *behaviorism.*

What is behaviorism? **Behaviorism** is the school of psychology that focuses on learning observable behavior. The term "observable" includes behaviors that are observable by means of instruments, such as the heart rate, blood pressure, and brain waves. These behaviors are *public* in that they can be measured easily and multiple observers would agree about their existence and features. Given their focus on behavior, behaviorists define psychology as the scientific study of *behavior,* not of *behavior and mental processes.*

B. F. Skinner (1904–1990) also contributed to behaviorism. He believed that organisms learn to behave in certain ways because they have been **reinforced** for doing so—that is, their behavior has a positive outcome. He demonstrated that laboratory animals can be trained to carry out behaviors through strategic use of reinforcers, such as food. He trained rats to turn in circles, climb ladders, and push toys across the floor. Because Skinner showed that he could teach animals remarkable combinations of behaviors by means of reinforcement, many psychologists adopted the view that, in principle, one could explain complex human behavior in terms of thousands of instances of learning through reinforcement (see Figure 1.2).

———■— Gestalt Psychology: Making Psychology Whole

In the 1920s, another school of psychology—**Gestalt psychology**—was prominent in Germany. In the 1930s, the three founders of the school—Max Wertheimer (1880–1943), Kurt Koffka (1886–1941), and Wolfgang Köhler (1887–1967)—left Europe to escape the Nazi threat. They carried on their work in the United States, giving further impetus to the growing American ascendance in psychology.

What is Gestalt psychology? Gestalt psychologists focused on perception and on how perception influences thinking and problem solving. The German word *Gestalt* translates as "pattern" or "organized whole." In contrast to the behaviorists, Gestalt psychologists argued that we cannot understand human nature by focusing only on observable behavior. In contrast to the structuralists, they claimed that we cannot explain human perceptions, emotions, or thought processes in terms of basic units. Perceptions are *more* than the sums of their parts: Gestalt psychologists saw our perceptions as wholes that give meaning to parts, as we see in Figure 1.3.

reflect & relate

Psychologist William James visited Helen Keller as a child and brought her an ostrich feather. If you had been Helen Keller, would you have appreciated this gift? Explain.

Archives of the History of American Psychology

■ **John B. Watson**
Watson's aim was to show how most human behavior and emotional reactions—other than a few inborn reflexes—resulted from conditioning. Following an academic career, Watson moved to New York, where he worked as a psychologist for the J. Walter Thompson advertising agency. He grew wealthy through successful ad campaigns for products such as Camel cigarettes, Johnson & Johnson baby powder, and Maxwell House coffee—in which he introduced the idea of the "coffee break."

Behaviorism The school of psychology that defines psychology as the study of observable behavior and studies relationships between stimuli and responses.

Reinforcement A stimulus that follows a response and increases the frequency of the response.

Gestalt psychology The school of psychology that emphasizes the tendency to organize perceptions into wholes and to integrate separate stimuli into meaningful patterns.

Tom McHugh/Photo Researchers, Inc.

Bob & Marian Breland-Bailey, Hot Springs AR

Figure 1.2
The Power of Reinforcement
In the photo on the left, we see a feathered friend that has learned to drop shapes into their proper places through reinforcement. In the photo on the right, "Air Raccoon" shoots a basket. Behaviorists teach animals complex behaviors such as shooting baskets by first reinforcing approximations to the goal (or target behavior). As time progresses, closer approximations are demanded before reinforcement is given.

reflect & relate

Why do behaviorists object to schools of psychology that use introspection? Do you agree with the behaviorist view? Why or why not?

Gestalt psychologists showed that we tend to perceive separate pieces of information as integrated wholes, depending on the contexts in which they occur. In part A of Figure 1.3, the dots in the centers of the drawings are the same size, yet we may perceive them as being different in size because of their surroundings. The second symbol in each line in part B is identical, but in the top row we may perceive it as a B and in the bottom row as the number 13. The symbol has not changed, but its context has. The inner squares in part C are equally bright, but they do not appear so because of their contrasting backgrounds. There are many examples of this in literature and everyday life. In *The Prince and the Pauper*, Mark Twain dressed a peasant boy as a prince, and the kingdom bowed to him. Do clothes sometimes make the man or woman? Try wearing cutoffs for a job interview!

Gestalt psychologists believed that learning could be active and purposeful, not merely responsive and mechanical as in Watson's and Skinner's experiments. They found that much learning, especially in problem solving, is accomplished by **insight**, not by mechanical repetition, as we see in a classic experiment that took place nearly a century ago.

Have you ever pondered a problem for quite a while and then, suddenly, seen the solution? Did the solution seem to come out of nowhere? In a "flash"? Consider Wolfgang Köhler's research with chimpanzees, as shown in Figure 1.4. At first, the chimpanzee is unsuccessful in reaching for bananas suspended from the ceiling. Then he suddenly stacks the boxes and climbs up to reach the bananas. It seems the chimp has experienced a sudden reorganization of the mental elements of the problem—that is, he has had a "flash of insight." Köhler's findings suggest that people too often manipulate the elements of prob-

Figure 1.3
The Importance of Context
Gestalt psychologists have shown that our perceptions depend not only on our sensory impressions but also on the context of our impressions. You will interpret a man running toward you very differently depending on whether you are on a deserted street at night or at a track in the morning.

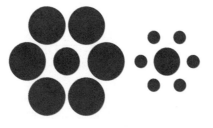

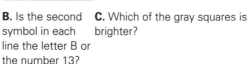

A. Are the dots in the center of the configurations the same size? Why not take a ruler and measure them?

B. Is the second symbol in each line the letter B or the number 13?

C. Which of the gray squares is brighter?

Figure 1.4
Some Insight into Insight
At first, the chimpanzee cannot reach the bananas hanging from the ceiling. After some time has passed, the chimp has an apparent "flash of insight" and piles the boxes on top of one another to reach the fruit.

lems until we group them in such a way that we believe we will be able to reach a goal. The manipulations may take quite some time as mental trial and error proceeds. But once the solution has been found, we seem to perceive it all of a sudden.

◼️ Psychoanalysis: Digging Beneath the Surface

Psychoanalysis, the school of psychology founded by Sigmund Freud (1856–1939), differs from other schools in background and approach. Freud's theory has invaded popular culture, and you may be familiar with a number of its concepts. For example, perhaps a friend has tried to "interpret" a slip of the tongue you made or has asked you what you thought might be the meaning of an especially vivid dream.

What is psychoanalysis? **Psychoanalysis** is the name of the theory of personality and of the method of therapy developed by Sigmund Freud. As a theory of personality, psychoanalysis was based on the idea that much of our lives is governed by unconscious ideas and impulses that originate in childhood conflicts. Psychoanalysts believe that verbal slips and dreams often represent unconscious wishes. Freud was an Austrian physician who fled to England in the 1930s to escape the Nazis. Whereas academic psychologists of the early 1900s were conducting their research in the laboratory, Freud gained his understanding of people by working with patients. He was astounded at how little insight his patients seemed to have into their motives. Some patients justified the most abominable behavior with absurd explanations. Others seized the opportunity to blame themselves for nearly every misfortune that had befallen the human species.

Psychoanalytic theory proposes that most of the mind is unconscious—a seething cauldron of conflicting impulses, urges, and wishes. People are motivated to gratify these impulses, ugly as some of them are. But at the same time, people are motivated to see themselves as decent, and hence may delude themselves about their true motives. Because Freud proposed that the motion of underlying forces of personality determines our thoughts, feelings, and behavior, his theory is referred to as **psychodynamic.**

As a physician, Freud's goal was to help individuals who were suffering from various psychological and social problems. His method of psychotherapy, psychoanalysis, aims to help patients gain insight into many of their deep-seated conflicts and to find socially acceptable ways of expressing wishes and gratifying needs (you will learn more about psychoanalysis in Chapter 13).

Psychoanalysis The school of psychology that emphasizes the importance of unconscious motives and conflicts as determinants of human behavior.

Psychodynamic Referring to Freud's theory, which proposes that the motion of underlying forces of personality determines our thoughts, feelings, and behavior.

CONCEPT REVIEW ■ CONCEPT REVIEW 1.1 ■ CONCEPT REVIEW

HISTORIC SCHOOLS OF PSYCHOLOGY

SCHOOL/MAJOR PROPONENT(S)	KEY CONCEPTS	CURRENT STATUS
Structuralism Wilhelm Wundt 	The mind can be studied scientifically by using introspection to discover the basic elements of experience. Conscious experience can be broken down into *objective* sensations such as sight or taste, and *subjective* feelings such as emotional responses, will, and mental images like memories or dreams.	We do not encounter structuralists today, but cognitive and experimental psychologists study related topics such as sensation and perception, emotion, memory, and states of consciousness (including dreams).
Functionalism William James 	There is a relationship between consciousness and behavior. Consciousness is fluid and streamlike. Experience cannot be broken down into objective sensations and subjective feelings. Functionalists focused on how experience helps us function more adaptively in our environments.	We do not have pure functionalists today, but functionalism preceded behaviorism in its interest in how habits are formed by experience and help us adapt. Behavior is seen as evolving: Adaptive behavior is maintained, whereas maladaptive behavior tends to drop out.
Behaviorism John B. Watson, B. F. Skinner John B. Watson B. F. Skinner	Psychology must limit itself to observable, measurable events—to behavior, not mental processes. Organisms learn to behave in certain ways because of the effects of their behavior.	Some "pure" behaviorists remain, but behaviorism more generally has contributed to experimental psychology, the psychology of learning, and methods of therapy (behavior therapy). Although many contemporary psychologists argue that it is desirable to study consciousness and mental processes, the behaviorist influence has encouraged them to base many of their conclusions on measurable behaviors.
Gestalt Psychology Max Wertheimer, Kurt Koffka, Wolfgang Köhler Are the center dots the same size?	Gestalt psychologists focused on perception, thinking, and problem solving. Whereas structuralists tried to isolate basic elements of experience, Gestalt psychologists focused on the tendency to see perceptions as wholes that give meaning to parts.	Gestalt principles continue to be studied in the field of sensations and perception. Other Gestalt ideas, such as those involving thinking and problem solving, continue to be studied by cognitive psychologists and experimental psychologists. Gestalt therapy—which aims to help people integrate conflicting parts of their personalities—remains in use.
Psychoanalysis Sigmund Freud, Carl Jung, Alfred Adler, Karen Horney, Erik Erikson Sigmund Freud Karen Horney Erik Erikson	Visible behavior and conscious thinking are influenced by unconscious ideas and conflicts. People are motivated to gratify primitive sexual and aggressive impulses, even if they are unaware of their true motives. Unconscious processes are more influential than conscious thought in determining human behavior.	Psychoanalytic thinking remains quite alive in the popular culture. Among psychologists, many discount psychoanalysis altogether, because many of its concepts cannot be studied by scientific means. Modern psychoanalytic therapists tend to place more emphasis on the roles of conscious motives, conscious thinking, and decision making.

( ) Learning Connections

◀◀ *Where Psychology Comes From—A History* ▶▶

REVIEW:

5 _____ proclaimed "Know thyself" and suggested the use of introspection to gain self-knowledge.
  (a) Aristotle,
  (b) Democritus,
  (c) Socrates,
  (d) Wertheimer.

6 William James founded the school of _____, which dealt with behavior as well as conscious experience.
  (a) structuralism,
  (b) functionalism,
  (c) Gestalt psychology,
  (d) psychoanalysis.

CRITICAL THINKING:
Do you believe that the richness and complexity of human behavior can be explained as the summation of so many instances of learning? Explain.

Go www
to
http://academic.cengage.com/psychology/rathus
for an interactive version of this review.

HOW TODAY'S PSYCHOLOGISTS VIEW BEHAVIOR AND MENTAL PROCESSES

Today we no longer find psychologists who describe themselves as structuralists or functionalists. Although the school of Gestalt psychology gave birth to current research approaches in perception and problem solving, few would label themselves Gestalt psychologists. But we do find Gestalt therapists who help clients integrate conflicting parts of their personality (making themselves "whole"). The numbers of behaviorists and psychoanalysts have been declining (Robins et al., 1999). Many contemporary psychologists in the behaviorist tradition look on themselves as social-cognitive theorists,[1] and many psychoanalysts consider themselves neoanalysts or ego analysts rather than traditional Freudians.

The history of psychological thought has taken many turns, and contemporary psychologists differ in their approaches. Today there are several broad, influential perspectives in psychology: evolutionary and biological, cognitive, humanistic–existential, psychodynamic, learning, and sociocultural. Each emphasizes different topics of investigation. Each approaches its topics in its own ways.

◼ The Evolutionary and Biological Perspectives: It's Only Natural

Psychologists are interested in the roles of evolution and heredity in behavior and mental processes such as psychological disorders, criminal behavior, and thinking. Generally speaking, our heredity provides a broad range of behavioral and mental possibilities. Environmental factors interact with inherited factors to determine specific behavior and mental processes. *What is the evolutionary perspective?*

Evolutionary psychologists focus on the evolution of behavior and mental processes. Charles Darwin argued that in the age-old struggle for existence, only the "fittest" (most

---

[1] Formerly termed *social-learning theorists.*

adaptive) organisms reach maturity and reproduce. For example, fish that swim faster or people who are naturally immune to certain diseases are more likely to survive and transmit their **genes** to future generations. Individuals die, but species tend to evolve in adaptive directions. Evolutionary psychologists suggest that much human social behavior, such as aggressive behavior and mate selection, has a hereditary basis. People may be influenced by social rules, cultural factors, even personal choice, but evolutionary psychologists believe that inherited tendencies sort of whisper in people's ears and tend to move them in certain directions.

When we ask the question "What evolves?" our answer is biological processes and structures. Psychologists assume that thoughts, fantasies, and dreams—and the inborn or **instinctive** behavior patterns of various species—are made possible by the nervous system and especially by the brain. *What is the biological perspective?* Psychologists with a biological perspective seek the links between the activity of the brain, the activity of hormones, and heredity, on the one hand, and behavior and mental processes on the other.

The biological perspective tends to focus on events that occur below the level of consciousness. As we see next, the cognitive perspective is the essence of consciousness. *What is the cognitive perspective?*

◼ The Cognitive Perspective: Keeping Psychology "In Mind"

Psychologists with a **cognitive** perspective venture into the realm of mental processes to understand human nature. They investigate the ways in which we perceive and mentally represent the world, how we learn, remember the past, plan for the future, solve problems, form judgments, make decisions, and use language. Cognitive psychologists, in short, study those things we refer to as the *mind*.

The cognitive tradition has roots in Socrates' advice to "know thyself" and in his suggested method of introspection. We also find cognitive psychology's roots in structuralism, functionalism, and Gestalt psychology, each of which, in its own way, addressed issues that are of interest to cognitive psychologists.

◼ The Humanistic–Existential Perspective: The Search for Meaning

The humanistic–existential perspective is cognitive in flavor, yet it emphasizes more the role of subjective (personal) experience. *What is the humanistic–existential perspective?* Let us consider each of the parts of this perspective: *humanism* and *existentialism*. **Humanism** stresses the human capacity for self-fulfillment and the central roles of consciousness, self-awareness, and decision making. Humanists believe that self-awareness, experience, and choice permit us, to a large extent, to "invent ourselves" as we progress through life. Consciousness—our sense of being in the world—is seen as the force that unifies our personalities. **Existentialism** views people as free to choose and as being responsible for choosing ethical conduct. Grounded in the work of Carl Rogers (1951) and Abraham Maslow (1970), the humanistic–existential perspective has many contemporary adherents (Moss, 2002; Schneider et al., 2003).

◼ The Psychodynamic Perspective: Still Digging

In the 1940s and 1950s, psychodynamic theory dominated the field of psychotherapy and influenced scientific psychology and the arts. Renowned artists and writers consulted psychodynamic therapists to liberate the expression of their unconscious ideas. Today, Freud's influence is still felt, although it no longer dominates psychotherapy. Contemporary psychologists who follow theories derived from Freud are likely to call themselves *neoanalysts*. Famous neoanalysts such as Karen Horney (1885–1952) and Erik Erikson (1902–1994) focused less on the unconscious and more on conscious choice and self-direction.

Genes The basic building blocks of heredity.

Instinctive An inborn pattern of behavior that is triggered by a particular stimulus.

Cognitive Having to do with mental processes such as sensation and perception, memory, intelligence, language, thought, and problem solving.

Humanism The philosophy and school of psychology that asserts that people are conscious, self-aware, and capable of free choice, self-fulfillment, and ethical behavior.

Existentialism The view that people are free and responsible for their own behavior.

Perspectives on Learning: From the Behavioral to the Cognitive

Many contemporary psychologists study the effects of experience on behavior. Learning, to them, is the essential factor in describing, explaining, predicting, and controlling behavior. The term *learning* has different meanings to psychologists of different persuasions, however. Some students of learning find roles for consciousness and insight. Others do not. This distinction is found today among those who adhere to the behavioral and social cognitive perspectives. *What are the two major perspectives on learning?*

For John B. Watson, behaviorism was an approach to life as well as a guideline for psychological research. He viewed people as doing things because of their learning histories, their situations, and rewards, not because of conscious choice. Like Watson, contemporary behaviorists emphasize environmental influences and the learning of habits through repetition and reinforcement. **Social-cognitive theorists,** in contrast, suggest that people can modify and create their environments. They note that people engage in intentional learning by observing others. Since the 1960s, social-cognitive theorists have gained influence in the areas of personality development, psychological disorders, and psychotherapy.

Chuck Savage /Corbis

■ **The Sociocultural Perspective**
The United States is a mosaic of people from various ethnic backgrounds. The sociocultural perspective teaches that we cannot understand the hopes and problems of people from a particular ethnic group without understanding that group's history and cultural heritage. The sociocultural perspective helps us understand and appreciate the scope of behavior and mental processes.

The Sociocultural Perspective: How Do You Complete the Sentence "I Am . . ."?

The profession of psychology focuses mainly on the individual and is committed to the dignity of the individual. However, many psychologists today believe we cannot understand people's behavior and mental processes without reference to their diversity (Basic Behavioral Science Task Force, 1996b).

What is the sociocultural perspective? The **sociocultural perspective** addresses many of the ways in which people differ from one another. It studies the influences of ethnicity, gender, culture, and socioeconomic status on behavior and mental processes. Studying cultures other than their own helps psychologists understand the roles of culture in behavior, beliefs, values, and attitudes (Chang et al., 2005; Edwards, 2005; Sabbagh, 2005). For example, what is often seen as healthful outspoken behavior by most U.S. women may be interpreted as brazen in Latino and Latina American or Asian American communities.

Ethnicity   One kind of diversity involves people's ethnicity. Members of an **ethnic group** share their cultural heritage, race, language, or history. The experiences of various ethnic groups in the United States highlight the impact of social, political, and economic factors on human behavior and development (Basic Behavioral Science Task Force, 1996b).

Individuals from various ethnic and racial groups have struggled for recognition in psychology as in society at large. In 1901, Gilbert Haven Jones was the first African American to receive a Ph.D. in psychology, but he had to do so in Germany. J. Henry Alston engaged in research on perception of heat and cold and in 1920 became the first African American psychologist to be published in a major psychology journal.

The most well-known African American psychologists may be Kenneth Clark (b. 1914) and Mamie Phipps Clark (1917–1983). The Clarks conducted research that showed the negative effects of school segregation on African American children. In one such study, African American children were shown white and brown dolls and asked to "Give me the pretty doll," or "Give me the doll that looks bad." Most children's choices showed that they preferred the white dolls over the brown ones. The Clarks concluded that the children had swallowed society's preference for European Americans. The Clarks' research was cited by

Social-cognitive theory A school of psychology in the behaviorist tradition that includes cognitive factors in the explanation and prediction of behavior. Formerly termed *social-learning theory.*

Sociocultural perspective The view that focuses on the roles of ethnicity, gender, culture, and socioeconomic status in behavior and mental processes.

Ethnic group A group characterized by common features such as cultural heritage, history, race, and language.

Library of Congress

■ **Mamie Phipps Clark and Kenneth B. Clark**

The Clarks earned their doctorates in psychology at Columbia University, promoted the welfare of children, and undertook research that was cited in the Supreme Court's decision to overturn the doctrine of "separate but equal" schools for African American and European American children.

Archives of the History of American Psychology

■ **Mary Whiton Calkins**

She just said no—to the doctorate from Radcliffe that was offered her, that is. She had completed her graduate work at Harvard, but Harvard was not admitting women as matriculated students at the time. Calkins went on to pioneer research in memory at Wellesley College and to become the first female president of the American Psychological Association.

Gender The culturally defined concepts of *masculinity* and *femininity.*

the Supreme Court in 1954 when it overturned the "separate but equal" schools doctrine that had allowed inequalities in school services for various ethnic groups.

Today African Americans continue to influence psychology. For example, psychologist Claude Steele (e.g., Blascovich et al., 2001) has shown that many African Americans inadvertently sabotage their own performance on intelligence tests because rather than focus on test items, they worry about the stereotype that African Americans are not as intelligent as European Americans (see Chapter 8). African American psychologist Nancy Boyd-Franklin (Franklin & Boyd-Franklin, 2000) studies group and family therapy with African Americans. African American psychologist Tony Strickland (Lawson & Strickland, 2004; Strickland & Gray, 2000) has discovered that people from different ethnic groups may respond to drugs in different ways.

Latino American Jorge Sanchez was among the first to show how intelligence tests are culturally biased—to the disadvantage of Mexican American children. Latina American Lillian Comas-Díaz (e.g., 2003) edits a journal on multicultural mental health. Asian American psychologist Stanley Sue (Chang & Sue, 2003; Lam & Sue, 2001) has shown that discrimination may be connected with racial differences in intelligence and achievement (see Chapter 8). Asian American psychologist Richard Suinn (Jenkins et al., 2003) studies mental health and the development of identity among Asians and Asian Americans.

Gender   **Gender** refers to the culturally defined concepts of *masculinity* and *femininity.* Gender is not fully defined by anatomic sex. It involves a complex web of cultural expectations and social roles that affect people's self-concepts and hopes and dreams as well as their behavior. Just as members of ethnic minority groups have experienced prejudice, so too have women.

Although American women have attended college only since 1833, when Oberlin College opened its doors to women, most American college students today are in fact women. Women now receive nearly three-quarters of the undergraduate degrees in psychology and two-thirds of the doctoral degrees (U.S. Department of Education, 2004). ◆ **Truth or Fiction Revisited:** Women now actually receive the majority of doctoral degrees in psychology.

Women have made indispensable contributions to psychology. Mary Whiton Calkins (1863–1930) introduced the method of paired associates to study memory (see Chapter 7), discovered the primacy and recency effects, and engaged in research into the role of the frequency of repetition in the vividness of memories. Calkins had studied psychology at Harvard University, which she had to attend as a "guest student," because Harvard was not yet admitting women. When she completed her Ph.D. requirements, Harvard would not award her the degree because of her sex. Instead, Harvard offered to grant her a doctorate from its sister school, Radcliffe. As a form of protest, Calkins declined the offer. Even without the Ph.D., Calkins went on to become president of the American Psychological Association. ◆ **Truth or Fiction Revisited:** It is therefore true that the first female president of the American Psychological Association turned down the doctoral degree that was offered to her.

Christine Ladd-Franklin (1847–1930), like Calkins, was born in an era in which women were expected to remain in the home and were excluded from careers in science (Minton, 2000). She nevertheless pursued a career in psychology, taught at Johns Hopkins and Columbia Universities, and formulated a theory of color vision.

Margaret Floy Washburn (1871–1939) was the first woman to receive a Ph.D. in psychology. Washburn wrote *The Animal Mind,* a work containing many ideas that would later become part of behaviorism. Helen Bradford Thompson (1874–1947) was the first psychologist to study psychological gender differences. Her 1903 book *The Mental Traits of Sex* analyzed the performance of 25 women and 25 men on tests of intellect, emotional response, and sensation and perception (Milar, 2000). Thompson was ahead of her time in her conclusion that gender differences in these areas appeared to be strongly influenced by the social environment from infancy through adulthood.

In more recent years, Mary Salter Ainsworth (1913–1999) revolutionized our understanding of attachment between parents and children by means of her cross-cultural studies. Elizabeth Loftus (e.g., Loftus, 2004; Loftus & Bernstein, 2005) has shown that our memories are not snapshots of the past. Instead, they often consist of something old (what actually happened), something new (that is, influenced by more recent events), something borrowed (for example, further shaped by our biases and prejudices), and something blue (altered by tinges of color or emotion). Susan Nolen-Hoeksema (e.g., Nolen-Hoeksema & Keita, 2003) is contributing to our understanding of the ways in which self-destructive ruminating (that is, going back and forth repeatedly over the same issues) prevents us from making decisions and heightens feelings of depression (see Chapter 12).

The contributions of members of diverse ethnic groups and women have broadened our understanding of the influences of ethnicity and gender on behavior and mental processes. They have taught us that what is true for men may not always be true for women. What is true for European Americans may not be true for people from other backgrounds. The inclusion of women and people from various ethnic backgrounds provides the mosaic that is psychology today.

By now we have a sense of the various fields of psychology, the history of psychology, and the ways in which today's psychologists look at behavior and mental processes. Basically, psychology has sought to be the scientific study of behavior and mental processes. Like other scientists, psychologists engage in critical thinking and conduct research to answer the questions that interest them. We address those topics next.

reflect & relate

Consider your own sex and ethnic background. What would it have been like for you to try to study psychology in the United States a century ago?

() Learning Connections

 ◀◀   *How Today's Psychologists View Behavior and Mental Processes*   ▶▶

REVIEW:

7 _____ psychologists note that only the fittest organisms reach maturity and reproduce, thereby transmitting their genes to future generations.
   (a) Evolutionary,
   (b) Behavioral,
   (c) Social cognitive,
   (d) Psychodynamic.

8 _____-existential psychologists stress the importance of self-awareness and people's freedom to make choices.
   (a) Psychodynamic,
   (b) Gestalt,
   (c) Biological,
   (d) Humanistic.

9 _____ revolutionized our understanding of attachment between parents and children,
   (a) Richard Suinn,
   (b) Mary Salter Ainsworth,
   (c) Jorge Sanchez,
   (d) Margaret Floy Washburn.

10 Kenneth Clark and Mamie Phipps Clark influenced a key United States Supreme Court decision on
   (a) desegregation in the schools,
   (b) psychotherapists' rights to privileged communications,
   (c) the Miranda law,
   (d) voting rights.

CRITICAL THINKING:
Should we teach Freud's ideas? Many psychologists argue that Freud's views have not been supported by research evidence and are thus of no more than historic interest. Therefore, Freud's ideas should not be emphasized in psychology textbooks. Some psychologists would even exclude Freud from a scientific textbook. What do you think?

Go to www

http://academic.cengage.com/psychology/rathus
for an interactive version of this review.

HOW PSYCHOLOGISTS STUDY BEHAVIOR AND MENTAL PROCESSES

Does alcohol cause aggression? Does watching violence on TV cause children to be violent? Why do some people hardly ever think of food, whereas others are obsessed with it and snack all day? Why do some unhappy people attempt suicide, whereas others work overtime coping with their problems? How does having people of different ethnic backgrounds collaborate in their work affect feelings of prejudice?

Many of us have expressed opinions—maybe strong opinions—on questions like these. But as we saw in our discussion of people who claim to be abducted by aliens from outer space, scientists insist on evidence. Psychologists, like other scientists, use careful means to observe and measure behavior and the factors that influence behavior.

The need for evidence is one of the keys to critical thinking. Critical thinking is a life tool for all of us as well as a pathway toward scientific knowledge. Let us now explain why it can be good to be critical. Then we'll talk about the scientific method and research methods.

▪— Critical Thinking: Sorting Out Truth from Fiction

Let us look at the world through the eyes of the psychologist. Psychologists are guided by scientific principles, and one hallmark of science is *critical thinking*. **What is critical thinking?** Critical thinking has many meanings. On one level, it means taking nothing for granted. It means not believing things just because they are in print or because they were uttered by authority figures or celebrities. It means not necessarily believing that it is healthful to express all of your feelings just because a friend in "therapy" urges you to do so. On another level, critical thinking refers to a process of thoughtfully analyzing and probing the questions, statements, and arguments of others. It means examining definitions of terms, examining the premises or assumptions behind arguments, and then scrutinizing the logic with which arguments are developed.

Principles of Critical Thinking   Let us consider principles of critical thinking that can be of help to you in college and beyond:

1. *Be skeptical.* Keep an open mind. Politicians and advertisers try to persuade you. Even research reported in the media or in textbooks may take a certain slant. Extend this principle to yourself. Are some of your own attitudes and beliefs superficial or unfounded? Accept nothing as the truth until you have examined the evidence.
2. *Insist on evidence.* It is not sufficient that an opinion is traditional, that it appears in print or on the Internet, or it is expressed by a doctor or a lawyer. Ask for evidence.
3. *Examine definitions of terms.* Some statements are true when a term is defined in one way but not when it is defined in another way. Consider the statement, "Head Start programs have raised children's IQs." The correctness of the statement depends on the definition of "IQ." (You will see later in the text that *IQ* has a specific meaning and is not the same thing as the broader concept of *intelligence*.)
4. *Examine the assumptions or premises of arguments.* Consider the statement that one cannot learn about human beings by engaging in research with animals. One premise in the statement seems to be that human beings are not animals. We are, of course. (Would you rather be a plant?)
5. *Be cautious in drawing conclusions from evidence.* For many years, studies had shown that most clients who receive psychotherapy improve. It was therefore generally assumed that psychotherapy worked. Then a psychologist named Hans Eysenck pointed out that most psychologically troubled people who did *not* receive psychotherapy also improved. The question thus becomes whether people receiving psychotherapy are *more* likely to improve than those who do not. Current research on the effectiveness of psychotherapy therefore carefully compares the benefits of therapy techniques to the benefits of other techniques or of no treatment at all. Be espe-

cially skeptical of anecdotes. When you hear "I know someone who . . .", ask yourself whether this one person's reported experience is satisfactory as evidence.

6. *Consider alternative interpretations of research evidence.* Does alcohol cause aggression? Later in the chapter we will report evidence that there is a clear *connection,* or correlation, between alcohol and aggression. For example, many people who commit violent crimes have been drinking. But does the evidence show that drinking causes aggression? Might other factors, such as gender, age, or willingness to take risks, account for both drinking and aggressive behavior?

7. *Do not oversimplify.* Most human behavior involves complex interactions of genetic and environmental influences. Also consider the issue of whether psychotherapy helps people with psychological problems. A broad answer to this question—a simple yes or no—might be oversimplifying. It is more worthwhile to ask, What *type* of psychotherapy, practiced by *whom,* is most helpful for *what kind of problem?*

8. *Do not overgeneralize.* Consider the statement that one cannot learn about human beings by engaging in research with nonhuman animals. Is the truth of the matter an all-or-nothing issue? Are there certain kinds of information we can obtain about people from research with animals? What kinds of things are you likely to be able to learn only through research with people?

9. *Apply critical thinking to all areas of life.* A skeptical attitude and a demand for evidence are not only useful in college, but are of value in all areas of life. Be skeptical when you are bombarded by TV commercials, when political causes try to sweep you up, when you see the latest cover stories about Elvis and UFO sightings in supermarket tabloids. How many times have you heard the claim "Studies have shown that . . ."? Perhaps such claims sound convincing, but ask yourself: Who ran the studies? Were the researchers neutral scientists, or were they biased toward obtaining certain results?

These are the kinds of principles that guide psychologists' thinking as they observe behavior, engage in research, or advise clients as to how to improve the quality of their lives. Perhaps applying these principles will improve the quality of your own life.

Life Connections
Critical Thinking and Astrology

Let's apply the principles of critical thinking to astrology. But first read this personality report. I wrote it about you:

> You have your strengths and your weaknesses, but much of the time, you do not give yourself enough credit for your strengths. You are one of those people who has the inner potential for change, but you need to pay more attention to your own feelings so that you can determine the right direction for yourself.
>
> You have many times found yourself to be in conflict as your inner impulses have run up against the limits of social rules and moral codes. Most of the time you manage to resolve conflict in a way that makes sense to you, but now and then you have doubts and wonder whether you have done the right thing. You would often like to be doing two or more things at the same time, and you occasionally resent the fact that you cannot.
>
> There is an inner you known to you alone, and you often present a face to the world that does not quite reflect your genuine thoughts and feelings. And now and then you look at the things you have done and the path that you have taken, and you have some doubt as to whether it is all worth it.

That's you to a T, isn't it? It probably sounds familiar enough. The tendency to believe a generalized (but phony) personality report is called the *Barnum effect,* after circus magnate P. T. Barnum, who once declared that a good circus had a "little something for everybody." ■

Bill Frymire/Masterfile

■ **The Lure of Astrology**

Astrology has been shown to be a pseudoscience, not a real science. How, then, do we account for its allure to so many millions of people?

◆ **Truth or Fiction Revisited:** The Barnum effect allows generalized personality reports to sound perfectly accurate and also allows fortune-tellers to make a living. That is, most of us have enough in common that a fortune-teller's "revelations" about us may ring true. A Mexican study found that students overwhelmingly endorse generalized personality reports about them, especially when they are favorable (Pulido & Marco, 2000).

Most of us have personality traits in common. But what do tea leaves, bird droppings, palms (of your hands, not on the tropical sands), and the stars have in common? Let us see.

P. T. Barnum also once declared, "There's a sucker born every minute." The tendency to believe generalized personality reports has made people vulnerable to phonies throughout history. This tendency enriches the pocketbooks of astrologists who offer to "read your personality" and predict your future based on the movements of the stars and planets.

Astrology is based on the notion that the positions of the sun, the moon, and the stars affect human temperament and human affairs. For example, people born under the sign of Jupiter are believed to be jovial, or full of playful good humor. People born under the sign of Saturn are thought to be gloomy and morose (saturnine). And people born under Mars are believed to be warlike (martial). One supposedly can also foretell the future by studying the positions of these bodies.

Astrologers maintain that the positions of the heavenly bodies at the time of our birth determine our personality and destiny. They prepare forecasts called *horoscopes* that are based on our birth dates and indicate what is safe for us to do. If you get involved with someone who asks for your "sign" (for example, Aquarius or Taurus), he or she is inquiring about your birth date in astrological terms. Astrologers claim that your sign, which reflects the month during which you were born, indicates who you will be compatible with. You may have been wondering whether you should date someone of another religion. If you start to follow astrology, you may also be wondering whether it is safe for a Sagittarius to be dating a Pisces or a Gemini.

Although psychologists and other scientists consider astrology to be a pseudoscience, it has millions of followers. One survey of 1,574 adults found that 28% of Americans believe in astrology (Newport & Strausberg, 2001). The National Science Foundation (2002) found that although 60% of Americans reject astrology, 43% still check their horoscopes now and then.

The allure of astrology is understandable. People want to know about themselves and the world. One could argue that understanding one's abilities and the nature of the world foster the survival of the individual. Evolutionary forces would thus favor the survival of individuals who are curious. People may be drawn to astrology and other pseudosciences as a way of understanding the self and the world—especially unexpected events (Wiseman & Smith, 2002). But it becomes self-serving, because people are most likely to believe in astrology when the descriptions they hear about their personalities are favorable (Hamilton, 2001; MacDonald & Standing, 2002; Wundar, 2003). It seems to go like this: The "validity" of astrology is confirmed when the astrologer—or palm reader, or reader of tea leaves, or reader of tarot cards, or even the reader of bird droppings—says something positive about the individual. If the message is bad, there goes the validity of the messenger!

Believers in astrology also tend to argue as follows:

■ Astrology has been practiced for centuries and is a cultural tradition.
■ Astrology seems to provide a path to meaning for people who are uneducated and, for a fortunate few with limited means, a road to riches.
■ People in high positions have followed the advice of astrologers. (Nancy Reagan is reported to have consulted an astrologer in arranging the schedule of her husband, President Regan.)

- The moon is powerful enough to sway the tides. Why shouldn't the pulls of heavenly bodies affect people's destinies?
- Astrology is a special art and not a science. Therefore, scientific testing is irrelevant.
- Astrology works.

Think critically about these arguments. Does the fact that astrology is traditional affect its scientific merit? Does Nancy Reagan's (or anyone else's) belief in astrology affect its scientific merit? In science, beliefs about the behavior of cosmic rays, chemical compounds, cells, people—or the meaning of bird droppings or the movements of the stars—must be supported by evidence. References to authority figures are *not* scientific evidence. And astrological predictions are no more likely to come true than predictions based on chance (Crowe, 1990; Munro & Munro, 2000). That is fact, but does it matter?

Perhaps. Perhaps not. Magical predictions tend to keep their allure. Many people want magic in their lives (Munro & Munro, 2000). Even in our age of scientific enlightenment, many people are more comfortable with fanciful stories and opinion than they are with evidence.

But what about you? Will you be more skeptical in the future?

The popular—but incorrect—belief in astrology helps point out why strong arguments, references to authority figures, even tightly knit theories are not adequate as scientific evidence. Psychologists, as scientists, use careful means to try to answer research questions. One of these is the scientific method, which involves ways of gathering evidence and ways of sharing evidence with the scientific community.

The Scientific Method: Putting Ideas to the Test

What is the scientific method? The scientific method is an organized way of using experience and testing ideas in an effort to expand and refine knowledge. Psychologists do not necessarily follow the steps of the scientific method as we might follow a recipe in a cookbook. However, modern research ideally is guided by certain principles.

Psychologists usually begin by *formulating a research question.* Our daily experiences, psychological theory, even folklore all help generate questions for research. Consider some questions that may arise from daily experience. Daily experience in using day-care centers may motivate us to conduct research on whether day care affects the development of social skills or the bonds of attachment between children and mothers. Social cognitive principles of observational learning may prompt research on the effects of TV violence. Research questions may also arise from common knowledge. Consider adages such as "misery loves company," "opposites attract," and "seeing is believing." Psychologists may ask, *Does* misery love company? *Do* opposites attract? *Can* people believe what they see?

A research question may be reworded as a hypothesis (see Figure 1.5). A **hypothesis** is a statement about behavior or mental processes that is tested through research. One hypothesis about day care might be that preschoolers who are placed in day care will acquire greater social skills in relating to peers than preschoolers who are cared for in the home.

Psychologists next examine the research question or *test the hypothesis* through controlled methods such as the experiment. For example, we could take a group of preschoolers who attend day care and another group who do not, and introduce each to a new child in a controlled setting such as a child-research center. We could then observe how children in each group interact with the new acquaintance.

Psychologists draw conclusions on the basis of their observations or findings. When their observations do not bear out their hypotheses, they may modify the theories from which the hypotheses were derived. Research findings often suggest refinements to psychological theories and, consequently, new avenues of research. In our research on day care, we would probably find that children in day care show greater social skills than children who are cared for in the home (Belsky et al., 2001).

As psychologists draw conclusions from research evidence, they are guided by principles of critical thinking. For example, they try not to confuse **correlations**—or associations—between findings with cause and effect. Although more aggressive children apparently spend more time watching violent TV shows, it may be erroneous to conclude from

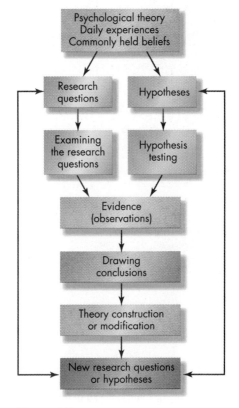

Figure 1.5
The Scientific Method
The scientific method is a systematic way of organizing and expanding scientific knowledge. Daily experiences, common beliefs, and scientific observations all contribute to the development of theories. Psychological theories explain observations and lead to hypotheses about behavior and mental processes. Observations can confirm the theory or lead to its refinement or abandonment.

Go to your student website to access an interactive version of this figure.

this kind of evidence that TV violence *causes* aggressive behavior. A **selection factor** may be at work because the children studied choose (select) for themselves what they will watch. Perhaps more aggressive children are more likely than less aggressive children to tune in to violent TV shows.

To better understand the effects of the selection factor, consider a study on the relationship between exercise and health. Imagine that we were to compare a group of people who exercised regularly with a group of people who did not. We might find that the exercisers were physically healthier than the couch potatoes. But could we conclude without doubt that exercise is a causal factor in good health? Perhaps not. The selection factor—the fact that one group chose to exercise and the other did not—could also explain the results. Perhaps healthy people are more likely to *choose* to exercise.

Some psychologists include publication of research reports in professional journals as part of the scientific method. Researchers are obligated to share enough details of their work so that others can repeat or **replicate** it to see whether the findings hold up over time and with different subjects. Publication of research also permits the scientific community at large to evaluate the methods and conclusions of other scientists.

━━■━ Samples and Populations: Hitting the Target Population

Consider a piece of history that never quite happened: The Republican candidate Alf Landon defeated the incumbent president, Franklin D. Roosevelt, in 1936. Or at least Landon did so in a poll conducted by a popular magazine of the day, the *Literary Digest*. In the actual election, however, Roosevelt routed Landon by a landslide of 11 million votes. ◁▷ **Truth or Fiction Revisited**: It is true that you could survey millions of voters and still not predict the outcome of a presidential election. In effect, the *Digest* accomplished something like this when they predicted a Landon victory. How was so great a discrepancy possible?

The *Digest*, you see, had surveyed voters by phone. Today telephone sampling is a widely practiced and reasonably legitimate polling technique. But the *Digest* poll was taken during the Great Depression, when people who had telephones were much wealthier than those who did not. People at higher income levels are also more likely to vote Republican. No surprise, then, that the overwhelming majority of those sampled said they would vote for Landon.

How do psychologists use samples to represent populations? The *Digest* poll failed because of its method of sampling. Samples must be drawn so that they accurately *represent* the population they are intended to reflect. Only representative samples allow us to **generalize**—or *extend*—our findings from research samples to populations.

In surveys such as that conducted by *Literary Digest*, and in other research methods, the individuals who are studied are referred to as a **sample**. A sample is a segment of a **population** (the group that is targeted for study). Psychologists and other scientists need to ensure that the people they observe represent their target population, such as U.S. voters, and not subgroups such as southern Californians or European American members of the middle class.

Problems in Generalizing from Psychological Research

> *All generalizations are dangerous, even this one.*
> —ALEXANDRE DUMAS

Many factors must be considered in interpreting the accuracy of the results of scientific research. One is the nature of the research sample. Later in the chapter we consider research in which the subjects were drawn from a population of college men who were social drinkers. That is, they tended to drink at social gatherings but not when alone. Who do college men represent, other than themselves? To whom can we extend, or generalize, the results? For one thing, the results may not extend to women, not even to college women. In the chapter on consciousness, for example, we see that alcohol affects women more quickly than men.

Hypothesis In psychology, a specific statement about behavior or mental processes that is tested through research.

Correlation An association or relationship among variables, as we might find between height and weight or between study habits and school grades.

Selection factor A source of bias that may occur in research findings when subjects are allowed to choose for themselves a certain treatment in a scientific study.

Replicate Repeat, reproduce, copy.

Generalize To extend from the particular to the general; to apply observations based on a sample to a population.

Sample Part of a population.

Population A complete group of organisms or events.

Facial Analysis—The Scientific Method in Action

LEARNING OBJECTIVES

- Use facial analysis as an example to explain how psychologists apply theories to real-world settings.
- Explain how this research in facial analysis provides a good example of how psychologists conduct research.
- Explain why objectivity is important in studying psychology and other sciences.

APPLIED LESSON

1 What might be some real-world applications of facial analysis?

2 Explain why facial analysis might be a more objective measure of emotions than our own perceptions.
3 Explain why the use of computers can be so important in research.

CRITICAL THINKING

Critical thinkers maintain an attitude of skepticism. It would be appropriate to be skeptical about the ability of computers to undertake facial analysis. How does the study shown here affect an attitude of skepticism toward the use of computers?

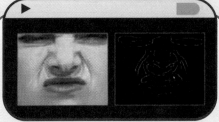

Will you soon be using your camera cell phone to snap a picture of someone, send it to an online lab for analysis, and get a report back on whether the person is trustworthy, telling the truth, or expressing genuine feelings? Facial analysis is just one example of how psychological research can be applied in real-world settings.

Watch this video!
Go to www
your companion website at
http://academic.cengage.com/psychology/rathus
Click on the Video Connections tab under this chapter.

Also, compared to the general adult male population, college men tend to be younger and score higher on intelligence tests. We cannot be certain that the findings extend to older men or to those with lower intelligence test scores. Social drinkers may even differ biologically and psychologically from alcoholics, who have difficulty controlling their drinking.

By and large, we must also question whether findings of research with men can be generalized to women and whether research with European American men can be extended to members of ethnic minority groups. For example, personality tests completed by European Americans and by African Americans may need to be interpreted in diverse ways if accurate conclusions are to be drawn.

Random and Stratified Sampling   One way to achieve a representative sample is by means of **random sampling.** In a random sample, each member of a population has an equal chance of being asked to participate. Researchers can also use a **stratified sample,** which is selected so that known subgroups in the population are represented proportionately in the sample. For instance, 13% of the American population is African American. A stratified sample would thus be 13% African American. As a practical matter, a large randomly selected sample will show accurate stratification. A random sample of 1,500 people will represent the broad American population reasonably well. A sample of 20,000 European Americans or men will not.

Large-scale magazine surveys of sexual behavior have asked readers to fill out and return questionnaires. Although many thousands of readers completed the questionnaires and sent them in, did the survey respondents represent the American population? Probably not. These studies and similar ones may have been influenced by **volunteer bias.** People

Random sample A sample drawn so that each member of a population has an equal chance of being selected to participate.

Stratified sample A sample drawn so that identified subgroups in the population are represented proportionately in the sample. How can stratified sampling be carried out to ensure that a sample represents the ethnic diversity we find in the population at large?

Volunteer bias A source of bias or error in research reflecting the prospect that people who offer to participate in research studies differ systematically from people who do not.

who offer or volunteer to participate in research studies differ systematically from people who do not. In the case of research on sexual behavior, volunteers may represent subgroups of the population—or of readers of the magazines in question—who are willing to disclose intimate information and therefore may also be likely to be more liberal in their sexual behavior (Rathus et al., 2005). Volunteers may also be more interested in research than other people, as well as have more spare time. How might such volunteers differ from the population at large? How might such differences slant or bias the research outcomes?

■ Methods of Observation: The Better to See You With

Many people consider themselves experts in psychology. How many times have you or someone else been eager to share a life experience that "proves" some point about human nature?

Even though we see much during our lifetimes, our personal observations tend to be fleeting and unsystematic. We sift through experience for the things that interest us. We often ignore the obvious because it does not fit our assumptions about the way things ought to be. Scientists, however, have devised more controlled ways of observing others. *What methods of observation are used by psychologists?* In this section we consider three methods of observation widely used by psychologists and other behavioral scientists: the case study, the survey, and naturalistic observation.

Case Study   **Case studies** collect information about individuals and small groups. Many case studies are clinical; that is, they are detailed descriptions of a person's psychological problems and how a psychologist treated the problems. Case studies are sometimes used to investigate rare occurrences, as in the case of Chris Sizemore, who was diagnosed with multiple personalities (technically termed *dissociative identity disorder*). A psychiatrist identified three distinct personalities in Chris. Her story was made into a more theatrical movie called *The Three Faces of Eve*. One personality, "Eve White," was a mousy, well-meaning woman who had two other "personalities" inside her. One was "Eve Black," a promiscuous personality who emerged now and then to take control of her behavior. The third personality, "Jane," was a well-adjusted woman who integrated parts of Eve White and Eve Black.

Case studies have various sources of inaccuracy. People's memories have gaps and factual inaccuracies (Loftus, 2004). People may also distort their pasts to please the interviewer or because they want to remember things in certain ways. Interviewers may also have certain expectations and subtly encourage subjects to fill in gaps in ways that are consistent with these expectations. Psychoanalysts, for example, have been criticized for guiding people who seek their help into viewing their own lives from the Freudian perspective (Hergenhahn, 2005). No wonder, then, that many people provide "evidence" that is consistent with psychodynamic theory—such as, "My parents' strictness during toilet training is the source of my compulsive neatness." However, interviewers and other kinds of researchers who hold *any* theoretical viewpoint run the risk of indirectly prodding people into saying what they want to hear.

The Survey   In the good old days, we had to wait until the wee hours of the morning to learn the results of local and national elections. Throughout the evening and early morning hours, suspense would build as ballots from distant neighborhoods and states were tallied. Nowadays, we are barely settled with an after-dinner cup of coffee on election night when reporters announce that a computer has examined the ballots of a "scientifically selected sample" and predicted the next president of the United States. This projection may occur with less than 1% of the vote tallied.

Just as computers and pollsters predict election results and report national opinion on the basis of scientifically selected samples, psychologists conduct **surveys** to learn about behavior and mental processes that cannot be observed in the natural setting or studied experimentally. Psychologists conducting surveys may employ questionnaires and interviews or examine public records. One of the advantages of the survey is that by distributing questionnaires and analyzing answers with a computer, psychologists can study many thousands of people at a time.

Case study A carefully drawn biography that may be obtained through interviews, questionnaires, and psychological tests.

Survey A method of scientific investigation in which a large sample of people answer questions about their attitudes or behavior.

The best-known surveys of all time, the so-called Kinsey reports, provided surprising information during the middle of the twentieth century, a time of relative sexual repression in the United States. Alfred Kinsey and his colleagues published two surveys of sexual behavior based on extensive interviews: *Sexual Behavior in the Human Male* (1948) and *Sexual Behavior in the Human Female* (1953). The nation was shocked to hear that masturbation among his sample of men was virtually universal in a day when masturbation was still widely thought to impair health. During this time, it was also widely believed that virtually all single women were virgins. Nonetheless, Kinsey found that about 1 woman in 3 who was still single at age 25 reported having engaged in sexual intercourse.

Surveys, like case studies, also have sources of inaccuracy. People may recall their behavior inaccurately or lie about it. Some people try to ingratiate themselves with their interviewers by answering in what they think to be the socially desirable direction. The Kinsey studies all relied on male interviewers, for example. It has been speculated that female interviewees might have been more open and honest with female interviewers. Similar problems may occur when interviewers and the people surveyed are from different ethnic or socioeconomic backgrounds. Other people may falsify their attitudes and exaggerate their problems to draw attention to themselves or to intentionally foul up the results.

Another bias in the case study and survey methods is social desirability. That is, many people involved in research studies tend to tell the interviewer what they think the interviewer would like to hear and not what they really think. For example, if people brushed their teeth as often as they claimed, and used the amount of toothpaste they indicated, three times as much toothpaste would be sold in the United States than is actually sold. People also appear to overreport church attendance and to underreport abortions (Barringer, 1993). You can gain insight into whether you tend to express your genuine feelings or socially desirable answers by completing the nearby Social-Desirability Scale.

Naturalistic Observation   You use **naturalistic observation**—that is, you observe people in their natural habitats—every day. So do psychologists and other scientists. Naturalistic observation has the advantage of allowing psychologists and other scientists to observe behavior where it happens, or "in the field." Observers use *unobtrusive* measures to avoid interfering with the behaviors they are observing. For example, Jane Goodall has observed the behavior of chimpanzees in their natural environment to learn about their social behavior, sexual behavior, use of tools, and other facts of chimp life. Her observations have shown us that (1) we were incorrect to think that only humans use tools; and (2) kissing on the lips, as a greeting, is apparently used by chimpanzees as well as by humans (Goodall, 2000).

reflect & relate
Why not try out the naturalistic observation method for yourself? The next time you eat at a fast-food restaurant, look around. Pick out slender people and overweight people and note whether they eat differently—even when they select the same foods. Do overweight people eat more rapidly? Do they chew less frequently? Do they leave less food on their plates? What conclusions can you draw?

Naturalistic observation A scientific method in which organisms are observed in their natural environments.

■ **The Naturalistic-Observation Method**
Jane Goodall has observed the behavior of chimpanzees—our closest genetic relatives—in the field, "where it happens." She has found that chimps use sticks to grub for food, and that they apparently kiss each other as a social greeting. Scientists who use this method try not to interfere with the animals or people they observe, even though this sometimes means allowing an animal to be mistreated by other animals or to die from a curable illness.

Karl Ammann /Corbis

Self-Assessment

Dare You Say What You Think? The Social-Desirability Scale

One of the problems researchers encounter during surveys and case studies is that of social desirability. That is, people being interviewed may tell the researcher what they think the researcher wants to hear and not what they really believe. In doing so, they may provide the so-called socially desirable answer—the answer they believe will earn the approval of the researcher. Falling prey to social desirability may cause us to distort our beliefs and experiences in interviews and psychological tests. The bias toward responding in socially desirable directions is a source of error in the case study and survey methods.

What about you? Do you say what you think, or do you tend to misrepresent your beliefs to earn the approval of others? Do you answer questions honestly, or do you say what you think other people want to hear?

You can complete the Social-Desirability Scale devised by Crowne and Marlowe to gain insight into whether you have a tendency to produce socially desirable responses.

Directions:

Read each item and decide whether it is true (T) or false (F) for you. Try to work rapidly and answer each question by circling the T or the F. Then turn to the scoring key in the appendix to interpret your answers.

- T F **1.** Before voting, I thoroughly investigate the qualifications of all the candidates.
- T F **2.** I never hesitate to go out of my way to help someone in trouble.
- T F **3.** It is sometimes hard for me to go on with my work if I am not encouraged.
- T F **4.** I have never intensely disliked anyone.
- T F **5.** On occasions I have had doubts about my ability to succeed in life.
- T F **6.** I sometimes feel resentful when I don't get my way.
- T F **7.** I am always careful about my manner of dress.
- T F **8.** My table manners at home are as good as when I eat out in a restaurant.
- T F **9.** If I could get into a movie without paying and be sure I was not seen, I would probably do it.
- T F **10.** On a few occasions, I have given up something because I thought too little of my ability.
- T F **11.** I like to gossip at times.
- T F **12.** There have been times when I felt like rebelling against people in authority even though I knew they were right.
- T F **13.** No matter who I'm talking to, I'm always a good listener.

- T F **14.** I can remember "playing sick" to get out of something.
- T F **15.** There have been occasions when I have taken advantage of someone.
- T F **16.** I'm always willing to admit it when I make a mistake.
- T F **17.** I always try to practice what I preach.
- T F **18.** I don't find it particularly difficult to get along with loudmouthed, obnoxious people.
- T F **19.** I sometimes try to get even rather than forgive and forget.
- T F **20.** When I don't know something I don't mind at all admitting it.
- T F **21.** I am always courteous, even to people who are disagreeable.
- T F **22.** At times I have really insisted on having things my own way.
- T F **23.** There have been occasions when I felt like smashing things.
- T F **24.** I would never think of letting someone else be punished for my wrongdoings.
- T F **25.** I never resent being asked to return a favor.
- T F **26.** I have never been irked when people expressed ideas very different from my own.
- T F **27.** I never make a long trip without checking the safety of my car.
- T F **28.** There have been times when I was quite jealous of the good fortune of others.
- T F **29.** I have almost never felt the urge to tell someone off.
- T F **30.** I am sometimes irritated by people who ask favors of me.
- T F **31.** I have never felt that I was punished without cause.
- T F **32.** I sometimes think when people have a misfortune they only got what they deserved.
- T F **33.** I have never deliberately said something that hurt someone's feelings.

SOURCE: "A New Scale of Social Desirability Independent of Pathology," by D. P. Crowne and D. A. Marlowe, 1960, *Journal of Consulting Psychology*, 24, p. 351. Copyright 1960 by the American Psychological Association. Reprinted by permission.

Go to www
http://academic.cengage.com/psychology/rathus
where you can fill out an interactive version of this Self-Assessment and automatically score your results.

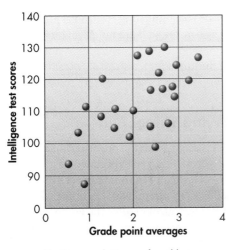

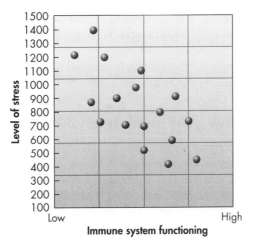

Positive correlation, as found between intelligence and academic achievement

Negative correlation, as found between stress and functioning of the immune system

Figure 1.6
Positive and Negative Correlations
When there is a positive correlation between variables, as there is between intelligence and achievement, one increases as the other increases. By and large, the higher people score on intelligence tests, the better their academic performance is likely to be, as in the diagram on the left. (Each dot represents an individual's intelligence test score and grade point average.) But there is a negative correlation between stress and health. As the amount of stress we experience increases, the functioning of our immune system tends to decrease. Correlational research may suggest but does not demonstrate cause and effect.

■ Correlation: On How Things Go Together—Or Not

Are people with higher intelligence more likely to do well in school? Are people with a stronger need for achievement likely to climb higher up the corporate ladder? What is the relationship between stress and health?

Such questions are often answered by the mathematical method of correlation. *What is the correlational method?* Correlation follows observation. By using the correlational method, psychologists investigate whether observed behavior or a measured trait is related to, or correlated with, another. Consider the variables of intelligence and academic performance. These variables are assigned numbers such as intelligence test scores and academic averages. Then the numbers are mathematically related and expressed as a **correlation coefficient.** A correlation coefficient is a number that varies between +1.00 and −1.00.

Studies report **positive correlations** between intelligence test scores and academic achievement, as measured, for example, by grade point averages. Generally speaking, the higher people score on intelligence tests, the better their academic performance is likely to be. The scores attained on intelligence tests tend to be positively correlated (about +0.60 to +0.70) with academic achievement (see the first panel in Figure 1.6). But factors *other* than performance on intelligence tests also contribute to academic success. These include achievement motivation and adjustment.

Many correlations are *negative;* that is, as one variable increases, the other variable decreases. There is a **negative correlation** between stress and health. As the amount of stress affecting us increases, the functioning of our immune system decreases (see Figure 1.6). Under high levels of stress, many people show poorer health.

What kinds of correlations (positive or negative) would you expect to find among behavior patterns such as the following: Churchgoing and crime? Language ability and musical ability? Level of education and incidence of teenage pregnancy? Grades in school and delinquency? Why?

Correlational research may suggest but does not prove cause and effect. For example, it may seem logical to assume that high intelligence makes it possible for children to profit from education. Research has also shown, however, that education contributes to higher

Correlational method A mathematical method of determining whether one variable increases or decreases as another variable increases or decreases. For example, there is a correlation between intelligence test scores and grades in school.

Correlation coefficient A number between + 1.00 and − 1.00 that expresses the strength and direction (positive or negative) of the relationship between two variables.

Positive correlation A relationship between variables in which one variable increases as the other also increases.

Negative correlation A relationship between two variables in which one variable increases as the other decreases.

scores on intelligence tests. Preschoolers who are placed in stimulating Head Start programs later attain higher scores on intelligence tests than age-mates who did not have this experience. The relationship between intelligence and academic performance may not be as simple as we might think (see Figure 1.7). What of the link between stress and health? Does stress impair health, or is it possible that people in poorer health encounter more stress?

◾ The Experimental Method: Trying Things Out

What is the experimental method? Most psychologists agree that the preferred method for answering questions about cause and effect is the experiment. In an **experiment,** a group of subjects receives a **treatment,** such as a dose of alcohol, a change in room temperature, perhaps an injection of a drug. The subjects are then observed carefully to determine whether the treatment makes a difference in their behavior. Does alcohol alter the ability to take tests, for example? What about differences in room temperatures and level of background noise?

Experiments are used when possible because they allow psychologists to control the experiences of subjects and draw conclusions about cause and effect. A psychologist may theorize that alcohol leads to aggression because it reduces fear of consequences. She or he may then hypothesize that a treatment in which subjects receive a specified dosage of alcohol will lead to increases in aggression. Let us follow the example of the effects of alcohol on aggression to further our understanding of the experimental method.

Independent and Dependent Variables   In an experiment to determine whether alcohol causes aggression, subjects are given an amount of alcohol and its effects are measured. In this case, alcohol is an **independent variable.** The presence of an independent variable is manipulated by the experimenters so that its effects may be determined. The independent variable of alcohol may be administered at different levels, or doses, from none or very little to enough to cause intoxication or drunkenness.

The measured results, or outcomes, in an experiment are called **dependent variables.** The presence of dependent variables presumably depends on the independent variables. In an experiment to determine whether alcohol influences aggression, aggressive behavior would be a dependent variable. Other dependent variables of interest might include sexual

Experiment A scientific method that seeks to confirm cause-and-effect relationships by introducing independent variables and observing their effects on dependent variables.

Treatment In experiments, a condition received by subjects so that its effects may be observed.

Independent variable A condition in a scientific study that is manipulated so that its effects may be observed.

Dependent variable A measure of an assumed effect of an independent variable.

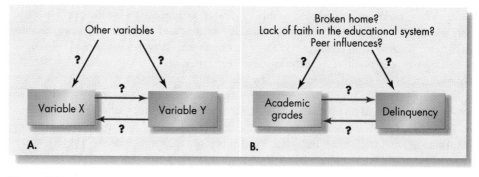

Figure 1.7
Correlational Relationships, Cause, and Effect
Correlational relationships may suggest but do not demonstrate cause and effect. In part A, there is a correlation between variables X and Y. Does this mean that either variable X causes variable Y or that variable Y causes variable X? Not necessarily. Other factors could affect both variables X and Y. Consider the examples of academic grades (variable X) and juvenile delinquency (variable Y) in part B. There is a negative correlation between the two. Does this mean that poor grades contribute to delinquency? Perhaps. Does it mean that delinquency contributes to poor grades? Again, perhaps. But there could also be other variables—such as a broken home, lack of faith in the educational system, or peer influences—that contribute both to poor grades and delinquency.

arousal, visual-motor coordination, and performance on cognitive tasks such as defining words.

In an experiment on the relationships between temperature and aggression, temperature would be an independent variable and aggressive behavior would be a dependent variable. We could set temperatures from below freezing to blistering hot, and study its effects on aggression. We could also use a second independent variable such as social provocation; we could insult some subjects but not others and see whether insults affect their level of aggression. This method would allow us to study the ways in which two independent variables—temperature and social provocation—affect aggression, by themselves and together.

We also need to specify what we will be measuring as aggressive behavior. In the experimental setting, pressing a lever to deliver an electric shock to another person is a useful definition of aggression, because the lever need not actually be connected to anything.

Experimental and Control Groups   Ideal experiments use "experimental groups" and "control groups." Subjects in **experimental groups** obtain the treatment. Members of **control groups** do not. Every effort is made to ensure that all other conditions are held constant for both groups. This method enhances the researchers' ability to draw conclusions about cause and effect. The researchers can be more confident that outcomes of the experiment are caused by the treatments and not by chance factors or chance fluctuations in behavior.

For example, in an experiment on the effects of alcohol on aggression, members of the experimental group would ingest alcohol, and members of the control group would not. The researcher would then measure how much aggression was expressed by each group.

Blinds and Double Blinds   One classic experiment on the effects of alcohol on aggression (Boyatzis, 1974) reported that men at parties where beer and liquor were served acted more aggressively than men at parties where only soft drinks were served. But subjects in the experimental group *knew* they had drunk alcohol, and those in the control group *knew* they had not. Aggression that appeared to result from alcohol might thus have reflected the subjects' *expectations* about the effects of alcohol. People tend to act in stereotypical ways when they believe they have been drinking alcohol. For instance, men tend to become less anxious in social situations, more aggressive, and more sexually aroused. To what extent do these behavior patterns reflect the direct effects of alcohol on the body, and to what extent do they affect people's *beliefs* about the effects of alcohol?

In medicine, physicians sometimes give patients **placebos** (a fake treatment, often sugar pills, that has the appearance of being genuine) when the patient insists on a medical cure but the physician does not believe that one is necessary. When patients report that placebos have helped them, it is because they expected the pills to be of help and not because of the biochemical effects of the pills. Placebos are not limited to pills made of sugar. As we will see, subjects in psychological experiments can be given placebos such as tonic water, but if the subjects think they have drunk alcohol, we can conclude that changes in their behavior stem from their beliefs about the effects of alcohol, not from the alcohol itself.

Well-designed experiments control for the effects of expectations by creating conditions under which subjects are unaware of, or **blind** to, the treatment. Placebos are one way of keeping subjects blind to whether they have received a treatment. Yet researchers may also have expectations. They may be "rooting for" a certain treatment. For example, tobacco company executives may wish to show that cigarette smoking is harmless. In such cases, it is useful if the people measuring the experimental outcomes are unaware of which subjects have received the treatment. Studies in which neither the subjects nor the experimenters know who has obtained the treatment are called **double-blind studies.**

◆ **Truth or Fiction Revisited:** It is true that neither the subjects nor the researchers know who is receiving the real treatment in many experiments. For example, the Food and Drug Administration requires double-blind studies before it allows the marketing of new drugs. The drug and the placebo look and taste alike. Experimenters assign the drug or placebo to subjects at random. Neither the subjects nor the observers know who is taking the drug and who is taking the placebo. After the final measurements have been made, a

Experimental groups In experiments, groups whose members obtain the treatment.

Control groups In experiments, groups whose members do not obtain the treatment, while other conditions are held constant.

Placebo A bogus treatment that has the appearance of being genuine.

Blind In experimental terminology, unaware of whether or not one has received a treatment.

Double-blind study A study in which neither the subjects nor the observers know who has received the treatment.

AP/Wide World Photos

■ **What Are the Effects of Alcohol?**
Psychologists have conducted numerous studies to determine the effects of alcohol. Questions have been raised about the soundness of research in which people *know* that they have drunk alcohol. Why would such research be questioned, and how can we keep people blind to the fact that they have drunk alcohol?

neutral panel (a group of people who have no personal stake in the outcome of the study) judges whether the effects of the drug differed from those of the placebo.

In one classic double-blind study on the effects of alcohol, Alan Lang and his colleagues (1975) pretested a cocktail of vodka and tonic water to make certain that it could not be discriminated by taste from tonic water alone. They recruited college male social drinkers as subjects. Some of the men drank vodka and tonic water. Others drank tonic water only. Of those who drank vodka, half were misled into believing they had drunk tonic water only (see Figure 1.8). Of those who drank tonic water only, half were misled into believing their drink contained vodka. Thus, half the subjects were blind to their treatment. Experimenters who measured the men's aggressive responses were also blind concerning which subjects had drunk vodka.

The research team found that men who believed that they had drunk vodka responded "more aggressively" (that is, they chose a higher level of shock and pressed a lever to deliver it) to a provocation than men who believed that they had drunk tonic water only. The actual content of the drink was immaterial. That is, the men's *belief* about what they drank affected their aggressive behavior more than what they actually consumed. The results of the Lang study differ dramatically from those reported by Boyatzis, perhaps be-cause the Boyatzis study did not control for the effects of expectations or beliefs about alcohol.

■ Ethics of Research with Humans

If the Lang group were running their experiment today rather than in the 1970s, they might have been denied permission to do so by a university ethics review committee. Why? Because the researchers in the Lang study gave some participants alcohol to drink and deceived the entire group about the purposes and methods of the study. Was their method **ethical?**

We'll return to this question, but let's first address a broader one. *What ethical issues affect research and practice with humans?*

Psychologists adhere to a number of ethical standards that are intended to promote individual dignity, human welfare, and scientific integrity. The standards are also intended to ensure that psychologists do not engage in harmful research methods or treatments. Because in virtually all institutional settings, including colleges, hospitals, and research foundations, ethics review committees help researchers consider the potential harm of their methods and review proposed studies according to ethical guidelines. When the committees find that proposed research might be unacceptably harmful to subjects, they may withhold approval. The committees also weigh the potential benefits of the research against the potential harm.

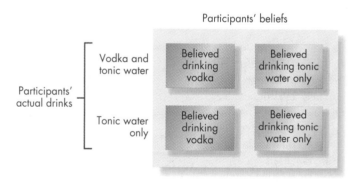

Participants' beliefs

Participants' actual drinks

Vodka and tonic water — Believed drinking vodka | Believed drinking tonic water only

Tonic water only — Believed drinking vodka | Believed drinking tonic water only

Figure 1.8
The Experimental Conditions in the Lang Study
The taste of vodka cannot be discerned when vodka is mixed with tonic water. For this reason, it was possible for subjects in the Lang study on the effects of alcohol to be kept "blind" as to whether or not they had actually drunk alcohol. Blind studies allow psychologists to control for the effects of subjects' expectations.

Today individuals must provide **informed consent** before they participate in research (American Psychological Association, 2002). A general overview of the research and the opportunity to choose not to participate apparently gives potential participants a sense of control and decreases stress (Sieber, 2004). Is there a way in which subjects in the Lang study could have provided informed consent? What do you think?

Psychologists keep the records of research subjects and clients confidential because they respect people's privacy and because people are more likely to express their true thoughts and feelings when researchers or therapists keep them confidential (Smith, 2003a, 2003c). Sometimes conflicts of interest arise, as when a client threatens to harm someone and the psychologist feels obligated to warn the victim (Follingstad & McCormick, 2002).

Some studies could not be carried out if subjects knew what the researchers were trying to learn, or which treatment they had received (e.g., a new medicine or a sugar pill). As you can imagine, psychologists have long debated the ethics of deceiving subjects. According to the American Psychological Association's (2002) *Ethical Principles of Psychologists and Code of Conduct*, psychologists may use deception only when they believe the benefits of the research outweigh its potential harm, when they believe the individuals might have been willing to participate if they had understood the benefits of the research, and when subjects are **debriefed.** Debriefing means that the purposes and methods of the research are explained afterward.

Return to the Lang (Lang et al., 1975) study on alcohol and aggression. In this study, the researchers (1) misinformed subjects about the beverage they were drinking and (2) misled them into believing they were giving other subjects electric shock when they were actually pressing switches on an unconnected control board. (*Aggression,* as explained earlier, was defined as pressing these switches.) In the study, students who believed they had drunk vodka selected higher levels of shock than students who believed they had not.

◀━■━ Ethics of Research with Animals

Psychologists and other scientists may use animals to conduct research that cannot be carried out with humans (Carroll & Overmier, 2001). For example, experiments on the effects of early separation from the mother have been done with monkeys and other animals. Such research has helped psychologists investigate the formation of attachment bonds between parent and child.

What ethical issues affect research with animals? Experiments with infant monkeys highlight some of the ethical issues faced by psychologists and other scientists who contemplate potentially harmful research. Psychologists and biologists who study the workings of the brain destroy sections of the brains of laboratory animals to learn how they influence behavior. For example, a lesion in one part of a brain structure causes a rat to overeat. A lesion elsewhere causes the rat to go on a crash diet. Psychologists generalize to humans from experiments such as these in the hope of finding solutions to problems such as eating disorders. Proponents of the use of animals in research argue that many advances in medicine and psychology could not have taken place without them (Bekoff, 2002). For example, we would know less about how drugs affect tumors or the brain.

According to the ethical guidelines of the American Psychological Association, animals may be harmed only when there is no alternative and when researchers believe that the benefits of the research justify the harm (American Psychological Association, 2002; Smith, 2003b, 2003c).

Now that we have an overview of psychology as a science, we will move on to the connections between psychology and biology in Chapter 2. Psychologists assume that our behaviors and our mental processes are related to biological events. In Chapter 2 we consider the evidence for this assumption.

What do you think? Was it ethical to deceive participants in the Lang study as to what they were drinking? Why or why not?

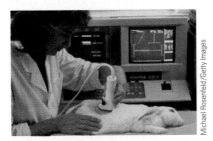

Michael Rosenfeld/Getty Images

■ **The Ethics of Using Animals in Research**
Is it ethical for researchers to harm animals to obtain knowledge that may benefit humans?

Ethical Referring to one's system of deriving standards for determining what is moral.

Informed consent A subject's agreement to participate in research after receiving information about the purposes of the study and the nature of the treatments.

Debrief To explain the purposes and methods of a completed procedure to a participant.

◯ Learning Connections

◀◀   *How Psychologists Study Behavior and Mental Processes*   ▶▶

Learning Connections

REVIEW:

11 The central idea in critical thinking is
 (a) skepticism,
 (b) challenging authority figures,
 (c) creating a hypothesis,
 (d) following tradition.

12 In a _____ sample, each member of a population has an equal chance of being asked to participate.
 (a) stratified,
 (b) random,
 (c) multicultural,
 (d) blind.

13 In the _____, a large number of people answer questions about attitudes or behavior.
 (a) field,
 (b) case study,
 (c) survey,
 (d) anecdote.

14 Correlational research does not reveal
 (a) the identities of subjects,
 (b) the purposes of the research to participants,
 (c) the natural habitat of the subjects,
 (d) cause and effect.

15 In experiments, blinds are used to defeat the effects of
 (a) expectations,
 (b) the selection factor,
 (c) volunteer bias,
 (d) the scientific method.

16 _____ standards help promote the dignity of the individual and protect subjects or clients from harm.
 (a) Scientific,
 (b) Research,
 (c) Committee,
 (d) Ethical.

CRITICAL THINKING:
People who exercise are generally healthier than people who do not. Does this fact show that exercise is a causal factor in good health? Why or why not?

Go to www
http://academic.cengage.com/psychology/rathus
for an interactive version of this review.

RECITE—*An Active Summary*™

Recite to Go!   *Don't have time to study right now? You can study on the go!*
Go to your companion website and download an audio version of this review section to your media player. You can also access an interactive flash-card version of this review from your website.

| 1. What is psychology? | Psychology is the scientific study of behavior and mental processes. Psychology seeks to describe, explain, predict, and control behavior and mental processes. |
| 2. What do psychologists do? | Psychologists engage in research, practice, and teaching. Clinical, health, and counseling psychologists help people optimize their psychological and physical health. School and educational psychologists enhance educational processes. Industrial and organizational psychologists improve the functioning of businesses and organizations. Person- |

ality, social, developmental, and experimental psychologists are mainly involved in research.

3. Who were some of the ancient contributors to psychology?	The ancient Greek philosopher Aristotle declared that people are motivated to seek pleasure and avoid pain. Democritus suggested that we could think of behavior in terms of a body and a mind and raised the question of whether there is free will. Socrates advised, "Know thyself."
4. What is structuralism?	Structuralism, founded by Wilhelm Wundt, used introspection to study the objective and subjective elements of experience.
5. What is functionalism?	Functionalism, founded by William James, dealt with behavior as well as conscious experience and focused on the importance of habit.
6. What is behaviorism?	Behaviorism, founded by John B. Watson, argues that psychology must limit itself to observable behavior and not attempt to deal with consciousness. B. F. Skinner introduced the concept of reinforcement.
7. What is Gestalt psychology?	Gestalt psychology, founded by Wertheimer, Koffka, and Köhler, is concerned with perception and argues that the wholeness of human experience is more than the sum of its parts.
8. What is psychoanalysis?	Psychoanalysis, founded by Sigmund Freud, asserts that people are driven by hidden impulses and distort reality to protect themselves from anxiety.
9. What is the evolutionary perspective?	The evolutionary perspective is based on the work of Charles Darwin, who argued that in the age-old struggle for survival, only the "fittest" organisms reach maturity and reproduce, thereby transmitting the traits that enable them to survive to their offspring.
10. What is the biological perspective?	The biological perspective studies the links between behavior and mental processes on the one hand, and heredity, the nervous system, and the endocrine system on the other.
11. What is the cognitive perspective?	The cognitive perspective is concerned with the ways in which we mentally represent the world and process information.
12. What is the humanistic–existential perspective?	Humanistic–existential psychologists stress the importance of subjective experience and assert that people have the freedom to make choices.
13. What are the two major perspectives on learning?	The key perspectives on learning are the behavioral perspective and the social-cognitive perspective. Behaviorism focuses on environmental influences on learning. Social-cognitive theory argues that psychologists can address cognition, that people engage in intentional learning, and that people are free to modify and create environments.
14. What is the sociocultural perspective?	The sociocultural perspective focuses on the roles of ethnicity, gender, culture, and socioeconomic status in behavior and mental processes.
15. What is critical thinking?	Skepticism is the hallmark of critical thinking. Critical thinking means insisting on evidence and analyzing arguments. It involves examining the definitions of terms, examining the premises or assumptions behind arguments, and scrutinizing the logic with which arguments are developed. Critical thinkers are cautious in drawing conclusions from evidence. They do not oversimplify or overgeneralize.
16. What is the scientific method?	The scientific method is an organized way of expanding and refining knowledge. Psychologists reach conclusions about their hypotheses on the basis of their research observations.
17. How do psychologists use samples to represent populations?	A sample is a part of a population. Samples must represent the population they are to reflect. In a *random sample*, each member of a population has an equal chance of be-

	ing selected to participate. A *stratified sample* is selected so that known subgroups in the population are represented proportionately in the sample.
18. What methods of observation are used by psychologists?	Case studies gather information about the lives of individuals. The survey method uses interviews, questionnaires, or public records to gather information that cannot be observed directly. The naturalistic observation method observes behavior "in the field."
19. What is the correlational method?	The correlational method is a means of showing whether variables are independent or vary with one another. Correlations can be positive or negative, varying between +1.00 (a perfect positive correlation) and −1.00 (a perfect negative correlation).
20. What is the experimental method?	Experiments are used to reveal cause and effect. Experimental groups receive a treatment, whereas control groups do not. Blinds may be used to control for the expectations of subjects and researchers.
21. What ethical issues affect research and practice with humans?	The ethical standards of psychologists are intended to protect subjects in research and clients in practice from harm. Ethics review committees judge the harmfulness of proposed research and help make it less harmful. Human subjects are required to give informed consent prior to participating in research and are debriefed afterward.
22. What ethical issues affect research with animals?	Some research can be conducted only with animals. Ethical standards require that animals may be harmed only if there is no alternative and if the benefits justify the harm.

Key Terms

Psychology   4
Theory   4
Pure research   5
Applied research   5
Introspection   7
Structuralism   8
Functionalism   8
Behaviorism   9
Reinforcement   9
Gestalt psychology   9
Insight   10
Psychoanalysis   11
Psychodynamic   11
Genes   14
Instinctive   14
Cognitive   14
Humanism   14

Existentialism   14
Social-cognitive theory   15
Sociocultural perspective   15
Ethnic group   15
Gender   16
Correlation   21
Hypothesis   21
Selection factor   22
Replicate   22
Generalize   22
Sample   22
Population   22
Random sample   23
Stratified sample   23
Volunteer bias   23
Case study   24
Survey   24

Naturalistic observation   25
Correlation coefficient   27
Positive correlation   27
Negative correlation   27
Experiment   28
Treatment   28
Independent variable   28
Dependent variable   28
Experimental groups   29
Control groups   29
Placebo   29
Blind   29
Double-blind study   29
Ethical   30
Informed consent   30
Debrief   31

Active Learning Resources

Visit Your Companion Website
for This Book

http://academic.cengage.com/psychology/rathus

Check out this companion website where you will find online resources directly linked to your book. This is where you'll access the videos highlighted in your Video Connections feature. You can answer the questions online and email them to your professor. In addition you'll find downloadable audio review material, interactive versions of the study aids, Power Visuals for mastering and reviewing key concepts, as well as quizzing, and much more!

CENGAGENOW™

http://academic.cengage.com

Need help studying? This site is your one-stop study shop. Take a Pre-Test and Cengage NOW will generate a Personalized Study Plan based on your test results. The Study Plan will identify the topics you need to review and direct you to online resources to help you master those topics. You can then take a Post-Test to help you determine the concepts you have mastered and what you still need to work on. In addition you can access interactive media including the videos highlighted in your Video Connections box.

Author Blog

What does your author Spence Rathus have to say about the state of psychology? Visit your companion website every Tuesday and click on "Author Blog." This is where he'll talk about the most recent controversies and hot topics in psychology. This will keep you up to date with what your author is thinking and give you great insight into modern psychology.

CHAPTER 2

Biology and Psychology

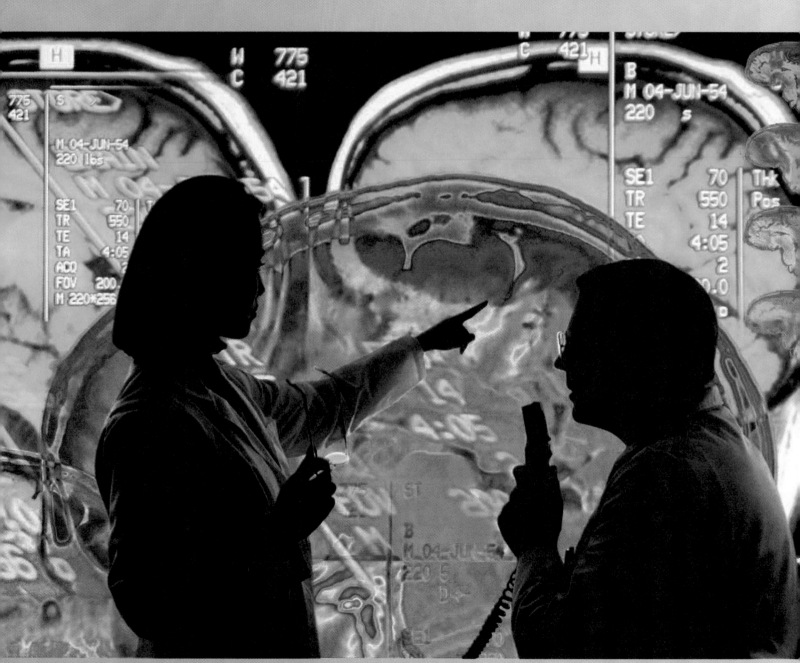

Pete Saloutos/Corbis

T	F	The human brain is larger than that of any other animal.
T	F	A single cell can stretch all the way from your spine to your toe.
T	F	Messages travel in the brain by means of electricity.
T	F	A brain cell can send out hundreds of messages each second—and manage to catch some rest in between.
T	F	Fear can give you indigestion.
T	F	If a surgeon were to stimulate a certain part of your brain electrically, you might swear that someone had stroked your leg.
T	F	A hormone turns a disinterested male rodent into a doting father.
T	F	Charles Darwin was nearly excluded from the voyage that led to the development of his theory of evolution because the captain of the ship did not like the shape of his nose.
T	F	Your genetic code overlaps 25% with that of a carrot.
T	F	Neanderthals are not necessarily extinct; they may be lurking in your genes.

Go to www
http://academic.cengage.com/pstchology/rathus
for an interactive version of this Truth or Fiction feature

"Gage is no longer Gage," said those who had known him before the accident.

There are many key characters in the history of psychology, and some of them did not arrive there intentionally. One of these was a promising railroad worker who was helping our young nation stretch from coast to coast. His name was Phineas Gage. Gage was highly admired by his friends and his coworkers. But all that changed one day in 1848. While he was tamping down the blasting powder for a dynamite charge, Gage accidentally set the powder off. The inch-thick metal tamping rod shot upward through his cheek and brain and out the top of his head.

If the trajectory of the rod had been slightly different, Gage would have died. Although Gage fell back in a heap, he was miraculously alive. His coworkers watched in shock as he stood up a few moments later and spoke. While the local doctor marveled at the hole through Gage's head, Gage asked when he'd be able to return to work. Two months later, Gage's external wounds had healed, but the psychological aspects of the wound were now obvious. His former employer, who had regarded him as "the most efficient and capable foreman in their employ previous to his injury" (Harlow, 1868), refused to rehire him because he had changed so much:

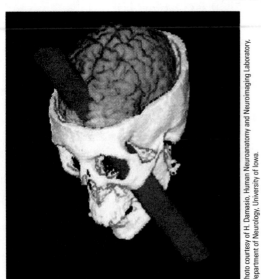

■ **Phineas Gage**
The railroad worker survived an accident in which a metal tamping rod shot through his head. But the brain damage affected his personality.
From H. Damasio, T. Grabowski, R. Frank, A. M. Galaburda, and A. R. Damasio, "The Return of Phineas Gage: Clues about the Brain from a Famous Patient, *Science*, 264:1102–1105. © 1994. American Association for the Advancement of Science. Reprinted with permission.

The equilibrium or balance, so to speak, between his intellectual faculties and animal propensities, seems to have been destroyed. He is . . . irreverent, indulging at times in the grossest profanity (which was not previously his custom). [He showed little consideration for other people, was] impatient of restraint or advice when it conflicts with his desires . . . obstinate, yet capricious and vacillating, devising many plans of future operation, which are no sooner arranged than they are abandoned in turn for others . . . But all had not been lost in Gage's brain. In fact, many of his intellectual skills were just fine, apparently untouched.

Harlow (1868)

Generations of researchers—psychologists, physicians, biologists, neuroscientists—have wondered how the changes in Gage's personality might have been caused by the damage to his brain. Perhaps the trajectory of the rod spared parts of the frontal lobes that are involved in language and movement but damaged areas connected with personality and emotional response (Damasio, 2000; Wagar & Thagard, 2004).

In this chapter, we will learn about the frontal lobes of the brain and much more. We will travel from the small to the large—from the microscopic brain cells that hold and transmit information, to the visible structures that provide the basis for functions such as memory, speech, sensation, thought, planning, and voluntary movement.

THE NERVOUS SYSTEM: ON BEING WIRED

As a child, I did not think it was a good thing to have a "nervous" system. After all, if your system were not jittery, you might be less likely to jump at strange noises. Later I learned that a nervous system is not a system that is nervous. It is a system of nerves involved in thought processes, heartbeat, visual-motor coordination, and so on. The nervous system contains the brain, the spinal cord, and other parts that make it possible for us to receive information from the world outside and to act on that world.

I also learned that the human nervous system is more complex than that of any other animal and that our brains are larger than those of any other animal. Now, this last piece of business is not quite true. A human brain weighs about 3 pounds, but the brains of elephants and whales may be four times as heavy. ◆ **Truth or Fiction Revisited:** Thus it is not true that the human brain is larger than that of any other animal. Still, our brains account for a greater part of our body weight than do those of elephants or whales. Our brains weigh about 1/60th of our body weight. Elephant brains weigh about 1/1,000th of their total weight, and whale brains are a paltry 1/10,000th of their weight. So, humans win the brain-as-a-percentage-of-body-weight contest.

The brain is only one part of the nervous system. We will see that the nervous system serves as the material base for our behaviors, emotions, and cognitions (our thoughts, images, and plans). The nervous system is composed of cells, most of which are neurons, which is where we will begin our study of the nervous system.

—■— Neurons: Into the Fabulous Forest

Within our brains lies a fabulous forest of nerve cells, or neurons. ***What are neurons?*** **Neurons** are cells that can be visualized as having branches, trunks, and roots—something like trees. As we voyage through this forest, we see that many nerve cells lie alongside one another like a thicket of trees. But neurons can also lie end to end, with their "roots" intertwined with the "branches" of the neurons that lie below. Trees receive sunlight, water, and nutrients from the soil. Neurons receive "messages" from a number of sources such as light, other neurons, and pressure on the skin, and they can pass these messages along in a complex biological dance.

We are born with more than 100 billion neurons. Most of them are found in the brain. The nervous system also contains **glial cells.** Glial cells remove dead neurons and waste products from the nervous system, nourish and insulate neurons, and direct their growth. But neurons occupy center stage in the nervous system. The messages transmitted by neurons somehow account for phenomena ranging from the perception of an itch from a mosquito bite to the coordination of a skier's vision and muscles to the composition of a concerto to the solution of an algebraic equation.

Neurons vary according to their functions and their location. Neurons in the brain may be only a fraction of an inch in length, whereas others in the legs are several feet long. Most neurons include a cell body, dendrites, and an axon (see Figure 2.1). The cell body contains the core or *nucleus* of the cell. The nucleus uses oxygen and nutrients to generate the energy needed to carry out the work of the cell. Anywhere from a few to several hundred short fibers, or **dendrites,** extend like roots from the cell body to receive incoming messages from thousands of adjoining neurons. Each neuron has an **axon** that extends like a trunk from the cell body. Axons are very thin, but those that carry messages from the toes to the spinal cord extend several feet.

Like tree trunks, axons can branch off in different directions. Axons end in small bulb-shaped structures called *terminals* or *terminal buttons.* Neurons carry messages in one direction only: from the dendrites or cell body through the axon to the axon terminals. The messages are then transmitted from the terminal buttons to other neurons, muscles, or glands.

As a child matures, the axons of neurons become longer, and the dendrites and terminals proliferate, creating vast interconnected networks for the transmission of complex

Neuron A nerve cell.

Glial cells Cells that nourish and insulate neurons, direct their growth, and remove waste products from the nervous system.

Dendrites Rootlike structures, attached to the cell body of a neuron, that receive impulses from other neurons.

Axon A long, thin part of a neuron that transmits impulses to other neurons from branching structures called *terminal buttons.*

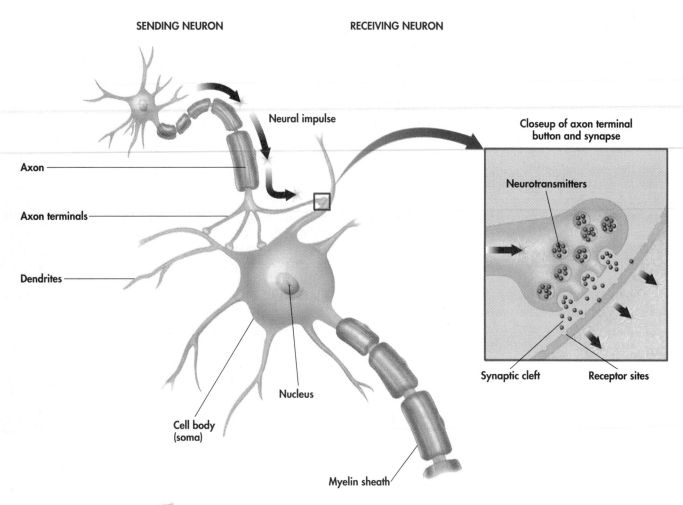

SENDING NEURON   RECEIVING NEURON

Neural impulse

Closeup of axon terminal
button and synapse

Axon

Axon terminals

Dendrites

Neurotransmitters

Synaptic cleft   Receptor sites

Nucleus

Cell body
(soma)

Myelin sheath

Go to your student
website to access
an interactive version
of this figure.

Figure 2.1
The Anatomy of a Neuron
"Messages" enter neurons through dendrites, are transmitted along the trunklike axon, and
then are sent from axon terminal buttons to muscles, glands, and other neurons. Axon terminal
buttons contain sacs of chemicals called *neurotransmitters*. Neurotransmitters are released
into the synaptic cleft, where many of them bind to receptor sites on the dendrites of the receiving neuron. Dozens of neurotransmitters have been identified.

messages. The number of glial cells also increases as the nervous system develops, contributing to its dense appearance.

Myelin: Miniature Bratwurst?   The axons of many neurons are wrapped tightly with
white, fatty **myelin** that makes them look like strings of sausages (bratwurst, actually) under the microscope. The fat insulates the axon from electrically charged atoms, or ions,
found in the fluids that surround the nervous system. The myelin sheath minimizes leakage
of the electrical current being carried along the axon, thereby allowing messages to be conducted more efficiently.

Myelination is part of the maturation process that leads to the child's ability to crawl
and walk during the first year. Infants are not physiologically "ready" to engage in visual–
motor coordination and other activities until the coating process reaches certain levels. In
people with the disease multiple sclerosis, myelin is replaced with a hard fibrous tissue that
throws off the timing of nerve impulses and disrupts muscular control.

Myelin   A fatty substance that encases
and insulates axons, facilitating transmission of neural impulses.

Afferent and Efferent Neurons: From There to Here and Here to There   If someone steps on your toes, the sensation is registered by receptors or sensory neurons near the

surface of your skin. Then it is transmitted to the spinal cord and brain through **afferent neurons,** which are perhaps two to three feet long. ◆ **Truth or Fiction Revisited**: Thus it is true that a single cell can stretch all the way from your spine to your toe. In the brain, subsequent messages might be conveyed by associative neurons that are only a few thousandths of an inch long. You experience the pain through this process and perhaps entertain some rather nasty thoughts about the perpetrator, who is now apologizing and begging for understanding. Long before you arrive at any logical conclusions, however, motor neurons (**efferent neurons**) send messages to your foot so that you withdraw it and begin an impressive hopping routine. Other efferent neurons stimulate glands so that your heart is beating more rapidly, you are sweating, and the hair on the back of your arms has become erect! Being a good sport, you say, "Oh, it's nothing." But considering all the neurons involved, it really is something, isn't it?

In case you think that afferent and efferent neurons will be hard to distinguish because they sound pretty much the SAME to you, remember that they *are* the "SAME." That is, *Sensory = Afferent*, and *Motor = Efferent.*

■ The Neural Impulse: Let Us "Sing the Body Electric" [1]

In the 18th century, the Italian physiologist Luigi Galvani (1737–1798) conducted a shocking experiment in a rainstorm. While his neighbors had the sense to remain indoors, Galvani and his wife were out on the porch connecting lightning rods to the heads of dissected frogs whose legs were connected by wires to a well of water. When lightning blazed above, the frogs' muscles contracted. This is not a recommended way to prepare frogs' legs. Galvani was demonstrating that the messages (**neural impulses**) that travel along neurons are electrochemical in nature.

What are neural impulses? Neural impulses are messages that travel within neurons at somewhere between 2 (in nonmyelinated neurons) and 225 miles an hour (in myelinated neurons). This speed is not impressive when compared with that of an electrical current in a toaster oven or a lamp, which can travel at close to the speed of light—over 186,000 miles per second. Distances in the body are short, however, and a message will travel from a toe to the brain in perhaps 1/50th of a second.

An Electrochemical Voyage (No Tickets Needed, Just "Charges")   The process by which neural impulses travel is electrochemical. Chemical changes take place within neurons that cause an electrical charge to be transmitted along their lengths. Neurons and body fluids contain ions—positively or negatively charged atoms. In a resting state—that is, when a neuron is not being stimulated by its neighbors—negatively charged chloride (Cl^-) ions are plentiful within the neuron, contributing to an overall negative charge in relation to the outside. The difference in electrical charge readies (**polarizes**) a neuron for firing by creating an internal negative charge in relation to the body fluid outside the cell membrane. The electrical potential across the neural membrane when it is not responding to other neurons—its **resting potential**—is about −70 millivolts in relation to the body fluid outside the cell membrane.

When an area on the surface of the resting neuron is adequately stimulated by other neurons, the cell membrane in the area changes its permeability to allow positively charged sodium ions to enter. Thus the area of entry becomes positively charged, or **depolarized** with respect to the outside (see Figure 2.2A). The permeability of the cell membrane then changes again, allowing no more sodium ions to enter (see Figure 2.2B).

The electrical impulse that provides the basis for the conduction of a neural impulse along an axon of a neuron is termed its **action potential.** The inside of the cell axon at the disturbed area has an action potential of 110 millivolts. This action potential, added to the −70 millivolts that characterize the resting potential, brings the membrane voltage to a positive charge of about +30 to +40 millivolts (see Figure 2.3). This inner change causes the next section of the cell to become permeable to sodium ions. At the same time, other

Afferent neurons Neurons that transmit messages from sensory receptors to the spinal cord and brain. Also called *sensory neurons.*

Efferent neurons Neurons that transmit messages from the brain or spinal cord to muscles and glands. Also called *motor neurons.*

Neural impulse The electrochemical discharge of a nerve cell, or neuron.

Polarize To ready a neuron for firing by creating an internal negative charge in relation to the body fluid outside the cell membrane.

Resting potential The electrical potential across the neural membrane when it is not responding to other neurons.

Depolarize To reduce the resting potential of a cell membrane from about −70 millivolts toward zero.

Action potential The electrical impulse that provides the basis for the conduction of a neural impulse along an axon of a neuron.

---

[1] From Walt Whitman's *Leaves of Grass.*

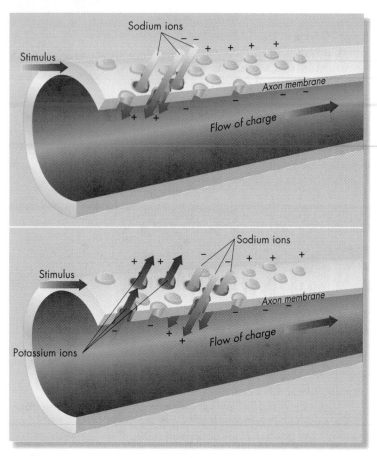

A. During an action potential, sodium gates in the neuron membrane open and sodium ions enter the axon, bringing a positive charge with them.

B. After an action potential occurs, the sodium gates close at that point, and open at the next point along the axon. When the sodium gates close, potassium gates open and potassium ions flow out of the axon, carrying a positive charge with them.

Figure 2.2

The Neural Impulse

When a section of a neuron is stimulated by other neurons, the cell membrane becomes permeable to sodium ions so that an action potential of about 40 millivolts is induced. This action potential is transmitted along the axon. The neuron fires according to the all-or-none principle.

positively charged (potassium) ions are being pumped out of the area of the cell that was previously affected, which returns the area to its resting potential. In this way, the neural impulse is transmitted continuously along an axon. Because the impulse is created anew as it progresses, its strength does not change.

◆ **Truth or Fiction Revisited:** Thus it is true that messages travel in the brain by means of electricity. These are messages *within* neurons. Communication *between* neurons, however, is carried out quite differently.

Firing: How Messages Voyage from Neuron to Neuron   The conduction of the neural impulse along the length of a neuron is what is meant by *firing*. When a rifle fires, it sends a bullet speeding through its barrel and discharges it at more than 1,000 feet per second. *What happens when a neuron fires?* Neurons also fire, but instead of a barrel, a neuron has an axon. Instead of discharging a bullet, it releases neurotransmitters.

Some neurons fire in less than 1/1,000th of a second. When they fire, neurons transmit messages to other neurons, muscles, or glands. However, neurons will not fire unless the incoming messages combine to reach a certain strength, which is defined as the *threshold* at which a neuron will fire. A weak message may cause a temporary shift in electrical charge at some point along the cell membrane, but this charge will dissipate if the neuron is not stimulated to its threshold.

Not only can a neuron fire in less than 1/1000th of a second, but a neuron may also transmit several hundred messages each second. Every time a neuron fires, it transmits an impulse of the same strength. This occurrence is known as the **all-or-none principle.** That

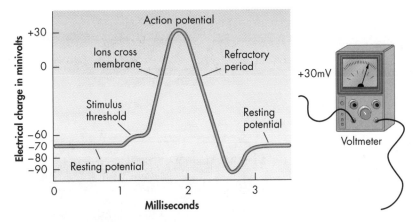

Figure 2.3

Changes in Electrical Charges as a Neural Impulse Is Transmitted Across an Axon
The resting potential of a segment of a cell axon is about −70 millivolts. But the inside of the cell axon at the disturbed area has an action potential of about 110 millivolts. When we add this figure to the −70 millivolts that characterize the resting potential, we bring the membrane voltage to a positive charge of about +30 to +40 millivolts. This inner change causes the next section of the cell to become permeable to sodium ions. In this way, the neural impulse is transmitted continuously along an axon.

is, either a neuron fires or it doesn't. Neurons fire more often when they have been stimulated by larger numbers of other neurons. Stronger stimuli cause more frequent firing, but again, the strength of each firing remains the same.

◇ **Truth or Fiction Revisited:** It is true that a single brain cell can send out hundreds of messages each second—and manage to catch some rest in between. For a few thousandths of a second after firing, a neuron is in a **refractory period;** that is, it is insensitive to messages from other neurons and will not fire. This period is a time of recovery during which sodium is prevented from passing through the neuronal membrane. Because such periods of "recovery" might occur hundreds of times per second, it seems a rapid recovery and a short rest indeed.

Stop and think for a moment: Billions of cells can each fire hundreds of times per second, sending different kinds of messages to different groups of cells each time. How can any humanmade computer we know of today begin to transmit such vast quantities of information? Our capacity to process information apparently helps us begin to understand the human capacities for insight and intuition.

The Synapse: On Being Well-Connected A neuron relays its message to another neuron across a junction called a **synapse.** *What is a synapse?* A synapse consists of an axon terminal button from the transmitting neuron, a dendrite or the body of a receiving neuron, and a fluid-filled gap between the two that is called the *synaptic cleft* (see Figure 2.1). Although the neural impulse is electrical, it does not jump across the synaptic cleft like a spark. Instead, when a nerve impulse reaches a synapse, axon terminals release chemicals into the synaptic cleft like myriad ships being cast into the sea. Scientists have identified a few dozen of these chemicals to date. In the following section, we consider a few of them that are usually of the greatest interest to psychologists.

▬■▬ Neurotransmitters: The Chemical Keys to Communication

Sacs called synaptic vesicles in the axon terminals contain neurotransmitters. When a neural impulse (action potential) reaches the axon terminal, the vesicles release varying amounts of **neurotransmitters**—the chemical keys to communication—into the synaptic

All-or-none principle The fact that a neuron fires an impulse of the same strength whenever its action potential is triggered.

Refractory period A phase following firing during which a neuron is less sensitive to messages from other neurons and will not fire.

Synapse A junction between the axon terminals of one neuron and the dendrites or cell body of another neuron.

Neurotransmitters Chemical substances involved in the transmission of neural impulses from one neuron to another.

The Action Potential

LEARNING OBJECTIVES
■ Define action potential.
■ Explain how an action potential travels along the axon of a neuron.
■ Explain the relationship between the action potential and the resting potential.

APPLIED LESSON
Can neurons partially fire? Why do you think that is?

CRITICAL THINKING
It has been said that the brain runs on electricity. Critical thinkers do not oversimplify or overgeneralize. Would you say this statement is true or false? Or is it partly true? Explain your answer by applying your knowledge of the action and resting potentials, and of neurotransmitters.

A neuron's action potential is the electrical impulse that travels along its axon, enabling the conduction of a neural impulse. The inside of the axon at the disturbed area has an action potential of 110 millivolts, providing the axon membrane with a positive charge. This change causes the next section of the axon to become permeable to sodium ions, while potassium ions are pumped out of the area previously affected, returning the area to its resting potential. In this way, the neural impulse is propagated continuously along an axon.

Watch this video!
Go to www
your companion website at
http://academic.cengage.com/psychology/rathus
Click on the Video Connections tab under this chapter.

---

cleft. From there, they influence the receiving neuron. *Which neurotransmitters are of interest to psychologists? What do they do?*

Dozens of neurotransmitters have been identified. Each has its own chemical structure, and each can fit into a specifically tailored harbor, or **receptor site,** on the receiving cell. The analogy of a key fitting into a lock is often used to describe this process. Once released, not all molecules of a neurotransmitter find their way into receptor sites of other neurons. "Loose" neurotransmitters are usually either broken down or reabsorbed by the axon terminal (a process called *reuptake*).

Some neurotransmitters act to *excite* other neurons—that is, to cause other neurons to fire. Other neurotransmitters act to *inhibit* receiving neurons. That is, they prevent the neurons from firing. The sum of the stimulation—excitatory and inhibitory—determines whether a neuron will fire and, if so, when neurotransmitters will be released.

Neurotransmitters are involved in physical processes such as muscle contraction and psychological processes such as thoughts and emotions. Excesses or deficiencies of neurotransmitters have been linked to psychological disorders such as depression and schizophrenia. Let us consider the effects of some neurotransmitters of interest to psychologists: acetylcholine (ACh), dopamine, norepinephrine, serotonin, GABA, and endorphins.

Acetylcholine (ACh) controls muscle contractions. It is excitatory at synapses between nerves and muscles that involve voluntary movement but inhibitory at the heart and some other locations. The effects of *curare* highlight the functioning of ACh. Curare is a poison that is extracted from plants by native South Americans and used in hunting. If an arrow

Receptor site   A location on a dendrite of a receiving neuron tailored to receive a neurotransmitter.

Acetylcholine (ACh)   A neurotransmitter that controls muscle contractions.

tipped with curare pierces the skin and the poison enters the body, it prevents ACh from binding to the receptor sites on neurons. Because ACh helps muscles move, curare causes paralysis. The victim is prevented from contracting the muscles used in breathing and therefore dies from suffocation. Botulism, a disease that stems from food poisoning, prevents the release of ACh and has the same effect as *curare.*

ACh is also normally prevalent in a part of the brain called the **hippocampus,** a structure involved in the formation of memories (Louie & Wilson, 2001). When the amount of ACh available to the brain decreases, as in Alzheimer's disease, memory formation is impaired (Chu et al., 2005). In one experiment, researchers (Egawa et al., 2002) decreased the ACh available to the hippocampus of laboratory rats. As a result, the rats could not learn to navigate a maze, apparently because they could not remember which way to turn at the choice points.

■ **Former Heavyweight Champion Muhammad Ali and Actor Michael J. Fox—Two of the Many Afflicted with Parkinson's Disease**

Parkinson's disease is connected with deficiencies in the neurotransmitter dopamine, and is characterized by tremors, loss of coordination, and jerky movement. In this photo, Ali and Fox meet with two senators in an effort to secure more funding for research on the disease.

Dopamine acts in the brain and affects ability to perceive pleasure, voluntary movement, and learning and memory (Davis et al., 2004; Heinz, 2004). Deficiencies of dopamine are linked to Parkinson's disease, in which people progressively lose control over their muscles (Olanow, 2000; Swerdlow et al., 2003). They develop muscle tremors and jerky, uncoordinated movements. The boxer Muhammad Ali and actor Michael J. Fox are two of the better-known individuals who are afflicted with Parkinson's disease.

The psychological disorder *schizophrenia* is characterized by confusion and false perceptions, and it has been linked to dopamine. People with schizophrenia may have more receptor sites for dopamine in an area of the brain that is involved in emotional responding. For this reason, they may "overutilize" the dopamine available in the brain (Butcher, 2000; Kapur, 2003). Overutilization is connected with hallucinations and disturbances of thought and emotion. The phenothiazines, a group of drugs used in the treatment of schizophrenia, inhibit the action of dopamine by blocking some dopamine receptors (Lidow et al., 2001). Because of their action, phenothiazines may have Parkinson's-like side effects, which are usually treated by lowering the dose, prescribing additional drugs, or switching to another drug.

Norepinephrine is produced largely by neurons in the brain stem, and acts both as a neurotransmitter and as a hormone. It is an excitatory neurotransmitter that speeds up the heartbeat and other body processes and is involved in general arousal, learning and memory, and eating. Excesses and deficiencies of norepinephrine have been linked to mood disorders. Deficiencies of both ACh and norepinephrine particularly impair memory formation (Egawa et al., 2002).

The stimulants cocaine and amphetamines ("speed") boost norepinephrine (as well as dopamine) production, increasing the firing of neurons and leading to persistent arousal. Amphetamines both facilitate the release of these neurotransmitters and prevent their reuptake. Cocaine also blocks reuptake.

Serotonin is involved in emotional arousal and sleep. Deficiencies of serotonin have been linked to eating disorders, alcoholism, depression, aggression, and insomnia. The drug LSD decreases the action of serotonin and may also influence the utilization of dopamine. With LSD, "two no's make a yes." By inhibiting an inhibitor, it increases brain activity, in this case often producing hallucinations.

Gamma-aminobutyric acid (GABA) is another neurotransmitter of great interest to psychologists. One reason is that GABA is an inhibitory neurotransmitter that may help calm anxiety reactions (Stroele et al., 2002). Tranquilizers and alcohol may quell anxiety by binding with GABA receptors and amplifying its effects. One class of antianxiety drug may also increase the sensitivity of receptor sites to GABA. Other studies link deficiencies of GABA to depression (Clénet et al., 2005).

Endorphins are inhibitory neurotransmitters. The word *endorphin* is the contraction of *endogenous morphine. Endogenous* means "developing from within." Endorphins occur

Hippocampus A part of the limbic system of the brain that is involved in memory formation.

Dopamine A neurotransmitter that is involved in Parkinson's disease and that appears to play a role in schizophrenia.

Norepinephrine A neurotransmitter whose action is similar to that of the hormone epinephrine and that may play a role in depression.

Serotonin A neurotransmitter, deficiencies of which have been linked to affective disorders, anxiety, and insomnia.

Gamma-aminobutyric acid (GABA) An inhibitory neurotransmitter that apparently helps calm anxiety.

Endorphins Neurotransmitters that are composed of amino acids and that are functionally similar to morphine.

naturally in the brain and in the bloodstream and are similar to the narcotic morphine in their functions and effects. They lock into receptor sites for chemicals that transmit pain messages to the brain. Once the endorphin "key" is in the "lock," the pain-causing chemicals are locked out. Endorphins may also increase our sense of competence, enhance the functioning of the immune system, and be connected with the pleasurable "runner's high" reported by many long-distance runners (Jonsdottir et al., 2000; Oktedalen et al., 2001). Concept Review 2.1 reviews much of the information on neurotransmitters.

There you have it—a fabulous forest of neurons in which billions upon billions of axon terminals are pouring armadas of neurotransmitters into synaptic clefts at any given time. The process occurs when you are involved in strenuous activity. It is taking place this moment as you are reading this page. It will happen later when you have a snack or watch TV. Moreover, the process is repeated several hundred times every second. The combined activity of all these neurotransmitters determines which messages will be transmitted and which ones will not. You experience your sensations, your thoughts, and your control over your body as psychological events, but the psychological events come from billions upon billions of electrochemical events.

We can think of neurons as the microscopic building blocks of the nervous system. Millions upon millions of these neurons gather together to form larger, visible structures that we think of as the parts of the nervous system. We discuss those parts next.

■ **Runner's High?**

Why have thousands of people taken up long-distance running? Running promotes cardiovascular conditioning, muscle strength, and weight control. But many long-distance runners also experience a "runner's high" that appears to be connected with the release of endorphins. Endorphins are naturally occurring substances that are similar in function to the narcotic morphine.

The Parts of the Nervous System

What are the parts of the nervous system? The nervous system consists of the brain, the spinal cord, and the **nerves** linking them to the sensory organs, muscles, and glands. As shown in Figure 2.4, the brain and spinal cord make up the **central nervous system.** If you compare your nervous system to a computer, your central nervous system would be your central processing unit (CPU).

The sensory (afferent) neurons, which receive and transmit messages to the brain and spinal cord, and the motor (efferent) neurons, which transmit messages from the brain or spinal cord to the muscles and glands, make up the **peripheral nervous system.** In the comparison of the nervous system to a computer, the peripheral nervous system makes up the nervous system's peripheral devices—keyboard, mouse, DVD drive, and so on. You would not be able to feed information to your computer's central processing unit without these *peripheral* devices. Other peripheral devices, such as your monitor and printer, allow you to follow what is happening inside your CPU and see what it has done.

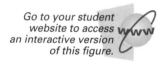

Go to your student website to access an interactive version of this figure.

Figure 2.4
The Divisions of the Nervous System
The nervous system contains two main divisions: the central nervous system and the peripheral nervous system. The central nervous system consists of the brain and spinal cord. The peripheral nervous system contains the somatic and autonomic systems. In turn, the autonomic nervous system has sympathetic and parasympathetic divisions.

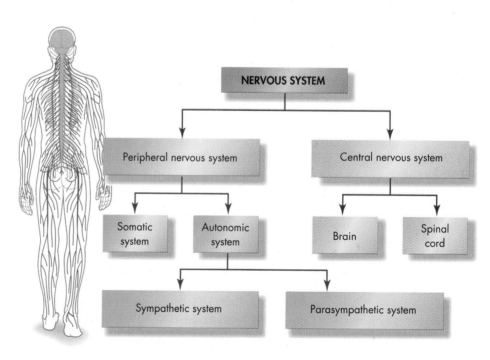

CONCEPT REVIEW 2.1

KEY NEUROTRANSMITTERS AND THEIR FUNCTIONS

NEUROTRANSMITTER	FUNCTIONS	COMMENTS
Acetylcholine (ACh)	Causes muscle contractions and is involved in formation of memories	Found at synapses between motor neurons and muscles; deficiencies linked with paralysis and Alzheimer's disease
Dopamine	Is involved in pleasure, addiction, movement, learning, attention, memory, and emotional response	Tremors of Parkinson's disease linked with low levels of dopamine; people with schizophrenia may overutilize dopamine
Norepinephrine	Accelerates the heart rate, affects eating, and is linked with activity levels, learning, and remembering	Imbalances linked with mood disorders such as depression and bipolar disorder
Serotonin	Is involved in behavior patterns and psychological problems, including obesity, depression, insomnia, alcoholism, and aggression	Drugs that block the reuptake of serotonin, helpful in the treatment of depression
Gamma-aminobutyric acid (GABA)	An inhibitory neurotransmitter that may lessen anxiety	Tranquilizers and alcohol may counter anxiety by binding with GABA receptors or increasing the sensitivity of receptor sites to GABA
Endorphins	Inhibit pain by locking pain-causing chemicals out of their receptor sites	Endorphins may be connected with some people's indifference to pain, the painkilling effects of acupuncture, and the "runner's high" experienced by many long-distance runners

The Peripheral Nervous System: The Body's Peripheral Devices   *What are the divisions and functions of the peripheral nervous system?* The peripheral nervous system consists of sensory and motor neurons that transmit messages to and from the central nervous system. Without the peripheral nervous system, our brains would be like isolated CPUs. There would be no keyboards, mouses, CDs, or other ways of inputting information. There would be no monitors, printers, modems, or other ways of displaying or transmitting information. We would be detached from the world: We would not be able to perceive it; we would not be able to act on it. The two main divisions of the peripheral nervous system are the *somatic nervous system* and the *autonomic nervous system.*

The **somatic nervous system** contains sensory (afferent) and motor (efferent) neurons. It transmits messages about sights, sounds, smells, temperature, body positions, and so on, to the central nervous system. As a result, we can experience the beauties and the horrors of the world, its physical ecstasies and agonies. Messages transmitted from the brain and spinal cord to the somatic nervous system control purposeful body movements such as raising a hand, winking, or running, as well as the tiny, almost imperceptible movements that maintain our balance and posture.

Autonomic means "automatic." The **autonomic nervous system (ANS)** regulates the glands and the muscles of internal organs. Thus, the ANS controls activities such as heartbeat, respiration, digestion, and dilation of the pupils of the eyes. These activities can occur automatically, while we are asleep. But some of them can be overridden by conscious control. You can breathe at a purposeful pace, for example. Methods like biofeedback and

Nerve   A bundle of axons from many neurons.

Central nervous system   The brain and spinal cord.

Peripheral nervous system   The part of the nervous system consisting of the somatic nervous system and the autonomic nervous system.

Somatic nervous system   The division of the peripheral nervous system that connects the central nervous system with sensory receptors, skeletal muscles, and the surface of the body.

Autonomic nervous system (ANS)   The division of the peripheral nervous system that regulates glands and activities such as heartbeat, respiration, digestion, and dilation of the pupils.

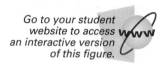

Go to your student website to access an interactive version of this figure.

Figure 2.5

The Parasympathetic and Sympathetic Branches of the Autonomic Nervous System (ANS)
The parasympathetic branch of the ANS generally acts to replenish stores of energy in the body. The sympathetic branch is most active during activities that expend energy. The two branches of the ANS frequently have antagonistic effects on the organs they service.

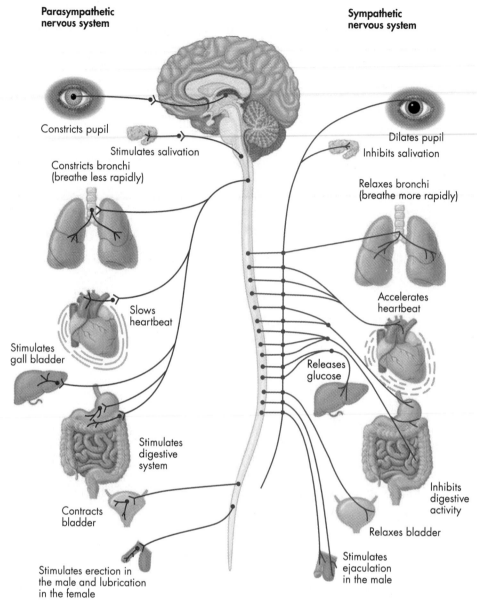

yoga also help people gain voluntary control of functions such as heart rate and blood pressure.

The ANS also has two branches, or divisions: **sympathetic** and **parasympathetic.** These branches have largely opposing effects. Many organs and glands are stimulated by both branches of the ANS (see Figure 2.5). When organs and glands are simultaneously stimulated by both divisions, their effects can average out to some degree. In general, the sympathetic division is most active during processes that involve spending body energy from stored reserves, such as a fight-or-flight response to a predator or when you find out that your rent is going to be raised. The parasympathetic division is most active during processes that replenish reserves of energy, such as eating. When we are afraid, the sympathetic division of the ANS accelerates the heart rate. When we relax, the parasympathetic division decelerates the heart rate. The parasympathetic division stimulates digestive processes, but the sympathetic branch inhibits digestion.

Have you ever tried to eat a meal when you're worried or anxious about something, like a big test or a speech you will have to present to the class? At such times, food usually has no appeal; and, if you force yourself to eat, the food may seem to land in your stomach like a rock. This is the sympathetic division of your ANS in action. The sympathetic division of the ANS predominates when we feel fear or anxiety, and these feelings can therefore cause indigestion. ◆ **Truth or Fiction Revisited:** Thus it is true that fear can give you indigestion.

Sympathetic   The branch of the ANS that is most active during emotional responses, such as fear and anxiety, that spend the body's reserves of energy.

Parasympathetic   The branch of the ANS that is most active during processes (such as digestion) that restore the body's reserves of energy.

The ANS is of particular interest to psychologists because its activities are linked to various emotions such as anxiety and love. Some people seem to have overly reactive sympathetic nervous systems. In the absence of threats, their bodies still respond as though they are faced with danger. Psychologists often help them learn to relax when there is no external reason for them to feel so "wound up tight."

The Central Nervous System: The Body's Central Processing Unit   It is your central nervous system that makes you so special. Other species see more sharply, smell more keenly, and hear more acutely. Other species run faster, or fly through the air, or swim underwater—without the benefit of artificial devices such as airplanes and submarines. But it is your central nervous system that enables you to use symbols and language, the abilities that allow people not only to adapt to their environment but to create new environments and give them names (Bandura, 1999). ***What are the divisions and functions of the central nervous system?*** The central nervous system consists of the spinal cord and the brain.

The **spinal cord** is a true "information superhighway"—a column of nerves as thick as a thumb. It transmits messages from sensory receptors to the brain and from the brain to muscles and glands throughout the body. The spinal cord also carries out some "local government." That is, it responds to some sources of external stimulation through **spinal reflexes.** A spinal reflex is an unlearned response to a stimulus that may require only two neurons—a sensory neuron and a motor neuron (see Figure 2.6).

The spinal cord and brain contain gray matter and white matter. **Gray matter** consists of nonmyelinated neurons. Some of these are involved in spinal reflexes. Others send their axons to the brain. **White matter** is composed of bundles of longer, myelinated (and thus whitish) axons that carry messages to and from the brain. A cross section of the spinal cord shows that the gray matter, which includes cell bodies, is distributed in a butterfly pattern (see Figure 2.6).

We have many reflexes. We blink in response to a puff of air in our faces. We swallow when food accumulates in the mouth. A physician may tap below the knee to elicit the knee-jerk reflex, a sign that the nervous system is operating adequately. Urinating and defecating are reflexes that occur in response to pressure in the bladder and the rectum. Parents typically spend weeks or months toilet-training infants—in other words, teaching them to involve their brains in the process of elimination. Learning to inhibit these reflexes makes civilization possible.

Sexual response also involves many reflexes. Stimulation of the genital organs leads to the reflexes of erection in the male and vaginal lubrication in the female (reflexes that make sexual intercourse possible), and to the reflexive muscle contractions of orgasm. As reflexes, these processes need not involve the brain, but most often they do. Feelings of passion, memories of an enjoyable sexual encounter, and sexual fantasies usually contribute to sexual response by transmitting messages from the brain to the genitals through the spinal cord.

reflect & relate

Reflexes are automatic, involuntary responses. Yet the great majority of the time we engage in sexual behavior voluntarily. How, then, do we explain the fact that sexual responses like erection, vaginal lubrication, and orgasm are reflexes?

Spinal cord A column of nerves within the spine that transmits messages from sensory receptors to the brain and from the brain to muscles and glands throughout the body.

Spinal reflex A simple, unlearned response to a stimulus that may involve only two neurons.

Gray matter In the spinal cord, the grayish neurons and neural segments that are involved in spinal reflexes.

White matter In the spinal cord, axon bundles that carry messages from and to the brain.

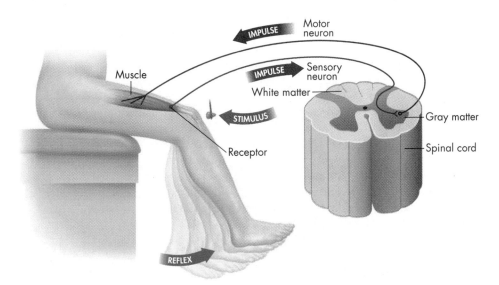

Figure 2.6

The Reflex Arc

Reflexes are inborn, stereotyped behavior patterns that have apparently evolved because they help individuals adapt to the environment even before they can understand and purposefully manipulate the environment. Here we see a cross-section of the spinal cord, highlighting a sensory neuron and a motor neuron, which are involved in the knee-jerk reflex. In some reflexes, interneurons link sensory and motor neurons.

A Closer Look

Of Spiderman, Dr. Octopus, and Brain–Machine Interfaces

A Closer Look

■ **Dr. Octopus and Your Friendly, Neighborhood Spiderman**

Dr. Octopus used a brain–machine interface to control artificial limbs he needed to handle radioactive substances. Unfortunately, the artificial limbs gained control of Dr. Octopus. Is such a brain–machine interface pure science fiction, or will we be using them to overcome disabilities, such as paralysis?

Melissa Moseley/Sony Pictures/Bureau L.A. Collections/Corbis

Dr. Octopus, the villain that terrorizes the city in the film of the Spiderman comic, is the ultimate characterization of a brain–machine interface (BMI) on the big screen. In Spiderman 2, the brain is that of nuclear physicist Dr. Otto Octavius, who dreams of harnessing nuclear fusion. The machine is a harness of four mechanical arms designed with tentacle-like flexibility, gripping and vision capabilities, and artificial intelligence that gives them some self-control. The interface between the machine and the brain is at the spinal cord level, with an "inhibitor chip" to prevent the artificial intelligence in the mechanical arms from taking over Octavius's brain. Controlling this mechanical device with his own thoughts, Octavius is able to manipulate hazardous materials during his fusion experiments. However, things go terribly wrong during the exhibition of one of these experiments: The mechanical arms fuse to Octavius's body while the inhibitor chip is disabled, resulting in the machine gaining partial control of his brain. Unable to subvert the machine to his will and conscience, Octavius, together with the BMI, becomes the villainous Dr. Octopus. At the end of the movie, in a flicker of sanity and heroism, Octavius dramatically sacrifices his life as the only way to terminate the evil machine and save the world.

Although Dr. Octopus is a fictional character, a figment of a vivid imagination, audiences are fascinated by the fact that he is a human BMI. BMIs straddle the worlds of fact and fiction. While the entertainment industry has focused primarily on applications for augmenting cognitive and sensorimotor function, as seen in Star Trek and many other science-fiction scenarios, the scientific community has targeted clinical applications, such as limbs that are controlled by radio signals from the brain for restoring motor function after traumatic lesion of the central nervous system. (Such a method could allow people with spinal cord damage to walk again.) The current BMI approach is based on the idea that a human user could enact voluntary motor intentions through a direct interface between his brain and an artificial effector in virtually the same way that we see, walk, or grab an object with our own limbs. It should be possible to achieve brain control of an external device or effector through training using any combination of visual, tactile, or auditory feedback. As a result of long-term use of the BMI, the brain should be able to "incorporate" (or adapt to) the artificial effector as an extension of its own body. With these goals in mind, the last five years have witnessed a dramatic increase in BMI-related studies in academic institutions around the world. Subjects have learned to utilize their brain activity for different purposes, ranging from electroencephalogram- and electrocorticographic-based systems (Leuthardt et al. 2004; Wolpaw et al. 2002), in which human subjects control computer cursors, to multielectrode-based systems, in which nonhuman primates control the movements of cursors and robots to perform different kinds of reaching and grasping tasks (Musallam et al. 2004; Serruya et al. 2002; Taylor et al. 2002). ■

Source: Adapted from "Brain versus Machine Control," by J. M. Carmena, 2004, PLoS Biol 2(12), p. e430. An open-access article distributed under the terms of the Creative Commons Attribution License.

() **Learning Connections**

 The Nervous System — On Being Wired

Learning Connections

REVIEW:

1 Neurons transmit messages to other neurons through chemical substances called
   (a) action potentials,
   (b) synapses,
   (c) axons,
   (d) neurotransmitters.

2 The _____ nervous system consists of the brain and spinal cord.
   (a) somatic,
   (b) central,
   (c) peripheral,
   (d) autonomic.

3 Deficiencies of _____ are linked to anxiety, depression, and insomnia.
   (a) acetylcholine,
   (b) norepinephrine,
   (c) serotonin,
   (d) epinephrine.

4 _____ is a fatty substance that insulates neurons.
   (a) Dendrite,
   (b) Myelin,
   (c) Axon,
   (d) Gamma aminobutyric acid.

CRITICAL THINKING:
Psychology is the study of behavior and mental processes. Why, then, are psychologists interested in the nervous system?

Go to www
http://academic.cengage.com/psychology/rathus
for an interactive version of this review.

THE BRAIN: WIDER THAN THE SKY

The Brain—is wider than the Sky—
For—put them side by side—
The one the other will contain
With ease—and you—beside—
—EMILY DICKINSON

Every show has a star, and the brain is the undisputed star of the human nervous system. The size and shape of your brain are responsible for your large, delightfully rounded head. In all the animal kingdom, you (and about 6 billion other people) are unique because of the capacities for learning and thinking residing in the human brain.

The brains of men average about 15% larger than those of women (Kimura, 2002), which is related to the difference in body size. However, it appears that being well-connected (in terms of synapses) is more important than size in the human brain. Moreover, women's brains "run hotter" than men's. Women metabolize more glucose (sugar) and appear to use more of their brains on a given task (Kimura, 2002).

Seeing the Brain Through the Eyes of the Psychologist

Philosophers and scientists have wondered about the functions of the brain throughout history. Scientists today generally agree that the mind is a function of the brain (Bogen, 1998; Dietrich, 2004; Hohwy & Frith, 2004; Roser & Gazzaniga, 2004). Some engage in research that attempts to pinpoint exactly what happens in certain parts of the brain when we are listening to music or trying to remember someone's face. At other times—as in the case of Phineas Gage—knowledge has almost literally fallen into their laps. From injuries to the head—some of them minimal, some horrendous—we have learned that brain damage can

Richard T. Nowitz/Corbis

Figure 2.7

The Electroencephalograph (EEG)
The EEG detects brain waves that pass between electrodes that are attached to the scalp. It has been used to reveal electrical activity associated with relaxation and the stages of sleep.

Electroencephalograph (EEG) A method of detecting brain waves by means of measuring the current between electrodes placed on the scalp.

Computerized axial tomography (CAT scan) A method of brain imaging that passes a narrow X-ray beam through the head and measures structures that reflect the rays from various angles, enabling a computer to generate a three-dimensional image.

Positron emission tomography (PET scan) A method of brain imaging that injects a radioactive tracer into the bloodstream and assesses activity of parts of the brain according to the amount of glucose they metabolize.

---

impair consciousness, perception, memory, and abilities to make plans and decisions. In some cases, the loss of large portions of the brain may result in little loss of function. But the loss of smaller portions in particular locations can cause language problems, memory loss, or death. It has been known for about two centuries that damage to the left side of the brain is connected with loss of sensation or movement on the right side of the body, and vice versa. Thus it has been assumed that the brain's control mechanisms cross over from right to left, and vice versa, as they descend into the body.

Accidents provide unplanned—and uncontrolled—opportunities of studying the brain. Nevertheless, they remain useful (e.g., Baldo et al., 2004; Eslinger et al., 2004). Still, scientists learn more about the brain through methods like experimentation, electroencephalography, and brain scans. *How do researchers learn about the functions of the brain?*

Experimenting with the Brain   The results of disease and accidents (as in the case of Phineas Gage) have shown us that brain injuries can be connected with changes in behavior and mental processes. Scientists have also purposefully damaged part of the brain in laboratory animals to observe the results. For example, damaging one part of the hypothalamus causes rats to overeat. Damaging another part of the hypothalamus causes them to stop eating. It is as if parts of the brain contain on–off switches for certain kinds of behavior, at least in lower animals.

Because the brain has no receptors for pain, surgeon Wilder Penfield (1969) was able to stimulate parts of human brains with electrical probes. As a result, his patients reported perceiving certain memories. Electrical stimulation of the brain has also shown that parts of the brain are connected with specific kinds of sensations (as of light or sound) or motor activities (such as movement of an arm or leg).

The Electroencephalograph   Penfield stimulated parts of the brain with an electrical current and asked people to report what they experienced. Researchers have also used the **electroencephalograph** (EEG) to record the natural electrical activity of the brain.

The EEG (see Figure 2.7) detects minute amounts of electrical activity—called brain waves—that pass between the electrodes. Certain brain waves are associated with feelings of relaxation, with various stages of sleep, and with neurological problems such as epilepsy.

Brain-Imaging Techniques   When Phineas Gage had his fabled accident, the only ways to look into the brain were to drill holes or crack it open, neither of which would have contributed to the well-being of the subject. But in the latter years of the 20th century, researchers developed imaging techniques that tap the computer's capacity to generate images of the parts of the brain from sources of radiation.

Computerized axial tomography (CAT or CT scan), shown in Figure 2.8A, passes X rays through the head and measures the structures that reflect the beams from various angles, generating a three-dimensional image. The CAT scan reveals deformities in shape and structure that are connected with blood clots, tumors, and other health problems.

A second method, **positron emission tomography (PET scan),** shown in Figure 2.8B, forms a computer-generated image of the activity of parts of the brain by tracing the amount of glucose used (or metabolized) by these parts. More glucose is metabolized in more active parts of the brain. To trace the metabolism of glucose, a harmless amount of a radioactive compound, called a *tracer,* is mixed with glucose and injected into the bloodstream. When the glucose reaches the brain, the patterns of activity are revealed by measurement of the positrons—positively charged particles—that are given off by the tracer. The PET scan has been used by researchers to see which parts of the brain are most active

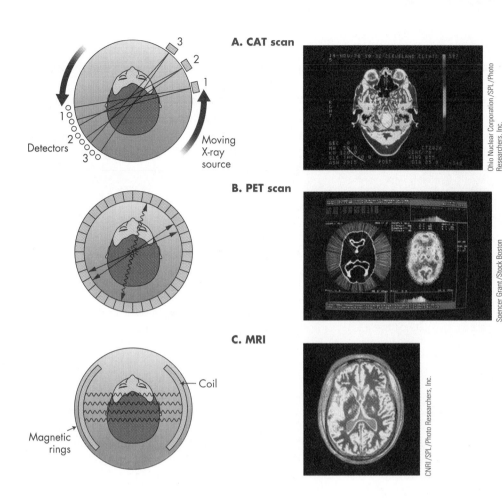

A. CAT scan

Ohio Nuclear Corporation/SPL/Photo Researchers, Inc.

B. PET scan

Spencer Grant/Stock Boston

C. MRI

CNRI/SPL/Photo Researchers, Inc.

A. Computerized axial tomography (the CAT scan) passes a narrow X-ray beam through the head and measures structures that reflect the rays from various angles, enabling a computer to generate a three-dimensional image.

B. Positron emission tomography (the PET scan) injects a radioactive tracer into the bloodstream and assesses activity of parts of the brain according to the amount of glucose they metabolize.

C. Magnetic resonance imaging (MRI) places a person in a magnetic field and uses radio waves to cause the brain to emit signals which reveal shifts in the flow of blood which, in turn, indicate brain activity.

Figure 2.8
Brain Imaging Techniques
Part A shows a CAT scan, part B a PET scan, and part C, MRI.

when we are, for example, listening to music, working out a math problem, using language, or playing chess.

A third imaging technique is **magnetic resonance imaging (MRI),** which is shown in Figure 2.8C. In MRI, the person lies in a powerful magnetic field and is exposed to radio waves that cause parts of the brain to emit signals, which are measured from multiple angles. MRI relies on subtle shifts in blood flow. (More blood flows to more active parts of the brain, supplying them with oxygen.) MRI can be used to show which parts of the brain are active when we are, say, solving math problems (Rickard et al., 2000) or speaking (Dogil et al., 2002). **Functional MRI (fMRI)** enables researchers to observe the brain "while it works" by taking repeated scans while subjects engage in activities such as mental processes and voluntary movements.

The tamping rod that shot through part of the prefrontal cortex of Phineas Gage impaired his ability to make decisions (Wagar & Thagard, 2004). Decision making is considered an executive function of the brain. Some researchers consider the prefrontal cortex to be the "executive center" of the brain, where decisions are made to keep information in working memory and to solve problems. Research with the PET scan and MRI supports the view that the prefrontal cortex is where we process much of the information involved in making plans and solving problems (Kroger et al., 2002; Rowe et al., 2001). Figure 2.9 shows the prefrontal cortex. One prefrontal region is found in each hemisphere, a bit above the outer edge of the eyebrow.

▬■ A Voyage Through the Brain: Revealing the Central Processing Unit

Perhaps you never imagined yourself as going off to foreign territory to unearth evidence about the history and functioning of the human species. But get your traveling gear, because we are about to go off on a voyage of discovery—a voyage within your own skull. We will be traveling through your brain—a fascinating archaeological site.

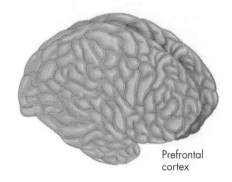

Prefrontal cortex

Figure 2.9
The Prefrontal Cortex of the Brain
The prefrontal cortex comes in pairs. One is found in each hemisphere, a bit above the outer edge of the eyebrow. The prefrontal cortex is highly active during visual and spatial problem solving. Your sense of self—your continuous sense of being in and operating on the world—may also reside largely in the prefrontal cortex.

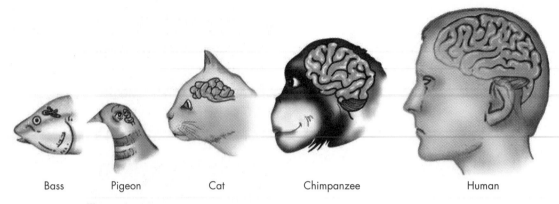

| Bass | Pigeon | Cat | Chimpanzee | Human |

Figure 2.10

Comparison of the Human Brain to the Brains of Other Species

Some parts of the human brain, especially the older parts, are quite similar to the corresponding parts of the brains of other mammals. They are even somewhat similar to those of birds and fish and are involved in survival functions such as breathing, feeding, and the regulation of the sleeping–waking cycle. However, the cerebrums, which are involved in cognitive processes, are quite different.

Magnetic resonance imaging (MRI) A method of brain imaging that places a person in a magnetic field and uses radio waves to cause the brain to emit signals that reveal shifts in the flow of blood which, in turn, indicate brain activity.

Functional MRI (fMRI) A form of MRI that enables researchers to observe the brain "while it works" by taking repeated scans.

Medulla An oblong area of the hindbrain involved in regulation of heartbeat and respiration.

Your brain reveals much of what is so special about you. It also holds a record of your connectedness with other animals that have walked, swum, and flown the Earth for hundreds of millions of years. In fact, some parts of your brain—those that we meet first on our tour—are not all that different from the corresponding parts of the brains of rats, cats, and monkeys. They even bear some resemblance to the brains of birds and fish (see Figure 2.10). The "older" parts of your brain—in terms of evolution—are found beneath your rounded skull and have functions very similar to those of these other species. These parts are involved in basic survival functions such as breathing, feeding, and the regulation of cycles of sleeping and waking. ***What are the structures and functions of the brain?***

Let us now begin our tour of the brain (see Figure 2.11). We begin with the oldest part of our "archaeological dig"—the hindbrain, where the spinal cord rises to meet the brain (refer to Figure 2.11). Here we find three major structures: the medulla, the pons, and the cerebellum. Many pathways pass through the **medulla** to connect the spinal cord to higher

■ **Supreme Balance and Coordination**
While we enjoy viewing the performances of acrobats and ballet dancers, their cerebellums are enabling them to manifest their excellent balance and coordination.

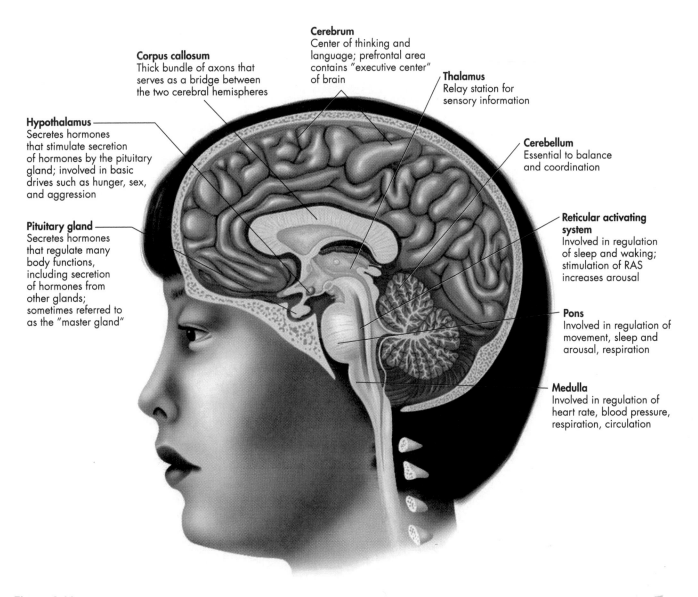

Corpus callosum
Thick bundle of axons that serves as a bridge between the two cerebral hemispheres

Cerebrum
Center of thinking and language; prefrontal area contains "executive center" of brain

Thalamus
Relay station for sensory information

Hypothalamus
Secretes hormones that stimulate secretion of hormones by the pituitary gland; involved in basic drives such as hunger, sex, and aggression

Pituitary gland
Secretes hormones that regulate many body functions, including secretion of hormones from other glands; sometimes referred to as the "master gland"

Cerebellum
Essential to balance and coordination

Reticular activating system
Involved in regulation of sleep and waking; stimulation of RAS increases arousal

Pons
Involved in regulation of movement, sleep and arousal, respiration

Medulla
Involved in regulation of heart rate, blood pressure, respiration, circulation

Figure 2.11

The Parts of the Human Brain

This view of the brain, split top to bottom, shows some of the most important structures. Note how close the hypothalamus is to the pituitary gland. The proximity allows the hypothalamus to readily influence the pituitary gland. The "valleys" in the cerebrum are called fissures.

Go to your student website to access an interactive version of this figure.

levels of the brain. The medulla regulates basic functions such as heart rate, blood pressure, and respiration. (In fact, Gage survived his accident because his medulla escaped injury.) The medulla also plays roles in sleeping, sneezing, and coughing. The **pons** is a bulge in the hindbrain that lies forward of the medulla. *Pons* is the Latin word for "bridge." The pons is so named because of the bundles of nerves that pass through it. The pons transmits information about body movement and is involved in functions related to attention, sleep and alertness, and respiration.

Behind the pons lies the **cerebellum** ("little brain" in Latin). The cerebellum has two hemispheres that are involved in maintaining balance and in controlling motor (muscle) behavior. You may send a command from your forebrain to get up and walk to the refrigerator, but your cerebellum is key to organizing the information that enables you to engage in these movements. The cerebellum allows you to place one leg in front of the other and reach your destination without tipping over. Injury to the cerebellum may impair motor coordination and cause stumbling and loss of muscle tone. Alcohol depresses the functioning of the cerebellum, so police often ask drivers suspected of drinking too much to engage in

Pons A structure of the hindbrain involved in respiration, attention, and sleep and dreaming.

Cerebellum A part of the hindbrain involved in muscle coordination and balance.

tasks that involve the cerebellum, such as touching their noses with their fingers or walking a straight line.

As we tour the hindbrain, we also find the lower part of the **reticular activating system (RAS).** That is where the RAS begins, but it ascends through the midbrain into the lower part of the forebrain. The RAS is vital in the functions of attention, sleep, and arousal. Injury to the RAS may result in a coma. Stimulation of the RAS causes it to send messages to the cerebral cortex (the large wrinkled mass that you think of as your brain), making us more alert to sensory information. In classic neurological research, Guiseppe Moruzzi and Horace Magoun (1949) discovered that electrical stimulation of the reticular formation of a sleeping cat caused it to awaken at once. But when the reticular formation was severed from higher parts of the brain, the animal fell into a coma from which it would not awaken. Drugs known as central nervous system depressants, such as alcohol, are thought to work, in part, by lowering RAS activity.

Sudden loud noises stimulate the RAS and awaken a sleeping animal or person. But the RAS may become selective through learning. That is, it comes to play a filtering role. It may allow some messages to filter through to higher brain levels and awareness while screening others out. For example, the parent who has primary responsibility for child care may be awakened by the stirring sounds of an infant, whereas the sounds of traffic or street noise are filtered out, even though they are louder. The other parent, in contrast, may sleep through loud crying by the infant. If the first parent must be away for several days, however, the second parent's RAS may quickly become sensitive to noises produced by the child. This sensitivity may rapidly fade again when the first parent returns.

Let's move onward and upward. Key areas of the forwardmost part of the brain, or forebrain, are the thalamus, the hypothalamus, the limbic system, and the cerebrum (see Figure 2.11). The **thalamus** is located near the center of the brain. It consists of two joined egg-shaped structures. The thalamus serves as a relay station for sensory stimulation. Nerve fibers from sensory systems enter from below; their information is then transmitted to the cerebral cortex by fibers that exit from above. For example, the thalamus relays sensory input from the eyes to the visual areas of the cerebral cortex. The thalamus also regulates sleep and attention in coordination with other brain structures, including the RAS.

The **hypothalamus** lies beneath the thalamus and above the pituitary gland. It weighs only 4 grams, yet it is vital in the regulation of body temperature, concentration of fluids, storage of nutrients, and motivation and emotion. Experimenters learn many of the functions of the hypothalamus by implanting electrodes in parts of it and observing the effects of electrical stimulation. They have found that the hypothalamus is involved in hunger, thirst, sexual behavior, caring for offspring, and aggression. Among lower animals, stimulation of various areas of the hypothalamus can trigger instinctual behaviors such as fighting, mating, or nest building.

Canadian psychologists James Olds and Peter Milner (1954) made a splendid mistake in the 1950s. They were attempting to implant an electrode in a rat's reticular formation to see how stimulation of the area might affect learning. Olds, however, was primarily a social psychologist and not a biological psychologist. He missed his target and found a part of the animal's hypothalamus instead. Olds and Milner dubbed this area the "pleasure center" because the animal would repeat whatever it was doing when it was stimulated. The term *pleasure center* is not used too frequently, because it appears to attribute human emotions to rats. Yet the "pleasure centers" must be doing something right, because rats stimulate themselves in these centers by pressing a pedal several thousand times an hour, until they are exhausted (Olds, 1969).

The hypothalamus is important to humans as well as lower animals. Unfortunately (or fortunately), our "pleasure centers" are not as clearly defined as those of the rat. Then, too, our responses to messages from the hypothalamus are less automatic and relatively more influenced by higher brain functions—that is, cognitive factors such as thought, choice, and value systems. It is all a part of being human.

The **limbic system** forms a fringe along the inner edge of the cerebrum and is fully evolved only in mammals. (Dig in from the surface a little to find it; see Figure 2.12.) It is made up of several structures, including the amygdala, hippocampus, and parts of the hy-

Reticular activating system (RAS) A part of the brain involved in attention, sleep, and arousal.

Thalamus An area near the center of the brain involved in the relay of sensory information to the cortex and in the functions of sleep and attention.

Hypothalamus A bundle of nuclei below the thalamus involved in body temperature, motivation, and emotion.

Limbic system A group of structures involved in memory, motivation, and emotion that forms a fringe along the inner edge of the cerebrum.

pothalamus. It is involved in memory and emotion and in the drives of hunger, sex, and aggression. People with hippocampal damage can retrieve old memories but cannot permanently store new information. As a result, they may reread the same newspaper day in and day out without recalling that they read it before. Or they may have to be perpetually reintroduced to people they have met just hours earlier (Squire, 2004).

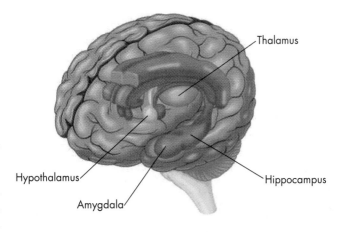

Figure 2.12
The Limbic System
The limbic system is made up of structures that include the amygdala, the hippocampus, and parts of the hypothalamus. It is evolved fully only in mammals and forms a fringe along the inner edge of the cerebrum. The limbic system is involved in memory and emotion, and in the drives of hunger, sex, and aggression.

Go to your student website to access an interactive version of this figure.

In the film *50 First Dates*, Drew Barrymore plays a woman whose hippocampus was damaged. Each day she must be reintroduced to her suitor, played by Adam Sandler, who eventually arranges for her to view an explanatory videotape each morning upon waking.

The **amygdala** is near the bottom of the limbic system and looks like two little almonds. Studies using lesioning and electrical stimulation show that the amygdala is connected with aggressive behavior in monkeys, cats, and other animals. Early in the 20th century, Heinrich Klüver and Paul Bucy (1939) lesioned part of the amygdala of a rhesus monkey. Rhesus monkeys are normally a scrappy lot and try to bite or grab at intruders, but destruction of this animal's amygdala made it docile. No longer did it react aggressively to people. It even allowed people to poke and pinch it. Electrical stimulation of the part of the amygdala that Klüver and Bucy had destroyed, however, triggers a "rage response." For example, it causes a cat to hiss and arch its back in preparation to attack. The amygdala is also connected with a fear response (LeDoux, 1998). If you electrically stimulate another part of the amygdala, the cat cringes in fear when you cage it with a mouse. Not very tigerlike.

The amygdala is also connected with vigilance. It is involved in emotions, learning, and memory, and it sort of behaves like a spotlight, focusing attention on matters that are novel and important to know more about. In studies reported in 2000, researchers used MRI to scan the amygdala while subjects were shown faces of European Americans and African Americans. One study flashed the photos by four men and four women, half European American and half African American (Hart et al., 2000). The subjects showed less activity in the amygdala when they viewed faces belonging to people of their own ethnic group, suggesting that they were more comfortable with "familiar" faces.

Now we journey upward to the cerebrum. The **cerebrum** is the crowning glory of the brain. Only in humans does the cerebrum make up such a large part of the brain (see Figure 2.13). The cerebrum is responsible for thinking and language. The surface of the cerebrum—the **cerebral cortex**—is wrinkled, or convoluted, with ridges and valleys. The convolutions allow a great deal of surface area to be packed into the brain—and surface area is apparently connected with cognitive ability. Valleys in the cortex are called *fissures*. A key fissure almost divides the cerebrum in half, creating two hemispheres with something of the shape of a walnut. The hemispheres are connected by the **corpus callosum** (Latin for "hard body"), a bundle of some 200 million nerve fibers.

Amygdala A part of the limbic system that apparently facilitates stereotypical aggressive responses.

Cerebrum The large mass of the forebrain, which consists of two hemispheres.

Cerebral cortex The wrinkled surface area (gray matter) of the cerebrum.

Columbia Pictures Corporation./ZUMA/Corbis

■ **Who Is He?**
In the film *50 First Dates*, Drew Barrymore plays a woman whose ability to form new memories has been compromised by brain damage. One day she falls in love with her suitor, Adam Sandler, but she fails to recognize him upon waking the following day. The relationship manages to survive when Sandler arranges for her to see a videotape each morning that explains her situation and reintroduces him.

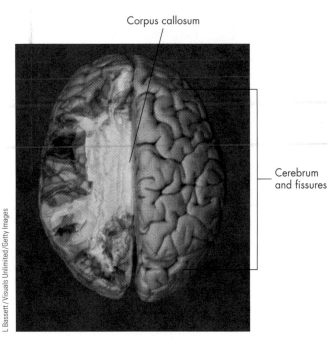

Corpus callosum

Cerebrum and fissures

L Bassett / Visuals Unlimited / Getty Images

Figure 2.13
A Human Brain, Showing the Cerebrum and the Corpus Callosum
The corpus callosum is a fiber bundle of some 200 million neurons that connects the left and right hemispheres.

Corpus callosum   A thick fiber bundle that connects the hemispheres of the cortex.

Somatosensory cortex   The section of cortex in which sensory stimulation is projected. It lies just behind the central fissure in the parietal lobe.

Motor cortex   The section of cortex that lies in the frontal lobe, just across the central fissure from the sensory cortex. Neural impulses in the motor cortex are linked to muscular responses throughout the body.

The Cerebral Cortex: The "Bark" That Reasons

The cerebral cortex is the part of the brain that you usually think of as your brain. *Cortex* is a Latin word meaning "bark," as in the bark of a tree. Just as the bark is the outer coating of a tree, the cerebral cortex is the outer coating of the cerebrum. Despite its extreme importance and its creation of a world of civilization and culture, it is only about one-eighth of an inch thick. It is the outer edge of the brain that brings humans to their outer limits.

The cerebral cortex is involved in almost every bodily activity, including most sensations and most responses. It is also the part of the brain that frees people from the tyranny of genetic dictates and instinct. It is the seat of thinking and language, and it enables humans to think deeply about the world outside and to make decisions. Other organisms run faster than we do, are stronger, or bite more sharply. Yet humans think faster, are intellectually "stronger," and, we might add, have a "biting" wit—all of which is made possible by the cerebral cortex. *What are the parts of the cerebral cortex?*

The cerebral cortex has two hemispheres, left and right. Each of the hemispheres is divided into four lobes, as shown in Figure 2.14. The *frontal lobe* lies in front of the central fissure and the *parietal lobe* behind it. The *temporal lobe* lies below the side, or lateral, fissure—across from the frontal and parietal lobes. The *occipital lobe* lies behind the temporal lobe and behind and below the parietal lobe.

When light strikes the eyes, neurons in the occipital lobe fire, and as a result, we "see" (that is, the image is projected in the brain). Direct artificial stimulation of the occipital lobe also produces visual sensations. If neurons in the occipital region of the cortex were stimulated with electricity, you would "see" flashes of light even if it were pitch black or your eyes were covered. The hearing or auditory area of the cortex lies in the temporal lobe along the lateral fissure. Sounds cause structures in the ear to vibrate. Messages are relayed from those structures to the auditory area of the cortex, and, when you hear a noise, neurons in this area are firing.

Just behind the central fissure in the parietal lobe lies an area called the **somatosensory cortex,** which receives messages from skin senses all over the body. These sensations include warmth and cold, touch, pain, and movement. Neurons in different parts of the sensory cortex fire, depending on whether you wiggle your finger or raise your leg.

But Figure 2.14 shows that the ways in which our bodies are situated or represented on the somatosensory cortex make for strange-looking humans, indeed. Our faces and our hands are huge compared with, say, our trunk and our legs. This overrepresentation is one of the reasons that our face, head, and hands are more sensitive to touch than other parts of the body.

Many years ago it was discovered that patients with injuries to one hemisphere of the brain would show sensory or motor deficits on the opposite side of the body below the head. This led to the recognition that sensory and motor nerves cross in the brain and elsewhere. The left hemisphere controls acts on, and receives inputs from, the right side of the body. The right hemisphere controls acts on, and receives inputs from, the left side of the body.

The **motor cortex** lies in the frontal lobe, just across the valley of the central fissure from the somatosensory cortex. Neurons firing in the motor cortex cause parts of our body to move. More than 100 years ago, German scientists electrically stimulated the motor cortex in dogs and observed that muscles contracted in response (Fritsch & Hitzig, 1870/1960). Since then, neuroscientists have mapped the motor cortex in people and lower animals by inserting electrical probes and seeing which muscles contract. For example, José Delgado (1969) caused one patient to make a fist even though he tried to prevent his hand from closing. The patient said, "I guess, doctor, that your electricity is stronger than my will" (Delgado, 1969, p. 114). Delgado also made a monkey smile in this manner, thousands of times in one session. If a surgeon were to stimulate a certain area of the right hemisphere of the motor cortex with an electrical probe, you would raise your left leg. This action would be sensed in the somatosensory cortex, and you might have a devil of a time trying to figure out whether you had intended to raise that leg! ◆ **Truth or Fiction Revisited:** It is quite true that, if a brain surgeon were to stimulate the proper area of your somatosensory cortex with an electrical probe, it might seem as if someone were touching your arm or leg. A Swedish MRI study found that just the expectation of being tickled in a certain part of the body activates the corresponding area of the somatosensory cortex (Carlsson et al., 2000).

We find overrepresentation of the face, head, and hands in the motor cortex as in the somatosensory cortex. The "detail" of these body parts on the cortex would appear to enable us to engage in fine muscle control over these areas of our bodies. Think of the possible human nuances of facial expression. Think of the fine motor control we can exert as our

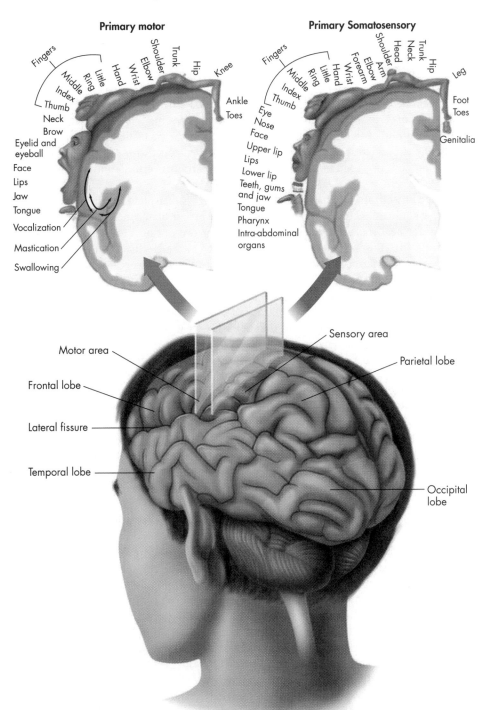

Figure 2.14
The Geography of the Cerebral Cortex
The cortex has four lobes: frontal, parietal, temporal, and occipital. The visual area of the cortex is in the occipital lobe. The hearing or auditory cortex lies in the temporal lobe. The motor and somatosensory areas—shown above—face each other across the central fissure. Note that the face and the hands are "super-sized" in the motor and somatosensory areas. Why do you think this is so?

fingers fly over the piano keyboard, or the fine motor control of the surgeon engaged in a delicate operation.

Thinking, Language, and the Cortex   Areas of the cerebral cortex that are not primarily involved in sensation or motor activity are called *association areas*. They make possible the breadth and depth of human learning, thought, memory, and language. *What parts of the cerebral cortex are involved in thinking and language?* The association areas in the *prefrontal* region of the brain—that is, in the frontal lobes, near the forehead—are the brain's executive center. It appears to be where we solve problems and make plans and decisions (Baldo et al., 2004; Buchanan et al., 2004; Shimamura, 2002).

Executive functions like problem solving also require memory, like the memory in your computer. Association areas also provide the core of your working memory (Chafee & Goldman-Rakic, 2000; Constantinidis et al., 2001). They are connected with various sensory areas in the brain and can tap whatever sensory information is needed or desired. The prefrontal region thus retrieves visual, auditory, and other memories and manipulates them; similarly, a computer retrieves information from files in storage and manipulates it in working memory.

Certain neurons in the visual area of the occipital lobe fire in response to the visual presentation of vertical lines. Others fire in response to presentation of horizontal lines. Although one group of cells may respond to one aspect of the visual field and another group of cells may respond to another, association areas put it all together. As a result, we see a box or an automobile or a road map and not a confusing array of verticals and horizontals.

Language Functions   In some ways, the left and right hemispheres of the brain duplicate each other's functions. In other ways, they differ. The left hemisphere contains language functions for nearly all right-handed people and for two out of three left-handed people (Pinker, 1994b). However, the brain remains "plastic," or changeable, through about the age of 13. As a result, children who lose the left hemisphere of the brain because of medical problems may transfer speech functions to the right hemisphere (Hertz-Pannier et al., 2002).

Two key language areas lie within the hemisphere of the cortex that contains language functions (usually the left hemisphere): Broca's area and Wernicke's area (see Figure 2.15). Damage to either area is likely to cause an **aphasia**—that is, a disruption of the ability to understand or produce language.

Wernicke's area lies in the temporal lobe near the auditory cortex. It responds mainly to auditory information (sounds). As you are reading this page, however, the visual information is registered in the visual cortex of your occipital lobe. It is then recoded as auditory information as it travels to Wernicke's area. Broca's area is located in the frontal lobe, near the section of the motor cortex that controls the muscles of the tongue, throat, and other areas of the face used when speaking. Broca's area processes the information and relays it to the motor cortex. The motor cortex sends the signals that cause muscles in your throat and mouth to contract. If you are "subvocalizing"—saying what you are reading "under your breath"—that is because Wernicke's area transmits information to Broca's area via nerve fibers.

People with damage to Wernicke's area may show **Wernicke's aphasia,** which impairs their abilities to comprehend speech and to think of the proper words to express their own thoughts. Ironically, they usually speak freely and with proper syntax. Wernicke's area is essential to understanding the relationships between words and their meanings. When Broca's area is damaged, people usually understand language well enough but speak slowly and laboriously, in simple sentences. This pattern is termed **Broca's aphasia.**

Some people with Broca's aphasia utter short, meaningful phrases that omit small but important grammatical words such as *is, and,* and *the.* Such an individual may laboriously say "walk dog." The phrase can have various meanings, such as "I want to take the dog for a walk" or "Take the dog out for a walk." Carroll (2004) reports the laborious, agrammatical speech of one individual with Broca's aphasia: "Yes . . . ah . . . Monday . . . er Dad and Peter H. . . . (his own name), and Dad . . . er hospital . . . and ah . . . Wednesday . . . Wednesday nine o'clock . . . and oh . . . Thursday . . . ten o'clock, ah doctors . . . two . . . an' doctors . . . and er . . . teeth . . . yah."

Broca's area   Wernicke's area

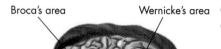
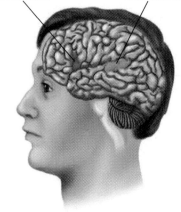

Figure 2.15

Broca's and Wernicke's Areas of the Cerebral Cortex

The areas that are most involved in speech are Broca's area and Wernicke's area. Damage to either area can produce an *aphasia*—a disruption of the ability to understand or produce language.

Aphasia   A disruption in the ability to understand or produce language.

Wernicke's aphasia   A language disorder characterized by difficulty comprehending the meaning of spoken language.

Broca's aphasia   A language disorder characterized by slow, laborious speech.

A part of the brain called the *angular gyrus* lies between the visual cortex and Wernicke's area. The angular gyrus "translates" visual information, as in perceiving written words, into auditory information (sounds) and sends it on to Wernicke's area. Brain imaging suggests that problems in the angular gyrus can seriously impair reading ability because it becomes difficult for the reader to segment words into sounds (Milne et al., 2002; Ruff et al., 2003).

Left Brain, Right Brain?

We often hear of being "left-brained" or "right-brained." ***What would it mean to be "left-brained" or "right-brained"?*** The notion is that the hemispheres of the brain are involved in very different kinds of intellectual and emotional functions and responses. According to this view, left-brained people would be primarily logical and intellectual. Right-brained people would be intuitive, creative, and emotional. Those of us who are fortunate enough to have our brains "in balance" would presumably have the best of it—the capacity for logic combined with emotional richness.

Like many other popular ideas, the left-brain–right-brain notion is exaggerated. Research does suggest that in right-handed individuals, the left hemisphere is relatively more involved in intellectual undertakings that require logical analysis and problem solving, language, and mathematical computation (Corballis et al., 2002; Shenal & Harrison, 2003). The other hemisphere (usually the right hemisphere) is usually superior in visual–spatial functions (it's better at putting puzzles together), recognition of faces, discrimination of colors, aesthetic and emotional responses, understanding metaphors, and creative mathematical reasoning. Despite these differences, the hemispheres of the brain do not act independently such that some people are truly left-brained and others right-brained (Colvin et al., 2005). The functions of the left and right hemispheres overlap to some degree, and they tend to respond simultaneously as we focus our attention on one thing or another.

Now let us consider another issue involving sidedness: left-handedness. People who are left-handed are different from people who are right-handed in terms of the way they write, throw a ball, and so on. But there are interesting questions as to whether people who are left-handed are psychologically different from "righties."

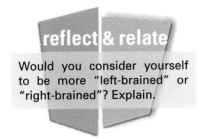

Would you consider yourself to be more "left-brained" or "right-brained"? Explain.

Handedness: Is Being Right-Handed Right?

What do Michelangelo, Leonardo da Vinci, and Steve Young all have in common? No, they are not all artists. Only one was a football player. But they are all left-handed. ***Does it matter whether one is left-handed? Why are people right-handed or left-handed?***

Despite the success of these examples, being left-handed was once seen as a deficiency. Left-handed students were made to learn to write with their right hands. The language still swarms with slurs on lefties. We speak of "left-handed compliments," of having "two left feet," of strange events as "coming out of left field." The word *sinister* derives from "left-hand or unlucky side" in Latin. The French word *gauche* is used to mean clumsy, but it literally means "left." The English word *adroit* mean "skillful" and derives from the French *à droit*, "to the right." Also consider positive usages such as being "righteous" or on one's "right side."

Overall, 8% to 10% of us are lefties. Left-handedness is more common in boys than girls (Rosenbaum, 2000). We are usually labeled right-handed or left-handed on the basis of our handwriting preferences, yet some people write with one hand and pass a football with the other. Some people even swing a tennis racket and pitch a baseball with different hands.

Being left-handed appears to be provide a somewhat-greater-than-average probability of language problems, such as dyslexia and stuttering, and health problems such as migraine headaches and allergies (Andreou et al., 2002; Geschwind & Galaburda, 1987; Habib & Robichon, 2003). But there may also be advantages to being left-handed. Left-handed people are more likely than right-handed people to be numbered among the ranks of gifted artists, musicians, and mathematicians (Kilshaw & Annett, 1983; Ostatníková et al., 2002).

The origins of handedness has a genetic component. Left-handedness runs in families. In the English royal family, Queen Elizabeth II, and Princes Charles and William are all left-handed, as was the Queen Mother (Rosenbaum, 2000). If both of your parents are right-handed, your chances of being right-handed are about 92%. If one of your parents is left-handed, your chances of being right-handed drop to about 80%. And if both of your parents are left-handed, your chances of also being left-handed are about 1 in 2 (Rosenbaum, 2000).

Whether we are talking about language functions, being "left-brained" or "right-brained," or handedness, we are talking about people whose hemispheres of the cerebral cortex communicate back and forth. Now let us see what happens when the major avenue of communication between the hemispheres shuts down.

◾ Split-Brain Experiments: How Many Brains Do You Have?

A number of people with severe cases of **epilepsy** have split-brain operations in which much of the corpus callosum is severed (refer back to Figure 2.11). The purpose of the operation is to confine seizures to one hemisphere of the cerebral cortex rather than allowing a neural tempest to reverberate. Split-brain operations do seem to help people with epilepsy. *What happens when the brain is split in two?*

Epilepsy Temporary disturbances of brain functions that involve sudden neural discharges.

People who have undergone split-brain operations can be thought of as winding up with two brains, yet under most circumstances their behavior remains ordinary enough. Still, some aspects of hemispheres that have stopped talking to each other are intriguing.

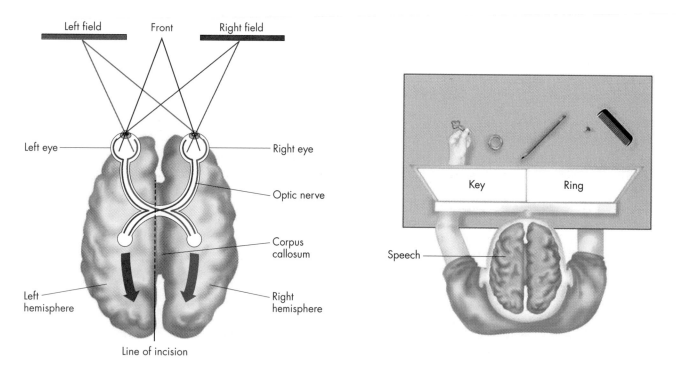

Figure 2.16

A Divided-Brain Experiment

In the drawing on the left, we see that visual sensations in the left visual field are projected in the occipital cortex of the right hemisphere. Visual sensations from the right visual field are projected in the occipital cortex in the left hemisphere. In the divided-brain experiment diagrammed on the right, a person with a severed corpus callosum handles a key with his left hand and perceives the written word *key* in his left visual field. The word "key" is projected in the right hemisphere. Speech, however, is usually a function of the left hemisphere. The written word "ring," perceived by the right visual field, is projected in the left hemisphere. So, when asked what he is handling, the divided-brain subject reports "ring," not "key."

As reported by pioneering brain surgeon Joseph Bogen (1969, 2000), each hemisphere may have a "mind of its own." One split-brain patient reported that her hemispheres frequently disagreed on what she should be wearing. What she meant was that one hand might undo her blouse as rapidly as the other was buttoning it. A man reported that one hemisphere (the left hemisphere, which contained language functions) liked reading but the other one did not. If he shifted a book from his right hand to his left hand, his left hand would put it down. The left hand is connected with the right hemisphere of the cerebral cortex, which in most people—including this patient—does not contain language functions.

Another pioneer of split-brain research, Roger Wolcott Sperry (1982), found that people with split brains whose eyes are closed may be able to verbally describe an object such as a key when they hold it in one hand, but not when they hold it in the other hand. If a person with a split brain handles a key with his left hand behind a screen, tactile impressions of the key are projected into the right hemisphere, which has little or no language ability (see Figure 2.16). Thus, he will not be able to describe the key. If he holds it in his right hand, he will have no trouble describing it because sensory impressions are projected into the left hemisphere of the cortex, which contains language functions. To further confound matters, if the word *ring* is projected into the left hemisphere while the person is asked what he is handling, he will say "ring," not "key."

However, this discrepancy between what is felt and what is said occurs only in people with split brains. Even so, people who have undergone split-brain operations tend to lead largely normal lives. And for the rest of us, the two hemispheres work together most of the time, even when we are playing the piano or solving math problems.

Now that we have discussed the structures and the functioning of the brain, we will return to matters of chemistry. In the next section, we see the effects on behavior and mental processes of chemicals—*hormones*—that are secreted by glands and poured directly into the bloodstream.

() Learning Connections

◀◀ *The Brain—Wider Than the Sky* ▶▶

REVIEW:

5 Which of the following records the electrical activity of the brain?
   (a) The PET scan,
   (b) The EEG,
   (c) MRI,
   (d) The CAT scan.

6 Which of the following is involved in balance and coordination?
   (a) The thalamus,
   (b) The hippocampus,
   (c) Broca's area,
   (d) The cerebellum.

7 The visual cortex is found in the _____ lobe.
   (a) occipital,
   (b) frontal,
   (c) parietal,
   (d) temporal.

8 The executive center of the brain is found in the _____ lobe.
   (a) occipital,
   (b) frontal,
   (c) parietal,
   (d) temporal.

CRITICAL THINKING:
In what ways does the research evidence reported in this section suggest that "the mind" is a function of the brain? Do you believe that the mind is based in the brain? If not, where or what do you think is the mind? What is your evidence?

Go to www
http://academic.cengage.com/psychology/rathus
for an interactive version of this review.

THE ENDOCRINE SYSTEM: CHEMICALS IN THE BLOODSTREAM

What is the endocrine system? The body contains two types of **glands:** glands with ducts and glands without ducts. A *duct* is a passageway that carries substances to specific locations. Saliva, sweat, tears, and breast milk all reach their destinations through ducts. Psychologists are interested in the substances secreted by a number of *ductless* glands because of their effects on behavior and mental processes. The ductless glands make up the **endocrine system,** and they release **hormones** into the bloodstream. Hormones are then picked up by specific receptor sites and regulate growth, metabolism, and some forms of behavior. That is, they act only on receptors in certain locations.

Much hormonal action helps the body maintain steady states—fluid levels, blood sugar levels, and so on. Bodily mechanisms measure current levels; when these levels deviate from optimal, they signal glands to release hormones. The maintenance of steady states requires feedback of bodily information to glands. This type of system is referred to as a *negative feedback loop.* When enough of a hormone has been secreted, the gland is signaled to stop.

The Pituitary and the Hypothalamus: Master and Commander

Gland An organ that secretes one or more chemical substances such as hormones, saliva, or milk.

Endocrine system The body's system of ductless glands that secrete hormones and release them directly into the bloodstream.

Hormone A substance secreted by an endocrine gland that regulates various body functions.

Pituitary gland The gland that secretes growth hormone, prolactin, antidiuretic hormone, and other hormones.

The pituitary gland and the hypothalamus work in close cooperation. The **pituitary gland** lies below the hypothalamus (see Concept Review 2.2 on page 66). Although the pituitary is only about the size of a pea, it is so central to the body's functioning that it has been dubbed the "master gland." The anterior (front) and posterior (back) lobes of the pituitary gland secrete many hormones. *Growth hormone* regulates the growth of muscles, bones, and glands. Children whose growth patterns are abnormally slow may catch up to their agemates when they obtain growth hormone. *Prolactin* regulates maternal behavior in lower mammals such as rats and stimulates production of milk in women. As a water conservation measure, *vasopressin* (also called *antidiuretic hormone*) inhibits production of urine when the body's fluid levels are low. Vasopressin is also connected with stereotypical paternal behavior in some mammals (see the nearby "A Closer Look"). *Oxytocin* stimulates labor

A Closer Look
Of Mice and Men: On Hormones, Attachment, and Fatherhood

Is vasopressin the "Daddy hormone"? Perhaps so, at least in meadow voles, a kind of tailless mouse. Vasopressin is connected with attachment between vole fathers and their young. ◁▷ **Truth or Fiction Revisited:** Increasing vasopressin levels transforms an indifferent male into a caring, monogamous, and protective mate and father (Lim et al., 2004; Parker & Lee, 2001).

Vasopressin is normally secreted by the pituitary gland, which secretes many hormones that are involved in reproduction and the nurturing of young. For example, prolactin regulates maternal behavior in lower mammals and stimulates the production of milk in women. Vasopressin enables the body to conserve water by inhibiting urine production when fluid levels are low; however, it is also connected with paternal behavior patterns in some mammals. For example, male prairie voles form pair-bonds with female prairie voles after mating with them (Balaban, 2004; Lim et al., 2004; Liu et al., 2001). Mating stimulates secretion of vasopressin, and vasopressin causes the previously promiscuous male to sing, "I only have eyes for you."

Despite its effects on voles, vasopressin has not yet been shown to be so tightly connected with the formation of bonds between men and women, and men and children. But what will further research bring to light? ■

in pregnant women and is connected with maternal behavior (cuddling and caring for young) in some mammals (Insel, 2000; Taylor et al., 2000b). Obstetricians can induce labor by injecting pregnant women with oxytocin. During nursing, stimulation of the nerve endings of the nipples signals the brain to secrete oxytocin which then causes the breasts to eject milk.

Although the pituitary gland may be the "master gland," the master has a "commander": the hypothalamus. We know today that the hypothalamus regulates much pituitary activity. The hypothalamus secretes a number of releasing hormones, or "factors," that stimulate the pituitary gland to secrete related hormones. For example, growth hormone releasing factor (hGRF) causes the pituitary to produce growth hormone. Blood vessels between the hypothalamus and the pituitary gland provide a direct route for these factors.

◾ The Pineal Gland

The pineal gland secretes the hormone *melatonin,* which helps regulate the sleep–wake cycle and may affect the onset of puberty. Melatonin may also be connected with aging. In addition, it appears that melatonin is a mild sedative and some people use it as a sleeping pill (Arendt, 2000; Nagtegaal et al., 2000). Melatonin may also help people adjust to jet lag (Takahashi et al., 2002).

◾ The Thyroid Gland: The Body's Accelerator

The thyroid gland could be considered the body's accelerator. It produces *thyroxin,* which affects the body's *metabolism*—the rate at which the body uses oxygen and produces energy. Some people are overweight because of *hypothyroidism,* a condition that results from too little thyroxin. Thyroxin deficiency in children can lead to *cretinism,* a condition characterized by stunted growth and mental retardation. Adults who secrete too little thyroxin may feel tired and sluggish and may put on weight. People who produce too much thyroxin may develop *hyperthyroidism,* which is characterized by excitability, insomnia, and weight loss.

◾ The Adrenal Glands: Coping with Stress

The adrenal glands, located above the kidneys, have an outer layer, or cortex, and an inner core, or medulla. The adrenal cortex is regulated by the pituitary hormone ACTH (adrenocorticotrophic hormone). The adrenal cortex secretes hormones known as *corticosteroids,* or cortical steroids. These hormones increase resistance to stress, promote muscle development, and cause the liver to release stored sugar, making more energy available in emergencies, as when you see another car veering toward your own. Epinephrine and norepinephrine are secreted by the adrenal medulla. *Epinephrine,* also known as adrenaline, is manufactured exclusively by the adrenal glands, but norepinephrine (noradrenaline) is also produced elsewhere in the body. (Norepinephrine acts as a neurotransmitter in the brain.) The sympathetic branch of the autonomic nervous system causes the adrenal medulla to release a mixture of epinephrine and norepinephrine that helps arouse the body to cope with threats and stress. Epinephrine is of interest to psychologists because it has emotional as well as physical effects. It intensifies most emotions and is central to the experience of fear and anxiety.

reflect & relate

Have you heard that adolescents are "hormonal" or affected by "glands"? If so, by which glands would they be affected?

◾ The Testes and the Ovaries

The testes and ovaries also produce steroids, among them testosterone and estrogen. If it were not for the secretion of the male sex hormone *testosterone* about six weeks after conception, we would all develop the external genital organs of females. Testosterone is produced not only by the testes but in smaller amounts by the ovaries and adrenal glands. A few weeks after conception, testosterone causes the male's sex organs to develop. During puberty, testosterone stokes the growth of muscle and bone and the development of primary

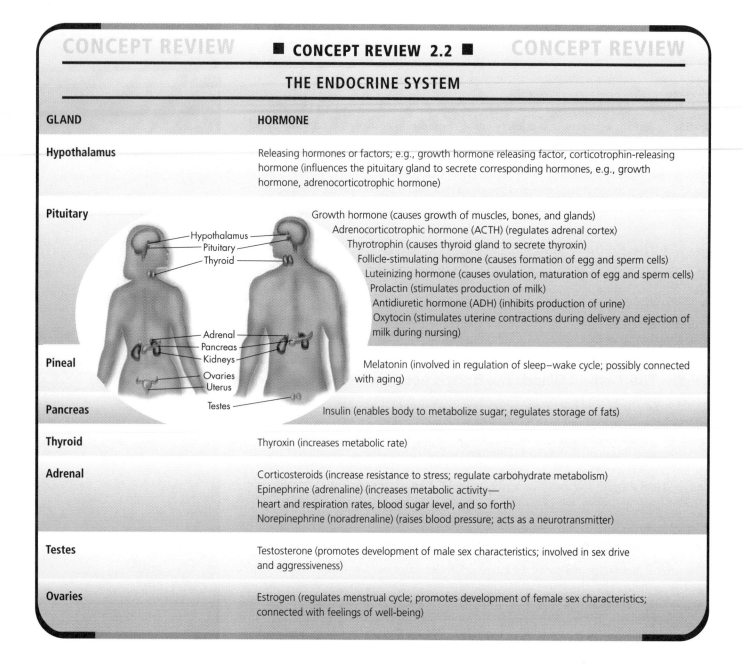

■ CONCEPT REVIEW 2.2 ■

THE ENDOCRINE SYSTEM

GLAND	HORMONE
Hypothalamus	Releasing hormones or factors; e.g., growth hormone releasing factor, corticotrophin-releasing hormone (influences the pituitary gland to secrete corresponding hormones, e.g., growth hormone, adrenocorticotrophic hormone)
Pituitary	Growth hormone (causes growth of muscles, bones, and glands) Adrenocorticotrophic hormone (ACTH) (regulates adrenal cortex) Thyrotrophin (causes thyroid gland to secrete thyroxin) Follicle-stimulating hormone (causes formation of egg and sperm cells) Luteinizing hormone (causes ovulation, maturation of egg and sperm cells) Prolactin (stimulates production of milk) Antidiuretic hormone (ADH) (inhibits production of urine) Oxytocin (stimulates uterine contractions during delivery and ejection of milk during nursing)
Pineal	Melatonin (involved in regulation of sleep–wake cycle; possibly connected with aging)
Pancreas	Insulin (enables body to metabolize sugar; regulates storage of fats)
Thyroid	Thyroxin (increases metabolic rate)
Adrenal	Corticosteroids (increase resistance to stress; regulate carbohydrate metabolism) Epinephrine (adrenaline) (increases metabolic activity—heart and respiration rates, blood sugar level, and so forth) Norepinephrine (noradrenaline) (raises blood pressure; acts as a neurotransmitter)
Testes	Testosterone (promotes development of male sex characteristics; involved in sex drive and aggressiveness)
Ovaries	Estrogen (regulates menstrual cycle; promotes development of female sex characteristics; connected with feelings of well-being)

In the illustration labels: Hypothalamus, Pituitary, Thyroid, Adrenal, Pancreas, Kidneys, Ovaries, Uterus, Testes

and secondary sex characteristics. *Primary sex characteristics* are directly involved in reproduction and include the increased size of the penis and the sperm-producing ability of the testes. *Secondary sex characteristics* such as the presence of a beard and a deeper voice differentiate males from females but are not directly involved in reproduction.

The ovaries produce *estrogen* and *progesterone* as well as small amounts of testosterone. Estrogen is also produced in smaller amounts by the testes. Estrogen fosters female reproductive capacity and secondary sex characteristics such as accumulation of fatty tissue in the breasts and hips. Progesterone stimulates growth of the female reproductive organs and prepares the uterus to maintain pregnancy.

Estrogen, like testosterone, has psychological effects as well as biological effects. For one thing, higher levels of estrogen seem to be connected with optimal cognitive functioning and feelings of well-being among women (Ross et al., 2000; Yaffe et al., 2000). Women are also more interested in sexual activity when estrogen levels are high—particularly during ovulation, when they are fertile. Older women placed on estrogen replacement showed improved memory functioning and visual–spatial abilities (Duka et al., 2000).

Life Connections
Steroids, Behavior, and Mental Processes

Steroids increase the muscle mass, heighten resistance to stress, and increase the body's energy supply by signaling the liver to release sugar into the bloodstream. The steroid testosterone is connected with the sex drive in both males and females (females secrete some testosterone in the adrenal glands) (Davis, 2000).

Anabolic steroids (synthetic versions of the male sex hormone testosterone) have been used, sometimes in tandem with growth hormone, to enhance athletic prowess. Not only do these steroids enhance athletic prowess, they are also connected with self-confidence, aggressiveness, even memory functioning (Janowsky et al., 2000). Anabolic steroids are generally outlawed in sports, however. The lure of steroids is understandable. Sometimes the difference between an acceptable athletic performance and a great one is rather small. Thousands of athletes try to make it in the big leagues, and the edge offered by steroids—even if minor—can spell the difference between a fumbling attempt and a smashing success. If steroids help, why the fuss? Some of it is related to the ethics of competition—the idea that athletes should "play fair." But steroid use is also linked to liver damage and other health problems. ■

Estrogen even affects women's perceptions of who is attractive. (Really.) One study found that British women prefer feminized male faces, as shown in Figure 2.17B, during most phases of the menstrual cycle (Penton-Voak & Perrett, 2000). Women apparently associate such facial features with personality traits like warmth and honesty. However, they prefer masculinized faces, as shown in Figure 2.17A, when they are ovulating. The evolutionary perspective might suggest that women unconsciously interpret such features as indicative of reproductive capacity—that is, they "instinctively" see these men as likely to father children.

Estrogen and progesterone levels vary and regulate the woman's menstrual cycle. Following menstruation—the monthly sloughing off of the lining of the uterus—estrogen levels increase, leading to the ripening of an ovum (egg cell) and the growth of the lining of the uterus. Ovulation (release of the ovum by an ovary) occurs when estrogens reach peak blood levels. Then the lining of the uterus thickens in response to the secretion of progesterone, gaining the capacity to support an embryo if fertilization should occur. If the ovum

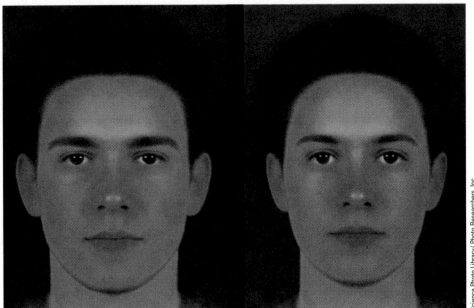

A.   B.

Science Photo Library/ Photo Researchers, Inc.

Figure 2.17
Which One Is Mr. Right?
The answer may depend on the phase of the woman's menstrual cycle. Women are apparently more attracted to men with masculinized features when they are capable of conceiving (part A), and men with more feminized features (part B) when they are not.

Symptoms of PMS

PMS is short for premenstrual syndrome, a cluster of symptoms that may affect women during eight days prior to and during menstruation. Research suggests that most women have some of these symptoms, but that they are usually not severe enough to interfere with their daily functioning. But some women experience severe symptoms, and they are advised to discuss their situations with their gynecologists.

Do you experience PMS? Complete the following Self-Assessment to gain insight into whether you do and, if so, how severely.

Directions:

Following is a list of various psychological and physical symptoms of PMS. Indicate whether you encounter these symptoms and how severe they are by checking the appropriate box. Then turn to the answer key in Appendix B to assess your responses.

PART I: PSYCHOLOGICAL SYMPTOMS OF PMS	DO NOT HAVE	MILD	MODERATE	SEVERE	DISABLING
Proneness to accidents					
Depression					
Anxiety					
Panic					
Mood swings					
Crying spells					
Sudden anger					
Irritability					
Loss of interest in usual activities					
Difficulty concentrating					
Lack of energy					
Excessive use of alcohol					
Frustration					
Overeating or cravings for certain foods					
Insomnia or excessive sleeping					
Feelings of being out of control or overwhelmed					
Paranoia					
PART II: PHYSICAL SYMPTOMS OF PMS	**DO NOT HAVE**	**MILD**	**MODERATE**	**SEVERE**	**DISABLING**
Migraines					
Breast tenderness					
Joint or muscle pain					
Stiffness					
Weight gain					
Feelings of bloating					
Blurred vision					
Poor motor coordination					
Exhaustion					
Dark circles under the eyes					
Runny eyes					

Go to www

http://academic.cengage.com/psychology/rathus
where you can fill out an interactive version of this
Self-Assessment and automatically score your results.

is not fertilized, estrogen and progesterone levels drop suddenly, triggering menstruation once more.

Some women experience premenstrual syndrome (PMS), which is discomfort in the days preceding and during menstruation. You can check the nearby Self-Assessment on Symptoms of PMS to evaluate whether you have PMS. If you do, check with your doctor. Many effective treatments are available.

There are thus important links between biological factors, behavior, and mental processes. Thoughts and mental images may seem to be intangible pictures that float in our heads, but they have substance. They involve billions of brain cells (neurons) and the transmission of thousands of chemicals from one neuron to another—repeated hundreds of times per second. These countless bits of microscopic activity give rise to feelings, plans, computation, art and music, and all the cognitive activities that make us human. We pour chemicals called hormones into our bloodstreams, and they affect our activity levels, our anxiety levels, even our sex drives. An understanding of biology helps us grasp many psychological events that might otherwise seem elusive and without substance.

() Learning Connections

◀◀ *The Endocrine System—Chemicals in the Bloodstream* ▶▶

REVIEW:

9 The _____ secretes releasing factors that influence the pituitary gland.
  (a) brain stem,
  (b) thalamus,
  (c) hypothalamus,
  (d) duct.

10 Which of the following is central to the emotions of anxiety and fear?
  (a) Epinephrine,
  (b) Corticosteroids,
  (c) Vasopressin,
  (d) Oxytocin.

CRITICAL THINKING:
If so many behaviors and mental processes are affected by glands, do people have free will?

Go to
http://academic.cengage.com/psychology/rathus
for an interactive version of this review.

EVOLUTION AND HEREDITY: THE NATURE OF NATURE

harles Darwin almost missed the boat. Literally. ◆ **Truth or Fiction Revisited**: It is true that the British scientist was nearly prevented from undertaking his historic voyage due to the shape of his nose. Darwin had volunteered to serve on an expeditionary voyage on the H.M.S. *Beagle,* but the captain, Robert Fitz-Roy, objected to Darwin because of the shape of his nose. Fitz-Roy believed that you could judge a person's character by the outline of his facial features, and Darwin's nose didn't fit the . . . bill. But Fitz-Roy relented, and in the 1830s, Darwin undertook the historic voyage to the Galápagos Islands that led to the development of his theory of evolution.

In 1871 Darwin published *The Descent of Man,* which made the case that humans, like other species, were a product of evolution. He argued that the great apes (chimpanzees, gorillas, and so on) and humans shared a common primate ancestor. Evidence from fossil remains suggests that such a common ancestor might have lived about 13 million years ago

A National Science Foundation (2002) survey of 1,574 American adults found that only a slim majority—53%—agreed with the statement, "Human beings developed from earlier species of animals." Do you believe that scientific texts, such as this book, should present the theory of evolution? Explain your point of view.

(Moyà-Solà et al., 2004). Many people ridiculed Darwin's views because they were displeased with the notion that they might share ancestry with apes. Others argued that Darwin's theory contradicted the book of Genesis, which stated that humans had been created in one day in the image of God.

What is Darwin's theory of evolution? The concept of a *struggle for existence* lies at the core of Darwin's theory of evolution. At the Galápagos Islands, Darwin found himself immersed in the unfolding of a huge game of "Survivor," with animals and plants competing for food, water, territory, even light. But here the game was for real, and the rewards had nothing to do with fame or fortune. The rewards were reaching sexual maturity and transmitting one's genes into subsequent generations.

Since the beginning of time, the universe has been changing. For billions of years, microscopic particles have been forming immense gas clouds in space. Galaxies and solar systems have been condensing from the clouds, sparkling for some eons, then winking out. Change has brought life and death and countless challenges to survival. As described by evolutionary theory, some creatures have adapted successfully to these challenges, and their numbers have increased. Others have not met the challenges and have fallen back into the distant mists of time. Evidence suggests that 99.99% of all species that ever existed are now extinct (Gould, 2002). Which species prosper and which fade away is determined by **natural selection;** that is, species that are better adapted to their environment are more likely to survive and reproduce.

When we humans first appeared on Earth, our survival required a different sort of struggle than it does today. We fought or fled from predators such as leopards. We foraged across parched lands for food. We might have warred with humanoid creatures very much like ourselves—creatures who have since become extinct. But because of the evolution of our intellect, not fangs nor wings nor claws, we prevailed. Our numbers have increased. We continue to transmit the traits that led to our selection down through the generations by means of genetic material whose chemical codes are only now being cracked.

Just what is handed down through the generations? The answer is biological, or physiological, structures and processes. Our biology serves as the material base for our behaviors, emotions, and cognitions (our thoughts, images, and plans). Biology somehow gives rise to specific behavioral tendencies in some organisms, such as the chick's instinctive fear of the shadow of the hawk. But the behavior of many species, especially higher species such as humans, is flexible and affected by experience and choice, as well as by heredity.

According to the theory of evolution, species and individuals compete for the same resources. Small variations—random genetic variations called **mutations**—lead to differences among individuals, differences which affect the ability to adapt to change. Those individuals whose traits are better adapted are more likely to survive (that is, to be "naturally selected"). Survival permits them to reach sexual maturity, to reproduce, and to transmit their features or traits to the next generation. What began as chance variation becomes embedded over the generations—if it fosters survival. Chance variations that hinder survival are likely to disappear from the gene pool.

Natural selection A core concept of the theory of evolution that holds that adaptive genetic variations among members of a species enable individuals with those variations to survive and reproduce. As a result, such variations tend to be preserved, whereas nonadaptive variations tend to drop out.

Mutation A sudden variation in an inheritable characteristic, as distinguished from a variation that results from generations of gradual selection.

Evolutionary psychology The branch of psychology that studies the ways in which adaptation and natural selection are connected with mental processes and behavior.

Evolutionary Psychology: "Doing What Comes Naturally"

These same concepts of *adaptation* and *natural selection* have also been applied to psychological traits and are key concepts in **evolutionary psychology.** *What is evolutionary psychology?* Evolutionary psychology studies the ways in which adaptation and natural selection are connected with mental processes and behavior (Buss, 2000; Cory, 2002). Over the eons evolution has provided organisms with advantages such as stronger fins and wings, sharper claws, and camouflage. Human evolution has given rise to various physical traits and also to such diverse activities as language, art, committed relationships, and warfare.

One of the concepts of evolutionary psychology is that not only physical traits but also many patterns of behavior, including social behavior, evolve and can be transmitted genetically from generation to generation. Behavior patterns that help an organism to survive and reproduce may be transmitted to the next generation. Such behaviors are believed to include aggression, strategies of mate selection, even altruism (that is, self-sacrifice of the individual to help perpetuate the family grouping) (Bruene & Ribbert, 2002; McAndrew, 2002). Such behavior patterns are termed *instinctive* or *species-specific* because they evolved within certain **species.**

What is meant by an "instinct"? An **instinct** is a stereotyped pattern of behavior that is triggered in a specific situation. Instinctive behavior is nearly identical among the members of the species in which it appears. It tends to resist modification, even when it serves no purpose (as in the interminable barking of some breeds of dogs) or results in punishment. Instinctive behavior also appears when the individual is reared in isolation from others of its kind and thus cannot learn the behavior from experience.

Consider some examples of instinctive behavior. If you place an egg from the nest of a goose a few inches in front of her, she will roll it back to the nest with her beak. However, she won't retrieve it if it's farther away—in the "not my egg" zone. If you rear a white-crowned sparrow in isolation from other sparrows, it will still sing a recognizable species-specific song when it matures. The male stickleback fish instinctively attacks fish (or pieces of painted wood) with the kinds of red bellies that are characteristic of other male stickle-backs. Many psychologists consider language to be "instinctive" among humans. Psychologists are trying to determine what other kinds of human behavior may be instinctive. However, even instinctive behavior can be modified to some degree by learning, and most psychologists agree that the richness and complexity of human behavior are made possible by learning.

Heredity, Genetics, and Behavioral Genetics

Consider some facts of life:

- People cannot breathe underwater (without special equipment).
- People cannot fly (again, without rather special equipment).
- Fish cannot learn to speak French or do an Irish jig even if you rear them in enriched environments and send them to finishing school.
- Chimpanzees and gorillas can use sign language but cannot speak.

People cannot breathe underwater or fly (without oxygen tanks, airplanes, or other devices) because of their **heredity.** ***What is meant by "heredity"?*** Heredity defines one's *nature*—which is based on biological structures and processes. Heredity refers to the biological transmission of traits that have evolved from generation to generation. Fish are limited in other ways by their natural traits. Chimpanzees and gorillas can understand many spoken words and express some concepts through nonverbal symbol systems such as American Sign Language. Apes cannot speak, however, apparently because of limitations in the speech areas of the brain.

Heredity makes behaviors possible and also places limits on them. ***What is meant by "genetics"?*** The subfield of biology that studies heredity is called **genetics.** *Behavioral genetics* bridges the sciences of psychology and biology. It is concerned with the genetic transmission of traits that give rise to patterns of behavior.

The field of genetics looks at both species-specific behavior patterns (instincts) and individual differences among the members of a species. Behavioral genetics focuses on individual differences (Plomin & Crabbe, 2000). Psychologists are thinking in terms of behavioral genetics when they ask about the inborn reasons why individuals may differ in their behavior and mental processes. For example, some children learn language more quickly than others. Part of the reason may lie in behavioral genetics—their heredity. But some children also experience a richer exposure to language at early ages.

Heredity appears to be a factor in almost all aspects of human behavior, personality, and mental processes (Bouchard & Loehlin, 2001). Examples include sociability, shyness, social dominance, aggressiveness, leadership, thrill seeking, effectiveness as a parent or a therapist, happiness, even interest in arts and crafts (Knafo et al., 2005; Lykken & Csik-szentmihalyi, 2001; Lykken et al., 1992).

Heredity is apparently involved in psychological disorders ranging from anxiety and depression to schizophrenia, bipolar disorder, alcoholism, and personality disorders

Have you known family pets that have engaged in instinctive behavior? What was the behavior? Why do you believe it was instinctive?

David Thompson /OSF/ Animals, Animals

■ Instinctive Behavior
The male stickleback instinctively attacks fish (or pieces of painted wood) with the kinds of red bellies that are characteristic of other male stickle-backs. Sticklebacks will show the stereotyped instinctive behavior even when they are reared in isolation from other members of their species. Rearing an organism in isolation prevents it from learning from another member of its species.

Species A category of biological classification consisting of related organisms who are capable of interbreeding. *Homo sapiens*—humans—make up one species.

Instinct A stereotyped pattern of behavior that is triggered by a particular stimulus and nearly identical among members of a species, even when they are reared in isolation.

Heredity The transmission of traits from parent to offspring by means of genes.

Genetics The area of biology that focuses on heredity.

(Gregory, 2004; Kendler et al., 2000b; Plomin & McGuffin, 2003; Sansone & Levitt, 2005; Sullivan et al., 2000). These disorders are discussed in Chapter 12, but here we can note that a study of 794 pairs of female twins by Kendler and his colleagues (2000a) found six aspects of psychological health that were connected with genetic factors: feelings of physical well-being, social relationships, anxiety and depression, substance abuse, use of social support, and self-esteem. The Kendler group also found, however, that the family environment contributed strongly to social relationships, substance abuse, and social support. Although psychological health is influenced by environmental factors, our understanding of the role of heredity continues to expand. Unlocking these mysteries depends on how well we understand genes and chromosomes.

Our genetic code (discussed in the next section) is made up of molecules. *Molecular genetics* attempts to identify specific genes that are connected with behavior and mental processes. Researchers are attempting to identify genes that are connected with physical and psychological disorders. It appears to be possible to cure some disorders by modifying the genetic code of affected individuals (Goldsmith et al., 2003). ***What are the roles of genes and chromosomes in heredity?***

Genes and Chromosomes: The Building Blocks of Heredity

Genes are the most basic building blocks of heredity. Genes regulate the development of specific traits. Some traits, such as blood type, are controlled by a single pair of genes. (One gene is derived from each parent.) Other traits are determined by combinations of genes. The inherited component of complex psychological traits, such as intelligence, is believed to be determined by combinations of genes. It is estimated that the cells within your body contain 20,000 to 25,000 genes (Human Genome Sequencing Consortium, 2004).

Genes are segments of **chromosomes.** That is, chromosomes are made up of strings of genes. Each cell in the body contains 46 chromosomes arranged in 23 pairs. Chromosomes are large complex molecules of **DNA** (short for *deoxyribonucleic acid*), which has several chemical components. The tightly wound structure of DNA was first demonstrated in the 1950s by James Watson and Francis Crick. DNA takes the form of a double helix—a twisting molecular ladder (see Figure 2.18). The "rungs" of the ladder are made up of chemicals whose names are abbreviated as A, T, C, and G. A always links up with T to complete a rung, and C always combines with G. Therefore, you can describe the *genetic code* in terms of the nucleotides you find along just one of the rungs—e.g., CTGAGTCAC and so on. A single gene can contain hundreds of thousands of base pairs. So if you think of a gene as a word, it can be a few hundred thousand letters long and completely unpronounceable. A group of scientists working together around the globe—referred to as the Human Genome Project—has learned that the sequencing of your DNA consists of about 3 billion DNA sequences spread throughout your chromosomes (Plomin & Crabbe, 2000). These sequences—the order of the chemicals we call A, T, C, and G—caused you to grow arms and not wings, and skin rather than scales. Psychologists debate the extent to which genes influence complex psychological traits such as intelligence, aggressiveness, and happiness, and the appearance of psychological disorders such as schizophrenia. Some traits, such as eye color, are determined by a single pair of genes. Other traits, especially complex psychological traits such as sociability and aggressiveness, are thought to be **polygenic**—that is, influenced by combinations of genes.

Your genetic code provides your **genotype**—that is, your full genetic potential, as determined by the sequencing of the chemicals in your DNA. But the person you see in the mirror was also influenced by your early experiences in the home, injuries, adequacy of nourishment, educational experiences, and numerous other environmental influences. Therefore, you see the outer appearance of your phenotype, including the hairstyles of the day. Your **phenotype** is the manner in which your genetic code manifests itself because of your experiences and environmental circumstances. Your genotype enables you to acquire language. Your phenotype reveals that you are likely to be speaking English if you were reared in the United States or Spanish if you were reared in Mexico (or both, if you are Mexican American).

Gene A basic unit of heredity, which is found at a specific point on a chromosome.

Chromosome A microscopic rod-shaped body in the cell nucleus carrying genes that transmit hereditary traits from generation to generation. Humans normally have 46 chromosomes.

DNA Acronym for deoxyribonucleic acid, the substance that forms the basic material of chromosomes. It takes the form of a double helix and contains the genetic code.

Polygenic Referring to traits that are influenced by combinations of genes.

Genotype One's genetic makeup, based on the sequencing of the nucleotides we term A, C, G, and T.

Phenotype One's actual development and appearance, as based on one's genotype and environmental influences.

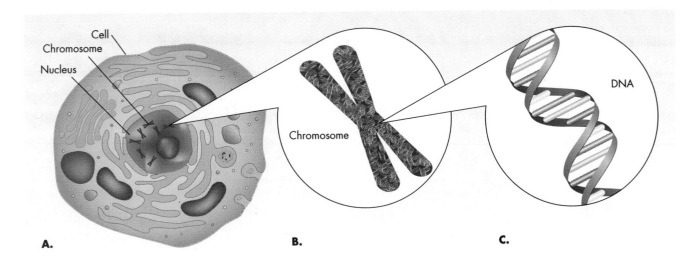

Figure 2.18
Cells, Chromosomes, and DNA
A. The nuclei of cells contain chromosomes. **B.** Chromosomes are made up of DNA. **C.** Segments of DNA are made up of genes that determine physical traits such as height, eye color, and whether pigs have wings (no, because of their genetic makeup, they don't). Genes are segments of chromosomes that are found with the nuclei of cells. The genetic code—that is the order of the chemicals A, G, T, and C—determines your species and all those traits that can be inherited, from the color of your eyes to predispositions toward many psychological traits and abilities, including sociability and musical talent.

Your genotype provides what psychologists refer to as your **nature.** Your phenotype represents the interaction of your nature (heredity) and your **nurture** (environmental influences) in the origins of your behavior and mental processes. Psychologists are especially interested in the roles of nature and nurture in intelligence and psychological disorders. Our genotypes provide us with physical traits that set the stage for certain behaviors. But none of us is the result of heredity alone. Environmental factors such as nutrition, learning opportunities, cultural influences, exercise, and (unfortunately) accident and illness also determine our phenotypes, and whether genetically possible behaviors will be displayed. Behavior and mental processes represent the interaction of nature and nurture. A potential Shakespeare who is reared in poverty and never taught to read or write will not create a *Hamlet.*

We normally receive 23 chromosomes from our father's sperm cell and 23 chromosomes from our mother's egg cell (ovum). When a sperm cell fertilizes an ovum, the chromosomes form 23 pairs (see Figure 2.19). The 23rd pair consists of **sex chromosomes,** which determine whether we are female or male. We all receive an X sex chromosome (so called because of the X shape) from our mother. If we also receive an X sex chromosome from our father, we develop into a female. If we receive a Y sex chromosome (named after the Y shape) from our father, we develop into a male. In the following section, we observe the unfortunate results that may occur when people do not receive the normal complement of chromosomes from their parents.

Down Syndrome   When people do not have the normal number of 46 chromosomes (23 pairs), physical and behavioral abnormalities may result. Most persons with **Down syndrome,** for example, have an extra, or third, chromosome on the 21st pair. The extra chromosome is usually contributed by the mother, and the condition becomes increasingly likely as the mother's age at the time of pregnancy increases. Persons with Down syndrome have a downward-sloping fold of skin at the inner corners of the eyes, a round face, a protruding tongue, and a broad, flat nose. They are cognitively impaired and usually have physical problems that cause death by middle age (Schupf, 2000).

Nature   The inborn, innate character of an organism.

Nurture   The sum total of the environmental factors that affect an organism from conception onward. (In another usage, *nurture* refers to the act of nourishing and otherwise promoting the development of youngsters.)

Sex chromosomes   The 23rd pair of chromosomes, whose genetic material determines the sex of the individual.

Down syndrome   A condition caused by an extra chromosome on the 21st pair and characterized by mental deficiency, a broad face, and slanting eyes.

Figure 2.19
The 23 Pairs of Human Chromosomes
People normally have 23 pairs of chromosomes. Sex is determined by the 23rd pair of chromosomes. Females have two X sex chromosomes, whereas males have an X sex chromosome and a Y sex chromosome.

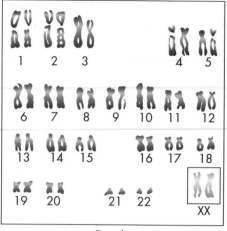

Female   Male

A Closer Look

Are You a Human or a Mouse (or a Chimp or a Carrot)? Some Fascinating Facts About Genes

◇ **Truth or Fiction Revisited:** Yes, it is true that your genetic code overlaps about 25% with that of a carrot. Don't be concerned. It doesn't mean you're going to turn orange or that you are about to enter your "salad days." So, to quote Bugs Bunny, "What's up, Doc?" What's "up" is that your genetic code, like the genetic codes of other life forms, is a sequence of four chemicals. By chance alone, then, one out of four in the sequence would be repeated in any randomly selected segments of carrot and human DNA.

The house mouse is not only in your pantry; much of it is in your genes. The genomes of humans and mice have been decoded and, of the 30,000 or so genes possessed by each, about 29,700 genes in one have some counterpart in the other (Gunter & Dhand, 2002). The counterparts are not necessarily the same; for example, the mouse has more genes related to odor detection and thus a better sense of smell. The genetic difference between mice and humans results from some 75 million years of evolution along different paths from a common mammalian ancestor. When we consider how different we appear to be from the mouse, it is remarkable how similar we are in genetic makeup. But only a few hundred genes apparently explain why mice are pests (and pets). The overlap also makes mice excellent stand-ins for humans in medical research.

Our closest genetic relatives are chimpanzees, with whom we may have shared a common ancestor some 6 to 9 million years ago. Only 1.58% of the genetic code of the chimpanzee differs from our own. Putting it another way: Our genetic codes overlap with those of chimps by more than 98% (Zimmer, 2002–2003)!

The sequence of your own DNA also overlaps about 99.9% with that of other humans (Plomin & Crabbe, 2000). Yet the difference of 0.1% accounts for the differences between Mozart and Nelson Mandela and between Michelle Kwan and Oprah Winfrey. Despite this enormous overlap, people differ greatly in their skin coloration, their body shape, and their psychological makeup, including their talents and skills. Some compose symphonies and others are tone-deaf. Some tackle differential equations and others cannot add or subtract. Some figure skate in the Olympics and others trip over their own feet. Even though we differ but 0.1% in genetic code from our fellows, it often seems easier to focus on how much we differ rather than on how much we have in common.

◇ **Truth or Fiction Revisited:** It is true that Neanderthals and some other ancient humanoids may not be quite as extinct as has been believed. In fact, they may be "lurking" in your own genetic code. Recent analysis of DNA suggests that modern humans—that's us—may have interbred with other humanoids rather than simply replacing them (Wilford, 2005). When you misbehave, you can now say it's the Neanderthal in you—although the truth could be quite the reverse. ■

━━■━ Kinship Studies: Is the Behavior of Relatives Related?

What are kinship studies? Kinship studies are ways in which psychologists compare the presence of traits and behavior patterns in people who are biologically related or unrelated to help determine the role of genetic factors in their occurrence. The more *closely* people are related, the more *genes* they have in common. Identical twins share 100% of their genes. Parents and children have 50% of their genes in common, as do siblings (brothers and sisters). Aunts and uncles related by blood have a 25% overlap with nieces and nephews. First cousins share 12.5% of their genes. If genes are involved in a trait or behavior pattern, people who are more closely related should be more likely to show similar traits or behavior. Psychologists and behavioral geneticists are especially interested in running kinship studies with twins and adopted individuals (Plomin, 2002).

Twin Studies: Looking into the Genetic Mirror   The fertilized egg cell (ovum) that carries genetic messages from both parents is called a *zygote*. Now and then, a zygote divides into two cells that separate, so that instead of developing into a single person, it develops into two people with the same genetic makeup. Such people are identical, or **monozygotic (MZ), twins.** If the woman releases two ova in the same month and they are both fertilized, they develop into fraternal, or **dizygotic (DZ), twins.** DZ twins, like other siblings, share 50% of their genes. MZ twins are important in the study of the relative influences of nature (heredity) and nurture (the environment) because differences between MZ twins are the result of nurture. (They do not differ in their heredity—that is, their nature—because their genetic makeup is the same.)

Twin studies compare the presence of traits and behavior patterns in MZ twins, DZ twins, and other people to help determine the role of genetic factors in their occurrence. If MZ twins show greater similarity on a trait or behavior pattern than DZ twins, a genetic basis for the trait or behavior is suggested.

Twin studies show how strongly genetic factors influence physical features. MZ twins are more likely to look alike and to be similar in height, even to have more similar cholesterol levels than DZ twins. These findings hold even when the MZ twins are reared apart and the DZ twins are reared together (Stunkard et al., 1990). Research shows that MZ twin sisters begin to menstruate about one to two months apart, whereas DZ twins begin to menstruate about a year apart. MZ twins are more alike than DZ twins in their blood pressure, brain wave patterns, even in their speech patterns, gestures, and mannerisms (Hansell et al., 2001; Lensvelt-Mulders & Hettema, 2001; Lykken et al., 1992).

MZ twins also resemble one another more strongly than DZ twins in intelligence and personality traits like sociability, anxiety, friendliness, and conformity, even happiness (Markon et al., 2002; McCourt et al., 1999; McCrae et al., 2000). David Lykken and Mike Csikszentmihalyi (2001) suggest that we inherit a tendency toward a certain level of happiness. Despite the ups and downs of life, we tend to drift back to our usual levels of cheerfulness (or irritability). We shall investigate the role of (happy?) genes in happiness in greater depth in Chapter 9. Heredity is also a key contributor to developmental factors such as cognitive functioning, autism, and early signs of attachment such as smiling, cuddling, and expression of fear of strangers (DiLalla, 2004; DiLalla et al., 1996; Scarr & Kidd, 1983).

MZ twins are more likely than DZ twins to share psychological disorders such as autism, depression, schizophrenia, and even vulnerability to alcoholism (McGue et al., 1992; Plomin, 2000; Veenstra-Vanderweele & Cook, 2003). In one study on autism, the concordance rate for MZ twins was about 60%. (That is, if one member of a pair of MZ twins was autistic, the other member had a 60% chance of being so.) The concordance rate for DZ twins was only 10% (Plomin et al., 1994).

Of course, twin studies are not perfect. MZ twins may resemble each other more closely than DZ twins partly because they are treated more similarly. MZ twins frequently are dressed identically, and parents sometimes have difficulty telling them apart.

One way to get around this difficulty is to find and compare MZ twins who were reared in different homes. Any similarities between MZ twins reared apart cannot be explained by a shared home environment and would appear to be largely a result of heredity. In the fas-

Michael Greenlar / The Image Works

■ **Down Syndrome**
Down syndrome is caused by an extra chromosome on the 21st pair and becomes more likely to occur as the mother's age at the time of pregnancy increases. Persons with Down syndrome have characteristic facial features including downward-sloping folds of skin at the inner corners of the eyes, are mentally retarded, and usually have health problems that lead to death by middle age.

Monozygotic (MZ) twins   Twins that develop from a single fertilized ovum that divides in two early in prenatal development. MZ twins thus share the same genetic code. Also called *identical twins.*

Dizygotic (DZ) twins   Twins that develop from two fertilized ova and who are thus as closely related as brothers and sisters in general. Also called *fraternal twins.*

reflect & relate

Which family members seem to be like you physically or psychologically? Which seem to be very different? How do you explain the similarities and differences?

cinating Minnesota Study of Twins Reared Apart (Bouchard et al., 1990; DiLalla et al., 1999; Markon et al., 2002), researchers have been measuring the physiological and psychological characteristics of 56 sets of MZ adult twins who were separated in infancy and reared in different homes.

In sum, MZ twins reared apart are about as similar as MZ twins reared together on a variety of measures of intelligence, personality, temperament, occupational and leisure-time interests, and social attitudes. These traits thus would appear to have a genetic underpinning.

Adoption Studies The results of kinship studies can be confused when relatives share similar environments as well as genes. Adoption studies overcome some of this problem by comparing children who have been separated from their parents at an early age (or in which identical twins are separated at an early age) and reared in different environments. Psychologists look for similarities between children and their adoptive and natural parents. When children reared by adoptive parents are more similar to their natural parents in a particular trait, strong evidence exists for a genetic role in the development of that trait.

In later chapters we will see that psychologists have been particularly interested in the use of adoption studies to sort out the effects of nature and nurture in the development of personality traits, intelligence, and various psychological disorders. Such traits and disorders apparently represent the interaction of complex groupings of genes as well as environmental influences.

Selective Breeding: The Nurture of Nature

Under natural selection, traits that enable animals and plants to adapt better to their environments are likely to be—in Darwin's wording—"preserved." But there is another kind of selection: selection not by nature, but by humans; and we call it *selective breeding*. *What is selective breeding?*

We selectively breed plants and animals to enhance desired physical and—in the case of animals—behavioral traits. We breed cattle and chickens to be bigger and fatter so that they provide more food calories for less feed.

Dogs have been selectively bred for size, gentleness, tendencies to protect their territory, and for ease of training, including housebreaking. We haven't tried to housebreak rats, but we have selectively bred rats for maze-learning ability. In classic research, an initial group of rats was tested for maze-learning ability, as measured by the number of errors they make in repeated trials to reach a food goal (Tryon, 1940). Rats making the fewest mistakes are labeled B1, indicating high maze-learning ability. Those making the most errors are labeled D1. The distribution of errors for the first or parent generation is shown in part A of Figure 2.20, which shows the number of blind-alley entrances (errors) over a series of 19 runs through the maze. Note that the distribution of errors for the parent generation (part A of Figure 2.20) is rather even, ranging from very few to about 200. Rats with high maze-learning ability are then bred with other rats with high maze-learning ability; rats with low maze-learning ability are similarly bred with other "maze-dull" rats. Their offspring, the second generation (part B of Figure 2.20), begins to show dramatic differences in maze-learning ability. The offspring of the maze-bright rats (B2) are beginning to form a group that differs distinctly from the offspring of the maze-dull rats (D2). Parts C and D of Figure 2.20 show that if we selectively breed subsequent generations of maze-bright and maze-dull rats, we begin to arrive at a point where the distributions of the brightest and the dullest hardly overlap at all. By the seventh generation, the maze-bright (B7) rats are making about 1 error per trial, whereas the maze-dull (D7) rats are making 9 to 10 errors per trial.

Maze-learning ability can be considered reflective of animal intelligence. It requires visual–motor skills and the ability to profit from experience. A key issue in psychology is the role of genetic factors in the behaviors and mental processes that make up intelligence in humans. We look more closely at that controversial issue in Chapter 8.

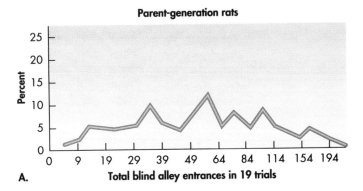

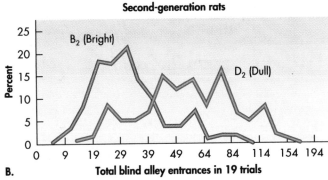

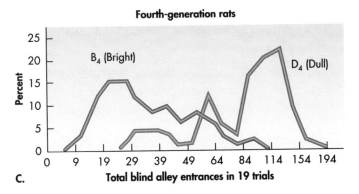

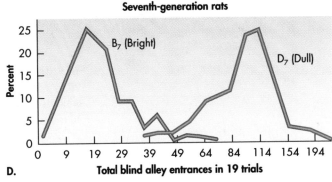

Figure 2.20

Selective Breeding for Maze-Learning Ability in Rats

Humans selectively breed animals and plants to achieve desired physical traits. In the case of animals, however, it is also possible to selectively breed for psychological traits and behaviors such as aggressiveness and trainability (in dogs) and maze-learning ability (in rats). In the classic Tryon (1940) study, "maze-bright" and "maze-dull" rats were selectively bred over several generations, until the distributions of their maze-learning ability barely overlapped.

() Learning Connections

◀◀ *Evolution and Heredity—The Nature of Nature* ▶▶

REVIEW:

11 Darwin believed that mutations occur at random but are maintained or lost by
(a) natural selection,
(b) neurotransmitters,
(c) the limbic system,
(d) maturation.

12 Species-specific behavior patterns are also called
(a) habits,
(b) traits,
(c) mutations,
(d) instincts.

13 _____ are the most basic building blocks of heredity.
(a) Atoms,
(b) Neurons,
(c) Genes,
(d) Chromosomes.

14 The behavior of _____ twins is of interest because they have the same genes.
(a) monozygotic,
(b) dizygotic,
(c) trizygotic,
(d) newborn.

CRITICAL THINKING:
What ethical, social, and political issues would be involved in attempting to selectively breed humans for desired traits?

Go to
http://academic.cengage.com/psychology/rathus
for an interactive version of this review.

RECITE—*An Active Summary*™

 Recite to Go! *Don't have time to study right now? You can study on the go!*
Go to your companion website and download an audio version of this review section to your media player. You can also access an interactive flash-card version of this review from your website.

1. What are neurons?	Neurons are cells that transmit information through neural impulses. Neurons have a cell body; dendrites, which receive messages; and axons, which conduct messages and transmit them to other cells by means of neurotransmitters. Myelin sheaths insulate many axons, allowing more efficient conduction of messages.
2. What are neural impulses?	Neural transmission is electrochemical. An electrical charge is conducted along an axon by a process that allows sodium ions to enter the cell and then pumps them out. The neuron has a resting potential of -70 millivolts and an action potential of about $+40$ millivolts.
3. What happens when a neuron fires?	Neurons fire (transmit messages to other neurons, muscles, or glands) by releasing neurotransmitters. They fire according to an all-or-none principle, up to hundreds of times per second. Each firing is followed by a refractory period.
4. What is a synapse?	Neurons fire across synapses, which consist of an axon terminal from the transmitting neuron, a dendrite or the body of a receiving neuron, and a fluid-filled synaptic cleft between the two.
5. Which neurotransmitters are of interest to psychologists? What do they do?	These include acetylcholine, which is involved in muscle contractions and memory; dopamine, which is involved in pleasure and addiction; norepinephrine, which accelerates body processes; serotonin, which is involved in eating, sleep, and emotional arousal; GABA, which inhibits anxiety; and endorphins, which are natural painkillers.
6. What are the parts of the nervous system?	A nerve is a bundle of axons and dendrites. The nervous system is one of the systems that regulates the body. It is involved in thought processes, emotional responses, heartbeat, motor activity, and so on.
7. What are the divisions and functions of the peripheral nervous system?	The peripheral nervous system has two main divisions: somatic and autonomic (the ANS). The somatic nervous system transmits sensory information about skeletal muscles, skin, and joints to the central nervous system. It also controls skeletal muscular activity. The ANS regulates glands and activities such as heartbeat and digestion.
8. What are the divisions and functions of the central nervous system?	The central nervous system consists of the brain and spinal cord. Reflexes involve the spinal cord but not the brain. The central nervous system has gray matter, which is composed of nonmyelinated neurons, and white matter, which is composed of bundles of myelinated axons.
9. How do researchers learn about the functions of the brain?	Researchers historically learned about the brain from the effects of accidents. They study the effects of intentional damage. They observe how animals respond to electrical stimulation of parts of the brain. They study brain waves with the EEG. CAT scans, PET scans, and MRI enable the creation of computer-generated images of the brain.
10. What are the structures and functions of the brain?	The hindbrain includes the medulla, the pons, and the cerebellum. The reticular activating system begins in the hindbrain and continues into the forebrain. Important structures of the forebrain include the thalamus, which serves as a relay station for sensory stimulation; the hypothalamus, which regulates body temperature and various aspects of motivation and emotion; the limbic system, which is involved in memory,

emotion, and motivation; and the cerebrum, which is the brain's center of thinking and language.

11. What are the parts of the cerebral cortex?	The outer fringe of the cerebrum is the cerebral cortex, which is divided into two hemispheres and four lobes: frontal, parietal, temporal, and occipital.
12. What parts of the cerebral cortex are involved in thinking and language?	Language areas of the cortex usually lie in the left hemisphere. Wernicke's area responds mainly to auditory information. Broca's area is mainly responsible for speech. Damage to either area can cause an aphasia.
13. What would it mean to be "left-brained" or "right-brained"?	The left hemisphere is usually relatively more involved in logical analysis and problem solving, whereas the right hemisphere is usually superior in visual–spatial functions and aesthetic and emotional responses. But the hemispheres generally work together.
14. Does it matter whether one is left-handed? Why are people right-handed or left-handed?	About 1 person in 10 is left-handed. Learning disabilities are somewhat more common among left-handed people, but so is creativity, as shown in the arts. Handedness appears to have a genetic component.
15. What happens when the brain is split in two?	The behavior of people who have had operations that sever most of the corpus callosum remains largely normal. On the other hand, they may be able to verbally describe a screened-off object such as a pencil held in the hand connected to the hemisphere that contains language functions but cannot do so when the object is held in the other hand.
16. What is the endocrine system?	The endocrine system consists of ductless glands that secrete hormones. The pituitary gland secretes growth hormone, prolactin, and oxytocin. Thyroxin affects the metabolism. The adrenal cortex produces steroids. The adrenal medulla secretes epinephrine, which increases the metabolic rate and is involved in general emotional arousal. The sex hormones are responsible for sexual differentiation. Female sex hormones regulate the menstrual cycle.
17. What is Darwin's theory of evolution?	Darwin's theory proposes that a struggle for existence between and within species results in the survival of the fittest individuals. According to the principle of natural selection, the fittest individuals survive to reproduce and transmit their genes to future generations.
18. What is evolutionary psychology?	Evolutionary psychology studies the ways in which natural selection is connected with mental processes and behavior. Evolutionary psychologists suggest that not only physical traits but also behavior evolves and is transmitted from generation to generation.
19. What is meant by an "instinct"?	An instinct is a stereotypical behavior pattern found among members of a species; it occurs even when the individual is reared in isolation.
20. What is meant by "heredity"?	Heredity involves the biological transmission of traits from generation to generation.
21. What is meant by "genetics"?	Genetics is the area of biology that studies heredity. Behavioral genetics is concerned with the genetic transmission of traits that give rise to behavior. Molecular genetics identifies genes that are connected with behavior and mental processes.
22. What are the roles of genes and chromosomes in heredity?	Genes are the biochemical materials that regulate the development of traits. Genes are segments of chromosomes. Humans have 46 chromosomes arranged in 23 pairs. Chromosomes are molecules of DNA, which takes the form of a twisting ladder. Sex chromosomes determine the sex of the child.
23. What are kinship studies?	Psychologists conduct kinship studies to help determine the influences of genetic and environmental factors. Twin studies are useful because identical (monozygotic) twins share the same genetic code; therefore, differences reflect environmental factors.
24. What is selective breeding?	In selective breeding, one breeds offspring that are closest to a desired trait, and continues to breed their offspring that are yet closer to the goal. Humans selectively breed many animals, including dogs, for physical and behavioral traits.

Key Terms

Neuron 39
Glial cells 39
Dendrites 39
Axon 39
Myelin 40
Afferent neurons 41
Efferent neurons 41
Neural impulse 41
Polarize 41
Resting potential 41
Depolarize 41
Action potential 41
All-or-none principle 42
Refractory period 43
Synapse 43
Neurotransmitters 43
Receptor site 44
Acetylcholine (ACh) 44
Hippocampus 45
Dopamine 45
Norepinephrine 45
Serotonin 45
Gamma-aminobutyric
　acid (GABA) 45
Endorphins 45
Nerve 46
Central nervous system 46
Peripheral nervous system 46

Somatic nervous system 47
Autonomic nervous system (ANS) 47
Sympathetic 48
Parasympathetic 48
Spinal cord 49
Spinal reflex 49
Gray matter 49
White matter 49
Electroencephalograph (EEG) 52
Computerized axial tomography
　(CAT scan) 52
Positron emission tomography
　(PET scan) 52
Magnetic resonance imaging
　(MRI) 53
Functional MRI (fMRI) 53
Medulla 54
Pons 55
Cerebellum 55
Reticular activating system (RAS) 56
Thalamus 56
Hypothalamus 56
Limbic system 56
Amygdala 57
Cerebrum 57
Cerebral cortex 57
Corpus callosum 58
Somatosensory cortex 58

Motor cortex 58
Aphasia 60
Wernicke's aphasia 60
Broca's aphasia 60
Epilepsy 62
Gland 64
Endocrine system 64
Hormone 64
Pituitary gland 64
Natural selection 70
Mutation 70
Evolutionary psychology 70
Species 71
Instinct 71
Heredity 71
Genetics 71
Gene 72
Chromosome 72
DNA 72
Polygenic 72
Genotype 72
Phenotype 72
Nature 73
Nurture 73
Sex chromosomes 73
Down syndrome 73
Monozygotic (MZ) twins 75
Dizygotic (DZ) twins 75

Active Learning Resources

Visit Your Companion Website
for This Book

http://academic.cengage.com/psychology/rathus

Check out this companion website where you will find online resources directly linked to your book. This is where you'll access the videos highlighted in your Video Connections feature. You can answer the questions online and email them to your professor. In addition you'll find downloadable audio review material, interactive versions of the study aids, Power Visuals for mastering and reviewing key concepts, as well as quizzing, and much more!

CENGAGENOW™   **http://academic.cengage.com**

Need help studying? This site is your one-stop study shop. Take a Pre-Test and Cengage NOW will generate a Personalized Study Plan based on your test results. The Study Plan will identify the topics you need to review and direct you to online resources to help you master those topics. You can then take a Post-Test to help you determine the concepts you have mastered and what you still need to work on. In addition you can access interactive media including the videos highlighted in your Video Connections box.

Author Blog

What does your author Spence Rathus have to say about the state of psychology? Visit your companion website every Tuesday and click on "Author Blog." This is where he'll talk about the most recent controversies and hot topics in psychology. This will keep you up to date with what your author is thinking and give you great insight into modern psychology.

CHAPTER 3

The Voyage Through the Life Span

Karen Kasmauski/National Geographic/Getty Images

| T | F | Your heart started beating when you were only one-fifth of an inch long and weighed a fraction of an ounce. |

| T | F | Prior to 6 months or so of age, "out of sight" is literally "out of mind." |

| T | F | Children who attend day-care programs are more aggressive than children who do not. |

| T | F | Child abusers were frequently abused themselves as children. |

| T | F | The architect Frank Lloyd Wright designed New York's innovative spiral-shaped Guggenheim Museum when he was 65 years old. |

| T | F | Alzheimer's disease is a normal part of aging. |

| T | F | "Successful aging" involves avoiding new challenges. |

Go to www

http://academic.cengage.com/pstchology/rathus
for an interactive version of this Truth or Fiction feature.

There is no cure for birth or death save to enjoy the interval.
—George Santayana

She went for the girl. Kathy had three boys—a pair of 10-year-old twins and a 5-year-old—and decided, "Enough is enough." How delightful it would be to have a little girl. Though she was in her early 40s and had some fertility problems, she would try. But was she going to leave the sex of her baby up to chance? You might think that after having three boys, the odds were now in her favor. But that's not the way it works. The more boys you have already, the more likely it is you'll have another boy if you try again. (That's because there may be something systematic—even if unknown—about the way the couple determine the sex of their child.)

So Kathy placed her fate in the hands of a company that touted a high success rate in helping couples have girls rather than boys. Kathy and her husband spent thousands of dollars, chemically induced her reluctant ovaries to produce ova, underwent artificial insemination to maximize the chances of conception, and—as it turns out—she didn't get pregnant.

But each year millions upon millions of women do. Developmental psychologists study the child's voyage through the life span for several reasons. The discovery of early influences and developmental sequences helps psychologists understand adults. Psychologists are also interested in the effects of genetic factors, early interactions with parents and siblings, and the school and community on traits such as aggressiveness and intelligence.

Developmental psychologists seek to learn the causes of developmental abnormalities. For example, should pregnant women abstain from smoking and drinking? (Yes.) Is it safe for a pregnant woman to take aspirin for a headache or tetracycline to ward off a bacterial invasion? (Perhaps not. Ask your obstetrician.) What factors contribute to child abuse? Some developmental psychologists focus on adult development. For example, what conflicts and disillusionments can we expect as we voyage through our 30s, 40s, and 50s? The information acquired by developmental psychologists can help us make decisions about how we rear our children and lead our own lives.

Let us now turn to prenatal developments—the changes that occur between conception and birth. They are spectacular, but they occur "out of sight."

PRENATAL DEVELOPMENT: THE BEGINNING OF OUR LIFE STORY

The most dramatic gains in height and weight occur during prenatal development. *What developments occur from conception through birth?* Within 9 months, the newly conceived organism develops from a nearly microscopic cell to a newborn child about 20 inches long. Its weight increases a billionfold!

During the months following conception, the single cell formed by the union of sperm and egg—the **zygote**—multiplies, becoming two cells, then four, then eight, and so on. By the time the infant is ready to be born, it contains trillions of cells.

The zygote divides repeatedly as it proceeds on its 3- to 4-day voyage to the uterus. The ball-like mass of multiplying cells wanders about the uterus for another 3 to 4 days before beginning to implant in the uterine wall. Implantation takes another week or so. The period from conception to implantation is called the **germinal stage.**

The **embryonic stage** lasts from implantation until about the eighth week of development. During this stage, the major body organ systems take form. As you can see from Figure 3.1, the growth of the head precedes that of other parts of the body. The growth of the organs—heart, lungs, and so on—also precedes the growth of the extremities. The relatively early **maturation** of the brain and the organ systems allows them to participate in the nourishment and further development of the embryo. ◆ **Truth or Fiction Revisited:** During the fourth week, a primitive heart begins to beat and pump blood—in an organism that is one-fifth of an inch long. The heart will continue to beat without rest every minute of every day for most of a century, perhaps longer.

By the end of the second month, the head has become rounded and the facial features distinct—all in an embryo that is about 1 inch long and weighs 1/30th of an ounce. During the second month, the nervous system begins to transmit messages. By 5 to 6 weeks, the embryo is only a quarter to half an inch long, yet nondescript sex organs have formed. By about the seventh week, the genetic code (XY or XX) begins to assert itself, causing the sex organs to differentiate. If a Y sex chromosome is present, testes form and begin to produce **androgens** (male sex hormones), which further masculinize the sex organs. In the absence of these hormones, the embryo develops sex organs typical of the female, regardless of its genetic code. However, individuals with a male genetic code would be sterile.

As it develops, the embryo is suspended within a protective **amniotic sac** in the mother's uterus. The sac is surrounded by a clear membrane and contains amniotic fluid.

Zygote A fertilized ovum (egg cell).

Germinal stage The first stage of prenatal development, during which the dividing mass of cells has not become implanted in the uterine wall.

Embryonic stage The baby from the third through the eighth weeks following conception, during which time the major organ systems undergo rapid differentiation.

Maturation The process of development as guided by the unfolding of the genetic code.

Androgens Male sex hormones.

Amniotic sac A sac within the uterus that contains the embryo or fetus.

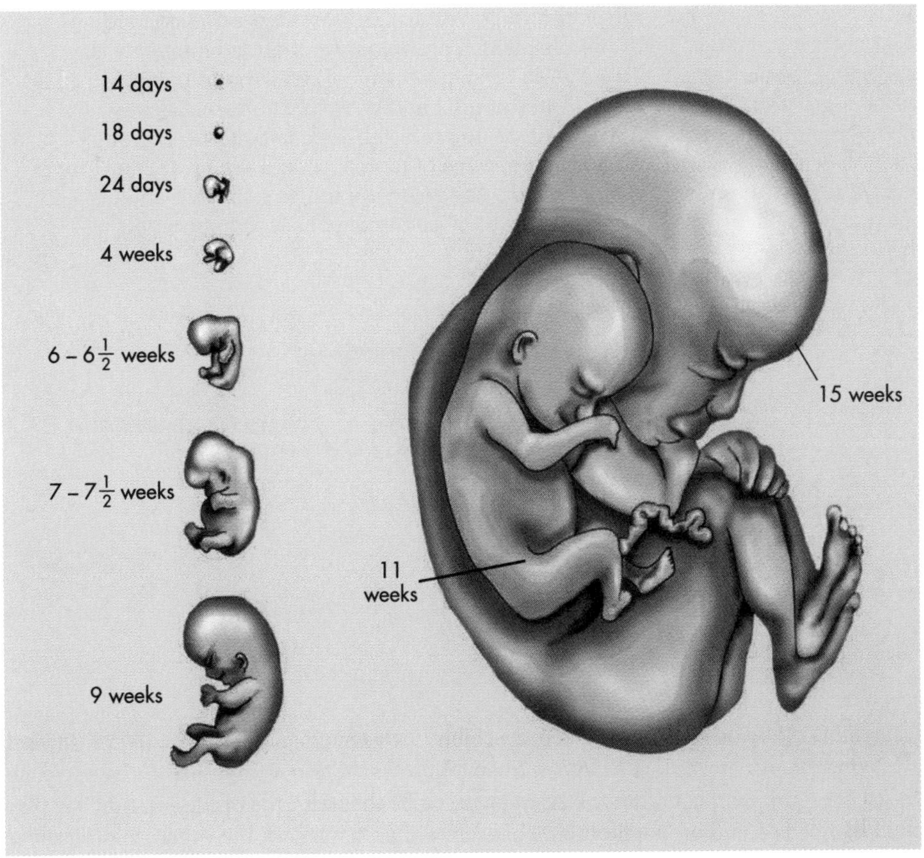

Figure 3.1

Embryos and Fetuses at Various Intervals of Prenatal Development
Development of the head (and brain) precedes that of other parts of the body. The development of the organs—heart, lungs, and so on—also precedes the development of the limbs. The relatively early maturation of the brain and the organ systems allows them to participate in the nourishment and further development of the embryo.

Placenta A membrane that permits the exchange of nutrients and waste products between the mother and her developing child but does not allow the maternal and fetal bloodstreams to mix.

Umbilical cord A tube between the mother and her developing child through which nutrients and waste products are conducted.

Fetal stage The baby from the third month following conception through childbirth, during which time there is maturation of organ systems and dramatic gains in length and weight.

The fluid is a sort of natural air bag, allowing the child to move or even jerk around without injury. It also helps maintain an even temperature.

From now until birth, the embryo exchanges nutrients and wastes with the mother through the **placenta.** The embryo is connected to the placenta by the **umbilical cord.** The placenta is connected to the mother by blood vessels in the uterine wall.

The **fetal stage** lasts from the beginning of the third month until birth. By the end of the third month, the major organ systems and the fingers and toes have formed. In the middle of the fourth month, the mother usually detects the first fetal movements. By the end of the sixth month, the fetus moves its limbs so vigorously that mothers often feel that they are being kicked. The fetus opens and shuts its eyes, sucks its thumb, alternates between periods of being awake and sleeping, and responds to light. It also turns somersaults, which can be perceived by the mother.

During the 3 months prior to birth, the organ systems of the fetus continue to mature. The heart and lungs become increasingly capable of sustaining independent life. The fetus gains about 5½ pounds and doubles in length. Newborn boys average about 7½ pounds and newborn girls about 7 pounds.

( ) Learning Connections

◄◄   *Prenatal Development—The Beginning of Our Life Story*   ►►

REVIEW:

1 The major body organ systems take form during the
   (a) prepubescent stage,   (c) fetal stage,
   (b) embryonic stage,   (d) germinal stage.

2 The embryo is connected to the placenta by the
   (a) umbilical cord,   (c) uterus,
   (b) amniotic sac,   (d) zygote.

CRITICAL THINKING:
A woman can bear a child of the desired sex by using preimplantation genetic diagnosis (PGD), in which health professionals surgically harvest a woman's ova and fertilize them in a laboratory dish, creating several embryos. After a few days of cell division, the sex chromosomal structure of each embryo is examined to determine whether it is female or male. Embryos of the desired sex are implanted in the woman's uterus, where one or more can grow to term. Sex selection raises moral and ethical issues. One is the discarding of the unselected embryos. Another is whether it is "right"—in religious terms or in terms of balancing the number of girls and boys in a culture. Because males tend to be preferred, sex selection can create an overabundance of males, as in India and China. Yet many believe that selecting the sex of one's child is purely a matter of personal choice. What do you think? Why?

Go to www
http://academic.cengage.com/psychology/rathus
for an interactive version of this review.

CHILDHOOD

Childhood begins with birth. When my children are enjoying themselves, I kid them and say, "Stop having fun. You're a child, and childhood is the worst time of life." I get a laugh because they know that childhood is supposed to be the best time of life—a time for play and learning and endless possibilities. For many children it is that, but other children suffer from problems such as malnutrition, low self-esteem, and child abuse.

Let us chronicle the events of childhood. The most obvious aspects of child development are physical, so we begin with these. Then we consider cognitive and social and emotional developments.

——■— Physical Development: The Drama Continues

Physical development includes gains in height and weight, maturation of the nervous system, and development of bones, muscles, and organs. *What physical developments occur during childhood?*

During infancy—the first two years of childhood—dramatic gains in height and weight continue. Babies usually double their birth weight in about 5 months and triple it by their first birthday (Kuczmarski et al., 2000). Their height increases by about 10 inches in the first year. Children grow another 4 to 6 inches during the second year and gain some 4 to 7 pounds. After that, they gain about 2 to 3 inches a year until they reach the adolescent growth spurt. Weight gains also remain fairly even at about 4 to 6 pounds per year until the spurt. Other aspects of physical development in childhood include reflexes and perceptual development.

Reflexes: Entering the World Prewired   Soon after you were born, a doctor or nurse probably pressed her fingers against the palms of your hands. Although you would have had no idea what to do in response, most likely you grasped the fingers firmly—so firmly that you could have been lifted from your cradle!

Grasping at birth is inborn, an example of the importance of nature in human development. Grasping is one of the baby's reflexes. **Reflexes** are simple, unlearned, stereotypical responses elicited by specific stimuli. Newborn children do not know that it is necessary to eat to survive. Fortunately, rooting and sucking reflexes cause them to eat. They turn their head toward stimuli that prod or stroke the cheek, chin, or corner of the mouth. This is termed **rooting**. They suck objects that touch their lips. Reflexes are essential to survival and occur automatically—that is, without thinking about them.

Newborns use the withdrawal reflex to avoid painful stimuli. In the startle, or Moro, reflex, they draw up their legs and arch their backs in response to sudden noises, bumps, or loss of support while being held. They grasp objects that press against the palms of their hands (the grasp, or palmar, reflex). They fan their toes when the soles of their feet are stimulated (the Babinski reflex). Pediatricians test these reflexes to assess babies' neural functioning.

Babies also breathe, sneeze, cough, yawn, and blink reflexively. And it is guaranteed that you will learn about the sphincter (anal muscle) reflex if you put on your best clothes and hold an undiapered baby on your lap for a while.

Motor Development   The motor development of the child refers to the progression from simple acts like lifting the head to running around. Maturation and experience both play key roles in motor development (Muir, 2000; Pryce et al., 2001; Roncesvalles et al., 2001). Maturation of the brain is a key to motor development. Motor development provides some of the most fascinating changes in infants, in part because so much seems to happen so quickly—and so much of it during the first year. Children go through a sequence that includes rolling over, sitting up, crawling, creeping, walking, and running. The ages at which infants first engage in these activities vary, but the sequence generally remains the same (see Figure 3.2). Invariant sequences suggest an unfolding of the genetic code (maturation).

The role of maturation in areas such as physical development (for example, gains in height and weight and the effects of puberty), language development, and motor development is clear. But environmental factors are also involved. Children may have certain genetic potentials for body size and growth rates, but they do not reach them unless environmental factors such as nutrition, relatively clean air, and so on are available. Children do not understand or produce language until their genetic codes spark the development of certain structures and processes in the brain. But the environment is also involved. Children learn

reflect & relate

During the fourth month most mothers begin to detect their baby's movements and feel that their baby is "alive." What is your view on when the baby is alive? What standard or standards do you use in forming your view?

Reflex A simple unlearned response to a stimulus.

Rooting The turning of an infant's head toward a touch, such as by the mother's nipple.

Figure 3.2
Motor Development
Motor development proceeds in an orderly sequence, which suggests that there is a strong maturational component. However, there is considerable variation in the timing of the marker events shown in this figure. An infant who is a bit behind will most likely develop without problems, and a precocious infant will not necessarily become a rocket scientist (or gymnast).

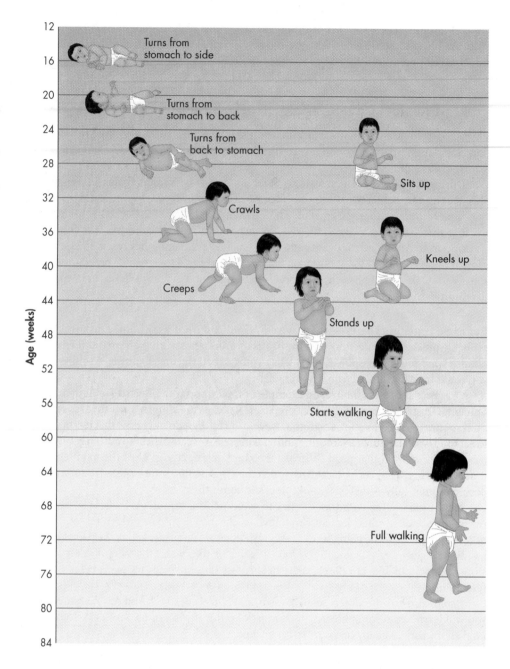

the languages used in their homes and communities. They do not speak foreign tongues without being exposed to them.

Perceptual Development: On *Not* Going Off the Deep End   Newborn children spend about 16 hours a day sleeping and do not have much opportunity to learn about the world. Yet they perceive the world reasonably well soon after birth. Within a couple of days, infants can follow, or "track," a moving light with their eyes (Kellman & von Hofsten, 1992). By 3 months, they can discriminate most colors (Banks & Shannon, 1993; Teller, 1998). Newborns are nearsighted, but by about 4 months, infants focus on distant objects about as well as adults do.

The visual preferences of infants are measured by the amount of time, termed **fixation time,** they spend looking at one stimulus instead of another. In classic research by Robert Fantz (1961), 2-month-old infants preferred visual stimuli that resembled the human face

Fixation time   The amount of time spent looking at a visual stimulus.

to newsprint, a bull's-eye, and featureless red, white, and yellow disks (see Figure 3.3).

Classic research has shown that infants tend to respond to cues for depth by the time they are able to crawl (at about 6 to 8 months). Most also have the good sense to avoid crawling off ledges and table tops into open space (Campos et al., 1978). Figure 3.4 shows the setup in the classic "visual cliff" experiment run by Walk and Gibson (1961). An 8-month-old infant crawls freely above the part of the glass with a checkerboard pattern immediately underneath, but hesitates to crawl over the part beneath which the checkerboard has been dropped a few feet. Because the glass would support the infant, this is a "visual cliff," not an actual cliff.

Normal newborns hear well. Most newborns reflexively turn their heads toward unusual sounds. This finding, along with findings about visual tracking, suggests that infants are pre-programmed to survey their environments. Speaking or singing softly in a low-pitched tone soothes infants. This is why lullabies help infants fall asleep.

Three-day-old babies prefer their mother's voice to those of other women, but they do not show a preference for their father's voice (DeCasper & Prescott, 1984; Freeman et al., 1993). Babies, of course, have had months of "experience" in the uterus. For at least 2 or 3 months before birth, they have been able to hear. Because they are predominantly exposed to sounds produced by their mother, learning may contribute to newborn preferences.

Babies' preferences for odors are similar to those of adults. Newborn infants spit, stick out their tongue, and literally wrinkle their nose at the odor of rotten eggs. They smile and make licking motions in response to chocolate, strawberry, vanilla, and honey. The sense of smell, like the sense of hearing, may provide a vehicle for mother–infant recognition. Within the first week, nursing infants prefer to turn toward their mother's nursing pads (which are detected by smell) rather than those of strange women (Macfarlane, 1975). By 15 days, nursing infants prefer their mother's underarm odor to those of other women (Porter et al., 1992). Newborn babies discriminate tastes. They eagerly suck liquid solutions of sugar and milk but grimace and refuse to suck salty or bitter solutions (Petrov et al., 2001; Rosenstein & Oster, 1988).

Newborns are sensitive to touch. Many reflexes including rooting and sucking are triggered by touch. Touch is an important avenue of learning and communication for babies. Sensations of skin against skin appear to provide feelings of comfort and security that may contribute to the formation of affectionate bonds between infants and their caregivers.

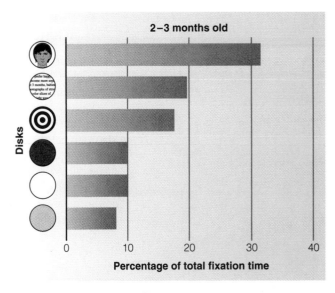

Figure 3.3
Two-Month-Olds' Preferences for Visual Stimuli
Infants appear to prefer complex to simple visual stimuli. By 2 months of age, they also show preference for the human face. Researchers debate whether the face draws attention because of its content (that is, being a face) or because of its stimulus characteristics (complexity, arrangement, and so on).

Figure 3.4
The Classic Visual Cliff Experiment
This young explorer has the good sense not to crawl out onto an apparently unsupported surface, even when Mother beckons from the other side. Rats, pups, kittens, and chicks also will not try to walk across to the other side. (So don't bother asking why the chicken crossed the visual cliff.)

Controversy in Psychology: Is Development Continuous or Discontinuous?

Do developmental changes tend to occur gradually (continuously)? Or do they tend to occur in major leaps (discontinuously) that dramatically alter our bodies and behavior? ***Does development occur gradually or in stages?***

John B. Watson and other behaviorists viewed development as a mainly continuous process in which the effects of learning mount gradually, with no major sudden changes. Maturational theorists, however, argue that people are prewired or preset to change dramatically at certain times of life. Rapid qualitative changes can be ushered in during new stages of development. They point out that the environment, even when enriched, profits us little until we are ready, or mature enough, to develop in a certain direction. For example, newborn babies do not imitate their parents' speech, even when the parents speak clearly and deliberately.

Certain aspects of physical development are clearly discontinuous, For example, the changes from the age of 2 to the onset of puberty (the period of development during which reproduction becomes possible) are continuous, with children gradually growing larger. Then a new stage of development begins with the adolescent growth spurt, which is triggered by hormones and characterized by rapid changes in structure and function, as in the development of the sex organ, as well as size.

Psychologists disagree more strongly on whether aspects of development such as cognitive development, attachment, and gender typing occur in stages. Stage theorists, such as Jean Piaget—whose theory of cognitive development we discuss next—and Sigmund Freud, saw development as discontinuous. Jean Piaget believed that cognitive development consisted of four stages of development. In this chapter we will also see that Lawrence Kohlberg's theory of moral development consists of three levels and two stages within each level. Erik Erikson's theory of psychosocial development consists of eight stages.

Cognitive Development: On the Edge of Reason?

The ways in which children mentally represent and think about the world—that is, their *cognitive development*—are explored in this section. Because cognitive functioning develops over many years, young children have ideas about the world that differ considerably from those of adults. Many of these ideas are charming but illogical—at least to adults. Let us consider three views of cognitive development. We will begin with Jean Piaget's stage theory of cognitive development. Then we will turn to the views of the Russian psychologist Lev Semenovich Vygotsky (1896–1934), whose approach is quite different from Piaget's but is enjoying a rebirth in popularity. Then we will focus on Lawrence Kohlberg's theory of moral development.

Jean Piaget's Cognitive–Developmental Theory   Jean Piaget (1896–1980) was offered the curatorship of a museum in Geneva, but he had to turn it down. After all, he was only 11 at the time. Piaget's first intellectual love was biology, and he published his first scientific article at the age of 10. He then became a laboratory assistant to the director of a museum of natural history and engaged in research on mollusks (oysters, clams, snails, and such). The director soon died, and Piaget published the research findings himself. On the basis of these papers, he was offered the curatorship.

Piaget earned his Ph.D. in biology. In 1920 he obtained a job at the Binet Institute in Paris, where work on intelligence tests was being conducted. His first task was to adapt English verbal reasoning items for use with French children. To do so, he had to try out the items on children in various age groups and see whether they could arrive at correct answers. The task was boring until Piaget became intrigued by the children's *wrong* answers. Another investigator might have shrugged them off, but Piaget perceived patterns in the children's "mistakes." The wrong answers reflected consistent, if illogical, cognitive processes. Piaget's observations led to his theory of cognitive development.

reflect & relate

How closely did your parents pay attention to your height and weight? Did they chart it? How did your physical development affect your self-esteem?

■ **Jean Piaget**

Farrell Grehan /Corbis

Assimilation   Piaget described human thought, or intelligence, in terms of the concepts of assimilation and accommodation. **Assimilation** means responding to a new stimulus through a reflex or existing habit. Infants, for example, usually try to place new objects in their mouth to suck, feel, or explore. Piaget would say that the child is assimilating a new toy to the sucking schema. A **schema** is a pattern of action or a "mental structure" involved in acquiring or organizing knowledge.

Piaget regarded children as natural physicists who seek to learn about and control their world. In the Piagetian view, children who squish their food and laugh enthusiastically are budding scientists. In addition to enjoying the responses of their parents, they are studying the texture and consistency of their food. (Parents, of course, might wish that their children would practice these experiments in the laboratory, not the dining room.)

Accommodation   **Accommodation** is the creation of new ways of responding to objects or looking at the world. In accommodation, children transform existing schemas to incorporate new events. Children (and adults) accommodate to objects and situations that cannot be integrated into existing schemas. For example, children who study biology learn that whales cannot be assimilated into the "fish" schema. They accommodate by constructing new schemas, such as "mammals without legs that live in the sea." The ability to accommodate to novel stimuli advances as a result of maturation and experience. Let us apply these concepts to the stages of cognitive development.

Piaget's Stages of Cognitive Development   *What are Piaget's stages of cognitive development?* Piaget hypothesized that children's cognitive processes develop in an orderly sequence. Some children may be more advanced than others, but the sequence remains the same. Piaget (1963) identified four major stages of cognitive development: sensorimotor, preoperational, concrete operational, and formal operational.

The Sensorimotor Stage   The newborn infant is capable of assimilating novel stimuli only to existing reflexes (or ready-made schemas) such as the rooting and sucking reflexes. But by the time an infant reaches the age of 1 month, he or she already shows purposeful behavior by repeating behavior patterns that are pleasurable, such as sucking his or her hand. During the first month or so, an infant apparently does not connect stimuli perceived through different senses. Reflexive turning toward sources of auditory and olfactory stimulation cannot be considered purposeful searching. But within the first few months the infant begins to coordinate vision with grasping to look at the object being held or touched.

A 3- or 4-month-old infant may be fascinated by her own hands and legs. The infant may become absorbed in watching herself open and close her fists. The infant becomes increasingly interested in acting on the environment to make interesting results (such as the sound of a rattle) last longer or occur again. Behavior becomes increasingly intentional and purposeful. Between 4 and 8 months of age, the infant explores cause-and-effect relationships such as the thump made by tossing an object or the swinging that results from kicking a hanging toy.

◆ **Truth or Fiction Revisited:** It is true that "out of sight" is literally "out of mind" prior to the age of 6 months or so. For most infants younger than 6 months, objects are not yet represented mentally. For this reason, as you can see in Figure 3.5, a child makes no effort to search for an object that has been removed or placed behind a screen. By the age of 8 to 12 months, however, infants realize that objects removed from sight still exist and attempt to find them. In this way, they show what is known as **object permanence,** thereby making it possible to play peek-a-boo.

Between 1 and 2 years of age, children begin to show interest in how things are constructed. It may be for this reason that they persistently touch and finger their parents' faces and their own. Toward the end of the second year, children begin to engage in mental trial and error before they try out overt behaviors. For example, when they look for an object you have removed, they will no longer begin their search in the last place they saw it. Rather, they may follow you, assuming you are carrying the object even though it is not visible. It is

Assimilation According to Piaget, the inclusion of a new event into an existing schema.

Schema According to Piaget, a hypothetical mental structure that permits the classification and organization of new information.

Accommodation According to Piaget, the modification of schemas so that information inconsistent with existing schemas can be integrated or understood.

Object permanence Recognition that objects removed from sight still exist, as demonstrated in young children by continued pursuit.

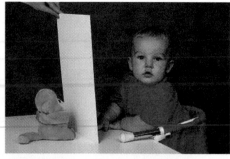

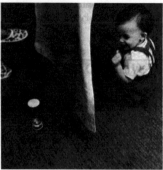

Figure 3.5

Object Permanence
To the infant at the top, who is in the early part of the sensorimotor stage, out of sight is truly out of mind. Once a sheet of paper is placed between the infant and the toy animal, the infant loses all interest in it. The toy is apparently not yet mentally represented. The photos on the bottom show a child later in the sensorimotor stage. This child does mentally represent objects and pushes through a curtain to reach one that has been screened from sight.

as though they are anticipating failure in searching for the object in the place where they last saw it.

Because the first stage of development is dominated by learning to coordinate perception of the self and of the environment with motor activity, Piaget termed it the **sensorimotor stage.** This stage comes to a close with the acquisition of the basics of language at about age 2.

The Preoperational Stage The **preoperational stage** is characterized by the use of words and symbols to represent objects and relationships among them. But be warned—any resemblance between the logic of children between the ages of 2 and 7 and your own logic may be coincidental. Children may use the same words as adults, but this does not mean their views of the world are the same. Preoperational children tend to think one-dimensionally—to focus on one aspect of a problem or situation at a time.

One consequence of one-dimensional thinking is **egocentrism.** Preoperational children cannot understand that other people do not see things the same way they do. When my daughter Allyn was 2½, I asked her to tell me about a trip to the store with her mother. "You tell me," she replied. It seemed she did not understand that I could not see the world through her eyes.

To egocentric preoperational children, all the world's a stage that has been erected to meet their needs and amuse them. When asked, "Why does the sun shine?" they may say, "To keep me warm." If asked, "Why is the sky blue?" they may respond, "'Cause blue's my favorite color." Preoperational children also show **animism.** They attribute life and consciousness to physical objects like the sun and the moon. They also show **artificialism.** They believe that environmental events like rain and thunder are human inventions. Asked why the sky is blue, 4-year-olds may answer, "'Cause Mommy painted it." Examples of egocentrism, animism, and artificialism are shown in Table 3.1.

To gain further insight into preoperational thinking, find a 3- or 4-year-old and try these mini-experiments:

■ Pour water from a tall, thin glass into a low, wide glass. Now, ask the child whether the low, wide glass contains more, less, or the same amount of water that was in the tall, thin glass. If the child says that they hold the same amount of water (with possible minor ex-

Sensorimotor stage The first of Piaget's stages of cognitive development, characterized by coordination of sensory information and motor activity, early exploration of the environment, and lack of language.

Preoperational stage The second of Piaget's stages, characterized by illogical use of words and symbols, spotty logic, and egocentrism.

Egocentrism According to Piaget, the assumption that others view the world as one does oneself.

Animism The belief that inanimate objects move because of will or spirit.

Artificialism The belief that natural objects have been created by human beings.

CONCEPT REVIEW ■ **CONCEPT REVIEW 3.1** ■ CONCEPT REVIEW

JEAN PIAGET'S STAGES OF COGNITIVE DEVELOPMENT

STAGE		APPROXIMATE	COMMENTS
Sensorimotor		Birth–2 years	At first, the child lacks language and does not use symbols or mental representations of objects. In time, reflexive responding ends, and intentional behavior—as in making interesting stimulation last—begins. The child develops the object concept and acquires the basics of language.
Preoperational		2–7 years	The child begins to represent the world mentally, but thought is egocentric. The child does not focus on two aspects of a situation at once and therefore lacks conservation. The child shows animism, artificialism, and objective responsibility for wrongdoing.
Concrete operational		7–12 years	Logical mental actions—called operations—begin. The child develops conservation concepts, can adopt the viewpoint of others, can classify objects in series, and shows comprehension of basic relational concepts (such as one object being larger or heavier than another).
Formal operational		12 years and older	Mature, adult thought emerges. Thinking is characterized by deductive logic, consideration of various possibilities (mental trial and error), abstract thought, and the formation and testing of hypotheses.

ceptions for spillage and evaporation), the child is correct. But if the child errs, why do you think this is so?

■ Now flatten a ball of clay into a pancake, and ask the child whether you wind up with more, less, or the same amount of clay? If the child errs again, why do you think this is so?

To arrive at the correct answers to these questions, children must understand the law of **conservation.** This law holds that basic properties of substances such as mass, weight, and volume remain the same—that is, are *conserved*—when one changes superficial properties such as their shape or arrangement.

Conservation requires the ability to think about, or **center** on, two aspects of a situation at once, such as height and width. Conserving the mass, weight, or volume of a substance requires the recognition that a change in one dimension can compensate for a change in another. But the preoperational boy in Figure 3.6 focuses on only one dimension at a time. First he is shown two tall, thin glasses of juice and agrees that they contain the same amount of juice. Then, while he watches, juice is poured from a tall glass into a squat glass. Now he is asked which glass contains more juice. After mulling over the problem, he points

Conservation According to Piaget, recognition that basic properties of substances such as weight and mass remain the same when superficial features change.

Center According to Piaget, to focus one's attention.

TABLE 3.1 ■ Examples of Preoperational Thought

TYPE OF THOUGHT	SAMPLE QUESTIONS	TYPICAL ANSWERS
Egocentrism	Why does it get dark out? Why does the sun shine? Why is there snow?	So I can go to sleep. To keep me warm. For me to play in.
Animism	Why do trees have leaves? Why do stars twinkle?	To keep them warm. Because they're happy and cheerful.
Artificialism	What makes it rain? Why is the sky blue? What is the wind?	Someone emptying a watering can. Somebody painted it. A man blowing.

to the tall glass. Why? Because when he looks at the glasses he is "overwhelmed" by the fact that the thinner glass is taller. The preoperational child focuses on the most apparent dimension of the situation—in this case, the greater height of the thinner glass. He does not realize that the increased width of the squat glass compensates for the decreased height. By the way, if you ask him whether any juice has been added or taken away in the pouring process, he readily says no. But if you then repeat the question about which glass contains *more* juice, he again points to the taller glass. If all this sounds rather illogical, that is because it is illogical—or, in Piaget's terms, preoperational.

Piaget (1997) found that the moral judgment of preoperational children is also one-dimensional. Five-year-olds tend to be slaves to rules and authority. When you ask them why something should be done in a certain way, they may insist, "Because that's the way to do it!" or "Because Mommy says so!" Right is right and wrong is wrong. Why? "Because!"—that's why.

According to most older children and adults, an act is a crime only when there is criminal intent. Accidents may be hurtful, but the perpetrators are usually seen as blameless. But in the court of the one-dimensional, preoperational child, there is **objective responsibility.** People are sentenced (and harshly!) on the basis of the amount of damage they have done, not their motives or intentions. To demonstrate objective responsibility, Piaget would tell children stories and ask them which character was naughtier and why. John, for example, accidentally breaks 15 cups when he opens a door. Henry breaks 1 cup when he sneaks into a kitchen cabinet to find forbidden jam. The preoperational child usually judges John to be naughtier. Why? Because he broke more cups.

Objective responsibility According to Piaget, the assignment of blame according to the amount of damage done rather than the motives of the actor.

Figure 3.6
Conservation
A. The boy in this illustration agreed that the amount of water in two identical containers is equal. **B.** He then watched as water from one container was poured into a tall, thin container. **C.** When asked whether the amounts of water in the two containers are now the same, he says no.

A.   B.   C.

Video Connections

Piaget's Stages of Development

LEARNING OBJECTIVES

- Explain what is meant by cognitive developmental theory.
- Provide the correct order of Piaget's stages of cognitive development.
- Describe tasks that indicate whether a child is showing behaviors characteristic of a given stage of cognitive development.

APPLIED LESSON

1 If you want to encourage a 4-year-old child to take a pill, would it be a better idea to bring it in a tiny cup or on a huge plate? Explain.

2 Why do you think Piaget was never particularly concerned about how early children enter a particular stage of development?

CRITICAL THINKING

One of the basic controversies in developmental psychology is whether development is continuous or discontinuous. What was Piaget's perspective on this debate? Do all psychologists agree with Piaget? What is an alternative to a stage theory of development?

Nine-month-old Hayden has learned that he can move the large toy (obstacle) to retrieve the more desirable toy underneath. Jean Piaget described children's cognitive development in terms of four stages. Which stage is suggested by Hayden's action? Explain.

Watch this video!

Go to www your companion website at http://academic.cengage.com/psychology/rathus Click on the Video Connections tab under this chapter.

The Concrete-Operational Stage   By about age 7, the typical child is entering the stage of **concrete operations.** In this stage, which lasts until about age 12, children show the beginnings of the capacity for adult logic. However, their logical thoughts, or *operations*, generally involve tangible objects rather than abstract ideas. Concrete operational children are capable of **decentration**; they can center on two dimensions of a problem at once. This attainment has implications for moral judgments, conservation, and other intellectual undertakings.

Children now become **subjective** in their moral judgments. When assigning guilt, they center on the motives of wrongdoers as well as on the amount of damage done. Concrete-operational children judge Henry more harshly than John because John's misdeed was an accident.

Concrete-operational children understand the laws of conservation. The boy in Figure 3.6, now a few years older, would say that the squat glass still contains the same amount of juice. If asked why, he might reply, "Because you can pour it back into the other one." Such an answer also suggests awareness of the concept of **reversibility**—the recognition that many processes can be reversed or undone so that things are restored to their previous condition. Centering simultaneously on the height and the width of the glasses, the boy recognizes that the loss in height compensates for the gain in width.

Children in this stage are less egocentric. They are able to take on the roles of others and to view the world, and themselves, from other people's perspectives. They recognize that people see things in different ways because of different situations and different sets of values.

During the concrete-operational stage, children's own sets of values begin to emerge and acquire stability. Children come to understand that feelings of love between them and their parents can endure even when someone is temporarily angry or disappointed. We continue our discussion of Piaget's theory—his stage of formal operations—later in the chapter in the section on adolescence.

Concrete-operational stage Piaget's third stage, characterized by logical thought concerning tangible objects, conservation, and subjective morality.

Decentration Simultaneous focusing on more than one dimension of a problem, so that flexible, reversible thought becomes possible.

Subjective moral judgment According to Piaget, moral judgment that is based on the motives of the perpetrator.

Reversibility According to Piaget, recognition that processes can be undone, that things can be made as they were.

Evaluation of Piaget's Theory   A number of questions have been raised concerning the accuracy of Piaget's views. Among them are these:

- *Was Piaget's timing accurate?* Some critics argue that Piaget's methods led him to underestimate children's abilities (Bjorklund, 2000; Meltzoff & Gopnik, 1997). Other researchers using different methods have found, for example, that preschoolers are less egocentric and that children are capable of conservation at earlier ages than Piaget thought.
- *Does cognitive development occur in stages?* Cognitive events such as egocentrism and conservation appear to develop more continuously than Piaget thought—that is, they may not occur in stages (Bjorklund, 2000; Flavell, 2000). Although cognitive developments appear to build on previous cognitive developments, the process may be more gradual than stagelike.
- *Are developmental sequences always the same?* Here, Piaget's views have fared better. It seems there is no variation in the sequence in which cognitive developments occur.

In sum, Piaget's theoretical edifice has been rocked, but it has not been reduced to rubble. Now let us consider the views of Vygotsky. Vygotsky, unlike Piaget, is not a stage theorist. Instead, he sees the transmission of knowledge from generation to generation as cumulative, and focuses on the ways in which children's interactions with their elders enhance their cognitive development.

Lev Vygotsky's Sociocultural Theory   The term *sociocultural theory* has different meanings. For example, the term can refer to the roles of factors such as ethnicity and gender in behavior and mental processes. Vygotsky's sociocultural theory focuses instead on the ways in which children's cognitive development is influenced by the cultures in which they are reared and the people who teach them.

Vygotsky's (1978) theory focuses on the transmission of information and cognitive skills from generation to generation. The transmission of skills involves teaching and learning, but Vygotsky is no behaviorist. He does not view learning as a mechanical process that can be described in terms of the conditioning of units of behavior. Rather, he focuses more generally on how the child's social interaction with adults, largely in the home, organizes a child's learning experiences in such a way that the child can obtain cognitive skills—such as computation or reading skills—and use them to acquire information. Like Piaget, Vygotsky sees the child's functioning as adaptive (Piaget & Smith, 2000), and the child adapts to his or her social and cultural interactions.

What are the key concepts of Vygotsky's theory of cognitive development? Key concepts in Vygotsky's theory include the *zone of proximal development* and *scaffolding*. The word *proximal* means "nearby" or "close," as in the words *approximate* and *proximity*. The **zone of proximal development (ZPD)** refers to a range of tasks that a child can carry out with the help of someone who is more skilled (Haenen, 2001). The "zone" refers to the relationship between the child's abilities and what she or he can do with help from others. Adults or older children best guide the child through this zone by gearing their assistance to the child's capabilities (Flavell et al., 2002).

Within the zone we find an apprenticeship in which the child works with, and learns from, others (Meijer & Elshout, 2001). When learning with others, the child tends to internalize—or bring inward—the conversations and explanations that help him or her gain skills (Prior & Welling, 2001; Vygotsky, 1962; Yang, 2000). Children not only learn the meanings of words from teachers but also learn ways of talking to themselves about solving problems within a cultural context (DeVries, 2000). Outer speech becomes inner speech. What was the teacher's becomes the child's. What was a social and cultural context becomes embedded within the child (Moro & Rodriguez, 2000); thus the term, *sociocultural theory.*

A *scaffold* is a temporary skeletal structure that enables workers to fabricate a building, bridge, or other, more permanent, structure. Cognitive **scaffolding** refers to the temporary support provided by a parent or teacher to a child who is learning to perform a task. Guidance decreases as the child becomes more skilled and self-sufficient (Clarke-Stewart & Beck, 1999; Maccoby, 1992). In Vygotsky's theory, teachers and parents provide children with

Davidson Films, Inc.

■ **Lev Semenovich Vygotsky**
The Russian psychologist is said to have possessed the genius of a Mozart but to have lived in a time and place that was deaf to genius. In his youth he was interested in literature and philosophy. He enrolled in medical school at Moscow University, switched to law school, then returned to literature, and later became interested in psychology. Vygotsky is known for showing how social speech becomes inner speech and how "scaffolding" by others assists children to develop the cognitive skills to succeed.

Zone of proximal development (ZPD) Vygotsky's term for the situation in which a child carries out tasks with the help of someone who is more skilled, frequently an adult who represents the culture in which the child develops.

Scaffolding Vygotsky's term for temporary cognitive structures or methods of solving problems that help the child as he or she learns to function independently.

problem-solving methods that serve as cognitive scaffolding while the child gains the ability to function independently. A child's instructors may offer advice on sounding out letters and words that provide a temporary support until reading "clicks" and the child no longer needs the device. Children may be offered scaffolding that enables them to use their fingers to do calculations. Eventually, the scaffolding is removed and the cognitive structures stand alone.

A Puerto Rican study found that students also use scaffolding when they are explaining to one another how they can improve school projects, such as essay assignments (De Guerrero & Villamil, 2000). Children at first even view the value of education in terms of their parents' verbalizations about school success (Bigelow, 2001). Vygotsky's theory points out that children's attitudes toward schooling are embedded within the parent–child relationship.

The concepts of scaffolding and the zone of proximal development are illustrated in a study in which 3- and 5-year-old children were given the task of sorting doll furniture into the rooms in which they belonged (Freund, 1990). Children who were allowed to interact with their mothers performed at a higher level than children who worked alone. Furthermore, mothers adjusted the amount of help they gave to fit the child's level of competence. They gave younger children more detailed, concrete suggestions than they gave older children. When the experimenters made the task more difficult, mothers gave more help to children of both ages.

Catherine Haden and her colleagues (2001) observed 21 mother–child pairs engage in various tasks when the children were 2 and 3 years of age. They analyzed the children's recall of their performance 1 and 3 days afterward. The children best recalled those aspects of the tasks they had both worked on and discussed with their mothers. Their memory under these circumstances exceeded that when the activities were (1) handled jointly but talked about only by the mother, or (2) handled jointly but not discussed at all.

Piaget's focus was largely maturational. It was assumed that maturation of the brain allowed the child to experience new levels of insights and suddenly develop new kinds of problem solving. Vygotsky focused on the processes in the teacher–learner relationship. To Vygotsky, cognitive development was about culture and social interaction. Let us now turn to another aspect of cognitive development—the ways in which children (and adults) arrive at judgments as to what is right and what is wrong.

Lawrence Kohlberg's Theory of Moral Development *How do children reason about right and wrong?* Cognitive–developmental theorist Lawrence Kohlberg (1981) used the following tale in his research into children's moral reasoning. Before going on, why not read the tale yourself?

> In Europe a woman was near death from a special kind of cancer. There was one drug that the doctors thought might save her. It was a form of radium that a druggist in the same town had recently discovered. The drug was expensive to make, but the druggist was charging ten times what the drug cost him to make. He paid $200 for the radium and charged $2,000 for a small dose of the drug. The sick woman's husband, Heinz, went to everyone he knew to borrow the money, but he could only get together about $1,000, which was half of what it cost. He told the druggist that his wife was dying and asked him to sell it cheaper or let him pay later. But the druggist said: "No, I discovered the drug, and I'm going to make money from it." So Heinz got desperate and broke into the man's store to steal the drug for his wife. (Kohlberg, 1969)

Heinz is caught in a moral dilemma. In such dilemmas, a legal or social rule (in this case, the law forbidding stealing) is pitted against a strong human need (his desire to save his wife). Children and adults arrive at yes or no answers for different reasons. According to Kohlberg, the reasons can be classified according to the level of moral development they reflect.

As a stage theorist, Kohlberg argues that the stages of moral reasoning follow a specific sequence (see Concept Review 3.2: Kohlberg's Levels and Stages of Moral Development). Children progress at different rates, and not all children (or adults) reach the highest stage. But the sequence is always the same: Children must go through stage 1 before they enter

■ CONCEPT REVIEW 3.2 ■

LAWRENCE KOHLBERG'S LEVELS AND STAGES OF MORAL DEVELOPMENT

STAGE OF DEVELOPMENT	EXAMPLES OF MORAL REASONING THAT SUPPORT HEINZ'S STEALING THE DRUG	EXAMPLES OF MORAL REASONING THAT OPPOSE HEINZ'S STEALING THE DRUG
Level I: Preconventional Stage 1: Judgments guided by obedience and the prospect of punishment (the consequences of the behavior)	It isn't wrong to take the drug. Heinz did try to pay the druggist for it, and it's worth only $200, not $2,000.	Taking things without paying is wrong because it's against the law. Heinz will get caught and go to jail.
Stage 2: Naively egoistic, instrumental orientation (things are right when they satisfy people's needs)	Heinz ought to take the drug because his wife really needs it. He can always pay the druggist back.	Heinz shouldn't take the drug. If he gets caught and winds up in jail, it won't do his wife any good.
Level II: Conventional Stage 3: Good-boy orientation (moral behavior helps others and is socially approved)	Stealing is a crime, so it's bad, but Heinz should take the drug to save his wife or else people would blame him for letting her die.	Stealing is a crime. Heinz shouldn't just take the drug, because his family will be dishonored and they will blame him.
Stage 4: Law-and-order orientation (moral behavior is doing one's duty and showing respect for authority)	Heinz must take the drug to do his duty to save his wife. Eventually, he has to pay the druggist for it, however.	If everyone took the law into his or her own hands, civilization would fall apart, so Heinz shouldn't steal the drug.
Level III: Postconventional Stage 5: Contractual, legalistic orientation (one must weigh pressing human needs against society's need to maintain social order)	This thing is complicated because society has a right to maintain law and order, but Heinz has to take the drug to save his wife.	I can see why Heinz feels he has to take the drug, but laws exist for the benefit of society as a whole and can't simply be cast aside.
Stage 6: Universal ethical principles orientation (people must follow universal ethical principles and their own conscience, even if it means breaking the law)	In this case, the law comes into conflict with the principle of the sanctity of human life. Heinz must take the drug because his wife's life is more important than the law.	If Heinz truly believes that stealing the drug is worse than letting his wife die, he should not take it. People have to make sacrifices to do what they think is right.

stage 2, and so on. According to Kohlberg, there are three levels of moral development and two stages within each level.

When it comes to the dilemma of Heinz, Kohlberg believed that people could justify Heinz's stealing of the drug or his decision not to steal it by the reasoning of any level or stage of moral development. In other words, Kohlberg was not as interested in the eventual "yes" or "no" as he was in *how a person reasoned* to arrive at yes or no.

The Preconventional Level   The **preconventional level** applies to most children through about the age of 9. Children at this level base their moral judgments on the consequences of behavior. For example, stage 1 is oriented toward obedience and punishment. Good behavior is obedient and allows one to avoid punishment. However, a child in stage 1 can decide that Heinz should or should not steal the drug.

In stage 2, good behavior allows people to satisfy their needs and those of others. (Heinz's wife needs the drug; therefore, stealing it—the only way of obtaining it—is not wrong.)

The Conventional Level   In the **conventional level** of moral reasoning, right and wrong are judged by conformity to conventional (familial, religious, societal) standards of

Preconventional level According to Kohlberg, a period during which moral judgments are based largely on expectation of rewards or punishments.

Conventional level According to Kohlberg, a period during which moral judgments largely reflect social conventions. A "law and order" approach to morality.

right and wrong. According to the stage 3, "good-boy orientation," moral behavior is that which meets the needs and expectations of others. Moral behavior is what is "normal"—what the majority does. (Heinz should steal the drug because that is what a "good husband" would do. It is "natural" or "normal" to try to help one's wife. *Or,* Heinz should *not* steal the drug because "good people do not steal.")

In stage 4, moral judgments are based on rules that maintain the social order. Showing respect for authority and doing one's duty are valued highly. (Heinz *must* steal the drug; it would be his fault if he let his wife die. He would pay the druggist later, when he had the money.) Many people do not mature beyond the conventional level.

The Postconventional Level Postconventional moral reasoning is more complex and focuses on dilemmas in which individual needs are pitted against the need to maintain the social order and on personal conscience. We discuss the postconventional level later in the chapter in the section on adolescence.

Thomas Hoeffgen/Getty Images

■ **Wrong, but *Why?***
Almost any observer would say that what the aggressor is doing is wrong, but *why* is it wrong? Can you think of answers that would reflect different levels of moral development, according to Kohlberg?

Evaluation of Kohlberg's Theory Consistent with Kohlberg's theory, research suggests that moral reasoning does follow a developmental sequence (Dawson, 2002). even though most people do not reach the level of postconventional thought. Postconventional thought, when found, begins in adolescence. It also seems that Piaget's stage of formal operations is a prerequisite for postconventional reasoning, which requires the capacities to understand abstract moral principles and to empathize with the attitudes and emotional responses of other people (Flavell et al., 2002).

Also consistent with Kohlberg's theory, children do not appear to skip stages as they progress (Flavell et al., 2002). Classic research shows that when children are exposed to adult models who exhibit a lower stage of moral reasoning, they can be enticed to follow along (Bandura & McDonald, 1963). But children who are exposed to examples of moral reasoning above and below their own stage generally prefer the higher stage (Rest, 1983). The direction of moral development would therefore appear to be as Kohlberg predicted, even if children can be influenced by the opinions of others.

——■► Social and Emotional Development

Social relationships are crucial to us as children. When we are infants, our very survival depends on them. Later in life, they contribute to our feelings of happiness and satisfaction. In this section we discuss aspects of social development, including Erikson's theory of psychosocial development, attachment, day care, styles of parenting, and child abuse.

Erik Erikson's Stages of Psychosocial Development According to Erik Erikson, we undergo several stages of psychosocial development (see Concept Review 3.3: Erikson's Stages of Psychosocial Development). *What are Erikson's stages of psychosocial development?* During Erikson's first stage, **trust versus mistrust,** we depend on our primary caregivers (usually our parents) and come to expect that our environments will—or will not—meet our needs. During early childhood and the preschool years, we begin to explore the environment more actively and try new things. At this time, our relationships with our parents and friends can encourage us to develop **autonomy** (self-direction) and initiative, or feelings of shame and guilt. During the elementary school years, friends and teachers take on more importance, encouraging us to become industrious or to develop feelings of inferiority. We will see that Erikson's theory includes eight stages that straddle the life span.

Trust versus mistrust Erikson's first stage of psychosocial development, during which children do—or do not—come to trust that primary caregivers and the environment will meet their needs.
Autonomy Self-direction.

CONCEPT REVIEW   ■ CONCEPT REVIEW 3.3 ■   CONCEPT REVIEW

ERIK ERIKSON'S STAGES OF PSYCHOSOCIAL DEVELOPMENT

TIME PERIOD	LIFE CRISIS	THE DEVELOPMENTAL TASK
Infancy (0–1)	Trust versus mistrust	Coming to trust the mother and the environment—to associate surroundings with feelings of inner goodness
Early childhood (1–3)	Autonomy versus shame and doubt	Developing the wish to make choices and the self-control to exercise choice
Preschool years (4–5)	Initiative versus guilt	Adding planning and "attacking" to choice, becoming active and on the move
Elementary school years (6–12)	Industry versus inferiority	Becoming eagerly absorbed in skills, tasks, and productivity; mastering the fundamentals of technology
Adolescence	Identity versus role diffusion	Connecting skills and social roles to formation of career objectives; developing a sense of who one is and what one stands for
Young adulthood	Intimacy versus isolation	Committing the self to another; engaging in sexual love
Middle adulthood	Generativity versus stagnation	Needing to be needed; guiding and encouraging the younger generation; being creative
Late adulthood	Integrity versus despair	Accepting the time and place of one's life cycle; achieving wisdom and dignity

Source: Erikson, 1963, pp. 247–269.

───■─ Attachment: Ties That Bind

At the age of 2, my daughter Allyn almost succeeded in preventing me from finishing a book. When I locked myself into my study, she positioned herself outside the door and called, "Daddy, oh Daddy." At other times, she would bang on the door or cry outside. When I would give in (several times a day) and open the door, she would run in and say, "I want you to pick up me," and hold out her arms or climb into my lap. Although we were separate human beings, it was as though she were very much *attached* to me. *Questions: How do feelings of attachment develop? What kinds of experiences affect attachment?*

Psychologist Mary D. Salter Ainsworth (1913–1999) defined **attachment** as an emotional tie that is formed between one animal or person and another specific individual. Attachment keeps organisms together—it is vital to the survival of the infant—and it tends to endure. The behaviors that define attachment include (1) attempts to maintain contact or nearness, and (2) shows of anxiety when separated. Babies and children try to maintain contact with caregivers to whom they are attached. They engage in eye contact, pull and tug at them, ask to be picked up, and may even jump in front of them in such a way that they will be "run over" if they are not picked up!

Attachment The enduring affectional tie that binds one person to another.

The Strange Situation and Patterns of Attachment   The ways in which infants behave in strange situations are connected with their bonds of attachment with their caregivers. Given this fact, Ainsworth and her colleagues (1978) innovated the *strange situation method* to learn how infants respond to separations and reunions with a caregiver (usually the mother) and a stranger. Using this method, Ainsworth and her colleagues identified three major types of attachment, including secure attachment and two types of insecure attachment:

1. *Secure attachment.* Securely attached infants mildly protest their mother's departure, seek interaction upon reunion, and are readily comforted by her.
2. *Avoidant attachment.* Infants who show avoidant attachment are least distressed by their mother's departure. They play by themselves without fuss and ignore their mothers when they return.
3. *Ambivalent/resistant attachment.* Infants with ambivalent/resistant attachment are the most emotional. They show severe signs of distress when their mother leaves and show ambivalence upon reunion by alternately clinging to and pushing their mother away when she returns.

Attachment is connected with the quality of care that infants receive. The parents of securely attached children are more likely to be affectionate and reliable caregivers (Isabella, 1998; Posada et al., 2002). A wealth of research literature speaks of the benefits of secure attachment. For example, secure children are happier, more sociable, and more cooperative than insecure children (Bohlin et al., 2000). At ages 5 and 6, securely attached children are liked better by their peers and teachers, are more competent, and have fewer behavior problems than insecurely attached children (Granot & Mayseless, 2001; Moss & St-Laurent, 2001). In this vein, we can also note that having the primary caregiver present during stressful situations, such as pediatric exams, helps children cope with these situations (Ybarra et al., 2000).

Stages of Attachment Ainsworth and her colleagues observed infants in many societies, including the African country of Uganda. She noted the efforts of infants to maintain contact with the mother, their protests when separated from her, and their use of her as a base for exploring their environment. At first, infants show *indiscriminate attachment.* That is, they prefer being held or being with someone to being alone, but they are generally willing to be held by unfamiliar people. Specific attachment to the primary caregiver begins to develop at about 4 months of age and becomes intense by about 7 months of age. Fear of strangers, which develops in some but not all children, follows 1 or 2 months later.

From studies such as these, Ainsworth identified three phases of attachment:

1. The *initial-preattachment phase,* which lasts from birth to about 3 months and is characterized by indiscriminate attachment.
2. The *attachment-in-the-making phase,* which occurs at about 3 or 4 months and is characterized by preference for familiar figures.
3. The *clear-cut-attachment phase,* which occurs at about 6 or 7 months and is characterized by intensified dependence on the primary caregiver.

John Bowlby (1988), a colleague of Mary Ainsworth, believed that attachment is also characterized by fear of strangers ("stranger anxiety"). At about 8 to 10 months of age, children may cry and cling to their parents when strangers try to befriend them. But not all children develop fear of strangers.

Theoretical Views of Attachment Early in the 20th century, behaviorists argued that attachment behaviors are learned through experience. Caregivers feed their infants and tend to their other physiological needs. Thus, infants associate their caregivers with gratification of needs and learn to approach them to meet their needs. The feelings of gratification associated with the meeting of basic needs generalize into feelings of security when the caregiver is present.

Classic research by psychologist Harry F. Harlow suggests that skin contact may be more important than learning experiences. Harlow noted that infant rhesus monkeys reared without mothers or companions became attached to pieces of cloth in their cages. They maintained contact with them and showed distress when separated from them. Harlow conducted a series of experiments to find out why (Harlow, 1959).

Courtesy of the Author

■ **Allyn**
At the age of 2, the author's daughter Allyn nearly succeeded in preventing the publication of a book by continually pulling him away from the computer when he was at work. Because of their mutual attachment, separation was painful.

Marvin S. Roberts

■ **Mary D. Salter Ainsworth**
Ainsworth's cross-cultural studies and her innovation of the strange situation method have made her a key figure in the development of theories of the formation of bonds of attachment between children and their caregivers.

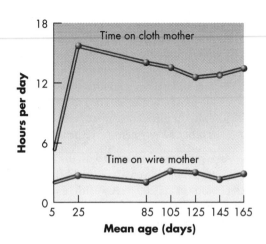

Figure 3.7
Attachment in Infant Monkeys
Although this rhesus monkey infant is fed by the wire "mother," it spends most of its time clinging to the soft, cuddly terry-cloth "mother." The monkey knows where to get a meal, but contact comfort is apparently more important than food in the development of attachment in infant monkeys (and infant humans?).

Figure 3.8
Security
With its terry-cloth surrogate mother nearby, this infant rhesus monkey apparently feels secure enough to explore the "bear monster" placed in its cage. But infants with wire surrogate mothers or no mothers at all cower in a corner when such "monsters" are introduced.

In one study, Harlow placed infant rhesus monkeys in cages with two surrogate mothers, as shown in Figure 3.7. One "mother" was made of wire mesh from which a baby bottle was extended. The other surrogate mother was made of soft, cuddly terry cloth. The infant monkeys spent most of their time clinging to the cloth mother, even though "she" did not gratify their need for food. Harlow concluded that monkeys—and perhaps humans—have an inborn need for **contact comfort** that is as basic as the need for food. Gratification of the need for contact comfort, rather than food, might be why infant monkeys (and humans) cling to their mothers.

Harlow and Zimmerman (1959) found that a surrogate mother made of terry cloth could also serve as a comforting base from which an infant monkey would explore its environment (see Figure 3.8). Toys such as stuffed bears and oversized wooden insects were placed in cages with infant monkeys and their surrogate mothers. When the infants were alone or had wire surrogate mothers for companions, they cowered in fear as long as the "bear monster" or "insect monster" was present. But when the terry cloth mothers were present, the infants clung to them for a while and then explored the intruding "monster." With human infants, too, bonds of mother–infant attachment appear to provide a secure base from which infants express their curiosity.

Other researchers, such as **ethologist** Konrad Lorenz, argue that for many animals, attachment is an instinct—inborn. (Ethologists study the behavioral characteristics of various species of animals.) Attachment, like other instincts, is theorized to occur in the presence of a specific stimulus and during a **critical period** of life—that is, a period during which the animal is sensitive to the stimulus.

Some animals become attached to the first moving object they encounter. The unwritten rule seems to be, "If it moves, it must be Mother." It is as if the image of the moving object becomes "imprinted" on the young animal. The formation of an attachment in this manner is therefore called **imprinting.**

Lorenz (1981) became well known when pictures of his "family" of goslings were made public (see Figure 3.9). How did Lorenz acquire his following? He was present when the goslings hatched and during their critical period, and he allowed them to follow him. The critical period for geese and some other animals is bounded, at the younger end, by the age at which they first walk and, at the older end, by the age at which they develop fear of strangers. The goslings followed Lorenz persistently, ran to him when frightened, honked with distress at his departure, and tried to overcome barriers between them. If you substitute crying for honking, it all sounds rather human.

Ainsworth and Bowlby (1991) consider attachment to be instinctive in humans. However, among humans attachment is less related to issues such as locomotion and fear of strangers (which is not universal). Moreover, the critical period with humans is quite extended. Having noted the nature of attachment, many parents wonder about the effects of day care on attachment.

Life Connections
Day Care—Blessing, Headache, or Both?

Looking for a phrase that can strike fear in the hearts of millions of American parents? Try "day care." Nowadays most parents, including most mothers of infants, work. As a result, millions of parents are obsessed with trying to find quality day care. What happens when children must be taken care of by others? Does day care affect children's bonds of attachment with their parents? Does it affect their social and cognitive development?

Some studies find that infants in full-time day care are somewhat more likely than children without day-care experience to be insecure. But most infants in both groups are securely attached (Booth et al., 2003; Sagi et al., 2002).

Day care has mixed effects on children's social and cognitive development. Infants in care are more peer oriented and play at higher developmental levels than home-reared infants, and are more independent, self-confident, outgoing, affectionate, helpful, and cooperative (Clarke-Stewart, 1991; Field, 1991).

A study funded by the National Institute on Child Health and Human Development compared the development of children in "high-quality" day care with that of children in "low-quality" day care, and with that of children reared in the home by their mothers. The quality of the day care was defined in terms of the richness of the learning environment (availability of toys, books, and other materials), the ratio of caregivers to children (high quality meant more caregivers), and the amount of individual attention received by the child (more was better). The researchers found high-quality day care resulted in scores on tests of language and cognitive skills that rivaled those of children reared in the home by their mothers (Belsky et al., 2001).

■ **Day Care**
Because most parents in the United States are in the workforce, day care is not a luxury—it's a necessity. What are the effects of day care on children's bonds of attachment with their parents, and on children's cognitive and social development?

Figure 3.9
Imprinting
Quite a following? Konrad Lorenz may not look like Mommy to you, but these goslings became attached to him because he was the first moving object they perceived and followed. This type of attachment process is referred to as *imprinting*. Imprinting among goslings is an instinctive pattern of behavior that is triggered by a specific stimulus (a moving object) and which occurs during a critical period of development.

Contact comfort A hypothesized primary drive to seek physical comfort through contact with another.

Ethologist A scientist who studies the characteristic behavior patterns of species of animals.

Critical period A period of time when an instinctive response can be elicited by a particular stimulus.

Imprinting A process occurring during a critical period in the development of an organism, in which that organism responds to a stimulus in a manner that will afterward be difficult to modify.

But the same study found that the more time preschoolers spent in child care, the more likely they were to be rated as defiant, aggressive, and disobedient in kindergarten (Belsky et al., 2001). Seventeen percent of children who were in child care for more than 30 hours a week received higher scores on rating items like "gets in lots of fights," "cruelty," "talking too much," "explosive behavior," "argues a lot," and "demands a lot of attention." Only 6% of children who were in child care for fewer than 10 hours a week had these problems. ◆ **Truth or Fiction Revisited:** It is true that children in day care are more aggressive than children who are not. Children who were cared for in traditional day-care settings, by a grandmother, by a nanny, even by their fathers received the higher ratings. Could it be that Mom was the only answer?

Most researchers involved in the study cautioned against reading too much into it. They noted that most of the children's behavior fell within the normal range; even most of the aggressive behavior was not out of bounds.

The researchers also noted the following:

- Although 17% of kindergartners who had been in child care acted more assertively and aggressively, that percentage is actually the norm for the general population of children. (And 9% of the children who spent most of their time with their mothers were also rated by teachers as showing aggression.)
- The nature of family–child interactions had more impact on children's behavior than the number of hours in child care.
- Demanding attention in kindergarten may actually be an adaptive social response to being placed in a situation in which many children are competing for limited resources.

In any case, millions of parents have to decide not about *whether* to place their children in day care, but *where* to do so.

Another issue in social and emotional development is parenting styles. Parental behavior not only contributes to the development of attachment, but also to the development of self-esteem, self-reliance, achievement motivation, and competence. ■

■ Parenting Styles: Strictly Speaking?

Many psychologists have been concerned about the relationships between parenting styles and the personality development of the child. *What types of parental behavior are connected with variables such as self-esteem, achievement motivation, and independence in children?* Diana Baumrind (1973) has been particularly interested in the connections between parental behavior and the development of **instrumental competence** in their children. (Instrumental competence refers to the ability to manipulate the environment to achieve one's goals.) Baumrind has focused largely on four aspects of parental behavior: (1) strictness; (2) demands for the child to achieve intellectual, emotional, and social maturity; (3) communication ability; and (4) warmth and involvement. She labeled the three parenting styles the *authoritative, authoritarian,* and *permissive* styles. Other researchers also speak of the *uninvolved* style. These four styles are defined in the following ways:

1. *Authoritative parents.* The parents of the most competent children rate high in all four areas of behavior (see Table 3.2). They are strict (restrictive) and demand mature behavior. But they temper their strictness with desire to reason with their children and with love and support (Galambos et al., 2003). They expect much, but they explain why and offer help. Baumrind labeled these parents **authoritative parents** to suggest that they know what they want but are also loving and respectful of their children.

2. *Authoritarian parents.* **Authoritarian parents** view obedience as a virtue for its own sake. They have strict guidelines about what is right and wrong, and they demand that their children stick to them. Both authoritative and authoritarian parents have strict standards, but authoritative parents explain their demands and are supportive, whereas authoritarian parents rely on force and communicate poorly with their

Instrumental competence Ability to manipulate one's environment to achieve one's goals.

Authoritative parents Parents who are strict and warm. Authoritative parents demand mature behavior but use reason rather than force in discipline.

Authoritarian parents Parents who are rigid in their rules and who demand obedience for the sake of obedience.

TABLE 3.2 ■ Parenting Styles

STYLE OF PARENTING	RESTRICTIVENESS	PARENTAL BEHAVIOR		
		DEMANDS FOR MATURE BEHAVIOR	COMMUNICATION ABILITY	WARMTH AND SUPPORT
Authoritative	High (use of reasoning)	High	High	High
Authoritarian	High (use of force)	Moderate	Low	Low
Permissive	Low (easygoing)	Low	Low	High
Uninvolved	Low (uninvolved)	Low	Low	Low

Note: Research suggests that the children of authoritative parents develop as the most competent.

children. Authoritarian parents do not respect their children's points of view, and they may be cold and rejecting. When children ask them why they should do this or that, authoritarian parents often answer, "Because I say so!"

3. *Permissive parents.* **Permissive parents** are generally easygoing with their children. As a result, the children do pretty much what the children want. Permissive parents are warm and supportive, but poor at communicating.

4. *Uninvolved parents.* **Uninvolved parents** tend to leave their children on their own. They make few demands and show little warmth or encouragement.

Research evidence shows that the children of warm parents are more likely to be socially and emotionally well adjusted. They are also more likely to internalize moral standards—that is, to develop a conscience (Grusec, 2002; Rudy & Grusec, 2001).

Strictness seems to pay off, provided it is tempered with reason and warmth. Children of authori*tative* parents have the greatest self-reliance, self-esteem, social competence, and achievement motivation (Galambos et al., 2003; Grusec, 2002; Kim & Rohner, 2002). Children of authori*tarian* parents are often withdrawn or aggressive and usually do not do as well in school as children of authoritative parents (Kim & Rohner, 2002; Steinberg, 2001). Children of permissive parents seem to be less mature. They are often impulsive, moody, and aggressive. In adolescence, lack of parental monitoring is often linked to delinquency and poor academic performance. Children of uninvolved parents tend to obtain poorer grades than children whose parents make demands on them. The children of uninvolved parents also tend to be more likely to hang out with crowds who "party" a good deal and use drugs (Durbin et al., 1993). The message? Simple enough: Children profit when parents make reasonable demands, show warmth and encouragement, and spend time with them.

━━■━ Child Abuse: Broken Bonds

The incidence of child abuse is underreported, but it is estimated that nearly 3 million American children are neglected or abused each year by their parents or caregivers (USDHHS, 2004). About one in six of these experiences serious injury. Thousands die. More than 150,000 are sexually abused (Letourneau et al., 2004; USDHHS, 2004).

Many factors contribute to child abuse: stress, a history of child abuse in at least one of the parents' families of origin, acceptance of violence as a way of coping with stress, failure to become attached to the children, substance abuse, and rigid attitudes toward child rearing (Burgess & Drais, 2001).

Children who are physically or sexually abused are likely to develop personal and social problems and psychological disorders (Katerndahl et al., 2005; Letourneau et al., 2004). They are less likely than other children to venture out to explore the world. As adults, they are more likely to be violent toward their intimate partners (Benda & Corwyn, 2002).

Permissive parents Parents who impose few, if any, rules and who do not supervise their children closely.

Uninvolved parents Parents who generally leave their children to themselves.

Research in the United States (Newcomb & Locke, 2001; Pears & Capaldi, 2001; Wilcox et al., 2004) and Mexico (Frias-Armenta, 2002) reveals that child abuse runs in families to some degree. ◇ **Truth or Fiction Revisited:** It is true that child abusers were frequently abused themselves as children. Even though child abusers are more likely to have been abused than the general population, *most children who are abused do* not *abuse their own children as adults* (Flores et al., 2005; Wilcox et al., 2004).

When abuse does run in families, why does it do so? There are several hypotheses. One is the generalization that child abuse is part of a poor parenting environment, and that children reared in such an environment are less likely to have resources later on that contribute to a better parenting environment (Frias-Armenta, 2002; Pears & Capaldi, 2001). Another is that parents serve as role models. According to Murray Straus (1995), "Spanking teaches kids that when someone is doing something you don't like and they won't stop doing it, you hit them." A third hypothesis is that children adopt parents' strict philosophies about discipline. Exposure to violence in their own home leads some children to view abuse as normal. A fourth is that being abused can create feelings of hostility that are then expressed against others, including one's own children.

But let us note that many children who are victimized by abuse develop into psychologically healthy adults. Some of these children simply rely on their own strong personal qualities, such as unflagging self-esteem, to develop rewarding relationships and careers (Wilcox et al., 2004). Some develop in families with abundant physical and social resources, despite instances of abuse (Katerndahl et al., 2005). Still others manage to form fruitful relationships with adults outside their families who provide them with emotional support that is unavailable within their families of origin (Flores et al., 2005).

( ) **Learning Connections**

◀◀   *Childhood*   ▶▶

REVIEW:

3 _____ causes newborns to fan their toes.
  (a) The Moro reflex,
  (b) Rooting,
  (c) Crawling,
  (d) The Babinski reflex.

4 According to Piaget, the _____ period is characterized by conservation and reversibility.
  (a) sensorimotor,
  (b) latency,
  (c) concrete-operational,
  (d) preoperational.

5 Vygotsky used the concepts of scaffolding and the _____ of proximal development to explain cognitive development.
  (a) stage,
  (b) zone,
  (c) phase,
  (d) style.

6 Kohlberg's stage _____ is oriented toward obedience and punishment.
  (a) 1,
  (b) 2,
  (c) 3,
  (d) 4.

7 The Harlow studies suggest that _____ is most important in the development of attachment.
  (a) imprinting,
  (b) exploration of the environment,
  (c) fear of strangers,
  (d) contact comfort.

8 Parents with a(n) _____ parenting style are most likely to have competent children.
  (a) permissive,
  (b) authoritative,
  (c) authoritarian,
  (d) uninvolved.

CRITICAL THINKING:
Refer to the findings of Vygotsky, Ainsworth, Harlow, Kohlberg, and Baumrind to develop a "plan" for rearing a child who is secure and competent.

Go www to
http://academic.cengage.com/psychology/rathus
for an interactive version of this review.

ADOLESCENCE

Perhaps no other period of life is as exciting—and as bewildering—as **adolescence.** Except for infancy, more changes occur during adolescence than during any other time of life.

In our society, adolescents are "neither fish nor fowl"—neither children nor adults. Adolescents may be old enough to reproduce and be as large as their parents, yet they are required to remain in school through age 16, may not be allowed to get drivers' licenses until they are 16 or 17, and cannot attend R-rated films without an adult. Given these restrictions, a growing yearning for independence, and a sex drive heightened by high levels of sex hormones, it is not surprising that adolescents can be in conflict with their parents. Like childhood, adolescence entails physical, cognitive, social, and emotional changes.

reflect & relate

There is a saying: "Adolescents are neither fish nor fowl." Can you apply this saying to your own experiences as an adolescent?

▬ Physical Development: Fanning the Flames

Following infancy, children grow about 2 to 3 inches a year. Weight gains remain fairly even at about 4 to 6 pounds per year. *What physical developments occur during adolescence?* One of the most noticeable physical developments of adolescence is a growth spurt that lasts 2 to 3 years and ends the gradual changes in height and weight that characterize most of childhood. Within this short span of years, adolescents grow some 8 to 12 inches. Most boys wind up taller and heavier than most girls.

In boys, the weight of the muscle mass increases notably. The width of the shoulders and circumference of the chest also increase. Adolescents may eat enormous quantities of food to fuel their growth spurt. Adults fighting the "battle of the bulge" stare at them in wonder as they wolf down french fries and shakes at the fast-food counter and later go out for pizza.

Puberty: More Than "Just a Phase"?   **Puberty** is the period during which the body becomes sexually mature. It heralds the onset of adolescence. Puberty begins with the appearance of **secondary sex characteristics** such as body hair, deepening of the voice in males, and rounding of the breasts and hips in females. In boys, pituitary hormones stimulate the testes to increase the output of testosterone, which in turn causes enlargement of the penis and testes and the appearance of body hair. By the early teens, erections become common, and boys may ejaculate. Ejaculatory ability usually precedes the presence of mature sperm by at least a year. Ejaculation thus is not evidence of reproductive capacity.

In girls, a critical body weight in the neighborhood of 100 pounds is thought to trigger a cascade of hormonal secretions in the brain that cause the ovaries to secrete higher levels of the female sex hormone, estrogen (Frisch, 1997). Estrogen stimulates the growth of breast tissue and tissue in the hips and buttocks. The pelvis widens, rounding the hips. Small amounts of androgens produced by the adrenal glands, along with estrogen, spur the growth of pubic and underarm hair. Estrogen and androgens also stoke the development of female sex organs. Estrogen production becomes cyclical during puberty and regulates the menstrual cycle. The beginning of menstruation, or **menarche,** usually occurs between 11 and 14. Girls cannot become pregnant until they ovulate, however, and ovulation may begin two years after menarche.

Plush Studios/Getty Images

■ **Adolescents**

In our culture, adolescents are "neither fish nor fowl." Although they may be old enough to reproduce and may be as large as their parents, they are often treated like children.

──■─ Cognitive Development: The Age of Reason?

I am a college student of extremely modest means. Some crazy psychologist interested in something called "formal operational thought" has just promised to pay me $20 if I can make a coherent logical argument for the proposition that the federal government should under no circumstances ever give or lend more to needy college students. Now what could people who believe that *possibly say by way of supporting argument? Well, I suppose they* could *offer this line of reasoning . . . (Adapted from Flavell et al., 2002)*

The adolescent thinker approaches problems differently from the elementary school child. ***What cognitive developments occur during adolescence?*** Let us begin to answer this question by comparing the child's thought processes to that of the adolescent. The child sticks to the facts, to concrete reality. Speculating about abstract possibilities and what might be is very difficult. The adolescent, on the other hand, is able to deal with the abstract and the hypothetical. As shown in the above example, adolescents realize that one does not have to believe in the truth or justice of a thing in order to argue for it (Flavell et al., 2002). In this section we explore some of the cognitive developments of adolescence by referring to the views of Piaget and Kohlberg.

The Stage of Formal Operations   According to Piaget, children undergo three stages of cognitive development prior to adolescence: sensorimotor, preoperational, and concrete operational. The stage of **formal operations** is the final stage in Piaget's theory, and it represents cognitive maturity. For many children in Western societies, formal operational thought begins at about the beginning of adolescence—the age of 11 or 12. Some people enter this stage later, however, and some never do.

The major achievements of the stage of formal operations involve classification, logical thought, and the ability to hypothesize. Central features are the ability to think about ideas as well as objects and to group and classify ideas—symbols, statements, entire theories. Adolescents can generally follow arguments from premises to conclusions and back again. They can generally appreciate both the outer environment and the world of the imagination: they engage in hypothetical thinking and deductive reasoning.

Formal-operational adolescents (and adults) think abstractly. They solve geometric problems about circles and squares without reference to what the circles and squares may represent in the real world. Adolescents in this stage derive rules for behavior from general principles and can focus, or center, on multiple aspects of a situation at once to solve problems.

In this stage, adolescents tend to emerge as theoretical scientists—even though they may think of themselves as having little interest in science. That is, they can deal with hypothetical situations. They realize that situations can have different outcomes, and they think ahead, imagining them. Adolescents also conduct social experiments to test their hypotheses. They may try out various tones of voice and of treating others to see what works best for them.

Adolescent Egocentrism: "You Just Don't Understand!"   Adolescents in the formal operational stage reason deductively. They classify objects or people and then draw conclusions about them. Adolescents can be proud of their new logical abilities, leading to a new sort of egocentrism: They demand acceptance of their logic without recognizing the exceptions or practical problems that may be considered by adults. Consider this example: "It is wrong to hurt people. Company A hurts people" (perhaps through pollution or economic pressures). "Therefore, Company A must be severely punished or shut down." This thinking is logical. But by impatiently demanding major changes or severe penalties, one may not fully consider various practical problems such as the thousands of workers who might be laid off. Adults have often had life experiences that encourage them to see shades of gray rather than black and white.

The thought of preschoolers is characterized by egocentrism in which they cannot take another's point of view. Adolescent thought is marked by an egocentrism in which they can understand the thoughts of others but still have trouble separating things that are of con-

Adolescence The period of life bounded by puberty and the assumption of adult responsibilities.

Puberty The period of physical development during which sexual reproduction first becomes possible.

Secondary sex characteristics Characteristics that distinguish the sexes, such as distribution of body hair and depth of voice, but that are not directly involved in reproduction.

Menarche The beginning of menstruation.

Formal-operational stage Piaget's fourth stage, characterized by abstract logical thought and deduction from principles.

cern to others and those that are of concern only to themselves (Elkind, 1967, 1985). Adolescent egocentrism gives rise to two interesting cognitive developments: the *imaginary audience* and the *personal fable*.

The concept of the **imaginary audience** refers to the belief that other people are as concerned with our thoughts and behavior as we are. Adolescents thus see themselves as the center of attention and assume that other people are also preoccupied with their appearance and behavior (Milstead et al., 1993). Adolescents may feel on stage with all eyes on them.

The concept of the imaginary audience may drive the intense adolescent desire for privacy. It helps explain why adolescents are so self-conscious, why they worry about every facial blemish and spend hours grooming. Self-consciousness seems to peak at about 13 and then decline. Girls tend to be more self-conscious than boys (Elkind & Bowen, 1979).

The **personal fable** is the belief that our feelings and ideas are special, even unique, and that we are invulnerable. Many adolescents seem to think they are invulnerable, like Superboy or Supergirl. The personal fable seems to underlie adolescent showing off and risk taking (Cohn et al., 1995; Milstead et al., 1993). Some adolescents adopt an "It can't happen to me" attitude: They assume they can smoke without risk of cancer or experiment with sex without risk of sexually transmitted infections or pregnancy. Another aspect of the personal fable is the idea that no one else has experienced or can understand one's "unique" feelings such as needing independence or being in love. The personal fable may underlie the common teenage lament, "You just don't understand me!"

■ **Adolescent Self-Consciousness**
The concept of the imaginary audience may help explain why adolescents are self-conscious about their appearance, why they worry about minor facial imperfections, and why they devote so much time to grooming.

The Postconventional Level of Moral Reasoning   Kohlberg's theory of moral reasoning involves three levels: preconventional, conventional, and postconventional (see Concept Review 3.2 on page 98). Individuals can arrive at the same decision as to whether or not Heinz should save his wife by taking the drug without paying for it for different reasons. Deciding not to steal the drug for fear of punishment is less complex than deciding not to because of the belief that doing so will weaken the social order.

None of Kohlberg's levels is tied to a person's age. Although postconventional reasoning is the highest level, most adolescents and adults never reach it. But if postconventional reasoning emerges, it usually does so in adolescence. Kohlberg's (1969) research found postconventional moral judgments were absent among 7- to 10-year-olds. But by age 16, stage 5 reasoning is shown by about 20% of adolescents, and stage 6 reasoning by about 5%.

At the **postconventional level,** moral reasoning is based on the person's own moral standards. Moral judgments are derived from personal values, not from conventional standards or authority figures. In the contractual, legalistic orientation characteristic of stage 5, it is recognized that laws stem from agreed-upon procedures and that the rule of law is in general good for society; therefore, laws should not be violated except under pressing circumstances. (Although it is illegal for Heinz to steal the drug, in this case it is the right thing to do.)

Stage 6 moral reasoning demands adherence to supposedly universal ethical principles such as the sanctity of human life, individual dignity, justice, and the Golden Rule ("Do unto others as you would have them do unto you"). If a law is unjust or contradicts the rights of the individual, it is wrong to obey it.

People at the postconventional level see their conscience as the highest moral authority. This point has created confusion. To some it suggests that it is right to break the law when it is convenient, but this interpretation is wrong. Kohlberg means that people at this level feel they must do what they think is right even if they break the law or must sacrifice themselves.

Imaginary audience An aspect of adolescent egocentrism; the belief that other people are as concerned with our thoughts and behaviors as we are.

Personal fable Another aspect of adolescent egocentrism; the belief that our feelings and ideas are special and unique and that we are invulnerable.

Postconventional level According to Kohlberg, a period during which moral judgments are derived from moral principles and people look to themselves to set moral standards.

Are There Gender Differences in Moral Development?   A number of studies using Heinz's dilemma have found that boys show higher levels of moral reasoning than girls. But Carol Gilligan (1982; Gilligan et al., 1989) argues that this gender difference reflects different patterns of socialization for boys and girls—not differences in morality. Gilligan considers 11-year-old Jake. Jake weighs the scales of justice like a math problem. He shows that life is worth more than property and concludes that it is Heinz's duty to steal the drug (stage 4 reasoning). Gilligan also points to 11-year-old Amy. Amy vacillates. Amy says that stealing the drug and letting Heinz's wife die are both wrong. So Amy looks for alternatives, such as getting a loan, because it wouldn't help Heinz's wife if he went to jail.

Gilligan finds Amy's reasoning to be as sophisticated as Jake's, yet Amy would be rated as having a lower level of moral development in Kohlberg's scheme. Gilligan argues that girls are socialized to focus on the needs of others and forgo simple judgments of right and wrong. Amy is therefore more likely to show stage 3 reasoning, which focuses in part on empathy—or caring for others. Jake has been socialized to make judgments based on logic. He wants to derive clear-cut conclusions from premises.

We could argue endlessly about which form of moral reasoning—Jake's or Amy's—is "higher." Instead, let us note a review of the research that shows only slight tendencies for boys to favor Jake's "justice" approach and girls to favor Amy's "caring" approach (Jaffee & Hyde, 2000). Thus, the justice orientation does not "belong" to boys and the care orientation does not "belong" to girls.

Social and Emotional Development: Storm and Stress, Smooth Sailing, or Both?

What social and emotional developments occur during adolescence? In terms of social and emotional development, adolescence has been associated with turbulence. In the 19th century, psychologist G. Stanley Hall described adolescence as a time of *Sturm und Drang*—storm and stress. Current views challenge the assumption that "storm and stress" is the norm (Griffin, 2001). Many adolescents experience a rather calm and joyous period of development. We need to consider individual differences and cultural variations (Arnett, 1999).

Certainly, many American teenagers abuse drugs, get pregnant, contract sexually transmitted infections, get involved in violence, fail in school, even attempt suicide (CDC, 2000b). The U.S. Centers for Disease Control and Prevention (CDC, 2000b) reported that 72% of all deaths among people aged 10 to 24 years result from just four causes: motor vehicle crashes (31%), other accidents (11%), homicide (18%), and suicide (12%). Nevertheless, the majority of Americans make it through adolescence quite well.

Striving for Independence   As these biological changes take place, adolescents strive to become more independent from parents, which may lead to bickering (Smetana et al., 2003). Bickering usually concerns homework, chores, money, appearance, curfews, and dating. Disagreements about clothes and friends are common.

Adolescents and parents are often in conflict because adolescents experiment with things that can be harmful to their health. Yet—apparently because of the personal fable—adolescents may not perceive such activities to be as risky as their parents do. Cohn and his colleagues (1995) found, for example, that parents perceived drinking, smoking, failure to use seat belts, drag racing, and a number of other activities to be riskier than did their teenagers.

Some distancing from parents is beneficial (Smetana et al., 2003). After all, adolescents do have to form relationships outside the family. But greater independence does not necessarily mean that adolescents become emotionally detached from parents or fall completely under the spell of peers. Most adolescents continue to feel love, respect, and loyalty toward parents (Eberly & Montemayor, 1999). Adolescents who feel close to their parents actually show more self-reliance and independence than do those who distance themselves. They fare better in school and have fewer adjustment problems (Flouri & Buchanan, 2003). De-

Ariel Skelley/Corbis

■ **Adolescent Relationships with Parents**

Adolescents strive for some independence from their parents, including some distancing. But most adolescents continue to feel love, respect, and loyalty toward their parents. Adolescents and parents also tend to share social, political, religious, and economic views.

spite conflict over issues of control, parents and adolescents tend to share social, political, religious, and economic views (Sagrestano et al., 1999). In sum, there are frequent differences between parents and adolescents on issues of personal control. However, there is apparently less of a "generation gap" on broader matters.

Ego Identity Versus Role Diffusion: "Who Am I?"   According to Erik Erikson, we undergo eight stages of psychosocial development. (See Concept Review 3.3 on page 100.) Four of them, beginning with trust versus mistrust, occur in childhood. The fifth, that of *ego identity versus role diffusion,* occurs in adolescence. **Ego identity** is a firm sense of who one is and what one stands for. It can carry one through difficult times and lend meaning to achievements. Adolescents who do not develop ego identity may experience **role diffusion.** They spread themselves too thin, running down one blind alley after another and placing themselves at the mercy of leaders who promise to give them the sense of identity they cannot find for themselves.

The creation of an adult identity is a key challenge, involving learning about one's interests and abilities and connecting them with occupations and roles in life. Identity also involves sexual, political, and religious beliefs and commitments. Will the individual be monogamous or sexually active with several people? Will he or she lean left or right along the political spectrum? What role will be played by religion?

Adolescent Sexuality—When? What? (How?) Who? Where? and Why?—Not to Mention, "Should I?"

> My first sexual experience occurred in a car after the high school junior prom. We were both virgins, very uncertain but very much in love. We had been going together since eighth grade. The experience was somewhat painful. I remember wondering if I would look different to my mother the next day. I guess I didn't because nothing was said. (Adapted from Morrison et al., 1980, p. 108)

Although many adolescents do not form enduring romantic relationships or support themselves, the changes of puberty ready their bodies for sexual activity. High hormone levels stir interest in sex. Adolescents therefore wrestle with issues of how and when to express their awakening sexuality. To complicate matters, Western culture sends mixed messages about sex. Teenagers may be advised to wait until they have married or entered into meaningful relationships, but they are also bombarded by sexual messages in films, TV, print advertising, and virtually every other medium.

All in all, about half of American high school students have engaged in sexual intercourse (CDC, 2000b). Adolescents usually obtain little advice at home or in school about how to handle their emerging sexuality. Peers also influence the sexual behavior of adolescents. When teenagers are asked why they do not wait to have sexual intercourse, the most common reason is peer pressure (Dickson et al., 1998). All in all, about 800,000 teenage girls get pregnant each year, resulting in 500,000 births ("Less Sex," 2004).

Still, there is encouraging news. The final decade of the 20th century saw a decline in the teenage pregnancy rate due largely to educational campaigns in the schools, the media, churches, and communities ("Less Sex," 2004).

Ego identity Erikson's term for a firm sense of who one is and what one stands for.

Role diffusion Erikson's term for lack of clarity in one's life roles (due to failure to develop ego identity).

Learning Connections

◀◀   *Adolescence*   ▶▶

REVIEW:

9 Which of the following is a primary sex characteristic?
(a) The growth of body hair,
(b) Reproductive capacity,
(c) Deepening of the voice in males,
(d) Rounding of the hips in females.

10 Adolescent _____ gives rise to the imaginary audience and the personal fable.
(a) hypothesis testing,
(b) postconventional reasoning,
(c) deductive logic,
(d) egocentrism.

11 In postconventional moral reasoning, people consider _____ as the standard for what is right.
(a) their own conscience,
(b) social rules,
(c) laws,
(d) tradition and folklore.

12 Erik Erikson considers the life crisis of adolescence to be ego identity versus
(a) despair,
(b) achievement orientation,
(c) mistrust,
(d) role diffusion.

CRITICAL THINKING:
Weigh the evidence and consider why many adolescents take risks and why many are in conflict with parents and authority figures.

Go to www
http://academic.cengage.com/psychology/rathus
for an interactive version of this review.

ADULTHOOD

Development continues throughout the life span. Many theorists believe that adult concerns and involvements follow observable patterns, so that we can speak of "stages" of adult development. Others argue that there may no longer be a standard life cycle with predictable stages or phases. Age now has an "elastic quality"—being 50, 60, 70, 80, or even 90 no longer necessarily means loss of cognitive or physical ability, or even wrinkling. People are living longer than ever before and are freer than ever to choose their own destiny.

■ Physical Development: A Lifetime of Change

The most obvious aspects of development during adulthood are physical. ***What physical developments occur during adulthood?*** Let us consider the physical developments that take place in young, or early, adulthood, which covers the ages between 20 and 40; middle adulthood, which spans the ages of 45 to 65; and late adulthood, which begins at 65.

Young Adulthood   Most young adults are at their height of sensory sharpness, strength, reaction time, and cardiovascular fitness. On the other hand, women gymnasts find themselves lacking a competitive edge in their 20s because they are accumulating (normal!) body fat and losing suppleness and flexibility. Other athletes, such as football, baseball, and basketball players, are more likely to experience a decline in their 30s. Most athletes retire by age 40. Sexually speaking, most people in early adulthood become readily aroused. They tend to attain and maintain erections as desired and to lubricate readily.

Middle Adulthood   In our middle years, we are unlikely to possess the strength, coordination, and stamina that we had during our 20s and 30s. The decline is most obvious in professional sports, where peak performance is at a premium. Gordie Howe still played hockey at 50, but most pros at those ages can no longer keep up with the "kids."

reflect & relate

Where do you fit into the chronicle of the adult years? Do events in your own life fit with any of the research findings or theories presented in this chapter?

The years between 40 and 60 are reasonably stable. There is gradual physical decline, but it is minor and only likely to be of concern if a person competes with young adults—or with idealized memories of oneself. There are exceptions. The 20-year-old couch potato occasionally becomes the 50-year-old marathoner. By any reasonable standard, people in middle adulthood can maintain excellent cardiorespiratory condition. Because the physical decline in middle adulthood is gradual, people who begin to eat more nutritious diets (e.g., decrease intake of animal fats and increase intake of fruits and vegetables) and to exercise may find themselves looking and feeling better than they did in young adulthood.

For women, **menopause** is usually considered to be the single most important change of life that occurs during middle adulthood. Menopause usually occurs during the late 40s or early 50s. Menopause is the final phase of the *climacteric,* which is caused by a decline in secretion of female sex hormones. Ovulation comes to an end, and there is some loss of breast tissue and of elasticity of the skin. Loss of bone density can lead to osteoporosis (brittle bones). During the climacteric, many women experience hot flashes, loss of sleep, and some anxiety and depression. Women's experiences during and following the climacteric reflect the intensity of their physical symptoms—which vary considerably—and the extent to which their self-concept was wrapped up with their reproductive capacity (Dennerstein, 2003; Hvas et al., 2004).

Late Adulthood   An *agequake* is coming. With improved health care and knowledge of the importance of diet and exercise, more Americans than ever before are 65 or older (Nuland, 2005). In 1900, only 1 American in 30 was over 65. By 2030, 1 American in 5 will be 65 or older.

Various changes—some of them troublesome—do occur during the later years (see Figure 3.10). Changes in calcium metabolism increase the brittleness of the bones and heighten the risk of breaks due to falls. The skin becomes less elastic and subject to wrinkles and folds. Older people see and hear less acutely. Because of a decline in the sense of smell, they may use more spice to flavor their food. Older people need more time to respond to stimuli. Older drivers, for example, need more time to respond to changing road conditions. As we grow older, our immune system functions less effectively, leaving us more vulnerable to disease.

Age-related changes impact sexual functioning, yet most people can enjoy sex for a lifetime if they remain generally healthy and adjust their expectations. Nevertheless, especially for many men, the question during late adulthood may shift from "Should I?" to "Can I?"

Menopause The cessation of menstruation.

A Closer Look
Aging, Sex, and Ethnicity: Diverse Patterns

Americans in general are living longer, but there are sex and ethnic differences in life expectancy. For example, women in our society outlive men by about six years (Health, United States, 2002). European Americans and Asian Americans live longer on average than do Latino and Latina Americans, African Americans, and Native Americans (Health, United States, 2002).

Why do women in the United States outlive men? For one thing, heart disease, the nation's leading killer, tends to develop later in women than in men. Men are also more likely to die because of accidents, cirrhosis of the liver, strokes, suicide, homicide, AIDS, and cancer (Health, United States, 2002). Many such deaths reflect excessive drinking

and risky behavior. Many men are also reluctant to have regular physical exams or to talk to their doctors about their health problems. "In their 20s, [men are] too strong to need a doctor; in their 30s, they're too busy, and in their 40s, too scared" (Courtenay, 2000).

There is a seven-year difference in life expectancy between people in the highest income brackets and those in the lowest. Members of certain ethnic minority groups in our society are likely to be poor. Poor people tend to eat less nutritious diets, encounter more stress, and have less access to health care. We may not be able to cannot control our sex and ethnic background, but we can choose whether or not to engage in more healthful behavior. ■

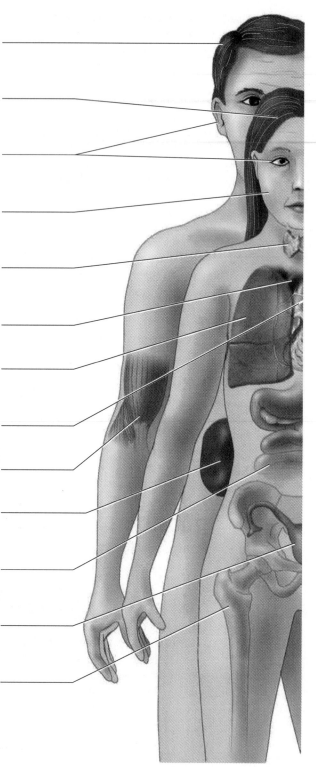

Hair and nails
Hair often turns gray and thins out. Men may go bald. Fingernails can thicken.

Brain
The brain shrinks, but it is not known if that affects mental functions.

The senses
The sensitivity of hearing, sight, taste, and smell can all decline with age.

Skin
Wrinkles occur as the skin thins and the underlying fat shrinks, and age spots often crop up.

Glands and hormones
Levels of many hormones drop, or the body becomes less responsive to them.

Immune system
The body becomes less able to resist some pathogens.

Lungs
It doesn't just seem harder to climb those stairs; lung capacity drops.

Heart and blood vessels
Cardiovascular problems become more common.

Muscles
Strength usually peaks in the 20s, then declines.

Kidneys and urinary tract
The kidneys become less efficient. The bladder can't hold as much, so urination is more frequent.

Digestive system
Digestion slows down as the secretion of digestive enzymes decreases.

Reproductive system
Women go through menopause, and testosterone levels drop for men.

Bones and joints
Wear and tear can lead to arthritic joints, and osteoporosis is common, especially in women.

Figure 3.10
The Relentless March of Time
A number of physical changes occur during the later years. The reasons for aging, however, are not yet completely understood. People can also affect the pace of their aging by eating properly, exercising, maintaining a positive outlook, and finding and meeting challenges that are consistent with their abilities.

Go to your student website to access www an interactive version of this figure.

Why Do We Age? Although it may be hard to believe it will happen to us, every person who has walked the Earth so far has aged. *Why do we age?* Aging, like other aspects of development, apparently involves a complex interaction of nature and nurture (or lack of nurture). There is evidence to support a role for nature—or genes—in aging. Different species have different life spans, and longevity runs in families. People whose parents and grandparents lived into their 80s and 90s have a better chance of reaching these ages themselves. But it is unclear exactly how genes involved in aging express themselves. There is also an obvious role for behavioral and environmental influences. Poor diet, lack of exercise, pollution, by-products of metabolism (e.g., "free radicals"), and disease contribute to aging (Kim et al., 2002). Issues such as the following provide a more detailed look at the aging process (Nuland, 2005):

1. Cells lose the ability to reproduce themselves.
2. There is an accumulation of unwanted cells, including fat cells and cells that accumulate in the joints.
3. Chromosomes mutate, leading to problems such as cancer.
4. The microscopic structures (mitochondria) in cells that produce energy for the cells mutate.
5. "Junk" accumulates within cells, leading to problems such as hardening of the arteries.
6. Junk also accumulates in the fluid outside cells, which may lead to problems such as Alzheimer's disease.
7. Proteins in the fluid outside cells undergo changes that may lead to problems such as high blood pressure.

Regular medical evaluations, proper diet (for example, consuming less animal fat), and exercise all help people live longer. Exercise helps older people maintain flexibility and cardiovascular condition. The exercise need not pound the body and produce rivers of sweat. Because older people tend to have more brittle bones and more rigid joints, fast or prolonged walking are excellent choices (Gill et al., 2000; Hakim et al., 1998; Tanasescu et al., 2002).

▬■ Cognitive Development: Maximizing Cognitive Powers

What cognitive developments occur during adulthood? As in the case of physical development, people are also at the height of their cognitive powers during early adulthood. Many professionals show the broadest knowledge of their fields at about the time they are graduating from college or graduate school. Their studies are freshest. As time goes on, specialized knowledge may deepen while understanding of related areas grows relatively superficial.

Cognitive development in adulthood has many aspects—creativity, memory functioning, and intelligence. People can be creative for a lifetime. At the age of 80, Merce Cunningham choreographed a dance that made use of computer-generated digital images (Teachout, 2000). Hans Hofmann created some of his most vibrant paintings at 85, and Pablo Picasso was painting in his 90s. Grandma Moses did not even begin painting until she was 78 years old. Giuseppe Verdi wrote his joyous opera *Falstaff* at the age of 79. ◈ **Truth or Fiction Revisited**: And it is *not* true that the architect Frank Lloyd Wright designed New York's innovative spiral-shaped Guggenheim Museum when he was 65 years old. He was actually 89.

Memory functioning does decline with age. Older people may have trouble recalling the names of common objects or people they know. Memory lapses can be embarrassing, and older people sometimes lose confidence in their memories, which may lower their motivation to remember things. But declines in memory are not usually as large as people assume and are often reversible (Villa & Abeles, 2000). Memory tests usually measure ability to recall meaningless information. Older people show better memory functioning in areas in which they can apply their experience, especially their specialties, to new challenges. For example, who would do a better job of learning and remembering how to solve problems in chemistry—a college history major or a retired professor of chemistry?

You might choose the chemistry professor because of his or her crystallized intelligence, not his or her fluid intelligence. **Crystallized intelligence** represents one's lifetime of intellectual attainments. We are using the example of knowledge of chemistry, but crystallized intelligence is shown more generally by vocabulary and accumulated facts about world affairs. Therefore, crystallized intelligence can increase over the decades. **Fluid intelligence** is defined as mental flexibility, demonstrated by the ability to process information rapidly, as in learning and solving problems in new areas. It is the sort of intellectual functioning that is typically measured on intelligence tests, especially with problems that have time limits.

Young adults obtain the highest intelligence test scores (Schaie et al., 2004). Yet people tend to retain verbal skills, as demonstrated by vocabulary and general knowledge, into advanced old age. The performance of older people on tasks that require speed and visual–spatial skills, such as piecing puzzles together, tends to decline (Schaie et al., 2004; Zimprich & Martin, 2002).

One of the most severe assaults on intellectual functioning, especially among older people, is Alzheimer's disease.

Alzheimer's Disease   What is Alzheimer's disease? What are its origins? **Alzheimer's disease** is a progressive form of mental deterioration that affects about 1% of people at age 60 and nearly half past age 85 (Brody, 2005). ◈ **Truth or Fiction Revisited**: Alzheimer's disease is *not* a normal part of aging. Although Alzheimer's is connected with aging, it is a disease rather than a normal progression (Yesavage et al., 2002).

AP/Wide World Photos

■ **Frank Lloyd Wright**
The innovative architect created New York's unique Solomon R. Guggenheim Museum at the age of 89.

Crystallized intelligence One's lifetime of intellectual achievement, as shown largely through vocabulary and knowledge of world affairs.

Fluid intelligence Mental flexibility as shown in learning rapidly to solve new kinds of problems.

Alzheimer's disease A progressive form of mental deterioration characterized by loss of memory, language, problem solving, and other cognitive functions.

Self-Assessment

How Long Will You Live? The Life-Expectancy Scale

Life-expectancy scales are used by the government and insurance companies to estimate how long people will live. Scales such as these are not precise—which is a good thing, if you think about it. But they do help reveal factors that contribute to longevity.

Directions: To complete the scale, begin with one of the following number of years, depending on your sex and ethnicity:

RACE	FEMALE	MALE
European American	79	72
African American	73	65
All races, combined	78	71

Now add or subtract years according to the following directions:

Running Total   Personal Facts

_____ 1. If you live in an urban area with a population over 2 million, **subtract 2.**

_____ 2. If you live in a town with under 10,000 people or on a farm, **add 2.**

_____ 3. If any grandparent lived to 85, **add 2.**

_____ 4. If all four grandparents lived to 80, **add 6.**

_____ 5. If either parent died of a stroke or heart attack before the age of 50, **subtract 4.**

_____ 6. If any parent, brother, or sister under 50 has (or had) cancer or a heart condition, or has had diabetes since childhood, **subtract 3.**

_____ 7. Do you earn over $100,000* a year? If so, **subtract 2.**

_____ 8. If you finished college, **add 1.** If you have a graduate or professional degree, **add 2 more.**

_____ 9. If you are 65 or over and still working, **add 3.**

_____ 10. If you live with a spouse or friend, **add 5.** If not, **subtract 1** for every ten years alone since age 25.

*This figure is an inflation-adjusted estimate.

Lifestyle Status

_____ 11. If you work behind a desk, **subtract 3.**

_____ 12. If your work requires regular, heavy physical labor, **add 3.**

_____ 13. If you exercise strenuously (tennis, running, swimming, and so forth) five times a week for at least a half-hour, **add 4.** If two or three times a week, **add 2.**

_____ 14. Do you sleep more than ten hours each night? **Subtract 4.**

_____ 15. Are you intense, aggressive, easily angered? **Subtract 3.**

_____ 16. Are you easygoing and relaxed? **Add 3.**

_____ 17. Are you happy? **Add 1.** Unhappy? **Subtract 2.**

_____ 18. Have you had a speeding ticket in the last year? **Subtract 1.**

_____ 19. Do you smoke more than two packs a day? **Subtract 8.** One or two packs? **Subtract 6.** One-half to one? **Subtract 3.**

_____ 20. Are you overweight by 50 lbs. or more? **Subtract 8.** By 30 to 50 lbs.? **Subtract 4.** By 10 to 30 lbs.? **Subtract 2.**

_____ 21. If you are a man over 40 and have annual checkups, **add 2.**

_____ 22. If you are a woman and see a gynecologist once a year, **add 2.**

Age Adjustment

_____ 23. If you are between 50 and 70, **add 4.**

_____ 24. If you are over 70, **add 5.**

_____ YOUR LIFE EXPECTANCY

Source: Based on "Life Expectancy at Birth, at 65 Years of Age, and at 75 Years of Age, According to Race and Sex: United States," by Centers for Disease Control, 2003, *Health, United States, 2003,* http://www.cdc.gov/nchs/data/hus/tables/2003/03hus027.pdf, Table 27; and *Lifegain,* by R. F. Allen with S. Linde, 1986, Morristown, NJ: Human Resources Institute Press, Tempe Wick Road.

Go to www http://academic.cengage.com/psychology/rathus where you can fill out an interactive version of this Self-Assessment and automatically score your results.

Alzheimer's disease is characterized by general, gradual deterioration in cognitive processes such as memory, language, and problem solving. As the disease progresses, people may fail to recognize familiar faces or forget their names. At the most severe stage, people with Alzheimer's disease become helpless. They become unable to communicate or walk and require help in toileting and feeding. Isolated memory losses, as in forgetting where one put one's glasses, may be a normal feature of aging (Qualls & Abeles, 2000). Alzheimer's, in contrast, seriously impairs vocational and social functioning.

Alzheimer's disease is characterized by reduced levels of the neurotransmitter acetylcholine (ACh) and by the buildup of a plaque that impairs neural functioning in the brain.

One form of drug therapy has aimed at boosting ACh levels by slowing its breakdown (Trinh et al., 2003). This approach achieves modest benefits with many people. The plaque is formed from fragments of a body protein called beta amyloid (Brody, 2005). Normally, the immune system prevents the buildup of plaque, but not so in the case of people with Alzheimer's disease. Thus another approach to the treatment of Alzheimer's is the development of a vaccine made from beta amyloid that will stimulate the immune system to recognize and attack the plaque more vigorously (Janus et al., 2000; Morgan et al., 2000).

Although Alzheimer's is not a normal part of aging, there are normal, gradual declines in intellectual functioning and memory among older people (Qualls & Abeles, 2000). Although we understand little about why these declines occur, they appear to be connected with biological problems (Yesavage et al., 2002). Depression and losses of sensory acuity and motivation may also contribute to lower cognitive test scores. B. F. Skinner (1983) argued that much of the falloff is due to an "aging environment" rather than an aging person. That is, the behavior of older people often goes unreinforced. This view is substantiated by a classic study of nursing home residents who were rewarded for remembering recent events and showed improved scores on tests of memory (Langer et al., 1979).

─■─ Social and Emotional Development: Growing Psychologically Healthier?

Changes in social and emotional development during adulthood are probably the most "elastic" or fluid. These changes are affected by cultural expectations and individual behavior patterns. As a result, there is much variety. Nevertheless, many developmental theorists suggest that there are enough commonalities that we can speak of trends. One trend is that the outlook for older people has become more optimistic over the past generation—not only because of medical advances but also because the behavior and mental processes of many older people are remaining younger than at any other time in history.

There is more good news. Research evidence suggests that people tend to grow psychologically healthier as they advance from adolescence through middle adulthood. Psychologists Constance Jones and William Meredith (2000) studied information on 236 participants in California growth studies who had been followed from early adolescence for about 50 years and found that they generally became more productive and had healthier relationships as time went on. Even some people with a turbulent adolescence showed better psychological health at age 62 than they had half a century earlier.

Let us now follow social and emotional developments throughout the course of adulthood, beginning with young adulthood.

Young Adulthood   *What social and emotional developments occur during young adulthood?* Many theorists suggest that young adulthood is the period of life during which people tend to establish themselves as independent members of society.

At some point during the 20s, many people become fueled by ambition. Many strive to advance in their careers. Those who seek professional careers may spend much of their 20s acquiring the skills that will enable them to succeed (Levinson et al., 1978; Levinson, 1996). It is largely during the 20s that people become generally responsible for their own support, make their own choices, and are freed from parental influences. Many young adults adopt what theorist Daniel Levinson and his colleagues (1978) call the **dream**—the drive to "become" someone, to leave their mark on history—which serves as a tentative blueprint for life.

During young adulthood, people tend to leave their families of origin and create families of their own. Erik Erikson (1963) characterized young adulthood as the stage of **intimacy versus isolation.** (For a summary of Erikson's stages, see Concept Review 3.3 on page 100.) Erikson saw the establishment of intimate relationships as central to young adulthood. Young adults who have evolved a firm sense of identity during adolescence are ready to "fuse" their identities with those of other people through marriage and abiding friendships. People who do not reach out to develop intimate relationships risk retreating into isolation and loneliness.

At age 30 or so, many people reassess their lives, asking themselves, "Where is my life going?" "Why am I doing this?" (Levinson et al., 1978). It is not uncommon for them to

■ **Establishing Intimate Relationships** According to Erik Erikson, establishing intimate relationships is a central task of young adulthood.

Dream In this usage, Levinson's term for the overriding drive of youth to become someone important, to leave one's mark on history.

Intimacy versus isolation Erikson's life crisis of young adulthood, which is characterized by the task of developing abiding intimate relationships.

switch careers or form new intimate relationships. The later 30s are often characterized by settling down—planting roots. Many young adults make a financial and emotional investment in their home. They become focused on career advancement, children, and long-term mortgages.

Middle Adulthood   A number of key changes in social and emotional development occur during middle adulthood. ***What social and emotional developments occur during middle adulthood?*** Consider Erikson's views on the middle years.

Erikson (1963) labeled the life crisis of the middle years **generativity versus stagnation.** *Generativity* involves doing things that we believe are worthwhile, such as rearing children or producing on the job. Generativity enhances and maintains self-esteem. Generativity also involves making the world a better place through joining church or civic groups. *Stagnation* means treading water, as in keeping the same job at the same pay for 30 years. Stagnation damages self-esteem.

According to Levinson and colleagues (1978), whose research involved case studies of 40 men, there is a **midlife transition** at about age 40 to 45. Previously, men had viewed their age in terms of the number of years that had elapsed since birth. Now they begin to think of their age in terms of the number of years they have left. Men in their 30s still think of themselves as older brothers to "kids" in their 20s. But at about 40 to 45, some marker event—illness, a change of job, the death of a friend or parent, or being beaten at tennis by one's son—leads men to realize that they are a full generation older. They realize they will never be president or chairperson of the board. They will never play shortstop for the Dodgers. They mourn the passing of their youth and begin to adjust to the specters of late adulthood and death.

Research suggests that women may undergo a midlife transition sooner than men do (Zucker et al., 2002). Why? Much of it has to do with the winding down of the "biological clock"—that is, the abilities to conceive and bear children. For example, once they turn 35, women are usually advised to have their fetuses routinely tested for Down syndrome and other chromosomal disorders. At age 35, women enter higher risk categories for side effects from birth control pills. Yet many women today are having children in their 40s and, now and then, beyond.

In both sexes, according to Levinson, the midlife transition may trigger a **midlife crisis.** The middle-level, middle-aged businessperson looking ahead to another 10 to 20 years of grinding out accounts in a Wall Street cubbyhole may encounter severe depression. The homemaker with two teenagers, an empty house from 8:00 AM to 4:00 PM, and a 40th birthday on the way may feel that she or he is coming apart at the seams. Both feel a sense of entrapment and loss of purpose.

Yet many Americans find that these years present opportunities for new direction and fulfillment. Many people are at the height of their productive powers during this period. Women often renew their sense of self in their 40s and 50s. Women in their early 40s are more likely than women in their early 30s to feel confident, exert an influence on their community, feel secure and committed; to feel productive, effective, and powerful, and to extend their interests beyond their family (Zucker et al., 2002). Many, perhaps most, of today's robust 45- to 55-year-olds can look forward to another 30 to 40 healthy years. Yet some people in this age group experience a midcourse correction (Zucker et al., 2002). And why not? Many decades remain for self-fulfillment.

Late Adulthood

> It's never too late to be what you might have been.
> —George Eliot

What social and emotional developments occur during late adulthood? Generativity does not end with middle age. Research suggests that many individuals in late adulthood continue to be creative and also to maintain a firm sense of who they are and what they stand for (Webster, 2003). The Greek philosopher Plato was so optimistic about late adulthood that he argued that one could achieve great pleasure in one's later years, engage in meaningful public service, and also achieve wisdom (McKee & Barber, 2001).

Generativity versus stagnation Erikson's term for the crisis of middle adulthood, characterized by the task of being productive and contributing to younger generations.

Midlife transition Levinson's term for the ages from 40 to 45, which are characterized by a shift in psychological perspective from viewing ourselves in terms of years lived to viewing ourselves in terms of the years we have left.

Midlife crisis A crisis experienced by many people during the midlife transition when they realize that life may be more than halfway over and they reassess their achievements in terms of their dreams.

According to psychologist Erik Erikson, late adulthood is the stage of **ego integrity versus despair.** The basic challenge is to maintain the belief that life is meaningful and worthwhile as one ages and faces the inevitability of death. Erikson, like Plato, spoke of the importance of wisdom. He believed that ego integrity derives from wisdom, which can be defined as expert knowledge about the meaning of life, balancing one's own needs and those of others, and pushing toward excellence in one's behavior and achievements (Baltes & Staudinger, 2000; Sternberg, 2000). Erikson also believed that wisdom enables people to accept their life span as occurring at a certain point in the sweep of history and as being limited. We spend most of our lives accumulating objects and relationships, and Erikson argues that adjustment in the later years requires the ability to let go of them. Other views of late adulthood stress the importance of creating new challenges; however, biological and social realities may require older people to become more selective in their pursuits.

Successful Aging   The later years were once seen mainly as a prelude to dying. Older people were viewed as crotchety and irritable. It was assumed that they reaped little pleasure from life. *No more.* Many stereotypes about aging are becoming less prevalent. How do people in the United States age today? Despite the changes that accompany aging, most people in their 70s report being generally satisfied with their lives (Volz, 2000). Americans are eating more wisely and exercising at later ages, so many older people are robust. According to a national poll of some 1,600 adults by the *Los Angeles Times,* 75% of older people feel younger than their age—19 years on average (Stewart & Armet, 2000).

One aspect of successful aging is subjective well-being. A sense of well-being in late adulthood is linked to more than physical health and feeling younger than one's years. An analysis of 286 studies noted three factors that are connected with a sense of well-being: socioeconomic status, social network, and competence (Pinquart & Sörensen, 2000). Having social contacts with friends and one's adult children is important. Competence enables one to fill one's days with meaningful activities and handle the problems that can arise at any age.

Developmental psychologists are using the term *successful aging* in their study of characteristics that enable older people to lead more enjoyable and productive lives. ◇ **Truth or Fiction Revisited**: It is not true that successful aging involves avoiding new challenges. There are three components of successful aging:

1. *Reshaping one's life to concentrate on what one finds to be important and meaningful.* Research with people aged 70 and above reveals that successful agers form emotional goals that bring them satisfaction (Löckenhoff & Carstensen, 2004). Researchers use terms like "selective optimization and compensation" to describe how successful agers lead their lives (Bajor & Baltes, 2003; Freund & Baltes, 2002). They no longer compete in arenas better left to younger people—such as certain athletic or business activities. Rather, they focus on matters that allow them to maintain a sense of control over their lives. Moreover, they use available resources to make up for losses. If their memory is not quite what it was, they write notes. If their senses are no longer as acute, they use hearing aids or allow themselves more time to take in information.

2. *A positive outlook.* For example, some older people attribute occasional health problems such as aches and pains to *specific* and *unstable* factors like a cold or jogging too long. Others attribute aches and pains to *global* and *stable* factors such as aging itself. Not surprisingly, those who attribute these problems to specific, unstable factors are more optimistic about surmounting them. Rakowski (1995) followed 1,400 people aged 70 or older with health problems such as aches and pains. He found that those who blamed the problems on aging were more likely to die in the near future than those who blamed them on specific, unstable factors.

■ **"Successful Aging"?**
The later years were once seen mainly as a prelude to dying. In the third millennium, however, many older people—termed "successful agers"—are seeking new challenges.

Ego integrity versus despair Erikson's term for the crisis of late adulthood, characterized by the task of maintaining one's sense of identity despite physical deterioration.

3. *Self-challenge.* Many people look forward to late adulthood as a time when they can rest from life's challenges. But sitting back and allowing the world to pass by is a prescription for vegetating, not for living life to its fullest. In one experiment, Sandman and Crinella (1995) randomly assigned people whose average age was 72 either to a foster grandparent program with neurologically impaired children or to a control group. They followed both groups for 10 years. The foster grandparents carried out physical challenges, such as walking a few miles each day, and also engaged in new kinds of social interactions. Those in the control group did not engage in these activities. After 10 years, the foster grandparents showed superior overall cognitive functioning, including memory, and better sleep patterns, as compared with controls.

The *Los Angeles Times* poll found that 25% of people who had retired believed that they had done so too soon (Stewart & Armet, 2000). Older adults today are returning to school in record numbers, becoming entrepreneurs, volunteering, and, in many cases, continuing to work. According to retirement specialist Helen Dennis (2000),

> Work is a tremendous social environment. Generally, people spend more time at work with colleagues and friends than they do with their families. Those people who are currently retiring have had long-term experiences with an employer. They've lived through marriages, births, deaths, Christmases, and Thanksgivings.

Nearly half (45%) of those polled by the *Los Angeles Times* agreed with the statement, "When you give up your job, you give up a large part of who you are" (Stewart & Armet, 2000).

"Lying Down to Pleasant Dreams . . ."

The American poet William Cullen Bryant is best known for his poem "Thanatopsis," which he composed at the age of 18. "Thanatopsis" expresses Erik Erikson's goal of ego integrity—optimism that we can maintain a sense of trust through life. By meeting squarely the challenges of our adult lives, perhaps we can take our leave with dignity. When our time

( ) Learning Connections

◀◀   *Adulthood*   ▶▶

REVIEW:

13 Most people are at their height in sensory acuteness, reaction time, and cardiovascular fitness during
(a) adolescence,
(b) young adulthood,
(c) middle adulthood,
(d) late adulthood.

14 _____ intelligence refers to one's lifetime of intellectual achievement.
(a) Crystallized,
(b) Fluid,
(c) Performance,
(d) Verbal.

15 Alzheimer's disease is characterized by reduced levels of
(a) acetylcholine,
(b) ACTH,
(c) adrenaline,
(d) thyroxin.

16 Erikson labeled the life crisis of the middle years
(a) ego identity versus role diffusion,
(b) intimacy versus isolation,
(c) generativity versus stagnation,
(d) ego integrity versus despair.

CRITICAL THINKING:
How do the factors that contribute to longevity demonstrate key roles for heredity, environmental factors, patterns of behavior, and attitudes?

Go to
http://academic.cengage.com/psychology/rathus
for an interactive version of this review.

comes to "join the innumerable caravan"—the billions who have died before us—perhaps we can depart life with integrity.

"Live," wrote the poet, so that

> . . . when thy summons comes to join
> The innumerable caravan that moves
> To that mysterious realm, where each shall take
> His chamber in the silent halls of death,
> Thou go not, like the quarry-slave at night,
> Scourged to his dungeon, but, sustained and soothed
> By an unfaltering trust, approach thy grave
> Like one that wraps the drapery of his couch
> About him, and lies down to pleasant dreams.

Bryant, of course, wrote "Thanatopsis" at age 18, not at 85, the age at which he died. At that advanced age, his feelings—and his verse—might have differed. But literature and poetry, unlike science, need not reflect reality. They can serve to inspire and warm us.

RECITE—*An Active Summary*™

 Recite to Go! *Don't have time to study right now? You can study on the go!*
Go to your companion website and download an audio version of this review section to your media player. You can also access an interactive flash-card version of this review from your website.

1. What developments occur from conception through birth?	Prenatal development occurs in stages: the germinal, embryonic, and fetal stages. During the germinal stage, the zygote divides and becomes implanted in the uterine wall. The major organ systems are formed during the embryonic stage. The fetal stage is characterized by maturation and gains in size.
2. What physical developments occur during childhood?	Reflexes such as sucking and swallowing are inborn. Motor development of the child involves the interaction of maturation and experience. Newborn babies can see quite well and show greater interest in complex visual stimuli than in simple ones. Infants can usually perceive depth by the time they crawl. Newborns can normally hear and prefer their mother's voice.
3. Does development occur gradually or in stages?	Stage theorists like Freud and Piaget view development as discontinuous. Learning theorists tend to view psychological development as more continuous. Some aspects of development, such as the adolescent growth spurt, are discontinuous. There is controversy as to whether cognitive development is continuous or discontinuous.
4. What are Piaget's stages of cognitive development?	Piaget saw children as budding scientists who actively strive to make sense of the perceptual world. He defined intelligence as involving assimilation and accommodation. Piaget's theory includes four stages: sensorimotor, preoperational, concrete operational, and formal operational.
5. What are the key concepts of Vygotsky's theory of cognitive development?	Vygotsky's concepts include the *zone of proximal development* (ZPD) and *scaffolding*. When learning with others, children internalize conversations and explanations that foster skills. Children learn ways to think about problems in a cultural context.
6. How do children reason about right and wrong?	Lawrence Kohlberg hypothesized that children's moral reasoning develops through three levels, with two stages each. Moral decisions develop from being based on pain and pleasure ("preconventional"), through necessity to maintain the social order ("conventional"), to reliance on one's conscience ("postconventional").

7. What are Erikson's stages of psychosocial development?	Erikson hypothesizes eight stages of psychosocial development. Each represents a life crisis. The first of these is "trust versus mistrust," during which the child learns that the world is a good place that meets her or his needs—or not.
8. How do feelings of attachment develop? What kinds of experiences affect attachment?	Ainsworth proposes three stages of attachment: the initial-preattachment phase, the attachment-in-the-making phase, and the clear-cut-attachment phase. Bowlby adds fear of strangers. Harlow's studies with monkeys suggest that contact comfort is a key to the development of attachment.
9. What types of parental behavior are connected with variables such as self-esteem, achievement motivation, and independence in children?	Styles of parental behavior include the authoritative, authoritarian, permissive, and uninvolved styles. The children of authoritative parents are the most achievement oriented and well adjusted.
10. What physical developments occur during adolescence?	Adolescence begins at puberty and ends with assumption of adult responsibilities. Changes that lead to reproductive capacity and secondary sex characteristics are stimulated by increased levels of sex hormones. Sex hormones stir interest in sex. Adolescents may spurt 6 or more inches in a year.
11. What cognitive developments occur during adolescence?	Formal operational thinking appears in adolescence, but not everyone reaches it. Two consequences of adolescent egocentrism are the imaginary audience and the personal fable.
12. What social and emotional developments occur during adolescence?	Adolescents are often in conflict with parents because adolescents desire independence and take risks. Yet most adolescents continue to respect their parents. According to Erikson, adolescents strive to forge an ego identity.
13. What physical developments occur during adulthood?	People are usually at the height of their physical powers during young adulthood. Middle adulthood is characterized by a gradual decline in strength. Older people show less sensory acuity, and the immune system weakens.
14. Why do we age?	Aging involves genetic and environmental factors. Longevity runs in families. Factors such as pollution and disease weaken the body. Exercise, diet, and smoking all affect longevity.
15. What cognitive developments occur during adulthood?	People are usually at the height of their cognitive powers during early adulthood, but people can be creative for a lifetime. Memory declines with age. People tend to retain verbal ability into advanced old age. Crystallized intelligence generally increases with age, whereas fluid intelligence declines.
16. What is Alzheimer's disease? What are its origins?	Alzheimer's disease is characterized by cognitive deterioration in memory, language, problem solving. It is connected with reduced acetylcholine and buildup of plaque in the brain.
17. What social and emotional developments occur during young adulthood?	Young adulthood is generally characterized by efforts to advance in the business world and the development of intimate ties.
18. What social and emotional developments occur during middle adulthood?	Many theorists view middle adulthood as a time of crisis (the "midlife crisis") and further reassessment. Many middle adults try to come to terms with the discrepancies between their achievements and the dreams of their youth.
19. What social and emotional developments occur during late adulthood?	Erikson saw the basic challenge of late adulthood as maintaining the belief that life is worthwhile in the face of physical deterioration.
20. How do people in the United States age today?	Most older Americans report being generally satisfied with their lives. "Successful agers" focus on what they find important, keep a positive outlook, and find new challenges.

Key Terms

Zygote 85

Germinal stage 85

Embryonic stage 85

Maturation 85

Androgens 85

Amniotic sac 85

Placenta 86

Umbilical cord 86

Fetal stage 86

Reflex 87

Rooting 87

Fixation time 88

Assimilation 91

Schema 91

Accommodation 91

Object permanence 91

Sensorimotor stage 92

Preoperational stage 92

Egocentrism 92

Animism 92

Artificialism 92

Conservation 93

Center 93

Objective responsibility 94

Concrete-operational stage 95

Decentration 95

Subjective moral judgment 95

Reversibility 95

Zone of proximal development (ZPD) 96

Scaffolding 96

Preconventional level 98

Conventional level 98

Trust versus mistrust 99

Autonomy 99

Attachment 100

Contact comfort 102

Ethologist 102

Critical period 102

Imprinting 102

Instrumental competence 104

Authoritative parents 104

Authoritarian parents 104

Permissive parents 105

Uninvolved parents 105

Adolescence 107

Puberty 107

Secondary sex characteristics 107

Menarche 107

Formal-operational stage 108

Imaginary audience 109

Personal fable 109

Postconventional level 109

Ego identity 111

Role diffusion 111

Menopause 113

Crystallized intelligence 115

Fluid intelligence 115

Alzheimer's disease 115

Dream 117

Intimacy versus isolation 117

Generativity versus stagnation 118

Midlife transition 118

Midlife crisis 118

Ego integrity versus despair 119

Active Learning Resources

Visit Your Companion Website for This Book

http://academic.cengage.com/psychology/rathus

Check out this companion website where you will find online resources directly linked to your book. This is where you'll access the videos highlighted in your Video Connections feature. You can answer the questions online and email them to your professor. In addition you'll find downloadable audio review material, interactive versions of the study aids, Power Visuals for mastering and reviewing key concepts, as well as quizzing, and much more!

CENGAGENOW™

http://academic.cengage.com

Need help studying? This site is your one-stop study shop. Take a Pre-Test and Cengage NOW will generate a Personalized Study Plan based on your test results. The Study Plan will identify the topics you need to review and direct you to online resources to help you master those topics. You can then take a Post-Test to help you determine the concepts you have mastered and what you still need to work on. In addition you can access interactive media including the videos highlighted in your Video Connections box.

Author Blog

What does your author Spence Rathus have to say about the state of psychology? Visit your companion website every Tuesday and click on "Author Blog." This is where he'll talk about the most recent controversies and hot topics in psychology. This will keep you up to date with what your author is thinking and give you great insight into modern psychology.

CHAPTER 4

Sensation and Perception

T	F	People have five senses.
T	F	If we could see waves of light with slightly longer wavelengths, warm-blooded animals would glow in the dark.
T	F	People sometimes hear what they want to hear.
T	F	When we mix blue and yellow light, we obtain green light.
T	F	The bodies of catfish are covered with taste buds.
T	F	The skin is a sensory organ as well as a protective coating for the body.
T	F	Many people experience pain "in" limbs that have been amputated.
T	F	You have a sense that keeps you an upright person.
T	F	Some people can read other people's minds.

Go to www

http://academic.cengage.com/pstchology/rathus
for an interactive version of this Truth or Fiction feature.

In *The Matrix* film series, our world is unreal. The people we touch, the food we taste, the distant hills we see, the sunshine we feel on our skin, the voices and traffic we hear, the perfumes and exhaust we smell, the buildings that shelter us from the wetness of the rain and the bite of winter ice—all these are nothing but software. We, too—that is, you and I—are also software.

We lead our lives in the early days of the 21st century. But according to the films, the real world is found 200 years in our future. Real people are plugged into devices that harvest their energy and provide them with simulated lives 200 years in the past. How are people given their make-believe lives? Cells in their brains are caused to fire in patterns that create illusions of reality. We think we see because the cells involved in vision are firing. We think we hear because the cells involved in hearing are firing. And so on for all our senses. The illusion is almost perfect. The great majority of us are content to dwell as software in an illusory world. Our interactions with computerized objects and other people's software selves are satisfying and convincing enough. Only a very few sense that something is wrong, but not even they are sure what it is.

The real world, such as it is, is a withered sunless specter of its former self. It is ruled by machines, whose artificial intelligence rivals or surpasses our own. People lie in pods, hooked into the virtual world of the early 2000s. The muscles in their limbs remain unused and weaken. Their eyes stay shut.

Yet sensory information is transmitted to their central nervous systems, and they piece it together to form their representations of the world outside. In *The Matrix*, the world outside is very different, but their virtual reality is created much as our "real reality" is.

Warner Bros./The Kobal Collection

■ **How Do Our Senses Connect Us with the World Outside?**

In *The Matrix* film series, our world is unreal. The people we touch, the food we taste, even the sun we feel on our skin are all software. In this photo, Keanu Reeves battles not only gravity, but also a software program (right) who is an expert in kung fu.

SENSATION AND PERCEPTION: YOUR TICKETS OF ADMISSION TO THE WORLD OUTSIDE

What are sensation and perception? **Sensation** is the stimulation of sensory receptors and the transmission of sensory information to the central nervous system (the spinal cord or brain). Sensory receptors are located in sensory organs such as the eyes and ears, the skin, and elsewhere in the body. Stimulation of the senses is an automatic process. It results from sources of energy, like light and sound, or from the presence of chemicals, as in smell and taste. In *The Matrix*, a step is skipped: There is no stimulation of sensory receptors in the eyes, the nose, the skin, and so on. There is, instead, direct transmission of sensory information to the central nervous system.

Perception is not automatic. Perception is an active process in which sensations are organized and interpreted to form an inner representation of the world. Perception may

Sensation The stimulation of sensory receptors and the transmission of sensory information to the central nervous system.

Perception The process by which sensations are organized into an inner representation of the world.

begin with sensation, but it also reflects our experiences and expectations as it makes sense of sensory stimuli. A person standing 15 feet away and a 12-inch-tall doll right next to you may cast similar-sized images on the back of your eye, but whether you interpret the shape to be a foot-long doll or a full-grown person 15 feet away is a matter of perception that depends on your experience with dolls, people, and distance.

In this chapter you will see that your personal map of reality—your ticket of admission to a world of changing sights, sounds, and other sources of sensory input—depends largely on the so-called five senses: vision, hearing, smell, taste, and touch. But touch is just one of several "skin senses," which also include pressure, warmth, cold, and pain. ◆ **Truth or Fiction Revisited:** People have many more than five senses. There are also senses that alert you to your own body position without your having to watch every step you take. As we explore each of these senses, we will find that similar sensations may lead to different perceptions in different people—or to different situations in the same person.

Before we begin our voyage through the senses, let us consider a number of concepts that apply to all of them: *absolute threshold, difference threshold, signal-detection theory,* and *sensory adaptation.* In doing so, we will learn why we can dim the lights gradually to near darkness without anyone noticing. (Sneaky?) We will also learn why we might become indifferent to the savory aromas of delightful dinners. (Disappointing?) *How do we know when something is there? How do we know when it has changed?*

◾ Absolute Threshold: So, Is It There or Not?

Nineteenth-century German psychologist Gustav Fechner used the term **absolute threshold** to refer to the weakest amount of a stimulus that a person can distinguish from no stimulus at all. For example, the absolute threshold for light would be the minimum brightness (physical energy) required to activate the visual sensory system.

Psychophysicists look for the absolute thresholds of the senses by exposing individuals to progressively stronger stimuli until they find the minimum stimuli that the person can detect 50% of the time. These absolute thresholds are not all that absolute, however. Some people are more sensitive than others, and even the same person might have a slightly different response at different times.

Nevertheless, under ideal conditions, our ability to detect stimuli are quite sensitive. The following are measures of the absolute thresholds for the senses of vision, hearing, taste, smell, and touch:

- Vision: a candle flame viewed from about 30 miles on a clear, dark night.
- Hearing: a watch ticking from about 20 feet away in a quiet room.
- Taste: 1 teaspoon of sugar dissolved in 2 gallons of water.
- Smell: about one drop of perfume diffused throughout a small house (1 part in 500 million).
- Touch: the pressure of the wing of a fly falling on a cheek from a distance of about 0.4 inch.

How different our lives would be if the absolute thresholds for the human senses differed! If your ears were sensitive to sounds that are lower in **pitch,** you might hear the collisions among molecules of air. If you could see light with slightly longer wavelengths, you would see infrared light waves. Your world would be transformed because heat generates infrared light. ◆ **Truth or Fiction Revisited:** If we could see waves of light with slightly longer wavelengths, warm-blooded animals—including other people—would glow in the dark.

◾ Difference Threshold: Is It the Same or Is It Different?

How much of a difference in intensity between two lights is required before you will detect one as being brighter than the other? The minimum difference in magnitude of two stimuli required to tell them apart is their **difference threshold.** As with the absolute threshold, psychologists agree to the standard of a difference in strength that can be detected 50% of the time.

Psychophysicist Ernst Weber discovered through laboratory research that the threshold for perceiving differences in the intensity of light is about 2% (actually closer to 1/60th) of

Absolute threshold The minimal amount of energy that can produce a sensation.

Pitch The highness or lowness of a sound, as determined by the frequency of the sound waves.

Difference threshold The minimal difference in intensity required between two sources of energy so that they will be perceived as being different.

their intensity. This fraction, 1/60th, is known as **Weber's constant** for light. A related concept is the **just noticeable difference (jnd)**—the minimum difference in stimuli that a person can detect. For example, at least 50% of the time, most people can tell if a light becomes just 1/60th brighter or dimmer. Weber's constant for light holds whether we are comparing moderately bright lights or moderately dull lights. But it becomes inaccurate when we compare extremely bright or extremely dull lights.

Weber's constant for noticing differences in lifted weight is 1/53rd. (Round it off to 1/50th, or 2%.) That means if you are strong enough to heft a 100-pound barbell, you would not notice that it was heavier until about 2 pounds were added. Yet if you are a runner who carries 1-pound dumbbells, you would definitely notice if someone slipped you dumbbells even a pound heavier because the increase would be 100%.

What about sound? People are most sensitive to changes in the pitch (frequency) of sounds. The Weber constant for pitch is 1/333, meaning that on average, people can tell when a tone rises or falls in pitch by an extremely small one-third of 1%. (Even a small error in pitch makes singers sound sharp or flat.) Remember this when friends criticize your singing—you may not be "tone deaf" but just slightly off. The sense of taste is much less sensitive. On average, people cannot detect differences in saltiness of less than 20%. That is why "low-salt" chips that have 15% less salt than your favorite chips do not taste so bad.

Signal-Detection Theory: Is Being Bright Enough?

From the discussion so far it might seem that people are simply switched on by certain amounts of stimulation. This is not quite so. People are also influenced by psychological factors. **Signal-detection theory** considers these factors. *What is signal-detection theory?*

According to signal-detection theory, the relationship between a physical stimulus and a sensory response is not fully mechanical. People's ability to detect stimuli such as blips on a radar screen depends not only on the intensity of the blips but also on their training (learning), motivation (desire to perceive blips), and psychological states such as fatigue or alertness.

The intensity of the signal is one factor that determines whether people will perceive sensory stimuli (signals) or a difference between signals. Another is the degree to which the signal can be distinguished from background noise. It is easier to hear a friend speaking in a quiet room than in a room in which people are singing and clinking glasses. The sharpness of a person's biological sensory system is still another factor. Is sensory capacity fully developed? Is it diminished by age?

◆ **Truth or Fiction Revisited:** It is true that people sometimes hear what they want to hear. That is, we tend to detect stimuli we are searching for. The place in which you are reading this book may be abuzz with signals. If you are outside, perhaps a breeze is blowing against your face. Perhaps the shadows of passing clouds darken the scene now and then. If you are inside, perhaps there are the occasional clanks and hums emitted by a heating system. Perhaps the aromas of dinner are hanging in the air, or there are voices from a television set. Yet, you are focusing your attention on this page (I hope). Thus, the other signals recede into the background. One psychological factor in signal detection is focusing on signals one considers important.

Feature Detectors in the Brain: Firing on Cue

Imagine you are standing by the curb of a busy street as a bus approaches. When neurons in your sensory organs—in this case, your eyes—are stimulated by the approach of the bus, they relay information to the sensory cortex in the brain. Nobel prize winners David Hubel and Torsten Wiesel (1979) discovered that various neurons in the visual cortex of the brain fire in response to particular features of the visual input. *What are feature detectors?* Many cells in the brain detect (i.e., fire in response to) lines presented at various angles—vertical, horizontal, and in between. Other cells fire in response to specific colors.

Because they respond to different aspects or features of a scene, these brain cells are termed **feature detectors.** In the example of the bus, visual feature detectors respond to the bus's edges, depth, contours, textures, shadows, speed, and kinds of motion (up, down,

reflect & relate

Think of times when you have been so involved in something that you didn't notice the heat or the cold. Think of times you have grown so used to sounds like those made by crickets or trains at night that you fall asleep without hearing them. How do these experiences relate to signal-detection theory?

David Oliver/Getty Images

■ **Signal Detection**
The detection of signals is determined not only by the physical characteristics of the signals but also by psychological factors such as motivation and attention. The people in this photo are tuned into their newspapers for the moment, and not to each other.

Weber's constant The fraction of the intensity by which a source of physical energy must be increased or decreased so that a difference in intensity will be perceived.

Just noticeable difference (jnd) The minimal amount by which a source of energy must be increased or decreased so that a difference in intensity will be perceived.

Signal-detection theory The view that the perception of sensory stimuli involves the interaction of physical, biological, and psychological factors.

Feature detectors Neurons in the sensory cortex that fire in response to specific features of sensory information such as lines or edges of objects.

forward, and back). There are also feature detectors for other senses. Auditory feature detectors, for example, respond to the pitch, loudness, and other aspects of the sounds of the bus.

Sensory Adaptation: Where Did It Go?

Our sensory systems are admirably suited to a changing environment. *How do our sensory systems adapt to a changing environment?* **Sensory adaptation** refers to the processes by which we become more sensitive to stimuli of low magnitude and less sensitive to stimuli that remain the same, such as the background noises outside the window.

Consider how the visual sense adapts to lower intensities of light. When we first walk into a darkened movie theater, we see little but the images on the screen. As we search for our seats, however, we become increasingly sensitive to the faces around us and to the features of the theater. The process of becoming more sensitive to stimulation is referred to as **sensitization,** or positive adaptation.

But we become less sensitive to constant stimulation. Sources of light appear to grow dimmer as we adapt to them. In fact, if you could keep an image completely stable on the retinas of your eyes, the image would fade in a few seconds. Similarly, at the beach we soon become less aware of the lapping of the waves. When we live in a city, we become desensitized to sounds of traffic except, perhaps, for the occasional backfire or siren. And, as you may have noticed from experiences with freshly painted rooms, sensitivity to disagreeable odors fades quite rapidly. The process of becoming less sensitive to stimulation is referred to as **desensitization,** or negative adaptation.

Our sensitivities to stimulation provide our brains with information that we use to understand and influence the world outside. Therefore, it is not surprising that psychologists study the ways in which we sense and perceive this information—through vision, hearing, the chemical senses, and still other senses, as we see throughout the remainder of the chapter.

Sensory adaptation The processes by which organisms become more sensitive to stimuli that are low in magnitude and less sensitive to stimuli that are constant or ongoing in magnitude.

Sensitization The type of sensory adaptation in which we become more sensitive to stimuli that are low in magnitude. Also called *positive adaptation.*

Desensitization The type of sensory adaptation in which we become less sensitive to constant stimuli. Also called *negative adaptation.*

() Learning Connections

◀◀ Sensation and Perception—Your Tickets of Admission to the World Outside ▶▶

REVIEW:

1. Which of the following discovered the threshold for perceiving differences in the intensity of light?
   (a) Fechner,
   (b) Young,
   (c) Hering,
   (d) Weber.

2. When we enter a darkened movie theater, the process of becoming more sensitive to low lighting is referred to as
   (a) positive adaptation,
   (b) negative adaptation,
   (c) stimulus control,
   (d) signal detection.

3. Which of the following is defined as the organization of sensations into an inner representation of the world?
   (a) Gestalt psychology,
   (b) the just noticeable difference,
   (c) psychophysics,
   (d) perception.

4. The absolute threshold for a stimulus is the intensity required for a person to sense the stimulus _____ percent of the time.
   (a) 25,
   (b) 50,
   (c) 67,
   (d) 100.

CRITICAL THINKING:
Which factors in sensation and perception reflect our nature? Which reflect nurture?

Go to

http://academic.cengage.com/psychology/rathus
for an interactive version of this review.

VISION: LETTING THE SUN SHINE IN

Our eyes are our biological "windows on the world." More than half of our brain's cerebral cortex is devoted to visual functions (Basic Behavioral Science Task Force, 1996b). Because vision is our dominant sense, blindness is considered by many to be the most debilitating sensory loss. To understand vision, let us first "look" at light.

Light: How Dazzling?

Light is fascinating stuff. It radiates. It illuminates. It dazzles. It glows. It beckons like a beacon. We speak of the "light of reason." We speak of genius as "brilliance." In almost all cultures, light is a symbol of goodness and knowledge. People who aren't in the know are said to be "in the dark." *Just what is light?*

It is visible light that triggers visual sensations. Yet visible light is just one small part of a spectrum of electromagnetic energy that surrounds us (see Figure 4.1). All forms of

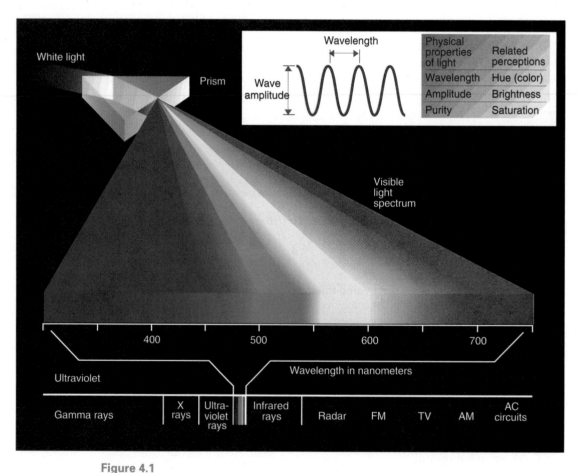

Figure 4.1

The Visible Spectrum

By passing a source of white light, such as sunlight, through a prism, we break it down into the colors of the visible spectrum. The visible spectrum is just a narrow segment of the electromagnetic spectrum. The electromagnetic spectrum also includes radio waves, microwaves, X rays, cosmic rays, and many others. Different forms of electromagnetic energy have wavelengths which vary from a few trillionths of a meter to thousands of miles. Visible light varies in wavelength from about 400 to 700 *billionths* of a meter. (One meter = 39.37 inches.)

electromagnetic energy move in waves, and different kinds of electromagnetic energy have signature wavelengths:

- Cosmic rays: The wavelengths of these rays from outer space are only a few *trillionths* of an inch long.
- Radio waves: Some radio signals extend for miles.
- Visible light: Roses are red, and violets are blue. Why? Different colors have different wavelengths, with violet the shortest at about 400 *billionths* of a meter in length and red the longest at 700 billionths of a meter.

Have you seen rainbows or light that has been broken down into several colors as it filtered through your windows? Sir Isaac Newton, the British scientist, discovered that sunlight could be broken down into different colors by means of a triangular solid of glass called a *prism* (see Figure 4.1). When I took introductory psychology, I was taught to remember the colors of the spectrum, from longest to shortest wavelengths, by using the mnemonic device *Roy G. Biv* (red, orange, yellow, green, blue, indigo, violet). The wavelength of visible light determines its color, or **hue.** The wavelength for red is longer than the wavelength for orange, and so on through the spectrum.

The Eye: The Better to See You With

Consider that magnificent invention called the camera, which records visual experiences. In traditional cameras, light enters an opening and is focused onto a sensitive surface. Chemicals on film or transistors create a lasting impression of the image that entered the camera.

How does the eye work? The eye—our living camera—is no less remarkable. Look at its major parts, as shown in Figure 4.2. As with a camera, light enters through a narrow opening and is projected onto a sensitive surface. Light first passes through the transparent **cornea,** which covers the front of the eye's surface. (The "white" of the eye, or *sclera,* is composed of hard protective tissue.) The amount of light that passes through the cornea is determined by the size of the opening of the muscle called the **iris,** which is the colored part of the eye. The opening in the iris is the **pupil.** The size of the pupil adjusts automatically to the amount of light present. Therefore, you do not have to purposefully open your eyes further to see better in low lighting. The more intense the light, the smaller the opening. In similar fashion, "point and shoot" cameras automatically adjust the amount of light allowed in according to its brightness. Pupil size is also sensitive to our emotions: We can be truly "wide-eyed with fear."

Hue The color of light, as determined by its wavelength.

Cornea Transparent tissue forming the outer surface of the eyeball.

Iris A muscular membrane whose dilation regulates the amount of light that enters the eye.

Pupil The black-looking opening in the center of the iris, through which light enters the eye.

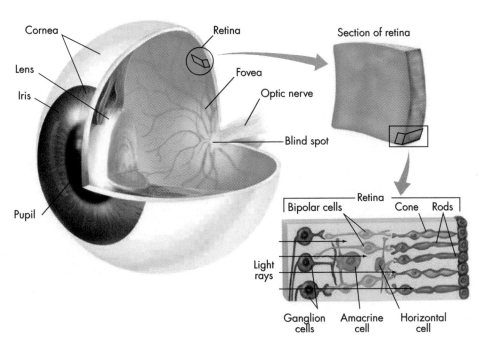

Go to your student website to access an interactive version of this figure.

Figure 4.2
The Human Eye
In both the eye and a camera, light enters through a narrow opening and is projected onto a sensitive surface. In the eye, the photosensitive surface is called the retina, and information concerning the changing images on the retina is transmitted to the brain. The retina contains photoreceptors called rods and cones. Rods and cones transmit sensory input back through the bipolar neurons to the ganglion neurons. The axons of the ganglion neurons form the optic nerve, which transmits sensory stimulation through the brain to the visual cortex of the occipital lobe.

Once light passes through the iris, it encounters the **lens.** The lens adjusts or accommodates to the image by changing its thickness. Changes in thickness permit a clear image of the object to be projected onto the retina. These changes focus the light according to the distance of the object from the viewer. If you hold a finger at arm's length and slowly bring it toward your nose, you will feel tension in the eye as the thickness of the lens accommodates to keep the retinal image in focus. When people squint to bring an object into focus, they are adjusting the thickness of the lens.

The **retina** is like the light-sensitive surface in the camera. The retina consists of cells called **photoreceptors** that are sensitive to light (photosensitive). There are two types of photoreceptors: *rods* and *cones*. The retina (see Figure 4.2) contains several layers of cells: the rods and cones, **bipolar cells,** and **ganglion cells.** All of these cells are neurons. The rods and cones respond to light with chemical changes that create neural impulses that are picked up by the bipolar cells. These then activate the ganglion cells. The axons of the million or so ganglion cells in our retina converge to form the **optic nerve.** The optic nerve conducts sensory input to the brain, where it is relayed to the visual area of the occipital lobe. As if this were not enough, the eye has additional neurons to enhance this process. Amacrine cells and horizontal cells make sideways connections at a level near the rods and cones and at another level near the ganglion cells. As a result, single bipolar cells can pick up signals from many rods and cones, and, in turn, a single ganglion cell is able to funnel information from multiple bipolar cells. In fact, rods and cones outnumber ganglion cells by more than 100 to 1.

Rods and Cones   Rods and **cones** are the photoreceptors in the retina (see Figure 4.3). About 125 million rods and 6.4 million cones are distributed across the retina. The cones are most densely packed in a small spot at the center of the retina called the **fovea** (see Figure 4.2). Visual acuity (sharpness and detail) is greatest at this spot. The fovea is composed almost exclusively of cones. Rods are most dense just outside the fovea and thin out toward the periphery of the retina.

Rods allow us to see in black and white. Cones provide color vision. In low lighting, it is possible to photograph a clearer image in black-and-white than in color. Similarly, rods are more sensitive to dim light than cones are. Therefore, as light grows dim during the evening hours, objects appear to lose their color before their outlines fade from view.

In contrast to the visual acuity of the fovea is the **blind spot,** which is insensitive to visual stimulation. It is the part of the retina where the axons of the ganglion cells converge to form the optic nerve (see Figure 4.2). Figure 4.4 will help you "view" your blind spot.

Lens A transparent body behind the iris that focuses an image on the retina.

Retina The area of the inner surface of the eye that contains rods and cones.

Photoreceptors Cells that respond to light.

Bipolar cells Neurons that conduct neural impulses from rods and cones to ganglion cells.

Ganglion cells Neurons whose axons form the optic nerve.

Optic nerve The nerve that transmits sensory information from the eye to the brain.

Rods Rod-shaped photoreceptors that are sensitive only to the intensity of light.

Cones Cone-shaped photoreceptors that transmit sensations of color.

Fovea An area near the center of the retina that is dense with cones and where vision is consequently most acute.

Blind spot The area of the retina where axons from ganglion cells meet to form the optic nerve.

Figure 4.3
Rods and Cones
A. You have about 125 million rods and 6.4 million cones distributed across the retina of each eye. Only cones provide sensations of color. The fovea of the eye is almost exclusively populated by cones, which are then distributed more sparsely as you work toward the periphery of the retina.
B. As shown in this color-enhanced photo, the rods are rod-shaped in appearance and the cones are cone-shaped.

A.

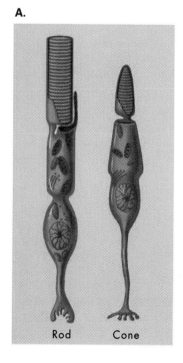

Rod   Cone

B.

Omikron/Photo Researchers, Inc.

Figure 4.4
The Blind Spot
To try a "disappearing act," close your left eye, hold the book close to your face, and look at the boy with your right eye. Slowly move the book away until the pie disappears. The pie disappears because it is being projected onto the blind spot of your retina, the point at which the axons of ganglion neurons collect to form the optic nerve. Note that when the pie disappears, your brain "fills in" the missing checkerboard pattern, which is one reason that you're not usually aware that you have blind spots.

Visual acuity (sharpness of vision) is connected with the shape of the eye. People who have to be unusually close to an object to discriminate its details are *nearsighted*. People who see distant objects unusually clearly but have difficulty focusing on nearby objects are *farsighted*. Nearsightedness can result when the eyeball is elongated such that the images of distant objects are focused in front of the retina. When the eyeball is too short, the images of nearby objects are focused behind the retina, causing farsightedness. Eyeglasses or contact lenses help nearsighted people focus distant objects on their retinas. Laser surgery can correct vision by changing the shape of the eye. Farsighted people usually see well enough without eyeglasses until they reach their middle years, when they may need glasses for reading.

Beginning in the late 30s to the mid-40s, the lenses start to grow brittle, making it more difficult to accommodate to, or focus on, objects. This condition is called **presbyopia**, from the Greek words for "old man" and "eyes." But presbyopia occurs by middle adulthood, not late adulthood. Presbyopia makes it difficult to perceive nearby visual stimuli. People who had normal visual acuity in their youth often require corrective lenses to read in middle adulthood.

Light Adaptation When we walk out onto a dark street, we may at first not be able to see people, trees, and cars clearly. But as time goes on, we are better able to discriminate the features of people and objects. The process of adjusting to lower lighting is called **dark adaptation.**

Figure 4.5 shows the amount of light needed for detection as a function of the amount of time spent in the dark. The cones and rods adapt at different rates. The cones, which permit

Visual acuity Sharpness of vision.

Presbyopia A condition characterized by brittleness of the lens.

Dark adaptation The process of adjusting to conditions of lower lighting by increasing the sensitivity of rods and cones.

Figure 4.5
Dark Adaptation
This illustration shows the amount of light necessary for detection as a function of the amount of time spent in the dark. Cones and rods adapt at different rates. Cones, which permit perception of color, reach maximum dark adaptation in about ten minutes. Rods, which permit perception of dark and light only, are more sensitive than cones. Rods continue to adapt for up to about 45 minutes.

Go to your student website to access an interactive version of this figure.
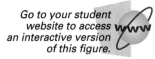

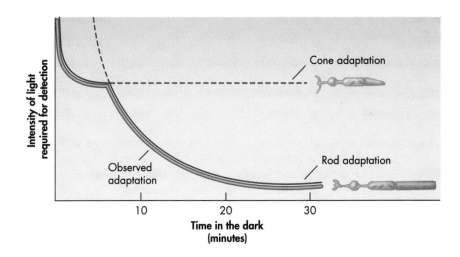

reflect & relate

Try a mini-experiment. Take a watch with a second hand and enter a walk-in closet that allows just the merest sliver of light to pass under the door. Close the door. How long does it take until you can see the objects in the closet?

perception of color, reach their maximum adaptation to darkness in about 10 minutes. The rods, which allow perception of light and dark only, are more sensitive to dim light and continue to adapt for 45 minutes or so.

Adaptation to brighter lighting conditions takes place more rapidly. When you emerge from the theater into the brilliance of the afternoon, you may at first be painfully surprised by the featureless blaze around you. The experience is not unlike turning up the brightness of the television set to maximum, at which the edges of objects seem to dissolve into light. But within a minute or so of entering the street, the brightness of the scene dims and objects regain their edges.

■ Color Vision: Creating an Inner World of Color

For most of us, the world is a place of brilliant colors—the blue–greens of the ocean, the red–oranges of the setting sun, the deepened greens of June, the glories of the purple rhododendron and red hibiscus. Color is an emotional and aesthetic part of our everyday lives. In this section we explore some of the dimensions of color and then examine theories about how we manage to convert different wavelengths of light into perceptions of color. *What are some perceptual dimensions of color?* These include hue, value, and saturation.

The wavelength of light determines its color, or *hue.* The value of a color is its degree of lightness or darkness. The saturation refers to how intense a color appears to us. A fire-engine red is more saturated than a pale pinkish red.

Colors also have psychological associations within various cultural settings. For example, in the United States a bride may be dressed in white as a sign of purity. In traditional India, the guests would be shocked, because white is the color for funerals. Here we mourn in black.

Complementary Descriptive of colors of the spectrum that when combined produce white or nearly white light.

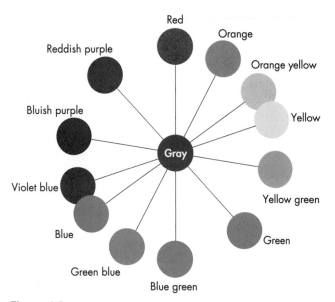

Figure 4.6
The Color Wheel
A color wheel can be formed by bending the colors of the spectrum into a circle and placing complementary colors across from one another. (A few colors between violet and red are not found in the spectrum and must be added to complete the circle.) When lights of complementary colors such as yellow and violet blue are mixed, they dissolve into neutral gray. The afterimage of a color is its complement.

Warm and Cool Colors If we bend the colors of the spectrum into a circle, we create a color wheel, as shown in Figure 4.6. Psychologically, the colors on the green–blue side of the color wheel are considered to be cool in temperature. Those colors on the yellow–orange–red side are considered to be warm. Perhaps greens and blues suggest the coolness of the ocean and the sky, whereas things that are burning tend to be red or orange. A room decorated in green or blue may seem more appealing on a hot July day than a room decorated in red or orange.

Complementary Colors The colors across from one another on the color wheel are labeled **complementary.** Red–green and blue–yellow are the major complementary pairs. If we mix complementary colors together, they dissolve into gray. ◆ **Truth or Fiction Revisited:** It is not true, therefore, that when we mix blue and yellow light, we obtain green light.

"But wait!" you say. "Blue and yellow cannot be complementary because by mixing pigments of blue and yellow we create green, not gray." True enough, but we have been talking about mixing *lights,* not *pigments.* Light is the source of all color. Pigments reflect and absorb different wavelengths of light selectively. The mixture of lights is an *additive* process. The mixture of pigments is *subtractive.* Figure 4.7 shows mixtures of lights and pigments of various colors.

Pigments gain their colors by absorbing light from certain segments of the spectrum and reflecting the rest. For example, we see most plant life as green because the pigment in chlorophyll absorbs most of the red, blue, and violet wavelengths of light. The remaining green is reflected. A red pigment absorbs most of the spectrum but reflects red. White pigments reflect all colors equally. Black pigments reflect very little light.

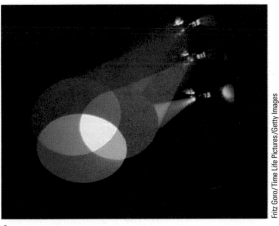

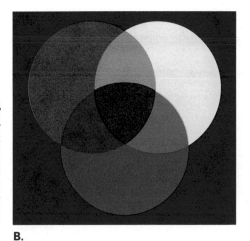

A.　　　　　　　　　　　　　　　　　　**B.**

Figure 4.7
Additive and Subtractive Color Mixtures Produced by Lights and Pigments
Thomas Young discovered that white light and all the colors of the spectrum could be produced
by adding combinations of lights of red, green, and violet blue and varying their intensities
(see part A). Part B shows subtractive color mixtures, which are formed by mixing pigments,
not light.

In *Sunday Afternoon on the Island of La Grande Jatte* (see Figure 4.8), French painter
Georges Seurat molded his figures and forms from dabs of color. Instead of mixing his
pigments, he placed points of pure color next to one another. When the painting is viewed
from very close (see the detail), the sensations are of pure color. But from a distance the
placement of pure colors creates the impression of mixtures of color.

Figure 4.8
Sunday Afternoon on the Island of La Grande Jatte
The French painter Georges Seurat molded his figures and forms from dabs of color. Instead
of mixing his pigments, he placed points of pure color next to one another. When the viewer is
close to the canvas (see the detail), the points of color are apparent. But from a distance, they
create the impression of color mixtures.

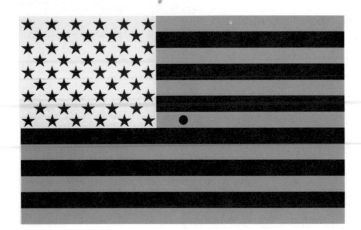

Figure 4.9
Three Cheers for the . . . Green, Black, and Yellow?
Don't be concerned. We can readily restore Old Glory to its familiar hues. Place a sheet of white paper beneath the book, and stare at the black dot in the center of the flag for at least 30 seconds. Then remove the book. The afterimage on the paper beneath will look familiar.

Afterimages Before reading on, why don't you try a brief experiment? Look at the strangely colored American flag in Figure 4.9 for at least half a minute. Try not to blink as you are doing so. Then look at a sheet of white or light gray paper. What has happened to the flag? If your color vision is working properly, and if you looked at the miscolored flag long enough, you should see a flag composed of the familiar red, white, and blue. The flag you perceive on the white sheet of paper is an **afterimage** of the first. (If you didn't look at the green, black, and yellow flag long enough the first time, try it again.) In afterimages, persistent sensations of color are followed by perception of the complementary color when the first color is removed. The same holds true for black and white. Staring at one will create an afterimage of the other. The phenomenon of afterimages has contributed to one of the theories of color vision, as we will see.

Theories of Color Vision: How Colorful?

Adults with normal color vision can discriminate thousands of colors across the visible spectrum. Different colors have different wavelengths. Although we can vary the physical wavelengths of light in a continuous manner from shorter to longer, many changes in color are discontinuous. Our perception of a color shifts suddenly from blue to green, even though the change in wavelength may be smaller than that between two blues!

How do we perceive color? Why are roses red and violets blue? Our perception of color depends on the physical properties of an object and on the eye's transmission of different messages to the brain when lights with different wavelengths stimulate the cones in the retina.

There are two main theories of color vision: the trichromatic theory and the opponent-process theory (Gegenfurtner & Kiper, 2003). **Trichromatic theory** is based on an experiment conducted by the British scientist Thomas Young in the early 1800s. As in Figure 4.7, Young projected red, green, and blue-violet lights onto a screen so that they partly overlapped. He found that he could create any color in the visible spectrum by varying the intensities of the three lights. When all three lights fell on the same spot, they created white light, or the appearance of no color at all.

The German physiologist Hermann von Helmholtz saw in Young's discovery an explanation of color vision. Helmholtz suggested that the retina in the eye must have three different types of color photoreceptors or cones. Some cones must be sensitive to red light, some to green, and some to blue. We see other colors when various color receptors are stimulated simultaneously. For example, we perceive yellow when the receptors for red and green are firing.

In 1870, another German physiologist Ewald Hering proposed the **opponent-process theory** of color vision: There are three types of color receptors, but they are not sensitive only to red, green, and blue, as Helmholtz had claimed. Hering suggested instead that afterimages (such as that of the American flag shown in Figure 4.9) are made possible by three types of color receptors: red–green, blue–yellow, and a type that perceives differences in brightness. According to Hering, a red–green cone cannot transmit messages for red and green at the same time. Therefore, staring at the green, black, and yellow flag for 30 seconds will disturb the balance of neural activity. The afterimage of red, white, and blue would represent the eye's attempt to reestablish a balance.

Afterimage The lingering visual impression made by a stimulus that has been removed.

Trichromatic theory The theory that color vision is made possible by three types of cones, some of which respond to red light, some to green, and some to blue.

Opponent-process theory The theory that color vision is made possible by three types of cones, some of which respond to red or green light, some to blue or yellow, and some to the intensity of light.

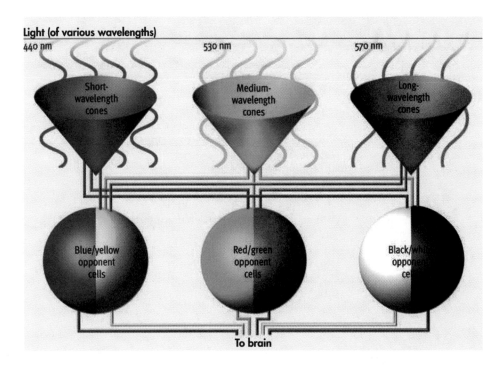

Figure 4.10
The Perception of Color
Perception of color actually requires elements of both trichromatic and opponent-process theory. Cones in the retina are sensitive to either blue, green, or red. Color mixtures (such as yellow) require the simultaneous firing of groups of cones (in this case, green and red). But higher levels of visual processing occur in opponent-process fashion, explaining the occurrence of afterimages.

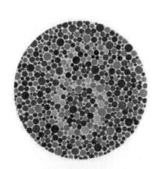

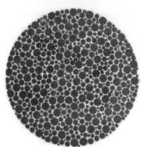

Figure 4.11
Plates from a Test for Color Blindness
Can you see the numbers in these plates from a test for color blindness? A person with red–green color blindness would not be able to see the 6, and a person with blue–yellow color blindness would probably not discern the 12. (Caution: These reproductions cannot be used for actual testing of color blindness.)

Research suggests that each theory of color vision is partially correct (Li & DeVries, 2004; Shapley & Hawken, 2002). For example, research shows that some cones are sensitive to blue, some to green, and some to red (see Figure 4.10). However, cones appear to be connected by bipolar and ganglion neurons such that the messages produced by the cones are transmitted to the brain in an opponent-process fashion (Hornstein et al., 2004; Suttle et al., 2002).

A neural rebound effect apparently helps explain the occurrence of afterimages. That is, a green-sensitive ganglion that had been excited by green light for half a minute or so might switch briefly to inhibitory activity when the light is shut off. The effect would be to perceive red even though no red light is present (Hornstein et al., 2004). Imagine looking at a green fir tree with red ornaments for a minute or so during the holidays, then turning your gaze to a white brick fireplace nearby. You might just see an image of a red tree with green ornaments!

Color Blindness: What Kind of "Chromat" Are You?

If you can discriminate among the colors of the visible spectrum, you have normal color vision and are labeled a **trichromat.** This means that you are sensitive to red–green, blue–yellow, and light–dark. *What is color blindness? Why are some people color-blind?* People who are totally color-blind, called **monochromats,** are sensitive only to lightness and darkness. Total color blindness is rare. Fully color-blind individuals see the world as trichromats would on a black-and-white television set or in a black-and-white movie.

Partial color blindness is a sex-linked trait that mostly affects males. Partially color-blind people are called **dichromats.** They can discriminate only between two colors—red and green or blue and yellow—and the colors that are derived from mixing these colors (Loop et al., 2003). Figure 4.11 shows the types of tests that are used to diagnose color blindness.

A dichromat might put on one red sock and one green sock, but would not mix red and blue socks. Monochromats might put on socks of any color. They would not notice a difference as long as the socks' colors did not differ in intensity—that is, brightness.

Trichromat A person with normal color vision.

Monochromat A person who is sensitive to black and white only and hence color-blind.

Dichromat A person who is sensitive to black–white and either red–green or blue–yellow and hence partially color-blind.

() Learning Connections

◀◀   *Vision—Letting the Sun Shine In*   ▶▶

Learning Connections

REVIEW:

5 The size of the opening of the _____ determines the amount of light that passes through the
   cornea.
   (a) pupil,
   (b) iris,
   (c) sclera,
   (d) lens.

6 The axons of _____ make up the optic nerve.
   (a) rods,
   (b) cones,
   (c) bipolar cells,
   (d) ganglion cells.

7 Opponent-process theory explains
   (a) dark adaptation,
   (b) negative adaptation,
   (c) afterimages,
   (d) color blindness.

8 Which of the following is a complementary pair of
   colors?
   (a) Red–green,
   (b) Blue–green,
   (c) Red–yellow,
   (d) Yellow–green.

CRITICAL THINKING:
Parents point out leaves and grass in summer to children and say,
"The leaves are green," and "The grass is green." After a while, children come to label other things that are the same or similar in color as
green. When two people agree that a piece of paper or a plant is green,
do we know whether or not they are visualizing the same color in their
minds? (And why might behaviorists object to asking this question?)

Go to www
http://academic.cengage.com/psychology/rathus
for an interactive version of this review.

VISUAL PERCEPTION: HOW PERCEPTIVE?

What do you see in Figure 4.12—meaningless splotches of ink or a rider on horseback?
If you perceive a horse and rider, it is not just because of the visual sensations provided by
the drawing. Each of the blobs is meaningless in and of itself, and the pattern is vague.
Despite the lack of clarity, however, you may still perceive a horse and rider.

Visual perception is the process by which we organize or make sense of the sensory impressions caused by the light that strikes our eyes. Visual perception involves our knowledge,
expectations, and motivations. Whereas sensation may be thought of as a mechanical process
(e.g., light stimulating the rods and cones of our retina), perception is an active process
through which we interpret the world around us. *How do we organize bits of visual information into meaningful wholes?* The answer has something to do with your general knowledge and your desire to fit incoming bits and pieces of information into familiar patterns.

In the case of the horse and rider, your integration of disconnected pieces of information into a meaningful whole also reflects the principle of **closure**—that is, the tendency to
perceive a complete or whole figure even when there are gaps in the sensory input. Put another way, in perception the whole can be much more than the mere sum of the parts.

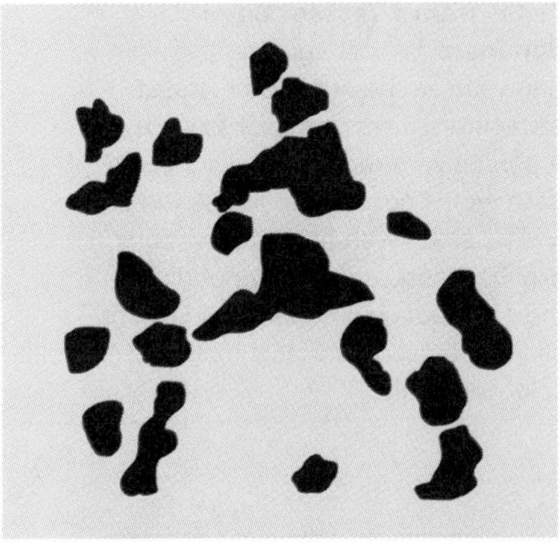

▅ Perceptual Organization: Getting It Together

Early in the 20th century, Gestalt psychologists noted certain consistencies in the way we integrate bits and pieces of sensory stimulation into meaningful wholes. They attempted to
identify the rules that govern these processes. Max Wertheimer, in particular, discovered

Figure 4.12
Closure
Meaningless splotches of ink, or a
horse and rider? This figure illustrates
the Gestalt principle of closure.

Closure The tendency to perceive a broken figure as being complete or whole.

many such rules. As a group, these rules are referred to as the laws of perceptual organization. We examine several of them, beginning with those concerning figure–ground perception.

Figure–Ground Perception   If you look out your window, you may see people, buildings, cars, and streets, or perhaps grass, trees, birds, and clouds. These objects tend to be perceived as figures against backgrounds. Individual cars seen against the background of the street are easier to pick out than cars piled on top of one another in a junkyard. Birds seen against the sky are more likely to be perceived than birds "in the bush."

When figure–ground relationships are *ambiguous,* or capable of being interpreted in various ways, our perceptions tend to be unstable and shift back and forth (Bull et al., 2003). Consider Figure 4.13. How many people, objects, and animals can you find? If your eye is drawn back and forth, so that now you perceive light figures on a dark ground and then dark figures on a light ground, you are experiencing figure–ground reversals. In other words, a shift is occurring in your perception of what is figure and what is ground, or background. The artist was able to have fun with us because of our tendency to try to isolate geometric patterns or figures from a background. In this case, however, the "background" is as meaningful and detailed as the "figure." Therefore, our perceptions shift back and forth.

Figure 4.14 shows a Rubin vase, one of psychologists' favorite illustrations of figure–ground relationships. The figure–ground relationship in part A of the figure is ambiguous. There are no cues that suggest which area must be the figure. For this reason, our perception may shift from seeing the vase to seeing two profiles. There is no such problem in part B. Because it seems that a white vase has been brought forward against a colored ground, we are more likely to perceive the vase than the profiles. In part C, we are more likely to perceive the profiles than the vase, because the profiles are complete and the vase is broken against the background. Of course, if we wish to, we can still perceive the vase in part C, because experience has shown us where it is. Why not have some fun with friends by covering up parts B and C and asking them what they see? (They'll catch on quickly if they see all three drawings at once.)

Figure 4.13
Figure and Ground
How many animals and demons can you find in this Escher print? Do we have white figures on a black background or black figures on a white background? Figure–ground perception is the tendency to perceive geometric forms against a background.

*Go to your student
website to access
an interactive version
of this figure.*

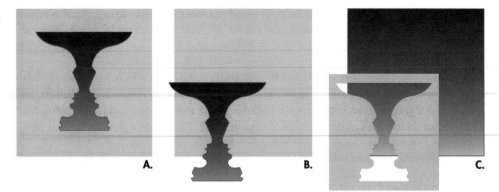

Figure 4.14
The Rubin Vase
A favorite drawing used by psychologists to demonstrate figure–ground perception. Part A is ambiguous, with neither the vase nor the profiles clearly the figure or the ground. In part B, the vase is the figure; in part C, the profiles are.

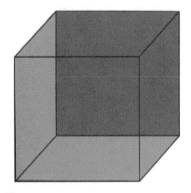

Figure 4.15
The Necker Cube
Ambiguity in the drawing of the cube makes perceptual shifts possible. Therefore, the darker tinted surface can become either the front or back of the cube.

*Go to your student
website to access
an interactive version
of this figure.*

Proximity Nearness; the perceptual tendency to group together objects that are near one another.

Similarity The perceptual tendency to group together objects that are similar in appearance.

Continuity The tendency to perceive a series of points or lines as having unity.

Common fate The tendency to perceive elements that move together as belonging together.

The Necker cube (see Figure 4.15) is another ambiguous drawing that can lead to perceptual shifts. Hold this page at arm's length and stare at the center of the figure for 30 seconds or so. Try to allow your eye muscles to relax. (You may feel your eyes "glazing over.") After a while you will notice a shift in your perception of the box. What was a front edge will become a back edge, and vice versa. The perceptual shift occurs because the outline of the drawing allows two interpretations.

Other Gestalt Rules for Organization   Gestalt psychologists have noted that our perceptions are also guided by rules or laws of *proximity, similarity, continuity,* and *common fate.*

Let's try a mini-experiment. Without reading further, describe part A of Figure 4.16. Did you say it consists of six lines or of three groups of two parallel lines? If you said three sets of lines, you were influenced by the **proximity,** or nearness, of some of the lines. There is no other reason for perceiving them in pairs or subgroups: All lines are parallel and equal in length.

Now describe part B of Figure 4.16. Did you perceive the figure as a 6 by 6 grid, or as three columns of *x*'s and three columns of *o*'s? According to the law of **similarity,** we perceive similar objects as belonging together. For this reason, you may have been more likely to describe part B in terms of columns than in terms of rows or a grid.

What of part C? Is it a circle with two lines stemming from it, or is it a (broken) line that goes through a circle? If you saw it as a single (broken) line, you were probably organizing your perceptions according to the rule of **continuity.** That is, we perceive a series of points or a broken line as having unity.

According to the law of **common fate,** elements seen moving together are perceived as belonging together. A group of people running in the same direction appears unified in purpose. Birds that flock together seem to be of a feather. (Did I get that right?) Part D of Figure 4.16 provides another example of the law of closure. The arcs tend to be perceived as a circle (or circle with gaps) rather than as just a series of arcs.

Figure 4.16
Some Gestalt Laws of Perceptual Organization
These drawings illustrate the Gestalt laws of proximity, similarity, continuity, and closure.

A. Proximity

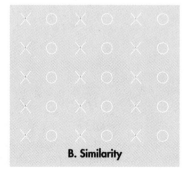

B. Similarity

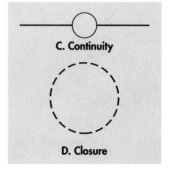

C. Continuity

D. Closure

Top-Down Versus Bottom-Up Processing   Imagine that you are trying to put together a 1,000-piece jigsaw puzzle—a task I usually avoid, despite the cajoling of my children. Now imagine that you are trying to accomplish it after someone has walked off with the box showing the picture formed by the completed puzzle.

When you have the box—when you know what the "big picture" or pattern looks like—the task of assembling the pieces is termed **top-down processing.** The "top" of the visual system refers to the image of the pattern in the brain. The top-down strategy for piecing the puzzle together is your use of the larger pattern to guide your placement of particular pieces. Without knowledge of the pattern (without the box), the assembly process is referred to as **bottom-up processing.** You begin with bits and pieces of information and become aware of the pattern they form only after you have worked at it for a while (Wilson & Farah, 2003).

Top-down and bottom-up processing can be applied to many matters, even politics. If you consider yourself to be a liberal or a conservative, you can "fill in" your attitude toward many specific issues by applying the liberal or conservative position. That is top-down processing. But many people do not label themselves liberal or conservative. They look at issues and form positions on an issue-by-issue basis. Eventually they may discover an overall pattern that places them more or less in the liberal or conservative camp. That is bottom-up processing.

Perception of Motion: Life on the Move

The motions of objects—people, animals, cars, or boulders plummeting down a hillside—is a vital source of sensory information. Objects in motion even capture the attention of newborn infants. *How do we perceive movement?* To understand perception of movement, think of what it is like to be on a train that has begun to pull out of the station while the train on the next track stays still. If your own train does not lurch as it accelerates, it might seem that the other train is moving. Or you might not be sure whether your train is moving forward or the other train is moving back.

The visual perception of movement is based on change of position relative to other objects. To early scientists, whose only tool for visual observation was the naked eye, it seemed logical that the sun circled the earth. You have to be able to imagine the movement of the earth around the sun as seen from a theoretical point in outer space; you cannot observe it directly.

How, then, can you be certain which train is moving? One way is to look for objects that you know are still, such as platform columns, houses, signs, or trees. If your position does not change in relation to them, your train is not moving. You might also try to sense the motion of the train in your body. You probably know from experience how to do these things quite well.

We have been considering the perception of real movement. Psychologists have also studied several types of apparent movement, or **illusions** of movement. One of these illusions is *stroboscopic motion.*

Stroboscopic Motion   So-called motion pictures do not really consist of images that move. Rather, the audience is shown 16 to 22 pictures, or *frames,* per second. Each frame differs slightly from the preceding one. Showing the frames in rapid succession provides the illusion of movement. This illusion of motion is termed **stroboscopic motion.**

At the rate of at least 16 frames per second, the "motion" in a film seems smooth and natural. With fewer than 16 or so frames per second, the movement looks jumpy and unnatural. That is why slow motion is usually achieved by filming 100 or more frames per second. When they are played back at about 22 frames per second, the movement seems slowed down, but still smooth and natural. Figure 4.17 suggests a series of photos shown in sequence to provide the perception of motion.

Depth Perception: How Far Is Far?

Think of the problems you might have if you could not judge depth or distance. You might bump into other people, believing them to be farther away. An outfielder might not be able to judge whether to run toward the infield or the fence to catch a fly ball. You might give

reflect & relate

Have you had the experience of being in a train and not knowing whether your train or one on the next track was moving? How do you explain your confusion? How did you figure out which one was really moving?

Top-down processing The use of contextual information or knowledge of a pattern in order to organize parts of the pattern.

Bottom-up processing The organization of the parts of a pattern to recognize, or form an image of, the pattern they compose.

Illusions Sensations that give rise to misperceptions.

Stroboscopic motion A visual illusion in which the perception of motion is generated by a series of stationary images that are presented in rapid succession.

Abe Rezmy/The Image Works

Figure 4.17
Stroboscopic Motion
In a motion picture, viewing a series of stationary images at the rate of about 16 to 22 frames per second provides an illusion of movement termed *stroboscopic motion*. The actual movement that is occurring is the rapid switching of stationary images.

Hogarth pinxt.   T. Cook & Son sc.

FRONTISPIECE TO KERBY.

Bettmann /Corbis

Figure 4.18
What Is Wrong with This Picture?
How does English artist William Hogarth use monocular cues for depth perception to deceive the viewer?

Monocular cues Stimuli suggestive of depth that can be perceived with only one eye.

Perspective A monocular cue for depth based on the convergence (coming together) of parallel lines as they recede into the distance.

your front bumper a workout in stop-and-go traffic. *How do we perceive depth?* Monocular and *binocular cues* help us perceive the depth of objects—that is, their distance from us.

Monocular Cues How does an artist portray three-dimensional objects on a two-dimensional surface? Artists use **monocular cues** called pictorial cues to create an illusion of depth. These cues can be perceived by one eye (*mono-* means "one"). They include perspective, relative size, clearness, overlapping, shadows, and texture gradient, and they cause some objects to seem more distant than others even though they are all drawn or painted on a flat surface.

Distant objects stimulate smaller areas on the retina than nearby ones, even though they may be the same size. The distances between far-off objects also appear to be smaller than equivalent distances between nearby objects. For this reason, the phenomenon known as **perspective** occurs. That is, we tend to perceive parallel lines as coming closer together, or converging, as they recede from us. As we will see when we discuss *size constancy*, however, experience teaches us that distant objects that look small are larger when they are close. In this way, their relative size also becomes a cue to their distance.

The engraving in Figure 4.18 represents an impossible scene in which the artist uses principles of perspective to fool the viewer. Artists normally use *relative size*—the fact that distant objects look smaller than nearby objects of the same size—to suggest depth in their works. The paradoxes in *Frontispiece to Kerby* are made possible because more distant objects are *not* necessarily depicted as smaller than nearby objects. Thus, what at first seems to be background suddenly becomes foreground, and vice versa.

The *clearness* of an object suggests its distance. Experience teaches us that we sense more details of nearby objects. For this reason, artists can suggest that objects are closer to the viewer by depicting them in greater detail. Note that the "distant" hill in the engraving in Figure 4.18 is given less detail than the nearby plants at the bottom of the picture. Our perceptions are mocked when a man "on" the distant hill in the background is shown conversing with a woman leaning out a window in the middle ground.

We also learn that nearby objects can block our view of more-distant objects. *Overlapping* is the placing of one object in front of another. Experience teaches us that partly covered objects are farther away than the objects that obscure them (see Figure 4.19). In Figure 4.18, which looks closer: the row of trees in the "background" or the moon sign hanging from the building (or is it buildings?) to the right? How does the artist use overlapping to mislead the viewer?

Additional information about depth is provided by *shadowing* and is based on the fact that opaque objects block light and produce shadows. Shadows and highlights give us information about an object's three-dimensional shape and its relationship to the source of light. For example, the left part of Figure 4.20 is perceived as a two-dimensional circle, but the right part tends to be perceived as a three-dimensional sphere because of the highlight on its surface and the shadow underneath. In the "sphere," the highlighted central area is perceived as closest to us, with the surface receding to the edges.

Another monocular cue is **texture gradient.** (A gradient is a progressive change.) Closer objects are perceived as having rougher textures. In Figure 4.18, the building just behind the large fisherman's head has a rougher texture and therefore seems to be closer than the building with the window from which the woman is leaning. Our surprise is heightened when the moon sign is seen as hanging from both buildings.

Motion cues are another kind of monocular cue. If you have ever driven in the country, you have probably noticed that distant objects such as mountains and stars appear to move along with you. Objects at an intermediate distance seem to be stationary, but nearby objects such as roadside markers, rocks, and trees seem to go by quite rapidly. The tendency of objects to seem to move backward or forward as a function of their distance is known as **motion parallax.** We learn to perceive objects that appear to move with us as being at greater distances.

Earlier we noted that nearby objects cause the lens of the eye to accommodate or bend more in order to bring them into focus. The sensations of tension in the eye muscles also provide a monocular cue to depth, especially when we are within about 4 feet of the objects.

Binocular Cues   **Binocular cues,** or cues that involve both eyes, also help us perceive depth. Two binocular cues are *retinal disparity* and *convergence*.

Try an experiment. Hold your right index finger at arm's length. Now hold your left index finger about a foot closer, but in a direct line. If you keep your eyes relaxed as you do so, you will see first one finger and then the other. An image of each finger will be projected onto the retina of each eye, and each image will be slightly different because the finger will be seen from different angles. The difference between the projected images is referred to as **retinal disparity** and serves as a binocular cue for depth perception. Note that in the case of the closer finger, the "two fingers" appear to be farther apart. Closer objects have greater retinal disparity.

If we try to maintain a single image of the closer finger, our eyes must turn inward, or converge on it, making us cross-eyed. **Convergence** causes feelings of tension in the eye muscles and provides another binocular cue for depth. (After convergence occurs, try looking at the finger first with one eye closed, then the other. You will readily see how different the images are in each eye.) The binocular cues of retinal disparity and convergence are strongest when objects are close. Concept Review 4.1 summarizes cues for depth perception.

Why are psychologists concerned about depth perception? On a fundamental level, sources of food and danger lie near or far. Evolutionary psychologists would note that organisms that have sophisticated systems for perceiving distance are more likely to survive into adulthood and reproduce, thus making these systems a stable element in their species. In the following section you will see that our methods of perception also help us keep the world a stable place, even though the shapes and colors and other properties of objects are perpetually shifting.

■ Perceptual Constancies: Is a Door a Rectangle When It Is Partly Open?

The world is a constantly shifting display of visual sensations. Think how confusing it would be if you believed that a door was a trapezoid and not a rectangle because it is ajar. Or what if we perceived a doorway to be a different doorway when seen from 6 feet away as

Figure 4.19
Overlapping as a Cue for Depth
The four circles are all the same size. Which circles seem closer? The complete circles or the circles with chunks bitten out of them?

Figure 4.20
Shadowing as a Cue for Depth
Shadowing makes the circle on the right look three-dimensional.

Texture gradient A monocular cue for depth based on the perception that closer objects appear to have rougher (more detailed) surfaces.

Motion parallax A monocular cue for depth based on the perception that nearby objects appear to move more rapidly in relation to our own motion.

Binocular cues Stimuli suggestive of depth that involve simultaneous perception by both eyes.

Retinal disparity A binocular cue for depth based on the difference in the image cast by an object on the retinas of the eyes as the object moves closer or farther away.

Convergence A binocular cue for depth based on the inward movement of the eyes as they attempt to focus on an object that is drawing nearer.

CONCEPT REVIEW ■ **CONCEPT REVIEW 4.1** ■ CONCEPT REVIEW

MONOCULAR CUES FOR DEPTH PERCEPTION

Pictorial Cues*

Clearness leads us to perceive the trees and signs and people with greater detail as being closer to us.

Relative size leads us to perceive the bicycles and people that are larger as being closer to us.

Perspective leads us to perceive the parallel lines on the sidewalk as coming closer together, or converging, as they recede from us.

Texture gradient leads us to perceive the tree trunks and handlebars with rougher (more detailed) textures as being closer.

Shadowing leads us to perceive the shadows and highlights in the seats of the bicycles as giving them depth (and curved surfaces) although the picture we are viewing is two-dimensional.

Overlapping leads us to perceive the bicycles that block our view of parts of other bicycles as being closer to us.

Richard Douglas Rose

Motion Cues   Motion parallax Perceiving objects that seem to move forward with us as distant and objects that seem to move backward as nearby

*These cues are commonly used by artists to create the impression of depth (a third dimension) in two-dimensional works such as drawings and paintings.

---

compared to 4 feet? As we neared it, we might think it was larger than the door we were seeking and become lost. Or consider the problems of the pet owner who recognizes his dog from the side but not from above because its shape is different when seen from above. Fortunately, these problems tend not to occur—at least with familiar objects—because perceptual constancies enable us to recognize objects even when their apparent shape or size differs. *What are perceptual constancies?*

Size Constancy   There are a number of perceptual constancies, including that of **size constancy.** We may say that people "look like ants" when viewed from the top of a tall building, but because of size constancy, we know they remain full-sized people even if the details of their forms are lost in the distance. We can thus say that we *perceive* people to be the same size, even when viewed from different distances.

The image of a dog seen from 20 feet away occupies about the same amount of space on your retina as an inch-long insect crawling on your hand. Yet you do not perceive the dog to

Size constancy The tendency to perceive an object as being the same size even as the size of its retinal image changes according to the object's distance.

be as small as the insect. Through your visual experiences you have acquired size constancy—that is, the tendency to perceive an object as the same size even though the size of its image on your retina varies as a function of its distance. Experience teaches us about perspective—that the same object seen at a distance appears to be smaller than when it is nearby.

A cross-cultural case study suggests that a person from another culture might indeed perceive people and cars to be insects from the vantage point of an airplane. This study also emphasizes the role of experience in the development of size constancy. Anthropologist Colin Turnbull (1961) found that an African Pygmy, Kenge, thought that buffalo perceived across an open field were some form of insect. Turnbull had to drive Kenge down to where the animals were grazing to convince him that they were not insects. During the drive, as the buffalo gradually grew in size, Kenge muttered to himself and moved closer to Turnbull in fear. Even after Kenge saw that these animals were, indeed, familiar buffalo, he still wondered how they could grow large so quickly. Kenge, you see, lived in a thick forest and normally did not view large animals from great distances. For this reason, he had not developed size constancy for distant objects. However, Kenge had no difficulty displaying size constancy with objects placed at various distances in his home.

Color Constancy   **Color constancy** is the tendency to perceive objects as retaining their color even though lighting conditions may alter their appearance. Your bright yellow car may edge toward gray as the hours wend their way through twilight. But when you finally locate the car in the parking lot, you may still think of it as yellow. You expect to find a yellow car and still judge it to be "more yellow" than the (twilight-faded) red and green cars on either side of it.

Brightness constancy is similar to color constancy. Consider Figure 4.21. The orange squares within the blue squares are equally bright, yet the one within the dark blue square is perceived as brighter. Why? Again, consider the role of experience. If it were nighttime, we would expect orange to fade to gray. The fact that the orange within the dark square stimulates the eye with equal intensity suggests that it must be much brighter than the orange within the lighter square.

Shape Constancy   **Shape constancy** is the tendency to perceive objects as maintaining their shape, even if we look at them from different angles so that the shape of their image on the retina changes dramatically. You perceive the top of a coffee cup or a glass to be a circle even though it is a circle only when seen from above. When seen from an angle, it is an ellipse. When the cup or glass is seen on edge, its retinal image is the same as that of a straight line. So why do you still describe the rim of the cup or glass as a circle? Perhaps for two reasons: First, experience has taught you that the cup will look circular when seen from above. Second, you may have labeled the cup as circular or round. Experience and labels help make the world a stable place. Can you imagine the chaos that would prevail if we described objects as they appear as they stimulate our sensory organs with each changing moment?

Let us return to the door that "changes shape" when it is ajar. The door is a rectangle only when viewed straight on (see Figure 4.22, part A). When we move to the side or open it, the left or right edge comes closer and appears to be larger, changing the retinal image to a trapezoid. Yet we continue to think of doors as rectangles. In part B of Figure 4.22, we see a woman with a very large hand, but because of experience, we recognize that the hand only appears to be out of proportion to the rest of her because it is pushed toward us.

▬■▬ Visual Illusions: Is Seeing Believing?

The principles of perceptual organization make it possible for our eyes to "play tricks" on us. Psychologists, like magicians, enjoy pulling a rabbit out of a hat now and then. Let me demonstrate how the perceptual constancies trick the eye through *visual illusions*.

The Hering–Helmholtz and Müller–Lyer illusions (see Figure 4.23) are named after the people who devised them. In the Hering–Helmholtz illusion (part A), the horizontal lines are straight and parallel. However, the radiating lines cause them to appear to be bent outward near the center. The two lines in the Müller–Lyer illusion (part B) are the same length, but the line on the right, with its reversed arrowheads, looks longer.

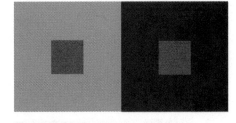

Figure 4.21
Brightness Constancy
The orange squares within the blue squares are the same hue, yet the orange within the dark blue square is perceived as brighter. Why?

Color constancy The tendency to perceive an object as being the same color even though lighting conditions change its appearance.

Brightness constancy The tendency to perceive an object as being just as bright even though lighting conditions change its intensity.

Shape constancy The tendency to perceive an object as being the same shape although the retinal image varies in shape as it rotates.

Video Connections

The Ames Room

LEARNING OBJECTIVES
- Explain the source of confusion in the Ames Room.
- Understand how illusions can fool our perceptions.

APPLIED LESSON
1. How do visual artists use illusions to create a sense of depth in two-dimensional drawings and paintings?
2. Have you ever been surprised at how large the moon looks when it is low on the horizon, "resting" atop buildings or trees in the distance? How do you explain why it looks larger under these circumstances than when it is high in the sky?

3. Can we rely on our past experience of rooms to make sense of the Ames Room? Why or why not?

CRITICAL THINKING
1. Have you heard the expression "looking at the world through rose-colored glasses"? How can you relate this saying to the concept of illusions?
2. Have you sat in a train and watched the train on the next track move backward, only to discover that you were actually moving forward? How do you explain this illusion?

The Ames Room shown here is named after Adelbert Ames, Jr., who first constructed one in 1946. The idea was originally conceived, however, by Hermann von Helmholtz. The illusions created by the Ames Room work because (1) the room looks cubic when viewed with one eye but it is actually trapezoidal, and (2) people or objects seem to grow or decrease in size when they move from one corner to another.

Watch this video!
Go to www
your companion website at
http://academic.cengage.com/psychology/rathus
Click on the Video Connections tab under this chapter.

A.

Enamul Hoque/Getty Images

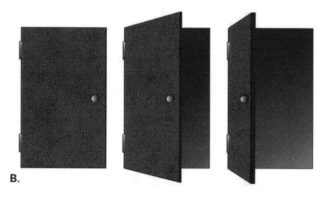

B.

Figure 4.22
Size Constancy and Shape Constancy
(A) Size Constancy. Although this woman's hand looks as though it is larger than her head, we recognize that this is an illusion created by the fact that her hand is closer to us than her head. (B) Shape Constancy. When closed, the door is a rectangle. When open, the retinal image is trapezoidal. But because of shape constancy, we still perceive it as rectangular.

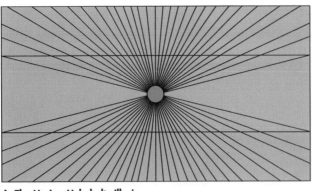

A. The Hering–Helmholtz Illusion

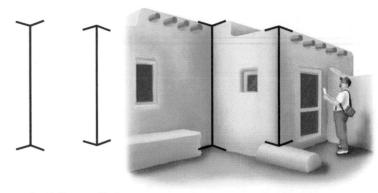

B. The Müller-Lyer Illusion

Figure 4.23

The Hering–Helmholtz and Müller–Lyer Illusions

In the Hering–Helmholtz illusion, are the horizontal lines straight or curved? In the Müller–Lyer illusion, are the vertical lines equal in length?

Go to your student website to access an interactive version of this figure.

Let us try to explain these illusions. Because of our experience and lifelong use of perceptual cues, we tend to perceive the Hering–Helmholtz drawing as three-dimensional. Because of our tendency to perceive bits of sensory information as figures against grounds, we perceive the white area in the center as a circle in front of a series of radiating lines, all of which lie in front of a white ground. Next, because of our experience with perspective, we perceive the radiating lines as parallel. We perceive the two horizontal lines as intersecting the "receding" lines, and we know that they would have to appear bent out at the center if they were to be equidistant at all points from the center of the circle.

Experience probably compels us to perceive the vertical lines in the Müller–Lyer illusion as the corners of a building (see Figure 4.23, part B). We interpret the length of the lines based on our experience with corners of buildings.

Figure 4.24 is known as the Ponzo illusion. In this illusion, the two monsters are equal in height (check with a ruler). However, do you perceive the top monster as being bigger? The rule of size constancy may give us some insight into this illusion as well. Perhaps the converging lines again strike us as being lines receding into the distance. Again, the rule of size constancy tells us that if two objects appear to be the same size and one is farther away, the object that looks farther away must be larger. So we perceive the top monster as being larger.

Figure 4.24

A Monstrous Illusion

The two monsters in this drawing are exactly the same height and width. Yet the top one appears to be much larger. Can you use the principle of size constancy to explain why?

Source: Ponzo Illusion from *Mind Sights* by Roger N. Shepard. © Roger N. Shepard. Reprinted by permission of Henry Holt and Company, LLC.

Learning Connections

◀◀   *Visual Perception—How Perceptive?*   ▶▶

REVIEW:

9 Perceptual _____ help make the world a stable place.
   (a) constancies,
   (b) shifts,
   (c) similarities,
   (d) cues.

10 The Rubin vase and Necker cube encourage perceptual shifts because
   (a) they are visual illusions,
   (b) of the rule of continuity,
   (c) they are ambiguous figures,
   (d) we adapt to them over time.

11 When we move, the moon appears to move with us because of
   (a) depth perception,
   (b) motion parallax,
   (c) stroboscopic motion,
   (d) binocular cues.

12 Which of the following is a binocular cue for depth perception?
   (a) Perspective,
   (b) Texture gradient,
   (c) Retinal disparity,
   (d) Overlapping.

CRITICAL THINKING:
How do we explain that Kenge, the African Pygmy, thought that buffalo perceived across an open field were some form of insect? Did you know that many of the stars that we sense as sparkling points of light in the night sky are many times larger and hotter than our sun? If you knew the answer, *how* did you know it? Can you relate the question about stars to Kenge's situation?

Go www
to
http://academic.cengage.com/psychology/rathus
for an interactive version of this review.

HEARING: MAKING SENSE OF SOUND

Consider the advertising slogan for the classic science fiction film *Alien:* "In space, no one can hear you scream." It's true. Space is an almost perfect vacuum. Hearing requires a medium through which sound can travel, such as air or water. *What is sound?*

Sound, or auditory stimulation, travels through the air like waves. If you could see them, they would look something like the ripples in a pond when you toss in a pebble. You hear the splash even if you can't see the sound of it. The sound of the splash is caused by changes in air pressure. The air is alternately compressed and expanded like the movements of an accordion. If you were listening under water, you would also hear the splash because of changes in the pressure of the water. In either case, the changes in pressure are vibrations that approach your ears in waves. These vibrations—sound waves—can also be created by a ringing bell (see Figure 4.25), your vocal cords, guitar strings, or the slam of a book thrown down on a desk. A single cycle of compression and expansion is one wave of sound. Sound waves can occur many (many!) times in 1 second. The human ear is sensitive to sound waves with frequencies of from 20 to 20,000 cycles per second.

Pitch and Loudness: All Sorts of Vibes

Hertz (Hz) A unit expressing the frequency of sound waves. One hertz equals one cycle per second.

Pitch and loudness are two psychological dimensions of sound. The pitch of a sound is determined by its frequency, or the number of cycles per second as expressed in the unit **hertz (Hz).** One cycle per second is 1 Hz. The greater the number of cycles per second (Hz), the higher the pitch of the sound.

The pitch of women's voices is usually higher than that of men's voices because women's vocal cords are usually shorter and therefore vibrate at a greater frequency. Also, the strings of a violin are shorter than those of a viola or bass violin. Pitch detectors in the brain allow us to tell differences in pitch.

The loudness of a sound roughly corresponds to the height, or amplitude, of sound waves. Figure 4.26 shows records of sound waves that vary in frequency and amplitude. Frequency and amplitude are independent. That is, both high- and low-pitched sounds can be either high or low in loudness. The loudness of a sound is expressed in **decibels (dB).** Zero dB is equivalent to the threshold of hearing—the lowest sound that the typical person can hear. How loud is that? It's about as loud as the ticking of a watch 20 feet away in a very quiet room.

The decibel equivalents of familiar sounds are shown in Figure 4.27. Twenty-five dB is equivalent in loudness to a whisper at 5 feet. Thirty dB is roughly the limit of loudness at which your librarian would like to keep your college library. You may suffer hearing damage if you are exposed to sounds of 85 to 90 dB for long periods. This is why (careful) carpenters wear ear covers while they are hammering away, and why young people risk permanent damage to their hearing when they attend loud rock concerts, which reach levels of above 140 dB. (Bring ear plugs.) The ear is the marvelous instrument that senses all these different "vibes."

The Ear: The Better to Hear You With

The human ear is good for lots of things—including catching dust, combing hair around, and hanging jewelry from. It is also well suited to sensing sounds. *How does the ear work?* The ear is shaped and structured to capture sound waves, vibrate in sympathy with them, and transmit them to the brain. In this way, you not only hear something, you can also figure out what it is. The ear has three parts: the outer ear, middle ear, and inner ear (see Figure 4.28).

The outer ear is shaped to funnel sound waves to the *eardrum,* a thin membrane that vibrates in response to sound waves and thereby transmits them to the middle and inner ears. The middle ear contains the eardrum and three small bones which also transmit sound by vibrating. These bones were given their Latin names (*malleus, incus,* and *stapes* [pronounced STAY-peas]), which translate as "hammer," "anvil," and "stirrup") because of their shapes. The middle ear functions as an amplifier, increasing the pressure of the air entering the ear.

The stirrup is attached to another vibrating membrane, the *oval window*. The oval window works in conjunction with the round window which balances the pressure in the inner ear (see Figure 4.28). The round window pushes outward when the oval window pushes in, and is pulled inward when the oval window vibrates outward.

The oval window transmits vibrations into the inner ear, the bony tube called the **cochlea** (from the Greek word for "snail"). The cochlea, which is shaped like a snail shell, contains two longitudinal membranes that divide it into three fluid-filled chambers. One of the membranes that lies coiled within the cochlea is called the **basilar membrane.** Vibrations in the fluids within the chambers of the inner ear press against the basilar membrane.

The **organ of Corti,** sometimes referred to as the "command post" of hearing, is attached to the basilar membrane. Some 25,000 receptor cells—called hair cells because they project like hair from the organ of Corti—are found in each ear. Hair cells "dance" in response to the vibrations of the basilar membrane. Their movements generate neural

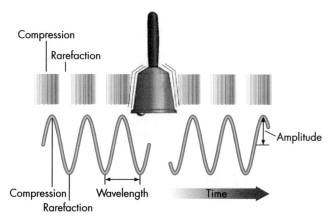

Figure 4.25
Creation of Sound Waves
The ringing of a bell compresses and expands (rarefies) air molecules, sending forth vibrations that stimulate the sense of hearing and are called sound waves.

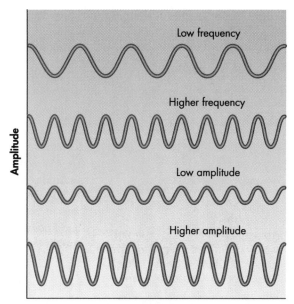

0.1 second

Figure 4.26
Sound Waves of Various Frequencies and Amplitudes
Which sounds have the highest pitch? Which are loudest?

Decibel (dB) A unit expressing the loudness of a sound.

Cochlea The inner ear; the bony tube that contains the basilar membrane and the organ of Corti.

Basilar membrane A membrane that lies coiled within the cochlea.

Organ of Corti The receptor for hearing that lies on the basilar membrane in the cochlea.

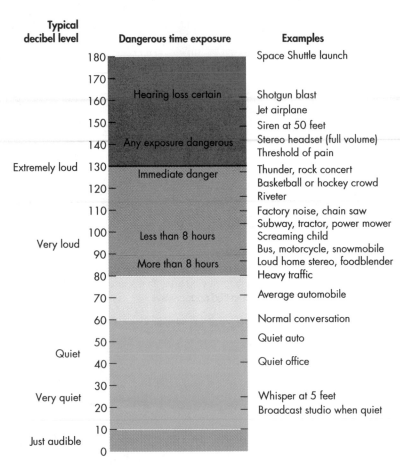

Typical decibel level	Dangerous time exposure	Examples
180	Hearing loss certain	Space Shuttle launch
170		
160		Shotgun blast
150		Jet airplane
140	Any exposure dangerous	Siren at 50 feet
		Stereo headset (full volume)
		Threshold of pain
Extremely loud 130	Immediate danger	Thunder, rock concert
120		Basketball or hockey crowd
		Riveter
110		Factory noise, chain saw
		Subway, tractor, power mower
Very loud 100	Less than 8 hours	Screaming child
90		Bus, motorcycle, snowmobile
	More than 8 hours	Loud home stereo, foodblender
80		Heavy traffic
70		Average automobile
60		Normal conversation
Quiet 50		Quiet auto
40		Quiet office
Very quiet 30		
20		Whisper at 5 feet
		Broadcast studio when quiet
10		
Just audible 0		

Figure 4.27
Decibel Ratings of Familiar Sounds
Zero dB is the threshold of hearing. You may suffer hearing loss if you incur prolonged exposure to sounds of 85 to 90 dB.

impulses, which are transmitted to the brain via the **auditory nerve.** Auditory input is then projected onto the hearing areas of the temporal lobes of the cerebral cortex.

Locating Sounds: Up, Down, and Around

How do you balance the loudness of a stereo set? You sit between the speakers and adjust the volume until the sound seems to be equally loud in each ear. If the sound to the right is louder, the musical instruments are perceived as being to the right rather than in front. *How do we locate sounds?* There is a resemblance between balancing a stereo set and locating sounds. A sound that is louder in the right ear is perceived as coming from the right. A sound coming from the right also reaches the right ear first. Both loudness and the sequence in which the sounds reach the ears provide directional cues.

But it may not be easy to locate a sound coming from directly in front or in back of you or above. Such sounds are equally distant from each ear and equally loud. So what do we do? Simple—usually we turn our head slightly to determine in which ear the sound increases. If you turn your head to the right and the loudness increases in your left ear, the sound is likely coming from in front. We also use vision and knowledge to locate the source of sounds. If you hear the roar of jet engines, you can usually assume that the airplane is overhead.

Perception of Loudness and Pitch

Sounds are heard because they cause vibration in parts of the ear and information about these vibrations is transmitted to the brain. *How do we perceive loudness and pitch?* The loudness and pitch of sounds appear to be related to the number of receptor neurons on the organ of Corti that fire and how often they fire. Psychologists generally agree that sounds are perceived as louder when more of these sensory neurons fire.

It takes two processes to explain perception of color: *trichromatic theory* and *opponent-process theory.* Similarly, it takes at least two processes to explain perception of sound waves that vary in frequency from 20 to 20,000 cycles per second: *place theory* and *frequency theory.*

Hermann von Helmholtz helped develop the place theory of pitch discrimination as well as the trichromatic theory of color vision. **Place theory** holds that the pitch of a sound is sensed according to the place along the basilar membrane that vibrates in response to it. In research with guinea pigs and cadavers that led to the award of a Nobel prize, Georg von Békésy (1957) found that receptors at different sites along the membrane fire in response to tones of differing frequencies. Receptor neurons appear to be lined up along the basilar membrane like piano keys. The higher the pitch of a sound, the closer the responsive neurons lie to the oval window (Larkin, 2000). However, place theory appears to apply only to

Are you familiar with the violin, viola, cello, and bass violin? How do their sounds differ? How can you use the information in this section to explain the differences?

Auditory nerve The axon bundle that transmits neural impulses from the organ of Corti to the brain.

Place theory The theory that the pitch of a sound is determined by the section of the basilar membrane that vibrates in response to the sound.

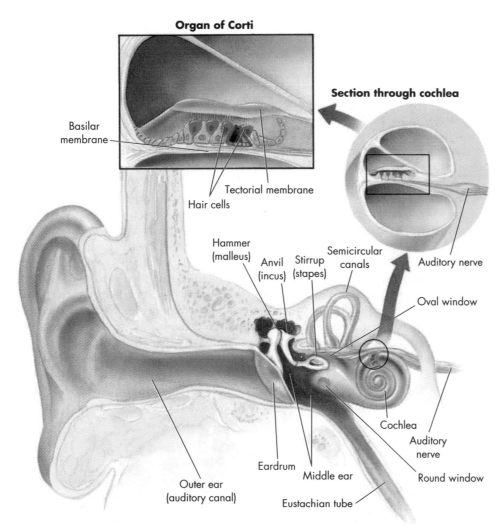

Organ of Corti

Section through cochlea

Basilar membrane

Tectorial membrane

Hair cells

Hammer (malleus)

Anvil (incus)

Stirrup (stapes)

Semicircular canals

Auditory nerve

Oval window

Cochlea

Auditory nerve

Round window

Eardrum

Middle ear

Outer ear (auditory canal)

Eustachian tube

Go to your student website to access an interactive version of this figure.

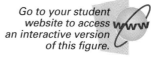

Figure 4.28
The Human Ear
The outer ear funnels sound to the eardrum. Inside the eardrum, vibrations of the hammer, anvil, and stirrup transmit sound to the inner ear. Vibrations in the cochlea transmit the sound to the auditory nerve by way of the basilar membrane and the organ of Corti.

pitches that are at least 5,000 Hz. But what about lower pitches? That's where frequency theory comes in.

Frequency theory notes that for us to perceive lower pitches, we need to match the frequency of the sound waves with our neural impulses. That is, in response to low pitches—say 20 to 1,000 cycles per second—hair cells on the basilar membrane fire at the same frequencies as the sound waves. However, neurons cannot fire more frequently. Therefore, frequency theory best explains perception of pitches between 20 and 1,000 cycles per second.

I noted that it takes *at least two processes* to explain how people perceive pitch. The perception of sounds between 1,000 and 5,000 cycles per second apparently depends both on the part of the basilar membrane that vibrates (as in place theory), and the frequency with which it vibrates (as in frequency theory). The processes apparently work together to enable us to hear pitches in the intermediate range (Goldstein, 2004).

━■━ Deafness: Navigating a World of Silence

More than 1 in 10 Americans have a hearing impairment, and 1 in 100 cannot hear at all (Canalis & Lambert, 2000). Deaf people are deprived of a key source of information about the world around them. In recent years, however, people have often been on hand to

Frequency theory The theory that the pitch of a sound is reflected in the frequency of the neural impulses that are generated in response to the sound.

reflect & relate

Do you know anyone with hearing problems? What is the source of the impairment? How does the person cope with the impairment?

convert political and other speeches into hand signs (such as those of American Sign Language) for hearing-impaired members of the audience. Many television shows are "closed captioned" so that they can be understood by people with hearing problems. ***What is deafness? What can we do about it?***

Two major types of deafness are conductive deafness and sensorineural deafness. *Conductive deafness* stems from damage to the structures of the middle ear—either to the eardrum or to the bones that conduct (and amplify) sound waves from the outer ear to the inner ear (Canalis & Lambert, 2000). This is the hearing impairment often found among older people. Hearing aids amplify sound and often help people with conductive deafness.

Sensorineural deafness usually stems from damage to the structures of the inner ear, most often the loss of hair cells. Sensorineural deafness can also stem from damage to the auditory nerve, caused by such factors as disease or exposure to very loud sounds. In sensorineural deafness, people tend to be more sensitive to some pitches than others. In so-called Hunter's notch, the loss is limited to the frequencies of the sound waves generated by a gun firing. Prolonged exposure to 85 dB can cause hearing loss. People who attend rock concerts, where sounds may reach 140 dB, risk damaging their ears, as do workers who run pneumatic drills or drive noisy vehicles. The ringing sensation that often follows exposure to loud sounds probably means that hair cells in the inner ear have been damaged. If you are suddenly exposed to loud sounds, your fingertips can serve as emergency ear protectors.

Cochlear implants, or "artificial ears," contain microphones that sense sounds and electronic equipment that transmits sounds past damaged hair cells to stimulate the auditory nerve. Such implants have helped many people with sensorineural deafness (Geers et al., 2002), but they cannot assume the functions of damaged auditory nerves.

☉ Learning Connections

◀◀ *Hearing—Making Sense of Sound* ▶▶

Learning Connections

REVIEW:

13 The human ear can hear sounds varying in frequency from 20 to _____ cycles per second (Hz).
(a) 200,
(b) 2,000,
(c) 20,000,
(d) 2 million.

14 The "command post" of hearing is the
(a) organ of Corti,
(b) basilar membrane,

(c) malleus,
(d) auditory nerve.

15 The threshold of hearing is defined as _____ dB.
(a) 0,
(b) 30,
(c) 85,
(d) 140.

CRITICAL THINKING:
Many young people—and some not-so-young people!—blare their stereos or attend loud concerts even though they know they are endangering their hearing. Why do you think they do this?

Go to www
http://academic.cengage.com/psychology/rathus
for an interactive version of this review.

THE CHEMICAL SENSES: SMELL AND TASTE

Smell and taste are the chemical senses. In vision and hearing, physical energy strikes our sensory receptors. In smell and taste, we sample molecules of substances.

Smell: Sampling Molecules in the Air

People are underprivileged when it comes to the sense of smell. Dogs, for example, devote about seven times as much of the cerebral cortex as we do to the sense of smell. Male dogs sniff to determine the boundaries of other dogs' territories and whether female dogs are sexually receptive. Some dogs earn a living sniffing out explosive devices or illicit drugs in suitcases.

Smell also has an important role in human behavior. It contributes to the **flavor** of foods, for example. If you did not have a sense of smell, an onion and an apple might taste the same to you! People's sense of smell may be deficient when compared with that of the dog, but we can detect the odor of 1 one-millionth of a milligram of vanilla in a liter of air.

How does the sense of smell work? Smell detects odors. An *odor* is a sample of molecules of a substance in the air. Odors trigger firing of receptor neurons in the olfactory membrane high in each nostril. Receptor neurons can detect even a few molecules of the substance in gaseous form. The receptor neurons transmit information about odors to the brain via the **olfactory nerve.**

It is unclear how many basic kinds of odors there are. In any event, olfactory receptors may respond to more than one kind. Mixtures of smell sensations produce the broad range of odors that we can perceive.

The sense of smell adapts rapidly to odors. You quickly lose awareness of them, even obnoxious odors. This might be fortunate if you are in a locker room or a latrine. It might not be so helpful if you are exposed to paint fumes or secondhand smoke, because you may lose awareness of them while danger remains. One odor can mask another, as do air "fresheners."

reflect & relate
Have you had the experience of growing accustomed to a noxious odor so that you have lost awareness of it?

Owen Franken/Corbis

■ **An Acute Sense of Smell**
Dogs devote a greater portion of their cerebral cortex to the sense of smell than humans do. Dogs have been trained to sniff out drugs, explosives, and, in this case, people.

Taste: Yes, You've Got Taste

Your cocker spaniel may jump at the chance to finish off your bowl of sherbet, but your Siamese cat may turn up her nose at the opportunity. Why? Dogs can perceive sweetness, as can pigs, but cats cannot. But when it comes to the sense of taste, the catfish may be the champ. According to Joseph Brand (2000) of the Monell Chemical Senses Center, catfish are "swimming tongues." ◆ **Truth or Fiction Revisited:** Catfish can detect food through murky water and across long distances because their bodies are studded with nearly 150,000 taste buds.

Animals, including humans, use the sense of taste in acquiring nutrients and avoiding poisons. A food may look good from a distance. It may trigger fond memories. It may even smell good, but if it tastes bad, we are likely not to swallow it (Scott, 2001).

How does the sense of taste work? As in the case of smell, taste samples molecules of a substance. Taste is sensed through **taste cells**—receptor neurons located on **taste buds.** You have about 10,000 taste buds, most of which are located near the edges and back of your tongue. Taste buds tend to specialize a bit. Some, for example, are more responsive to sweetness, whereas others react to several tastes. Other taste receptors are found in the roof, sides, and back of the mouth, and in the throat. Some taste buds are even found in the stomach, although we only perceive tastes in the mouth and top of the throat. Buds in the mouth are evolutionarily adaptive because they can warn of bad food before it is swallowed (Brand, 2000).

Flavor A complex quality of food and other substances that is based on their odor, texture, and temperature as well their taste.

Olfactory nerve The nerve that transmits information concerning odors from olfactory receptors to the brain.

Taste cells Receptor cells that are sensitive to taste.

Taste buds The sensory organs for taste. They contain taste cells and are mostly located on the tongue.

A Closer Look
Advances in Science? The Case of the Aromatic T-Shirts

A Closer Look

Readers may be familiar with perfume and cologne as aids to sexual attraction, but how about body odor? Body odor? Yes, body odor.

A group of researchers (Jacob et al., 2002) had a sample of men wear T-shirts for two days. Throughout that period they kept their aromas "pure" by avoiding deodorants, spicy foods (no garlic, please), pets, and sex. They then placed the T-shirts in boxes where they could not be seen but could clearly be smelled. Women in the study then made a sacrifice for science which may have been greater than the men's. They were asked to smell each of the boxes and choose the one they would be most willing to live with—that is, the one they would choose "if they had to smell it all the time."

Now, the women were kept blind as to the purpose of the study and also blind to the fact that they were smelling "ripe" T-shirts. By and large, the women rated the odors as mildly pleasant. The women had no difficulty telling the "boxes" apart and easily selected a favorite.

The T-shirt study apparently has something to do with evolution and genes. The shirts selected as favorites had been worn by men who were similar in genetic makeup to the women's fathers. The genes that seem to do the trick are called M.H.C. genes, and they produce proteins that identify cells within one's body as "self," not foreign. Cells that reap the stamp of approval are not attacked by the body's immune system. But why the father? Here the researchers become speculative. Perhaps by finding odors that are suggestive of genetic similarity to the father, but not the mother, women are enticed to mate with men who are similar but not overly similar to themselves.

This is not to suggest that the major factor in modern mate selection is, well, nasal inspiration. Visual appearance, education, interests, and socioeconomic status may have more to do with it. But it could be that the nose also knows something about what it takes for a woman to live comfortably with a man year after year. ■

reflect & relate

Has food ever seemed to lose its flavor when you had a cold or an allergy attack? Why did it happen?

Researchers generally agree on at least four primary taste qualities: sweet, sour, salty, and bitter. Some argue for a fifth basic taste, which is termed *umami* (pronounced *ooh-mommy*) in Japanese and means "meaty" or "savory." Others suggest that there are still more basic tastes (Schiffman, 2000; Schiffman et al., 2003). Regardless of the number of basic tastes, the flavor of a food is more complex than taste alone. *Flavor* depends on odor, texture, and temperature as well as on taste. Apples and onions are similar in taste, but their flavors differ greatly. (Would you chomp into a nice cold onion on a warm day?) If it were not for odor, heated tenderized shoe leather might pass for steak.

Just as some people see better than others, some people taste better than others—but their superiority may be limited to one or more basic tastes. Those of us with low sensitivity for sweetness may require twice the sugar to sweeten our food as those who are more sensitive. Those of us who claim to enjoy bitter foods may actually be taste blind to them (Lanier et al., 2005). Sensitivities to various tastes have a genetic component (Bartoshuk, 2000; Duffy et al., 2004).

By eating hot foods and scraping your tongue with forks and rough pieces of food, you regularly kill off many taste cells. But you need not be alarmed at this inadvertent oral aggression. Taste cells are the rabbits of the sense receptors. They reproduce rapidly enough to completely renew themselves about once a week.

Although older people often complain that their food has little or no "taste," they are more likely to experience a decline in the sense of smell. Because the flavor of a food represents both its tastes and its odors or aromas, older people experience loss in the *flavor* of their food. Therefore, older people might spice their food heavily to enhance its flavor.

() **Learning Connections**

◀◀ *The Chemical Senses — Smell and Taste* ▶▶

Learning Connections

REVIEW:

16 Flavor includes all of the following except for the _____ of food.
    (a) aroma,
    (b) appearance,
    (c) texture,
    (d) temperature.

17 Of the following, _____ reproduce most rapidly.
    (a) receptor neurons in the olfactory membrane,
    (b) the structures of the middle ear,
    (c) hair cells of the inner ear,
    (d) taste cells.

CRITICAL THINKING:
Critical thinkers pay close attention to definitions. What is the difference between the *taste* and the *flavor* of food?

Go to
http://academic.cengage.com/psychology/rathus
for an interactive version of this review.

THE SKIN SENSES (YES, IT DOES)

The skin is much more than a protective coating for your body. As you may know from lying on the sand beneath a broiling sun, and perhaps from touching the person lying next to you, the skin also discriminates among many kinds of sensations. ◆ **Truth or Fiction Revisited:** It is true that the skin is a sensory organ as well as a protective coating for the body. *What are the skin senses? How do they work?* The skin senses include touch, pressure, warmth, cold, and pain. We have distinct sensory receptors for pressure, temperature, and pain, but some nerve endings may receive more than one type of sensory input. Here let's focus on touch, pressure, temperature, and pain.

▬ Touch and Pressure: Making Contact

Sensory receptors embedded in the skin fire when the surface of the skin is touched. There may be several kinds of receptors for touch, some that respond to constant pressure, some that respond to intermittent pressure, as in tapping the skin. *Active touching* means continually moving your hand along the surface of an object so that you continue to receive sensory input from the object (O'Dell & Hoyert, 2002). If you are trying to "get the feel of" a fabric or the texture of a friend's hair, you must move your hand over it. Otherwise the sensations quickly fade. If you pass your hand over the fabric or hair and then hold it still, the sensations of touching will fade. Active touching receives information concerning pressure, temperature, texture, and feedback from the muscles involved in movements of our hands.

Different parts of the body are more sensitive to touch and pressure than others. If you take another look at Figure 2.14 on page 59, you'll see that the parts of the body that "cover" more than their fair share of somatosensory cortex are most sensitive to touch. These parts include the hands, face, and some other regions of the body. Our fingertips, lips, noses, and cheeks are more sensitive than our shoulders, thighs, and calves. Why the difference in sensitivity? First, nerve endings are more densely packed in the fingertips and face than in other locations. Second, more sensory cortex is devoted to the perception of sensations in the fingertips and face (see Figure 2.14 on page 59).

The sense of pressure, like the sense of touch, undergoes rapid adaptation. For example, you may have undertaken several minutes of strategic movements to wind up with

reflect & relate

Your can assess the sensitivity of your sense of touch by trying a mini-experiment suggested by Cynthia O'Dell and Mark Hoyert (2002): Set out a series of cookie cutter outlines, close your eyes, and see how many you can identify from your sense of touch alone.

your hand on the arm or leg of your date, only to discover that adaptation to this delightful source of pressure reduces the sensation.

Temperature: Sometimes Everything Is Relative

reflect & relate

Have you ever entered a swimming pool and felt cold even though the water temperature was in the 70s? How can you explain the experience?

The receptors for temperature are neurons located just beneath the skin. When skin temperature increases, the receptors for warmth fire. Decreases in skin temperature cause receptors for cold to fire.

Sensations of temperature are relative. When we are at normal body temperature, we might perceive another person's skin as warm. When we are feverish, though, the other person's skin might seem cool. We also adapt to differences in temperature. When we walk out of an air-conditioned house into the July sun, we feel intense heat at first. Then the sensations of heat tend to fade. Similarly, when we enter a swimming pool, the water may seem cold because it is below body temperature. Yet after a few moments an 80°F pool may seem quite warm. In fact, we may chide a newcomer for not diving right in.

Pain: Too Much of a Good Thing?

For most people, pain is a frequent visitor. Headaches, backaches, toothaches—these are only a few of the types of pain that most of us encounter from time to time. According to a national Gallup survey of more than 2,000 adults (Arthritis Foundation, 2000), 89% experience pain at least once a month. More than half (55%) of people aged 65 and above say they experience pain daily. People aged 65 and above are most likely to attribute pain to getting older (88%) and to assume they can do nothing about disabilities such as arthritis. By contrast, people aged 18 to 34 are more likely to attribute pain to tension or stress (73%), overwork (64%), or their lifestyle (51%). When we assume that there is nothing we can do about pain, we are less likely to try. Yet 43% of Americans say that pain curtails their activities, and 50% say that pain puts them in a bad mood. What is pain? What can we do about it?

Pain results when neurons called *nociceptors* in the skin are stimulated. Evolutionary psychologists would point out that pain is adaptive, if unpleasant, because it motivates us to do something about it. For some of us, however, chronic pain—pain that lasts once injuries or illnesses have cleared—saps our vitality and interferes with the pleasures of everyday life (Turk & Okifuji, 2002).

We can sense pain throughout most of the body, but pain is usually sharpest where nerve endings are densely packed, as in the fingers and face. Pain can also be felt deep within the body, as in the cases of abdominal pain and back pain. Even though headaches may seem to originate deep inside the head, there are no nerve endings for pain in the brain.

Pain usually originates at the point of contact, as when you bang a knee (see Figure 4.29). But it reverberates throughout the nervous system. The pain message to the brain is initiated by the release of chemicals such as prostaglandins, bradykinin, and P (yes, P stands for "pain"). *Prostaglandins* facilitate transmission of the pain message to the brain and heighten circulation to the injured area, causing the redness and swelling that we call inflammation. Inflammation attracts infection-fighting blood cells to the injury to protect it against invading germs. Pain-relieving drugs such as aspirin and ibuprofen help by inhibiting production of prostaglandins.

The pain message is relayed from the spinal cord to the thalamus and then projected to the cerebral cortex, making us aware of the location and intensity of the damage. Ronald Melzack (1999) speaks of a "neuromatrix" that includes these chemical reactions but involves other aspects of our physiology and psychology in our reaction to pain. For example, visual and other sensory inputs tell us what is happening and affect our interpretation of the situation. Our emotional response affects the degree of pain, and so do the ways in which we respond to stress. For example, if the pain derives from an object we fear, perhaps a knife or needle, we may experience more pain. If we perceive that there is nothing we can do to change the situation, perception of pain may increase. If we have self-confidence and a history of successful responding to stress, perception of pain may diminish.

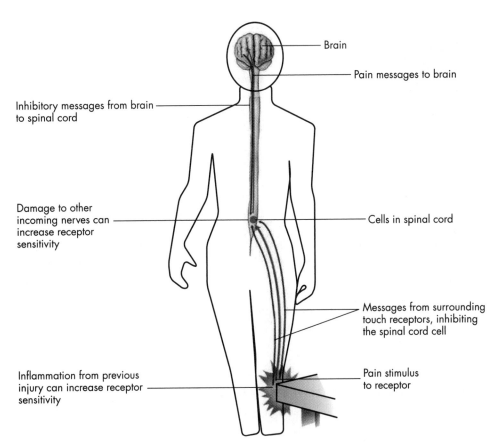

Brain

Pain messages to brain

Inhibitory messages from brain to spinal cord

Damage to other incoming nerves can increase receptor sensitivity

Cells in spinal cord

Messages from surrounding touch receptors, inhibiting the spinal cord cell

Inflammation from previous injury can increase receptor sensitivity

Pain stimulus to receptor

Figure 4.29
Perception of Pain
Pain originates at the point of contact, and the pain message to the brain is initiated by the release of prostaglandins, bradykinin, and substance *P*.

Phantom Limb Pain   One of the more intriguing topics in the study of pain is phantom limb pain. ◈ **Truth or Fiction Revisited:** Many people do experience pain "in" limbs that have been amputated (Horgan & MacLachlan, 2004). About 2 out of 3 combat veterans with amputated limbs report feeling pain in such missing, or "phantom," limbs (Kooijman et al., 2000). Although the pain occurs in the absence of the limb, it is real enough. It sometimes involves activation of nerves in the stump of the missing limb, but local anesthesia does not always eliminate the pain. Researchers have found that many people who experience phantom limb pain have also undergone reorganization of the motor and somatosensory cortex that is consistent with the pain (Mackert et al., 2003).

Gate Theory   Simple remedies like rubbing a banged knee frequently help relieve pain. Why? One possible answer lies in the *gate theory* of pain originated by Ronald Melzack and Patrick Wall (Sufka & Price, 2002). Gate theory proposes that the nervous system can process only a limited amount of stimulation at a time. Rubbing the knee transmits sensations to the brain that "compete" for the attention of neurons. Many nerves are thus prevented from transmitting pain messages to the brain. It is like shutting down a "gate" in the spinal cord, or like a switchboard being flooded with calls. Flooding prevents any calls from getting through.

Acupuncture   Thousands of years ago, the Chinese began mapping the body to learn where pins might be placed to deaden pain. This practice is termed acupuncture. Traditional acupuncturists believe that the practice balances the body's flow of energy, but research has shown that it stimulates nerves that reach the hypothalamus and may also cause the release of *endorphins* (Ulett & Wedding, 2003). Endorphins are neurotransmitters that are similar to the narcotic morphine in their chemical structure and effects.

The following "Life Connections" section describes psychological methods for coping with pain.

Life Connections
Pain, Pain, Go Away—Don't Come Again Another Day

Coping with that age-old enemy—pain—has traditionally been a medical issue. The primary treatment has been chemical, as in the use of painkilling drugs. Psychology, however, has dramatically expanded our arsenal of weapons for fighting pain.

Accurate Information

Giving people accurate and thorough information about their condition often helps them manage pain (Tait, 2005). Most people in pain try *not* to think about why things hurt. Physicians, too, often fail to discuss with patients the meaning of the pain and what the patient can expect. Yet when uncomfortable procedures are used, such as cardiac catheterization or chemotherapy for cancer, knowledge of the details of the treatment, including how long it will last and how much discomfort there will be, can help people cope with the pain. But some people do not *want* information about painful medical procedures. Their attitude is, "Do what you have to do and get it over with." It is helpful to match the amount of information provided with the amount desired (Ludwick-Rosenthal & Neufeld, 1993).

Distraction and Fantasy: The Playstation Approach to Coping With Pain?

Diverting attention from pain helps many people cope with it (L. L. Cohen, 2002; Dehghani et al., 2004). Psychologists frequently recommend that people use distraction or fantasy as ways of coping with pain. For example, imagine that you've injured your leg

Brooklyn Production /Corbis

■ **The Playstation Approach to Coping with Pain?**
Psychologists have found that distraction and fantasy help individuals cope with pain. Yes, it may hurt, but perhaps we can focus our attention elsewhere.

and you're waiting to see the doctor in an emergency room. You can distract yourself by focusing on details of your environment. You can count ceiling tiles or the hairs on the back of a finger. You can describe (or criticize) the clothes of medical personnel or passersby. Playing video games also distracts people from the pain and discomfort of medical procedures (Robbins, 2000). Child cancer patients can become wrapped up in video games while they receive chemotherapy. Blowing on a noisemaker and purposeful coughing help children deal with injections.

Hypnosis

In 1842 London physician W. S. Ward amputated a man's leg after using a rather strange anesthetic: hypnosis. According to reports, the man experienced no discomfort. Today hypnosis is often used to reduce chronic pain (Gay et al., 2002; Mamtani & Cimino, 2002) and as an anesthetic in dentistry, childbirth, even some forms of surgery (Montgomery et al., 2000).

In using hypnosis to manage pain, the hypnotist usually instructs the person that he or she feels nothing or that pain is distant and slight. Hypnosis also aids in the use of distraction and fantasy (McGrath, 2004; Patterson, 2004). For example, the hypnotist can guide the person to imagine that he or she is relaxing on a warm, exotic shore.

Relaxation Training

When we are in pain, we often tense up. Tensing muscles is uncomfortable in itself, arouses the sympathetic nervous system, and focuses attention on the pain (Hamilton et al., 2004). Relaxation counteracts these behavior patterns. Some psychological methods of relaxation focus on relaxing muscle groups (Gay et al., 2002). Some involve breathing exercises. Others use relaxing imagery, which distracts the person and deepens feelings of relaxation. Relaxation training may be as effective as most medications for headaches (Martin, 2002) and for chronic pain in the lower back and jaw.

Challenging Irrational Beliefs

Irrational beliefs can heighten pain. For example, telling oneself that the pain is unbearable and will never cease increases discomfort (Turk & Okifuji, 2002). Some people seem to feel obligated to focus on things that distress them. They may be unwilling to allow themselves to be distracted from pain and discomfort. Psychotherapy that challenges irrational beliefs is helpful (Stroud et al., 2000).

Other Methods

Pain is a source of stress, and many factors moderate the effects of stress. One is a sense of commitment. For example, if we are undergoing a painful medical procedure to diagnose or treat an illness, it might help if we recall that we *chose* to participate, rather than see ourselves as helpless victims. Thus, we are in control of the situation, and a sense of control enhances the ability to cope with pain (Peters et al., 2004; Turk & Okifuji, 2002).

Supportive social networks help as well (Peters et al., 2004). The benefits of having friends visit us—or visiting friends who are unwell—are as consistent with psychological findings as they are with folklore.

Don't forget gate theory. When you feel pain in a toe, squeeze all your toes. When you feel pain in your calf, rub your thighs. People around you may wonder what you're doing, but you're entitled to try to "flood the switchboard" so that some pain messages don't get through. ■

◯ Learning Connections

  ◀◀   *The Skin Senses (Yes, It Does)*   ▶▶

Learning Connections

REVIEW:

18 Of the following, our _____ are most sensitive
  to touch.
  (a) thighs,
  (b) shoulders,
  (c) calves,
  (d) lips.

19 All of the following stimulate perception of pain,
  except for
  (a) substance *P*,
  (b) endorphins,

  (c) bradykinin,
  (d) prostaglandins.

20 Which of the following is a psychological method
  for managing pain?
  (a) Acupuncture,
  (b) Painkilling medication,
  (c) Challenging irrational beliefs,
  (d) Amputation.

CRITICAL THINKING:
People who have had amputations frequently complain of "phantom
limb pain." Where is the pain actually located?

Go www
to
http://academic.cengage.com/psychology/rathus
for an interactive version of this review.

■ **Kinesthesis**
This young acrobat receives information about the position and movement
of the parts of his body through the
sense of kinesthesis. Information is
fed to his brain from sensory organs in
the joints, tendons, and muscles. This
allows him to follow his own movements without looking at himself.

Andy Levin / Photo Researchers, Inc.

Kinesthesis The sense that informs us
about the positions and motion of parts
of our bodies.

KINESTHESIS AND THE VESTIBULAR SENSE

Try an experiment. Close your eyes, and then touch your nose with your finger. If you
weren't right on target, I'm sure you came close. But how? You didn't see your hand moving, and you didn't hear your arm swishing through the air. Humans and many other animals have senses that alert them to their movements and body position without relying on
vision, including *kinesthesis* and the *vestibular sense*.

■ Kinesthesis: How Moving?

What is kinesthesis? **Kinesthesis** is the sense that informs you about the position and
motion of parts of the body. The term is derived from the ancient Greek words for "motion" (*kinesis*) and "perception" (*aisthesis*). In kinesthesis, sensory information is fed back
to the brain from sensory organs in the joints, tendons, and muscles. You were able to
bring your finger to your nose easily by employing your kinesthetic sense. When you
make a muscle in your arm, the sensations of tightness and hardness are also provided by
kinesthesis.

Imagine going for a walk without kinesthesis. You would have to watch the forward motion of each leg to be certain you had raised it high enough to clear the curb. And if you had
tried the nose-to-finger brief experiment without the kinesthetic sense, you would have had
no sensory feedback until you felt the pressure of your finger against your nose (or cheek,
or eye, or forehead), and you probably would have missed dozens of times.

Are you in the mood for another mini-experiment? Close your eyes again. Then "make
a muscle" in your right arm. Could you sense the muscle without looking at it or feeling it
with your left hand? Of course you could. Kinesthesis also provides information about
muscle contractions.

A Closer Look

How Did the Animals Know the Tsunami Was Coming?

A Closer Look

The tsunami that in late 2004 hit the southern coast of south central Asia—in countries from Indonesia to Sri Lanka to India—killed as many as one quarter of a million people. The people were caught off guard. But not the animals.

Along the western coast of Thailand, elephants giving rides to tourists began to trumpet agitatedly hours before the tsunami, just about when the earthquake that fractured the ocean floor sent the big waves rushing toward the shore. An hour before the waves slammed into the area, the elephants began wailing. Just before the waves struck, they trooped off to higher ground.

There were reports that dogs refused to go outdoors. In one Sri Lankan town, dogs who usually enjoyed a run on the beach might have saved their owner's life. "They are usually excited to go on this outing," he said (cited in Mott, 2005). But on the day of the tsunami, they refused to go out. A survivor in Thailand said, "Dogs are smarter than all of us. . . . [They] started running away up to the hilltops long before we even realized what was coming" (cited in Oldenburg, 2005).

Paul Souders/Getty Images

■ Do Elephants Sense What Humans Can't

Research indicates that elephants can sense vibrations in the ground over vast distances. This might be one way they can detect an earthquake or a tsunami before a human becomes aware of it. Other animals use other senses to detect tsunamis, earthquakes, and other impending disasters.

Flamingos usually breed in low-lying areas at this time of year, but on the day of the tsunami, they abandoned their sanctuary on the coast of India and headed into safer forests before the waves hit shore (Oldenburg, 2005).

The Yala National Park in Sri Lanka was hit hard by the waves, but wildlife officials were surprised to find that hundreds of elephants, tigers, leopards, deer, wild boar, water buffalo, monkeys, and reptiles had escaped the tsunami unharmed.

People have noticed that animals appear to have a "sixth sense" for detecting earthquakes, hurricanes, volcanic eruptions, and tsunamis before the earth starts shaking. Rats, for example, evacuate buildings. Sparrows take flight. Dogs howl. Some animals are apparently supersensitive to sound, others to temperature, touch, or vibration, which gives them advance warning. Alan Rabinowitz of the Wildlife Conservation Society in New York says that many animals can detect subtle or abrupt changes in the environment. "Earthquakes bring vibrational changes on land and in water while storms cause electromagnetic changes in the atmosphere," he said. "Some animals have acute senses of hearing and smell that allow them to determine something coming towards them long before humans might know" (cited in Mott, 2005).

Research shows that many kinds of fish detect shakes long before humans do. Elephants are particularly sensitive to ground vibrations and probably sensed the earthquake that caused the tsunami in their feet and trunks. Some birds, dogs, tigers, and elephants can detect sound waves whose frequencies are too low for humans to hear ("infrasound"). Dogs' superior sense of smell might detect subtle chemical changes in the air that warn them of calamities.

Researcher Michelle Heupel of the Mote Marine Laboratory in Florida concludes, "I think these animals are more attuned to their environment than we give them credit for. When things change, they may not understand why it's happening, but the change itself may trigger some instinct to move to an area that is safer for them" (cited in Oldenburg, 2005). ■

Vestibular sense The sense of equilibrium that informs us about our bodies' positions relative to gravity.

▪— The Vestibular Sense: How Upright?

◇ **Truth or Fiction Revisited:** It is true that you have a sense that keeps you an upright person. It is your **vestibular sense,** which provides your brain with information as to whether or not you are upright (physically, not morally). ***How does the vestibular sense work?*** Sensory organs located in the semicircular canals and elsewhere in the ears monitor your body's motion and position in relation to gravity. They tell you whether you are falling and provide cues to whether your body is changing speed, such as when you are in an accelerating airplane or automobile. It is thus the vestibular sense that keeps us physically upright. Now, you may recall episodes when you have been spun around blindfolded at a party or in the spinning "Teacups" amusement park ride. Afterward, it might have been difficult for you to locate yourself in space (if you remained blindfolded) or to retain your balance. The reason is that the fluid in the semicircular canals was tossed about so fiercely that you lost your ability to monitor or control your position in relation to gravity.

Concept Review 4.2 summarizes key points about the senses.

CONCEPT REVIEW   ■ **CONCEPT REVIEW 4.2** ■   **CONCEPT REVIEW**

THE SENSES

SENSE	WHAT WE SENSE	RECEPTOR ORGANS	NATURE OF SENSORY RECEPTORS
Vision	Visible light (part of the spectrum of electromagnetic energy; different colors have different wavelengths)	Eyes	Photoreceptors in the retinas (*rods,* which are sensitive to the intensity of light; and *cones,* which are sensitive to color)
Hearing	Changes in air pressure (or in another medium, such as water) that result from vibrations called *sound waves*	Ears	"Hair cells" in the organ of Corti, which is attached to a membrane (the *basilar membrane*) within the inner ear (the *cochlea*)
Smell	Molecules of the substance	Nose	Receptor neurons in the olfactory membrane high in each nostril

(continued)

CONCEPT REVIEW ■ **CONCEPT REVIEW 4.2** ■ CONCEPT REVIEW

THE SENSES (CONTINUED)

SENSE	WHAT WE SENSE	RECEPTOR ORGANS	NATURE OF SENSORY RECEPTORS
Taste	Molecules of the substance	Tongue	Taste cells located on taste buds on the tongue
Touch, Pressure	Pushing or pulling of the surface of the body	Skin	Nerve endings in the skin, some of which are located around the hair follicles
Kinesthesis	Muscle contractions	Sensory organs in joints, tendons, and muscles	Receptor cells in joints, tendons, and muscles
The Vestibular Sense	Movement and position in relation to gravity	Sensory organs in the ears (e.g., in the *semicircular canals*)	Receptor cells in the ears

Andy Levin/Photo Researchers, Inc.

⟨⟩ Learning Connections

◀◀ *Kinesthesis and the Vestibular Sense* ▶▶

REVIEW:

21 In kinesthesis, sensory information is fed back to the brain from sensory organs in the
(a) muscles,
(b) eyes,
(c) ears,
(d) skin.

22 The vestibular sense is housed mainly in the _____ of the ear.
(a) cochlea,
(b) basilar membrane,
(c) incus,
(d) semicircular canals.

CRITICAL THINKING:
Why are some people "natural athletes"? Might there be genetic factors related to kinesthesis and the vestibular sense that contribute to their abilities?

Go to www
http://academic.cengage.com/psychology/rathus
for an interactive version of this review.

VIRTUAL REALITY AND ESP: SENSATION AND PERCEPTION ON THE EDGE

Sensation is the peripheral device that feeds information into our central processing unit—the brain. Topics on the edge of psychology explore fascinating things that might happen if—as in *The Matrix*—the sensations we perceive do not represent reality, or if sensation were bypassed altogether and we directly perceived things in the world outside. Make no mistake:

Warner Bros./Photofest

■ **Virtual Reality or "Real" Reality?**
In *The Matrix* film series, the characters enter our world by being "plugged in." Computer technology—fortunately or unfortunately—has not yet advanced to the point where we cannot distinguish what is real from what is virtual.

These topics are indeed on the edge. For the time being there is little chance of mistaking virtual reality and, well, real reality. Also, research evidence fails to support perception in the absence of sensation. Nevertheless, these topics arouse a good deal of interest and are worthy of our attention.

■ Virtual Reality

"Seeing is believing," or so goes the saying. But can we always believe what we see—or smell or hear or taste or feel? Not necessarily.

In *The Matrix* series, we envision a world in which we are deceived into believing that the world we sense every day is real, when it is actually a vanished dream. *The Matrix* is science fiction on the theme of virtual reality. *What is virtual reality?* Virtual reality is the perception of events that are fed directly into the senses via electronic technology.

Virtual reality may sound purely like the stuff of science fiction, but it is in use today, employing computer-generated imagery. Although few would be fooled into believing a virtual visual world is real, psychologists are now using computer-generated images to help people overcome phobias such as fear of public speaking (Harris et al., 2002), spiders (Garcia-Palacios et al., 2002), flying (Maltby et al., 2002; Muehlberger et al., 2001), and heights (Rothbaum & Hodges, 1999). In the case of fear of heights, individuals view images in which they perceive themselves as gradually rising to greater heights, even though they are remaining still. Because the images are computer generated rather than real, they are referred to as *virtual reality*. Children (and many adults?) also use virtual reality—often in the form of virtual reality goggles or helmets—to feel that they are participating more fully in computer games.

Cybersex   Also consider *cybersex* or *virtual sex* (Harton & Boedeker, 2005; Mustanski, 2004). Users wear headphones, 3-D glasses, and a bodysuit with detectors that follow their movements and stimulators for their skin. The detectors and stimulators are connected to computers that record users' responses and create the impression of being touched by textures such as satin or skin. They can interact with another online person who is outfitted with similar gear or be connected with a "canned" program.

What are the psychological and social implications of virtual sex? If we could at a moment's notice access a satisfying virtual sexual encounter with an appealing person (or program) who was concerned only with meeting our needs, would we become less sensitive to the needs of our real partners? What would be the implications for family life?

━━■━ ESP: Is There Perception Without Sensation?

Our sensory organs are the peripheral devices that feed information into our central processing units—our brains. Our second topic on the edge of psychology asks the question: What if there were such as thing as extrasensory perception (ESP)? What if sensation were bypassed, and we directly perceived things in the world outside? Although the hard research evidence comes down hard against ESP, 60% of the American public believes that some people have psychic powers or ESP (National Science Foundation, 2002). Therefore, it is useful to understand the issue and examine the type of research that psychologists conduct to determine whether it has validity. Let us begin by defining precognition and other topics in ESP.

Precognition, Psychokinesis, Telepathy, and Clairvoyance   Imagine the wealth you could amass if you had *precognition,* that is, if you were able to perceive future events in advance. Perhaps you would check the next week's stock market reports and know what to buy or sell. Or you could bet with confidence on who would win the next Super Bowl or World Series. Or think of the power you would have if you were capable of *psychokinesis,* that is, of mentally manipulating or moving objects. You may have gotten a glimpse of the possibilities in films like *The Matrix, The Sixth Sense,* and *Star Wars.* Precognition and psychokinesis are two concepts associated with ESP. Two other theoretical forms of ESP are *telepathy,* or direct transmission of thoughts or ideas from one person to another, and *clairvoyance,* or the perception of objects that do not stimulate the sensory organs. An example of clairvoyance is "seeing" what card will be dealt next, even though it is still in the deck and unseen even by the dealer.

Does anyone you know believe that some people are "psychics"? What kind of evidence is required to support the existence of ESP? Why do you think that many readers of this textbook will continue to believe in ESP despite the lack of scientific evidence?

Now that we have made some definitions, let us note that many psychologists do not believe that ESP is an appropriate area for scientific inquiry. Scientists study natural events, but ESP smacks of the supernatural, even the occult. ESP also has the flavor of a nightclub act in which a blindfolded "clairvoyant" calls out the contents of an audience member's pocketbook. Other psychologists, however, believe that there is nothing wrong with investigating ESP. The issue for them is not whether ESP is sensationalistic but whether its existence can be demonstrated in the laboratory. *Does ESP really exist?*

A well-known ESP researcher was Joseph Banks Rhine of Duke University, who studied ESP for several decades, beginning in the 1920s. In a typical experiment in clairvoyance, Rhine would use a pack of 25 cards, which contained 5 sets of the cards shown in Figure 4.30. Pigeons pecking patterns at random to indicate which one was about to be turned up would be "correct" 20% of the time. Rhine found that some people guessed correctly significantly more often than the 20% chance rate. He concluded that these people might have some degree of ESP.

A more current method for studying telepathy is the *ganzfeld procedure* (Dalkvist, 2001; Parker, 2001). In this method, one person acts as a "sender" and the other as a "receiver." The sender views randomly selected visual stimuli such as photographs or videotapes, while the receiver, who is in another room and whose eyes are covered and ears are blocked, tries to mentally tune in to the sender. After a session, the receiver is shown four visual stimuli and asked to select the one transmitted by the sender. A person guessing which stimulus was "transmitted" would be correct 25% of the time (1 time in 4) by chance alone. An analysis of 28 experiments using the ganzfeld procedure, however, found that receivers correctly

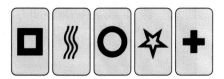

Figure 4.30
Zener Cards
Joseph Banks Rhine used these cards in research on clairvoyance. Participants are asked to predict which card will be turned up.

Corbis Sygma

■ *The Sixth Sense?*
In the fictional film of that name, Bruce Willis portrays a psychologist who treats a boy who has a "sixth sense." Why are psychologists skeptical about the existence of ESP?

identified the visual stimulus 38% of the time (Honorton, 1985), a percentage unlikely to be due to chance. A series of 11 more studies with the ganzfeld procedure obtained similar results (Bem & Honorton, 1994; Honorton et al., 1990).

Overall, however, there are reasons to be skeptical. First is the *file-drawer problem.* Buyers of supermarket tabloids tend to forget the predictions of "psychics" when the predictions fail to come true (that is, they have "filed" them away). Similarly, ESP researchers are more likely to "file away" research results that show failure. Therefore, we would expect unusual findings (for example, a subject with a high success rate on experimental tasks over a few days) to appear in the research literature. In other words, if you flip a coin indefinitely, eventually you will flip 10 heads in a row. The odds against it are high, but if you report your eventual success and do not report the weeks of failure, you may give the impression that you have unique coin-flipping ability.

It has also been difficult to replicate experiments in ESP. People who have "demonstrated" ESP with one researcher have failed to do so with another, or they have refused to participate in other studies. Also, the findings in one study are usually absent in follow-ups or under careful analysis. For example, Milton and Wiseman (1999) reviewed the research reported by Bem and Honorton (1994). They weighed the results of 30 ganzfeld ESP studies from seven laboratories. They found no evidence—zero—that subjects in these studies scored above chance levels on the ESP task. Critiques of the Milton and Wiseman (1999) review once more present conflicting conclusions (Bem et al., 2001; Storm & Ertel, 2001, 2002).

Let's make one point clear: From all of these studies, *not one person has emerged who can reliably show ESP from one occasion to another and from one researcher to another.* ◈ **Truth or Fiction Revisited**: There is no adequate scientific evidence that people can read other people's minds. Research has not identified one single indisputable telepath or clairvoyant. In sum, most psychologists do not grant ESP research much credibility. They prefer to study perception that involves sensation. After all, what is life without sensation?

( ) Learning Connections

◀◀ *Virtual Reality and ESP—Sensation and Perception on the Edge* ▶▶

REVIEW:

23 Virtual reality is the perception of events that are fed directly into the senses by means of
(a) a sixth sense,
(b) the semicircular canals,
(c) electronic technology,
(d) ESP.

24 When researchers do not report research results that show failure, we encounter the _____ problem.
(a) ganzfeld,
(b) file-drawer,
(c) Rhine,
(d) Zener.

CRITICAL THINKING:
Why do many psychologists believe that it is inappropriate to conduct research into ESP? Do you agree with them? Explain your point of view.

Go to
http://academic.cengage.com/psychology/rathus
for an interactive version of this review.

RECITE—*An Active Summary*™

 Recite to Go!   *Don't have time to study right now? You can study on the go!*
Go to your companion website and download an audio version of this review section to your media player. You can
also access an interactive flashcard version of this review from your website.

1. What are sensation and perception?	Sensation involves the stimulation of sensory receptors and the transmission of sensory information to the central nervous system. Perception is the organization of sensations to represent the outside world.
2. How do we know when something is there? How do we know when it has changed?	We know something is present when the intensity of the stimulus exceeds the absolute threshold for that stimulus. The absolute threshold is the lowest intensity at which the stimulus can be detected. We know that something has changed when the change in intensity exceeds the difference threshold. Difference thresholds are expressed in Weber's constants.
3. What is signal-detection theory?	Signal-detection theory explains how stimulus characteristics and psychological factors—such as motivation and attention—interact to influence whether a stimulus is detected.
4. What are feature detectors?	Feature detectors are neurons that fire in response to specific features of sensed stimuli. For example, feature detectors in the visual cortex fire in response to lines sensed at certain angles.
5. How do our sensory systems adapt to a changing environment?	We become more sensitive to stimuli of low magnitude and less sensitive to stimuli that remain the same. Growing more sensitive to stimulation is termed sensitization, or positive adaptation. Growing less sensitive is called desensitization, or negative adaptation.
6. What is light?	Visible light is the part of the range of electromagnetic energy that triggers visual sensations. Light is made up of waves of energy. White sunlight can be broken down into the colors of the rainbow by a prism.
7. How does the eye work?	The eye senses and transmits visual stimulation to the occipital lobe. The size of the pupil determines the amount of light that can pass through the lens. The lens focuses light onto the retina, which is composed of photoreceptors called rods and cones. Cones permit perception of color. Rods transmit sensations of light and dark. Light is transmitted from the retina to the brain by the optic nerve.
8. What are some perceptual dimensions of color?	These include hue, value, and saturation. The wavelength of light determines its hue. Colors across from one another on the color wheel are complementary. In afterimages, sensations of color are followed by perception of the complementary color when the first color is removed.
9. How do we perceive color? Why are roses red and violets blue?	According to the trichromatic theory, there are three types of cones—some sensitive to red, others to green, still others to blue. The opponent-process theory proposes three types of color receptors: red–green, blue–yellow, and light–dark.
10. What is color blindness? Why are some people color-blind?	People with normal color vision are called trichromats. Monochromats see no color, and dichromats are blind to some parts of the spectrum. Partial color blindness is a sex-linked trait.
11. How do we organize bits of visual information into meaningful wholes?	Perceptual organization involves recognizing relationships between parts and the whole. Gestalt rules of perceptual organization involve figure–ground relationships, proximity, similarity, continuity, common fate, and closure. Perception of a whole

followed by perception of parts is top-down processing. Perception of the parts that leads to perception of a whole is bottom-up processing.

12. How do we perceive movement?	We perceive movement when the light reflected by moving objects moves across the retina, and also when objects shift in relation to one another. Stroboscopic motion occurs through the presentation of a rapid progression of images of stationary objects (frames).
13. How do we perceive depth?	Depth perception involves monocular and binocular cues. Monocular cues include perspective, clearness, interposition, shadows, texture gradient, and motion parallax. Binocular cues include retinal disparity and convergence.
14. What are perceptual constancies?	Perceptual constancies are acquired through experience and make the world a stable place. We learn that objects retain their size, shape, brightness, and color despite their distance from us, their position, or changes in lighting conditions.
15. What is sound?	Sound waves require a medium such as air or water. Sound waves alternately compress and expand molecules of the medium, creating vibrations. The human ear can hear sounds varying in frequency from 20 to 20,000 cycles per second (Hz). The greater the frequency, the higher the pitch. The loudness of a sound corresponds to the amplitude of sound waves as measured in decibels.
16. How does the ear work?	The ear captures sound waves, vibrates in sympathy with them, and transmits auditory information to the brain. The outer ear funnels sound waves to the eardrum which transmits the auditory information through the bones of the middle ear to the cochlea of the inner ear. From there, sound travels to the brain via the auditory nerve.
17. How do we locate sounds?	We locate sounds by determining in which ear they are louder. We may turn our heads to pin down that information.
18. How do we perceive loudness and pitch?	Sounds are perceived as louder when more sensory neurons fire. Place theory holds that the pitch of a sound is sensed according to the place along the basilar membrane that vibrates in response to it. Frequency theory states that pitch perception depends on the stimulation of neural impulses that match the frequency of the sound.
19. What is deafness? What can we do about it?	Conductive deafness is caused by damage to the middle ear and is often ameliorated by hearing aids, which amplify sounds. Sensorineural deafness is caused by damage to neurons in the inner ear.
20. How does the sense of smell work?	The sense of smell is chemical. It samples molecules of substances called odors through the olfactory membrane in each nostril. Odor contributes to the flavor of foods.
21. How does the sense of taste work?	Taste is sensed through taste cells, which are located in taste buds. Flavor involves the odor, texture, and temperature of food, as well as taste.
22. What are the skin senses? How do they work?	The skin senses include touch, pressure, warmth, cold, and pain. Touches and pressure are sensed by receptors located around the roots of hair cells. We have separate receptors for warmth and cold.
23. What is kinesthesis?	Kinesthesis is the sensation of body position and movement. It relies on sensory organs in the joints, tendons, and muscles.
24. How does the vestibular sense work?	The vestibular sense is mostly housed in the semicircular canals of the ears and tells us whether we are in an upright position.
25. What is virtual reality?	Virtual reality is the perception of events that are fed directly into the senses via electronic technology.
26. Does ESP really exist?	ESP refers to the perception through means other than sensory organs. The ganzfeld procedure studies telepathy by having one person try to mentally transmit visual information to a receiver in another room. There is no reliable evidence for the existence of ESP.

Key Terms

Sensation   126
Perception   126
Absolute threshold   127
Pitch   127
Difference threshold   127
Weber's constant   128
Just noticeable difference (jnd)   128
Signal-detection theory   128
Feature detectors   128
Sensory adaptation   129
Sensitization   129
Desensitization   129
Hue   131
Cornea   131
Iris   131
Pupil   131
Lens   132
Retina   132
Photoreceptors   132
Bipolar cells   132
Ganglion cells   132
Optic nerve   132
Rods   132
Cones   132

Fovea   132
Blind spot   132
Visual acuity   133
Presbyopia   133
Dark adaptation   133
Complementary   134
Afterimage   136
Trichromatic theory   136
Opponent-process theory   136
Trichromat   137
Monochromat   137
Dichromat   137
Closure   138
Proximity   140
Similarity   140
Continuity   140
Common fate   140
Top-down processing   141
Bottom-up processing   141
Illusions   141
Stroboscopic motion   141
Monocular cues   142
Perspective   142
Texture gradient   143

Motion parallax   143
Binocular cues   143
Retinal disparity   143
Convergence   143
Size constancy   144
Color constancy   145
Brightness constancy   145
Shape constancy   145
Hertz (Hz)   148
Decibel (dB)   149
Cochlea   149
Basilar membrane   149
Organ of Corti   149
Auditory nerve   150
Place theory   150
Frequency theory   151
Flavor   153
Olfactory nerve   153
Taste cells   153
Taste buds   153
Kinesthesis   160
Vestibular sense   162

Active Learning Resources

Visit Your Companion Website for This Book

http://academic.cengage.com/psychology/rathus

Check out this companion website where you will find online resources directly linked to your book. This is where you'll access the videos highlighted in your Video Connections feature. You can answer the questions online and email them to your professor. In addition you'll find downloadable audio review material, interactive versions of the study aids, Power Visuals for mastering and reviewing key concepts, as well as quizzing, and much more!

CENGAGENOW™

http://academic.cengage.com

Need help studying? This site is your one-stop study shop. Take a Pre-Test and Cengage NOW will generate a Personalized Study Plan based on your test results. The Study Plan will identify the topics you need to review and direct you to online resources to help you master those topics. You can then take a Post-Test to help you determine the concepts you have mastered and what you still need to work on. In addition you can access interactive media including the videos highlighted in your Video Connections box.

Author Blog

What does your author Spence Rathus have to say about the state of psychology? Visit your companion website every Tuesday and click on "Author Blog." This is where he'll talk about the most recent controversies and hot topics in psychology. This will keep you up to date with what your author is thinking and give you great insight into modern psychology.

CHAPTER 5

Consciousness

Jonathan Andrew/Corbis

T	F	We act out our forbidden fantasies in our dreams.
T	F	Many people have insomnia because they try too hard to fall asleep at night.
T	F	It is dangerous to awaken a sleepwalker.
T	F	You can be hypnotized against your will.
T	F	You can teach a rat to raise or lower its heart rate.
T	F	Some people visit cyberspace with virtual bodies.
T	F	A drink a day is good for you.
T	F	Heroin was once used as a cure for addiction to morphine.
T	F	Many health professionals calm down hyperactive children by giving them a stimulant.
T	F	Coca-Cola once "added life" to its signature drink through the use of a powerful—but now illegal—stimulant.
T	F	The number of people who die from smoking-related causes is greater than the number lost to motor vehicle accidents, abuse of alcohol and all other drugs, suicide, homicide, and AIDS *combined*.

Go to www
*http://academic.cengage.com/pstchology/rathus
for an interactive version of this Truth or Fiction feature.*

I fired up the computer, logged on, and immediately aimed my browser at the Alta Vista search engine on the Web. I entered in the keyword "Self" and hit the search button. In a matter of seconds, after furiously scanning all of cyberspace, the engine came back with a reply . . . 2.5 million hits! Looks like the self is everywhere! Maybe that meant something. Or maybe I just needed to narrow my search. So I entered in the keywords "True Self." This time I got 11,000 hits. Better. I was on the right track. How about "Essence of Self?" The search engine hummed away and returned 245 hits. Now I was definitely zooming in on the target. I could tell this was the right path because a lot of the hits included web sites devoted to philosophy, spirituality, and poetry— although it also turned up the American Legion Magazine and a web page called "Understanding Diarrhea in Travelers." No, really! . . . Finally, I entered in the keywords "The True and Essential Self" and clicked the search button. Once again Alta Vista went out into the vast Netherland of global electronified knowledge and came back with . . . zero hits. Nothing! The void! The True and Essential Self was nowhere to be found, well at least not in cyberspace.

So psychologist John Suler (2005) describes one of his journeys into cyberspace. Thinking that his search engine was a bit slow, I thought I'd Google "self." It took Google 0.17 seconds to find 215 million hits. "True self"? I got 702,000 hits in 0.19 seconds. There were 54 hits for "true and essential self," but it did take Google nearly one second to come up with them. So, the True and Essential Self is now to be found in cyberspace. I wonder where it is in the real world.

WHAT IS CONSCIOUSNESS?

Psychologists are quite interested in the self, which is one aspect of consciousness. Psychologists are also becoming more and more interested in people's experiences on the Internet, which some psychologists consider to create an altered state of consciousness. Consciousness, altered states of consciousness . . . let us begin this most intriguing area of psychology by posing this question: *What is consciousness?*

Consciousness is a familiar word, and we probably all have ideas about what it means. Psychologists use the word in a variety of ways.

■ Consciousness as Awareness

One meaning of consciousness is *sensory awareness* of the environment. The sense of vision enables us to see, or be *conscious* of, the sun gleaming on the snow. The sense of hearing allows us to hear, or be conscious of, a concert. Yet sometimes we are not aware of sensory stimulation. We may be unaware, or unconscious, of sensory stimulation when we do not pay attention to it. The world is abuzz with signals, yet you are conscious of, or focusing on, only the words on this page (I hope).

Therefore, another aspect of consciousness is **selective attention.** Selective attention means focusing one's consciousness on a particular stimulus. The concept of selective attention is important to self-control. To pay attention in class, you must screen out the pleasant aroma of the cologne or perfume wafting toward you from the person in the next seat.

Selective attention The focus of consciousness on a particular stimulus.

To keep your car on the road, you must pay more attention to driving conditions than to your hunger pangs or your feelings about an argument with a friend. If you are out in the woods at night, attending to rustling sounds in the brush nearby may be crucial to your survival.

Adaptation to our environment involves learning which stimuli must be attended to and which ones can be safely ignored. Selective attention makes our senses keener (Vorobyev et al., 2004). This is why we can pick out the speech of a single person across a room at a cocktail party, a phenomenon aptly termed the *cocktail party effect.*

Although we can decide where and when we will focus our attention, various kinds of stimuli also tend to capture attention. Among them are these:

- Sudden changes, as when a cool breeze enters a sweltering room or we receive a particularly high or low grade on an exam.
- Novel stimuli, as when a dog enters the classroom or a person shows up with an unusual hairdo.
- Intense stimuli, such as bright colors, loud noises, sharp pain, or extremely attractive people.
- Repetitive stimuli, as when the same TV commercial is played a dozen times throughout the course of a football game.

How do advertisers of running shoes, automobiles, beer, or cologne use these facts to get "into" our consciousness and, they hope, into our pocketbooks? Think of some TV commercials that captured your attention. What kinds of stimuli made them front and center in your awareness?

Yet another meaning of consciousness is that of **direct inner awareness.** Close your eyes and imagine spilling a can of bright red paint across a black tabletop. Watch it spread across the black, shiny surface and then spill onto the floor. Although this image may be vivid, you did not "see" it literally. Neither your eyes nor any other sensory organs were involved. You were *conscious* of the image through direct inner awareness.

We are conscious of—or have direct inner awareness of—thoughts, images, emotions, and memories. However, we may not be able to measure direct inner awareness scientifically. Nevertheless, many psychologists argue, if you have it, you know it. Self-awareness is connected with the firing of billions of neurons hundreds of times per second. Even so, we detect psychological processes but not neural events (Roth, 2000).

◾ Conscious, Preconscious, Unconscious, and Nonconscious

Sigmund Freud, the founder of psychoanalysis, differentiated between the thoughts and feelings of which we are conscious, or aware, and those that are preconscious and unconscious. **Preconscious** material is not currently in awareness but is readily available. For example, if you answer the following questions, you will summon up "preconscious" information: What did you eat for breakfast? What is your phone number? You can make these preconscious bits of information conscious by directing your attention to them.

Still other mental events are **unconscious,** or unavailable to awareness under most circumstances. Freud believed that some painful memories and sexual and aggressive impulses are unacceptable to us, so we *automatically* (unconsciously) eject them from awareness. That is, we *repress* them. **Repression** of these memories and impulses allows us to avoid feelings of anxiety, guilt, or shame.

People can also *choose* to stop thinking about unacceptable ideas or distractions. When we consciously eject unwanted mental events from awareness, we are engaging in **suppression.** We may, for example, suppress thoughts of an upcoming party when we need to study for a test. We may also try to suppress thoughts of a test while we are at the party!

Some bodily processes, such as the firings of neurons, are **nonconscious.** They cannot be experienced through sensory awareness or direct inner awareness. The growing of hair and the carrying of oxygen in the blood are nonconscious. We can see that our hair has grown, but we have no sense receptors that give us sensations of growing. We can feel the need to breathe but do not directly experience the exchange of carbon dioxide and oxygen.

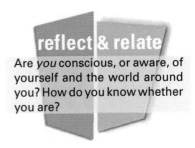

reflect & relate

Are *you* conscious, or aware, of yourself and the world around you? How do you know whether you are?

Direct inner awareness Knowledge of one's own thoughts, feelings, and memories.

Preconscious In psychodynamic theory, descriptive of material that is not in awareness but can be brought into awareness by focusing one's attention.

Unconscious In psychodynamic theory, descriptive of ideas and feelings that are not available to awareness. Also: without consciousness.

Repression In psychodynamic theory, the unconscious ejection of anxiety-evoking ideas, impulses, or images from awareness.

Suppression The deliberate, or conscious, placing of certain ideas, impulses, or images out of awareness.

Nonconscious Descriptive of bodily processes such as the growing of hair, of which we cannot become conscious. We may "recognize" that our hair is growing but cannot directly experience the biological process.

A Closer Look
Terri Schiavo, Consciousness, and Biological Functioning

In 1990, 25-year-old Terri Schiavo collapsed from cardiac arrest, stopped breathing, and suffered brain damage due to lack of oxygen. For the next 15 years, she lay in what her doctors diagnosed as a vegetative state. An electroencephalogram (EEG) showed that her cerebral cortex, the seat of consciousness, was largely inactive (see Table 5.1). After the collapse, Terri began breathing on her own again, but she was sustained by a feeding tube. In 2005, Terri's doctors removed the feeding tube, following a protracted court battle between her husband, who had custody and wanted the tube removed, and her parents, who wanted her to remain alive. The battle reached state and federal courts, and even led to the passing of a special law involving only Terri by the United States Congress. Nevertheless, the tube was removed and within two weeks, Terri's life functions had ceased.

Many issues are involved in the Terri Schiavo case: medical, psychological, legal, religious, and philosophical. We will address a few of them here.

First, the medical: As you can see in Table 5.1, Terri's state was considered to be unconscious ("persistently vegetative") by the majority of the medical profession (Annas, 2005; Quill, 2005). If that diagnosis was correct, Terri had no real chance of regaining consciousness after 15 years. But if, as a few doctors suggested, Terri might instead be suffering from a "minimally conscious state," there was some possibility of recovery, even at this late stage. An auto mechanic named Terry Wallis regained awareness from a minimally conscious state more than 18 years after he fell unconscious due to an auto accident. A Kansas resident named Sarah Scantlin, another crash victim, emerged from a minimally conscious state after 19 years.

From a psychological perspective, it would appear that Terri's EEG argued in favor of the diagnosis of vegetative state. Wallis and Scantlin's brains showed nearly normal activity on occasion when they were socially stimulated. Terri's did not. Terri's continued breathing and conduct of other bodily functions could be explained by the continued functioning of lower parts of her brain. These parts could also explain intermittent reflexive smiling and other behaviors that gave some hope to people who cared for her.

Legally speaking, Terri's husband had custody, and state and federal courts found no reason why custody should be removed from him. He argued that Terri would not have

■ **Terri Schiavo**

Terri Schiavo collapsed from cardiac arrest, damaging her brain due to oxygen deprivation. She lay in what most health professionals labeled a vegetative state for 15 years, before her feeding tube was disconnected. Her case touched off a conflict that polarized the nation into opposing camps—one of which insisted that all life was inviolate, and the other which insisted that biological functions in the absence of consciousness were not inviolate.

wanted to remain indefinitely in such a state. The Supreme Court refused to hear the case, which allowed the judgments of the lower courts to stand.

Now, the difficult religious and philosophical issues: Terri's parents and the Catholic Church, to which Terri belonged, believe that every human life is precious and sacred, regardless of how disabled. The church's view is also consistent with the teachings of the Greek philosopher Aristotle, who believed that no person's existence should ever be violated (Leland, 2005). Those who supported Ms. Schiavo's husband in effect agreed with the French philosopher Descartes, who argued that psychological self-awareness or consciousness was more important than biological functioning. These views are also relevant to the controversies over abortion, stem-cell research, the death penalty—even animal rights (Annas, 2005; Leland, 2005).

Critical thinkers will have to weigh the issues and decide for themselves where they stand on the Terri Schiavo case. Certainly, it's an issue we hope we'll never have to personally face. ■

TABLE 5.1 ■ Conscious, Partially Conscious, and Unconscious States

STATE	CONSCIOUS	ASLEEP**	MINIMALLY CONSCIOUS	COMATOSE*	VEGETATIVE*
Awareness	Full	Little to none	Partial	None	None
Motor functions	Full range of voluntary movements and reflexes available	Variable: May be still, may move limbs, occasionally walks	Reaches for object; may grasp objects and hold them	Variable: Some reflexes available; may withdraw from pain	May make random movements; may withdraw from pain
Hearing	Normal hearing	Little to none	May respond to commands to grasp objects, blink, and so on	None	Shows startle reflex to sudden loud noises
Vision	Normal vision	Eyes may wince at bright light or when startled	May track moving objects with eyes	None	Eyes may wince at bright light or when startled
Communication	Full range of language and body language available	May talk or shout during dreams	May produce understandable sounds or gestures	None	None
Emotional response	Full range of emotional responses available	May show horror at nightmare	May smile or cry in response to visitor's behavior	None	May show reflexive or random smiling or crying
Brain activity	High level of activity in cortex and elsewhere; memory functions	Varies from high during REM sleep to low during deep sleep; little memory	Voice of loved one may spur almost normal cortical activity; may remember surroundings	Control of primitive basic life functions by parts of the hindbrain such as the pons and the medulla (see Figure 2.11 on p. 55)	Minimal, random activity in the cortex
Cause	(Normal waking state)	Fatigue; normal variation in consciousness	Brain injury; lack of oxygen	Brain injury; lack of oxygen	Brain injury; lack of oxygen
Comments	(Normal waking state)	Movements and utterances may reflect dream content; can be awakened	May recover rapidly or after many years; may be aware of surroundings	Most people recover in 2–3 weeks	May regain some awareness in few months; after 2 years, none recover

*Unconscious states. **Variable: Unconscious–partially conscious states.

Let us now journey all the way back to the most conscious aspects of our being—our sense of self.

▪ Consciousness as Personal Unity: The Sense of Self

As we develop, we differentiate ourselves from that which is not us. We develop a sense of being persons, individuals. There is a totality to our impressions, thoughts, and feelings that makes up our conscious existence—our continuing sense of self in a changing world. That self forms intentions and guides its own behavior. In this usage of the word, consciousness *is* self. Later we will see that the sense of self seems to change when people venture online, or become wrapped up in being online.

▪ Consciousness as the Waking State

The word *conscious* also refers to the waking state as opposed, for example, to sleep. From this perspective, sleep, meditation, the hypnotic "trance," and the distorted perceptions that can accompany use of consciousness-altering drugs are considered *altered states of consciousness*.

In the remainder of this chapter, we explore various types of altered states of consciousness, including sleep, dreams, and daydreams; hypnosis, meditation, and biofeedback; going online; and, finally, the effects of psychoactive drugs.

■ **Consciousness as the Sense of Self**
The concept of *consciousness* has many meanings in psychology and in general usage. One is the sense of self. The concept of consciousness also refers to sensory awareness, the selective aspect of attention, direct inner awareness, and the waking state.

( ) Learning Connections

◀◀ *What Is Consciousness?* ▶▶

REVIEW:

1 When we unconsciously eject threatening material from consciousness, we are engaging in
   (a) repression,
   (b) suppression,
   (c) selective attention,
   (d) the cocktail party effect.

2 The growing of hair is
   (a) minimally conscious,
   (b) preconscious,
   (c) conscious,
   (d) nonconscious.

CRITICAL THINKING:
Where do you stand on the Terri Schiavo case? Why?

Go to www
http://academic.cengage.com/psychology/rathus
for an interactive version of this review.

SLEEP AND DREAMS: OTHER WORLDS WITHIN?

Sleep is a fascinating topic. After all, we spend about one-third of our adult lives asleep. Sleep experts recommend that adults get eight hours of sleep a night, but according to the National Sleep Foundation (2005b), adults in the United States typically get a bit less than seven. About one-third get six hours or less of sleep a night during the work week. One-third admit that lack of sleep impairs their ability to function during the day, and nearly one in five admits to falling asleep at the wheel some time during the past year.

Figure 5.1
Sleep Times for Mammals
Different mammals require different amounts of sleep. Reasons remain uncertain, but evolution apparently plays a role: Animals more prone to being attacked by predators sleep less.

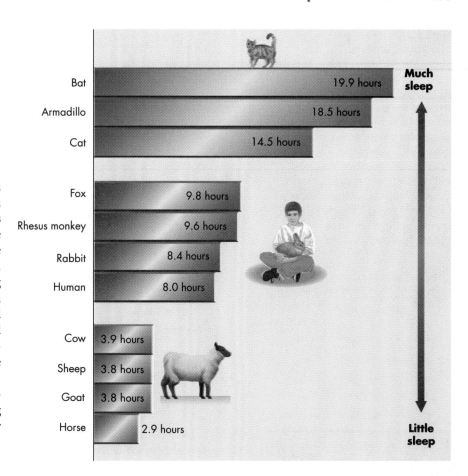

Bat	19.9 hours
Armadillo	18.5 hours
Cat	14.5 hours
Fox	9.8 hours
Rhesus monkey	9.6 hours
Rabbit	8.4 hours
Human	8.0 hours
Cow	3.9 hours
Sheep	3.8 hours
Goat	3.8 hours
Horse	2.9 hours

Much sleep

Little sleep

Yes, we spend one-third of our lives in sleep—or would if we could. As you can see in Figure 5.1, however, some animals get much more sleep than we do, and some obtain much less. Why? It might have something to do with evolutionary forces. Animals who are most at risk of being hunted by predators tend to sleep less—an adaptive response to the realities of life and death. Those individuals who required more sleep might have been killed by predators, eliminating their genes from the gene pool of their species.

The amount of sleep we and other animals need is but one of the fascinating aspects of sleep and wakefulness. Another involves the rhythms of sleep.

Biological and Circadian Rhythms

Our lives are connected with the rhythms of the universe at large. Planet Earth rotates in about 24 hours. The earth revolves around the sun once a year. It takes many millions of years for the sun to revolve around the Milky Way galaxy, of which it is a part.

We and other animals are also subject to rhythms, and they are related to the rotation and revolutions of the planet. Many birds (and people who can afford it!) migrate south in the fall and north in the spring. A number of animals hibernate for the winter and emerge when buds again are about to blossom. Women's menstrual cycles normally run 28 days, similar to the length of the cycle of the phases of the moon. (The root of the word *menses* is "moon.")

Alternating periods of wakefulness and sleep provide an example of an internally generated *circadian rhythm.* ***What is a circadian rhythm?*** A **circadian rhythm** is a cycle that is connected with the 24-hour period of the earth's rotation. A cycle of wakefulness and sleep is normally 24 hours long. When people are removed from cues that signal day or night, however, a cycle tends to become extended to about 25 hours, and people sleep nearly 10 of them (National Sleep Foundation, 2005b). Why? We do not know. And during a night of sleep, we typically undergo a series of 90-minute cycles in which we run through the stages of sleep.

Some of us, "morning people," function best in the morning, others in the afternoon. Some of us are "night owls," who are at our best when most neighbors are sound asleep.

Why do we sleep? Why do we dream? What are daydreams? Let us explore the nature of sleep, dreams, sleep disorders, and daydreams and fantasies.

The Stages of Sleep: How Do We Sleep?

When we sleep, we slip from consciousness to unconsciousness. When we are conscious, our brains emit waves characterized by certain *frequencies* (numbers of waves per second) and *amplitudes* (heights—an index of strength). Brain waves are rough indicators of the activity of neurons. The strength or energy of brain waves is expressed in volts (an electrical unit). Likewise, when we sleep our brains emit waves that differ from those emitted when

Circadian rhythm A cycle that is connected with the 24-hour period of the earth's rotation. (From the Latin *circa*, meaning "about," and *dies*, meaning "day.")

Figure 5.2
The Stages of Sleep
This figure illustrates typical EEG patterns for the stages of sleep. During REM sleep, EEG patterns resemble those of the waking state. For this reason, REM sleep is often termed *paradoxical sleep*. As sleep progresses from stage 1 to stage 4, brain waves become slower, and their amplitude increases. Dreams, including normal nightmares, are most vivid during REM sleep. More disturbing sleep terrors tend to occur during deep stage 4 sleep.

Go to your student website to access an interactive version of this figure.

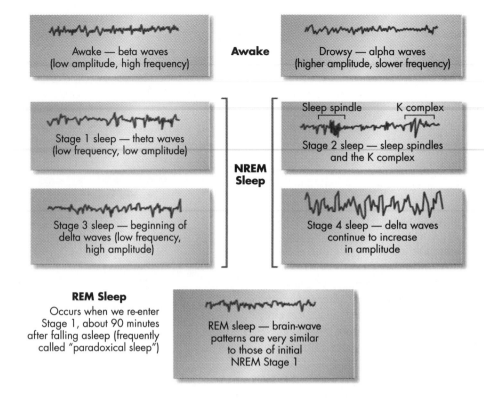

Alpha waves Rapid low-amplitude brain waves that have been linked to feelings of relaxation.

Non-rapid-eye-movement (NREM) sleep Stages of sleep 1 through 4.

Rapid-eye-movement (REM) sleep A stage of sleep characterized by rapid eye movements, which have been linked to dreaming.

Theta waves Slow brain waves produced during the hypnagogic state.

we are conscious. The electroencephalograph (EEG; see Figure 2.7 on page 52) has helped researchers identify the different brain waves during the waking state and when we are sleeping. Figure 5.2 shows EEG patterns that reflect the frequency and strength of brain waves during the waking state, when we are relaxed, and when we are in the various stages of sleep. Brain waves, like other waves, are cyclical. The printouts in Figure 5.2 show what happens during a period of 15 seconds or so. *How do we describe the various stages of sleep?*

High-frequency brain waves are associated with wakefulness. When we move deeper into sleep, their frequency decreases and their amplitude (strength) increases. When we close our eyes and begin to relax before going to sleep, our brains emit many **alpha waves.** Alpha waves are low-amplitude brain waves of about 8 to 13 cycles per second.

Figure 5.2 shows five stages of sleep. The first four sleep stages are considered **non-rapid-eye-movement (NREM)** sleep. These contrast with the fifth stage, **rapid-eye-movement (REM)** sleep, so called because our eyes dart back and forth beneath our eyelids.

As we enter stage 1 sleep, our brain waves slow down from the alpha rhythm and enter a pattern of **theta waves.** Theta waves, with a frequency of about 6 to 8 cycles per second, are accompanied by slow, rolling eye movements. The transition from alpha waves to theta waves may be accompanied by a *hypnagogic state* during which we may experience brief but vivid dreamlike images. Stage 1 sleep is the lightest stage of sleep. If we are awakened from stage 1 sleep, we may deny that we were asleep or feel that we have not slept at all.

After 30 to 40 minutes of stage 1 sleep, we undergo a steep descent into stages 2, 3, and 4 (see Figure 5.3). During stage 2, brain waves are medium in amplitude with a frequency of about 4 to 7 cycles per second, but these are punctuated by *sleep spindles*. Sleep spindles have a frequency of 12 to 16 cycles per second and represent brief bursts of rapid brain activity.

Figure 5.3
Sleep Cycles
This figure illustrates the alternation of REM and non-REM sleep for the typical sleeper. There are about five periods of REM sleep during an 8-hour night. Sleep is deeper earlier in the night, and REM sleep tends to become prolonged toward morning.

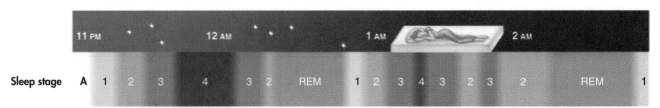

During deep sleep stages 3 and 4, our brains produce slower **delta waves,** which reach relatively great amplitude. During stage 3, the delta waves have a frequency of 1 to 3 cycles per second. Stage 4 is the deepest stage of sleep, from which it is the most difficult to be awakened. During stage 4 sleep, the delta waves slow to about 0.5 to 2 cycles per second, and their amplitude is greatest.

After perhaps half an hour of deep stage 4 sleep, we begin a relatively rapid journey back upward through the stages until we enter REM sleep (see Figure 5.3). During REM sleep, we produce relatively rapid, low-amplitude brain waves that resemble those of light stage 1 sleep. REM sleep is also called *paradoxical sleep* because the EEG patterns observed suggest a level of arousal similar to that of the waking state (see Figure 5.2). However, it is difficult to awaken a person during REM sleep. When people are awakened during REM sleep, they report dreaming about 80% of the time. We also dream during NREM sleep but only about 20% of the time.

Each night we tend to undergo five cycles through the stages of sleep (see Figure 5.3). Five cycles include five periods of REM sleep. Our first journey through stage 4 sleep is usually longest. Sleep tends to become lighter as the night wears on. Periods of REM sleep tend to become longer. Toward morning our last period of REM sleep may last about half an hour.

Now that we have some idea of what sleep is like, let us consider *why* we sleep.

━━▪━ The Functions of Sleep: Why Do We Sleep?

Why do we sleep? Researchers do not have all the answers as to why we sleep, but sleep seems to serve a number of purposes: It rejuvenates the body, helps us recover from stress, helps us consolidate learning and memories, and may promote development of infants' brains.

Consider the hypothesis that sleep helps rejuvenate a tired body. Most of us have had the experience of going without sleep for a night and feeling "wrecked" or "out of it" the following day. Perhaps the next evening we went to bed early to "catch up on our sleep." What happens to you if you do not sleep for one night? For several nights? Compare people who are highly sleep deprived with people who have been drinking heavily. Sleepless people's abilities to concentrate and perform may be seriously impaired, but they may be the last ones to recognize their limitations.

Many students can pull "all-nighters" in which they cram for a test through the night and perform reasonably well the following day (Horowitz et al., 2003). But they begin to show deficits in psychological functions such as learning and memory if they go sleepless for more than one night (Ohno et al., 2002; Taylor & McFatter, 2003). Sleep deprivation makes for dangerous driving (Stutts et al., 2003). The National Sleep Foundation (2005b) estimates that sleep deprivation is connected with 100,000 vehicular crashes and 1,500 deaths each year. To combat sleep deprivation during the week, many people sleep late or nap on their days off (National Sleep Foundation, 2005b).

Why Do You Need the Amount of Sleep You Need?   The amount of sleep we need seems to be in part genetically determined (National Sleep Foundation, 2005b). People also need more sleep when they are under stress, such as a change of job, an episode of depression, or a terrorist attack (National Sleep Foundation, 2001). Sleep helps us recover from stress.

reflect & relate
How much sleep do you need? (How do you know?) Did you ever "pull an all-nighter"? What were the effects?

reflect & relate
The next time you pull an all-nighter, why not keep a diary of your feelings the following day? This activity could help you the next time you are faced with the decision of whether to stay awake and study or get some sleep.

Delta waves Strong, slow brain waves usually emitted during stage 4 sleep.

Newborn babies may sleep 16 hours a day, and teenagers may sleep "around the clock" (12 hours or more). It is widely believed that older people need less sleep than younger adults do, but sleep in older people is often interrupted by physical discomfort or the need to go to the bathroom. To make up for sleep lost at night, older people may "nod off" during the day.

Sleep, Learning, and Memory   REM sleep and deep sleep are both connected with the consolidation of learning and memory (Gais & Born, 2004; Rauchs et al., 2004; Ribeiro & Nicolelis, 2004). In some studies, animals or people have been deprived of REM sleep. Fetuses have periods of waking and sleeping, and REM sleep may foster the development of the brain before birth (Fifer & Moon, 2003). Deprivation of REM sleep is accomplished by monitoring EEG records and eye movements and waking people during REM sleep. Under these conditions animals and people learn more slowly and forget what they have learned sooner (Kennedy, 2002; Ribeiro & Nicolelis, 2004). In any event, people and other animals that are deprived of REM sleep tend to show *REM rebound,* meaning that they spend more time in REM sleep during subsequent sleep periods. They "catch up." Let us now consider dreams, a mystery about which philosophers, poets, and scientists have theorized for centuries.

◾ Dreams: What Is the "Stuff" of Dreams?

To quote from Shakespeare's *The Tempest,* just what is the "stuff" of dreams? *What are dreams?* Dreams are imagery in the absence of external stimulation and can seem real. In college I had repeated "anxiety dreams" the night before a test. I would dream that I had taken the test and it was all over. (Imagine my disappointment when I awakened and realized the test still lay before me!)

Dreams are most likely to be vivid during REM sleep. Images are vaguer and more fleeting during NREM sleep. If you sleep for eight hours and undergo five sleep cycles, you may have five dreams. Dreams may compress time the way a movie does, by skipping hours or days to a future time, but the actual action tends to take place in "real time." Fifteen minutes of events fills about 15 minutes of dreaming. Furthermore, your dream theater is quite flexible. You can dream in black and white or in full color.

Some dreams are nightmares. One common nightmare is that something heavy is sitting on your chest and watching you as you breathe. Another is that you are trying to run away from a threat but cannot gain your footing or coordinate your legs. Nightmares, like most pleasant dreams, are products of REM sleep.

Why do we dream what we dream? There are many theories about why we dream what we dream. Some are psychological and others are more biologically oriented.

Dreams as "the Residue of the Day"   You may recall dreams involving fantastic adventures, but most dreams involve memories of the day gone by—or, poetically, "the residue of the day" (Domhoff, 2001, 2003). If we are preoccupied with illness or death, sex or aggression, or moral dilemmas, we are likely to dream about them. The characters in our dreams are more likely to be friends and neighbors than spies, monsters, and princes.

Traumatic events, however, can spawn nightmares, as reported in the aftermath of the terrorist attacks on the World Trade Center and Pentagon in 2001 (Gorman, 2001; Singareddy & Balon, 2002). People who have frequent nightmares are more likely than others to also have feelings of anxiety and depression (Blagrove et al., 2004; Levin & Fireman, 2002).

Dreams as the Expression of Unconscious Desires   In the Disney film *Cinderella,* a song lyric goes, "A dream is a wish your heart makes." Freud theorized that dreams reflect unconscious wishes and urges. He argued that dreams express impulses we would censor during the day. Moreover, he said that the content of dreams is symbolic of unconscious fantasized objects such as the genitals. In his method of psychoanalysis, Freud would interpret his clients' dreams. ◂▸ **Truth or Fiction Revisited:** But there is no evidence we act out forbidden fantasies in our dreams. Dreams do, however, seem to be consistent with gender

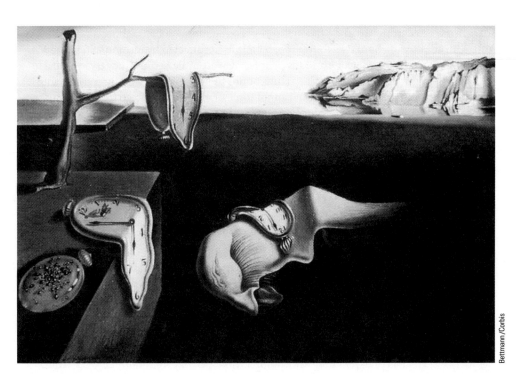

Bettmann/Corbis

■ **Dream Images?**
In *The Persistence of Memory,*
Salvador Dali seems to depict images
born in dreams. What is "such stuff
as dreams are made on"? "Where"
do dreams come from? Why do they
contain what they contain? Are most
dreams exciting adventures or dull
recurrences of the events of the day?

roles; that is, males are more likely than females to have dreams with aggressive content (Schredl et al., 2004).

The Activation–Synthesis Model of Dreams   There are also biological views of the "meanings" of dreams (Domhoff, 2003). According to the **activation–synthesis model,** acetylcholine (a neurotransmitter) and the pons (see Figure 2.11 on page 55) stimulate responses that lead to dreaming (Hobson, 2003; Ogawa et al., 2002). One is *activation* of the reticular activating system (RAS; see Figure 2.11), which arouses us, but not to waking. During the waking state, firing of these cells is linked to movement, particularly in walking, running, and other physical acts. But during REM sleep, neurotransmitters tend to inhibit activity so we usually do not thrash about (Bassetti et al., 2000). In this way, we save ourselves— and our bed partners—wear and tear. But the eye muscles are stimulated and show the REM activity associated with dreaming. The RAS also stimulates parts of the cortex involved in memory. The cortex then *synthesizes,* or pieces together, these sources of stimulation to yield the stuff of dreams (Anderson & Horne, 2004). Because recent events are most likely to be reverberating in our brains, we are most like to dream about them. With the brain cut off from the world outside, learning experiences and memories are replayed and consolidated during sleep (Siegel, 2002; Stickgold et al., 2001). It's useful to get a night of sleep between studying and test-taking, if you can.

There is no absolute agreement on the origins of the functions of sleep or the content of dreams, but many—perhaps most—of us either live with or encounter sleep disorders now and then.

──■- Sleep Disorders

Although nightmares are unpleasant, they do not qualify as sleep disorders. The term *sleep disorder* is reserved for other problems that can seriously interfere with our functioning. *What kinds of sleep disorders are there?* Some sleep disorders, like insomnia, are all too familiar, experienced by at least half of American adults. Others, like apnea (pauses in breathing) affect fewer than 10% of us (National Sleep Foundation, 2005b). In this section we discuss insomnia and less common sleep disorders: narcolepsy, apnea, sleep terrors, bed-wetting, and sleepwalking.

Activation–synthesis model The view that dreams reflect activation of cognitive activity by the reticular activating system and synthesis of this activity into a pattern by the cerebral cortex.

Insomnia   According to the National Sleep Foundation (2005b), more than half of American adults and about two-thirds of older adults are affected by insomnia in any given year.   ◇ **Truth or Fiction Revisited:** Many people have insomnia because they try too hard to fall asleep at night. Trying to get to sleep compounds their sleep problems by creating autonomic activity and muscle tension. You cannot force or will yourself to go to sleep. You can only set the stage for sleep by relaxing when you are tired. You will find strategies for tackling insomnia—and winning—in the following "Life Connections" feature.

Life Connections
Getting to Sleep Without Drugs

Do you have a problem with insomnia? The nearby self-assessment, "Are You Getting Your Z's?", may offer some insight. If you decide that you do have a problem, what can you do about it?

The most common medical method for getting to sleep in the United States is popping pills (National Sleep Foundation, 2005a). Sleeping pills may work—for a while. So may tranquilizers. They reduce arousal and may distract you from trying to *get* to sleep. Expectations of success may also help.

But there are problems with sleeping pills. First, many people may attribute success to the pill and not to themselves and thus come to depend on the pill. Second, a person may develop tolerance for sleeping pills with regular use and then need higher doses to achieve the same effects. Third, high doses of these chemicals can be dangerous, especially if mixed with alcohol. Fourth, sleeping pills do not enhance your skills at handling insomnia. When you stop taking them, insomnia is likely to return (National Sleep Foundation, 2005a).

There are excellent psychological methods for coping with insomnia. Some, like muscle relaxation exercises, reduce tension directly. Psychological methods also divert us from the "task" of trying somehow to *get* to sleep, which, as noted, is one of the ways in which we keep ourselves awake (National Sleep Foundation, 2005a). One or more of the following psychological methods may work for you:

- *Relax.* Take a hot bath at bedtime or meditate. Releasing muscle tension reduces the amount of time needed to fall asleep and the incidence of waking during the night (Gatchel & Oordt, 2003).
- *Challenge exaggerated fears.* Thinking that the next day will be ruined unless you get to sleep *right now* may increase, rather than decrease, bedtime tension. We often exaggerate the problems that will befall us if we do not sleep (Gatchel & Oordt, 2003). Table 5.2 shows a number of beliefs that can increase our tension at bedtime and possible alternative, calming beliefs.
- *Don't ruminate in bed.* Don't plan or worry about tomorrow in bed (National Sleep Foundation, 2005a). When you lie down, you may organize your thoughts for a few minutes, but then allow yourself to relax or engage in a soothing fantasy. If an important idea comes to you, jot it down on a handy pad so that you don't worry about forgetting it. If thoughts or inspirations persist, however, get up and think about them elsewhere. Let your bed be a place for relaxation and sleep—not your second office. A bed—even a waterbed—should not be a think tank.
- *Establish a regular routine.* Sleeping late can end up causing problems in falling asleep. Set your alarm for the same time each morning and get up, regardless of how long you have slept (Gatchel & Oordt, 2003; National Sleep Foundation, 2005a). By rising at a regular time, you'll encourage yourself to fall asleep at a regular time.

TABLE 5.2 ■ Beliefs That Increase Tension and Alternatives

BELIEFS THAT INCREASE TENSION	ALTERNATIVES
If I don't get to sleep, I'll feel wrecked tomorrow.	Not necessarily. If I'm tired, I can go to bed early tomorrow night.
It's unhealthy for me not to get more sleep.	Not necessarily. Some people do very well on only a few hours of sleep.
I'll wreck my sleeping schedule for the whole week if I don't get to sleep very soon.	Not at all. If I'm tired, I'll just go to bed a bit earlier. I'll get up about the same time with no problem.
If I don't get to sleep, I won't be able to concentrate on that big test/conference tomorrow.	Possibly, but my fears may be exaggerated. I may just as well relax or get up and do something enjoyable for a while.

■ *Try fantasy.* Fantasies tend to occur naturally when we are falling asleep. Allow yourself to "go with" soothing, relaxing fantasies that occur at bedtime, or use pleasant imagery to get to sleep. Fantasize a sun-drenched beach with waves lapping on the shore or a walk through a mountain meadow on a summer day. Construct your own "mind trips" and paint in the details. No passport or credit cards needed.

Above all: Accept the idea that it really doesn't matter if you don't get to sleep early *this night.* You will survive. In fact, you'll do just fine. ■

Narcolepsy   A person with **narcolepsy** suddenly falls asleep. Narcolepsy afflicts as many as 100,000 people in the United States and seems to run in families. The "sleep attack" may last 15 minutes or so, after which the person feels refreshed. Nevertheless, sleep attacks are dangerous and upsetting. They can occur while driving or working with sharp tools. They may be accompanied by the collapse of muscle groups or of the entire body—a condition called *sleep paralysis.* In sleep paralysis, the person cannot move during the transition from consciousness to sleep, and hallucinations (as of a person or object sitting on the chest) occur.

Narcolepsy is thought to be a disorder of REM-sleep functioning. Stimulants and antidepressant drugs have helped many people with the problem (Schwartz, 2004).

Apnea   **Apnea** is a dangerous sleep disorder in which the air passages are obstructed. People with apnea stop breathing periodically, up to several hundred times per night (National Sleep Foundation, 2005b). Obstruction may cause the sleeper to sit up and gasp for air before falling back asleep. People with apnea are stimulated nearly, but not quite, to waking by the buildup of carbon dioxide. Some 10 million Americans have apnea, and it is associated with obesity and chronic snoring (National Sleep Foundation, 2005b). Apnea can lead to high blood pressure, heart attacks, and strokes.

Causes of apnea include anatomical deformities that clog the air passageways, such as a thick palate, and problems in the breathing centers in the brain. Apnea is treated by such measures as weight loss, surgery, and *continuous positive airway pressure,* which is supplied by a mask that provides air pressure that keeps the airway open during sleep.

Deep-Sleep Disorders: Sleep Terrors, Bed-Wetting, and Sleepwalking   Sleep terrors, bed-wetting, and sleepwalking all occur during deep (stage 3 or 4) sleep. They are more common among children and may reflect immaturity of the nervous system (Kataria, 2004). **Sleep terrors** are similar to, but more severe than, nightmares, which occur during REM sleep. Sleep terrors usually occur during the first two sleep cycles of the night, whereas

Narcolepsy A "sleep attack" in which a person falls asleep suddenly and irresistibly.

Apnea Temporary absence or cessation of breathing. (From Greek and Latin roots meaning "without" and "breathing.")

Sleep terrors Frightening dreamlike experiences that occur during the deepest stage of NREM sleep. Nightmares, in contrast, occur during REM sleep.

Self-Assessment

Sleep Quiz—Are You Getting Your Z's?

This Self-Assessment can help you learn whether you are getting enough sleep. Circle the *T* if an item is true or mostly true, or the *F* if an item is false or mostly false for you. Then check the meaning of your answers in Appendix B.

[T] [F] 1. I need an alarm clock in order to wake up at the appropriate time.

[T] [F] 2. It's a struggle for me to get out of bed in the morning.

[T] [F] 3. Weekday mornings I hit the snooze button several times to get more sleep.

[T] [F] 4. I feel tired, irritable, and stressed out during the week.

[T] [F] 5. I have trouble concentrating and remembering.

[T] [F] 6. I feel slow with critical thinking, problem solving, and being creative.

[T] [F] 7. I often fall asleep watching television.

[T] [F] 8. I often fall asleep after heavy meals or after a low dose of alcohol.

[T] [F] 9. I often fall asleep while relaxing after dinner.

[T] [F] 10. I often fall asleep within five minutes of getting into bed.

[T] [F] 11. I often feel drowsy while driving.

[T] [F] 12. I often sleep extra hours on weekend mornings.

[T] [F] 13. I often need a nap to get through the day.

[T] [F] 14. I have dark circles around my eyes.

SOURCE: *Power Sleep* by James Maas (New York: Villard 1998). Copyright 1998 by James B. Maas, Ph.D. Used by permission of Villard Books, a division of Random House, Inc.

Go to www http://academic.cengage.com/psychology/rathus where you can fill out an interactive version of this Self-Assessment and automatically score your results.

■ **Narcolepsy**
In an experiment on narcolepsy, the dog barks, nods its head, and then falls suddenly asleep.

nightmares are more likely to occur toward morning. Experiencing a surge in the heart and respiration rates, the person may suddenly sit up, talk incoherently, and thrash about. He or she is never fully awake, returns to sleep, and may recall a vague image as of someone pressing on his or her chest. (Memories of nightmares tend to be more detailed.) Sleep terrors are often decreased by a minor tranquilizer at bedtime. The drug reduces the amount of time spent in stage 4 sleep.

Bed-wetting most likely reflects immaturity of the nervous system. In most cases it resolves itself before adolescence, often by age 8. Methods that condition children to awaken when they are about to urinate have been helpful (Kainz, 2002; Mellon & McGrath, 2000). The drug imipramine often helps. Sometimes all that is needed is reassurance that no one is to blame for bed-wetting and that most children "outgrow" it.

Perhaps half of children talk in their sleep now and then. Adults occasionally do so, too. Surveys suggest that some 7% to 15% of children walk in their sleep (Neveus et al., 2002). Only 2% of adults do (Ohayon et al., 1999). Sleepwalkers may roam about nightly while their parents fret about accidents that might befall them. Sleepwalkers typically do not remember their excursions, although they may respond to questions while they are up and about. ◁▶ **Truth or Fiction Revisited:** Contrary to myth, there is no evidence that sleepwalkers become violent if they are awakened, although they may be confused and upset. Mild tranquilizers and maturity typically put an end to it.

○ Learning Connections

◀◀ *Sleep and Dreams — Other Worlds Within?* ▶▶

REVIEW:

 3 REM sleep is also referred to as
   (a) deep sleep,
   (b) the hypnagogic state,
   (c) paradoxical sleep,
   (d) stage 3 sleep.

 4 Sleep terrors
   (a) occur during deep sleep,
   (b) are less upsetting than nightmares,
   (c) are caused by problems in breathing,
   (d) are another name for nightmares.

CRITICAL THINKING:
How do you think parents should respond to children's bed-wetting? Explain.

Go www
to
http://academic.cengage.com/psychology/rathus
for an interactive version of this review.

ALTERING CONSCIOUSNESS THROUGH HYPNOSIS, MEDITATION, AND BIOFEEDBACK

Perhaps you have seen films in which Count Dracula hypnotized resistant victims into a stupor. Then he could give them a bite in the neck with no further nonsense. Perhaps you have watched a fellow student try to place a friend in a "trance" after reading a book on hypnosis. Or perhaps you have seen an audience member hypnotized in a nightclub act. If so, chances are the person acted as if he or she had returned to childhood, imagined that a snake was about to have a nip, or lay rigid between two chairs for a while. In this section we deal

AP/Wide World Photos

■ **Hypnosis**

Hypnotized people become passive and follow the suggestions of the hypnotist. Only recently has hypnosis become a respectable subject for psychological inquiry.

with three altered states of consciousness: hypnosis, meditation, and biofeedback. In each of these, we focus on stimuli that are not common parts of our daily lives.

▬■▬ Hypnosis: How Entrancing?

Of these altered states, the one we hear of most is hypnosis. *What is hypnosis?* The word **hypnosis** is derived from the Greek word for sleep. It is an altered state of consciousness in which people are suggestible and behave as though they are in a trance. Modern hypnosis evolves from the ideas of Franz Mesmer in the 18th century. Mesmer asserted that everything in the universe was connected by forms of magnetism—which may not be far from the mark. However, he also claimed that people, too, could be drawn to one another by "animal magnetism." Not so. Mesmer used bizarre props to bring people under his "spell" and managed a respectable cure rate for minor ailments. Scientists now attribute his successes to the placebo effect, not animal magnetism.

Today hypnotism is more than a nightclub act. It is also used as an anesthetic in dentistry, childbirth, and medical procedures (Patterson, 2004; Shenefelt, 2003). Some psychologists use hypnosis to help clients reduce anxiety, overcome fears, or lessen the perception of chronic pain (Jensen et al., 2005; Pinnell & Covino, 2000). A study with 241 surgery patients shows how hypnosis can help people deal with pain and anxiety. The patients had procedures with local anesthetics (Lang et al., 2000). They could use as much pain medication as they wished. Patients who were hypnotized needed less additional pain medication and experienced less anxiety as measured by blood pressure and heart rate. The hypnotized patients focused on pleasant imagery rather than the surgery. Hypnosis helps people relax to cope with stress and enhance the functioning of their immune systems (Kiecolt-Glaser et al., 2001). Hypnosis can also be useful in helping people control their weight and stop smoking (Lynn et al., 2003). Some police departments use hypnosis to prompt the memories of witnesses.

The state of consciousness called the *hypnotic trance* has traditionally been induced by asking people to narrow their attention to a small light, a spot on the wall, an object held by the hypnotist, or the hypnotist's voice. The hypnotist usually suggests that the person's limbs are becoming warm, heavy, and relaxed. People may also be told that they are becoming sleepy or falling asleep. But hypnosis is *not* sleep, as shown by differences between EEG recordings for the hypnotic trance and the stages of sleep. But subjects understand that the word *sleep* suggests a hypnotic trance. Researchers are also studying changes in the brain that result from hypnotic induction. For example, Rainville and his colleagues (2002) used PET scans on people being hypnotized and found that mental absorption and mental relaxation are associated with changes in blood flow in the cerebral cortex (absorption) and parts of the brain involved in arousal and attention (relaxation).

People who are easily hypnotized are said to have *hypnotic suggestibility*. Part of "suggestibility" is knowledge of what is expected during the "trance state." Generally speaking, suggestible people are prone to fantasy and want to cooperate with the hypnotist (Barber, 2000). As a result, they pay close attention to the instructions. ◆▷ **Truth or Fiction Revisited:** It is therefore extremely unlikely that someone could be hypnotized against his or her will (Barber, 2000). Hypnotists and people who have been hypnotized report that hypnosis can bring about the changes shown in Table 5.3.

Hypnosis A condition in which people are highly suggestible and behave as though they are in a trance.

Explaining Hypnosis   Hypnotism is no longer explained in terms of animal magnetism, but psychodynamic and learning theorists have offered explanations. According to Freud, hypnotized adults permit themselves to return to childish modes of responding that emphasize fantasy and impulse rather than fact and logic. Modern views of hypnosis are quite different. *How do psychologists explain the effects of hypnosis?*

TABLE 5.3 ■ Changes in Consciousness Attributed to Hypnosis*

CHANGE	COMMENTS
Passivity	Awaiting instructions, suspending planning.
Narrowed attention	Focusing on the hypnotist's instructions, not attending to background noise or intruding thoughts.
Pseudomemories and hypermnesia	Reporting pseudomemories (false memories) or highly detailed memories (hypermnesia).
Suggestibility	Responding to suggestions that an arm is becoming lighter and will rise, or that the eyelids are becoming heavier and must close.
Playing unusual roles	In *age regression,* people may play themselves as infants or children. A person may speak a language forgotten since childhood.
Perceptual distortions	Acting as though hypnotically induced hallucinations and delusions are real. Behaving as if one cannot hear loud noises, smell odors, or feel pain.
Posthypnotic amnesia	Acting as though one cannot recall events that take place under hypnosis.
Posthypnotic suggestion	Following commands given while hypnotized after one "awakens," such as falling back into a trance when given the command "Sleep!" or—in the case of a would-be quitter— finding cigarette smoke aversive.

SOURCES: Barber, 2000; Green & Lynn, 2000; Lancaster et al., 2000; Patterson, 2004; Woody & Szechtman, 2000.

*Research evidence in support of these changes in consciousness is mixed.

Theodore Sarbin offers a **role theory** view of hypnosis (Sarbin & Coe, 1972). He points out that the changes in behavior attributed to the hypnotic trance can be successfully imitated when people are instructed to behave *as though* they were hypnotized. For example, people can lie rigid between two chairs whether they are hypnotized or not. Also, people cannot be hypnotized unless they are familiar with the hypnotic "role"—the behavior that constitutes the trance. Sarbin is not saying that subjects *fake* the hypnotic role. Instead, Sarbin is suggesting that people *allow* themselves to enact this role under the hypnotist's directions.

The **response set theory** of hypnosis is related to role theory. It suggests that expectations play a role in the production of experiences suggested by the hypnotist (Kirsch, 2000). A positive response to each suggestion of the hypnotist sets the stage—creates a *response set*—in which the subject is more likely to follow further suggestions (Barrios, 2001).

Role theory and response set theory appear to be supported by research evidence that "suggestible" people want to be hypnotized, are good role players, have vivid imaginations, and know what is expected of them (Barber, 2000; Kirsch, 2000). The fact that the behaviors shown by hypnotized people can be mimicked by people who know what is expected of them means that we need not resort to the concept of the "hypnotic trance"—an unusual and mystifying altered state of awareness—to explain hypnotic events.

reflect & relate

Has anybody tried to hypnotize you or someone you know? How did he or she do it? What were the results? How do the results fit with the theories of hypnosis discussed here?

Role theory A theory that explains hypnotic events in terms of the person's ability to act *as though* he or she were hypnotized.

Response set theory The view that response expectancies play a key role in the production of the experiences suggested by the hypnotist.

Let us now consider two other altered states of consciousness that involve different ways of focusing our attention: meditation and biofeedback.

◼ Meditation: The World Fades Away

What is meditation? The dictionary defines *meditation* as the act or process of thinking. But the concept usually suggests thinking deeply about the universe or about one's place in the world, often within a spiritual context. As the term is commonly used by psychologists, however, meditation refers to various ways of focusing one's consciousness to alter one's relationship to the world. In thus use, ironically, *meditation* can also refer to a process by which people seem to suspend thinking and allow the world to fade away.

The kinds of meditation that psychologists speak of are *not* the first definitions you find in the dictionary. Rather, the kinds psychologists speak of tend to refer to rituals, exercises, even passive observation—activities that alter the normal relationship between the person and the environment. They are methods of suspending problem solving, planning, worries, and awareness of the events of the day. These methods alter consciousness—the normal focus of attention—and help people cope with stress by inducing feelings of relaxation.

One common form of meditation, **transcendental meditation (TM),** was brought to the United States by the Maharishi Mahesh Yogi in 1959. People practice TM by concentrating on *mantras*—words or sounds that are claimed to help the person achieve an altered state of consciousness. TM has some goals that cannot be assessed scientifically, such as expanding consciousness to encompass spiritual experiences, but there are also measurable goals, such as reducing anxiety and blood pressure. For example, Herbert Benson (1975) found that TM lowered the heart and respiration rates and also produced what he labeled a *relaxation response.* The blood pressure of people with hypertension—a risk factor in cardiovascular disease—decreased.

A research program at the College of Maharishi Vedic Medicine in Fairfield, Iowa, has focused on older African Americans, a group prone to hypertension (Ready, 2000). Two studies compared the effects of TM, muscle relaxation, and a "health education" placebo on high blood pressure (Alexander et al., 1996; Schneider et al., 1995). They found that TM was significantly more effective at reducing high blood pressure than relaxation or the placebo. A third study reported that TM practiced by African American adults for several months was significantly more likely than the health education placebo to slow hardening of the arteries (Castillo-Richmond et al., 2000).

Psychologist Jon Kabat-Zinn, founder of the Stress Reduction Clinic at the University of Massachusetts Medical Center, has promoted the use of **mindfulness meditation (MM)** in cognitive and behavior therapy. MM, as opposed to TM, makes no pretense of achieving spiritual goals. Instead, MM provides clients with mantra-like techniques they can use to focus on the present moment rather than ruminate about problems (Heidenreich & Michalak, 2003; Salmon et al., 2004). MM holds promise for helping clients cope with problems such as depression as well as reducing stress (Ramel et al., 2004). Brain imaging also shows that meditation activates neural structures involved in attention and in control of the autonomic nervous system, helping produce feelings of relaxation (Lazar et al., 2000).

◼ Biofeedback: In Touch with the Untouchable

Psychologist Neal E. Miller (1909–2002) trained laboratory rats to increase or decrease their heart rates. How? His procedure was simple but ingenious. As discovered by James Olds and Peter Milner (1954), there is a "pleasure center" in the rat's hypothalamus. A small burst of electricity in this center is strongly reinforcing: Rats learn to do what they can, such as pressing a lever, to obtain this "reward."

Miller (1969) implanted electrodes in the rats' pleasure centers. Some rats were then given a burst of electricity whenever their heart rate happened to increase. Other rats received the burst when their heart rate went lower. In other words, one group of rats was

◼ Meditation

People use many forms of meditation to try to expand their inner awareness and experience inner harmony. Although practitioners of some forms of meditation claim that it has spiritual effects, research does suggest that meditation can have healthful effects on the blood pressure and other health-related bodily functions.

Mika/Zefa/Corbis

Transcendental meditation (TM) The simplified form of meditation brought to the United States by the Maharishi Mahesh Yogi and used as a method for coping with stress.

Mindfulness meditation (MM) A form of meditation that provides clients with techniques they can use to focus on the present moment rather than ruminate about problems.

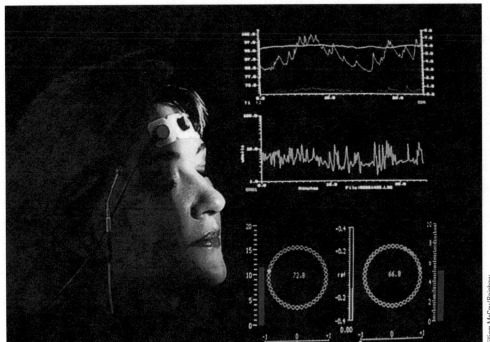

■ **Biofeedback**
Biofeedback is a system that provides, or "feeds back," information about a bodily function to an organism. Through biofeedback training, people have learned to gain voluntary control over a number of functions that are normally automatic, such as heart rate and blood pressure.

"rewarded" when their heart rate increased; the other, when their heart rate decreased. After a 90-minute training session, the rats learned to alter their heart rates by as much as 20% in the direction for which they had been rewarded. ◆▶ **Truth or Fiction Revisited**: It is true that you can teach a rat to raise or lower its heart rate.

Miller's research was an example of **biofeedback training (BFT)**. *What is biofeedback training?* Biofeedback is a system that provides, or "feeds back," information about a bodily function. Miller used electrical stimulation of the brain to feed back information to rats when they had engaged in a targeted bodily response—in this case, raised or lowered their heart rates. Somehow the rats used this feedback to raise or lower their heart rates voluntarily.

Similarly, people have learned to change some bodily functions voluntarily, including heart rate, that were once considered beyond conscious control. Electrodes are not implanted in people's brains. Rather, people hear a "blip" or receive some other signal that informs them when they are showing the targeted response.

How is biofeedback training used? BFT is used in many ways, including helping people combat stress, tension, and anxiety. For example, people can learn to emit alpha waves through EEG feedback and feel more relaxed. A blip may blink faster whenever alpha waves are being emitted. The psychologist's asks the person to "make the blip go faster." An **electromyograph (EMG)** monitors muscle tension. The EMG is also used to help people become more aware of muscle tension in the forehead, fingers, and elsewhere and to learn to lower the tension (Martin, 2002). Through the use of other instruments, people have learned to lower their heart rate, blood pressure, and sweating (Nagourney, 2002). All of these changes are relaxing. Biofeedback is widely used by sports psychologists to teach athletes how to relax muscle groups that are unessential to the task at hand so that the athletes can control anxiety and tension.

Sleep, hypnosis, meditation, and biofeedback training all involve ways of focusing our consciousness or allowing it to wander. Another way of focusing our consciousness, familiar to millions of Americans, involves going with the world online.

Biofeedback training (BFT) The systematic feeding back to an organism information about a bodily function so that the organism can gain control of that function.

Electromyograph (EMG) An instrument that measures muscle tension.

( ) Learning Connections

◀◀ *Altering Consciousness Through Hypnosis, Meditation,*
    and Biofeedback ▶▶

REVIEW:

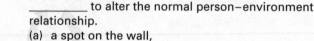

5 According to _____ theory, knowledge of what
   one is expected to do is a key component of being
   hypnotized.
   (a) response set,
   (b) mental,
   (c) magnetic,
   (d) psychoanalytic.

6 In meditation, one focuses "passively" on
   _____ to alter the normal person–environment
   relationship.
   (a) a spot on the wall,
   (b) a song,
   (c) instructions in a booklet,
   (d) a mantra.

CRITICAL THINKING:
Is it possible to explain the behavior of the rats in Miller's research on
biofeedback by referring to what the animals were "thinking" when
they learned to increase or decrease their heart rates? Explain.

Go
to
http://academic.cengage.com/psychology/rathus
for an interactive version of this review.

ALTERING CONSCIOUSNESS BY CONNECTING WITH THE INTERNET

Going online, like hypnosis, biofeedback, and meditation, alters the normal relationship between the person and the environment. Psychologist John Suler (2005), like many others, refers to the online realm as *cyberspace.* Cyberspace, he notes, is a psychological space, one with unique psychological features. Going online alters one's sensory experiences, allows one to go beyond his or her spatial boundaries—to casinos, stores, chat rooms, business meetings, and the like, allows one to hide or change his or her identity, to develop and access numerous relationships simultaneously, and to "save" his or her experiences. There is also a "disinhibition effect"; people say and do things in the virtual world that they would not do in the real world. "As a virtual reality," writes Suler, the virtual world "stretches across a wide range from the simulated true-to-life experiences of webcams to the highly imaginative environments of avatar communities." ◀ **Truth or Fiction Revisited: Avatars** are virtual bodies you "wear." You can use them to merge with your character in a video game or to chat with others. Perhaps you will not be surprised that people tend to choose avatars that are more powerful or attractive than they are (Lee & Shin, 2004; Rique, 2004).

Cyberspace is akin to an altered state of consciousness. It is a dreamlike world that enables people to experience reality and themselves from a different perspective. Cyberspace becomes an extension of one's consciousness.

By going online, you can access the great works of art and the great museums. You can observe busy highways through webcams 6,000 miles away. You can explore resources that you can use to write papers and learn more about academic topics, reference libraries (e.g., encyclopedias, thesauri), and the like. This virtual library makes visiting the real library optional for most students (see Table 5.4). You can play games that millions of other people join in. You also have the opportunity to interact with other students or new acquaintances in forums or chat rooms. Changing your sex in the real world requires hormone treatments and surgery. In the virtual world, you need only lie about your sex.

Avatar An image representing a user in a multi-user virtual reality space.

The Concept of "Flow": Another Altered State?

"Going with the flow" is more than just a saying. **Flow** is defined as the riveting of attention so that one becomes wrapped up in what she or he is doing and may lose track of time. If you're carrying out assignments or writing a paper, flow is a good thing. But flow is also one of the factors that keeps people returning to cyberspace. The word *flow* is used to refer to an altered state of consciousness that people may experience when they are deeply involved in a pleasant activity (Pace, 2004). Flow is likely to develop when people are experiencing challenges—such as those involved in video games or making online stock trades—and mastering them. Flow can lessen self-awareness and become motivating for its own sake. Many people want to continue to go with the flow, whether it involves communicating, playing games, exploring, gambling, even shopping (Koufaris, 2002; Waterman et al., 2003).

Some online game players adopt the virtual world as a key part of their lives (Whang & Chang, 2004). Millions of people, for example, spend hours each day playing the online game *Lineage*. Their lifestyle in cyberspace assumes great importance. Can the quest for flow be addictive?

■ **Visiting the Virtual World**

Going online has so many appeals: a sense of power, community, aesthetic experience, shaping of one's virtual identity, diversion from problems in the real world, shopping, gambling, stock trading, game playing . . . and on and on. Is it any wonder that some people find themselves spending more and more time online, to the detriment of their responsibilities and relationships in the real world?

Internet Addiction

When we are speaking about being addicted to drugs, we are referring to bodily changes that make having the drug within one's system the normal state of affairs. The concept of **Internet addiction** refers to a self-defeating behavior pattern in which one is preoccupied with going online to the extent that it disrupts one's functioning in the real world (Suler, 2004). As with drug addiction, people who are "addicted" to the Internet may perceive it as an extremely important part of their lives, use it excessively, experience lack of control over going online, and neglect their studies or work and their flesh-and-blood social lives (Widyanto & McMurran, 2004).

Some Internet addictions involve gaming and competition (Suler, 2004). Others fulfill social needs. Loneliness and boredom in the real world seem to increase the risk that

reflect & relate

How often do you go online? For what purposes? Are you at all concerned about the amount of time you spend online? Explain.

TABLE 5.4 ■ College Students Online

- Nearly 9 out of 10 college students have gone online at one time or another.
- Nearly 3 out of 4 college students check their email at least once a day.
- About 3 out of 5 college students have downloaded music files from the Internet.
- College Internet users are about twice as likely to "IM"—that is, use instant messaging—as other Internet users.
- About 4 out of 5 college students say that the Internet has had a positive influence on their college academic experience. The Internet is more than a medium for entertainment.
- Nearly half of college students say that email has enabled them to communicate things to a professor that they would not have been able to say in person, either in class, or even privately. Email allows you to keep a safe psychological distance.
- About 3 out of 4 college students agree that they do research more frequently on the Internet than at the library. Only about 1 student in 10 uses the library more often than the Internet.
- About half of college students have been required to share information with other students in their classes via the Internet.
- More than 2 out of 3 college students subscribe to at least one mailing list to carry on email discussions about topics brought up in class.
- Nearly half of students say they use the Internet most often to communicate socially.

SOURCE: Jones et al., 2002.

Flow An altered state of consciousness that people may experience when deeply involved in an enjoyable activity.

Internet addiction A self-defeating behavior pattern in which one is preoccupied with going online to the extent that it disrupts one's functioning in the real world.

one might become trapped online (Chak & Leung, 2004; Morahan-Martin & Schumacher, 2003; Nichols & Nicki, 2004). Other forms of Internet gratification include belonging to a virtual community, aesthetic experience, diversion from problems in the real world, and the status gained by adding some fictional assets to one's true identity (Song et al., 2004).

The nearby self-assessment will afford you insight as to whether you may be "addicted" to the Internet. If you are concerned about your responses to the self-assessment, the Life Connections section on "Handling Addiction to the Internet" may be of use.

Self-Assessment

Are You "Addicted" to the Internet?

Some people have difficulty controlling the amount of time they spend online. Some are emailing or IMing nearly everyone they know. Some of them are hopping from news item to news item. Some of them are surfing for the best prices on CDs, airline fares, whatever. Some are into "cybersex." Unfortunately, the time spent detracts from the completion of college assignments.

Are you concerned about the amount of time you spend online, or the nature of the websites you are visiting? Respond to the following items by circling the *T* if an item is true or mostly true for you or the *F* if an item is false or mostly false for you. Then check the answer key in Appendix B.

T F 1. I find myself needing to spend more time online to enjoy it as much.

T F 2. I feel uptight, depressed, or nervous when I can't go online.

T F 3. I find myself spending more time online than I planned to do.

T F 4. I take great pride in the Internet navigational skills I have acquired.

T F 5. I have a desire to cut down or control the amount of time I am spending online.

T F 6. The truth is I'd rather email or IM most people rather than talk to them on the phone or see them in person.

T F 7. I find myself impatient for others to leave so I can go online.

T F 8. After I have gone online, I carefully delete my online history and unwanted temporary Internet files.

T F 9. I would rather shop online than go to a "bricks and mortar" store.

T F 10. I am a completely different person when I am online.

T F 11. I sometimes experience a feeling of great satisfaction when I use my user name and my password to log in to a website.

T F 12. I spend a good deal of time in activities directed toward going online.

T F 13. I have lost track of time when I go online.

T F 14. Shopping online sometimes gives me a sense of power.

T F 15. The fact is that I have reduced social, educational, or recreational activities so that I could spend more time online.

T F 16. The truth is that I have continued to spend a great deal of time online despite evidence of persistent or recurrent emotional or social problems caused or exacerbated by its use.

T F 17. I sometimes feel that my virtual community is more important to me than my flesh-and-blood community.

T F 18. Spending the same amount of time online is less satisfying than it was.

T F 19. The challenges of finding new things and going new places on the Internet excite me as much as a real outing or trip.

T F 20. Going online for long periods of time has become a habit.

T F 21. I find myself hiding or lying about the amount of time I spend online or the nature of the websites I visit.

T F 22. When I'm online, I sometimes feel as though I'm connected with the computer or the Internet in a way that is hard to put into words.

T F 23. When I cannot find a way to go online, I feel a great sense of loss.

T F 24. I find myself unable to exercise self-control over how much time I spend online.

Go to www http://academic.cengage.com/psychology/rathus where you can fill out an interactive version of this Self-Assessment and automatically score your results.

Life Connections
Handling Addiction to the Internet

Some students are concerned that they go online too often, or spend too much time online, or that the urge to go online is too strong. Here are some suggestions about things you can do if you are concerned that you have become "addicted" to the Internet:

- Give yourself strict limits on the amount of time you allow yourself to spend online for recreational use. Reward yourself for sticking to the limit by putting some money toward something you really want—like a camera or an iPod. Punish yourself for going over the limit by taking money out of the fund.
- Shut your computer off (don't just put it on standby) after you have spent your allotted amount of time online, or finished with your legitimate purposes. Then you will have to go through rebooting your computer before you can use it to go online again.
- Do something else rather than going online or visiting a website that consumes too much time or encourages you to waste money. Read a book, go for a walk, check your assignments, or chat (offline!) with a friend.
- Go online only in a public place, so that you're reluctant to visit "adult" websites. For example, use the library or the student center or the cafeteria.
- Spend time you would have spent at adult websites in developing interpersonal relationships. ■

◌ Learning Connections

◀◀   *Altering Consciousness by Connecting with the Internet*   ▶▶

REVIEW:

7 The altered state of consciousness that people may experience when they are deeply involved in a pleasant activity is termed
   (a) browsing,
   (b) surfing,
   (c) biofeedback,
   (d) flow.

8 According to the text, Internet addiction refers to
   (a) doing research online rather than in the library,
   (b) emailing for more than an hour a day,
   (c) a self-defeating behavior pattern,
   (d) gambling online.

CRITICAL THINKING:
Which uses of the Internet do you consider to be positive? Which do you consider to be negative? Explain.

Go to WWW
http://academic.cengage.com/psychology/rathus
for an interactive version of this review.

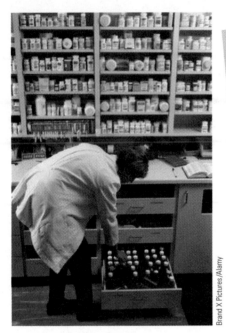

Brand X Pictures/Alamy

■ The Deluge of Drugs
The lives of many Americans are flooded with drugs—licit and illicit. People use drugs to get going in the morning, to get to sleep at night, and to feel better about themselves and other people in between. When does substance use become substance abuse? When does substance abuse become substance dependence? Why do so many deceive themselves about the nature of their use of drugs?

Depressant A drug that lowers the rate of activity of the nervous system.

Stimulant A drug that increases activity of the nervous system.

Substance abuse Persistent use of a substance even though it is causing or compounding problems in meeting the demands of life.

Substance dependence Loss of control over use of a substance. Biologically speaking, dependence is typified by tolerance, withdrawal symptoms, or both.

Tolerance Habituation to a drug, with the result that increasingly higher doses of the drug are needed to achieve similar effects.

Withdrawal symptoms A characteristic cluster of symptoms that results from sudden decrease in an addictive drug's level of usage.

ALTERING CONSCIOUSNESS THROUGH DRUGS

The world is a supermarket of drugs. The United States is flooded with drugs that distort perceptions and change mood—drugs that take you up, let you down, and move you across town. Some of these drugs are legal, others illegal. Some are used recreationally, others medically. Some are safe if used correctly and dangerous if they are not. Some people use drugs because their friends do or because their parents tell them not to. Some are seeking pleasure; others are seeking inner truth or escape.

Young people often become involved with drugs that impair their ability to learn at school and are connected with reckless behavior (Wills et al., 2002). Alcohol is the most popular drug on high school and college campuses (Johnston et al., 2003). More than 40% of college students have tried marijuana, and 1 in 6 or 7 smokes it regularly (Johnston et al., 2003). Many Americans take **depressants** to get to sleep at night and **stimulants** to get going in the morning. Cocaine was once a toy of the well-to-do, but price breaks have brought it into the lockers of high school students.

Substance Abuse and Dependence: Crossing the Line

Where does drug use end and abuse begin? *What are substance abuse and dependence?* The American Psychiatric Association (2000) defines **substance abuse** as repeated use of a substance despite the fact that it is causing or compounding social, occupational, psychological, or physical problems. If you are missing school or work because you are drunk or "sleeping it off," you are abusing alcohol. The amount you drink is not as crucial as the fact that your pattern of use disrupts your life.[1]

Substance dependence is more severe than substance abuse and has behavioral and biological aspects (American Psychiatric Association, 2000). Behaviorally, dependence is characterized by loss of control over use of the substance. Dependent people may organize their lives around getting and using a substance. Biological or physiological dependence is typified by tolerance, withdrawal symptoms, or both. **Tolerance** is the body's habituation to a substance so that, with regular usage, higher doses are needed to achieve similar effects. There are **withdrawal symptoms** when the level of usage suddenly drops off. Withdrawal symptoms for alcohol include anxiety, tremors, restlessness, rapid pulse, and high blood pressure.

When doing without a drug, people who are *psychologically* dependent show signs of anxiety such as shakiness, rapid pulse, and sweating that may be similar to withdrawal symptoms. Because of these signs, they may believe that they are physiologically dependent on—or addicted to—a drug when they are psychologically dependent. But symptoms of withdrawal from some drugs are unmistakably physiological. One is delirium tremens ("the DTs"), experienced by some chronic alcoholics when they suddenly lower their intake of alcohol. People with DTs have heavy sweating, restlessness, disorientation, and frightening hallucinations—often of crawling animals.

Causal Factors in Substance Abuse and Dependence   *What are the causes of substance abuse and dependence?* Substance abuse and dependence usually begin with experimental use in adolescence (Chassin et al., 2000; Lewinsohn et al., 2000a). People experiment with drugs for various reasons, including curiosity, conformity to peer pressure, parental use, rebelliousness, escape from boredom or pressure, and excitement or pleasure (Griffin et al., 2004; Wilkinson & Abraham, 2004; Zand et al., 2004). Let us have a look at some theories of substance abuse.

---

[1] By this definition, one might label a self-defeating preoccupation with the Internet to be "Internet abuse," rather than "Internet addiction."

Social–cognitive theorists suggest that people often try alcohol and tranquilizers such as Valium (the generic name is diazepam) on the basis of a recommendation or observation of others. Expectations about the effects of a substance predict its use (Cumsille et al., 2000).

Use of a substance may be reinforced by peers or by the drug's positive effects on mood and its reduction of anxiety, fear, and stress (Griffin et al., 2004; Wills et al., 2002). Many people use drugs as a form of self-medication for anxiety and depression, even low self-esteem (Beitchman et al., 2001; Dierker et al., 2001). For people who are physiologically dependent, avoidance of withdrawal symptoms is also reinforcing. Carrying a supply of the substance is reinforcing because one need not worry about going without it. Parents who use drugs may increase their children's knowledge of drugs. They also, in effect, show their children when to use them—for example, by drinking alcohol to cope with tension or to lessen the anxiety associated with meeting people at parties and other get-togethers (Fournier et al., 2004; Power et al., 2005).

Certain people apparently have a genetic predisposition toward physiological dependence on certain substances, such as alcohol, opioids, cocaine, and nicotine (Chen et al., 2004; Kalivas, 2003; Nurnberger et al., 2004; Radel et al., 2005; Wall et al., 2003). The biological children of alcoholics who are reared by adoptive parents are more likely to develop alcohol-related problems than the biological children of the adoptive parents. An inherited tendency toward alcoholism may involve greater sensitivity to alcohol (that is, greater enjoyment of it) and greater tolerance (Pihl et al., 1990; Schuckit et al., 2001). Greater tolerance is shown by studies in which college students with alcoholic parents show better muscular control and visual–motor coordination when they drink than other college students do (Pihl et al., 1990). People with a family history of alcoholism are also more sensitive to the stimulating effects of alcohol, which occur at lower levels of intoxication (Conrad et al., 2001).

Now that we have learned about substance abuse and dependence, let us turn to a discussion of the different kinds of psychoactive drugs. Some are depressants, others stimulants, and still others hallucinogens. Let us consider the effects of these drugs on consciousness, beginning with depressants.

Depressants

Depressants generally act by slowing the activity of the central nervous system. There are also effects specific to each depressant. In this section we consider the effects of alcohol, opiates, and barbiturates.

Alcohol—The Swiss Army Knife of Psychoactive Substances   No drug has meant so much to so many as alcohol. Alcohol is our dinnertime relaxant, our bedtime sedative, our cocktail-party social facilitator. We use alcohol to celebrate holy days, applaud our accomplishments, and express joyous wishes. The young assert their maturity with alcohol. Alcohol is used at least occasionally by the majority of high school and college students (Johnston et al., 2003; Wilgoren, 2000). Alcohol even kills germs on surface wounds.

People use alcohol like a Swiss Army knife. It does it all. It is the all-purpose medicine you can buy without prescription. It is the relief from anxiety, depression, or loneliness that you can swallow in public without criticism or stigma (Bonin et al., 2000; Swendsen et al., 2000). A man who takes a Valium tablet may look weak. It is "macho" to down a bottle of beer.

But the army knife also has a sharp blade. No drug has been so abused as alcohol. Ten million to 20 million Americans are alcoholics. In contrast, 750,000 to 1 million use heroin regularly, and about 800,000 use cocaine regularly (O'Brien, 1996). Excessive drinking has been linked to lower productivity, loss of employment, and downward movement in social status. Yet, half of all Americans use alcohol regularly.

About four college students die *each day* from alcohol-related causes (Hingson et al., 2002). Binge drinking—having five or more drinks in a row for a male, or four or more for a female (Naimi et al., 2003b)—is connected with aggressive behavior, poor grades, sexual promiscuity, and accidents (Abbey et al., 2001; Vik et al., 2000; Zand et al., 2004). Nevertheless, 44% of college students binge at least twice a month (Hingson et al., 2002). The media pay more attention to deaths due to heroin and cocaine overdoses, but more college students die each year from causes related to drinking, including accidents and overdoses (Hingson et al., 2002; Li et al., 2001). Alcohol is the drug of choice on campus.

What are the effects of alcohol? The effects of alcohol vary with the dose and duration of use. Low doses may be stimulating because alcohol dilates blood vessels, which ferry sugar through the body. Higher doses have a sedative effect, which is why alcohol is classified as a depressant. Alcohol relaxes people and deadens minor aches and pains. Alcohol also intoxicates: It impairs cognitive functioning, slurs the speech, and impairs coordination.

Alcohol lowers inhibitions. Drinkers may do things they would not do if they were sober, such as having unprotected sex (Cooper, 2002; MacDonald et al., 2000; Vik et al., 2000). Why? Perhaps alcohol impairs the thought processes needed to inhibit impulses (Steele & Josephs, 1990). When drunk, people may be less able to foresee the consequences of their behavior. They may also be less likely to summon up their moral beliefs. Then, too, alcohol induces feelings of elation and euphoria that may wash away doubts. Alcohol is also associated with a liberated social role in our culture. Drinkers may place the blame on alcohol ("It's the alcohol, not me"), even though they choose to drink.

Adolescent drinking has been repeatedly linked to poor school grades (Wills et al., 2002). Drinking can, of course, contribute to poor grades, but adolescents may drink to reduce academic stress.

Men are more likely than women to become alcoholics. Why? A cultural explanation is that tighter social constraints are usually placed on women. A biological explanation is that alcohol hits women harder, discouraging them from overindulging. Alcohol "goes to women's heads" faster than to men's, because women metabolize less of it in the stomach (Lieber, 1990). Alcohol reaches women's bloodstreams and brains relatively intact. Asians and Asian Americans are less likely than Europeans and European Americans to drink to excess because they are more likely to show a "flushing response" to alcohol, as evidenced by redness of the face, rapid heart rate, dizziness, and headaches (Fromme et al., 2004; Luczak et al., 2002).

Regardless of how or why one starts drinking, regular drinking can lead to physiological dependence. People are then motivated to drink to avoid withdrawal symptoms. Still, even when alcoholics have "dried out"—withdrawn from alcohol—many return to drinking. Perhaps they still want to use alcohol as a way of coping with stress or as an excuse for failure.

Opiates   **Opiates** are a group of **narcotics** derived from the opium poppy, from which they obtain their name. The ancient Sumerians gave the opium poppy its name: It means "plant of joy." **Opioids** are similar in chemical structure but made in a laboratory. Opiates include morphine, heroin, codeine, Demerol, and similar drugs. *What are the effects of opiates?* The major medical application of opiates is relief from pain.

Heroin can provide a strong euphoric "rush." Users claim that it is so pleasurable it can eradicate thoughts of food or sex. High doses can cause drowsiness and stupor, alter time perception, and impair judgment. With regular use of opiates, the brain stops producing neurotransmitters that are chemically similar to opiates—the pain-relieving endorphins. As a result, people can become physiologically dependent on opiates, such that going without them can be agonizing. Withdrawal syndromes may begin with flu-like symptoms and progress through tremors, cramps, chills alternating with sweating, rapid pulse, high blood pressure, insomnia, vomiting, and diarrhea. This information seems to have gotten through to high school students; most disapprove of using heroin (Johnston et al., 2003).

◆ **Truth or Fiction Revisited:** Ironically, heroin was in fact once used as a cure for addiction to morphine. Now we have methadone, a humanmade opioid that is used to treat physiological dependence on heroin. Methadone is slower acting than heroin and does not provide the thrilling rush, but it does prevent withdrawal symptoms (Fiellin et al., 2001).

Barbiturates   *What are the effects of barbiturates?* **Barbiturates** like Nembutal and Seconal are depressants with several medical uses, including relief from anxiety, tension,

The next time you are at a social occasion, note the behavior of people who are drinking and those who are not. What do you think are individuals' motives for drinking? Does drinking visibly affect their behavior? If you drink, how does it affect your behavior?

AP/Wide World Photos

■ **Why Does Alcohol Affect Women More Quickly Than Men?**
Alcohol "goes to women's heads" more quickly, even when researchers control for body weight.

Opiates A group of narcotics derived from the opium poppy that provide a euphoric rush and depress the nervous system.

Narcotics Drugs used to relieve pain and induce sleep. The term is usually reserved for opiates.

Opioids Chemicals that act on opiate receptors but are not derived from the opium poppy.

Barbiturate An addictive depressant used to relieve anxiety or induce sleep.

Life Connections
Is a Drink a Day Good for You?

The effects of alcohol on health are complex. Light drinking can be beneficial. Having a drink or two a day increases levels of high-density lipoprotein (HDL, or "good" cholesterol) in the bloodstream, decreasing the risk of cardiovascular disorders (Mukamal et al., 2001). Another positive effect is cognitive: Studies of older adults find that those who had been having a drink a day are less likely to see their cognitive abilities decline with age (Cervilla et al., 2000; Stampfer et al., 2005). A drink or two a day may even cut the risk of Alzheimer's disease (Norton, 2000). The path to positive cognitive results from alcohol may be through the heart: Small doses of alcohol may help maintain a healthful flow of oxygen-laden blood to the brain. ◆ **Truth or Fiction Revisited**: Therefore, a drink a day is apparently good for you. Most health professionals, however, do not advise that people drink regularly, though lightly, for fear they may run into problems with self-control. The positive effects of alcohol disappear in heavy drinkers (Cervilla et al., 2000).

Now, the negative. As a food, alcohol is fattening. Even so, chronic drinkers may be malnourished. Although alcohol is high in calories, it does not contain vitamins and proteins. Chronic drinking can lead to health problems caused by protein deficiency and vitamin B deficiency. Chronic heavy drinking has been linked to cardiovascular disorders and cancer. In particular, heavy drinking places women at risk for breast cancer (American Cancer Society, 2005; Singletary & Gapstur, 2001). Drinking by a pregnant woman may harm the embryo. ■

and pain, and treatment of epilepsy, high blood pressure, and insomnia. With regular use, barbiturates lead rapidly to physiological and psychological dependence. Physicians therefore provide them with caution.

Barbiturates are popular as street drugs because they are relaxing and produce mild euphoria. High doses result in drowsiness, motor impairment, slurred speech, irritability, and poor judgment. A highly physiologically dependent person who is withdrawn abruptly from barbiturates may experience convulsions and die. Because of additive effects, it is dangerous to mix alcohol and other depressants.

Stimulants

Stimulants increase the activity of the nervous system. Some of their effects can be positive. For example, amphetamines stimulate cognitive activity and apparently help people control impulses (Feola et al., 2000; de Wit et al., 2000). Some stimulants are appealing as street drugs because they contribute to feelings of euphoria and self-confidence. But they also have their risks. In this section we discuss amphetamines, cocaine, and nicotine.

Amphetamines and Related Stimulants   *What are the effects of amphetamines?*
Amphetamines were first used by soldiers during World War II to help them stay alert at night. Truck drivers also use them to drive through the night. Students use amphetamines for all-night cram sessions. Dieters use them because they reduce hunger.

Amphetamines are often abused for the euphoric rush high doses can produce. Some people swallow amphetamines in pill form or inject liquid Methedrine, the strongest form, into their veins. As a result, they may stay awake and high for days on end. But such highs must end. People who have been on prolonged highs sometimes "crash," or fall into a deep sleep or depression. Some commit suicide when crashing.

◆ **Truth or Fiction Revisited:** It is true that many health professionals calm hyperactive children by giving them a stimulant—the stimulant methylphenidate (Ritalin). Although

Amphetamines Stimulants derived from *alpha-methyl-beta-phenyl-ethyl-amine,* a colorless liquid consisting of carbon, hydrogen, and nitrogen.

some critics believe that Ritalin is prescribed too freely, Ritalin has been shown to increase the attention span, decrease aggressive and disruptive behavior, and lead to academic gains (Evans et al., 2001; Pelham et al., 2002). Why should Ritalin, a stimulant, calm children? Hyperactivity may be connected with immaturity of the cerebral cortex, and Ritalin may stimulate the cortex to exercise control over more primitive parts of the brain.

Tolerance for amphetamines develops quickly, and users can become dependent on them, especially when they use them to self-medicate themselves for depression. Whether amphetamines cause physical addiction has been a subject of controversy (Volkow et al., 2001a, 2001b). High doses can cause restlessness, insomnia, loss of appetite, hallucinations, paranoid delusions (e.g., false ideas that others are eavesdropping or intend them harm), and irritability.

Cocaine Cocaine is derived from coca leaves—the plant from which the soft drink took its name. Do you recall commercials claiming that "Coke adds life"? Given its caffeine and sugar content, "Coke"—Coca-Cola, that is—should provide quite a lift. ◆ **Truth or Fiction Revisited:** It is true that Coca-Cola once "added life" through the use of a powerful then legal but now illegal stimulant: cocaine. But Coca-Cola hasn't been "the real thing" since 1906, when the company stopped using cocaine in its formula.

What are the effects of cocaine? The stimulant cocaine produces euphoria, reduces hunger, deadens pain, and boosts self-confidence. As shown in Figure 5.4, cocaine apparently works by binding to sites on sending neurons that normally reuptake molecules of the neurotransmitters norepinephrine, dopamine, and serotonin. As a result, molecules of these transmitter remain longer in the synaptic cleft, enhancing their mood-altering effects

A Closer Look
"Rophies"—The Date Rape Drug

A Closer Look

Rophies, roofies, R2, roofenol, roachies, la rocha, rope, or whatever you call it is dubbed the "date rape" drug because it has been slipped into the drinks of unsuspecting women, lowering inhibitions, lessening their ability to resist a sexual assault, and, when mixed with alcohol, often causing blackouts that prevent victims from remembering what happened to them. For this reason, Rohypnol has also been called the "Forget Pill," "Trip-and-Fall," and "Mind-Erasers." The drug has no taste or odor, so the victims don't realize what is happening when an assailant slips it into a drink. About ten minutes after taking it, the woman may feel dizzy and disoriented, simultaneously too hot and too cold, or nauseated. She may have difficulty speaking and moving and then pass out. She may "black out" for 8 to 24 hours, having little or no memory of what happened.

Rohypnol is not manufactured or sold legally in the United States, but it is prescribed as a treatment for insomnia and as a sedative hypnotic in other countries. It is in the same class of drugs as the tranquilizer Valium, but about 10 times stronger.

Rohypnol is often used with other drugs, such as alcohol, to create a dramatic "high." Rohypnol intoxication is generally associated with impaired judgment, memory, and motor skills, and can make a victim unable to resist or recall a sexual attack. Effects begin within 30 minutes, peak within 2 hours, and can persist for 8 hours or more.

Here are some ideas for avoiding problems with Rohypnol:

- Be wary about accepting drinks from anyone you don't know well or long enough to trust.
- Don't put your drink down and leave it unattended, even to go to the restroom.
- If you think that you have been a victim, notify authorities immediately. ■

Source: Fact sheets prepared by the National Institute on Drug Abuse (Rohypnol and GHB), Office on Women's Health in the U. S. Department of Health and Human Services, http://165.112.78.61/Infofax/RohypnolGHB.html.

and producing a "rush." But when cocaine levels drop, lower absorption of neurotransmitters by receiving neurons causes the user's mood to "crash."

Cocaine may be brewed from coca leaves as a "tea," snorted in powder form, or injected in liquid form. Repeated snorting constricts blood vessels in the nose, drying the skin and sometimes exposing cartilage and perforating the nasal septum. These problems require cosmetic surgery. The potent cocaine derivatives known as "crack" and "bazooka" are inexpensive because they are unrefined. Physical dangers include sudden rises in blood pressure, which constricts the coronary arteries and thickens the blood, decreases the oxygen supply to the heart, and quickens the heart rate (Kollins & Rush, 2002). These events can lead to respiratory and cardiovascular

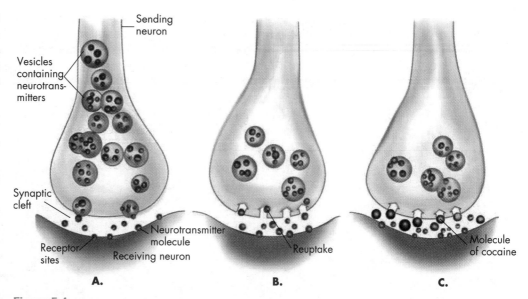

Figure 5.4

How Cocaine Produces Euphoria and Why People "Crash"

A. In the normal functioning of the nervous system, neurotransmitters are released into the synaptic cleft by vesicles in terminal buttons of sending neurons. Many are taken up by receptor sites in receiving neurons.
B. In the process called reuptake, sending neurons typically reabsorb excess molecules of neurotransmitters.
C. Molecules of cocaine bind to the sites on sending neurons that normally reuptake molecules of neurotransmitters. As a result, molecules of norepinephrine, dopamine, and serotonin remain longer in the synaptic cleft, increasing their typical mood-altering effects and providing a euphoric "rush." When the person stops using cocaine, the lessened absorption of neurotransmitters by receiving neurons causes his or her mood to "crash."

Go to your student website to access an interactive version of this figure.

collapse, as in the sudden deaths of some young athletes (Foltin et al., 2003; Hicks et al., 2003). Overdoses can cause restlessness and insomnia, tremors, headaches, nausea, convulsions, hallucinations, and delusions. Use of crack has been connected with strokes. Only about 4% of adolescents aged 15 to 19 use cocaine regularly, and most believe that it is harmful (Johnston et al., 2003). Cocaine causes physiological as well as psychological dependence.

Cocaine—also called *snow* and *coke*—has been used as a local anesthetic since the early 1800s. In 1884 it came to the attention of Sigmund Freud, who used it to fight his own depression and published an article about it: "Song of Praise." Freud's early ardor was tempered when he learned that cocaine is habit-forming and can cause hallucinations and delusions.

Nicotine   Nicotine is the stimulant in tobacco smoke. ***What are the effects of nicotine?*** Nicotine stimulates discharge of the hormone adrenaline and the release of neurotransmitters, including dopamine and acetylcholine (Arnold et al., 2003). Adrenaline creates a burst of autonomic activity that accelerates the heart rate and pours sugar into the blood. Acetylcholine is vital in memory formation, and nicotine appears to enhance memory and attention; improve performance on simple, repetitive tasks; and enhance the mood (Gentry, et al., 2000; Rezvani & Levin, 2001). Although it is a stimulant, nicotine appears to reduce stress (O'Brien, 1996). Nicotine depresses the appetite and raises the metabolic rate. Thus, some people smoke cigarettes to control their weight (Jeffery et al., 2000).

Nicotine creates the physiological dependence on tobacco products (American Lung Association, 2005). Symptoms of withdrawal include nervousness, drowsiness, loss of energy, headaches, irregular bowel movements, lightheadedness, insomnia, dizziness, cramps, palpitations, tremors, and sweating.

It's no secret. Cigarette packs sold in the United States carry messages like "Warning: The Surgeon General Has Determined That Cigarette Smoking Is Dangerous to Your

Video Connections

Why Is Nicotine So Addictive?

LEARNING OBJECTIVES

■ Explain the role of reinforcement in addiction.

■ Explain why nicotine is so addictive, and how understanding cues may help people quit smoking.

APPLIED LESSON

1 How reinforcing is nicotine compared to other drugs?

2 If people are partly attracted to smoking cigarettes at social gatherings because it gives them something to do with their hands, what kinds of other things might they do instead? If you're trying to quit smoking, what might you say to someone who offers you a cigarette? What if the person is insistent?

CRITICAL THINKING

We are taught to think of the illicit drugs of heroin and cocaine as potentially extremely harmful, and few would argue that they should be legalized. Why are cigarettes—which cause so many diseases and contain an addictive substance (nicotine)—legal when these others are not? Should the legal system treat cigarettes and nicotine equally as compared with drugs such as heroin and cocaine—that is, restrict none of them, or to be consistent, restrict all of them?

Nicotine is one of the most widely used psychoactive substances. Why is smoking alluring to so many? Why can it be so difficult to quit smoking?

Watch this video!

Go to www
your companion website at
http://academic.cengage.com/psychology/rathus
Click on the Video Connections tab under this chapter.

Health." Cigarette advertising has been banned on radio and television. Nearly 430,000 Americans die from smoking-related illnesses each year (American Lung Association, 2005). This number is greater than the equivalent of two jumbo jets colliding in midair each day with all passengers lost. ◆ **Truth or Fiction Revisited:** It is higher than the number of people who die each year from motor vehicle accidents, alcohol and drug abuse, suicide, homicide, and AIDS *combined.*

The carbon monoxide in cigarette smoke impairs the blood's ability to carry oxygen, causing shortness of breath. The **hydrocarbons** ("tars") in cigarette and cigar smoke lead to lung cancer (American Lung Association, 2005). Cigarette smoking also stiffens arteries (Mahmud & Feely, 2003) and is linked to death from heart disease, chronic lung and respiratory diseases, and other health problems. Women who smoke show reduced bone density, increasing the risk of fracture of the hip and back (Werner et al., 2003; Yarbrough et al., 2004). Pregnant women who smoke have a higher risk of miscarriage, preterm births, stillborn babies, and children with learning problems (American Lung Association, 2005).

Second-hand smoke—smoke inhaled from other people's tobacco products—is also connected with respiratory illnesses, asthma, and other health problems. Prolonged exposure to second-hand smoke during childhood is a risk factor for lung cancer (American Cancer Society, 2003). Because of the effects of second-hand smoke, smoking has been banished from many airplanes and restaurants.

Why, then, do people smoke? For many reasons—such as the desire to look sophisticated (although these days smokers may be more likely to be judged foolish than sophisticated), to have something to do with their hands, and—of course—to take in nicotine.

The incidence of smoking is connected with gender and level of education (see Table 5.5). Better-educated people are less likely to smoke and more likely to quit, if they do smoke.

Hydrocarbons Chemical compounds consisting of hydrogen and carbon.

Second-hand smoke Smoke from the tobacco products and exhalations of other people.

■ Cigarettes: Smoking Guns?

The perils of cigarette smoking are widely known today. One surgeon general declared that cigarette smoking is the chief preventable cause of death in the United States. The numbers of Americans who die from smoking are comparable to the number of lives that would be lost if two jumbo jets crashed *every day.* If flying were that unsafe, would the government ground all flights? Would the public continue to make airline reservations?

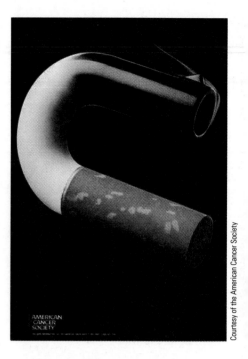

Courtesy of the American Cancer Society

TABLE 5.5 ■ Snapshot, U.S.A.: Gender, Level of Education, and Smoking

FACTOR	GROUP	PERCENT WHO SMOKE
Gender	Women	20
	Men	25.2
Level of education	Fewer than 12 years	38
	16 years and above	14

SOURCES: Centers for Disease Control/National Center for Health Statistics, May 28, 2004, *Morbidity and Mortality Weekly Report, 53*(20), pp. 427–431; Smoking Fact Sheet, American Lung Association, 2000, http://www.lungusa.org.

A Closer Look
On the Edge with Ecstasy

Ecstasy—also known as MDMA (acronym for 3, 4-methyl-enedioxymethamphetamine)—is a popular "party drug" or "club drug." Ecstasy is "on the edge" in more ways than one. For example, its chemical formula has similarities both to amphetamines, the stimulant, and mescaline, the hallucinogen (Concar, 2002; Freese et al., 2002). As a result, Ecstasy gives users the boost of a stimulant and, as a mild hallucinogen, also removes users a bit from reality. The combination appears to free users to some degree from inhibitions and awareness of the possible results of risky behavior, such as unprotected sex.

MDMA was first used legally in the 1970s, and even prescribed by psychiatrists to help with therapy (Rosenbaum, 2002). By the 1980s it had become part of the recreational drug scene and was criminalized. Today there remain some efforts to conduct research into the therapeutic uses of MDMA, but there is much resistance, just as there is to studying the medical uses of marijuana (Doblin, 2002; Pentney, 2001). While the medical debate goes on, MDMA appears to be increasing in popularity among high school (Yacoubian, 2003) and college students (Strote et al., 2002).

MDMA may also mean living on the edge because of a few known risks and some potential risks. For one thing, experiments with laboratory animals such as mice show that MDMA can increase anxiety (Navarro & Maldonado, 2002). Experiments with laboratory animals show that MDMA reduces the activity of the neurotransmitters serotonin and dopamine in the brain (Cassaday et al., 2003; Parrott, 2003; Taffe et al., 2002). Depletion of serotonin impairs the functioning of working memory (Cassaday et al., 2003; Taffe et al., 2002) and causes problems with eating, sleeping, and mood (leading to depression, for example). Some researchers are concerned that even occasional MDMA users could be setting themselves up for problems related to depletion of serotonin and dopamine later in life (Parrott, 2003; Taffe et al., 2002). ■

Houston Scott/Corbis Sygma

■ Ecstasy—A Popular Party Drug

If Ecstasy—also known as MDMA—is enjoyable for most users, why are health professionals concerned about its possible short- and long-term effects?

Anne Marie Rousseau / The Image Works

■ An LSD Trip?

This hallucinogen can give rise to a vivid parade of colors and visual distortions. Some users claim to have achieved great insights while "tripping," but typically they have been unable to recall or apply them afterward.

Hallucinogen A substance that causes hallucinations.

Marijuana The dried vegetable matter of the *Cannabis sativa* plant.

LSD Lysergic acid diethylamide; a hallucinogen.

Flashbacks Distorted perceptions or hallucinations that occur days or weeks after LSD usage but mimic the LSD experience.

Mescaline A hallucinogen derived from the mescal (peyote) cactus.

Phencyclidine (PCP) Another hallucinogen whose name is an acronym for its chemical structure.

──■── Hallucinogens

Hallucinogens are so named because they produce hallucinations—that is, sensations and perceptions in the absence of external stimulation. Hallucinogens may also have additional effects such as relaxation, euphoria, or, in some cases, panic.

Marijuana   **Marijuana** is produced from the *Cannabis sativa* plant, which grows wild in many parts of the world.   *What are the effects of marijuana?* Marijuana helps some people relax and can elevate their mood. It also sometimes produces mild hallucinations, which is why we discuss it in the section on hallucinogens. The major psychedelic substance in marijuana is delta-9-tetrahydrocannabinol, or THC. THC is found in the branches and leaves of the plant, but it is highly concentrated in the resin. *Hashish,* or "hash," is derived from the resin and is more potent than marijuana.

In the 19th century, marijuana was used much as aspirin is used today for headaches and minor aches and pains. It could be bought without a prescription in any drugstore. Today marijuana use and possession are illegal in most states. Marijuana also carries a number of health risks. For example, it impairs the perceptual–motor coordination used in driving and operating machines. It impairs short-term memory and slows learning (Ashton, 2001). Although it causes positive mood changes in many people, there are also disturbing instances of anxiety and confusion and occasional reports of psychotic reactions (Johns, 2001).

Some users report that marijuana helps them socialize. Moderate to strong intoxication is linked to reports of sharpened perceptions, increases in self-insight, creative thinking, and empathy for others. Time seems to slow. A song might seem to last an hour rather than minutes. There is increased awareness of bodily sensations such as heartbeat. Marijuana users also report that strong intoxication heightens sexual sensations. Visual hallucinations may occur, and strong intoxication may cause disorientation. If the smoker's mood is euphoric, loss of personal identity may be interpreted as "harmony" with the universe, but some users find disorientation threatening and fear they will not regain their identity. Accelerated heart rate and heightened awareness of bodily sensations leads some users to fear their hearts will "run away" with them. Strong intoxication can cause nausea and vomiting. Research suggests that regular users may experience both tolerance and withdrawal symptoms (American Psychiatric Association, 2000; Johns, 2001).

LSD and Other Hallucinogens   **LSD** is the abbreviation for lysergic acid diethylamide, a synthetic hallucinogen. *What are the effects of LSD and other kinds of hallucinogens?* Users of "acid" claim that it "expands consciousness" and opens up new worlds to them. Sometimes people say they have achieved great insights while using LSD, but when it wears off they cannot apply or recall them. LSD produces vivid, colorful hallucinations.

Some LSD users have **flashbacks**—distorted perceptions or hallucinations that mimic the LSD "trip" but occur days, weeks, or longer after usage. The experiencing of flashbacks is more techni-cally termed hallucinogen persisting perception disorder (HPPD) by the American Psychiatric Association (2000). The psychological explanation of "flashbacks" is that people who would use LSD regularly are also more likely to allow flights of fancy. But research with 38 people with HPPD suggests that following extensive use of LSD, the brain may fail to inhibit internal sources of visionlike experiences when the eyes are closed (Abraham & Duffy, 2001).

Other hallucinogens include **mescaline** (derived from the peyote cactus) and **phencyclidine** (PCP). PCP was developed as an anesthetic and an animal tranquilizer. It goes by the street names "angel dust," "ozone," "wack," and "rocket fuel." The street terms "killer joints" and "crystal supergrass" refer to PCP combined with marijuana.

Regular use of hallucinogens may lead to tolerance and psychological dependence, but is not known to create physiological dependence. High doses may impair coordination, cloud judgment, change the mood, and cause frightening hallucinations and delusions.

() **Learning Connections**

◀◀ *Altering Consciousness Through Drugs* ▶▶

Learning Connections

REVIEW:

9 Physiological dependence on a substance is evidenced by _____ when one discontinues use of the substance.
   (a) a seizure,
   (b) anxiety,
   (c) withdrawal symptoms,
   (d) euphoria.

10 The group most likely to show a flushing response to alcohol is
   (a) African Americans,
   (b) Asian Americans,
   (c) European Americans,
   (d) Latino and Latina Americans.

11 _____ is used to treat hyperactivity in children.
   (a) Valium,
   (b) Alcohol,
   (c) Barbiturates,
   (d) Ritalin.

12 _____ is the stimulant found in tobacco smoke.
   (a) 3, 4-methylenedioxymethamphetamine,
   (b) Cocaine,
   (c) Nicotine,
   (d) Dihydrotestosterone.

CRITICAL THINKING:
Many students complain that they are tired of "phony horror stories" about drugs. Does this textbook's presentation of information about the effects of drugs seem to be straightforward or biased? What is the evidence for your view?

Go to
http://academic.cengage.com/psychology/rathus
for an interactive version of this review.

RECITE—*An Active Summary*™

 Recite to Go! *Don't have time to study right now? You can study on the go!*
Go to your companion website and download an audio version of this review section to your media player. You can also access an interactive flash-card version of this review from your website.

1. What is consciousness?	*Consciousness* has several meanings, including sensory awareness, direct inner awareness, selective attention, the sense of self, and the waking state.
2. What is a circadian rhythm?	A circadian rhythm is a cycle that is connected with the 24-hour period of the earth's rotation, such as the sleep–wake cycle.
3. How do we describe the stages of sleep?	According to EEG records, each stage of sleep is characterized by different brain waves. There are four stages of non-rapid-eye-movement (NREM) sleep and one stage of REM sleep. Stage 1 sleep is the lightest, and stage 4 is the deepest.
4. Why do we sleep?	Sleep serves a restorative function. People who have been deprived of REM sleep learn more slowly and forget what they have learned more quickly.
5. What are dreams?	Dreams are cognitive activity that occurs while we are sleeping. Most dreaming, including nightmares, occurs during REM sleep.

6. Why do we dream what we dream?	The activation–synthesis model suggests that dreams reflect automatic biological activity by the pons and the synthesis of subsequent sensory stimulation by the frontal lobes of the brain. Most dream content reflects the events of the day.
7. What kinds of sleep disorders are there?	Insomnia is most often encountered by people who are anxious and tense. Deep sleep disorders include sleep terrors, bed-wetting, and sleepwalking.
8. What is hypnosis?	Hypnosis is an altered state of consciousness in which people are suggestible and behave as though they are in a trance.
9. How do psychologists explain the effects of hypnosis?	Current theories do not rely on a trance state. Rather, they emphasize people's ability to role-play the "trance" (role theory) and do what is expected of them (response set theory).
10. What is meditation?	People meditate by focusing on an object or a mantra to alter the normal relationship between the self and the environment. Meditation can help people cope with stress and normalize the blood pressure. Research is under way on its usefulness with depression and other psychological problems.
11. What is biofeedback training?	Biofeedback is a method for increasing consciousness of bodily functions. The organism is provided with information about a biological response and gains some control over it.
12. How is biofeedback training used?	People can learn to control heart rate, blood pressure, even the emission of certain brain waves.
13. What are substance abuse and dependence?	Substance abuse is use of a substance that persists even though it impairs one's functioning. Dependence may be characterized by organizing one's life around using the substance and by the development of tolerance, withdrawal symptoms, or both.
14. What are the causes of substance abuse and dependence?	People usually try drugs out of curiosity, but usage can be reinforced by anxiety reduction and feelings of euphoria. People are also motivated to avoid withdrawal symptoms once they become dependent. People may have genetic predispositions to become dependent on certain drugs.
15. What are the effects of alcohol?	Alcohol is a depressant that slows the activity of the central nervous system. Alcohol is also intoxicating and can lead to physiological dependence. It provides an excuse for failure or for antisocial behavior, but does not directly cause such behavior.
16. What are the effects of opiates?	The opiates morphine and heroin are depressants that reduce pain, but they are also bought on the street because of the euphoric "rush" they provide. Their use can lead to dependence.
17. What are the effects of barbiturates?	Barbiturates are depressants with medical uses, including relaxation, pain management, and treatment of epilepsy, high blood pressure, and insomnia. Barbiturates lead rapidly to dependence.
18. What are the effects of amphetamines?	Stimulants act by increasing the activity of the nervous system. Amphetamines produce feelings of euphoria when taken in high doses. But high doses may also cause restlessness, insomnia, psychotic symptoms, and a "crash" upon withdrawal. Ritalin is commonly used to treat hyperactive children.
19. What are the effects of cocaine?	The stimulant cocaine provides feelings of euphoria and bolsters self-confidence. Physically, it causes spikes in blood pressure and constricts blood vessels. Overdoses can lead to restlessness, insomnia, psychotic reactions, and cardiorespiratory collapse.
20. What are the effects of nicotine?	Nicotine is the addictive stimulant in tobacco smoke. Cigarette smoke also contains carbon monoxide and hydrocarbons. Smoking has been linked to death from heart disease and cancer.

21. What are the effects of marijuana?	Marijuana is a hallucinogen whose active ingredients, including THC, may produce relaxation, heightened and distorted perceptions, feelings of empathy, and reports of new insights. Marijuana elevates the heart rate and the smoke is harmful.
22. What are the effects of LSD and other kinds of hallucinogens?	LSD and other hallucinogens produce hallucinations. Some LSD users have "flashbacks" to earlier experiences. "Ecstasy" often combines a stimulant with a hallucinogen.

Key Terms

Active Learning Resources

Visit Your Companion Website for This Book

http://academic.cengage.com/psychology/rathus

Check out this companion website where you will find online resources directly linked to your book. This is where you'll access the videos highlighted in your Video Connections feature. You can answer the questions online and email them to your professor. In addition you'll find downloadable audio review material, interactive versions of the study aids, Power Visuals for mastering and reviewing key concepts, as well as quizzing, and much more!

CENGAGENOW™   **http://academic.cengage.com**

Need help studying? This site is your one-stop study shop. Take a Pre-Test and Cengage NOW will generate a Personalized Study Plan based on your test results. The Study Plan will identify the topics you need to review and direct you to online resources to help you master those topics. You can then take a Post-Test to help you determine the concepts you have mastered and what you still need to work on. In addition you can access interactive media including the videos highlighted in your Video Connections box.

Author Blog

Tues

What does your author Spence Rathus have to say about the state of psychology? Visit your companion website every Tuesday and click on "Author Blog." This is where he'll talk about the most recent controversies and hot topics in psychology. This will keep you up to date with what your author is thinking and give you great insight into modern psychology.

CHAPTER 6

Learning

Randy Faris/Corbis

truth or fiction?

[T] [F] A single nauseating meal can give rise to a taste aversion that lasts for years.

[T] [F] Psychologists helped a young boy overcome his fear of rabbits by having him eat cookies while a rabbit was brought closer and closer.

[T] [F] During World War II, a psychologist created a missile that would use pigeons to guide the missile to its target.

[T] [F] Slot-machine players pop coins into the machines most rapidly when they have no idea when they might win.

[T] [F] You can train a rat to climb a ramp, cross a bridge, climb a ladder, pedal a toy car, and do several other tasks—all in proper sequence.

[T] [F] Scientists have implanted electrodes in the brains of rats and guided them through mazes by means of remote control.

[T] [F] You have to make mistakes to learn.

[T] [F] Despite all the media hoopla, no scientific connection has been established between violence in the media and real-life aggression.

Go to www

http://academic.cengage.com/pstchology/rathus
for an interactive version of this Truth or Fiction feature.

preview

Dylan Klebold and Eric Harris were engrossed in violent video games for hours at a time. They were particularly keen on a game named *Doom*. Harris had managed to reprogram *Doom* so that he, the player, became invulnerable and had an endless supply of weapons. He would "mow down" all the other characters in the game. His program caused some of the characters to ask God why they had been shot as they lay dying. Later on, Klebold and Harris asked some of their shooting victims at Columbine High School in Colorado whether they believed in God. One of the killers also referred to his shotgun as Arlene, the name of a character in *Doom* (Saunders, 2003).

In the small rural town of Bethel, Alaska, Evan Ramsey would play *Doom, Die Hard,* and *Resident Evil* for endless hours. Ramsey shot four people, killing two and wounding two. Afterward, he said the video games taught him that being shot would reduce a player's "health factor" but probably not be lethal.

Michael Carneal was also a fan of *Doom*—and another video game, *Redneck Revenge.* He showed up at school one morning with a semiautomatic pistol, two shotguns, and two rifles. He aimed them at people in a prayer group. Before he was finished, three of them lay dead and five were wounded. Although Carneal had had no appreciable experience with firearms, authorities noted that his aim was uncannily accurate. He fired just once at each person's head, as one would do to rack up points in a video game—especially a game that offers extra points for head shots.

The debate about whether violence in media such as films, television, and video games fuels violence in the real world has been going on for more than 40 years. Psychologist Craig A. Anderson (2003, 2004), who has carried out extensive research in this area, argues that studies show that media violence is

■ **What Are the Effects of Playing Violent Video Games?**

Do violent video games provide a safe outlet for aggressive impulses? Do they encourage aggressive behavior? Do they teach players aggressive skills? Do they do some or all of the above?

Midway Games/Getty Images

a risk factor for increasing emotional arousal, aggressive behavior, and violent thoughts.

One reason to be particularly concerned about violent video games is that they require audience participation (Anderson et al., 2004). Players don't passively watch; they *participate*. Violent games like *Grand Theft Auto* have grown increasingly popular. Some games reward players for killing police, prostitutes, and bystanders. Virtual weapons include guns, knives, flamethrowers, swords, clubs, cars, hands, and feet. Sometimes the player assumes the role of a hero, but it is also common for the player to assume the role of a criminal.

What do we *learn* from video games and other media, such as television, films, and books? The research suggests that we learn a great deal—not only aggressive skills, but also the idea that violence is the normal state of affairs.

We will return to this controversial issue later in the chapter. This is the chapter that deals with the psychology of learning. Most of what we learn may be helpful and adaptive. But there are exceptions, as in the case of violent video games.

What* is *learning? Learning as defined in psychology is more than listening to teachers, honing skateboard jumps, or mastering the use of an iPod. From the behaviorist perspective, **learning** is a relatively permanent change in behavior that arises from practice or experience. The behaviorist perspective plays down the roles of cognition and choice. It suggests that players of violent video games went on rampages because they had been rewarded or reinforced for similar behavior in games.

Cognitive psychologists define learning as a mental change that may or may not be associated with changes in behavior. These mental changes may affect, but do not directly cause, changes in behavior. From this perspective, the participants in the video games had acquired skills that enabled them to attack people, but they had then chosen to attack others. Learning, for cognitive psychologists, may be *shown* by changes in behavior, but learning itself is a mental process. Cognitive psychologists suggest that people choose whether or not to imitate the aggressive and other behaviors they observe, and that people are most likely to imitate behaviors that are consistent with their values.

In many animals, much behavior is instinctive, or inborn, rather than learned. For example, tadpoles start out life swimming, but, after they develop legs, they hop on land in appropriate frog fashion—without taking hopping lessons. Salmon instinctively use the sense of smell to find, and return to spawn in, the stream where they were hatched after they have spent years roaming the seas. Robins instinctively know how to sing the song of their species and to build nests.

Among humans, however, the variety and complexity of behavior patterns are largely products of experience. We learn to read, to compute numbers, and to surf the Internet. It is natural to experience hunger, but humans learn to seek out the foods that are preferred in their culture. We learn which behavior patterns are deemed socially acceptable and which are considered wrong. We also unfortunately learn prejudices and stereotypes and negative behaviors such as using violence to deal with conflict. Our families and communities use verbal guidance, set examples, and apply rewards and punishments to teach us and transmit cultural values.

Learning (1) According to behaviorists, a relatively permanent change in behavior that results from experience. (2) According to cognitive theorists, the process by which organisms make relatively permanent changes in the way they represent the environment because of experience. These changes influence the organism's behavior but do not fully determine it.

Sometimes learning experiences are direct, as when we are praised for doing something properly. But we can also learn from the experiences of others. We learn about the past, other peoples, and how to put things together from other people, books, and audiovisual media. In this chapter we consider various kinds of learning, including conditioning and learning in which cognition plays a more central role.

CLASSICAL CONDITIONING: LEARNING WHAT IS LINKED TO WHAT

Classical conditioning involves some of the ways in which we learn to associate events with other events. Consider this: We have a distinct preference for a grade of A rather than F. We are also (usually) more likely to stop for a red light than for a green light. Why? We are not born with instinctive attitudes toward the letters *A* and *F*. Nor are we born knowing that red means stop and green means go. We learn the meanings of these symbols because they are associated with other events. A's are associated with instructor approval and the likelihood of getting into graduate school. Stopping at red lights is associated with avoiding accidents and traffic citations.

What is classical conditioning? **Classical conditioning** is a simple form of associative learning that enables organisms to anticipate events. If the name Ivan Pavlov rings a bell with us, it is most likely because of his research in learning with dogs. ***What is the contribution of Ivan Pavlov to the psychology of learning?*** Ivan Pavlov (1927) made his great contribution to the psychology of learning by accident. Pavlov was actually attempting to identify neural receptors in the mouth that triggered a response from the salivary glands. But his efforts were hampered by the dogs' annoying tendency to salivate at undesired times, such as when a laboratory assistant was clumsy and banged the metal food trays.

Just as you salivate after you've taken a big bite of cake, a dog salivates if meat powder is placed on its tongue. Pavlov was dosing his dogs with meat powder for his research because he knew that salivation in response to meat powder is a reflex. Reflexes are unlearned and evoked by certain **stimuli.** Pavlov discovered that reflexes can also be learned, or *conditioned,* by association. His dogs began salivating in response to clanging food trays because clanging, in the past, had been repeatedly paired with arrival of food. The dogs would also salivate when an assistant entered the laboratory. Why? In the past, the assistant had brought food.

Classical conditioning A simple form of learning in which an organism comes to associate or anticipate events. A neutral stimulus comes to evoke the response usually evoked by another stimulus by being paired repeatedly with the other stimulus. (Cognitive theorists view classical conditioning as the learning of relationships among events so as to allow an organism to represent its environment.) Also referred to as *respondent conditioning* or *Pavlovian conditioning.*

Stimulus An environmental condition that elicits a response.

■ **Ivan Pavlov and His Associates—Including a Professional Furry Salivator (the Dog), Early in the Twentieth Century**

Bettmann /Corbis

Pavlov at first viewed the extra salivation of his dogs as a hindrance to his research. But then it dawned on him that this "problem" might be worth looking into. He found out that he could train, or condition, his dogs to salivate in response to any stimulus.

In his initial experiments, Pavlov trained dogs to salivate when he sounded a tone. Pavlov termed these trained salivary responses "conditional reflexes." The reflexes were *conditional* on the repeated pairing of a previously neutral stimulus (such as the clanging of a food tray) and a stimulus (in this case, food) that evoked the target response (in this case, salivation). Today, conditional reflexes are generally referred to as *conditioned responses*.

Pavlov demonstrated conditioned responses by strapping a dog into a harness like the one shown in Figure 6.1. When meat powder was placed on the dog's tongue, the dog salivated. Pavlov repeated the process several times, with one difference. He preceded the meat powder by half a second or so with the sounding of a tone on each occasion. After several pairings of the meat powder and the tone, Pavlov sounded the tone but did *not* follow it with the meat powder. Still the dog salivated. It had learned to salivate in response to the tone.

Why Did Pavlov's Dogs Learn to Salivate in Response to the Tone?

Behaviorists explain the outcome of *classical conditioning* in terms of the publicly observable conditions of learning. For them, classical conditioning is a simple form of learning in which one stimulus comes to evoke the response usually evoked by another stimulus. Why? Because the stimuli are paired repeatedly. In Pavlov's demonstration, the dog learned to salivate in response to the tone *because* the tone had been paired with meat powder. Behaviorists do *not* say that the dog "knew" food was on the way. How can we guess what a dog "knows"? We can only outline the conditions under which targeted behaviors occur.

Cognitive psychologists view classical conditioning as the learning of relationships among events. The relationships allow organisms to mentally represent their environments and make predictions (Pickens & Holland, 2004). In Pavlov's demonstration, the dog salivated in response to the tone *because* the tone became mentally connected with the meat. The cognitive focus is on *the information learned by the organism*. Organisms are seen as seekers of information that generate and test rules about relationships among events.

Kirsch and his colleagues (2004) suggest that both views have something to offer. That is, conditioning can occur automatically, simply by pairing stimuli. But in many cases, and especially among higher animals, representations of the environment are also created.

Stimuli and Responses in Classical Conditioning

In Pavlov's experiment, the meat powder is an unlearned or **unconditioned stimulus (UCS).** Salivation in response to the meat powder is an unlearned or **unconditioned response (UCR).** The tone was at first a meaningless or neutral stimulus. It might have caused the dog to look in the direction of the sound—an **orienting reflex.** But the tone was not yet associated with food. Then, through repeated association with the meat powder, the tone became a learned or **conditioned stimulus (CS)** for the salivation response. Salivation in response to the tone (or conditioned stimulus) is a learned or **conditioned response (CR).** Therefore, salivation can be either a conditioned response or an unconditioned response, depending on the method used to evoke the response (see Figure 6.2).

Here is a mini-experiment that many adults have tried. They smile at infants, say something like "kitchie-coo" (don't ask me why), and then tickle the infant's foot. Perhaps the infant laughs and perhaps curls or retracts the foot. After a few repetitions—which psychologists call "trials"—the adult's simply saying "kitchie-coo" is likely to be enough to cause the infant to laugh and retract its foot.

Taste Aversion: Are All Stimuli Created Equal?

When I was a child in the Bronx, my friends and I would go to the movies on Saturday mornings. One day my friends dared me to eat two huge containers of buttered popcorn by myself. I had no problem with the first enormous basket of buttered popcorn. More

Figure 6.1

Pavlov's Demonstration of Conditioned Reflexes in Laboratory Dogs
From behind a one-way mirror, a laboratory assistant sounds a tone and then places meat powder on the dog's tongue. After several pairings, the dog salivates in response to the tone alone. A tube collects saliva and passes it to a vial. The quantity of saliva is taken as a measure of the strength of the animal's response.

Unconditioned stimulus (UCS) A stimulus that elicits a response from an organism prior to conditioning.

Unconditioned response (UCR) An unlearned response to an unconditioned stimulus.

Orienting reflex An unlearned response in which an organism attends to a stimulus.

Conditioned stimulus (CS) A previously neutral stimulus that elicits a conditioned response because it has been paired repeatedly with a stimulus that already elicited that response.

Conditioned response (CR) In classical conditioning, a learned response to a conditioned stimulus.

Figure 6.2

A Schematic Representation of Classical Conditioning

Prior to conditioning, food elicits salivation. The tone, a neutral stimulus, elicits either no response or an orienting response. During conditioning, the tone is rung just before meat powder is placed on the dog's tongue. After several repetitions, the tone, now a CS, elicits salivation, the CR.

Go to your student website to access an interactive version of this figure.

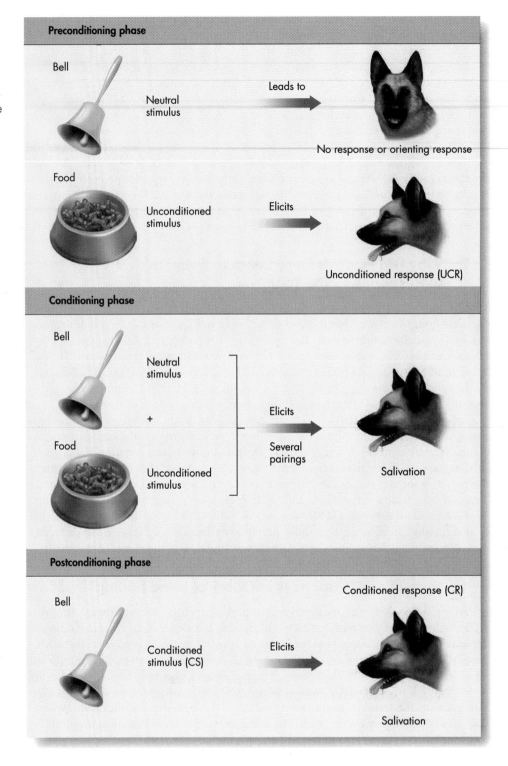

Preconditioning phase

Bell — Neutral stimulus — Leads to — No response or orienting response

Food — Unconditioned stimulus — Elicits — Unconditioned response (UCR)

Conditioning phase

Bell — Neutral stimulus + Food — Unconditioned stimulus — Elicits / Several pairings — Salivation

Postconditioning phase

Bell — Conditioned stimulus (CS) — Elicits — Conditioned response (CR) / Salivation

slowly—much more slowly—I forced down the second basket. I felt bloated and nauseated. The taste of the butter, corn, and salt lingered in my mouth and nose, and my head spun. It was obvious to me that no one could talk me into even another handful of popcorn that day. But I was surprised that I couldn't face buttered popcorn again for a year.

Years later I learned that psychologists refer to my response to buttered popcorn as a *taste aversion.* ***What are taste aversions? Why are they of special interest to psychologists?*** Many decades have now passed, and the distinctive odor of buttered popcorn still turns my stomach. ◆ **Truth or Fiction Revisited:** A single nauseating meal can give rise to a taste aversion that lasts for years.

Taste aversions are intriguing examples of classical conditioning. They are adaptive because they motivate organisms to avoid harmful foods. Taste aversions differ from other kinds of classical conditioning in a couple of ways. First, only one association may be required. A single overdose of popcorn left me with a lifetime aversion. Second, whereas most kinds of classical conditioning require that the unconditioned stimulus and conditioned stimulus be close together in time, in taste aversion the unconditioned stimulus (in this case, nausea) can occur hours after the conditioned stimulus (in this case, the flavor of food).

The Evolution of Taste Aversion   Research on taste aversion also challenges the view that organisms learn to associate any stimuli that are linked in time. In reality, not all stimuli are created equal. The evolutionary perspective suggests that animals (and humans) would be biologically predisposed to develop aversions that are adaptive in their environments (Garcia et al., 1989). Those of us who acquire taste aversions quickly are less likely to eat bad food, more likely to survive, and more likely to contribute our genes to future generations.

In a classic study, Garcia and Koelling (1966) conditioned two groups of rats. Each group was exposed to the same three-part conditioned stimulus: a taste of sweetened water, a light, and a clicker. Afterward, one group was presented with an unconditioned stimulus of nausea (induced by poison or radiation), and the other group was presented with an unconditioned stimulus of electric shock. After conditioning, the rats who had been nauseated showed an aversion for sweetened water but not to the light or clicker. Although all three stimuli had been presented at the same time, *the rats had acquired only the taste aversion.* After conditioning, the rats that had been shocked avoided both the light and the clicker, *but they did not show a taste aversion to the sweetened water.* For each group of rats, learning was adaptive. In the natural scheme of things, nausea is more likely to stem from poisoned food than from lights or sounds. So, for nauseated rats, acquiring the taste aversion was appropriate. Sharp pain, in contrast, is more likely to stem from natural events involving lights (e.g., fire, lightning) and sharp sounds (e.g., twigs snapping, things falling). Therefore, it was more appropriate for the shocked animals to develop an aversion to the light and the clicker than the sweetened water.

In classical conditioning, organisms learn to connect stimuli, such as the sounding of a tone with food. Now let us consider various factors in classical conditioning, beginning with what happens when the connection between stimuli is broken.

■ **Formation of a Taste Aversion?**
Taste aversions can be acquired by means of a single pairing of the US and the CS. Evolutionary psychologists point out that the rapid acquisition of a taste aversion makes it more likely that a human or an animal will survive and reproduce.

⬛ Extinction and Spontaneous Recovery

Extinction and spontaneous recovery are aspects of conditioning that help us adapt by updating our expectations or representations of a changing environment. For example, a child may learn to connect hearing a car pull into the driveway (a conditioned stimulus) with the arrival of his or her parents (an unconditioned stimulus). Thus, the child may squeal with delight when he hears the car.

What is the role of extinction in classical conditioning? **Extinction** enters the picture when times—and the relationships between events—change. After moving to a new house, the child's parents may commute by public transportation. The sound of a car in a nearby driveway may signal a neighbor's, not a parent's, homecoming. When a conditioned stimulus (such as the sound of a car) is no longer followed by an unconditioned stimulus (a parent's homecoming), the conditioned stimulus loses its ability to elicit a conditioned response. The organism adapts to change.

In classical conditioning, extinction is the process by which conditioned stimuli lose the ability to elicit conditioned responses, because the conditioned stimuli are no longer associated with unconditioned stimuli. That is, the toddler is no longer gleeful at the sounds of the car in the driveway. From the cognitive perspective, extinction changes the animal's mental representation of its environment, because the conditioned stimulus no longer allows it to make the same prediction.

In experiments on the extinction of conditioned responses, Pavlov found that repeated presentations of the conditioned stimulus (in this case, the tone) without the unconditioned stimulus (in this case, meat powder) led to extinction of the conditioned response (salivation in response to the tone). Basically, the dog stopped salivating at the sound of the

Extinction An experimental procedure in which stimuli lose their ability to evoke learned responses because the events that had followed the stimuli no longer occur. (The learned responses are said to be *extinguished.*)

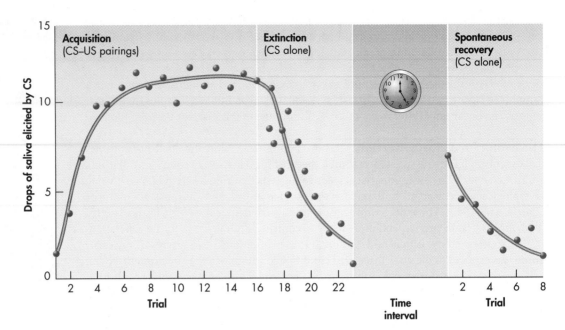

Figure 6.3

Learning and Extinction Curves

Actual data from Pavlov (1927) is illustrated by the dots, and the curved lines are idealized. In the acquisition phase, a dog salivates (shows a CR) in response to a tone (CS) after a few trials in which the tone is paired with meat powder (the UCS). Afterward, the CR is extinguished in about 10 trials during which the CS is not followed by the UCS. After a rest period, the CR recovers spontaneously. A second series of extinction trials leads to more rapid extinction of the CR.

tone. Interestingly, Figure 6.3 shows that a dog was conditioned to begin to salivate in response to a tone after 2 or 3 pairings of the tone with meat powder. Continued pairings of the stimuli led to increased salivation (measured in number of drops of saliva). After 7 or 8 trials, salivation leveled off at 11 to 12 drops.

In the next series of experiments, salivation in response to the tone was extinguished by trials in which the tone was presented without the meat powder. After about 10 extinction trials, the animal no longer salivated. It no longer showed the conditioned response when the tone was sounded. Now, what will happen if we allow a couple of days to pass and then sound the tone again?

What is the role of spontaneous recovery in classical conditioning? We asked what would happen if we were to allow a day or two to pass after we had extinguished salivation in Pavlov's dog and then again sounded the tone. Where would you place your bet? Would the dog salivate or not?

If you bet that the dog would again show the conditioned response (in this case, salivation in response to the tone), you were correct. Organisms tend to show **spontaneous recovery** of extinguished conditioned responses as a function of the passage of time. For this reason, the term *extinction* may be a bit misleading. When a species of animal becomes extinct, all members of that species capable of reproducing have died. The species vanishes. But the experimental extinction of conditioned responses does not lead to their permanent eradication. Rather, it seems to *inhibit* them. The response remains available for the future under the "right" conditions.

Evolutionary psychologists note that spontaneous recovery, like extinction, is adaptive. What would happen if the child heard no car in the driveway for several months? It could be that the next time a car entered the driveway, the child would associate the sounds with a parent's homecoming rather than with the arrival of a neighbor. This expectation could be appropriate. After all, *something* had changed when no car entered the driveway for so long. In the wild, a water hole may contain water for only a couple of months during the year. Evolution would favor the survival of animals that associate the water hole with the thirst drive from time to time so that they return to it when it once more holds water.

Spontaneous recovery The recurrence of an extinguished response as a function of the passage of time.

Boyd Norton / The Image Work

■ **Spontaneous Recovery of the Tendency to Visit a Water Hole After Time Has Passed**
If a water hole dries up, animals' tendencies to go to the water hole in a given season may be extinguished. When another season rolls around, however, the tendency to visit the water hole may spontaneously recover. Evolution would favor the survival of animals that associate the water hole with reduction of the thirst drive from time to time so that they are likely to return to it when it again holds water.

As time passes and seasons change, things sometimes follow circular paths and arrive where they were before. Spontaneous recovery helps organisms adapt to situations that recur from time to time.

─■─ Generalization and Discrimination

No two things are exactly alike. Traffic lights are hung at slightly different heights, and shades of red and green differ a little. The barking of two dogs differs, and the sound of the same animal differs slightly from one bark to the next. Rustling sounds in the undergrowth differ, but evolution would favor the survival of rabbits and deer that flee when they perceive any one of many possible rustling sounds. Adaptation requires us to respond similarly (or *generalize*) to stimuli that are equivalent in function and to respond differently to (or *discriminate* between) stimuli that are not.

What is the role of generalization in classical conditioning? Pavlov noted that responding to different stimuli as though they are functionally equivalent—*generalizing*— is adaptive for animals. **Generalization** is the tendency for a conditioned response to be evoked by stimuli that are similar to the stimulus to which the response was conditioned. For example, Pavlov demonstrated generalization by getting his dog to salivate when it was shown a circle. Then later the dog salivated in response to being shown closed geometric figures—even squares! The more closely the figure resembled a circle, however, the greater the *strength* of the response (as measured by drops of saliva).

But what happens if food follows the presentation of a circle but not a square? ***What is the role of discrimination in classical conditioning?*** Organisms must also learn that (1) many stimuli perceived as being similar are functionally different, and (2) they must respond adaptively to each. During the first couple months of life, for example, babies can discriminate their mother's voice from those of other women. They often stop crying when they hear their mother but not when they hear a stranger.

Pavlov showed that a dog conditioned to salivate in response to circles could be trained *not* to salivate in response to ellipses. After a while, the dog no longer salivated in response to the ellipses. Instead, it showed **discrimination**: It salivated only in response to circles. Pavlov found that increasing the difficulty of the discrimination task apparently tormented the dog. After the dog was trained to salivate in response to circles but not ellipses, Pavlov showed it a series of progressively rounder ellipses. Eventually the dog could no longer distinguish the ellipses from circles. The animal was so stressed that it urinated, defecated, barked profusely, and snapped at laboratory personnel.

Generalization In conditioning, the tendency for a conditioned response to be evoked by stimuli that are similar to the stimulus to which the response was conditioned.

Discrimination In conditioning, the tendency for an organism to distinguish between a conditioned stimulus and similar stimuli that do not forecast an unconditioned stimulus.

■ Generalization at the Crossroads
Chances are that you have never seen this particular traffic light in this particular setting. Because of generalization, however, we can safely bet that you would know what to do—stop or go—if you were to drive up to it.

Higher-order conditioning (1) According to behaviorists, a classical conditioning procedure in which a previously neutral stimulus comes to elicit the response brought forth by a *conditioned* stimulus by being paired repeatedly with that conditioned stimulus. (2) According to cognitive psychologists, the learning of relationships among events, none of which evokes an unlearned response.

Counterconditioning A fear-reduction technique in which pleasant stimuli are associated with fear-evoking stimuli so that the fear-evoking stimuli lose their aversive qualities.

How do we explain the dog's belligerent behavior? In *Frustration and Aggression,* a classic work written more than 65 years ago, a group of behaviorally oriented psychologists suggested that frustration induces aggression (Dollard et al., 1939). Rewards—such as food—are usually contingent on correct discrimination. That is, if the dog errs, it doesn't eat. Cognitive theorists, however, disagree (Rescorla, 1988). They would say that in Pavlov's experiment, the dog's loss of the ability to adjust its mental map of the environment was frustrating.

Daily life requires generalization and discrimination. No two hotels are alike, but when we travel from one city to another it is adaptive to expect to stay in a hotel. It is encouraging that a green light in Washington has the same meaning as a green light in Paris. Returning home requires the ability to discriminate our home from others. Imagine the confusion that would reign if we could not discriminate our friends, mates, or coworkers from other people.

■ Higher-Order Conditioning

Consider a child who is burned by touching a hot stove. After this experience, the sight of the stove may evoke fear. And because hearing the word *stove* may evoke a mental image of the stove, just hearing the word may evoke fear.

Do you recall the mini-experiment in which an adult smiles, says "kitchie-coo," and then tickles an infant's foot? After a few repetitions, just smiling at the infant may cause the infant to retract its foot. In fact, just walking into the room may have the same effect! The experiences with touching the hot stove and tickling the infant's foot are examples of higher-order conditioning. *What is higher-order conditioning?*

In **higher-order conditioning,** a previously neutral stimulus (for example, hearing the word *stove* or seeing the adult who had done the tickling enter the room) comes to serve as a learned or conditioned stimulus after being paired repeatedly with a stimulus that has already become a learned or conditioned stimulus (for example, seeing the stove or hearing the phrase "kitchie-coo"). Pavlov demonstrated higher-order conditioning by first conditioning a dog to salivate in response to a tone. He then repeatedly paired the shining of a light with the sounding of the tone. After several pairings, shining the light (the higher-order conditioned stimulus) came to evoke the response (salivation) that had been elicited by the tone (the first-order conditioned stimulus).

Life Connections
Applications of Classical Conditioning

In the nearby Video Connections, we meet one of the celebrities of the science of psychology, "Little Albert." Albert did not seek his fame; after all, he was under a year old at the time. At that tender age he was conditioned by John B. Watson to fear rats (a loud clanging sound was presented with the rat), and, by generalization, furry animals. Soon afterward, a colleague of Watson carried out a well-known experiment in counterconditioning of fears. ■

Counterconditioning The reasoning behind counterconditioning is this: If fears, as Watson had shown, could be conditioned by painful experiences like a clanging noise, perhaps fears could be *counterconditioned* by substituting pleasant experiences. In 1924, Watson's protégé Mary Cover Jones attempted to countercondition fear in a two-year-old boy called Peter.

"Little Albert"

LEARNING OBJECTIVES

- Explain the learning theory of fear that underlies the experiment by John B. Watson and his future wife, Rosalie Rayner.
- Explain the processes of classical conditioning and stimulus generalization.

APPLIED LESSON

1 How would you go about reversing Little Albert's conditioning?
2 Explain how classical conditioning and stimulus generalization might be related to the development of phobias.

CRITICAL THINKING

1 Critical thinkers do not over-generalize. The Watson and Rayner experiment suggests that fears can be conditioned. If this is so, does it mean that all fears are conditioned? Can you think of rival explanations for many people's fears of heights or snakes?
2 Many psychologists have criticized Watson and Rayner's conduct of the experiment with Little Albert for ethical reasons. Do you believe that it was ethical of the investigators to conduct this experiment? Why or why not?

Behaviorists believe that much behavior—even human behavior—can be explained by principles of conditioning. Watson and Rayner used classical conditioning to teach an 11-month-old boy, "Little Albert," to fear rats. After conditioning, Albert's fear generalized to other furry animals and the fur collar on his mother's coat. Albert also avoided rats, apparently in an effort to reduce his conditioned fear response. Are all fears acquired by conditioning? Was this experiment ethical?

Watch this video!

Go to www your companion website at http://academic.cengage.com/psychology/rathus Click on the Video Connections tab under this chapter.

Peter had an intense fear of rabbits. Jones had a rabbit gradually brought closer to Peter while he munched candy and cookies. ◆ **Truth or Fiction Revisited:** Thus, it is true that psychologists helped a young boy overcome his fear of rabbits by having him eat cookies while a rabbit was brought progressively closer. Jones first placed the rabbit in a far corner of the room while Peter munched and crunched. Peter cast a wary eye, but he continued to consume the treats. Gradually the animal was brought closer until Peter simultaneously ate and touched the rabbit. Jones theorized that the joy of eating was incompatible with fear and counterconditioned it.

Flooding and Systematic Desensitization If Mary Cover Jones simply plopped the rabbit on Peter's lap rather than bring it gradually closer, she would have been using the method of **flooding.** Had she done so, the cookies on the plate, and those already eaten, might have decorated the walls—even if the method eventually worked.

Flooding and systematic desensitization, like counterconditioning, are behavior therapy methods for reducing fears. They are based on the classical conditioning principle of extinction. In flooding, the client is exposed to the fear-evoking stimulus until fear is extinguished. Little Albert, for example, might have been placed in close contact with a rat until his fear had become extinguished. In extinction, the conditioned stimulus (in this case,

Michael Newman/PhotoEdit

■ **Can Chocolate Chip Cookies Countercondition Fears?**
In the 1920s Mary Cover Jones helped a boy overcome his fear of rabbits by having him munch on cookies as the animal was brought closer.

the rat) is presented repeatedly in the absence of the unconditioned stimulus (the clanging of the steel bars) until the conditioned response (fear) is no longer evoked.

A German study of 75 people aged 18 to 54 evaluated the effectiveness of a flooding-type treatment for agoraphobia, which is the fear of being out in busy, open areas (Fischer et al., 1998). Agoraphobic participants were exposed all day for two to three weeks to densely populated, open places. They showed reductions in anxiety and in avoidance of busy, open places immediately after treatment. Gains remained in place several years afterward.

Although flooding is usually effective, it is unpleasant. (When you are fearful of rats, being placed in a room with one is no picnic.) For this reason, behavior therapists frequently prefer to use **systematic desensitization,** in which the client is gradually exposed to fear-evoking stimuli under circumstances in which he or she remains relaxed. For example, while feeling relaxed, Little Albert might have been given an opportunity to look at photos of rats or to see rats from a distance before they were brought closer. Systematic desensitization takes longer than flooding but is not as unpleasant.

In any event, people can learn by means of simple association. In terms of the evolutionary perspective, organisms that can learn by several routes—including conditioning and conscious reflection—would stand a greater chance of survival than organisms whose learning is limited to conditioning.

Flooding A behavioral fear-reduction technique based on principles of classical conditioning. Fear-evoking stimuli (CSs) are presented continuously in the absence of actual harm so that fear responses (CRs) are extinguished.

Systematic desensitization A behavioral fear-reduction technique in which a hierarchy of fear-evoking stimuli is presented while the person remains relaxed.

( ) Learning Connections

◀◀   *Classical Conditioning—Learning What Is Linked to What*   ▶▶

Learning Connections

REVIEW:

1 A response to an unconditioned stimulus is called a(n)
  (a) conditioned response,
  (b) conditioned stimulus,
  (c) unconditioned response,
  (d) unconditioned stimulus.

2 In Pavlov's experiments, repeated presentation of a tone without being followed by meat powder extinguished the
  (a) conditioned response,
  (b) conditioned stimulus,
  (c) unconditioned response,
  (d) unconditioned stimulus.

3 In stimulus _____, organisms show a conditioned response in response to a range of stimuli similar to the conditioned stimulus.
  (a) recovery,
  (b) discrimination,

  (c) generalization,
  (d) conditioning.

4 In _____, a client is continuously exposed to a fear-evoking stimulus until the fear response is extinguished.
  (a) stimulus generalization,
  (b) stimulus discrimination,
  (c) aversive conditioning,
  (d) flooding.

5 In systematic _____, the client is gradually exposed to fear-evoking stimuli under circumstances in which he or she remains relaxed.
  (a) desensitization,
  (b) sensitization,
  (c) recovery,
  (d) flooding.

CRITICAL THINKING:
Critical thinkers attend to the definitions of terms. How do behaviorists and cognitive psychologists define learning? Why do they have these different approaches?
   Would behaviorists say that after a few pairings of a tone with food that a dog "knows" that the tone "means" food is on its way? Why or why not?

Go to

http://academic.cengage.com/psychology/rathus
for an interactive version of this review.

OPERANT CONDITIONING: LEARNING WHAT DOES WHAT TO WHAT

Through classical conditioning, we learn to associate stimuli. As a result, a simple, usually passive, response made to one stimulus is then made in response to the other. In the case of Little Albert, clanging noises were associated with a rat. As a result, the rat came to elicit the fear caused by the clanging. However, classical conditioning is only one kind of learning that occurs in these situations. After Little Albert acquired his fear of the rat, his voluntary behavior changed: He tried to avoid the rat. Thus, Little Albert engaged in another kind of learning—*operant conditioning*. In operant conditioning, organisms learn to do things—or *not* to do things—because of the consequences of their behavior. For example, I avoided buttered popcorn to prevent nausea. But we also seek fluids when we are thirsty, sex when we are aroused, and an ambient temperature of 68° to 70° F when we feel too hot or too cold. *Classical conditioning focuses on how organisms form anticipations about their environments. Operant conditioning focuses on what they do about them.* Let us consider the key contributions of B. F. Skinner to operant conditioning.

◾ B. F. Skinner and Reinforcement

When it comes to unusual war stories, few will top that of B. F. Skinner. One of Skinner's wartime efforts was "Project Pigeon." *What is the contribution of B. F. Skinner to the psychology of learning?*

◈ **Truth or Fiction Revisited:** During World War II, Skinner proposed that pigeons be trained to guide missiles to their targets. In their training, the pigeons would be **reinforced** with food pellets for pecking at targets projected onto a screen (see Figure 6.4). Once trained, the pigeons would be placed in missiles. Their pecking at similar targets displayed on a screen would correct the missile's flight path, resulting in a "hit" and a sacrificed pigeon. Plans for building the necessary missile—for some reason called the *Pelican* and not the *Pigeon*—were scrapped, however. The pigeon equipment was too bulky and Skinner's suggestion was not taken seriously. Might one conclude that the Defense Department decided that Project Pigeon was—forgive me—for the birds?

Annabella Bluesky/Photo Researchers, Inc.

◾ **Will Fear of Busy, Open Places Be Extinguished by Persistent Exposure?**
Research results are encouraging. It seems that persistent exposure of agoraphobic individuals to busy, open areas reduces their anxiety and their avoidance of such places.

Reinforce To follow a response with a stimulus that increases the frequency of the response.

     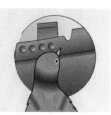

Figure 6.4
Project Pigeon
During World War II, B. F. Skinner suggested using operant conditioning to train pigeons to guide missiles to their targets. The pigeons would first be reinforced for pecking targets projected on a screen. Afterward, in combat, pecking the on-screen target would keep the missile on course.

■ **B. F. Skinner**

Project Pigeon may have been scrapped, but Skinner's ideas have found wide application. In operant conditioning, an organism learns to *do* something because of the effects or consequences of the behavior.

Skinner taught pigeons and other animals to engage in **operant behavior,** behavior that operates on, or manipulates, the environment. In classical conditioning, involuntary responses such as salivation or eyeblinks are often conditioned. In operant conditioning, *voluntary* responses such as pecking at a target, pressing a lever, or skills required for playing tennis are acquired, or conditioned. *What is operant conditioning?*

Operant conditioning is defined as a simple form of learning in which an organism learns to engage in certain behavior because of the effects of that behavior. In operant conditioning, we learn to engage in behaviors that result in presumably desirable consequences such as food, a hug, an A on a test, attention, or social approval. Some children learn to conform to social rules to earn the attention and approval of their parents and teachers. Other children, ironically, may learn to "misbehave," because misbehavior also gets attention. In particular, children may learn to be "bad" when their "good" behavior is routinely ignored. Some children who do not do well in school seek the approval of deviant peers (Patterson et al., 2000).

■ Methods of Operant Conditioning

Skinner (1938) made many theoretical and technological innovations. Among them was his focus on discrete behaviors such as lever pressing as the *unit,* or type, of behavior to be studied. Other psychologists might focus on how organisms think or "feel." Skinner focused on measurable things they do. Many psychologists have found these kinds of behavior inconsequential, especially when it comes to explaining and predicting human behavior. But Skinner's supporters point out that focusing on discrete behavior creates the potential for helpful changes. For example, in helping people combat depression, one psychologist might focus on their "feelings." A Skinnerian would focus on cataloguing (and modifying) the types of things that "depressed people" *do.* Directly modifying depressive behavior might also brighten clients' self-reports about their "feelings of depression."

■ **Depressed Is as Depressed Does?**
Behaviorist B. F. Skinner explained psychological problems like depression in terms of people's observable behaviors, not their self-reported feelings. A Skinnerian therapist might focus on modifying this client's depressive behavior patterns rather than on talking about feelings. The therapist might even give the client a concrete schedule for getting out and doing things.

Operant behavior Voluntary responses that are reinforced.

Operant conditioning A simple form of learning in which an organism learns to engage in behavior because it is reinforced.

To study operant behavior, Skinner devised an animal cage (or "operant chamber") that has been dubbed the *Skinner box.* (Skinner himself repeatedly requested that his operant chamber *not* be called a Skinner box, but history has thus far failed to honor his wishes.) Such a box is shown in Figure 6.5. The cage is ideal for laboratory experimentation because experimental conditions can be carefully introduced and removed, and their effects on laboratory animals can be observed.

The rat in Figure 6.5 was deprived of food and placed in a Skinner box with a lever at one end. At first it sniffed its way around the cage and engaged in random behavior. The rat's first pressing of the lever was accidental. But because of this action, a food pellet dropped into the cage. The arrival of the food pellet increased the probability that the rat would press the lever again. The pellet is thus said to have *reinforced* lever pressing.

Skinner's methodology even works when pigeons can fly in and out of feeders in the wild. Japanese researcher Ken'ichi Fuji (2002) poured grain into a feeder, and several hundred pigeons flew in and out over a 3-month period. Although the pigeons generally learned to peck a key to obtain the grain, one pair of pigeons showed a fascinating variation on the theme. One of them always pecked while the other one ate the grain!

In operant conditioning, it matters little why or how the first "correct" response is made. The animal can happen on it by chance or be physically guided to make the response. You may command your dog to "Sit!" and then press its backside down until it is sitting. Finally you reinforce sitting with food or a pat on the head and a kind word. Animal trainers use physical guiding or coaxing to bring about the first "correct" response. Can you imagine how long it would take to train your dog if you waited for it to sit or roll over and then seized the opportunity to command it to sit or roll over?

People, of course, can be verbally guided into desired responses when they are learning tasks such as spelling, adding numbers, or operating a machine. But they need to be informed when they have made the correct response. Knowledge of results often is all the reinforcement people need to learn new skills.

◼ Types of Reinforcers

A reinforcer is any stimulus that increases the probability that responses preceding it— whether pecking a button in a Skinner box or studying for a quiz—will be repeated. ***What are the various kinds of reinforcers?*** Reinforcers include food pellets when an animal has been deprived of food; water when it has been deprived of liquid; the opportunity to mate; and the sound of a tone that has previously been associated with eating. Skinner distinguished between positive and negative reinforcers.

Positive and Negative Reinforcers **Positive reinforcers** increase the probability that a behavior will occur when they are applied. Food and approval usually serve as positive reinforcers. **Negative reinforcers** increase the probability that a behavior will occur when the reinforcers are *removed* (see Figure 6.6). People often learn to plan ahead so that they need not fear that things will go wrong. In such cases fear acts as a negative reinforcer; *removal* of fear increases the probability that planning ahead will be repeated.

Some reinforcers have more impact than others. For example, pigeons who learn that one food tray has more food than another choose the tray with more food (Olthof & Roberts, 2000). Similarly, you would probably choose a job that paid $1,000 over a similar job that paid $10. (If not, get in touch with me—I have some chores for you.) With sufficient reinforcement, behaviors become *habits.* That is, they have a high probability of recurrence.

Immediate Versus Delayed Reinforcers Immediate reinforcers are more effective than delayed reinforcers. Therefore, the short-term consequences of behavior often provide more of an incentive than the long-term consequences.

Some students socialize when they should be studying because the pleasure of socializing is immediate. Studying may not pay off until the final exam or graduation. (This is why younger students do better with frequent tests.) It is difficult to quit smoking cigarettes

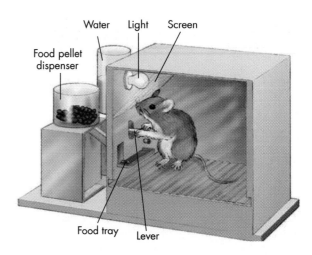

Figure 6.5
The Effects of Reinforcement
One of the celebrities of modern psychology, a laboratory rat, earns its keep in a Skinner box. The animal presses a lever because of reinforcement—in the form of food pellets— delivered through the feeder. The habit strength of this behavior is defined as the frequency of lever pressing.

Positive reinforcer A reinforcer that when *presented* increases the frequency of an operant.

Negative reinforcer A reinforcer that when *removed* increases the frequency of an operant.

Go to your student website to access an interactive version of this figure.

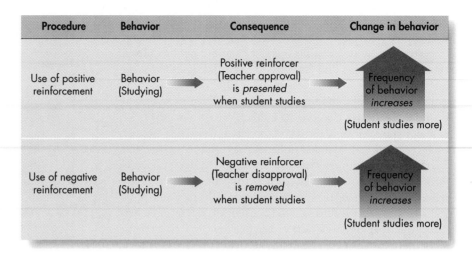

Figure 6.6
Positive Versus Negative Reinforcers
All reinforcers *increase* the frequency of behavior. Negative reinforcers, however, are aversive stimuli that increase the frequency of behavior when they are *removed*. In these examples, teacher approval functions as a positive reinforcer when students study harder because of it. Teacher *disapproval* functions as a negative reinforcer when its *removal* increases the frequency of studying. Can you think of situations in which teacher approval might function as a negative reinforcer?

because the reinforcement of nicotine is immediate and the health hazards of smoking more distant. Focusing on short-term reinforcement is also connected with risky sex, such as engaging in sexual activity with a stranger or failing to prevent pregnancy (Caffray & Schneider, 2000; Fuertes et al., 2002). One of the aspects of being human is the ability to foresee the long-range consequences of one's behavior and to make choices. But immediate reinforcers—such as those cookies staring in the face of the would-be dieter—can be powerful temptations indeed.

Primary and Secondary Reinforcers   We can also distinguish between primary and secondary, or conditioned, reinforcers. **Primary reinforcers** are effective because of the organism's biological makeup. For example, food, water, warmth (positive reinforcers), and pain (a negative reinforcer) all serve as primary reinforcers. **Secondary reinforcers** acquire their value through being associated with established reinforcers. For this reason they are also termed **conditioned reinforcers.** We may seek money because we have learned that it may be exchanged for primary reinforcers.

Extinction and Spontaneous Recovery in Operant Conditioning

Keisha's teacher writes "Good" on all of her homework assignments before returning them. One day, her teacher no longer writes anything on the assignments—the reinforcement ends. Reinforcers are used to strengthen responses. What happens when reinforcement stops? *What is the role of extinction in operant conditioning?*

In Pavlov's experiment, the meat powder was the event that followed and confirmed the appropriateness of salivation. In Keisha's situation, seeing "Good" written on her assignments confirmed the appropriateness of the way in which she did her homework. In operant conditioning, the ensuing events are reinforcers. In operant conditioning the extinction of learned responses results from the repeated performance of operant behavior without reinforcement. Keisha might stop doing her homework if she is not reinforced for completing it. In other words, reinforcers maintain operant behavior or strengthen habitual behavior in operant conditioning. With humans, fortunately, people can reinforce themselves for desired behavior by telling themselves they did a good job—or, in Keisha's case, she may tell herself that she is doing the right thing regardless of whether or not her teacher recognizes it.

What is the role of spontaneous recovery in operant conditioning? Spontaneous recovery of learned responses occurs in operant conditioning as well as in classical condi-

Primary reinforcer An unlearned reinforcer.

Secondary reinforcer A stimulus that gains reinforcement value through association with established reinforcers.

Conditioned reinforcer Another term for a secondary reinforcer.

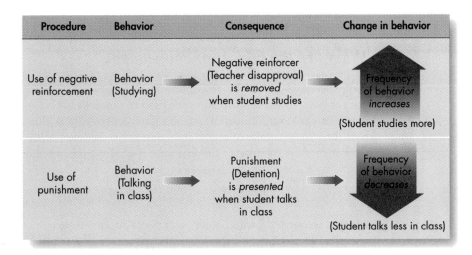

Procedure	Behavior	Consequence	Change in behavior
Use of negative reinforcement	Behavior (Studying)	Negative reinforcer (Teacher disapproval) is *removed* when student studies	Frequency of behavior *increases* (Student studies more)
Use of punishment	Behavior (Talking in class)	Punishment (Detention) is *presented* when student talks in class	Frequency of behavior *decreases* (Student talks less in class)

Go to your student website to access an interactive version of this figure.

Figure 6.7
Negative Reinforcers Versus Punishments
Negative reinforcers and punishments both tend to be aversive stimuli. Reinforcers, however, *increase* the frequency of behavior. Punishments *decrease* the frequency of behavior. Negative reinforcers increase the frequency of behavior when they are *removed*. Punishments decrease or suppress the frequency of behavior when they are *applied*. Can you think of situations in which punishing students might have effects other than those desired by the teacher?

tioning. Spontaneous recovery is adaptive in operant conditioning as well as in classical conditioning. Reinforcers may once again become available after time elapses, just as there are new tender sprouts on twigs when the spring arrives.

Reinforcers Versus Rewards and Punishments

Reinforcers are defined as stimuli that increase the frequency of behavior. *Why did Skinner make a point of distinguishing between reinforcers on the one hand and rewards and punishments on the other?* Reinforcers are known by their effects, whereas **rewards** and punishments are known by how they feel. It may be that most reinforcers—food, hugs, having the other person admit to starting the argument, and so on—feel good, or are pleasant events. Yet things that we might assume would feel bad, such as a slap on the hand, disapproval from a teacher, even suspensions and detention may be positively reinforcing to some people—perhaps because such experiences confirm negative feelings toward teachers or one's belonging within a deviant subculture (Atkins et al., 2002).

Skinner preferred the concept of reinforcement to that of reward because reinforcement does not suggest trying to "get inside the head" of an organism (whether a human or lower animal) to guess what it would find pleasant or unpleasant. A list of reinforcers is arrived at scientifically and *empirically*—that is, by observing what sorts of stimuli increase the frequency of the behavior.

Punishments are defined as aversive events that suppress or decrease the frequency of the behavior they follow (see Figure 6.7). Punishment can rapidly suppress undesirable behavior (Gershoff, 2002) and may be warranted in "emergencies," such as when a child tries to run into the street.

Discriminative Stimuli: Do You Step on the Accelerator When the Light Is Green or Red?

B. F. Skinner might not have been able to get his pigeons into the drivers' seats of missiles, but he had no problem training them to respond to traffic lights. Imagine yourself trying the following experiment.

You find a pigeon. Or you sit on a park bench, close your eyes, and one finds you. You place it in a Skinner box with a button on the wall. You drop a food pellet into the cage whenever the pigeon pecks the button. (Soon it will learn to peck the button whenever it has not eaten for a while.) Now you place a small green light in the cage and turn it on and

Reward A pleasant stimulus that increases the frequency of the behavior it follows.

Punishment An unpleasant stimulus that suppresses the behavior it follows.

Courtesy of Charles Patrick France and Christopher Cruz

■ **A Discriminative Stimulus**
You might not think that pigeons are very discriminating, yet they readily learn that pecking will not bring food in the presence of a discriminative stimulus such as a red light.

Life Connections
What Are the Effects of Punishment?

Many psychologists argue that punishment—especially corporal punishment—often fails to achieve the goals of parents, teachers, and others. Psychologist Elizabeth Gershoff (2002) analyzed 88 studies of more than 36,000 children and found connections between physical punishment (e.g., spanking) and various behavior patterns in childhood and adulthood. For example:

- Children who are physically punished are less likely to develop internal moral standards.
- Physical punishment is connected with poorer parent–child relationships.
- Physically punished children are more likely to be aggressive toward other children and to engage in criminal behavior later in life.
- Physically punished children are more likely as adults to abuse their spouses or their own children.

Gershoff (2002) adds that punishment tends to suppress undesirable behavior only under circumstances in which its delivery is guaranteed. It does not take children long to learn that they can "get away with murder" with one parent or teacher but not with another. Moreover, punishment does not in itself suggest an alternative acceptable form of behavior.

There are some other reasons for not using physical punishment:

- It hurts.
- Punished individuals may withdraw from the situation. Severely punished children may run away, cut class, or drop out of school.
- Children also *learn* responses that are punished. Whether or not children choose to perform punished responses, punishment rivets the children's attention on them.

Gershoff's research findings have not gone unchallenged. Diana Baumrind and her colleagues (2002) point out, for example, that most of the studies examined by Gershoff were correlational, not experimental. Therefore, we cannot be certain about cause and effect. Consider the connection between parental punishment and childhood aggression. Does parental punishment contribute to childhood aggression, or are more aggressive children likely to frustrate their parents, leading their parents to use physical punishment? In any event, most psychologists tend to prefer rewarding children for desirable behavior to punishing them for unwanted behavior. By ignoring misbehavior, or by using **time out** from positive reinforcement, one can avoid reinforcing misbehavior.

To reward or positively reinforce children for desired behavior takes time and care. Avoiding the use of punishment is not enough. First, we must pay attention to children when they are behaving well. If we take their desirable behavior for granted and respond to them only when they misbehave, we may be encouraging misbehavior. Second, we must be certain that children are aware of, and capable of performing, desired behavior. It is harmful and fruitless merely to punish children for unwanted behavior. We must also carefully guide them, either physically or verbally, into making the desired responses, and then reward them. We cannot teach children table manners by waiting for them to exhibit proper responses at random and then reinforcing them for their responses. Try holding a reward of ice cream behind your back and waiting for a child to exhibit proper manners. You will have a slippery dining room floor long before the child develops good table manners. ■

Time out Removal of an organism from a situation in which reinforcement is available when unwanted behavior is shown.

off intermittently throughout the day. Reinforce button pecking with food whenever the green light is on, but not when the light is off. It will not take long for this clever city pigeon to learn that it will gain as much by grooming itself or cooing and flapping around as it will by pecking the button when the light is off.

The green light has become a discriminative stimulus. *What are discriminative stimuli?* **Discriminative stimuli,** such as green or red lights, indicate whether behavior (in the case of the pigeon, pecking a button) will be reinforced (by a food pellet being dropped into the cage). Behaviors that are not reinforced tend to be extinguished. For the pigeon in our experiment, the behavior of pecking the button *when the light is off* is extinguished.

A moment's reflection will suggest many ways in which discriminative stimuli influence our behavior. Isn't it more efficient to answer the telephone when it is ringing? Do you think it is wise to ask someone for a favor when she or he is displaying anger and disapproval toward you?

We noted that a pigeon learns to peck a button if food drops into its cage when it does so. What if you want the pigeon to continue to peck the button, but you're running out of food? Do not despair. As we see in the following section, you can keep that bird pecking away indefinitely, even as you hold up on most of the food.

Schedules of Reinforcement: How Often? Under What Conditions?

In operant conditioning, some responses are maintained by means of **continuous reinforcement.** You probably become warmer every time you put on heavy clothing. You probably become less thirsty every time you drink water. Yet if you have ever watched people toss their money down the maws of slot machines, you know that behavior can also be maintained by means of **partial reinforcement.** *What are the various schedules of reinforcement? How do they affect behavior?*

Folklore about gambling is consistent with learning theory. You can get a person "hooked" on gambling by fixing the game to allow heavy winnings at first. Then you gradually space out the winnings (reinforcements) until gambling is maintained by infrequent winning—or even no winning at all. Partial reinforcement schedules can maintain gambling, like other behavior, for a great deal of time, even though it goes unreinforced (Pulley, 1998).

Responses that have been maintained by partial reinforcement are more resistant to extinction than responses that have been maintained by continuous reinforcement (Rescorla, 1999). From the cognitive perspective, we could suggest that organisms that have experienced partial reinforcement do not expect reinforcement every time they engage in a response. Therefore, they are more likely to persist in the absence of reinforcement.

There are four basic reinforcement schedules: *fixed-interval, variable-interval, fixed-ratio,* and *variable-ratio.*

Interval Schedules In a **fixed-interval schedule,** a fixed amount of time—say, a minute—must elapse before the correct response will result in a reinforcer. With a fixed-interval schedule, an organism's response rate falls off after each reinforcement and then picks up again as the time when reinforcement will occur approaches. For example, in a 1-minute fixed-interval schedule, a rat is reinforced with, say, a food pellet for the first operant—for example, the first pressing of a lever—that occurs after a minute has elapsed. After each reinforcement, the rat's rate of lever pressing slows down, but as the end of the 1-minute interval draws near, lever pressing increases in frequency, as suggested in Figure 6.8. It is as if the rat has learned that it must wait a while before it is reinforced. The resultant record on the cumulative recorder shows a typical series of upward waves, or scallops, which are called *fixed-interval scallops.*

Car dealers use fixed-interval reinforcement schedules when they offer incentives for buying up the remainder of the year's line in summer and fall. In a sense, they are

Discriminative stimulus In operant conditioning, a stimulus that indicates that reinforcement is available.

Continuous reinforcement A schedule of reinforcement in which every correct response is reinforced.

Partial reinforcement One of several reinforcement schedules in which not every correct response is reinforced.

Fixed-interval schedule A schedule in which a fixed amount of time must elapse between the previous and subsequent times that reinforcement is available.

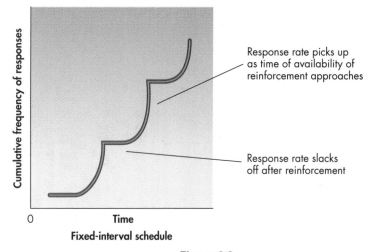

Response rate picks up as time of availability of reinforcement approaches

Response rate slacks off after reinforcement

Cumulative frequency of responses

Time

Fixed-interval schedule

Figure 6.8

The "Fixed-Interval Scallop"

Organisms who are reinforced on a fixed-interval schedule tend to slack off responding after each reinforcement. The rate of response picks up as they near the time when reinforcement will become available. The results on the cumulative recorder look like upward-moving waves, or scallops.

■ Slot Machines Pay Off on Unpredictable Variable-Ratio Schedules
Because "one-armed bandits" make unpredictable payoffs, people tend to maintain a high response rate—that is, to drop coins into them in rapid succession.

suppressing buying at other times, except for consumers whose current cars are in their death throes or those with little self-control. Similarly, you learn to check your email only at a certain time of day if your correspondent writes at that time each day.

Reinforcement is more unpredictable in a **variable-interval schedule.** Therefore, the response rate is steadier but lower. If the boss calls us in for a weekly report, we probably work hard to pull things together just before the report is to be given, just as we might cram the night before a weekly quiz. But if we know that the boss might call us in for a report on the progress of a certain project at any time (variable-interval schedule), we are likely to keep things in a state of reasonable readiness at all times. However, our efforts are unlikely to have the intensity they would in a fixed-interval schedule (for example, a weekly report). Similarly, we are less likely to cram for unpredictable pop quizzes than to study for regular quizzes. But we are likely to do at least some studying on a regular basis. Likewise, if you receive email from your correspondent irregularly, you are likely to check your email regularly, but with less eagerness.

A Closer Look
Robo Rats? Using Operant Conditioning to Teach Rats How to Search for Survivors of Disasters

City dwellers know that rats rustle through garbage, but will we one day be using rats to search through rubble where people cannot go to find survivors of disasters? The results of a study carried out in Brooklyn, New York, suggest that this is a real possibility.

◆ **Truth or Fiction Revisited:** Sanjiv Talwar and his colleagues (2002) used operant conditioning to guide rats through mazes by means of "remote control." They were inspired to test out the method by an earthquake in India and the terrorist attacks of September 11, 2001. The tsunami

■ Robo-Rat?
Part A of the figure shows how Talwar and his colleagues guided a rat through a zigzag course. They cued the rat to turn left (L) or right (R), then reinforced it with a burst of electricity in the rat's pleasure center for doing so. Part B shows a more complex 3-D course through which a rat was guided. The goal is to shape rats to rustle through rubble to help find survivors of a disaster.
Source: "Behavioural neuroscience: Rat navigation guided by remote control" by Sanjiv K. Talwar et al., *Nature* 417 (2002), fig. 1, p. 37. Reprinted by permission of Nature Publishing Group.

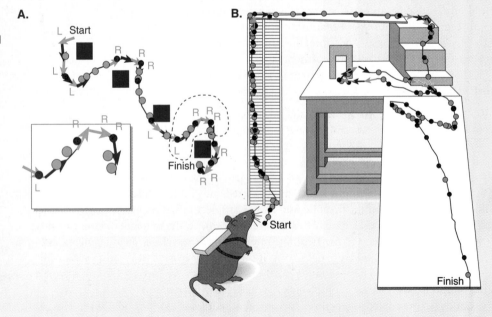

Ratio Schedules   In a **fixed-ratio schedule,** reinforcement is provided after a fixed number of correct responses have been made. In a **variable-ratio schedule,** reinforcement is provided after a variable number of correct responses have been made. In a 10:1 variable-ratio schedule, the mean number of correct responses that would have to be made before a subsequent correct response would be reinforced is 10, but the ratio of correct responses to reinforcements might be allowed to vary from, say, 1:1 to 20:1 on a random basis.

Fixed- and variable-ratio schedules maintain a high response rate. With a fixed-ratio schedule, it is as if the organism learns that it must make several responses before being reinforced. It then "gets them out of the way" as rapidly as possible. Consider the example of piecework. If a worker must sew five shirts to receive $10, he or she is on a fixed-ratio (5:1) schedule and is likely to sew at a uniformly high rate, although there might be a brief pause after each reinforcement. With a variable-ratio schedule, reinforcement can come at any time.   ◁▷ **Truth or Fiction Revisited:** The unpredictability of winnings also maintains a high response rate. Slot machines tend to pay off on variable-ratio schedules, and players can be seen popping coins into them and yanking their "arms" with barely a pause. I have seen players who do not even stop to pick up their winnings. Instead, they continue to pop in the coins, either from their original stack or from the winnings tray.

Variable-interval schedule A schedule in which a variable amount of time must elapse between the previous and subsequent times that reinforcement is available.

Fixed-ratio schedule A schedule in which reinforcement is provided after a fixed number of correct responses.

Variable-ratio schedule A schedule in which reinforcement is provided after a variable number of correct responses.

of 2004 provides an additional incentive for this type of experimentation.

The researchers outfitted five rats with electrodes in their brains and backpacks containing various electronic devices. One goal was to inform the rats whether they should turn right or left. Another was to reinforce them for doing so. To point the rats in the right direction, the team sent electric signals to brain regions that receive sensations from whiskers. The researchers inserted electrodes in the animals pleasure centers to provide reinforcement.

The researchers placed the rats in a maze. As the animals approached a choice point where they could turn left or right, the researchers stimulated their brains as would a whisker touch on the left or right side of the head. When the animals turned in the direction of the "virtual touches," the researchers zapped their brains' pleasure centers.

Courtesy of Dr. Sanjiv Talwar

Not only did the bursts of electricity teach the rats which way to turn, but they also apparently motivated the rats to move faster, even if it meant climbing steps or hopping from a shelf. The rat is apparently seeking the next burst. Talwar says that "the rats figure it out in 5 or 10 minutes" (Milius, 2002). The researchers steered the rats across a jagged pile of concrete, an area that was so brightly lit that rats would normally avoid it, even up a tree.

Robin Murphy, who is developing search-and-rescue robots in Florida, is skeptical. She admits that the rats seem to work out in experiments, but she wonders how people can guide a rat that is out of sight (a small video camera strapped to the animal's head?) and whether bursts of electricity will keep the rat going through areas with high temperatures and little or no oxygen. Murphy also worries about sending animals, even rats, into such environments. "One of the reasons many of us are in robotics is because robots can reduce the risk to living things," she says (Milius, 2002).

What do you think? ∎

Shaping

If you are teaching hip-hop dancing to people who have never danced, do not wait until they have performed it precisely before telling them they're on the right track. The foxtrot will be back in style before they have learned a thing.

We can teach complex behaviors by **shaping**. *How can we use shaping to teach complex behavior patterns?* Shaping reinforces progressive steps toward the behavioral goal. At first, for example, it may be wise to smile and say, "Good," when a reluctant newcomer gathers the courage to get out on the dance floor, even if your feet are flattened by his initial clumsiness. If you are teaching someone to drive a car with a standard shift, at first generously reinforce the learner simply for shifting gears without stalling.

But as training proceeds, we come to expect more before we are willing to provide reinforcement. We reinforce **successive approximations** of the goal. If you want to train a rat to climb a ladder, first reinforce it with a food pellet when it turns toward the ladder. Then wait until it approaches the ladder before giving it a pellet. Then do not drop a pellet into the cage until the rat touches the ladder. In this way, the rat will reach the top of the ladder more quickly than if you had waited for the target behavior to occur at random. ◇ **Truth or Fiction Revisited:** Through use of shaping, one can indeed train a rat to climb a ramp, cross a bridge, climb a ladder, and so on in a desired sequence. As you see in the nearby "A Closer Look" on "RoboRats," rats can also be trained to make certain movements by "remote control."

Learning to drive a new standard-shift automobile to a new job also involves a complex sequence of operant behaviors. At first we actively seek out all the discriminative stimuli or landmarks that give us cues for when to turn—signs, buildings, hills, valleys. We also focus on shifting to a lower gear as we slow so the car won't stall. After many repetitions, these responses, or chains of behavior, become habitual, and we need to pay very little attention to them.

Have you ever driven home and suddenly realized that you couldn't recall exactly how you got there? Your entire trip may seem "lost." Were you in great danger? How could you allow such a thing to happen? Actually, your driving and your responses to the demands of the route may have become so habitual that you did not have to focus on them. As you drove, you were able to think about dinner, work, or the weekend. But if something unusual had occurred on the way, such as an engine problem or a rainstorm, you would have devoted as much attention to your driving as was needed to arrive home. Your trip was probably quite safe after all.

Shaping A procedure for teaching complex behaviors that at first reinforces approximations of the target behavior.

Successive approximations Behaviors that are progressively closer to a target behavior.

Life Connections
Applications of Operant Conditioning

Operant conditioning, like classical conditioning, is not just an exotic laboratory procedure. We use it every day in our efforts to influence other people. Parents and peers induce children to acquire so-called gender-appropriate behavior patterns through rewards and punishments. Parents also tend to praise their children for sharing their toys and to punish them for being too aggressive. Peers participate in the socialization process by playing with children who are generous and nonaggressive and, often, by avoiding those who are not (Warman & Cohen, 2000).

Operant conditioning also plays a role in attitude formation. Adults often reward children for expressing attitudes that coincide with their own and punish or ignore them for expressing contradictory attitudes. Let us now consider some specific applications of operant conditioning. ■

Biofeedback Training?　Biofeedback training (BFT) is based on principles of operant conditioning. BFT has enabled people and lower animals to learn to control autonomic responses to attain reinforcement (Miller, 1969; Vernon et al., 2003).

Through BFT, people can gain control of autonomic functions such as the flow of blood in a finger. They can also learn to improve their control over functions that can be manipulated voluntarily, such as muscle tension. When people receive BFT, reinforcement is given in the form of *information*. Perhaps a sound changes in pitch or frequency of occurrence to signal that they have modified the autonomic function in the desired direction. For example, we can learn to emit alpha waves—the kind of brain wave associated with feelings of relaxation—through feedback from an electroencephalograph (EEG; an instrument that measures brain waves). People use other instruments to learn to lower their muscle tension, heart rates, and blood pressure.

BFT is also used with people who have lost neuromuscular control of parts of their body as a result of an accident. A "bleep" sound informs them when they have contracted a muscle or sent an impulse down a neural pathway. By concentrating on changing the bleeps, they may gradually regain voluntary control over the damaged function.

Principles of operant conditioning have also enabled psychologists and educators to develop many beneficial innovations, such as behavior modification in the classroom and programmed learning.

Behavior Modification in the Classroom: Accentuating the Positive　Remember that reinforcers are defined as stimuli that increase the frequency of behavior—not as pleasant events. Ironically, adults frequently reinforce undesirable behavior in children by paying attention to them, or punishing them, when they misbehave but ignoring them when they behave in desirable ways. Similarly, teachers who raise their voices when children misbehave may be unintentionally conferring hero status on those pupils in the eyes of their peers. To the teacher's surprise, some children may then go out of their way to earn disapproval.

Teacher preparation and in-service programs show teachers how to use behavior modification to reverse these response patterns. Teachers are taught to reinforce children when they are behaving appropriately and, when possible, to extinguish misbehavior by ignoring it.

Among older children and adolescents, peer approval may be a more powerful reinforcer than teacher approval. Peer approval may maintain misbehavior, and ignoring misbehavior may only allow students to become more disruptive. In such cases it may be necessary to separate troublesome children.

reflect & relate
How have teachers in your own experience maintained— or failed to maintain—control over their classrooms?

Bob Daemmrich/The Image Works

■ **Praise**
Praise from the teacher reinforces desirable behavior in most children. Behavior modification in the classroom applies principles of operant conditioning.

Teachers also frequently use time out from positive reinforcement to discourage misbehavior. In this method, children are placed in a drab, restrictive environment for a specified period, usually about 10 minutes, when they behave disruptively. While they are isolated, they cannot earn the attention of peers or teachers, and no reinforcers are present.

Programmed Learning: Step by Step   B. F. Skinner developed an educational method called *programmed learning* that is based on operant conditioning. This method assumes that any complex task involving conceptual learning as well as motor skills can be broken down into a number of small steps. These steps can be shaped individually and then combined in sequence to form the correct behavioral chain.

Programmed learning does not punish errors. Instead, correct responses are reinforced. Every child earns "100," but at her or his own pace. Programmed learning also assumes it is the task of the teacher (or program) to structure the learning experience in such a way that errors will not be made. ◆ **Truth or Fiction Revisited:** Actually, one can learn *without* making mistakes.

( ) Learning Connections

◀◀   *Operant Conditioning—Learning What Does What to What*   ▶▶

REVIEW:

6 One removes _____ reinforcers to increase the probability that operant behavior will occur.
(a) positive,
(b) negative,
(c) conditional,
(d) unconditional.

7 In operant conditioning, repeated performance of a learned response in the absence of reinforcement leads to
(a) spontaneous recovery,
(b) extinction,
(c) punishment,
(d) stimulus discrimination.

8 A(n) _____ stimulus indicates when operant behavior will be reinforced.
(a) discriminative,
(b) conditioned,
(c) unconditioned,
(d) primary.

9 Slot machines pay off on a _____ schedule.
(a) fixed-interval,
(b) fixed-ratio,
(c) variable-interval,
(d) variable-ratio.

10 _____ training enables organisms to gain control of autonomic responses to attain reinforcement.
(a) Relaxation,
(b) Medical,
(c) Biofeedback,
(d) Interval.

11 _____ learning breaks down learning tasks into small steps and reinforces correct performance of each step.
(a) Cognitive,
(b) Fixed,
(c) Variable,
(d) Programmed.

CRITICAL THINKING:
Every time I tell my classes that many psychologists frown on the use of punishment, many students chide me for being unrealistic and "goody-goody." Let's try some critical thinking: What are the effects of punishment? Does it stop undesirable behavior? If so, when? Are there other ways of encouraging desirable behavior? Which is preferable? How can we judge?

Go
to www
http://academic.cengage.com/psychology/rathus
for an interactive version of this review.

COGNITIVE FACTORS IN LEARNING

Classical and operant conditioning were originally conceived of as relatively simple forms of learning. Much of conditioning's appeal is that it can be said to meet the behaviorist objective of explaining behavior in terms of observable events—in this case, laboratory conditions. Building on this theoretical base, some psychologists have suggested that the most complex human behavior involves the summation of a series of instances of conditioning. Many psychologists believe, however, that conditioning is too mechanical a process to explain all instances of learned behavior, even in laboratory rats. They turn to cognitive factors to describe and explain additional findings in the psychology of learning. *How do we explain what happens during classical conditioning from a cognitive perspective?*

In addition to concepts such as *association* and *reinforcement*, cognitive psychologists use concepts such as *mental structures, schemas, templates,* and *information processing.* Cognitive psychologists see people as searching for information, weighing evidence, and making decisions. Let us consider some classic research that points to cognitive factors in learning, as opposed to mechanical associations. These cognitive factors are not necessarily limited to humans—although, of course, people are the only species that can talk about them.

⬛ Latent Learning: Forming Cognitive Maps

I'm all grown up. I know the whole mall.
—The Author's Daughter Jordan at Age 7

Many behaviorists argue that organisms acquire only responses for which they are reinforced. E. C. Tolman, however, showed that rats also learn about their environment in the absence of reinforcement. In doing so, he showed that rats must form cognitive maps of their surroundings. *What is the evidence that people and lower animals form cognitive maps of their environments?*

Latent Hidden or concealed.

Tolman trained some rats to run through mazes for food goals. Other rats were allowed to explore the same mazes for several days without food goals or other rewards. After the unrewarded rats had been allowed to explore the mazes for ten days, food rewards were placed in a box at the far end of the maze. The previously unrewarded rats reached the food box as quickly as the rewarded rats after only one or two trials (Tolman & Honzik, 1930).

Tolman concluded that the rats had learned about the mazes by exploring them even when they went unrewarded by food. He distinguished between *learning* and *performance.* Rats apparently created a cognitive map of a maze. Even though they were not externally motivated to follow a rapid route through the maze, they would learn fast routes just by exploring it. Yet this learning might remain hidden, or **latent,** until food motivated them to take the rapid routes.

Stephen Johnson /Getty Images

⬛ How Do They Learn Their Way Around the Mall?
Have these shoppers simply been conditioned to turn left or right at various choice points like so many rats in a maze, or have they learned to mentally represent the mall? (And do rats also learn to mentally represent mazes?)

⬛ Contingency Theory: Does Conditioning Work Because It Provides Information?

Behaviorists and cognitive psychologists interpret classical conditioning in different ways. Behaviorists explain it in terms of the pairing of stimuli. Cognitive psychologists explain classical conditioning in terms of the ways in which stimuli provide information that allows organisms to form or revise mental representations of their environment. Robert Rescorla's

contingency theory suggests that learning occurs only when the conditioned stimulus (CS) provides *information* about the unconditioned stimulus (US).

In classical conditioning of dogs, Rescorla (1967) obtained some results that are difficult to explain without reference to cognitive concepts. Each phase of his work paired a tone (a CS) with an electric shock (a US), but in different ways. With one group of animals, the shock was consistently presented after the tone. The dogs in this group learned to show a fear response when the tone was presented.

A second group of dogs heard an equal number of tones and received an equal number of electric shocks, but the shock did not immediately follow the tone. In other words, the tone and the shock were not paired. Now, from the behaviorist perspective, the dogs should not have learned to associate the tone and the shock, because one did not predict the other. Actually, the dogs learned quite a lot: They learned that they had nothing to fear when the tone was sounded! They showed vigilance and fear when the laboratory was quiet—for the shock might come at any time—but they were calm in the presence of the tone itself.

The third group of dogs also received equal numbers of tones and shocks, but the stimuli were presented at random. Occasionally they were paired, but most often they were not. According to Rescorla, behaviorists might argue that intermittent pairing of the tones and shocks should have brought about some learning. Yet it did not. The animals showed no fear in response to the tone. Rescorla suggests that the animals in this group learned nothing because the tones did not allow them to make predictions about electric shock. Rescorla concluded that learning occurs only when the CS (in this case, the tone) provides information about the US (in this case, the shock).

■ Observational Learning: Monkey See, Monkey May *Choose* to Do?

How many things have you learned from watching other people in real life, in films, and on television? From films and television, you may have gathered vague ideas about how to sky-dive, ride a surfboard, climb sheer cliffs, run a pattern to catch a touchdown pass in the Super Bowl, and dust for fingerprints, even if you have never tried them yourself. How do people learn by observing others?

In experiments on **observational learning,** Albert Bandura and his colleagues conducted experiments (e.g., Bandura et al., 1963) that show that we can acquire skills by observing the behavior of others. Observational learning occurs when, as children, we watch our parents cook, clean, or repair a broken appliance. Observational learning takes place

---

Contingency theory The view that learning occurs when stimuli provide information about the likelihood of the occurrence of other stimuli.

Observational learning The acquisition of knowledge and skills through the observation of others (who are called *models*) rather than by means of direct experience.

■ **Observational Learning**
Cognitive psychologists note that people usually do not learn complex skills on the basis of the summation of so many instances of conditioning. Rather, we can intend to learn, focus on models, and imitate and adapt the behaviors we observe.

Tom McCarthy/PhotoEdit

■ CONCEPT REVIEW 6.1 ■

KINDS OF LEARNING

KIND OF LEARNING		WHAT IS LEARNED	HOW IT IS LEARNED
Classical conditioning Major proponents: Ivan Pavlov (known for basic research with dogs) John B. Watson (known as originator of behaviorism)	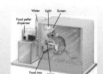	Association of events; anticipations, signs, expectations; automatic responses to new stimuli	A neutral stimulus is repeatedly paired with a stimulus (an unconditioned stimulus, or UCS) that elicits a response (an unconditioned response, or UCR) until the neutral stimulus produces a response (conditioned response, or CR) that anticipates and prepares for the unconditioned stimulus. At this point, the neutral stimulus has become a conditioned stimulus (CS).
Operant conditioning Major proponent: B. F. Skinner		Behavior that operates on, or affects, the environment to produce consequences	A response is rewarded or reinforced so that it occurs with greater frequency in similar situations.
Observational learning Major proponents: Albert Bandura Julian Rotter Walter Mischel	Tom McCarthy/PhotoEdit	Expectations (if–then relationships), knowledge, and skills	A person observes the behavior of another person (live or through media such as films, television, or books) and its effects.

when we watch teachers solve problems on the blackboard or hear them speak in a foreign language. Observational learning is not mechanically acquired through reinforcement. We can learn through observation without engaging in overt responses at all. It appears sufficient to pay attention to the behavior. We may need some practice to refine the skills we acquire. We may also allow these skills to lie dormant or latent. For example, we may not imitate aggressive behavior unless we are provoked and believe that we are more likely to be rewarded than punished for it.

In the terminology of observational learning, a person who engages in a response that is imitated is a **model.** When we see modeled behavior being reinforced, we are said to be *vicariously* reinforced. Engaging in the behavior thus becomes more likely for us as well as for the model. Concept Review 6.1 summarizes various kinds of learning.

Have you ever studied an atlas, a road map, a cookbook, or a computer manual for the pleasure of doing so? What kind of learning were you engaging in? Was there any reinforcement? If so, what was it? When did it occur?

■ Violence in the Media and Aggression

We learn by observing parents and peers, attending school, reading books, and watching media such as television and films. Nearly all of us have been exposed to television, videotapes, and films in the classroom. Children in day-care centers often watch *Sesame Street.* There are filmed and electronic versions of great works of literature such as Orson Welles's *Macbeth* or Laurence Olivier's *Hamlet.*

But what of our exposure to the media *outside* the classroom? Television and the Internet are key sources of informal observational learning. Children are routinely exposed to scenes of murder, beating, and sexual assault—just by turning on the TV set (Huesmann et al., 2003). If a child watches 2 to 4 hours of TV a day, she or he will have seen 8,000 murders

Model An organism that engages in a response that is then imitated by another organism.

Michael Newman/PhotoEdit

■ What Are the Effects of Media Violence?

Preschool children in the United States watch TV an average of four hours a day. Schoolchildren spend more hours at the TV set than in the classroom. Is it any wonder psychologists, educators, and parents express concern about the effects of media violence?

and another 100,000 acts of violence *by the time she or he has finished elementary school* (Eron, 2000). Are kids less likely to be exposed to violence by going to the movies? No. One study found that virtually all G-rated animated films have scenes of violence, with a mean duration of 9 to 10 minutes per film (Yokota & Thompson, 2000). Other media with violent content include films, music, music videos, video games, the Internet, and comic books (Anderson, 2004).

Bandura: Effects of Violence in the Media   A classic experiment by Bandura, Ross, and Ross (1963) suggests the influence of aggressive models. One group of preschool children observed a film of an adult model hitting and kicking an inflated Bobo doll, while a control group saw an aggression-free film. The experimental and control groups were then left alone in a room with the same doll, as hidden observers recorded their behavior. The children who had observed the aggressive model showed significantly more aggressive behavior toward the doll themselves (see Figure 6.9). Many children imitated bizarre attacks they would not have thought up themselves. ◆ **Truth or Fiction Revisited:** Actually, numerous scientific connections have been established between violence in the media and real-life aggression.

Violence tends to be glamorized in the media. Superheroes battle villains who are trying to destroy or take over the world. Violence is often portrayed as having only temporary or minimal effects. (How often has Wile E. Coyote fallen from a cliff and been pounded into the ground by a boulder, only to bounce back and pursue the Road Runner once more?) In the great majority of violent TV shows, there is no remorse, criticism, or penalty for violent behavior. Few TV programs show harmful long-term consequences of aggressive behavior.

Albert Bandura

Figure 6.9
Classic Research on the Imitation of Aggressive Models
Albert Bandura and his colleagues found evidence that children frequently imitate the aggressive behavior that they observe. In the top row, an adult model strikes a clown doll. The lower rows show a boy and a girl imitating the aggressive behavior.

Seeing the perpetrator of the violence go unpunished increases the chances that the child will act aggressively (Krcmar & Cooke, 2001). Children may not even view death as much of a problem. As killer Evan Ramsey said, being shot might reduce a person's "health factor." How often do video-game characters "die"—only to be reborn to fight again?

Why all this violence? Simple: Violence sells. But does violence do more than sell? That is, does media violence *cause* real violence? If so, what can parents and educators do to prevent the fictional from spilling over into the real world?

Consensus on the Effects of Violence in the Media?   In any event, most organizations of health professionals agree that media violence contributes to aggression (Anderson, 2004; Huesmann et al., 2003). Consider a number of ways in which depictions of violence make such a contribution:

- *Observational learning.* Children learn from observation (Anderson, 2003, 2004). TV violence models aggressive "skills," which children may acquire. Media violence also provides viewers with aggressive *scripts*—that is, ideas about how to behave in situations like those they have observed (Huesmann et al., 2003).
- *Disinhibition.* Punishment inhibits behavior. Conversely, media violence may disinhibit aggressive behavior, especially when media characters "get away" with violence or are rewarded for it (Haridakis, 2002).
- *Increased arousal.* Media violence and aggressive video games increase viewers' emotional arousal (Bushman & Anderson, 2001). That is, media "work them up." We are more likely to be aggressive when we are aroused.
- *Priming of aggressive thoughts and memories.* Media violence triggers aggressive ideas and memories (Bushman & Anderson, 2002).
- *Habituation.* We become "habituated to," or used to, repeated stimuli. Repeated exposure to TV violence may decrease viewers' sensitivity to real violence. If children come to perceive violence as the norm, they may become more tolerant of it and place less value on restraining aggressive urges (Anderson et al., 2003).

On the other hand, viewers are more likely to imitate media violence when they identify with the characters and when the portrayal of violence is realistic (Huesmann et al., 2003). Therefore, viewers may be more likely to imitate violence when the perpetrator looks like them and lives in a similar environment than when it is perpetrated by Wile E. Coyote.

Playing violent video games increases aggressive thoughts and behavior in the laboratory (Anderson, 2003, 2004). It is also connected with a history of juvenile delinquency. However, males are relatively more likely than females to act aggressively after playing violent video games and are more likely to see the world as a hostile place (Bartholow & Anderson, 2002). But students who obtain higher grades are *less* likely than their lower-achieving peers to act aggressively after exposure to violent media games. Thus, gender roles, possible biological gender differences, and psychological factors such as achievement motivation also figure into the effects of media violence.

There seems to be a circular relationship between exposure to media violence and aggressive behavior (Anderson & Dill, 2000; Anderson et al., 2003; Haridakis, 2002). Yes, violence in the media contributes to aggressive behavior, but aggressive youngsters are also more likely to seek out this kind of entertainment. Figure 6.10 explores the possible connections between media violence and aggressive behavior.

The family also affects the likelihood that children will imitate media violence. Studies find that parental substance abuse, paternal physical punishments, and single parenting contribute to the likelihood of aggression in early childhood (Brook et al., 2001; Gupta et al., 2001). Parental rejection and use of physical punishment further increase the likelihood of aggression in children (Eron, 1982). These family factors suggest that the parents of aggressive children may be absent or unlikely to help young children understand that the kinds of socially inappropriate behaviors they see in the media are not for them. A harsh home life may also confirm the TV viewer's or game player's vision of the world as a violent place.

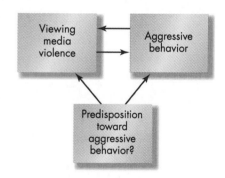

Figure 6.10

What Are the Connections Between Media Violence and Aggressive Behavior?
Does media violence cause aggressive behavior? Do aggressive children prefer to tune into violent shows? Or do third factors, such as personality traits that create a disposition toward aggression, contribute both to aggressive behavior and the interest in media violence?

Life Connections
Teaching Children Not to Imitate Media Violence

Children are going to be exposed to media violence—if not in Saturday morning cartoon shows, then in evening dramas and in the news. Or they'll hear about violence from friends, watch other children get into fights, or read about violence in the newspapers. If all those sources of violence were somehow hidden from view, they would learn about violence in *Hamlet*, *Macbeth*, even the Bible. It may be impossible to prevent children from being exposed to violent models.

What, then, can be done? Parents and educators can do many things to tone down the impact of media violence (Huesmann et al., 2003). Children who watch violent shows act less aggressively when they are informed that:

- The violent behavior they observe in the media does *not* represent the behavior of most people.
- The apparently aggressive behaviors they watch are not real. They reflect camera tricks, special effects, and stunts.
- Most people resolve conflicts by nonviolent means.
- The real-life consequences of violence are harmful to the victim and, often, the aggressor.

If children believe violence to be inappropriate for them, they will be less likely to act aggressively, even if they have acquired aggressive skills from exposure to the media or other sources.

It would be of little use to talk about learning if we couldn't remember what we learn from second to second or from day to day. In the next chapter, we turn our attention to memory. In Chapter 8, we see how learning is intertwined with thinking, language, and intelligence. ■

() Learning Connections

◀◀ Cognitive Factors in Learning ▶▶

REVIEW:

12 Tolman labels learning without performing
(a) stimulus generalization,
(c) conditioning,
(c) latent learning,
(d) spontaneous recovery.

13 Bandura found that observers are likely to imitate the behavior of models when the models
(a) are rewarded,
(b) are unlike the observers,
(c) know they are being watched,
(d) are on film or television.

Learning Connections

CRITICAL THINKING:
Critical thinkers pay attention to the definitions of terms. Does violence in the media *cause* violence in real life? Look up the definition of the word *cause* and explain why some scientists prefer to say that violence in the media is a *risk factor* for violence in real life.

Go to
http://academic.cengage.com/psychology/rathus
for an interactive version of this review.

RECITE—*An Active Summary*™

 Recite to Go! *Don't have time to study right now? You can study on the go!*
Go to your companion website and download an audio version of this review section to your media player. You can also access an interactive flash-card version of this review from your website.

1. What is learning?	Learning is the process by which experience leads to relatively permanent changes in behavior.
2. What is classical conditioning?	Classical conditioning is a simple form of associative learning in which a previously neutral stimulus (CS) comes to elicit the response evoked by a second stimulus (UCS) as a result of repeatedly being paired with the second stimulus.
3. What is the contribution of Ivan Pavlov to the psychology of learning?	Pavlov happened upon conditioning by chance, as he was studying salivation in laboratory dogs. Pavlov discovered that reflexes can be learned, or *conditioned*, through association.
4. What are taste aversions? Why are they of special interest to psychologists?	Taste aversions are instances of classical conditioning in which organisms learn that a food is noxious on the basis of a nauseating experience. Taste aversions are of interest because learning may occur from a single association and because the UCS (nausea) can occur hours after the CS (the flavor of food).
5. What is the role of extinction in classical conditioning?	Extinction helps organisms adapt to environmental changes. After a UCS–CS association has been learned, repeated presentation of the CS without the UCS extinguishes the CR.
6. What is the role of spontaneous recovery in classical conditioning?	Extinguished responses may show spontaneous recovery as a function of the time that has elapsed since extinction occurred.
7. What is the role of generalization in classical conditioning?	Generalization and discrimination are also adaptive. Generalization helps organisms adapt to new events by responding to a range of stimuli similar to the CS.
8. What is the role of discrimination in classical conditioning?	In discrimination, organisms learn to show a CR in response to a more limited range of stimuli by pairing only the limited stimulus with the US.
9. What is higher-order conditioning?	In higher-order conditioning, a previously neutral stimulus comes to serve as a CS after being paired repeatedly with another CS.
10. What is the contribution of B. F. Skinner to the psychology of learning?	Skinner developed the concept of reinforcement and innovated techniques for studying operant conditioning such as the "Skinner box" and the cumulative recorder. He developed behavior modification and programmed learning.
11. What is operant conditioning?	Operant conditioning is a simple form of learning in which organisms learn to engage in behavior that is reinforced. Reinforced responses occur with greater frequency.
12. What are the various kinds of reinforcers?	These include positive, negative, primary, and secondary reinforcers.
13. What is the role of extinction in operant conditioning?	In operant conditioning, learned responses are extinguished as a result of repeated performance in the absence of reinforcement.
14. What is the role of spontaneous recovery in operant conditioning?	As in classical conditioning, spontaneous recovery occurs as a function of the passage of time.

15. Why did Skinner make a point of distinguishing between reinforcers on the one hand, and rewards and punishments on the other?	Rewards and punishments are defined, respectively, as pleasant and aversive events that affect behavior. Skinner preferred the concept of *reinforcement* because lists of reinforcers are obtained by observing their effects on behavior.
16. Why do many psychologists disapprove of punishment?	Many psychologists recommend not using punishment because it hurts, does not suggest acceptable behavior, and may create feelings of hostility.
17. What are discriminative stimuli?	Discriminative stimuli (such as green lights) indicate when operants (such as pecking a button) will be reinforced.
18. What are the various schedules of reinforcement? How do they affect behavior?	Continuous reinforcement leads to the most rapid acquisition of new responses, but behavior is maintained most economically through partial reinforcement. The four reinforcement schedules are fixed-interval, variable-interval, fixed-ratio, and variable-ratio schedules.
19. How can we use shaping to teach complex behavior patterns?	In shaping, successive approximations of the target response are reinforced, leading to the performance of a complex sequence of behaviors.
20. How do we explain what happens during classical conditioning from a cognitive perspective?	According to contingency theory, organisms learn associations between stimuli when stimuli provide new information about each other.
21. What is the evidence that people and lower animals form cognitive maps of their environments?	Some evidence is derived from Tolman's research on latent learning. He demonstrated that rats can learn—that is, they can modify their cognitive map of the environment—in the absence of reinforcement.
22. How do people learn by observing others?	Bandura has shown that people can learn to do things simply by observing others; they need not emit responses that are reinforced. Learners may then choose whether to perform the observed behaviors.

Key Terms

Learning   209
Classical conditioning   210
Stimulus   210
Unconditioned stimulus (UCS)   211
Unconditioned response (UCR)   211
Orienting reflex   211
Conditioned stimulus (CS)   211
Conditioned response (CR)   211
Extinction   213
Spontaneous recovery   214
Generalization   215
Discrimination   215
Higher-order conditioning   216
Counterconditioning   216

Flooding   217
Systematic desensitization   218
Reinforce   219
Operant behavior   220
Operant conditioning   220
Positive reinforcer   221
Negative reinforcer   221
Primary reinforcer   222
Secondary reinforcer   222
Conditioned reinforcer   222
Reward   223
Punishment   223
Time out   224
Discriminative stimulus   225

Continuous reinforcement   225
Partial reinforcement   225
Fixed-interval schedule   225
Variable-interval schedule   226
Fixed-ratio schedule   227
Variable-ratio schedule   227
Shaping   228
Successive approximations   228
Latent   231
Contingency theory   232
Observational learning   232
Model   233

Active Learning Resources

Visit Your Companion Website for This Book

http://academic.cengage.com/psychology/rathus

Check out this companion website where you will find online resources directly linked to your book. This is where you'll access the videos highlighted in your Video Connections feature. You can answer the questions online and email them to your professor. In addition you'll find downloadable audio review material, interactive versions of the study aids, Power Visuals for mastering and reviewing key concepts, as well as quizzing, and much more!

CENGAGENOW™

http://academic.cengage.com

Need help studying? This site is your one-stop study shop. Take a Pre-Test and Cengage NOW will generate a Personalized Study Plan based on your test results. The Study Plan will identify the topics you need to review and direct you to online resources to help you master those topics. You can then take a Post-Test to help you determine the concepts you have mastered and what you still need to work on. In addition you can access interactive media including the videos highlighted in your Video Connections box.

Author Blog

What does your author Spence Rathus have to say about the state of psychology? Visit your companion website every Tuesday and click on "Author Blog." This is where he'll talk about the most recent controversies and hot topics in psychology. This will keep you up to date with what your author is thinking and give you great insight into modern psychology.

CHAPTER 7

Memory: Remembrance of Things Past—and Future

J Price/Getty Images

T F	A woman who could not remember who she was automatically dialed her mother's number when the police gave her a telephone.
T F	Oh say, can you see? If the answer is yes, you have a photographic memory.
T F	Learning must be meaningful if we are to remember it.
T F	It may be easier for you to recall the name of your first-grade teacher than the name of someone you just met at a party.
T F	All of our experiences are permanently imprinted on the brain, so the proper stimulus can cause us to remember them exactly.
T F	You may always recall where you were and what you were doing on the morning of September 11, 2001.
T F	If you study with the stereo on, you would probably do better to take the test with the stereo on.
T F	Learning Spanish can make it harder to remember French—and vice versa.
T F	After part of his hippocampus was surgically removed, a man could not form new memories. Each time he was reminded of his uncle's dying, he grieved as he had when he first heard of it.
T F	You may improve your memory by sniffing a hormone.

Go to www
http://academic.cengage.com/pstchology/rathus
for an interactive version of this Truth or Fiction feature.

J eff would never forget his sudden loss of memory. He watched in horror as his flip phone slipped from his pocket and fell to the floor of the Blockbuster store in Boston. Before he could grab it, it shattered into pieces. A New York college student, Jeff experienced the trauma of phone loss on his winter break.

Why was the loss traumatic? Why was it a memory problem? Simple: There was no way for Jeff to retrieve his phone book. "I was at the store and it was snowing out and I suddenly realized that I had no way of getting in touch with anyone," he explains (Metz, 2005). The worst part of the loss was that Jeff had been seeing someone in New York, and now he had no way to contact her. Because her cell phone was her only phone, he could not call information. A day later he showed up on her doorstep, hoping she wouldn't think he had been avoiding her calls. She forgave him but had him write her number down—on paper. Still, Jeff would not forget the day his cell phone lost its memory.

Jeff now copies every cell-phone entry in a little black book—made of paper. Other people back up their phone books—and their pictures and downloads—on servers provided by cellular telephone operating companies or cell-phone manufacturers. Verizon Wireless, for example, offers "Backup Assistant." Motorola's brand is "MyBackup." Most people provide their old cell phone when obtaining a new one so that its memory can be transferred. But if, like Jeff, you suffer memory loss . . .

Why is that phone book so crucial? Is it because you'd rather speed dial or voice dial than press all those little buttons? Speed dialing is useful enough, but if you're like many millions of others, a more important reason is that you don't want to deal with memorizing all those numbers—especially when you've got your family, your friends, your coworkers, your drugstore, your pizza-delivery service, your tutor, your auto repair shop, your hairdresser, your yoga center, and perhaps your pet groomer in it.

What's the problem with remembering all those phone numbers? The answer lies partly in their length. Psychologist George Miller (1956) researched the amount of information people can keep in mind at once, and he found that the average person is comfortable with digesting about seven digits at a time. Most people have little trouble recalling five pieces of information, as in a zip code. Some can remember nine, which is, for most, an upper limit. So seven pieces of information, plus or minus one or two, is the "magic" number.

But when you add in area codes, the number is ten digits long, not seven. And when you consider that we put people's home numbers, mobile numbers, and work numbers in our phone books, we have several entries to remember for many people.

There's more. Numbers may struggle with one another for attention. Or, to put it more scientifically, similar numbers may "pop in" when we are trying to remember a number. One source of confusion is that many people keep the same mobile number even when they move, so their area code may not represent where they live, work, or go to college. Then there's the friend whose last four digits are 5015, but someone else's are 5105. You tell yourself, "Okay it's *not* the same as Lataya's," but then (a) you can't remember which one was Lataya's, or (b) you're not absolutely certain whether it *was* or *was not* the same as Lataya's. After you mess it up a few times, you give up.

If you know a number "cold"—for example, 5015—and then you learn a new, similar number—for example, 5105—the first number might interfere with your ability to recall the second. Psychologists call that memory problem *proactive interference*. Or perhaps learning the second phone number— 5105—interferes with your ability to remember the first number—5015. That memory problem is called *retroactive interference*.

This chapter is all about the "backup assistant" in your brain—your memory. Without your memory, there is no past. Without your memory, experience is trivial and learning is lost. Let us see what psychologists have learned about the ways in which we remember things—other than keying them into a cell-phone phone book. First, however, try to meet the challenges to your memory we pose in the nearby Self-Assessment. We'll be talking about your responses throughout the chapter.

Self-Assessment

Self-Assessment

Self-Assessment

Five Challenges to Your Memory

Let's challenge your memory. This is not an actual memory test of the sort used by psychologists to determine whether people's memory functioning is within normal limits. Instead, it will provide you with some insight into how your memory works and may also be fun.

Directions: Find four sheets of blank paper and number them 1 through 4. Also use a watch with a second hand. Then follow these instructions:

1. Following are ten letters. Look at them for 15 seconds. Later in the chapter, I will ask you if you can write them on sheet number 1. (No cheating! Don't do it now.)

THUNSTOFAM

2. Look at these nine figures for 30 seconds. Then try to draw them in the proper sequence on sheet number 2. (Yes, right after you've finished looking at them. We'll talk about your drawings later.)

3. Okay, here's another list of letters, 17 this time. Look at the list for 60 seconds and then see whether you can reproduce it on sheet number 3. (I'm being generous this time—a full minute.)

GMC-BSI-BMA-TTC-IAF-BI

4. Which of these pennies is an accurate reproduction of the Lincoln penny you see every day? This time there's nothing to draw on another sheet; just circle or put a checkmark by the penny that you think resembles the ones you throw in the back of the drawer.

5. Examine the following drawings for 1 minute. Then copy the names of the figures on sheet number 4. When you're finished, just keep reading. Soon I'll be asking you to draw those figures.

 eyeglasses   hourglass   seven   gun

Go to www *http://academic.cengage.com/psychology/rathus where you can fill out an interactive version of this Self-Assessment and automatically score your results.*

That's it. You'll find out about the results of this Self-Assessment as you read through the chapter.

MEMORY SYSTEMS: PRESSING THE "REWIND" AND "FAST-FORWARD" BUTTONS

Jeff remembered things he had personally done, like drop his cell phone in Boston and show up at his girlfriend's doorstep on a blustery day in January. Remembering dropping one's cell phone is an *episodic memory*—a memory of an event in one's life. According to psychologists who have extensively researched memory, episodic memory is one kind of memory system (Dobbins et al., 2004; Schacter, 2000; Zola et al., 2003). And when I learned of Jeff's experience, I tried to remind myself repeatedly not to forget to jot down notes about it and write it up as soon as I could. (I was trying to jog my *prospective memory*—to remember to do something in the future.) Let us consider several memory systems.

Explicit Versus Implicit Memories

What is meant by explicit memory? **Explicit memory**—also referred to as *declarative memory*—is memory for specific information. Things that are *explicit* are clear, or clearly stated or explained. The use of the term *declarative* indicates that these memories state or reveal (i.e., *declare*) specific information. The information may be autobiographical or refer to general knowledge. ("Well, I declare!")

Implicit memory—also referred to as *nondeclarative memory*—is memory of how to perform a procedure or skill; it is the act itself, *doing* something, like riding a bike, accessing your cell-phone phone book, and texting a message (Schacter et al., 1993). While Jeff was talking excitedly about his experiences, he was also demonstrating implicit memories: how to talk and, for that matter, how to prance about the room.

First let us talk more about two kinds of explicit memories described by psychologist Endel Tulving (1985; Tulving & Markowitsch, 1998): episodic and semantic. They are identified according to the type of information they hold.

Episodic Memory *What is meant by episodic memory?* **Episodic memories** are kinds of explicit memories. They are memories of the things that happen to us or take place in our presence (Eichenbaum & Fortin, 2003). Episodic memory is also referred to as *autobiographical memory*. Your memories of what you ate for breakfast and of what your professor said in class today are episodic memories.

Semantic Memory: On *Not* Getting Personal *What is meant by semantic memory?* General knowledge is referred to as **semantic memory**. *Semantics* concerns meanings. You can "remember" that the United States has 50 states without visiting them and personally adding them up. You "remember" who authored *Hamlet*, although you were not looking over Shakespeare's shoulder as he did so. These are examples of semantic memory.

Your future recollection that there are several memory systems is more likely to be semantic than episodic. In other words, you are more likely to "know" that there are several types of memory than to recall the date on which you learned about them, where you were, how you were sitting, and whether you were also thinking about dinner at the time. We tend to use the phrase "I remember . . . " when we are referring to episodic memories, as in "I *remember* the blizzard of 2004." But we are more likely to say "I know . . . " in reference to semantic memories, as in "I *know* about—" (or, "I heard about—") "—the blizzard of 1898." Put it another way: You may *remember* that you wrote to your mother, but you *know* that Shakespeare wrote *Hamlet*.

Implicit Memory: Remembering as Doing *What is meant by implicit memory?* As the term *implicit* implies (should I start this sentence again?), implicit memories are suggested (or implied) but not plainly stated or verbally expressed. Implicit memories are illustrated by the things that people *do* but not by the things they state clearly. Implicit memories involve procedures and skills, cognitive and physical, and are also referred to as *procedural* or *skill memories*.

■ An Example of an Implicit Memory Memories of how to ride a bicycle, how to type, how to turn the lights on and off, and how to drive a car are implicit memories. Implicit memories tend to persist even when we do not use them for many years. This photo of the older Jean Piaget, the cognitive-developmental theorist discussed in Chapter 3, suggests that we may never forget how to ride a bicycle.

Explicit memory Memory that clearly and distinctly expresses (explicates) specific information.

Implicit memory Memory that is suggested (implied) but not plainly expressed, as illustrated in the things that people *do* but do not state clearly.

Episodic memory Memories of events experienced by a person or that take place in the person's presence.

Semantic memory General knowledge, as opposed to episodic memory.

Here are some implicit memories: You have probably learned and now remember how to speak at least one language, how to ride a bicycle, how to swim or swing a bat, how to type, how to turn on the lights, how to drive a car, and how to text-message a friend. It is said that you never "forget" how to ride a bicycle. Implicit memories can endure even when we have not used them for years. Getting to class "by habit"—without paying attention to landmarks or directions—is another instance of implicit memory. If someone asked you what 2 times 2 is, the number 4 would probably "pop" into mind without conscious calculation. After going over the alphabet or multiplication tables hundreds of times, our memory of them becomes automatic or implicit. We need not focus on them to use them.

Your memory of the alphabet or the multiplication tables reflects repetition that makes associations automatic. This phenomenon is called **priming.** Brain imaging shows that priming makes it possible for people to carry out mental tasks with less neural activity (Savage et al., 2001; Schacter & Badgaiyan, 2001; Schacter et al., 2004). Years of priming helps people make complete words out of the word fragments (Schacter et al., 1999). Even though the cues in the following fragments are limited, you might make them into words:

PYGY   MRCA   TXT   BUFL

Sample answers are "Pygmy," "merchant," "text," and "buffalo." Let us jump ahead to the next chapter ("Thinking, Language, and Intelligence") to mention factors that affect how many words you can make out of these fragments. One is your expertise with English. If English is your second language, you will probably make fewer associations to these fragments than if English is your first language. Another factor is creativity. Can you think of other factors?

Daniel Schacter (1992) illustrates implicit memory with the story of a woman with amnesia who was wandering the streets. The police picked her up and found that she could not remember her identity or anything about her life and that she had no identification. After fruitless interviewing, the police hit on the idea of asking her to dial phone numbers—"any number at all." ◆ **Truth or Fiction Revisited:** Although the woman did not "know" what she was doing, she dialed her mother's number. When asked for the phone numbers of people she knew, she had had no answer. She could not *declare* her mother's phone number. She could not make the number *explicit.* She could not even remember her mother's name, or whether she had a mother. All this explicit information was gone. But dialing her mother's phone number was a habit, and she did it "on automatic pilot." She had been *primed* for the task by dialing the number thousands of times.

▅ Retrospective Memory Versus Prospective Memory

What is the difference between retrospective memory and prospective memory? **Retrospective memory** is the recalling of information that has been previously learned. *Episodic, semantic,* and *implicit memories* all involve remembering things that were learned. **Prospective memory** refers to remembering to do things in the future, such as remembering to brush your teeth before going out, to pay your bills (yuck), to take out some cash, and to make a list of things to do so you won't forget what to do! And if you do make a list of things to do, you must remember where you put it.

I tried to remember to jot down Jeff's cell-phone saga. Most of us have had failures of prospective memory in which we feel we were supposed to do something but can't remember what. Prospective memory may fail when we are preoccupied (caught up in surfing the Net or fantasizing about you-know-who), distracted (we get a text message just as we are about to do something), or "stressed out" about time (Schacter, 1999; Trafton et al., 2003).

There are various kinds of prospective memory tasks. *Habitual tasks* such as getting to class on time are easier to remember than occasional tasks such as meeting someone for coffee at an arbitrary time (d'Ydewalle et al., 1999). Motivation also plays a role. You are more likely to remember the coffee date if the person you are meeting excites you. Psychologists also distinguish between event-based and time-based prospective memory tasks (Fortin et al., 2002). *Event-based tasks* are triggered by events, such as remembering to take one's medicine at breakfast or to brush one's teeth after eating. *Time-based tasks* are to be performed at a certain time or after a certain amount of time has elapsed between occurrences,

Try a mini-experiment. Take out a pen or pencil and write your name. (Or, if you are using a keyboard, key in your name.) Now reflect: You remembered how to hold and write with the pen or pencil, or how to type. Did you have to "think" about how to do these things or were they "right there"? What type of memory is involved?

Priming The activation of specific associations in memory, often as a result of repetition and without making a conscious effort to access the memory.

Retrospective memory Memory for past events, activities, and learning experiences, as shown by explicit (episodic and semantic) and implicit memories.

Prospective memory Memory to perform an act in the future, as at a certain time or when a certain event occurs.

CONCEPT REVIEW   CONCEPT REVIEW

■ CONCEPT REVIEW 7.1 ■

MEMORY SYSTEMS

Looking Back, Looking Ahead

Memories can address past events (*retrospective memories*) or future events (*prospective memories*). Memories of the past can be *explicit* (declarative) or *implicit* (nondeclarative). Explicit memories include memories of personal episodes (which are called *episodic* or *autobiographical memories*) or of general information (*semantic memories*).

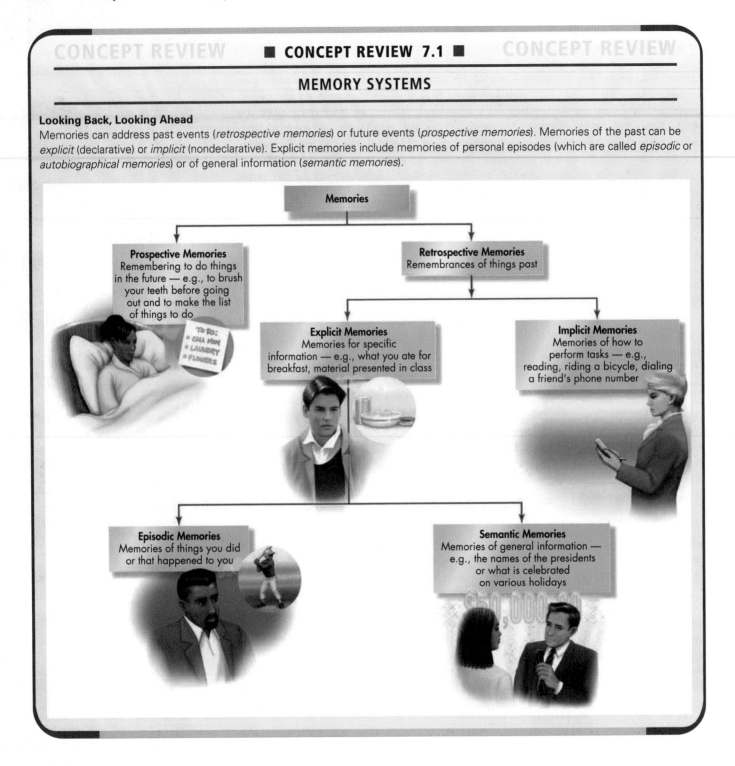

Memories

Prospective Memories
Remembering to do things in the future — e.g., to brush your teeth before going out and to make the list of things to do

Retrospective Memories
Remembrances of things past

Explicit Memories
Memories for specific information — e.g., what you ate for breakfast, material presented in class

Implicit Memories
Memories of how to perform tasks — e.g., reading, riding a bicycle, dialing a friend's phone number

Episodic Memories
Memories of things you did or that happened to you

Semantic Memories
Memories of general information — e.g., the names of the presidents or what is celebrated on various holidays

such as tuning in to a favorite news program at 7:30 PM or taking a pill every four hours (Marsh et al., 2005).

An age-related decline takes place in retrospective and prospective memories (Brigman & Cherry, 2002; Reese & Cherry, 2002). The decline in older adults may be related to their speed of cognitive processing rather than the "loss" of information per se. In the case of prospective memory, older adults take longer to respond to the cues or reminders (West & Craik, 1999). If they meet with a friend, they may remember that they were supposed to ask something, but they may take time to recall the question. Older adults with greater verbal ability and occupational status, however, are better able to keep intentions in mind (Reese & Cherry, 2002).

Moods and attitudes affect prospective memory (Villa & Abeles, 2000). For example, depressed people are less likely to push to remind themselves to do what they intend to do (Marsh et al., 2005; Rude et al., 1999). The various memory systems are summarized in Concept Review 7.1.

Before moving to the next section, turn to the piece of paper on which you wrote the names of the four figures in the Self-Assessment—that is, sheet number 4—and draw the figures from memory. Hold on to the drawings. We'll talk about them soon.

◯ Learning Connections

◄◄ *Memory Systems—Pressing the "Rewind" and "Fast-Forward" Buttons* ►►

REVIEW:

1 Remembering how to use a keyboard or ride a bicycle is a(n) _____ memory.
   (a) explicit,
   (b) implicit,
   (c) episodic,
   (d) semantic.

2 Memories of the events that happen to a person are _____ memories.
   (a) repressed,
   (b) implicit,
   (c) episodic,
   (d) semantic.

3 _____ memories concern generalized knowledge.
   (a) Retrospective,
   (b) Implicit,
   (c) Episodic,
   (d) Semantic.

CRITICAL THINKING:
Critical thinkers pay close attention to definitions. Does it seem strange that we can speak of using memory to remember to do things in the future? Explain your answer.

Go to www http://academic.cengage.com/psychology/rathus for an interactive version of this review.

PROCESSES OF MEMORY: PROCESSING INFORMATION IN OUR MOST PERSONAL COMPUTERS

Both psychologists and computer scientists speak of processing information. Think of using a computer to write a term paper. Once the system is up and operating, you begin to enter information. You can enter information into the computer's memory by, for example, typing alphanumeric characters on a keyboard or—in the case of voice recognition technology—speaking. But if you were to do some major surgery on your computer (which I am often tempted to do) and open up its memory, you wouldn't find these characters or sounds inside it. This is because the computer is programmed to change the characters or sounds—that is, the information you have entered—into a form that can be placed in its electronic memory. Similarly, when we perceive information, we must change it into a form that can be remembered if we are to place it in our memory.

Encoding: The Memory's "Transformer"

Information about the outside world reaches our senses in the form of physical and chemical stimuli. The first stage of information processing is changing information so that we can place it in memory: **encoding**. *What is the role of encoding in memory?* When we encode information, we transform it into psychological formats that can be represented mentally. To do so, we commonly use visual, auditory, and semantic codes.

Let us illustrate the uses of coding by referring to the list of letters you first saw in the section on challenges to memory. Try to write the letters on sheet number 1. Go on, take a minute and then come back.

If you had used a **visual code** to try to remember the list, you would have mentally represented it as a picture. That is, you would have maintained—or attempted to maintain—a mental image of the letters. Some artists and art historians seem to maintain marvelous visual mental representations of works of art. This enables them to quickly recognize whether a work is authentic.

You may also have decided to read the list of letters to yourself—that is, to silently say them in sequence: "t," "h," "u," and so on. By so doing, you would have been using an **acoustic code,** or representing the stimuli as a sequence of sounds. You may also have read the list as a three-syllable word, "thun-sto-fam." This is an acoustic code, but it also involves the "meaning" of the letters, in the sense that you are interpreting the list as a word. This approach has elements of a semantic code.

Semantic codes represent stimuli in terms of their meaning. Our 10 letters were meaningless in and of themselves. However, they can also serve as an acronym—a term made up of the first letters of a phrase—for the familiar phrase "THe UNited STates OF AMerica." This observation lends them meaning.

Storage: The Memory's "Save" Function

The second memory process is **storage**. *What is the role of storage in memory?* Storage means maintaining information over time. If you were given the task of storing the list of letters—that is, told to remember it—how would you attempt to place it in storage? One way would be by **maintenance rehearsal**—by mentally repeating the list, or saying it to yourself. Our awareness of the functioning of our memory, referred to by psychologists as **metamemory,** becomes more sophisticated as we develop.

You could also have condensed the amount of information you were rehearsing by reading the list as a three-syllable word; that is, you could have rehearsed three syllables (said "thun-sto-fam" over and over again) rather than 10 letters. In either case, repetition would have been the key to memory. (We talk more about such condensing, or "chunking," very soon.)

You could also encode the list of letters by relating it to something that you already know. This coding is called **elaborative rehearsal.** You are "elaborating" or extending the semantic meaning of the letters you are trying to remember. For example, as mentioned above, the list of 10 letters is an acronym for "The United States of America." (That is, you take the first 2 letters of each of the words in the phrase and string them together to make up the 10 letters of THUNSTOFAM.) If you had recognized this, storage of the list of letters might have been almost instantaneous, and it would probably have been permanent.

Adequate maintenance rehearsal, however, can do the job. ◇ **Truth or Fiction Revisited:** Therefore, it is not true that learning must be meaningful if we are to remember it.

Retrieval: The Memory's "Search" Function

The third memory process is **retrieval**. *What is the role of retrieval in memory?* The retrieval of stored information means locating it and returning it to consciousness. With well-known information such as our names and occupations, retrieval is effortless and, for all practical purposes, immediate. But when we are trying to remember large amounts of information, or information that is not perfectly understood, retrieval can be difficult or can fail. It is easiest to retrieve information stored in a computer by using the name of the file. Similarly, retrieval of information from our memories requires knowledge of the proper cues.

Encoding Modifying information so that it can be placed in memory. The first stage of information processing.

Visual code Mental representation of information as a picture.

Acoustic code Mental representation of information as a sequence of sounds.

Semantic code Mental representation of information according to its meaning.

Storage The maintenance of information over time. The second stage of information processing.

Maintenance rehearsal Mental repetition of information to keep it in memory.

Metamemory Self-awareness of the ways in which memory functions, allowing the person to encode, store, and retrieve information effectively.

Elaborative rehearsal The kind of coding in which new information is related to information that is already known.

Retrieval The location of stored information and its return to consciousness. The third stage of information processing.

If you had encoded THUNSTOFAM as a three-syllable word, your retrieval strategy would involve recollection of the word and rules for decoding. In other words, you would say the "word" *thun-sto-fam* and then decode it by spelling it out. You might err in that "thun" sounds like "thumb" and "sto" could also be spelled "stow." However, using the semantic code, or recognition of the acronym for "The United States of America," could lead to flawless recollection.

I stuck my neck out by predicting that you would immediately and permanently store the list if you recognized it as an acronym. Here, too, there would be recollection (of the name of a nation) and rules for decoding. That is, to "remember" the 10 letters, you would have to envision the phrase ("The United States of America") and read off the first 2 letters of each word. In this case, you are actually reconstructing the list of 10 letters.

Now, what if you were not able to remember the list of 10 letters? What would have gone wrong? In terms of the three processes of memory, it could be that you had (1) not encoded the list in a useful way, (2) not entered the encoded information into storage, or (3) stored the information but forgotten the cues for remembering it—such as the phrase "The United States of America" or the rule for decoding the phrase.

You may have noticed that we have come a long way into this chapter, but I have not yet *defined* memory. No apologies—we weren't ready. Now that we have explored some basic concepts, let us give it a try: **Memory** is the processes by which information is encoded, stored, and retrieved.

Memory The processes by which information is encoded, stored, and retrieved.

◯ Learning Connections

◀◀ *Processes of Memory—Processing Information in Our Most Personal Computers* ▶▶

REVIEW:

4 _____ is the transforming of information so that we can remember it.
   (a) Storage,
   (b) Processing,
   (c) Encoding,
   (d) Rehearsal.

5 Mental repetition of a stimulus is called
   (a) transformation,
   (b) discrimination,
   (c) priming,
   (d) maintenance rehearsal.

6 According to the text, the best way to remember *thunstofam* is by
   (a) elaborative rehearsal,
   (b) rote,
   (c) a visual code,
   (d) an auditory code.

CRITICAL THINKING:
Why would an author—like me—compare the functioning of memory to the functioning of a computer? Do you find the comparison to be helpful or misleading?

Go to
http://academic.cengage.com/psychology/rathus
for an interactive version of this review.

STAGES OF MEMORY: MAKING *SENSE* OF THE *SHORT* AND THE *LONG* OF IT

William James (1890) was intrigued by the fact that some memories are unreliable. They would "go in one ear and out the other," while other memories stuck for a lifetime. The world is a dazzling array of sights and sounds and other sources of sensory information, but only some of it is remembered. Psychologists Richard Atkinson and Richard Shiffrin (1968) suggested a model for how some information is lost immediately, other information is held

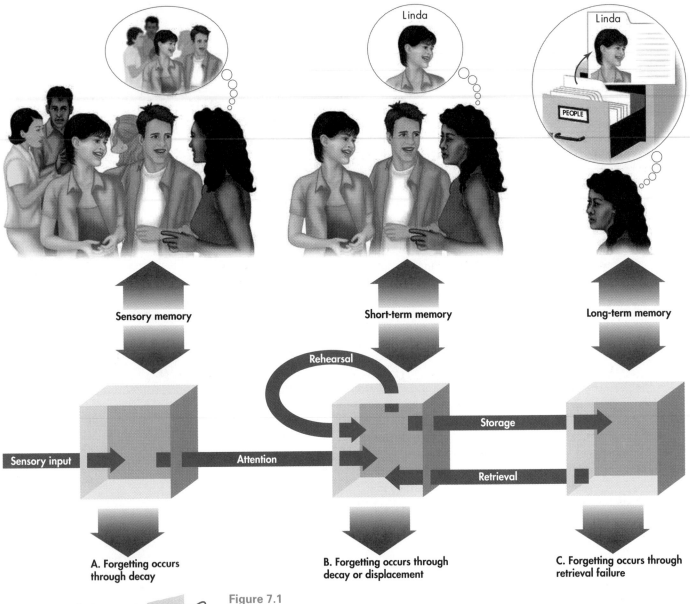

A. Forgetting occurs through decay

B. Forgetting occurs through decay or displacement

C. Forgetting occurs through retrieval failure

Go to your student website to access an interactive version of this figure.

Figure 7.1

Three Stages of Memory

The Atkinson–Shiffrin model proposes that there are three stages of memory: (a) sensory memory, (b) short-term memory, and (c) long-term memory. Part A shows that sensory information impacts on the registers of sensory memory. Memory traces are held briefly in sensory memory before decaying. If we attend to the information, much of it can be transferred to short-term memory (STM). Part B: Information may be maintained in STM through maintenance rehearsal or elaborative rehearsal. Otherwise, it may decay or be displaced. Part C: Once information is transferred to long-term memory (LTM), it may be filed away indefinitely. However, if the information in LTM is organized poorly, or if we cannot find cues to retrieve it, it can be lost.

briefly, and still other information is held for a lifetime. *What is the Atkinson–Shiffrin model of memory?* As shown in Figure 7.1, they proposed three stages of memory that determine whether (and how long) information is retained: *sensory memory, short-term memory* (STM), and *long-term memory* (LTM).

There is a saying that when you cover a topic completely, you are talking about "the long and short of it." In the case of the stages of memory, we could say that we are trying to "make *sense* of the *short* and the *long* of it."

Sensory Memory: Flashes on the Mental Monitor

When we look at a visual stimulus, our impressions may seem fluid enough. Actually, however, they consist of a series of eye fixations referred to as **saccadic eye movements.** These movements jump from one point to another about four times each second. Yet the visual sensations seem continuous, or streamlike, because of **sensory memory.** Sensory memory is the type or stage of memory that is first encountered by a stimulus. Although sensory memory holds impressions briefly, it is long enough so that a series of perceptions seem to be connected. *How does sensory memory function?*

To explain the functioning of sensory memory, let us return to our list of letters: THUNSTOFAM. If the list were flashed on a screen for a fraction of a second, the visual impression, or **memory trace,** of the stimulus would also last for only a fraction of a second afterward. Psychologists speak of the memory trace of the list as being held in a visual **sensory register.**

If the letters had been flashed on a screen for, say, 1/10th of a second, your ability to remember them on the basis of sensory memory alone would be limited. Your memory would be based on a single eye fixation, and the trace of the image would vanish before a single second had passed. A century ago, psychologist William McDougall (1904) engaged in research in which he showed people 1 to 12 letters arranged in rows—just long enough to allow a single eye fixation. Under these conditions, people could typically remember only 4 or 5 letters. Thus recollection of THUNSTOFAM, a list of 10 letters arranged in a single row, would probably depend on whether one had encoded it so that it could be processed further.

George Sperling (1960) modified McDougall's experimental method and showed that there is a difference between what people can see and what they can report. McDougall had used a *whole-report procedure,* in which people were asked to report every letter they saw in the array. Sperling used a modified *partial-report procedure,* in which people were asked to report the contents of one of three rows of letters. In a typical procedure, Sperling flashed three rows of letters like the following on a screen for 50 milliseconds (1/20th of a second):

A G R E
V L S B
N K B T

Using the whole-report procedure, people could report an average of 4 letters from the entire display (1 out of 3). But if immediately after presenting the display Sperling pointed an arrow at a row he wanted viewers to report, they usually reported most of the letters in the row successfully.

If Sperling presented 6 letters arrayed in two rows, people could usually report either row without error. If people were flashed three rows of 4 letters each—a total of 12—they reported correctly an average of 3 of 4 letters in the designated row, suggesting that about 9 of the 12 letters had been perceived.

Sperling found that the amount of time that elapsed before he pointed to the row to be reported affected people's memory. If he delayed pointing for a few fractions of a second after showing the letters, people were less successful in reporting the letters in the row. If he allowed a full second to elapse, the arrow did not help people remember at all. Sperling concluded that the memory trace of visual stimuli *decays* within a second (see Figure 7.1). With a single eye fixation, people can *see* most of a display of 12 letters clearly, as shown by their ability to immediately read off most of the letters in a designated row. Yet as fractions of a second are elapsing, the trace of the letters is fading. By the time a full second elapses, the trace is gone.

Iconic Memory   Psychologists believe we possess a sensory register for each sense. The mental representations of visual stimuli are referred to as **icons.** The sensory register that holds icons is labeled **iconic memory.** Iconic memories are accurate, photographic memories. ◆ **Truth or Fiction Revisited:** Those of us who see and mentally represent visual stimuli do have "photographic memories." But these memories are brief. What most of us

Saccadic eye movement The rapid jumps made by a person's eyes as they fixate on different points.

Sensory memory The type or stage of memory first encountered by a stimulus. Sensory memory holds impressions briefly, but long enough so that series of perceptions are psychologically continuous.

Memory trace An assumed change in the nervous system that reflects the impression made by a stimulus. Memory traces are said to be "held" in sensory registers.

Sensory register A system of memory that holds information briefly, but long enough so that it can be processed further. There may be a sensory register for every sense.

Icon A mental representation of a visual stimulus that is held briefly in sensory memory.

Iconic memory The sensory register that briefly holds mental representations of visual stimuli.

Ed Kashi /Corbis

■ **Memorizing a Script by Rehearsing Echoic Memories**

As actors work on memorizing scripts, they first encode visual information (printed words) as echoes (their corresponding sounds within the brain). Then they commit the echoes to memory by rehearsing (repeating) them, referring back to the visual information as necessary. Eventually, the lines of other actors become cues that trigger memory of an actor's own lines.

Eidetic imagery The maintenance of detailed visual memories over several minutes.

Echo A mental representation of an auditory stimulus (sound) that is held briefly in sensory memory.

Echoic memory The sensory register that briefly holds mental representations of auditory stimuli.

Short-term memory The type or stage of memory that can hold information for up to a minute or so after the trace of the stimulus decays. Also called *working memory.*

Working memory Same as *short-term memory.*

usually think of as a photographic memory—the ability to retain exact mental representations of visual stimuli over long periods—is technically termed **eidetic imagery.** Although all people who can see have photographic memories (that is, icons), only a few have eidetic imagery.

Iconic Memory and Saccadic Eye Movements   Iconic memory smooths out the bumps in the visual ride. Saccadic eye movements occur about four times a second. But iconic memory holds icons up to a second. For this reason, the flow of visual information seems smooth and continuous. Your impression that the words you are reading flow across the page, rather than jumping across in spurts, is a product of your iconic memory. Similarly, motion pictures present 16 to 22 separate frames, or still images, each second. Iconic memory allows you to perceive the imagery in the film as being seamless (G. R. Loftus, 1983).

Echoic Memory   Mental representations of sounds, or auditory stimuli, are called **echoes. Echoic memory** is the sensory register that holds echoes.

The memory traces of auditory stimuli—echoes—can last for several seconds, many times longer than the traces of visual stimuli (icons). This difference is one of the reasons that acoustic codes aid in the retention of information that has been presented visually—or why saying the letters or syllables of THUNSTOFAM makes the list easier to remember.

But echoes, like icons, fade with time. If they are to be retained, we must pay attention to them. By selectively attending to certain stimuli, we sort them out from background noise. For example, children have been shown photographs of rooms full of toys and been asked to recall as many as they can. One such study found that 2-year-old boys are more likely to attend to and remember toys such as cars, puzzles, and trains. Two-year-old girls are more likely to attend to and remember dolls, dishes, and teddy bears (Renninger & Wozniak, 1985). Even by this early age, the things that children attend to may fall into stereotypical patterns.

■ Short-Term Memory: Keeping Things "In Mind"

Imagine that you are completing a writing assignment and you keyboard or speak words and phrases into your word-processing program. They appear on your monitor as a sign that your computer has them in *memory.* Your word-processing program allows you to add words, delete words, check whether they are spelled correctly, add images, and move paragraphs from place to place. Although you can manipulate the information in your computer's memory, it isn't saved. It hasn't been entered into storage. If the program or the computer crashes, the information is gone. The computer's memory is a short-term affair. To maintain a long-term connection with the information, you have to save it. Saving it means naming it—hopefully with a name that you will remember so that you can later find and retrieve the information—and instructing your computer to save it (keep it in storage until told otherwise).

If you focus on a stimulus in the sensory register, you will tend to retain it in your own **short-term memory**—also referred to as **working memory**—for a minute or so after the trace of the stimulus decays. *How does short-term memory function?* As one researcher describes it, "Working memory is the mental glue that links a thought through time from its beginning to its end" (Goldman-Rakic, 1995). When you are given a phone number by the information operator and write it down or immediately dial the number, you are retaining the number in your short-term memory. When you are told the name of someone at a party and then use that name immediately in addressing that person, you are retaining the name in short-term memory. In short-term memory, the image tends to fade significantly after 10 to 12 seconds if it is not repeated or rehearsed. It is possible to focus on maintaining a visual image in the short-term memory, but it is more common to encode visual stimuli as sounds, or auditory stimuli. Then the sounds can be rehearsed, or repeated.

Most of us know that one way of retaining information in short-term memory—and possibly storing it permanently—is to repeat it either out loud or mentally. When an information operator tells me a phone number, I usually repeat it continuously while I am dialing it or scrambling for a pencil and scrap of paper so that I can "save" it. The more times we repeat information, the more likely we are to remember it. We have the capacity (if not the will or the time) to repeat information and maintain it in short-term memory indefinitely.

Once information is in our short-term memories, we can work on it. Like the information in the word-processing program, we can manipulate it. But it isn't necessarily saved. If we don't do something to save it (like write down the telephone number on paper as well as in a cell-phone phone book), it can be gone forever. We can try to reconstruct it, but it may never be the same. Getting most of the digits in someone's phone number right doesn't get you a date for the weekend—at least not with the person you were thinking of!

◇ **Truth or Fiction Revisited:** It is true that it may be easier for you to recall the name of your first-grade teacher than the name of someone you just met at a party. You need to rehearse new information to "save" it, but you may need only the proper cue to retrieve information from long-term memory.

Let us now return to the task of remembering the first list of letters in the challenges to memory at the beginning of the chapter. If you had encoded the letters as the three-syllable word THUN-STO-FAM, you would probably have recalled them by mentally rehearsing (saying to yourself) the three-syllable "word" and then spelling it out from the sounds. A few minutes later, if someone asked whether the letters had been uppercase (THUNSTOFAM) or lowercase (thunstofam), you might not have been able to answer with confidence. You used an acoustic code to help recall the list, and uppercase and lowercase letters sound alike.

Because it can be pronounced, THUNSTOFAM is not too difficult to retain in short-term memory. But what if the list of letters had been TBXLFNTSDK? This list of letters cannot be pronounced as it is. You would have to find a complex acronym to code these letters, and do so within a fraction of a second—most likely an impossible task. To aid recall, you would probably choose to try to repeat the letters rapidly—to read each one as many times as possible before the memory trace fades. You might visualize each letter as you say it and try to get back to it (that is, to run through the entire list) before it decays.

Let us assume that you encoded the letters as sounds and then rehearsed the sounds. When asked to report the list, you might mistakenly say T-V-X-L-F-N-T-S-T-K. This would be an understandable error because the incorrect *V* and *T* sounds are similar, respectively, to the correct *B* and *D* sounds.

The Serial-Position Effect   If asked to recall the list of letters TBXLFNTSDK, you would be likely to recall the first and last letters in the series, *T* and *K,* more accurately than the others. *Why are we most likely to remember the first and last items in a list?* The tendency to recall the first and last items in a series is known as the **serial-position effect.** This effect may occur because we pay more attention to the first and last stimuli in a series. They serve as the visual or auditory boundaries for the other stimuli. It may also be that the first items are likely to be rehearsed more frequently (repeated more times) than other items. The last items are likely to have been rehearsed most recently and hence are most likely to be retained in short-term memory.

Chunking   Rapidly rehearsing ten meaningless letters is not an easy task. With TBXLFNTSDK there are ten discrete elements, or **chunks,** of information that must be kept in short-term memory. When we encode THUNSTOFAM as three syllables, there are only three chunks to swallow at once—a memory task that is easier on the digestion.

As noted at the beginning of the chapter, psychologist George Miller (1956) found that the average person is comfortable with digesting about seven integers at a time, the number of integers in a telephone number: "My problem is that I have been persecuted by an integer [the number *seven*]. For seven years this number has followed me around, has intruded in my most private data, and has assaulted me from the pages of our most public journals" (1956). *Is seven a magic number, or did the phone company get lucky?*

Research shows that most people have little trouble recalling five chunks of information, as in a zip code. Some can remember nine, which is, for all but a few, an upper limit.

Serial-position effect The tendency to recall more accurately the first and last items in a series.

Chunk A stimulus or group of stimuli that are perceived as a discrete piece of information.

So seven chunks, plus or minus one or two, is a "magic" number in the sense that the typical human can remember that many chunks of information and not much more.

So how, you ask, do we manage to include area codes in our recollections of telephone numbers, hence making them 10 digits long? Actually, we usually don't. We tend to recall the area code as a single chunk of information derived from our general knowledge of where a person lives. So we are more likely to remember (or "know") the 10-digit numbers of acquaintances who reside in locales with area codes that we use often.

Businesses pay the phone company hefty premiums so that they can attain numbers with two or three zeroes or repeated digits—for example, 592-2000 or 277-3333. These numbers include fewer chunks of information and hence are easier to remember. Customer recollection of business phone numbers increases sales. One financial services company uses the toll-free number CALL-IRA, which reduces the task to two chunks of information that also happen to be meaningfully related (semantically coded) to the nature of the business. Similarly, a clinic that helps people quit smoking arranged for a telephone number that can be reached by dialing the letters NO SMOKE.

Return to the third challenge to memory presented earlier. Were you able to remember the six groups of letters? Would your task have been simpler if you had grouped them differently? How about moving the dashes forward by a letter, so that they read GM-CBS-IBM-ATT-CIA-FBI? If we do this, we have the same list of letters, but we also have six chunks of information that can be coded semantically (according to what they mean). You may have also been able to generate the list by remembering a rule, such as "big corporations and government agencies."

If we can recall seven or perhaps nine chunks of information, how do children remember the alphabet? The alphabet contains 26 discrete pieces of information. How do children learn to encode the letters of the alphabet, which are visual symbols, as spoken sounds? There is nothing about the shape of an *A* that suggests its sound. Nor does the visual stimulus *B* sound "B-ish." Children learn to associate letters with their spoken names by **rote.** It is mechanical associative learning that takes time and repetition. If you think that learning the alphabet by rote is a simple task, try learning the Russian alphabet.

If you had recognized THUNSTOFAM as an acronym for the first two letters of each word in the phrase "THe UNited STates OF AMerica," you would also have reduced the number of chunks of information that had to be recalled. You could have considered the phrase to be a single chunk of information. The rule that you must use the first two letters of each word of the phrase would be another chunk.

Reconsider the second challenge to memory presented earlier. You were asked to remember nine chunks of visual information. Perhaps you could have used the acoustic codes "L" and "Square" for chunks 3 and 5, but no obvious codes are available for the seven other chunks. Now look at Figure 7.2. If you had recognized that the elements in the challenge could be arranged as the familiar tic-tac-toe grid, remembering the nine elements might have required two chunks of information. The first would have been the mental image of the grid, and the second would have been the rule for decoding: Each element corresponds to the shape of a section of the grid if read like words on a page (from upper left to lower right). The number sequence 1 through 9 would not in itself present a problem, because you learned this series by rote many years ago and have rehearsed it in countless calculations since then.

Interference in Short-Term Memory   I mentioned that I often find myself scrambling for a pencil and a scrap of paper to write down a telephone number. If I keep on rehearsing the number while I'm looking, I'm okay. But I have also often cursed myself for failing to keep a pad and pencil by the telephone, and sometimes this has interfered with my recollection of the number. (The moral of the story? Avoid self-reproach.) It has also happened that I have actually looked up a phone number and been about to dial it when someone has asked me for the time or where I said we were going to dinner. Unless I say, "Hold on a minute!" and manage to jot down the number on something, it's back to the phone book or the information service. Attending to distracting information, even briefly, prevents me from rehearsing the number, so it falls through the cracks of my short-term memory.

In a classic experiment with college students, Lloyd and Margaret Peterson (1959) demonstrated how prevention of rehearsal can wreak havoc with short-term memory. They

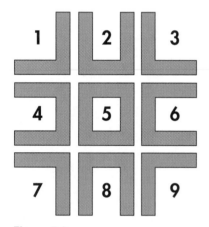

Figure 7.2
A Familiar Grid
The nine drawings in the second challenge to memory form this familiar tic-tac-toe grid when the numbers are placed inside them and they are arranged in order. This method for recalling the shapes collapses nine chunks of information into two. One is the tic-tac-toe grid. The second is the rule for decoding the drawings from the grid.

Rote Mechanical associative learning that is based on repetition.

asked students to remember three-letter combinations such as HGB—normally, three easy chunks of information. They then had the students count backward from an arbitrary number, such as 181, by threes (that is, 181, 178, 175, 172, and so on). The students were told to stop counting and to report the letter sequence after the intervals of time shown in Figure 7.3. The percentage of correctly recalled letter combinations fell dramatically within seconds. After 18 seconds of interference, counting had dislodged the letter sequences in almost all students' memories.

Psychologists say that the appearance of new information in short-term memory **displaces** the old information. Remember: Only a few bits of information can be retained in short-term memory at the same time. (Unfortunately we cannot pay a few dollars more to upgrade our human memories from, say, 512 megabytes to 1 or 2 gigabytes.) Think of short-term memory as a shelf or workbench. Once it is full, some things fall off it when new items are shoved onto it. Here we have another possible explanation for the recency effect: The most recently learned bit of information is least likely to be displaced by additional information.

Displacement occurs at cocktail parties, and I'm not referring to jostling by the crowd. The point is this: When you meet Linda or Latrell at the party, you should have little trouble remembering the name. But then you may meet Tamara, Travis, or Timothy, and, still later, Keith, Kevin, Keisha, or LaToya. By that time you may have a hard time dredging up Jennifer or Jonathan's name—unless, of course, you were very, very attracted to one of them. A passionate response would set a person apart and inspire a good deal of selective attention. According to signal-detection theory, if you were enamored enough, you might "detect" the person's name (sensory signals) with a vengeance, and other names would dissolve into background noise.

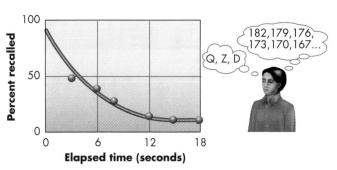

Figure 7.3
The Effect of Interference on Short-Term Memory
In this experiment, college students were asked to remember a series of three letters while they counted backward by threes. After just 3 seconds, retention was cut by half. Ability to recall the words was almost completely lost by 15 seconds.

◼ Long-Term Memory: Your Memory's "Hard Drive"

Long-term memory is the third stage of information processing. Think of your long-term memory as a vast storehouse of information containing names, dates, places, what Johnny did to you in second grade, and what Susan said about you when you were 12. *How does long-term memory function?*

Some psychologists (Freud was one) used to believe that nearly all of our perceptions and ideas are stored permanently. We might not be able to retrieve all of them, however. Some memories might be "lost" because of lack of proper cues, or they might be kept unconscious by the forces of **repression**. Adherents to this view often pointed to the work of neurosurgeon Wilder Penfield (1969). When parts of their brains were electrically stimulated, many of Penfield's patients reported the appearance of images that had something of the feel of memories.

Today most psychologists view this notion as exaggerated. Memory researcher Elizabeth Loftus, for example, notes that the "memories" stimulated by Penfield's probes lacked detail and were sometimes incorrect (Loftus & Loftus, 1980; E. F. Loftus, 1983). ◈ **Truth or Fiction Revisited:** It has therefore *not* been shown that all of our experiences are permanently imprinted on the brain. Now let us consider some other questions about long-term memory.

How Accurate Are Long-Term Memories? Psychologist Elizabeth Loftus notes that memories are distorted by our biases and needs—by the ways in which we conceptualize our worlds. We represent much of our world in the form of **schemas.**

To understand what is meant by the term *schema,* consider the problems of travelers who met up with Procrustes, the legendary highwayman of ancient Greece. Procrustes had a quirk. He was interested not only in travelers' pocketbooks but also in their height. He had a concept—a schema—of how tall people should be, and when people did not fit his schema, they were in trouble. You see, Procrustes also had a bed, the famous "Procrustean bed." He made his victims lie down in the bed, and if they were too short for it, he stretched them to make them fit. If they were too long for the bed, he practiced surgery on their legs.

Displace In memory theory, to cause information to be lost from short-term memory by adding new information.

Long-term memory The type or stage of memory capable of relatively permanent storage.

Repression In Freud's psychodynamic theory, the ejection of anxiety-evoking ideas from conscious awareness.

Schema A way of mentally representing the world, such as a belief or an expectation, that can influence perception of persons, objects, and situations.

Figure 7.4

Memory as Reconstructive
In their classic experiment, Carmichael, Hogan, and Walter (1932) showed people the figures in the left-hand box and made remarks as suggested in the other boxes. For example, the experimenter might say, "This drawing looks like eyeglasses [or a dumbbell]." When people later reconstructed the drawings, they were influenced by the labels.

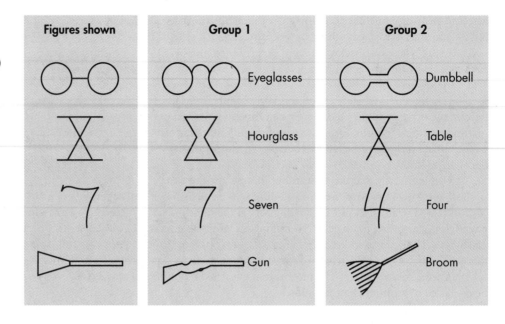

Although the myth of Procrustes may sound absurd, it reflects a quirky truth about each of us. We all carry our cognitive Procrustean beds around with us—our unique ways of perceiving the world—and we try to make things and people fit them. Let me give you an example. "Retrieve" the fourth sheet of paper you prepared according to the Self-Assessment in the beginning of the chapter. You drew the figures "from memory" according to instructions on page 247. Now look at Figure 7.4. Are your drawings closer in form to those in group 1 or to those in group 2? I wouldn't be surprised if they were more like those in group 1—if, for example, your first drawing looked more like eyeglasses than a dumbbell. After all, they were labeled like the drawings in group 1. The labels serve as *schemas* for the drawings—ways of organizing your knowledge of them—and these schemas may have influenced your recollections.

Consider another example of the power of schemas in processing information. Loftus and Palmer (1974) showed people a film of a car crash and then asked them to fill out questionnaires that included a question about how fast the cars were going at the time. The language of the question varied in subtle ways, however. Some people were asked to estimate

Figure 7.5

How Fast Were These Cars Going When They Collided?
Our schemas influence our processing of information. When shown pictures such as these, people who were asked how fast the cars were going when they *smashed* into each other offer higher estimates than people who were told that the cars *hit* each other.

Source: Based on "Reconstruction of Automobile Destruction: An Example of Interaction Between Language and Memory," by E. F. Loftus & J. C. Palmer (1974), *Journal of Verbal Learning and Verbal Behavior, 13,* 585–589. Academic Press, Inc. Adapted by permission of the author.

how fast the cars were going when they "hit" each other. Others were asked to estimate the cars' speed when they "smashed into" each other. On average, people who reconstructed the scene on the basis of the cue "hit" estimated a speed of 34 mph. People who watched the same film but reconstructed the scene on the basis of the cue "smashed" estimated a speed of 41 mph! (See Figure 7.5.) The use of the words *hit* or *smashed* caused people to organize their knowledge about the crash in different ways. The words served as schemas that fostered the development of different ways of processing information about the crash.

Subjects in the same study were questioned again a week later: "Did you see any broken glass?" Because there was no broken glass shown in the film, an answer of "yes" would

A Closer Look
Can We Trust Eyewitness Testimony?

Jean Piaget, the investigator of children's cognitive development, distinctly remembered an attempt to kidnap him from his baby carriage as he was being wheeled along the Champs Élysées. He recalled the excited throng, the abrasions on the face of the nurse who rescued him, the police officer's white baton, and the flight of the assailant. Although they were graphic, Piaget's memories were false. Years later, the nurse admitted that she had made up the tale.

Can eyewitness testimony be trusted? Is there reason to believe that the statements of eyewitnesses are any more factual than Piaget's? Legal professionals are concerned about the accuracy of our long-term memories as reflected in eyewitness testimony (Wells & Olsen, 2003). Let us consider what can go wrong—and what can go right—with eyewitness testimony.

Royalty Free/Corbis

■ **Eyewitness Testimony?**
How trustworthy is eyewitness testimony? Memories are reconstructive rather than photographic. The wording of questions also influences the content of the memory. Attorneys therefore are sometimes instructed not to phrase questions in such a way that they "lead" the witness.

One problem with eyewitness testimony is that the words chosen by an experimenter—and those chosen by a lawyer interrogating a witness—have been shown to influence the reconstruction of memories (Wells & Olsen, 2003). For example, as in the experiment described earlier, an attorney for the plaintiff might ask the witness, "How fast was the defendant's car going when it *smashed into* the plaintiff's car?" In such a case, the car might be reported as going faster than if the question had been: "How fast was the defendant's car going when the accident occurred?" (Loftus & Palmer, 1974). Could the attorney for the defendant claim that use of the word *smashed* biased the witness? What about jurors who heard the word *smashed*? Would they be biased toward assuming that the driver had been reckless?

Children tend to be more suggestible witnesses than adults, and preschoolers are more suggestible than older children (Ceci & Bruck, 1993; Erskine et al., 2001). But when questioned carefully, even young children may be able to provide accurate testimony (Ceci & Bruck, 1993; Gordon et al., 2001).

There are cases in which the memories of eyewitnesses have been "refreshed" by hypnosis. Sad to say, hypnosis does more than amplify memories; it can also distort them (Loftus, 1994). One problem is that witnesses may accept and embellish suggestions made by the hypnotist. Another is that hypnotized people may report fantasized occurrences as compellingly as if they were real (Loftus, 1994).

Problems also arise in the identification of criminals by eyewitnesses. For one thing, witnesses may pay more attention to the suspect's clothing than to more meaningful characteristics such as facial features, height, and weight. In one experiment, viewers of a videotaped crime incorrectly identified a man as the criminal because he wore the eyeglasses and T-shirt that had been worn by the perpetrator on the tape. The man who had actually committed the crime was identified less often (Sanders, 1984). ■

Reconstructive Memory

LEARNING OBJECTIVES

- Explain what is meant by the view that memory is reconstructive and not like accessing a snapshot of an event.
- Explain what happened in the "Lost in the Mall" study.

APPLIED LESSON

1 What kinds of factors influence a person's memory? How could these factors affect eyewitness testimony?
2 What is a "leading" question? Why does it "lead"?

CRITICAL THINKING

1 The video suggests that we cannot always rely on people's accounts of what happened. What shall we do about it? What would be the consequences of disallowing eyewitness testimony in the apprehension and prosecution of criminals?
2 It was once believed that exact images of external events are somehow imprinted on the mind, and that they can be recovered, in detail, by the appropriate cues. Does the video support or oppose this view?

Do our long-term memories consist of accurate snapshots of the past, or do we reconstruct them according to our own biases and the suggestions of other people? How might a false memory of being separated from your parents when you were a child be planted?

Watch this video!

Go to www your companion website at http://academic.cengage.com/psychology/rathus Click on the Video Connections tab under this chapter.

be wrong. Of those who had earlier been encouraged to process information about the accident in terms of one car "hitting" the other, 14% incorrectly answered yes. But 32% of the subjects who had processed information about the crash in terms of one car "smashing into" the other reported, incorrectly, that they had seen broken glass.

How Much Information Can Be Stored in Long-Term Memory? How many gigabytes of storage are there in your most personal computer—your brain? Unlike a computer, the human ability to store information is, for all practical purposes, unlimited (Goldman-Rakic et al., 2000b). Even the largest hard drives fill up when we save Web pages, photos, songs, and movies. Yet how many "movies" of the past have you saved in your own long-term memory? How many thousands of scenes and stories can you rerun at will? And, assuming that you have an intact sensory system, the movies in your personal storage bins not only have color and sound, but also aromas, tactile sensations, and more. *Your long-term memory is a biochemical "hard drive" with no known limits on the amount of information it can store.*

Yes, new information may replace older information in short-term memory, but there is no evidence that long-term memories—those in "storage"—are lost by displacement. Long-term memories may endure a lifetime. Now and then it may seem that we have forgotten, or "lost," a long-term memory such as the names of elementary school classmates. Yet it may be that we cannot find the proper cues to retrieve them. It is like forgetting the name of a file stored on a computer. If long-term memories are lost, they may be lost in the same way that a misplaced object or computer file is lost. Although we cannot retrieve it, we sense that it is still somewhere in the room or on the hard drive. For example, you may drive by your elementary school and suddenly recall the long-lost names of schoolteachers and streets in your old neighborhood.

Transferring Information from Short-Term to Long-Term Memory: Using the "Save" Function How can you transfer information from short-term to long-term memory? By and large, the more often chunks of information are rehearsed, the more likely they are to be transferred to long-term memory. Repeating information over and over to prevent it from decaying or being displaced is termed *maintenance rehearsal.* But maintenance rehearsal is not necessarily the best way to store information (Simpson et al., 1994).

A more effective method is to make information more meaningful—to purposefully relate new information to things that are already well known (Woloshyn et al., 1994). For example, to better remember the components of levers, physics students might use seesaws, wheelbarrows, and oars as examples (Scruggs & Mastropieri, 1992). The nine chunks of information in our second challenge to memory were made easier to reconstruct once they were associated with the familiar tic-tac-toe grid in Figure 7.2. Relating new material to well-known material is known as **elaborative rehearsal.** For example, have you seen the following word before?

FUNTHOSTAM

Say it aloud. Do you know it? If you had used an acoustic code alone to memorize THUNSTOFAM, the list of letters you first saw on page 243, it might not have been easy to recognize FUNTHOSTAM as an incorrect spelling. Let us assume, however, that by now you have used elaborative rehearsal and encoded THUNSTOFAM semantically (according to its "meaning") as an acronym for "The United States of America." Then you would have been able to mentally scan the spelling of the words in the phrase "The United States of America" to determine that FUNTHOSTAM is an incorrect spelling.

Rote repetition of a meaningless group of syllables, such as *thun-sto-fam,* relies on maintenance rehearsal for permanent storage. The process might be tedious (continued rehearsal) and unreliable. Elaborative rehearsal—tying THUNSTOFAM to the name of a country—might make storage instantaneous and retrieval foolproof.

Levels of Processing Information People who use elaborative rehearsal to remember things are *processing information at a deeper level* than people who use maintenance rehearsal. *What is the levels-of-processing model of memory?* Fergus Craik and Robert Lockhart (1972) pioneered the levels-of-processing model of memory, which holds that memories tend to endure when information is processed *deeply*—attended to, encoded carefully, pondered, and related to things we already know. Remembering relies on how *deeply* people process information, not on whether memories are transferred from one *stage* of memory to another.

Evidence for the importance of levels of processing information is found in an experiment with three groups of college students, all of whom were asked to study a picture of a living room for one minute (Bransford et al., 1977). The groups' examination of the picture entailed different approaches. Two groups were informed that small *x*'s were imbedded in the picture. The first of these groups was asked to find the *x*'s by scanning the picture horizontally and vertically. The second group was informed that the *x*'s could be found in the edges of the objects in the room and was asked to look for them there. The third group was asked, instead, to think about how it would use the objects pictured in the room. As a result of the divergent sets of instructions, the first two groups (the *x* hunters) processed information about the objects in the picture superficially. But the third group rehearsed the objects elaboratively—that is, members of this group thought about the objects in terms of their meanings and uses. It should not be surprising that the third group remembered many times more objects than the first two groups.

Language arts teachers encourage students to use new vocabulary words in sentences to process them more deeply. Each new usage is an instance of elaborative rehearsal. Usage helps build semantic codes that make it easier to retrieve the meanings of words in the future. When I was in high school, teachers of foreign languages told us that learning classical languages "exercises the mind" so that we would understand English better. Not exactly. The mind is not analogous to a muscle that responds to exercise. The meanings of many English words, however, are based on foreign ones. A person who recognizes that *retrieve* stems from roots meaning "again" (*re-*) and "find" (*trouver* in French) is less likely to forget that *retrieval* means "finding again" or "bringing back."

Elaborative rehearsal A method for increasing retention of new information by relating it to information that is well known.

AP/Wide World Photos

■ **Flashbulb Memories**

Where were you and what were you doing on the morning of September 11, 2001? Many older Americans never forgot where they were and what they were doing when they learned about the attack on Pearl Harbor on December 7, 1941, or when they learned of the assassination of President John F. Kennedy in 1963. Major events can illuminate everything about them so that we recall everything that was happening at the time.

Think, too, of all the math problems we solved in high school. Each problem is an application of a procedure and, perhaps, of certain formulas. By repeatedly applying the procedures and formulas in slightly different contexts, we rehearse them elaboratively. As a result, we are more likely to remember them.

Biologically oriented research connects deep processing with activity in certain parts of the brain, notably the prefrontal area of the cerebral cortex (Constantinidis et al., 2001). One reason that older adults show memory loss is that they tend not to process information quite as deeply as younger people do (Grady et al., 1999). Deep processing requires sustained attention, and older adults, along with people who have suffered brain injuries and strokes, apparently cannot focus as well as they once did (Iidaka et al., 2000; Winocur et al., 2000).

Before going to the next section, cover the preceding paragraph with your hand. Which of the following is spelled correctly: *retrieval* or *retreival*? The spellings sound alike, so an acoustic code for reconstructing the proper spelling would fail. Yet a semantic code, such as the rule "*i* before *e* except after *c*," would allow you to reconstruct the proper spelling: retr*ie*val.

Flashbulb Memories ◆ **Truth or Fiction Revisited:** Many of us will never forget where we were or what we were doing when we learned of the attacks on the World Trade Center and the Pentagon on September 11, 2001 (Weaver & Krug, 2004). We may also have a detailed memory of what we were doing when we learned of a loved one's death.

Why is it that some events, like the attack of September 11, 2001, can be etched in memory for a lifetime? It appears that we tend to remember events that are surprising, important, and emotionally stirring more clearly. Such events can create "flashbulb memories," which preserve experiences in detail (Finkenauer et al., 1998; Otani et al., 2005). Why is the memory etched when the "flashbulb" goes off? One factor is the distinctness of the memory. It is easier to discriminate stimuli that stand out. Such events are striking in themselves. The feelings caused by them are also special. It is thus relatively easy to pick them out from the storehouse of memories. Major events such as the assassination of a president or the loss of a close relative also tend to have important effects on our lives. We are likely to dwell on them and form networks of associations. That is, we are likely to rehearse them elaboratively. Our rehearsal may include great expectations, or deep fears, for the future.

Biology is intimately connected with psychology. Strong feelings are connected with the secretion of stress hormones, and stress hormones help carve events into memory—"as almost to leave a scar upon the cerebral tissues," as noted by William James.

Organization in Long-Term Memory The storehouse of long-term memory is usually well organized. Items are not just piled on the floor or thrown into closets. *How is knowledge organized in long-term memory?* We tend to gather information about rats and cats into a certain section of the storehouse, perhaps the animal or mammal section. We put information about oaks, maples, and eucalyptus into the tree section. Such categorization of stimuli is a basic cognitive function. It allows us to make predictions about specific instances and to store information efficiently.

We tend to organize information according to a *hierarchical structure*, as shown in Figure 7.6. A *hierarchy* is an arrangement of items (or chunks of information) into groups or classes according to common or distinct features. As we work our way up the hierarchy shown in Figure 7.6, we find more encompassing, or *superordinate*, classes to which the items below them belong. For example, all mammals are animals, but there are many types of animals other than mammals.

When items are correctly organized in long-term memory, you are more likely to recall—or know—accurate information about them. For example, do you "remember" whether whales breathe underwater? If you did not know that whales are mammals (or, in Figure 7.6, *subordinate* to mammals), or if you knew nothing about mammals, a correct answer might depend on some remote instance of rote learning. That is, you might be depending on chancy episodic memory rather than on reliable semantic memory. For example, you might recall some details from a TV documentary on whales. If you *did* know that whales are mammals, however, you would also know—or remember—that whales do not breathe underwater. How? You would reconstruct information about whales from knowledge about mammals, the group to which whales are subordinate. Similarly, you

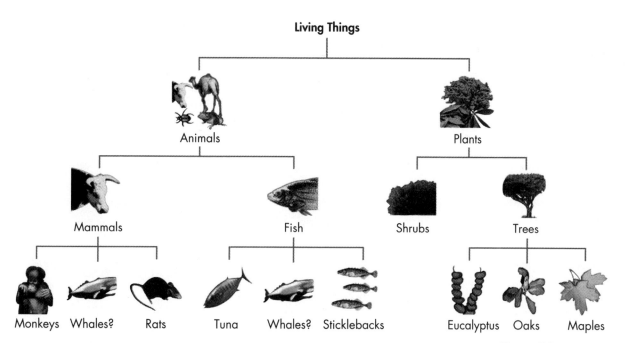

Living Things

Animals — Plants

Mammals — Fish | Shrubs — Trees

Monkeys | Whales? | Rats | Tuna | Whales? | Sticklebacks | Eucalyptus | Oaks | Maples

Figure 7.6
The Hierarchical Structure of Long-Term Memory
Where are whales filed in the hierarchical cabinets of your memory? Your classification of whales may influence your answers to these questions: Do whales breathe underwater? Are they warm-blooded? Do they nurse their young? A note to biological purists: This figure is not intended to represent phyla, classes, orders, and so on accurately. Rather, it shows how an individual's classification scheme might be organized.

would know, or remember, that because they are mammals, whales are warm-blooded, nurse their young, and are a good deal more intelligent than, say, tunas and sharks, which are fish. Had you incorrectly classified whales as fish, you might have searched your memory and constructed the incorrect answer that they do breathe underwater.

Your memory is thus organized according to a remarkably complex filing system that has a certain internal logic. If you place a piece of information into the wrong file, it is probably not the fault of the filing system itself. Nevertheless, you may "lose" the information in the sense of not being able to find the best cues to retrieve it.

The Tip-of-the-Tongue Phenomenon   Having something on the tip of your tongue can be a frustrating experience. It is like reeling in a fish but having it drop off the line just before it breaks the surface of the water. Psychologists term this experience the **tip-of-the-tongue (TOT) phenomenon,** or the **feeling-of-knowing experience.** *Why do we sometimes feel that the answer to a question is on the tip of our tongue?*

Research provides insight into the TOT phenomenon (Brown & McNeill, 1966; James & Burke, 2000). In classic research, Brown and McNeill (1966) defined some rather unusual words for students, such as *sampan,* a small riverboat used in China and Japan. The students were then asked to recall the words they had learned. Some of the students often had the right word "on the tip of their tongue" but reported words with similar meanings such as *junk, barge,* or *houseboat.* Still other students reported words that sounded similar, such as *Saipan, Siam, sarong,* and *sanching.* Why?

To begin with, the words were unfamiliar, so elaborative rehearsal did not take place. The students did not have an opportunity to relate the words to other things they knew. Brown and McNeill also suggested that our storage systems are indexed according to cues that include both the sounds and the meanings of words—that is, according to both acoustic and semantic codes. By scanning words similar in sound and meaning to the word on the tip of the tongue, we sometimes find a useful cue and retrieve the word for which we are searching.

The feeling-of-knowing experience also seems to reflect incomplete or imperfect learning. In such cases, our answers may be "in the ballpark" if not on the mark. In some feeling-of-knowing experiments, people are often asked trivia questions. When they do not recall an answer, they are then asked to guess how likely it is that they will recognize the right answer if it is among a group of possibilities. People turn out to be very accurate in their estimations about whether or not they will recognize the answer. Similarly, Brown and McNeill found that the students in their TOT experiment proved to be very good at estimating the number of syllables in words that they could not recall. The students often correctly guessed the initial sounds of the words. They sometimes recognized words that rhymed with them.

Tip-of-the-tongue (TOT) phenomenon The feeling that information is stored in memory although it cannot be readily retrieved. Also called the *feeling-of-knowing experience.*

Feeling-of-knowing experience Same as *tip-of-the-tongue phenomenon.*

A Closer Look

Life is Pleasant—and Memory Helps to Keep It That Way!

A Closer Look

Surveys conducted in the United States and around the world consistently show that people are generally happy with their lives, even people with physical and mental disabilities and people without much money. Researchers reviewing several studies on autobiographical memory and happiness have found that human memory is biased toward happiness and that mild depression can disrupt this bias for good over bad. The findings are published in the *Review of General Psychology*.

In their article "Life Is Pleasant—and Memory Helps to Keep It That Way!", W. Richard Walker of Winston-Salem State University, John J. Skowronski of Northern Illinois University, and Charles P. Thompson of Kansas State University find two causes for people's recollection of the past to be positively biased. The first cause seems to be that pleasant events do in fact outnumber unpleasant events because people seek positive experiences and avoid negative ones. Across 12 studies conducted by five different research teams, people of different ethnic backgrounds and ages consistently reported experiencing more positive events than negative events.

The other cause involves our memory system treating pleasant emotions differently from unpleasant emotions. Seven studies reviewed by the researchers provide support for a fading affect for negative emotions. Pleasant emotions fade more slowly than unpleasant emotions. One mechanism for uneven fading may be minimization. To return to our normal level of happiness, we try to minimize the impact of life events. Minimization is usually stronger for negative events than for positive events.

"This implies that there is a tendency to 'deaden' the emotional impact of negative events relative to the impact of positive events," according to Dr. Walker. "Such deadening occurs directly because people are motivated to view their life events in a relatively positive light."

This fading bias represents genuine emotional fading rather than an error in memory, and it should be viewed as evidence of healthy coping processes operating in memory,

■ **Is Life This Pleasant, or Does Memory Help Us to Remember It This Way?**

Surveys find that most people characterize their lives as pleasant, in part because they seek out pleasant experiences. On the other hand, research evidence also suggests that we tend to distort our memories by tamping down the negative emotions associated with unpleasant memories.

according to the authors. They add that this should not be confused with repression, a theory proposed by Sigmund Freud. This research suggests that people do remember negative events; they just remember them less negatively.

Of course, life is not pleasant for everyone. Of the 229 participants involved in eight reviewed studies in which diary entries were tracked, 17 reported more unpleasant than pleasant events, indicating that the fading affect does not work for everyone. Among those with mild depression, unpleasant and pleasant emotions tend to fade evenly. The more depressed people are, the more they are likely to recall negative events. ■

Source: Adapted from "Remembering the Good Times, Putting the Bad Times in Perspective—How Our Memory Helps Make Life Pleasant: Research Explains Why Most People Are Happy With Their Lives," by David Partenheimer, June 8, 2003, APA press release, Washington, DC: Public Affairs Office.

Sometimes an answer seems to be on the tip of our tongue because our learning of the topic is incomplete. We may not know the exact answer, but we know something. (As a matter of fact, if we have good writing skills, we may present our incomplete knowledge so forcefully that we earn a good grade on an essay question on the topic!) At such times, the problem lies not in retrieval but in the original processes of learning and memory—that is, encoding and storage.

Context-Dependent Memory: Been There, Done That?

It's déjà vu *all over again.*
—YOGI BERRA

The context in which we acquire information can also play a role in retrieval. I remember walking down the halls of the apartment building where I had lived as a child. Cooking odors triggered a sudden assault of images of playing under the staircase, of falling against a radiator, of the shrill voice of a former neighbor calling for her child at dinnertime. Have you ever walked the halls of an old school building and been assaulted by memories of faces and names that you had thought would be lost forever? Odors, it turns out, are particularly likely to trigger related memories (Pointer & Bond, 1998).

My experience was an example of a **context-dependent memory.** My memories were particularly clear in the context in which they were formed. *Why may it be useful to study in the room in which we will be tested?* One answer is that being in the proper context— for example, studying in the exam room or under the same conditions—can dramatically enhance recall (Isarida & Isarida, 1999). ◆ **Truth or Fiction Revisited:** Therefore, if you study with the stereo on, you would probably do better to take the test with the stereo on. One fascinating experiment in context-dependent memory included a number of people who were "all wet." Members of a university swimming club were asked to learn lists of words either while they were submerged or while they were literally high and dry (Godden & Baddeley, 1975). Students who learned the list underwater showed superior recall of the list when immersed. Similarly, those who had rehearsed the list ashore showed better retrieval on terra firma.

According to a study with 20 bilingual Cornell students, the "context" for memory extends to language (Marian & Neisser, 2000). The students were in their early 20s and had emigrated from Russia an average of eight years earlier. They were asked to recall the details of experiences in Russia and the United States. When they were interviewed in Russian, they were better able to retrieve experiences from their lives in Russia. Similarly, when they were interviewed in English, they were better able to recall events that happened in the United States.

Students do better on tests when they study under the same conditions—either in silence or with the stereo on (Grant et al., 1998). When police are interviewing witnesses to crimes, they ask the witnesses to paint the scene verbally as vividly as possible, or they visit the scene of the crime with the witnesses. People who mentally place themselves in the context in which they encoded and stored information frequently retrieve it more accurately.

One of the more eerie psychological experiences is *déjà vu* (French for "already seen"). Sometimes we meet someone new or find ourselves in a strange place, yet we have the feeling that we know this person or have been there before. All in all, about 60% of us believe we have had a déjà vu experience (Brown, 2003). Déjà vu seems to occur when we are in a context similar to one we have been in before—or when we meet someone who has a way of talking or moving similar to that of someone we know or once knew. Yet we do not recall the specific place or person. Nevertheless, familiarity with the context leads us to think, "I've been here before." Other explanations for the déjà vu experience run from the neurological (for example, a disruption in normal neural transmission) to the cognitive (for example, dual cognitive processes that are temporarily out of synchrony) (Brown, 2003). In any event, the sense that one has been there before, or done this thing before, can be so strong that one just stands back and wonders.

State-Dependent Memory **State-dependent memory** is an extension of context-dependent memory. We sometimes retrieve information better when we are in a biological or emotional state similar to the one in which we encoded and stored the information. Feeling

Context-dependent memory Information that is better retrieved in the context in which it was encoded and stored, or learned.

State-dependent memory Information that is better retrieved in the physiological or emotional state in which it was encoded and stored, or learned.

David Young-Wolff/PhotoEdit

■ **Should This Student Bring the TV to Class to Take the Test?**
Research on context-dependent memory suggests that we remember information better when we attempt to recall it in the context in which we learned it. If we study with the TV or stereo on, should we also take the test within the "context" of the TV or stereo?

the rush of love may trigger other images of falling in love. The grip of anger may prompt memories of incidents of frustration. The research in this area extends to states in which we are sober or inebriated.

Gordon Bower (1981) induced happy or sad moods in subjects by hypnotic suggestion. The subjects then learned lists of words. People who learned a list while in a happy mood showed better recall when happiness was induced again. People who had learned the list while in a sad mood showed better recall in a saddened state.

A happy mood influences us to focus on positive events (Eich, 1995; Matt et al., 1992). As a result, we have better recall of these events in the future. A sad mood, unfortunately, leads us to focus on and recall the negative. Happiness may feed on happiness, but sadness can develop into a vicious cycle and lead to depression.

() Learning Connections

◀◀ *Stages of Memory—Making Sense of the Short and the Long of It* ▶▶

REVIEW:

7 According to Atkinson and Shiffrin, long-term memories are typically lost by
(a) decay of the memory trace,
(b) lack of retrieval cues,
(c) displacement,
(d) being in a state that differs from the one in which the information was encountered.

8 _____ are the mental representations of visual stimuli.
(a) Icons,
(b) Echoes,
(c) Engrams,
(d) Saccadic eye movements.

9 According to the serial-position effect, we are most likely to recall
(a) only the first item in a series,
(b) only the last item in a series,
(c) the first and last items in a series,
(d) items that follow one another in a series.

10 We are likely to remember flashbulb memories because of the secretion of
(a) melatonin,
(b) dopamine,
(c) myelin,
(d) stress hormones.

CRITICAL THINKING:
Were you ever convinced that you were remembering something accurately, only to discover, later, that your memory was incorrect? How do you account for the distorted memory? Can we know whether our own memories are accurate? How is it possible to function in a world of uncertain memory?

Go www to
http://academic.cengage.com/psychology/rathus
for an interactive version of this review.

FORGETTING: WILL YOU REMEMBER HOW WE FORGET?

What do DAL, RIK, BOF, and ZEX have in common? They are all **nonsense syllables.** Nonsense syllables are meaningless sets of two consonants with a vowel sandwiched in between. They were first used by Hermann Ebbinghaus (1885/1913) to study memory and forgetting. Because nonsense syllables are intended to be meaningless, remembering them should depend on simple acoustic coding and maintenance rehearsal rather than on elaborative rehearsal, semantic coding, or other ways of making learning meaningful. They are thus well-suited for use in the measurement of forgetting. *What types of memory tasks are used in measuring forgetting?*

Nonsense syllables Meaningless sets of two consonants, with a vowel sandwiched in between, that are used to study memory.

■ Memory Tasks Used in Measuring Forgetting

Three basic memory tasks have been used by psychologists to measure forgetting: recognition, recall, and relearning. Nonsense syllables have been used in studying each of them. The study of these memory tasks has led to several conclusions about the nature of forgetting.

Recognition One aspect of forgetting is failure to recognize something we have experienced. There are many ways of measuring **recognition.** In many studies, psychologists ask subjects to read a list of nonsense syllables. The subjects then read a second list of nonsense syllables and indicate whether they recognize any of the syllables as having appeared on the first list. Forgetting is defined as failure to recognize a syllable that has been read before.

In another kind of recognition study, Harry Bahrick and his colleagues (1975) studied high-school graduates who had been out of school for various lengths of time. They interspersed photos of the graduates' classmates with four times as many photos of strangers. Recent graduates correctly recognized former classmates 90% of the time. Those who had been out of school for 40 years recognized former classmates 75% of the time. A chance level of recognition would have been only 20% (1 photo in 5 was of an actual classmate). Thus even older people showed rather solid long-term recognition ability.

Recognition is the easiest type of memory task. This is why multiple-choice tests are easier than fill-in-the-blank or essay tests. We can recognize correct answers more easily than we can recall them unaided.

Recall In his own studies of **recall,** another kind of memory task, Ebbinghaus (1885/ 1913) would read lists of nonsense syllables aloud to the beat of a metronome and then see how many he could produce from memory. After reading through a list once, he usually would be able to recall seven syllables—the typical limit for short-term memory.

Psychologists also often use lists of pairs of nonsense syllables, called **paired associates,** to measure recall. A list of paired associates is shown in Figure 7.7. Subjects read through the lists pair by pair. Later they are shown the first member of each pair and asked to recall the second. Recall is more difficult than recognition. In a recognition task, one simply indicates whether an item has been seen before or which of a number of items is paired with a stimulus (as in a multiple-choice test). In a recall task, the person must retrieve a syllable, with another syllable serving as a cue.

Retrieval is made easier if the two syllables can be meaningfully linked—that is, encoded semantically—even if the "meaning" is stretched a bit. Consider the first pair of nonsense syllables in Figure 7.7. The image of a WOMan smoking a CEG-arette may make CEG easier to retrieve when the person is presented with the cue WOM.

It is easier to recall vocabulary words from foreign languages if you can construct a meaningful link between the foreign and English words (Atkinson, 1975). The *peso*, pronounced *pay-so*, is a unit of Mexican money. A link can be formed by finding a part of the foreign word, such as the *pe-* (pronounced *pay*), and constructing a phrase such as "You pay with money." When you read or hear the word *peso* in the future, you recognize the *pe-* and retrieve the link or phrase. From the phrase, you then reconstruct the translation, "a unit of money."

Relearning: Is Learning Easier the Second Time Around? **Relearning** is a third method of measuring retention. Do you remember having to learn all of the state capitals in grade school? What were the capitals of Wyoming and Delaware? Even when we cannot recall or recognize material that had once been learned, such as Cheyenne for Wyoming and Dover for Delaware, we can relearn it more rapidly the second time. Similarly, as we go through our 30s and 40s we may forget a good deal of our high-school French or geometry. Yet the second time around we could learn what previously took months or years much more rapidly.

To study the efficiency of relearning, Ebbinghaus (1885/1913) devised the **method of savings.** First he recorded the number of repetitions required to learn a list of nonsense syllables or words. Then he recorded the number of repetitions required to relearn the list after a certain amount of time had elapsed. Next he computed the difference in the number of

Figure 7.7
Paired Associates
Psychologists often use paired associates to measure recall. Retrieving the syllable CEG in response to the cue WOM is made easier by an image of a WOMan smoking a "CEG-arette."

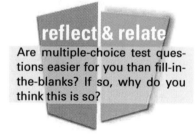

Are multiple-choice test questions easier for you than fill-in-the-blanks? If so, why do you think this is so?

Recognition In information processing, the easiest memory task, involving identification of objects or events encountered before.

Recall Retrieval or reconstruction of learned material.

Paired associates Nonsense syllables presented in pairs in experiments that measure recall.

Relearning A measure of retention. Material is usually relearned more quickly than it is learned initially.

Method of savings A measure of retention in which the difference between the number of repetitions originally required to learn a list and the number of repetitions required to relearn the list after a certain amount of time has elapsed is calculated.

Figure 7.8
Ebbinghaus's Classic Curve of Forgetting
Recollection of lists of words drops precipitously during the first hour after learning. Losses of learning then becomes more gradual. Retention drops by half within the first hour. It takes a month (31 days), however, for retention to be cut in half again.

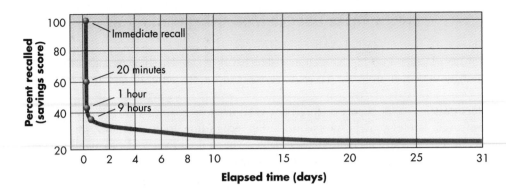

repetitions to determine the **savings.** If a list had to be repeated 20 times before it was learned, and 20 times again after a year had passed, there were no savings. Relearning, that is, was as tedious as the initial learning. If the list could be learned with only 10 repetitions after a year had elapsed, however, half the number of repetitions required for learning had been saved.

Figure 7.8 shows Ebbinghaus's classic curve of forgetting. As you can see, there was no loss of memory as measured by savings immediately after a list had been learned. However, recollection dropped quite a bit, by half, during the first hour after learning a list. Losses of learning then became more gradual. It took a month (31 days) for retention to be cut in half again. In other words, forgetting occurred most rapidly right after material was learned. We continue to forget material as time elapses, but at a slower pace.

Before leaving this section, I have one question for you: What are the capitals of Wyoming and Delaware?

━━■━ Interference Theory

When we do not attend to, encode, and rehearse sensory input, we may forget it through decay of the trace of the image. Material in short-term memory, like material in sensory memory, can be lost through decay. It can also be lost through displacement, as may happen when we try to remember several new names at a party.

Why can learning Spanish make it harder to remember French? The answer may be found in **interference theory.** According to this view, we also forget material in short-term and long-term memory because newly learned material interferes with it. The two basic types of interference are retroactive interference (also called *retroactive inhibition*) and proactive interference (also called *proactive inhibition*).

Retroactive Interference   In **retroactive interference,** new learning interferes with the retrieval of old learning. For example, a medical student may memorize the names of the bones in the leg through rote repetition. Later he or she may find that learning the names of the bones in the arm makes it more difficult to retrieve the names of the leg bones, especially if the names are similar in sound or in relative location on each limb.

Proactive Interference   In **proactive interference,** older learning interferes with the capacity to retrieve more recently learned material. High-school Spanish may pop in when you are trying to retrieve college French or Italian words. All three are Romance languages, with similar roots and spellings. Previously learned Japanese words probably would not interfere with your ability to retrieve more recently learned French or Italian, because the roots and sounds of Japanese differ considerably from those of the Romance languages. ◆ **Truth or Fiction Revisited:** It is therefore true that learning Spanish can make it harder to remember French—and vice versa.

Consider motor skills. You may learn to drive a standard shift on a car with three forward speeds and a clutch that must be let up slowly after shifting. Later you may learn to drive a car with five forward speeds and a clutch that must be released rapidly. For a while, you may make errors on the five-speed car because of proactive interference. (Old learning interferes with new learning.) If you return to the three-speed car after driving the five-speed car has become natural, you may stall it a few times. This is because of retroactive interference (new learning interferes with the old).

Savings The difference between the number of repetitions originally required to learn a list and the number of repetitions required to relearn the list after a certain amount of time has elapsed.

Interference theory The view that we may forget stored material because other learning interferes with it.

Retroactive interference The interference of new learning with the ability to retrieve material learned previously.

Proactive interference The interference by old learning with the ability to retrieve material learned recently.

▬■▬ Repression: Ejecting the Unwanted from Consciousness

According to Sigmund Freud, we are motivated to forget painful memories and unacceptable ideas because they produce anxiety, guilt, and shame. *What is the Freudian concept of repression?* Repression, according to Freud, is the automatic ejection of painful memories and unacceptable urges from conscious awareness. It is motivated by the desire to avoid facing painful memories and emotions. Psychoanalysts believe that repression is at the heart of disorders such as **dissociative amnesia** (see Chapter 12). There is a current controversy in psychology about whether repression (motivated forgetting) exists and, if it does, how it works. One interesting finding is that stress hormones—the kind we secrete when we experience extremes of anxiety, guilt, and shame—*heighten* memory formation (Clayton & Williams, 2000; McGaugh et al., 2002). But supporters of the concept of repression do not claim that repressed memories were ill-formed; they say, rather, that we do not focus on them.

There is much research on repression, often in the form of case studies that are found in psychoanalytic journals (e.g., Eagle, 2000). Much has been made of case studies in which veterans have supposedly forgotten traumatic battlefield experiences, developed posttraumatic stress disorder (once called "battlefield neurosis"), and then "felt better" once they recalled and discussed the traumatic events (Karon & Widener, 1998). Critics argue that the evidence for such repression and recovery of memories is weak and that this kind of "memory" can be implanted by the suggestions of interviewers (Loftus, 2001; Thomas & Loftus, 2002; van de Wetering et al., 2002). The issue remains controversial, as we see next.

Do People Really Recover Repressed Memories of Childhood? There may be little doubt that memory of traumatic events can be repressed. But there is also little doubt that many "recovered memories" of childhood sexual abuse may be induced by a therapist.[1]

A woman in therapy "recovered" the memory that she was raped by her teacher at the age of 13, got pregnant, and had an abortion. But there was no evidence for the event. And since the woman had not begun to ovulate until age 15, she could not have become pregnant at 13. Nevertheless, she filed charges against the teacher, and he had to pay lawyers his life savings to defend himself. Eventually, the court ruled in his favor—that the recovery of repressed memories had little scientific support.

Despite shaky scientific support, there are cases of so-called recovered memories, especially memories of childhood sexual abuse by a relative, teacher, or friend. The question is whether these memories are induced by therapists who foster beliefs that become so deeply ingrained they seem like authentic memories. "We don't know what percent of these recovered memories are real and what percent are pseudomemories," notes psychiatrist Harold Lief (cited in Brody, 2000), one of the first to challenge such memories.

Psychologist Elizabeth Loftus has engaged in numerous studies that show how easy it is to implant false memories through leading questions. In one study, researchers were able to readily convince half the subjects that they had been lost in a mall or hospitalized with severe pain as children.

▬■▬ Infantile Amnesia

Can children remember events from the first couple of years of life? When he interviewed people about their early experiences, Freud discovered that they could not recall episodes that had happened prior to the age of 3 or so and that recall was cloudy through the age of 5. This phenomenon is referred to as **infantile amnesia.**

Infantile amnesia has little to do with the fact that the episodes occurred in the distant past. Middle-aged and older people have vivid memories from the ages of 6 through 10, yet the events happened many decades ago. But 18-year-olds show steep declines in memory when they try to recall episodes that occurred earlier than the age of 6, even though they happened less than 18 years earlier (Wetzler & Sweeney, 1986).

---

[1] Adapted from Jane E. Brody. (2000, April 25). Memories of things that never were. *The New York Times*, p. F8.

Dissociative amnesia Amnesia thought to stem from psychological conflict or trauma.

Infantile amnesia Inability to recall events that occur prior to the age of 2 or 3. Also termed *childhood amnesia*.

Life Connections
Using the Psychology of Memory to Enhance Your Memory

Humans have survived the Ice Age, the Stone Age, the Iron Age, and, a bit more recently, the Industrial Revolution. Now we are trying to cope with the so-called Age of Information, in which there has been an explosion of information. Computers have been developed to process it. Humans, too, process information, and there is more of it to process than ever before. We can always add more memory to our computers, but how can people improve their memory? Fortunately, psychologists have helped devise methods for improving memory. Let us consider some of them.

Drill and Practice: "A, B, C, D . . . "

Repetition (rote maintenance rehearsal) helps transfer information from short-term to long-term memory. Does maintenance rehearsal seem too mechanical for you as a college student? If so, don't forget that this is how you learned the alphabet and how to count!

You can try the following methods for remembering a person's name:

1. Say the name aloud.
2. Ask the person a question, using her or his name.
3. Use the person's name as many times as you can during your conversation.
4. Write down the name when the conversation has ended.

Relate New Information to What Is Already Known

Relating new information to what is already known is a form of elaborative rehearsal (Willoughby et al., 1994). Herrmann (1991) suggests that you can better remember the name of a new acquaintance by thinking of a rhyme for it. Now you have done some thinking about the name, and you also have two tags for the person, not one. If you are trying to retrieve the spelling of the word *retrieve,* do so by retrieving the rule "*i* before *e* except after *c.*" There are exceptions, of course: Remember that "weird" doesn't follow the rule because it's a "weird" word.

Form Unusual, Exaggerated Associations

Psychologist Charles L. Brewer uses an interesting method to teach psychology students the fundamentals of shaping:

> Dr. Brewer first danced on his desk, then bleated like a sheep and finally got down on "all fours and oinked like a pig," he said. His antics were in response to a session he teaches on "successive approximation"—shaping behavior into a desired response.
>
> To get students to "shape" him, he told them he would try to figure out what they wanted him to do. If he guessed wrong, they'd "boo and hiss," while if he did what they wanted, they'd applaud him—which is why he eventually acted like a pig. "I'll do anything to get them to learn," he said. (DeAngelis, 1994a, p. 40)

It is easier to recall stimuli that stand out from the crowd. We pay more attention to them. Sometimes, therefore, we are better able to remember information when we create unusual, exaggerated associations.

Use the Method of Loci: Meatloaf in the Pocket

Another way to form unusual associations is the *method of loci* (pronounced LOW-sigh). Select a series of related images such as the parts of your body or the furniture in your home. Then imagine an item from your shopping list, or another list you want to remember, as being attached to each image. Consider this meaty application: Remember your shop-

Figure 7.9
The Method of Loci
By imagining meatloaf in your jacket pocket, you can combine several items into a single chunk of information. Once at the supermarket, recall the ingredients for meatloaf and ask yourself which ones you need to buy.

ping list by imagining meatloaf in your jacket pocket and balancing a breakfast plate on your head.

By placing meatloaf or a favorite complete dinner in your pocket, rather than a single item such as ground beef, you can combine several items into one chunk of information (see Figure 7.9). At the supermarket, you recall the ingredients for meatloaf and consider whether you need each one. The breakfast plate can remind you whether you need juice, bread for toast, eggs, cereals, fruit for the cereals, coffee or tea, milk for the coffee or lemons for the tea, and so on.

Use Mediation: Build a Conceptual Bridge

The method of mediation also relies on forming associations: You link two items with a third one that ties them together.

I used a combination of mediation and formation of unusual associations to help me remember foreign vocabulary words in high school. For example, the Spanish word *mujer* (pronounced moo-hair [almost]), means "woman" in English. Women have mo' hair than I do. Woman → mo' hair → *mujer*. This particular example would no longer work for me because now most men also have more hair than me, but the association was so outlandish that it stuck with me.

Use Mnemonic Devices

Broadly speaking, methods for jogging memory can all be termed *mnemonics*, or systems for remembering information. But *mnemonic devices* usually combine chunks of information into a format such as an acronym, jingle, or phrase. (By the way, the word *mnemonic* is derived from Mnemosyne, the Greek goddess of memory. Her name is pronounced *Nee-MOS-uh-nee*. How can you remember the pronunciation? Why not think of the goddess getting down on her two knees [*nee-nee*] to worship? End of commercial for mnemonic devices.) For example, recalling the phrase "Every Good Boy Does Fine" has helped many people remember the lines in the musical staff: E, G, B, D, F. In Chapter 3, we saw that the acronym *SAME* serves as a mnemonic device for distinguishing between afferent and efferent neurons. Most psychology students use the acronym *Roy G. Biv* to remember the colors of the rainbow.

And how can you math students ever be expected to remember the reciprocal of pi (that is, 1 divided by 3.14)? Simple: Just remember the question "Can I remember the reciprocal?" and count the number of letters in each word. The reciprocal of pi, it turns out, is 0.318310. (Remember the last two digits as 10, not as 1 and 0.)

Finally, how can you remember how to spell *mnemonics*? Easy—be willing to grant "aMNesty" to those who cannot. ■

Freud believed that young children have aggressive impulses and perverse lusts toward their parents. He attributed infantile amnesia to repression of these impulses. The episodes lost to infantile amnesia, however, are not weighted in the direction of such "primitive" impulses. In fact, infantile amnesia probably reflects the interaction of physiological and cognitive factors. For example, a structure of the limbic system (the **hippocampus**) that is involved in the storage of memories does not become mature until we are about 2 years old (Squire, 2004). Also, myelination of brain pathways is incomplete for the first few years, contributing to the inefficiency of information processing and memory formation.

There are also cognitive explanations for infantile amnesia:

- Infants are not particularly interested in remembering the past (Neisser, 1993).
- Infants, in contrast to older children, tend not to weave episodes together into meaningful stories of their own lives. Information about specific episodes thus tends to be lost. Research shows that when parents reminisce about the past with children, the children's memories of being infants are strengthened (Harley & Reese, 1999; Peterson, 2002; Wang, 2003). (Of course, one could question the accuracy of some of these reminiscences.)
- Infants do not make reliable use of language to symbolize or classify events (Wang, 2003). Their ability to *encode* sensory input—that is, to apply the auditory and semantic codes that facilitate memory formation—is therefore limited. Yet research shows that young infants can recall events throughout the period when infantile amnesia is presumed to occur if they are now and then exposed to objects they played with or photos of events (Rovee-Collier, 1999).

In any event, we are unlikely to remember episodes from the first two years of life unless we are reminded of them from time to time as we develop. Many early childhood memories that seem so clear today might be reconstructed and hold many inaccuracies. They might also be memories of events that occurred later than we thought. Yet there is no evidence that such early memories are systematically repressed.

━━■━ Anterograde and Retrograde Amnesia

Adults also experience amnesia, although usually for biological reasons, as in the cases of anterograde and retrograde amnesia (Kopelman, 2002). *Why do people frequently have trouble recalling being in accidents?* In so-called **anterograde amnesia,** there are memory lapses for the period following a trauma such as a blow to the head, an electric shock, or an operation. In some cases the trauma seems to interfere with all the processes of memory. The ability to pay attention, the encoding of sensory input, and rehearsal are all impaired. A number of investigators have linked certain kinds of brain damage—such as damage to the hippocampus (see Figure 7.10)—to amnesia (Eichenbaum & Fortin, 2003; Spiers et al., 2001).

Consider the classic case of a man called "H. M." Parts of the brain are sometimes lesioned to help people with epilepsy. In H. M.'s case, a section of the hippocampus was removed (Milner, 1966). Right after the operation, H. M.'s mental functioning appeared normal. As time went on, however, it became clear that he had problems processing new information. For example, two years after the operation, H. M. believed he was 27—his age at the time of the operation. When his family moved to a new address, H. M. could not find his new home or remember the new address. He responded with appropriate grief to the death of his uncle, yet he then began to ask about his uncle and why he did not visit. ◆ **Truth or Fiction Revisited:** It is true that a man could not form new memories after part of his hippocampus was surgically removed. Each time he was reminded of his uncle's passing, he grieved as if he were hearing it for the first time. H. M.'s operation apparently prevented him from transferring information from short-term to long-term memory.

In **retrograde amnesia,** the source of trauma prevents people from remembering events that took place before the accident (Wheeler & McMillan, 2001). A football player who is knocked unconscious or a person in an auto accident may be unable to recall events that occurred for several minutes prior to the trauma. The football player may not recall

Hippocampus A structure in the limbic system that plays an important role in the formation of new memories.

Anterograde amnesia Failure to remember events that occur after physical trauma because of the effects of the trauma.

Retrograde amnesia Failure to remember events that occur prior to physical trauma because of the effects of the trauma.

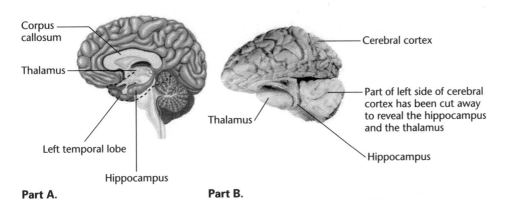

Figure 7.10
The Hippocampus
The hippocampus is essential to the formation of new memories. Part A shows the location of the hippocampus in the brain. Part B is a photo of a human brain as seen from above. The upper part of the left side of the cerebral cortex has been cut away, revealing the hippocampus. The hippocampus loops over the thalamus, runs behind it, and then underneath it.
Courtesy of Dana Copeland

taking the field. The person in the accident may not recall entering the car. It also sometimes happens that the individual cannot remember events that occurred for several years prior to the trauma.

In one well-known case of retrograde amnesia, a man received a head injury in a motorcycle accident (Baddeley, 1982). When he regained consciousness, he had lost memory for all events that had occurred after the age of 11. In fact, he appeared to believe that he was still 11 years old. During the next few months he gradually recovered more knowledge of his past. He moved toward the present year by year, up until the critical motorcycle ride. But he never did recover the events just prior to the accident. The accident had apparently prevented the information that was rapidly unfolding before him from being transferred to long-term memory. In terms of stages of memory, it may be that our perceptions and ideas need to consolidate, or rest undisturbed for a while, if they are to be transferred to long-term memory (Nader et al., 2000).

( ) Learning Connections

Forgetting—Will You Remember How We Forget?

REVIEW:

11 The classic curve of forgetting was constructed by
(a) the Petersons,
(b) Craik,
(c) Schacter,
(d) Ebbinghaus.

12 In _____, new learning interferes with the retrieval of old learning.
(a) proactive interferences,
(b) retroactive interference,
(c) dissociative amnesia,
(d) infantile amnesia.

13 Freud believed that infantile amnesia reflected
(a) immaturity of the hippocampus,
(b) lack of language,
(c) lack of interest in autobiographical memory,
(d) repression.

14 A football player who is knocked unconscious is most likely to experience
(a) retrograde amnesia,
(b) anterograde amnesia,
(c) proactive interference,
(d) retroactive interference.

CRITICAL THINKING:
Critical thinkers avoid overgeneralizing. According to the concept of infantile amnesia, children remember little or nothing from the first two years of life. But is this view of children's memory an overgeneralization? Don't children recognize their caregivers? Don't they acquire and remember language? Don't they remember how to crawl and sit up and walk? To what kinds of memories does the concept of infantile amnesia apply?

Go to www http://academic.cengage.com/psychology/rathus for an interactive version of this review.

THE BIOLOGY OF MEMORY: THE BRAIN AS A LIVING TIME MACHINE

Joel and Clementine didn't meet on Match.com. In fact, they are anything but well-matched. In the film *Eternal Sunshine of the Spotless Mind*, Joel (Jim Carrey) is a sort of cautious, depressed male who runs into Clementine (Kate Winslet), a volatile and offbeat book clerk. Clementine divides her time between dying her hair blue and blood orange. When the relationship fails, Clementine is miserable. She visits a doctor who erases all memory of Joel from her mind—making it "spotless"—so that she will feel the warmth of the sun once more rather than the lonely dread of darkness. Joel is dumbfounded by Clementine's failure to recognize him. He learns of the process she underwent and decides to have Clementine erased from his mind as well.

The main part of the film follows the erasing process that takes place inside Joel's mind. One image of Clementine after another dissolves as the world around them dissolves as well. Erasure is possible because the doctor has "mapped" Joel's memories of Clementine. They are all interconnected, and he can follow their paths through the brain and zap them.

Are memories in fact interconnected in the brain? Psychologists assume that mental processes such as the encoding, storage, and retrieval of information—that is, memory—are accompanied by changes in the brain. Early in the 20th century, many psychologists used the concept of the **engram** in their study of memory. Engrams were viewed as electrical circuits in the brain that corresponded to memory traces—neurological processes that paralleled experiences. Yet biological psychologists such as Karl Lashley (1950) spent many fruitless years searching for such circuits or for the structures of the brain in which they might be housed. Much research on the biology of memory focuses today on the roles of stimulants, neurons, neurotransmitters, hormones, and structures in the brain. For example, nicotine—the habit-forming stimulant that is found in tobacco products—appears to aid in the formation of memories. No one suggests that students smoke as a way of studying for tests, but as we see in the following section, there are fascinating suggestions of chemicals that may someday be used to promote the consolidation of memories.

Kate Winslet and Jim Carrey play Clementine and Joel, a pair of mismatched lovers in *Eternal Sunshine of the Spotless Mind.* When the relationship doesn't work out, Clementine has memories of Joel mapped and then erased from her brain. Joel follows suit. Can memories be mapped? Can they be erased?

Steve Sands/New York Newswire/Corbis

◆ Neural Activity and Memory: "Better Living Through Chemistry"

What neural events are connected with memory? The story of Joel and Clementine is fictional but may hold a kernel of truth. Rats who are reared in stimulating environments provide some answers. The animals develop more dendrites and synapses in the cerebral cortex than rats reared in impoverished environments (Neisser, 1997a). Moreover, visually stimulating rats increases the number of synapses in their visual cortex (Battaglia et al., 2004; Bilkey, 2004). Therefore, the storage of experience does involve avenues of communication among brain cells.

Information received through other senses is just as likely to lead to corresponding changes in the cortical regions that represent them. For example, sounds may similarly cause changes in the auditory cortex. Experiences perceived by several senses are apparently stored in numerous parts of the cortex. The recall of sensory experiences apparently involves neural activity in related regions of the brain.

Research with sea snails such as *Aplysia* and *Hermissenda* offers more insight into the biology of memory. *Aplysia* only has some 20,000 neurons compared with humans' billions. As a result, researchers have been able to study how experience is reflected at the synapses

Engram (1) An assumed electrical circuit in the brain that corresponds to a memory trace. (2) An assumed chemical change in the brain that accompanies learning. (From the Greek *en-,* meaning "in," and *gramma,* meaning "something that is written or recorded.")

of specific neurons. The sea snail will reflexively withdraw its gills when it receives electric shock, in the way a person will reflexively withdraw a hand from a hot stove or a thorn. In one kind of experiment, researchers precede the shock with a squirt of water. After a few repetitions, the sea snail becomes conditioned to withdraw its gills when squirted with the water. When sea snails are conditioned, they release more serotonin at certain synapses. As a consequence, transmission at these synapses becomes more efficient as trials (learning) progress (Kandel, 2001). This greater efficiency is termed **long-term potentiation** (LTP). As shown in Figure 7.11, dendrites can also participate in LTP by sprouting new branches that attach to the transmitting axon. Rats who are given substances that enhance LTP learn mazes with fewer errors; that is, they are less likely to turn down the wrong alley (Uzakov et al., 2005).

Serotonin and many other naturally occurring chemical substances, including adrenaline, noradrenaline, acetylcholine, glutamate, antidiuretic hormone, even the sex hormone estrogen have been shown to play roles in memory:

- Serotonin. This neurotransmitter increases the efficiency of conditioning in sea snails (Kandel, 2001). It is released when stimuli are paired repeatedly, increasing the efficiency of neural transmission (LTP) at certain synapses and creating neural circuits that contain the information.
- Acetylcholine (ACh). This neurotransmitter is vital in memory formation; low levels of ACh are connected with Alzheimer's disease. Increased levels of ACh promote conditioning in mice (Farr et al., 2000a).
- Glutamate. Glutamate, like serotonin, increases the efficiency of conditioning. Agents that increase the action of glutamate promote conditioning in mice (Farr et al., 2000a, 2000b).
- Adrenaline and noradrenaline (also called *epinephrine* and *norepineprhine*). The hormone adrenaline and the related hormone and neurotransmitter noradrenaline both strengthen memory when they are released into the bloodstream following learning. Stressful events stimulate release of stress hormones from the adrenal glands—adrenaline and steroids—which, in turn, stimulate a structure in the limbic system (the amygdala) to release noradrenaline. These hormones and neurotransmitter, acting together, heighten memory for stressful events (McGaugh, 2005).
- Vasopressin. Also known as *antidiuretic hormone,* vasopressin affects fluid retention. Like many other chemical substances in the body, it has multiple tasks, one of which is facilitating memory functioning, particularly working memory (Paban et al., 2003). ◆ **Truth or Fiction Revisited:** Sniffing vasopressin in the form of a nasal spray generally benefits memory functioning (Perras et al., 1997).
- Estrogen and testosterone. The sex hormones estrogen and testosterone boost working memory in, respectively, females and males (Janowsky et al., 2000). Estrogen replacement may help older, postmenopausal women retain cognitive functioning.

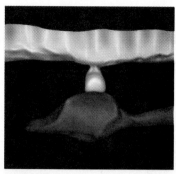

Part A.

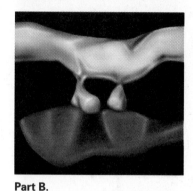

Part B.

Figure 7.11

One Avenue to Long-Term Potentiation (LTP)

LTP can occur via the action of neurotransmitters such as serotonin and glutamate at synapses. Structurally, LTP can also occur as shown in Parts A and B, when dendrites sprout new branches that connect with transmitting axons, increasing the amount of stimulation they receive.

⬛ Brain Structures and Memory

What structures in the brain are connected with memory? Memory does not reside in a single structure of the brain. As suggested in *Eternal Sunshine of the Spotless Mind,* it relies on complex neural networks that draw on various parts of the brain (Nyberg et al., 2000).

But some parts of the brain play more specific roles in memory. The hippocampus is vital in storing new information even if we can retrieve old information without it (Fields, 2005). But the hippocampus is not a storage bin. Rather, it is involved in relaying sensory information to parts of the cortex.

Where are the storage bins? The brain stores parts of memories in the appropriate areas of the sensory cortex. Sights are stored in the visual cortex, sounds in the auditory cortex, and so on. The limbic system is largely responsible for integrating these pieces of information when we recall an event. The frontal lobes apparently store information about where and when events occur (Chafee & Goldman-Rakic, 2000; Goldman-Rakic et al., 2000a).

Long-term potentiation (LTP) Enhanced efficiency in synaptic transmission that follows brief, rapid stimulation.

But what of the decision to try to recall something? What of the spark of consciousness that drives us to move backward in time or to strive to remember to do something in the future? The prefrontal cortex is the executive center in memory (Buckner et al., 2001; Wheeler & Treisman, 2002). It appears to empower people with consciousness—the ability to mentally represent and become aware of experiences that occur in the past, present, and future. It enables people to mentally travel back in time to reexperience the personal, autobiographical past. It enables people to focus on the things they intend to do in the future, such as mail a letter on the way to class or brush their teeth before going to bed (Fuster, 2000; McDaniel et al., 1999).

The hippocampus is also involved in the where and when of things (Eichenbaum & Fortin, 2003). The hippocampus does not become mature until we are about 2 years old. Immaturity may be connected with infantile amnesia. Adults with hippocampal damage may be able to form new procedural memories, even though they cannot form new episodic ("where and when") memories (Fields, 2005). They can develop new skills even though they cannot recall the practice sessions (Reed & Squire, 1997).

The thalamus (see Figure 7.10) is involved in the formation of verbal memories. Part of the thalamus of an Air Force cadet known as N. A. was damaged in a fencing accident. Afterward, N. A. could no longer form verbal memories, but he could form visual memories (Squire, 2004). (One might measure visual memory by showing people pictures, allowing time to pass, and then asking them to point out those they have been shown.)

The encoding, storage, and retrieval of information thus involve biological activity. As we learn, new synapses are developed, and changes occur at existing synapses. Parts of the brain are also involved in the formation of memories. In the next chapter, we see how people manipulate information they have stored to adapt to the environment or create new environments.

( ) Learning Connections

◀◀ *The Biology of Memory—The Brain as a Living Time Machine* ▶▶

REVIEW:

15 The decision to retrieve a memory is most likely made in the _____ of the brain.
   (a) hippocampus,
   (b) visual cortex,
   (c) prefrontal lobes,
   (d) amygdala.

16 Researchers use _____ to study LTP because they have only about 20,000 neurons.
   (a) sea snails,
   (b) rats,
   (c) monkeys,
   (d) pigeons.

17 _____ is vital in the storage of new information.
   (a) Broca's area,
   (b) The ganglion cell,
   (c) Nicotine,
   (d) The hippocampus.

18 The _____ seems to be involved in the formation of verbal memories.
   (a) thalamus,
   (b) hippocampus,
   (c) visual cortex,
   (d) amygdala.

CRITICAL THINKING:
Think about the evidence concerning the relationships between various kinds of chemicals—including stimulants, neurotransmitters, and hormones—and memory. How would you design an experiment to whether or not a chemical had an effect on memory functioning? How would you determine a safe dose of the chemical? How would you measure memory functioning? How might your methods differ if you were using people or animals?

Go www
to
http://academic.cengage.com/psychology/rathus
for an interactive version of this review.

RECITE—*An Active Summary*™

 Recite to Go!   *Don't have time to study right now? You can study on the go!*
Go to your companion website and download an audio version of this review section to your media player. You can also access an interactive flash-card version of this review from your website.

1. What is meant by explicit memory?	Explicit memories contain specific information—information that can be clearly stated or declared. The information can be autobiographical or general.
2. What is meant by episodic memory?	An episodic memory is a memory of an event that one has observed or participated in.
3. What is meant by semantic memory?	Semantic memory is general knowledge, as in remembering that the United States has 50 states or that Shakespeare wrote *Hamlet*.
4. What is meant by implicit memory?	Implicit or procedural memory means knowing how to do things like write with a pencil or ride a bicycle.
5. What is the difference between retrospective memory and prospective memory?	Retrospective memories concern events in the past that can be explicit or implicit. Prospective memories involve remembering to do things in the future. Prospective memory is affected by factors such as distraction, mood, and age.
6. What is the role of encoding in memory?	Encoding information transforms it so that we can place it in memory. We may use visual, auditory, and semantic codes to convert stimuli into formats that can be remembered.
7. What is the role of storage in memory?	Storage is the maintenance of information over time. The main methods of storing information are maintenance rehearsal and elaborative rehearsal.
8. What is the role of retrieval in memory?	Retrieval means locating stored information and bringing it back into consciousness. Retrieval requires use of the proper cues (just as to retrieve information from a hard drive, we need to know the file name).
9. What is the Atkinson–Shiffrin model of memory?	Atkinson and Shiffrin propose that there are three stages of memory—sensory memory, short-term memory, and long-term memory. The progress of information through these stages determines whether and how long it is remembered.
10. How does sensory memory function?	Each sense is believed to have a sensory register that briefly holds the memory traces of stimuli in sensory memory. The traces then decay. Icons represent visual stimuli. Echoes represent auditory stimuli.
11. How does short-term memory function?	Focusing on a stimulus allows us to maintain it in short-term memory—also called *working memory*—for a minute or so after the trace decays. Rehearsal allows us to maintain information indefinitely. New information in short-term memory can displace older information.
12. Why are we most likely to remember the first and last items in a list?	This phenomenon is referred to as the serial-position effect. The initial items in a list are rehearsed most often, and the final items are least likely to have been displaced by new information.
13. Is seven a magic number, or did the phone company get lucky?	Seven may not be a magic number, but it seems that the typical person can remember about seven chunks of information.

14. How does long-term memory function?	There is no known limit to the amount of information that can be stored in long-term memory. Long-term "memories" are reconstructed. The memories of eyewitnesses can be distorted by leading questions. Information can be transferred from short-term to long-term memory by rehearsal.
15. What is the levels-of-processing model of memory?	This model views memory in terms of a single dimension—not three stages. It is hypothesized that we encode, store, and retrieve information better when we process it more deeply.
16. Why is it that some events, like the attack of September 11, 2001, can be etched in memory for a lifetime?	So-called *flashbulb memories* tend to occur within a web of unusual and emotionally arousing circumstances. We may elaborate them extensively—that is, relate them to many things.
17. How is knowledge organized in long-term memory?	We tend to place information in hierarchies. We classify chunks of information into groups according to common features.
18. Why do we sometimes feel that the answer to a question is on the tip of our tongue?	Research suggests that the tip-of-the-tongue phenomenon often reflects incomplete learning.
19. Why may it be useful to study in the room in which we will be tested?	Memories are frequently dependent on the context in which they were formed. We retrieve information more efficiently when we are in the same context as when we acquired the information.
20. What types of memory tasks are used in measuring forgetting?	Nonsense syllables were developed by Ebbinghaus in the 19th century as a way of measuring memory. Retention is often tested through recognition, recall, and relearning.
21. Why can learning Spanish make it harder to remember French?	This is an example of retroactive interference, in which new learning interferes with old learning. In proactive interference, on the other hand, old learning interferes with new learning.
22. What is the Freudian concept of repression?	Repression is Freud's concept of motivated forgetting. Freud believed we are motivated to forget threatening material.
23. Can children remember events from the first couple of years of life?	Probably not. Modern psychologists believe that infantile amnesia reflects immaturity of the hippocampus and failure to encode events.
24. Why do people frequently have trouble recalling being in accidents?	Physical trauma can interfere with memory formation. In anterograde amnesia, trauma prevents formation of new memories. In retrograde amnesia, trauma prevents retrieval of previously known information.
25. What neural events are connected with memory?	Learning is connected with the proliferation of dendrites and synapses in the brain. Learning and memory are also connected with the release of the neurotransmitters and hormones.
26. What structures in the brain are connected with memory?	The hippocampus relays sensory information to the cortex and is therefore vital in formation of new memories. Visual memories appear to be stored in the visual cortex, auditory memories in the auditory cortex, and so on.

Key Terms

Explicit memory   244

Implicit memory   244

Episodic memory   244

Semantic memory   244

Priming   245

Retrospective memory   245

Prospective memory   245

Encoding   248

Visual code   248

Acoustic code   248

Semantic code   248

Storage   248

Maintenance rehearsal   248

Metamemory   248

Elaborative rehearsal   248

Retrieval   248

Memory   249

Saccadic eye movement   251

Sensory memory   251

Memory trace   251

Sensory register   251

Icon   251

Iconic memory   251

Eidetic imagery   252

Echo   252

Echoic memory   252

Short-term memory   252

Working memory   252

Serial-position effect   253

Chunk   253

Rote   254

Displace   255

Long-term memory   255

Repression   255

Schema   255

Elaborative rehearsal   259

Tip-of-the-tongue (TOT) phenomenon   261

Feeling-of-knowing experience   261

Context-dependent memory   263

State-dependent memory   263

Nonsense syllables   264

Recognition   265

Recall   265

Paired associates   265

Relearning   265

Method of savings   265

Savings   266

Interference theory   266

Retroactive interference   266

Proactive interference   266

Dissociative amnesia   267

Infantile amnesia   267

Hippocampus   270

Anterograde amnesia   270

Retrograde amnesia   270

Engram   272

Long-term potentiation (LTP)   273

Active Learning Resources

Visit Your Companion Website for This Book

http://academic.cengage.com/psychology/rathus

Check out this companion website where you will find online resources directly linked to your book. This is where you'll access the videos highlighted in your Video Connections feature. You can answer the questions online and email them to your professor. In addition you'll find downloadable audio review material, interactive versions of the study aids, Power Visuals for mastering and reviewing key concepts, as well as quizzing, and much more!

CENGAGENOW™

http://academic.cengage.com

Need help studying? This site is your one-stop study shop. Take a Pre-Test and Cengage NOW will generate a Personalized Study Plan based on your test results. The Study Plan will identify the topics you need to review and direct you to online resources to help you master those topics. You can then take a Post-Test to help you determine the concepts you have mastered and what you still need to work on. In addition you can access interactive media including the videos highlighted in your Video Connections box.

Author Blog

What does your author Spence Rathus have to say about the state of psychology? Visit your companion website every Tuesday and click on "Author Blog." This is where he'll talk about the most recent controversies and hot topics in psychology. This will keep you up to date with what your author is thinking and give you great insight into modern psychology.

CHAPTER 8

Thinking, Language, and Intelligence

Steve Prezant /Corbis

| T | F | You are most likely to find the answer to a frustrating problem by continuing to plug away at it. |

| T | F | Only humans can use insight to solve problems. |

| T | F | If a couple has five sons, the sixth child is likely to be a daughter. |

| T | F | People change their opinions when the opinions are shown to be wrong. |

| T | F | Crying is an early form of language. |

| T | F | Young children say things like "Daddy goed away" and "Mommy sitted down" because they *do* understand rules of grammar. |

| T | F | "Street smarts" are a sign of intelligence. |

| T | F | Creative people are highly intelligent. |

| T | F | Highly intelligent people are creative. |

| T | F | Two children can answer exactly the same items on an intelligence test correctly, yet one child can be above average in IQ, and the other can be below average. |

| T | F | Intelligence tests measure many things other than intelligence. |

| T | F | Head Start programs have raised children's IQs. |

Go to

http://academic.cengage.com/pstchology/rathus
for an interactive version of this Truth or Fiction feature.

Science has brought us many artificial objects—artificial sweeteners, designer drugs, and artificial limbs, to name a few. But one of the major scientific achievements lies in the realm of artificial intelligence. Artificial intelligence, or *AI,* is the duplication of human intellectual functioning in computers.

The concept of AI has a long history both in science fiction and in practice. The robot C3PO in *Star Wars* not only mimics human intelligence but also displays human anxieties and self-doubts. The programming in the artificial combination of flesh and metal portrayed by Arnold Schwarzenegger in the *Terminator* films presented him with options that enabled him to size up any situation and efficiently curse, kill, or utter Arnoldisms such as "I'll be back."

So much for Hollywood. The idea that human intelligence could be copied in computer form originated half a century ago. It was predicted that machines with AI would "one day" be able to understand spoken language, decipher bad handwriting, search their memories for information, reason, solve problems, make decisions, write books, and explain themselves out loud. At the time, these predictions were visionary. No longer. "One day" is today. Today's computers are very, very good at encoding storing, retrieving, and manipulating information to solve problems and make decisions. We even speak of them as having neural networks that can learn from experience (Nugent, 2004a, 2004b).

In some ways, AI goes beyond human intelligence. "Deep Blue," the IBM computer that defeated Russian grandmaster Garry Kasparov in chess, examined 200 million possible chess moves a *second.* Yet in 2003, Kasparov played an even more powerful computer, "Deep Junior," to a draw. But, said Kasparov, "I give us only a few years. Then they'll win every match, and we may have to struggle to win even a single game" (cited in Hoffman, 2003).

AI can solve problems that would take people years to solve, if they could solve them at all. Given clear direction and the right formulas, computers can carry out complex intellectual functions in a flash. "Who," asks University of Illinois professor Patrick Hayes, "can keep track of 10,000 topics like a computer?"

Moreover, when a computer learns something, it can rapidly share the information with other computers. But when you learn Spanish or calculus, other people cannot readily "download" the information from you. If they could (as in *The Matrix,* the science-fiction film series), education as we know it would vanish.

Mario Tama/Getty Images

■ **Russian Chess Champion Garry Kasparov**
Kasparov has played against computers that can analyze millions of possible moves per second and held his own. How "intelligent" are computers? What is "intelligence"?

Even so, Deep Blue and Deep Junior are baby steps. Despite their skill at chess, in other ways they are much less than human. They do not have human insight, intuition, and creativity. Although Ray Kurzweil (2004; Kurzweil & Keklak, 2003) is developing artificial intelligence that can write poetry and create art, the sparks of brilliance we find in today's computers turn into dense wood when we compare them to Shakespeare and Picasso. (I hope my computer's not reading this.)

Some futurists speak of the merging of human and computer intelligence. They speak of things like "chipping" the human brain (installing microchips that would boost our knowledge and processing power) or of microscopic robots that could set up shop at synapses and boost communication among neurons or supplant it with virtual realities that would have the immediacy of true experience.

It's all stimulating and somewhat scary. We're making computers that think more like people, and we may use computers to boost our own intellectual powers. What the worlds of natural and artificial intelligence will look like a century from now is anybody's guess. But for the moment at least, the qualities that make our psychological processes fully human have not been captured by computer science. That thought doesn't bother me a byte.

In this chapter, we look at three related areas of human psychological processes: thinking, language, and intelligence.

THINKING

The Greek philosopher Aristotle pointed out that people differ from lower organisms in their capacity for rational thinking. Thinking enables us to build skyscrapers, create computers, and scan the interior of the body without surgery. Some people even manage to keep track of their children and balance their checkbooks.

What is thinking? **Thinking** means attending to information, representing it mentally, reasoning about it, and making judgments and decisions about it. Thinking refers to conscious, planned attempts to make sense of and change the world. Mental processes such as dreaming and daydreaming may be unplanned and seem to proceed more or less on their own.

In this chapter we explore thinking and the related topics of language and intelligence. Humans tend to use language not only in communicating, but also in thinking. Intelligence provides the foundation for our capacity to think and solve problems. We begin with concepts, which provide many of the building blocks for thinking.

■ Concepts: The Building Blocks of Thinking

Here's a riddle from my own childhood: "What's black and white and read all over?" Because this riddle was spoken, not written, and involved the colors black and white, you would probably assume that "read" meant "red." Thus, in seeking an answer, you might scan your memory for an object that was red although it also somehow managed to be black and white. The answer to the riddle—"newspaper"—was usually met with a groan.

The word *newspaper* is a concept. *Red, black,* and *white* are also concepts—color concepts. *What are concepts?* **Concepts** are mental categories used to group together objects, relations, events, abstractions, or qualities that have common properties. Concepts are crucial to cognition. Concepts can represent objects, events, and activities—and visions of things that never were or cannot be measured, such as "Middle Earth" in Tolkien's *Lord of the Rings* novels or the land of Oz in *The Wizard of Oz.*

Labels for objects depend on experience with them and on one's cultural setting (Sloman et al., 2002). Concepts such as *square, circle,* and *triangle* are not all that common in nature, and some peoples who do not construct houses with these shapes, such as the Himba of Northern Namibia, have no words for them (Roberson et al., 2002). But these concepts

Thinking Paying attention to information, mentally representing it, reasoning about it, and making decisions about it.

Concept A mental category that is used to class together objects, relations, events, abstractions, or qualities that have common properties.

are basic to geometry. Much thinking has to do with categorizing new concepts and manipulating relationships among concepts, as in geometric proofs.

We tend to organize concepts in *hierarchies* (see Figure 8.1). The newspaper category includes objects such as your school paper and the *Los Angeles Times.* Newspapers, college textbooks, novels, and merchandise catalogs can be combined into higher-order categories such as *printed matter* or *printed devices that store information.* If you add hard drives and DVDs, you can create a still higher category, *objects that store information.* Now consider a question that requires categorical thinking: How are a newspaper and a DVD alike? Answers to such questions entail supplying the category that includes both objects. In this case, we can say that both objects store information. Their functions are alike, even if their technology differs.

Prototypes are good examples. They best match the key features of categories. Which animal seems more birdlike to you: a robin or an ostrich? Why? Which better fits the prototype of a fish: a sea horse or a tuna? Why?

Many simple prototypes, such as *dog* and *red,* are taught by means of examples, or **exemplars.** Research suggests that it is more efficient for most of us to learn what *fruits* and *vegetables* are from experience with exemplars of each, rather than by working from definitions of them (Smits et al., 2002). We point to a dog and tell a child "dog" or "This is a dog." Dogs are *positive instances* of the dog concept. *Negative instances*—things that are *not* dogs—are then shown to the child while we say, "This is *not* a dog." Negative instances of one concept may be positive instances of another. So, in teaching a child, we may be more likely to say, "This is not a dog—it's a cat" than simply, "This is not a dog."

Children may at first include horses and other four-legged animals within the dog concept until the differences between dogs and horses are pointed out. In language development,

■ **Words and Concepts, Concepts and Words**

Circles, squares, and triangles are found only rarely in nature and not among the Himba of Northern Namibia. It is not surprising, then, that they have no words for these concepts.

Prototype A concept of a category of objects or events that serves as a good example of the category.

Exemplar A specific example.

Figure 8.1
Organization of Concepts into Hierarchies
People may have a concept, "Objects that store information." This concept may include concepts such as MP3 files, DVD, and printed matter. Within the concept of printed matter, people may include newspapers, college textbooks (certainly the most important object that stores information!), novels, and catalogs. The concept of newspaper may include one's school newspaper and various commercial newspapers.

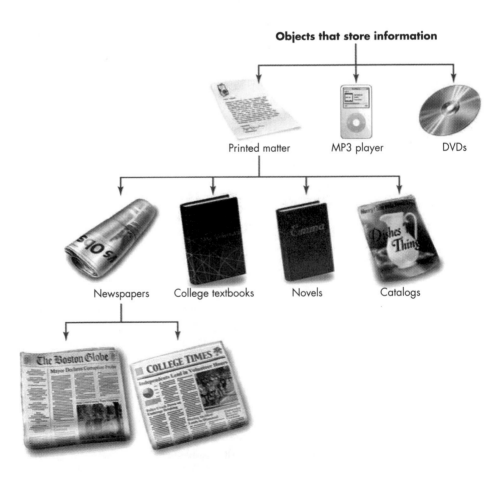

such overinclusion of instances in a category (reference to horses as dogs) is labeled *over-extension*. Children's prototypes become refined after children are shown positive and negative instances and given explanations. Abstract concepts such as *bachelor* or *square root* tend to be formed through explanations that involve more basic concepts.

Gale Zucker/Stock Boston LLC

■ **A Goat or a Dog?**
Yes, yes, you know the answer, but little children may at first include goats, horses, and other four-legged animals within the dog concept until they understand the differences among the animals.

■ Problem Solving: Getting from Here to There

Problem solving is an important aspect of thinking. Here's a problem for you to solve. What are the next two letters in this series?

OTTFFSSE__?

How did you try to find the answer? Did you search your personal memory banks and ask yourself what *O* can stand for, then *T,* and so on? Did you try to think of some phrase the letters might represent? Perhaps the first letters of the stars in a constellation?

Try this: Go to Google or Yahoo and enter the letters in the search window. Then click "Search." I used Google in Chapter 5, so I decided to first try www.yahoo.com this time. It took Yahoo 0.13 seconds to retrieve 132 hits, most of which held the answer. Thinking this was rather a little, I switched to Google. Google took a bit longer—0.17 seconds—but came up with 676 hits. The answer is . . . scroll down to the next few pages (or use a search engine).

When the first edition of this book was written, this solution—going to an online search engine—would not have been possible. There was no Google. In fact, there was no Internet. This section is about the ways in which we solve problems, on our own or with Google and Yahoo.

Now I would like to share something personal with you. One of the pleasures I derived from my own introductory psychology course lay in showing friends the textbook and getting them involved in the problems in the section on problem solving. First, of course, I struggled with them myself. Now it's your turn. Get some scrap paper, take a breath, and have a go at the problems in the nearby Self-Assessment. The answers will be discussed in the following pages, but don't peek. *Try* the problems first.

How do people solve problems? To answer this question, begin by considering the steps you used to try to solve parts a and b of problem 1 in the Self-Assessment. Did you first make sure you understood the problem by rereading the instructions? Or did you dive in as soon as you saw them on the page? Perhaps the solutions to 1a and 1b came easily, but I'm sure you studied 1c very carefully. Let's review what you may have been thinking when you attempted to solve these problems and how your cognitive processes might have led you to or away from solutions.

After you believed you understood what was required in each problem, you probably tried to discover the structure of the cycles in each series. Series 1a has repeated cycles of two letters: *AB, AB,* and so on. Series 1b may be seen as having four cycles of two consecutive letters: *AB, DE, BC,* and so on.

Again, did you solve 1a and 1b in a flash of insight, or did you try to find rules that govern each series? In series 1a, the rule is simply to repeat the cycle. Series 1b is more complicated, and different sets of rules can be used to describe it. One correct set of rules is that odd-numbered cycles (*1* and *3,* or *AB* and *BC*) simply repeat the last letter of the previous cycle (in this case *B*) and then advance by one letter in the alphabet. The same rule applies to even-numbered cycles (*2* and *4,* or *DE* and *EF*).

If you found rules for problems 1a and 1b, you used them to produce the next letters in the series: *AB* in series 1a and *CD* in series 1b. Perhaps you then evaluated the effectiveness of your rules by checking your answers against the solutions in the preceding paragraphs.

Now, the question is whether your solutions to problems 1a and 1b helped you to understand 1c or whether they interfered with your ability to solve 1c. Let us consider what psychologists mean by "understanding" a problem. Then let us see whether you applied an *algorithm* to solve 1a and 1b. As we read on, we'll also consider the roles of *heuristics, insight,* and *mental sets,* among other cognitive processes. You'll see that solving 1a and 1b might have made it more difficult rather than less difficult to solve 1c.

Self-Assessment

Self-Assessment

Puzzles, Problems, and Just Plain Fun

Self-Assessment

Are you ready for some mind benders? Following are a number of problems I came across in my own psychology courses. They were challenging and mostly enjoyable, except that I think I scratched my head a bit too hard over a couple of them. (The hair still hasn't grown back, although people unfamiliar with my past attribute it to male-pattern baldness.)

Have some fun with them. If the answer doesn't come immediately, why not stand back from the problem for a while and see if the answer comes to you in a "flash of insight." (I confess that I was suffering from a deficiency of insight when I tried to solve them.)

You will find the answers to Problem 1 as you read along in the text. You will find the answers to the others in the figure on page 563.

1. Provide the next two letters in the series for each of the following:
   a. ABABABAB??
   b. ABDEBCEF??
   c. OTTFFSSE??

2. Draw straight lines through all the points in the following figure, using only *four* lines. Do not lift your pencil from the paper or retrace your steps. (See Appendix B, p. 563 for answer.)

3. Move three matches in the following figure to make four squares of the same size. You must use *all* the matches. (See page 563 for answer.)

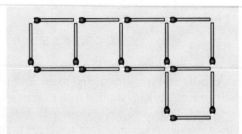

4. You have three jars—A, B, and C—which hold the amounts of water, in ounces, shown in the following table. For each of the seven problems, use the jars in any way you wish to arrive at the indicated amount of water. Fill or empty any jar as often as you wish. How do you obtain the desired amount of water in each problem? (The solutions are discussed on p. 289.)

Water Jar Problems

	THREE JARS ARE PRESENT WITH THE LISTED CAPACITY (IN OUNCES)			
PROBLEM	JAR A	JAR B	JAR C	GOAL
1	21	127	3	100
2	14	163	25	99
3	18	43	10	5
4	9	42	6	21
5	20	59	4	31
6	23	49	3	20
7	10	36	7	3

SOURCE: Adapted from *Rigidity of Behavior* (p. 109), by Abraham S. Luchins and Edith H. Luchins, 1959, Eugene: University of Oregon Press.

Go to www http://academic.cengage.com/psychology/rathus where you can fill out an interactive version of this *Self-Assessment and automatically score your results.*

Understanding the Problem   Let us begin our discussion of understanding problems by considering a bus driver problem my 9-year-old daughter Jordan gave me. Because I believe in exposing students to the tortures I have endured, see what you can do with it:

You're driving a bus that's leaving from Pennsylvania. To start off with, there were 32 people on the bus. At the next bus stop, 11 people got off and 9 people got on. At the next bus stop, 2 people got off, and 2 people got on. At the next bus stop, 12 people got on, and 16 people got off. At the next bus stop, 5 people got on and 3 people got off. What color are the bus driver's eyes?

I was not about to be fooled when I was listening to this problem. Although it seemed that I should be tracking the number of people who were on the bus, I sensed there was a trick. Therefore, I told myself to remember that the bus was leaving from Pennsylvania. Being clever, I also kept track of the number of stops rather than the number of people getting on and off. When I was finally hit with the question about the bus driver's eyes, I was at a loss. I protested that Jordan had said nothing about the bus driver's eyes, but she insisted that she had given me enough information to answer the question.

One of the requirements of problem solving is attending to relevant information. To do that, you need some familiarity with the type of problem. I classified the bus driver problem as a trick question and paid attention to silly details, but I wasn't on target.

How about you? What color were the bus driver's eyes?

If we assume it is crucial to keep track of the number of people getting on and off the bus, we focus on information that turns out to be nonessential. In fact, it distracts us from the key information.

When we are faced with a novel problem, how can we know which information is relevant and which is not? Background knowledge helps. If you are given a chemistry problem, it helps if you have taken courses in chemistry. If Jordan gives you a problem, it is helpful to expect the unexpected. (In case you still haven't gotten it, the critical information you need to solve the bus driver problem is provided in the first sentence.)

Successful understanding of a problem generally requires three features:

1. *The parts or elements of our mental representation of the problem relate to one another in a meaningful way.* If we are trying to solve a problem in geometry, our mental triangles, like actual triangles, should have angles that total 180 degrees.
2. *The elements of our mental representation of the problem correspond to the elements of the problem in the outer world.* If we are meeting a patient in the emergency room of a hospital, we want to arrive at a diagnosis of what might be wrong before we make a treatment plan. To do so, we take the patient's "vital signs," including heart rate, temperature, and blood pressure, so that our mental picture of the patient conforms to what is going on in his or her body.
3. *We have a storehouse of background knowledge that we can apply to the problem.* We have the necessary experience or course work to solve the problem.

The Use of Algorithms: Finding the Right Formula   An **algorithm** is a specific procedure for solving a type of problem. An algorithm invariably leads to the solution—if it is used properly, that is. Mathematical formulas like the Pythagorean theorem are examples of algorithms. They yield correct answers to problems *as long as the right formula is used.* Finding the right formula to solve a problem may require scanning one's memory for all formulas that contain variables that represent one or more of the elements in the problem. The Pythagorean theorem concerns right triangles. Therefore, it is appropriate to consider using this formula for problems concerning right triangles, but not others.

If you are going to be meeting someone for the first time and want to make a good impression, you consider the nature of the encounter (for example, a job interview or a "blind date") and then consider how to dress and behave for the encounter. If it's a job interview, the algorithm may be to dress neatly, be well-groomed, and not to wear too much cologne or perfume. If it's a date, you may ditch the suit but hike up the cologne or perfume a notch. In either case, smile and make eye contact—it's all part of the formula.

Anagrams are scrambled words. *Korc* is an anagram for *rock* or *cork*. The task in anagram problems is to try to reorganize jumbles or groups of letters into words. Some anagram problems require us to use every letter from the pool of letters; others allow us to use only some of the letters. How many words can you make from the pool of letters *DWARG*? If you were to use the **systematic random search** algorithm, you would list every possible letter combination, using from one to all five letters. You could use a dictionary or a spell-checking program to see whether each result is, in fact, a word. The method might take a while, but it would work.

Algorithm A systematic procedure for solving a problem that works invariably when it is correctly applied.

Systematic random search An algorithm for solving problems in which each possible solution is tested according to a particular set of rules.

Video Connections

Problem Solving

LEARNING OBJECTIVES

- To understand problem solving techniques and how they are related to intelligence.
- To be able to explain the elevator and match riddles, as well as their solutions.
- To understand the role of insight in problem solving.

APPLIED LESSON

1 Can you think of times you have engaged in divergent thinking? Give examples. What are the roles of divergent thinking and convergent thinking in problem solving?

What kinds of problem solving processes would you use to obtain the answers to the elevator and match riddles?

CRITICAL THINKING

2 Critical thinkers pay attention to definitions. What are the roles of "creativity" and "intelligence" in problem solving? Is there a way to sort out their roles, or are they intertwined?

3 What does it mean to be "clever" in solving riddles? Can you relate your answer to these video clips and concepts in the chapter such as creativity and intelligence?

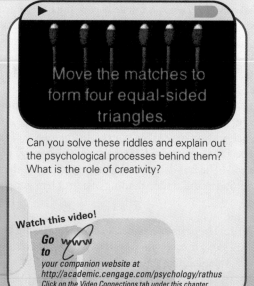

Move the matches to form four equal-sided triangles.

Can you solve these riddles and explain out the psychological processes behind them? What is the role of creativity?

Watch this video!

Go to www
your *companion website* at
http://academic.cengage.com/psychology/rathus
Click on the Video Connections tab under this chapter.

The Use of Heuristic Devices: If It Works, Just Do It?   *Is it best to use a tried-and-true formula to solve a problem?* Sometimes people use shortcuts to "jump to conclusions"—and these are often correct conclusions. The shortcuts are called **heuristics,** or heuristic devices—rules of thumb that help us simplify and solve problems. Heuristics are often based on strategies that worked in the past (Klaczynski, 2001).

In contrast to algorithms, heuristics do not guarantee a correct solution. But when they work, they permit more rapid solutions. A heuristic device for solving the anagram problem would be to look for familiar letter combinations and then check the remaining letters for words that include these combinations. In *DWARG,* for example, we find some familiar combinations: *dr* and *gr.* We may then quickly find *draw, drag,* and *grad.* The drawback to this method is that we might miss some words.

One type of heuristic device is the **means–end analysis.** In using this heuristic device, we assess the difference between our current situation and our goals and do what we can to reduce this difference. Let's say that you are out in your car and have gotten lost. One heuristic device based on analysis of what you need to do to get to where you want to go might be to ask for directions. This approach requires no "sense of direction." An algorithm might be more complicated and require some geographical knowledge. For example, let us say that you know your destination is west of your current location and on the other side of the railroad tracks. You might therefore drive toward the setting sun (west) and, at the same time, watch for railroad tracks. If the road comes to an end and you must turn left or right, you can scan in both directions for tracks. If you don't see any, turn right or left, but at the next major intersection turn toward the setting sun. Eventually you should get there. If not, you can ask for directions.

Heuristics Rules of thumb that help us simplify and solve problems.

Means–end analysis A heuristic device in which we try to solve a problem by evaluating the difference between the current situation and the goal.

The Use of Analogies: This Is Just Like . . . ? An *analogy* is a partial similarity among things that are different in other ways. The analogy heuristic applies the solution of an earlier problem to the solution of a new one. We use the analogy heuristic whenever we try to solve a new problem by referring to a previous problem (Halpern et al., 1990). Consider the water jar problems on page 284. Problem 2 is analogous to problem 1. Therefore, the approach to solving problem 1 works with problem 2. (Later we consider what happens when the analogy heuristic fails.)

Let us see whether you can use the analogy heuristic to your advantage in the following number series problem: To solve letter problems 1a, 1b, and 1c of the Self-Assessment on page 284, you had to figure out the rules that govern the order of the letters. Scan the following series of numbers and find the rule that governs their order:

8, 5, 4, 9, 1, 7, 6, 3, 2, 0

This is rather abstract and mathematical. Actually, you use the analogy heuristic regularly. For example, when you begin a new term with a new instructor, you probably consider who the instructor reminds you of. Then, perhaps, you recall the things that helped you get along with the analogous instructor and try them on the new one. We tend to look for things that helped us in the past in similar situations. When we considered OTTFFSSENT, we used the first letters of the numbers 1 through 10. When we consider the first 10 digits in the following order—8, 5, 4, 9, 1, 7, 6, 3, 2, and 0—we can again think of their first letters when they are spelled out. It happens that they are in alphabetical order (*eight, five, four,* and so on).

reflect & relate
Have you ever gotten lost and asked for directions? Is asking for directions an algorithm or a heuristic device?

Factors That Affect Problem Solving: Making Ruts, Climbing Out The way you approach a problem is central to how effective you are at solving it. Other factors also influence your effectiveness. ***What factors make it easier or harder to solve problems?*** Three such factors reside within you: your level of expertise, whether you fall prey to a mental set, and whether you develop insight into the problem.

Expertise To appreciate the role of expertise in problem solving, unscramble the following anagrams, taken from Novick and Coté (1992). In each case use all of the letters to form an actual English word:

DNSUO
RCWDO
IASYD

How long did it take you to unscramble each anagram ("sound," "crowd," and "daisy")? Would a person whose native language is English—that is, an "expert"—unscramble each anagram more efficiently than a bilingual person who spoke another language in the home? Why or why not?

Experts solve problems more efficiently and rapidly than novices do. Generally speaking, people who are experts at solving a certain kind of problem share the following characteristics:

- They know the particular area well.
- They have a good memory for the elements in the problems.
- They form mental images or representations that facilitate problem solving (Szala, 2002).
- They relate the problem to similar problems (Gorodetsky & Klavir, 2003).
- They are more goal-directed and have efficient methods for problem solving (Gorodetsky & Klavir, 2003).

These factors are interrelated. Art historians, for example, acquire a database that permits them to understand the intricacies of paintings. As a result, their memory for details of paintings mushrooms.

Novick and Coté (1992) found that the solutions to the anagram problems seemed to "pop out" in under two seconds among experts. The experts apparently used more efficient methods than the novices. Experts seemed to use *parallel processing*. That is, they dealt simultaneously with two or more elements of the problems. In the case of DNSUO, for example, they may have played with the order of the vowels (*UO* or *OU*) at the same time that they tested which consonant (D, N, or S) was likely to precede them, arriving quickly at *sou* and *sound*. Novices were more likely to engage in *serial processing*—that is, to handle one element of the problem at a time.

Mental Sets   Jordan hit me with another question: "A farmer had 17 sheep. All but 9 died. How many sheep did he have left?" Being a victim of a mental set, I assumed that this was a subtraction problem and gave the answer 8. She gleefully informed me that she hadn't said "9 died." She had said *"all but 9 died."* Therefore, the correct answer was 9. (Get it?) Put it another way: I had not *understood* the problem. My mental representation of the problem did not correspond to the actual elements of the problem.

Return to problem 1, part c in the Self-Assessment (page 284). To try to solve this problem, did you seek a pattern of letters that involved cycles and the alphabet? If so, it may be because this approach worked in solving parts a and b.

The tendency to respond to a new problem with the same approach that helped solve similar problems is termed a **mental set.** Mental sets usually make our work easier, but they can mislead us when the similarity between problems is illusory, as in part c of problem 1. Here is a clue: Part c is not an alphabet series. Each of the letters in the series *stands for* something. If you can discover what they stand for (that is, if you can discover the rule), you will be able to generate the 9th and 10th letters. (See page 563 for the answer.)

Insight: Aha!   To gain insight into the role of **insight** in problem solving, consider the following problem, posed by Metcalfe (1986):

> A stranger approached a museum curator and offered him an ancient bronze coin. The coin had an authentic appearance and was marked with the date 544 BCE. The curator had happily made acquisitions from suspicious sources before, but this time he promptly called the police and had the stranger arrested. Why?

I'm not going to give you the answer to this problem just yet. (You'll find it in Appendix B on page 563 under Puzzles, Problems, and Just Plain Fun.) But I'll make a guarantee. When you arrive at the solution, it will hit you all at once. You'll think "Of course!" (or something less polite). It will seem as though the pieces of information in the problem have suddenly been reorganized so that the solution leaps out—in a flash.

Bismarck, one of psychologist N. R. F. Maier's rats, provided evidence of insight in his species (Maier & Schneirla, 1935). Bismarck had been trained to climb a ladder to a tabletop where food was placed. On one occasion Maier used a mesh barrier to prevent the rat from reaching his goal. But, as shown in Figure 8.2, a second ladder was provided and was

■ **Jordan**
The author's daughter, Jordan, posed the problem, "A farmer had 17 sheep. All but 9 died. How many sheep were left?" What is the answer?

Mental set The tendency to respond to a new problem with an approach that was successfully used with similar problems.

Insight In Gestalt psychology, a sudden perception of relationships among elements of the "perceptual field," permitting the solution of a problem.

Figure 8.2
Bismarck Uses a Cognitive Map to Claim His Just Desserts
Bismarck has learned to reach dinner by climbing ladder *A*. But now the food goal (*F*) is blocked by a wire mesh barrier *B*. Bismarck washes his face for a while, but then, in an apparent flash of insight, he runs back down ladder *A* and up new ladder *N* to reach the goal.

visible to the animal. At first Bismarck sniffed and scratched and tried to find a path through the mesh. Then he spent some time washing his face, an activity that may signal frustration in rats. Suddenly he jumped into the air, turned, ran down the familiar ladder and around to the new ladder, ran up the new ladder, and claimed his just desserts. Did Bismarck suddenly perceive the relationships between the elements of the problem so that the solution occurred by insight? He seems to have had what Gestalt psychologists have termed an "Aha! experience." ◆ **Truth or Fiction Revisited:** It thus appears that humans are not the only species who use insight to solve problems.

Incubation   Let us return to the problems in the Self-Assessment. How did you do with problem 1, part c, and problems 2 and 3? Students tend to fiddle around with them for a while. The solutions, when they come, appear to arrive in a flash. Students set the stage for the flash of insight by studying the elements in the problems carefully, repeating the rules to themselves, and trying to imagine what a solution might look like. If you tried out solutions that did not meet the goals, you may have become frustrated and thought, "The heck with it! I'll come back to it later." ◆ **Truth or Fiction Revisited:** Standing back from the problem, rather than continuing to plug away at it, may allow for the **incubation** of insight. An incubator warms chicken eggs so that they will hatch. Incubation in problem solving refers to standing back from the problem for a while as some process within may continue to work on it. Later, the answer may come to us in a flash of insight. Standing back from the problem may help by distancing us from unprofitable but persistent mental sets (Both et al., 2004; Segal, 2004).

Have another look at the role of incubation in helping us overcome mental sets. Consider the seventh water jar problem on page 284. What if we had tried several solutions involving the three water jars and none had worked? We could distance ourselves from the problem for a day or two. At some point we might recall a 10, a 7, and a 3—three elements of the problem—and suddenly realize that we can arrive at the correct answer by using only two water jars!

Functional Fixedness   **Functional fixedness** may hinder problem solving. For example, first ask yourself what a pair of pliers is. Is it a tool for grasping, a paperweight, or a weapon? A pair of pliers could function as any of these, but your tendency to think of it as a grasping tool is fostered by your experience with it. You have probably used pliers only for grasping things. Functional fixedness is the tendency to think of an object in terms of its name or its familiar function. It can be similar to a mental set in that it makes it difficult to use familiar objects to solve problems in novel ways.

Now that you know what functional fixedness is, try to overcome it by solving the Duncker candle problem. You find these objects on a table: a candle, a box of matches, and some thumbtacks (see Figure 8.3). How do you use the objects on the table to attach the candle to the wall of the room so that it will burn properly? (See the answer on page 563.)

Figure 8.3
The Duncker Candle Problem
Can you use the objects shown on the table to attach the candle to the wall of the room so that it will burn properly?

——■— Judgment and Decision Making

Decisions, decisions. Should you go to breakfast before classes begin or catch a few extra winks? Should you rent or buy? For whom should you vote? What should you eat? Should you take a job or go on for advanced training when you complete your college program? If you opt for the job, cash will soon be jingling in your pockets. Yet later you may wonder if you have enough education to reach your full potential. By furthering your education, you may have to delay independence and gratification, but you may find a more fulfilling position later on. Decisions, decisions.

How do people make judgments and decisions?   You might like to think that people are so rational that they carefully weigh the pros and cons when they make judgments or decisions. Or you might think that they insist on finding and examining all the relevant information. Actually, people make most of their decisions on the basis of limited information.

Incubation   In problem solving, a hypothetical process that sometimes occurs when we stand back from a frustrating problem for a while and the solution "suddenly" appears.

Functional fixedness   Tendency to view an object in terms of its name or familiar usage.

They take shortcuts. They use heuristic devices—rules of thumb—in judgments and decision making just as they do in problem solving (Gilovich et al., 2002). For example, they may let a financial advisor select stocks for them rather than research the companies themselves. Or they may see a doctor recommended by a friend rather than look at the doctor's credentials. In this section we consider various factors in judgment and decision making.

Heuristics in Decision Making: If It Works, Must It Be Logical?   Let us begin by asking you to imagine that you flip a coin six times. In the following three possible outcomes, H stands for head and T for tail. Circle the most likely sequence:

H H H H H H

H H H T T T

T H H T H T

Did you select T H H T H T as the most likely sequence of events? Most people do. Why? There are two reasons. First, people recognize that the sequence of six heads in a row is unlikely. (The probability of achieving it is $1/2 \times 1/2 \times 1/2 \times 1/2 \times 1/2 \times 1/2$, or 1/64th.) Three heads and three tails are more likely than six heads (or six tails). Second, people recognize that the sequence of heads and tails ought to appear random. T H H T H T has a random look to it, whereas H H H T T T does not.

People tend to select T H H T H T because of the **representativeness heuristic.** According to this decision-making heuristic, people make judgments about events (samples) according to the populations of events that they appear to represent (Kahneman & Frederick, 2002; Shepperd & Koch, 2005). In this case, the sample of events is six coin tosses. The "population" is an infinite number of random coin tosses. But guess what? *Each* sequence is equally likely (or unlikely). If the question had been whether six heads or three heads and three tails had been more likely, the correct answer would have been three and three. If the question had been whether heads and tails would be more likely to be consecutive or in random order, the correct answer would have been random order. But each of the three sequences is a *specific* sequence. What is the probability of attaining the *specific* sequence T H H T H T? The probability that the first coin toss will result in a tail is 1/2. The probability that the second will result in a head is 1/2, and so on. Thus, the probability of attaining the exact sequence T H H T H T is identical to that of achieving any other specific sequence: $1/2 \times 1/2 \times 1/2 \times 1/2 \times 1/2 \times 1/2 = 1/64$th. (Try this out on a friend.)

Or consider this question: If a couple has five children, all of whom are boys, is their sixth child more likely to be a boy or a girl? Use of the representativeness heuristic might lead us to imagine that the couple is due for a girl. That is, five boys and one girl is closer to the assumed random distribution that accounts for roughly equal numbers of boys and girls in the world. But people with some knowledge of reproductive biology might predict that another boy is actually more likely because five boys in a row may be too many to be a random biological event. ◆ **Truth or Fiction Revisited:** Therefore, it is not true that the sixth child of a couple with five sons is likely to be a daughter. If the couple's conception of a boy or girl were random, however, what would be the probability of conceiving another boy? Answer: 1/2.

Another heuristic device used in decision making is the **availability heuristic.** According to this heuristic, our estimates of frequency or probability are based on how easy it is to find examples of relevant events. Let me ask you whether there are more art majors or sociology majors at your college. Unless you are familiar with the enrollment statistics, you will probably answer on the basis of the numbers of art majors and sociology majors that you know.

The **anchoring and adjustment heuristic** suggests that there can be a good deal of inertia in our judgments. In forming opinions or making estimates, we have an initial view, or presumption. This is the anchor. As we receive additional information, we make adjustments, sometimes grudgingly. That is, if you grow up believing that one religion or one political party is the "right" one, that belief serves as a cognitive anchor. When inconsistencies

Representativeness heuristic
A decision-making heuristic in which people make judgments about samples according to the populations they appear to represent.

Availability heuristic
A decision-making heuristic in which our estimates of frequency or probability of events are based on how easy it is to find examples.

Anchoring and adjustment heuristic A decision-making heuristic in which a presumption or first estimate serves as a cognitive anchor. As we receive additional information, we make adjustments but tend to remain in the proximity of the anchor.

show up in your religion or political party, you may adjust your views of them, but perhaps not very willingly.

Let us illustrate further by means of a math problem. Write each of the following multiplication problems on a separate piece of paper:

A. $8 \times 7 \times 6 \times 5 \times 4 \times 3 \times 2 \times 1$
B. $1 \times 2 \times 3 \times 4 \times 5 \times 6 \times 7 \times 8$

Show problem A to a few friends. Give them each 5 seconds to estimate the answer. Show problem B to some other friends and give them 5 seconds to estimate the answer.

The answers to the multiplication problems are the same because the order of quantities being multiplied does not change the outcome. When Tversky and Kahneman (1982) showed these problems to high school students, the average estimate given by students who were shown version A was significantly higher than that given by students who were shown version B. Students who saw 8 in the first position offered an average estimate of 2,250. Students who saw 1 in the first position gave an average estimate of 512. That is, the estimate was larger when 8 served as the anchor. By the way, what is the correct answer to the multiplication problems? Can you use the anchoring and adjustment heuristic to explain why both groups were so far off?

The Framing Effect: Say That Again? If you were on a low-fat diet, would you be more likely to choose an ice cream that is 97% fat free or one whose fat content makes up 10% of its calorie content? On one shopping excursion I was impressed with an ice cream package's claims that the product was 97% fat free. Yet when I read the label closely, I noticed that a 4-ounce serving had 160 calories, 27 of which were contributed by fat. Fat, then, accounted for 27/160ths, or about 17%, of the ice cream's calorie content. But fat accounted only for 3% of the ice cream's *weight*. The packagers of the ice cream knew all about the *framing effect*. They understood that labeling the ice cream as "97% fat free" would make it sound more healthful than "Only 17% of calories from fat." This is an example of the framing effect.

What is the framing effect? The **framing effect** refers to the way in which wording, or the context in which information is presented, affects decision making (Gonzalez et al., 2005; Tetlock & McGraw, 2005). Political groups, like advertisers, are aware of the framing effect and choose their words accordingly. For example, proponents of legalized abortion refer to themselves as "pro-choice" and opponents refer to themselves as "pro-life." Each group frames itself in a positive way ("pro" something) and refers to a popular value (freedom or life).

Parents also use the framing effect. My preschooler, Taylor, was invited to a play date at Abigail's house. I asked Taylor, "Would you like to play with Abigail at her house?" The question met with a resounding no. I thought things over and reframed the question: "Would you like to play at Abigail's house and have a real fun time? She has lots of toys and games, and I'll pick you up really soon." This time Taylor said yes.

Overconfidence: Is Your Hindsight 20–20? Whether our decisions are correct or incorrect, most of us tend to be overconfident about them. Overconfidence applies to judgments as wide-ranging as whether one will be infected by the virus that causes AIDS, predicting the outcome of elections, boasting that one's answers on a test are correct, and selecting stocks (McGraw et al., 2004; Soll & Klayman, 2004). ◆ **Truth or Fiction Revisited:** It is not true that people change their opinions when the opinions are shown to be wrong. (Have you ever known someone to maintain unrealistic confidence in a candidate who was far behind in the polls?)

We also tend to view our situations with 20–20 hindsight. When we are proven wrong, we frequently find a way to show that we "knew it all along." We also become overconfident that we would have known the actual outcome if we had had access to the information that became available after the event. For example, if we had known that a key player would pull a hamstring muscle, we would have predicted a different outcome for the football game. If

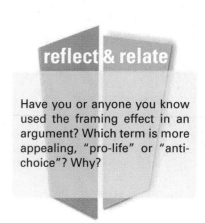

reflect & relate

Have you or anyone you know used the framing effect in an argument? Which term is more appealing, "pro-life" or "anti-choice"? Why?

Framing effect The influence of wording, or the context in which information is presented, on decision making.

we had known that it would be blustery on Election Day, we would have predicted a smaller voter turnout and a different outcome.

Why do people tend to be convinced that they are right, even when they are dead wrong? There are several reasons for overconfidence, even when our judgments are wrong. Here are some of them:

- We tend to be unaware of how flimsy our assumptions may be.
- We tend to focus on examples that confirm our judgments and ignore those that do not.
- Because our working memories have limited space, we tend to forget information that runs counter to our judgments.
- We work to bring about the events we believe in, so they sometimes become self-fulfilling prophecies.

Before leaving the section on thinking, I have a final problem for you:

You're driving a bus that's leaving from Pennsylvania. To start off with, there were 32 people on the bus. At the next bus stop, 11 people got off and 9 people got on. At the next bus stop, 2 people got off and 2 people got on. At the next bus stop, 12 people got on and 16 people got off. At the next bus stop, 5 people got on and 3 people got off. How many people are now on the bus?

() Learning Connections

◀◀   *Thinking—The Most Human Aspect of Our Psychology?*   ▶▶

REVIEW:

1 A _____ is an example that best matches the key features of a category.
(a) concept,
(b) positive example,
(c) negative example,
(d) prototype.

2 A(n) _____ is a specific procedure for solving a type of problem.
(a) heuristic,
(b) analogy,
(c) algorithm,
(d) concept.

3 What method do people use when they are evaluating the difference between their current situation and their goals and what they can to reduce this difference?
(a) means–end analysis,
(b) representativeness heuristic,
(c) formula search,
(d) probability estimation.

4 Some problems are solved by rapid "perception of relationships" among the elements of the problem, which is called
(a) incubation,
(b) insight,
(c) heuristics,
(d) analogue tracking.

5 In forming opinions or making estimates, our initial view serves as a(n)
(a) frame,
(b) mental set,
(c) means to an end,
(d) cognitive anchor.

6 The _____ effect refers to the fact that wording, or the context in which information is presented, can influence decision making.
(a) adjustment,
(b) framing,
(c) linguistic,
(d) emotional.

CRITICAL THINKING:
Research suggests that people are reluctant to change their views, even when the views are shown to be incorrect. What are the implications of these research findings for professors who desire to encourage their students to become critical thinkers? How does this fact color your perception of your own attitudes?

Go to www
http://academic.cengage.com/psychology/rathus
for an interactive version of this review.

LANGUAGE

"The time has come," the Walrus said,
 "To talk of many things
Of shoes—and ships—and sealing wax—
 Of cabbages—and kings—
And why the sea is boiling hot—
 And whether pigs have wings."
 —LEWIS CARROLL, THROUGH THE LOOKING-GLASS

Lewis Carroll wasn't quite telling the truth. The sea is not boiling hot. At the risk of alienating walrus fans across the land, let me boldly assert that walruses neither speak nor use other forms of language to communicate. On the other hand, the time has come indeed to talk of how talking—of how language—permits us to communicate about shoes and ships and . . . you get the idea.

---■- Going Ape over Language?

In recent years our exclusive claim to language has been questioned because apes have been taught to use symbols to communicate. (*Symbols* such as words stand for or represent other objects, events, or ideas.) Chimpanzees and gorillas have been taught to communicate by making signs with their hands.

Chimpanzees are our closest genetic relatives, sharing an estimated 98.42% of their genetic code with humans (Zimmer, 2002–2003). MRI studies with chimpanzees and gorillas show that most of them, like humans, show enlargement in the left hemisphere of the cerebral cortex, in part of Broca's area (Cantalupo & Hopkins, 2001; see Figure 8.4). The differences that remain between humans and chimps are at least in part associated with capabilities such as fine control of the mouth and larynx that are not found in apes (Enard et al., 2002). The genetic codes of chimps and humans are apparently similar enough to give chimps some ability to use language, but different enough to explain why chimps cannot articulate speech (Gibson, 2002; Mazur, 2002).

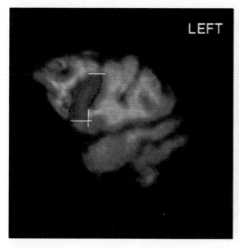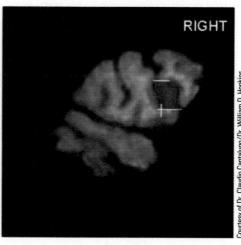

Courtesy of Dr. Claudio Cantalupo/Dr. William D. Hopkins

Figure 8.4

MRI Results of the Left and Right Hemispheres of the Cerebral Cortexes of a Great Ape
In their MRI study of the brains of 25 chimpanzees and 2 gorillas, Cantalupo and Hopkins found that the great majority, 20, showed larger areas similar to Broca's area in the left hemisphere. So do most humans. Six apes showed larger areas in the right hemisphere. Only one showed no difference. It would thus appear that chimpanzees and gorillas have some rudimentary language structures in their brains, even if they are not "wired" for speech.

Susan Kulkin/Photo Researchers, Inc.

■ A Chimpanzee Uses Signs to Communicate

We share more than 98% of our genetic codes with chimpanzees and apparently also some ability to communicate using symbols. Although chimpanzees and other apes cannot articulate speech, they have enlarged areas on the left side of the brain that correspond to Broca's area in humans. There is no question that chimpanzees learn signs for objects and actions; however, many psychologists and linguists question whether they share the inborn human ability to order them according to rules of grammar.

Language The communication of information by means of symbols arranged according to rules of grammar.

Do Apes Really Use Language?   Although apes do not speak, they have been taught to use American Sign Language and other symbol systems. For example, a chimpanzee named Washoe, who was a pioneer in the effort to teach apes to use language, was using 181 signs by the age of 32. Loulis, a baby chimp adopted by Washoe, gained the ability to use signs just by observing Washoe and some other chimps who had been trained in sign language (Fouts, 1997). Other chimps have used plastic symbols or pressed keys on a computer keyboard to communicate.

Sue Savage-Rumbaugh and her colleagues (1993; Brakke & Savage-Rumbaugh, 1996; Shanker et al., 1999) believe that pygmy chimpanzees can understand some of the semantic subtleties of language. She claims that one chimp, Kanzi, picked up language from observing another chimp being trained and has the grammatical abilities of a 2½-year-old child. Kanzi also understands several spoken words (spoken by humans, that is). Kanzi held a toy snake to a toy dog's mouth when asked to make the dog bite the snake.

Critics of the view that apes can learn to produce language, such as Herbert Terrace (1979) and Steven Pinker (1994a), note the following:

■ Apes can string together signs in a given sequence to earn rewards, but animals lower on the evolutionary ladder, such as pigeons, can also peck buttons in a certain sequence to obtain a reward.

■ It takes apes longer to learn new signs than it takes children to learn new words.

■ Apes are unreliable in their sequencing of signs, suggesting that by and large they do not comprehend rules of grammar.

■ People observing apes sign may be subject to *observer bias*—that is, they may be seeing what they want to see.

Scientists will continue to debate how well chimpanzees and gorillas understand and produce language, but there is little doubt that they have learned to use symbols to communicate (Hixon, 1998; Savage-Rumbaugh & Fields, 2000). Moreover, it is clear that chimps understand many of the subtleties of communication. For example, when they are behind a human, they make noises to get the person's attention. As soon as the person turns to them, they begin to sign (Bodamar & Gardner, 2002). Yet most researchers continue to consider that language emerges spontaneously only in people (Enard et al., 2002).

──■─ What Is Language?

As you can see from the discussion of apes and language, the way in which one defines language is no small matter. *Just how do we define language?* If we define language simply as a system of communication, many animals have language, including the birds and the bees. Dogs may communicate their possession of a territory by barking at an intruder, but they are not saying, "Excuse me, but you are too close for comfort." Birds warn other birds of predators. And, through particular chirps and shrieks, they may communicate that they have taken possession of a tree or bush. The waggle dances of bees inform other bees of the location of a food source or a predator. Vervet monkeys make sounds that signal the distance and species of predators. All of these are instinctive communication patterns, but not what we mean by language.

In language, sounds or signs are symbols for objects and actions. There is apparently no doubt that apes have learned to use symbols to communicate. But is the use of symbols to communicate an adequate definition of language? Many language experts require one more piece. They define **language** as the communication of thoughts and feelings by means of symbols *that are arranged according to rules of grammar.* Instinctive waggle dances and barks have no symbols and no grammar, even though, in the case of a dog that needs to go for a walk, they may carry hints of desperation. By this rigorous definition, only humans clearly use language. Whether apes can handle rules of grammar is under debate.

Language makes it possible for one person to communicate knowledge to another and for one generation to communicate to another. It creates a vehicle for recording experiences. It allows us to put ourselves in the shoes of other people, to learn more than we could learn from direct experience. Language also provides many units of thinking.

What are the properties of a "true" language? True language is distinguished from the communication systems of lower animals by properties such as semanticity, infinite creativity, and displacement (Hoff, 2005).

- **Semanticity:** The sounds (or signs) of a language have meaning. Words serve as symbols for actions, objects, relational concepts (*over, in, more,* and so on), and other ideas. The communications systems of the birds and the bees lack semanticity.
- **Infinite creativity:** The capacity to create rather than imitate sentences.
- **Displacement:** The capacity to communicate information about events and objects in another time or place. Language makes it possible to transmit knowledge from one person to another and from one generation to another, furthering human adaptation.

──■─ Language and Cognition: Do We Need Words to Think?

Let us discuss language in terms of the broader picture: What are the relationships between language and thinking? The relationships between language and thinking are complex and not always obvious. For example, can you think *without* using language? (The answer seems to be yes, but of course you would not be able to use thoughts that entail symbols that are arranged according to rules of grammar.) Would you be able to solve problems without using words or sentences? (That depends on the problem.)

Jean Piaget (Inhelder & Piaget, 1958) believed that language reflects knowledge of the world but that much knowledge can be acquired without language. For example, it is possible to understand the concepts of roundness or redness even when we do not know or use the words *round* or *red.*

──■─ Language and Culture

Different languages have different words for the same concepts, and concepts do not necessarily overlap. Concepts expressed in our own language (such as *square* and *triangle*) may not exist in the language of another culture—and vice versa. Is it possible for English speakers to share the thoughts experienced by people who speak other languages? The answer is probably yes in many or most cases, but in some cases, no. In any event, the question brings us to the linguistic-relativity hypothesis.

The Linguistic-Relativity Hypothesis   The **linguistic-relativity hypothesis** was proposed by Benjamin Whorf (1956). Whorf believed that language structures the way we perceive the world. That is, the categories and relationships we use to understand the world are derived from our language. Therefore, speakers of various languages conceptualize the world in different ways.

Thus most English speakers' ability to think about snow may be limited compared with that of the Inuit (Eskimos). We have only a few words for snow. The Inuit have many words for snow. The words differ according to whether the snow is hard packed, falling, melting, covered by ice, and so on. When we think about snow, we have fewer words to choose from and have to search for descriptive adjectives. The Inuit, however, can readily find a single

reflect & relate

Have you ever known someone to claim that a pet could "speak" or understand English or another language? *Did* the pet really "speak"? *Did* the pet "understand" language? What was the nature of the evidence? What is your conclusion?

Semanticity Meaning. The quality of language in which words are used as symbols for objects, events, or ideas.

Infinite creativity The capacity to combine words into original sentences.

Displacement The quality of language that permits one to communicate information about objects and events in another time and place.

Linguistic-relativity hypothesis The view that language structures the way in which we view the world.

A Closer Look
"U R a QT" and Other Internet Lingo

A Closer Look

Languages, like people, adapt to circumstances. Consider the words "text" and "message." Any English teacher will be happy to insist that these words are nouns, referring to the names of things. ("This sentence is made up of text." "Got the message?")

As anyone who writes emails, IM's, or sends text messages by means of cell phones (BTW, cell phones = cellular telephones) is well aware, however, the written and spoken languages have been changing. For example, both "text" and "text message" are used as verbs. Why say a college student "sends a text message" to a friend, when it's easier to say the student "*text messages* a friends" or simply "*texts* a friend"? (Doing much *texting* lately?)

Because it isn't easy to send text messages using a telephone keypad, the language has also been condensing. It took me a while, but sometime after I received the text message "u r a qt" from a daughter, the light bulb above my head went off. ("You are a cutie.") And BTW quite naturally = "by the way."

Being a qt, I thought I'd share with you some of my favorite adjustments to the evolving English lexicon:

ur = your
ur l8 = you're late
FYI = for your information
LOL = laughing out loud
LOL :) = like really LOL for sure
2 = to/too/two
4 = for (or four)
4get = forget
4N = foreign
ADN = any day now (yeah, like it's really gonna
    happen)
B = be
Bf = boyfriend
B4 = before (yes, I know you guessed it)
B4N = bye for now
BB = bye-bye
BTDT = been there, done that
CB = call back
CUL or CU l8r = see you later
C U = see you
G2G = got to go
Gf = girlfriend
Gr8 = great

Richard Douglas Rose

■ **Language, Like People, Adapts**
Cell-phone "texting" has led users to condense the language. Some think it's GR8. Others think it's NAGI. B4N. CU L8R, Gf or Bf.

IC = I see
ICCL = I couldn't care less
ILU = I love you (sweet?)
KISS = keep it simple, stupid
KUTGW = keep up the good work (what I write
    on excellent test papers)
@ = at (of course)
MSG = message
W = with
W/O = without
XLNT = excellent
NAGI = not a good idea
XOXO = hugs and kisses
PLS = please
PCM = please call me . . .
. . . and, finally, ttfn = ta ta for now ■

word that describes a complex weather condition. Is it therefore easier for them to think about this variety of snow? Similarly, the Hanunoo people of the Philippines use 92 words for rice, depending on whether the rice is husked or unhusked and on how it is prepared. And whereas we have one word for camel, Arabs have more than 250.

In English, we have hundreds of words to describe colors. There is about a 95% overlap in perception and labeling of colors between English speakers and Chinese people (Moore et al., 2002). It has been pointed out, however, that Shona-speaking people use only three words for colors, and Bassa speakers use only two words for colors, corresponding to light and dark. Nevertheless, a study of 100 languages spoken in nonindustrialized societies finds overlaps for white, black, red, green, yellow, and blue (Regier et al., 2005). Moreover, people who use only a few words to distinguish among colors seem to perceive the same color variations as people with more words. For example, the Dani of New Guinea have just two words for colors: one that refers to yellows and reds and one that refers to greens and blues. Yet performance on matching and memory tasks shows that the Dani can discriminate the many colors of the spectrum.

The Hopi Indians had two words for flying objects, one for birds and an all-inclusive word for anything else that might be found traveling through the air. Does this mean that the Hopi were limited in their ability to think about bumblebees and airplanes? Are English speakers limited in their ability to think about skiing conditions? Probably not. English-speaking skiers who are concerned about different skiing conditions have developed a comprehensive vocabulary about snow, including the terms *powder, slush, ice, hard packed,* and *corn snow,* that allows them to communicate and think about snow with the facility of the Inuit. When a need to expand a language's vocabulary arises, the speakers of that language apparently have little trouble meeting the need.

Most cognitive scientists no longer accept the linguistic-relativity hypothesis (Pinker, 1990). For one thing, adults use images and abstract logical propositions, as well as words, as units of thought. Infants, moreover, display considerable intelligence before they have learned to speak. Another criticism is that a language's vocabulary suggests the range of concepts that the speakers of the language have traditionally found important, not their cognitive limits. For example, people who were magically lifted from the 19th century and placed inside an airplane probably would not think they were flying inside a bird or a large insect, even if their language lacked a word for airplane.

━━■━ Language Development: The Two-Year Explosion

How does language develop? Languages around the world develop in a specific sequence of steps, beginning with the *prelinguistic* vocalizations of crying, cooing, and babbling. These sounds are not symbols. That is, they do not represent objects or events. Therefore, they are *pre*linguistic, not linguistic.

Prelinguistic Vocalizations: Sounds Without Meaning?   As parents are well aware, newborn children have one inborn, highly effective form of verbal expression: crying—and more crying. ◆ **Truth or Fiction Revisited:** But crying does not represent language; it is a prelinguistic event. During the second month, babies begin *cooing,* another form of prelinguistic expression which appears to be linked to feelings of pleasure. By the fifth or sixth month, children begin to *babble.* Children babble sounds that occur in many languages, including the throaty German *ch,* the clicks of certain African languages, and rolling *r*'s. Babies' babbling frequently combines consonants and vowels, as in "ba," "ga," and, sometimes, the much-valued "dada." "Dada" at first is purely coincidental (sorry, dads), despite the family's delight over its appearance.

Babbling, like crying and cooing, is inborn and prelinguistic. Deaf children babble, and children from cultures whose languages sound very different all seem to babble the same sounds (Hoff, 2005). But children single out the sounds used in the home within a few months. By the age of 9 or 10 months they are repeating the sounds regularly, and foreign sounds are dropping out. In fact, early experience in acquiring the phonemes native to one's own language can make it difficult to pronounce and even discriminate the phonemes used in other languages later in life (Iverson et al., 2003).

Children tend to utter their first word at about 1 year of age, but many parents miss it, often because it is not pronounced clearly or because pronunciation varies from one usage to the next (Nelson et al., 1993). The growth of vocabulary is slow at first. It may take children 3 to 4 months to achieve a 10-word vocabulary after they have spoken their first word. By about 18 months, children are producing a couple of dozen words.

Development of Grammar   The first linguistic utterances of children around the globe are single words that can express complex meanings. These initial utterances of children are called **holophrases.** For example, *mama* may be used by the child to signify meanings as varied as "There goes Mama," "Come here, Mama," and "You are my Mama." Similarly, *cat* can signify "There is a cat," "That stuffed animal looks just like my cat," or "I want you to give me my cat right now!" Most children readily teach their parents what they intend by augmenting their holophrases with gestures, intonations, and reinforcers. That is, they act delighted when parents do as requested and howl when they do not.

Toward the end of the second year, children begin to speak two-word sentences. These sentences are termed *telegraphic speech* because they resemble telegrams. Telegrams cut out the "unnecessary" words. "Home Tuesday" might stand for "I expect to be home on Tuesday." Two-word utterances seem to appear at about the same time in the development of all languages (Slobin, 1983). Two-word utterances are brief but grammatically correct. The child says, "Sit chair" to tell a parent to sit in a chair, not "Chair sit." The child says, "My shoe," not "Shoe my," to show possession. "Mommy go" means Mommy is leaving. "Go Mommy" expresses the wish for Mommy to go away.

There are different kinds of two-word utterances. Some, for example, contain nouns or pronouns and verbs ("Daddy sit"). Others contain verbs and objects ("Hit ball"). The sequence of emergence of the various kinds of two-word utterances is also apparently the same in all languages—languages diverse as English, Luo (an African tongue), German, Russian, and Turkish (Slobin, 1983). The invariance of this sequence has implications for theories of language development, as we will see.

Overregularization   **Overregularization** is an important development for understanding the roles of nature and nurture in language development. In English, we add *d* or *ed* to make the past tense of regular verbs and *s* or *z* sounds to make regular nouns plural. Thus, *walk* becomes *walked*, and *look* becomes *looked. Cat* becomes *cats*, and *doggy* becomes *doggies*. There are also irregular verbs and nouns. For example, *see* becomes *saw, sit* becomes *sat*, and *go* becomes *went. Sheep* remains *sheep* (plural) and *child* becomes *children*.

At first children learn irregular verbs and nouns by imitating older people. Two-year-olds tend to form them correctly—at first! Then they become aware of the grammatical rules for forming the past tense and plurals. As a result, they tend to make charming errors (Pinker, 1997). A 3- to 5-year-old, for example, may be more likely to say "I seed it" than "I saw it," and more likely to say "Mommy sitted down" than "Mommy sat down." They are likely to talk about the "gooses" and "sheeps" they "seed" on the farm and about all the "childs" they ran into at the playground. This tendency to regularize the irregular is what is meant by overregularization. ◆ **Truth or Fiction Revisited:** Young children *do* say things like "Daddy goed away" and "Mommy sitted down" because they understand rules of grammar.

Should parents be concerned about overregularization? Not at all. Overregularization reflects knowledge of grammar, not faulty language development. In another year or two, *mouses* will be boringly transformed into *mice*, and Mommy will no longer have *sitted* down. Parents might as well enjoy overregularization while they can.

Other Developments   By the age of 6, children's vocabularies have expanded to 10,000 words, give or take a few thousand. By 7 to 9, most children realize that words can have more than one meaning, and they are entertained by riddles and jokes that require some sophistication with language ("What's black and white, but read all over?").

Holophrase A single word used to express complex meanings.

Overregularization The application of regular grammatical rules for forming inflections (e.g., past tense and plurals) to irregular verbs and nouns.

Between the elementary school and high school years, language grows more complex, and children rapidly add on to their vocabularies. Vocabulary, in fact, can grow for a lifetime, especially in one's fields of specialization and interest.

Nature and Nurture in Language Development

> *Since all normal humans talk but no house pets or house plants do, no matter how pampered, heredity must be involved in language. But since a child growing up in Japan speaks Japanese whereas the same child brought up in California would speak English, the environment is also crucial.*
> —STEVEN PINKER

Billions of children have acquired the languages spoken by their parents and passed them down, with minor changes, from generation to generation. Language development, like many other areas of development, apparently reflects the interactions between nature and nurture. ***What are the roles of nature and nurture in language development?***

Learning Theory and Language Development: Infant Hear, Infant Say?   Learning theorists see language as developing according to laws of learning (Hoff, 2005). They usually refer to the concepts of imitation and reinforcement. From a social-cognitive perspective, parents serve as *models*. Children learn language, at least in part, through observation and imitation. Many words, especially nouns and verbs (including irregular verbs), are apparently learned by imitation.

At first children accurately repeat the irregular verb forms they observe. This repetition can probably be explained by modeling, but modeling does not explain all the events involved in learning. Children later begin to overregularize irregular verb forms *because of* knowledge of rules of grammar, and not imitation. Nor does imitative learning explain how children come to utter phrases and sentences they have *not* observed. Parents, for example, are unlikely to model utterances such as "Bye-bye sock" and "Allgone Daddy," but children say them.

Learning theory cannot account for the unchanging sequence of language development and the spurts in children's language acquisition. Even the types of two-word utterances emerge in a consistent pattern in diverse cultures. Although timing differs from one child to another, the types of questions used, passive versus active sentences, and so on, all emerge in the same order.

The Nativist Approach to Language Development: Speaking from the Genes?
The nativist theory of language development holds that the innate factors—which make up children's *nature*—cause children to attend to and acquire language in certain ways. From this perspective, children bring neurological "prewiring" to language learning (Baker, 2001; Newport, 1998; Pinker, 1994a, 1999).

According to **psycholinguistic theory,** language acquisition involves the interaction of environmental influences—such as exposure to parental speech and reinforcement—and the inborn tendency to acquire language. Noam Chomsky (1980, 1991) refers to the inborn tendency as a **language acquisition device (LAD).** Evidence for an LAD is found in the universality of human language abilities and in the specific sequence of language development (Baker, 2001).

The LAD prepares the nervous system to learn grammar. On the surface, languages differ a great deal. However, the LAD serves children all over the world because languages share what Chomsky refers to as a "universal grammar"—an underlying set of rules for turning ideas into sentences (Pinker, 1994a). Consider an analogy with computers: According to psycholinguistic theory, the universal grammar that resides in the LAD is the same as a computer's basic operating system (Baker, 2001). The particular language that a child learns to use is the same as a word-processing program.

In the following section we see that some aspects of language development—particularly vocabulary development—are strongly related to intelligence.

Psycholinguistic theory The view that language learning involves an interaction between environmental factors and an inborn tendency to acquire language.

Language acquisition device (LAD) In psycholinguistic theory, neural "prewiring" that facilitates the child's learning of grammar.

( ) Learning Connections

◀◀   *Language*   ▶▶

REVIEW:

7 Which of the following is not a feature of
language?
(a) Following commands,
(b) Semanticity,
(c) Infinite creativity,
(d) Displacement.

8 The major source of skepticism about whether
apes can truly use language concerns their
ability to
(a) make signs,
(b) speak,
(c) understand grammar,
(d) string signs together in a pattern.

9 Crying, cooing, and babbling are
(a) prelinguistic events,
(b) grammatically correct utterances,
(c) infant speech,
(d) universal grammar.

10 Children's use of sentences such as "I standed up"
and "Mommy sitted down" are examples of
(a) bad grammar,
(b) overextension,
(c) overregularization,
(d) linguistic relativity.

11 _____ are one-word utterances that have the
meanings of sentences.
(a) Holograms,
(b) Holographics,
(c) Hololinguistics,
(d) Holophrases.

12 The LAD prepares the nervous system to learn
(a) grammar,
(b) vocabulary,
(c) inflections,
(d) the sounds of speech.

CRITICAL THINKING:
How can we explain why (most) children who grow up in the United
States speak English and why (most) children growing up in Japan
speak Japanese? And how can we explain why dogs and cats who
grow up in the United States do *not* speak English?

Go to www
http://academic.cengage.com/psychology/rathus
for an interactive version of this review.

INTELLIGENCE: THE MOST CONTROVERSIAL TOPIC IN PSYCHOLOGY?

What form of life is so adaptive that it can survive in desert temperatures of 120° F or Arctic climes of −40° F? What form of life can run, walk, climb, swim, live underwater for months on end, and fly to the moon and back? I won't keep you in suspense any longer. We are that form of life. Yet our unclad bodies do not allow us to adapt to these extremes of temperature. Brute strength does not allow us to live underwater or travel to the moon. Rather, it is our **intelligence** that permits us to adapt to these conditions and to challenge our physical limitations.

Intelligence is one of the human assets that has enabled humans to survive and prosper. Other species may be stronger, run faster, smell more keenly, even live longer, but only humans have produced literature, music, mathematics, and science. Intelligence is believed to make these achievements possible.

Just what is intelligence? The concept of intelligence is closely related to thinking. Whereas thinking involves the understanding and manipulating of information, *intelligence*

Intelligence A complex and controversial concept. According to David Wechsler (1975), the "capacity . . . to understand the world [and] resourcefulness to cope with its challenges."

is considered to be the underlying ability to understand the world and cope with its challenges. In other words, intelligence is seen as making thinking possible.

Although these concepts overlap, psychologists tend to be concerned with *how* we think, but laypeople and psychologists are often concerned with *how much* intelligence we have. At an early age, we gain impressions of how intelligent or bright we are compared to other people.

Intelligence provides the basis for academic achievements. Intelligence allows people to think—to understand complex ideas, reason, and solve problems—and to learn from experience and adapt to the environment (Neisser et al., 1996). As we see in architecture and space travel, intelligence also permits people to create environments. Although intelligence, like thinking, cannot be directly seen or touched, psychologists tie the concept to achievements such as school performance and occupational status (Pind et al., 2003; Wagner, 1997).

Although psychologists have engaged in thousands of studies on intelligence, they do not quite agree on what it is. Psychologists have therefore developed theories to help them understand and define intelligence. In this section we discuss these theories of the nature of intelligence. Then we see how intelligence is measured and discuss group differences in intelligence. Finally, we examine the determinants of intelligence: heredity and the environment. Along the way, you will see why intelligence may just be the most controversial concept in the science of psychology. *What are the various theories of intelligence?*

Theories of Intelligence

Theories of intelligence have taken the concept apart and then put it back together again. But like Humpty-Dumpty, the pieces don't necessarily fit together easily. Let us begin with factor theories.

Factor Theories Many investigators have viewed intelligence as consisting of one or more *factors*. Factor theories argue that intelligence is made up of a number of mental abilities, ranging from one kind of ability to hundreds.

In 1904, British psychologist Charles Spearman suggested that the behaviors we consider intelligent have a common underlying factor. He labeled this factor **g,** for "general intelligence" or broad reasoning and problem-solving abilities. Spearman supported his view by noting that people rarely score very high in one area (such as knowledge of the meaning of words) and very low in another (such as the ability to compute numbers). People who excel in one area are also likely to excel in others. But he also noted that even the most capable people are relatively superior in some areas—such as music or business or poetry. For this reason, he suggested that specific, or **s,** factors account for specific abilities.

To test his views, Spearman developed **factor analysis.** Factor analysis is a statistical technique that allows researchers to determine which items on tests seem to be measuring the same things. When he compared relationships among test scores of verbal, mathematical, and spatial reasoning, Spearman repeatedly found evidence supporting the existence of *s* factors. The evidence for *g* was more limited. Interestingly, recent research continues to find a key role for *g* in performance on many intelligence tests. A number of cognitive psychologists (e.g., Colom et al., 2003) find evidence that connects *g* with *working memory*—that is, the ability to keep various elements of a problem in mind at once. Contemporary psychologists continue to use the term *g* in research, speaking, for example, of the extent to which they believe a particular kind of test, such as the SATs, measure *g* (Gignac & Vernon, 2003; Pyryt, 2000; Rushton et al., 2003).

The American psychologist Louis Thurstone (1938) used factor analysis with tests of specific abilities and concluded that Spearman had oversimplified intelligence. Thurstone's data suggested the presence of nine specific factors, which he labeled **primary mental abilities** (see Table 8.1). Thurstone's primary mental abilities contain the types of items measured on the most widely used intelligence tests today. The question remains as to whether his primary mental abilities are distinct or whether they are different ways of assessing *g*.

The Theory of Multiple Intelligences Thurstone wrote about various factors or components of intelligence. Howard Gardner (1983/1993), instead, proposes that there are a number of *intelligences,* not just one. *What is meant by multiple intelligences?* Gardner

When did you form an impression of how intelligent you are? Has this impression helped you or hurt you? How?

NASA/Stone/Getty Images

■ **Going for a Walk?**
It is our intelligence and not our brute strength or other physical skills that allows us to develop art and commerce, live underwater in submarine environments, fly through the air in machines, or "walk" in the vacuum of outer space.

g Spearman's symbol for general intelligence, which he believed underlay more specific abilities.

s Spearman's symbol for *specific* factors, or *s factors,* which he believed accounted for individual abilities.

Factor analysis A statistical technique that allows researchers to determine the relationships among large number of items such as test items.

Primary mental abilities According to Thurstone, the basic abilities that make up intelligence.

TABLE 8.1 ■ Primary Mental Abilities, According to Thurstone

ABILITY	DEFINITION
Visual and spatial abilities	Visualizing forms and spatial relationships
Perceptual speed	Grasping perceptual details rapidly, perceiving similarities and differences between stimuli
Numerical ability	Computing numbers
Verbal meaning	Knowing the meanings of words
Memory	Recalling information (e.g., words and sentences)
Word fluency	Thinking of words quickly (e.g., rhyming and doing crossword puzzles)
Deductive reasoning	Deriving examples from general rules
Inductive reasoning	Inferring general rules from examples

refers to each kind of intelligence in his theory as "an intelligence" because they can differ so much (see Figure 8.5). He also believes that each kind of intelligence is based in a different part of the brain. Two of these "intelligences" are familiar ones: language ability and logical–mathematical ability. Gardner also refers, however, to bodily–kinesthetic talents (of the sort shown by dancers and athletes), musical talent, spatial–relations skills, and two kinds of personal intelligence: awareness of one's own inner feelings and sensitivity to other people's

Figure 8.5
Gardner's Theory of Multiple Intelligences

According to Gardner, there are not one but several *intelligences,* each based in a different area of the brain. Language ability and logic are familiar aspects of intelligence. But Gardner also refers to bodily talents, musical ability, spatial–relations skills, and two kinds of personal intelligence— sensitivity to one's own feelings (intrapersonal sensitivity) and sensitivity to the feelings of others (interpersonal sensitivity)—as *intelligences.* Gardner's critics ask whether such special talents are truly "intelligences" or specific talents.

feelings. Gardner (2001) has recently added "naturalist intelligence" and "existential intelligence." Naturalist intelligence refers to the ability to look at natural events, such as kinds of animals and plants, or the stars above, and to develop insights into their nature and the laws that govern their behavior. Existential intelligence means dealing with the larger philosophical issues of life. According to Gardner, one can compose symphonies or advance mathematical theory yet be average in, say, language and personal skills. (Are not some academic "geniuses" foolish in their personal lives?)

Critics of Gardner's view agree that people function more intelligently in some aspects of life than in others. They also agree that many people have special talents, such as bodily–kinesthetic talents, even if their overall intelligence is average. But these critics question whether such special intellectual skills are best thought of as "intelligences" or special talents (Neisser et al., 1996). Language skills, reasoning ability, and ability to solve math problems seem to be more closely related than musical or gymnastic talent to what most people mean by intelligence. If people have no musical ability, do we really think of them as *unintelligent?* It is difficult to define intelligence in a way that everyone agrees on.

The Triarchic Theory of Intelligence   Psychologist Robert Sternberg (2000; Sternberg et al., 2003) has constructed a three-pronged, or *triarchic*, theory of intelligence that resembles a view proposed by the Greek philosopher Aristotle (Tigner & Tigner, 2000). ***What is Sternberg's triarchic model of intelligence?*** These types of intelligence are *analytical, creative,* and *practical* (see Figure 8.6).

Analytical intelligence is similar to Aristotle's "theoretical intelligence" and can be defined as academic ability. It enables us to solve problems and acquire new knowledge. It is the type of intelligence measured by standard intelligence tests. Problem-solving skills include encoding information, combining and comparing bits of information, and generating a solution. Consider Sternberg's analogy problem:

Washington is to *1* as *Lincoln* is to (a) 5, (b) 10, (c) 15, (d) 50?

To solve the analogy, we must first correctly *encode* the elements—*Washington, 1,* and *Lincoln*—by identifying them and comparing them to other information. We can first

Analytical intelligence
(Academic ability)
Abilities to solve problems,
compare and contrast, judge,
evaluate, and criticize

Creative intelligence
(Creativity and insight)
Abilities to invent, discover,
suppose, or theorize

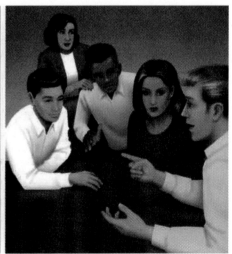

Practical intelligence
("Street smarts")
Abilities to adapt to the demands
of one's environment, apply
knowledge in practical situations

Figure 8.6
Sternberg's Theory of Intelligence
According to Robert Sternberg, there are three types of intelligence: analytical (academic ability), creative, and practical ("street smarts"). Psychologists discuss the relationships between intelligence and creativity, but within Sternberg's model, creativity is a *type* of intellectual functioning.

encode *Washington* and *Lincoln* as the names of presidents and then try to combine *Washington* and *1* in a meaningful manner. (There are other possibilities: Both are also the names of memorials and cities, for example.) If we do encode the names as presidents, two possibilities quickly come to mind. Washington was the first president, and his picture is on the $1 bill. We can then generate two possible solutions and try them out. First, was Lincoln the 5th, 10th, 15th, or 50th president? Second, on what bill is Lincoln's picture found? (Do you need to consult a history book or peek into your wallet at this point?) The answer is (a) 5, because Lincoln's likeness is found on the $5 bill. (He was the nation's 16th president, not 15th president.)

Creative intelligence is similar to Aristotle's "productive intelligence" and is defined by the abilities to cope with novel situations and generate many possible solutions to problems. It is creative to quickly relate novel situations to familiar situations (that is, to perceive similarities and differences). Psychologists who consider creativity to be separate from analytical intelligence or academic ability note that there is only a moderate relationship between academic ability and creativity (Simonton, 2000). To Sternberg, however, creativity *is* a form of intelligence.

Aristotle and Sternberg both speak of practical intelligence, or "street smarts." ◆ **Truth or Fiction Revisited:** It is therefore true that street smarts are a sign of intelligence— at least according to Aristotle and Sternberg. Practical intelligence enables people to deal with other people, including difficult people, and to meet the demands of their environment. For example, keeping a job by adapting one's behavior to the employer's requirements is adaptive. But if the employer is making unreasonable demands, finding a more suitable job is also adaptive. Street smarts appear to help people get by in the real world, especially with other people, but are not particularly predictive of academic success (Heng, 2000).

Emotional Intelligence Psychologists Peter Salovey and John Mayer developed the theory of emotional intelligence, which was popularized by psychologist Daniel Goleman (1995). The theory holds that social and emotional skills, like academic skills, are a form of intelligence. *Just what is "emotional intelligence"?* Emotional intelligence resembles two of Gardner's "intelligences"—intrapersonal skills and interpersonal skills (including insight into the feelings of other people). It also involves self-insight and self-control—the abilities to recognize and regulate one's moods (Salovey et al., 2002).

Failure to develop emotional intelligence is connected with poor ability to cope with stress, depression, and aggressive behavior (Salovey et al., 2002; Wang, 2002). Therefore, some psychologists wish for schools to teach skills related to emotional intelligence as well as academic ability. "I can foresee a day," wrote Goleman (1995), "when education will routinely [teach] human competencies such as self-awareness, self-control and empathy, and the arts of listening, resolving conflicts and cooperation."

But *is* emotional intelligence a form of intelligence? Psychologist Ulric Neisser (1997b) says that "the skills that Goleman describes . . . are certainly important for determining life outcomes, but nothing is to be gained by calling them forms of intelligence."

There are thus many views of intelligence—what intelligence is and how many kinds of intelligence there may be. We do not yet have the final word on the nature of intelligence, but I would like to share David Wechsler's definition. Wechsler originated the most widely used series of intelligence tests, and he defined intelligence as the "capacity of an individual to understand the world [and the] resourcefulness to cope with its challenges" (1975, p. 139).

◼ Creativity and Intelligence

Think of artists, musicians, poets, scientists who innovate research methods, and other creative individuals. *What is creativity? How is it connected to intelligence?*

Like the concept of intelligence, the concept of creativity has been difficult to define. One issue is whether creativity is distinct from intelligence, or is, as Sternberg suggests, a type of intelligence. For example, we would not ask the question, "Do creative people tend to be intelligent?" unless we saw creativity as distinct from intelligence. ◆ **Truth or Fiction Revisited:** The answer to whether an intelligent person is creative or a creative person is intelligent thus partly depends on definitions. If you consider creativity to be an aspect of intelligence, then the two concepts—intelligence and creativity—overlap. But if you think of intelligence as more closely related to academic ability, it is not always true that a highly intelligent person is creative or that a creative person is highly intelligent. Research findings suggest that the relationship between intelligence test scores and standard measures of creativity is only moderate (Simonton, 2000; Sternberg & Williams, 1997).

Within his triarchic theory, Sternberg defines **creativity** as the ability to do things that are novel and useful (Sternberg, 2001). Other psychologists note that creative people can solve problems to which there are no preexisting solutions and no tried and true formulas (Simonton, 2000). According to Sternberg and Lubart (1995, 1996), creative people take chances. They refuse to accept limitations. They appreciate art and music. They use common materials to make unique things. They challenge social norms and take unpopular stands. They challenge ideas that other people accept at face value.

Many psychologists see creativity as the ability to make unusual, sometimes remote, associations to the elements of a problem to generate new combinations. An essential aspect of a creative response is the leap from the elements of the problem to the novel solution.

Creative problem solving demands divergent rather than convergent thinking. In **convergent thinking,** thought is limited to present facts; the problem solver narrows his or her thinking to find the best solution. (You use convergent thinking to arrive at the right answer to a multiple-choice question.) In **divergent thinking,** the problem solver associates freely to the elements of the problem, allowing "leads" to run a nearly limitless course. (You may use divergent thinking when you are trying to generate ideas to answer an essay question on a test.) Problem solving can involve both kinds of thinking. At first divergent thinking helps generate many possible solutions. Convergent thinking is then used to select likely solutions and reject others. The nearby Remote Associates Test may afford you insight into your creativity.

Intelligence test questions usually require analytical, convergent thinking to focus in on the one right answer. Tests of creativity determine how flexible a person's thinking is (Simonton, 2000). Here is an item from a test used by Getzels and Jackson (1962) to measure associative ability, a factor in creativity: "Write as many meanings as you can for

reflect & relate

Do you know any creative people? Do they challenge social norms and take unpopular stands? Are they "conformists"? Does your personal experience fit the discussion in the text?

Creativity The ability to generate novel and useful solutions to problems.

Convergent thinking A thought process that narrows in on the single best solution to a problem.

Divergent thinking A thought process that attempts to generate multiple solutions to problems.

Self-Assessment

The Remote Associates Test

One aspect of creativity is the ability to associate freely to all aspects of a problem. Creative people take far-flung ideas and piece them together in novel combinations. Following are items from the Remote Associates Test, which measures the ability to find words that are distantly related to stimulus words. For each set of three words, try to think of a fourth word that is related to all three words. For example, the words *rough, resistance,* and *beer* suggest the word *draft*, as in the phrases *rough draft, draft resistance,* and *draft beer*. The answers are given in Appendix B.

1. food	catcher	hot	_____
2. hearted	feet	bitter	_____
3. dark	shot	sun	_____
4. Canadian	golf	sandwich	_____

5. tug	gravy	show	_____
6. attorney	self	spending	_____
7. magic	pitch	power	_____
8. arm	coal	peach	_____
9. type	ghost	story	_____

Go to www

http://academic.cengage.com/psychology/rathus where you can fill out an interactive version of this Self-Assessment and automatically score your results.

each of the following words: (a) duck; (b) sack; (c) pitch; (d) fair." Those who write several meanings for each word, rather than only one, are rated as potentially more creative.

Another measure of creativity asks people to produce as many words as possible that, say, begin with T and end with N within a minute. Still another item might give people a minute to classify a list of names in as many ways as possible. How many ways can you group the following names?

MARTHA PAUL JEFFRY SALLY PABLO JOAN

One way would be to classify them as men's names or women's names. Another would be English names versus Spanish names. Still another would be six-letter names, five-letter names, and four-letter names. The ability to do well on these kinds of items is connected with scores on standard intelligence tests, but only moderately so.

Now that we have begun speaking of scores on intelligence tests, let's see how psychologists go about measuring intelligence. We will also see how psychologists attempt to *validate* their measures of intelligence—that is, how they try to demonstrate that they are in fact measuring intelligence.

The Measurement of Intelligence

Although psychologists disagree about the nature of intelligence, laypeople and educators are concerned with "how much" intelligence people have, because the issue affects educational and occupational choices. In this section we consider two of the most widely used intelligence tests.

The Stanford–Binet Intelligence Scale   Many of the concepts of psychology have their origins in common sense. The commonsense notion that academic achievement depends on children's intelligence led Alfred Binet and Theodore Simon to invent measures of intelligence.

What is the Stanford–Binet Intelligence Scale? Early in the 20th century, the French public school system was looking for a test that could identify children who were unlikely to benefit from regular classroom instruction. If these children were identified, they could be given special attention. The first version of that test, the Binet–Simon scale, came into use in 1905. Since that time it has undergone extensive revision and refinement. The current version is the Stanford–Binet Intelligence Scale (SBIS).

Binet assumed that intelligence increases with age, so older children should get more items right than younger children. Binet therefore included a series of age-graded questions, as in Table 8.2, arranged in order of difficulty.

The Binet–Simon scale yielded a score called a **mental age (MA).** The MA shows the intellectual level at which a child is functioning. For example, a child with an MA of 6 is functioning intellectually like the average 6-year-old. In taking the test, children earned "months" of credit for each correct answer. Their MA was determined by adding up the years and months of credit they attained.

Louis Terman adapted the Binet–Simon scale for use with American children at Stanford University. The first version of the resultant Stanford–Binet Intelligence Scale was published in 1916. The SBIS included more items than the original test and was used with children aged 2 to 16. The SBIS also yielded an **intelligence quotient (IQ)** rather than an MA. As a result, American educators developed interest in learning the IQs of their pupils. The SBIS is used today with children from the age of 2 upward and with adults.

The IQ reflects the relationship between a child's mental age and his or her actual or chronological age (CA). Use of this ratio reflects the fact that the same MA score has different implications for children of different ages. That is, an MA of 8 is an above-average score for a 6-year-old but below average for a 10-year-old. In 1912 the German psychologist Wilhelm Stern suggested the IQ as a way to deal with this problem. Stern computed IQ using the formula

$$IQ = \frac{\text{Mental Age (MA)}}{\text{Chronological Age (CA)}} \times 100.$$

Mental age (MA) The accumulated months of credit that a person earns on the Stanford–Binet Intelligence Scale.

Intelligence quotient (IQ) (1) Originally, a ratio obtained by dividing a child's score (or mental age) on an intelligence test by chronological age. (2) Generally, a score on an intelligence test.

TABLE 8.2 ■ Items Similar to Those on the Stanford–Binet Intelligence Scale

LEVEL (YEARS)	ITEM
2	1. Children show knowledge of basic vocabulary words by identifying parts of a doll, such as the mouth, ears, and hair. 2. Children show counting and spatial skills along with visual–motor coordination by building a tower of four blocks to match a model.
4	1. Children show word fluency and categorical thinking by filling in the missing words when they are asked questions such as: "Father is a man; mother is a _____?" "Hamburgers are hot; ice cream is _____?" 2. Children show comprehension by answering correctly when they are asked questions such as: "Why do people have automobiles?" "Why do people have medicine?"
9	1. Children can point out verbal absurdities, as in this question: "In an old cemetery, scientists unearthed a skull which they think was that of George Washington when he was only 5 years of age. What is silly about that?" 2. Children display fluency with words, as shown by answering these questions: "Can you tell me a number that rhymes with snore?" "Can you tell me a color that rhymes with glue?"
Adult	1. Adults show knowledge of the meanings of words and conceptual thinking by correctly explaining the differences between word pairs like "sickness and misery," "house and home," and "integrity and prestige." 2. Adults show spatial skills by correctly answering questions like: "If a car turned to the right to head north, in what direction was it heading before it turned?"

According to this formula, a child with an MA of 6 and a CA of 6 would have an IQ of 100. Children who can handle intellectual problems as well as older children do have IQs above 100. For example, an 8-year-old who does as well on the SBIS as the average 10-year-old would attain an IQ of 125. Children who do not answer as many items correctly as other children of the same age attain MAs lower than their CAs. Thus, their IQ scores are below 100.

IQ scores on the SBIS today are derived by comparing their results to those of other people of the same age. People who answer more items correctly than the average for people of the same age attain IQ scores above 100. People who answer fewer items correctly than the average for their age attain scores below 100. ◆ **Truth or Fiction Revisited:** Therefore, two children can answer exactly the same items on an intelligence test correctly, yet one can be above average and the other below average in IQ. This is because the ages of the children may differ. The more intelligent child would be the younger of the two.

The Wechsler Scales   In contrast to the SBIS, David Wechsler developed a series of scales for use with children and adults. *What is different about the Wechsler scales of intelligence?* The Wechsler scales group test questions into a number of separate subtests (see Figure 8.7). Each subtest measures a different intellectual task. For this reason, the test shows how well a person does on one type of task (such as defining words) as compared with another (such as using blocks to construct geometric designs). In this way, the Wechsler scales highlight children's relative strengths and weaknesses, as well as measure overall intellectual functioning.

Wechsler described some of his scales as measuring *verbal* tasks and others as assessing *performance* tasks. In general, verbal subtests require knowledge of verbal concepts, whereas performance subtests require familiarity with spatial–relations concepts. But it is not that

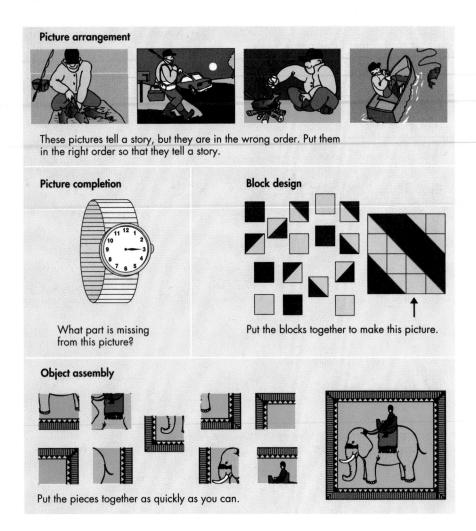

Picture arrangement

These pictures tell a story, but they are in the wrong order. Put them in the right order so that they tell a story.

Picture completion

What part is missing from this picture?

Block design

Put the blocks together to make this picture.

Object assembly

Put the pieces together as quickly as you can.

Figure 8.7
Items Similar to Those on the Wechsler Adult Intelligence Scale

easy to distinguish between the two groupings. For example, associating to the name of the object being pieced together in subtest 11—a sign of word fluency and general knowledge as well as of spatial–relations ability—helps the person construct it more rapidly. In any event, Wechsler's scales permit the computation of verbal and performance IQs. Nontechnically oriented college students often attain higher verbal than performance IQs. Less-well-educated people often obtain higher performance than verbal IQs.

Wechsler also introduced the concept of the *deviation IQ.* Instead of dividing mental by chronological age to compute an IQ, he based IQ scores on how a person's answers compared with those attained by people in the same age group. The average test result at any age level is defined as an IQ score of 100. Wechsler distributed IQ scores so that the middle 50% were defined as the "broad average range" of 90 to 110.

As you can see in Figure 8.8, IQ scores cluster around the average. Only 4% of the population have IQ scores of above 130 or below 70.

Group Tests The SBIS and Wechsler scales are administered to one person at a time. This one-to-one ratio is optimal because it allows the examiner to observe the test taker closely. Examiners are alerted to factors that impair performance, such as language difficulties, illness, or a noisy or poorly lit room. But large institutions with few trained examiners, such as the public schools and armed forces, require tests that can be administered simultaneously to large groups.

Group tests for children were first developed during World War I. At first these tests were hailed as remarkable instruments because they helped school administrators place children. As the years passed, however, group tests came under attack because many administrators relied on them exclusively and did not seek other sources of information about children's abilities.

At their best, intelligence tests provide just one source of information about individual children. Numbers alone, and especially IQ scores, cannot adequately define children's special abilities and talents.

━━■━ Differences in Intellectual Functioning

The average IQ score in the United States is very close to 100. Yet for some socioeconomic and ethnic groups in the United States, the average is higher, and for others, it is lower. Questions have also been raised about whether males or females are more intelligent overall, and whether there are gender differences in the kinds of intellectual or cognitive skills

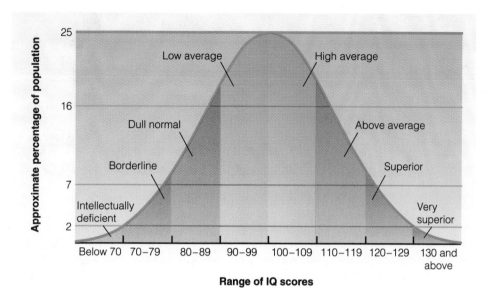

Figure 8.8
Approximate Distribution of IQ Scores
Wechsler defined the deviation IQ so that 50% of scores fall within the broad average range of 90 to 110. This bell-shaped curve is referred to as a *normal curve* by psychologists. It describes the distribution of many traits, including height.

valued in society. Tests of intellectual functioning have thus been seen as divisive and as maintaining a class system or social order that is based on prejudices and "tradition" as much as on science. In this section we discuss (1) socioeconomic and ethnic differences and (2) gender differences in cognitive skills.

Socioeconomic and Ethnic Differences   There is a body of research suggestive of differences in intelligence—or, more precisely, intelligence test scores—between socioeconomic and ethnic groups. *What are the socioeconomic and ethnic differences in intelligence?* Lower-class U.S. children obtain IQ scores some 10 to 15 points lower than those obtained by middle- and upper-class children. African American children tend to obtain IQ scores some 15 points lower than those obtained by their European American age-mates (Neisser et al., 1996). Latino and Latina American and Native American children also tend to score below the norms for European Americans (Neisser et al., 1996).

Many studies of IQ confuse the factors of social class and ethnicity because disproportionate numbers of African Americans, Latino and Latina Americans, and Native Americans are found among the lower socioeconomic classes (Neisser et al., 1996). When we limit our observations to particular ethnic groups, however, we still find an effect for social class. That is, middle-class European Americans outscore poorer European Americans. Middle-class African Americans, Latino and Latina Americans, and Native Americans also outscore poorer members of their own ethnic groups.

There may also be intellectual differences between Asians and Caucasians. Asian Americans, for example, frequently outscore European Americans on the math portion of the Scholastic Aptitude Test. Students in China (Taiwan) and Japan also outscore European Americans on achievement tests in math and science (Stevenson et al., 1986). In the United States, moreover, people of Asian Indian, Korean, Japanese, Filipino, and Chinese descent are more likely than European Americans, African Americans, and Latino and Latina Americans to graduate high school and complete college (Xie & Goyette, 2003; Yeh & Chang, 2004). They are also highly overrepresented in competitive colleges and universities.

■ **Who's Smart?**
Asian children and Asian American children frequently outperform European American children on tests of cognitive skills. Many psychologists believe that Asian Americans place greater value on education because they have been discriminated against in careers that do not require advanced education.

Figure 8.9

Sample Items from Cattell's Culture-Fair Intelligence Test
Culture-fair tests attempt to use items that do not discriminate against ethnic groups on the basis of their cultural background.

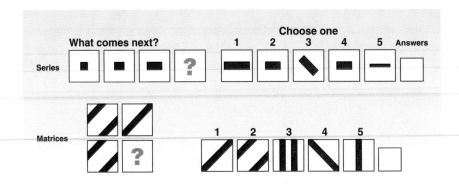

There are differences in mathematics ability between high school students in Germany and Japan. Japanese students, who are Asian, outscore European German students (Randel et al., 2000). Most psychologists believe that such ethnic differences reflect cultural attitudes toward education rather than inborn racial differences (Neisser et al., 1996). That is, the Asian children may be more motivated to work in school (Fuligni & Witkow, 2004; Xie & Goyette, 2003). Research shows that Chinese and Japanese students and their mothers tend to attribute academic successes to hard work (Randel et al., 2000). European Americans are more likely to attribute their children's academic successes to "natural" ability (Basic Behavioral Science Task Force, 1996b). Steinberg and his colleagues (1996) claim that parental encouragement and supervision in combination with peer support for academic achievement partially explain the superior performances of European Americans and Asian Americans as compared with African Americans and Latino and Latina Americans.

These ethnic differences lead us to ask, ***Do intelligence tests contain cultural biases against ethnic minority groups and immigrants?*** Are the tests valid when used with ethnic minority groups or people who are poorly educated? ◀▶ **Truth or Fiction Revisited:** Some psychologists and social critics argue that intelligence tests measure many things other than intelligence—including familiarity with the dominant middle-class culture in the United States and motivation to perform well.

Because children reared in African American or Latino and Latina American neighborhoods may be at a cultural disadvantage in intelligence testing (Helms, 1992; Kwate, 2001), many psychologists, including Raymond B. Cattell (1949) and Florence Goodenough (Goodenough & Harris, 1950), have tried to construct culture-free intelligence tests. Cattell's Culture-Fair Intelligence Test evaluates reasoning through the child's ability to understand and use the rules that govern a progression of geometric designs (see Figure 8.9). Goodenough's Draw-A-Person test is based on the premise that children from all cultural backgrounds have had the opportunity to observe people and note the relationships between the parts and the whole. Her instructions simply require children to draw a picture of a man or woman.

Ironically, European American children outperform African American children on "culture-free" tests (Rushton et al., 2003), perhaps because they are more likely to be familiar with materials such as blocks and pencils and paper. They are more likely than disadvantaged children to have played with blocks (practice relevant to the Cattell test) and to have sketched animals, people, and things (practice relevant to the Goodenough test). Nor do culture-free tests predict academic success as well as other intelligence tests.

Gender Differences   It was once widely believed that males were more intelligent than females because of their greater knowledge of world affairs and their skills in science and industry. But these differences did not reflect differences in cognitive ability. Rather, they reflected exclusion of females from world affairs, science, and industry. Moreover, intelligence tests do not show overall gender differences in cognitive abilities (Halpern & LaMay, 2000).

Do males and females differ in intellectual functioning? Reviews of the research suggest that girls are somewhat superior to boys in verbal abilities, such as vocabulary, ability to generate sentences and words that are similar in meaning to other words, spelling, knowledge of foreign languages, and pronunciation (Halpern, 2003). Girls seem to acquire language somewhat faster than boys do. Also, in the United States, more boys than girls have reading problems, ranging from reading below grade level to severe disabilities (Liederman et al., 2005; Skelton, 2005).

Males seem to do somewhat better at manipulating visual images in working memory. Males as a group excel in visual–spatial abilities of the sort used in math, science, and reading maps (Collaer & Nelson, 2002; Grön et al., 2000; Halpern & LaMay, 2000). One study compared the navigation strategies of 90 male and 104 female university students (Dabbs et al., 1998). In giving directions, men more often referred to miles and directional coordinates (north, south, east, and west). Women were more likely to refer to landmarks and turning right or left.

Studies find that males generally obtain higher scores on math tests than females do (Beller & Gafni, 2000; Gallagher et al., 2000; Halpern & LaMay, 2000; Leahey & Guo, 2001). Boys largely outperform girls on the math section of the SAT.

But note that the reported gender differences are *group* differences. There is greater variation in these skills between individuals *within* the groups than between males and females (Halpern, 2003). That is, there may be a greater difference in, say, verbal skills between two women than between the typical woman and the typical man. Millions of females outdistance the "average" male in math and spatial abilities. Men have produced their verbally adept Shakespeares. Moreover, Hyde and Plant (1995) assert that in most cases, differences in cognitive skills are small. Differences in verbal, math, and visual–spatial abilities also appear to be narrowing as more females pursue course work in fields that had been typically populated by males.

While scholars sit around and debate gender differences in intellectual functioning, women are voting on the issue by flooding fields once populated almost exclusively by men (Cox & Alm, 2005). Table 8.3 and Figure 8.10 show

TABLE 8.3 ■ Women as a Percentage of College Students Receiving Bachelor's Degrees in the Sciences

FIELD	1971	2002
Biology	29%	61%
Chemistry	18	48
Computer science	14	28
Engineering	1	19
Geology	11	45
Mathematics	38	47
Physics	7	23

Source: From "Scientists Are Made, Not Born," by W. Michael Cox and Richard Alm, February 25, 2005, *New York Times online.*

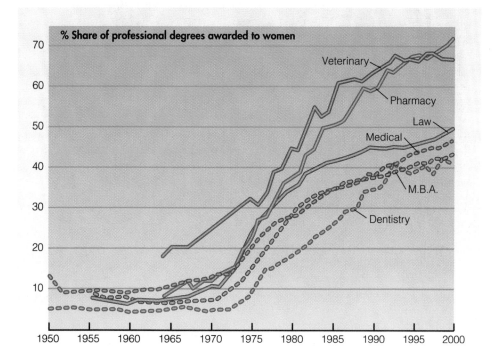

Figure 8.10
Women Flood Professions Once Populated Almost Exclusively by Men

that women are tossing these stereotypes out the window by entering the sciences and professional fields ranging from business to law to medicine in increasing numbers.

NATURE AND NURTURE IN INTELLIGENCE: WHERE DOES INTELLIGENCE COME FROM?

If different ethnic groups tend to score differently on intelligence tests, psychologists—like educators and other people involved in public life—want to know why. We will see that this is one debate that can make use of key empirical findings. Psychologists can point with pride to a rich mine of research on the roles of nature (genetic influences) and nurture (environmental influences) in the development of intelligence.

■ Genetic Influences on Intelligence

What are the genetic influences on intelligence? Research on genetic influences has employed kinship studies, twin studies, and adoptee studies (Neisser et al., 1996). Let us consider each of these to see whether heredity affects intellectual functioning.

We can examine the IQ scores of closely and distantly related people who have been reared together or apart. If heredity is involved in human intelligence, closely related people ought to have more similar IQs than distantly related or unrelated people, even when they are reared separately (Petrill & Deater-Deckard, 2004).

Figure 8.11 is a composite of the results of more than 100 studies of IQ and heredity in human beings (Bouchard et al., 1990). The IQ scores of identical (monozygotic, or MZ) twins are more alike than scores for any other pairs, even when the twins have been reared apart. There are moderate correlations between the IQ scores of fraternal (dizygotic, or DZ) twins, between those of siblings, and between those of parents and their children.

Figure 8.11

Findings of Studies of the Relationship between IQ Scores and Heredity

The data are a composite of studies summarized in the journal *Science*. By and large, correlations are greater between pairs of people who are more closely related. Yet people who are reared together also have more similar IQ scores than people who are reared apart. Such findings suggest that both genetic and environmental factors contribute to IQ scores.

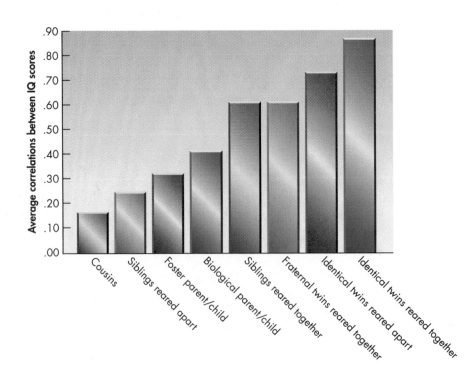

Correlations between the scores of children and their foster parents and between those of cousins are weak.

The results of large-scale twin studies are consistent with the data in Figure 8.11. A classic study of 500 pairs of MZ and DZ twins in Louisville, Kentucky (Wilson, 1983), found that the correlations in intelligence between MZ twins were about the same as that for MZ twins in Figure 8.11. The correlations in intelligence between DZ twin pairs was the same as that between other siblings. The MacArthur Longitudinal Twin Study examined the intellectual abilities of 200 14-month-old pairs of twins (Plomin et al., 1993). The study found that MZ twins were more similar than DZ twins in spatial memory, ability to categorize things, and word comprehension.

In sum, studies generally suggest that the **heritability** of intelligence is between 40% and 60% (Neisser et al., 1996). In other words, about half of the difference between your IQ score and the IQ scores of other people can be explained by heredity.

Note, too, that genetic pairs (such as MZ twins) who were reared together show higher correlations in their IQ scores than similar genetic pairs (such as other MZ twins) who were reared apart. This finding holds for DZ twins, siblings, parents and their children, and unrelated people. Being reared together is therefore related with similarities in IQ. *For this reason, the same group of studies used to demonstrate a role for the heritability of IQ scores also suggests that the environment plays a role in determining IQ scores.*

Another strategy for exploring genetic influences on intelligence is to compare the correlations between the IQ scores of adopted children and those of their biological and adoptive parents. When children are separated from their biological parents at an early age, one can argue that strong relationships between their IQs and those of their natural parents reflect genetic influences. Strong relationships between the children's IQs and those of their adoptive parents might reflect environmental influences.

Several studies with 1- and 2-year-old children in Colorado (Baker et al., 1983), Texas (Horn, 1983), and Minnesota (Scarr & Weinberg, 1983) have found a stronger relationship between the IQ scores of adopted children and those of their biological parents than between the children's scores and those of their adoptive parents.

Brain imaging has been used to explore possible gender differences in intellectual functioning. This avenue of research suggests that the brain hemispheres may be more specialized in males than in females (Shaywitz et al., 1995). For example, men with damage to the left hemisphere are more likely than women with similar damage to have difficulty in verbal functioning. Men with damage to the right hemisphere are more likely to have problems with spatial relations than women with similar injuries. Women appear more able to use both hemispheres for these functions and hence have a greater chance of recovery.

Environmental factors (nurture) also affect intellectual functioning on intelligence tests and in life.

——■— Environmental Influences on Intelligence

What are the environmental influences on intelligence? To answer this question we must consider studies of environmental influences, which also employ a variety of research strategies. These include observation of the role of the home environment and evaluation of the effects of educational programs.

The HOME Environment   The home environment and styles of parenting also affect IQ scores (Han et al., 2004; Molfese et al., 2003). Children of parents who are emotionally and verbally responsive, furnish appropriate play materials, are involved with their children, encourage independence, and provide varied daily experiences obtain higher IQ scores later on (Molfese et al., 1997). Organization and safety in the home have also been linked to higher IQs and achievement test scores (Bradley et al., 1989; Petrill et al., 2004).

reflect & relate

Does your own family seem to be generally similar in overall intellectual functioning? Are there one or more family members who appear to stand out from the others because of intelligence? If so, in what ways? How do you account for the difference?

Heritability The degree to which the variations in a trait from one person to another can be attributed to, or explained by, genetic factors.

■ Head Start
Preschoolers who are placed in Head Start programs have shown dramatic improvements in readiness for elementary school and in IQ scores.

Other studies support the view that children's early environment is linked to IQ scores and academic achievement. For example, Victoria Molfese and her colleagues (1997) found that the home environment was the single most important predictor of scores on IQ tests among children aged 3 to 8.

Education Although intelligence is viewed as permitting people to profit from education, education also apparently contributes to intelligence. Government-funded efforts to provide preschoolers with enriched early environments have led to intellectual gains. Head Start programs, for example, enhance the IQ scores, achievement test scores, and academic skills of disadvantaged children (Barnett, 1998; Zigler, 1999) by exposing them to materials and activities that middle-class children take for granted. These include letters and words, numbers, books, exercises in drawing, pegs and pegboards, puzzles, toy animals, and dolls. Head Start also helps poor children get medical and dental care, serves nutritious meals, and helps children develop the social skills necessary to succeed in school (Zigler, 1999).
◆ **Truth or Fiction Revisited:** It is therefore true that Head Start programs have raised children's IQs.

Preschool intervention programs can have long-term positive effects on children. During the elementary and high school years, graduates of preschool programs are less likely to be left back or placed in classes for slow learners. They are more likely to graduate from high school, go on to college, and earn higher incomes.

Later schooling also contributes to IQ. When children of about the same age start school a year apart because of admissions standards related to their date of birth, children who have been in school longer obtain higher IQ scores (Neisser et al., 1996). Moreover, test scores tend to decrease during the summer vacation (Neisser et al., 1996).

The findings on intelligence, the home environment, and educational experiences show that much indeed can be done to enhance intellectual functioning in children. Now let us return to research on the intellectual development of adopted children.

Adoptee Studies The Minnesota adoption studies reported by Scarr and Weinberg suggest a genetic influence on intelligence. But the same studies (Scarr & Weinberg, 1976, 1977) also suggest a role for environmental influences. African American children who were adopted during their first year by European American parents with above-average income and education obtained IQ scores some 15 to 25 points higher than those obtained by African American children reared by their natural parents (Scarr & Weinberg, 1976).

All in all, intellectual functioning appears to reflect the interaction of a complex web of genetic, physical, personal, and sociocultural factors (Bartels et al., 2002; Bishop et al., 2003), as suggested by Figure 8.12.

Perhaps we need not be so concerned with whether we can sort out exactly how much of a person's IQ is due to heredity and how much is due to environmental influences. Psychology has traditionally supported the dignity of the individual. It might be more appropriate for us to try to identify children *of all ethnic groups* whose environments place them at risk for failure and do what we can to enrich their environments. As noted by Paul Ehrlich (2000), professor of biology and population studies at Stanford University:

There is no such thing as a fixed human nature, but rather an interaction between our genotypes—the genetic information we have—and the different environments we live in, with the result that all our natures are unique.

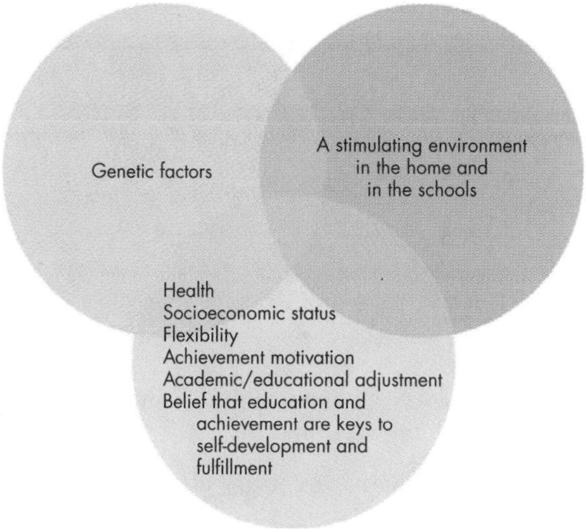

Genetic factors

A stimulating environment
in the home and
in the schools

Health
Socioeconomic status
Flexibility
Achievement motivation
Academic/educational adjustment
Belief that education and
     achievement are keys to
     self-development and
     fulfillment

Figure 8.12
The Complex Web of Factors That Affect Intellectual Functioning
Intellectual functioning appears to be influenced by the interaction of genetic factors, health, personality, and sociocultural factors.

( ) Learning Connections

◀◀ *Intelligence* ▶▶

REVIEW:

13 The originator of the concept of general intelligence, or *g,* is
(a) Thurstone,
(b) Spearman,
(c) Wechsler,
(d) Binet.

14 _____ is one of Gardner's multiple intelligences.
(a) existential intelligence,
(b) emotional intelligence,
(c) creativity,
(d) practical intelligence.

15 Creativity appears to be associated with
(a) divergent thinking,
(b) convergent thinking,
(c) mathematical ability,
(d) social conformity.

16 Wechsler originated the concept of
(a) intelligence,
(b) emotional intelligence,
(c) mental age,
(d) deviation IQ.

17 Approximately ____ percent of the population obtain IQ scores within the broad average range (90–110).
(a) 14,
(b) 50,
(c) 67,
(d) 98.

18 Estimates place the heritability of intelligence at about ____ percent.
(a) 14,
(b) 50,
(c) 67,
(d) 98.

CRITICAL THINKING:
Answering many of the questions we find on intelligence tests requires knowledge of vocabulary, skills in math, and a solid fund of general information. Because intelligence is supposed to be ability that underlies academic achievements—and not academic achievements themselves—does it make sense to find these types of items on intelligence tests? Explain.

Go to
http://academic.cengage.com/psychology/rathus
for an interactive version of this review.

RECITE—*An Active Summary*™

 Recite to Go! *Don't have time to study right now? You can study on the go!*
Go to your companion website and download an audio version of this review section to your media player. You can also access an interactive flash-card version of this review from your website.

1. What is thinking?	Thinking is conscious mental activity that involves attending to information, representing it, reasoning about it, and making judgments about it.
2. What are concepts?	Concepts are mental categories for grouping objects, events, or ideas with common properties.
3. How do people solve problems?	People first try to understand the problem. Then they use strategies such as including algorithms, heuristic devices, and analogies.
4. Is it best to use a tried-and-true formula to solve a problem?	Not necessarily. Heuristic devices can help us "jump" to right answers. Heuristics are rules of thumb that help us simplify and solve problems. Heuristics are less reliable than algorithms.
5. What factors make it easier or harder to solve problems?	Key factors include level of expertise, mental sets, insight, incubation, and functional fixedness.
6. How do people make judgments and decisions?	People sometimes make decisions by weighing the pluses and minuses, but most make decisions with limited information and heuristic devices.
7. What is the framing effect?	People often phrase or frame arguments in ways to persuade others.
8. Why do people tend to be convinced that they are right, even when they are dead wrong?	People tend to retain their convictions because they are unaware of the flimsiness of their assumptions, they focus on events that confirm their judgments, and they work to bring about results that fit their judgments.
9. How do we define language?	Language is the communication of thoughts and feelings by means of symbols that are arranged according to rules of grammar.
10. What are the properties of a "true" language?	True language is distinguished from the communication systems of lower animals by properties such as semanticity, infinite creativity, and displacement.
11. What are the relationships between language and thinking?	Language is not necessary for thinking, but language makes possible cognitive activity that involves use of symbols arranged according to rules of grammar.
12. Is it possible for English speakers to share the thoughts experienced by people who speak other language?	Perhaps it is. According to the linguistic-relativity hypothesis, the concepts we use to understand the world are derived from our language. But the vocabulary of a language may suggest the range of concepts users have found to be useful, not their cognitive limits.
13. How does language develop?	Children make the prelinguistic sounds of crying, cooing, and babbling before true language develops. Single-word utterances occur at about 1 year; two-word utterances by 2. Early language is characterized by overextension and overregularization.
14. What are the roles of nature and nurture in language development?	The two main theories of language development are learning theories and nativist theories. Learning theories focus on reinforcement and imitation. Nativist theories assume that innate factors enable children to attend to and perceive language.
15. What is intelligence?	Intelligence provides the cognitive basis for academic achievement. Wechsler defined it as the "capacity . . . to understand the world . . . and . . . cope with its challenges."

16. What are the various theories of intelligence?	Spearman and Thurstone believed that intelligence is composed of factors. Spearman believed that a common factor, *g*, underlies all intelligent behavior but that people also have specific abilities, or *s* factors.
17. What is meant by multiple intelligences?	Gardner believes that people have several intelligences, not one, and that each is based in a different area of the brain.
18. What is Sternberg's triarchic model of intelligence?	Sternberg's triarchic theory proposes three kinds of intelligence: academic ability, creativity, and practical intelligence.
19. What is "emotional intelligence"?	The theory of emotional intelligence holds that social and emotional skills are a form of intelligence that helps children avert violence and depression.
20. What is creativity? How is it connected to intelligence?	Creative people take chances, defy limits, and appreciate art and music. Creative problem solving involves divergent thinking.
21. What is the Stanford-Binet Intelligence Scale?	This is the test originated by Binet in France and developed by Terman at Stanford University. It includes age-graded questions and compares mental age with chronological age.
22. What is different about the Wechsler scales of intelligence?	The Wechsler scales use deviation IQs, which compare a person's performance with that of age-mates. The Wechsler scales contain verbal and performance subtests.
23. What are the socioeconomic and ethnic differences in intelligence?	Middle- and upper-class children outscore lower-class children by 10 to 15 points on intelligence tests. Asian Americans tend to outscore European Americans, and European Americans tend to outscore African Americans and Latino and Latina Americans.
24. Do males and females differ in intellectual functioning?	Females would appear to excel in verbal skills, and males in math and spatial relations. These group differences, however, are small and narrowing. Moreover, many males excel in verbal skills and many females in math and spatial relations.
25. Do intelligence tests contain cultural biases against ethnic minority groups and immigrants?	Many psychologists believe that intelligence tests are biased against African Americans and people in the lower classes because the tests require familiarity with concepts that reflect middle-class European American culture.
26. What are the genetic influences on intelligence?	Kinship studies find a stronger relationship between the IQ scores of adopted children and their biological parents than between the children's scores and those of their adoptive parents. The heritability of intelligence is estimated at 40% to 60%.
27. What are the environmental influences on intelligence?	Environmental influences on intelligence include the home environment and education.

Key Terms

Thinking   281

Concept   281

Prototype   282

Exemplar   282

Algorithm   285

Systematic random search   285

Heuristics   286

Means–end analysis   286

Mental set   288

Insight   288

Incubation   289

Functional fixedness   289

Representativeness heuristic   290

Availability heuristic   290

Anchoring and adjustment heuristic   290

Framing effect   291

Language   294

Semanticity   295

Infinite creativity   295

Displacement   295

Linguistic-relativity hypothesis   295

Holophrase   298

Overregularization   298

Psycholinguistic theory   299

Language acquisition device (LAD)   299

Intelligence   300

g   301

s   301

Factor analysis   301

Primary mental abilities   301

Creativity   305

Convergent thinking   305

Divergent thinking   305

Mental age (MA)   306

Intelligence quotient (IQ)   306

Heritability   313

Active Learning Resources

Visit Your Companion Website
for This Book

http://academic.cengage.com/psychology/rathus

Check out this companion website where you will find online resources directly linked to your book. This is where you'll access the videos highlighted in your Video Connections feature. You can answer the questions online and email them to your professor. In addition you'll find downloadable audio review material, interactive versions of the study aids, Power Visuals for mastering and reviewing key concepts, as well as quizzing, and much more!

CENGAGENOW™

http://academic.cengage.com

Need help studying? This site is your one-stop study shop. Take a Pre-Test and Cengage NOW will generate a Personalized Study Plan based on your test results. The Study Plan will identify the topics you need to review and direct you to online resources to help you master those topics. You can then take a Post-Test to help you determine the concepts you have mastered and what you still need to work on. In addition you can access interactive media including the videos highlighted in your Video Connections box.

Author Blog

What does your author Spence Rathus have to say about the state of psychology? Visit your companion website every Tuesday and click on "Author Blog." This is where he'll talk about the most recent controversies and hot topics in psychology. This will keep you up to date with what your author is thinking and give you great insight into modern psychology.

CHAPTER 9

Motivation and Emotion

Tim Wimborne/Reuters/Corbis

truth or fiction?

| T | F | Siamese fighting fish who have been reared without ever seeing another fish assume stereotypical threatening stances and attack other males when they are introduced into their tanks. |

| T | F | Getting away from it all by going on a vacation from all sensory input for a few hours is relaxing. |

| T | F | People feel hunger due to contractions ("pangs") in the stomach. |

| T | F | You can never be too rich or too thin. |

| T | F | Fashion magazines can contribute to eating disorders among women. |

| T | F | Males behave more aggressively than females do. |

| T | F | Money can't buy you happiness. |

| T | F | You may be able to fool a lie detector by squiggling your toes. |

Go to www
http://academic.cengage.com/pstchology/rathus
for an interactive version of this Truth or Fiction feature.

preview

C assie emailed me:

From: Cassie
To: Prof Rathus
Subject: **%-)**
Hey Prof! **:-V**
Sorry I couldn't make it to Intro Psych yesterday. **:-(**
You may have heard that that big retaining wall on the Henry Hudson collapsed.
8-o It was a mean slide and I was stuck behind a thousand cars and nobody
could move. **}:-[** I wasn't hurt but do you need a note from my doctor? **%-6** Just
kidding.
Did I miss anything important? **:\'(**
CU L8R! **:^D**
Cassie

If I had not been a psychologist, I would just have clicked Reply and written,
"Glad you weren't hurt, but every class is important. Drop by during office
hours in the morning. CU tomorrow **:-)**." But being a psychologist, I had
to ask myself *why* Cassie had written this email in the way she had. The
first answer that came to mind was that she wanted to stay in my "good
graces."

That didn't sound very scientific. I had to get to the bottom of her motivation. Did the evolutionary perspective suggest that she might have recognized
that students who show their professors they are trying to meet their course
requirements are more likely to survive and pass their genes along to the
next generation? Or that Cassie had a "Keep Dr. Rathus on my side" instinct?
Perhaps not. Did drive-reduction theory suggest that Cassie experienced
fear when she missed class, and that fear drove her to do something—namely,
email me—that would reduce the discomforting emotion? Perhaps. Did
Cassie thrive on the exciting stimulation of introductory psychology and wish
to make certain that nothing would prevent her from returning to class so she
could experience that stimulation again? Knowing full well the joy (another
emotion, but very different from fear) of psychology, I figured there might be
something to that. Now, humanistic theory might suggest that Cassie was attempting to meet various needs, such as the need to survive introductory psychology. Or what of the need to belong to the class? The need to have the approval of her professor? The need to experience the cognitive stimulation of
psychology? The need to actualize herself fully as a human being, which nothing but psychology could do so well?

As a psychologist, I also noted her methods of expressing her emotions:
for example,

}:-[and **:^D.** Don't look at me; you can interpret these for yourself.

Perhaps I was getting too embroiled in this train of thought.

I clicked Reply, wrote, "Glad you weren't hurt, but every class is important. Drop by during office hours in the morning. CU tomorrow **:-)**" and
clicked Send.

She had obviously wanted to remain in my good graces—whatever those are.

All of this quite naturally leads to an exploration of the psychology of motivation and emotion. Let us begin our journey with some definitions.

THE PSYCHOLOGY OF MOTIVATION: THE *WHYS* OF WHY

The psychology of motivation concerns the *whys* of behavior. Why do people do this or that? ***What are motives, needs, drives, and incentives?*** **Motives** are hypothetical states that activate behavior, propelling one toward goals. Why do we say "hypothetical states"? Because motives are not seen and measured directly. They are inferred from behavior. We may infer that Cassie was motivated to stay in my good graces by observing her behavior—in this case, her writing-email-behavior. Motives may take the form of *needs, drives,* and *incentives,* which are also inferred from behavior.

Psychologists speak of physiological and psychological **needs.** We must meet physiological needs to survive. Examples include the needs for oxygen, food, drink, pain avoidance, proper temperature, and elimination of waste products. Some physiological needs, such as hunger and thirst, are states of physical deprivation. When we have not eaten or drunk for a while, we develop needs for food and water. The body also needs oxygen, vitamins, minerals, and so on.

Psychological needs include needs for achievement, power, self-esteem, social approval, and belonging. Many psychological needs might have motivated Cassie's email, including needs for social approval and good grades. Psychological needs differ from physiological needs in two ways. First, psychological needs are not necessarily based on states of deprivation. A person with a need for achievement—like Cassie—may already have a history of successful achievements. Second, psychological needs may be acquired through experience, or learned. By contrast, physiological needs reside in the physical makeup of the organism. Because people's biological makeups are similar, we share similar physiological needs. But we are influenced by our cultural settings, and our needs may be expressed in various ways. All people need food, but some prefer a vegetarian diet whereas others prefer meat. Because learning enters into psychological needs, they can differ markedly from one person to another.

Needs give rise to **drives.** Depletion of food gives rise to the hunger drive, and depletion of liquids gives rise to the thirst drive. **Physiological drives** are the counterparts of physiological needs. When we have gone without food and water, our body may *need* these substances. Our *experience* of the drives of hunger and thirst, however, is psychological. Drives arouse us to action. Drives tend to be stronger when we have been deprived longer. We are usually hungrier when we haven't eaten for five hours than if it was just five minutes ago.

Psychological needs for approval, achievement, and belonging also give rise to drives. We can have a drive to get ahead in the business world just as we have a drive to eat. Psychologists are working to learn more about the origins of these drives. We do know that we can also be driven to obtain *incentives.*

An **incentive** is an object, person, or situation that is viewed as capable of satisfying a need or as desirable for its own sake. Money, food, a sexually attractive person, social approval, and attention can all act as incentives that motivate behavior.

In the following section, we explore theories of motivation. We ask: Just what is so motivating about motives?

reflect & relate

What are some of the key motives in your own life? What are your needs? What drives you? What incentives do you work for? Can you think of any needs or drives that motivate you but might not motivate other people?

Motive A hypothetical state within an organism that propels the organism toward a goal. (From the Latin *movere,* meaning "to move.")

Need A state of deprivation.

Drive A condition of arousal in an organism that is associated with a need.

Physiological drives Unlearned drives with a biological basis, such as hunger, thirst, and avoidance of pain.

Incentive An object, person, or situation perceived as being capable of satisfying a need.

⟨⟩ Learning Connections

◄◄   *The Psychology of Motivation—The Whys of Why*   ►►

Learning Connections

REVIEW:

1 Which of the following is a hypothetical state that activates behavior and directs organisms toward goals?
   (a) A drive,
   (b) An incentive,
   (c) A motive,
   (d) A need.

2 Which of the following is an object, person, or situation that is perceived as being capable of satisfying a need?
   (a) A drive,
   (b) An incentive,
   (c) A motive,
   (d) A need.

CRITICAL THINKING:
What is meant by the term hypothetical state? What purpose does the use of the term serve in psychology? Can you think of a hypothetical state discussed in the previous chapter?

Go to www

http://academic.cengage.com/psychology/rathus
for an interactive version of this review.

THEORIES OF MOTIVATION: WHICH WHY IS WHICH?

Although psychologists agree that it is important to understand why humans and lower animals do things, they do not agree about the precise nature of motivation. Let us consider various theoretical perspectives on motivation.

▬ The Evolutionary Perspective: The Fish, the Spiders, and the Bees

The evolutionary perspective notes that many animals are neurally "prewired"—that is, born with preprogrammed tendencies—to respond to certain situations in certain ways. ◈ **Truth or Fiction Revisited:** It is true that Siamese fighting fish reared in isolation from other fish assume stereotypical threatening stances and attack other males when they are introduced into their tank. Spiders spin webs instinctively. Bees "dance" instinctively to communicate the location of food to other bees.

These instinctive behaviors are found in particular species. They are *species-specific*. *What is meant by species-specific behaviors?* Species-specific behaviors are also called **instincts,** or *fixed-action patterns* (FAPs). Such behavior patterns are inborn. That is, they are genetically transmitted from generation to generation.

Psychologists have asked whether humans have instincts, and if so, how many. A century ago, psychologists William James (1890) and William McDougall (1908) argued that humans have instincts that foster survival and social behavior. James numbered love, sympathy, and modesty among his social instincts. McDougall compiled 12 "basic" instincts, including hunger, sex, and self-assertion. Other psychologists have made longer lists, and still others deny that people have any instincts. The question of whether people have instincts—and what they might be—remains unresolved.

■ A Fixed-Action Pattern

In the presence of another male, Siamese fighting fish assume threatening stances in which they extend their fins and gills and circle each other. If neither male retreats, there will be a conflict.

Comstock

Instinct An inherited disposition to activate specific behavior patterns that are designed to reach certain goals.

▬ Drive-Reductionism and Homeostasis: "Steady, Steady . . ."

Sigmund Freud believed that tension motivates us to behave in ways that restore us to a resting state. His views are similar to those of the **drive-reduction theory** of learning, as set forth by psychologist Clark Hull in the 1930s. *What is drive-reduction theory?*

According to Hull, **primary drives** such as hunger, thirst, and pain trigger arousal (tension) and activate behavior. We learn to engage in behaviors that reduce the tension. We also acquire drives through experience. These drives are called **acquired drives.** We may acquire a drive for money because money enables us to obtain food, drink, and homes, which protect us from predators and extremes of temperature. We might acquire drives for social approval and affiliation because other people, and their goodwill, help us reduce primary drives, especially when we are infants. In all cases, reduction of tension is the goal. Yet some people appear to acquire what could be considered excessive drives for money or affiliation. They gather money long after their material needs have been met, and some people find it difficult to be alone, even briefly.

Primary drives like hunger are triggered when we are in a state of deprivation. Sensations of hunger motivate us to act in ways that will restore the bodily balance. This tendency to maintain a steady state is called **homeostasis.** Homeostasis works much like a thermostat. When the temperature in a room drops below the set point, the heating system is triggered. The heat stays on until the set point is reached. Similarly, most animals eat until they are no longer hungry. The fact that many people eat "recreationally"—for example, when they see an appealing dessert—suggests there is more to eating than drive reduction.

▬ The Search for Stimulation: Is Downtime a Downer?

Physical needs give rise to drives like hunger and thirst. In such cases, we are motivated to *reduce* the tension or stimulation that impinges on us. *Are all motives aimed at the reduction of tension?* No, in the case of *stimulus motives,* organisms seek to *increase* stimulation.

For example, a classic study conducted at McGill University in Montreal during the 1950s suggests the importance of sensory stimulation and activity. Some "lucky" students were paid $20 a day (which, with inflation, would now be more like $200) for doing nothing—literally. Would you like to "work" by doing nothing for $200 a day? Don't answer too quickly. According to the results of classic research on sensory deprivation, you might not like it at all.

In that experiment, student volunteers were placed in quiet cubicles and blindfolded (Bexton et al., 1954). Their arms were bandaged; they could hear nothing but the dull, continuous hum of air conditioning. Many slept for a while, but after a few hours of sensory-deprived wakefulness, most felt bored and irritable. As time went on, many grew more uncomfortable. Many students quit the experiment during the first day despite the financial incentive. ◈ **Truth or Fiction Revisited:** Therefore, it is not true that getting away from it all by going on a vacation from all sensory input for a few hours is relaxing. Many of those who remained for a few days found it hard to concentrate on simple problems days afterward. For many, the experiment did not provide a relaxing vacation. Instead, it produced boredom and disorientation.

Lower animals and humans appear motivated to seek novel stimulation. Even when they have been deprived of food, rats may explore unfamiliar arms of mazes rather than head straight for the spot where they have learned to expect food. Animals that have just copulated and thereby reduced their primary sex drives often show renewed interest in sexual behavior when presented with a new sex partner—a novelty. People (and nonhumans) take in more calories at buffets and smorgasbords than when fewer kinds of food are available (Raynor & Epstein, 2001). Children spend hour after hour playing video games for the pleasure of zapping virtual people or monsters. Infants play with "busy boxes"—boxes filled with objects that honk, squeak, rattle, and buzz when manipulated in certain ways. Finding ways to control the gadgets is apparently reinforcing, even though learning is not rewarded with desserts or parental hugs.

Stimulus motives provide an evolutionary advantage. Animals that are active and motivated to learn about and manipulate their environment are more likely to survive. If you

■ **Monkeying Around**
Do organisms have innate drives to obtain sensory stimulation, manipulate objects (like these young rhesus monkeys), and explore the environment? The monkeys appear to monkey around with gadgets just for the fun of it. No external incentives are needed. Children similarly enjoy manipulating gadgets that honk, squeak, rattle, and buzz, even though the resultant honks and squeaks do not satisfy physiological drives such as hunger or thirst.

Drive-reduction theory The view that organisms learn to engage in behaviors that have the effect of reducing drives.

Primary drives Unlearned, or physiological, drives.

Acquired drives Drives acquired through experience, or learned.

Homeostasis The tendency of the body to maintain a steady state.

Self-Assessment

The Sensation-Seeking Scale

Self-Assessment

Self-Assessment

Some people seek higher levels of stimulation and activity than others. John is a couch potato, content to watch TV all evening. Marsha doesn't feel right unless she's out on the tennis court or jogging. Cliff isn't content unless he has ridden his motorcycle over back trails at breakneck speeds, and Angelina feels great when she's catching the big wave.

What about you? Are you content to read or watch TV all day? Or must you catch the big wave or bounce the bike across the dunes of the desert? Sensation-seeking scales measure the level of stimulation or arousal a person will seek.

Marvin Zuckerman (1971) identified four factors that are involved in sensation seeking: (1) seeking thrill and adventure, (2) disinhibition (that is, tendency to express impulses), (3) seeking experience, and (4) susceptibility to boredom.

A shortened version of one of Zuckerman's scales follows. To gain insight into your own sensation-seeking tendencies, circle the choice, A or B, that best describes you. Then compare your answers to those in the answer key in Appendix B.

1. **A.** I would like a job that requires a lot of traveling.
    B. I would prefer a job in one location.
2. **A.** I am invigorated by a brisk, cold day.
    B. I can't wait to get indoors on a cold day.
3. **A.** I get bored seeing the same old faces.
    B. I like the comfortable familiarity of everyday friends.
4. **A.** I would prefer living in an ideal society in which everyone is safe, secure, and happy.
    B. I would have preferred living in the unsettled days of our history.
5. **A.** I sometimes like to do things that are a little frightening.
    B. A sensible person avoids activities that are dangerous.

6. **A.** I would not like to be hypnotized.
    B. I would like to have the experience of being hypnotized.
7. **A.** The most important goal in life is to live it to the fullest and experience as much as possible.
    B. and happiness.
8. **A.** I would like to try parachute jumping.
    B. I would never want to try jumping out of a plane, with or without a parachute.
9. **A.** I enter cold water gradually, giving myself time to get used to it.
    B. I like to dive or jump right into the ocean or a cold pool.
10. **A.** When I go on a vacation, I prefer the change of camping out.
    B. When I go on a vacation, I prefer the comfort of a good room and bed.
11. **A.** I prefer people who are emotionally expressive even if they are a bit unstable.
    B. I prefer people who are calm and even tempered.
12. **A.** A good painting should shock or jolt the senses.
    B. A good painting should give one a feeling of peace and security.
13. **A.** People who ride motorcycles must have some kind of unconscious need to hurt themselves.
    B. I would like to drive or ride a motorcycle.

Go to http://academic.cengage.com/psychology/rathus *where you can fill out an interactive version of this Self-Assessment and automatically score your results.*

---

reflect & relate

Do you enjoy roller coasters? If so, why? Where would you place yourself in Maslow's hierarchy? Where do you see yourself as being headed in the hierarchy? Why?

Self-actualization According to Maslow and other humanistic psychologists, self-initiated striving to become what one is capable of being. The motive for reaching one's full potential and for expressing one's unique capabilities.

know where the nearest tall tree is, you're more likely to escape a lion. If you've foraged for food and water, you're more likely to pass your genes to future generations.

■ Humanistic Theory: "I've Got to Be Me"?

Humanistic psychologists such as Abraham Maslow (1908–1970) suggest that human behavior is more than mechanical and more than aimed toward tension-reduction and survival. *How does humanistic theory differ from other theories of motivation?* Maslow believed that people are also motivated by a conscious desire for personal growth. Humanists note that people tolerate pain, hunger, and many other sources of tension to obtain personal fulfillment.

Maslow believed that we are separated from so-called lower animals by our capacity for **self-actualization,** or self-initiated striving to become whatever we believe we are capable of being. Maslow considered self-actualization to be as vital a need in humans as hunger. The need for self-actualization pushes people to strive to become concert pianists, chief executive officers, or best-selling authors—even when they have plenty of money to live on.

Maslow (1970) organized human needs into a hierarchy. *What is Maslow's hierarchy of needs?* Maslow's hierarchy ranges from physiological needs such as hunger and thirst, through self-actualization (see Figure 9.1). He believed that we naturally strive to climb this hierarchy.

Critics of Maslow's theory argue that there is too much individual variation for the hierarchy of motives to apply to everyone. Some people whose physiological, safety, and love needs are met show little interest in achievement and recognition. And some artists devote themselves fully to their craft, even if they have to pass up the comforts of a warm home or alienate their families. Many people seek distant, self-actualizing goals, even when more basic needs, as outlined by Maslow, have not been met.

Each theory of motivation may have something to offer. Drive-reduction theory may explain why we drink when thirsty, but stimulus motives might explain why we go clubbing and drink alcohol. Each theory might apply to certain aspects of behavior. As the chapter progresses, we will describe research that lends support to each theory. Let us first consider the hunger drive. Hunger is based on physiological needs, and drive reduction would appear to explain some—although not all—eating behavior. Then we consider two powerful motives that push us ahead in life and sometimes to the front of the line: aggression and achievement. Psychologist Henry Murray (1938) called aggression and achievement *social motives*. He believed that people acquired aggressive and achievement-oriented behavior patterns to meet psychological needs. But evolutionary psychologists believe that "genetic whisperings" also influence aggression, achievement, and other aspects of personality and social behavior (Buss, 2003; Filley et al., 2001; Plomin, 2002).

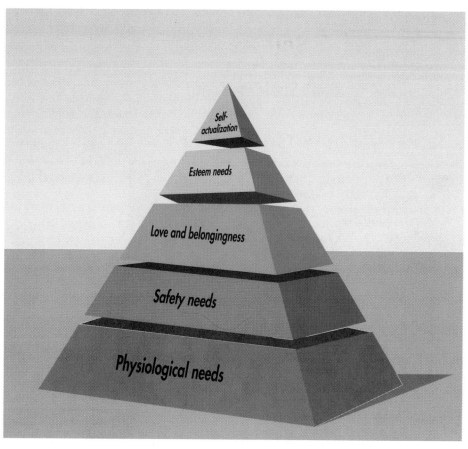

Figure 9.1
Maslow's Hierarchy of Needs
Maslow believed we progress toward higher psychological needs once basic survival needs have been met. Where do you fit in this picture?

Go to your student website to access an interactive version of this figure.

◯ Learning Connections

◀◀   *Theories of Motivation—Which Why Is Which?*   ▶▶

REVIEW:

3 The concept of homeostasis best explains why
(a) adolescents become more interested in peer relationships,
(b) monkeys spend time manipulating gadgets,
(c) people go on roller coasters,
(d) animals eat when they are hungry.

4 According to the _____ perspective, animals are born with instinctive tendencies to behave in certain ways.
(a) humanistic,
(b) evolutionary,
(c) drive-reductionist,
(d) stimulation-seeking.

CRITICAL THINKING:
How does rearing an animal in isolation from others of its kind help researchers learn about what behaviors are instinctive? Would it be possible to run such an experiment with humans? Why or why not?

Go to
http://academic.cengage.com/psychology/rathus
for an interactive version of this review.

HUNGER: DO YOU GO BY "TUMMY-TIME"?

We need food to survive, but food means more than survival. Food is a symbol of family togetherness and caring. We associate food with the nurturance of the parent–child relationship, with visits home on holidays. Friends and relatives offer us food when we enter their homes, and saying no may be viewed as a personal rejection. Bacon and eggs, coffee with cream and sugar, meat and mashed potatoes—all seem to be part of sharing American values and abundance. *How is the hunger drive regulated?*

■ **What Does Food Mean to You?**
In almost every culture, eating is a social event. Food is a means of survival, but there are many other interesting questions about food. Why do we feel hungry or satiated? Why do many people continue to eat when they have already supplied their bodies with the needed nutrients? Why do others starve themselves?

Robert van der Hilst /Corbis

■ Biological Influences on Hunger

I go by tummy-time and I want my dinner.
—SIR WINSTON CHURCHILL

In considering the bodily mechanisms that regulate hunger, let us begin with the mouth. (After all, we are talking about eating.) After we chew and swallow a certain amount, we receive signals of satiety. We also get signals of **satiety** from the digestive tract, although these signals take longer to reach the brain. Therefore, if we did not receive signals of satiety from chewing and swallowing, we might eat for a long time after we had taken in enough food.

In classic "sham feeding" experiments with dogs, researchers implanted a tube in the animals' throats so that any food swallowed fell out of the body. Even though no food reached the stomach, the animals stopped feeding after a while (Janowitz & Grossman, 1949). Thus sensations of chewing and swallowing must provide some feelings of satiety. The dogs in the study, however, resumed feeding sooner than animals whose food did reach the stomach. Let us proceed to the stomach, too, as we seek further regulatory factors in hunger.

An empty stomach leads to stomach contractions, which we call *hunger pangs*. Classic research suggested that stomach contractions are crucial to hunger. A man (A. L. Washburn) swallowed a balloon that was inflated in his stomach. His stomach contractions squeezed the balloon, so the contractions could be recorded by observers. Washburn also pressed a key when he felt hungry, and the researchers found a correspondence between his stomach contractions and his feelings of hunger (Cannon & Washburn, 1912).

◈ **Truth or Fiction Revisited:** It is true that pangs in the stomach are connected with feelings of hunger, *but* stomach contractions are not as influential as formerly thought. We apparently go by more than "tummy-time." Medical observations and classic research find that humans and nonhumans whose stomachs have been removed still regulate food intake so as to maintain a normal weight (Tsang, 1938). (Food is absorbed through their intestines.) This finding led to the discovery of other mechanisms that regulate hunger, including the hypothalamus, blood sugar level, and receptors in the liver. When we are deprived of food, the level of sugar in the blood drops. The drop is communicated to the hypothalamus, which stokes the hunger drive.

If you were just reviving from a surgical operation, fighting your way through the fog of the anesthesia, food would probably be the last thing on your mind. But when a researcher uses a probe to destroy the **ventromedial nucleus** (**VMN**) of a rat's hypothalamus, the rat will grope toward food as soon as its eyes open. Then it eats vast quantities of Purina Rat Chow or whatever.

The VMN seems to be able to function like a "stop-eating center" in the rat's brain. If the VMN is electrically stimulated—that is, "switched on"—the rat stops eating until the current is turned off. When the VMN is destroyed, the rat becomes **hyperphagic** (see Figure 9.2).

Satiety The state of being satisfied; fullness.

Ventromedial nucleus (VMN) A central area on the underside of the hypothalamus that appears to function as a stop-eating center.

Hyperphagic Characterized by excessive eating.

That is, it continues to eat until it has about doubled its normal weight. Then it will level off its eating rate and maintain the higher weight. It is as if the set point of the stop-eating center has been raised to a higher level, like turning up the thermostat in a house from 65°F degrees to 80°F. Other research suggests that the hyperphagic rats are also more finicky. They eat more fats or sweet-tasting food, but if their food is salty or bitter they eat less. Some people develop tumors near the base of the brain that damage the VMN and apparently cause them to overeat (Miller, 1995).

The **lateral hypothalamus** may function like a "start-eating center" by producing molecules that signal the rat to eat (Chua, 2004). If you destroy the lateral hypothalamus, the rat may stop eating altogether—that is, become **aphagic.**

▬ Psychological Influences on Hunger

Although many areas of the body work in concert to regulate the hunger drive, this is only part of the story. In human beings, the hunger drive is more complex. Psychological as well as physiological factors play an important role. How many times have you been made hungry by the sight or aroma of food? How many times have you eaten not because you were hungry but because you were at a relative's home or hanging around in a cafeteria? Or because you felt anxious or depressed? Or simply because you were bored?

▬ Obesity: A Serious and Pervasive Problem

There is no sincerer love than the love of food.
—George Bernard Shaw

The two biggest sellers in any bookstore are the cookbooks and the diet books. The cookbooks tell you how to prepare the food and the diet books tell you how not to eat any of it.
—Andy Rooney

Consider some facts about obesity:

- More than three out of ten adult Americans are obese, according to the National Body Mass Index (BMI[1]) guidelines (Flegal et al., 2002).
- More than half of African American women aged 40 or above are obese, possibly because they have lower metabolic rates than European American women (Flegal et al., 2002).
- Americans eat more than a total of 800 billion calories of food each day (200 billion calories more than they need to maintain their weights). The extra calories could feed the nation of Germany—80 million people.
- About 300,000 Americans die each year because of health problems related to obesity (Pinel et al., 2000).
- Weight control is elusive for most people; even those who have dieted "successfully" regain most of the weight they have lost (Cooper & Fairburn, 2001).

Figure 9.2
A Hyperphagic Rat
This rodent winner of the basketball look-alike contest went on a binge after it received a lesion in part of the hypothalamus. It is as if the lesion pushed the "set point" for body weight up several notches; the rat's weight is now about five times normal. But now it eats only enough to maintain its pleasantly plump stature, so you need not be concerned that it will eventually burst.

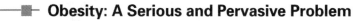

reflect & relate

Why do *you* eat? How do you experience the hunger drive? Have you ever eaten because you were anxious or bored or because you passed a bakery window with some enticing pastries? What are the effects on your health?

---

[1] You can calculate your body mass index as follows. Write down your weight in pounds. Multiply it by 703. Divide the product by your height in inches squared. For example, if you weigh 160 lbs. and are 5'8" tall, your BMI is $(160 \times 703)/68^2$, or 24.33. You will find an online BMI calculator at www.cdc.gov/nccdphp/dnpa/bmi/calc-bmi.htm. A BMI of 25 or higher is defined as overweight. A BMI of 30 or higher is defined as obese.

Lateral hypothalamus An area at the side of the hypothalamus that appears to function as a start-eating center.

Aphagic Characterized by undereating.

TABLE 9.1 ■ Years of Life Lost Due to Obesity for European American and African American Young Adults		
	FEMALE	**MALE**
European American	8	13
African American	5	20

American culture idealizes slender heroes and heroines. For those who "more than measure up" to TV and film idols, food may have replaced sex as the central source of guilt. Obese people encounter more than their fair share of health problems, including hypertension, heart disease, diabetes, gallbladder disease, osteoarthritis, sleep apnea and respiratory problems, and certain kinds of cancer (Centers for Disease Control and Prevention, 2005a). A study using data collected by the federal government found that severely obese young adults (those with a BMI above 45) live shorter lives than people who are normal in weight (Fontaine et al., 2003; see Table 9.1). Why are so many people obese? What can we do about it?

Origins of Obesity

We are in real trouble. Having a culture bombarded with rushed lifestyles, fast foods, and physical inactivity has caught up with us.
—CARMEN NEVAREZ, VICE PRESIDENT OF THE BERKELEY, CALIFORNIA, PUBLIC HEALTH INSTITUTE

Many biological and psychological factors are involved in obesity. On the biological side, we can point to the influences of heredity, adipose tissue (body fat), and metabolism (the rate at which the individual converts calories to energy).

Obesity runs in families. It was once assumed that obese parents encouraged their children to be overweight by serving fattening foods and setting poor examples. A study of Scandinavian adoptees, however, found that children bear a closer resemblance in weight to their biological parents than to their adoptive parents (Stunkard et al., 1990). Today it is widely accepted that heredity plays a role in obesity (Wadden et al., 2002).

If heredity is a factor in obesity, just what might be inherited? There are various possibilities. One is a mutation in the melanocortin 4 receptor gene, which makes a protein that influences the hypothalamus. If the gene makes too little of the protein, the person experiences too much hunger and is thus vulnerable to binge eating. A typical study of the gene, published in the *New England Journal of Medicine* (Farooqi et al., 2003), recruited 469 severely obese adults and found that the binge eaters among them were more likely to possess the gene. Even so, the gene was found among only 5% of the people in the sample. Therefore, many genes may contribute to obesity.

Efforts by obese people to maintain a slender profile may be sabotaged by microscopic units of life in their own bodies: fat cells. No, fat cells are not overweight cells. They are cells that store fat. Hunger might be related to the amount of stored fat. As time passes after a meal, the blood sugar level drops. Fat is then drawn from these cells for nourishment. At some point, referred to as the *set point,* the lower level of fat is communicated to the hypothalamus, triggering the hunger drive.

People with more fat cells feel food-deprived earlier, even though they may be equal in weight. Why? More signals are sent to the hypothalamus. Obese and *formerly* obese people tend to have more fat cells than people of normal weight. Thus many people who have lost weight complain that they always feel hungry when they try to maintain their losses.

Fatty tissue also metabolizes (burns) food more slowly than muscle does. For this reason, a person with a high fat-to-muscle ratio metabolizes food more slowly than a person of the same weight with a lower fat-to-muscle ratio. That is, two people who are identical in weight may metabolize food at different rates, depending on the distribution of muscle and fat in their bodies. Obese people therefore are doubly handicapped in their efforts to lose weight—not only by their extra weight but by the fact that they have so many fat cells.

The normal distribution of fat cells is different for men and women. The average man is 40% muscle and 15% fat. The average woman is 23% muscle and 25% fat. If a man and a woman with typical distributions of muscle and fat are of equal weight, therefore, the woman—who has more fat cells—has to eat less to maintain that weight.

Ironically, dieting itself makes it more difficult to lose weight. This is because people on diets and those who have lost substantial amounts of weight burn fewer calories. That is,

Life Connections
The Skinny on Weight Control

Many factors—biological, psychological, and sociocultural—contribute to obesity. People can do many things to fight weight gain, but first be advised that psychologists warn that not everyone should be trying to slim down. Women in the United States today are under social pressure to conform to an unnaturally slender female ideal. As a result, they tend to set unrealistic weight loss goals (Linde et al., 2004). For many overweight people, however, especially those who are obese, shedding excess pounds lowers the risks of health problems such as diabetes and heart disease.

Research on motivation and on methods of therapy has enhanced our knowledge of healthful ways to lose weight. Sound weight-control programs do not involve fad diets such as fasting, eliminating carbohydrates, or eating excessive amounts of one particular food (Brownell & Horgen, 2003). Nor do we have effective and safe drugs to treat obesity (Yanovski & Yanovski, 2002). Today's most effective weight-control programs involve improving nutritional knowledge, decreasing calorie intake, exercising, and changing eating habits.

Most health professionals believe that people in the United States eat too much animal fat and not enough fruits and vegetables (see www.mypyramid.gov). Studies have shown that eating foods low in saturated fats and cholesterol is not only good for the heart but can also contribute to weight loss. Eating fewer calories also lowers weight. Eating fewer calories does not just mean eating smaller portions. It means switching to some lower-calorie foods—relying more on fresh, unsweetened fruits and vegetables (eating apples rather than apple pie), fish and poultry, and skim milk and cheese (see Figure 9.3).

Figure 9.3
Federal Government Guidelines for Healthier Eating
The 2005 guidelines available at www.mypyramid.gov call for eating more whole grains, fruits, and vegetables, and less fat, particularly solid fats. The person climbing the stairs indicates that exercise is also part of a healthy lifestyle.

Orange = GRAINS. Make half your grains whole. Eat at least 3 ounces of whole grain bread, cereal, crackers, rice, or pasta every day.

Green = VEGETABLES. Eat more dark green veggies. Eat more orange veggies. Eat more dry beans and peas.

Red = FRUITS. Eat a variety of fruit. Choose fresh, frozen, canned, or dried fruit.

Yellow = OILS. Know your fats. Make most of your fat sources from fish, nuts, and vegetable oils. Limit solid fats like butter, stick margarine, shortening, and lard.

Blue = MILK. Get your calcium-rich foods. Go low-fat or fat-free. If you don't or can't consume milk, choose lactose-free products or other calcium sources such as green leafy vegetables, like kale and broccoli, or fish like salmon and sardines.

Purple = MEAT & BEANS. Go lean on protein. Choose low-fat or lean meats and poultry. Bake it, broil it, or grill it. Vary your choices—with more fish, beans, peas, nuts, and seeds.

It can mean cutting down on—or eliminating—butter, margarine, oils derived from animals, and sugar. The same foods that help control weight also tend to be high in vitamins and fiber and low in fats. Most health experts agree that such foods therefore reduce the risk of heart disease; almost all agree that they reduce the risk of cancer and some other illnesses (see Chapter 11).

Dieting plus exercise is more effective than dieting alone for shedding pounds and keeping them off (Centers for Disease Control and Prevention, 2005b). When we restrict our intake of calories, our metabolic rate compensates by slowing down (Wadden et al., 2002). Exercise burns calories and builds muscle tissue, which metabolizes more calories than fatty tissue does (Dubbert, 2002).

Cognitive-behavioral methods also provide strategies for losing weight. Among them are the following:

- Establish calorie-intake goals and keep track of whether you are meeting them. Go to a website (e.g., www.healthierus.gov/dietaryguidelines) or book that shows how many calories are found in foods. Keep a diary of your calorie intake.
- Substitute low-calorie foods for high-calorie foods. Fill your stomach with celery rather than cheesecake and enchiladas. Eat preplanned low-calorie snacks instead of binge eating peanuts or ice cream.
- Take a five-minute break between helpings. Ask yourself, "Am I still hungry?" If not, stop eating.
- Avoid temptations that have sidetracked you in the past. Shop at the mall with the Alfalfa Sprout Café, not the Cheesecake Factory. Plan your meal before entering a restaurant. (Avoid ogling that tempting full-color menu.) Attend to your own plate, not to the sumptuous dish at the next table. (Your salad probably looks greener to them, anyhow.) Shop from a list. Walk briskly through the supermarket, preferably after dinner when you're less hungry. Don't be sidetracked by pretty packages (fattening things may come in them). Don't linger in the kitchen. Study, watch TV, write emails, and surf the Internet elsewhere. Don't bring fattening foods into the house. Prepare only enough food to meet your calorie goals.
- Exercise to burn more calories and increase your metabolic rate. Reach for your mate, not your plate (to coin a phrase). Take a brisk walk instead of eating an unplanned snack. Build exercise routines by adding a few minutes each week.
- Reward yourself for meeting calorie goals (but not with food). Imagine how great you'll look in that new swimsuit next summer. Do not go to the latest movie unless you have met your weekly calorie goal. When you meet your weekly calorie goal, put cash in the bank toward a vacation or a new camera.
- Use imagery to help yourself lose weight. Tempted by a fattening dish? Imagine that it's rotten, that you would be nauseated by it and have a sick taste in your mouth for the rest of the day.
- Mentally walk through solutions to problem situations. Consider what you will do when cake is handed out at the office party. Rehearse your next visit to relatives who tell you how painfully thin you look and try to stuff you with food. Imagine how you will politely (but firmly) refuse seconds and thirds, despite their objections.
- Above all, if you slip from your plan for a day, don't blow things out of proportion. Dieters are often tempted to binge, especially when they rigidly see themselves either as perfect successes or as complete failures or when they experience powerful emotions—either positive or negative. Consider the weekly or monthly trend, not just a single day. Credit yourself for the long-term trend. If you do binge, resume dieting the next day.

Losing weight—and keeping it off—is not easy, but it can be done. Making a commitment to losing weight and establishing a workable plan for doing so are two of the keys. ■

their metabolic rates slow down (Wadden et al., 2002). The slowdown appears to be a built-in mechanism that helps preserve life in times of famine. It also, however, makes it more difficult for dieters to continue to lose weight. The pounds come off more and more reluctantly.

Psychological factors, such as observational learning, stress, and emotional states also contribute to obesity (Canetti et al., 2002; Henker et al., 2002). Children in the United States are exposed to an average of 10,000 food commercials a year. More than 9 out of 10 of these commercials are for fast foods (like McDonald's fries), sugared cereals, candy, and soft drinks (Wadden et al., 2002). Situations also play a role. Family celebrations, watching TV, arguments, and tension at work can all lead to overeating or falling off a diet (Brownell & Horgen, 2003). Negative emotions such as depression and anxiety can lead to binge eating (Stice et al., 2000a).

As we have seen, millions upon millions of Americans are eating too much and becoming obese. But now let us turn our attention to the hundreds of thousands of people—mainly adolescent girls and young women, but also some boys and men—who are obtaining too little nutrition. Some eat too little. Some eat too much and then purposefully throw it up. Eating has become a traumatic experience for many Americans, a continuous test of willpower—or won't-power. Dieting has become the "normal"—at least in the statistical sense of the word—way of eating for women in the United States today. But for some people, especially young women, dieting becomes so extreme that their health is in jeopardy, as we see in the following section on eating disorders. ***What are the eating disorders?***

■ **Is Everyone Dieting?**
At any given time, at least half of the adult American population is on a diet. Dieting has become the "normal" pattern of eating for women. Dozens of diets vie for attention on bookstore shelves. How can we know which ones contain truth and which ones contain fiction?

■ Eating Disorders

The **eating disorders** are characterized by persistent, gross disturbances in eating patterns. In this section we focus on an eating disorder in which individuals are too thin, *anorexia nervosa,* and one in which the person may be normal in weight, but certainly not in the methods used to maintain that weight—*bulimia nervosa.*

Anorexia Nervosa   The Duchess of Windsor famously said, "You can never be too rich or too thin." ◆ **Truth or Fiction Revisited:** Most people make no objection to having a fat bank account, but the fact is that one can certainly be too thin, as in the case of **anorexia nervosa.** Anorexia nervosa is a life-threatening eating disorder characterized by extreme fear of being too heavy, dramatic weight loss, a distorted body image, and resistance to eating enough to reach or maintain a healthful weight, as we see in the nearby "Closer Look" on the case of Rachel.

Rachel, like other people with anorexia nervosa, weighed less than 85% of her desirable body weight. By and large, anorexia nervosa afflicts women during adolescence and young adulthood (Winzelberg et al., 2000; Zagar & Rubenstein, 2002). The typical person with anorexia is a young European American female of higher socioeconomic status (McLaren, 2002). A study of 985 European American women and 1,061 African American women found that 1.5% of the European Americans and none of the African Americans had met the diagnostic standards for anorexia nervosa at some time during their lives (Striegel-Moore et al., 2003). Affluent females have greater access to fitness centers and health clubs and are more likely to subscribe to the magazines that idealize slender bodies and shop in the boutiques that cater to svelte women. All in all, they are regularly confronted with unrealistic standards of slimness that make them dissatisfied with their own figures (McLaren, 2002; Neumark-Sztainer et al., 2002a). The incidences of anorexia nervosa and bulimia nervosa have increased markedly in recent years.

We also find eating disorders among some males, particularly among males who are compelled by their chosen activities—for example, wrestling or dancing—to keep their weight at a certain limit (Bailey, 2003a; Goode, 2000). But women with these disorders outnumber men who have them by more than 6 to 1 (Goode, 2000; Striegel-Moore & Cachelin, 2001).

Females with anorexia nervosa can drop 25% or more of their weight within a year. Severe weight loss triggers abnormalities in the endocrine system (that is, with hormones) that prevent ovulation (Golden, 2002). General health deteriorates. Females with anorexia are

Eating disorders A group of disorders marked by persistent, gross disturbances in eating patterns.

Anorexia nervosa A life-threatening eating disorder characterized by dramatic weight loss and a distorted body image.

also at risk for premature development of osteoporosis, a condition characterized by loss of bone density that usually afflicts people in late adulthood (Jacoangeli et al., 2002). Given these problems, the mortality rate for females with anorexia nervosa is approximately 5%.

In one common pattern, the girl sees that she has gained some weight after reaching puberty, and she resolves that she must lose it. But even after the weight is gone, she maintains her pattern of dieting and, in many cases, exercises at a fever pitch. This pattern continues as she plunges below her "desirable" weight—according to standardized weight charts—and even after those who care about her tell her that she is becoming "all skin and bones." Girls with the disorder tend to deny that they are losing too much weight. They are in denial about health problems; some point to feverish exercise routines as evidence of strength. Distortion of the body image is a major feature of the disorder (Striegel-Moore et al., 2004). Friends, coworkers, and families see females with anorexia nervosa as skin and bones. Meanwhile, the women gaze in the mirror and believe that they are looking at a body shape that is too heavy.

Ironically, individuals with anorexia do not literally distance themselves from food. They may become as preoccupied with food as they are with their own body shape. They may develop a fascination with cookbooks, shop for their families, and prepare gourmet feasts—for other people, that is.

Bulimia Nervosa

> Nicole awakens in her cold dark room and already wishes it was time to go back to bed. She dreads the thought of going through this day, which will be like so many others in her recent past. She asks herself the question every morning, "Will I be able to make it through the day without being totally obsessed by thoughts of food, or will I blow it again and spend the day [binge eating]"? She tells herself that today she will begin a new life, today she will start to live like a normal human being. However, she is not at all convinced that the choice is hers. (Boskind-White & White, 1983, p. 29)

So, does Nicole begin a new life today? No. Despite her pledge to herself, Nicole begins the day with eggs and toast—butter included. Then she downs cookies; bagels smothered with

Anorexia Nervosa

LEARNING OBJECTIVES

- To develop a better understanding of why people eat—or refuse to eat.
- To understand some of the motives connected with eating disorders.

APPLIED LESSON

1. What pressures do you observe in society and in the media that motivate people to be slender?
2. What does it mean to have a distorted body image? How does the woman in the video view herself?

3. Why does the woman in the video eat, even though she would prefer not to?

CRITICAL THINKING

1. The majority of women in the United States diet continuously. Do you see dieting as a normal or abnormal pattern of eating? Explain your view. (Hint: What are some different ways of defining "normal"?)
2. Which do you see as a more serious eating problem: obesity or anorexia nervosa? What standards are you using to arrive at your answer?

Eating disorders affect many Americans, especially women. Why?

Watch this video!

Go to your companion website at http://academic.cengage.com/psychology/rathus
Click on the Video Connections tab under this chapter.

A Closer Look
Anorexia Nervosa—The Case of Rachel

I wanted to be a runner. Runners were thin and I attributed this to dieting, not training. So I began restricting my diet: No butter, red meat, pork, dessert, candy, or snacking. If I ate any of the forbidden items I obsessed about it and felt guilty for days.

As a high school freshman, I wanted to run with the fastest girls so I trained hard, really hard and ate less. Lunch was lettuce sandwiches, carrots, and an apple. By my senior year, I was number three on the team and lunch was a bagel and an orange.

I maintained a rigid schedule—running cross country and track, having a seat on student council, volunteering, and maintaining a 3.9 GPA throughout high school—while starving myself (1,000 calories per day), trying to attain the impossible perfection I thought couldn't be far away if I only slimmed down a little bit more.

Several teammates were concerned, but I shrugged them off saying family members were tall and slender; I was a health nut; I didn't like fatty foods; I was a vegetarian; I didn't like sweets; I wasn't hungry; I wasn't starving.

A psychiatrist didn't help at all. I went in, sat on the couch and told her what she wanted to hear: I would eat more, run less, stop restricting myself, and quit obsessing about being thin. I was very good at knowing exactly what to tell others.

I dropped 10 pounds my freshman year—from 125 to 115 lbs. I was 5'8" tall and wore a size five. I hated my body so I starved myself and ran like a mad woman.

In quiet moments, I was sad and worried about what might be going on inside me.

I was already taking birth control to regain my menstrual cycle; my weight was 15% below what was recommended for my height; I was always cold; I had chest pains and an irregular heartbeat; my hair was limp and broke off; my skin was colorless.

It wasn't until I came to the University of Iowa and joined the varsity women's cross country team that I began to see what I was doing to myself. A teammate had an eating problem. Every time I saw her, I felt sick to my stomach. She had sunken cheeks, eyes so big they swallowed her face. She was an excellent student and a college-level varsity athlete. Many people wondered at her determination, but I understood. She used the same excuses I did.

For one sick instant, I wondered if I would be happier if I were that thin. That is when I started to realize I was slowly killing myself.

At the urging of my coach, I saw the team nutritionist who recommended a psychiatrist who felt no pity for me and made me take a brutally honest look at who I was and why I was starving myself. She didn't accept any of my excuses. She helped me realize that there are other things to think about besides food and body image. About this time I decided to quit the cross country team. The pressure I felt to be thin and competition at the college level were too much when I needed to focus on getting well.

After two months of therapy, my weight had dropped again. I'm not sure how far because I refused to step on a scale, but my size five pants were falling off. My psychiatrist required weekly weigh-ins.

I wasn't putting into practice any of the things my nutritionist and counselor suggested. They told me that if I wanted to have children someday I needed to eat. They warned me of osteoporosis at age 30. Then my psychiatrist scared me to death. She told me I needed to start eating more or I would be checked into the hospital and hooked up to an IV. That would put me on the same level as my Iowa teammate. I had looked at her with such horror and never realized that I was in the same position.

My psychiatrist asked how my family would feel if they had to visit me in the hospital because I refused to eat. It was enough to make me think hard the next time I went through the food service lines.

Of course, I didn't get better the next day. But it was a step in the right direction. It's taken me three years to get where I am now. At 5'8-¾" (I even grew as I got healthier) and 145 lbs., I look and feel healthier, have better eating and exercise habits, and I don't obsess about food as much as I used to. On rare occasions, I think about controlling my food intake. My eating disorder will haunt me for the rest of my life. If I'm not careful, it could creep back. ■

Source: From *Well & Good*, 2002, University of Iowa Health Care. Used by permission.

cream cheese, butter, and jelly; doughnuts; candy bars; bowlfuls of cereal and milk—all in less than an hour. When her body cries "No more!" she turns to the next step in her routine: purging. In the bathroom, she ties back her hair. She runs the shower to mask noise, drinks some water, and then makes herself throw it all up. Afterward she makes another pledge to herself: "Starting tomorrow, I'm going to change." Will she change? In truth, she doubts it.

Nicole has **bulimia nervosa,** which entails repeated cycles of binge eating and purging. Binge eating often follows efforts to diet (Corwin, 2000). There are various methods of purging. Nicole vomited. Other people use strict dieting or fasting, laxatives, and prolonged exercise. Individuals with eating disorders, like Rachel and Nicole, tend to be perfectionistic about their bodies (Shafran et al., 2002; Tyrka et al., 2002). They will not settle for less than their idealized body shape and weight. Bulimia, like anorexia, triggers hormonal imbalances: One study found that nearly half of women with bulimia nervosa have irregular menstrual cycles (Gendall et al., 2000).

Bulimia nervosa, like anorexia nervosa, tends to afflict women during adolescence and young adulthood (Lewinsohn et al., 2000b; Winzelberg et al., 2000). The study by Striegel-Moore and her colleagues (2003) found that 2.4% of the European American women in their sample reported symptoms of bulimia nervosa, as compared with 0.4% of the African Americans.

Origins of the Eating Disorders *What are the origins of the eating disorders?* Health professionals have done a great deal of research into the origins of eating disorders, but they admit that many questions about them remain unanswered (Striegel-Moore & Cachelin, 2001).

Many parents are obsessed with getting their children—especially their infants—to eat. Thus some psychologists suggest that children may use refusal to eat as a way of resisting or punishing parents. ("You have to eat something!" "I'm not hungry!") Parents in such families often have issues with eating and dieting themselves. They also "act out" against their daughters—letting them know that they consider them unattractive and that they should slim down (Baker et al., 2000; Cooper et al., 2001).

A particularly disturbing risk factor for eating disorders in adolescent females is a history of child abuse, particularly sexual abuse (Ackard et al., 2001; K. P. Anderson et al., 2000; Leonard et al., 2003; Nagata et al., 2001). One study found a history of childhood sexual abuse in about half of women with bulimia nervosa, as opposed to a rate of about 7% among women without the disorder (Deep et al., 1999). Another study compared 45 pairs of sisters, in which one of each pair was diagnosed with anorexia nervosa (Karwautz et al., 2001). Those with anorexia were significantly more likely to be exposed to high parental expectations *and* to sexual abuse.

The sociocultural climate also affects eating behavior (Williams et al., 2003). Slimness is idealized in the United States. When you check out *Cosmopolitan, Glamour,* or the Victoria's Secret catalog, you are looking at models who, on average, are 9% taller and 16% thinner than the typical female—and who still manage to have ample bustlines. Miss America, the annually renewed American role model, has also been slenderizing across the years. Over the past 80 years, the winner has added only 2% in height but has lost 12 lbs. in weight. In the 1920s, Miss America's weight relative to her height yielded a Body Mass Index (BMI) of 20 to 25, which is considered normal by the World Health Organization (WHO). WHO labels people as malnourished when their BMIs are lower than 18.5. Recent Miss Americas, however, come in at a BMI near 17 (Rubinstein & Caballero, 2000). So Miss America adds to the woes of "normal" young women.

Eric Ryan/Getty Images

■ **The Ideal?**
Most women cannot achieve today's ideal figure without extreme self-deprivation. The images of women in films, TV, and fashion magazines apparently contribute to eating disorders and women try to measure up—or, should we say, "measure down"?

Bulimia nervosa An eating disorder characterized by repeated cycles of binge eating and purging.

◆ **Truth or Fiction Revisited:** Thus it is true that fashion magazines can contribute to eating disorders among women. As the cultural ideal slenderizes, women with average body weights according to the health charts feel overweight, and more-than-average women feel gargantuan (Utter et al., 2003; Williams et al., 2003).

A survey of 4,746 junior high and high school students by Dianne Neumark-Sztainer (2002b) and her colleagues found that 57% of the girls had made serious efforts to lose weight—for example, dieting, using food substitutes like Slim-Fast, or upping their cigarette usage. Twelve percent had used more extreme measures: vomiting, using diet pills, or taking laxatives or diuretics. Even one-third of the boys had attempted to lose weight, although their tactics were usually not as severe as the girls'.

Eating disorders tend to run in families, which raises the possibility of genetic involvement (Bergen et al., 2003; DeAngelis, 2002; Kaye et al., 2004). A genetic mutation might be involved in binge eating in some people (Farooqi et al., 2003). Genetic factors might also be involved in the obsessionistic and perfectionistic personality traits that often accompany the need to be superthin (Favaro, 2005; Kaye et al., 2004; Speranza et al., 2001). Perfectionism, cultural emphasis on slimness, and family conflict may be a recipe for development of eating disorders (Baker et al., 2000).

( ) Learning Connections

◀◀　　*Hunger—Do You Go by "Tummy-Time"?*　　▶▶

REVIEW:

5　As time passes after a meal, the _____ sugar level drops and fat is drawn from fat cells to provide nourishment.
   (a) hypothalamic,
   (b) blood,
   (c) ventromedial,
   (d) body mass index.

6　Anorexia nervosa and bulimia nervosa are related to the personality trait of
   (a) openness to new experience,
   (b) paranoia,
   (c) agreeableness,
   (d) perfectionism.

7　Most people with anorexia nervosa or bulimia nervosa are
   (a) female,
   (b) dancers,

   (c) college graduates,
   (d) middle-aged.

8　"Sham feeding" experiments with dogs suggest that
   (a) removal of the stomach causes animals to stop eating,
   (b) sensations of chewing and swallowing provide some feelings of satiety,
   (c) the hypothalamus has start-eating and stop-eating centers,
   (d) stomach "pangs" are the most important contributors to the hunger drive.

CRITICAL THINKING:
It is possible that genetic factors are involved in the development of eating disorders. If they are, is there any purpose to trying to challenge the cultural idealization of the extremely thin female? Explain.

Go
to
http://academic.cengage.com/psychology/rathus
for an interactive version of this review.

■ **How Powerful Is the Sex Drive?**
The sex drive is quite powerful among late adolescents and young adults, when sex hormones are at their peak. However, the modes of sexual expression they choose—and whether they express sexual impulses at all—is greatly influenced by cultural factors.

SEXUAL MOTIVATION: ATTITUDES AND BEHAVIOR

What turns people on? What makes the sex drive click? What springs people's hearts into their mouths, tightens their throats, and stirs their sex organs? Is it the sight of a lover undressing, a jpeg file on an adult website, a sniff of velvety perfume, a sip of wine? Some people become aroused by remembrances of lovers past. Some are stimulated by fantasies of flings with strangers.

Many factors contribute to the sex drive. People vary greatly in the cues that excite them sexually and in the frequency with which they experience sexual thoughts and feelings. Sex hormones also play their part. In adolescence, when we are flooded with sex hormones, we may seem perpetually aroused or arousable. Yet some people rarely or never entertain sexual thoughts or fantasies. Cultural beliefs also influence sexual behavior and the pleasure people find—or do not find—in sex. Sexual motivation may be natural, but this natural function is strongly influenced by religious and moral beliefs, cultural tradition, folklore, and superstition.

Regardless of our ethnicity, our levels of education, and cultural influences, our sex drives are connected with sex hormones. *What are the effects of sex hormones on sexual motivation?*

Hormones and Sexual Motivation: Adding Fuel to the Fire

Sex hormones can be said to fuel the sex drive. Research with men who produce little testosterone—due to age or health problems—shows that their sex drive increases when they receive testosterone replacement therapy (Seidman, 2003). The most common sexual problem among women is lack of sexual desire or interest, and the sex drive in women is also connected with testosterone levels (Apperloo et al., 2003). Although men produce 10 to 20 times the testosterone produced by women, women produce androgens ("male" sex hormones) in the adrenal glands. Testosterone injections, patches, or pills can heighten the sex drive in women who do not produce enough of the hormone (Van Anders et al., 2005).

Sex hormones promote the development of male and female sex organs and regulate the menstrual cycle. They also have activating and organizing effects on sexual behavior. **Activating effects** involve the sex drive. Female mice, rats, cats, and dogs are receptive to males only during **estrus,** when female sex hormones are plentiful. During estrus, female rats respond to males by hopping, wiggling their ears, and arching their backs with their tails to one side, thus enabling males to penetrate them.

Sex hormones also have directional or **organizing effects.** That is, they predispose lower animals toward stereotypical masculine or feminine mating patterns. Sex hormones are thus likely candidates for influencing the development of sexual orientation, as we see later (Lalumière et al., 2000).

Sex hormones may further "masculinize" or "feminize" the brain by creating predispositions consistent with some gender-role tendencies (Collaer & Hines, 1995; Crews, 1994). For example, male rats are generally superior to females in maze-learning ability, a task that requires spatial skills. But female rats that are exposed to androgens in the uterus (e.g., because they have several male siblings in the uterus with them) or soon after birth learn maze routes as rapidly as males (Vandenbergh, 1993).

First let us ask, *What happens to the body when people are sexually aroused?*

Sexual Response

According to various measures, men show more interest in sex than women do (Peplau, 2003). Women are more likely to want to combine sex with a romantic relationship (Fisher, 2000; Peplau, 2003). A survey of more than 1,000 undergraduates found that men reported

Activating effect The arousal-producing effects of sex hormones that increase the likelihood of sexual behavior.

Estrus The periodic sexual excitement of many female mammals, as governed by levels of sex hormones.

Organizing effect The directional effect of sex hormones—for example, along stereotypically masculine or feminine lines.

being more interested than women in casual sex and multiple sex partners (Schmitt et al., 2001).

Although we may be more culturally attuned to focus on sex differences rather than similarities, William Masters and Virginia Johnson (1966) found that the biological responses of males and females to sexual stimulation are quite similar. Masters and Johnson use the term *sexual response cycle* to describe the changes that occur in the body as men and women become sexually aroused. Masters and Johnson divide the **sexual response cycle** into four phases: *excitement, plateau, orgasm,* and *resolution.*

The sexual response cycle is characterized by *vasocongestion* and *myotonia.* **Vasocongestion** is the swelling of the genital tissues with blood. It causes erection of the penis and swelling of the area surrounding the vaginal opening. The testes, the nipples, even the earlobes swell as blood vessels dilate in these areas. **Myotonia** is muscle tension. It causes facial grimaces, spasms in the hands and feet, and then the spasms of orgasm.

Erection, vaginal lubrication, and orgasm are all reflexes. That is, they occur automatically in response to adequate sexual stimulation. Of course, the decision to enter a sexual relationship is voluntary, as are the decisions to kiss and pet and so on.

Excitement Phase   Vasocongestion during the **excitement phase** can cause erection in young men within a few seconds after sexual stimulation begins. The scrotal skin thickens, becoming less baggy. The testes increase in size and become elevated.

In the female, excitement is characterized by vaginal lubrication, which may start 10 to 30 seconds after sexual stimulation begins. Vasocongestion swells the **clitoris** and flattens and spreads the vaginal lips. The inner part of the vagina expands. The breasts enlarge, and blood vessels near the surface become more prominent. The nipples may become erect in both men and women. Heart rate and blood pressure increase.

Plateau Phase   The level of sexual arousal remains somewhat stable during the **plateau phase** of the cycle. Because of vasocongestion, men show some increase in the circumference of the head of the penis, which also takes on a purplish hue. The testes are elevated into position for **ejaculation** and may reach one and a half times their unaroused size.

In women, vasocongestion swells the outer part of the vagina, contracting the vaginal opening in preparation for grasping the penis. The inner part of the vagina expands further. The clitoris withdraws beneath the clitoral hood and shortens.

Breathing becomes rapid, like panting. Heart rate may increase to 100 to 160 beats per minute. Blood pressure continues to rise.

Orgasmic Phase   During **orgasm** in the male, muscle contractions propel the ejaculate out of the body. Sensations of pleasure tend to be related to the strength of the contractions and the amount of seminal fluid present. The first 3 to 4 contractions are generally most intense and occur at 0.8-second intervals (5 contractions every 4 seconds). Additional contractions occur more slowly.

Orgasm in the female is manifested by 3 to 15 contractions of the pelvic muscles that surround the vaginal barrel. The contractions first occur at 0.8-second intervals. As in the male, they release sexual tension. Weaker and slower contractions follow.

Blood pressure and heart rate reach a peak, with the heart beating up to 180 times per minute. Respiration may increase to 40 breaths per minute.

Resolution Phase   After orgasm, the body returns to its unaroused state. This is called the **resolution phase.** After orgasm, blood is released from engorged areas, so that erection and clitoral swelling disappear. Blood pressure, heart rate, and breathing return to normal levels. Partners usually feel relaxed and satisfied.

Unlike women, men enter a **refractory period** during which they cannot experience another orgasm or ejaculate. The refractory period of adolescent males may last only minutes, whereas that of men age 50 and above may last from several minutes to a day. Women do not undergo a refractory period and therefore can become quickly rearoused to the point of repeated (multiple) orgasm if they desire and receive continued sexual stimulation.

Sexual response cycle   Masters's and Johnson's model of sexual response, which consists of four stages or phases.

Vasocongestion   Engorgement of blood vessels with blood, which swells the genitals and breasts during sexual arousal.

Myotonia   Muscle tension.

Excitement phase   The first phase of the sexual response cycle, which is characterized by muscle tension, increases in the heart rate, and erection in the male and vaginal lubrication in the female.

Clitoris   The female sex organ that is most sensitive to sexual sensation; a smooth, round knob of tissue that is situated above the urethral opening.

Plateau phase   The second phase of the sexual response cycle, which is characterized by increases in vasocongestion, muscle tension, heart rate, and blood pressure in preparation for orgasm.

Ejaculation   Propulsion of seminal fluid (semen) from the penis by contraction of muscles at the base of the penis.

Orgasm   The height or climax of sexual excitement, involving involuntary muscle contractions, release of sexual tensions, and, usually, subjective feelings of pleasure.

Resolution phase   The fourth phase of the sexual response cycle, during which the body gradually returns to its pre-aroused state.

Refractory period   In the sexual response cycle, a period of time following orgasm during which an individual is not responsive to sexual stimulation.

The sexual response cycle describes what happens when females and males are exposed to sexual stimulation. But what kinds of sexual experiences do people seek? How many sex partners do they have? Who are their partners? *What do we know about the sex lives of people in the United States?* Let us begin to answer some of these questions by reporting the results of some key surveys of sexual behavior.

Surveys of Sexual Behavior

The well-known Kinsey reports (Kinsey et al., 1948, 1953) carefully interviewed 5,300 males and 5,940 females in the United States between 1938 and 1949. Interviewers asked about sexual experiences including masturbation, oral sex, and premarital sex. The nation was astounded to be informed that the majority of males masturbated and had engaged in sexual intercourse prior to marriage. Moreover, significant minorities of females reported engaging in these behaviors. But Kinsey had not obtained a random sample of the population. His samples underrepresented people of color, people in rural areas, older people, poor people, Catholics, and Jews. There is thus no way of knowing whether or not Kinsey's results accurately mirrored general American sexual behavior at the time. But the *relationships* Kinsey uncovered, such as the positive link between level of education and premarital sex, may be accurate enough.

A more recent survey—the National Health and Social Life Survey (NHSLS)—interviewed 3,432 people (Laumann et al., 1994) and may provide our most accurate information. Of this number, 3,159 were English-speaking adults aged 18 to 59. The other 273 respondents were obtained by purposefully oversampling African American and Hispanic American households to obtain more information about these ethnic groups. The sample probably represents the overall U.S. adult population quite well, but it may include too few Asian Americans, Native Americans, and Jews to offer much information about these groups. The NHSLS team identified households in various locales and obtained an overall participation rate of close to 80%.

The NHSLS considered the sociocultural factors of sex, level of education, religion, and race/ethnicity in many aspects of people's sexual behavior, including their number of sex partners (see Table 9.2). Males in the survey reported higher numbers of sex partners than females did. For example, 1 male in 3 (33%) reported having 11 or more sex partners since the age of 18. This compares with fewer than 1 woman in 10 (9%). On the other hand, most Americans limit their sex partners to a handful or fewer.

Education appears to be a liberating influence on sexual behavior. People with some college, or who have completed college, report more sex partners than those who attended only grade school or high school. Conservative religious experience, on the other hand, acts as a restraint. Liberal Protestants (for example, Methodists, Lutherans, Presbyterians, Episcopalians, and United Churches of Christ) and people who say they have no religion report higher numbers of sex partners than Catholics and more conservative Protestants (such as Baptists, Pentecostals, and member of Churches of Christ and Assemblies of God).

Ethnicity is also connected with sexual behavior. The research findings in Table 9.2 suggest that European Americans and African Americans have the highest numbers of sex partners. Latino and Latina Americans are mostly Catholic, and Catholicism may restrain sexual behavior. Asian Americans appear to be the most sexually restrained ethnic group. However, the sample sizes of Asian Americans and Native Americans are small.

reflect & relate

What are the attitudes of most people from your cultural background toward gay males and lesbians? Do you share these attitudes? Why or why not?

Heterosexual Referring to people who are sexually aroused by, and interested in forming romantic relationships with, people of the other sex.

Homosexual Referring to people who are sexually aroused by, and interested in forming romantic relationships with, people of the same sex. (Derived from the Greek *homos*, meaning "same," not from the Latin *homo*, meaning "man.")

Sexual Orientation

The great majority of people have a **heterosexual** orientation. That is, they are sexually attracted to, and interested in forming romantic relationships with, people of the other sex. Some people, however, have a **homosexual** orientation. They are attracted to and interested in forming romantic relationships with people of their own sex. Males with a homosexual orientation are referred to as *gay males*. Females with a homosexual orientation are referred to as *lesbians*. But homosexual males and females are sometimes categorized together as "gay people," or "gays." *Bisexual* people are attracted to both females and males.

TABLE 9.2 ■ Number of Sex Partners Since Age 18 as Found in the National Health and Social Life Survey *

SOCIOCULTURAL FACTORS	NUMBER OF SEX PARTNERS (%)					
	0	1	2–4	5–10	11–20	21+
Gender						
Male	3	20	21	23	16	17
Female	3	32	36	20	6	3
Education						
Less than high school	4	27	36	19	9	6
High school graduate	3	30	29	20	10	7
Some college	2	24	29	23	12	9
College graduate	2	24	26	24	11	13
Advanced degree	4	25	26	23	10	13
Religion						
None	3	16	29	20	16	16
Liberal, moderate Protestant	2	23	31	23	12	8
Conservative Protestant	3	30	30	20	10	7
Catholic	4	27	29	23	8	9
Race/Ethnicity						
European American	3	26	29	22	11	9
African American	2	18	34	24	11	11
Latino and Latina American	3	36	27	17	8	9
Asian American**	6	46	25	14	6	3
Native American**	5	28	35	23	5	5

SOURCE: Adapted from *The Social Organization of Sexuality: Sexual Practices in the United States* (table 5.1C, p. 179), by E. O. Laumann, J. H. Gagnon, R. T. Michael, & S. Michaels, 1994, Chicago: University of Chicago Press. Adapted by permission of Chicago University Press.

*Conducted by a research team centered at the University of Chicago.

**These sample sizes are quite small.

Sexual orientation The directionality of one's sexual and romantic interests; that is, whether one is sexually attracted to, and desires to form a romantic relationship with, members of the other sex or of one's own sex.

Surveys find that about 3% of the males and 2% of the females in the United States identify themselves as homosexual (Laumann et al., 1994). Theories of the origins of **sexual orientation** look both at nature and nurture—the biological makeup of the individual and environmental influences. Several theories bridge the two. *What do we know about the origins of gay male and lesbian sexual orientations?*

Learning theorists look for the roles of factors such as reinforcement and observational learning. From this perspective, reinforcement of sexual behavior with members of one's own sex—as in reaching orgasm with them when members of the other sex are unavailable—might affect one's sexual orientation. Similarly, childhood sexual abuse by someone of the same sex could lead to fantasies about sex with people of one's own sex and affect sexual orientation. Observation of others engaged in enjoyable male–male or female–female sexual encounters could also affect the development of sexual orientation. But critics point out that most individuals become aware of their sexual orientation before they have sexual contacts with other people of either sex (Laumann et al., 1994). Moreover, in a society that generally condemns homosexuality, young people are unlikely to believe that male–male or female–female contacts will have positive effects for them.

Randy Gregory holds his daughter Laura Jewel Gregory, 1, with life partner, Kevin Boynton, outside their home.

Michael Mulvey/Dallas Morning News/Corbis

A Closer Look
Pheromones and Sexual Orientation

Vision is normally the dominant sense in humans. We tend to gather more information about other people by looking at them than by smelling them or touching them (Wade, 2005). In the film "Scent of a Woman," however, Al Pacino played a blind man who was drawn to women by their odor. Are there odors that are characteristic of the other sex? If so, how important are they in determining sexual attraction?

Some answers are suggested by a study by Swedish researchers (Savic et al., 2005) who used PET scans to show that gay and heterosexual men respond differently to smelling chemicals that may affect sexual arousal, and that the gay men respond similarly to women (see Figure 9.4). The study involved suspected **pheromones,** which are chemicals emitted by a member of a species to evoke a response in another member of the species. Previously, researchers had found that pheromones may enhance people's moods, have effects on fertility, and provide a basis for sexual communication at a level below conscious awareness.

The Swedish study investigated the effects of two chemicals: a testosterone derivative produced in men's sweat and an estrogen-like compound found in women's urine. Most odors activate neurons in specific regions of the brain, increasing the blood flow to these regions and causing them to "light up" when imaged by the PET scan. The estrogen-like compound activated the usual smell-related areas in women, but it lighted up the hypothalamus—a structure involved in sexual behavior—in heterosexual men. The chemical extracted from male sweat, in contrast, did the opposite; it activated the hypothalamus in women and the usual smell-related areas in men. Each chemical seemed to be just another odor with one sex but a pheromone with the other. Gay men in the study, however, responded to the chemicals as women did. That is, their hypothalamus was lighted up by the chemical drawn from male sweat. Lesbians were also studied, but the data were complex and not ready for publication (Wade, 2005).

It must be noted that the Swedish study does not reveal cause and effect. A "snapshot" was taken of brain functioning at a point in time. The snapshot did not show how the brain's responses develop. Were the activity patterns in heterosexual and gay men a cause of their sexual orientation or an effect of their sexual orientation? If sexual orientation has a genetic basis, or is influenced by hormones in the womb or at puberty, it might be that the neurons in the hypothalamus become hardwired in a way that shapes sexual orientation. Conversely, the findings could mean that experience leads straight and gay men to respond in different ways.

In any event, the study does suggest a role for pheromones in human sexual response and lays the groundwork for further research. ■

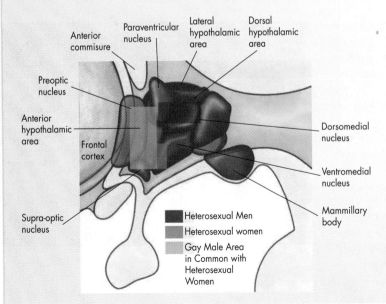

Figure 9.4

Who Lights Up Your Hypothalamus?
Certain areas of the hypothalamus "light up" when heterosexual males smell an estrogen-like compound (estratetraenol) found in women's urine, when heterosexual women smell an androgen-like compound (androstadienone), and when gay males smell the androstadienone. The hypothalamus of gay males responds similarly to that of heterosexual women when the person is presented with the odor of androstadienone. Note the locations of the ventromedial nucleus and the lateral hypothalamus, which are relevant to the chapter's earlier discussion of the hunger drive.
Source: Savic et al., "Brain response to putative pheromones in homosexual men," *Proceedings of the National Association of Sciences, 102,* fig. 3, p. 7539. Reprinted by permission.

There is evidence for genetic factors in sexual orientation (Bailey, 2003b; Dawood et al., 2000; Kendler et al., 2000c; Rahman & Wilson, 2003). One study found that 22% of the brothers of 51 gay men were gay or bisexual, although one would expect to find only 3% of the brothers to also be gay if the relationship were coincidental (Pillard & Weinrich, 1986). Twin studies also support a role for genes. About 52% of identical (MZ) twin pairs are "concordant" (in agreement) for a gay male sexual orientation, as compared with 22% for fraternal (DZ) twins (Bailey & Pillard, 1991). Monozygotic (MZ) twins fully share their genetic heritage, whereas dizygotic (DZ) twins, like other pairs of siblings, overlap 50%. Bear in mind that MZ twins are more likely to be dressed alike and treated alike than DZ twins. Thus, their greater concordance for a gay sexual orientation may at least in part reflect environmental factors (Kendler et al., 2000c).

In many species, there is little room for thinking about sex and deciding whether an individual will pursue sexual relationships with males or females. Sexual motivation comes under the governance of sex hormones (Hill et al., 2005; Holmes et al., 2005; Sartor et al., 2005). And much sexual motivation is determined by whether the brains and sex organs of fetuses are bathed in large doses of testosterone in the uterus. In male fetuses, testosterone is normally produced by the developing testes. Yet female fetuses may also be exposed to testosterone. They can be flooded with testosterone naturally if they share the uterus with many male siblings. Researchers can also inject male sex hormones into the uterus. When they do, the sex organs of females become masculinized in appearance, and their brains become organized in the male direction, creating a tendency toward masculine-typed behavior patterns at maturity, including mating with other females (Crews, 1994).

It has been shown, then, that sex hormones predispose nonhumans to stereotypical masculine or feminine mating patterns. Do sex hormones influence the developing human embryo and fetus as they affect rodents? This possibility continues to receive intensive study (Rahman et al., 2004; Van Anders & Hampson, 2005). And if prenatal hormone levels affect the sexual orientation of the fetus, what causes the fluctuation in hormone levels? We're not sure. Hormone levels in utero are affected by genetic factors and maternal stress, along with other factors. How does maternal stress fit into the equation? Stressful experiences trigger the release of stress hormones including *epinephrine* and *cortisol*. Cortisol is a steroid that is chemically similar to testosterone. Cortisol could thus affect the prenatal development of the brain, especially if the mother is under continuous stress. It is possible that the brains of some gay males were feminized in utero and that the brains of some lesbians were masculinized in utero (Collaer & Hines, 1995).

We have to conclude by confessing that much about the development of sexual orientation remains speculative. There are possible roles for prenatal exposure to certain hormones. Exposure to these hormones, in turn, may be related to genetic factors, use of drugs, and maternal stress. Moreover, the possibility that childhood experiences play a role has not been ruled out. But the interactions among these factors largely remain a mystery. Nor is there reason to believe that the development of sexual orientation follows the same pattern for all people (Garnets, 2002).

We noted that testosterone is connected with the sex drive. In the following section we see that testosterone also appears to be connected with aggression.

reflect & relate

Have you heard the term *sexual preference?* How does it differ from *sexual orientation?* The word *preference* implies that people choose their sexual orientation. Do you believe that people *decide* whether to be heterosexual or gay? Explain.

Pheromone A chemical secretion detected by other members of the same species that stimulates stereotypical behaviors.

◯ Learning Connections

◀◀ *Sexual Motivation—Attitudes and Behavior* ▶▶

Learning Connections

REVIEW:

9 _____ has/have a restraining effect on sexual behavior.
 (a) Higher education,
 (b) Television,
 (c) Testosterone,
 (d) Conservative religious beliefs.

10 The most common sexual problem among women is
 (a) painful sex,
 (b) lack of sexual desire or interest,
 (c) greater interest in sex than men have,
 (d) confusion about their sexual orientation.

11 Researchers suspect that sex hormones are most likely to affect sexual orientation
 (a) prenatally,

 (b) during childhood,
 (c) at puberty,
 (d) during adulthood.

12 Twin studies
 (a) show that sexual orientation is not inherited,
 (b) suggest that genetic factors play a role in sexual orientation,
 (c) show that children reared in the same way develop the same sexual orientation,
 (d) show that heredity is involved in sexual orientation among women but not men.

CRITICAL THINKING:
If sex is a natural function, do cultures have the right to restrict the expression of sexual impulses? Explain your view.

Go to www
http://academic.cengage.com/psychology/rathus
for an interactive version of this review.

AGGRESSION: THE DARK SIDE OF MOTIVATION

There are armed conflicts of one kind or another on every continent. There is suicide terrorism. There is murder and battering, often by people's most intimate partners. There is rape. *What have psychologists learned about biological and psychological influences on aggressive behavior?*

■ Biology, Chemistry, Aggression, and Gender Differences

Although there are exceptions, in most cultures, it is the males who march off to war and battle for glory (and sneaker commercials). Numerous biological structures and chemicals appear to be involved in aggression. In response to certain stimuli, many nonhumans show instinctive aggressive reactions. For example, the male robin responds aggressively to the red breast of another robin. Such behavior is automatic, although it can be modified by learning. The hypothalamus appears to be involved in this inborn reaction pattern. Electrical stimulation of part of the hypothalamus triggers stereotypical aggressive behaviors in many nonhumans. However, in humans, whose brains are more complex, other brain structures, such as the prefrontal cortex, normally moderate aggressive impulses (Elliott & Mirsky, 2002; Silver et al., 2005).

Chemistry is involved in aggression, especially testosterone (Rilling et al., 2004). Testosterone appears to affect the tendencies to dominate and control other people. For example, aggressive boys and adolescents are likely to have higher testosterone levels than their less aggressive peers (Chance et al., 2000). Members of so-called "rambunctious" fraternities have higher testosterone levels, on average, than members of more "well-behaved" fraternities (Dabbs et al., 1996).

◆ **Truth or Fiction Revisited:** Males have higher testosterone levels than women do and are also (usually) more aggressive than women, especially toward male strangers (Felson, 2002; Hines & Saudino, 2003; Pope et al., 2000; Zeichner et al., 2003). Yet all is not biological. In her classic review of the research on gender differences in aggression, Ann Frodi and her colleagues (1977) found that females behave as aggressively as males do when they have the means to do so and believe that aggression is justified. The Frodi group also found that:

■ Females are more likely to feel anxious or guilty about aggression. Such feelings inhibit aggressive behavior.
■ Females are more likely to empathize with the victim. Empathy encourages helping behavior, not aggression.
■ Gender differences in aggression tend to decrease when the victim is anonymous. Anonymity may prevent females from empathizing with their victims.

Let us look more deeply into psychological aspects of aggression.

■ **Aggressive Behavior**
Is human aggression instinctive or is it learned? Do people just "explode" in certain situations, or do they decide to behave aggressively?

Psychological Perspectives on Aggression

Psychologists have recognized the importance of understanding (and curbing) human aggressiveness. Let us consider various psychological views of aggression.

Psychodynamic Theory and Aggression Sigmund Freud believed that aggressive impulses are inevitable reactions to the frustrations of daily life. According to Freud, children (and adults) naturally desire to vent aggressive impulses on other people, including parents, because even the most attentive parents cannot gratify all their demands immediately. Yet children also fear punishment and loss of love, so they repress most aggressive impulses.

Cognitive Psychology and Aggression Cognitive psychologists assert that people naturally try to understand their environment and make decisions. Frustration and discomfort may set the stage for aggression, but aggression is *not* automatic. Cognitive factors intervene (Berkowitz, 2004a). Our behavior is influenced not only by our feelings, but also by our values, our interpretation of our situations, and by personal choice. Thus people who believe that aggression is necessary and justified—as during wartime—are likely to act aggressively. People who believe that a war or act of aggression is unjust, or who oppose aggression under all circumstances, are unlikely to be aggressive (Archer, 2001; Lotufo & Martins, 2004).

Cognitive researchers also find that some people who act aggressively distort other people's motives. They may assume that other people intend them harm when they actually do not (Dodge et al., 2002). People are also more likely to respond aggressively to a provocation when they magnify the importance of the "insult" (Lochman & Wells, 2002). How do you respond when someone bumps into you? If you see it as an intentional insult to your "honor," you may respond aggressively. If you view it as an accident or a social problem in need of a solution, you are less likely to be aggressive.

Learning and Aggression From the behavioral perspective, learning is acquired through reinforcement. Organisms that are reinforced for aggressive behavior are more likely to behave aggressively in similar situations. Environmental consequences make it more likely that an animal will be rewarded for aggression if it "picks on" a smaller, weaker animal. Strong, agile organisms are likely to be reinforced for aggressive behavior.

Among most animals, reinforcement is physical, for example, food, mating, or escaping a predator. Humans also respond to social reinforcers, such as social approval. Research shows that children are less likely to behave aggressively when teachers and fellow students disapprove of aggression (Henry et al., 2000).

Aggressive behaviors themselves may either be instinctive, as in the case of many nonhumans, or acquired by reinforcement. However, social cognitive theorists—like other cognitive theorists—believe that consciousness and choice play key roles in human aggression.

reflect & relate

Consider people whom you would label "explosive." Do you believe that they actually explode or that they *decide* where and when to behave violently? Explain.

Andre Ringuette/Getty Images

Social cognitive theorists believe that we are not likely to act aggressively unless we believe that aggression is appropriate under the circumstances and likely to be reinforced.

■ Environmental Factors and Aggression: When the Heat Is On

Environmental factors can contribute to the likelihood of aggressive behavior. Bad-smelling pollutants decrease feelings of attraction and heighten aggression (Baron et al., 2006; Zala & Penn, 2004). Extremes of noise can also trigger violence. If you and your partner have had a fight and are then exposed to a tire blowout, look out. Angry people are more likely to behave aggressively when exposed to a sudden noise of 95 dB than one of 55 dB (Donnerstein & Wilson, 1976).

Extreme heat also apparently makes some people hot under the collar (Anderson, 2001; Simister & Cooper, 2005). That is, high temperatures are connected with aggression. The frequency of honking at traffic lights in Phoenix increases with the temperature (Kenrick & MacFarlane, 1986). In Raleigh, North Carolina, the incidence of rape and aggravated assault rises with the average monthly temperature (Simpson & Perry, 1990).

Some psychologists suggest that the probability of aggressive behavior continues to increase as the temperature soars (Bushman et al., 2005). Others argue that once temperatures become extremely aversive, people tend to avoid aggressive behavior so that they will not be doubly struck by hot temperature and a hot temper (Cohn & Rotton, 2005; Rotton & Cohn, 2000, 2004).

The overall message seems to be something like this: Human survival on planet Earth no longer requires physical aggressiveness in the way it once may have. Yes, aggression may be affected by testosterone levels and other biological factors, but that does not mean that human aggression is mechanical or automatic. Yes, aggressive behaviors may be learned, but people appraise their situations and decide whether or not to act aggressively. People's cultural milieus are one source of information people use in making decisions. When aggression is valued within a culture, or seen as "normal," people are more likely to choose to act aggressively. Environmental factors such as unpleasant odors and sudden noises also affect the likelihood that people will behave aggressively.

() Learning Connections

◀◀   *Aggression — The Dark Side of Motivation*   ▶▶

REVIEW:

13 The hormone _____ affects tendencies to dominate and control other people.
    (a) melatonin,
    (b) thyroxin,
    (c) testosterone,
    (d) prolactin.

14 Cognitive psychologists assert that people are likely to behave aggressively when
    (a) they appraise the situation and decide aggression is appropriate,
    (b) their hypothalamus is stimulated,
    (c) reinforcement is available for aggressive behavior,
    (d) they are frustrated.

CRITICAL THINKING:
If aggression is "natural" throughout the animal kingdom, are societies justified in setting limits on human aggression? Explain.

Go to
http://academic.cengage.com/psychology/rathus
for an interactive version of this review.

ACHIEVEMENT MOTIVATION: "JUST DO IT"?

Many students persist in studying despite being surrounded by distractions. Many people strive relentlessly to get ahead, to "make it," to earn large sums of money, to invent, to accomplish the impossible. ***Why do some people strive to get ahead?*** Psychological research has pointed to these people having something called *achievement motivation* (Robbins et al., 2005).

Psychologist David McClelland (1958) helped pioneer the assessment of achievement motivation through evaluation of fantasies. One method involves the Thematic Apperception Test (TAT), developed by Henry Murray. The TAT contains cards with pictures and drawings that are subject to various interpretations. Individuals are shown one or more TAT cards and asked to construct stories about the pictured theme: to indicate what led up to it, what the characters are thinking and feeling, and what is likely to happen.

One TAT card is similar to that in Figure 9.5. The meaning of the card is ambiguous—unclear. Is the girl sleeping, thinking about the book, wishing she were out with friends? Consider two stories that could be told about this card:

Story 1: "She's upset that she's got to read the book because she's behind in her assignments and doesn't particularly like to work. She'd much rather be out with her friends, and she may very well sneak out to do just that."

Story 2: "She's thinking, 'Someday I'll be a great scholar. I'll write books like this, and everybody will be proud of me.' She reads all the time."

The second story suggests the presence of more achievement motivation than the first. Classic studies find that people with high achievement motivation earn higher grades than people with comparable learning ability but lower achievement motivation. They are more likely to earn high salaries and be promoted than less motivated people with similar opportunities (Aronoff & Litevin, 1971; Orpen, 1995).

McClelland (1965) used the TAT to sort college students into groups—students with high achievement motivation and students with low achievement motivation. He found that 83% of college graduates with high achievement motivation found jobs in occupations characterized by risk, decision making, and the chance for great success, such as business management, sales, or self-employment. Most (70%) of the graduates who chose nonentrepreneurial positions showed low achievement motivation. People with high achievement motivation seem to prefer challenges and are willing to take moderate risks to achieve their goals.

Figure 9.5

Tapping Fantasies in Personality Research

This picture is similar to a Thematic Apperception Test card used to measure the need for achievement. What is happening in this picture? What is the person thinking and feeling? What is going to happen? Your answers to these questions reflect your own needs as well as the content of the picture itself.

■ Extrinsic Versus Intrinsic Motives: What Flavor Is Your Achievement Motivation?

Do you want to do well in this course? If you do, why? Carol Dweck (e.g., Molden & Dweck, 2000) finds that achievement motivation can be driven by performance or learning goals, or both. For example, are you motivated mainly by performance goals? That is, is your grade in the course of most importance? If it is, it may be in part because your motives concern tangible rewards such as getting into graduate school, landing a good job, reaping approval from parents or your instructor, or avoiding criticism. Performance goals are usually met through extrinsic rewards such as praise and income. Research suggests that tangible rewards, such as money, can serve as an incentive for maintaining good grades. These rewards

reflect & relate

Do you seem to be driven mainly by performance goals or learning goals in this course and in your other courses? Explain.

tend to have a more lasting effect, however, when students look upon incentives as signs that they are intelligent and capable (Spencer et al., 2005).

Or is it learning goals that mainly motivate you to do well? That is, is your central motive the enhancing of your knowledge and skills—your ability to understand and master the subject matter? Learning goals usually lead to intrinsic rewards, such as satisfaction with oneself. Students who develop learning goals often have parents with strong achievement motivation who encourage their children to think and act independently. Parents and teachers help children develop learning goals by showing warmth and praising them for their efforts to learn, exposing them to novel and stimulating experiences, and encouraging persistence (Dweck, 2002a). Children who are stimulated in this way tend to set high standards for themselves, associate their achievements with self-worth, and attribute their achievements to their own efforts rather than to chance or to the intervention of others (Dweck, 2002b; Grouzet et al., 2004; Marshall & Brown, 2004).

Many of us strive to meet both performance and learning goals in our courses as well as in other areas of life. Grades are important because they are connected with (very) tangible benefits, but learning for its own sake is also of value—and can provide great pleasure!

( ) Learning Connections

◀◀ *Achievement Motivation—"Just Do It"?* **▶▶**

REVIEW:

15 McClelland assessed achievement motivation by means of
 (a) interviews,
 (b) observing behavior,
 (c) comparing salaries,
 (d) evaluating fantasies.

16 Money works best as an incentive for students to achieve when
 (a) it leads students to believe that they are capable,
 (b) it is provided on a fixed-interval schedule,
 (c) it is given only when students raise their grade point averages,
 (d) students are mainly influenced by learning goals.

CRITICAL THINKING:
Some people strive harder to get ahead than others. Is it circular reasoning to "explain" the difference in terms of more or less achievement motivation?

Go to
http://academic.cengage.com/psychology/rathus
for an interactive version of this review.

EMOTION: ADDING COLOR TO LIFE

Emotions color our lives. We are green with envy, red with anger, blue with sorrow. Positive emotions such as love and desire can fill our days with pleasure. Negative emotions such as fear, depression, and anger can fill us with dread and make each day a chore. *Just what is an emotion?*

An emotion can be a response to a situation, in the way that fear is a response to a threat. An emotion can motivate behavior (e.g., anger can motivate us to act aggressively). An emotion can also be a goal in itself. We may behave in ways that will lead us to experience happiness or feelings of love. Emotions are thus intertwined with motivation. We are driven by emotions and meeting—or failing to meet—our needs can have powerful emotional results.

TABLE 9.3 ■ Components of Emotions

EMOTION	PHYSIOLOGICAL	COGNITIVE	BEHAVIORAL
Fear	Sympathetic arousal	Belief that one is in danger	Avoidance tendencies
Anger	Sympathetic and parasympathetic arousal	Frustration or belief that one is being mistreated	Attack tendencies
Depression	Parasympathetic arousal	Thoughts of helplessness, hopelessness, worthlessness	Inactivity, possible self-destructive tendencies

Emotions are defined as feeling states with physiological, cognitive, and behavioral components (Carlson & Hatfield, 1992). In terms of physiology, strong emotions arouse the autonomic nervous system (Gomez et al., 2005; see Chapter 2). The greater the arousal, the more intense the emotion. It also appears that the type of arousal affects the emotion being experienced. Although the word *emotion* might seem to be about feeling and not about thinking, cognitions—particularly interpretations of the meanings of events—are important aspects of emotions. *Fear,* which usually occurs in response to a threat, involves cognitions that one is in danger as well as arousal of the **sympathetic nervous system** (e.g., rapid heartbeat and breathing, sweating, muscle tension). Emotions also involve behavioral tendencies. Fear is connected with behavioral tendencies to avoid or escape from a particular situation (see Table 9.3). As a response to a social provocation, *anger* involves cognitions that the provocateur should be paid back, arousal of both the sympathetic and **parasympathetic nervous systems,** and tendencies to attack. *Depression* usually involves cognitions of helplessness and hopelessness, parasympathetic arousal, and tendencies toward inactivity—or, sometimes, self-destruction. *Happiness, grief, jealousy, disgust, embarrassment, liking*—all have cognitive, physiological, and behavioral components.

The Expression of Emotions: The Smile Seen Around the World?

Happiness and sadness are found in all cultures, but, *How can we tell when other people are happy or sad?* It turns out that the expression of many emotions may be universal (Ekman, 2003). Smiling is apparently a universal sign of friendliness and approval. Baring the teeth, as noted by Charles Darwin (1872) in the 19th century, may be a universal sign of anger. As the originator of the theory of evolution, Darwin believed that the universal recognition of facial expressions would have survival value. For example, in the absence of language, facial expressions could signal the approach of enemies (or friends).

Most investigators (e.g., Buss, 1992; Ekman, 2003; Izard, 1994) concur that certain facial expressions suggest the same emotions in all people. Moreover, people in diverse cultures recognize the emotions manifested by certain facial expressions. Paul Ekman (1999) describes his classic research in which he took photographs of people exhibiting anger, disgust, fear, happiness, sadness, and surprise (see Figure 9.6). He then asked people around the world to indicate what emotions were being depicted. Those queried ranged from European college students to members of the Fore, a tribe that dwells in the New Guinea highlands. All groups, including the Fore, who had almost no contact with Western culture, agreed on the emotions being portrayed. The Fore also displayed familiar facial expressions when asked how they would respond if they were the characters in stories that called for basic emotional responses. Ekman and his colleagues (1987) obtained similar results in a study of ten cultures. In that study, participants were allowed to identify more than one emotion in facial expressions. The participants generally agreed on which two emotions were being shown and which emotion was more intense.

Emotion A feeling state with cognitive, physiological, and behavioral components.

Sympathetic nervous system The branch of the autonomic nervous system that is most active during processes that spend body energy from stored reserves, such as in a fight-or-flight reaction to a predator or when you are anxious about a big test. When people experience fear, the sympathetic nervous system accelerates the heart rate, raises the blood pressure, tenses muscles, and so on.

Parasympathetic nervous system The branch of the autonomic nervous system that is most active during processes that restore reserves of energy to the body, such as relaxing and eating. When people relax, the parasympathetic nervous system decelerates the heart rate, normalizes the blood pressure, relaxes muscles, and so on. The parasympathetic division also stimulates digestion.

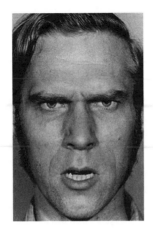
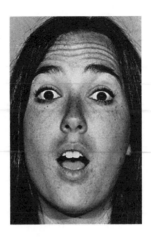
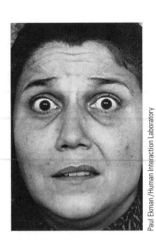

Paul Ekman/Human Interaction Laboratory

Figure 9.6
Photographs Used in Research by Paul Ekman
Ekman's research suggests that the facial expressions connected with several important emotions such as happiness, anger, surprise, and fear are universally recognized.

Richard Ellis/The Image Works

■ **Christopher Reeve: Poster Boy for Positive Psychology**
The actor, who played *Superman* in several films, turned out not to be invulnerable when he was thrown from a horse. The accident paralyzed Reeve but did not destroy his fighting spirit or his tendency toward happiness. Reeve was a perfect exemplar of positive psychology. Upon his death, his physicians suggested that Reeve's positive outlook may have helped him survive for nearly a decade following his paralysis.

Positive psychology The field of psychology that is about personal well-being and satisfaction; joy, sensual pleasure, and happiness; and optimism and hope for the future.

An interesting study found that women's college yearbook pictures predicted life outcomes as much as 30 years later. LeeAnne Harker and Dacher Keltner (2001) found that women who showed more positive emotions in yearbook photos—such as by smiling—were more likely to show social competence, personal well-being, and even happier marriages as the years went by. By the way, their physical attractiveness did not seem to matter; it was the display of positive emotions that told the lifelong tale.

On the other hand, there is no perfect one-to-one relationship between facial expressions and emotions. Facial expressions sometimes occur in the absence of the emotion they are thought to accompany (Camras, 2000). As noted by psychologist Joseph Campos (2000), the voice, posture, and gestures also provide clues as to what people are feeling and about to do.

Many psychologists help individuals cope with negative emotions such as fear, anger, and depression. But psychologists have also studied positive emotions, such as happiness, and considered ways in which you might increase your own feelings of happiness.

■— "Is Evvvvrybody Happy?" An Excursion into Positive Psychology

Ted Lewis, the Great Depression–era bandleader, used to begin his act by asking, "Is evvvvrybody happy?" Well, everybody is not happy, but surveys do suggest that most people in developed nations are satisfied with their lives (Cummins & Nistico, 2002). Many people might think that psychologists are interested only in negative emotions such as anxiety, depression, and anger. Not at all. An area of psychology called **positive psychology** deals with positive emotions such as happiness and love, optimism and hope, and joy and sensual pleasures (Aspinwall & Staudinger, 2003; Hendrick & Hendrick, 2002; Keyes & Haidt, 2003).

What factors contribute to happiness? Are some people just "born happy" or do life experiences determine happiness? What factors interfere with happiness? Some psychologists, such as David Lykken (Lykken & Csikszentmihalyi, 2001), believe that genetic factors play a powerful role in happiness. They note that happiness tends to run in families and that we tend to have a more or less stable level of happiness throughout much of our lives (Easterlin, 2002). Positive events such as learning that the person we love also loves us, having a loved one support our goals, or recognition at work can certainly raise our level of happiness at the moment (Feeney, 2004). Similarly, negative life events, such as the loss of a loved one, financial reverses, or injuries can depress us—and understandably so. Yet we may tend to bounce back to a more or less characteristic level of happiness, as did the actor Christopher Reeve following the accident—being thrown from a horse—that paralyzed him.

Following Reeve's death in 2004, his physicians suggested that Reeve's positive outlook helped him survive in his paralyzed condition for nearly a decade.

Which life experiences contribute to happiness? ◆▶ **Truth or Fiction Revisited**: Despite the saying that "money can't buy you happiness," surveys in the United States, Russia, China, and Latin America suggest that people tend to be happier when they live in affluent societies or earn decent incomes (Frey & Stutzer, 2000; Graham & Pettinato, 2001; Lever, 2004; Schyns, 2001; Tsou & Liu, 2001). It may not be that money makes people happy in itself, but when we have enough money, at least we don't have to worry about money (Cummins, 2000).

U.S. surveys reveal more evidence for a role for social and socioeconomic factors in happiness. For example, European Americans tend to be happier than African Americans, and more educated people tend to be happier than less well educated people (Easterlin, 2001). The persistence of differences according to race and education suggests that socio-economic circumstances are in fact important contributors to happiness (Easterlin, 2001).

People who are married (Tsou & Liu, 2001) and who have social support (Feeney, 2004; Lu, 1999) tend to be happier than "loners." Happy people also tend to be open to new experiences; they are more willing to risk becoming involved in new relationships (Rath, 2002).

Research has also suggested that religious people are happier than those who are not, as was found to be the case in studies of Americans, Chinese people, and Israelis (Francis et al., 2004; Swinyard et al., 2001). The Swinyard study found that one's inner life—one's feeling of connectedness to important things outside oneself—was found to be a greater contributor to happiness than material possessions. Chinese college students tend to think about happiness in terms of feelings of contentment, inner harmony, personal achievement, physical wellness, spiritual enrichment, hopefulness about the future, generosity, and self-development (Lu, 2001).

reflect & relate

Do you know anyone who almost always seems to be happy? How do you explain his or her happiness?

Life Connections
"Come On! Get Happy!" A Possible or Impossible Dream?

Are there lessons for you in these research findings on happiness? Perhaps. But keep in mind that the studies are correlational; for example, not one of them provided individuals with money to determine whether affluence would affect their mood. Nor did any of them manipulate people's attitudes toward life and measure the outcomes. Still, there might be no harm in placing oneself within the groups of people who are more likely to be happy. Here are some suggestions:

- Take advantage of your education to develop knowledge and skills that can help you be free from want. Even if money does not make you happy in itself, it is good not to have to worry about money.
- Do not let the idea that other people have more prevent you from appreciating what you have.
- Value social relationships. Be open to new friends.
- Think about the meaning of your life and whether you can make your life more meaningful to yourself.
- Consider whether you are generally optimistic or pessimistic about your future. If you are pessimistic, examine the reasons for your pessimism and work to overcome them. If you cannot find reasons for your pessimism, challenge yourself to change your outlook.
- Consider whether you blame yourself too much when things go wrong or give yourself too little credit when things go right.

Noshir Desai/Corbis

■ **An Indian Laughing Club**
Are they laughing because they are happy, or are they happy because they are laughing? Or are both true? These people are part of a club in India where over 50 people gather together to laugh and become happier.

In the section on the facial-feedback hypothesis, we see that you may also find it worthwhile to "put on a happy face." ■

Facial-feedback hypothesis The view that stereotypical facial expressions can contribute to stereotypical emotions.

DPA/RS3/The Image Works

■ **Is Smiling Caused by Feeling Good, or Does Smiling Cause Us to Feel Good?**
Smiling is usually a response to feeling good within, but experimental research into the facial-feedback hypothesis suggests that the act of smiling can also enhance our moods.

Then there are the attitudinal aspects of happiness (Cheng & Furnham, 2001; Cummins & Nistico, 2002). Numerous studies have shown that people at any income level can make themselves miserable when they compare their incomes to those who bring in more (Schyns, 2001; Stutzer, 2004). Happiness also tends to be accompanied by optimism—a cognitive bias toward assuming that things will work out (Aspinwall & Staudinger, 2003; Diener et al., 2000; Keyes & Haidt, 2003). But the "bias" is not groundless, because happy people often believe in their ability to effect change. Thus they try harder. They are also willing to pat themselves on the back for their successes and are not quick to blame themselves when things go wrong. These attitudes contribute to self-esteem, yet another factor in happiness.

■ The Facial-Feedback Hypothesis: Does Smiling Make You Happy?

The face has a special place among visual stimuli. Social animals like humans need to be able to differentiate and recognize members of their group and, in people, the face is the most distinctive key to identity (Parr et al., 2000). Faces are also a key to social communication. Facial expressions reflect emotional states, and our ability to "read" these expressions enables us to interact appropriately with other people.

It is known that various emotional states give rise to certain patterns of electrical activity in the facial muscles and in the brain (Cacioppo et al., 1988). But can it work the other way around? The **facial-feedback hypothesis** argues that facial expressions can also affect our emotional state, and that the causal relationship between emotions and facial expressions can work in the opposite direction. ***Can smiling give rise to feelings of good will? Can frowning produce anger?*** Perhaps they can.

Psychological research has yielded some interesting findings concerning the facial-feedback hypothesis. Inducing people to smile, for example, leads them to report more positive feelings and to rate cartoons as more humorous (Basic Behavioral Science Task Force, 1996c; Soussignan, 2002). When induced to frown, they rate cartoons as more aggressive. When they exhibit pain through facial expressions, they rate electric shocks as more painful.

What are the possible links between facial feedback and emotion? One is arousal. Intense contraction of facial muscles such as those used in signifying fear heightens arousal, which, in turn, boosts emotional response. Feedback from the contraction of facial muscles may also induce emotions. Engaging in the "Duchenne smile," characterized by "crow's feet wrinkles around the eyes and a subtle drop in the eye cover fold so that the skin above the eye moves down slightly toward the eyeball" (Ekman, 2003) can induce pleasant feelings (Soussignan, 2002).

You may have heard the British expression "Keep a stiff upper lip" as a recommendation for handling stress. It might be that a "stiff" lip suppresses emotional response—as long as the lip is relaxed rather than quivering with fear or tension. But when the lip is stiffened through strong muscle tension, facial feedback may heighten emotional response.

Theories of Emotion: "How Do You Feel?"

David, 32, is not sleeping well. He wakes before dawn and cannot get back to sleep. His appetite is off, his energy level is low, he has started smoking again. He has a couple of drinks at lunch and muses that it's lucky that any more alcohol makes him sick to his stomach—otherwise, he'd probably be drinking too much, too. Then he thinks, "So what difference would it make?" Sometimes he is sexually frustrated; at other times he wonders whether he has any sex drive left. Although he's awake, each day it's getting harder to drag himself out of bed in the morning. This week he missed one day of work and was late twice. His supervisor has suggested in a nonthreatening way that he "do something about it." David knows that her next warning will not be nonthreatening. It's been going downhill since Sue walked out. Suicide has even crossed David's mind. He wonders if he's going crazy.

David is experiencing the emotion of depression, seriously so. Depression is to be expected following a loss, such as the end of a relationship, but David's feelings have lingered. His friends tell him that he should get out and do things, but David is so down that he hasn't the motivation to do much at all. After much prompting by family and friends, David consults a psychologist who, ironically, also pushes him to get out and do things—the things he used to enjoy. The psychologist also shows David that part of his problem is that sees himself as a failure who cannot make meaningful changes.

How do the physiological, situational, and cognitive components of emotions interact to produce feelings and behavior? Some psychologists argue that physiological arousal is a more basic component of emotional response than cognition and that the type of arousal we experience strongly influences our cognitive appraisal and our labeling of the emotion (e.g., Izard, 1984). For these psychologists, the body takes precedence over the mind. Do David's bodily reactions—for example, his loss of appetite and energy—take precedence over his cognitions? Other psychologists argue that cognitive appraisal and physiological arousal are so strongly intertwined that cognitive processes may determine the emotional response. Are David's ideas that he is helpless to change things more at the heart of his feelings of depression?

The "commonsense theory" of emotions is that something happens (a situation) that is cognitively appraised (interpreted) by the person, and the feeling state (a combination of arousal and thoughts) follows. For example, you meet someone new, appraise that person as delightful, and feelings of attraction follow. Or, as in the case of David, a social relationship comes to an end, you recognize your loss, feel powerless to change it, and feel down in the dumps.

Go to your student website to access an interactive version of this figure.

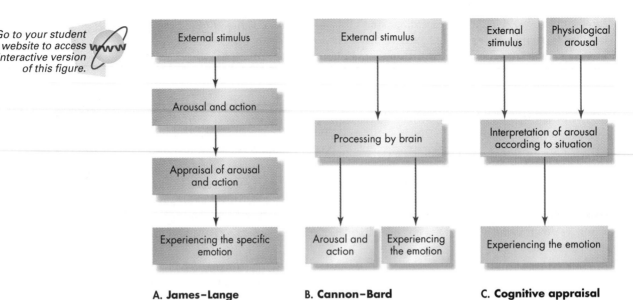

Figure 9.7
Theories of Emotion
Several theories of emotion have been advanced, each of which proposes a different role for the components of emotional response. According to the James–Lange theory (part A), events trigger specific arousal patterns and actions. Emotions result from our appraisal of our body responses. According to the Cannon–Bard theory (part B), events are first processed by the brain. Body patterns of arousal, action, and our emotional responses are then triggered simultaneously. According to the theory of cognitive appraisal (part C), events and arousal are appraised by the individual. The emotional response stems from the person's appraisal of the situation and his or her level of arousal.

However, both historic and contemporary theories of how the components of emotions interact are at variance with this commonsense view. Let us consider a number of theories and see whether we can arrive at some useful conclusions.

The James–Lange Theory A century ago, William James suggested that our emotions follow, rather than cause, our behavioral responses to events. At about the same time this view was also proposed by the Danish physiologist Karl G. Lange. It is therefore termed the James–Lange theory of emotion.

According to James and Lange, certain external stimuli instinctively trigger specific patterns of arousal and action, such as fighting or fleeing (see Figure 9.7, part A). We then become angry *because* we are acting aggressively or become afraid *because* we are running away. Emotions are simply the cognitive representations (or by-products) of automatic physiological and behavioral responses.

The James–Lange theory is consistent with the facial-feedback hypothesis. That is, smiling apparently can induce pleasant feelings, even if the effect may not be strong enough to overcome feelings of sadness (Ekman, 1993). The theory also suggests that we may be able to change our feelings by changing our behavior. Changing one's behavior to change one's feelings is one aspect of behavior therapy. When David's psychologist urges him to get out and do things, she is assuming that by changing his behavior, David can have a positive effect on the way he feels.

Walter Cannon (1927) criticized the James–Lange assertion that each emotion has distinct physiological correlates. He argued that the physiological arousal associated with emotion A is not as distinct from the arousal associated with emotion B as the theory asserts. Note that the James–Lange view downplays the importance of human cognition; it denies the roles of cognitive appraisal, personal values, and personal choice in our behavioral and emotional responses to events.

The Cannon–Bard Theory Walter Cannon (1927) and Philip Bard (1934) suggested that an event might *simultaneously* trigger bodily responses (arousal and action) and the experience of an emotion. As shown in Figure 9.7 (part B), when an event is perceived (processed by the brain), the brain stimulates autonomic and muscular activity (arousal and action) *and* cognitive activity (experience of the emotion). Thus, according to the Cannon–Bard theory, emotions *accompany* bodily responses. They are not *produced by* bodily changes, as in the James–Lange theory.

The central criticism of the Cannon–Bard theory focuses on whether bodily responses (arousal and action) and emotions are actually stimulated simultaneously. For example, pain or the perception of danger may trigger arousal before we begin to feel distress or fear. Also, many of us have had the experience of having a "narrow escape" and becoming aroused and shaky afterward, when we have had time to consider the damage that might have occurred. What is needed is a theory that allows for an ongoing interaction of external events, physiological changes (such as autonomic arousal and muscular activity), and cognitive activities.

The Theory of Cognitive Appraisal More recent theoretical approaches to emotion stress cognitive factors. Among those who argue that thinking comes first are Gordon Bower, Richard Lazarus, Stanley Schachter, Jerome Singer, and Robert Zajonc.

Schachter asserts that emotions are associated with similar patterns of bodily arousal that vary in strength, but that the way we label an emotion depends largely on our appraisal of the situation. Cognitive appraisal is based on many factors, including our perception of events and the ways other people respond to those events (see Figure 9.7, part C). When other people are present, we engage in social comparison to arrive at a response.

In a classic experiment, Schachter and Singer (1962) showed that arousal can be labeled quite differently, depending on the situation. The investigators told participants they wanted to determine the effects of a vitamin on vision. Half the participants received an injection of adrenaline, a hormone that stimulates the sympathetic branch of the autonomic nervous system. A control group received an injection of a placebo. Those who had been given adrenaline received one of three "cognitive manipulations." Group 1 was told nothing about possible emotional effects of the "vitamin." Group 2 was deliberately misinformed; members of this group were led to expect itching, numbness, or other irrelevant symptoms. Group 3 was informed accurately about the increased arousal they would experience. Group 4 was a control group injected with a placebo and given no information about its effects.

After receiving injections and cognitive manipulations, the participants were asked to wait in pairs while the experimental apparatus was being set up. The participants did not know that the person with whom they were waiting was a confederate of the experimenter. The confederate's purpose was to respond in a way that the participant would believe was caused by the injection.

Some participants waited with a confederate who acted happy-go-lucky. He flew paper airplanes about the room and tossed paper balls into a wastebasket. Other participants waited with a confederate who acted angry. He complained about the experiment, tore up a questionnaire, and stormed out of the room. As the confederates worked for their Oscar awards, the real participants were observed through a one-way mirror.

The people in groups 1 and 2 were likely to imitate the behavior of the confederate. Those who were exposed to the happy-go-lucky confederate acted jovial and content. Those who were exposed to the angry confederate imitated that person's complaining, aggressive behavior. But those in groups 3 and 4 were less influenced by the confederate's behavior.

Schachter and Singer concluded that participants in groups 1 and 2 were in an ambiguous situation. Members of these groups felt arousal from the adrenaline injection but couldn't label it as a specific emotion. Social comparison with a confederate led them to

Corbis/Sygma

■ **Fear, and Behavior, and Cognitive Appraisal, and . . . Fear!**
Yes, this film still from one of the *Godzilla* films may look silly, but it raises the question of how we experience fear. Do we run from a dangerous stimulus and feel fear as a result? Does a dangerous stimulus trigger fear and running simultaneously? Or do we appraise our situation, decide that it is dangerous, and then feel fear and choose to run away?

attribute their arousal either to happiness or to anger. Members of group 3 expected arousal from the injection, but no particular emotional consequences. These participants did not imitate the confederate's display of happiness or anger because they were not in an ambiguous situation; they knew their arousal was caused by adrenaline. Members of group 4 had no arousal for which they needed an attribution, except perhaps for some arousal induced by observing the confederate. Nor did they imitate the behavior of the confederate.

Now, happiness and anger are very different emotions. Happiness is a positive emotion, whereas anger, for most of us, is a negative emotion. Yet Schachter and Singer suggest that the bodily differences between these two emotions are slight so that different views of the situation can lead one person to label arousal as happiness and another person to label it as anger. The Schachter–Singer view could not be further removed from the James–Lange theory, which holds that each emotion is associated with specific and readily recognized body sensations. The truth, it happens, may lie somewhere in between.

In science, it must be possible to replicate experiments and attain identical or similar results; otherwise, a theory cannot be considered valid. The Schachter and Singer study has been replicated, but with *different* results (Ekman, 1993). For example, some studies found that participants were less likely to imitate the behavior of the confederate and were likely to perceive unexplained arousal negatively, attributing it to nervousness or anger (Zimbardo et al., 1993).

The connections between arousal and emotions have led to the development of many kinds of lie detection, as we see in the following section.

The Polygraph: Just What Do Lie Detectors Detect? Since the attacks of September 11, 2001, the United States has become more concerned about security and the need to determine whether people being interrogated are presenting truth or lies (*Nature* editorial, 2004). The connection between autonomic arousal and emotions has led to the development of many kinds of lie detectors. Such instruments detect something, but do they detect specific emotional responses that signify lies? Let us take a closer look at the problem of lying.

Lying—for better or worse—is a part of life. A *New York Times* poll found that 60% of American adults believe that it is sometimes necessary to lie, especially to protect people's feelings (Smiley, 2000). Political leaders lie to get elected. Many people lie to get dates or initiate sexual relations—for example, about other relationships, making professions of love, or in the case of the Internet, about one's appearance or age (Suler, 2005). People also lie about their qualifications to get jobs, and, of course, some people lie in denying guilt for crimes. Although we are unlikely to subject political leaders and lovers to lie detector tests, such tests are frequently used in hiring and in criminal investigations.

Facial expressions often offer clues to deceit, but some people can lie with a straight face—or a smile. As Shakespeare pointed out in *Hamlet,* "One may smile, and smile, and be a villain." The use of devices to detect lies has a long, if not laudable, history:

> The Bedouins of Arabia . . . until quite recently required conflicting witnesses to lick a hot iron; the one whose tongue was burned was thought to be lying. The Chinese, it is said, had a similar method for detecting lying: Suspects were forced to chew rice powder and spit it out; if the powder was dry, the suspect was guilty. (Kleinmuntz & Szucko, 1984, pp. 766–767)

These methods may sound primitive, even bizarre, but they are broadly consistent with modern psychological knowledge. Anxiety about being caught in a lie is linked to arousal of the sympathetic division of the autonomic nervous system. One sign of sympathetic arousal is lack of saliva, or dryness in the mouth. The emotions of fear and guilt are also linked to sympathetic arousal and, hence, to dryness in the mouth.

How do lie detectors work? How reliable are they? Modern polygraphs monitor indicators of sympathetic arousal during an interrogation: heart rate, blood pressure, respiration rate, and electrodermal response (sweating) (see Figure 9.8). But questions have been raised about the validity of assessing truth or fiction by means of polygraphs (Berntson, 2004; Branaman & Gallagher, 2005).

The American Polygraph Association claims that use of the polygraph is 85% to 95% accurate. Critics find polygraph testing to be less accurate and claim that it is sensitive to

reflect & relate
Do you see yourself as being good at knowing when people are lying to you? What cues do you look for?

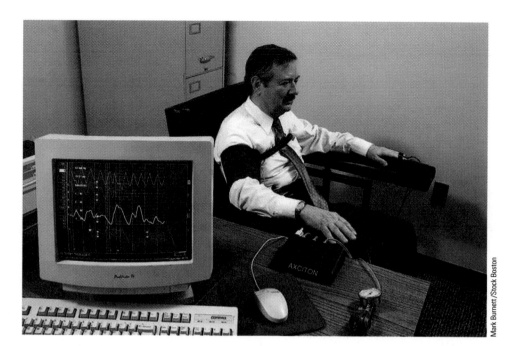

Figure 9.8
What Do "Lie Detectors" Detect?
The polygraph monitors heart rate, blood pressure, respiration rate, and sweat in the palms of the hands. Is the polygraph sensitive to lying only? Is it foolproof? Because of the controversy surrounding these questions, many courts no longer admit polygraph evidence.

more than lies (Saxe & Ben-Shakhar, 1999). Factors such as tense muscles, drugs, and previous experience with polygraph tests can significantly reduce their accuracy rate. In one experiment, people were able to reduce the accuracy of polygraph-based judgments to about 50% by biting their tongue (to produce pain) or pressing their toes against the floor (to tense muscles) while being interrogated (Honts et al., 1985). You might thus give the examiner the impression that you are lying even when you are telling the truth, throwing off the test's results. ◆▶ **Truth or Fiction Revisited:** Thus it is true that you might be able to fool a lie detector by wiggling your toes.

Iacono and Lykken (1997) conducted a mail survey of members of the Society for Psychophysiological Research and the General Psychology division of the American Psychological Association. Response rates were high—91% and 74%, respectively. Most respondents replied that polygraph lie detection was not theoretically sound, that claims for its validity were overstated, that people can easily learn to beat the test, and that polygraph results should not be admitted as evidence in courts of law.

It appears that no specific pattern of bodily responses pinpoints lying (Fiedler et al., 2002; *Nature* editorial, 2004). Because of validity problems, results of polygraph examinations are no longer admitted as evidence in many courts. But the lure of technology to determine lying remains strong. Research is underway in the development of techniques that measure brain waves, heat patterns in the face, and other biological events (Miller et al., 2002; *Nature* editorial, 2004; Soskins et al., 2001).

Evaluation   What can we make of all this? What do we make of research into the connections between lie detection and arousal? First of all, stronger emotions are connected with higher levels of arousal (Gomez et al., 2005), but research by Paul Ekman (1993) suggests that the patterns of arousal connected with various emotions are more specific than suggested by Schachter and Singer. They are, however, apparently less specific than suggested by James and Lange. Brain imaging suggests that different emotions, such as happiness and sadness, involve different structures within the brain (Goleman, 1995). Moreover, lack of control over our emotions and lack of understanding of what is happening to us are disturbing experiences (Zimbardo et al., 1993). Thus our cognitive appraisals of situations affect our emotional responses, even if not quite in the way envisioned by Schachter.

In sum, various components of an experience—cognitive, physiological, and behavioral—contribute to our emotional responses. Our bodies may become aroused in a given situation, but as we saw in the classic research of Schachter and Singer, people also appraise those situations so that arousal alone does not appear to directly cause one emotion or another. The fact that none of the theories of emotion we have discussed applies to all people in all situations is comforting. Apparently our emotions are not quite as easily understood, manipulated, or—as in the case of the polygraph—even detected as some theorists have suggested.

() Learning Connections

◀◀ *Emotion—Adding Color to Life* ▶▶

REVIEW:

17 The emotion of anxiety mainly involves arousal of the
 (a) sympathetic division of the autonomic nervous system,
 (b) parasympathetic division of the autonomic nervous system,
 (c) sympathetic division of the somatic nervous system,
 (d) parasympathetic division of the somatic nervous system.

18 The facial expression of emotions such as anger, fear, happiness, and surprise appears to be
 (a) learned,
 (b) culture-specific,
 (c) universal,
 (d) similar only in developed nations.

19 The view that a person runs from a threat and then feels fear is consistent with the _____ theory of emotions.
 (a) James–Lange,
 (b) Cannon–Bard,
 (c) Schacter–Singer,
 (d) commonsense.

20 Polygraphs assess all of the following except for
 (a) heart rate,
 (b) brain waves,
 (c) blood pressure,
 (d) electrodermal response.

CRITICAL THINKING:
Should lie detectors be used in screening candidates for mortgages or jobs? Explain your view.

Go to www
http://academic.cengage.com/psychology/rathus
for an interactive version of this review.

RECITE—*An Active Summary*™

 Recite to Go!   *Don't have time to study right now? You can study on the go!*
Go to your companion website and download an audio version of this review section to your media player. You can also access an interactive flash-card version of this review from your website.

1. What are motives, needs, drives, and incentives?	Motives are hypothetical states within an organism that propel the organism toward goals. Physiological needs include those for oxygen and food. Psychological needs include those for achievement and self-esteem. Needs give rise to drives; for example, depletion of food gives rise to the hunger drive. An incentive is a desirable object, person, or situation.
2. What is meant by species-specific behaviors?	Organisms are born with preprogrammed tendencies—called instincts, species-specific behaviors, or fixed-action patterns (FAPs)—to behave in certain ways in certain situations. FAPs occur in the presence of stimuli called releasers.
3. What is drive-reduction theory?	According to drive-reduction theory, we are motivated to engage in behavior that reduces drives. The body has a tendency called homeostasis to maintain a steady state; food deprivation thus leads to the hunger drive and eating, which reduces hunger.
4. Are all motives aimed at the reduction of tension?	Apparently not. Stimulus motives aim to increase rather than decrease the amount of stimulation acting on the organism. We apparently have needs for stimulation, activity, exploration, and manipulation.
5. How does humanistic theory differ from other theories of motivation?	Instincts and drives are mainly defensive, aimed at survival and reproduction. Humanistic psychologists argue that people are self-aware and that behavior can be growth oriented; people are motivated to strive for self-actualization.
6. What is Maslow's hierarchy of needs?	Maslow hypothesized that people have a hierarchy of needs. Once lower-level needs such as physiological and safety needs are met, people strive to meet needs for love, esteem, and self-actualization.
7. How is the hunger drive regulated?	Hunger is regulated by several internal factors, including stomach contractions, blood sugar level, receptors in the mouth and liver, and the hypothalamus. External stimuli such as the aroma of food can also trigger hunger.
8. What are the eating disorders?	The eating disorders, anorexia nervosa and bulimia nervosa, involve gross disturbances in normal patterns of eating. Anorexia is characterized by refusal to eat and extreme thinness. Bulimia is characterized by cycles of binge eating and purging.
9. What are the origins of the eating disorders?	Most psychologists consider cultural idealization of the slender female to be a major contributor to eating disorders. Eating disorders may have a genetic component involving perfectionistic personality traits.
10. What are the effects of sex hormones on sexual motivation?	Sex hormones have activating and organizing effects on behavior. "Male" sex hormones appear to fuel the sex drive, even in women, who produce much less of them. Many female animals are receptive to males only during estrus, when female sex hormones are plentiful.
11. What happens to the body when people are sexually aroused?	Vasocongestion and myotonia take people through a four-phase sexual response cycle: excitement, plateau, orgasm, and resolution.

12. What do we know about the sex lives of people in the United States?	Sexual behavior is influenced by religious beliefs and tradition. Males are more likely than females to masturbate, engage in premarital sex, and have multiple sex partners. Education has a liberating influence on sexual behavior; conservative religious beliefs have a restraining effect.
13. What is sexual orientation?	Sexual orientation is the directionality of erotic interests. People with a homosexual orientation are attracted to and interested in forming romantic relationships with people of their own sex.
14. What do we know about the origins of gay male and lesbian sexual orientations?	Learning theorists explain sexual orientation in terms of reinforcement and observational learning. Biological psychologists find evidence for genetic factors in sexual orientation, as found in comparisons of MZ and DZ twins. In many species, sexual motivation is almost completely regulated by sex hormones.
15. What have psychologists learned about biological and psychological influences on aggressive behavior?	Testosterone is involved in aggression. Freud believed that frustrations could trigger aggression. Cognitive and social cognitive psychologists assert that our behavior is influenced by our values, our interpretation of our situations, and by choice.
16. Why do some people strive to get ahead?	One reason may be that they have more achievement motivation than others. Academic achievement may be motivated by performance or learning goals.
17. What is an emotion?	An emotion is a feeling state with physiological, cognitive, and behavioral components.
18. How can we tell when other people are happy or sad?	Facial expressions are one factor in the expression of emotion. According to Ekman, the expression of several basic emotions is recognized in cultures around the world.
19. What factors contribute to happiness?	Happiness may have a genetic component, but environmental and attitudinal factors also make their contributions. Affluence helps, and so do social relationships, optimism, and self-esteem.
20. Can smiling give rise to feelings of good will? Can frowning produce anger?	Facial expressions might influence one's experience of emotion. The contraction of facial muscles might be influential.
21. How do the physiological, situational, and cognitive components of emotions interact to produce feelings and behavior?	According to the James–Lange theory, emotions reflect specific patterns of arousal and action that are triggered by certain external events. The emotion follows the behavioral response. The Cannon–Bard theory proposes that processing of events by the brain gives rise simultaneously to feelings and bodily responses. According to Schachter and Singer's theory of cognitive appraisal, emotions reflect arousal and appraisal of the situation.
22. How do lie detectors work? How reliable are they?	Lie detectors—also called polygraphs—monitor heart rate, blood pressure, respiration rate, and sweating while a person is being interrogated. Critics find polygraph testing to be unreliable.

Key Terms

Active Learning Resources

Visit Your Companion Website for This Book

http://academic.cengage.com/psychology/rathus

Check out this companion website where you will find online resources directly linked to your book. This is where you'll access the videos highlighted in your Video Connections feature. You can answer the questions online and email them to your professor. In addition you'll find downloadable audio review material, interactive versions of the study aids, Power Visuals for mastering and reviewing key concepts, as well as quizzing, and much more!

CENGAGENOW™

http://academic.cengage.com

Need help studying? This site is your one-stop study shop. Take a Pre-Test and Cengage NOW will generate a Personalized Study Plan based on your test results. The Study Plan will identify the topics you need to review and direct you to online resources to help you master those topics. You can then take a Post-Test to help you determine the concepts you have mastered and what you still need to work on. In addition you can access interactive media including the videos highlighted in your Video Connections box.

Author Blog

What does your author Spence Rathus have to say about the state of psychology? Visit your companion website every Tuesday and click on "Author Blog." This is where he'll talk about the most recent controversies and hot topics in psychology. This will keep you up to date with what your author is thinking and give you great insight into modern psychology.

CHAPTER 10

Stress, Health, and Adjustment

| T | F | Some stress is good for us. |

| T | F | Because variety is the spice of life, the more change the better. |

| T | F | Going on vacation is stressful. |

| T | F | Searching for social approval or perfection is an excellent way of making yourself miserable. |

| T | F | Type A people achieve more than Type B people, but they are less satisfied with themselves. |

| T | F | Humor helps us cope with stress. |

| T | F | At any given moment, countless microscopic warriors within our bodies are carrying out search-and-destroy missions against foreign agents. |

| T | F | If you have a family history of heart disease or cancer, there is little or nothing you can do to prevent developing the illness yourself. |

| T | F | Blowing things out of proportion can give you a headache. |

Go to www
http://academic.cengage.com/pstchology/rathus
for an interactive version of this Truth or Fiction feature.

atrina came through the door of a home in a New Orleans suburb at 10 o'clock on Monday morning. She didn't knock. She flowed underneath the door and then she began to come in through the windows, the rising waters of a tempest whose winds had tossed torrents against the shore at close to 150 miles per hour.

Gail, a nurse, and her husband Earl, a machinist, had socked away some money for the future and nearly owned their one-story brick home free and clear. They had been looking forward to spending more time with their grandchildren.

But in minutes Katrina changed their lives forever. Before they fully comprehended what was happening, water was sloshing up against their waists.

The front door normally opened out, but Katrina held it shut. Gail and Earl managed to climb out a window against Katrina's onrushing fury.

Gail and Earl, like many of their neighbors, owned a boat—a 17-foot Sunbird. They slogged to the boat through the sudden river and the pouring rain, to where it was parked under the roof of the carport. They pulled themselves up onto it, and then they realized that the keys to the engine were still in the house.

Gail and Earl looked at each other. Earl knew what he had to do. He slid back into the water. There was no more reaching the ground to walk through it. He swam back to the house. Once he was in the house, the water continued to rise.

"The boat was just about touching the roof of the carport," Gail said. "I'm screaming for him to hurry up. Because if we got stuck under there, you know, we would have died" (Herbert, 2005).

Somehow Earl found the keys and worked his way back to the boat and they got the engine going. By the time they left the carport, the water was up to the roof of the house. They could barely see through the rain, much less maneuver, but they managed to move the boat two blocks to the shelter of the roof of the drive-through lane of a bank. But about an hour later they had to return to the storm because the boat was bouncing up against the roof of the drive-through.

Fortunately, the rain eased and Gail and Earl piloted the Sunbird out across the alien waterscape. There was no refilling the engine with gasoline. The gas stations were underwater. Even locating themselves had turned eerie, with the street signs underwater. Cars and trucks bobbed by like strange logs in a stream.

Then it dawned on them that people around them were screaming for help. Drenched people stood on rooftops or leaned out of upper-story windows, waving and yelling. Gail and Earl took as many as they could in the Sunbird and found their way to a shelter in a local high school.

Then they turned about and went out for more people. Others—police, firefighters, civilians—were also out in boats doing their part. Local officials managed to find them gasoline. They rode the waters and ferried people to the shelter for two days, bringing in 150. Hungry, unwashed despite the flooding, and exhausted, Gail and Earl were then evacuated themselves to Baton Rouge,

Chris Graythen/Getty Images

■ Katrina

Hurricane Katrina flooded some 80% of New Orleans by means of rain, the storm surge, and the breaking of levees. Natural disasters such as Katrina expose people to countless life changes in addition to the danger itself. For many, life will never be the same. For hundreds who were caught in the storm surge or in collapsing buildings, life ended prematurely.

where they rested for a couple of days and then made their way to relatives in Florida. It never occurred to them that they were heroes.

Their home is gone. So, too, are their jobs. They lost a car and a truck. Yet they were lucky. "If we did not have family," Gail said, "we'd be living under a bridge."

When asked how the ordeal had affected her psychologically, Gail said, "Don't ask me now. It's too early." Later she added, "Listen, everybody's depressed and kind of still in shock. Everybody who's been through this thing. It's hard to believe it happened" (Herbert, 2005).

Disasters like Katrina have their emotional toll as well as their physical toll (Carey, 2005; Leitch, 2005). Studies of communities devastated by fires, earthquakes, tsunamis, hurricanes, and other disasters suggest that most survivors eventually come to live with their memories and their grief. But many have lingering nightmares, flashbacks, depression, and irritability that suggest deeper effects of stress.

This chapter is about stress—its origins, its psychological and physical effects, and ways of coping. *What is stress?*

STRESS: WHAT IT IS, WHERE IT COMES FROM

In physics, stress is defined as a pressure or force exerted on a body. Tons of rock pressing on the earth, one car smashing into another, a rubber band stretching—all are types of physical stress. Psychological forces, or stresses, also press, push, or pull. We may feel "crushed" by the weight of a big decision, "smashed" by adversity, or "stretched" to the point of snapping. In the case of the victims of Katrina, physical events had psychological as well as physical consequences. As we will see throughout the chapter, those psychological consequences can also affect our health.

Psychologists define **stress** as the demand made on an organism to adapt, cope, or adjust. ◆ **Truth or Fiction Revisited:** Some stress is healthful and necessary to keep us alert and occupied. Stress researcher Hans Selye (1980) referred to such healthful stress as **eustress.** We may experience eustress when we begin a sought-after job or are trying to choose the color of an iPod. But intense or prolonged stress, such as that caused by Hurricane Katrina or social or financial problems, can overtax our adjustive capacity, affect our moods, impair our ability to experience pleasure, and harm the body (Kiecolt-Glaser et al., 2002a, 2002b; Schneiderman et al., 2005).

Stress is one of the key topics in health psychology. *What is health psychology?* **Health psychology** studies the relationships between psychological factors and the prevention and treatment of physical health problems. Health psychologists investigate how

- psychological factors such as stress, behavior patterns, and attitudes can lead to or aggravate illness;
- people can cope with stress;
- stress and **pathogens** (disease-causing organisms such as bacteria and viruses) interact to influence the immune system;
- people decide whether or not to seek health care; and
- psychological interventions such as health education (for example, concerning nutrition, smoking, and exercise) and behavior modification can contribute to physical health.

Stress The demand that is made on an organism to adapt.

Eustress (YOU-stress) Stress that is healthful.

Health psychology The field of psychology that studies the relationships between psychological factors (e.g., attitudes, beliefs, situational influences, and behavior patterns) and the prevention and treatment of physical illness.

Pathogen A microscopic organism (e.g., bacterium or virus) that can cause disease.

In this chapter we consider sources of stress, factors that moderate the impact of stress, and the body's response to stress. We consider various physical health issues that overlap with the science of psychology, including headaches, heart disease, and cancer. We have seen how disasters create stress. Let us consider less severe but more common sources of stress: daily hassles, life changes, conflict, irrational beliefs, and Type A behavior.

Daily Hassles: The Stress of Everyday Life

Which straw will break the camel's back? The last straw, according to the saying. Similarly, stresses can pile up until we can no longer cope with them. Some of these stresses are daily hassles. *What are daily hassles?* **Daily hassles** are regularly occurring conditions and experiences that can threaten or harm our well-being. Others are life changes. Lazarus and his colleagues (1985) analyzed a scale that measures daily hassles and their opposites—termed **uplifts**—and found that hassles could be grouped as follows:

1. *Household hassles:* preparing meals, shopping, and home maintenance.
2. *Health hassles:* physical illness, concern about medical treatment, and side effects of medication.
3. *Time-pressure hassles:* having too many things to do, too many responsibilities, and not enough time.
4. *Inner concern hassles:* being socially isolated, lonely (Cacioppo et al., 2003).
5. *Environmental hassles:* crime, neighborhood deterioration, and traffic noise.
6. *Financial responsibility hassles:* concern about owing money such as mortgage payments and loan installments.
7. *Work hassles:* job dissatisfaction, not liking one's duties at work, and problems with coworkers.
8. *Security hassles:* concerns about job security, terrorism, taxes, property investments, stock market swings, and retirement.

An Israeli study of Israeli Jews and Arabs found that uplifts were related to family satisfaction among both groups and to general life satisfaction among Jews (Lavee & Ben-Ari, 2003). Daily hassles, by contrast, are linked to variables such as nervousness, worrying, inability to get started, feelings of sadness, and feelings of loneliness.

Life Changes: Variety May Be the Spice of Life, But Does Too Much Spice Leave a Bad Taste?

You might think that marrying Mr. or Ms. Right, finding a good job, and moving to a better neighborhood all in the same year would propel you into a state of bliss. It might. ◆ **Truth or Fiction Revisited:** Although variety adds spice to life, too much variety might lead to physical illness. *How can too much of a good thing make you ill?* It is because the events that add variety to life are changes. Even pleasant changes require adjustment. Piling one atop the another, even positive changes can lead to headaches, high blood pressure, and other health problems.

Life changes differ from daily hassles in two key ways:

1. Many life changes are positive and desirable. Hassles, by definition, are negative.
2. Hassles occur regularly. Life changes occur at irregular intervals.

Peggy Blake and her colleagues (1984) constructed a scale to measure the impact of life changes among college students. Surveys with students revealed that death of a spouse or parent were considered the most stressful life changes (94 and 88 life-change units, respectively; see Table 10.1). Academic failure (77 units) and graduation from college (68 units) were also considered highly stressful, even though graduation from college is a positive event—considering the alternative. Positive life changes such as an outstanding personal achievement (49 units) and going on vacation (30 units) also made the list. ◆ **Truth or Fiction Revisited:** Although vacations can be good for your health (Gump & Matthews, 2000), they are life changes, and changes require adjustment.

Richard Douglas Rose

■ A Daily Hassle

Daily hassles are notable daily conditions and experiences that are threatening or harmful to a person's well-being. Here we see a daily hassle for some commuters in the Philippines. What are some of the daily hassles in your life?

reflect & relate

How many daily hassles do you experience? Are they temporary or permanent? How many are connected with your role as a student? What can you do about them?

Daily hassles Notable daily conditions and experiences that are threatening or harmful to a person's well-being.

Uplifts Notable pleasant daily conditions and experiences.

TABLE 10.1 ■ Life-Change Units Connected with Various Events

EVENT	LIFE-CHANGE UNITS
1. Death of a spouse, lover, or child	94
2. Death of a parent or sibling	88
3. Beginning formal higher education	84
4. Jail sentence	82
5. Divorce or marital separation	82
6. Unwanted pregnancy of self, spouse, or lover	80
7. Abortion of unwanted pregnancy of self, spouse, or lover	80
8. Academic failure	77
9. Marrying or living with lover against parents' wishes	75
10. Change in love relationship or important friendship	74
11. Change in marital status of parents	73
12. Hospitalization of a parent or sibling	70
13. Graduation from college	68
14. Major personal injury or illness	68
15. Wanted pregnancy of self, spouse, or lover	67
16. Preparing for an important exam or writing a major paper	65
17. Major financial difficulties	65
18. Change in academic status	64
19. Change in relationship with members of your immediate family	62
20. Hospitalization of yourself or a close relative	61
21. Change in course of study, major field, vocational goals, or work status	60
22. Change in own financial status	59
23. Beginning or ceasing service in the armed forces	57
24. Change in living arrangements, conditions, or environment	55
25. Change in frequency or nature of sexual experiences	55
26. Change in degree of interest in college or attitudes toward education	55
27. Academic success	54
28. Change to a new college or university	54
29. Change in number or type of arguments with roommate	52
30. Change in responsibility at work	50
31. Change in amount or nature of social activities	50
32. Change in routine at college or work	49
33. Change in amount of leisure time	49
34. Outstanding personal achievement	49
35. Improvement of own health	47
36. Change in study habits	46
37. Change in religious affiliation	44
38. Change in address or residence	43
39. Change in weight or eating habits	39
40. Vacation or travel	30

SOURCE: Adapted from *Self-Assessment and Behavior Change Manual* (pp. 43–47), by Peggy Blake, Robert Fry, and Michael Pesjack. Copyright 1984 by McGraw-Hill. Adapted by permission of The McGraw-Hill Companies, Inc.

Hassles, Life Changes, and Health Problems   Hassles and life changes—especially negative life changes—affect us psychologically. They can cause us to worry and affect our moods (Harkness & Luther, 2001). Stressors such as hassles and life changes also predict health problems such as heart disease and cancer, even athletic injuries (Perna et al., 2003). Holmes and Rahe (1967) found that people who "earned" 300 or more life-change units within a year, according to their scale, were at greater risk for health problems. Eight of 10 developed health problems, compared with only 1 of 3 people whose totals of life-change units for the year were below 150.

■ Life Changes

Life changes differ from daily hassles in that they tend to be more episodic. Also, life changes can be positive, such as graduation (above), as well as negative, such as the tsunami of 2004 (right). Whether positive or negative, life changes require adjustment and are sources of stress—although some sources of stress are not harmful and others can be deadly. What is the relationship between life changes and illness? Is the relationship causal?

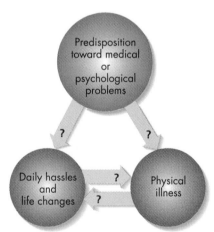

Figure 10.1

What Are the Relationships Among Daily Hassles, Life Changes, and Physical Illness?

Do daily hassles and life events cause illness, or are people who are predisposed toward medical or psychological problems encounter or generate more hassles and amass more life-change units?

How Are Hassles Connected with Health Problems? The links between daily hassles, life changes, and health problems are supported by research (Schneiderman et al., 2005). But what leads to what? Although it may appear obvious that hassles and life changes should *cause* health problems, what is obvious can be incomplete, even wrong. In this case, researchers are not even certain that stress causes illness. Let us consider a number of limitations in the research on the connections between daily hassles, life changes, and health problems:

1. The Nature of the Links Critical thinkers are cautious in their interpretation of research results. The nature of the links between hassles, life changes, and illness are open to question. It may seem logical that the hassles and life changes caused the disorders, but other explanations of the data are also possible (see Figure 10.1). One possible explanation is that people who are *predisposed* toward medical or psychological problems encounter more hassles and amass more life-change units (Harkness & Luther, 2001). For example, undiagnosed medical disorders may contribute to sexual problems, arguments with spouses or in-laws, changes in living conditions and personal habits, and changes in sleeping habits.

2. Positive Versus Negative Life Changes Other aspects of the research on the relationship between life changes and illness have also been challenged. For example, positive life changes may be less disturbing than hassles and negative life changes, even though the number of life-change units assigned to them is high (Lefcourt et al., 1981). Consider a change in one's amount of leisure time. More leisure, as less leisure, requires adjustment, but would you find it to be as stressful?

3. Personal Differences People with different personal traits respond to stress in different ways. People who are easygoing or psychologically hardy are less likely to become ill under the impact of stress. Optimism also helps people cope with stress. An optimistic outlook helps people marshal social support and find other ways of coping with stress (Brissette et al., 2002).

4. Cognitive Appraisal The stress of an event reflects the meaning of the event to the individual (CNS Spectrums, 2005; Gaab et al., 2005). Pregnancy, for example, can be a positive or negative life change, depending on whether one wants a child. We appraise the life changes we encounter. Our response to them depends on their perceived danger, our values and goals, our beliefs in our coping ability, our social support, and so on. The same event will be less taxing to someone with greater coping ability and support than to someone who lacks these advantages.

▬■▬ Conflict—Darned If You Do, Darned If You Don't?

Should you eat dessert or try to stick to your diet? Should you live on campus, which is more convenient, or should you rent an apartment, where you may have more independence? Choices like these can place us in **conflict**. *What is conflict?* In psychology, conflict is the feeling of being pulled in two or more directions by opposing motives. Conflict is frustrating and stressful. Psychologists often classify conflicts into four types: approach–approach, avoidance–avoidance, approach–avoidance, and multiple approach–avoidance.

Classic experimental research by Neal E. Miller (1944) and others suggests that the **approach–approach conflict** (see Figure 10.2, part A) is the least stressful type of conflict. Here, each of two goals is desirable, and both are within reach. You may not be able to decide between pizza or tacos, or a trip to Nassau or Hawaii. I recently had such a conflict in which I was "forced" to choose between triple-chocolate fat-free frozen yogurt and coffee-chocolate-chip fat-free frozen yogurt. Such conflicts are usually resolved by making a decision (I took the triple chocolate!). Those who experience this type of conflict may vacillate until they make a decision, as shown by people who put off decisions and ruminate about conflicting goals (Emmons & King, 1988).

Conflict Being torn in different directions by opposing motives. Feelings produced by being in conflict.

Approach–approach conflict A type of conflict in which the goals that produce opposing motives are positive and within reach.

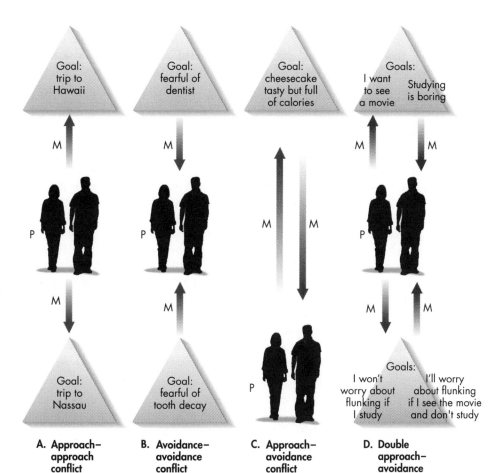

A. Approach–approach conflict ("Where should I vacation?")

B. Avoidance–avoidance conflict ("Should I see the dentist?")

C. Approach–avoidance conflict ("Should I eat the cheesecake?")

D. Double approach–avoidance conflict ("Should I study or go to a movie?")

Figure 10.2
Models for Conflict
Part A shows an approach–approach conflict, in which a person (P) has motives (M) to reach two goals that are desirable, but approach of one requires exclusion of the other. Part B shows an avoidance–avoidance conflict in which both goals are negative, but avoiding one requires approaching the other. Part C shows an approach–avoidance conflict, in which the same goal has desirable and undesirable properties. Part D shows a double approach–avoidance conflict, which is the simplest kind of *multiple* approach–avoidance conflict. In a multiple approach–avoidance conflict, two or more goals have mixed properties.

Avoidance–avoidance conflict (see Figure 10.2, part B) is more stressful because you are motivated to avoid each of two negative goals. But avoiding one requires approaching the other. You may be fearful of visiting the dentist but also afraid that your teeth will decay if you do not make an appointment and go. Each potential outcome in an avoidance–avoidance conflict is undesirable. When an avoidance–avoidance conflict is highly stressful and no resolution is in sight, some people withdraw from the conflict by focusing on other matters or doing nothing.

When the same goal produces both approach and avoidance motives, we have an **approach–avoidance conflict** (see Figure 10.2, part C). People and things have their pluses and minuses, their good points and their bad points. Cheesecake may be delicious, but oh, the calories! Goals that produce mixed motives may seem more attractive from a distance but undesirable from up close (Miller, 1944). Many couples who repeatedly break up and reunite recall each other fondly when apart and swear that they could make the relationship work if they got together again. But after they do spend time together, they again wonder, "How could I ever have believed that this so-and-so would change?"

The most complex form of conflict is the **multiple approach–avoidance conflict,** in which each of several alternative courses of action has pluses and minuses. An example with two goals is shown in Figure 10.2, part D. This sort of conflict might arise on the eve of an examination, when you are faced with the choice of studying or, say, going to a film. Each alternative has both positive and negative aspects: "Studying's a bore, but I won't have to worry about flunking. I'd love to see the movie, but I'd just be worrying about how I'll do tomorrow."

Research by Robert Emmons and Laura King has connected internal conflict with various health problems. In one study (Emmons & King, 1988), the researchers enlisted 88 college undergraduates and surveyed their personal goals and the degree of conflict experienced between them. They used diaries to assess the students' emotional lives and physical symptoms. Students who reported more conflict and more ambivalence about conflict more often reported feeling anxious and depressed, reported more physical complaints, and made significantly more visits to the college health center over the course of two years.

▬▬ Irrational Beliefs: Ten Doorways to Distress

Psychologist Albert Ellis notes that our beliefs about events, as well as the events themselves, can be stressors (Ellis, 2002, 2004a, 2004b). Consider a case in which a person is fired from a job and is anxious and depressed about it. It may seem logical that losing the job is responsible for the misery, but Ellis points out how the individual's beliefs about the loss compound his or her misery.

How do irrational beliefs create or compound stress? Let us examine this situation according to Ellis's A → B → C approach: Losing the job is an *activating event* (A). The eventual outcome, or *consequence* (C), is misery. Between the activating event (A) and the consequence (C), however, lie *beliefs* (B), such as these: "This job was the most important thing in my life," "What a no-good failure I am," "My family will starve," "I'll never find a job as good," "There's nothing I can do about it." Beliefs such as these compound misery, foster helplessness, and divert us from planning and deciding what to do next. The belief that "There's nothing I can do about it" fosters helplessness. The belief that "I am a no-good failure" internalizes the blame and may be an exaggeration. The belief that "My family will starve" may also be an exaggeration.

Let's diagram the situation:

$$\text{Activating events} \rightarrow \text{Beliefs} \rightarrow \text{Consequences}$$
$$\text{or A} \rightarrow \text{B} \rightarrow \text{C}$$

Anxieties about the future and depression over a loss are normal and to be expected. The beliefs of the person who lost the job, however, tend to **catastrophize** the extent of the loss and contribute to anxiety and depression—and thus raise the person's blood pressure (Dunkley et al., 2003; Melmed, 2003). By heightening the individual's emotional reaction to

---

Avoidance–avoidance conflict A type of conflict in which the goals are negative, but avoidance of one requires approaching the other.

Approach–avoidance conflict A type of conflict in which the same goal produces approach and avoidance motives.

Multiple approach–avoidance conflict A type of conflict in which each of a number of goals produces approach and avoidance motives.

Catastrophize To interpret negative events as being disastrous; to "blow out of proportion."

TABLE 10.2 ■ Irrational Beliefs: Cognitive Doorways to Distress

Irrational Belief 1:	You must have sincere love and approval almost all the time from the people who are important to you.
Irrational Belief 2:	You must prove yourself to be thoroughly competent, adequate, and achieving at something important.
Irrational Belief 3:	Things must go the way you want them to go. Life is awful when you don't get your first choice in everything.
Irrational Belief 4:	Other people must treat everyone fairly and justly. When people act unfairly or unethically, they are rotten.
Irrational Belief 5:	When there is danger or fear in your world, you must be preoccupied with and upset by it.
Irrational Belief 6:	People and things should turn out better than they do. It's awful and horrible when you don't find quick solutions to life's hassles.
Irrational Belief 7:	Your emotional misery stems from external pressures that you have little or no ability to control. Unless these external pressures change, you must remain miserable.
Irrational Belief 8:	It is easier to evade life's responsibilities and problems than to face them and undertake more rewarding forms of self-discipline.
Irrational Belief 9:	Your past influenced you immensely and must therefore continue to determine your feelings and behavior today.
Irrational Belief 10:	You can achieve happiness by inertia and inaction, or by just enjoying yourself from day to day.

reflect & relate

Do you have an excessive need for social approval? Are you perfectionistic? How do these needs affect you?

the loss and fostering feelings of helplessness, these beliefs also impair coping ability. They lower the person's self-efficacy expectations.

Ellis proposes that many of us carry with us the irrational beliefs shown in Table 10.2. They are our personal doorways to distress. In fact, they can give rise to problems in themselves. When problems assault us from other sources, these beliefs can magnify their effect.

Ellis finds it understandable that we would want the approval of others but irrational to believe that we cannot survive without it. It would be nice to be competent in everything we do, but it's unreasonable to *expect* it. Sure, it would be nice to be able to serve and volley like a tennis pro, but most of us haven't the time or natural ability to perfect the game. Demanding perfection prevents us from going out on the court on weekends and batting the ball back and forth just for fun (Ciarrochi, 2004). Belief number 5 is a prescription for perpetual emotional upheaval. Beliefs numbers 7 and 9 lead to feelings of helplessness and demoralization. Sure, Ellis might say, childhood experiences can explain the origins of irrational beliefs, but it is our own cognitive appraisal—here and now—that causes us to be miserable.

Truth or Fiction Revisited: Research findings confirm the connections between irrational beliefs (e.g., excessive dependence on social approval and perfectionism) and feelings of anxiety and depression (Ciarrochi, 2004; Rice & Dellwo, 2001; Wiebe & McCabe, 2002).

——■— The Type A Behavior Pattern

Some people create stress for themselves through the **Type A behavior** pattern. *What is Type A behavior?* Type A people are highly driven, competitive, impatient, hostile, and

Type A behavior Behavior characterized by a sense of time urgency, competitiveness, and hostility.

Bill Bachman / The Image Works

■ **Type A Behavior Pattern**
The Type A behavior pattern is characterized by a sense of time urgency, competitiveness, and hostility.

aggressive—so much so that they are prone to getting into auto accidents (Ben-Zur, 2002; Karlberg et al., 1998; Magnavita et al., 1997). They feel rushed and pressured and keep one eye glued to the clock (Conte et al., 2001). They are not only prompt for appointments but often early. They eat, walk, and talk rapidly. They grow restless when others work slowly. They attempt to dominate group discussions. Type A people find it difficult to surrender control or share power. They are reluctant to delegate authority in the workplace and thus increase their own workloads.

Type A people find it difficult just to go out on the tennis court and bat the ball back and forth (Masters et al., 2003). They watch their form, perfect their strokes, and strive for continual self-improvement. They require themselves to achieve in everything they do.

reflect & relate

Are you Type A, Type B, or somewhere in between? How does your "type" affect your life?

Type B   ◇ **Truth or Fiction Revisited:** It is true that Type A people achieve more than Type B people but are less satisfied with themselves. Type B people relax more readily than Type A people and focus more on the quality of life. They are less ambitious and less impatient, and they pace themselves. Type A people earn higher grades and more money than Type B's who are equal in intelligence, but Type A people are more likely to continue to strive for more and more.

Self-Assessment

Are You Type A or Type B?

Complete the questionnaire by circling the yes if the behavior pattern described is typical of you, or the no if it is not. Try to work rapidly and leave no items blank. Then read the section on Type A behavior and turn to the scoring key in Appendix B.

Do you:

yes no **1.** strongly accent key words in your everyday speech?
yes no **2.** eat and walk quickly?
yes no **3.** believe that children should be taught to be competitive?
yes no **4.** feel restless when watching a slow worker?
yes no **5.** hurry other people to get on with what they're trying to say?
yes no **6.** find it highly aggravating to be stuck in traffic or waiting for a seat at a restaurant?
yes no **7.** continue to think about your own problems and business even when listening to someone else?
yes no **8.** try to eat and shave, or drive and jot down notes at the same time?
yes no **9.** catch up on your work while on vacations?
yes no **10.** bring conversations around to topics of concern to you?
yes no **11.** feel guilty when you spend time just relaxing?
yes no **12.** find that you're so wrapped up in your work that you no longer notice office decorations or the scenery when you commute?

yes no **13.** find yourself concerned with getting more *things* rather than developing your creativity and social concerns?
yes no **14.** try to schedule more and more activities into less time?
yes no **15.** always appear for appointments on time?
yes no **16.** clench or pound your fists or use other gestures to emphasize your views?
yes no **17.** credit your accomplishments to your ability to work rapidly?
yes no **18.** feel that things must be done *now* and quickly?
yes no **19.** constantly try to find more efficient ways to get things done?
yes no **20.** insist on winning at games rather than just having fun?
yes no **21.** interrupt others often?
yes no **22.** feel irritated when others are late?
yes no **23.** leave the table immediately after eating?
yes no **24.** feel rushed?
yes no **25.** feel dissatisfied with your current level of performance?

Go to www
http://academic.cengage.com/psychology/rathus *where you can fill out an interactive version of this Self-Assessment and automatically score your results.*

⟨⟩ Learning Connections

◀◀   *Stress—What It Is, Where It Comes From*   ▶▶

REVIEW:

1 Life changes differ from daily hassles in that they are
(a) pleasant,
(b) brief,
(c) less regular,
(d) stressful.

2 The feeling of being pulled in two or more directions by opposing motives is called
(a) frustration,
(b) conflict,
(c) irrational,
(d) eustress.

3 Albert Ellis notes that our _____ events, as well as the events themselves, can be stressors.
(a) emotional responses to,
(b) flashbacks to,
(c) dreams about,
(d) beliefs about.

4 Type A behavior is characterized by a sense of
(a) time urgency,
(b) fairness,
(c) loss,
(d) social responsibility.

CRITICAL THINKING:
Life changes are stressful. Should people therefore avoid life changes?

Go to www
http://academic.cengage.com/psychology/rathus
for an interactive version of this review.

PSYCHOLOGICAL MODERATORS OF STRESS

There is no one-to-one relationship between stress and physical or psychological health problems. Physical factors account for some of the variability in our responses: Some people inherit predispositions toward specific disorders. Psychological factors also play a role, however (Melmed, 2003). They can influence, or *moderate,* the effects of stress. In this section we discuss several psychological moderators of stress: self-efficacy expectations, psychological hardiness, humor, predictability and control, and social support.

Self-Efficacy Expectations: "The Little Engine That Could"

Self-efficacy is the ability to make things happen. Our **self-efficacy expectations** affect our ability to withstand stress (Basic Behavioral Science Task Force, 1996a; Maciejewski et al., 2000). *How do our self-efficacy expectations affect our ability to withstand stress?*

A classic experiment by Albert Bandura and his colleagues (1985) shows that high self-efficacy expectations are accompanied by relatively *lower* levels of adrenaline and noradrenaline in the bloodstream when we are faced with fear-inducing objects. The Bandura group assessed subjects' self-efficacy, exposed them to fearful stimuli, and monitored the levels of adrenaline and noradrenaline in their bloodstreams as they did so. Adrenaline and noradrenaline are secreted when we are under stress. They arouse the body in several ways, such as accelerating the heart rate and releasing glucose from the liver. As a result, we may have "butterflies in the stomach" and feel nervous. Excessive arousal can also distract us from coping with the tasks at hand.

People who are self-confident are less prone to be disturbed by adverse events (Kaslow et al., 2002; Lang & Heckhausen, 2001). People with higher self-efficacy expectations

Self-efficacy expectations Our beliefs that we can bring about desired changes through our own efforts.

Javier Soriano/AFP/Getty Images

■ Self-Efficacy Expectations and Performance
Outstanding athletes such as Lance Armstrong tend to have high self-efficacy expectations. That is, they believe in themselves. Self-efficacy expectations are one of the psychological factors that moderate the effects of stress.

are more likely to lose weight or quit smoking and less likely to relapse afterward (E. S. Anderson et al., 2000, 2001; Shiffman et al., 2000). They are better able to function in spite of pain (Lackner et al., 1996). A study of Native Americans found that alcohol abuse was correlated with self-efficacy expectations (M. J. Taylor, 2000). That is, individuals with feelings of powerlessness were more likely to abuse alcohol, perhaps as a way of lessening stress.

People are more likely to comply with medical advice when they believe that it will work (Schwartzer & Renner, 2000). Women, for example, are more likely to engage in breast self-examination when they believe that they will really be able to detect abnormal growths (Miller et al., 1996). People are more likely to try to quit smoking when they believe that they can do so successfully (Segan et al., 2002).

▬▶ Psychological Hardiness: Tough Enough?

Psychological hardiness also helps people resist stress (Kaddour, 2003; Richardson, 2002). Our understanding of hardiness is derived largely from the pioneering work of Suzanne Kobasa and her colleagues (1994). They studied business executives who seemed able to resist illness despite stress. In one phase of the research, executives completed a battery of psychological tests. Kobasa (1990) found that the psychologically hardy executives had three key characteristics. *What characteristics are connected with psychological hardiness?* The characteristics include commitment, challenge, and control.

1. Kobasa found that psychologically hardy executives were high in *commitment.* They tended to involve themselves in, rather than feel alienated from, whatever they were doing or encountering. A Slovakian study found that psychologically hardy secondary school students try to actively solve problems rather than avoid them (Baumgartner, 2002).
2. They were also high in *challenge.* They believed that change, rather than stability, is normal in life. They appraised change as an interesting incentive to personal growth, not as a threat to security.
3. They were high in perceived *control* over their lives. A sense of control is one of the keys to psychological hardiness (Folkman & Moskowitz, 2000b; Tennen & Affleck, 2000). Hardy participants felt and behaved as though they were influential, rather than helpless, in facing the various rewards and punishments of life. Psychologically hardy people tend to have what Julian B. Rotter (1990) terms an internal **locus of control.** The nearby Self-Assessment contains a Locus of Control Scale that will offer you insight as to how psychologically hardy you may be.

Hardy people may be more resistant to stress because they *choose* to face it (Baumgartner, 2002; Kobasa, 1990). They also interpret stress as making life more interesting. For example, they see a conference with a supervisor as an opportunity to persuade the supervisor rather than as a risk to their position.

▬▶ Sense of Humor: Does Humor Help One Cope with Stress?

The idea that humor lightens the burdens of life and helps people cope with stress has been with us for millennia. Consider the biblical maxim, "A merry heart doeth good like a medicine" (Proverbs 17:22).

Is there any evidence that humor helps us cope with stress? ◆ **Truth or Fiction Revisited:** Research suggests that humor can indeed moderate the effects of stress (Godfrey, 2004). In one classic study, for example, students completed a checklist of negative life events and a measure of mood disturbance (Martin & Lefcourt, 1983). The measure of

reflect & relate

Are you committed to your undertakings—including college? Do you seek or avoid challenges? Are you in control of your life? What do your answers suggest about your psychological hardiness?

Psychological hardiness A cluster of traits that buffer stress and are characterized by commitment, challenge, and control.

Locus of control The place (locus) to which an individual attributes control over the receiving of reinforcers—either inside or outside the self.

Self-Assessment

The Locus of Control Scale

Self-Assessment

Self-Assessment

Psychologically hardy people tend to have an internal locus of control. They believe that they are in control of their own lives. In contrast, people with an external locus of control tend to see their fate as being out of their hands.

Are you "internal" or "external"? To learn about your perception of your locus of control, complete this questionnaire, which was developed by Stephen Nowicki and Bonnie Strickland (1973). Circle the yes or no for each question. Then check the answer key in Appendix B.

yes no **1.** Do you believe that most problems will solve themselves if you just don't fool with them?

yes no **2.** Do you believe that you can stop yourself from catching a cold?

yes no **3.** Are some people just born lucky?

yes no **4.** Most of the time, do you feel that getting good grades means a great deal to you?

yes no **5.** Are you often blamed for things that just aren't your fault?

yes no **6.** Do you believe that if somebody studies hard enough, he or she can pass any subject?

yes no **7.** Do you feel that most of the time it doesn't pay to try hard because things never turn out right anyway?

yes no **8.** Do you feel that if things start out well in the morning, it's going to be a good day no matter what you do?

yes no **9.** Do you feel that most of the time parents listen to what their children have to say?

yes no **10.** Do you believe that wishing can make good things happen?

yes no **11.** When you get punished, does it usually seem it's for no good reason at all?

yes no **12.** Most of the time, do you find it hard to change a friend's opinion?

yes no **13.** Do you think cheering more than luck helps a team win?

yes no **14.** Did you feel that it was nearly impossible to change your parents' minds about anything?

yes no **15.** Do you believe that parents should allow children to make most of their own decisions?

yes no **16.** Do you feel that when you do something wrong there's very little you can do to make it right?

yes no **17.** Do you believe that most people are just born good at sports?

yes no **18.** Are most other people your age stronger than you are?

yes no **19.** Do you feel that one of the best ways to handle most problems is just not to think about them?

yes no **20.** Do you feel that you have a lot of choice in deciding who your friends are?

yes no **21.** If you find a four-leaf clover, do you believe that it might bring you good luck?

yes no **22.** Did you often feel that whether or not you did your homework had much to do with what kind of grades you got?

yes no **23.** Do you feel that when a person your age is angry with you, there's little you can do to stop him or her?

yes no **24.** Have you ever had a good luck charm?

yes no **25.** Do you believe that whether or not people like you depends on how you act?

yes no **26.** Did your parents usually help you if you asked them to?

yes no **27.** Have you ever felt that when people were angry with you, it was usually for no reason at all?

yes no **28.** Most of the time, do you feel that you can change what might happen tomorrow by what you did today?

yes no **29.** Do you believe that when bad things are going to happen they are just going to happen no matter what you try to do to stop them?

yes no **30.** Do you think that people can get their own way if they just keep trying?

yes no **31.** Most of the time do you find it useless to try to get your own way at home?

yes no **32.** Do you feel that when good things happen, they happen because of hard work?

yes no **33.** Do you feel that when somebody your age wants to be your enemy there's little you can do to change matters?

yes no **34.** Do you feel that it's easy to get friends to do what you want them to do?

yes no **35.** Do you usually feel that you have little to say about what you get to eat at home?

yes no **36.** Do you feel that when someone doesn't like you, there's little you can do about it?

yes no **37.** Did you usually feel it was almost useless to try in school, because most other children were just plain smarter than you were?

yes no **38.** Are you the kind of person who believes that planning ahead makes things turn out better?

yes no **39.** Most of the time, do you feel that you have little to say about what your family decides to do?

yes no **40.** Do you think it's better to be smart than to be lucky?

Go to www

http://academic.cengage.com/psychology/rathus where you can fill out an interactive version of this Self-Assessment and automatically score your results.

mood disturbance also yielded a stress score. The students also rated their sense of humor. Students were asked to try to produce humor in an experimental stressful situation, and their ability to do so was rated by the researchers. Students who had a greater sense of humor and were capable of producing humor in the stressful experimental condition were less affected by the stress than other students. In other experiments, Lefcourt (1997) found that exposing students to humorous videotapes raised the level of immunoglobin A (a measure of the functioning of the immune system) in their saliva.

How does humor help people cope with stress? We are uncertain, but there are many possibilities. One is that laughter stimulates the output of endorphins, which might enhance the functioning of the immune system. Another is that the benefits of humor may be explained in terms of the positive cognitive shifts they entail and the positive emotions that accompany them.

——■— Predictability and Control: "If I Can Stop the Roller Coaster, I Don't Want to Get Off"

The ability to predict a stressor apparently moderates its impact. ***How do predictability and control help us cope with stress?*** Predictability allows us to brace ourselves for the inevitable and, in many cases, plan ways of coping with it. Control—even the illusion of being in control—allows us to feel that we are not at the mercy of the fates (Folkman & Moskowitz, 2000b; Tennen & Affleck, 2000). There is also a relationship between the desire to assume control over one's situation and the usefulness of information about impending stressors. Predictability is of greater benefit to **internals**—that is, to people who wish to exercise control over their situations—than to **externals.** People who want information about medical procedures and what they will experience cope better with pain when they undergo those procedures (Ludwick-Rosenthal & Neufeld, 1993).

——■— Social Support: Being in It Together

People are social beings, and social support also seems to act as a buffer against the effects of stress (Cohen et al., 2003; Folkman & Moskowitz, 2000a).

The concept of social support has many definitions:

1. *Emotional concern*—listening to people's problems and expressing feelings of sympathy, caring, understanding, and reassurance.
2. *Instrumental aid*—the material supports and services that facilitate adaptive behavior. For example, after a disaster the government may arrange for low-interest loans so that survivors can rebuild. Relief organizations may provide foodstuffs, medicines, and temporary living quarters.
3. *Information*—guidance and advice that enhance people's ability to cope.
4. *Appraisal*—feedback from others about how one is doing. This kind of support involves helping people interpret, or "make sense of," what has happened to them.
5. *Socializing*—conversation, recreation, going shopping with someone. Socializing is beneficial even when it is not oriented toward solving problems.

Does social support help people cope with stress? Yes, research does support the value of social support. Introverts, people who lack social skills, and people who live by themselves seem more prone to developing infectious diseases such as colds under stress (Cohen et al., 2003). Social support helps Mexican Americans and other immigrants to cope with the stresses of acculturation (Hovey, 2000). Social support helped children cope with the stresses of Hurricane Andrew (Vernberg et al., 1996) and Chinese villagers cope with an earthquake (X. Wang et al., 2000). Stress is less likely to lead to high blood pressure or alcohol abuse in people who have social support (Linden et al., 1993). Even online social support helps people cope with the stresses of cancer and other health problems (Broom, 2005; Hoybye et al., 2005).

How does stress contribute to the development of physical health problems? In the next section, we consider the effects of stress on the body.

Internals People who perceive the ability to attain reinforcements as being largely within themselves.

Externals People who perceive the ability to attain reinforcements as being largely outside themselves.

◯ Learning Connections

◄◄ *Psychological Moderators of Stress* ▶▶

REVIEW:

5 Bandura and his colleagues (1985) found that high self-efficacy expectations are accompanied by relatively lower levels of _____ in the bloodstream when we are faced with fear-inducing objects.
(a) adrenaline,
(b) myelin,
(c) endorphins,
(d) melatonin.

6 According to Kobasa, psychologically hardy executives are high in
(a) courtesy,
(b) courage,
(c) commitment,
(d) endorphins.

7 Predictability is of greater benefit to _____ in helping them cope with stress.
(a) people who wish to exercise control over their situations,
(b) Type B people,
(c) people who are not psychologically hardy,
(d) people with a sense of humor.

CRITICAL THINKING:
Social support helps most people cope with stress. What does this research finding suggest about human nature?

Go to
http://academic.cengage.com/psychology/rathus
for an interactive version of this review.

STRESS AND THE BODY: THE WAR WITHIN

Stress is more than a psychological event. It is more than "knowing" it is there; it is more than "feeling" pushed and pulled. Stress also has very definite effects on the body which, as we will see, can lead to psychological and physical health problems. Stress researcher Hans Selye outlined a number of the bodily effects in his concept of the general adaptation syndrome (GAS).

─■─ The General Adaptation Syndrome

Hans Selye suggested that under stress the body is like a clock with an alarm that does not shut off until the clock shakes apart or its energy has been depleted. The body's response to different stressors shows certain similarities whether the stressor is a bacterial invasion, perceived danger, or a major life change (Selye, 1976). For this reason, Selye labeled this response the **general adaptation syndrome (GAS)**. *What is the general adaptation syndrome?* The GAS is a group of bodily changes that occur in three stages: an alarm reaction, a resistance stage, and an exhaustion stage. These changes mobilize the body for action and—like that alarm that goes on ringing—can eventually wear out the body.

The Alarm Reaction   The **alarm reaction** is triggered by perception of a stressor. This reaction mobilizes or arouses the body, biologically speaking. Early in the 20th century, physiologist Walter B. Cannon (1932) argued that this mobilization was the basis for an instinctive **fight-or-flight reaction.** But contemporary psychologists question whether

General adaptation syndrome (GAS) Selye's term for a hypothesized three-stage response to stress.

Alarm reaction The first stage of the GAS, which is triggered by the impact of a stressor and characterized by sympathetic activity.

Fight-or-flight reaction An innate adaptive response to the perception of danger.

Keith Brofsky/Getty Images

■ **Are Their Alarm Systems Ringing as They Take Out a Loan?**
The alarm reaction of the general adaptation syndrome can be triggered by daily hassles and life changes—such as taking out a large loan—as well as by physical threats. When the stressor persists, diseases of adaptation may develop.

the fight-or-flight reaction is instinctive in humans (Updegraff et al., 2002). In any event, the alarm reaction involves bodily changes that are initiated by the brain and regulated by the endocrine system and the sympathetic division of the autonomic nervous system (ANS).

Stress has a domino effect on the endocrine system (Bauer et al., 2003; Melmed, 2003; see Figure 10.3). The hypothalamus secretes corticotrophin-releasing hormone (CRH). CRH causes the pituitary gland to secrete adrenocorticotrophic hormone (ACTH). ACTH then causes the adrenal cortex to secrete cortisol and other corticosteroids (steroidal hormones produced by the adrenal cortex). Corticosteroids help protect the body by combating allergic reactions (such as difficulty in breathing) and producing inflammation (Leonard, 2005). (However, corticosteroids can be harmful to the cardiovascular system, which is one reason that chronic stress can impair one's health and why athletes who use steroids to build the muscle mass can experience cardiovascular problems.) Inflammation increases circulation to parts of the body that are injured. It ferries in hordes of white blood cells to fend off invading pathogens.

Two other hormones that play a major role in the alarm reaction are secreted by the adrenal medulla. The sympathetic division of the ANS activates the adrenal medulla, causing it to release a mixture of adrenaline and noradrenaline. This mixture arouses the body by accelerating the heart rate and causing the liver to release glucose (sugar). This provides the energy that fuels the fight-or-flight reaction, which activates the body so that it is prepared to fight or flee from a predator.

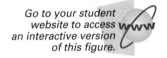

Go to your student website to access an interactive version of this figure.

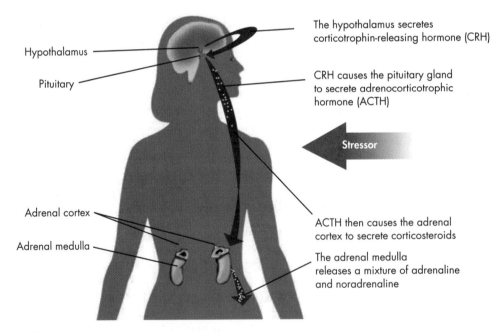

Hypothalamus

Pituitary

Adrenal cortex

Adrenal medulla

The hypothalamus secretes corticotrophin-releasing hormone (CRH)

CRH causes the pituitary gland to secrete adrenocorticotrophic hormone (ACTH)

Stressor

ACTH then causes the adrenal cortex to secrete corticosteroids

The adrenal medulla releases a mixture of adrenaline and noradrenaline

Figure 10.3
Stress and the Endocrine System
Stress has a domino effect on the endocrine system, leading to the release of corticosteroids and a mixture of adrenaline and noradrenaline. Corticosteroids combat allergic reactions (such as difficulty in breathing) and cause inflammation. Adrenaline and noradrenaline arouse the body to cope by accelerating the heart rate and providing energy for the fight-or-flight reaction.

A Closer Look
Gender Differences in Response to Stress?

A Closer Look

For nearly a century, it has been widely believed that people experience what Harvard University physiologist Walter Cannon labeled a "fight-or-flight" reaction to stress. Cannon believed that the body is prewired to either become mobilized for combat when faced with a predator or a competitor, or, if the predator is threatening enough, to flee. Although the biology of his day did not allow Cannon to be as precise as we can be, we now know that the fight-or-flight reaction includes bodily changes that involve the brain (perceptions, neurotransmitters), the endocrine system (hormones), and the sympathetic division of the autonomic nervous system (rapid heart beat, rapid breathing, muscle tension). These changes pump us up to fight like demons or, when advisable, to beat a hasty retreat.

Or do they?

According to a review of the literature by UCLA psychologist Shelley E. Taylor and her colleagues (2000b), women under stress are more likely to tend to the kids or "interface" with family and friends than either fight or flee. Her review was prompted by a student who made the offhand remark that nearly all of the rats in studies of stress were male. Taylor's review found that prior to 1995, when federal agencies began requiring more equal representation of women in funded studies, only 17% of subjects were female. The gender gap allowed researchers to ignore the question of whether females responded to stress in the same way as males.

Taylor and her colleagues (2000b) then dug more deeply into the literature and found that "men and women do have some reliably different responses to stress." Taylor notes, "I think we've really been missing the boat on one of the most important responses."

The "woman's response" to stress can be called the "tend-and-befriend" response. It involves nurturing and seeking social support rather than fighting or fleeing. When females faced a threat, a disaster, or even an especially bad day at the office, they often responded by caring for their children and seeking social contact and support from others, especially other women. After a bad day at the office, men were more likely to withdraw from the family or start arguments.

Evolutionary psychologists suggest that the tend-and-befriend response might have become sealed in human genes because it promotes the survival of females who are tending to their offspring. Females who choose to fight may often die or at least be separated from their offspring—no evolutionary brass ring here.

Gender differences in behavior are frequently connected with gender differences in hormones and other biological factors. This one is no different. Taylor and her colleagues point to the effects of the pituitary hormone oxytocin. Oxytocin is connected with nurturing behaviors such as affiliat-

■ **"Fight-or-Flight" or "Tend-and-Befriend"?**
Walter Cannon labeled the body's response to stress the "fight-or-flight" reaction.

Bonnie Kamin/PhotoEdit

ing with and cuddling one's young in many mammals (Taylor et al., 2000b). When oxytocin is released during stress, it tends to have a calming effect on both rats and humans. It makes them less afraid and more social.

But wait a minute! Men also release oxytocin when they are under stress. So why the gender difference? The answer may lie in the presence of other hormones, the sex hormones estrogen and testosterone. Female have more estrogen than males do, and estrogen appears to enhance the effects of oxytocin. Males, on the other hand, have more testosterone than females, and testosterone may mitigate the effects of oxytocin by prompting feelings of self-confidence (which may be exaggerated) and fostering aggression (Sullivan, 2000).

Males may thus be more aggressive than females under stress because of the genetic balance of hormones in their bodies, while females are more affiliative and nurturant. Due to such differences, women tend to outlive men. "Men are more likely than women to respond to stressful experiences by developing certain stress-related disorders, including hypertension, aggressive behavior, or abuse of alcohol or hard drugs," Taylor added in a UCLA press release (May, 2000). "Because the tend-and-befriend regulatory system may, in some ways, protect women against stress, this biopsychosocial pattern may provide insights into why women live an average of seven and a half years longer than men."

Not all psychologists agree with a biological explanation. Psychologist Alice H. Eagly (2000) allows that gender differences in response to stress may be rooted in hormones but suggests that the differences may reflect cultural conditioning. "I think we have a certain amount of evidence that women are in some sense more affiliative, but what that's due to becomes the question. Is it biologically hard-wired? Or is it because women have more family responsibility and preparation for that in their development? That is the big question for psychologists."

A big question, indeed. ■

TABLE 10.3 ■ Components of the Alarm Reaction*
Corticosteroids are secreted.
Adrenaline is secreted.
Noradrenaline is secreted.
Respiration rate increases.
Heart rate increases.
Blood pressure increases.
Muscles tense.
Blood shifts from internal organs to the skeletal musculature.
Digestion is inhibited.
Sugar is released from the liver.
Blood coagulability increases.

*The alarm reaction is triggered by stressors. It is defined by the release of corticosteroids and adrenaline and by activity of the sympathetic branch of the autonomic nervous system.

reflect & relate

What do you experience happening in your body when you are under stress? How do those sensations fit the description of the general adaptation syndrome?

Resistance stage The second stage of the GAS, characterized by prolonged sympathetic activity in an effort to restore lost energy and repair damage. Also called the *adaptation stage.*

Exhaustion stage The third stage of the GAS, characterized by weakened resistance and possible deterioration.

Immune system The system of the body that recognizes and destroys foreign agents (antigens) that invade the body.

Leukocytes White blood cells. (Derived from the Greek words *leukos,* meaning "white," and *kytos,* literally meaning "a hollow" but used to refer to cells.)

Antigen A substance that stimulates the body to mount an immune system response to it. (The contraction for *anti*body *generator.*)

Antibodies Substances formed by white blood cells that recognize and destroy antigens.

The fight-or-flight reaction stems from a period in human prehistory when many stressors were life threatening. It was triggered by the sight of a predator at the edge of a thicket or by a sudden rustling in the undergrowth. Today it may be aroused when you are caught in stop-and-go traffic or learn that your mortgage payments are going to increase. Once the threat is removed, the body returns to a lower state of arousal. Many of the bodily changes that occur in the alarm reaction are outlined in Table 10.3.

Many contemporary theorists do not believe that the fight-or-flight reaction is universal. In the nearby "A Closer Look," Shelley Taylor and her colleagues report evidence that many women engage in a tend-and-befriend response to threats, rather than a fight-or-flight response. Margaret Kemeny and her colleagues (e.g., Updegraff et al., 2002) also observe that some people attempt to respond productively to stress by pulling back from the situation to better appraise it and conserve their resources while they are doing so. This response pattern to stress is described by two theories that are currently under development: cognitive adaptation theory and conservation of resources theory.

The Resistance Stage   According to Selye's theory, if the alarm reaction mobilizes the body and the stressor is not removed, we enter the adaptation or **resistance stage** of the GAS. Levels of endocrine and sympathetic activity are lower than in the alarm reaction but still higher than normal. (It's as if the alarm is still on, but a bit softer.) But make no mistake: The person feels tense, and the body remains under a heavy burden.

The Exhaustion Stage   If the stressor is still not dealt with adequately, we may enter the **exhaustion stage** of the GAS. Individual capacities for resisting stress vary, but anyone will eventually become exhausted when stress continues indefinitely. The muscles become fatigued. The body is depleted of the resources required for combating stress. With exhaustion, the parasympathetic division of the ANS may predominate. As a result, our heartbeat and respiration rate slow down, and many aspects of sympathetic activity are reversed. It might sound as if we would profit from the respite, but remember that we are still under stress—possibly an external threat. Continued stress in the exhaustion stage may lead to what Selye terms "diseases of adaptation." These are connected with constriction of blood vessels and alternation of the heart rhythm, and can range from allergies to hives and coronary heart disease (CHD)—and, ultimately, death.

Discussion of the effects of stress on the immune system paves the way for understanding the links between psychological factors and physical illness.

▬■▬ Effects of Stress on the Immune System

Research shows that stress suppresses the **immune system,** as measured by the presence of various substances in the blood that make up the immune system (Antoni et al., 2005; Hawkley & Cacioppo, 2004). Psychological factors such as feelings of control and social support moderate these effects (Cohen et al., 2001a).

The Immune System   Given the complexity of the human body and the fast pace of scientific change, we often feel that we are dependent on trained professionals to cope with illness. Yet we actually do most of this coping by ourselves, by means of the immune system. *How does the immune system work?*

The immune system combats disease in several ways (Delves & Roitt, 2000; Leonard, 2005). One way is the production of white blood cells, which engulf and kill pathogens such as bacteria, fungi, and viruses, and worn-out and cancerous body cells. The technical term for white blood cells is **leukocytes.** ◆▷ **Truth or Fiction Revisited:** Leukocytes carry on microscopic warfare. They engage in search-and-destroy missions in which they "recognize" and eradicate foreign agents and unhealthy cells.

Leukocytes recognize foreign substances by their shapes. The foreign substances are termed **antigens** because the body reacts to them by generating specialized proteins, or **antibodies.** Antibodies attach themselves to the foreign substances, deactivating them and

Video Connections

Health and Stress

LEARNING OBJECTIVES

■ To better understand the links between health and stress; for example, to understand what happens to the immune system when a person is exposed to stress.

■ To better understand how investigators study the links between stress and health.

APPLIED LESSON

1 Explain what happens to the immune system when a person becomes stressed. What is the role of cytokine?

2 What are the sources of stress in your life? Your hassles? Your life changes? Conflicts?

3 What can you do to reduce some of the stress in your own life?

CRITICAL THINKING

1 How can you differentiate between "good stress" and "bad stress" in your own life? What standards would you use to decide?

2 Critical thinkers do not overgeneralize. An elevated heart rate is one part of the "alarm reaction" we experience is response to stress. Is elevating the heart rate always unhealthful? Explain.

3 Why is research into the correlation between stress and illness considered inadequate to explain cause and effect?

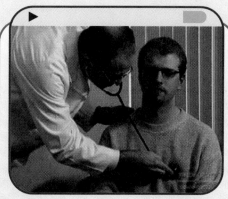

Stress is a huge problem in our society and has far-reaching effects on our health.

Watch this video!

Go to **www**

your companion website at
http://academic.cengage.com/psychology/rathus
Click on the Video Connections tab under this chapter.

---

marking them for destruction. The immune system "remembers" how to battle antigens by maintaining their antibodies in the bloodstream, often for years.[1]

Inflammation is another function of the immune system. When injury occurs, blood vessels in the area first contract (to stem bleeding) and then dilate. Dilation increases the flow of blood, cells, and natural chemicals to the damaged area, causing the redness, swelling, and warmth that characterize inflammation (Leonard, 2005). The increased blood supply also floods the region with white blood cells to combat invading microscopic life forms such as bacteria, which otherwise might use the local damage as a port of entry into the body.

Stress and the Immune System   Psychologists, biologists, and medical researchers have combined their efforts in a field of study that addresses the relationships among psychological factors, the nervous system, the endocrine system, the immune system, and disease. This field is called **psychoneuroimmunology.** One of its major concerns is the effect of stress on the immune system (Antoni et al., 2005). *How does stress affect the immune system?*

One of the reasons that stress eventually exhausts us is that it stimulates the production of steroids. Steroids suppress the functioning of the immune system. Suppression has negligible effects when steroids are secreted occasionally. But persistent secretion of steroids decreases inflammation and interferes with the formation of antibodies. As a consequence, we

---

[1] A vaccination introduces a weakened form of an antigen (usually a bacteria or a virus) into the body to stimulate the production of antibodies. Antibodies can confer immunity for many years, in some cases for a lifetime.

Inflammation Increased blood flow to an injured area of the body, resulting in redness, warmth, and an increased supply of white blood cells.

Psychoneuroimmunology The field that studies the relationships between psychological factors (e.g., attitudes and overt behavior patterns) and the functioning of the immune system.

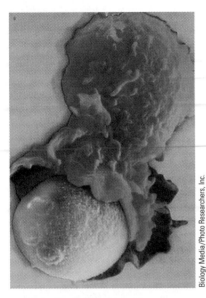

■ **Microscopic Warfare**
The immune system helps us to combat disease. It produces white blood cells (leukocytes), such as that shown here, which routinely engulf and kill pathogens like bacteria and viruses.

become more vulnerable to infections, including the common cold (Barnard et al., 2005; Cohen et al., 2001b, 2003).

In one study, dental students showed lower immune system functioning, as measured by lower levels of antibodies in their saliva, during stressful periods of the school year than immediately following vacations (Jemmott et al., 1983). In contrast, social support buffers the effects of stress and enhances the functioning of the immune system (Cohen et al., 2001a, 2001b). In the Jemmott study, students who had many friends showed less suppression of immune system functioning than students with few friends.

Other studies with students show that the stress of exams depresses the immune system's response to the Epstein-Barr virus, which causes fatigue and other problems (Glaser et al., 1993). Here, too, lonely students showed greater suppression of the immune system than students who had social support. All in all, however, there is only modest evidence that psychological interventions enhance the functioning of the immune system. A review of the research found that hypnosis (intended to help people relax), stress management methods, and conditioning methods were of some use, but less than reliable (Miller & Cohen, 2001).

Life Connections
Coping with Stress

Health psychologists have engaged in a wealth of research concerning the ways in which mental processes and behavior can help people cope with stress. Because stress depresses the functioning of the immune system, it may be that alleviating stress has beneficial effects on the immune system, thus making us less vulnerable to some health problems. At the very least, stress reduction reduces feelings of stress!

Here are some ways of coping with stress.

Controlling Irrational Thoughts People often feel pressure from their own thoughts. Consider the experiences in Table 10.4. How do we change the irrational thoughts that create and compound stress? The answer is deceptively simple, as you can see in the table: We just change them. This may require work, however.

Cognitive-behavioral psychologists (e.g., Marks & Dar, 2000) outline a procedure for controlling irrational or catastrophizing thoughts that often accompany feelings of anxiety, conflict, or tension:

1. Develop awareness of the thoughts that seem to be making you miserable by careful self-examination. Study the examples in Table 10.4 to see if they apply to you. (Also consider Ellis's list of irrational beliefs in Table 10.2 and ask yourself whether any of them governs your behavior.) Also: When you encounter anxiety or frustration, pay close attention to your thoughts.
2. Evaluate the accuracy of the thoughts. Are they guiding you toward a solution, or are they compounding your problems? Do they reflect reality or do they blow things out of proportion? Do they misplace the blame for failure or shortcomings?
3. Prepare thoughts that are incompatible with the irrational or catastrophizing thoughts and practice saying them firmly to yourself.
4. Reward yourself with a mental pat on the back for making effective changes in your beliefs and thought patterns.

Lowering Arousal: Turning Down the Inner Alarm Stress tends to trigger intense activity in the sympathetic branch of the autonomic nervous system—in other words, arousal. Psychologists and other scientists have developed many methods for teaching

TABLE 10.4 ■ **Controlling Irrational Beliefs and Thoughts**

IRRATIONAL (UPSETTING) THOUGHTS	RATIONAL (CALMING) THOUGHTS
"Oh my God, I'm going to completely lose control!"	"This is painful and upsetting, but I don't have to go to pieces over it."
"This will never end."	"This will end even if it's hard to see the end right now."
"It'll be awful if Mom gives me that look again."	"It's more pleasant when Mom's happy with me, but I can live with it if she isn't."
"How can I go out there? I'll look like a fool."	"So you're not perfect. That doesn't mean that you're going to look stupid. And so what if someone thinks you look stupid? You can live with that, too. Just stop worrying and have some fun."
"My heart's going to leap out of my chest! How much can I stand?"	"Easy—hearts don't leap out of chests. Stop and think! Breathe slowly, in and out."
"What can I do? There's nothing I can do!"	"Easy—stop and think. Just because you can't think of a solution right now doesn't mean there's nothing you can do. Take it a minute at a time. Breathe easy."

Do irrational beliefs or catastrophizing thoughts compound your feelings of anxiety and tension? Cognitive-behavioral psychologists suggest that you can cope with stress by becoming aware of your irrational, upsetting thoughts and replacing them with rational, calming thoughts.

people to reduce arousal. These include meditation, biofeedback, and progressive relaxation. In progressive relaxation, people purposefully tense a particular muscle group before relaxing it. This sequence allows them to develop awareness of their muscle tensions and also to differentiate between feelings of tension and relaxation.

The following instructions will help you try meditation:

■ Begin by meditating once or twice a day for 10 to 20 minutes.
■ In meditation, what you *don't* do is more important than what you *do* do. Adopt a passive, "what happens, happens" attitude.
■ Create a quiet, nondisruptive environment. For example, don't face a light directly.
■ Do not eat for an hour beforehand; avoid caffeine for at least two hours.
■ Assume a comfortable position.
■ As a device to aid concentrating, you may focus on your breathing or seat yourself before a calming object such as a plant or burning incense.
■ If you are using a mantra (like the syllable "om," pronounced aummm), you can prepare for meditation and say the mantra out loud several times. Enjoy it. Then say it more and more softly. Close your eyes and only think the mantra. Allow yourself to perceive, rather than actively think, the mantra. Again, adopt a passive attitude. Continue to perceive the mantra. It may grow louder or softer, disappear for a while, then return.
■ If disruptive thoughts enter your mind as you are meditating, you can allow them to "pass through." Don't get wrapped up in trying to squelch them, or you may raise your level of arousal.
■ Allow yourself to drift. (You won't go too far.) What happens, happens.

■ Above all, take what you get. You cannot force the relaxing effects of meditation. You can only set the stage for it and allow it to happen.

Exercising: Run for Your Life?

I like long walks, especially when they are taken by people who annoy me.
—FRED ALLEN

Exercise, particularly aerobic exercise, enhances the functioning of the immune system, contributes to our psychological well-being, and helps us cope with stress (Jonsdottir et al., 2000; Tkachuk & Martin, 1999). *Aerobic exercise* refers to exercise that requires a sustained increase in consumption of oxygen. Aerobic exercise promotes cardiovascular fitness. Aerobic exercises include, but are not limited to, running and jogging, running in place, walking (at more than a leisurely pace), aerobic dancing, jumping rope, swimming, bicycle riding, basketball, racquetball, and cross-country skiing.

Anaerobic exercises, in contrast, involve short bursts of muscle activity. Examples of anaerobic exercises are weight training, calisthenics (which usually allow rest periods between exercises), and sports such as baseball, in which there are infrequent bursts of strenuous activity. Anaerobic exercises can strengthen muscles and improve flexibility.

Exercise helps people cope by enhancing their physical fitness, or "condition." Fitness includes muscle strength; muscle endurance; suppleness or flexibility; cardiorespiratory, or aerobic, fitness; and a higher ratio of muscle to fat (usually due to both building muscle and reducing fat). Fitness also enhances our natural immunity and boosts our levels of endorphins (Jonsdottir et al., 2000). Cardiovascular fitness, or "condition," means that the body can use more oxygen during vigorous activity and pump more blood with each heartbeat. Because conditioned athletes' hearts pump more blood with each beat, they usually have a slower pulse rate—that is, fewer heartbeats per minute. During aerobic exercise, however, they may double or triple their resting heart rate for minutes at a time.

Aerobic exercise raises blood levels of high-density lipoproteins (HDL, or "good cholesterol") (Stampfer et al., 2000). HDL lowers the amount of low-density lipoproteins (LDL, or "bad cholesterol") in the blood. This is another way in which exercise may reduce the risk of heart attacks.

How about you? Are you thinking of climbing onto the exercise bandwagon? If so:

■ Unless you have engaged in sustained and vigorous exercise recently, seek the advice of a medical expert. If you smoke, have a family history of heart disease, are overweight, or are over 40, get a stress test.

■ Consider joining a beginner's aerobics class. Group leaders are not usually experts in physiology, but at least they "know the steps." You'll also be among other beginners and derive the benefits of social support.

■ Get the proper equipment to facilitate performance and avert injury.

■ Read up on the activity you are considering. Books, magazines, and newspaper articles will give you ideas as to how to get started and how fast to progress.

■ Consider activities you can sustain for a lifetime. Don't worry about building yourself up rapidly. Enjoy yourself. Your strength and endurance will progress on their own. If you do not enjoy what you're doing, you're not likely to stick to it.

■ If you feel severe pain, don't try to exercise "through" it. Soreness is to be expected for beginners (and for old-timers now and then). In that sense, soreness, at least when it is intermittent, is normal. But sharp pain is abnormal and a sign that something is wrong.

■ Have fun! ■

( ) **Learning Connections**

◀◀ *Stress and the Body—The War Within* ▶▶

REVIEW:

8 The first stage of the general adaptation
syndrome is
(a) anger,
(b) alarm,
(c) resistance,
(d) flight.

9 Under stress, the hypothalamus secretes
(a) corticotrophin-releasing hormone,
(b) adrenocorticotrophic hormone,
(c) cortisol,
(d) adrenaline.

10 A tend-and-befriend response to stress is most
likely to be shown by
(a) children,
(b) men,
(c) women,
(d) older people.

11 Some leukocytes produce _____ that bind to
foreign agents and mark them for destruction.
(a) antibodies,
(b) antigens,
(c) pathogens,
(d) steroids.

CRITICAL THINKING:
Prolonged stress is connected with health problems. Must you avoid
stress to remain healthy, or can you do something to become psychologically hardy?

Go to
http://academic.cengage.com/psychology/rathus
for an interactive version of this review.

PSYCHOLOGY AND HEALTH

Why do people become ill? Why do some people develop cancer? Why do others have heart attacks? Why do still others seem to be immune to these illnesses? Why do some of us seem to come down with everything that is going around, while others ride out the roughest winters with nary a sniffle? *What is the biopsychosocial approach to health?* The **biopsychosocial** approach recognizes that there is no single, simple answer to these questions. The likelihood of contracting an illness—be it a case of the flu or cancer—can reflect the interaction of many factors, including biological, psychological, and sociocultural factors (Schneiderman et al., 2005).

Biological factors such as pathogens, inoculations, injuries, age, gender, and a family history of disease may strike us as the most obvious causes of illness. Genetics, in particular, tempts some people to assume that there is little they can do about their health. Some cases of health problems are unavoidable for people with certain genes. ◁▷ **Truth or Fiction Revisited:** But it is not true that if you have a family history of heart disease or cancer, there is little or nothing you can do to prevent developing the illness yourself. In many cases, especially with heart problems and cancer, genes only create *predispositions* toward the health problem. The life choices we make—the behaviors we select—also affect our likelihood of becoming ill (Hoover, 2000).

Genetic predispositions interact with the environment to express themselves (Kéri, 2003). For example, genetic factors are involved in breast cancer. However, rates of breast cancer among women who have recently immigrated to the United States from rural Asia are similar to those in their countries of origin and nearly 80% lower than the rates among

Biopsychosocial Having to do with the interactions of biological, psychological, and sociocultural factors.

TABLE 10.5 ■ Annual Preventable Deaths in the United States*

■ Elimination of tobacco use could prevent 400,000 deaths each year from cancer, heart and lung diseases, and stroke.

■ Improved diet and exercise could prevent 300,000 deaths from conditions like heart disease, stroke, diabetes, and cancer.

■ Control of underage and excess drinking of alcohol could prevent 100,000 deaths from motor vehicle accidents, falls, drownings, and other alcohol-related injuries.

■ Immunizations for infectious diseases could prevent up to 100,000 deaths.

■ Safer sex or sexual abstinence could prevent 10,000–20,000 deaths from sexually transmitted infections (STIs).

*Other measures for preventing needless deaths include improved worker training and safety to prevent accidents in the workplace, wider screening for breast and cervical cancer, and control of high blood pressure and elevated blood cholesterol levels.

third-generation Asian American women, whose rates are similar to those of European American women (Hoover, 2000). Thus factors related to one's lifestyle are also intimately connected with the risk of breast cancer—and most other kinds of cancer.

Biological, psychological (behavior and personality), sociocultural factors, and stressors all play roles in health and illness. Many health problems are affected by psychological factors, such as attitudes, emotions, and behavior (Kiecolt-Glaser et al., 2002b; Salovey et al., 2000). Table 10.5 reveals that nearly 1 million deaths each year in the United States are preventable (Health, United States, 2002). Stopping smoking, eating right, exercising, and controlling alcohol use would prevent nearly 80% of these. Psychological states such as anxiety and depression can impair the functioning of the immune system, rendering us more vulnerable to physical disorders ranging from viral infections to cancer (McGuire et al., 2002; Salovey et al., 2000).

Let us now discuss some health problems, including headaches, heart disease, and cancer. Each of them involves biological, psychological, and environmental factors—including the social and technological environments. Although these are medical problems, we also explore ways in which psychologists have contributed to their prevention and treatment.

──■─ Headaches: When Stress Presses and Pounds

Headaches are among the most common stress-related physical ailments. Nearly 20% of people in the United States suffer severe headaches. *How has psychology contributed to the understanding and treatment of headaches?* To answer this question, let us consider the common tension headache and the more severe migraine headache.

Tension Headache   The single most frequent kind of headache is the tension headache. During the first two stages of the GAS we are likely to contract muscles in the shoulders, neck, forehead, and scalp. Persistent stress can lead to constant contraction of these muscles, causing muscle tension headaches.   ◆ **Truth or Fiction Revisited:** Psychological factors, such as the tendency to catastrophize negative events—that is, to blow them out of proportion—can bring on a tension headache (Ukestad & Wittrock, 1996). A combination of stress and feelings of anxiety or depression also tends to trigger them (Huber & Henrich, 2003; Janke et al., 2004). Tension headaches often come on gradually. They are most often characterized by dull, steady pain on both sides of the head and feelings of tightness or pressure.

Migraine Headache   The **migraine headache** usually has a sudden onset and is identified by severe throbbing pain on one side of the head. Migraines affect 1 American in 10 (Mulvihill, 2000). They may last for hours or days. Sensory and motor disturbances often precede the pain; a warning "aura" may include vision problems and perception of unusual odors. The migraines themselves are often accompanied by sensitivity to light, loss of

Migraine headaches Throbbing headaches that are connected with changes in the supply of blood to the head.

appetite, nausea, vomiting, sensory and motor disturbances such as loss of balance, and changes in mood. Imaging techniques suggest that when something triggers a migraine, neurons at the back of the brain fire in waves that ripple across the top of the head then down to the brainstem, the site of many pain centers.

Triggers for migraines include barometric pressure; pollen; certain drugs; monosodium glutamate (MSG), a chemical that is often used to enhance flavor; chocolate; aged cheese; beer, champagne, and red wine; the hormonal changes connected with menstruation; and stress-related anxieties (Goadsby et al., 2002; Huber & Henrich, 2003; Mulvihill, 2000).

The behaviors connected with migraine headaches serve as a mini-textbook in health psychology (Holroyd, 2002). For example, the Type A behavior pattern apparently contributes to migraines. In one study, 53% of people who had migraine headaches showed the Type A behavior pattern, compared with 23% of people who had muscle tension headaches (Rappaport et al., 1988). Another study compared 26 women who had regular migraines with women who had none. The migraine sufferers were more sensitive to pain, more self-critical, more likely to catastrophize stress and pain, and less likely to seek social support when under stress (Hassinger et al., 1999).

Regardless of the source of the headache, we can unwittingly propel ourselves into a vicious cycle. Headache pain is a stressor that can lead us to increase, rather than relax, muscle tension in the neck, shoulders, scalp, and face.

Life Connections
Preventing and Coping with Headaches

Because many headaches are related to stress, one way to fight headaches is to lessen the stress in your life. All the methods mentioned here—challenging irrational beliefs, lowering the physical alarm, and exercising—may be of help (Astin, 2004). We described the method of meditation for lowering arousal. Progressive relaxation focuses on decreasing muscle tension and has been shown to be highly effective in relieving muscle tension headaches (Blanchard et al., 1990; Holden et al., 1999). Biofeedback training has also helped many people with migraine headaches (Powers et al., 2001; Scharff et al., 2002).

Aspirin, acetaminophen, ibuprofen, and many prescription drugs also fight headaches. Some inhibit the production of the prostaglandins that help initiate transmission of pain messages to the brain. Newer prescription drugs can help prevent many migraines; ask your doctor. People who are sensitive to MSG or red wine can request meals without MSG and switch to white wine. ▪

──▪── Coronary Heart Disease: Taking Stress to Heart

Coronary heart disease (CHD) is the leading cause of death in the United States, most often from heart attacks (American Heart Association, 2005b). *What are the major risk factors for coronary heart disease?* Let us begin by considering the risk factors for CHD.

- ▪ *Family history:* People with a family history of CHD are more likely to develop the disease themselves (American Heart Association, 2005a; Nabel, 2003).
- ▪ *Physiological conditions:* Obesity, high **serum cholesterol** levels, and **hypertension** are risk factors for CHD (American Heart Association, 2005a; Stamler et al., 2000; R. B. Williams et al., 2003). About one American in five has hypertension, or abnormally high blood pressure (Blumenthal et al., 2002), which can lead to CHD. When high blood pressure has no identifiable cause, it is referred to as *essential hypertension.* This condition has a genetic component (Levy et al., 2000; S. M. Williams et al.,

Serum cholesterol Cholesterol in the blood.

Hypertension High blood pressure.

2000). Blood pressure is also, however, connected with emotions like depression and anxiety (Kazuomi Kario et al., 2001). It also rises when we inhibit the expression of strong feelings or are angry or on guard against threats (Jorgensen et al., 1996). When we are under stress, we may believe that we can feel our blood pressure "pounding through the roof," but this notion is usually false. Most people cannot recognize hypertension. Therefore it is important to check the blood pressure regularly.

- *Patterns of consumption:* Patterns include heavy drinking, smoking, and overeating (Stampfer et al., 2000; Xin et al., 2001). On the other hand, a little alcohol seems to be good for the heart (Blanco-Colio et al., 2000).

- *Type A behavior:* Most studies suggest that there is at least a modest relationship between Type A behavior and CHD (Le Melledo et al., 2001; Smith & Ruiz, 2002). Research suggests that alleviating Type A behavior may reduce the risk of *recurrent* heart attacks (Friedman & Ulmer, 1984).

- *Hostility and holding in feelings of anger:* Hostility seems to be the component of the Type A behavior pattern that is most harmful to physical health (Birks & Roger, 2000; Smith & Ruiz, 2002; R. B. Williams et al., 2003). One study that controlled for the influences of other risk factors, like high blood pressure and cholesterol levels, smoking, and obesity, found that people who are highly prone to anger are about three times as likely as other people to have heart attacks (Williams et al., 2000). The stress hormones connected with anger can constrict blood vessels to the heart, leading to a heart attack. Chronically hostile and angry people also have higher cholesterol levels (Richards et al., 2000). Highly hostile young adults—as young as 18 to 30—are already at greater risk for hardening of the arteries, which increases the risk of heart attacks (Iribarren et al., 2000).

- *Job strain:* Overtime work, assembly line labor, and exposure to conflicting demands can all contribute to CHD. High-strain work, which makes heavy demands on workers but gives them little personal control, puts workers at the highest risk (Bishop et al., 2003; Krantz et al., 1988; Smith & Ruiz, 2002). As shown in Figure 10.4, the work of food servers may best fit this description.

Figure 10.4
The Job-Strain Model
This model highlights the psychological demands made by various occupations and the amount of personal (decision) control they allow. Occupations characterized by high demand and low decision control place workers at greatest risk for heart disease.

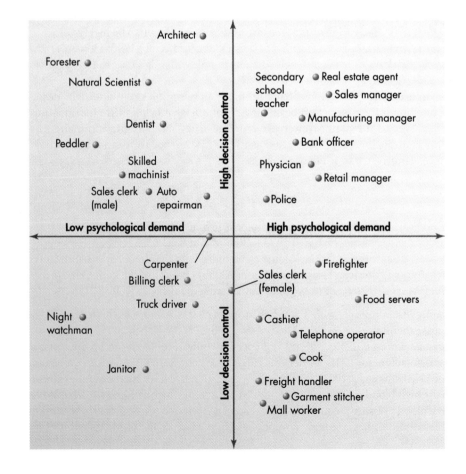

- *Chronic fatigue, stress, anxiety, depression, and emotional strain* (Heinz et al., 2003; Pasic et al., 2003; Tacon et al., 2003). Depression is connected with irregularities in the heart rate and may make blood platelets "sticky," which may, in turn, cause clots (Kramer, 2003).
- *Sudden stressors:* For example, after the 1994 Los Angeles earthquake there was an increased incidence of death from heart attacks in people with heart disease (Leor et al., 1996).
- *A physically inactive lifestyle* (Stampfer et al., 2000).

African Americans are more likely than European Americans to have heart attacks and to die from them (American Heart Association, 2005a; Malkin, 2004). Figure 10.5 compares the death rates from heart disease of African American women and women from other ethnic backgrounds in the United States (Smith, 2000). Early diagnosis and treatment might help decrease the racial gap. However, African Americans with heart disease are less likely than European Americans to obtain complex procedures such as bypass surgery and to take simple measures such as aspirin, even when they would benefit equally from them (Freeman & Payne, 2000; Rathore et al., 2000). Moreover, when European Americans and African Americans show up in the emergency room with heart attacks and other severe cardiac problems, physicians are more likely to misdiagnose the conditions among the African Americans (J. H. Pope et al., 2000).

Figure 10.5

Deaths from Heart Disease per 100,000 Women Aged 35 and Above

African American women have experienced a higher annual death rate from heart attacks (553 per 100,000) than women from any other ethnic group in the United States.

reflect & relate

Does coronary heart disease or cancer run in your family? If so, what can you do about it?

Life Connections
Reducing the Risk of CHD Through Behavior Modification

Once CHD has been diagnosed, a number of medical treatments, including surgery and medication, are available. People who have not had CHD (as well as those who have), however, can profit from behavior modification techniques designed to reduce the risk factors. These methods include the following.

- *Stopping smoking.* See Chapter 5.
- *Dietary change.* See Chapter 9 for strategies for maintaining a healthful body weight. Most health experts agree on three dietary strategies that are helpful in preventing CHD (Mozaffarian et al., 2003; Willett, 2002; www.mypyramid.gov): Substitute nonhydrogenated unsaturated fats for saturated fats; increase consumption of omega-3 fatty acids, which are found in fish, fish oil supplements, and plant sources; and eat a diet high in fruits, vegetables, nuts (unsalted), and whole grains.
- *Reducing hypertension.* Medication reduces hypertension, but behavioral changes, including the dietary changes outlined above, are sometimes enough: meditation (Labiano & Brusasca, 2002), aerobic exercise (Blumenthal et al., 2005), and consuming less salt (Sacks et al., 2001).
- *Lowering low-density lipoprotein (harmful) serum cholesterol.* There is also medication for lowering LDL, but behavioral methods involve exercise, medication, and cutting down on foods that are high in cholesterol and saturated fats (Stampfer et al., 2000).
- *Modifying Type A behavior.*
- *Managing feelings of anger.*
- *Exercising.* Sustained physical activity protects people from CHD and helps them cope with stress (Blumenthal et al., 2005; Stampfer et al., 2000). ■

──■─ Cancer: Swerving Off Course

Cancer is the number-one killer of women in the United States and the number-two killer of men (American Cancer Society, 2005a). Cancer is characterized by the development of abnormal, or mutant, cells that may take root anywhere in the body: in the blood, bones, digestive tract, lungs, and sex organs. If their spread is not controlled early, the cancerous cells may *metastasize*—that is, establish colonies elsewhere in the body. It appears that our bodies develop cancerous cells frequently. However, these are normally destroyed by the immune system. People whose immune system is damaged by physical or psychological factors may be more likely to develop tumors (Antoni, 2003).

What are the major risk factors for cancer?

Risk Factors   As with many other disorders, people can inherit a disposition toward cancer (American Cancer Society, 2005a; Hoover, 2000). Carcinogenic genes may remove the brakes from cell division, allowing cells to multiply wildly. Or they may allow mutations to accumulate unchecked. Many behavior patterns, however, markedly heighten the risk for cancer. These include smoking, drinking alcohol (especially in women), and sunbathing (which may cause skin cancer due to exposure to ultraviolet light). Prolonged psychological conditions such as depression or stress may heighten the risk of some kinds of cancer by depressing the functioning of the immune system (Bauer et al., 2003; McGuire et al., 2002; Salovey et al., 2000).

African Americans are more likely than European Americans to contract most forms of cancer (American Cancer Society, 2005b). Possibly because of genetic factors, the incidence of lung cancer is significantly higher among African Americans than European Americans (American Cancer Society, 2005b). Once they contract cancer, African Americans are more likely than European Americans to die from it (American Cancer Society, 2005b). The results for African Americans are connected with their lower socioeconomic status and relative lack of access to health care (Altman, 2005; Whitfield et al., 2002).

Also consider cultural differences in health. Death rates from cancer are higher in such nations as the Netherlands, Denmark, England, Canada, and—yes—the United States, where average rates of animal fat intake are high (Bray & Atkin, 2004). Death rates from cancer are lower in such nations as Thailand, the Philippines, and Japan, where fat intake is lower and people eat more fruits and vegetables. However, studies in the United States have brought into question the usefulness of eating fruits and vegetables in preventing cancer. For example, Karin Michels and her colleagues (2000) followed some 80,000 women and 40,000 men over several years and found little connection between eating fruits and vegetables and the risk of colon and rectal cancers. Arthur Schatzkin and his colleagues (2000) studied some 2,000 women and men who had had precancerous growths removed from their colons. The subjects were randomly assigned to eat low-fat diets that were high in fiber, fruits, and vegetables and were assessed four years later. There were no differences in the incidence of new precancerous growths in the colons of the two groups.

Researchers have also suggested possible links between stress and cancer (Salovey et al., 2000). For example, Rachel Yehuda (2003) suggests that stress sometimes lowers levels of cortisol and impairs the ability of the immune system to destroy cancer cells. But here, too, the research evidence calls these theoretical links into question.

For example, Polly Newcomb (2005), head of a Seattle cancer prevention program, interviewed nearly 1,000 women, some of whom had developed breast cancer and others who had not. The women were asked about the incidence of major life changes over a five-year period. There were no differences in the incidence of these life events between the cancer patients and the other women.

Does stress cause cancer, then? "I have no idea, and nobody else does, either," replies Ohio State psychologist Barbara Andersen (2005), who researches stress reduction in cancer patients. "If somebody suggested that they know, I would question them."

Concept Review 10.1 summarizes the possible biopsychosocial factors in heart disease and cancer.

CONCEPT REVIEW ■ CONCEPT REVIEW 10.1 ■ CONCEPT REVIEW

BIOPSYCHOSOCIAL FACTORS IN HEART DISEASE AND CANCER

HEART DISEASE	CANCER

HEART DISEASE

Biological:
Family history
Physiological conditions:
   Obesity
   High serum cholesterol
   Hypertension

Psychological (personality and behavior):
Type A behavior
Hostility and holding in feelings of anger
Job strain
Chronic fatigue, stress, anxiety, depression,
   and emotional strain
Patterns of consumption:
   Heavy drinking (but a drink a day may be
      helpful with heart disease)
   Smoking
   Overeating
Sudden stressors
Physical inactivity

Sociocultural:
African Americans are more prone to hyper-
   tension and heart disease than Euro-
   pean Americans
Access to health care
Timing of diagnosis and treatment

CANCER

Biological:
Family history
Physiological conditions:
   Obesity

Psychological (personality and behavior):
Patterns of consumption:
   Smoking
   Drinking alcohol (especially in women)
   Eating animal fats?
Sunbathing (skin cancer)
Prolonged depression
Stress? Especially prolonged stress

Sociocultural: .
Socioeconomic status
Access to health care
Timing of diagnosis and treatment
Higher death rates are found in nations with
   higher rates of fat intake

Life Connections
Preventing and Coping with Cancer

People with cancer not only must cope with the biological aspects of their illnesses, but they may also face psychological problems such as feelings of anxiety and depression, changes in body image after the removal of a breast or testicle, feelings of vulnerability, and family problems. For example, some families criticize members with cancer for feeling sorry for themselves or not fighting the disease hard enough (Andersen et al., 1994; Rosenthal, 1993). Psychological stress due to cancer can weaken the immune system, setting the stage for other health problems, such as respiratory tract infections (Andersen, 2002). Even training physicians to listen more attentively and convey warmth can help (Andersen, 2002). ■

There are psychological treatments for the discomfort and stress that often accompany medical procedures such as chemotherapy and surgery. People undergoing chemotherapy who also obtain relaxation training and guided imagery techniques experience significantly less nausea and vomiting than patients who do not use these methods (Wang et al., 2002). Distraction helps (L. L. Cohen, 2002). Research with children suggests that virtual reality distracts them from the effects of chemotherapy (Gershon et al., 2004). Playing video games apparently calms children being prepared for surgery (Video games calm kids before surgery, 2004).

Cancer requires medical treatment, and in many cases, there are few treatment options. But people with cancer can still choose how they will deal with the disease. Patients' moods are connected with the functioning of the immune system, and we know that prolonged stress and depression and feelings of tension depress the immune system (McGuire et al., 2002). The literature is mixed, however, about whether patients' attitudes and moods can actually affect the course of cancer (Kiecolt-Glaser et al., 2002b). Some studies, however, suggest that there may be a somewhat higher survival rate for women with breast cancer who show a fighting spirit rather than feelings of depression (Faller et al., 1999; Hjerl et al., 2003; Watson et al., 1999).

Psychologists are teaching coping skills to people with cancer to relieve psychological distress as well as pain. One study of 235 women with metastatic breast cancer found that group therapy aimed at providing support and helping the women express their feelings enhanced the women's moods and decreased the amount of pain they experienced (Goodwin et al., 2001). Unfortunately, the therapy did not affect their survival rate.

We can also take measures such as the following:

- Exercise regularly. Exercise not only helps us cope with stress, it also lowers the risk of developing CHD.
- Have regular medical checkups so that cancer will be detected early. Cancer is most treatable in the early stages.
- If we are struck by cancer, we can fight it energetically.

We conclude this section with good news for readers of this book: *Better-educated* people—that means *you*—are more likely to modify health-impairing behavior and reap the benefits of change (Pappas et al., 1993).

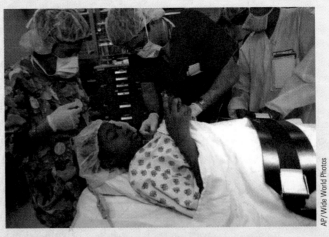

■ The PlayStation Approach to Coping with Discomfort?
Nykia Crawford, 10, distracts herself as she is prepped for surgery by playing a video game.

Learning Connections

◀◀ *Psychology and Health* ▶▶

REVIEW:

12 Which of the following is not a trigger for migraine headaches?
 (a) Hormonal changes connected with menstruation,
 (b) Eating fruits and vegetables,
 (c) Barometric pressure,
 (d) Stress-related anxieties.

13 A risk factor for coronary heart disease is a high level of serum
 (a) imipramine,
 (b) dopamine,
 (c) cholesterol,
 (d) leukocytes.

14 _____ is a risk factor for CHD, but not for cancer.
 (a) Family history,
 (b) Consumption of saturated fats,
 (c) Cigarette smoking,
 (d) Hostility.

15 People who live in _____ are least likely to develop cancer.
 (a) the United States,
 (b) Denmark,
 (c) England,
 (d) Thailand.

CRITICAL THINKING:

Health problems such as headaches, coronary disorders, and cancer are usually conceptualized as medical problems. What are the roles of psychologists in understanding and treating these problems?

Go to http://academic.cengage.com/psychology/rathus for an interactive version of this review.

RECITE—*An Active Summary*™

 Recite to Go! *Don't have time to study right now? You can study on the go!*
Go to your companion website and download an audio version of this review section to your media player. You can also access an interactive flash-card version of this review from your website.

1. What is health psychology?	Health psychology studies relationships between psychological factors and the prevention and treatment of physical illness.
2. What is stress?	Stress is the demand made on an organism to adjust. Some stress keeps us alert and occupied, but too much can tax our adjustive capacities and contribute to health problems.
3. What are daily hassles?	Daily hassles are regularly occurring experiences that threaten or harm our well-being, such as household, health, time pressure, inner concern, environmental, financial responsibility, work, and future security hassles.
4. How can too much of a good thing make you ill?	Too many positive life changes can affect health because life changes require adjustment. Hassles and life changes are connected with health problems.

5. What is conflict?	Conflict is feeling pulled in two or more directions by opposing motives.
6. How do irrational beliefs create or compound stress?	Negative activating events can be made more aversive when irrational beliefs compound their effects. Sample irrational beliefs include high need for social approval and perfectionism.
7. What is Type A behavior?	Type A behavior involves time urgency, competitiveness, impatience, and hostility.
8. How do our self-efficacy expectations affect our ability to withstand stress?	Self-efficacy expectations encourage us to persist in difficult tasks and to endure discomfort. Self-efficacy expectations are also connected with lower levels of adrenaline and noradrenaline, thus moderating bodily arousal.
9. What characteristics are connected with psychological hardiness?	Psychological hardiness is characterized by commitment, challenge, and control.
10. Is there any evidence that humor helps us cope with stress?	Research evidence shows that students who produce humor under adversity experience less stress. Watching humorous videos may enhance the functioning of the immune system.
11. How do predictability and control help us cope with stress?	Predictability allows us to brace ourselves, and control permits us to plan ways of coping with stress.
12. Does social support help people cope with stress?	Social support has been shown to help people resist infectious diseases such as colds. It also helps people cope with the stress of cancer and other health problems.
13. What is the general adaptation syndrome?	The GAS describes bodily changes triggered by stressors. There are three stages: alarm, resistance, and exhaustion. Corticosteroids resist stress by fighting inflammation and allergic reactions. Adrenaline mobilizes the body. The parasympathetic division of the ANS predominates during the exhaustion stage and is connected with depression and inactivity.
14. How does the immune system work?	Leukocytes engulf and kill pathogens, worn-out body cells, and cancerous cells. The immune system "remembers" how to battle antigens by maintaining their antibodies in the bloodstream. The immune system also facilitates inflammation, increasing the number of leukocytes transported to an injury.
15. How does stress affect the immune system?	Stress depresses the functioning of the immune system by stimulating the release of corticosteroids. Steroids interfere with the formation of antibodies.
16. What is the biopsychosocial approach to health?	This view recognizes that many factors, including biological, psychological, and sociocultural factors, affect our health.
17. How has psychology contributed to the understanding and treatment of headaches?	Psychologists participate in research concerning the origins of headaches, including stress and tension, and help people alleviate headaches by reducing tension. Biofeedback training methods help many people cope with migraines.
18. What are the major risk factors for coronary heart disease?	The major risk factors include family history; conditions such as hypertension and high levels of serum cholesterol; behavior patterns such as heavy drinking, smoking, eating fatty foods, and Type A behavior; work overload; chronic tension and fatigue; and physical inactivity.
19. What are the major risk factors for cancer?	The major risk factors for cancer include family history, smoking, drinking alcohol, eating animal fats, sunbathing, and stress.

Key Terms

Stress   365

Eustress   365

Health psychology   365

Pathogen   365

Daily hassles   366

Uplifts   366

Conflict   369

Approach–approach conflict   369

Avoidance–avoidance conflict   370

Approach–avoidance conflict   370

Multiple approach–avoidance
conflict   370

Catastrophize   370

Type A behavior   371

Self-efficacy expectations   373

Psychological hardiness   374

Locus of control   374

Internals   376

Externals   376

General adaptation syndrome
(GAS)   377

Alarm reaction   377

Fight-or-flight reaction   377

Resistance stage   380

Exhaustion stage   380

Immune system   380

Leukocytes   380

Antigen   380

Antibodies   380

Inflammation   381

Psychoneuroimmunology   381

Biopsychosocial   385

Migraine headaches   386

Serum cholesterol   387

Hypertension   387

Active Learning Resources

Visit Your Companion Website
for This Book

http://academic.cengage.com/psychology/rathus

Check out this companion website where you will find online resources directly linked to your book. This is where you'll access the videos highlighted in your Video Connections feature. You can answer the questions online and email them to your professor. In addition you'll find downloadable audio review material, interactive versions of the study aids, Power Visuals for mastering and reviewing key concepts, as well as quizzing, and much more!

CENGAGENOW™   **http://academic.cengage.com**

Need help studying? This site is your one-stop study shop. Take a Pre-Test and Cengage NOW will generate a Personalized Study Plan based on your test results. The Study Plan will identify the topics you need to review and direct you to online resources to help you master those topics. You can then take a Post-Test to help you determine the concepts you have mastered and what you still need to work on. In addition you can access interactive media including the videos highlighted in your Video Connections box.

Author Blog

What does your author Spence Rathus have to say about the state of psychology? Visit your companion website every Tuesday and click on "Author Blog." This is where he'll talk about the most recent controversies and hot topics in psychology. This will keep you up to date with what your author is thinking and give you great insight into modern psychology.

CHAPTER 11

Personality: Theory and Measurement

truth or fiction?

| T | F | Biting one's fingernails or smoking cigarettes as an adult is a sign of conflict experienced during early childhood. |

| T | F | Bloodletting and vomiting were once recommended as ways of coping with depression. |

| T | F | 2,500 years ago, a Greek physician devised a way of looking at personality that—with a little "tweaking"—remains in use today. |

| T | F | Actually, there are no basic personality traits. We are all conditioned by society to behave in certain ways. |

| T | F | The most well-adjusted immigrants are those who abandon the language and customs of their country of origin and become like members of the dominant culture in their new host country. |

| T | F | Psychologists can determine whether a person has told the truth on a personality test. |

| T | F | There is a psychological test made up of inkblots, and test-takers are asked to say what the blots look like to them. |

Go to www

http://academic.cengage.com/pstchology/rathus
for an interactive version of this Truth or Fiction feature.

As a psychologist, I see it as my duty to keep abreast of all developments in my field. So I Googled "personality tests online." Google retrieved 2.3 million hits in 0.22 seconds (slowpoke). There was certainly quantity, but how about quality?

Consider the eight "sponsored links":

Employment Testing	Hire right with Brainbench skills, aptitude & personality assessments. **www.brainbench.com**
College & Career Plan . . .	Take a Personality Assessment Explore Suggested Careers & Majors **www.CollegeBoard.com**
Ultimate Personality Test	The Real You: A Scientific Analysis It's Fun, Accurate & Free! **www.Tickle.com**
Knowing Your Personality	Most detailed Personality Assessment on the Internet! **www.personality100.com**
Are You Hot?	Does your personality make you Hot? Take this fun test to find out! **www.ruhotquiz.com**
Are You Normal?	A fun test to see how your personality compares to the rest! **www.runormal.com**
Online Testing	Free information and resources on online testing. **www.snap.com**
Your Name Is No Accident	See Why the Amazing Truth of Your Numerology Chart Cannot Tell a Lie **www.123Numerology.com**

Image 100/Getty Images

■ **R U Hot?**
Because people may want to check out whether they're "hot" now and then, entrepreneurs have posted tests that they claim will give people the answer online. Is "hotness" a common personality trait? Are the tests that measure "hotness" reliable and valid? Stay tuned to this chapter for some answers and speculations.

I was rather, well, sort of tickled to see the traditional College Board, administrator of the beloved SATs, in the same cyberspace as www.tickle.com and www.ruhotquiz.com. The test at www.tickle.com was made up of 50 multiple-choice questions. I answered them, but then would have had to give them my personal info to get results. I decided to live without them, although the website quotes "Mark" of Boston as saying, "I could NOT believe that the results of my personality test were, 'Mark, you're a rock star.' I've been writing songs on my guitar my entire adult life. How did you know?!" Mark won; I guess I lose.

Now every psychology professor secretly craves to know whether she or he is hot, right? So I gave www.ruhotquiz.com a shot. After all, it was supposed to be a "fun test." I completed the multiple-choice questions, one of which asked me whether

I'd prefer to be with Ashlee Simpson or Jennifer Aniston. (My secret.) But then the website refused to tell me whether I was steaming hot or just tepid unless I would give them my email address. No way, José.

I didn't go to www.runormal.com. They might not have given me the answer I wanted. And as far as www.123Numerology.com is concerned, I really don't care whether my name is an accident, and I'm sure my numerology chart (whatever that is) would always tell the truth.

Just about every website listed on the first few pages of hits was a .com (commercial) website. They all wanted my money, which is understandable. But I didn't want any of their information badly enough to pay for it. True, I didn't check out all 2.3 million websites, but at least I took an unfair sample.

Now, I took the SATs long ago and I have already selected my college majors and my career, so I didn't try to take anything that the College Board was offering. But for students who aren't sure what they want to major in, or what they'd like to do after college, the College Board has useful assessments that are worth a look.

This is the chapter that many students think makes up the core of psychology—the chapter that talks about what personality is and how psychologists measure personality.

Just what** is **personality? But people do not necessarily even agree on how to use the word **personality.** Many equate personality with liveliness, as in "She's got a lot of personality." Others characterize a person's personality as consisting of one's most striking traits, as in a "shy personality" or a "happy-go-lucky personality." Psychologists define personality as the reasonably stable patterns of emotions, motives, and behavior that distinguish one person from another.

In this chapter, we lay the foundations for the understanding of personality. We see how psychologists seek to explain the development of personality and to predict how people with certain personality traits respond to the demands of life. We explore five perspectives on personality: the psychoanalytic, trait, learning, humanistic, and sociocultural perspectives. We also discuss personality tests—the methods used to measure whether people are introverted, agreeable, and, perhaps, "hot." In Chapter 12 we consider the connections between personality and psychological disorders.

THE PSYCHOANALYTIC PERSPECTIVE: EXCAVATING THE ICEBERG

Where do we get the idea that the "unconscious" can exert control over our behavior? One source is psychoanalytic theory.

There are several **psychoanalytic theories** of personality, each of which owes its origin to Sigmund Freud. Each teaches that personality is characterized by conflict. At first the conflict is external: Drives like sex, aggression, and the need for superiority come into

Personality The distinct patterns of behavior, thoughts, and feelings that characterize a person's adaptation to life.

Psychoanalytic theory Sigmund Freud's perspective, which emphasizes the importance of unconscious motives and conflicts as forces that determine behavior.

■ Sigmund Freud
Freud is one of the key figures in the history of psychology—the first person that comes to mind when most people are asked to name a psychologist. Today many see his teachings as unscientific and even question whether they should be included in a scientific psychology textbook.

Conscious Self-aware.

Preconscious Capable of being brought into awareness by the focusing of attention.

Unconscious In psychoanalytic theory, not available to awareness by simple focusing of attention.

Repression A defense mechanism that protects the person from anxiety by ejecting anxiety-evoking ideas and impulses from awareness.

Psychoanalysis In this usage, Freud's method of exploring human personality.

Psychic structure In psychoanalytic theory, a hypothesized mental structure that helps explain different aspects of behavior.

Id The psychic structure, present at birth, that represents physiological drives and is fully unconscious.

Ego The second psychic structure to develop, characterized by self-awareness, planning, and delay of gratification.

conflict with laws, social rules, and moral codes. But at some point laws and social rules are brought inward—that is, *internalized*. The conflict is then between opposing *inner* forces. At any given moment our behavior—including the behavior of our fictional serial killer—our thoughts, and our emotions represent the outcome of these inner contests. **What is Freud's psychoanalytic theory?**

■ Sigmund Freud's Theory of Psychosexual Development

Sigmund Freud (1856–1939) was a mass of contradictions. Some have lauded him as one of the greatest thinkers of the 20th century. Others have criticized him as overrated. He preached liberal views on sexuality but was himself a model of sexual restraint. He invented a popular form of psychotherapy but experienced lifelong psychologically related problems such as migraine headaches, fainting under stress, hatred of the telephone, and an addiction to cigars. He smoked 20 cigars a day and could not or would not break the habit even after he developed cancer of the jaw.

Freud was trained as a physician. Early in his practice, he was surprised to find that some people apparently experienced loss of feeling in a hand or paralysis of the legs even though they have no medical disorder. These odd symptoms often disappeared once the person recalled and discussed stressful events and feelings of guilt or anxiety that seemed to be related to the symptoms. Although these events and feelings lay hidden beneath the surface of awareness, they could influence behavior.

From this sort of clinical evidence, Freud concluded that the mind is like an iceberg. Only the tip of an iceberg rises above the surface of the water; the great mass of it lies hidden in the deep (see Figure 11.1). Freud came to believe that people, similarly, are aware of only a small part of the ideas and impulses that dwell within their minds. He thought that a larger portion of the mind—one that contained our deepest images, thoughts, fears, and urges—lies beneath the surface of awareness, where little light illumines them.

Freud labeled the region that pokes into the light of awareness the **conscious** part of the mind. He called the regions below the surface the *preconscious* and the *unconscious*. The **preconscious** mind contains ideas that are out of awareness but can be made conscious simply by focusing on them. The **unconscious** mind contains primitive instincts such as sex and aggression. Some unconscious urges cannot be experienced consciously because mental images and words cannot portray them in all their color and fury. Other unconscious urges may be kept below the surface by repression because they would create anxiety. **Repression** is defined as the automatic ejection of anxiety-evoking ideas from awareness. People forget many ugly experiences, and some research evidence suggests that people *might* repress them (Furnham et al., 2003; Myers & Brewin, 1994). Other investigators allow that forgetting and distortion of memory occurs, but view the concept of repression as nothing but a myth (Kihlstrom, 2002).

In the unconscious mind, primitive drives seek expression, while learned values try to keep them in check. The conflict can arouse emotional outbursts and psychological problems. To explore the unconscious mind, Freud used a form of mental detective work called **psychoanalysis.** In psychoanalysis, people are encouraged to talk about anything that pops into their mind while they remain comfortable and relaxed.

The Structure of Personality   Freud spoke of mental or **psychic structures** to describe the clashing forces of personality. Psychic structures cannot be seen or measured directly, but their presence is suggested by behavior, expressed thoughts, and emotions. Freud believed there are three psychic structures: the id, the ego, and the superego.

The **id** is present at birth. It represents biological drives and is unconscious. Freud described the id as "a chaos, a cauldron of seething excitations" (1927/1964, p. 73). The conscious mind might find it inconsistent to love and hate the same person, but such conflicting emotions can dwell side by side in the id. In the id, one can hate one's mother for failing to gratify immediately all of one's needs, while also loving her. The id seeks instant gratification of instincts without consideration for law, social custom, or other people.

The **ego** begins to develop during the first year of life, largely because a child's demands for gratification cannot all be met immediately. The ego stands for reason and good

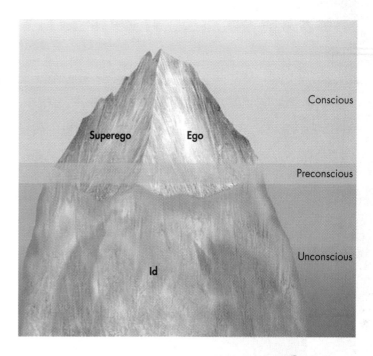

Figure 11.1
The Human Iceberg According to Freud
According to psychoanalytic theory, only the tip of human personality rises above the surface of the mind into conscious awareness. Material in the preconscious can become conscious if we direct our attention to it. Unconscious material tends to remain shrouded in mystery.

sense, for rational ways of coping with frustration. It curbs the appetites of the id and seeks ways to find gratification yet avoid social disapproval. The id informs you that you are hungry, but the ego decides to microwave enchiladas. The ego takes into account what is practical along with what is urged by the id. The ego also provides the conscious sense of self.

Although most of the ego is conscious, some of its business is carried out unconsciously. For example, the ego also acts as a censor that screens the impulses of the id. When the ego senses that improper impulses are rising into awareness, it may use psychological defenses to prevent them from surfacing. Repression is one such psychological defense, or **defense mechanism.** Several defense mechanisms are described in Table 11.1.

The **superego** develops as the child incorporates the moral standards and values of parents and other members of the community. The child does so through **identification,** by trying to become like these people. The superego holds up shining models of an ideal self and monitors the intentions of the ego, handing out judgments of right and wrong. It floods the ego with feelings of guilt and shame when the verdict is negative.

Freud believed that a healthy personality has found ways to gratify most of the id's demands without seriously offending the superego. Most of these demands are contained or repressed. If the ego is not a good problem solver, or if the superego is too stern, the ego will have a hard time of it.

According to psychoanalytic theory, identification is a means by which people usually incorporate the moral standards and values of parents and members of the community. As we see in the nearby "Closer Look," "members of the community" can include sports teams.

Stages of Psychosexual Development Freud stirred controversy by arguing that sexual impulses are a central factor in personality development, even among children. Freud believed that sexual feelings are closely linked to children's basic ways of relating to the world, such as nursing and moving their bowels.

Freud believed that a major instinct, *eros,* aims to preserve and perpetuate life. Eros is fueled by psychological, or psychic, energy, which Freud labeled **libido.** Libidinal energy involves sexual impulses, so Freud considered it to be *psychosexual.* As the child develops, this energy is expressed through sexual feelings in different parts of the body, or **erogenous zones.** To Freud, human development involves the transfer of libidinal energy from one erogenous zone to another. He hypothesized five periods of **psychosexual development:** oral, anal, phallic, latency, and genital.

During the first year of life a child experiences much of her or his world through the mouth. If it fits, into the mouth it goes. This is the **oral stage.** Freud argued that oral activities such as sucking and biting give the child sexual gratification as well as nourishment.

Freud believed that children encounter conflict during each stage of psychosexual development. During the oral stage, conflict centers on the nature and extent of oral gratification. Early weaning (cessation of breast feeding) can lead to frustration. Excessive gratification, on the other hand, can lead an infant to expect that it will routinely get anything it wants. Insufficient or excessive gratification in any stage could lead to **fixation** in that stage and to the development of traits that are characteristic of the stage. Oral traits include

Go to your student website to access an interactive version of this figure.

Defense mechanism In psychoanalytic theory, an unconscious function of the ego that protects it from anxiety-evoking material by preventing accurate recognition of this material.

Superego The third psychic structure, which functions as a moral guardian and sets forth high standards for behavior.

Identification In psychoanalytic theory, the unconscious adoption of another person's behavior.

Libido Sexual interest or drive.

Erogenous zone An area of the body that is sensitive to sexual sensations.

Psychosexual development In psychoanalytic theory, the process by which libidinal energy is expressed through different erogenous zones during different stages of development.

Oral stage The first stage of psychosexual development, during which gratification is hypothesized to be attained primarily through oral activities.

Fixation In psychoanalytic theory, arrested development. Attachment to objects of an earlier stage.

TABLE 11.1 ■ Defense Mechanisms

DEFENSE MECHANISM	DEFINITION	EXAMPLES
Repression	Ejection of anxiety-evoking ideas from awareness.	• A student forgets that a difficult term paper is due. • A person in therapy forgets an appointment when anxiety-evoking material is to be discussed.
Regression	Return, under stress, to a form of behavior characteristic of an earlier stage of development.	• An adolescent cries when forbidden to use the family car. • An adult becomes highly dependent on his parents after the breakup of his marriage.
Rationalization	Use of self-deceiving justifications for unacceptable behavior.	• A student blames her cheating on her teacher's leaving the room during a test. • A man explains his cheating on his income tax by saying, "Everyone does it."
Displacement	Transfer of ideas and impulses from threatening or unsuitable objects to less threatening objects.	• A worker picks a fight with her spouse after being sharply criticized by her supervisor.
Projection	Thrusting one's own unacceptable impulses onto others so that others are believed to have those impulses.	• A hostile person perceives the world as a dangerous place. • A sexually frustrated person interprets innocent gestures as sexual advances.
Reaction formation	Engaging in behavior that opposes one's genuine impulses to keep those impulses repressed.	• A person who is angry with a relative behaves in a "sickly sweet" manner toward that relative. • A sadistic individual becomes a physician.
Denial	Refusal to face the true nature of a threat.	• Belief that one will not contract cancer or heart disease even though one smokes heavily. • "It can't happen to me."
Sublimation	Channeling primitive impulses into positive, constructive efforts.	• A person paints nudes for the sake of "beauty" and "art." • A hostile person becomes a tennis star.

Laura Dwight/Corbis

■ The Oral Stage?
According to Sigmund Freud, during the first year the child is in the oral stage of development. If it fits, into the mouth it goes. What, according to Freud, are the effects of insufficient or excessive gratification during the oral stage? Is there evidence to support his views?

reflect & relate

If you were fixated in a stage of psychosocial development, which stage would it be? Explain.

dependency, gullibility, and excessive optimism or pessimism (depending on the child's experiences with gratification).

Freud theorized that adults with an *oral fixation* could experience exaggerated desires for "oral activities," such as smoking, overeating, alcohol abuse, and nail biting. Like the infant whose survival depends on the mercy of an adult, adults with oral fixations may desire clinging, dependent relationships.

A Closer Look
Who's Really "Number One"? On the "Persistent American Itch to Create Heroes"

Who are the NASCAR fans? Are they us, with "our insatiable craving for celebrity and our ache for fable and our need to live vicariously in the glamour and accomplishment of others and our persistent American itch to create heroes" (MacGregor, 2005)? Or are they, as described in Steve Rushin's pointedly humorous and acerbic *Sports Illustrated* column, "tattooed, shirtless, sewer-mouthed drunks; and their husbands" (Miles, 2005)?

Rushin is being clever, but what, we might ask, have psychologists learned about the appeal of celebrities, and especially sports celebrities? Many people form deep and enduring bonds of attachment with athletes and sports teams. Once they identify with a team, their self-esteem rises and falls with the team's wins and losses (Wann et al., 2000). Wins lead to a surge of testosterone in males (Bernhardt et al., 1998), which is connected with aggressiveness and self-confidence. Wins increase the optimism of both males and females.

Psychoanalytic theory suggests that children identify with parents and other "big" people in their lives because big people seem to hold the keys to the resources they need for sustenance and stimulation or excitement. Athletes and entertainers—the rich and famous—have their fan clubs, filled with people who tie their own lights to the brilliant suns of their stars.

Teams and sports heroes provide both entertainment and the kind of gutsy competition that evolutionary psychologists believe whispers to us from our genes, pushing us toward aggression and dominance. If we can't do it on our own, we can do it *through* someone else. In some kind of psychological sense, we can *be* someone who is more effective at

■ **NASCAR Hero Dale Earnhardt, Jr.**
Why do fans idolize sports heroes and heroines? How do we explain the "persistent American itch to create heroes"?

climbing the heap of humankind into the sun. Evolutionary psychologists also connect adoration of sports heroes to a time when humans lived in tribes and their warrior-protectors were their true genetic representatives. Today, college and professional athletes may differ from fans in a genetic sense, but fans can still identify with and worship their heroes, even if they recognize that it's sort of silly. "Our sports heroes are our warriors," notes Arizona State psychologist Robert Cialdini (2000), who has deeply studied fans' identification with athletes. "The self is centrally involved in the outcome of the event. Whoever you root for represents you." ■

During the **anal stage,** gratification is attained through contraction and relaxation of the muscles that control elimination of waste products. Elimination, which is reflexive during most of the first year, comes under voluntary muscular control, even if such control is not reliable at first. The anal stage begins in the second year.

During the anal stage children learn to delay the gratification that comes from eliminating whenever they feel the urge. The general issue of self-control may bring conflict between parent and child. *Anal fixations* may stem from this conflict and lead to either of two sets of traits in adulthood. *Anal-retentive* traits involve excessive use of self-control: perfectionism, a strong need for order, and exaggerated neatness and cleanliness. *Anal-expulsive* traits, on the other hand, "let it all hang out": carelessness, messiness, even sadism.

Children enter the **phallic stage** during the third year. During this stage the major erogenous zone is the penis in boys and the clitoris in girls. Parent–child conflict is likely to develop over masturbation, to which parents may respond with threats or punishment. During the phallic stage children may develop strong sexual attachments to the parent of the other sex and begin to view the parent of the same sex as a rival for the other parent's affections. Thus boys may want to marry their mothers, and girls may want to marry their fathers.

Children have difficulty dealing with feelings of lust and jealousy. These feelings, therefore, remain unconscious, but their influence is felt through fantasies about marriage with

Anal stage The second stage of psychosexual development, when gratification is attained through anal activities.

Phallic stage The third stage of psychosexual development, characterized by a shift of libido to the phallic region. (From the Greek *phallos,* referring to an image of the penis. However, Freud used the term *phallic* to refer both to boys and girls.)

Oedipus complex A conflict of the phallic stage in which the boy wishes to possess his mother sexually and perceives his father as a rival in love.

Electra complex A conflict of the phallic stage in which the girl longs for her father and resents her mother.

Gender-typing The process by which people acquire the traits considered appropriate for people of their sex in a given cultural setting.

Gender role A cluster of behaviors that characterizes traditional "feminine" or "masculine" behaviors within a cultural setting.

Displaced Transferred.

Latency A phase of psychosexual development characterized by repression of sexual impulses.

Genital stage The mature stage of psychosexual development, characterized by preferred expression of libido through intercourse with an adult of the other gender.

Incest taboo The cultural prohibition against marrying or having sexual relations with a close blood relative.

Analytical psychology Jung's psychoanalytic theory, which emphasizes the collective unconscious and archetypes.

Collective unconscious Jung's hypothesized store of vague memories that represent the history of humankind.

Archetypes Basic, primitive images or concepts hypothesized by Jung to reside in the collective unconscious.

Inferiority complex Feelings of inferiority hypothesized by Adler to serve as a central motivating force.

Drive for superiority Adler's term for the desire to compensate for feelings of inferiority.

the parent of the other sex and hostility toward the parent of the same sex. In boys, this conflict is labeled the **Oedipus complex,** after the legendary Greek king who unwittingly killed his father and married his mother. Similar feelings in girls give rise to the **Electra complex.** According to Greek legend, Electra was the daughter of the king Agamemnon. She longed for him after his death and sought revenge against his slayers—her mother and her mother's lover.[1]

The Oedipus and Electra complexes are resolved by about the ages of 5 or 6. Children repress their hostilities toward the parent of the same sex and begin to identify with her or him. In psychoanalytic theory, identification is the key to **gender-typing:** It leads children to play the **gender roles** of the parent of the same sex and to internalize his or her values. Sexual feelings toward the parent of the other sex are repressed for several years. When the feelings reemerge during adolescence, they are **displaced,** or transferred, to socially appropriate members of the other sex.

Freud believed that by the age of 5 or 6, children have been in conflict with their parents over sexual feelings for several years. The pressures of the Oedipus and Electra complexes cause them to repress all sexual urges. In so doing, they enter a period of **latency,** during which their sexual feelings remain unconscious, they prefer playmates of their own sex, and they focus on schoolwork.

Freud believed that we enter the final stage of psychosexual development, the **genital stage,** at puberty. Adolescent males again experience sexual urges toward their mother, and adolescent females experience such urges toward their father. But the **incest taboo** causes them to repress these impulses and displace them onto other adults or adolescents of the other sex. Boys might seek girls "just like the girl that married dear old Dad." Girls might be attracted to boys who resemble their fathers.

People in the genital stage prefer to find sexual gratification through intercourse with a member of the other sex. In Freud's view, oral or anal stimulation, masturbation, and sexual activity with people of the same sex all represent *pregenital* fixations and immature forms of sexual conduct.

Other Psychoanalytic Theorists

Freud had several intellectual heirs. Their theories, like his, include conflict and defense mechanisms. In other respects, they differ considerably. ***Who are some other psychoanalytic theorists? What are their views on personality?***

Carl Jung Carl Jung (1875–1961) was a Swiss psychiatrist who had been a member of Freud's inner circle. He fell into disfavor with Freud when he developed his own psychoanalytic theory—**analytical psychology.** In contrast to Freud (by whom, Jung said, "the brain is viewed as an appendage of the genital organs"), Jung downplayed the importance of sex. He saw sex as one of several important instincts.

Jung, like Freud, was intrigued by unconscious processes. He believed that we not only have a *personal* unconscious that contains repressed memories and impulses, but also a **collective unconscious** containing primitive images, or **archetypes,** that reflect the history of our species. Examples of archetypes are the all-powerful God, the young hero, the fertile and nurturing mother, the wise old man, the hostile brother—even fairy godmothers, wicked witches, and themes of rebirth or resurrection. Archetypes themselves remain unconscious, but Jung believed they affect our thoughts and feelings and cause us to respond to cultural themes in the media.

Alfred Adler Alfred Adler (1870–1937), another follower of Freud, also felt that Freud had placed too much emphasis on sex. Adler believed that people are basically motivated by an **inferiority complex.** In some people, feelings of inferiority may be based on physical problems and the need to compensate for them. Adler believed, however, that all of us encounter some feelings of inferiority because of our small size as children, and that these feelings give rise to a **drive for superiority.** As a child, Adler was crippled by rickets and

[1] No, the movie *Troy* got it wrong. Agamemnon's wife, and not the Trojans, was responsible for his death.

suffered from pneumonia, and it may be that his theory developed in part from his own striving to overcome bouts of illness.

Adler believed that self-awareness plays a major role in the formation of personality. He spoke of a **creative self,** a self-aware aspect of personality that strives to overcome obstacles and develop the person's potential. Because each person's potential is unique, Adler's views have been termed **individual psychology.**

Karen Horney   Karen Horney (1885–1952) was criticized by the New York Psychoanalytic Institute because she took issue with the way in which psychoanalytic theory portrayed women. Early in the century, psychoanalytic theory taught that a woman's place was in the home. Women who sought to compete with men in the business world were assumed to be suffering from unconscious penis envy. Psychoanalytic theory taught that little girls feel inferior to boys when they learn that boys have a penis and they do not. But Horney argued that little girls do *not* feel inferior to boys and that these views were founded on Western cultural prejudice, not scientific evidence.

Horney agreed with Freud that childhood experiences are important in psychological development. Like other neoanalysts, however, she asserted that unconscious sexual and aggressive impulses are less important than social relationships. She also believed that genuine and consistent love can alleviate the effects of a traumatic childhood.

Erik Erikson   Like many other modern psychoanalysts, Erik Erikson (1902–1994) believed that Freud had placed undue emphasis on sex. Like Horney, he believed that social relationships are more important than sex. Erikson also believed that to a large extent we are the conscious architects of our own personalities.

Erikson, like Freud, is known for devising a comprehensive theory of personality development. But whereas Freud proposed stages of psycho*sexual* development, Erikson proposed stages of psycho*social* development. Rather than label stages for various erogenous zones, Erikson labeled them for the traits that might be developed during them (see Concept Review 3.3 on page 100). Each stage is named according to its possible outcomes. For example, the first stage of **psychosocial development** is labeled the stage of trust versus mistrust because two outcomes are possible: (1) a warm, loving relationship with the mother and others during infancy might lead to a sense of basic trust in people and the world; or (2) a cold, ungratifying relationship with the mother and others might generate a general sense of mistrust. Erikson believed that most people would wind up with some blend of trust and mistrust—hopefully more trust than mistrust. A basic sense of mistrust could interfere with the formation of relationships unless it was recognized and challenged.

For Erikson, the goal of adolescence is the attainment of **ego identity,** not genital sexuality. The focus is on who we see ourselves as being and what we stand for, not on sexual interests.

▶ Evaluation of the Psychoanalytic Perspective

Psychoanalysis has tremendous appeal. It is rich in concepts and seems to explain many human traits. ***What are the strengths and weaknesses of the psychoanalytic perspective?***

On the positive side, Freud fought for the idea that personality is subject to scientific analysis. He developed his theories at a time when many people viewed psychological problems as signs of possession by the devil or evil spirits. Freud argued that psychological disorders stem from problems within the person—not spirits. His views contributed to the development of compassion for people with psychological disorders and to methods of psychotherapy.

Psychoanalytic theory also focused attention on the far-reaching effects of childhood events. Psychoanalytic theorists suggested that parents respond to the emotional needs of their children.   ◆ **Truth or Fiction Revisited:** But there is no adequate evidence that biting one's nails in adulthood or smoking cigarettes signifies an oral fixation.

Freud taught us that sexual and aggressive urges are common, and that recognizing them is not the same as acting on them. As W. Bertram Wolfe put it, "Freud found sex an outcast in the outhouse, and left it in the living room an honored guest."

UPI/Bettmann/Corbis

■ **Karen Horney**
Horney, like many of Freud's intellectual descendants, took issue with Freud on many issues. For one thing, Horney did not believe that little girls had penis envy or felt inferior to boys in any other way. She also believed that children's social relationships are more important in their development than unconscious sexual and aggressive impulses.

Creative self According to Adler, the self-aware aspect of personality that strives to achieve its full potential.

Individual psychology Adler's psychoanalytic theory, which emphasizes feelings of inferiority and the creative self.

Psychosocial development Erikson's theory of personality and development, which emphasizes social relationships and eight stages of growth.

Ego identity A firm sense of who one is and what one stands for.

UPI/Bettmann/Corbis

■ **Erik Erikson**
Like other modern-day analysts, Erikson believed that Freud had placed too much emphasis on sex and unconscious conflict. Erikson believed that social relationships were the key to healthful development.

Freud also noted that people have defensive ways of looking at the world. His defense mechanisms have become part of everyday speech. Whether or not we attribute these cognitive distortions to defense mechanisms, our thinking might be twisted by efforts to avoid anxiety and guilt. Because defense mechanisms are unconscious, they are difficult to assess and were rejected by academic psychologists in the 1950s and 1960s. But the cognitive revolution has again made them the subject of scientific investigation, and psychologists believe they might have found some evidence for their existence (Cramer, 2000; Somerfield & McCrae, 2000). The debate continues.

Critics note that "psychic structures"—id, ego, and superego—are too vague to measure scientifically (Hergenhahn, 2005). Nor can they be used to predict behavior with precision. They are little more than useful fictions—poetic ways to express inner conflict.

Nor have the stages of psychosexual development escaped criticism. Children begin to masturbate as early as the first year, not in the phallic stage. As parents know from discovering their children play "doctor," the latency stage is not as sexually latent as Freud believed. The evidence for Erikson's developmental views seems sturdier. For example, people who fail to develop ego identity in adolescence seem to have problems with intimate relationships later on.

Freud's clinical method of gathering evidence is also suspect (Hergenhahn, 2005). Therapists may subtly guide clients into producing memories and feelings they expect to find. Also, Freud and many other psychoanalytic theorists restricted their evidence gathering to case studies with individuals who sought help, particularly Europeans and European Americans from the middle and upper classes. People who seek therapy—and who can afford to pay for protracted therapy—differ from the general population.

Psychoanalytic theory focused on reasons that people develop certain traits. We next discuss trait theory, which is not so much concerned with the origins of traits as with their description and categorization.

◖◗ Learning Connections

◀◀   *The Psychoanalytic Perspective—Excavating the Iceberg*   ▶▶

REVIEW:

Learning Connections

1 According to Freud, _____ is the automatic ejection of anxiety-provoking ideas from consciousness.
  (a) rejection,
  (b) regression,
  (c) repression,
  (d) displacement.

2 According to Freud, the _____ is the moral sense.
  (a) libido,
  (b) id,
  (c) ego,
  (d) superego.

3 Jung believed that in addition to a personal unconscious mind, people also have a _____ unconscious.
  (a) collective,
  (b) group,
  (c) preconscious,
  (d) species.

4 Erikson extended Freud's five developmental stages to
  (a) 6,
  (b) 7,
  (c) 8,
  (d) 10.

CRITICAL THINKING:
If Freud's theory is riddled with scientific shortcomings, why do you think it remains popular among the general population?

 Go to www
http://academic.cengage.com/psychology/rathus
for an interactive version of this review.

THE TRAIT PERSPECTIVE: THE MULTIDIMENSIONAL UNIVERSE

In most of us by the age of thirty, the character has set like plaster, and will never soften again.
—WILLIAM JAMES

The notion of **traits** is familiar enough. If I asked you to describe yourself, you would probably do so in terms of traits such as bright, sophisticated, and witty. (That is you, is it not?) We also describe other people in terms of traits. *What are traits?*

Traits are reasonably stable elements of personality that are inferred from behavior. If you describe a friend as "shy," it may be because you have observed anxiety or withdrawal in that person's social encounters. Traits are assumed to account for consistent behavior in different situations. You probably expect your "shy" friend to be retiring in most social confrontations—"all across the board," as the saying goes.

From Hippocrates to the Present

What is the history of the trait perspective? The trait perspective dates at least to the Greek physician Hippocrates (ca. 460–377 BCE). It has generally been assumed that traits are embedded in people's bodies, but *how?* Hippocrates believed that traits are embedded in bodily fluids. In his view, a person's personality depends on the balance of four basic fluids, or "humors," in the body. Yellow bile is associated with a choleric (quick-tempered) disposition; blood with a sanguine (warm, cheerful) one; phlegm with a phlegmatic (sluggish, calm, cool) disposition; and black bile with a melancholic (gloomy, pensive) temperament. Disease was believed to reflect an imbalance among the humors. Depression, for example, represented an excess of black bile. ◆ **Truth or Fiction Revisited:** Methods such as bloodletting and vomiting were thus recommended to restore the balance (Maher & Maher, 1994). Although Hippocrates' theory was speculative, the terms *choleric, sanguine,* and so on are still in use today.

More contemporary trait theories assume that traits are heritable and are embedded in the nervous system. These theories rely on the mathematical technique of factor analysis, developed by Charles Spearman to study intelligence (see Chapter 8). The goal is to determine which traits are basic to others.

Early in the 20th century, Gordon Allport and a colleague (Allport & Oddbert, 1936) catalogued some 18,000 human traits from a search through word lists like dictionaries. Some were physical traits such as *short, weak,* and *brunette.* Others were behavioral traits such as *shy* and *emotional.* This exhaustive list has served as the basis for personality research by many other psychologists—but "hotness" was not included. *How have contemporary psychologists reduced the universe of traits to more manageable lists?*

Hans Eysenck's Trait Theory: A Two-Dimensional View

British psychologist Hans J. Eysenck (1916–1997) developed the first British training program for clinical psychologists and focused much of his research on the relationships between two personality traits: **introversion–extraversion** and emotional stability–instability (Eysenck & Eysenck, 1985). (Emotional *in*stability is also called **neuroticism**). Carl Jung was the first to distinguish between introverts and extraverts. Eysenck added the dimension of emotional stability–instability to introversion–extraversion. He catalogued various personality traits according to where they are situated along these dimensions or factors

Trait A relatively stable aspect of personality that is inferred from behavior and assumed to give rise to consistent behavior.

Introversion A trait characterized by intense imagination and the tendency to inhibit impulses.

Extraversion A trait characterized by tendencies to be socially outgoing and to express feelings and impulses freely.

Neuroticism Eysenck's term for emotional instability.

Figure 11.2

Eysenck's Personality Dimensions and Hippocrates' Personality Types
Various personality traits shown in the outer ring fall within the two major dimensions of personality suggested by Hans Eysenck. The inner circle shows how Hippocrates' four major personality types—choleric, sanguine, phlegmatic, and melancholic—fit within Eysenck's dimensions.

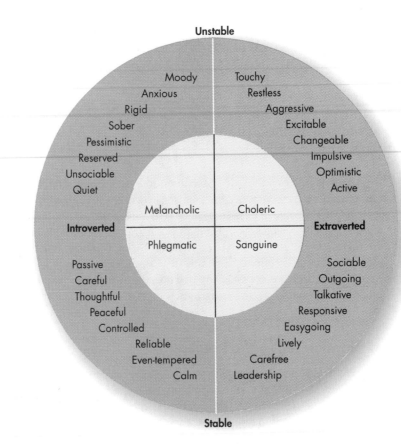

reflect & relate

How would you describe yourself in terms of traits? Where would you place yourself in Eysenck's two-dimensional scheme? Where would you stand, according to the five-factor model? Are you pleased with your self-evaluation? Why or why not?

Denis Felix/Getty Images

■ **Are They Extraverted or Just Responding to the "Photo Op"?**
Hans Eysenck based much of his research on the relationships between two personality traits: introversion–extraversion and emotional stability–instability. Extraversion is characterized by tendencies to be socially outgoing and to freely express feelings and impulses. Some people are mostly extraverted, others mostly introverted, and some are balanced—both outgoing (extraverted) and reflective (introverted).

(see Figure 11.2). For example, an anxious person would be high in both introversion and neuroticism—that is, preoccupied with his or her own thoughts and emotionally unstable.

Eysenck acknowledged that his scheme is similar to Hippocrates'. According to Eysenck's dimensions, the choleric type would be extraverted and unstable; the sanguine type, extraverted and stable; the phlegmatic type, introverted and stable; and the melancholic type, introverted and unstable. ◆ **Truth or Fiction Revisited:** It is true that some 2,500 years ago, Hippocrates, the Greek physician, devised a way of looking at personality that could be said to remain in use today.

▬▬ The "Big Five": The Five-Factor Model

More recent research suggests that there may be five basic personality factors, not two. These include the two found by Eysenck—extraversion and neuroticism—along with conscientiousness, agreeableness, and openness to experience (see Table 11.2). ("Hotness" remains among the missing.) Many personality theorists, especially Robert McCrae and Paul T. Costa, Jr., have played a role in the development of the five-factor model. Cross-cultural research has found that these five factors appear to define the personality structure of American, German, Portuguese, Israeli, Chinese, Korean, Japanese, and Philippine people (Katigbak et al., 2002; McCrae & Costa, 1997). A study of more than 5,000 Ger-

TABLE 11.2 ■ The "Big Five": The Five-Factor Model

FACTOR	NAME	TRAITS
I	Extraversion	Contrasts talkativeness, assertiveness, and activity with silence, passivity, and reserve
II	Agreeableness	Contrasts kindness, trust, and warmth with hostility, selfishness, and distrust
III	Conscientiousness	Contrasts organization, thoroughness, and reliability with carelessness, negligence, and unreliability
IV	Neuroticism	Contrasts nervousness, moodiness, and sensitivity to negative stimuli with coping ability
V	Openness to experience	Contrasts imagination, curiosity, and creativity with shallowness and lack of perceptiveness

man, British, Spanish, Czech, and Turkish people suggests that the factors are related to people's basic temperaments, which are considered to be largely inborn (McCrae et al., 2000). The researchers interpreted the results to suggest that our personalities tend to mature over time rather than be shaped by environmental conditions, although the expression of personality traits is certainly affected by culture. (A person who is "basically" open to new experience is likely to behave less openly in a restrictive society than in an open society.)

The five-factor model—also known as the "Big Five" model—wins an "Are You Hot?" award. That is, it is quite popular right now. There are hundreds of studies correlating scores on the five factors, according to a psychological test constructed by Costa and McCrae (the *NEO Five-Factor Inventory*), with various behavior patterns, psychological disorders, and kinds of "personalities." Consider driving. Significant negative correlations have been found between the numbers of tickets people get and accidents people get into, on the one hand, and the factor of agreeableness on the other (Cellar et al., 2000). As we have long suspected, it's safer to share the freeway with agreeable people. People who are not judgmental—who will put up with your every whim, like puppy dogs—tend to score low on conscientiousness (they don't examine you too closely) and high on agreeableness (you can be yourself; that's cool) (Bernardin et al., 2000). Despite the stereotype that older people, especially men, are "crotchety," assessment of 65- to 100-year-olds using the *NEO Five-Factor Inventory* suggests that people, especially men, become more agreeable as they grow older (Weiss et al., 2005). People who are anxious or depressed tend to score higher on the trait of neuroticism (Bienvenu et al., 2005). Introverts are more likely than extraverts to fear public gatherings and public speaking (Bienvenu et al., 2005). A firm handshake is positively correlated with extraversion and negatively correlated with neuroticism (Chaplin et al., 2000).

The five-factor model is being used in the realm of politics. For example, studies in the United States (Butler, 2000) and Belgium and Poland (van Hiel et al., 2000) show that people who are right-wing authoritarians ("Do it the way it's always been done! Why? Because I say so!") score low on openness to experience ("Turn off that TV! Get off the 'Net now!").

Teachers and group-care workers who rate children as being high in behavior problems are also more likely to be emotionally unstable, introverted, and closed to new experience themselves (Kroes et al., 2005). Do we need to administer the *NEO Five-Factor Inventory* to workers in day-care centers we are considering? In the realm of psychological disorders,

Personality Theory and Measurement

LEARNING OBJECTIVES

- To learn how the reasonably stable patterns of behavior we term personality "traits" may change, depending on one's situation.
- To learn what meant by the "person-in-the-situation" phenomenon.
- To understand how "if-then" signatures differ from traditional theories of personality.

APPLIED LESSON

1 What is the "person-in-the-situation" phenomenon? How does the situation affect, for example, the behavior of the recruit into the armed forces?

2 Can you think of a time you were in a social situation and behaved in such a way that you surprised yourself? Can you explain your behavior in terms of the requirements of the situation?

CRITICAL THINKING

1 Critical thinkers are concerned about definitions. How would you define "personality trait"? Are traits stable or unstable features of personality? Does the situation change one's personality or one's behavior? Can you distinguish between the two? Explain your view.

2 If a person acts one way in one situation and another way in another situation, how can we determine what are the "genuine" personality traits of that person? (Is there such a thing as a genuine or "real" personality trait?)

The "person-in-the-situation" phenomenon offers one explanation of why we may be shy in one situation and uninhibited in another.

Watch this video!

Go to www

your companion website at
http://academic.cengage.com/psychology/rathus
Click on the Video Connections tab under this chapter.

---

researchers are studying links between the factors and disorders such as anxiety disorders (Rector et al., 2005; Watanabe et al., 2005), hypochondriasis (Cox et al., 2000), depression and suicide attempts (Cuijpers et al., 2005), schizophrenia (Gurrera et al., 2000), and personality disorders (Widiger & Costa, 1994). The five-factor model is apparently helping us describe these disorders. It remains to be seen how well the model will enable us to explain and predict them and control them (that is, prevent them or assist people who develop them).

▬■▬ Evaluation of the Trait Perspective

What are the strengths and weaknesses of trait theory? Trait theorists have focused much attention on the development of personality tests. They have also given rise to theories about the fit between personality and certain kinds of jobs (Holland, 1996). The qualities that suit a person for various kinds of work can be expressed in terms of abilities, personality traits, and interests. By using interviews and tests to learn about an individual's abilities and traits, testing and counseling centers can make helpful predictions about that person's chances of success and personal fulfillment in certain kinds of jobs.

One limitation of trait theory is that it has tended to be more descriptive than explanatory. It has historically focused on describing traits rather than on tracing their origins or finding out how they may be modified. Moreover, the "explanations" provided by trait theory are sometimes criticized as being circular. That is, they restate what is observed but do not explain it. Saying that John failed to ask Marsha on a date *because* of shyness is an example of a circular explanation: We have merely restated John's (shy) behavior as a trait (shyness).

A Closer Look
Virtuous Traits—Positive Psychology and Trait Theory

Curious. Open-minded. Persistent. Zestful. Kind. Fair. Modest. Hopeful. Humorous. That's you to a T, isn't it?

Trait theory has recently found applications within positive psychology, a field that studies character strengths and virtues, such as those just listed—how they come into being and how they are related to life satisfaction. Psychologists are also developing psychological methods that help people increase their happiness and life satisfaction, as we saw in Chapter 9.

Christopher Peterson and Martin E. P. Seligman (2004) summarized many of the research findings in their book, *Character Strengths and Virtues: A Handbook and Classification* (known as the *CSV*). The handbook lists six major virtues that were found in 40 different countries as different as Azerbaijan and Venezuela, along with the United States and other developed nations (see Table 11.3). These virtues were traitlike in that they were reasonably stable individual differences (Seligman et al., 2005). Research has also found that these virtues are related to life satisfaction and personal fulfillment (Peterson et al., 2005). These virtues are also defined by a number of character strengths. The strengths of zest, gratitude, hope, and love were most closely related to life satisfaction. Although the researchers did not isolate the causes of the development of these virtues, they did find that they were widely recognized and valued, despite cultural and religious differences, and that they were generally promoted by institutions in the cultures studied (Park et al., 2005).

The CSV was partly developed as a counterpoint to the DSM, which is the *Diagnostic and Statistical Manual of the Mental Disorders* developed by the American Psychiatric Association (2000). Whereas the DSM is a catalogue of (nearly) everything that can go wrong with people, the CSV is a catalogue of things that can, and do, go right. Fortunately, there are many of them. ■

TABLE 11.3 ■ Character Strengths and Virtues

VIRTUE	CORRESPONDING CHARACTER STRENGTHS
Wisdom and knowledge	Creativity, curiosity, open-mindedness, love of learning, perspective (ability to provide other people with sound advice)
Courage	Authenticity (speaking one's mind), bravery, persistence, zest
Humanity	Kindness, love, social intelligence (see emotional intelligence, discussed in Chapter 8)
Justice	Fairness, Leadership, teamwork
Temperance	Forgiveness, modesty, prudence, self-regulation
Transcendence	Appreciation of beauty and excellence, gratitude (when appropriate), hope, humor, religiousness (having a belief system about the meaning of life)

Source: Peterson & Seligman, 2004.

 # Learning Connections

◀◀   *The Trait Perspective — The Multidimensional Universe*   ▶▶

REVIEW:

5 Hippocrates' "choleric" personality type is best described as
  (a) depressed,
  (b) cheerful,
  (c) quick-tempered,
  (d) calm.

6 Which of Eysenck's two personality dimensions overlaps with a dimension found in five-factor theory?
  (a) introversion–extraversion,
  (b) agreeableness,
  (c) openness to experience,
  (d) conscientiousness.

CRITICAL THINKING:
What is a circular explanation of behavior? What does it mean to say that some critics view trait theory as offering a circular explanation of behavior?

Go to
http://academic.cengage.com/psychology/rathus
for an interactive version of this review.

LEARNING-THEORY PERSPECTIVES: ALL THE THINGS YOU DO

Trait theory focused on enduring personality characteristics that were generally presumed to be embedded in the nervous system. Learning theorists tend not to theorize in terms of traits. They focus, instead, on behaviors and presume that those behaviors are largely learned. That which is learned is also, in principle, capable of being unlearned. As a result, learning theory and personality theory may not be a perfect fit. Nevertheless, learning theorists—both behaviorists and social cognitive theorists—have contributed to the discussion of personality. *What does behaviorism contribute to our understanding of personality?*

▬ Behaviorism

At Johns Hopkins University in 1924, John B. Watson sounded the battle cry of the behaviorist movement:

> Give me a dozen healthy infants, well-formed, and my own specified world to bring them up in and I'll guarantee to take any one at random and train him to become any type of specialist I might suggest—doctor, lawyer, merchant-chief and, yes, even beggar-man and thief, regardless of his talents, penchants, tendencies, abilities, vocations, and the race of his ancestors. (p. 82)

This proclamation underscores the behaviorist view that personality is plastic—that situational or environmental influences, not internal, individual variables, are the key shapers of personality. In contrast to the psychoanalysts and structuralists of his day, Watson argued that unseen, undetectable mental structures must be rejected in favor of that which can be seen and measured. In the 1930s Watson's flag was carried onward by B. F. Skinner, who agreed that psychologists should avoid trying to see into the "black box" of the organism and instead emphasized the effects of external influences called *reinforcements* on behavior.

The views of Watson and Skinner largely ignored the notions of personal freedom, choice, and self-direction. Most of us assume that our wants originate within us. Watson and Skinner suggested that environmental influences such as parental approval and social custom shape us into *wanting* certain things and *not wanting* others.

In his novel *Walden Two,* Skinner (1948) described a Utopian society in which people are happy and content because they are allowed to do as they please. From early childhood, however, they have been trained or conditioned to be cooperative. Because of their reinforcement histories, they *want* to behave in decent, kind, and unselfish ways. They see themselves as free because society makes no effort to force them to behave in particular ways. The American poet Robert Frost wrote, "You have freedom when you're easy in your harness." Society in Skinner's *Walden Two* made children "easy" in their "harnesses," but the harnesses were very real.

Some object to behaviorist notions because they play down the importance of consciousness and choice. Others argue that humans are not blindly ruled by pleasure and pain. In some circumstances people have rebelled against the so-called necessity of survival by choosing pain and hardship over pleasure, or suicide. Many people have sacrificed their own lives to save those of others; and some commit suicide as a weapon. The behaviorist "defense" might be that the apparent choice of pain or death is forced on some just as conformity to social custom is forced on others.

■ **What Do These Children Want, and Why Do They Want It?**
According to Skinner, societies socialize individuals into *wanting* what is good for society. Are the music, the color, and the excitement of the patriotic gathering socializing this child into wanting to belong to the group?

————■— Social Cognitive Theory: Is Determinism a Two-Way Street?

Social cognitive theory[2] was developed by Albert Bandura (1986, 1999, 2002) and other psychologists (e.g., Mischel & Shoda, 1995). *How does social cognitive theory differ from the behaviorist view?* In contrast to behaviorism, which focuses on observable behavior and the situations in which these behaviors occur, social cognitive theory focuses on learning by observation and on the cognitive processes that underlie personal differences. Social cognitive theorists see people as influencing their environment just as their environment affects them. Social cognitive theorists agree with behaviorists that discussions of human nature should be tied to observable behaviors, but they assert that variables within people— which they call *person variables*—must also be considered if we are to understand people. *Situational variables* include rewards and punishments. Person variables include knowledge and skills, ways of interpreting experience, expectancies, emotions, and self-regulatory systems and plans (Bandura & Locke, 2003; Mischel & Shoda, 1995; see Figure 11.3).

We cannot predict behavior from situational variables alone. Whether a person will behave in a certain way also depends on the person's **expectancies** about the outcomes of that behavior and the perceived or **subjective values** of those outcomes. There are various kinds of expectancies. Some are predictions about what will follow what. For example, people might predict other people's behavior on the basis of body language such as "tight lips" or "shifty eyes." **Self-efficacy expectations** are beliefs that we can accomplish certain things, such as doing a backflip into a swimming pool or solving math problems (Bandura et al., 2001; Bandura & Locke, 2003). People with positive self-efficacy expectations tend to have high self-esteem (Sanna & Meier, 2000) and achievement motivation (Dweck, 2002a, 2002b; Heimpel et al., 2002). Psychotherapy often motivates people to try new things by changing their self-efficacy expectations from "I can't" to "Perhaps I can" (Bandura, 1999).

Observational Learning Observational learning (also termed **modeling** or *cognitive learning*) is one of the foundations of social cognitive theory. It refers to acquiring knowledge by observing others. For operant conditioning to occur, an organism must first engage in a response, and that response must be reinforced. But observational learning occurs even when the learner does not perform the observed behavior. Direct reinforcement is not required either. Observing others extends to reading about them or seeing what they do and what happens to them in books, TV, film, and the 'Net.

Self-efficacy is a key concept in social cognitive theory. Do you expect that you will succeed in this course and others? Do you believe in your abilities? How do your attitudes toward yourself affect your self-esteem and your achievement motivation?

Social cognitive theory A cognitively oriented learning theory in which observational learning and person variables such as values and expectancies play major roles in individual differences.

Expectancies Personal predictions about the outcomes of potential behaviors.

Subjective value The desirability of an object or event.

Self-efficacy expectations Beliefs to the effect that one can handle a task.

Model In social cognitive theory, an organism that exhibits behaviors that others will imitate or acquire through observational learning.

[2] The name of this theory is in flux. It was formerly referred to as social–learning theory. Today it is also sometimes referred to as *cognitive social theory* (Miller et al., 1996).

Sean Cayton/The Image Works

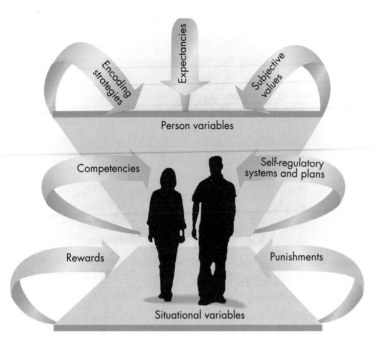

Figure 11.3

Situational and Personal Variables
Social cognitive theorists believe that we must consider both situational variables and variables within the person if we are going to understand people and predict behavior.

Photo by Pierre Tostee/ASP via Getty Images

■ **How Do Competencies Contribute to Performance?**
What factors contribute to this surfer's performance? Individual differences in competencies stem from variations in genetic endowment, nutrition, and learning opportunities.

Gender-schema theory A cognitive view of gender-typing that proposes that once girls and boys become aware of their anatomic sex, they begin to blend their self-expectations and self-esteem with the ways in which they fit the gender roles prescribed in a given culture.

Social Cognitive Theory and Gender-Typing

There seems to be little question that hormonal influences and organization of the brain contribute to gender typing. Social cognitive theorists, however, suggest that children also learn what is considered masculine or feminine by observational learning. Research evidence shows that children's views of what is masculine and feminine are related to those of their parents (Tenenbaum & Leaper, 2002).

Parents and other adults—even other children—inform children about how they are expected to behave. They reinforce or reward children for behavior they consider appropriate for their anatomic sex. They punish (or fail to reinforce) children for behavior they consider inappropriate. Girls, for example, are given dolls while they are still sleeping in their cribs. They are encouraged to use the dolls to rehearse caretaking behaviors in preparation for traditional feminine adult roles. Reinforcement helps, but, according to social cognitive theorists, not mechanically. Rather, reinforcement provides information about what behaviors people consider to be proper for girls and boys.

Gender-schema theory further emphasizes the role of cognition in gender-typing (Martin et al., 2002; Martin & Ruble, 2004). Cultures tend to polarize males and females into opposing groups because social life is organized around exclusive gender roles. For example, girls often accept their roles as nurturant (playing with dolls). Unless parents or unusual events encourage them to challenge the validity of gender polarization, children attempt to construct identities that are consistent with the "proper" script. Most children reject behavior that deviates. Children's self-esteem becomes wrapped up in the ways in which they measure up to the gender schema. For example, many boys tie their self-esteem to prowess in sports.

Once children understand the labels *boy* and *girl,* they have a basis for blending their self-concepts with the gender schema of their culture. No external pressure is required. Children who have developed a sense of being male or being female, which usually occurs by the age of 3, seek to learn what is considered appropriate for them by observing other people (Tenenbaum & Leaper, 2002).

■ Evaluation of the Learning Perspective

Learning theorists have made many contributions to the understanding of behavior, but the theories have left some psychologists dissatisfied. *What are the strengths and weaknesses of learning theories as they apply to personality?*

Psychoanalytic theorists and trait theorists propose the existence of psychological structures that cannot be seen and measured directly. Learning theorists—particularly behaviorists—have dramatized the importance of referring to publicly observable variables, or behaviors, if psychology is to be accepted as a science.

Similarly, psychoanalytic theorists and trait theorists focus on internal variables such as unconscious conflict and traits to explain and predict behavior. Learning theorists emphasize the importance of environmental conditions, or situational variables, as determinants of behavior. They have also elaborated on the conditions that foster learning, including automatic kinds of learning. They have shown that we can learn to do things because of reinforcements and that many behaviors are learned by observing others.

On the other hand, behaviorism avoids any attempt to describe, explain, or suggest the richness of inner human experience. We experience thoughts and feelings and browse our inner maps of the world, but behaviorism does not deal with these (Kendler, 2005). To be fair, the limitations of behaviorism are self-imposed. Personality theorists have traditionally

Myrleen Ferguson /PhotoEdit

Andy Sacks

■ Acquiring Gender Roles

How do gender roles develop? What contributions are made by evolutionary and genetic factors? What is the role of experience? Social cognitive theory notes that children obtain information about what kinds of preferences and behaviors are considered masculine or feminine in their cultures. This information plus some use of rewards and punishments by family members and others apparently encourages most children to imitate the behavior of people of the same sex. But is learning the whole story, or does learning interact with evolutionary and genetic factors to fashion likes and dislikes and patterns of behavior?

dealt with thoughts, feelings, and behavior, whereas behaviorism, which studies only that which is observable and measurable, deals with observable behavior.

Critics of social cognitive theory cannot accuse its supporters of denying the importance of cognitive activity and feelings. But some contend that social cognitive theory has not come up with satisfying statements about the development of traits or accounted for self-awareness. Also, social cognitive theory—like its intellectual forebear, behaviorism—may not pay enough attention to genetic variation in explaining individual differences in behavior. ◆ **Truth or Fiction Revisited:** Actually, there may be some basic personality traits, as suggested by trait theory. We may be conditioned by society to behave in certain ways, but conditioning is unlikely to fully explain individual differences in personality.

reflect & relate

Did your parents or caregivers expose you to any particular early learning experiences to ensure that you would develop to be a "proper" woman or man? Would you feel comfortable giving your son a doll to play with? Why or why not?

◯ Learning Connections

◀◀ Learning-Theory Perspectives—All the Things You Do ▶▶

Learning Connections

REVIEW:

7 Watson claimed that he could make any child into a doctor, lawyer, businessperson, or beggar by means of
   (a) psychological testing,
   (b) observational learning,
   (c) making repressed ideas conscious,
   (d) conditioning.

8 People in Skinner's novel *Walden Two* come to act in a way that benefits society because of
   (a) shaping at an early age,
   (b) development of the superego,

   (c) the trait of altruism,
   (d) discussions of right and wrong.

9 _____ are an example of a situational variable in social cognitive theory.
   (a) Self-efficacy expectancies,
   (b) Punishments,
   (c) Encoding strategies,
   (d) Competencies.

CRITICAL THINKING:
In *Walden Two,* children are conditioned to *want* what is good for the group. Given the cultural and social conditioning we experience as we develop, do you think that true freedom is possible? Could it be that free will is merely an illusion? Explain your views.

Go to

http://academic.cengage.com/psychology/rathus
for an interactive version of this review.

THE HUMANISTIC PERSPECTIVE: HOW BECOMING?

You are unique, and if that is not fulfilled, then something has been lost.
—MARTHA GRAHAM

Humanists and existentialists dwell on the meaning of life. Self-awareness is the hub of the humanistic search for meaning. **What is humanism?**

The term **humanism** has a long history and many meanings. It became a third force in American psychology in the 1950s and 1960s, partly in response to the predominant psychoanalytic and behavioral models. Psychoanalysis put people at the mercy of unconscious conflict, and behaviorism argued that people were shaped by the environment. Humanism puts people and self-awareness at the center of consideration and argues that they are capable of free choice, self-fulfillment, and ethical behavior.

Abraham Maslow and the Challenge of Self-Actualization

Humanists see Freud as preoccupied with the "basement" of the human condition. Freud wrote that people are basically motivated to gratify biological drives and that their perceptions are distorted by their psychological needs. **How do humanistic psychologists differ from psychoanalytic theorists?** The humanistic psychologist Abraham Maslow—whose hierarchy of needs we described in Chapter 9—argued that people also have a conscious need for **self-actualization,** or to become all that they can be. Because people are unique, they must follow unique paths to self-actualization. People are not at the mercy of unconscious, primitive impulses. Rather, the main threat to individual personality development is control by other people. We must each be free to get in touch with and actualize ourselves. But self-actualization requires taking risks. Many people are more comfortable with the familiar. But people who adhere to the "tried and true" may find their lives slipping into monotony and mediocrity.

Let us learn more about the nature of the self by examining Carl Rogers's self theory. Rogers offers insights into the ways in which the self develops—or fails to develop—in the real social world.

Carl Rogers's Self Theory

The humanistic psychologist Carl Rogers (1902–1987) wrote that people shape themselves through free choice and action. **What is your self ?** Rogers defined the *self* as the center of experience. Your self is your ongoing sense of who and what you are, your sense of how and why you react to the environment and how you choose to act on the environment. Your choices are made on the basis of your values, and your values are also part of your self. **What is self theory?** Rogers's self theory focuses on the nature of the self and the conditions that allow the self to develop freely. Two of his major concerns are the self-concept and self-esteem.

The Self-Concept and Frames of Reference   Our self-concepts consist of our impressions of ourselves and our evaluations of our adequacy. It may be helpful to think of us as rating ourselves according to various scales or dimensions such as good–bad, intelligent–unintelligent, strong–weak, and tall–short.

Rogers believed that we all have unique ways of looking at ourselves and the world—that is, unique **frames of reference.** It may be that we each use a different set of dimensions in defining ourselves and that we judge ourselves according to different sets of values. To one person, achievement–failure may be the most important dimension. To another person, the most important dimension may be decency–indecency. A third person may not even think in these terms.

Manchau/Getty Images

■ Unique
According to humanistic psychologists like Carl Rogers, each of us views the world from a unique frame of reference. What matters to one person may mean little to another.

Humanism The view that people are capable of free choice, self-fulfillment, and ethical behavior.

Self-actualization In humanistic theory, the innate tendency to strive to realize one's potential.

Frame of reference One's unique patterning of perceptions and attitudes according to which one evaluates events.

Self-Assessment   **Self-Assessment**

Self-Assessment

Do You Strive to Be All That You Can Be?

Self-Assessment

Are you a self-actualizer? Do you strive to be all that you can be? Psychologist Abraham Maslow attributed the following eight characteristics to the self-actualizing individual. How many of them describe you? Why not check them and undertake some self-evaluation?

yes no 1. *Do you fully experience life in the present—the here and now?* (Self-actualizers do not focus excessively on the lost past or wish their lives away as they stride toward distant goals.)

yes no 2. *Do you make growth choices rather than fear choices?* (Self-actualizers take reasonable risks to develop their unique potentials. They do not bask in the dull life of the status quo. They do not "settle.")

yes no 3. *Do you seek to acquire self-knowledge?* (Self-actualizers look inward. They search for values, talents, and meaningfulness. It might be enlightening to take an interest inventory—a test frequently used to help make career decisions—at your college testing and counseling center.)

yes no 4. *Do you strive toward honesty in interpersonal relationships?* (Self-actualizers strip away the social facades and games that stand in the way of self-disclosure and the formation of intimate relationships.)

yes no 5. *Do you behave self-assertively and express your own ideas and feelings, even at the risk of occasional social disapproval?* (Self-actualizers do not bottle up their feelings for the sake of avoiding social disapproval.)

yes no 6. *Do you strive toward new goals? Do you strive to be the best that you can be in a chosen life role?* (Self-actualizers do not live by the memory of past accomplishments. Nor do they present second-rate efforts.)

yes no 7. *Do you seek meaningful and rewarding life activities?* Do you experience moments of actualization that humanistic psychologists call *peak experiences*? (Peak experiences are brief moments of rapture filled with personal meaning. Examples might include completing a work of art, falling in love, redesigning a machine tool, suddenly solving a complex problem in math or physics, or having a baby. Note that we differ as individuals; one person's peak experience might bore another person silly.)

yes no 8. *Do you remain open to new experiences?* (Self-actualizers do not hold themselves back for fear that novel experiences might shake their views of the world, or of right and wrong. Self-actualizers are willing to revise their expectations, values, and opinions.)

Go to www
http://academic.cengage.com/psychology/rathus where you can fill out an interactive version of this Self-Assessment and automatically score your results.

Self-Esteem and Positive Regard   Rogers assumed that we all develop a need for self-regard, or self-esteem. At first, self-esteem reflects the esteem in which others hold us. Parents help children develop self-esteem when they show them **unconditional positive regard**—that is, when they accept them as having intrinsic merit regardless of their behavior at the moment. But when parents show children **conditional positive regard**—that is, when they accept them only when they behave in a desired manner—children may develop **conditions of worth.** Therefore, children may come to think that they have merit only if they behave as their parents wish them to behave.

Because each individual has a unique potential, children who develop conditions of worth must be somewhat disappointed in themselves. They cannot fully live up to the wishes of others and be true to themselves. This does not mean that the expression of the self inevitably leads to conflict. Rogers believed that we hurt others or act in antisocial ways only when we are frustrated in our efforts to develop our potential. When parents and others are loving and tolerant of our differentness, we, too, are loving—even if our preferences, abilities, and values differ from those of our parents.

Children in some families, however, learn that it is bad to have ideas of their own, especially about sexual, political, or religious matters. When they perceive their caregivers' disapproval, they may come to see themselves as rebels and label their feelings as selfish, wrong, or evil. If they wish to retain a consistent self-concept and self-esteem, they may have to deny their feelings or disown parts of themselves. In this way their self-concept becomes

Unconditional positive regard A persistent expression of esteem for the value of a person, but not necessarily an unqualified acceptance of all of the person's behaviors.

Conditional positive regard Judgment of another person's value on the basis of the acceptability of that person's behaviors.

Conditions of worth Standards by which the value of a person is judged.

Think of how your own frame of reference is unique, how it differs even from those of family members, friends, and, perhaps, love interests. Then consider some of the things that earn the approval or disapproval of these important people in your life. Can you explain their responses to you in terms of their frames of reference?

Self-ideal A mental image of what we believe we ought to be.

distorted. According to Rogers, anxiety often stems from recognition that people have feelings and desires that are inconsistent with their distorted self-concept. Because anxiety is unpleasant, people may deny the existence of their genuine feelings and desires.

Rogers believed that the path to self-actualization requires getting in touch with our genuine feelings, accepting them, and acting on them. This is the goal of Rogers's method of psychotherapy, *client-centered therapy.* Rogers also believed that we have mental images of what we are capable of becoming. These are termed **self-ideals.** We are motivated to reduce the difference between our self-concepts and our self-ideals.

Evaluation of the Humanistic Perspective

What are the strengths and weaknesses of humanistic theory? The humanistic perspective has tremendous appeal for college students because of its focus on the importance of personal experience. We tend to treasure our conscious experiences (our "selves"). For most nonhumans, to live is to move, to process food, to exchange oxygen and carbon dioxide, and to reproduce. But for humans, an essential aspect of life is conscious experience—the sense of oneself as progressing through space and time.

Ironically, the primary strength of the humanistic approach—its focus on conscious experience—is also its main weakness. Conscious experience is private and subjective. Therefore, the validity of formulating theories in terms of consciousness has been questioned.

Self-actualization, like trait theory, yields circular explanations for behavior. When we see someone engaging in what seems to be positive striving, we gain little insight by attributing this behavior to a self-actualizing force. We have done nothing to account for the origins of the force. And when we observe someone who is not engaging in growth-oriented striving, it seems arbitrary to "explain" this outcome by suggesting that the self-actualizing tendency has been stunted.

Humanistic theories, like learning theories, have little to say about the development of traits and personality types. They assume that we are all unique, but they do not predict the sorts of traits, abilities, and interests we will develop.

() Learning Connections

 The Humanistic Perspective—How Becoming?

REVIEW:

10 According to humanistic theory, freedom
   (a) requires coming to recognize and come to terms with unconscious conflict,
   (b) is only an illusion,
   (c) requires coming into conflict with parents and society,
   (d) is real.

11 According to Rogers, we all have unique
   (a) conditions of worth,
   (b) positive regard,
   (c) frames of reference,
   (d) social settings.

CRITICAL THINKING:
If humanistic theory is less scientific than some other views of personality, how do we explain its enduring popularity?

Go www
to

http://academic.cengage.com/psychology/rathus
for an interactive version of this review.

THE SOCIOCULTURAL PERSPECTIVE: PERSONALITY IN CONTEXT

Thirteen-year-old Hannah brought her lunch tray to the table in the cafeteria. Her mother, Julie, eyed with horror the french fries, the plate of mashed potatoes in gravy, the bag of potato chips, and the large paper cup brimming with soda. "You can't eat that!" she said. "It's garbage!"

"Oh come on, Mom! Chill, okay?" Hannah rejoined before taking her tray to sit with some friends rather than with us.

This scene occurred one Saturday at the Manhattan School of Music. I was sitting with other parents whose children studied piano, voice, or another instrument.

Julie and Hannah are Korean Americans. Flustered, Julie shook her head and said, "I've now been in the United States longer than I was in Korea, and I still can't get used to the way children act here." Dimitri, a Russian American parent, chimed in, "I never would have spoken to my parents the way Michael speaks to me. I would have been . . . whipped or beaten."

"I try to tell Hannah she is part of the family," Julie continued. "She should think of other people. When she talks that way, it's embarrassing."

"Over here children are not part of the family," said Ken, an African American parent. "They are either part of their own crowd or they are 'individuals.'"

"Being an individual does not mean you have to talk back to your mother," Julie said. "What do you think, Spencer? You're the psychologist."

I think I made some unhelpful comments about the ketchup on the french fries having antioxidants and lycopene, and some slightly helpful comments about what is typical of teenagers in the United States. But I'm not sure, because I was thinking deeply about Hannah at the time. Not about her lunch, but about the formation of her personality and the influences on her behavior.

Why is the sociocultural perspective important to the understanding of personality? As I thought about Hannah, I realized that in our multicultural society, personality cannot be understood without reference to the **sociocultural perspective.** According to a *New York Times* poll, 91% of people in the United States agree that "being an American is a big part" of who they are (Powers, 2000). Seventy-nine percent say that their religion has played a big role or some role in making them who they are, and 54% say that their race has played either a big role or some role (Powers, 2000). Different cultural groups within the United States have different attitudes, beliefs, norms, self-definitions, and values (Phinney, 2000, 2005).

Back to Hannah. Perhaps there were some unconscious psychoanalytic influences operating on her. Her traits included exceptional academic ability and musical talent, which were at least partly determined by her heredity. Clearly, she was consciously striving to become a great violinist. We could also detail the ways in which she had learned to play the violin and made complex motions habitual. We could gather information about her observations of her teachers and of great violinists. But we could not fully understand her personality without also considering the sociocultural influences acting on her.

Hannah, a teenager, was strongly influenced by her peers—she was completely at home with blue jeans and french fries. She was also a daughter in an Asian American immigrant group that views education as the key to success in our culture (Leppel, 2002). Belonging to this ethnic group had probably contributed to her ambition. But being a Korean American had not prevented her from becoming an outspoken American teenager. (Would she have been outspoken if she had been reared in Korea? I wondered. Of course, this question cannot be answered with certainty.) Her outspoken behavior had struck her mother as brazen and inappropriate. Julie was deeply offended by behavior that I consider normal in my own children. She reeled off the things that were "wrong" with Hannah from her Korean American perspective. I listed some things that were very right with Hannah and encouraged Julie to worry less.

Let us consider how sociocultural factors can affect one's sense of self.

reflect & relate

How do the values and customs of your home or home community fit with those of U.S. culture at large?

Sociocultural perspective The view that focuses on the roles of ethnicity, gender, culture, and socioeconomic status in personality formation, behavior, and mental processes.

Figure 11.4

The Self in Relation to Others from the Individualist and Collectivist Perspectives

To an individualist, the self is separate from other people (part A). To a collectivist, the self is complete only in terms of relationships to other people (part B). (Based on Markus & Kitayama, 1991).

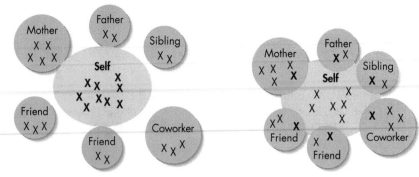

A. Independent view of self   B. Interdependent view of self

Do you see yourself as being individualistic or collectivistic? Explain.

Individualism Versus Collectivism: Who Am I (in This Cultural Setting)?

One could say that Julie's complaint was that Hannah saw herself as an individual and an artist to a greater extent than as a family member and a Korean girl. *What is meant by individualism and collectivism?* Cross-cultural research reveals that people in the United States and many northern European nations tend to be individualistic. **Individualists** tend to define themselves in terms of their personal identities and to give priority to their personal goals (Triandis, 2001). When asked to complete the statement "I am . . . ," they are likely to respond in terms of their personality traits ("I am outgoing," "I am artistic") or their occupations ("I am a nurse," "I am a systems analyst") (Triandis & Suh, 2002). In contrast, many people from cultures in Africa, Asia, and Central and South America tend to be collectivistic (Basic Behavioral Science Task Force, 1996c). **Collectivists** tend to define themselves in terms of the groups to which they belong and to give priority to the group's goals (Bandura, 2003; Triandis, 2001). They feel complete in terms of their relationships with others (Markus & Kitayama, 1991; see Figure 11.4). They are more likely than individualists to conform to group norms and judgments (Okazaki, 1997; Triandis & Suh, 2002). When asked to complete the statement "I am. . . ," collectivists are more likely to respond in terms of their families, gender, or nation ("I am a father," "I am a Buddhist," "I am a Japanese") (Triandis, 2001).

The seeds of individualism and collectivism are found in the culture in which a person grows up. The capitalist system fosters individualism to some degree. It assumes that individuals are entitled to amass personal fortunes and that the process of doing so creates jobs and wealth for large numbers of people. The individualist perspective is found in the self-reliant heroes and antiheroes of Western literature and mass media—from Homer's Odysseus to Clint Eastwood's gritty cowboys and Walt Disney's Pocahontas. The traditional writings of the East have exalted people who resist personal temptations to do their duty and promote the welfare of the group.

Another issue from the sociocultural perspective is *acculturation*. Just how much acculturation is good for you? *How does acculturation affect the psychological well-being of immigrants and their families?*

Acculturation, Adjustment, and Self-Esteem: Just How Much Acculturation Is Enough?

Should Hindu women who emigrate to the United States surrender the sari in favor of California Casuals? Should Russian immigrants try to teach their children English at home? Should African American children be acquainted with the music and art of African peoples or those of Europe? Such activities are examples of **acculturation,** the process by which immigrants become acclimated to the customs and behavior patterns of their new host culture.

Self-esteem has been shown to be connected with patterns of acculturation among immigrants (Phinney, 2003, 2005). Those patterns take various forms. Some immigrants are completely assimilated by the dominant culture. They lose the language and customs of their country of origin and identify with the dominant culture in the new host country.

Individualist A person who defines herself or himself in terms of personal traits and gives priority to her or his own goals.

Collectivist A person who defines herself or himself in terms of relationships to other people and groups and gives priority to group goals.

Acculturation The process of adaptation in which immigrants and native groups identify with a new, dominant culture by learning about that culture and making behavioral and attitudinal changes.

Others maintain almost complete separation. They retain the language and customs of their country of origin and never acclimate to those of the new country. Still others become bicultural (Ryder et al., 2000). They remain fluent in the language of their country of origin but also become conversant in the language of their new country. They blend the customs and values of both cultures. They can switch "mental gears"; they apply the values of one culture under some circumstances and apply the values of the other culture under others (Hong et al., 2000). Perhaps they relate to other people in one way at work or in school, and in another way at home or in the neighborhood.

◇ **Truth or Fiction Revisited:** Research evidence suggests that people who do not surrender their traditional backgrounds have relatively higher self-esteem than those who do. In one study, Chinese Americans who either identified with Chinese tradition or biculturalism had fewer psychological health problems (Yip & Cross, 2004). Other studies find that African American and Mexican Americans who are bicultural are less likely to be anxious and depressed than their peers who identify completely either with the culture at large or their subculture (Kim et al., 2003; Phinney et al., 1997; Phinney & Devich-Navarro, 1997). These studies might seem at odds with one another, but they seem to agree that there is little value in completely scuttling one's traditions or frame of reference.

Rob Lewine /Corbis

■ **Personality and Acculturation**
This family appears acculturated to life in the United States. Some immigrants are completely assimilated by the dominant culture and abandon the language and customs of their country of origin. Others retain the language and customs of their country of origin and never become comfortable with those of their new country. Still others become bicultural. They become fluent in both languages and blend the customs and values of both cultures.

─■─ Evaluation of the Sociocultural Perspective

The sociocultural perspective provides valuable insights into the roles of ethnicity, gender, culture, and socioeconomic status in personality formation. When we ignore sociocultural factors, we deal only with the core of the human being—the potentials that allow the person to adapt to external forces. Sociocultural factors are external forces that are internalized. They run through us deeply, touching many aspects of our cognitions, motives, emotions, and behavior. Without reference to sociocultural factors, we may be able to understand generalities about behavior and cognitive processes. We will not, however, be able to understand how individuals think, behave, and feel about themselves within a given cultural setting. The sociocultural perspective enhances our sensitivity to cultural differences and expectations and allows us to appreciate the richness of human behavior and mental processes.

Concept Review 11.1 (on pages 422 and 433) summarizes the various theories of personality.

() Learning Connections

◀◀ *The Sociocultural Perspective—Personality in Context* ▶▶

REVIEW:

12 Collectivists
   (a) feel complete in terms of their relationships with others,
   (b) are found only in Eastern nations,
   (c) find it difficult to become assimilated in new host nations,
   (d) do not see human life as being valuable.

13 Immigrants appear to be least well adjusted when they
   (a) learn the language of their new host nation,
   (b) adopt clothing styles of the new host nation,
   (c) retain traditional customs,
   (d) completely drop traditional customs.

CRITICAL THINKING:
Can one "believe in" more than one theory of personality? For example, could one accept the sociocultural perspective *along with* another perspective?

Go to
http://academic.cengage.com/psychology/rathus
for an interactive version of this review.

CONCEPT REVIEW ■ **CONCEPT REVIEW 11.1** ■ CONCEPT REVIEW

PERSPECTIVES OF PERSONALITY

	PSYCHODYNAMIC PERSPECTIVE	**TRAIT PERSPECTIVE**
Perspective	Preconscious and unconscious elements drive personality. 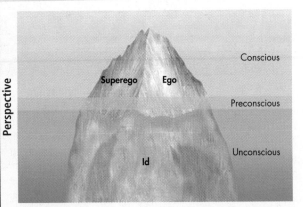	Personality is determined by a limited number of fundamental inherent traits. Hippocrates divides these traits into four types (inner circle), while Eysenck groups them into two major dimensions—extraversion/introversion and neuroticism (unstable/stable). 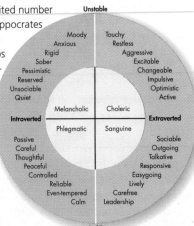 The current five-factor theory includes the two factors found by Eysenck, along with conscientiousness, agreeableness, and openness to experience. **THE BIG FIVE** Extraversion Neuroticism Conscientiousness Agreeableness Openness to Experience
Key Theorists	Sigmund Freud (1856–1939) Carl Jung (1875–1961) Alfred Adler (1870–1937) Karen Horney (1885–1952) Erik Erikson (1902–1994) Margaret Mahler (1897–1985)	Hippocrates (460–366 BCE) Hans Eysenck (1916–1997) Paul T. Costa, Jr. Robert McCrae
Focus of Research	■ Unconscious conflict ■ Drives such as sex, aggression, and the need for superiority come into conflict with law, social rules, and moral codes	■ Use of mathematical techniques to catalogue and organize basic human personality traits
View of Personality	■ Three structures of personality—id, eg., superego ■ Five stages of psychosexual development—oral, anal, phallic, latency, genital ■ Ego analysts—or *neoanalysts*—focus more on the role of the ego in making meaningful, conscious decisions	■ Based on theory of Hippocrates and work of Gordon Allport ■ Eysenck's two-dimensional model—Introversion–extraversion and emotional stability–instability ■ Current emphasis on the five-factor model (the "Big Five")—Extraversion, agreeableness, conscientiousness, neuroticism, openness to experience

(continued)

■ **CONCEPT REVIEW 11.1** ■

PERSPECTIVES OF PERSONALITY (CONTINUED)

LEARNING-THEORY PERSPECTIVE	HUMANISTIC-EXISTENTIAL PERSPECTIVE	SOCIOCULTURAL PERSPECTIVE
Situation and personal variables mold personality.	Maslow believed we progress toward higher psychological needs once basic survival needs have been met.	To a collectivist, the self is complete only in terms of relationships to other people.

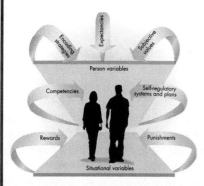

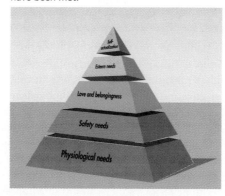

A. Independent view of self

B. Interdependent view of self

John B. Watson (1878–1958) B. F. Skinner (1904–1990) Albert Bandura	Abraham Maslow (1908–1970) Carl Rogers (1902–1987)	Martha Bernal Jean Phinney Harry Triandis Lillian Comas-Diaz Stanley Sue Richard Suinn
■ Behaviorist focus on situational factors that determine behavior ■ Social cognitive emphasis on observational learning and person variables—competencies, encoding strategies, expectancies, emotions, and self-regulation	■ The experience of being human and developing one's unique potential within an often hostile environment	■ The roles of ethnicity, gender, culture, and socioeconomic status in personality formation and behavior
■ Watson saw personality as plastic and determined by external, situational variables ■ Skinner believed that society conditions individuals into wanting what is good for society ■ Bandura believes in reciprocal determinism— that people and the environment influence one another—and in the role of making conscious choices	■ People have inborn drives to become what they are capable of being ■ Unconditional positive regard leads to self-esteem, which facilitates individual growth and development	■ Development differs in individualistic and collectivist societies ■ Discrimination, poverty, and acculturation affect the self-concept and self-esteem

reflect & relate

When you think about completing a questionnaire online or in a magazine, do you seek information about its validity, reliability, and standardization? Do you think you should? Explain.

reflect & relate

Have you ever taken a personality test? What were the results? Do you believe that the results were valid? Why or why not?

Validity In psychological testing, the degree to which a test measures what it is supposed to measure.

Reliability In psychological testing, the consistency or stability of test scores from one testing to another.

Standardization In psychological testing, the process by which one obtains and organizes test scores from various population groups, so that the results of a person completing a test can be compared to those of others of his or her sex, in his or her age group, and so on.

Behavior-rating scale A systematic means for recording the frequency with which target behaviors occur.

Aptitude A natural ability or talent.

Objective tests Tests whose items must be answered in a specified, limited manner. Tests whose items have concrete answers that are considered correct.

Forced-choice format A method of presenting test questions that requires a respondent to select one of a number of possible answers.

MEASUREMENT OF PERSONALITY

Well, then, shall we go online to find out whether we are "hot"? Probably not. Oh, we can go online to enjoy the cleverness of the test; some of the items are fun. But is the test *valid* and *reliable*? How was it *standardized*? **What are the characteristics of scientific personality tests?**

The **validity** of a test is the extent to which it measures what it is supposed to measure. We usually assess the validity of personality tests by comparing test results to external criteria or standards. For example, a test of hyperactivity might be compared with teachers' reports about whether or not children in their classes are hyperactive. The **reliability** of a test is the stability of one's test results from one testing to another. We usually determine the reliability of tests by comparing testing results on different occasions or at different ages. A reliable IQ test should provide scores during childhood that remain reasonably similar in adolescence and adulthood. Test **standardization** is a process that checks out the scores, validity, and reliability of a test with people of various ages and from various groups. As noted in Chapter 8, one cannot assess the intellectual functioning of an individual without relating it to other people in the same age group. Such information is made available when tests are professionally developed and scored.

Behavior-rating scales assess behavior in settings such as classrooms or mental hospitals. With behavior-rating scales, trained observers usually check off each occurrence of a specific behavior within a certain time frame—say, 15 minutes. Behavior-rating scales are growing in popularity, especially for use with children (Kamphaus et al., 2000). Standardized objective and projective tests, however, are used more frequently, and we focus on them in this section.

How are personality measures used? Measures of personality are used to make important decisions, such as whether a person is suited for a certain type of work, a particular class in school, or a drug to reduce agitation. As part of their admissions process, graduate schools often ask professors to rate prospective students on scales that assess traits such as intelligence, emotional stability, and cooperation. Students may take tests to measure their **aptitudes** and interests to gain insight into whether they are suited for certain occupations. It is assumed that students who share the aptitudes and interests of people who function well in certain positions are also likely to function well in those positions.

Let us consider the two most widely used types of personality tests: objective tests and projective tests.

Objective Tests

What are objective personality tests? **Objective tests** present respondents with a standardized group of test items in the form of a questionnaire. Respondents are limited to a specific range of answers. One test might ask respondents to indicate whether items are true or false for them. Another might ask respondents to select the preferred activity from groups of three.

Some tests have a **forced-choice format,** in which respondents are asked to indicate which of two or more statements is more true for them or which of several activities they prefer. The respondents are not usually given the option of answering "none of the above." Forced-choice formats are frequently used in interest inventories, which help predict whether the person would function well in a certain occupation. They are typically the only means of responding to online assessments because the test-taker is usually required to "click" a hot spot that represents the chosen answer. The following item is similar to those found in occupational interest inventories:

I would rather
a. be a forest ranger.
b. work in a busy office.
c. play a musical instrument.

TABLE 11.4 ■ Minnesota Multiphasic Personality Inventory (MMPI) Scales

SCALE	ABBREVIATION	POSSIBLE INTERPRETATIONS
Validity scales		
Question	?	Corresponds to number of items left unanswered
Lie	L	Lies or is highly conventional
Frequency	F	Exaggerates complaints or answers items haphazardly; may have bizarre ideas
Correction	K	Denies problems
Clinical scales		
Hypochondriasis	Hs	Has bodily concerns and complaints
Depression	D	Is depressed; has feelings of guilt and helplessness
Hysteria	Hy	Reacts to stress by developing physical symptoms; lacks insight
Psychopathic deviate	Pd	Is immoral, in conflict with the law; has stormy relationships
Masculinity/femininity	Mf	High scores suggest interests and behavior considered stereotypical of the other gender
Paranoia	Pa	Is suspicious and resentful, highly cynical about human nature
Psychasthenia	Pt	Is anxious, worried, high-strung
Schizophrenia	Sc	Is confused, disorganized, disoriented; has bizarre ideas
Hypomania	Ma	Is energetic, restless, active, easily bored
Social introversion	Si	Is introverted, timid, shy; lacks self-confidence

The Minnesota Multiphasic Personality Inventory (MMPI[3]) contains hundreds of items presented in a true–false format. The MMPI is designed to be used by clinical and counseling psychologists to help diagnose psychological disorders. Accurate measurement of an individual's problems should point to appropriate treatment. The MMPI is the most widely used psychological test in clinical work and is a widely used instrument for personality measurement in psychological research.

The MMPI is usually scored for the 4 **validity scales** and 10 **clinical scales** described in Table 11.4. The validity scales suggest whether answers actually represent the person's thoughts, emotions, and behaviors. ◆ **Truth or Fiction Revisited:** Psychologists cannot guarantee, however, that they can detect deception on a personality test.

The validity scales in Table 11.4 assess different **response sets,** or biases, in answering the questions. People with high L scores, for example, may be attempting to present themselves as excessively moral and well-behaved individuals. People with high F scores may be trying to seem bizarre or are answering haphazardly. Many personality measures have some kind of validity scale. The clinical scales of the MMPI assess the problems shown in Table 11.4, as well as stereotypical masculine or feminine interests and introversion.

The MMPI scales were constructed and validated *empirically*—that is, on the basis of actual clinical data rather than psychological theory. A test-item bank of several hundred items was derived from questions that are often asked in clinical interviews. Here are some examples of the kinds of items that were used:

My father was a good man.	T	F
I am very seldom troubled by headaches.	T	F
My hands and feet are usually warm enough.	T	F
I have never done anything dangerous for the thrill of it.	T	F
I work under a great deal of tension.	T	F

The items were administered to people with previously identified symptoms, such as depressive or schizophrenic symptoms. Items that successfully set these people apart were included on scales named for these conditions. Confidence in the MMPI has developed because of its extensive use.

Now that we have defined objective tests and surveyed the MMPI, we may ask—*How do projective tests differ from objective tests?*

[3] Currently the updated MMPI-2.

Photodisc Collection /Getty Images

■ **Is This Test Taker Telling the Truth?** How can psychologists determine whether or not people answer test items honestly? What are the validity scales of the MMPI?

Validity scales Groups of test items that indicate whether a person's responses accurately reflect that individual's traits.

Clinical scales Groups of test items that measure the presence of various abnormal behavior patterns.

Response set A tendency to answer test items according to a bias—for example, to make oneself seem perfect or bizarre.

Projective Tests

In **projective tests** there are no clear, specified answers. People are shown ambiguous stimuli such as inkblots or ambiguous drawings and asked to say what they look like or to tell stories about them. There is no one correct response. It is assumed that people *project* their own personalities into their responses. The meanings they attribute to these stimuli are assumed to reflect their personalities as well as the drawings or blots themselves.

The Rorschach Inkblot Test ◆ **Truth or Fiction Revisited:** There are actually a number of psychological tests made up of inkblots, and test-takers are indeed asked to say what the blots look like to them. The best known of these is the Rorschach inkblot test, named after its originator, Hermann Rorschach.

People are given the inkblots, one by one, and are asked what they look like or what they could be. A response that reflects the shape of the blot is considered a sign of adequate **reality testing.** A response that richly integrates several features of the blot is considered a sign of high intellectual functioning. Supporters of the Rorschach believe that it provides insight into a person's intelligence, interests, cultural background, personality traits, psychological disorders, and many other variables. Critics argue that there is little empirical evidence to support the test's validity (Garb et al., 2005).

Although there is no single "correct" response to the Rorschach inkblot shown in Figure 11.5, some responses are not in keeping with the features of the blots. Figure 11.5 could be a bat or a flying insect, the pointed face of an animal, the face of a jack o'lantern, or many other things. But responses like "an ice cream cone," "diseased lungs," or "a metal leaf in flames" are not suggested by the features of the blot and may indicate personality problems.

The Thematic Apperception Test The Thematic Apperception Test (TAT) was developed in the 1930s by Henry Murray and Christiana Morgan. It consists of drawings, like the one shown in Figure 9.5 (see p. 347), that are open to various interpretations. Individuals are given the cards one at a time and asked to make up stories about them.

The TAT is widely used in research on motivation and in clinical practice. The assumption is that we are likely to project our own needs into our responses to ambiguous situations, even if we are unaware of them or reluctant to talk about them. The TAT is also widely used to assess attitudes toward other people, especially parents, lovers, and spouses.

Figure 11.5
A Rorschach Inkblot
The Rorschach is the most widely used projective personality test. What does this inkblot look like to you? What could it be?

Projective test A psychological test that presents ambiguous stimuli onto which the test taker projects his or her own personality in making a response.

Reality testing The capacity to perceive one's environment and oneself according to accurate sensory impressions.

 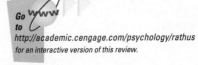

Learning Connections

◀◀ *Measurement of Personality* ▶▶

REVIEW:

14 According to the text, personality tests sample
(a) patterns of "surfing" the Internet,
(b) behavior,
(c) unconscious ideas,
(d) personality traits.

15 An online test is typically presented
(a) in a projective format,
(b) in a fill-in-the-blanks format,
(c) as an ambiguous stimulus,
(d) in a forced-choice format.

16 The MMPI seeks to detect deception by
(a) use of validity scales,
(b) human observation of the test-taker during the test,
(c) interviewing the test-taker after the test,
(d) comparing test results with those of other psychological tests.

CRITICAL THINKING:
Do you think that personality tests should be required as part of completing an application for a job? Why or why not?

Go to www http://academic.cengage.com/psychology/rathus for an interactive version of this review.

RECITE—*An Active Summary*™

 Recite to Go! *Don't have time to study right now? You can study on the go!*
Go to your companion website and download an audio version of this review section to your media player. You can also access an interactive flash-card version of this review from your website.

1. What *is* personality?	Personality refers to the reasonably stable patterns of behavior, thoughts, and emotions that distinguish one person from another.
2. What is Freud's psychoanalytic theory?	Freud's theory assumes we are driven by unconscious forces. People experience conflict between primitive instincts and social forces. The psychic structures are the id, ego, and superego. Defense mechanisms protect the ego from anxiety. The five stages of psychosexual development are oral, anal, phallic, latency, and genital.
3. Who are some other psychoanalytic theorists? What are their views on personality?	Jung's theory features a collective unconscious and archetypes. Adler's theory features the inferiority complex and a drive for superiority. Horney's theory focuses on parent–child relationships. Erikson's theory of psychosocial development extends Freud's five developmental stages to eight, including three in adulthood.
4. What are the strengths and weaknesses of the psychoanalytic perspective?	Freud argued that personality is subject to scientific analysis at a time when many still viewed psychological problems as signs of demonic possession. He focused attention on the importance of sexuality, the effects of child rearing, and people's distortion of perceptions to meet their needs. There is no evidence for the existence of psychic structures, and the theory holds inaccuracies about child development.
5. What are traits?	Traits are personality elements that are inferred from behavior and account for behavioral consistency.
6. What is the history of the trait perspective?	Hippocrates, the Greek physician, believed that personality reflects the balance of liquids ("humors") in the body. Allport surveyed traits by studying words in dictionaries.
7. How have contemporary psychologists reduced the universe of traits to more manageable lists?	Eysenck used factor analysis to arrive at two personality dimensions: introversion–extraversion and emotional stability–instability. Current factor analyses suggest there are five factors: extraversion, agreeableness, conscientiousness, emotional stability, and openness to experience.
8. What are the strengths and weaknesses of trait theory?	Trait theorists have developed personality tests and used them to predict adjustment in various lines of work. Critics argue that trait theory is descriptive, not explanatory.
9. What does behaviorism contribute to our understanding of personality?	Behaviorists believe that we should focus on the determinants of observable behavior rather than hypothetical unconscious forces. Skinner argued that environmental contingencies shape people into wanting to do things that society requires.
10. How does social cognitive theory differ from the behaviorist view?	Social cognitive theory has a cognitive orientation and focuses on learning by observation. To predict behavior, social cognitive theorists consider situational variables and person variables.
11. What are the strengths and weaknesses of learning theories as they apply to personality?	Learning theorists highlight the importance of referring to publicly observable behaviors in theorizing. Behaviorism does not, however, address the richness of inner human experience. Critics of social cognitive theory note that it does not account for the development of traits.
12. What is humanism?	Humanism argues that we are capable of free choice, self-fulfillment, and ethical behavior.

13. How do humanistic psychologists differ from psychoanalytic theorists?	Freud wrote that people are motivated to gratify unconscious drives. Humanistic psychologists believe that people have a conscious need for self-actualization.
14. What is your *self*? What is self theory?	According to Rogers, the self is an organized and consistent way in which a person perceives his or her "I" in relation to others. Self theory assumes the existence of the self and each person's unique frame of reference. The self attempts to actualize and does so when the person receives unconditional positive regard.
15. What are the strengths and weaknesses of humanistic theory?	Humanistic theory is appealing because of its focus on self-awareness and freedom, but critics argue that concepts such as conscious experience and self-actualization are unscientific.
16. Why is the sociocultural perspective important to the understanding of personality?	One cannot fully understand an individual without understanding the cultural beliefs and socioeconomic conditions that affect that individual. We need to consider the roles of ethnicity, gender, culture, and socioeconomic status in personality.
17. What is meant by individualism and collectivism?	Individualists define themselves in terms of their personal identities and give priority to their personal goals. Collectivists define themselves in terms of the groups to which they belong and give priority to the group's goals.
18. How does acculturation affect the psychological well-being of immigrants and their families?	Immigrants who blend the customs and values of their country of origin with those of their new host country have higher self-esteem than immigrants who become fully assimilated or remain apart from the new culture.
19. What are the characteristics of scientific personality tests?	Scientific personality tests have adequate validity, reliability, and standardization.
20. How are personality measures used?	Personality measures are used in many ways, including assessing psychological disorders, predicting the likelihood of adjustment in various lines of work, and measuring aptitudes.
21. What are objective personality tests?	Objective tests present test takers with a standardized set of test items to which they must respond in specific, limited ways (as in multiple-choice or true–false tests).
22. How do projective tests differ from objective tests?	Projective tests such as the Rorschach inkblot test have no specific correct answers. They present ambiguous stimuli and allow the test taker to give a range of responses that reflect individual differences.

Key Terms

Personality   399
Psychoanalytic theory   399
Conscious   400
Preconscious   400
Unconscious   400
Repression   400
Psychoanalysis   400
Psychic structure   400
Id   400
Ego   400
Defense mechanism   401
Superego   401
Identification   401
Libido   401
Erogenous zone   401
Psychosexual development   401
Oral stage   401
Fixation   401
Anal stage   403
Phallic stage   403
Oedipus complex   404
Electra complex   404
Gender-typing   404
Gender role   404

Displaced   404
Latency   404
Genital stage   404
Incest taboo   404
Analytical psychology   404
Collective unconscious   404
Archetypes   404
Inferiority complex   404
Drive for superiority   404
Creative self   405
Individual psychology   405
Psychosocial development   405
Ego identity   405
Trait   407
Introversion   407
Extraversion   407
Neuroticism   407
Social cognitive theory   413
Expectancies   413
Subjective value   413
Self-efficacy expectations   413
Model   413
Gender-schema theory   414
Humanism   416

Self-actualization   416
Frame of reference   416
Unconditional positive regard   417
Conditional positive regard   417
Conditions of worth   417
Self-ideal   418
Sociocultural perspective   419
Individualist   420
Collectivist   420
Acculturation   420
Validity   424
Reliability   424
Standardization   424
Behavior-rating scale   424
Aptitude   424
Objective tests   424
Forced-choice format   424
Validity scales   425
Clinical scales   425
Response set   425
Projective test   426
Reality testing   426

Active Learning Resources

Visit Your Companion Website for This Book

http://academic.cengage.com/psychology/rathus

Check out this companion website where you will find online resources directly linked to your book. This is where you'll access the videos highlighted in your Video Connections feature. You can answer the questions online and email them to your professor. In addition you'll find downloadable audio review material, interactive versions of the study aids, Power Visuals for mastering and reviewing key concepts, as well as quizzing, and much more!

CENGAGENOW™

http://academic.cengage.com

Need help studying? This site is your one-stop study shop. Take a Pre-Test and Cengage NOW will generate a Personalized Study Plan based on your test results. The Study Plan will identify the topics you need to review and direct you to online resources to help you master those topics. You can then take a Post-Test to help you determine the concepts you have mastered and what you still need to work on. In addition you can access interactive media including the videos highlighted in your Video Connections box.

Author Blog

What does your author Spence Rathus have to say about the state of psychology? Visit your companion website every Tuesday and click on "Author Blog." This is where he'll talk about the most recent controversies and hot topics in psychology. This will keep you up to date with what your author is thinking and give you great insight into modern psychology.

CHAPTER 12

Psychological Disorders

T	F	In the Middle Ages, innocent people were drowned as a way of proving that they were not possessed by the devil.
T	F	Anxiety is abnormal.
T	F	People with schizophrenia may see and hear things that are not really there.
T	F	A man shot the president of the United States in front of millions of television witnesses, yet he was found not guilty by a court of law.
T	F	Feeling elated may not be a good thing.
T	F	People who threaten to commit suicide are only seeking attention.
T	F	Some people have more than one personality dwelling within them, and each one may have different allergies and eyeglass prescriptions.
T	F	Some people can kill or maim others without any feelings of guilt.

Go to
http://academic.cengage.com/pstchology/rathus
for an interactive version of this Truth or Fiction feature.

L et's listen in on part of an interview with Etta:

Etta: Well . . . , ah . . . , Jesus was giving me all these cracks, window cracks, and screen crack sounds telling me that they was going to break into the house. So I put the camera stereo in the room where they jiggled the window off to come through the window. And the camera stereo, the security guards picked that up, the message by putting that camera in that room.

Interviewer: Were you in danger?

Etta: Well, if anyone gets into the house they said I'd get shot.

Interviewer: Who said?

Etta: That's The Eagle.

Interviewer: Can you say a little something about The Eagle?

Etta: The Eagle works through General Motors. It has something to do with my General Motors check I get every month.

Interviewer: And you get that check because it's part of your husband's work with GM?

Etta: Yes.

Interviewer: Say something about the relationship between GM and The Eagle.

Etta: Well . . . , ah . . . , when you do the 25 of the clock it means that you leave the house after one to mail letters so that they can check on you what how you're mailing the mail and they know when you're at that time.

Interviewer: And who's "they"?

Etta: That's The Eagle.

If you have the feeling that Etta is not making sense, you are quite correct. Etta has been diagnosed with the psychological disorder termed **schizophrenia.** Schizophrenia is a thought disorder—meaning that Etta's thoughts are not coherent. Normally our thoughts are rather tightly knit, having a beginning, a middle, and an end. Etta's thoughts—the way things are associated with one another—have come loose. She jumps from Jesus to cracks in the window to her "camera stereo" to "The Eagle" to General Motors to 25 o'clock (which does not exist) and the mail.

Etta also sees herself as being under attack. "They" are trying to break into the house. There's some kind of plot afoot having to do with The Eagle and General Motors. "They" are checking on her. Etta has false beliefs, or **delusions,** that she is being observed and persecuted. Yet for someone who believes she is being persecuted, Etta doesn't appear to be all that upset. Her **affect**—that is, her emotional response—is "flat" and inappropriate to the situation.

Schizophrenia is a psychological disorder, perhaps the most severe of psychological disorders. Fortunately—or unfortunately—it affects only about 1% of the population.

If Etta had lived in Salem, Massachusetts, in 1692, just 200 years after Columbus set foot in the New World, she might have been hanged as a witch.

Schizophrenia A psychotic disorder characterized by loss of control of thought processes and inappropriate emotional responses.

Delusions False, persistent beliefs that are unsubstantiated by sensory or objective evidence.

Affect (AFF-ekt) Feeling or emotional response, particularly as suggested by facial expression and body language.

At that time, most people assumed that the strange behaviors associated with psychological disorders were caused by possession by the devil. A score of people were executed in Salem that year for allegedly practicing the arts of Satan.

Possession could stem from retribution, in which God caused the devil to possess a person's soul as punishment for committing certain kinds of sins. Agitation and confusion were ascribed to such retribution. Possession was also believed to result from deals with the devil, in which people traded their souls for earthly gains. Such individuals were called witches. Witches were held responsible for unfortunate events ranging from a neighbor's infertility to a poor harvest. During the Middle Ages in Europe, as many as 500,000 accused witches were killed (Hergenhahn, 2005). The goings on at Salem were trivial by comparison.

◆ **Truth or Fiction Revisited**: A document authorized by Pope Innocent VIII, *The Hammer of Witches,* proposed ingenious "diagnostic" tests, such as the water-float test, to identify those who were possessed. The water-float test was based on the principle that pure metals sink to the bottom during smelting. Impurities float to the surface. Suspects were thus placed in deep water. Those who sank to the bottom (and drowned) were judged to be pure. Those who managed to keep their heads above water were assumed to be "impure" and in league with the devil. Then they were in real trouble. This ordeal is the origin of the phrase, "Damned if you do, and damned if you don't."

Few people in the United States today would claim that unusual or unacceptable behavior is caused by demons. Still, we continue to use "demonic" language. How many times have you heard the expressions "Something got into me" or "The devil made me do it"?

Etta was diagnosed with a psychological disorder. *What, exactly, are psychological disorders?*

■ **Exorcism**
This medieval woodcut represents the practice of exorcism, in which a demon is expelled from a person who has been "possessed."

reflect & relate

Have you ever heard anyone say, "Something got into me," or, "The devil made me do it"? What were the circumstances? Was the person trying to evade responsibility for wrongdoing?

WHAT ARE PSYCHOLOGICAL DISORDERS?

Psychology is the study of behavior and mental processes. **Psychological disorders** are behaviors or mental processes that are connected with distress or disability. They are not predictable responses to specific events.

◆ **Truth or Fiction Revisited**: Some psychological disorders are characterized by anxiety, but many people are anxious now and then without being considered disordered. It is appropriate to be anxious before an important date or on the eve of a midterm exam. When, then, are feelings like anxiety deemed to be abnormal or signs of a psychological disorder? For one thing, anxiety may suggest a disorder when it does not fit the situation. For example, there is (usually) little or no reason to be anxious when entering an elevator or looking out of a fourth-story window. The magnitude of the problem may also suggest disorder. Some anxiety can be expected before a job interview. However, feeling that your

Psychological disorders Patterns of behavior or mental processes that are connected with emotional distress or significant impairment in functioning.

heart is pounding so intensely that it might leap out of your chest—and then avoiding the interview—are not.

Behaviors or mental processes are suggestive of psychological disorders when they meet some combination of the following standards:

1. *Is the behavior unusual?* Etta's thoughts and her speech patterns were quite unusual, found only among a small minority of the population. Yet uncommon behavior or mental processes are not necessarily abnormal in themselves. Only one person holds the record for running or swimming the fastest mile. That person is different from you and me but is not abnormal. Thus rarity or statistical deviance is not sufficient for behavior or mental processes to be labeled abnormal. We must also consider the situation. Although many of us feel "panicked" when we realize that a term paper or report is due the next day, most of us do not have panic attacks "out of the blue." Unpredictable panic attacks are thus a psychological disorder.

2. *Does the behavior suggest faulty perception or interpretation of reality?* Etta's beliefs about The Eagle and General Motors suggested faulty interpretation of reality. Hearing voices and seeing things that are not there are considered **hallucinations. Ideas of persecution,** such as believing that the Mafia or the FBI are "out to get you," are also considered signs of disorder. (Unless, of course, they *are* out to get you.)

3. *Is the person's emotional response appropriate to the situation?* Irrational fears, such as intense fear of injections, and depression among people with "good lives" may be considered inappropriate and thus abnormal. Etta, on the other hand, showed **flat affect**—too little emotional response—when she reported imaginary events that should have been frightening.

4. *Is the behavior self-defeating?* Behavior or mental processes that cause misery rather than happiness and fulfillment may suggest psychological disorder. Chronic drinking impairs one's health and may therefore be deemed abnormal. Fear of needles is more likely to be considered abnormal if it prevents one from receiving necessary medical treatment.

5. *Is the behavior dangerous?* Behavior or mental processes that are hazardous to the self or others may be considered suggestive of psychological disorders. People who threaten or attempt suicide may be considered abnormal, as may people who threaten or attack others. But aggressive behavior in athletics—within certain limits, as in contact sports—is not considered disordered.

6. *Is the behavior socially unacceptable?* We must consider the cultural context of a behavior pattern in judging whether or not it is normal (Lopez & Guarnaccia, 2000). In the United States, it is deemed normal for males to be aggressive in sports and in combat. In other situations, warmth and tenderness are valued. Many people in the United States admire women who are self-assertive, yet Latino and Latina American, Asian American, and some conservative European American groups may see outspoken women as disrespectful.

Classifying Psychological Disorders

Classification is at the heart of science. Without classifying psychological disorders, investigators would not be able to communicate with each other and scientific progress would come to a halt. The most widely used classification scheme for psychological disorders[1] is the *Diagnostic and Statistical Manual* (DSM) of the American Psychiatric Association (2000). *How are psychological disorders classified?*

The current edition of the DSM is the DSM-IV-TR (fourth edition, text revision), and it provides information about a person's overall functioning as well as a diagnosis. People may receive diagnoses for clinical syndromes or personality disorders, or for both. It also includes information about people's medical conditions, psychosocial problems, and a

Hallucination A perception in the absence of sensory stimulation that is confused with reality.

Ideas of persecution Erroneous beliefs that one is being victimized or persecuted.

Flat affect A severe reduction in emotional expressiveness, found among many people with schizophrenia or serious depression.

---

[1] The American Psychiatric Association refers to psychological disorders as *mental disorders*.

global assessment of functioning. Medical conditions include physical disorders or problems that may affect people's response to psychotherapy or drug treatment. Psychosocial and environmental problems include difficulties that may affect the diagnosis, treatment, or outcome of a psychological disorder. The global assessment of functioning allows the clinician to compare the client's current level of functioning with her or his highest previous level of functioning to help set goals for restoring functioning.

Although the DSM is widely used, researchers have some concerns about it. Two of them concern the **reliability** and **validity** of the diagnostic standards. The DSM might be considered *reliable* if different interviewers or raters would make the same diagnosis when they evaluate the same people. The DSM might be considered *valid* if the diagnoses described in the manual correspond to clusters of behaviors observed in the real world. In the case of Etta, the DSM might be considered reliable if various evaluators who were using the manual arrived at the same diagnosis—schizophrenia. Referring once more to Etta, the DSM might be considered valid if the diagnosis of schizophrenia, described in the manual, fits Etta's actual behavior. A specific type of validity, called **predictive validity,** means that if a diagnosis is valid, we should be able to predict what will happen to the person over time (that is, the *course* of the disorder) and what type of treatment may be of help. In the case of Etta, as we will see in the section on schizophrenia, we would predict that the course of her disorder might be variable and that she might profit from drugs that affect her use of the neurotransmitter dopamine. These factors affect the clinical usefulness of the DSM (First et al., 2004).

The DSM contains various kinds of psychological disorders, many of which are discussed in this chapter. The standards for assessing these disorders are rather strict—so strict that some actual cases of disorders might be left out. Moreover, the reliability and validity of various diagnoses differs (Hilsenroth et al., 2004). For example, the diagnosis of schizophrenia might be more reliable and valid than the diagnosis of borderline personality disorder (Johansen et al., 2004). All in all, in evaluating the DSM, we should consider whether it improves clinical decision making and whether it enhances the clinical outcome for people with psychological disorders. The DSM, now in a revised version of its fourth edition, is less than perfect but appears to be making progress toward these goals.

━━■━ Explaining Psychological Disorders

How should we interpret Etta's behavior? *How do we explain psychological disorders?* Psychological disorders are explained according to various perspectives. The most common perspective throughout history has been belief in demons and possession. Scientific perspectives include the biological, psychological, and biopsychosocial perspectives.

The Biological Perspective   The biological perspective explains psychological disorders in terms of factors such as genetics, evolution, the brain, neurotransmitters, and hormones. We will see that heredity appears to play a role in several psychological disorders and that biological treatments tend to act on various neurotransmitters and the nervous system at large.

The Psychological Perspective   The psychological perspective focuses on behavior and mental processes in the description, origins, and treatment of psychological disorders. The great traditions of psychology—psychodynamic, behavioral, cognitive, humanistic, and sociocultural—all provide ways of viewing psychological disorders and appropriate treatment.

Psychodynamic theory views psychological disorders as symptoms of underlying unconscious processes that generally stem from childhood conflicts. From this viewpoint, anxiety disorders reflect difficulty repressing primitive sexual and aggressive urges, and schizophrenia represents the overwhelming of the ego by the id.

The behavioral perspective views disorders as reflecting the learning of maladaptive responses, such as running from feared objects and situations, or failure to learn adaptive responses, such as how to calm oneself after one has had a traumatic experience. From this

Reliability The consistency of a method of assessment, such as a psychological test or a manual describing the symptoms of psychological disorders.

Validity The extent to which a method of assessment, such as a psychological test or a manual describing the symptoms of psychological disorders measures the traits or behavior patterns it is supposed to assess.

Predictive validity In this usage, the extent to which a diagnosis permits one to predict the course of a disorder and the type of treatment that may be of help.

perspective, psychological disorders are not symptomatic of anything. The disordered behavior itself is the problem that can profit from treatment.

The cognitive perspective is deeply involved in the description and treatment of psychological disorders. Some researchers focus on ways in which people develop or worsen their psychological problems by blowing them out of proportion or blaming themselves for things that are not their fault. Social cognitive theorists study the ways in which people's belief in their ability to meet the challenges of their lives affects their optimism and perseverance in the face of difficulty. Researchers into schizophrenia outline the disorder's cognitive impairments, including the slowness of consolidating memories (Docherty, 2005; Fuller et al., 2005). Cognitive behavioral researchers are also developing promising techniques for helping people with schizophrenia distinguish between faulty beliefs and reality (Cather et al., 2005; Pinkham et al., 2004; Valmaggia et al., 2005).

Humanistic theory believes that people develop psychological disorders when their tendencies toward self-actualization are frustrated (Maslow, 1970; Rogers, 1951). People who disown their genuine feelings, for example, might erroneously experience them as coming from other people or unnamed sources.

According to the sociocultural perspective, social ills such as poverty, racism, and unemployment contribute to the development of psychological disorders. Moreover, some disorders are culture-bound, occurring within certain cultures and reflecting the preoccupations of people within those cultures. For example, some Japanese young adults experience an abnormal fear of offending or embarrassing other people, called *taijin-kuofu-sho*. Pacific islanders sometimes develop a sudden change in consciousness in which otherwise normal people lose control of their behavior and strike out at others. The condition is called *amok*, and the expression "to run amok" is derived from it.

The Biopsychosocial Perspective   Psychological disorders may be described from various perspectives, and their origins may involve a number of factors. For this reason, the **biopsychosocial perspective** comes into play. A person with an anxiety disorder may have a highly reactive nervous system, but he or she may also make matters worse by thinking things like "I've got to get out of here!" and "This is awful!" My nervous system is a gift from the genetic basement; it overreacts to many things, including injections and blood tests. But somewhere along the line I approached these issues from the cognitive perspective: I started arguing with myself, convincing myself that my overreactions were out of line with the "threat" imposed by these common medical procedures. By changing the way I thought about these procedures, I calmed my bodily responses as well. Throughout this chapter, we will see that multiple factors apply to most psychological disorders.

Now we know how we will be looking at psychological disorders. *How common are psychological disorders?*

▬ Prevalence of Psychological Disorders

At first glance, psychological disorders might seem to affect only a few of us. Relatively few people are admitted to psychiatric hospitals. Most people will never seek the help of a psychologist or psychiatrist. And the insanity plea—though well publicized—is a rarity in the criminal justice system. Many of us have "eccentric" relatives or friends, but most of them are not considered to be literally "crazy." Nonetheless, psychological disorders affect us all in one way or another.

About half of us will meet the criteria for a *DSM-IV* disorder at some time or another in our lives, with the disorder most often first beginning in childhood or adolescence (Kessler et al., 2005a; see Table 12.1). Slightly more than one-quarter of us will experience a psychological disorder in any given year (Kessler et al., 2005c; see Table 12.1). But if we include the problems of family members, friends, and coworkers, add in the number of those who foot the bill in terms of health insurance and taxes, and factor in increased product costs due to lost productivity, perhaps everyone is affected.

Let us now consider the various kinds of psychological disorders. We begin with schizophrenia, the disorder with which Etta was diagnosed.

Biopsychosocial perspective Description or explanation of psychological disorders in terms of the interactions of biological, psychological, and sociocultural factors.

TABLE 12.1 ■ Past-Year and Lifetime Prevalences of Psychological Disorders

	ANXIETY DISORDERS	MOOD DISORDERS	SUBSTANCE USE DISORDERS	ANY DISORDERS
Prevalence during past year	18.1%	9.5%	3.8%	26.2%
Lifetime prevalence	28.8%	20.8%	14.6%	46.4%
Median age of onset	11 years	30 years	20 years	14 years

SOURCES: Kessler et al., 2005a; Kessler et al., 2005c.

Note: The data in this table are based on a nationally representative sample of 9,282 English-speaking U.S. residents aged 18 and above. Respondents could report symptoms of more than one type of disorder. For example, anxiety and mood disorders are often "comorbid"—that is, go together. Anxiety and mood disorders are discussed in this chapter. Substance use disorders include abuse of, or dependence on, alcohol or other drugs, as described in Chapter 5.

◯ Learning Connections

◀◀ *What Are Psychological Disorders?* ▶▶

REVIEW:

1 Seeing or hearing something that is not there is considered a(n)
   (a) hallucination,
   (b) delusion,
   (c) lie,
   (d) sensitive sensation.

2 About one person in _____ will experience a psychological disorder at some time in her or his lifetime.
   (a) two,
   (b) three,
   (c) five,
   (d) ten.

CRITICAL THINKING:
When does a psychological problem become a "psychological disorder"? Is the border clearly defined?

Go to
http://academic.cengage.com/psychology/rathus
for an interactive version of this review.

SCHIZOPHRENIA: WHEN THINKING RUNS AMOK

When interviewers listened to Etta's incoherent story about Jesus and cracks in the window and her "camera stereo," they suspected that she could be diagnosed with schizophrenia. *What is schizophrenia?* Schizophrenia is a severe psychological disorder that touches every aspect of a person's life. It is characterized by disturbances in thought and language, perception and attention, motor activity, and mood, and by social withdrawal and absorption in daydreams or fantasy (Heinrichs, 2005).

Schizophrenia has been referred to as the worst disorder affecting people. It afflicts nearly 1% of the population worldwide. Its onset occurs relatively early in life, and it tends to endure.

People with schizophrenia have problems in memory, attention, and communication. Their thinking and communication ability becomes unravelled (Kerns & Berenbaum, 2002). Unless we allow our thoughts to wander, our thinking is normally tightly knit. We start at a certain point, and thoughts are logically connected. But people with schizophrenia often think illogically. As with Etta, their speech may be jumbled. They may combine parts of words into new words or make meaningless rhymes. They may jump from topic to topic, conveying little useful information. They usually do not recognize that their thoughts and behavior are abnormal.

Many people with schizophrenia, like Etta, have delusions—for example, delusions of grandeur, persecution, or reference. In the case of delusions of grandeur, a person may believe that he is a famous historical figure such as Jesus, or a person on a special mission. He may have grand, illogical plans for saving the world. Delusions tend to be unshakable even in the face of evidence that they are not true. People with delusions of persecution, like Etta, may believe that they are sought by the Mafia, CIA, FBI, or some other group. A woman with delusions of reference said that news stories contained coded information about her. A man with such delusions complained that neighbors had "bugged" his walls with "radios." Other people with schizophrenia have had delusions that they have committed unpardonable sins, that they were rotting away from disease, or that they or the world did not exist.

◈ **Truth or Fiction Revisited:** It is true that people with schizophrenia may see and hear things that are not really there. Their perceptions often include hallucinations—imagery in the absence of external stimulation that the person cannot distinguish from reality. Other people who experience hallucinations may see colors or even obscene words spelled out in midair. Auditory hallucinations are most common.

In individuals with schizophrenia, motor activity may become wild or so slowed that the person is said to be in a **stupor**—that is, a condition in which the senses, thought, and movement are inhibited. There may be strange gestures and grimaces. The person's emotional responses may be flat or blunted, or inappropriate—as in giggling upon hearing bad news. People with schizophrenia tend to withdraw from social contacts, and become wrapped up in their own thoughts and fantasies.

Stupor A condition in which the senses, thought, and movement are dulled.

Positive symptoms The excessive and sometimes bizarre symptoms of schizophrenia, including hallucinations, delusions, and loose associations.

─■─ Positive Versus Negative Symptoms

Many investigators find it useful to distinguish between positive and negative symptoms of schizophrenia. *What are the positive and negative symptoms of schizophrenia?* The **positive symptoms** are the excessive and sometimes bizarre symptoms, including

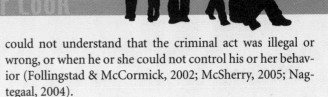

A Closer Look
The Insanity Plea

In 1982, John Hinckley was found not guilty of the assassination attempt on President Reagan's life, even though the shooting was witnessed by millions on television. Expert witnesses testified that he should be diagnosed with schizophrenia. ◈ **Truth or Fiction Revisited:** Hinckley was found not guilty by reason of insanity and committed to a psychiatric institution, where he remains to this day. What does it mean to be "insane"? What is the "insanity plea"?

In pleading insanity, lawyers use the M'Naghten rule, named after Daniel M'Naghten, who tried to assassinate the British prime minister, Sir Robert Peel, in 1843. M'Naghten had delusions that Peel was persecuting him, and he killed Peel's secretary in the attempt. The court found M'Naghten not guilty by reason of insanity, referring to what has become the M'Naghten rule. This rule states that the accused did not understand what she or he was doing at the time of the act, did not realize it was wrong, or was succumbing to an irresistible impulse. Today the insanity plea tends to be used in much the same way—when the person accused of the crime could not understand that the criminal act was illegal or wrong, or when he or she could not control his or her behavior (Follingstad & McCormick, 2002; McSherry, 2005; Nagtegaal, 2004).

Many people would like to ban the insanity plea because they equate it with people's "getting away with murder." But there may not be all that much cause for concern. Although the public estimates that the insanity defense is used in about 37% of felony cases, it is actually raised in only about 1% (Silver, 1994). Moreover, the insanity plea may be no bargain for people who use it. People found to be not guilty by reason of insanity, like John Hinckley, are institutionalized for indefinite terms—supposedly until they are no longer insane. If it can be difficult to prove that someone is insane, it can also be difficult to prove that he or she is no longer insane. Hinckley remains institutionalized more than two decades after he attempted to kill President Reagan. If he had been convicted of attempted murder, he might already have completed a limited sentence. ■

hallucinations, delusions, and looseness of associations. The **negative symptoms** are the deficiencies we find among people with schizophrenia, such as lack of emotional expression and motivation, loss of pleasure in activities, social withdrawal, and poverty of speech. Etta showed an abundance of positive symptoms, including delusions, along with negative symptoms, such as flat affect. The distinction is useful not only in terms of description, but also in terms of development of the disorder and likely outcome. For example, people with mainly positive symptoms are more likely to experience an abrupt onset of the disorder and tend to preserve their intellectual abilities. The positive symptoms also respond more favorably to antipsychotic medication (Roth et al., 2004; Walker et al., 2004). People with mainly negative symptoms tend to experience a more gradual development of the disorder and severe intellectual impairments in attention, memory, and so on. The negative symptoms also respond more poorly to antipsychotic drugs.

It may be that positive and negative symptoms represent different but related biological processes. Positive symptoms may involve deficiency in the brain mechanisms that normally inhibit excessive or bizarre behaviors. They may reflect a disturbance in regulation of dopamine in the brain, because drugs that regulate dopamine levels generally reduce bizarre behavior. Negative symptoms may reflect structural damage to the brain. Even so, positive and negative symptoms can coexist in the same person. Thus, these groups of symptoms have descriptive value but do not appear to represent distinct types of schizophrenia. *What types of schizophrenia are there?*

All types of schizophrenia involve a thought disorder. There are, however, various "types" with different emphases on positive and negative symptoms, including paranoid, disorganized, and catatonic schizophrenia.

Everett Collection

■ **Schizophrenia in *A Beautiful Mind***
In the film *A Beautiful Mind*, Russell Crowe played the role of John Forbes Nash, Jr. Nash struggled with schizophrenia for more than three decades and was eventually awarded a Nobel Prize in mathematics for work he had done decades earlier. People with paranoid schizophrenia may have hallucinations and systematized delusions, often involving the idea that they are being persecuted or are on a special mission. Nash's hallucinations are presented as being just as real to him as the actual external world.

◀━■━ Paranoid Schizophrenia

People with **paranoid schizophrenia,** such as Etta, have systematized delusions and, frequently, related auditory hallucinations. They usually have delusions of grandeur and persecution, but they may also have delusions of jealousy, in which they believe that a spouse or lover has been unfaithful. They may show agitation, confusion, and fear, and may experience vivid hallucinations that are consistent with their delusions. People with paranoid schizophrenia often construct complex or systematized delusions involving themes of wrongdoing or persecution. John Nash, whose life was depicted in the movie *A Beautiful Mind,* believed that the government was recruiting him to decipher coded messages by our Cold War enemies.

◀━■━ Disorganized Schizophrenia

People with **disorganized schizophrenia** show incoherence, loosening of associations, disorganized behavior, disorganized delusions, fragmentary delusions or hallucinations, and flat or highly inappropriate emotional responses. Extreme social impairment is common. People with this type of schizophrenia may also exhibit silliness and giddiness of mood, giggling, and nonsensical speech. They may neglect their appearance and personal hygiene and lose control of their bladder and bowels.

◀━■━ Catatonic Schizophrenia

Catatonic schizophrenia is one of the most unusual psychological disorders (Taylor & Fink, 2003). People with **catatonic schizophrenia** show striking impairment in motor activity. It is characterized by a slowing of activity into a stupor that may suddenly change into an agitated phase. Catatonic people may maintain unusual and even difficult postures for hours, even as their limbs grow swollen or stiff. A striking feature of this condition is **waxy flexibility,** in which the person maintains positions into which he or she has been manipulated by others. Catatonic individuals may also show **mutism,** but afterward they usually report that they heard what others were saying at the time.

Negative symptoms The deficiencies among people with schizophrenia, such as flat affect, lack of motivation, loss of pleasure, and social withdrawal.

Paranoid schizophrenia A type of schizophrenia characterized primarily by delusions—commonly of persecution—and vivid hallucinations.

Disorganized schizophrenia A type of schizophrenia characterized by disorganized delusions, vivid hallucinations, and inappropriate affect.

Catatonic schizophrenia A type of schizophrenia characterized by striking motor impairment.

Waxy flexibility A feature of catatonic schizophrenia in which people can be molded into postures that they maintain for quite some time.

Mutism Refusal to talk.

Schizophrenia is thus characterized by extremely unusual behavior. *What is known about the origins of schizophrenia?*

Explaining Schizophrenia

Biological, psychological, and sociocultural factors may all contribute to schizophrenia.

Biological Perspectives   Schizophrenia appears to be a brain disorder (Heinrichs, 2005). Many studies have been done to determine how the brains of schizophrenic people may differ from those of others. Studies have focused on the amount of gray matter in the brain, the size of ventricles (hollow spaces), activity levels in the brain, and brain chemistry.

One avenue of brain research connects the major deficits we find in schizophrenia—problems in attention, working memory, abstract thinking, and language—with dysfunction in the prefrontal cortex of the brain (Heinrichs, 2005). Brain imaging has shown that some but not all people with schizophrenia have less gray matter than other people (Heinrichs, 2005; Kasai et al., 2003; Thompson et al., 2001; see Figure 12.1). Many have smaller brains and, in particular, a smaller prefrontal region of the cortex (Heinrichs, 2005; Selemon et al., 2002, 2003). They also tend to have larger ventricles in the brain than other people (Keller et al., 2003). Brain scans suggest that people with schizophrenia also tend to have a lower level of activity in the frontal region of the brain (Lahti, et al., 2001; Meyer-Lindenberg

Grunnitus/Photo Researchers, Inc.

■ **Catatonic Schizophrenia**
People with catatonic schizophrenia show striking motor impairment and may hold unusual positions for hours.

Figure 12.1
Average Rates of Loss of Gray Matter Among Normal Adolescents and Adolescents Diagnosed with Schizophrenia
High-resolution MRI scans show rates of gray matter loss in normal 13- to 18-year-olds and among adolescents of the same age diagnosed with schizophrenia. Maps of brain changes reveal profound, progressive loss in schizophrenia (right). Loss also occurs in normal adolescents (left), but at a slower rate.
Source: Thompson et al., 2001.

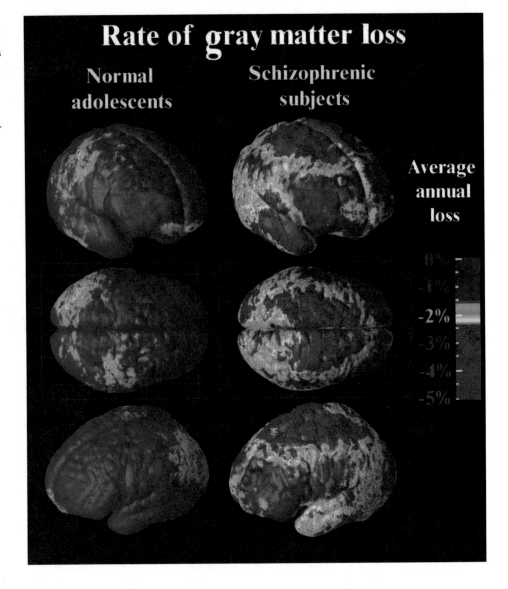

et al., 2001). Still other research connects the lower activity levels with a loss in synapses in the region (Glantz & Lewis, 2000; Selemon et al., 2002, 2003; Wolkin et al., 2003).

What might account for differences in brain structure and functioning? Heredity, complications during pregnancy and birth, and birth during winter are all risk factors for schizophrenia (Andreasen, 2003; Buckley et al., 2000; Jablensky & Kalaydjieva, 2003; Sawa & Snyder, 2002). Schizophrenia, like many other psychological disorders, runs in families (Conklin & Iacono, 2002; Hwu et al., 2003). People with schizophrenia make up about 1% of the population. Yet children with one parent who has been diagnosed with schizophrenia have about a 10% chance of being diagnosed with schizophrenia themselves. Children with two such parents have about a 35% to 40% chance of being so diagnosed (Gottesman, 1991; Straube & Oades, 1992). Twin studies also find about a 45% matching rate for the diagnosis among pairs of identical (MZ) twins, whose genetic codes are the same, compared with a 17% rate among pairs of fraternal (DZ) twins, who share half their genetic code (Plomin & Crabbe, 2000). Moreover, adoptee studies find that the biological parent typically places the child at greater risk for schizophrenia than the adoptive parent—even though the child has been reared by the adoptive parent (Gottesman, 1991). Sharing genes with relatives who have schizophrenia apparently places a person at risk of developing the disorder. Many studies have been carried out to try to isolate the gene or genes involved in schizophrenia. Some studies find locations for multiple genes on several chromosomes.

Many people with schizophrenia have undergone complications during pregnancy and birth (Heinrichs, 2005). For example, the mothers of many people with schizophrenia had the flu during the sixth or seventh month of pregnancy (Brown & Susser, 2002). An interaction between biology and the sociocultural setting is found in the link between poor maternal nutrition and schizophrenia (Hulshoff et al., 2000; Pol et al., 2000). Complications during childbirth, especially prolonged labor, seem to be connected with the larger ventricles we find among people with schizophrenia (McNeil et al., 2000). People with schizophrenia are also somewhat more likely to have been born during winter than would be predicted by chance (Pol et al., 2000; Suvisaari et al., 2002). Alcohol abuse may also lead to differences in brain structures among people with schizophrenia (E. V. Sullivan et al., 2000). On the other hand, research evidence is mixed about whether viral infections in childhood are connected with schizophrenia (Suvisaari et al., 2003). But taken together, these risk factors suggest that schizophrenia involves faulty development of the central nervous system.

Problems in the nervous system may involve brain chemistry as well as brain structures, and research along these lines has led to the dopamine theory of schizophrenia. According to the dopamine theory, people with schizophrenia overutilize dopamine (use more of it than other people do) although they may not produce more of it (Gijsman et al., 2002; Tsai & Coyle, 2002). Why? Research suggests that people with schizophrenia have increased concentrations of dopamine at the synapses in the brain and also larger numbers of dopamine receptors (Butcher, 2000). It's a sort of "double hit" of neural transmission that may be connected with the confusion that characterizes schizophrenia.

Psychological Perspectives   Most learning theorists have explained schizophrenia in terms of conditioning and the social setting. They have suggested that people engage in schizophrenic behavior when it is more likely to be reinforced than normal behavior. This may occur when a person is reared in a socially unrewarding or punitive situation. Inner fantasies then become more reinforcing than social realities. Patients in a psychiatric hospital may learn what is "expected" by observing others. Hospital staff may reinforce schizophrenic behavior by paying more attention to patients who behave bizarrely. This view is consistent with folklore that the child who disrupts the class attracts more attention from the teacher than the "good" child. Family discord and stress also appear to contribute to schizophrenia.

Sociocultural Perspectives   Many investigators have considered whether and how social and cultural factors such as poverty, discrimination, and overcrowding contribute to schizophrenia—especially among people with a genetic vulnerability. Classic research in New Haven, Connecticut, showed that the rate of schizophrenia was twice as high in the lowest socioeconomic class as in the next-higher class on the socioeconomic ladder (Hollingshead & Redlich, 1958). Poor-quality housing may contribute to schizophrenia

reflect & relate

There is evidence for genetic factors in schizophrenia. What would you tell the son or daughter of a person with schizophrenia about the likelihood of his or her developing schizophrenia? Explain.

(Mueser & McGurk, 2004). Some sociocultural theorists therefore suggest that "treatment" of schizophrenia requires alleviation of poverty and other social ills.

Critics of this view suggest that low socioeconomic status may be a result, rather than a cause, of schizophrenia. People with schizophrenia may drift toward low social status because they lack the social skills and cognitive abilities to function at higher social-class levels. Thus, they may wind up in poor neighborhoods or among the homeless in disproportionately high numbers.

Evidence for the hypothesis that people with schizophrenia drift downward in socioeconomic status is mixed. Many people with schizophrenia do drift downward occupationally in comparison with their fathers' occupations. Many others, however, were reared in families in which the father came from the lowest socioeconomic class. Because poverty may play a role in the development of schizophrenia, many researchers are interested in the possible interactions between biological and psychosocial factors (Buckley et al., 2000; Sawa & Snyder, 2002).

Quality of parenting is also connected with the development of schizophrenia (Buckley et al., 2000), but critics note that many people who are reared in socially punitive settings are apparently immune to the extinction of socially appropriate behavior. Other people develop schizophrenic behavior without having had opportunities to observe other people with schizophrenia.

The Biopsychosocial Perspective   Because biological, psychological, and sociocultural factors are implicated in schizophrenia, most investigators today favor the biopsychosocial model. According to this model, genetic factors create a predisposition toward or vulnerability to schizophrenia (see Figure 12.2). Genetic vulnerability to the disorder interacts with other factors, such as complications of pregnancy and birth, stress, quality of parenting, and social conditions to give rise to the disorder (Buckley et al., 2000; Sawa & Snyder, 2002).

Figure 12.2
The Biopsychosocial Model of Schizophrenia
According to the biopsychosocial model of schizophrenia, people with a genetic vulnerability to the disorder experience increased risk for schizophrenia when they encounter problems such as viral infections, birth complications, stress, and poor parenting. People without the genetic vulnerability would not develop schizophrenia despite psychological and social/sociocultural problems.

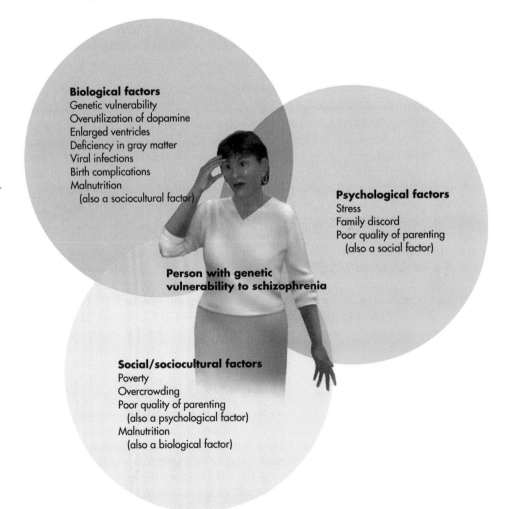

Biological factors
Genetic vulnerability
Overutilization of dopamine
Enlarged ventricles
Deficiency in gray matter
Viral infections
Birth complications
Malnutrition
   (also a sociocultural factor)

Psychological factors
Stress
Family discord
Poor quality of parenting
   (also a social factor)

Person with genetic vulnerability to schizophrenia

Social/sociocultural factors
Poverty
Overcrowding
Poor quality of parenting
   (also a psychological factor)
Malnutrition
   (also a biological factor)

Woman with *Schizophrenia*

LEARNING OBJECTIVES

- To be able to describe symptoms of paranoid schizophrenia.
- To understand how environmental factors may affect the course of schizophrenia.

APPLIED LESSON

1 When did Etta's episodes of schizophrenia begin? What environmental stressors apparently acted as a catalyst? If you were to try to "calculate" your own odds of developing schizophrenia, what kinds of factors would you consider?

2 What type of psychotherapy or counseling might you want to try to help a person diagnosed with paranoid schizophrenia? Why?

CRITICAL THINKING

What types of methods do clinicians and researchers use to determine whether a person is experiencing hallucinations? Do you consider these methods to be valid or foolproof? Explain your view.

Schizophrenia afflicts about 1% of the population worldwide. It is considered the most severe of the psychological disorders. In this video Etta discusses her own struggles with schizophrenia.

Watch this video!
Go to
your companion website at
http://academic.cengage.com/psychology/rathus
Click on the Video Connections tab under this chapter.

( ) Learning Connections

◀◀   *Schizophrenia—When Thinking Runs Amok*   ▶▶

REVIEW:

3 Schizophrenia is primarily a(n) _____ disorder.
  (a) cognitive,
  (b) emotional,
  (c) motor,
  (d) personality.

4 Which of the following is/are symptomatic of paranoid schizophrenia?
  (a) Feelings of depression,
  (b) Ideas of persecution,
  (c) Insight into the nature of one's disorder,
  (d) Silliness and giddiness.

5 Brain imaging suggests that there is a tendency for people with schizophrenia to have larger _____ than normal people do.
  (a) synapses,
  (b) prefrontal regions of the cortex,
  (c) ventricles,
  (d) limbic systems.

6 People with schizophrenia tend to utilize more of the neurotransmitter _____ than normal people do.
  (a) dopamine,
  (b) serotonin,
  (c) norepinephrine,
  (d) GABA.

CRITICAL THINKING:
Critical thinkers pay close attention to definitions of terms. Most researchers believe that schizophrenia is a disease of the brain. Why, then, is it considered a psychological or mental disorder?

Go to
http://academic.cengage.com/psychology/rathus
for an interactive version of this review.

MOOD DISORDERS: UP, DOWN, AND AROUND

Mood disorders are characterized by disturbance in expressed emotions. The disruption generally involves sadness or elation. Most instances of sadness are normal, or "run-of-the-mill." If you have failed an important test, if you have lost money in a business venture, or if your closest friend becomes ill, it is understandable and fitting for you to be sad about it. It would be odd, in fact, if you were *not* affected by adversity.

What kinds of mood disorders are there? In this section we discuss two mood disorders: major depression and bipolar disorder.

Major Depression

People with run-of-the-mill depression may feel sad, blue, or "down in the dumps." They may complain of lack of energy, loss of self-esteem, difficulty concentrating, loss of interest in activities and other people (Nezlek et al., 2000), pessimism, crying, and thoughts of suicide.

These feelings are more intense in people with **major depressive disorder (MDD).** According to a nationally representative sample of 9,282 English-speaking adults in the United States, MDD affects 6% to 7% of men and about 12% of women within any given year, and 1 person in 5 to 6 over the course of a lifetime (Kessler et al., 2005a, 2005c). About half of those with MDD experience severe symptoms such as poor appetite, serious weight loss, and agitation or **psychomotor retardation.** They may be unable to concentrate and make decisions. They may say that they "don't care" anymore and in some cases attempt suicide. A minority may display faulty perception of reality—so-called psychotic behaviors. These include delusions of unworthiness, guilt for imagined wrongdoings, even the notion that one is rotting from disease. There may also be delusions, as of the devil administering deserved punishment, or hallucinations, as of strange bodily sensations.

Bipolar Disorder

People with **bipolar disorder,** formerly known as *manic–depressive disorder,* have mood swings from ecstatic elation to deep depression. The cycles seem to be unrelated to external events. ◈ **Truth or Fiction Revisited:** In the case of bipolar disorder, feeling elated is not a good thing because in the elated, or **manic** phase, the person may show excessive excitement or silliness, carrying jokes too far. The manic person may also be argumentative. He or she may show poor judgment, destroying property, making huge contributions to charity, or giving away expensive possessions. People often find manic individuals abrasive and avoid them. They are often oversexed and too restless to sit still or sleep restfully. They often speak rapidly (showing "pressured speech") and jump from topic to topic (showing **rapid flight of ideas**). It can be hard to get a word in edgewise.

Depression is the other side of the coin. People with bipolar depression often sleep more than usual and are lethargic. People with major (or unipolar) depression are more likely to have insomnia and agitation. Those with bipolar depression also exhibit social withdrawal and irritability. Some people with bipolar disorder attempt suicide when the mood shifts from the elated phase toward depression (Jamison, 2000). They will do almost anything to escape the depths of depression that lie ahead.

Explaining Mood Disorders

What is known about the origins of mood disorders?

Biological Perspectives Researchers are searching for biological factors in mood disorders. Depression, for example, is often associated with the trait of **neuroticism,** which is heritable (Chioqueta & Stiles, 2005; Khan et al., 2005). Anxiety is also connected with

Major depressive disorder (MDD) A serious to severe depressive disorder in which the person may show loss of appetite, psychomotor retardation, and impaired reality testing.

Psychomotor retardation Slowness in motor activity and (apparently) in thought.

Bipolar disorder A disorder in which the mood alternates between two extreme poles (elation and depression). Also referred to as *manic depression.*

Manic Elated, showing excessive excitement.

Rapid flight of ideas Rapid speech and topic changes, characteristic of manicky behavior.

Neuroticism A personality trait characterized largely by persistent anxiety.

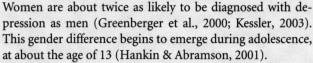

A Closer Look
The Case of Women and Depression

A Closer Look

Women are about twice as likely to be diagnosed with depression as men (Greenberger et al., 2000; Kessler, 2003). This gender difference begins to emerge during adolescence, at about the age of 13 (Hankin & Abramson, 2001).

Many people assume that biological gender differences largely explain why women are more likely to become depressed. Low levels of estrogen are widely seen as the culprit. As noted in Chapter 2, estrogen levels plummet prior to menstruation. How often do we hear degrading remarks such as "It must be that time of the month" when a woman expresses feelings of anger or irritation? But part of the gender difference may reflect the fact that men are less likely than women to admit to depression or seek treatment for it. "I'm the John Wayne generation," admitted one man, a physician. "'It's only a flesh wound'; that's how you deal with it. I thought depression was a weakness—there was something disgraceful about it. A real man would just get over it" (cited in Wartik, 2000).

Still, in any given year about 12% of women and 7% of men in the United States are diagnosable with depression (Depression Research, 2000). It was once assumed that depression was most likely to accompany menopause in women, because women could no longer carry out their "natural" function of childbearing. Women are more likely, however, to encounter depression during the childbearing years (Depression Research, 2000).

Yes, hormonal changes during adolescence, the menstrual cycle, and childbirth may contribute to depression in women (Cyranowski et al., 2000; McGrath et al., 1990). The bodies and brains of males, on the other hand, are stoked by testosterone during adolescence. High testosterone levels are connected with feelings of self-confidence, high activity levels, and aggressiveness, a cluster of traits and behaviors that are more connected with elation (even if sometimes misplaced) than with depression (H. G. Pope et al., 2000; Sullivan, 2000). Some theorists suggest, however, that women may also have a "cognitive vulnerability" to depression, connected with greater tendencies than men to ruminate about stresses and other negative events (Hankin & Abramson, 2001).

Some of the gender difference may also reflect the greater stresses placed on women, which tend to be greatest when they are working a double shift—one in the workforce

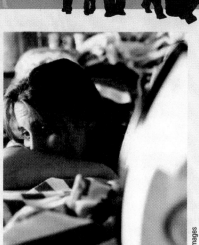

Peter Cade/Stone/Getty Images

■ **Women and Depression**
About twice as many women as men are likely to be diagnosed with depression. Does the gender difference reflect biases among the mental-health professionals who make the diagnoses, women's (frequent) status as second-class citizens, the fact that women are often expected to take care of the family as well as earn a living, hormonal and other biological differences between women and men, other factors—or all of the above or some of the above?

and the other meeting the demands of homemaking, childbearing, and child rearing (Kasen et al., 2005; Stapley, 2005). Women are more likely to experience physical and sexual abuse, poverty, single parenthood, and sexism. Single mothers, in particular, have lower socioeconomic status than men, and depression and other psychological disorders are more common among poor people (Cairney & Wade, 2002). Women are also more likely than men to help other people who are ill or under stress. Supporting other people heaps additional caregiving burdens on oneself. A part of "therapy" for depressed women, then, is to modify the overwhelming demands on women. The pain may lie in the individual, but the cause often lies in society. ■

neuroticism, and mood and anxiety disorders are frequently found in the same person (Khan et al., 2005; Nowakowska et al., 2005).

Genetic factors appear to be involved in major depression and bipolar disorder (Evans et al., 2005; Farmer et al., 2005). Twin and adoption studies suggest a powerful role for genetic factors in bipolar disorder (Faraone et al., 2004; Farmer et al., 2005).

Research into depression also focuses on underutilization of serotonin (Yatham et al., 2000; Young et al., 2003). People diagnosed with depression often respond to drugs that heighten the action of serotonin.

Psychological Perspectives   Many learning theorists suggest that depressed people behave as though they cannot obtain reinforcement. For example, they appear to be inactive and apathetic. Many people with depressive disorders have an *external locus of control*. That is, they do not believe they can control events so as to achieve reinforcements (Tong, 2001; Weinmann et al., 2001).

Research conducted by learning theorists has also found links between depression and **learned helplessness.** In classic research, psychologist Martin Seligman taught dogs that they were helpless to escape an electric shock. The dogs were prevented from leaving a cage in which they received repeated shocks. Later, a barrier to a safe compartment was removed, offering the animals a way out. When they were shocked again, however, the dogs made no effort to escape. They had apparently learned that they were helpless. Seligman's dogs were also, in a sense, reinforced for doing nothing. That is, the shock *eventually* stopped when the dogs were showing helpless behavior—inactivity and withdrawal. "Reinforcement" might have increased the likelihood of repeating the "successful behavior"— that is, doing nothing—in a similar situation. This helpless behavior resembles that of people who are depressed.

Other cognitive factors contribute to depression. For example, perfectionists set themselves up for depression by making irrational demands on themselves. They are likely to fall short of their (unrealistic) expectations and to feel depressed as a result (Flett & Hewitt, 2002; Flett et al., 2002).

Cognitive psychologists also note that people who ruminate about feelings of depression are more likely to prolong the feelings (Nolen-Hoeksema, 2000; Spasojevic & Alloy, 2001; A. Ward et al., 2003). Women are more likely than men to ruminate about feelings of depression (Nolen-Hoeksema, 2001). Men are more likely than women to fight negative feelings by distracting themselves or turning to alcohol (Nolen-Hoeksema, 2001). They thus expose themselves and their families to further problems.

Still other cognitions involve the ways in which people explain their failures and shortcomings to themselves (Hankin et al., 2005). Seligman (1996) suggests that when things go wrong we may think of the causes of failure as either *internal* or *external*, *stable* or *unstable*, *global* or *specific*. These various **attributional styles** can be illustrated using the example of having a date that does not work out. An internal attribution involves self-blame, as in "I really loused it up." An external attribution places the blame elsewhere (as in "Some couples just don't take to each other," or, "She was the wrong sign for me"). A stable attribution ("It's my personality") suggests a problem that cannot be changed. An unstable attribution ("It was because I had a head cold") suggests a temporary condition. A global attribution of failure ("I have no idea what to do when I'm with other people") suggests that the problem is quite large. A specific attribution ("I have problems making small talk at the beginning of a relationship") chops the problem down to a manageable size. Research has shown that people who are depressed are more likely to attribute the causes of their failures to internal, stable, and global factors—factors that they are relatively powerless to change (Lewinsohn et al., 2000b; Riso et al., 2003; Ziegler & Hawley, 2001).

Let's add one remarkable note about attributional styles and the mind–body connection. Shelley Taylor and her colleagues (2000a) found that self-blame for negative events is connected with poorer functioning of the immune system. Too much self-blame, in other words, is not only depressing; it may also be able to make us physically ill.

The Biopsychosocial Perspective   Relationships between mood disorders and biological factors are complex and under intense study. Even if people are biologically predisposed toward depression, self-efficacy expectations and attitudes—particularly attitudes about whether one can change things for the better—may also play a role.

Although the mood disorders are connected with processes within the individual, many kinds of situations are also connected with depression. For example, depression may be a reaction to loss or stress (Cowen, 2002; Mazure et al., 2000). Sources of chronic strain

Karim Shamsi-Basha/The Image Works

■ Why Did He Miss That Tackle?
This football player is compounding his feelings of depression by attributing his shortcomings on the field to factors that he cannot change. For example, he tells himself that he missed the tackle out of stupidity and lack of athletic ability. He ignores the facts that his coaching was poor and his teammates failed to support him.

reflect & relate

When you fall short of your goals, do you tend to be merciless in your self-criticism or do you tend to blame other people or "circumstances"? Are you accurate in your attributions? Do your views of your shortcomings tend to worsen or lessen your feelings of failure and depression?

Learned helplessness A model for the acquisition of depressive behavior, based on findings that organisms in aversive situations learn to show inactivity when their operants go unreinforced.

Attributional style The tendency to attribute one's behavior to internal or external factors, stable or unstable factors, and so on.

such as marital discord, physical discomfort, incompetence, and failure or pressure at work all contribute to depression. We tend to be more depressed by things we bring on ourselves, such as academic problems, financial problems, unwanted pregnancy, conflict with the law, arguments, and fights (Greenberger et al., 2000). Some people recover from depression less readily than others, however. People who remain depressed have lower self-esteem (Sherrington et al., 2001), are less likely to be able to solve social problems (Reinecke et al., 2001), and have less social support.

Suicide: When the "Psychache" Becomes Impossible to Bear

Why do people commit suicide? We will deal with suicide terrorism in Chapter 14. Here let us talk about people who choose to take their lives to escape feelings of depression, hopelessness, and helplessness. We may think many of these people have "so much to live for." Apparently, they disagree. So do the other thousands of others who take their own lives each year.

In any given year, about 3% of the American population considers suicide (Kessler et al., 2005b). About 31,000 Americans commit suicide each year (National Center for Injury Prevention and Control, 2005). Suicide is the third- or fourth-leading cause of death among older teenagers (National Center for Health Statistics, 2005). Who is most at risk of attempting or committing suicide?

Risk Factors in Suicide   Most suicides are linked to feelings of depression and hopelessness (Beautrais, 2003; Leslie et al., 2002; Sampaio et al., 2001). My daughter Jill Rathus and her colleagues (Miller et al., 2000; Velting et al., 2000) found that suicidal adolescents experience four areas of psychological problems: (1) confusion about the self, (2) impulsiveness, (3) emotional instability, and (4) interpersonal problems. Some suicidal teenagers, like suicidal adults, are highly achieving, rigid perfectionists who have set impossibly high expectations for themselves (Miller et al., 2000; Wu et al., 2001). Many people throw themselves into feelings of depression and hopelessness by comparing themselves negatively with others, even when the comparisons are inappropriate (Barber, 2001). For example, some people criticize themselves for being hired at a lower salary than others were, even though the financial climate of a company has changed.

Suicide attempts are more common following stressful life events, especially "exit events" (Beautrais, 2003). Exit events entail loss of social support, as in the death of a parent or friend, divorce, or a family member's leaving home. These exit events result in what Shneidman (2001) refers to as psychological pain, or "psychache." Other contributors to suicidal behavior among adolescents include concerns over sexuality, grades in school, problems at home, and substance abuse (Beautrais, 2003; Miller et al., 2000; Wu et al., 2001). It is not always a stressful event itself that precipitates suicide but can also be the individual's anxiety or fear of being "found out" about something, such as failing a course or getting arrested (Marttunen, 1998). Problem-solving ability—or lack of it—is connected with suicide. People who consider suicide are apparently less capable of solving their problems, especially their social problems, than others (Miller et al., 2000; Townsend et al., 2001). People contemplating suicide are thus less likely to find productive ways to change the stressful situation. They have borne the "psychache"; now they want a magical solution or a quick way out (Shneidman, 2001).

There is a tendency for suicide to run in families (Bongar, 2002; Joiner, 2002; Qin et al., 2003). Many suicide attempters have family members with serious psychological problems, and about 25% have family members who have taken their lives (Segal & Roy, 2001; Sorenson & Rutter, 1991). The causal connections are unclear, however. Do people who attempt suicide inherit disorders that can lead to suicide? Does the family environment subject family members to feelings of hopelessness? Does the suicide of a family member give a person the idea of committing suicide, or create the impression that he or she is destined to commit suicide? These possibilities and others—such as poor problem-solving ability—form a complex web of contributors.

Sociocultural Factors in Suicide   Suicide is connected not only with feelings of depression and stressful events, but also with age, educational status, ethnicity, and gender. Consider some facts about suicide:

- Suicide is the third-leading cause of death among young people aged 15 to 24 (National Center for Health Statistics, 2005). More teenagers and young adults die from suicide than from cancer, heart disease, AIDS, birth defects, stroke, pneumonia and influenza, and chronic lung disease combined (National Center for Health Statistics, 2005).
- Suicide is more common among college students than among people of the same age who do not attend college.
- Although teenage suicides loom large in the media spotlight, older people are actually more likely to commit suicide (National Center for Health Statistics, 2005). The suicide rate among older people who are single is twice that of older people who are married (National Center for Injury Prevention and Control, 2005).

Rates of suicide and suicide attempts also vary among different ethnic groups and according to gender. For example, about 1 in 6 Native Americans (17%) has attempted suicide— a rate higher than that of other Americans (Blum et al., 1992). About 1 in 8 Latino and Latina Americans has attempted suicide and 3 in 10 have considered it (National Center for Health Statistics, 2005). European Americans are next, with 8% attempting and 28% contemplating suicide. African Americans are least likely to attempt suicide (6.5%) or to consider it (20%). The suicide rates for African Americans are only about two-thirds of those for European Americans, even though African Americans are more likely to live in poverty and suffer discrimination (National Center for Health Statistics, 2005). How can we explain this "disconnect" between hope for the future and suicide rates? One possibility is that the support offered by extended families and the role of religion may have a protective effect on African Americans. Yet another possibility is that when African Americans are feeling low, they tend to blame social circumstances, including discrimination. European Americans, on the other hand, may feel that there is no one to blame but themselves.

About three times as many females as males attempt suicide, but about four times as many males "succeed," in part because males are likely to choose more deadly methods (National Center for Injury Prevention and Control, 2005). Males are more likely to shoot or hang themselves; females more often use drugs, such as overdoses of tranquilizers or sleeping pills, or poisons. Females often do not take enough of these chemicals. It also takes a while for the chemicals to work, giving others the opportunity to find the person and intervene.

Now let us consider some myths about suicide.

Myths About Suicide   You may have heard that individuals who threaten suicide are only seeking attention. Those who are serious just do it. ◆ **Truth or Fiction Revisited**: Actually, most people who commit suicide did give warnings about their intentions (Jackson & Nuttall, 2001; Waters, 2000).

Some believe that those who fail at suicide attempts are only seeking attention. But many people who commit suicide have made prior attempts (Jackson & Nuttall, 2001; Waters, 2000). Contrary to widespread belief, discussing suicide with a person who is depressed does not prompt the person to attempt suicide (National Center for Injury Prevention and Control, 2005). Extracting a promise not to commit suicide before calling or visiting a helping professional seems to prevent some suicides.

Some believe that only "insane" people (meaning people who are out of touch with reality) would take their own lives. However, suicidal thinking is not necessarily a sign of bizarre thinking. Instead, people may consider suicide when they think they have run out of options (Nock & Kazdin, 2002; Townsend et al., 2001).

Warning Signs of Suicide   The great majority of people who commit suicide send out signals beforehand (Bongar, 2002; Hendin et al., 2001). Sad to say, these signals often are overlooked, sometimes because other people do not recognize them, sometimes because other people do not have adequate access to health care (MacDonald, 1999; Wu et al., 2001). Sometimes people do not receive help until they actually attempt suicide, and sometimes not even then (Gili-Planas et al., 2001; Wu et al., 2001). Here are some clues that a person may be at risk of committing suicide (Bongar, 2002; Hendin et al., 2001):

- changes in eating and sleeping patterns
- difficulty concentrating on school or the job
- a sharp decline in performance and attendance at school or on the job
- loss of interest in previously enjoyed activities
- giving away prized possessions
- complaints about physical problems when no medical basis for the problems can be found
- withdrawal from social relationships
- personality or mood changes
- talking or writing about death or dying
- abuse of drugs or alcohol
- an attempted suicide
- availability of a handgun
- a precipitating event such as an argument, a broken romantic relationship, academic difficulties, problems on the job, loss of a friend, or trouble with the law
- in the case of adolescents, knowing or hearing about another teenager who has committed suicide (which can lead to so-called "cluster" suicides)
- threatening to commit suicide

Life Connections
Preventing Suicide

Imagine that you are having a heart-to-heart talk with Jamie, one of your best friends. Things haven't been going well. Jamie's grandmother died a month ago, and they were very close. Jamie's course work has been suffering, and things have also been going downhill with the person Jamie has been seeing. But you are not prepared when Jamie looks you in the eye and says, "I've been thinking about this for days, and I've decided that the only way out is to kill myself."

If someone tells you that he or she is considering suicide, you may become frightened and flustered or feel that an enormous burden has been placed on you. You are right: It has. In such a case your objective should be to encourage the person to consult a health-care provider, or to consult one yourself, as soon as possible. But if the person refuses to talk to anyone else and you feel that you can't break free for a consultation, there are a number of things you can do (Hendin et al., 2001; Omer & Elitzur, 2001; Shneidman, 2001):

1. Keep talking. Encourage the person to talk to you or to some other trusted person (Los Angeles Unified School District, 2000). Draw the person out with questions like, "What's happening?" "Where do you hurt?" "What do you want to happen?" Questions like these may encourage the person to express frustrated needs and provide some relief. They also give you time to think.
2. Be a good listener. Be supportive with people who express suicidal thoughts or feel depressed, hopeless, or worthless. They may believe their condition is hopeless and will never improve, but let them know that you are there for them and

■ A Suicide-Prevention Hotline

At suicide-prevention centers, staff members stand by hotlines around the clock. If you know someone who is threatening to commit suicide, consult a professional as soon as possible.

willing to help them get help. Show that you understand how upset the person is. Do *not* say, "Don't be silly."

3. Suggest that something other than suicide might solve the problem, even if it is not evident at the time. Many suicidal people see only two solutions—either death or a magical resolution of their problems. Therapists try to "remove the mental blinders" from suicidal people.

4. Emphasize as concretely as possible how the person's suicide would be devastating to you and to other people who care.

5. Ask how the person intends to commit suicide. People with concrete plans and a weapon are at greater risk. Ask if you might hold on to the weapon for a while. Sometimes the answer is yes.

6. Suggest that the person go *with you* to obtain professional help *now*. The emergency room of a general hospital, the campus counseling center or infirmary, or the campus or local police station will do. Some campuses and cities have suicide prevention centers with hotlines.

7. Extract a promise that the person will not commit suicide before seeing you again. Arrange a specific time and place to meet. Get professional help as soon as you are apart.

8. Do *not* tell people threatening suicide that they're silly or crazy. Do *not* insist on contact with specific people, such as parents or a spouse. Conflict with these people may have led to the suicidal thinking in the first place.

You can also check out the following resources:

■ The national suicide hotline: 1-800-SUICIDE (1-800-784-2433).

■ American Association of Suicidology: Their website, www.suicidology.org, provides information on ways to prevent suicide. You will also find a list of crisis centers.

■ American Foundation for Suicide Prevention: Their website, www.afsp.org, offers information about suicide and links to other suicide and mental health sites. ■

⟨⟩ Learning Connections

◀◀   *Mood Disorders—Up, Down, and Around*   ▶▶

REVIEW:

7 _____ is a symptom of bipolar disorder.
(a) Rapid flight of ideas,
(b) La belle indifférence,
(c) Waxy flexibility,
(d) Stupor.

8 Depressed people are more likely than other people to make _____ attributions for failures.
(a) external,
(b) specific,
(c) internal,
(d) unstable.

9 Research suggests there is a positive relationship between depression and
(a) openness to experience,
(b) neuroticism,

(c) extraversion,
(d) agreeableness.

10 Which of the following is true about one's gender and suicide?
(a) Males are more likely than females to use tranquilers in suicide attempts,
(b) Males are more likely than females to attempt suicide,
(c) Males who attempt suicide are more likely to be angry than depressed,
(d) Males succeed more often than females at suicide attempts.

CRITICAL THINKING:
Critical thinkers pay close attention to the definitions of terms. When is depression considered a psychological disorder? How does bipolar disorder differ from responses to the "ups and downs" of life?

Go to www
http://academic.cengage.com/psychology/rathus
for an interactive version of this review.

ANXIETY DISORDERS: REAL-LIFE FEAR FACTORS

Why is *Fear Factor* so riveting to some viewers? Perhaps the fact that many of us, perhaps most of us, could not imagine participating in activities such as allowing spiders to crawl over us for fame or fortune. Extreme fears of spiders, heights, and so on are examples of phobias, which are a type of anxiety disorder.

Anxiety has psychological and physical features. Psychological features include worrying, fear of the worst things happening, fear of losing control, nervousness, and inability to relax. Physical features reflect arousal of the sympathetic branch of the autonomic nervous system. They include trembling, sweating, a pounding or racing heart, elevated blood pressure (a flushed face), and faintness. Anxiety is an appropriate response to a real threat. It can be abnormal, however, when it is excessive or when it comes out of nowhere—that is, when events do not seem to warrant it. *What kinds of anxiety disorders are there?*

There are different kinds of anxiety disorders, but all of them are characterized by excessive or unwarranted anxiety. The anxiety disorders include phobias, panic disorder, generalized anxiety, obsessive–compulsive disorder, and stress disorders.

▬ Phobias

Phobias include specific phobias, social phobia, and agoraphobia. They can be detrimental to one's quality of life (Stein & Kean, 2000). **Specific phobias** are irrational fears of specific objects or situations, such as spiders, snakes, or heights. One specific phobia is fear of

Specific phobia Persistent fear of a specific object or situation.

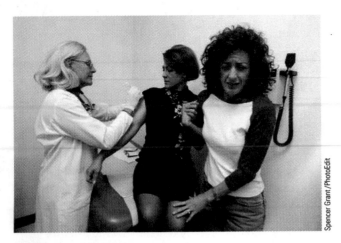

Spencer Grant/PhotoEdit

■ A Person with a Phobia

Phobias are excessive, irrational fears that can interfere with the person's functioning. A phobia for needles can prevent a person from seeking needed medical assistance.

elevators. Some people will not enter elevators despite the hardships they incur as a result (such as walking up 10 flights of steps). Yes, the cable *could* break. The ventilation *could* fail. One *could* be stuck in midair waiting for repairs. But these problems are uncommon, and it affects one's quality of life to walk up and down several flights of stairs to elude them. Similarly, some people with a specific phobia for hypodermic needles will not have injections, even to treat serious illness. Injections can be painful, but most people with a phobia for needles would gladly suffer an even more painful pinch if it would help them fight illness. Other specific phobias include **claustrophobia** (fear of tight or enclosed places), **acrophobia** (fear of heights), and fear of mice, snakes, and other creepy-crawlies. (Fear of spiders is technically called *arachnophobia*.) **Social phobias** are persistent fears of scrutiny by others or of doing something that will be humiliating or embarrassing. Fear of public speaking is a common social phobia.

Agoraphobia is also widespread among adults. Agoraphobia is derived from the Greek words meaning "fear of the marketplace," or fear of being out in open, busy areas. Persons with agoraphobia fear being in places from which it might be difficult to escape or in which help might not be available if they get upset. In practice, people who receive this diagnosis often refuse to venture out of their homes, especially by themselves. They find it difficult to hold a job or to maintain an ordinary social life.

——■▶ Panic Disorder

The following represents a first-person account of a panic attack:

> My heart would start pounding so hard I was sure I was having a heart attack. I used to go to the emergency room. Sometimes I felt dizzy, like I was going to pass out. I was sure I was about to die. —Kim

Panic disorder is an abrupt attack of acute anxiety that is not triggered by a specific object or situation. People with panic disorder have strong physical symptoms such as shortness of breath, heavy sweating, tremors, and pounding of the heart. Like Kim, they are particularly aware of cardiac sensations (Wilhelm et al., 2001). It is not unusual for them to think they are having a heart attack. Saliva levels of cortisol (a stress hormone) are elevated during attacks (Bandelow et al., 2000). People with the disorder may also experience choking sensations; nausea; numbness or tingling; flushes or chills; and fear of going crazy or losing control. Panic attacks may last minutes or hours. Afterwards, the person usually feels drained.

Many people panic now and then. The diagnosis of panic disorder is reserved for those who undergo a series of attacks or live in fear of attacks.

Panic attacks seem to come from nowhere. Thus, some people who have had them stay home for fear of having an attack in public. They are diagnosed as having panic disorder with agoraphobia.

Claustrophobia Fear of tight, small places.

Acrophobia Fear of high places.

Social phobia An irrational, excessive fear of public scrutiny.

Agoraphobia Fear of open, crowded places.

Panic disorder The recurrent experiencing of attacks of extreme anxiety in the absence of external stimuli that usually elicit anxiety.

Generalized anxiety disorder Feelings of dread and foreboding and sympathetic arousal of at least 6 months' duration.

——■▶ Generalized Anxiety Disorder

The central feature of **generalized anxiety disorder** is persistent anxiety. As with panic disorder, the anxiety cannot be attributed to a phobic object, situation, or activity. Rather, it seems to be free floating. The core of the disorder appears to be pervasive worrying about numerous problems (Aikins & Craske, 2001). Features of the disorder include motor tension (shakiness, inability to relax, furrowed brow, fidgeting); autonomic overarousal (sweating, dry mouth, racing heart, light-headedness, frequent urinating, diarrhea); and excessive vigilance, as shown by irritability, insomnia, and a tendency to be easily distracted.

Obsessive–Compulsive Disorder

Obsessions are recurrent, anxiety-provoking thoughts or images that seem irrational and beyond control. They are so compelling and recurrent that they disrupt daily life. They may include doubts about whether one has locked the doors and shut the windows, or images such as one mother's repeated fantasy that her children had been run over on the way home from school. One woman became obsessed with the idea that she had contaminated her hands with Sani-Flush and that the chemicals were spreading to everything she touched. A 16-year-old boy complained that he was distracted by "numbers in my head" when he was about to study or take a test. The more he tried to ignore them, the louder they became.

Compulsions are thoughts or behaviors that tend to reduce the anxiety connected with obsessions. They are seemingly irresistible urges to engage in specific acts, often repeatedly, such as elaborate washing after using the bathroom or repeatedly checking that one has locked the door or turned off the gas burners before leaving home. The impulse is recurrent and forceful, interfering with daily life. The woman who felt contaminated by Sani-Flush spent 3 to 4 hours at the sink each day and complained, "My hands look like lobster claws."

Stress Disorders

Sharia dreamed of a man assaulting her in the night at the Superdome in New Orleans, after she had been moved to this "refuge" following Hurricane Katrina in the summer of 2005. Darla, who lives in Oregon, dreamed that she was trapped in a World Trade Center tower when it was hit by an airplane on September 11, 2001. About one in six Iraq or Afghanistan veterans has nightmares and flashbacks to buddies being killed by snipers or explosive devices (Hoge et al., 2004). These all-too-real nightmarish events have caused many bad dreams. Such dreams are part of the experience of posttraumatic stress disorder.

Posttraumatic stress disorder (PTSD) is characterized by a rapid heart rate and feelings of anxiety and helplessness that are caused by a traumatic experience. Such experiences may include a natural or humanmade disaster, a threat or assault, or witnessing a death. PTSD may occur months or years after the event. It frequently occurs among firefighters, combat veterans, and people whose homes and communities have been swept away by natural disasters or who have been victims of accidents or violence (Blanchard et al., 2003; Vasterling et al., 2002).

The traumatic event is revisited in the form of intrusive memories, recurrent dreams, and flashbacks—the sudden feeling that the event is recurring (Rutkowski, 2001; Yehuda, 2002). People with PTSD typically try to avoid thoughts and activities connected to the traumatic event. They may find it more difficult to enjoy life (Beckham et al., 2000) and have sleep problems (Lavie, 2001), irritable outbursts, difficulty concentrating, extreme vigilance, and an intensified "startle" response (Shayley et al., 2000). The attacks of September 11, 2001, took their toll on sleep. According to a poll taken by the National Sleep Foundation (2001) two months afterward, nearly half of Americans had difficulty falling asleep, as compared with about one-quarter of Americans before the attacks (see Figure 12.3). Women respondents were somewhat more likely than men to report sleep problems such as trouble falling asleep (50% vs. 37%).

Acute stress disorder, like PTSD, is characterized by feelings of anxiety and helplessness that are caused by a traumatic event. PTSD, however, can occur 6 months or more after the traumatic event and tends to persist. Acute stress disorder occurs within a month of the event and lasts from 2 days to 4 weeks. Women who have been raped, for example, experience acute distress that tends to peak in severity a few weeks after the assault. Yet the same women often go on to experience PTSD (Koss et al., 2002; Street et al., 2003).

Mark Schuster and his colleagues (2001) conducted a telephone survey of a nationally representative sample of 560 American adults—not just those who lived near the attacks— three to five days following September 11, 2001. They found that 90% of respondents reported at least one stress-related symptom, and 44% reported more severe symptoms of

Obsession A recurring thought or image that seems beyond control.

Compulsion An irresistible urge to repeat an act or engage in ritualistic behavior such as hand washing.

Posttraumatic stress disorder (PTSD) A disorder that follows a distressing event outside the range of normal human experience and that is characterized by features such as intense fear, avoidance of stimuli associated with the event, and reliving of the event.

Acute stress disorder A disorder, like PTSD, that is characterized by feelings of anxiety and helplessness and caused by a traumatic event. Acute stress disorder occurs within a month of the event and lasts from 2 days to 4 weeks.

Sandy Huffaker/Getty Images

■ **A Traumatic Experience**
Approximately one in six soldiers returning from Afghanistan and Iraq experiences posttraumatic stress disorder (PTSD) (Hoge et al., 2004). PTSD is characterized by intrusive memories of the experience, recurrent dreams about it, and the sudden feeling that it is, in fact, recurring (as in "flashbacks"). Some soldiers flash back to buddies being blown up by improvised explosive devices (IEDs) or being shot by snipers.

Figure 12.3

Sleep Problems Among Americans Before and After September 11, 2001

Insomnia is one of the symptoms of stress disorders. A poll by the National Sleep Foundation found that Americans had a greater frequency of sleep problems after the terrorist attacks of September 11, 2001.

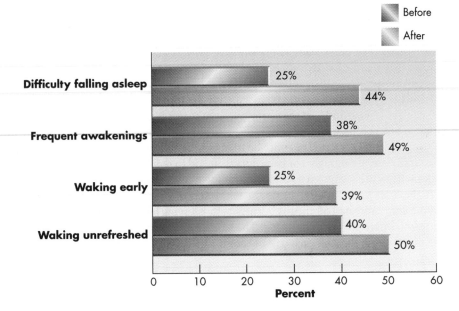

stress. Respondents coped by seeking social support, such as talking with others (98%) or participating in group activities (60%), by turning to religion (90%), and by making donations (36%). The great majority of parents of children aged 5 to 18 (84%) reported that they had talked with their children about the attacks for at least an hour, and about one-third (34%) restricted their children's exposure to television coverage of the attacks.

Explaining Anxiety Disorders

There are thus several kinds of anxiety disorders. *What is known about the origins of anxiety disorders?*

Biological Perspectives   Biological factors play a role in anxiety disorders. Genetic factors are implicated in most psychological disorders, including anxiety disorders (Kendler et al., 2001; Nestadt et al., 2000; Schmidt et al., 2000). Anxiety disorders tend to run in families. Twin studies find a higher rate of match for anxiety disorders among identical twins than among fraternal twins (Kendler et al., 2001). Studies of adoptees who are anxious similarly show that the biological parent places the child at risk for anxiety and related traits.

Psychological and Social Perspectives   Some learning theorists—particularly behaviorists—consider phobias to be conditioned fears that were acquired in early childhood. Therefore, their origins are beyond memory. Avoidance of feared stimuli is reinforced by the reduction of anxiety.

Other learning theorists—social cognitive theorists—dwell on the social aspects of developing phobias (Basic Behavioral Science Task Force, 1996b). If parents squirm, grimace, and shudder at the sight of mice, blood, or dirt on the kitchen floor, children might assume that these stimuli are awful and imitate their parents' behavior.

Cognitive theorists suggest that people maintain anxiety by thinking that they are in a terrible situation and helpless to change it. People with anxiety disorders may be cognitively biased toward focusing on threats (Fox et al., 2001; Sookman et al., 2001). Psychoanalysts and learning theorists agree that compulsive behavior reduces anxiety.

Cognitive theorists note that people's appraisals of the magnitude of threats help determine whether they are traumatic and can lead to PTSD (Folkman & Moskowitz, 2000a; Koss et al., 2002). People with panic attacks tend to overreact to physical sensations. Obsessions and compulsions may serve to divert attention from more frightening issues, such as "What am I going to do with my life?" When anxieties are acquired at a young age, we may later interpret them as enduring traits and label ourselves as "people who fear _____" (you fill it in). We then live up to the labels. We also entertain thoughts that heighten and perpetuate anxiety such as "I've got to get out of here," or "My heart is going to leap out of my chest." Such ideas intensify physical features of anxiety, disrupt planning, make stimuli seem worse than they are, motivate avoidance, and lower self-efficacy expectations. The belief that we will not be able to handle a threat heightens anxiety. The belief that we are in control reduces anxiety (Bandura et al., 1985).

Perhaps a predisposition toward anxiety—in the form of a highly reactive autonomic nervous system—can be inherited. What might make a nervous system "highly reactive"? In the case of panic disorder, faulty regulation of levels of serotonin and norepinephrine may be involved. Other anxiety disorders may involve the neurotransmitter glutamate, and receptor sites in the brain may not be sensitive enough to gamma-aminobutyric acid (GABA), a neurotransmitter that may counteract glutamate (Kalin, 2003; Lydiard, 2003; Stroele et al., 2002). The benzodiazepines, a class of drugs that reduce anxiety, may work by increasing the sensitivity of receptor sites to GABA.

The Biopsychosocial Perspective   Many cases of anxiety disorders reflect the interaction of biological, psychological, and social factors. In panic disorder, biological imbalances may initially trigger attacks. However, subsequent fear of attacks—and of the bodily cues that

A Closer Look
Fear Factor and Evolutionary Psychology

A Closer Look

Here are a couple of questions for you: How would you like to go bobbing for plums in a container filled with snakes? If that doesn't sound like your cup of tea, how would you like to have (approximately) 400 rats running over your body?

Now, before you turn thumbs down on these stunts, let us note that they were carried out on the TV show *Fear Factor* for the chance to win thousands of dollars and 15 minutes of fame. And these weren't just any rats. According to a *Fear Factor* producer, the rats were raised in laboratories, and like other lab rats, they were "as clean as rats can be."

These are only a few of the fears triggered by *Fear Factor*. As noted by a fan in Woodbridge Township, New Jersey: "In the Playmates Edition, one segment had the participants eating strawberries in a case full of flies; most of the playmates swallowed several flies. Other segments had similar feats, one with cockroaches. Now is that sick or what? In others the object is itself to swallow worms, crickets, and other insects" (www.imdb.com/title/tt0278191/usercomments).

A viewer in Santa Monica notes: "Mostly they get contestants to eat such disgusting things as live beetles, live worms, pig anuses, bull testicles and penises, goat spinal cords and whatever other else that is worse one could imagine. But tonight they outdid themselves by having each of the contestants suffer through 20 piercings of their arms with needles of various sizes, producing, not only squeamishness, but pain and blood" (www.imdb.com/title/tt0278191/usercomments).

How do we interpret people's reactions to having rats crawl over them, eating animals' genitals, having needles pierce their skin, and—in other episodes—cozying up to spiders and worms, and "climb[ing] around the water-slicked hood of a car suspended hundreds of feet in the air from a crane" (www.realitytvplanet.com/fearfactor_frontpage.php)? Why do these things elicit so many "yucks"? Why do

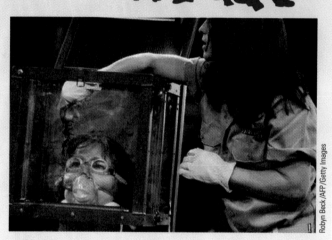

Robyn Beck/AFP/Getty Images

■ **What Are Your "Fear Factors"?**
Millions have been drawn to the TV show *Fear Factor*. Did they want to confront their own fears? Did they enjoy seeing others in apparent jeopardy? Why would you watch—or not?

audience members get queasy in the stomach? The contestants are (presumably) in no real danger, so why are viewers astonished?

Evolutionary psychologists suggest that fears such as those highlighted in *Fear Factor* may reflect natural selection. Susan Mineka (Oehman & Mineka, 2001) suggests that humans (and nonhuman primates) are genetically predisposed to fear stimuli that may have threatened their ancestors. Evolutionary forces would have favored the survival of individuals who were predisposed toward acquiring fears of large animals, spiders, snakes, heights, entrapment, sharp objects, and strangers. Thus individuals who fearlessly encounter the potentially harmful stimuli we see on *Fear Factor* may be at a disadvantage, evolutionarily speaking, rather than at an advantage. ■

signal their onset—may heighten discomfort and give one the idea that nothing can be done about them (Craske & Zucker, 2001). Moreover, panic attacks are likely to occur in social situations, especially in crowds. Feelings of helplessness increase fear. People with panic disorder can be helped by methods that reduce physical discomfort—including regular breathing—and show them that there are ways to cope with attacks (Craske & Zucker, 2001). They are also sometimes taken into social settings, such as crowded streets or stores, by psychologists who offer them social support and show them that they can tolerate such situations.

 ## Learning Connections

◀◀ Anxiety Disorders—Real-Life "Fear Factors"? ▶▶

REVIEW:

11 _____ disorder is characterized by sudden attacks in which people are highly sensitive to cardiac sensations and fear that they may be losing control or going crazy.
   (a) Obsessive–compulsive,
   (b) Panic,
   (c) Phobic,
   (d) Generalized anxiety.

12 Biological psychologists hypothesize that receptor sites in the brains of people with some anxiety disorders may not be sensitive enough to
   (a) gamma-aminobutyric acid (GABA),
   (b) glutamate,
   (c) dopamine,
   (d) adrenaline.

13 Flashbacks and recurrent dreams are common features of
   (a) phobic disorders,
   (b) panic attacks,
   (c) posttraumatic stress disorder,
   (d) obsessive–compulsive disorder.

14 _____ theorists speculate that there is survival value in fearing potentially harmful objects and situations.
   (a) Psychodynamic,
   (b) Learning,
   (c) Evolutionary,
   (d) Cognitive.

CRITICAL THINKING:
Critical thinkers attend to the definitions of terms. For example, is anxiety abnormal? What is the difference between run-of-the-mill anxiety and an *anxiety disorder*?

Go www
to
http://academic.cengage.com/psychology/rathus
for an interactive version of this review.

SOMATOFORM DISORDERS: WHEN THE BODY EXPRESSES STRESS

Somatoform disorders Disorders in which people complain of physical (somatic) problems even though no physical abnormality can be found.

Conversion disorder A somatoform disorder in which anxiety or unconscious conflicts are "converted" into physical symptoms that often have the effect of helping the person cope with anxiety or conflict.

People with **somatoform disorders** complain of physical problems such as paralysis, pain, or a persistent belief that they have a serious disease. But health professionals can find no evidence of a physical abnormality. *What kinds of somatoform disorders are there?* In this section we discuss two somatoform disorders: conversion disorder and hypochondriasis.

━■━ Conversion Disorder

Conversion disorder is characterized by a major change in, or loss of, physical functioning, although there are no medical findings to explain the loss of functioning. The behaviors are not intentionally produced. That is, the person is not faking. Conversion disorder is so named because it appears to "convert" a source of stress into a physical difficulty.

If you lost the ability to see at night, or if your legs became paralyzed, you would understandably show concern. But some people with conversion disorder show indifference to their symptoms, a remarkable feature referred to as **la belle indifférence.**

During World War II, some bomber pilots developed night blindness. They could not carry out their nighttime missions, although no damage to the optic nerves was found. In rare cases, women with large families have been reported to become paralyzed in the legs, again with no medical findings. More recently, a Cambodian woman who had witnessed atrocities became blind as a result.

Hypochondriasis

Another more common type of somatoform disorder is **hypochondriasis** (also called *hypochondria*). People with this disorder insist that they are suffering from a serious physical illness, even though no medical evidence of illness can be found. They become preoccupied with minor physical sensations and continue to believe that they are ill despite the reassurance of physicians that they are healthy. They may run from doctor to doctor, seeking the one who will find the causes of the sensations. Fear of illness may disrupt their work or home life.

Body Dysmorphic Disorder

People with **body dysmorphic disorder** are preoccupied with a fantasized or exaggerated physical defect in their appearance (Hildebrandt et al., 2004). They may spend hours examining themselves in the mirror and go to extreme lengths to correct the "problem," including cosmetic surgery (Sarwer & Crerand, 2004). Others remove all mirrors from their homes so as not to be reminded of the "flaw." People with the disorder may assume that others see them as deformed (Veale, 2004). They may compulsively groom themselves or pay close attention to styling every strand of hair.

What is known about the origins of somatoform disorders?

Explaining Somatoform Disorders

The somatoform disorders offer a fascinating study in the biopsychosocial perspective. Psychologically speaking, the somatoform disorders have much to do with what one focuses on—actual social and financial problems, for example, or one's body. Some investigators consider conversion disorder to be a form of self-hypnosis (Roelofs et al., 2002), and they note that there is research evidence that people with conversion disorder are highly susceptible to being hypnotized. The idea here would be that people with conversion disorder focus on an imaginary physical problem to the point where they exclude conflicting information.

In the case of hypochondriasis, people may misinterpret run-of-the-mill physical sensations—or symptoms—as signifying deadly illness. There is research evidence that people who develop hypochondriasis are particularly sensitive to bodily sensations and tend to ruminate about them (Lecci & Cohen, 2002). Moreover, enacting the role of a sick person has the "benefits" of relieving one of ordinary responsibilities and concerns. For example, how can one focus on work or family life when one believes he or she is rotting away with disease?

Certainly the social value of personal attractiveness can contribute to dissatisfaction with one's body. Physically attractive people are stereotyped as being good and socially skilled from an early age (Ramsey & Langlois, 2002; Ramsey et al., 2004). But people with body dysmorphic disorder may focus irrationally on an exaggerated blemish or other minor feature, suggestive of perfectionistic and ruminative tendencies.

Biologically speaking, tendencies toward perfectionism and rumination, which are found among many people with somatoform disorders, are thought to be at least partly heritable. Squeamishness about one's body may be too much of a good thing from the evolutionary perspective. That is, concern about bodily harm will presumably encourage one to avoid danger and provide advantages in survival and reproduction. But too much concern may lead to useless preoccupations.

Bald Headed Pictures/Taxi/Getty Images

■ Hypochondriasis

People with hypochondriasis are irrationally concerned that they have contracted illnesses. Such people appear to be unusually sensitive to physical sensations. Do they also focus on their physical symptoms to avoid dealing with the real problems in their lives?

La belle indifférence A French term descriptive of the lack of concern for their (imagined) medical problem sometimes shown by people with conversion disorders.

Hypochondriasis A somatoform disorder characterized by persistent belief that one is ill despite lack of medical findings.

Body dysmorphic disorder A somatoform disorder characterized by preoccupation with an imagined or exaggerated physical defect in one's appearance.

◯ Learning Connections

◀◀ *Somatoform Disorders—When the Body Expresses Stress* ▶▶

REVIEW:

15 What is unusual about "la belle indifférence"?
   (a) The term refers to physical symptoms,
   (b) People with la belle indifférence are uncon-
       cerned about potentially dangerous physical
       conditions,
   (c) It applies only to men who try to be "tough"
       when they are facing physical problems,
   (d) It is a medical term rather than a psychological
       term.

16 People who develop hypochondriasis tend to
    _____ bodily sensations.
   (a) ruminate about,
   (b) ignore,
   (c) fake,
   (d) repress or suppress.

CRITICAL THINKING:
It is healthful to be aware of changes in bodily functioning. How does
one distinguish between a healthful concern about one's body and the
somatoform disorder of hypochondriasis?

Go to www
http://academic.cengage.com/psychology/rathus
for an interactive version of this review.

DISSOCIATIVE DISORDERS: SPLITTING CONSCIOUSNESS

During one long fall semester, the Ohio State University campus lived in terror. Four college women were kidnapped, forced to take out cash from ATMs, and raped. A mysterious phone call led to the arrest of a 23-year-old drifter—let's call him "William"—who had been dismissed from the Navy.

William was not the boy next door.

Psychologists and psychiatrists who interviewed William concluded that 10 personalities—8 male and 2 female—dwelled in him (Keyes, 1995). His personality had been "fractured" by an abusive childhood. His several personalities displayed distinct facial expressions, speech patterns, and memories. They performed differently on psychological tests.

Arthur, the most rational personality, spoke with a British accent. Danny and Christopher were quiet adolescents. Christine was a 3-year-old girl. Tommy, a 16-year-old, had enlisted in the Navy. Allen was 18 and smoked. Adelena, a 19-year-old lesbian personality, had committed the rapes. Who had placed the mysterious phone call? Probably David, 9, an anxious child.

The defense claimed that William's behavior was caused by *dissociative identity disorder.* Of the identities or personalities dwelling within him, some were aware of the others. Some believed they were unique. As a child, Billy, the core identity, had learned to sleep to avoid his father's abuse. A psychiatrist asserted that Billy had also been "asleep," or in a "psychological coma," during the abductions. Billy should therefore be found not guilty by reason of insanity.

William was found not guilty. He was committed to a psychiatric institution and released six years later.

Dissociative identity disorder is one of the **dissociative disorders.** In dissociative disorders, there is a separation of psychological processes such as thoughts, emotions, identity,

Dissociative disorders Disorders in which there are sudden, temporary changes in consciousness or self-identity.

memory, or consciousness—the processes that make the person feel whole. ***What kinds of dissociative disorders are there?*** The dissociative disorders include dissociative amnesia, dissociative fugue, and William's disorder: dissociative identity disorder (also termed *multiple personality disorder*).

Dissociative Amnesia

In **dissociative amnesia,** the person is suddenly unable to recall important personal information (that is, explicit episodic memories). The loss of memory cannot be attributed to biological problems such as a blow to the head or excessive drinking. It is thus a psychological disorder and not an organic one. In the most common example, the person cannot recall events for a number of hours after a stressful incident, as in warfare or in the case of an uninjured survivor of an accident. In generalized amnesia, people forget their entire lives. Amnesia may last for hours or years.

Dissociative Fugue

In **dissociative fugue,** the person abruptly leaves his or her home or place of work and travels to another place, having lost all memory of his or her past life. While at the new location, the person either does not think about the past or reports a past filled with invented memories. The new personality is often more outgoing and less inhibited than the "real" identity. Following recovery, the events that occurred during the fugue are not recalled.

Dissociative Identity Disorder

In **dissociative identity disorder** (formerly termed **multiple personality disorder**), two or more identities or personalities, each with distinct traits and memories, "occupy" the same person. Each identity may or may not be aware of the others or of events experienced by the others (Huntjens et al., 2003).

◈ **Truth or Fiction Revisited:** The personalities of people with dissociative identity disorder can be very different from one another. They might have different eyeglass prescriptions (Braun, 1988). Braun reports cases in which assorted identities showed different allergic responses. In one person, an identity named Timmy was not sensitive to orange juice. But when another identity drank orange juice, he would break out with hives. Hives would also erupt if another identity emerged while the juice was being digested. If Timmy reappeared when the allergic reaction was present, the itching of the hives would cease and the blisters would start to subside. In other cases reported by Braun, different identities within a person might show various responses to the same medicine. Or one identity might exhibit color blindness while others have normal color vision.

A few celebrated cases of this disorder have been portrayed in the popular media. One of them became the subject of the film *The Three Faces of Eve*. In the film, a timid housewife named Eve White harbored two other identities. One was Eve Black, a sexually aggressive, antisocial personality. The third was "Jane," an emerging identity who was able to accept the existence of her primitive impulses yet engage in socially appropriate behavior. Finally the three faces merged into one—Jane. Ironically, later on, the real-life "Jane" (a woman named Chris Sizemore) reportedly split into 22 identities. Another well-publicized case is that of Sybil, a woman with 16 identities who was portrayed by Sally Field in the film *Sybil*.

Dissociative amnesia A dissociative disorder marked by loss of memory or self-identity; skills and general knowledge are usually retained.

Dissociative fugue A dissociative disorder in which one experiences amnesia and then flees to a new location.

Dissociative identity disorder A disorder in which a person appears to have two or more distinct identities or personalities that may alternately emerge.

Multiple personality disorder The previous term for *dissociative identity disorder*.

Dissociative Identity Disorder
In the film *The Three Faces of Eve*, Joanne Woodward played three personalities in the same woman: the shy, inhibited Eve White (lying on couch), the flirtatious, promiscuous Eve Black (in dark dress); and a third personality (right) who could accept her sexual and aggressive impulses and still maintain her sense of identity.

Museum of Modern Art/Film Stills Archive

reflect & relate

Have you seen a film or a TV show in which a character was supposed to have dissociative identity disorder (perhaps it was called "multiple personality")? What kind of behavior did the character display? Does the behavior seem consistent with the description of the disorder in the text? In the film or TV show, what were the supposed origins of the disorder?

■ Explaining Dissociative Disorders

The dissociative disorders are some of the odder psychological disorders. *What is known about the origins of dissociative disorders?*

Biopsychosocial factors may well be involved in dissociative disorders. According to learning and cognitive psychologists, people with dissociative disorders may have learned *not to think* about bad memories or disturbing impulses in an effort to avoid feelings of anxiety, guilt, and shame. Dissociative disorders may help people keep disturbing ideas out of mind.

What might such memories contain? The answer is painful interpersonal—or social—information. Research suggests that many cases of dissociative disorders involve memories of sexual or physical abuse during childhood, usually by a relative or caretaker (Banyard et al., 2003; Martinez-Taboas & Bernal, 2000; Migdow, 2003).

On a biological level, research with abused children and adolescents suggests that the trauma-related dissociation observed in dissociative disorders may have a neurological basis (Diseth, 2005). Child abuse may lead to some permanent neurochemical and structural abnormalities in parts of the brain involved in cognition and memory. Although it seems that the nature of the trauma in such cases is interpersonal, it need not necessarily be sexual in nature. In any event, one might expect resultant impairments in the recall of personal information.

( ) Learning Connections

◀◀ *Dissociative Disorders—Splitting Consciousness* ▶▶

Learning Connections

REVIEW:

17 Dissociative _____ is also known as multiple personality disorder.
(a) personality disorder,
(b) identity disorder,
(c) fugue,
(d) amnesia.

18 Many people with dissociative disorders have a history of
(a) tax evasion,
(b) multiple marriages,
(c) sleep disorders,
(d) childhood sexual abuse.

CRITICAL THINKING:
How does research into the origins of dissociative disorders support the biopsychosocial perspective?

 Go to
http://academic.cengage.com/psychology/rathus
for an interactive version of this review.

PERSONALITY DISORDERS: MAKING ONESELF OR OTHERS MISERABLE

Personality disorders, like personality traits, are characterized by enduring patterns of behavior. Personality disorders, however, are inflexible and maladaptive. They impair personal or social functioning and are a source of distress to the individual or to other people. *What kinds of personality disorders are there?*

There are a number of personality disorders. They include the paranoid, schizotypal, schizoid, antisocial, and avoidant personality disorders.

rs Enduring pat-
behavior that are
he individual or

Paranoid Personality Disorder

The defining trait of the **paranoid personality disorder** is a tendency to interpret other people's behavior as threatening or demeaning. People with the disorder do not show the grossly disorganized thinking of paranoid schizophrenia. They are mistrustful of others, however, and their relationships suffer for it. They may be suspicious of coworkers and supervisors, but they can generally hold a job.

Schizotypal and Schizoid Personality Disorders

Schizotypal personality disorder is characterized by peculiarities of thought, perception, or behavior, such as excessive fantasy and suspiciousness, feelings of being unreal, or odd usage of words. The bizarre behaviors that characterize schizophrenia are absent, so this disorder is schizo*typal,* not schizophrenic.

The **schizoid personality** is defined by indifference to relationships and flat emotional response. People with this disorder are "loners." They do not develop warm, tender feelings for others. They have few friends and rarely maintain long-term relationships. Some people with schizoid personality disorder do very well on the job provided that continuous social interaction is not required. They do not have hallucinations or delusions.

Borderline Personality Disorder

People with **borderline personality disorder** show instability in their relationships, self-image, and mood, and lack of control over impulses (Johansen et al., 2004; Yen et al., 2002). They tend to be uncertain of their values, goals, loyalties, careers, choices of friends, sometimes even their sexual orientations (Sokolova et al., 2002). Instability in self-image or identity may leave them with feelings of emptiness and boredom. Many cannot tolerate being alone and make desperate attempts to avoid feelings of abandonment. They may be clinging and demanding in social relationships, but clinging often pushes away the people on whom they depend. They alternate between extremes of adulation in their relationships (when their needs are met) and loathing (when they feel scorned). They tend to view other people as all good or all bad, shifting abruptly from one extreme to the other (Butler et al., 2002). As a result, they may flit from partner to partner in brief and stormy relationships. People whom they had idealized are treated with contempt when they feel the other person has failed them.

Instability of moods is a central characteristic of borderline personality disorder. Moods run the gamut from anger and irritability to depression and anxiety, with each lasting from a few hours to a few days. People with the disorder have difficulty controlling anger and are prone to fights or smashing things. They often act on impulse, such as eloping with someone they have just met. This impulsive and unpredictable behavior is often self-destructive and linked to a risk of suicidal attempts and gestures. It may involve spending sprees, gambling, drug abuse, engaging in unsafe sexual activity, reckless driving, binge eating, or shoplifting. People with the disorder may also engage in self-mutilation, such as scratching their wrists or burning cigarettes on their arms (Sachsse et al., 2002). Self-mutilation is sometimes a means of manipulating others, particularly in times of stress. Frequent self-mutilation is also associated with suicide attempts.

Antisocial Personality Disorder

◇ **Truth or Fiction Revisited:** It is true that some people can kill or maim others with no feelings of guilt at all. When these people also persistently violate the rights of others and are in repeated conflict with the law, they may be diagnosed with **antisocial personality disorder** (see Table 12.2). People with antisocial personality disorder often show a superficial charm and are at least average in intelligence. They fail to learn to improve their behavior from punishment, and they do not form meaningful bonds with other people (Levenston et al., 2000; Romero et al., 2001). Though they are often heavily punished by their parents and rejected by peers, they continue in their impulsive, careless styles of life. Women are more likely than men to have anxiety and depressive disorders. Men are more likely than women to have antisocial personality disorder (K. G. Anderson et al., 2001).

■ **A Person with Borderline Personality Disorder?**
Many well-known individuals such as Marilyn Monroe (seen here with her husband, playwright Arthur Miller) may have had borderline personality disorder. The disorder is characterized by instability in relationships, self-image, and mood, and by problems in impulse control.

Paranoid personality disorder A personality disorder characterized by persistent suspiciousness, but not involving the disorganization of paranoid schizophrenia.

Schizotypal personality disorder A personality disorder characterized by oddities of thought and behavior, but not involving bizarre psychotic behaviors.

Schizoid personality disorder A personality disorder characterized by social withdrawal.

Borderline personality disorder A personality disorder characterized by instability in relationships, self-image, mood, and lack of impulse control.

Antisocial personality disorder The diagnosis given a person who is in frequent conflict with society, yet who is undeterred by punishment and experiences little or no guilt and anxiety.

TABLE 12.2 ■ Characteristics of People Diagnosed with Antisocial Personality Disorder

Key Characteristics
History of delinquency and truancy
Persistent violation of the rights of others
Impulsiveness
Poor self-control
Lack of remorse for misdeeds
Lack of empathy
Deceitfulness and manipulativeness
Irresponsibility
Glibness; superficial charm
Exaggerated sense of self-worth

Other Common Characteristics
Lack of loyalty or of formation of enduring relationships
Failure to maintain good job performance over the years
Failure to develop or adhere to a life plan
Sexual promiscuity
Substance abuse
Inability to tolerate boredom
Low tolerance for frustration
Irritability

SOURCES: Levenston et al., 2000; Romero et al., 2001.

Do you know anyone whom you consider to have a "bad personality"? What characteristics lead you to describe him or her in this way? What is the difference between people with "bad personalities" and people with personality disorders?

Avoidant personality disorder A personality disorder in which the person is unwilling to enter relationships without assurance of acceptance because of fears of rejection and criticism.

Avoidant Personality Disorder

People with **avoidant personality disorder** are generally unwilling to enter a relationship without some assurance of acceptance because they fear rejection and criticism. As a result, they may have few close relationships outside their immediate families. Unlike people with schizoid personality disorder, however, they have some interest in, and feelings of warmth toward, other people. *What is known about the origins of personality disorders?*

Explaining Personality Disorders

Numerous biological, psychological, and sociocultural factors have been implicated in the personality disorders.

Biological Factors   Genetic factors are apparently involved in some personality disorders (Eaves et al., 2000; Rutter & Silberg, 2002). Personality traits are to some degree heritable (Plomin, 2000), and many personality disorders seem to be extreme variations of normal personality traits. An analysis of 51 twin and adoption studies estimated that genetic factors were the greatest influences on antisocial behavior (Rhee & Waldman, 2002). Referring to the five-factor model of personality, people with schizoid personalities tend to be highly introverted (Ross et al., 2002; Widiger & Costa, 1994). People with avoidant personalities tend to be both introverted and emotionally unstable (Ross et al., 2002; Widiger & Costa, 1994).

Perhaps the genetics of antisocial personality involve the prefrontal cortex of the brain, a part of the brain connected with emotional responses. There is some evidence that people with antisocial personality, as a group, have less gray matter (associative neurons) in the prefrontal cortex of the brain than other people do (Damasio, 2000; Raine et al., 2000; Yang et al., 2005). The lesser amount of gray matter could lessen the level of arousal of the nervous system. As a result, it could be more difficult to condition fear responses (Blair & James, 2001, 2003). People with the disorder would then be unlikely to show guilt for their misdeeds and would seem to be unafraid of punishment. But a biological factor such as a lower-than-normal level of arousal might not in itself cause the development of an antisocial personality (Rutter & Silberg, 2002). Perhaps a person must also be reared under conditions that do not foster the self-concept of a law-abiding citizen.

Psychological Factors   Learning theorists suggest that childhood experiences can contribute to maladaptive ways of relating to others in adulthood—that is, can lead to personality disorders. Cognitive psychologists find that antisocial adolescents encode social information in ways that bolster their misdeeds. For example, they tend to interpret other people's behavior as threatening, even when it is not (Crick & Dodge, 1994; Lochman & Dodge, 1994). Aggressive individuals often find it difficult to solve social problems in useful ways (McMurran et al., 2002). Cognitive therapists have encouraged some antisocial male adolescents to view social provocations as problems to be solved rather than as threats to their "manhood," with some favorable initial results (Lochman & Dodge, 1994).

Sociocultural Factors   The label of borderline personality has been applied to people as diverse as Marilyn Monroe and Lawrence of Arabia. Some theorists believe we live in fragmented and alienating times that tend to create problems in forming a stable identity and stable relationships. "Living on the edge," or border, can be seen as a metaphor for an unstable society.

The psychological disorders discussed in the chapter are summarized in Concept Review 12.1. Although the causes of many psychological disorders remain in dispute, various methods of therapy have been devised to deal with them. Those methods are the focus of Chapter 13.

■ CONCEPT REVIEW 12.1 ■

PSYCHOLOGICAL DISORDERS LISTED IN THE DSM-IV-TR

DISORDER	MAJOR SUBTYPES	SYMPTOMS	BIOPSYCHOSOCIAL PERSPECTIVES
Schizophrenia 	• Paranoid schizophrenia • Disorganized schizophrenia • Catatonic schizophrenia	• Disturbances in language and thought (e.g., delusions, hallucinations, loose associations) • Disturbances in motor activity • Flat or inappropriate affect • Withdrawal and absorption in daydreams or fantasy	• Genetic factors implicated due to high concordance rate among MZ twins • People with schizophrenia may have larger ventricles, smaller prefrontal cortexes, and fewer synapses than others • Overutilization of dopamine • Complications during pregnancy and birth connected with schizophrenia • Schizophrenic behavior can be imitated in the hospital setting and reinforced by staff attention • Poor parenting
Mood Disorders	• Major depression • Bipolar disorder	• Excessive feelings of sadness, helplessness, worthlessness • Excessive elation	• Genetic factors implicated in major depression and bipolar disorder • Depression connected with underutilization of serotonin • In depression, people learn that they are helpless to change their situations • Perfectionism, rumination, and attributional style—internal, stable, and global attributions for failures and shortcomings—lead to depression
Anxiety Disorders 	• Phobic disorder • Panic disorder • Generalized anxiety disorder • Obsessive–compulsive disorder • Stress disorders	• Worrying • Fear of the worst happening • Fear of losing control • Nervousness • Inability to relax	• Genetic factors are implicated • Phobias may have contributed to survival of human species • Receptor sites in the brain may not be sensitive enough to the neurotransmitter GABA, which quells anxiety reactions • Phobias may have been acquired by conditioning or observational learning • People with anxiety disorders may be biased toward attending too much to threats

In the schizophrenia image: Biological factors, Genetic vulnerability, Overutilization of dopamine, Enlarged ventricles, Deficiency in gray matter, Viral infections, Birth complications, Malnutrition (also a sociocultural factor); Psychological factors, Stress, Family discord, Poor quality of parenting (also a social factor); Person with genetic vulnerability to schizophrenia; Social/sociocultural factors, Poverty, Overcrowding, Poor quality of parenting (also a psychological factor), Malnutrition (also a biological factor).

In the anxiety disorders image: Genetic vulnerability?, Learning through conditioning or observational learning?, Anxiety Disorders, Failure to repress childhood conflicts?, Cognitive distortion?

Peter Cade /Stone /Getty Images

(continued)

CONCEPT REVIEW ■ CONCEPT REVIEW 12.1 ■ CONCEPT REVIEW

PSYCHOLOGICAL DISORDERS LISTED IN THE DSM-IV-TR (CONTINUED)

DISORDER	MAJOR SUBTYPES	SYMPTOMS	BIOPSYCHOSOCIAL PERSPECTIVES
Somatoform Disorders 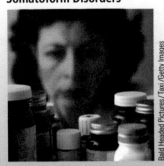 *Bald Headed Pictures /Taxi /Getty Images*	• Conversion disorder • Hypochondriasis • Body dysmorphic disorder	• Complaints of physical problems such as paralysis or pain • Persistent belief that one has a serious disease in the absence of medical findings • Excessive dissatisfaction with one's body	• High hypnotizability among people with conversion disorder • Misinterpretation of physical sensations as signs of serious illness in hypochondriasis • Relief from ordinary responsibilities and concerns due to playing a "sick role" • Sociocultural emphasis on perfection in body shape connected with dissatisfaction with one's body
Dissociative Disorders  *Museum of Modern Art / Film Stills Archive*	• Dissociative amnesia • Dissociative fugue • Dissociative identity disorder (multiple personality disorder)	• Separation of mental processes such as thoughts, emotions, identity, memory, or consciousness • Forgetting personal information	• People learn not to think about improper impulses or ugly memories, such as of childhood sexual abuse • Childhood trauma may affect parts of the brain involved in cognition and memory, leading to permanent chemical and structural changes
Personality Disorders  *Bettmann /Corbis*	• Paranoid • Schizotypal • Schizoid • Borderline • Antisocial • Avoidant	• Inflexible, maladaptive patterns of behavior • Impaired personal or social functioning • Give rise to personal or social distress	• Exaggerated personality traits, which are assumed to be partly heritable • Antisocial individuals may have less gray matter, lowering arousal, feelings of guilt, and the effects of punishment • Children learn maladaptive ways of relating to other people • Antisocial people misinterpret others' behavior as threatening

 **Learning Connections**

◀◀   *Personality Disorders—Making Oneself or Others Miserable*   ▶▶

REVIEW:

19 The defining trait of the _____ personality is suspiciousness.
(a) social withdrawal,
(b) anxiety,
(c) paranoid,
(d) confusion.

20 Instability of moods is a central characteristic of _____ personality disorder.
(a) avoidant,
(b) schizoid,
(c) antisocial,
(d) borderline.

21 Research suggests that people with _____ personalities have lower-than-normal levels of arousal than most people.
(a) antisocial,
(b) avoidant,
(c) borderline,
(d) schizoid.

CRITICAL THINKING:
Sick people may be excused from school or work. If some criminals are "sick" in the sense of being diagnosed with antisocial personality disorder, does the disorder relieve them of responsibility for criminal behavior? Explain.

Go to www

http://academic.cengage.com/psychology/rathus
for an interactive version of this review.

RECITE—*An Active Summary*™

Recite to Go! *Don't have time to study right now? You can study on the go!*
Go to your companion website and download an audio version of this review section to your media player. You can also access an interactive flash-card version of this review from your website.

1. What are psychological disorders?	Psychological disorders are characterized by unusual behavior, socially unacceptable behavior, faulty perception of reality, personal distress, dangerous behavior, or self-defeating behavior.
2. How are psychological disorders classified?	The most widely used classification scheme is found in the *Diagnostic and Statistical Manual (DSM)* of the American Psychiatric Association. The current edition of the DSM—the DSM-IV-TR—groups disorders on the basis of clinical syndromes and factors related to adjustment.
3. How do we explain psychological disorders?	Psychological disorders are explained, scientifically, by means of the biological, psychological, and biopsychosocial perspectives. Many nonscientists, however, have turned to demonology throughout much of history.
4. How common are psychological disorders?	About half of us will experience a psychological disorder at one time or another. About a quarter of us will do so in any given year.
5. What is schizophrenia?	Schizophrenia is a severe psychological disorder that is characterized by disturbances in thought and language, such as loosening of associations and delusions; in perception and attention, as found in hallucinations; in motor activity; in mood, as in flat or inappropriate emotional responses; and in social interaction, as in social withdrawal and absorption in daydreams or fantasy.
6. What are the positive and negative symptoms of schizophrenia?	Positive symptoms include excessive and bizarre symptoms such as hallucinations and delusions. The negative symptoms are deficiencies such as lack of emotional response and motivation.
7. What types of schizophrenia are there?	The DSM categorizes the three major types as paranoid, disorganized, and catatonic. Paranoid schizophrenia is characterized largely by systematized delusions; disorganized schizophrenia by incoherence; and catatonic schizophrenia by motor impairment.
8. What is known about the origins of schizophrenia?	Schizophrenia is connected with smaller brains in some people, especially fewer synapses in the prefrontal region, and larger ventricles. A genetic vulnerability to schizophrenia may interact with other factors, such as stress, complications during pregnancy and childbirth, and quality of parenting, to cause the disorder to develop. According to the dopamine theory of schizophrenia, people with schizophrenia apparently use more dopamine than other people do.
9. What kinds of mood disorders are there?	Mood disorders involve disturbances in expressed emotions. Major depression is characterized by persistent feelings of sadness, loss of interest, feelings of worthlessness or guilt, and inability to concentrate. Bipolar disorder is characterized by mood swings between elation and depression; manic episodes include rapid flight of ideas.
10. What is known about the origins of mood disorders?	Genetic factors may be involved in mood disorders, especially bipolar disorder. Research emphasizes possible roles for learned helplessness, attributional styles, and underutilization of serotonin in depression. People who are depressed are more likely than other people to make internal, stable, and global attributions for failures.

11. Why do people commit suicide?	Most people who commit suicide do so because of severe feelings of depression, hopelessness, helplessness, and worthlessness. (Suicide terrorism is another matter and is dealt with in Chapter 14.)
12. What kinds of anxiety disorders are there?	Anxiety disorders are characterized by tension, feelings of dread, and sympathetic arousal. They include irrational, excessive fears, or phobias; panic disorder, characterized by sudden anxiety attacks; generalized anxiety; obsessive–compulsive disorder, in which people are troubled by intrusive thoughts or impulses to repeat some activity; and stress disorders, in which a stressful event is followed by persistent fears and intrusive thoughts.
13. What is known about the origins of anxiety disorders?	Some people may be genetically predisposed to acquire certain fears. Anxiety disorders tend to run in families. Many learning theorists view phobias as conditioned fears. Cognitive theorists focus on ways in which people interpret threats.
14. What kinds of somatoform disorders are there?	People with somatoform disorders exhibit or complain of physical problems, although no medical evidence for them can be found. The somatoform disorders include conversion disorder, hypochondriasis, and body dysmorphic disorder. In conversion disorder, stress is converted into a physical symptom, and the individual may show la belle indifférence.
15. What is known about the origins of somatoform disorders?	Somatoform disorders may reflect the relative benefits of focusing on physical symptoms or features rather than psychological and social concerns and conflicts that most people would consider to be more important. Persons with these disorders tend toward exaggerated awareness of physical symptoms, perfectionism, and rumination.
16. What kinds of dissociative disorders are there?	Dissociative disorders are characterized by sudden, temporary changes in consciousness or self-identity. They include dissociative amnesia; dissociative fugue, which involves forgetting plus fleeing and adopting a new identity; and dissociative identity disorder (multiple personality), in which a person behaves as if more than one personality occupies his or her body.
17. What is known about the origins of dissociative disorders?	Many psychologists suggest that dissociative disorders help people keep disturbing memories or ideas out of mind. These memories may involve episodes of childhood sexual or physical abuse. It is possible that early trauma leads to chemical and structural changes in the brain.
18. What kinds of personality disorders are there?	Personality disorders are inflexible, maladaptive behavior patterns that impair personal or social functioning. The paranoid personality is defined by suspiciousness. People with schizotypal personality disorders show oddities of thought, perception, and behavior. Social withdrawal is the major characteristic of schizoid personality disorder. People with antisocial personality disorder persistently violate the rights of others and are in conflict with the law. They show no guilt and are largely undeterred by punishment. People with avoidant personality disorder tend to avoid relationships for fear of rejection.
19. What is known about the origins of personality disorders?	Genetic factors may be involved in personality disorders. Antisocial personality disorder may develop from some combination of genetic vulnerability (less gray matter in the prefrontal cortex of the brain, which may provide lower-than-normal levels of arousal), inconsistent discipline, and cynical processing of social information.

Key Terms

Schizophrenia 432

Delusions 432

Affect 432

Psychological disorders 433

Hallucination 434

Ideas of persecution 434

Flat affect 434

Reliability 435

Validity 435

Predictive validity 435

Biopsychosocial perspective 436

Stupor 438

Positive symptoms 438

Negative symptoms 439

Paranoid schizophrenia 439

Disorganized schizophrenia 439

Catatonic schizophrenia 439

Waxy flexibility 439

Mutism 439

Major depressive disorder (MDD) 444

Psychomotor retardation 444

Bipolar disorder 444

Manic 444

Rapid flight of ideas 444

Neuroticism 444

Learned helplessness 446

Attributional style 446

Specific phobia 451

Claustrophobia 452

Acrophobia 452

Social phobia 452

Agoraphobia 452

Panic disorder 452

Generalized anxiety disorder 452

Obsession 453

Compulsion 453

Posttraumatic stress disorder
   (PTSD) 453

Acute stress disorder 453

Somatoform disorders 456

Conversion disorder 456

La belle indifférence 457

Hypochondriasis 457

Body dysmorphic disorder 457

Dissociative disorders 458

Dissociative identity disorder 459

Multiple personality disorder 459

Dissociative amnesia 459

Dissociative fugue 459

Personality disorders 460

Paranoid personality disorder 461

Schizotypal personality disorder 461

Schizoid personality disorder 461

Borderline personality disorder 461

Antisocial personality disorder 461

Avoidant personality disorder 462

Active Learning Resources

Visit Your Companion Website
for This Book

http://academic.cengage.com/psychology/rathus

Check out this companion website where you will find online resources directly linked to your book. This is where you'll access the videos highlighted in your Video Connections feature. You can answer the questions online and email them to your professor. In addition you'll find downloadable audio review material, interactive versions of the study aids, Power Visuals for mastering and reviewing key concepts, as well as quizzing, and much more!

CENGAGENOW™

http://academic.cengage.com

Need help studying? This site is your one-stop study shop. Take a Pre-Test and Cengage NOW will generate a Personalized Study Plan based on your test results. The Study Plan will identify the topics you need to review and direct you to online resources to help you master those topics. You can then take a Post-Test to help you determine the concepts you have mastered and what you still need to work on. In addition you can access interactive media including the videos highlighted in your Video Connections box.

Author Blog

What does your author Spence Rathus have to say about the state of psychology? Visit your companion website every Tuesday and click on "Author Blog." This is where he'll talk about the most recent controversies and hot topics in psychology. This will keep you up to date with what your author is thinking and give you great insight into modern psychology.

CHAPTER 13

Methods of Therapy

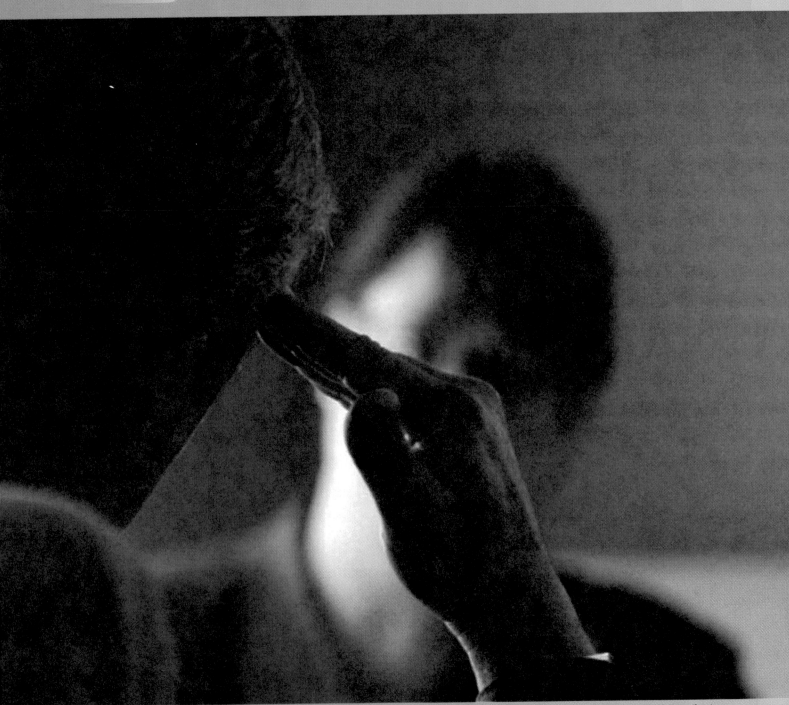

David Buffington /Getty Images

truth or fiction?

T	F	Residents of London used to visit the local insane asylum for a fun night out on the town.
T	F	Some psychotherapists interpret clients' dreams.
T	F	Some psychotherapists let their clients take the lead in psychotherapy.
T	F	Some psychotherapists tell their clients exactly what to do.
T	F	Lying in a reclining chair and fantasizing can be an effective way of confronting fears.
T	F	Smoking cigarettes can be an effective method for helping people stop smoking cigarettes.
T	F	There is no scientific evidence that psychotherapy helps people with psychological disorders.
T	F	The originator of a surgical technique to reduce violence learned that it was not always successful when one of his patients shot him.

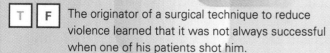

Go to www
http://academic.cengage.com/pstchology/rathus
for an interactive version of this Truth or Fiction feature.

Some things are too painful to bear. One of them, for New York Fire Chief Stephen King, was 9/11. His experiences at the World Trade Center that day led him to retire from the department, avoid bridges and tunnels, and stay out of Manhattan.

"I was in the north tower, the one that got hit first," King (2005) explains. "Where I was and what I saw that day—the many people that jumped, the magnitude of it—was just overwhelming." Many who witnessed the events of that day developed stress disorders.

But a new tool in the treatment of anxiety disorders, **virtual therapy,** has helped King face the past—and his future. Using the technology we find in video games, programs mimic traumatic settings and events, whether they be public speaking in an auditorium, flying in an airplane, spiders, or, in King's case, images of the World Trade Center.

JoAnn Difede, director of Anxiety and Traumatic Stress Studies Program at Weill Cornell Medical College, is using virtual therapy to help World Trade Center survivors cope with their memories (Difede & Hoffman, 2002). "The idea behind the treatment," Difede explains, "is to systematically expose the patient to aspects of their experience in a graded fashion so they can confront their fear of the trauma."

University of Southern California psychologist Albert Rizzo has developed scenes from classrooms and parties to help people overcome social anxieties. "'To help people deal with their problems, you must get them exposed to what they fear most," Rizzo (2004) notes.

Drs. Difede and Rizzo use programs like 3D Studio MAX and DeepPaint to create the necessary software. Atlanta-based company Virtually Better has developed scenes of a bridge and a glass elevator to desensitize patients to fear of heights, a virtual airplane cabin for people who fear flying, and a virtual thunderstorm to help people lessen their fear of tempestuous weather. The U.S. Army has asked Virtually Better to use its 3D imaging software to create programs that will help soldiers returning from theaters like Iraq and Afghanistan.

Virtually Better is working on programs to help treat addictions. Psychologists are studying whether virtual exposure to alcohol, drugs, and cigarettes can evoke cravings that patients can learn to resist. Virtually Better's contributions include scenes of a virtual crack house and a virtual bar.

Virtual therapy was also used to help desensitize Joanne Cartwright, who had a fear of spiders that impaired the quality of her life. "I washed my truck every night before I went to work in case there were webs," says Cartwright (cited in Robbins, 2000). "I put all my clothes in plastic bags and taped duct tape around my doors so spiders couldn't get in. I thought I was going to have

Christian Witkin

■ Former Firefighter Stephen King and Dr. JoAnn Difede, Who Treated Him with Virtual Therapy
King was in the World Trade Center tower that got hit first on September 11, 2001, and he developed post-traumatic stress disorder.

Virtual therapy The use of a virtual environment to assist people overcome fears and phobias. (Also: the use of tele-communications and computer links to carry out a psychologist–patient therapy session.)

Image and copyright by Hunter Hoffman, U.W. Virtual World programmed by Howard Abrams.

■ A Program Containing Images of the World Trade Center Intended to Help People with Posttraumatic Stress Disorder, like Firefighter Stephen King
After being exposed to virtual stimuli that represent people's sources of anxiety and stress, virtual-therapy clients are better able to be exposed to the actual stimuli.

a mental breakdown. I wasn't living." Twelve virtual therapy desensitization sessions changed her life. "I'm amazed," notes Cartwright, "because I am doing all this stuff I could never do," such as camping and hiking.

Writing in *Scientific American,* psychologist Hunter Hoffman (2004) describes an elaborate virtual environment called *SpiderWorld* that helps people with spider phobias overcome their aversion by gradually approaching virtual spiders and reaching out to touch them. A toy spider and a device that tracks the patient's hand movements provide tactile sensations akin to touching a real spider. Virtual immersion in *SpiderWorld* and similar virtual environments has also helped people cope with pain by distracting them from it.

Chief Stephen King received virtual therapy to learn to cope with his traumatic experience at the World Trade Center. If he had chosen a different kind of therapist, he might have been:

- lying on a couch, talking anything that popped into awareness, and exploring the possible meaning of his recurrent dreams;
- sitting face to face with a warm, gentle therapist who expressed faith in King's ability to manage his problems;
- listening to a frank, straightforward therapist assert that King was compounding his emotional problems by demanding that he be "man enough" to face the trauma of 9/11 and just move on;
- taking medication; or
- participating in some combination of these approaches.

These methods, although different, all represent methods of therapy. In this chapter we explore various methods of psychotherapy and biological therapy. *What is psychotherapy?*

■ **Dr. Hunter Hoffman of the University of Washington Uses Virtual Therapy to Treat "Miss Muffet"**
Miss Muffet is the name playfully given by Hoffman to a woman with a phobia for spiders. She is wearing virtual-reality headgear and sees the scene displayed on the monitor, which shows a large and hairy— but virtual—tarantula.

WHAT IS PSYCHOTHERAPY?

There are many kinds of psychotherapy, but they all have certain common characteristics. **Psychotherapy** is a systematic interaction between a therapist and a client that applies psychological principles to affect the client's thoughts, feelings, or behavior in an effort to help the client overcome psychological disorders, adjust to problems in living, or develop as an individual.

Quite a mouthful? True. But note the essentials:

1. *Systematic interaction.* Psychotherapy is a systematic interaction between a client and a therapist. The therapist's theoretical point of view interacts with the client's to determine how the therapist and client relate to each other.
2. *Psychological principles.* Psychotherapy is based on psychological theory and research in areas such as personality, learning, motivation, and emotion.
3. *Thoughts, feelings, and behavior.* Psychotherapy influences clients' thoughts, feelings, and behavior. It can be aimed at any or all of these aspects of human psychology.

Psychotherapy A systematic interaction between a therapist and a client that brings psychological principles to bear on influencing the client's thoughts, feelings, or behavior to help the client overcome abnormal behavior or adjust to problems in living.

4. *Psychological disorders, adjustment problems, and personal growth.* Psychotherapy is often used with people who have psychological disorders. Other people seek help in adjusting to problems such as shyness, weight problems, or loss of a life partner. Still other clients want to learn more about themselves and to reach their full potential as individuals, parents, or creative artists.

The History of Therapies

Historically speaking, "treatments" of psychological disorders often reflected the assumption that people who behaved in strange ways were possessed by demons. *How, then, have people with psychological problems and disorders been treated throughout the ages?* Because of this belief, treatment tended to involve cruel practices such as exorcism and execution. Some people who could not meet the demands of everyday life were tossed into prisons. Others begged in the streets, stole food, or became prostitutes. A few found their way to monasteries or other retreats that offered a kind word and some support. Generally speaking, they died early.

Asylums   **Asylums** originated in European monasteries. They were the first institutions meant primarily for people with psychological disorders. But their function was warehousing, not treatment. Their inmate populations mushroomed until the stresses created by noise, overcrowding, and disease aggravated the problems they were meant to ease. Inmates were frequently chained and beaten.

The word *bedlam* derives from St. Mary's of *Bethlehem,* the London asylum that opened its gates in 1547. Here unfortunate people with psychological disorders were chained, whipped, and allowed to lie in their own waste. ◈ **Truth or Fiction Revisited:** And here the ladies and gentlemen of the British upper class might stroll by on a lazy afternoon to be amused by inmates' antics. The price of admission was one penny.

Humanitarian reform movements began in the 18th century. In Paris, the physician Philippe Pinel unchained the patients at La Bicêtre. Rather than run amok, as had been feared, most patients profited from kindness and freedom. Many eventually reentered society. Later movements to reform institutions were led by William Tuke in England and Dorothea Dix in America.

Mental Hospitals   In the United States mental hospitals gradually replaced asylums. In the mid-1950s more than a million people resided in state, county, Veterans Administration, or private facilities. The mental hospital's function is treatment, not warehousing. Still, because of high patient populations and understaffing, many patients received little attention. Even today, with somewhat improved conditions, one psychiatrist may be responsible for the welfare of several hundred residents on the weekend when other staff are absent.

Culver Pictures

■ **The Unchaining of the Patients at La Bicêtre**
Philippe Pinel sparked the humanitarian reform movement by unchaining the patients at this asylum in Paris.

The Community Mental Health Movement   Since the 1960s, efforts have been made to maintain people with serious psychological disorders in their communities. Community mental health centers attempt to maintain new patients as outpatients and to serve patients who have been released from mental hospitals. Today most people with chronic psychological disorders live in the community, not the hospital. Social critics note that many people who had resided in hospitals for decades were suddenly discharged to "home" communities that seemed foreign and forbidding to them. Many do not receive adequate follow-up care. Many join the ranks of the homeless (Drury, 2003; Gulcur et al., 2003).

Asylum (uh-SIGH-lum). An institution for the care of the mentally ill.

◯ Learning Connections

Learning Connections

◀◀ *What Is Therapy?* ▶▶

REVIEW:

1 People seek psychotherapy to
   (a) cope with adjustment problems,
   (b) overcome psychological disorders,
   (c) learn about themselves,
   (d) all of the above.

2 The word *bedlam* derives from
   (a) the name of a British asylum,
   (b) an American mental hospital,
   (c) a famous psychologist,
   (d) the Greek word for "noise."

CRITICAL THINKING:
Critical thinkers pay attention to definitions. Is psychotherapy what you thought it was before you took this course? Explain.

Go to www
http://academic.cengage.com/psychology/rathus
for an interactive version of this review.

PSYCHOANALYTIC THERAPIES: DIGGING DEEP WITHIN

Psychoanalytic therapies are based on the thinking of Sigmund Freud, the founder of psychoanalytic theory. These therapies assume that psychological problems reflect early childhood experiences and internal conflicts. According to Freud, these conflicts involve the shifting of psychic, or libidinal, energy among the three psychic structures—the id, ego, and superego. These shifts of psychic energy determine our behavior. When primitive urges threaten to break through from the id or when the superego floods us with excessive guilt, defenses are established and distress is created. Freud's therapy method—psychoanalysis—aims to modify the flow of energy among these structures, largely to bulwark the ego against the torrents of energy loosed by the id and the superego. With impulses and feelings of guilt and shame placed under greater control, clients are freer to develop adaptive behavior. *How, then, do psychoanalysts conduct a traditional Freudian psychoanalysis?*

■ Traditional Psychoanalysis

Imagine your therapist asking you to lie on a couch in a slightly darkened room. She or he would sit behind you and encourage you to talk about anything that comes to mind, no matter how trivial, no matter how personal. To avoid interfering with your self-exploration, she or he might say little or nothing for session after session. That would be par for the course. A traditional **psychoanalysis** can extend for months, even years.

Psychoanalysis is the clinical method devised by Sigmund Freud. It aims to provide *insight* into the conflicts that are presumed to lie at the roots of a person's problems. Insight means many things, including knowledge of the experiences that lead to conflicts and maladaptive behavior, recognition of unconscious feelings and conflicts, and conscious evaluation of one's thoughts, feelings, and behavior.

Psychoanalysis also aims to help the client express feelings and urges that have been repressed. By so doing, Freud believed that the client spilled forth the psychic energy that had been repressed by conflicts and guilt. He called this spilling forth **catharsis.** Catharsis would provide relief by alleviating some of the forces assaulting the ego. Freud also sought to

Psychoanalysis Freud's method of psychotherapy. (Also the name of Freud's theory of personality.)

Catharsis Release of emotional tension, as after a traumatic experience, that has the effect of restoring one's psychological well-being.

■ A View of Freud's Consulting Room
Freud would sit in a chair by the head of the couch while a client free-associated. The basic rule of free association is that no thought is censored. Freud did not believe that free association was really "free"; he assumed that significant feelings would rise to the surface and demand expression.

replace impulsive and defensive behavior with coping behavior. In this way, for example, a man with a phobia for knives might discover that he had been repressing the urge to harm someone who had taken advantage of him. He might also find ways to confront the person verbally.

Early in his career as a therapist, Freud found that hypnosis allowed his clients to focus on repressed conflicts and talk about them. He also found, however, that some clients denied the accuracy of this material once they were out of the trance. Others found the memories to be brought out into the open prematurely and painfully. Freud therefore turned to **free association,** a more gradual method of breaking through the walls of defense that block a client's insight into unconscious processes. In free association, the client is made comfortable—for example, by lying on a couch—and asked to talk about any topic that comes to mind. No thought is to be censored—that is the basic rule. Psychoanalysts ask their clients to wander "freely" from topic to topic, but they do not believe that the process occurring *within* the client is fully free. Repressed impulses clamor for release.

The ego persists in trying to repress unacceptable impulses and threatening conflicts. As a result, clients might show **resistance** to recalling and discussing threatening ideas. The therapist observes the dynamic struggle between the compulsion to talk about disturbing ideas and resistance. Through discreet comments and questions, the analyst hopes to encourage the client to discuss his or her problems. Talking helps the client gain insight into his or her true wishes and explore ways of fulfilling them.

Transference   Freud believed that clients not only responded to him as an individual but also in ways that reflected their attitudes and feelings toward other people in their lives. He labeled this process **transference.** For example, a young woman client might respond to him as a father figure and displace her feelings toward her father onto Freud, perhaps seeking affection and wisdom.

Analyzing and working through transference has been considered a key aspect of psychoanalysis. Freud believed that clients reenact their childhood conflicts with their parents when they are in therapy. The following therapeutic dialogue illustrates the way in which an analyst may interpret a client's inability to communicate his needs to his wife as a function of transference. The purpose is to provide his client, a Mr. Arianes, with insight into how his relationship with his wife has been colored by his childhood relationship with his mother:

Arianes: I think you've got it there, Doc. We weren't communicating. I wouldn't tell [my wife] what was wrong or what I wanted from her. Maybe I expected her to understand me without saying anything.
Therapist: Like the expectations a child has of its mother.
Arianes: Not my mother!
Therapist: Oh?
Arianes: No, I always thought she had too many troubles of her own to pay attention to mine. I remember once I got hurt on my bike and came to her all bloodied up. When she saw me she got mad and yelled at me for making more trouble for her when she already had her hands full with my father.
Therapist: Do you remember how you felt then?
Arianes: I can't remember, but I know that after that I never brought my troubles to her again.
Therapist: How old were you?
Arianes: Nine, I know that because I got that bike for my ninth birthday. It was a little too big for me still, that's why I got hurt on it.
Therapist: Perhaps you carried this attitude into your marriage.
Arianes: What attitude?

Free association In psychoanalysis, the uncensored uttering of all thoughts that come to mind.

Resistance The tendency to block the free expression of impulses and primitive ideas—a reflection of the defense mechanism of repression.

Transference Responding to one person (such as a spouse or the psychoanalyst) in a way that is similar to the way one responded to another person (such as a parent) in childhood.

Therapist: The feeling that your wife, like your mother, would be unsympathetic to your difficulties. That there was no point in telling her about your experiences because she was too preoccupied or too busy to care.

Arianes: But she's so different from my mother. I come first with her.

Therapist: On one level you know that. On another, deeper level there may well be the fear that people—or maybe only women, or maybe only women you're close to—are all the same, and you can't take a chance at being rejected again in your need.

Arianes: Maybe you're right, Doc, but all that was so long ago, and I should be over that by now.

Therapist: That's not the way the mind works. If a shock or a disappointment is strong enough it can permanently freeze our picture of ourselves and our expectations of the world. The rest of us grows up—that is, we let ourselves learn about life from experience and from what we see, hear, or read of the experiences of others, but that one area where we really got hurt stays unchanged. So what I mean when I say you might be carrying that attitude into your relationship with your wife is that when it comes to your hopes of being understood and catered to when you feel hurt or abused by life, you still feel very much like that nine-year-old boy who was rebuffed in his need and gave up hope that anyone would or could respond to him. (Basch, 1980, pp. 29–30)

Dream Analysis ◆ **Truth or Fiction Revisited:** Some therapists do interpret clients' dreams. Freud often asked clients to jot down their dreams upon waking so they could discuss them in therapy. Freud considered dreams the "royal road to the unconscious." He believed that the content of dreams is determined by unconscious processes as well as by the events of the day. Unconscious impulses were expressed in dreams as **wish fulfillment.**

▬■▬ Short-Term Dynamic Therapies

How do modern psychoanalytic approaches differ from traditional psychoanalysis? Although some psychoanalysts still adhere to Freud's techniques, shorter-term dynamic therapies have been devised. Modern psychoanalytic therapy is briefer and less intense and makes treatment available to clients who do not have the time or money to make therapy part of their lifestyle.

Some modern psychoanalysts continue to focus on revealing unconscious material and breaking through psychological defenses. Nevertheless, they differ from traditional psychoanalysis in several ways (Prochaska & Norcross, 2003). One is that the client and therapist usually sit face to face (i.e., the client does not lie on a couch). The therapist may be directive. That is, modern therapists often suggest helpful behavior instead of focusing on insight alone. Finally, there is more focus on the ego as the "executive" of personality and less emphasis on the id. For this reason, many modern psychoanalysts are called **ego analysts.**

Many of Freud's followers, the "second generation" of psychoanalysts—from Jung and Adler to Horney and Erikson—believed that Freud had placed too much emphasis on sex and aggression and underestimated the role of the ego. For example, Freud aimed to establish conditions under which clients could spill forth psychic energy and eventually shore up the ego. Erikson, in contrast, spoke to clients directly about their values and concerns, encouraging them to develop desired traits and behavior patterns. Even Freud's daughter, the psychoanalyst Anna Freud (1895–1982), was more concerned with the ego than with unconscious conflict.

Interpersonal Psychotherapy One contemporary dynamic therapy, **interpersonal psychotherapy (ITP),** focuses on clients' current relationships rather than their childhoods and usually lasts no longer than 9 to 12 months. Developers of ITP view problems such as anxiety and depression as often occurring within social relationships. They therefore focus on clients' relationships and also try to directly alleviate feelings of anxiety and depression (de Mello et al., 2005; Kirschenbaum & Jourdan, 2005).

reflect & relate
Does it make you feel good to talk with other people about problems? Are there some "deep secrets" you are unwilling to talk about or share with others? How do you think a psychoanalyst would respond if you brought them up? Why?

Wish fulfillment A primitive method used by the id to attempt to gratify basic instincts.

Ego analyst A psychoanalyst therapist who focuses on the conscious, coping behavior of the ego instead of the hypothesized, unconscious functioning of the id.

Interpersonal psychotherapy (ITP) A short-term dynamic therapy that focuses on clients' relationships and direct alleviation of negative emotions such as anxiety and depression.

⟨⟩ Learning Connections

◀◀ *Psychoanalytic Therapies—Digging Deep Within* ▶▶

REVIEW:

3 The chief psychoanalytic method is
   (a) dream analysis,
   (b) free association,
   (c) hypnosis,
   (d) resistance.

4 Freud considered _____ to be the "royal road
   to the unconscious."
   (a) conflicts,
   (b) transference,

   (c) dreams,
   (d) resistance.

5 Modern analysts believe that the _____ plays
   a stronger role in behavior than Freud believed.
   (a) ego,
   (b) id,
   (c) libido,
   (d) superego.

CRITICAL THINKING:
According to psychoanalytic theory, is free association really "free"?
Explain your point of view.

Go to www
http://academic.cengage.com/psychology/rathus
for an interactive version of this review.

Learning Connections

■ **Carl Rogers**

Client-centered therapy Carl Rogers's method of psychotherapy, which emphasizes the creation of a warm, therapeutic atmosphere that frees clients to engage in self-exploration and self-expression.

HUMANISTIC THERAPIES: STRENGTHENING THE SELF

Psychoanalytic therapies focus on internal conflicts and unconscious processes. Humanistic therapies focus on the quality of the client's subjective, conscious experience. Traditional psychoanalysis focuses on early childhood experiences. Humanistic therapies are more likely to focus on what clients are experiencing here and now.

━■ Client-Centered Therapy: Removing Roadblocks to Self-Actualization

What is Carl Rogers's method of client-centered therapy? Rogers believed that we are free to make choices and control our destinies, despite the burdens of the past. He also believed that we have natural tendencies toward health, growth, and fulfillment. Psychological problems arise from roadblocks placed in the path of self-actualization—that is, what Rogers believed was an inborn tendency to strive to realize one's potential. If, when we are young, other people only approve of us when we are doing what they want us to do, we may learn to disown the parts of ourselves to which they object. We may learn to be seen but not heard—not even by ourselves. As a result, we may experience stress and discomfort and the feeling that we—or the world—are not real.

Client-centered therapy aims to provide insight into the parts of us that we have disowned so that we can feel whole. It creates a warm, therapeutic atmosphere that encourages self-exploration and self-expression. The therapist's acceptance of the client is thought to foster self-acceptance and self-esteem. Self-acceptance frees the client to make choices that develop his or her unique potential.

Bettmann/Corbis

Client-centered therapy is nondirective. ◆ **Truth or Fiction Revisited:** It is true that the client takes the lead, stating and exploring problems. An effective client-centered therapist has several qualities:

- **Unconditional positive regard:** respect for clients as human beings with unique values and goals.
- **Empathy:** recognition of the client's experiences and feelings. Therapists view the world through the client's **frame of reference** by setting aside their own values and listening closely.
- **Genuineness:** Openness and honesty in responding to the client. Client-centered therapists must be able to tolerate differentness because they believe that every client is different in important ways.

The following excerpt from a therapy session shows how Carl Rogers uses empathetic understanding and paraphrases a client's (Jill's) feelings. His goal is to help her recognize feelings that she has partially disowned:

Jill: I'm having a lot of problems dealing with my daughter. She's 20 years old; she's in college; I'm having a lot of trouble letting her go. . . . And I have a lot of guilt feelings about her; I have a real need to hang on to her.

C. R.: A need to hang on so you can kind of make up for the things you feel guilty about. Is that part of it?

Jill: There's a lot of that. . . . Also, she's been a real friend to me, and filled my life. . . . And it's very hard. . . . a lot of empty places now that she's not with me.

C. R.: The old vacuum, sort of, when she's not there.

Jill: Yes. Yes. I also would like to be the kind of mother that could be strong and say, you know, "Go and have a good life," and this is really hard for me, to do that.

C. R.: It's very hard to give up something that's been so precious in your life, but also something that I guess has caused you pain when you mentioned guilt.

Jill: Yeah. And I'm aware that I have some anger toward her that I don't always get what I want. I have needs that are not met. And, uh, I don't feel I have a right to those needs. You know. . . . she's a daughter; she's not my mother. Though sometimes I feel as if I'd like her to mother me . . . it's very difficult for me to ask for that and have a right to it.

C. R.: So, it may be unreasonable, but still, when she doesn't meet your needs, it makes you mad.

Jill: Yeah I get very angry, very angry with her.

C. R.: (*Pauses*) You're also feeling a little tension at this point, I guess.

Jill: Yeah. Yeah. A lot of conflict. . . . (C. R.: M-hm.) A lot of pain.

C. R. A lot of pain. Can you say anything more about what that's about? (Farber et al., 1996, pp. 74–75)

Client-centered therapy is practiced widely in college and university counseling centers, not just to help students experiencing, say, anxieties or depression but also to help them make decisions. Many college students have not yet made career choices or wonder whether they should become involved with particular people or in sexual activity. Client-centered therapists do not tell clients what to do. Instead, they help clients arrive at their own decisions.

■ Gestalt Therapy: Getting It Together

Gestalt therapy was originated by Fritz Perls (1893–1970). *What is Fritz Perls's method of Gestalt therapy?* Like client-centered therapy, Gestalt therapy assumes that people disown parts of themselves that might meet with social disapproval or rejection. People also don social masks, pretending to be things that they are not. Therapy aims to help individuals integrate conflicting parts of their personality. Perls used the term *Gestalt* to signify his

Unconditional positive regard Acceptance of the value of another person, although not necessarily acceptance of everything the person does.

Empathy Ability to perceive a client's feelings from the client's frame of reference. A quality of a good client-centered therapist.

Frame of reference One's unique patterning of perceptions and attitudes, according to which one evaluates events.

Genuineness Recognition and open expression of the therapist's own feelings.

Gestalt therapy Fritz Perls' form of psychotherapy, which attempts to integrate conflicting parts of the personality through directive methods designed to help clients perceive their whole selves.

reflect & relate

Carl Rogers believed that our psychological well-being is connected with our freedom to develop our unique frames of reference and potentials. Do you think you can separate your "real self" from your sociocultural experiences and religious training?

David Buffington/Getty Images

■ Client-Centered Therapy
By showing the qualities of unconditional positive regard, empathic understanding, and genuineness, client-centered therapists create an atmosphere in which clients can explore their feelings.

interest in giving the conflicting parts of the personality an integrated form or shape. He aimed to have his clients become aware of inner conflict, accept the reality of conflict rather than deny it or keep it repressed, and make productive choices despite misgivings and fears.

Although Perls's ideas about conflicting personality elements owe much to psychoanalytic theory, his form of therapy, unlike psychoanalysis, focuses on the here and now. Exercises heighten their awareness of their current feelings and behavior. Perls also believed, along with Rogers, that people are free to make choices and to direct their personal growth. But the charismatic and forceful Perls was unlike the gentle and accepting Rogers in temperament (Prochaska & Norcross, 2003). Thus, unlike client-centered therapy, Gestalt therapy is directive. The therapist leads the client through planned experiences.

◯ Learning Connections

◀◀ *Humanistic Therapies—Strengthening the Self* ▶▶

REVIEW:

6 The client-centered therapist's ability to accurately reflect clients' feelings is termed
  (a) unconditional positive regard,
  (b) empathy,
  (c) genuineness,
  (d) frame of reference.

7 What do client-centered and Gestalt therapy have in common?
  (a) They are both directive,
  (b) They are both nondirective,
  (c) They both focus on clients' subjective, conscious experience,
  (d) They both provide specific exercises to help clients develop self-insight.

CRITICAL THINKING:
Why are the therapies of Rogers and Perls placed in the same category? What do they have in common? How do they differ?

Go to WWW
http://academic.cengage.com/psychology/rathus
for an interactive version of this review.

BEHAVIOR THERAPY: ADJUSTMENT IS WHAT YOU DO

Psychoanalytic and humanistic forms of therapy tend to focus on what people think and feel. Behavior therapists tend to focus on what people *do*. **What is behavior therapy?** **Behavior therapy**—also called *behavior modification*—applies principles of learning to directly promote desired behavioral changes (Rachman, 2000). Behavior therapists rely heavily on principles of conditioning and observational learning. They help clients discontinue self-defeating behavior patterns such as overeating, smoking, and phobic avoidance of harmless stimuli. They help clients acquire adaptive behavior patterns such as the social skills required to start social relationships or say no to insistent salespeople. ◆ **Truth or Fiction Revisited:** In both cases, they may use specific procedures—telling their clients what to do.

Behavior therapists may help clients gain "insight" into maladaptive behaviors such as feelings of anxiety by helping the person become aware of the circumstances in which the behaviors occur. They do not help unearth the childhood origins of problems and the symbolic meanings of maladaptive behaviors as psychoanalysts do. Behavior therapists, like

Behavior therapy Systematic application of the principles of learning to the direct modification of a client's problem behaviors.

other therapists, may also build warm, therapeutic relationships with clients, but they see the effectiveness of behavior therapy as deriving from specific, learning-based procedures (Rachman, 2000). They insist that their methods be established by experimentation and that results be assessed in terms of measurable behavior. In this section we consider some frequently used behavior-therapy techniques.

—■— Fear-Reduction Methods

Many people, like firefighter Stephen King, seek therapy because of fears and phobias that interfere with their functioning. This is one of the areas in which behavior therapy has made great inroads. *What are some behavior-therapy methods for reducing fears?* These include flooding (see Chapter 6), systematic desensitization, and modeling.

Rainer Jensen /dpa /Landov

■ Overcoming Fear of Flying
Cognitive-behavioral therapists help clients reduce fear of flying in many ways, but each requires that clients be exposed to the objects and situations that disturb them. The people shown here are becoming accustomed to the interior of a plane while also learning what they can do in case there is a problem with the landing. Psychotherapists also use virtual therapy and other cognitive-behavioral methods.

Systematic Desensitization　Adam has a phobia for receiving injections. His behavior therapist treats him as he reclines in a comfortable padded chair. In a state of deep muscle relaxation, Adam observes slides projected on a screen. A slide of a nurse holding a needle has just been shown three times, 30 seconds at a time. Each time Adam has shown no anxiety. So now a slightly more discomforting slide is shown: one of the nurse aiming the needle toward someone's bare arm. After 15 seconds, our armchair adventurer notices twinges of discomfort and raises a finger as a signal (speaking might disturb his relaxation). The projector operator turns off the light, and Adam spends 2 minutes imagining his "safe scene"—lying on a beach beneath the tropical sun. Then the slide is shown again. This time Adam views it for 30 seconds before feeling anxiety.

◆ **Truth or Fiction Revisited:**　Adam is in effect confronting his fear while lying in a recliner and relaxing. Adam is undergoing **systematic desensitization,** a method for reducing phobic responses originated by psychiatrist Joseph Wolpe (1915–1997). Systematic desensitization is a gradual process in which the client learns to handle increasingly disturbing stimuli while anxiety to each one is being counterconditioned. About 10 to 20 stimuli such as slides are arranged in a sequence, or **hierarchy,** according to their "fear factor"—their capacity to trigger anxiety. In imagination or by being shown photos, the client travels gradually up through this hierarchy, approaching the target behavior. In Adam's case, the target behavior was the ability to receive an injection without undue anxiety. *Virtual therapy* uses more elaborate equipment than slides, but the principle is much the same (Winerman, 2005).

Wolpe developed systematic desensitization on the assumption that anxiety responses, like other behaviors, are learned or conditioned (Rachman, 2000). He reasoned that they can be unlearned by means of counterconditioning or extinction. In counterconditioning, a response that is incompatible with anxiety is made to appear under conditions that usually elicit anxiety. Muscle relaxation is incompatible with anxiety. For this reason, Adam's therapist is teaching him to relax in the presence of pictures of needles.

Remaining in the presence of phobic imagery, rather than running away from it, is also likely to enhance self-efficacy expectations. Self-efficacy expectations are negatively correlated with levels of adrenaline in the bloodstream (Bandura et al., 1985). Raising clients' self-efficacy expectations thus may help lower their adrenaline levels and reduce feelings of nervousness.

Modeling　Modeling relies on observational learning. In this method clients observe, and then imitate, people who approach and cope with the objects or situations that the clients fear. Bandura and his colleagues (1969) found that modeling worked as well as systematic desensitization—and more rapidly—in reducing fear of snakes. Like systematic desensitization, modeling is likely to increase self-efficacy expectations in coping with feared stimuli.

reflect & relate

Would any of the methods for reducing fears be helpful to you in your life? If so, which method would you prefer? Why?

Systematic　desensitization Wolpe's method for reducing fears by associating a hierarchy of images of fear-evoking stimuli with deep muscle relaxation.

Hierarchy An arrangement of stimuli according to the amount of fear they evoke.

Modeling A behavior-therapy technique in which a client observes and imitates a person who approaches and copes with feared objects or situations.

Virtual Reality Therapy

LEARNING OBJECTIVES

- To understand the use and effectiveness of virtual reality therapy ("virtual therapy") in the treatment of anxiety disorders.
- To understand how various psychologists might undertake different methods of therapy to help people with the same kinds of problems.

APPLIED LESSON

1 Can you think of any use of virtual therapy in your own life?
2 Do you think virtual therapy is appropriate for problems and disorders other than anxiety disorders? How might you apply it to teach social skills or alleviate feelings of depression?

CRITICAL THINKING

1 How does virtual reality therapy compare with other modes of therapy in helping people who have a fear of flying? What is the evidence concerning its effectiveness? What are its advantages and disadvantages?
2 Explain how virtual reality therapy is both similar and dissimilar to other cognitive-behavioral methods of psychotherapy for anxiety.
3 Agree or disagree with the following statement and support your answer: Virtual therapy is basically a variation of systematic desensitization.

Virtual reality therapy harnesses cutting-edge technology to help people overcome anxiety and phobias.

Watch this video!

Go www
to
your companion website at
http://academic.cengage.com/psychology/rathus
Click on the Video Connections tab under this chapter.

Aversive conditioning A behavior-therapy technique in which undesired responses are inhibited by pairing repugnant or offensive stimuli with them.

Rapid smoking An aversive conditioning method for quitting smoking in which the smoker inhales rapidly, thus rendering once-desirable cigarette smoke aversive.

Lester Sloan/Woodfin Camp & Associates

◾ Aversive Conditioning

Many people also seek behavior therapy because they want to break bad habits, such as smoking, excessive drinking, nail biting, and the like. One behavior-therapy approach to helping people do so is **aversive conditioning.** *How do behavior therapists use aversive conditioning to help people break bad habits?* Aversive conditioning is a controversial procedure in which painful or aversive stimuli are paired with unwanted impulses, such as desire for a cigarette or desire to engage in antisocial behavior, in an effort to make the impulse less appealing. For example, to help people control alcohol intake, tastes of different alcoholic beverages can be paired with drug-induced nausea and vomiting or with electric shock.

Aversive conditioning has been used with problems as diverse as cigarette smoking, sexual abuse, and retarded children's self-injurious behavior. **Rapid smoking** is an aversive-conditioning method designed to help smokers quit. In this method, the would-be quitter inhales every 6 seconds. In another method the hose of a hair dryer is hooked up to a chamber containing several lit cigarettes. Smoke is blown into the quitter's face as he or she also smokes a cigarette. A third method uses branching pipes so that the smoker draws in smoke from several cigarettes at the same time. In these methods, overexposure makes once-desirable cigarette smoke aversive. The quitter becomes motivated to avoid, rather than seek, cigarettes. ◇ **Truth or Fiction Revisited:** Therefore, smoking can be a way to stop smoking. Interest in

◾ Aversive Conditioning

In aversive conditioning, unwanted behaviors take on a noxious quality as a result of being repeatedly paired with aversive stimuli. Overexposure is making cigarette smoke aversive to this smoker.

A Closer Look
Eye-Movement Desensitization and Reprocessing

A Closer Look

Helping professionals are often inspired to develop therapy methods based on their personal experiences. A troubled young man named Carl Rogers discovered that his strict authoritarian father had coldly communicated values that were preventing him from becoming his own person. Rogers developed a therapy method that provides a warm atmosphere to help clients learn about and act on their genuine feelings. Aaron Beck found that he could argue himself out of his fear of driving through tunnels. Thus he developed cognitive therapy methods based on encouraging clients to recognize and challenge irrational fears and concerns.

So, too, with Francine Shapiro. As she paints it, Shapiro (1989) had troubling thoughts on her mind when she strolled into a park one day. But as her eyes darted about, taking in the scene, she found her troubled thoughts disappearing. Thus she developed a therapy method called **eye-movement desensitization and reprocessing (EMDR),** which has joined the arsenal of therapeutic weapons against stress disorders. Shapiro has trained thousands of helping professionals to use EMDR. In this method, the client is asked to imagine a traumatic scene while the therapist moves a finger rapidly back and forth before his or her eyes for about 20–30 seconds. The client follows the finger while keeping the troubling scene in mind. The client tells the therapist what he or she was thinking and how he or she felt during the procedure. The procedure is repeated until the client's feelings of anxiety are dissipated. Treatment takes about three 90-minute sessions.

Evidence from a number of studies suggests that EMDR helps decrease the anxiety associated with traumatic events.

One study, for example, compared the effectiveness of EMDR with two alternative treatments: exposure therapy (used, for example, with firefighter Stephen King to reduce his anxieties over the attacks of 9/11) and relaxation training (Taylor et al., 2003). Another study looked at the effectiveness of EMDR on numerous people following 9/11 (Silver et al., 2005). These studies and others (such as Sikes's & Sikes's [2005] study with college students and Devilly's [2002] review of the literature) suggest that EMDR is effective. But there are questions, including just *how* effective EMDR is and *why* it works (May, 2005). Devilly (2002), as noted, allows that EMDR is often effective, but his review finds other exposure therapies to be more effective. Research even challenges the idea that eye movements are a necessary part of therapy (May, 2005; Devilly, 2002). Skeptics have tried EMDR—or a cousin of it—using finger tapping rather than finger wagging, or instructing clients to keep their eyes straight ahead, and the results have remained the same.

It may be that the effects of EMDR can be attributed to a combination of nonspecific therapy factors and to exposure. Clients receiving EMDR may profit from a "therapeutic alliance" with the helping professional and from expectations of success. Moreover, the client *is* to some degree being exposed to the trauma that haunts him or her, and under circumstances in which the client believes he or she will be able to manage the trauma.

Conclusion? Exposure helps people cope with trauma. Eye movements may not be needed. ∎

---

aversive conditioning for quitting smoking has waned, however, because of side effects such as raising blood pressure and the availability of nicotine-replacement techniques.

In one study of aversive conditioning in the treatment of alcoholism, 63% of the 685 people treated remained abstinent for 1 year afterward, and about one third remained abstinent for at least 3 years (Wiens & Menustik, 1983). It may seem ironic that punitive aversive stimulation is sometimes used to stop children from punishing themselves, but people sometimes hurt themselves to obtain sympathy and attention. If self-injury leads to more pain than anticipated and no sympathy, it might be discontinued.

■ Operant Conditioning Procedures

We usually prefer to relate to people who smile at us rather than ignore us and to take courses in which we do well rather than fail. We tend to repeat behavior that is reinforced. Behavior that is not reinforced tends to become extinguished. Behavior therapists have used these principles of operant conditioning with psychotic patients as well as with clients with milder problems. *How do behavior therapists apply principles of operant conditioning in behavior modification?*

The staff at one mental hospital was at a loss about how to encourage withdrawn schizophrenic patients to eat regularly. Ayllon and Haughton (1962) observed that staff members

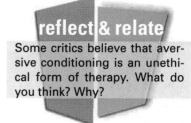

reflect & relate

Some critics believe that aversive conditioning is an unethical form of therapy. What do you think? Why?

Eye-movement desensitization and reprocessing (EMDR) A method of treating stress disorders by having clients visually follow a rapidly oscillating finger while they think of the traumatic events connected with the disorders.

were making the problem worse by coaxing patients into the dining room and even feeding them. Staff attention apparently reinforced the patients' lack of cooperation. Some rules were changed. Patients who did not arrive at the dining hall within 30 minutes after serving were locked out. Staff could not interact with patients at mealtime. With uncooperative behavior no longer reinforced, patients quickly changed their eating habits. Then patients were required to pay one penny to enter the dining hall. Pennies were earned by interacting with other patients and showing other socially appropriate behaviors. These target behaviors also became more frequent.

Health professionals are concerned about whether people who are, or have been, dependent on alcohol can exercise control over their drinking. One study showed that rewards for remaining abstinent from alcohol can exert a powerful effect (Petry et al., 2000). In the study, one group of alcohol-dependent veterans was given a standard treatment while another group received the treatment *plus* the chance to win prizes for remaining alcohol-free, as measured by a Breathalyzer test. By the end of the 8-week treatment period, 84% of the veterans who could win prizes remained in the program, as compared with 22% of the standard treatment group. The prizes had an average value of $200, far less than what alcohol-related absenteeism from work and other responsibilities can cost.

The Token Economy   Many psychiatric wards and hospitals use **token economies** in which patients need tokens such as poker chips to purchase TV viewing time, extra visits to the canteen, or a private room (Comaty et al., 2001). The tokens are dispensed as reinforcers for productive activities such as making beds, brushing teeth, and socializing. Token economies have not eliminated all symptoms of schizophrenia but have increased patients' activity and cooperation. Tokens have also been used to modify the behavior of children with conduct disorders.

Successive Approximations   The operant conditioning method of **successive approximations** is often used to help clients build good habits. Let us use a (not uncommon!) example: You want to study 3 hours each evening but can concentrate for only half an hour. Rather than attempting to increase your study time all at once, you could do so gradually by adding, say, 5 minutes each evening. After every hour or so of studying, you could reinforce yourself with 5 minutes of people-watching in a busy section of the library.

Biofeedback Training   Through **biofeedback training (BFT)**, therapists help clients become more aware of, and gain control over, various bodily functions. Therapists attach clients to devices that measure bodily functions such as heart rate. "Bleeps" or other electronic signals are used to indicate (and thereby reinforce) changes ("operants") in the desired direction—for example, a slower heart rate. (Knowledge of results is a powerful reinforcer.) One device, the electromyograph (EMG), monitors muscle tension. It has been used to increase control over muscle tension in the forehead and elsewhere, thereby alleviating anxiety, stress, and headaches.

BFT also helps clients voluntarily regulate functions once thought to be beyond conscious control, such as heart rate and blood pressure. Hypertensive clients use a blood pressure cuff and electronic signals to gain control over their blood pressure. The electroencephalograph (EEG) monitors brain waves and can be used to teach people how to produce alpha waves, which are associated with relaxation. Some people have overcome insomnia by learning to produce the kinds of brain waves associated with sleep.

■ Social Skills Training

In social skills training, behavior therapists decrease social anxiety and build social skills through operant-conditioning procedures that employ **self-monitoring**, coaching, modeling, role-playing, **behavior rehearsal**, and **feedback**. Social skills training has been used to help formerly hospitalized mental patients maintain jobs and apartments in the community. For example, a worker can rehearse politely asking a supervisor for assistance or asking a landlord to fix the plumbing in an apartment. Social skills training is effective in groups. Group members can role-play important people—such as parents, spouses, or potential dates—in the lives of other members.

Token economy A controlled environment in which people are reinforced for desired behaviors with tokens (such as poker chips) that may be exchanged for privileges.

Successive approximations In operant conditioning, a series of behaviors that gradually become more similar to a target behavior.

Biofeedback training (BFT) The systematic feeding back to an organism of information about a bodily function so that the organism can gain control of that function.

Self-monitoring Keeping a record of one's own behavior to identify problems and record successes.

Behavior rehearsal Practice.

Feedback In assertiveness training, information about the effectiveness of a response.

Assertive Training One form of social skills training is assertive training. In this method, also often carried out in a group, clients learn to speak up to express their genuine feelings and refuse unreasonable requests. You can learn whether you are as assertive as most college students by completing the assertiveness schedule in the following Self-Assessment.

Self-Assessment

Self-Assessment

Self-Assessment

Do You Demand Your Rights or Do You Wimp Out? The Assertiveness Schedule

What about you? Do you enrich the pockets of every telemarketer, or do you say no? Do you stick up for your rights, or do you allow others to walk all over you? Do you say what you feel or what you think other people want you to say? Do you initiate relationships with attractive people, or do you shy away from them?

One way to gain insight into how assertive you are is to take the following assertiveness schedule. Once you have finished, turn to Appendix B to find out how to calculate your score. A table in the appendix will also allow you to compare your assertiveness to that of a sample of 1,400 students drawn from 35 college campuses across the United States.

If you believe that you are not assertive enough, assertive training may be in order for you. You need not spend your life imitating a doormat.

Directions: Indicate how well each item describes you by using this code:

    3 = very much like me
    2 = rather like me
    1 = slightly like me
   −1 = slightly unlike me
   −2 = rather unlike me
   −3 = very much unlike me

_____ 1. Most people seem to be more aggressive and assertive than I am.

_____ 2. I have hesitated to develop social relationships because of "shyness."

_____ 3. When the food served at a restaurant is not done to my satisfaction, I complain about it to the waiter or waitress.

_____ 4. I am careful to avoid hurting other people's feelings, even when I feel that I have been injured.

_____ 5. If a salesperson has gone to considerable trouble to show me merchandise that is not quite suitable, I have a difficult time saying "No."

_____ 6. When I am asked to do something, I insist upon knowing why.

_____ 7. There are times when I look for a good, vigorous argument.

_____ 8. I strive to get ahead as well as most people in my position.

_____ 9. To be honest, people often take advantage of me.

_____ 10. I enjoy starting conversations with new acquaintances and strangers.

_____ 11. I often don't know what to say to people who are sexually attractive to me.

_____ 12. I will hesitate to make phone calls to business establishments and institutions.

_____ 13. I would rather apply for a job or for admission to a college by writing letters than by going through with personal interviews.

_____ 14. I find it embarrassing to return merchandise.

_____ 15. If a close and respected relative were annoying me, I would smother my feelings rather than express my annoyance.

_____ 16. I have avoided asking questions for fear of sounding stupid.

_____ 17. During an argument I am sometimes afraid that I will get so upset that I will shake all over.

_____ 18. If a famed and respected lecturer makes a comment which I think is incorrect, I will have the audience hear my point of view as well.

_____ 19. I avoid arguing over prices with clerks and salespeople.

_____ 20. When I have done something important or worthwhile, I manage to let others know about it.

_____ 21. I am open and frank about my feelings.

_____ 22. If someone has been spreading false and bad stories about me, I see him or her as soon as possible and "have a talk" about it.

_____ 23. I often have a hard time saying "No."

_____ 24. I tend to bottle up my emotions rather than make a scene.

_____ 25. I complain about poor service in a restaurant and elsewhere.

_____ 26. When I am given a compliment, I sometimes just don't know what to say.

_____ 27. If a couple near me in a theater or at a lecture were conversing rather loudly, I would ask them to be quiet or to take their conversation elsewhere.

_____ 28. Anyone attempting to push ahead of me in a line is in for a good battle.

_____ 29. I am quick to express an opinion.

_____ 30. There are times when I just can't say anything.

SOURCE: Reprinted from Rathus, 1973, pp. 398–406.

Go to www

http://academic.cengage.com/psychology/rathus where you can fill out an interactive version of this Self-Assessment and automatically score your results.

() Learning Connections

◀◀ *Behavior Therapy—Adjustment Is What You Do* ▶▶

REVIEW:

8 _____ is an example of the application of operant conditioning to psychotherapy.
   (a) Flooding,
   (b) The dialogue,
   (c) The prefrontal lobotomy,
   (d) Biofeedback training.

9 Behavior rehearsal is most similar in meaning to
   (a) social skills,
   (b) modeling,

   (c) practice,
   (d) assertive training.

10 Systematic desensitization was originated by
   (a) Joseph Wolpe,
   (b) Aaron Beck,
   (c) Albert Ellis,
   (d) Albert Bandura.

CRITICAL THINKING:
Behavior therapists argue that their methods are more scientific than
those of other therapists. How do they attempt to ensure that their
methods are scientific?

Go to www ▶▶
http://academic.cengage.com/psychology/rathus
for an interactive version of this review.

COGNITIVE THERAPIES: ADJUSTMENT IS WHAT YOU THINK (AND DO)

What thoughts do you have when things go wrong at school or on the job? Do you tell yourself that you're facing a problem that needs a solution? That you've successfully solved problems before and will be able to create a solution this time? Or do you think, "Oh no! This is awful! It's going to get worse, and I'm going to flunk (or get fired)!" If you go the "This is awful" route, you are probably heightening your discomfort and impairing your coping ability. Cognitive therapy focuses directly on your thoughts and encourages ideas that will help you solve problems rather than blow them out of proportion and magnify your discomfort.

What is cognitive therapy? **Cognitive therapy** focuses on changing the beliefs, attitudes, and automatic types of thinking that create and compound people's problems (Berk et al., 2004; Ellis, 2004a, 2004b). Cognitive therapists, like psychoanalytic and humanistic therapists, aim to foster self-insight, but they mainly aim to help make people more aware of their *current cognitions*. Cognitive therapists also aim to directly change maladaptive thoughts in an effort to reduce negative feelings and help clients solve problems.

Many behavior therapists incorporate cognitive procedures in their methods. For example, techniques such as systematic desensitization, covert sensitization, and covert reinforcement ask clients to focus on visual imagery. Behavioral methods for treating bulimia nervosa focus on clients' irrational attitudes toward their weight and body shape as well as foster good eating habits. Let us look at the approaches and methods of the cognitive therapists Aaron Beck and Albert Ellis.

Cognitive therapy A form of therapy that focuses on how clients' cognitions (e.g., expectations, attitudes, beliefs) lead to distress and may be modified to relieve distress and promote adaptive behavior.

■ Cognitive Therapy: Correcting Cognitive Errors

Psychiatrist Aaron Beck began his professional life as a psychoanalyst. He became impatient, however, with analysis's lengthy methods and reluctance to offer specific advice. In his own life he had successfully defeated fear of blood by assisting in surgical operations and argued himself out of irrational fear of driving through tunnels. Similarly, his methods of cognitive therapy focus on arguing clients out of beliefs that are making them miserable and exposing them to situations they avoid because of irrational fear (Berk et al., 2004; Warman et al., 2005). ***What is Aaron Beck's method of cognitive therapy?*** Beck encourages clients to become their own personal scientists and challenge feelings and beliefs that make no sense.

Beck encourages clients to see the irrationality of their ways of thinking. For example, depressed people tend to minimize their accomplishments and to assume that the worst will happen. Minimizing accomplishments and expecting the worst are (usually) distortions of reality that lead to feelings of depression. Cognitive distortions can be fleeting and automatic, difficult to detect. Beck's methods help clients become aware of such distortions and challenge them.

Beck notes a number of "cognitive errors" that contribute to clients' miseries:

■ **Aaron Beck (left) and Albert Ellis (right)**

Michael Fenichel, www.fenichel.com

1. Clients may *selectively perceive* the world as a harmful place and ignore evidence to the contrary.
2. Clients may *overgeneralize* on the basis of a few examples. For example, they may perceive themselves as worthless because they were laid off at work or as unattractive because they were refused a date.
3. Clients may *magnify*, or blow out of proportion, the importance of negative events. They may catastrophize failing a test by assuming they will flunk out of college or catastrophize losing a job by believing that they will never find another one and that serious harm will befall their family as a result.
4. Clients may engage in *absolutist thinking*, or looking at the world in black and white rather than in shades of gray. In doing so, a rejection on a date takes on the meaning of a lifetime of loneliness; an uncomfortable illness takes on life-threatening proportions.

The concept of pinpointing and modifying errors may become clearer from the following excerpt from a case in which a 53-year-old engineer obtained cognitive therapy for severe depression. The engineer had left his job and become inactive. As reported by Beck and his colleagues, the first goal of treatment was to foster physical activity—even things like raking leaves and preparing dinner—because activity is incompatible with depression. Then,

[the engineer's] cognitive distortions were identified by comparing his assessment of each activity with that of his wife. Alternative ways of interpreting his experiences were then considered.

In comparing his wife's résumé of his past experiences, he became aware that he had (1) undervalued his past by failing to mention many previous accomplishments, (2) regarded himself as far more responsible for his "failures" than she did, and (3) concluded that he was worthless since he had not succeeded in attaining certain goals in the past. When the two accounts were contrasted, he could discern many of his cognitive distortions. In subsequent sessions, his wife continued to serve as an "objectifier."

In midtherapy, [he] compiled a list of new attitudes that he had acquired since initiating therapy. These included:

1. "I am starting at a lower level of functioning at my job, but it will improve if I persist."

2. "I know that once I get going in the morning, everything will run all right for the rest of the day."
3. "I can't achieve everything at once."
4. "I have my periods of ups and downs, but in the long run I feel better."
5. "My expectations from my job and life should be scaled down to a realistic level."
6. "Giving in to avoidance [e.g., staying away from work and social interactions] never helps and only leads to further avoidance."

He was instructed to reread this list daily for several weeks even though he already knew the content. (Rush et al., 1975)

The engineer gradually became less depressed and returned to work and an active social life. Along the way, he learned to combat inappropriate self-blame for problems, perfectionistic expectations, magnification of failures, and overgeneralization from failures.

Becoming aware of cognitive errors and modifying catastrophizing thoughts helps us cope with stress. Internal, stable, and global attributions of failure lead to depression and feelings of helplessness. Cognitive therapists also alert clients to cognitive errors such as these so that the clients can change their attitudes and pave the way for more effective overt behavior.

Rational Emotive Behavior Therapy: Overcoming "Musts" and "Shoulds"

In **rational emotive behavior therapy (REBT)**, Albert Ellis (2002) points out that our beliefs *about* events, not only the events themselves, shape our responses to them. Moreover, many of us harbor a number of irrational beliefs that can give rise to problems or magnify their impact. Two of the most important ones are the belief that we must have the love and approval of people who are important to us and the belief that we must prove ourselves to be thoroughly competent, adequate, and achieving. *What is Albert Ellis's method of rational emotive behavior therapy (REBT)?*

Albert Ellis, like Aaron Beck, began his career as a psychoanalyst. And, also like Beck, he became disturbed by the passive role of the analyst and by the slow rate of obtaining results—if they were obtained at all. Ellis's REBT methods are active and directive. He does not sit back like the traditional psychoanalyst and occasionally offer an interpretation. Instead, he urges clients to seek out their irrational beliefs, which can be unconscious, though not as deeply buried as Freud believed. Nevertheless, they can be hard to pinpoint without some direction. Ellis shows clients how those beliefs lead to misery and challenges clients to change them. When Ellis sees clients behaving according to irrational beliefs, he may refute the beliefs by asking "Where is it written that you must . . . ?" or "What evidence do you have that . . . ?" According to Ellis, we need less misery and less blaming in our lives, and more action.

Toward a Cognitive-Behavioral Therapy

Many theorists consider cognitive therapy to be a collection of techniques that are a part of behavior therapy. Aaron Beck himself appears to be comfortable referring to his approach as *cognitive* in one article and *cognitive-behavioral* in another (Berk et al., 2005; Brown et al., 2004; Turkington et al., 2004; Warman & Beck, 2003). We may be headed toward an integration of the two approaches that will be termed **cognitive-behavioral therapy (CBT)**.

Ellis straddles behavioral and cognitive therapies. He originally dubbed his method of therapy *rational-emotive therapy,* because his focus was on the cognitive—irrational beliefs and how to change them. However, Ellis has also always promoted behavioral changes to cement cognitive changes. In keeping with his broad philosophy, he recently changed the name of rational-emotive therapy to rational emotive *behavior* therapy.

reflect & relate

Do you believe that you must have the love and approval of people who are important to you? Do you believe that you must prove yourself to be thoroughly competent, adequate, and achieving? Do such beliefs make you miserable? What can you do about them?

Rational emotive behavior therapy (REBT) Albert Ellis's form of therapy that encourages clients to challenge and correct irrational expectations and maladaptive behaviors.

Cognitive-behavior therapy (CBT) An approach to therapy that uses cognitive and behavioral techniques that have been validated by research.

Life Connections
Tackling Depression with Rational Thinking

Cognitive therapists note that depressed people often blame themselves for failures and problems, even when they are not at fault. Depressed people *internalize* blame and see their problems as *stable* and *global*—as all but impossible to change. Depressed people also make cognitive errors such as *catastrophizing* their problems and *minimizing* their accomplishments.

Column 1 in Table 13.1 illustrates a number of irrational, depressing thoughts. How many of them have you had? Column 2 indicates the type of cognitive error being made (such as internalizing or catastrophizing), and column 3 shows examples of rational alternatives.

You can pinpoint irrational, depressing thoughts by identifying the kinds of thoughts you have when you feel low. Look for the fleeting thoughts that can trigger mood changes. It helps to jot them down. Then challenge their accuracy. Do you characterize difficult situations as impossible and hopeless? Do you expect too much from yourself and minimize your achievements? Do you internalize more than your fair share of blame?

TABLE 13.1 ■ Irrational, Depressing Thoughts and Rational Alternatives

Many of us create or compound feelings of depression because of cognitive errors such as those in this table. Have you had any of these irrational, depressing thoughts? Are you willing to challenge them?

IRRATIONAL THOUGHT	TYPE OF THOUGHT	RATIONAL ALTERNATIVE
"There's nothing I can do."	Catastrophizing (the size of the problem), minimizing (one's coping ability), stabilizing	"I can't think of anything to do right now, but if I work at it, I may."
"I'm no good."	Internalizing, globalizing, stabilizing	"I did something I regret, but that doesn't make me evil or worthless as a person."
"This is absolutely awful."	Catastrophizing	"This is pretty bad, but it's not the end of the world."
"I just don't have the brains for college."	Stabilizing, globalizing	"I guess I really need to go back over the basics in that course."
"I just can't believe I did something so disgusting!"	Catastrophizing	"That was a bad experience. Well, I won't be likely to try that again soon."
"I can't imagine ever feeling right."	Stabilizing, catastrophizing	"This is painful, but if I try to work it through step by step, I'll probably eventually see my way out of it."
"It's all my fault."	Internalizing	"I'm not blameless, but I wasn't the only one involved. It may have been my idea, but he went into it with his eyes open."

continued

TABLE 13.1 ■ Irrational, Depressing Thoughts and Rational Alternatives—*continued*

IRRATIONAL THOUGHT	TYPE OF THOUGHT	RATIONAL ALTERNATIVE
"I can't do anything right."	Globalizing, stabilizing, catastrophizing, minimizing	"I sure screwed this up, but I've done a lot of things well, and I'll do other things well."
"I hurt everybody who gets close to me."	Internalizing, globalizing, stabilizing	"I'm not totally blameless, but I'm not responsible for the whole world. Others make their own decisions, and they have to live with the results, too."
"If people knew the real me, they would have it in for me."	Globalizing, minimizing (the positive in yourself)	"I'm not perfect, but nobody's perfect. I have positive as well as negative features, and I am entitled to self-interests."

You can use Table 13.1 to classify your cognitive errors and construct rational alternatives. Write these next to each irrational thought. Review them from time to time. When you are alone, you can read the irrational thought aloud. Then follow it by saying to yourself firmly, "No, that's irrational!" Then read the rational alternative aloud twice, *emphatically*.

After you have thought or read aloud the rational alternative, think, "That makes more sense! That's a more accurate view of things! I feel better now that I have things in perspective." ■

( ) Learning Connections

◀◀ *Cognitive Therapies—Adjustment Is What You Think (and Do)* ▶▶

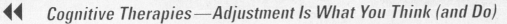

REVIEW:

11 According to Albert Ellis, the central factors in our problems are
(a) genetic factors,
(b) maladaptive habits,
(c) unconscious conflicts,
(d) irrational beliefs.

12 Looking at the world in black and white rather than in shades of gray is an example of
(a) selective perception,
(b) overgeneralization,
(c) absolutist thinking,
(d) magnification.

CRITICAL THINKING:
What is the difference between behavior therapy and cognitive therapy? Many therapists call themselves cognitive-behavioral therapists. Does it seem possible to combine behavior therapy and cognitive therapy? Explain.

Go to

http://academic.cengage.com/psychology/rathus
for an interactive version of this review.

GROUP THERAPIES

When a psychotherapist has several clients with similar problems—anxiety, depression, adjustment to divorce, lack of social skills—it often makes sense to treat them in a group rather than in individual sessions. The methods and characteristics of the group reflect the needs of the members and the theoretical orientation of the leader. In group psychoanalysis, clients might interpret one another's dreams. In a client-centered group, they might provide an accepting atmosphere for self-exploration. Members of behavior therapy groups might be jointly desensitized to anxiety-evoking stimuli or might practice social skills together. *What are the advantages and disadvantages of group therapy?*

Group therapy has the following advantages:

1. It is economical. It allows the therapist to work with several clients at once.
2. Compared with one-to-one therapy, group therapy provides more information and life experience for clients to draw upon.
3. Appropriate behavior receives group support. Clients usually appreciate an outpouring of peer approval.
4. When we run into troubles, it is easy to imagine that we are different from other people or inferior to them. Affiliating with people with similar problems is reassuring.
5. Group members who show improvement provide hope for other members.
6. Many individuals seek therapy because of problems in relating to other people. People who seek therapy for other reasons also may be socially inhibited. Members of groups have the opportunity to practice social skills in a relatively nonthreatening atmosphere. In a group consisting of men and women of different ages, group members can role-play one another's employers, employees, spouses, parents, children, and friends. Members can role-play asking one another out on dates, saying no (or yes), and so on.

But group therapy is not for everyone. Some clients fare better with individual treatment. Many prefer not to disclose their problems to a group. They may be overly shy or want individual attention. It is the responsibility of the therapist to insist that group disclosures be kept confidential, to establish a supportive atmosphere, and to ensure that group members obtain the attention they need.

Many types of therapy can be conducted either individually or in groups. Couple therapy and family therapy are conducted only with groups.

reflect & relate

Do you think you could share your intimate problems with a group of strangers? Can you see any advantages or disadvantages to doing so?

Couple Therapy

Couple therapy helps couples enhance their relationship by improving their communication skills and helping them manage conflict (Prochaska & Norcross, 2003). There are often power imbalances in relationships, and couple therapy helps individuals find "full membership" in the couple. Correcting power imbalances increases happiness and can decrease the incidence of domestic violence. Ironically, in situations of domestic violence, the partner with *less* power in the relationship is usually the violent one. Violence sometimes appears to be a way of compensating for inability to share power in other aspects of the relationship (Rathus & Sanderson, 1999).

Today the main approach to couple therapy is cognitive-behavioral (Rathus & Sanderson, 1999). It teaches couples communications skills (such as how to listen and how to express feelings), ways of handling feelings like depression and anger, and ways of solving problems.

Bob Daemmrich/Stock Boston LLC

■ **Group Therapy**

Group therapy has a number of advantages over individual therapy for many clients. It's economical, provides a fund of experience for clients to draw upon, elicits group support, and provides an opportunity to relate to other people. On the other hand, some clients do need individual attention.

─■─ Family Therapy

What is family therapy? Family therapy is a form of group therapy in which one or more families constitute the group. Family therapy may be undertaken from various theoretical viewpoints. One is the systems approach, in which family interaction is studied and modified to enhance the growth of individual family members and of the family unit as a whole (Prochaska & Norcross, 2003).

Family members with low self-esteem often cannot tolerate different attitudes and behaviors in other family members. Faulty communication within the family also creates problems. In addition, it is not uncommon for the family to present an "identified patient"—that is, the family member who has *the* problem and is *causing* all the trouble. Yet family therapists usually assume that the identified patient is a scapegoat for other problems within and among family members. It is a sort of myth: Change the bad apple—or identified patient—and the barrel—or family—will be functional once more. The family therapist—often a specialist in this field—attempts to teach the family to communicate more effectively and encourage growth and autonomy in each family member.

() **Learning Connections**

◄◄ *Group Therapies* ►►

REVIEW:

13 Today the main approach to couple therapy is
(a) Gestalt,
(b) client-centered,
(c) humanistic,
(d) cognitive-behavioral.

14 In the _____ approach to family therapy, family interaction is modified to enhance the

growth of family members and the family unit as a whole.
(a) group,
(b) individual,
(c) systems,
(d) psychoanalytic.

CRITICAL THINKING:
Critical thinkers avoid overgeneralization. Is it accurate to say that individual therapy is preferable to group therapy, or is the statement an overgeneralization?

Go to www
http://academic.cengage.com/psychology/rathus
for an interactive version of this review.

DOES PSYCHOTHERAPY WORK?

In 1952, the British psychologist Hans Eysenck published a review of psychotherapy research—"The Effects of Psychotherapy"—that sent shock waves through the psychotherapy community. On the basis of his review of the research, Eysenck concluded that the rate of improvement among people in psychotherapy was no greater than the rate of "spontaneous remission"—that is, the rate of improvement that would be shown by people with psychological disorders who received no treatment at all. Eysenck was not addressing people with schizophrenia, who typically profit from biological forms of therapy, but he argued that whether or not people with problems such as anxiety and depression received therapy, two of three reported substantial improvement within two years.

That was half a century ago. ◆ **Truth or Fiction Revisited:** There is now quite a bit of research evidence—with many studies employing a sophisticated statistical averaging method called **meta-analysis**—that show that psychotherapy is effective (Luborsky et al.,

Meta-analysis A method for combining and averaging the results of individual research studies.

2002; Shadish et al., 2000). *What, then, has research shown about the effectiveness of psychotherapy?*

In their classic early use of meta-analysis, Mary Lee Smith and Gene Glass (1977) analyzed the results of dozens of outcome studies of various types of therapies. They concluded that people who obtained psychoanalytic therapy showed greater well-being, on the average, than 70% to 75% of those who did not obtain treatment. Similarly, nearly 75% of the clients who obtained client-centered therapy were better off than people who did not obtain treatment. Psychoanalytic and client-centered therapies appear to be most effective with well-educated, verbal, strongly motivated clients who report problems with anxiety, depression (of light to moderate proportions), and interpersonal relationships. Neither form of therapy appears to be effective with people with psychotic disorders such as major depression, bipolar disorder, and schizophrenia. Smith and Glass (1977) found that people who obtained Gestalt therapy showed greater well-being than about 60% of those who did not obtain treatment. The effectiveness of psychoanalysis and client-centered therapy thus was reasonably comparable. Gestalt therapy fell behind.

Smith and Glass (1977) did not include cognitive therapies in their meta-analysis because at the time of their study many cognitive approaches were relatively new. Because behavior therapists also incorporate many cognitive techniques, it can be difficult to sort out which aspects—cognitive or otherwise—of behavioral treatments are most effective. Many meta-analyses of cognitive–behavioral therapy have been conducted since the early work of Smith and Glass, however. Their results are encouraging (e.g., DeRubeis et al., 2005; Hollon et al., 2005).

A meta-analysis of 90 studies by William R. Shadish and his colleagues (2000) concurred that psychotherapy is generally effective. Generally speaking, the more therapy the better; that is, people who have more psychotherapy tend to fare better than people who have less of it. Therapy also appears to be more effective when the outcome measures reflect the treatment (e.g., when the effects of treatment aimed at fear-reduction are measured in terms of people's ability to approach fear-inducing objects and situations).

Studies of cognitive therapy have shown that modifying irrational beliefs of the type described by Albert Ellis helps people with problems such as anxiety and depression (Engels et al., 1993; Haaga & Davison, 1993). Modifying self-defeating beliefs of the sort outlined by Aaron Beck also frequently alleviates anxiety and depression (Butler & Beck, 2001; Frank & Kupfer, 2003). Cognitive therapy has also helped people with personality disorders (Beck et al., 2001; Brown et al., 2004; Trull et al., 2003).

Behavioral and cognitive therapies have provided strategies for treating anxiety disorders, social skills deficits, and problems in self-control. These therapies—which are often integrated as cognitive-behavioral therapy (CBT)—have also provided empirically supported methods for helping couples and families in distress (Baucom et al., 1998), and for modifying behaviors related to health problems such as headaches (Blanchard, 1992), smoking, chronic pain, and bulimia nervosa (Agras et al., 2000; Compas et al., 1998). Cognitive-behavioral therapists have also innovated treatments for sexual dysfunctions for which there were no effective treatments. One meta-analysis of psychoanalytic therapy and CBT found both treatments to be helpful with personality disorders (Leichsenring & Leibing, 2003). Interestingly, of literally hundreds of studies reviewed, the researchers found only 25 studies that were rigorous enough to be included in the meta-analysis.

Cognitive-behavioral therapy has been used to help anorexic and bulimic individuals challenge their perfectionism and their attitudes toward their bodies. It has also been used to systematically reinforce appropriate eating behavior. Studies that compare the effectiveness of CBT and antidepressants find them to be comparably effective, with CBT sometimes showing a slight advantage (e.g., Jacobi et al., 2002). Drugs, after all, do not directly "attack" people's perfectionist attitudes and their distorted body images. They ease the presence of negative feelings and may help individuals enlist their own psychological resources, but pills do not offer advice or even a sympathetic ear.

The combination of cognitive therapy or CBT and drug therapy has helped many people with schizophrenia modify their delusional beliefs and behave in more socially acceptable ways (Turkington et al., 2004; Warman et al., 2005). But psychological therapy alone is apparently inadequate to treat the quirks of thought exhibited in people with severe psychotic disorders.

reflect & relate

If a psychiatrist or psychologist recommended a course of treatment for a problem, would you be reluctant to ask the professional about evidence as to whether that form of treatment has been shown to be effective? Why or why not?

A Closer Look
Psychotherapy and Ethnicity

The United States is changing. The numbers of African Americans, Asian Americans, and Latino and Latina Americans are growing rapidly, yet most of the "prescriptions" for psychotherapy discussed in this chapter were originated by, and intended for use with, European Americans. People from ethnic minority groups are less likely than European Americans to seek therapy for reasons such as the following:

- unawareness that therapy would help
- lack of information about the availability of professional services, or inability to pay for them (Anger-Díaz et al., 2004)
- distrust of professionals, particularly European American professionals and (for women) male professionals (Mittal & Wieling, 2004; Culture gaps, 2005)
- language barriers (Anger-Díaz et al., 2004)
- reluctance to open up about personal matters to strangers—especially strangers who are not members of one's own ethnic group (Chen & Davenport, 2005; Mittal & Wieling, 2004)
- cultural inclinations toward other approaches to problem solving, such as religious approaches and psychic healers (Cervantes & Parham, 2005).
- negative experiences with professionals and authority figures

Clinicians need to be sensitive to the cultural heritage, language, and values of the people they see in therapy (Chen & Davenport, 2005). They need to develop *multicultural competence* (Sue, 1999). Let us consider some of the issues involved in conducting psychotherapy with African Americans, Asian Americans, Latino and Latina Americans, and Native Americans.

African Americans
In addition to addressing the psychological problems of African American clients, therapists often need to help them cope with the effects of prejudice and discrimination. Some

Bill Aron/PhotoEdit

■ **Does the Ethnicity of the Psychotherapist Make a Difference?**
Some studies show that people from ethnic minority groups are uncomfortable sharing intimate information with therapists from different ethnic groups—especially with those from the dominant European American culture.

---

reflect & relate
Consider your part of the country and your sociocultural background. Do people in your area and from your background frequently go for "therapy"? Is psychotherapy considered a normal option for people having problems in your area, or is it stigmatized?

Specific factors Those factors in psychotherapy that are specific to a given approach, such as free association in psychoanalysis or systematic desensitization in behavior therapy.

Nonspecific factors Those factors in psychotherapy that are common to many approaches, such as the "therapeutic alliance" with the client.

Thus, it is not enough to ask which type of therapy is most effective. We must ask which type is most effective for a particular problem and a particular patient. What are its advantages? Its limitations? Clients may successfully use systematic desensitization or virtual therapy to overcome stage fright, but if they also want to know *why* they have stage fright, behavior therapy alone will not provide the answer. But, then again, insight-oriented forms of therapy might also not be able to provide the answer.

All in all, despite Han Eysenck's skepticism, noted at the beginning of the section, research suggests that psychotherapy appears to be effective more often than not. But, we might wonder, does psychotherapy help because of **specific factors** and treatment methods or because a client is receiving the support of an educated and trained helping professional? So-called **nonspecific factors** in therapy, such as the formation of the client-therapist "alliance," are connected with better therapeutic results (Klein et al., 2003; Meyer et al., 2002; Scaturo, 2005). However, specific techniques—such as specific cognitive and behavioral methods—appear to be much more effective than the therapist-client relationship in bringing about helpful changes (Stevens et al., 2000).

Another issue in the effectiveness of psychotherapy is multiculturalism, as we see in the nearby "A Closer Look" on psychotherapy and ethnicity. Do people from different backgrounds have equal access to psychotherapy? How can psychotherapy be made more effective with people from different backgrounds?

African Americans develop low self-esteem because they internalize negative stereotypes (Boyd-Franklin, 2001).

African Americans often are reluctant to seek psychological help because of cultural assumptions that people should manage their own problems and because of mistrust of the therapy process. They tend to assume that people are supposed to solve their own problems. Signs of emotional weakness such as tension, anxiety and depression are stigmatized (Ivey & Brooks-Harris, 2005).

Many African Americans are also suspicious of their therapists—especially when the therapist is a European American. They may withhold personal information because of the society's history of racial discrimination.

Asian Americans

Asian Americans tend to stigmatize people with psychological disorders. As a result, they may deny problems and refuse to seek help for them (Chen & Davenport, 2005). Asian Americans, especially recent immigrants, also may not understand or believe in Western approaches to psychotherapy. For example, Western psychotherapy typically encourages people to express their feelings openly. This mode of behavior may conflict with the Asian tradition of restraint in public. Many Asians prefer to receive concrete advice rather than Western-style encouragement to develop their own solutions (Chen & Davenport, 2005).

Because of a cultural tendency to deny painful thoughts, many Asians experience and express psychological problems as physical symptoms (Chen & Davenport, 2005). Rather than thinking of themselves as being anxious, they may focus on physical features of anxiety such as a pounding heart and heavy sweating. Rather than thinking of themselves as depressed, they may focus on fatigue and low energy levels.

Latino and Latina Americans

Therapists need to be aware of potential conflicts between the traditional Latino and Latina American value of interdependency in the family and the typical European American belief in independence and self-reliance (Anger-Díaz et al., 2004). Measures like the following may help bridge the gaps between psychotherapists and Latino and Latina American clients:

1. Interacting with clients in the language requested by them or, if this is not possible, referring them to professionals who can do so.
2. Using methods that are consistent with the client's values and levels of acculturation, as suggested by fluency in English and level of education.
3. Developing therapy methods that incorporate clients' cultural values (Cervantes & Parham, 2005). Malgady and his colleagues (1990), for example, use *cuento therapy* with Puerto Ricans. *Cuento therapy* uses Latino and Latina folktales (*cuentos*) with characters who serve as models for adaptive behavior.

Native Americans

Many psychological disorders experienced by Native Americans involve the disruption of their traditional culture caused by European colonization (Walle, 2004). Native Americans have also been denied full access to key institutions in Western culture. Loss of cultural identity and social disorganization have set the stage for problems such as alcoholism, substance abuse, and depression (Walle, 2004). If psychologists are to help Native Americans cope with psychological disorders, they need to do so in a way that is sensitive to their culture, customs, and values. Efforts to prevent such disorders should focus on strengthening Native American cultural identity, pride, and cohesion. ■

( ) Learning Connections

◀◀ *Does Psychotherapy Work?* ▶▶

REVIEW:

15 According to the studies analyzed by Smith and Glass, the *least* effective form of therapy is
(a) Gestalt therapy,
(b) psychoanalysis,
(c) cognitive therapy,
(d) behavior therapy.

16 Cognitive therapy is probably best used along with drug therapy in the treatment of
(a) personality disorders,
(b) depression,
(c) anxiety,
(d) schizophrenia.

CRITICAL THINKING:
Justin swears he feels much better because of psychoanalysis. "I feel so much better now," he claims. Deborah swears by her experience with Gestalt therapy. Are these anecdotal endorsements acceptable as scientific evidence? Why or why not?

Go to
http://academic.cengage.com/psychology/rathus
for an interactive version of this review.

BIOLOGICAL THERAPIES

The kinds of therapy we have discussed are psychological in nature—forms of *psychotherapy*. Psychotherapies apply *psychological* principles to treatment, principles based on psychological knowledge of matters such as learning and motivation. People with psychological disorders are also often treated with biological therapies. Biological therapies apply what is known of people's *biological* structures and processes to the amelioration of psychological disorders. For example, they may work by altering events in the nervous system, as by changing the action of neurotransmitters. In this section, we discuss three biological, or medical, approaches to treating people with psychological disorders: drug therapy, electroconvulsive therapy, and psychosurgery. *What kinds of drug therapy are available for psychological disorders?*

─■─ Drug Therapy: In Search of the Magic Pill?

In the 1950s Fats Domino popularized the song "My Blue Heaven." Fats was singing about the sky and happiness. Today "blue heavens" is one of the street names for the 10-milligram dose of the antianxiety drug Valium. Clinicians prescribe Valium and other drugs for people with various psychological disorders.

Antianxiety Drugs Most antianxiety drugs, such as Valium and Serax, belong to the chemical class known as *benzodiazepines*. Antianxiety drugs are usually prescribed for outpatients who complain of generalized anxiety or panic attacks, although many people also use them as sleeping pills. Valium and other antianxiety drugs depress the activity of the central nervous system (CNS). The CNS, in turn, decreases sympathetic activity, reducing the heart rate, respiration rate, and nervousness and tension.

Many people come to tolerate antianxiety drugs very quickly. When tolerance occurs, dosages must be increased for the drug to remain effective.

Sedation (feelings of being tired or drowsy) is the most common side effect of antianxiety drugs. Problems associated with withdrawal from these drugs include **rebound anxiety.** That is, some people who have been using these drugs regularly report that their anxiety becomes worse than before once they discontinue them. Antianxiety drugs can induce physical dependence, as evidenced by withdrawal symptoms such as tremors, sweating, insomnia, and rapid heartbeat.

Antipsychotic Drugs People with schizophrenia are often given antipsychotic drugs (also called *major tranquilizers*). In most cases these drugs reduce agitation, delusions, and hallucinations. Many antipsychotic drugs, including phenothiazines (e.g., Thorazine) and clozapine (Clozaril) are thought to act by blocking dopamine receptors in the brain (Buckley et al., 2000; Sawa & Snyder, 2002). Research along these lines supports the theory that schizophrenia is connected with overactivity of the neurotransmitter dopamine.

Antidepressants People with major depression often take so-called **antidepressant** drugs. These drugs are also helpful for some people with eating disorders, panic disorder, obsessive–compulsive disorder, and social phobia (Bacaltchuk et al., 2000; Barlow et al., 2000; McElroy et al., 2000; Santonastaso et al., 2001). Problems in the regulation of noradrenaline and serotonin may be involved in eating and panic disorders as well as in depression. Antidepressants are believed to work by increasing levels of these neurotransmitters, which can affect both depression and the appetite (Schneider et al., 2003; C. L. White et al., 2000b). As noted in the section on the effectiveness of psychotherapy, however, cognitive therapy addresses irrational attitudes concerning weight and body shape, fosters normal

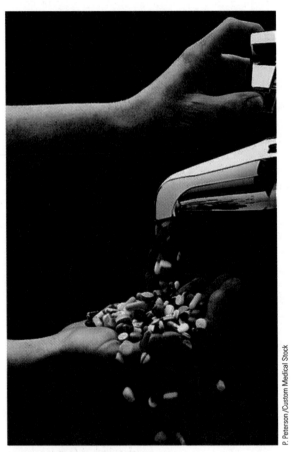

P. Peterson /Custom Medical Stock

■ **An Arsenal of Chemical Therapies**
Many drugs have been developed to combat psychological disorders. They include antianxiety drugs, antipsychotic drugs, antidepressants, and lithium.

Rebound anxiety Anxiety that can occur when one discontinues use of a tranquilizer.

Antidepressant Acting to relieve depression.

eating habits, and helps people resist the urges to binge and purge, often making therapy more effective than drugs for people with bulimia (Wilson et al., 2002). But when cognitive therapy does not help people with bulimia nervosa, drug therapy may do so (Walsh et al., 2000).

There are various antidepressants. Each increases the concentration of noradrenaline or serotonin in the brain (Frank & Kupfer, 2003). **Selective serotonin-reuptake inhibitors (SSRIs)** such as Prozac and Zoloft block the reuptake of serotonin by presynaptic neurons. As a result, serotonin remains in the synaptic cleft longer, influencing receiving neurons.

Antidepressant drugs must usually build up to a therapeutic level over several weeks. Because overdoses can be lethal, some people stay in a hospital during the buildup to prevent suicide attempts. There are also side effects, some of which are temporary, such as nausea, agitation, and weight gain.

Lithium   The ancient Greeks and Romans were among the first to use the metal lithium as a psychoactive drug. They prescribed mineral water—which contains lithium—for people with bipolar disorder. They had no inkling as to why this treatment sometimes helped. A salt of the metal lithium (lithium carbonate), in tablet form, flattens out cycles of manic behavior and depression in most people. It is not known exactly how lithium works, although it affects the functioning of neurotransmitters.

People with bipolar disorder may have to use lithium indefinitely, as a person with diabetes must use insulin to control the illness. Lithium also has been shown to have side effects such as hand tremors, memory impairment, and excessive thirst and urination (Kleindienst & Greil, 2003). Memory impairment is reported as the main reason why people discontinue lithium.

Does Drug Therapy Work?   There are thus a number of drugs available to treat psychological disorders. There is little question that drug therapy has helped many people with severe psychological disorders. For example, antipsychotic drugs largely account for the reduced need for the use of restraint and supervision (e.g., padded cells, straitjackets, hospitalization, and so on) with people diagnosed with schizophrenia. Antipsychotic drugs have allowed hundreds of thousands of former mental hospital residents to lead largely normal lives in the community, hold jobs, and maintain family lives. Most of the problems related to these drugs concern their side effects.

But many comparisons of psychotherapy (in the form of cognitive therapy) and drug therapy for depression suggest that cognitive therapy is as effective as, or more effective than, antidepressants (DeRubeis et al., 2005; Jacobi et al., 2002). Cognitive therapy appears to provide coping skills that reduce the risk of recurrence of depression once treatment ends (Hollon et al., 2005). Then again, at least one study suggests that a combination of cognitive therapy and antidepressant medication is superior to either treatment alone with chronically depressed people (Keller et al., 2000). On the other hand, SSRIs may also help prevent subsequent heart attacks in depressed people who have had prior heart attacks (Writing Committee for the ENRICHD Investigators, 2003).

A similar story holds for experiments comparing the effectiveness of cognitive-behavioral therapy and antidepressant medication in the treatment of panic disorder, obsessive–compulsive disorder, and bulimia nervosa. One study found that cognitive-behavioral therapy and the antidepressant imipramine are both helpful in treating panic disorder, but a combination of the psychological and biological treatments appears to be somewhat more helpful in the long run (Barlow et al., 2000). An Italian pilot study with 20 patients found that cognitive therapy was more likely than drug therapy to prevent relapse in the treatment of obsessive–compulsive disorder (Biondi & Picardi, 2005). A third study found that cognitive-behavioral therapy, antidepressant medication, and the combination of the two were all helpful in treating bulimia nervosa. At least in this study, cognitive-behavioral therapy was the most helpful of the three treatments, superior even to the combination of cognitive-behavioral therapy and the medicine (Jacobi et al., 2002). Perhaps patients who received cognitive-behavioral therapy alone developed higher beliefs in their own abilities to manage their problems (i.e., higher self-efficacy expectations).

Many psychologists and psychiatrists are comfortable with the short-term use of antianxiety drugs in helping clients manage periods of unusual anxiety or tension. Many

reflect & relate

Consider your own sociocultural background. In your experience, do people from your background express any particular attitudes toward people who use antianxiety drugs or antidepressants? Explain.

Selective serotonin-reuptake inhibitors (SSRIs) Antidepressant drugs that work by blocking the reuptake of serotonin by presynaptic neurons.

METHODS OF THERAPY

PSYCHOANALYTIC THERAPIES	HUMANISTIC THERAPIES	BEHAVIOR THERAPIES
Assume disorders stem from unresolved unconscious conflict (traditional) or within the context of disturbed social relationships (interpersonal psycho-therapy)	Assume disorders reflect feelings of alienation from one's genuine beliefs and feelings	Assume disorders reflect learning of mal-adaptive responses (such as maladaptive fear responses) or failure to learn adaptive responses (such as social skills)

Freud's consulting room.

Client-centered therapists provide a warm atmosphere in which clients feels free to explore their genuine feelings.

One way in which behavior therapists help clients overcome fears is to expose them to the feared object or situation under circumstances in which they remain relaxed.

Goals

• To strengthen ego functioning • To provide insight into unconscious conflict	• To help clients get in touch with parts of themselves that they have "disowned" • To help clients actualize their unique desires and abilities • To help clients integrate conflicting parts of their personality	• To help clients extinguish inappropriate fears • To help clients approach situations they have avoided • To help clients learn social skills

Methods

• "Talk therapy"—nondirective in traditional analysis; more direction in ego analysis and interpersonal psychotherapy (ITP) • Free association • Analysis of dreams	• Client-centered therapy is nondirective • Client-centered therapists provide atmosphere of unconditional positive regard, empathy, and genuineness • Gestalt therapists are directive	• Exposure therapies (including systematic desensitization, virtual therapy, modeling) • Operant methods (including token economy) • Aversive conditioning for self-defeating habits • Social skills training (including assertive training)

Comments

• Most effective with educated, highly verbal clients • Ego analysts and interpersonal therapists find value in directly encouraging changes in self-defeating behavior	• Client-centered therapy widely used in college and university counseling centers to help students make personal and academic decisions • Gestalt therapy popular during "human potential movement" of 1960s and 1970s; still practiced	• Developed treatment for problems for which there were previously no effective treatments (e.g., smoking, phobias) • Virtual therapy is new "wrinkle" in methods that have been used for half a century • Possibly heading toward integration with cognitive therapies (cognitive-behavioral therapy, or CBT)

Principal proponent:
Sigmund Freud (1856–1939) formulated his theory of personality a century ago. method of therapy, psychoanalysis, His achieved greatest prominence in the 1940s and 1950s.

Principal proponents:
Carl Rogers (1902–1970) developed client-centered therapy in the mid-20th century. Fritz Perls (1893–1970) originated Gestalt therapy, which reached its greatest prominence in the 1960s and 1970s.

Principal Proponents:
Joseph Wolpe (1915–1997) introduced systematic desensitization in the 1950s. Albert Bandura integrated behavioral and cognitive factors in forming his therapeutic methods, such as modeling.

Sigmund Freud

Carl Rogers

Albert Bandura

(continued)

METHODS OF THERAPY (CONTINUED)

COGNITIVE THERAPIES

Assume disorders reflect cognitive distortions or errors such as excessive self-blame, pessimism, perfectionism, and rumination about negative events

David Buffington/Getty Images

Cognitive therapists encourage clients to become aware of and correct cognitive errors and distortions, and to challenge irrational beliefs.

Goals
- To help clients become aware of self-defeating beliefs and attitudes that create and compound their problems
- To help clients challenge and change the self-defeating beliefs and attitudes to reduce negative feelings and solve problems

Methods
- Teach clients to focus on and become aware of "automatic" cognitive errors/irrational beliefs
- Teach clients to scientifically evaluate their faulty logic and irrational beliefs
- Help clients change cognitive errors and irrational beliefs
- Provide behavioral "homework" consistent with more helpful beliefs

Comments
- Possibly as or more effective than drug therapy in treatment of depression
- Making inroads into treatment of schizophrenia and personality disorders
- Possibly heading toward integration with behavior therapy

Principal proponents:
Aaron Beck introduced his approach, "cognitive therapy," in the 1960s. Albert Ellis first developed rational-emotive therapy (RET) in the 1950s and 1960s. He recently changed the name to rational emotive behavior therapy (REBT).

Michael Fenichel, www.fenichel.com

Aaron Beck and Albert Ellis

BIOLOGICAL THERAPIES

Assume that disorders reflect the interaction of genetic vulnerability with other factors, such as imbalance of neurotransmitters or hormones, or situational stressors; for example, depression may reflect the interaction of a genetic vulnerability with low serotonin levels and a failure experience

P. Peterson/Custom Medical Stock

Many drugs have been used to combat psychological disorders.

Goals
- To decrease feelings of anxiety and depression
- To lessen mood swings in bipolar disorder
- To lessen or remove the symptoms of schizophrenia—especially the positive or bizarre symptoms

Methods
- Antianxiety drugs
- "Antidepressant" drugs (also used with panic disorder, eating disorders, and others)
- Lithium compounds for bipolar disorder
- Antipsychotic drugs for schizophrenia
- Electroconvulsive shock therapy (ECT) for treatment of depression that resists psychotherapy and drug therapy
- Psychosurgery (rarely used)

Comments
- "Antidepressants" are finding applications with a wide variety of disorders
- More effective with positive than negative symptoms of schizophrenia
- Psychologists generally prefer psychotherapy to biological therapies

Najilah Feamy/Stock Boston, LLC

Electroconvulsive therapy (ECT) is mainly used for severe cases of depression in which other therapies have failed.

people, however, use antianxiety drugs routinely to dull the arousal stemming from anxiety-producing lifestyles or interpersonal problems. Rather than make the often painful decisions required to confront their problems and change their lives, they prefer to take a pill.

One study found that both tranquilizers and CBT (stress management training plus imagined exposure to the fearful stimuli) helped phobic people get through a dental session. However, 70% of those who received cognitive-behavioral therapy continued to go for dental treatment, as compared with only 20% of those who took the tranquilizer (Thom et al., 2000). CBT apparently taught people in the study coping skills, whereas the tranquilizers afforded only temporary relief.

In sum, drug therapy is effective for some disorders that do not respond to psychotherapy alone. Yet common sense and research evidence suggest that psychotherapy is preferable for problems such as anxiety and mild depression. No chemical can show a person how to change an idea or solve an interpersonal problem.

——■— Electroconvulsive Therapy

What is electroconvulsive therapy? **Electroconvulsive therapy (ECT)** is a biological form of therapy for psychological disorders that was introduced by the Italian psychiatrist Ugo Cerletti in 1939. Cerletti had noted that some slaughterhouses used electric shock to render animals unconscious. The shocks also produced convulsions. Along with other European researchers of the period, Cerletti erroneously believed that convulsions were incompatible with schizophrenia and other major psychological disorders.

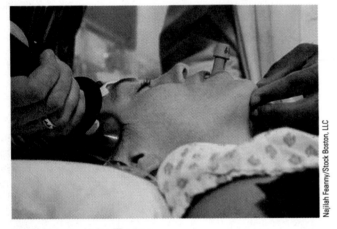

ECT was originally used for a variety of psychological disorders. Because of the advent of antipsychotic drugs, however, it is now used mainly for people with major depression who do not respond to antidepressants (Thase, 2004).

People typically obtain one ECT treatment three times a week for up to 10 sessions. Electrodes are attached to the temples and an electrical current strong enough to produce a convulsion is induced. The shock causes unconsciousness, so the patient does not recall it. Nevertheless, patients are given a **sedative** so that they are asleep during the treatment.

ECT is controversial for many reasons, such as the fact that many professionals are distressed by the thought of passing an electric shock through a patient's head and producing convulsions. There are also side effects, including memory problems (Lisanby et al., 2000; Weiner, 2000). Research suggests that for most people, however, cognitive impairment tends to be temporary (Eranti & McLoughlin, 2003).

Najilah Feanny/Stock Boston, LLC

■ Electroconvulsive Therapy
In ECT, electrodes are placed on each side of the patient's head and a current is passed between them, inducing a seizure. ECT is used mainly in cases of major depression when antidepressant drugs and psychotherapy are not sufficient.

Electroconvulsive therapy (ECT) Treatment of disorders like major depression by passing an electric current (that causes a convulsion) through the head.

Sedative A drug that relieves nervousness or agitation or puts one to sleep.

Psychosurgery Surgery intended to promote psychological changes or to relieve disordered behavior.

Prefrontal lobotomy The severing or destruction of a section of the frontal lobe of the brain.

——■— Psychosurgery

Psychosurgery is more controversial than ECT. *What is psychosurgery? How is it used to treat psychological disorders?* The best-known modern technique, **prefrontal lobotomy,** has been used with people with severe disorders. In this method, a picklike instrument severs the nerve pathways that link the prefrontal lobes of the brain to the thalamus. It is intended to sever thought from emotion and enable severely disturbed patients to regain control.

The method was pioneered by the Portuguese neurologist Antonio Egas Moniz and was brought to the United States in the 1930s. The theoretical rationale for the operation was vague and misguided and Moniz's reports of success were exaggerated. Nevertheless, by 1950 prefrontal lobotomies had been performed on thousands of people in an effort to reduce violence and agitation. Anecdotal evidence of the method's unreliable outcomes is found in an ironic footnote to history. ◆ **Truth or Fiction Revisited:** One of Dr. Moniz's "failures" did indeed shoot him, leaving a bullet lodged in his spine and paralyzing his legs.

Prefrontal lobotomy also has side effects, including hyperactivity and distractibility, impaired learning ability, overeating, apathy and withdrawal, epileptic-type seizures, reduced creativity, and, now and then, death. Because of these side effects, and because of the advent of antipsychotic drugs, this method has been largely discontinued in the United States.

() **Learning Connections**

 Biological Therapies

REVIEW:

17 Memory impairment is reported as the main reason that people stop using
 (a) antianxiety medication,
 (b) lithium,
 (c) antidepressants,
 (d) major tranquilizers.

18 Of the following treatments for psychological disorders, the least likely to be used is
 (a) antianxiety medication,
 (b) antidepressant medication,
 (c) electroconvulsive therapy,
 (d) prefrontal lobotomy.

Learning Connections

19 Antidepressants heighten the action of
 (a) GABA,
 (b) dopamine,
 (c) serotonin,
 (d) corticosteroids.

20 ECT is mainly used to treat severe cases of
 (a) depression,
 (b) anxiety,
 (c) bipolar disorder,
 (d) schizophrenia.

CRITICAL THINKING:
Why are psychologists concerned about prescribing antianxiety drugs for the stresses, anxieties, and tension of daily life? Are there times when it is appropriate to prescribe medical treatment for a psychological disorder?

Go to www
http://academic.cengage.com/psychology/rathus
for an interactive version of this review.

RECITE—*An Active Summary*™

 Recite to Go! *Don't have time to study right now? You can study on the go!*
Go to your companion website and download an audio version of this review section to your media player. You can also access an interactive flash-card version of this review from your website.

1. What is psychotherapy?	Psychotherapy is a systematic interaction between a therapist and a client that uses psychological principles to help the client overcome psychological disorders or adjust to problems in living.
2. How have people with psychological problems and disorders been treated throughout the ages?	Mostly badly. It has been generally assumed that psychological disorders represented possession due to witchcraft or divine retribution, and cruel methods such as exorcism were used to try to rid the person of evil spirits. Compassionate treatment is a relatively recent development.
3. How do psychoanalysts conduct a traditional Freudian psychoanalysis?	The main method of psychoanalysis is free association, but dream analysis and interpretations are also used.
4. How do modern psychoanalytic approaches differ from traditional psychoanalysis?	Modern approaches are briefer and more directive, and the therapist and client usually sit face to face.

5. What is Carl Rogers's method of client-centered therapy?	Client-centered therapy uses nondirective methods: The therapist shows unconditional positive regard, empathy, and genuineness.
6. What is Fritz Perls's method of Gestalt therapy?	Perls's directive method aims to help people integrate conflicting parts of their personality. He aimed to make clients aware of conflict and make choices despite fear.
7. What is behavior therapy?	Behavior therapy relies on principles of learning (e.g., conditioning and observational learning) to help clients develop adaptive behavior patterns and discontinue maladaptive ones.
8. What are some behavior-therapy methods for reducing fears?	These include flooding, systematic desensitization, and modeling. Virtual therapy is a new method for desensitizing patients to fears.
9. How do behavior therapists use aversive conditioning to help people break bad habits?	Aversive conditioning repeatedly pairs clients' self-defeating behaviors (e.g., excessive drinking or smoking) with aversive stimuli so that the goals become repulsive rather than tempting.
10. How do behavior therapists apply principles of operant conditioning in behavior modification?	These are behavior therapy methods that foster adaptive behavior through principles of reinforcement. Examples include token economies, successive approximation, social skills training, and biofeedback training.
11. What is cognitive therapy?	Cognitive therapy aims to give clients insight into irrational beliefs and cognitive distortions and replace these cognitive errors with rational beliefs and accurate perceptions.
12. What is Aaron Beck's method of cognitive therapy?	Aaron Beck notes that clients develop emotional problems such as depression because of cognitive errors that lead them to minimize accomplishments and catastrophize failures. Beck teaches clients how to scientifically dispute cognitive errors.
13. What is Albert Ellis's method of rational emotive behavior therapy (REBT)?	Ellis originated rational emotive behavior therapy, which holds that people's beliefs *about* events shape their responses to them. Irrational beliefs, such as the beliefs that we must have social approval or achieve perfection, can worsen problems. Ellis argues clients out of such beliefs.
14. What are the advantages and disadvantages of group therapy?	Group therapy is more economical than individual therapy. Moreover, group members benefit from the social support and experiences of other members. However, some clients cannot disclose their problems to a group or risk group disapproval.
15. What is family therapy?	In family therapy, one or more families make up the group. Family therapy undertaken from the "systems approach" modifies family interactions to enhance the growth of individuals in the family and the family as a whole.
16. What has research shown about the effectiveness of psychotherapy?	Statistical analyses such as meta-analysis show that people who obtain most forms of psychotherapy fare better than people who do not. Psychoanalytic and client-centered approaches are most helpful with highly verbal and motivated individuals. Cognitive and behavior therapies are probably most effective.
17. What kinds of drug therapy are available for psychological disorders?	Antipsychotic drugs help many people with schizophrenia by blocking the action of dopamine receptors. Antidepressants help many people with depression by raising levels of serotonin available to the brain. Lithium often helps people with bipolar disorder.
18. What is electroconvulsive therapy (ECT)?	In ECT an electrical current is passed through the temples, inducing a seizure and frequently relieving severe depression. ECT is controversial because of side effects such as loss of memory and because nobody knows why it works.
19. What is psychosurgery? How is it used to treat psychological disorders?	The prefrontal lobotomy, a type of psychosurgery, attempts to alleviate agitation by severing nerve pathways in the brain. The best-known psychosurgery technique, prefrontal lobotomy, has been largely discontinued because of side effects.

Key Terms

Virtual therapy   472

Psychotherapy   473

Asylum   474

Psychoanalysis   475

Catharsis   475

Free association   476

Resistance   476

Transference   476

Wish fulfillment   477

Ego analyst   477

Interpersonal psychotherapy
(ITP)   477

Client-centered therapy   478

Unconditional positive regard   479

Empathy   479

Frame of reference   479

Genuineness   479

Gestalt therapy   479

Behavior therapy   480

Systematic desensitization   481

Hierarchy   481

Modeling   481

Aversive conditioning   482

Rapid smoking   482

Eye-movement desensitization and
reprocessing (EMDR)   483

Token economy   484

Successive approximations   484

Biofeedback training (BFT)   484

Self-monitoring   484

Behavior rehearsal   484

Feedback   484

Cognitive therapy   486

Rational emotive behavior therapy
(REBT)   488

Cognitive-behavior therapy
(CBT)   488

Meta-analysis   492

Specific factors   494

Nonspecific factors   494

Rebound anxiety   496

Antidepressant   496

Selective serotonin-reuptake
inhibitors (SSRIs)   497

Electroconvulsive therapy (ECT)   500

Sedative   500

Psychosurgery   500

Prefrontal lobotomy   500

Active Learning Resources

Visit Your Companion Website for This Book

http://academic.cengage.com/psychology/rathus

Check out this companion website where you will find online resources directly linked to your book. This is where you'll access the videos highlighted in your Video Connections feature. You can answer the questions online and email them to your professor. In addition you'll find downloadable audio review material, interactive versions of the study aids, Power Visuals for mastering and reviewing key concepts, as well as quizzing, and much more!

CENGAGENOW™

http://academic.cengage.com

Need help studying? This site is your one-stop study shop. Take a Pre-Test and Cengage NOW will generate a Personalized Study Plan based on your test results. The Study Plan will identify the topics you need to review and direct you to online resources to help you master those topics. You can then take a Post-Test to help you determine the concepts you have mastered and what you still need to work on. In addition you can access interactive media including the videos highlighted in your Video Connections box.

Author Blog

What does your author Spence Rathus have to say about the state of psychology? Visit your companion website every Tuesday and click on "Author Blog." This is where he'll talk about the most recent controversies and hot topics in psychology. This will keep you up to date with what your author is thinking and give you great insight into modern psychology.

CHAPTER 14

Social Psychology

Steve Raymer/Corbis

truth or fiction?

Go to

Go to http://academic.cengage.com/pstchology/rathus for an interactive version of this Truth or Fiction feature.

preview

Consider some news from Iraq. On May 4, a suicide bomber in the Kurdish city of Erbil targets police recruits. He kills himself along with another 60 people, and wounds 150. Victims' bodies are loaded into ambulances, pickup trucks, and onto the backs of donkeys. Dozens of the wounded are taken to hospitals. Two days later, a suicide bomber detonates the explosives strapped around his torso in a crowded market at midday in a town 25 miles southeast of Baghdad. Sixteen people die and more than 40 are wounded. On July 25, a bomber wrapped in explosives ignites himself next to an oil tanker south of Baghdad, killing 59. In an orgy of a dozen suicide bombings in Baghdad on September 14, more than 160 Iraqis are killed and another 600 wounded.

As noted by political scientist Mark Danner of the University of California, "There have been suicide truck bombs, suicide tanker bombs, suicide police cars, suicide bombers on foot, suicide bombers posing as police officers, suicide bombers posing as soldiers, even suicide bombers on bicycles" (2005, p. 52). And in the United States, of course, there have been suicide terrorists using fully fueled airplanes as bombs.

Although you might think of suicide terrorism as a recent phenomenon, it dates back thousands of years (Pastor, 2004). But we have become most recently aware of suicide terrorism by strikes throughout the Muslim world, in Israel, and—with the attacks on New York, Washington, D.C., Madrid, and London—in the Western world. The word "suicide" in the phrase "suicide bomber" leads people to turn to psychologists for understanding, with the idea that something must be very wrong psychologically with these terrorists (Pastor, 2004). But many social scientists assert that suicide terrorists have no telltale psychological profile (Consortium of Social Science Associations, 2003; Lester et al., 2004). Social psychologist Philip Zimbardo (2004) argues that we must look to the situationist perspective to understand suicide terrorism.

The **situationist perspective** studies the ways in which people can be goaded by social influences into doing things that are not necessarily consistent with their personalities. In particular, Zimbardo (2004) has investigated the relative ease with which "ordinary" men and women can be incited to behave in evil ways.

The situationist perspective is part of the field of **social psychology.** *What is social psychology?* Social psychology studies the nature and causes of behavior and mental processes in social situations. The social psychological topics we discuss in this chapter include attitudes, social perception, social influence, and group behavior. As we explore each of these, we will ask what they might offer to those of us who have difficulty imagining why people would surrender their own lives to take the lives of others.

AP/Wide World Photos

■ **London, July 7, 2005**
Commuters coming into London on this summer morning were accompanied by four suicide bombers, who detonated the bombs, and themselves, at the peak of rush hour on three subway trains and aboard a bus. More than 50 people died, along with the bombers, and 700 were wounded. The bombers were apparently expressing their displeasure over Britain's support of the United States in Iraq.

Situationist perspective The view that social influence can goad people into doing things that are inconsistent with their usual behavior.

Social psychology The field of psychology that studies the nature and causes of people's thoughts and behavior in social situations.

ATTITUDES: "THE GOOD, THE BAD, AND THE UGLY"

How do you feel about abortion, stem cell research, and exhibiting the Ten Commandments in courthouses? These are hot-button topics because people have strong **attitudes** toward them. They each give rise to cognitive evaluations (such as approval or disapproval), feelings (such as liking, disliking, or something stronger), and behavioral tendencies (such as approach or avoidance). *What are attitudes?* Attitudes are behavioral and cognitive tendencies that are expressed by evaluating particular people, places, or things with favor or disfavor. Although I asked you how you "feel," attitudes are not just feelings or emotions. Many psychologists view thinking—or judgment—as more basic. Feelings and behavior follow.

Attitudes are largely learned, and they affect behavior. They can foster love or hate. They can give rise to helping behavior or to mass destruction. They can lead to social conflict or to the resolution of conflicts. Attitudes can change, but not easily. Most people do not change their religion or political affiliation without serious reflection or coercion.

reflect & relate

What attitudes are likely to be held by suicide terrorists?

The A–B Problem: Do We Act in Accord with Our Beliefs?

Is our behavior consistent with our attitudes—that is, with our beliefs and feelings? *Do people do as they think? (For example, do people really vote their consciences?)* When we are free to do as we wish, the answer is often yes. But, as indicated by the term **A–B problem,** there are exceptions. ◆ **Truth or Fiction Revisited:** In fact, the links between attitudes (A) and behaviors (B) tend to be weak to moderate. For example, research reveals that attitudes toward health-related behaviors such as excessive drinking, smoking, and drunken driving do not necessarily predict these behaviors (Stacy et al., 1994).

Several factors affect the likelihood that we can predict behavior from attitudes:

1. *Specificity.* We can better predict specific behavior from specific attitudes than from global attitudes. For example, we can better predict church attendance by knowing people's attitudes toward church attendance than by knowing whether they are Christian.

2. *Strength of attitudes.* Strong attitudes are more likely to determine behavior than weak attitudes (Huskinson & Haddock, 2004; Petty et al., 1997). A person who believes that the nation's destiny depends on Democrats taking control of Congress is more likely to vote than a person who leans toward that party but does not believe that elections make much difference.

3. *Vested interest.* People are more likely to act on their attitudes when they have a vested interest in the outcome (Lehman & Crano, 2002). People are more likely to vote for (or against) unionization of their workplace when they believe that their job security depends on it.

4. *Accessibility.* People are more likely to behave in accord with their attitudes when they are accessible—that is, when they are brought to mind (Kallgren et al., 2000; Petty et al., 1997). This is why politicians attempt to "get out the vote" by means of media blitzes just prior to an election. It does little good to have supporters who forget them on election day. Attitudes with a strong emotional impact are more accessible, which is one reason that politicians strive to get their supporters "worked up" over issues.

■ **Do People Always Vote Their "Conscience"?**
The A–B problem refers to the research finding that people do not always act in accord with their attitudes.

AP/Wide World Photos

reflect & relate

Can you think of recent elections in which politicians have tried to get out the vote by working people up over the issues? What issues?

Attitude Formation

You were not born a Republican or a Democrat. You were not born a Catholic, Jew, or Muslim—although your parents may have practiced one of these religions when you came along. *Where do attitudes come from?* Political, religious, and other attitudes are learned

Attitude An enduring mental representation of a person, place, or thing that evokes an emotional response and related behavior.

A–B problem The issue of how well we can predict behavior on the basis of attitudes.

or derived from cognitive processes (Bizer et al., 2004; Dovidio et al., 2004). In this section we describe some of those processes.

Conditioning may play a role in attitude formation (Walther et al., 2005). Laboratory experiments have shown that attitudes toward national groups can be influenced by associating them with positive words (such as *gift* or *happy*) or negative words (such as *ugly* or *failure*) (De Houwer et al., 2001). Parents often reward children for saying and doing things that agree with their own attitudes. Patriotism is encouraged by showing children approval when they sing the national anthem or wave the flag.

Attitudes formed through direct experience may be stronger and easier to recall, but we also acquire attitudes by observing, listening to, or reading the works of other people. The approval or disapproval of peers leads adolescents to prefer short or long hair, baggy jeans, or preppy sweaters. How do the things you read in newspapers or hear on the radio influence your attitudes?

Cognitive Appraisal   Nevertheless, attitude formation is not fully mechanical. People are also motivated to understand the environment so that they can make predictions and exercise some control over it (Bizer et al., 2004; Wood, 2000). People also sometimes form or change attitudes on the basis of new information (Dovidio et al., 2004; Petty et al., 1999; Walther et al., 2005). For example, we may believe that a car is more reliable than we had thought if a survey by *Consumer Reports* finds that it has an excellent repair record. Even so, initial attitudes act as cognitive anchors (Wegener et al., 2001; Wood, 2000). We often judge new ideas in terms of how much they deviate from our existing attitudes. Accepting larger deviations requires more information processing—in other words, more intellectual work (Petty et al., 1999; Tormala & Petty, 2004). For this reason, perhaps, great deviations—such as changes from liberal to conservative attitudes, or vice versa—are apt to be resisted.

Changing Attitudes Through Persuasion

Let advertisers spend the same amount of money improving their product that they do on advertising and they wouldn't have to advertise it.
—WILL ROGERS

Rogers's comment sounds on the mark, but he was probably wrong. It does little good to have a wonderful product if it remains a secret. *Can you really change people's attitudes and behavior?*

The **elaboration likelihood model** describes the ways in which people respond to persuasive messages (Crano, 2000; Salovey & Wegener, 2003). Consider two routes to persuading others to change attitudes. The first, or central, route inspires thoughtful consideration of arguments and evidence. The second, or peripheral, route associates objects with positive or negative cues. When politicians avow, "This bill is supported by liberals (or conservatives)," they are seeking predictable, knee-jerk reactions rather than careful consideration of a bill's merits. Other cues are rewards (such as a smile or a hug), punishments (such as parental disapproval), and such factors as the trustworthiness and attractiveness of the communicator.

Advertisements, which are a form of persuasive communication, also rely on central and peripheral routes. Some ads focus on the quality of the product (central route). Others attempt to associate the product with appealing images (peripheral route). Ads for Total cereal, which highlight its nutritional benefits, provide information about the quality of the product. So, too, did the "Pepsi Challenge" taste-test ads, which claimed that Pepsi tastes better than Coca-Cola. Marlboro cigarette ads that focus on the masculine, rugged image of the "Marlboro man"[1] offer no information about the product itself. Nor do ads that show football players heading for Disney World or choosing a brand of beer.

reflect & relate

How do you think cultural conditioning has influenced the attitudes of suicide terrorists?

reflect & relate

Would it be easy to change your attitudes toward your own religion or the religions of other people? How do your early religious experiences serve as "cognitive anchors"?

Elaboration likelihood model The view that persuasive messages are evaluated (elaborated) on the basis of central and peripheral cues.

---

[1] The actor in the original TV commercials died of lung cancer.

In this section we look at one central factor in persuasion—the nature of the message—and three peripheral factors: the messenger, the context of the message, and the audience.

The Persuasive Message: Say What? Say How? Say How Often? How do we respond when TV commercials are repeated until we have memorized the dimples on the actors' faces? Research suggests that familiarity breeds content, not contempt (Macrae et al., 2002; Zajonc, 2001; Zizak & Reber, 2004). ◆ **Truth or Fiction Revisited:** It appears that repeated exposure to people and things as diverse as the following enhances their appeal:

- political candidates (who are seen in repeated TV commercials)
- photos of African Americans
- photos of college students
- abstract art
- classical music

When trying to persuade someone, is it helpful or self-defeating to alert them to the arguments presented by the opposition? In two-sided arguments, the communicator recounts the arguments of the opposition in an effort to refute them. In research concerning a mock trial, college undergraduates were presented with two-sided arguments—those of the prosecution and those of the defendant (McKenzie et al., 2002). When one argument was weak, the college "jurors" expressed more confidence in their decision than when they did not hear the other side at all. Theologians and politicians sometimes forewarn their followers about the arguments of the opposition and then refute each one. Forewarning creates a kind of psychological immunity to them (Jacks & Devine, 2000).

It would be nice to think that people are too sophisticated to be persuaded by emotional factors in attitude formation, but they usually aren't (DeSteno et al., 2004). Consider the **fear appeal:** Women who are warned of the dire risk they run if they fail to be screened for breast cancer are more likely to obtain mammograms than women who are informed of the *benefits* of mammography (Ruiter et al., 2001). Interestingly, although sun tanning has been shown to increase the likelihood of skin cancer, warnings against suntanning were shown to be more effective when students were warned of risks to their *appearance* (e.g., premature aging, wrinkling, and scarring of the skin) than when the warning dealt with the risk to their health (Jones & Leary, 1994). That is, students informed of tanning's cosmetic effects were more likely to say they would protect themselves from the sun than were students informed about the risk of cancer. Fear appeals are most effective when the audience believes that the risks are serious—as in causing wrinkles!—and that the audience members can change their behavior to avert the risks—as in preventing cancer or wrinkling (Schneider et al., 2001).

Audiences also tend to believe arguments that appear to run counter to the vested interests of the communicator (Lehman & Crano, 2002). If the president of Chrysler or General Motors said that Toyotas and Hondas were superior, you can bet that we would prick up our ears.

The Persuasive Communicator: Whom Do You Trust? Would you go to a doctor who admitted he or she was behind the times? Would you buy a used car from a person who had been convicted of larceny? Research shows that persuasive communicators are characterized by expertise, trustworthiness, attractiveness, or similarity to their audiences (Petty et al., 1997). Because of the adoration of their fans, sports superstars such as Tiger Woods are the most valuable endorsers.

TV news anchors enjoy high prestige. One study (Mullen et al., 1987) found that before the

Fear appeal A type of persuasive communication that influences behavior on the basis of arousing fear instead of rational analysis of the issues.

■ **Most Valuable Endorsers?**
Advertisers use a combination of central and peripheral cues to sell their products. Why do advertisers enlist Tiger Woods and Catherine Zeta-Jones to promote their products and services?

1984 presidential election, the late ABC newscaster Peter Jennings had shown significantly more favorable facial expressions when reporting on Ronald Reagan than when reporting on Walter Mondale. Tom Brokaw of NBC showed no favoritism. The researchers also found that a higher percentage of viewers of ABC News voted for Reagan than viewers of NBC News. Did Jennings subtly persuade viewers to vote for Reagan? Perhaps he did in a number of cases. But viewers do not simply absorb everything the media feed them. People find it painful when they are confronted with information that counters their own views (Foerster et al., 2000). Therefore, they often show **selective avoidance** and **selective exposure** (Lavine et al., 2005). That is, they switch channels when the news coverage counters their own attitudes. They also seek communicators who share their views. Thus, Reagan supporters may have favored Jennings over Brokaw.

The Context of the Message: "Get 'Em in a Good Mood"   You are too shrewd to let someone persuade you by buttering you up, but perhaps someone you know would be influenced by a sip of wine, a bite of cheese, and a sincere compliment. Aspects of the immediate environment, such as music, increase the likelihood of persuasion. When we are in a good mood, we apparently are less likely to evaluate the situation carefully (Park & Banaji, 2000; Petty et al., 1997).

It is also counterproductive to call your friends idiots when they differ with you—even though their ideas are bound to be "foolish" if they do not agree with yours. Agreement and praise are more effective ways to encourage others to embrace your views. Appear sincere, or else your compliments will look manipulative. (It seems unfair to let out this information.)

The Persuaded Audience   Why can some people say no to salespeople? Why do others enrich the lives of every door-to-door salesperson? It may be that people with high self-esteem and low social anxiety are more likely to resist social pressure (Ellickson et al., 2001).

A classic study by Schwartz and Gottman (1976) describes the cognitive nature of the social anxiety that can make it difficult to refuse requests. They found that people who comply with unreasonable requests are more apt to report thoughts such as:

- "I was worried about what the other person would think of me if I refused."
- "It is better to help others than to be self-centered."
- "The other person might be hurt or insulted if I refused."

People who refuse unreasonable requests reported thoughts like these:

- "It doesn't matter what the other person thinks of me."
- "I am perfectly free to say no."
- "This request is unreasonable."

Changing Attitudes and Behavior by Means of Cognitive Dissonance: "I Think, Therefore I Am . . . Consistent"?

What is cognitive-dissonance theory? According to **cognitive-dissonance theory,** people are thinking creatures who seek consistency in their behaviors and their attitudes—that is, their views of the world (Albarracín & Wyer, 2000). People must apparently mentally represent the world accurately to predict and control events. Consistency in beliefs, attitudes, and behavior helps make the world seem like a predictable place. Therefore, if we find ourselves in the uncomfortable spot where two cherished ideas conflict, we are motivated to reduce the discrepancy.

In the first and still one of the best-known studies on cognitive dissonance, one group of participants received $1 (worth about $10 today) for telling someone else that a boring task was interesting (Festinger & Carlsmith, 1959). Members of a second group received $20 (worth about $200 today) to describe the chore positively. Both groups were paid to engage in **attitude-discrepant behavior**—that is, behavior that ran counter to what they actually thought. After presenting their fake enthusiasm for the boring task, the participants were asked to rate their own liking for it. Ironically, those who were paid *less* rated the task as actually more interesting than their better-paid colleagues reported. Similarly, being

Selective avoidance Diverting one's attention from information that is inconsistent with one's attitudes.

Selective exposure Deliberately seeking and attending to information that is consistent with one's attitudes.

Cognitive-dissonance theory The view that we are motivated to make our cognitions or beliefs consistent.

Attitude-discrepant behavior Behavior inconsistent with an attitude that may have the effect of modifying an attitude.

compelled by the law to recycle can lead to people's supporting recycling as opposed to throwing out all trash and garbage in a bundle.

Learning theorists (see Chapter 6) might predict a different outcome—that the more we are reinforced for doing something (given more money, for example), the more we should like it (not find the task quite as boring, that is). But that is not what happened here. Cognitive-dissonance theorists rightly predicted that because the ideas (cognitions) of (a) "I was paid very little" and (b) "I told someone that this assignment was interesting" are dissonant, people will tend to engage in **effort justification.** The discomfort of cognitive dissonance motivates people to explain their behavior to themselves in such a way that unpleasant undertakings seem worth it. Participants who were paid only $1 may have justified their lie by concluding that they may not have been lying in the first place. ◆ **Truth or Fiction Revisited:** As another example of effort justification, we do tend to appreciate things more when we have to work for them.

━━■━ Prejudice and Discrimination

Prejudice is an attitude toward a group that leads people to evaluate members of that group negatively—even though they have never met them. ◆ **Truth or Fiction Revisited:** Prejudiced people have in fact condemned billions of other people without ever meeting them or learning their names. On a cognitive level, prejudice is linked to expectations that members of the target group will behave poorly, say, in the workplace, or engage in criminal behavior or terrorism. On an emotional level, prejudice is associated with negative feelings such as fear, dislike, or hatred (No, 2004). In behavioral terms, prejudice is connected with avoidance, aggression, and discrimination. Prejudice is the most troubling kind of attitude. It is connected with the genocide of millions of people.

One form of behavior that results from prejudice is discrimination. Discrimination takes many forms, including denial of access to jobs, housing, and the voting booth.

Stereotypes   Are Jewish Americans shrewd and ambitious? Are African Americans superstitious and musical? Are gay men and lesbians unfit for military service? Such ideas are **stereotypes**—fixed, conventional attitudes toward certain groups that lead people to view members of those groups in a biased fashion.

Some stereotypes are positive rather than negative, such as the cultural stereotypes about physically attractive people. By and large, we assume that "good things come in pretty packages." Attractive children and adults are judged and treated more positively than their unattractive peers (Langlois et al., 2000). We expect attractive people to be poised, sociable, popular, intelligent, mentally healthy, fulfilled, persuasive, and successful in their jobs and marriages (Eagly et al., 1991; Feingold, 1992b).

Attractive people are more likely to be judged innocent of crimes in mock jury experiments and observational studies (Mazzella & Feingold, 1994). When they are found guilty, they are given less severe sentences. Perhaps we assume that attractive people have less need to resort to deviant behavior to achieve their goals. Even when they have erred, perhaps they will be more likely to change their evil ways.

Sources of Prejudice   The sources of prejudice are many and varied:

1. *Dissimilarity.* We are apt to like people who share our attitudes. In forming impressions of others, we are influenced by attitudinal similarity and dissimilarity (Duckitt et al., 2002). People of different religions and races often have different backgrounds, however, giving rise to dissimilar attitudes. Even when people of different races share important values, they may assume that they do not.
2. *Social conflict.* There is often social and economic conflict between people of different races and religions (Duckitt & Fisher, 2003). For example, Californian Mexican Americans and Africans Americans compete for many jobs, giving rise to harsh attitudes (Rosales et al., 2001).
3. *Social learning.* Children acquire some attitudes from other people, especially their parents. Children tend to imitate their parents, and parents reinforce their children

Effort justification In cognitive-dissonance theory, the tendency to seek justification (acceptable reasons) for strenuous efforts.

Stereotype A fixed, conventional idea about a group.

Video Connections

Stereotype Threat

LEARNING OBJECTIVES

■ To understand some of the stereotypes that exist in our society, and how they affect people's behavior.

■ To understand the theory of stereotype threat and how it is applied.

■ Explain how Claude Steele induced and reduced stereotype threat in his experiments.

APPLIED LESSON

1 What is the theory of stereotype threat, and what is its effect on people?

2 Have you ever wondered whether people from your ethnic background or gender can do something as well as people from another ethnic background or gender? How did your uncertainty make you feel?

CRITICAL THINKING

Agree or disagree with the following statement and support your answer: The solution to stereotype threat lies in society and not in the individual. (Watch out for overgeneralizations.)

"Nobody ever takes it for granted that I am very skilled at what I do," says this young mathematician. Just about everybody has experienced stereotype threat at one time or another. How does it affect us, and what can we do to combat it?

Watch this video!

Go to www

your companion website at
http://academic.cengage.com/psychology/rathus
Click on the Video Connections tab under this chapter.

---

for doing so (Duckitt et al., 2002). In this way prejudices can be transmitted from generation to generation.

The mass media also perpetuate stereotypes. TV commercials tend to portray European Americans, especially men, as more prominent and wielding more authority than African Americans (Coltraine & Messineo, 2000). In general, European American men tend to be portrayed as powerful, European American women as sex objects, African American men as aggressive, and African American women as unimportant.

4. *Information processing.* Prejudices act as cognitive filters through which we view the social world. We tend to think of people as "familiar" or "foreign," or "good" or "bad." Our feelings and reactions toward others may be biased by these perceptions (Crisp & Nicel, 2004; Förster et al., 2004). It is also easier to remember instances of behavior that are consistent with our biases than it is to reconstruct our mental categories (Kashima, 2000; Sherman & Frost, 2000). If you believe that Jewish Americans are stingy, it is easier to recall a Jewish American's negotiation of a price than a Jewish American's charitable donation. If you believe that Californians are airheads, it may be easier to recall TV images of surfing than of scientific conferences at Cal Tech and Berkeley.

5. *Social categorization.* We also tend to divide our social world into "us" and "them." People usually view those who belong to their own groups—the "in-group"—more favorably than those who do not—the "out-group" (Förster et al., 2004; Smith & Weber, 2005). Moreover, there is a tendency to assume that members of the out-group are more similar in their attitudes and behavior than members of our own groups (Mussweiler & Bodenhausen, 2002). Our isolation from the out-group makes it easier to maintain our stereotypes.

reflect & relate

How have the media in our country and in the Middle East used the following factors to influence attitudes toward out-groups: dissimilarity, social conflict, social learning, information processing, and social categorization?

Life Connections
Combating Prejudice

Prejudice has been with us throughout history, and it is unlikely that a miracle cure is at hand. Yet we need not stand idly by when we witness prejudice. We can create "mini-miracles"—changes in our own behavior and the behavior of people around us. For example, we can do the following:

1. *Encourage intergroup contact and cooperation.* Prejudice encourages us to avoid other groups, which is unfortunate because contact is one way of breaking down prejudices (Crisp & Nicel, 2004; Förster et al., 2004). Intergroup contact reveals that members of religious and racial groups have various values, abilities, interests, and personalities (Miller et al., 2004). Contact heightens awareness of individual differences, and this knowledge can lead us to abandon stereotypical thinking (Hewstone & Hamberger, 2000; Sherman & Frost, 2000). Intergroup contact is especially effective when people are striving to meet common goals, as in playing on the same team or working together on the yearbook.

2. *Present examples of admired individuals within groups that are often stigmatized.* Nilanjana Dasgupta and Anthony G. Greenwald (2001) found that they could modify negative attitudes toward African Americans by presenting photographs of admired African American individuals. Similarly, they could combat automatic preference for European Americans by presenting pictures of Europeans who were disliked. The effects of bringing admired individuals to mind will presumably work with verbal reminders as well.

3. *Attack discriminatory behavior.* It is sometimes easier to change people's behavior than to alter their feelings. Yet cognitive dissonance theory suggests that when we change people's behavior, their feelings may follow along. It is illegal to deny access to an education and jobs on the basis of gender, religion, race, or disability. Seek legal remedies if you have been discriminated against. Have you been denied access to living accommodations or a job because of prejudice? Talk about it to your academic advisor, the college equal opportunity office, or the dean of students. Unfortunately, many members of ethnic minority groups are reluctant to discuss

Thomas Hoeffgen /Getty Images

■ **Intergroup Contact**
Intergroup contact can reduce feelings of prejudice when people work together toward common goals.

A.

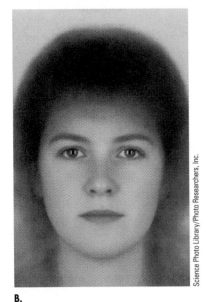

Science Photo Library/Photo Researchers, Inc.

B.

Figure 14.1

What Features Contribute to Facial Attractiveness?

In both England and Japan, features such as large eyes, high cheekbones, and narrow jaws contribute to perceptions of the attractiveness of women. Part A shows a composite of the faces of 15 women rated as the most attractive of a group of 60. Part B is a composite in which the features of these 15 women are exaggerated—that is, developed further in the direction that separates them from the average of the entire 60.

Attraction In social psychology, an attitude of liking or disliking (negative attraction).

instances of discrimination with members of majority groups, such as European American males (Stangor et al., 2002).

4. *Hold discussion forums.* Many campuses conduct workshops and discussion groups on gender, race, and diversity. Talk to your dean of students about holding such workshops.

5. *Examine your own beliefs.* Prejudice isn't "out there." Prejudice dwells within us. It is easy to focus on the prejudices of others, but what about our own? Have you examined your own attitudes and rejected stereotyping and prejudice?

Even if we do not personally harbor feelings of racial or religious enmity, are we doing anything to counter such feelings in others? Do we belong to organizations that deny access to members of other racial and religious groups? Do we strike up conversations with people from other groups or avoid them? College is meant to be a broadening experience, and we deny ourselves much of the education we could be receiving when we limit our encounters to people who share our own backgrounds.

Prejudices encourage us to avoid members of out-groups. As we see in the following section, attitudes of liking and loving have the opposite effect: They encourage us to develop relationships. ■

Interpersonal Attraction: On Liking, Loving, and Pairing Off

Attitudes of liking and loving can lead to important, lasting relationships. They are the flip side of the coin of prejudice—positive attitudes that are associated with interpersonal **attraction** rather than avoidance. *What factors contribute to attraction in our culture?* Among the factors contributing to attraction are physical appearance, similarity, and reciprocity (Smith & Weber, 2005).

Physical Appearance: How Important Is Looking Good? Physical appearance is a key factor in attraction and in the consideration of romantic partners (Langlois et al., 2000; Sangrador & Yela, 2000). What determines physical allure? Are our standards subjective—that is, "in the eye of the beholder"? Or is there general agreement on what is appealing?

◇ **Truth or Fiction Revisited:** Although there may be individual preferences, it does not seem that standards for beauty are so flexible that they are fully "in the eye of the beholder." Many standards for beauty appear to be cross-cultural (Langlois et al., 2000; Little & Perrett, 2002). For example, a study of people in England and Japan found that both British and Japanese men consider women with large eyes, high cheekbones, and narrow jaws to be most attractive (Perrett, 1994). In his research, Perrett created computer composites of the faces of 60 women and, as shown in part A of Figure 14.1, of the 15 women who were rated the most attractive. He then used computer enhancement to exaggerate the differences between the composite of the 60 and the composite of the 15 most attractive women. He arrived at the image shown in part B of Figure 14.1. Part B, which shows higher cheekbones and a narrower jaw than Part A, was rated as the most attractive image. Similar results were found for the image of a Japanese woman. Works of art suggest that the ancient Greeks and Egyptians favored similar facial features.

In our society, tallness is an asset for men (Hensley, 1994; Pierce, 1996). Although women may be less demanding than men concerning a variety of physical feature, height—that is, tallness—is more important to women in the selection of dates and mates than it is to men.

Although preferences for facial features may transcend time and culture, preferences for body weight and shape may be more culturally determined. For example, plumpness has been valued in many cultures. Grandmothers who worry that their granddaughters are starving themselves often come from cultures in which stoutness is acceptable or desirable.

In contemporary Western society, there is pressure on both males and females to be slender (Goode, 2000; Wade et al., 2000). Women generally favor men with a V-taper—broad shoulders and a narrow waist.

Gender Differences in Selection of a Partner Physical appearance may be a major factor in the selection of a romantic partner, but cross-cultural studies on mate selection find that women tend to place greater emphasis on traits such as professional status, consideration, dependability, kindness, and fondness for children. Men tend to place relatively greater emphasis on physical allure, cooking ability (can't they turn on the microwave oven themselves?), even thrift (Buss, 1994; Feingold, 1992a). A study of some 600 university students in China agreed that females place relatively more emphasis on earning potential in selecting a mate, and males place more emphasis on physical attractiveness (Chuang, 2002).

Susan Sprecher and her colleagues (1994) surveyed more than 13,000 Americans, attempting to represent the ethnic diversity we find in the United States. They asked how willing their subjects would be to marry someone who was older, younger, of a different religion, unlikely to hold a steady job, not good looking, and so on. Each item was answered by checking off a 7-point scale in which 1 meant "not at all" and 7 meant "very willing." Women were more willing than men to marry someone who was not good-looking, but less willing to marry someone who did not hold a steady job (see Figure 14.2).

Jeff Greenberg/Rainbow/PictureQuest

■ **"Looking Good"**
Models like these are among those who set the standards for beauty in contemporary American culture. How important is physical attractiveness in interpersonal attraction and social and vocational success?

How willing would you be to marry someone who . . .

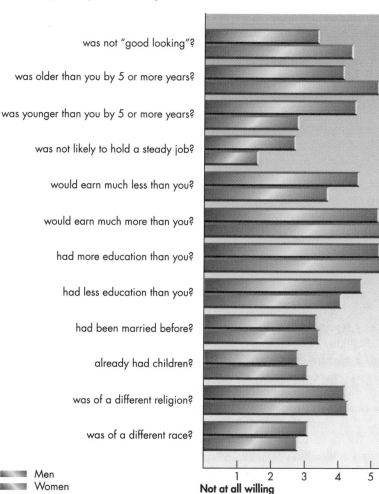

was not "good looking"?
was older than you by 5 or more years?
was younger than you by 5 or more years?
was not likely to hold a steady job?
would earn much less than you?
would earn much more than you?
had more education than you?
had less education than you?
had been married before?
already had children?
was of a different religion?
was of a different race?

Men
Women

1   2   3   4   5   6   7
Not at all willing   Very willing

Figure 14.2
Gender Differences in Preferences for Mates
The study by Sprecher and her colleagues find that women are more likely than men to be willing to marry someone who is older, makes more money, is better educated, but not good-looking. Men, on the other hand, are less willing to marry someone who is not good-looking. Men are also more willing to have partners who are younger, earn less, and are less well-educated. How would you interpret these findings?

Why do males tend to place relatively more emphasis than females on physical appearance in mate selection? Why do females tend to place relatively more emphasis on personal factors such as financial status and reliability? Evolutionary psychologists believe that evolutionary forces favor the survival of women who desire status in their mates and men who emphasize physical allure because these preferences provide reproductive advantages. According to the "parental investment model," a woman's appeal is more strongly connected with her age and health, both of which are markers of reproductive capacity. The value of men as reproducers, however, is more intertwined with factors that contribute to a stable environment for child rearing—such as social standing and reliability (Schmitt, 2003).

Men and women are perceived as more attractive when they are smiling (Reis et al., 1990). When you're smiling, observers expect to have positive social interactions with you (Harker & Keltner, 2001). There is thus ample reason to, as the song goes, "put on a happy face" when you are meeting people or going out with someone you like.

The Matching Hypothesis: Do "Opposites Attract" or Do "Birds of a Feather Flock Together"?

Although we may rate highly attractive people as most desirable, most of us also find partners. According to the **matching hypothesis,** we tend to get together with people who are similar to ourselves in physical attractiveness rather than the local Will Smith or Cameron Diaz look-alike. One motive for approaching "matches" seems to be fear of rejection by more attractive people (Bernstein et al., 1983). ◆ **Truth or Fiction Revisited:** Despite the familiar saying "Opposites attract," it seems that people who are similar are more likely than opposites to be attracted to one another.

The quest for similarity extends beyond physical attractiveness. Our marital and sex partners tend to be similar to us in race/ethnicity, age, level of education, and religion. Consider some findings of the National Health and Social Life Survey (Michael et al., 1994, pp. 45–47):

- Nearly 94% of single European American men have European American women as their sex partners; 2% are partnered with Latina Americans, 2% with Asian American women, and less than 1% with African American women.
- About 82% of African American men have African American women as their sex partners; nearly 8% are partnered with European American women and almost 5% with Latina Americans.
- About 83% of the women and men in the study chose partners within five years of their own age and of the same or a similar religion.
- Of nearly 2,000 women in the study, not one with a graduate college degree had a partner who had not finished high school.

The Matching Hypothesis
Do opposites attract, or do we tend to pair off with people who look and think the way we do? As suggested by these photographs, similarity often runs at least skin-deep.

Why do most people have partners from the same background as their own? One reason is that marriages are made in the neighborhood and not in heaven (Michael et al., 1994). We tend to live among people who are similar to us in background, and we therefore come into contact with them more often than with people from other backgrounds. Another reason is that we are drawn to people whose attitudes are similar to ours (Michinov & Michinov, 2001; Singh & Ho, 2000; Watson et al., 2000). Regardless of why we seek similarity, it turns out that similarity appears to be connected with satisfaction with a relationship (Lucas et al., 2004).

Other Factors in Attraction: Reciprocity and the Nearness of You?

Has anyone told you how good-looking, brilliant, and mature you are? That your taste is refined? That all in all, you are really something special? If so, have you been impressed by his or her fine judgment? **Reciprocity** is a powerful determinant of attraction (Bruce & Sanders, 2001; Sprecher, 1998). We tend to return feelings of admiration. We tend to be more open, warm, and helpful when we are interacting with strangers who seem to like us (Curtis & Miller, 1986).

Deb Levine (2000), writing in *CyberPsychology & Behavior,* compares attraction online ("virtual attraction") with attraction in the real world. She notes that proximity, or nearness, is a factor online and offline, but proximity online can mean visiting the same chat room a number of times even though people live thousands of miles apart. Self-disclosure and reciprocity occur more quickly online, perhaps because people think they are operating from a safe distance. It is more difficult, she asserts, to check out similarities in interests

Matching hypothesis The view that people tend to choose persons similar to themselves in attractiveness and attitudes in the formation of interpersonal relationships.

Reciprocity In interpersonal attraction, the tendency to return feelings and attitudes that are expressed about us.

Figure 14.3

The Triangular Model of Love

According to this model, love has three components: intimacy, passion, and commitment. The ideal of consummate love consists of romantic love plus commitment.

Source: From *The Psychology of Love* by R. J. Sternberg. Copyright 1988 Yale University Press. Reprinted by permission of the publisher

Liking = Intimacy alone (true friendships without passion or long-term commitment)

Romantic love = Intimacy + Passion (lovers physically and emotionally attracted to each other but without commitment, as in a summer romance)

Intimacy

Companionate love = Intimacy + Commitment (long-term committed friendship such as a marriage in which the passion has faded)

Consummate love = Intimacy + Passion + Commitment (a complete love consisting of all three components—an ideal difficult to attain)

Passion

Commitment

Infatuation = Passion alone (passionate, obsessive love at first sight without intimacy or commitment)

Fatuous love = Passion + Commitment (commitment based on passion but without time for intimacy to develop—shallow relationship such as a whirlwind courtship)

Empty love = Commitment alone (commitment to remain together without intimacy or passion)

because people are more or less free to present themselves as they wish. She suggests that people exchange biographies and photos within a month or so of when they meet online and meet in person, if possible, to dispel unrealistic expectations.

Whether online or offline, feelings of attraction are influenced by factors such as physical appearance and similarity. Let us explore what we mean when we say that feelings of attraction have blossomed into love.

Love "All you need is love," according to the Beatles song. Apparently, producers of films and television shows agree, at least in part. That is, nearly every movie, TV show, and novel has a love story in it. Even action films like *The Matrix,* the *Star Wars* series, *Spider-Man,* and *Collateral* have their love stories. Love is beautiful and elusive. Passion and romantic love are also lusty, surging with sexual desire. *Just what is love?*

Love is a strong positive emotion. We had a look at love between children and parents in Chapter 3. Here we will focus on that most dramatic, heated, passionate love we label *romantic love.*

There are a number of theories about romantic love. One theory is Robert Sternberg's (1988) **triangular model of love,** which can be thought of as a love triangle. This love triangle does not refer to two men wooing the same woman. It refers to Sternberg's view that love involves three components: intimacy, passion, and commitment (see Figure 14.3).

Intimacy refers to a couple's closeness, to their mutual concern and sharing of feelings and resources. **Passion** means romance and sexual feelings. **Commitment** is the decision to maintain a relationship. Passion is most crucial in short-term relationships. Intimacy and commitment are more important in enduring relationships. The ideal form of love combines all three: **consummate love.** Consummate love is made up of romantic love plus commitment.

Romantic love, in Sternberg's scheme, is characterized by passion and intimacy. Passion involves fascination (preoccupation with the loved one); sexual craving; and the desire for exclusiveness (a special relationship with the loved one). Intimacy involves caring—championing the interests of the loved one, even if it entails sacrificing one's own. People are cognitively biased toward evaluating their partners positively (Loving & Agnew, 2001). That is, we idealize those we love. People tend to attend to information that confirms their romantic interests. Lovers often magnify each other's positive features and overlook their flaws.

Even though romantic love and sexual desire tend to go together, evolutionary psychologist Lisa Diamond (2004) notes that they are different experiences and have different biological features. Diamond believes that sexual desire evolved as a means of ensuring mating, but that romantic love evolved from infant–caregiver relationships, in which the caregiver is self-sacrificing and engrossed in every aspect of the infant's development. Diamond also argues that the hormone **oxytocin** (see Chapter 2), which is connected with maternal behaviors such as cuddling, is more prevalent in women than men—suggesting at least one biochemical reason why women may be more likely than men to want to engage in sexual activity within the context of a relationship.

Triangular model of love Sternberg's view that love involves combinations of three components: intimacy, passion, and commitment.

Intimacy Close acquaintance and familiarity; a characteristic of a relationship in which partners share their inmost feelings.

Passion Strong romantic and sexual feelings.

Commitment The decision to maintain a relationship.

Consummate love The ideal form of love within Sternberg's model, which combines passion, intimacy, and commitment.

Romantic love An intense, positive emotion that involves sexual attraction, feelings of caring, and the belief that one is in love.

Oxytocin A pituitary hormone that stimulates labor in pregnant women and is connected with maternal behaviors such as cuddling and caring for young.

Self-Assessment

The Love Scale

Self-Assessment

Which are the strongest components of your love relationship? Intimacy? Passion? Commitment? All three components? Two of them?

To complete the following scale, fill in the blank spaces with the name of one person you love or care about deeply. Then rate your agreement with each of the items by using the 9-point scale in which 1 = "not at all," 5 = "moderately," and 9 = "extremely." Use points in between to indicate intermediate levels of agreement between these values. Then consult the scoring key in Appendix B.

Intimacy Component

1 2 3 4 5 6 7 8 9   **1.** I am actively supportive of _____'s well-being.

1 2 3 4 5 6 7 8 9   **2.** I have a warm relationship with _____.

1 2 3 4 5 6 7 8 9   **3.** I am able to count on _____ in times of need.

1 2 3 4 5 6 7 8 9   **4.** _____ is able to count on me in times of need.

1 2 3 4 5 6 7 8 9   **5.** I am willing to share myself and my possessions with _____.

1 2 3 4 5 6 7 8 9   **6.** I receive considerable emotional support from _____.

1 2 3 4 5 6 7 8 9   **7.** I give considerable emotional support to _____.

1 2 3 4 5 6 7 8 9   **8.** I communicate well with _____.

1 2 3 4 5 6 7 8 9   **9.** I value _____ greatly in my life.

1 2 3 4 5 6 7 8 9   **10.** I feel close to _____.

1 2 3 4 5 6 7 8 9   **11.** I have a comfortable relationship with _____.

1 2 3 4 5 6 7 8 9   **12.** I feel that I really understand _____.

1 2 3 4 5 6 7 8 9   **13.** I feel that _____ really understands me.

1 2 3 4 5 6 7 8 9   **14.** I feel that I can really trust _____.

1 2 3 4 5 6 7 8 9   **15.** I share deeply personal information about myself with _____.

Passion Component

1 2 3 4 5 6 7 8 9   **16.** Just seeing _____ excites me.

1 2 3 4 5 6 7 8 9   **17.** I find myself thinking about _____ frequently during the day.

1 2 3 4 5 6 7 8 9   **18.** My relationship with _____ is very romantic.

1 2 3 4 5 6 7 8 9   **19.** I find _____ to be very personally attractive.

1 2 3 4 5 6 7 8 9   **20.** I idealize _____.

1 2 3 4 5 6 7 8 9   **21.** I cannot imagine another person making me as happy as _____ does.

1 2 3 4 5 6 7 8 9   **22.** I would rather be with _____ than anyone else.

1 2 3 4 5 6 7 8 9   **23.** There is nothing more important to me than my relationship with _____.

1 2 3 4 5 6 7 8 9   **24.** I especially like physical contact with _____.

1 2 3 4 5 6 7 8 9   **25.** There is something almost "magical" about my relationship with _____.

1 2 3 4 5 6 7 8 9   **26.** I adore _____.

1 2 3 4 5 6 7 8 9   **27.** I cannot imagine life without _____.

1 2 3 4 5 6 7 8 9   **28.** My relationship with _____ is passionate.

1 2 3 4 5 6 7 8 9   **29.** When I see romantic movies and read romantic books, I think of _____.

1 2 3 4 5 6 7 8 9   **30.** I fantasize about _____.

Commitment Component

1 2 3 4 5 6 7 8 9   **31.** I know that I care about _____.

1 2 3 4 5 6 7 8 9   **32.** I am committed to maintaining my relationship with _____.

1 2 3 4 5 6 7 8 9   **33.** Because of my commitment to _____, I would not let other people come between us.

1 2 3 4 5 6 7 8 9   **34.** I have confidence in the stability of my relationship with _____.

1 2 3 4 5 6 7 8 9   **35.** I could not let anything get in the way of my commitment to _____.

1 2 3 4 5 6 7 8 9   **36.** I expect my love for _____ to last for the rest of my life.

1 2 3 4 5 6 7 8 9   **37.** I will always feel a strong responsibility for _____.

1 2 3 4 5 6 7 8 9   **38.** I view my commitment to _____ as a solid one.

1 2 3 4 5 6 7 8 9   **39.** I cannot imagine ending my relationship with _____.

1 2 3 4 5 6 7 8 9   **40.** I am certain of my love for _____.

1 2 3 4 5 6 7 8 9   **41.** I view my relationship with _____ as permanent.

1 2 3 4 5 6 7 8 9   **42.** I view my relationship with _____ as a good decision.

1 2 3 4 5 6 7 8 9   **43.** I feel a sense of responsibility toward _____.

1 2 3 4 5 6 7 8 9   **44.** I plan to continue my relationship with _____.

1 2 3 4 5 6 7 8 9   **45.** Even when _____ is hard to deal with, I remain committed to our relationship.

SOURCE: From *The Psychology of Love* by R. J. Sternberg. Copyright 1988 Yale University Press. Reprinted by permission of the publisher.

Go to www

http://academic.cengage.com/psychology/rathus where you can fill out an interactive version of this Self-Assessment and automatically score your results.

Learning Connections

◀◀ *Attitude—"The Good, the Bad, and the Ugly"* ▶▶

REVIEW:

1 Which of the following best expresses the relation-ship between attitudes and behaviors?
   (a) People always behave in ways that are consis-tent with their attitudes,
   (b) People always change their attitudes so that they are consistent with their behavior,
   (c) There is no relationship between attitudes and behaviors,
   (d) People are likely to act in accord with strong, specific attitudes.

2 Which of the following is a *central cue* for persuad-ing people to choose Coke or Pepsi?
   (a) Providing information about the taste of the drink,
   (b) Having a rock star deliver a television commercial,
   (c) Showing attractive, slender people drinking the soda,
   (d) Using a person with a fine voice to sell the product.

3 Research concerning persuasion shows that two-sided arguments have the advantage of
   (a) providing peripheral cues,
   (b) conditioning the audience,

   (c) appealing to the emotions rather than the intellect,
   (d) showing the audience how to refute the opposition's arguments.

4 Which source of prejudice is reflected in the statement, "It is easier to remember instances of behavior that are consistent with our prejudices."
   (a) Assumptions of dissimilarity,
   (b) Social conflict,
   (c) The three-stage theory of memory,
   (d) Information processing.

5 One motive for seeking "matches" rather than more attractive people seems to be
   (a) propinquity,
   (b) reciprocity of feelings,
   (c) fear of rejection,
   (d) sexual arousal.

CRITICAL THINKING:
How might the features found attractive by males and females provide humans with an evolutionary advantage? Can you think of other reasons why people might find these features attractive?

Go to

http://academic.cengage.com/psychology/rathus for an interactive version of this review.

SOCIAL PERCEPTION: LOOKING OUT, LOOKING WITHIN

An important area of social psychology concerns the ways in which we perceive other people—for example, the importance of the first impressions they make on us. Next we explore some factors that contribute to **social perception:** the primacy and recency effects, attribution theory, and body language.

◾ Primacy and Recency Effects: The Importance of First Impressions

Why do you wear a suit to a job interview? Why do defense attorneys make sure that their clients dress neatly and get their hair cut before they are seen by the jury? *Do first im-pressions really matter?* Apparently first impressions do matter—a great deal.

Social perception A subfield of so-cial psychology that studies the ways in which we form and modify im-pressions of others.

■ **First Impressions**
Why is it important to make a good first impression? What are some ways of doing so?

reflect & relate
Did you ever try to "make a good first impression"? What was the occasion? What did you do? Did it work out? Explain.

Whether we are talking about the business or social worlds, or even the relationship between a therapist and a client, first impressions are important (Bidell et al., 2002; Laungani, 2002). First impressions are an example of the primacy effect. Let's have a look at the primacy and recency effects.

Katie, a ballet student, got her nose pierced and sported a tiny stud. Her teachers, who had known her for three years, were astounded. Katie had always seemed traditional and conservative, and here she was, "going off the deep end." I overheard them conferring about Katie, and most concluded that friends at school must have instigated the change. The "real" Katie, they seemed convinced, would never have chosen to get the piercing.

Katie's teachers might have been influenced by the **primacy effect**. *What are the primacy and recency effects?* The teachers' initial impressions of Katie suggested to them that her nose pierce was out of character. The vision of Katie they had formed—their first impression—was of a serious student more interested in study and hard work, not in a social or subcultural fad. "This isn't Katie," one teacher said.

The primacy effect suggests that first impressions often make or break us. A former student of mine removed his earring, got a haircut, shaved, and bought a suit for an interview at a financial firm. ◁▷ **Truth or Fiction Revisited:** Ít is apparently not true that you should just "be yourself" in a job interview. Dressing down or cursing may very well cost you the job.

Why are first impressions important? The answer may be because we infer traits from behavior. If we act considerately at first, we are labeled considerate. The *trait* of consideration is used to explain and predict our future behavior. If, after being labeled considerate, one does something selfish or a bit nasty, this lapse may be seen as an exception to a rule—excused by circumstances or external causes. If one is first labeled as inconsiderate, however, months of considerate behavior may be perceived as a cynical effort to "make up for it."

Subjects in a classic experiment on the primacy effect read different stories about "Jim" (Luchins, 1957). The stories consisted of one or two paragraphs. The one-paragraph stories portrayed Jim as either friendly or unfriendly. These paragraphs were also used in the two-paragraph stories, but in this case the paragraphs were read in the reverse order. Of those reading only the "friendly" paragraph, 95% rated Jim as friendly. Of those who read just the "unfriendly" paragraph, 3% rated him as friendly. Seventy-eight percent of those who read two-paragraph stories in the "friendly-unfriendly" order labeled Jim as friendly. When they read the paragraphs in the reverse order, only 18% rated Jim as friendly.

How can we encourage people to pay more attention to impressions occurring after the first encounter? Abraham Luchins accomplished this by allowing time to elapse between the presentations of the two paragraphs. In this way, fading memories allowed more recent information to take precedence. This is known as the **recency effect.** Luchins found a second way to counter first impressions: He simply asked subjects to avoid making snap judgments and to weigh all the evidence. One of Katie's teachers apparently focused on the recency effect: She suggested that the "real Katie" might finally be "coming out."

There is some interesting research on the role of the handshake in making a first impression. In our culture, a firm handshake is a key to making a good first impression, by women as well as men. Researchers find that a firm handshake is perceived as an indication of being outgoing and open to new experience. A weak handshake was perceived as indicative of shyness and social anxiety (Chaplin et al., 2000). Thus both women and men in the business world are well advised to shake the hands of new acquaintances firmly.

Primacy effect The tendency to evaluate others in terms of first impressions.

Recency effect The tendency to evaluate others in terms of the most recent impression.

Attribution A belief concerning why people behave in a certain way.

■■- **Attribution Theory: You're Free to Choose, but I'm Caught in the Middle?**

When she was 3 years old, one of my daughters believed that a friend's son was a boy because he *wanted* to be a boy. Because she was 3 at the time, this error in my daughter's **attribution** of the boy's gender is understandable. Adults tend to make somewhat similar attribution errors, however. Although they do not believe that people's preferences have much to do with their gender, they do tend to exaggerate the role of choice in their behavior. *What is attribution theory? Why do we assume that other people intend the mischief that they do?*

An attribution is an assumption about why people do things. When you assume that one child is mistreating another child because she is "mean," you are making an attribution. The process by which we make inferences about the motives and traits of others through observation of their behavior is the **attribution process.** This section focuses on *attribution theory,* or the processes by which people draw conclusions about the factors that influence one another's behavior. Attribution theory is important because attributions lead us to perceive others either as purposeful actors or as victims of circumstances.

Dispositional and Situational Attributions   Social psychologists describe two types of attributions. **Dispositional attributions** ascribe a person's behavior to internal factors such as personality traits and free will. **Situational attributions** attribute a person's actions to external factors such as social influence or socialization. If you assume that one child is mistreating the other because her parents have given her certain attitudes toward the other child, you are making a situational attribution.

The Fundamental Attribution Error   In cultures that view the self as independent, such as ours, people tend to attribute other people's behavior primarily to internal factors such as personality, attitudes, and free will (Gilovich & Eibach, 2001; Reeder, 2001). This bias in the attribution process is known as the **fundamental attribution error.** In such individualistic societies, people tend to focus on the behavior of others rather than on the circumstances surrounding their behavior. For example, if a teenager gets into trouble with the law, individualistic societies are more likely to blame the teenager than the social environment in which the teenager lives. ◆▶ **Truth or Fiction Revisited:** Therefore, we do tend to hold others responsible for their misdeeds but to see ourselves as victims of circumstances when we misbehave.

One reason for the fundamental attribution error is that we tend to infer traits from behavior. But in collectivist cultures that stress interdependence, such as Asian cultures, people are more likely to attribute other people's behavior to that person's social roles and obligations (Basic Behavioral Science Task Force, 1996c). For example, Japanese people might be more likely to attribute a businessperson's extreme competitiveness to the "culture of business" rather than to his or her personality.

The Actor–Observer Effect   When we see people (including ourselves) doing things that we do not like, we tend to see the others as willful actors but to see ourselves as victims of circumstances (Baron et al., 2006; Stewart, 2005). The tendency to attribute other people's behavior to dispositional factors and our own behavior to situational influences is called the **actor–observer effect.**

One of my editors noted that when someone cut her off on the freeway, she would make a disposition attribution: "What a jerk!" (I'm being kind in my choice of language.) But if *she* cut someone off, she would make a situational attribution: "This road is so crowded I just didn't see them."

Parents and teenagers often argue about the teen's choice of friends or partners. When they do, the parents tend to infer traits from behavior and to see the teens as stubborn and resistant. The teenagers also infer traits from behavior. Thus they may see their parents as bossy and controlling. Parents and teens alike attribute the others' behavior to internal causes. That is, both make dispositional attributions about other people's behavior.

How do the parents and teenagers perceive themselves? The parents probably see themselves as being forced into combat by their children's foolishness. If they become insistent, it is in response to the teens' stubbornness. The teenagers probably see themselves as responding to peer pressures and, perhaps, to sexual urges that may have come from within but seem like a source of outside pressure. Both parents and children tend to see their own behavior as motivated by external forces. That is, they make situational attributions for their own behavior.

■ The Actor–Observer Effect
Who is at fault here? People tend to make dispositional attributions for other people's behavior, but they tend to see their own behavior as motivated by situational factors. Thus people are aware of the external forces acting on themselves when they behave, but tend to attribute other people's behavior to choice and will.

Attribution process The process by which people draw inferences about the motives and traits of others.

Dispositional attribution An assumption that a person's behavior is determined by internal causes such as personal attitudes or goals.

Situational attribution An assumption that a person's behavior is determined by external circumstances such as the social pressure found in a situation.

Fundamental attribution error The assumption that others act predominantly on the basis of their dispositions, even when there is evidence suggesting the importance of their situations.

Actor–observer effect The tendency to attribute our own behavior to situational factors but to attribute the behavior of others to dispositional factors.

The actor–observer effect extends to our perceptions of both the in-group (an extension of ourselves) and the out-group. Consider conflicts between nations, for example. Both sides may engage in brutal acts of violence. Each side usually considers the other to be calculating, inflexible, and—not infrequently—sinister. Each side also typically views its own people as victims of circumstances and its own violent actions as justified or dictated by the situation. After all, we may look at the other side as being in the wrong, but can we expect them to agree with us?

The Self-Serving Bias   There is also a **self-serving bias** in the attribution process. We are likely to ascribe our successes to internal, dispositional factors but our failures to external, situational influences (Duval & Silvia, 2002; Smith & Weber, 2005). When we have done well on a test, we are likely to credit our intelligence and hard work. But when we fail, we are likely to blame bad luck, the professor's making up an unfair test, or the noisy construction work going on outside.

We can extend the self-serving bias to sports. A study with 27 college wrestlers found that they tended to attribute their wins to stable and internal conditions such as their abilities, but their losses to unstable and external conditions such as an error by a referee (De Michele et al., 1998). Sports fans fall into the same trap. They tend to attribute their team's victories to internal conditions and their losses to external conditions (Wann & Shrader, 2000).

There are exceptions to the self-serving bias. In accord with the bias, when we work in groups, we tend to take the credit for the group's success but to pin the blame for group failure on someone else. But the outcome is different when we are friends with other group members—then we tend to share the credit for success or the blame for failure (Campbell et al., 2000). Another exception is found in the fact that depressed people are more likely than other people to ascribe their failures to internal factors, even when external forces are mostly to blame.

Another interesting attribution bias is a gender difference in attributions for friendly behavior. Men are more likely than women to interpret a woman's smile or friendliness toward a man as flirting (Abbey, 1987; Buss, 2000).

Factors Contributing to the Attribution Process   Our attribution of behavior to internal or external causes can apparently be influenced by three factors: *consensus, consistency,* and *distinctiveness* (Kelley & Michela, 1980). When few people act in a certain way—that is, when **consensus** is low—we are likely to attribute behavior to dispositional (internal) factors. **Consistency** refers to the degree to which the same person acts in the same way on other occasions. Highly consistent behavior can often be attributed to dispositional factors. **Distinctiveness** is the extent to which the person responds differently in different situations. If the person acts similarly in different situations, distinctiveness is low. We therefore are likely to attribute his or her behavior to dispositional factors.

Let us apply the criteria of consensus, consistency, and distinctiveness to the behavior of a customer in a restaurant. She takes one bite of her strawberry cheesecake and calls the waiter. She tells him that her food is inedible and demands that it be replaced. Now, has she complained as a result of internal causes (for example, because she is hard to please) or external causes (that is, because the food really is bad)? Under the following circumstances, we are likely to attribute her behavior to internal, dispositional causes: (1) No one else at the table is complaining, so consensus is low. (2) She has returned her food on other occasions, so consistency is high. (3) She complains in other restaurants also, so distinctiveness is low (see Table 14.1).

But under the following circumstances, we are likely to attribute the customer's behavior to external, situational causes: (1) Everyone else at the table is also complaining, so consensus is high. (2) She does not usually return food, so consistency is low. (3) She usually does not complain at restaurants, so distinctiveness is high. Given these conditions, we are likely to believe that the cheesecake really is awful and that the customer is justified in her response.

Self-serving bias The tendency to view one's successes as stemming from internal factors and one's failures as stemming from external factors.

Consensus General agreement.

Consistency In attribution theory, the degree to which the same person acts in the same way on different occasions.

Distinctiveness In attribution theory, the extent to which the person responds differently in different situations.

Body Language: The Body Speaks

Body language is important in social perception. ***What is body language?*** Body language is nonverbal language; it refers to the meanings we infer from the ways in which people carry themselves and the gestures they make (Greenlees et al., 2005; McClave, 2000). At an early age we learn that the way people carry themselves provides cues to how they feel and are likely to behave. You may have noticed that when people are "uptight" they may also be rigid and straight-backed. People who are relaxed are more likely to "hang loose." Factors such as eye contact, posture, and the distance between two people provide cues to the individuals' moods and their feelings toward their companions. When people face us and lean toward us, we may assume that they like us or are interested in what we are saying. If we overhear a conversation between a couple and observe that the woman is leaning toward the man while the man is sitting back and toying with his hair, we are likely to infer that he is not interested in what she is saying.

TABLE 14.1 ■ Factors Leading to Internal or External Attributions of Behavior		
	INTERNAL ATTRIBUTION	**EXTERNAL ATTRIBUTION**
Consensus	Low: Few people behave this way.	High: Most people behave this way.
Consistency	High: The person behaves this way frequently.	Low: The person does not behave this way frequently.
Distinctiveness	Low: The person behaves this way in many situations.	High: The person behaves this way in few situations.

Touching: Put the Arm on People (Literally)   Touching also communicates. Women are more likely than men to touch other people when they are interacting with them (Stier & Hall, 1984). In one "touching" experiment, Kleinke (1977) showed that appeals for help can be more effective when the distressed person makes physical contact with people who are asked for aid. A woman obtained more coins for phone calls when she touched the arm of the person she was asking for money. In another experiment, waitresses obtained higher tips when they touched patrons on the hand or the shoulder while making change (Crusco & Wetzel, 1984).

In these experiments, the touching was noncontroversial. It was usually gentle, brief, and done in familiar settings. When touching suggests greater intimacy than is desired, however, it can be seen as negative. A study in a nursing home found that responses to being touched depended on factors such as the status of the staff member, the type of touch, and the part of the body that was touched (Hollinger & Buschmann, 1993). Touching was considered positive when it was appropriate to the situation and did not appear to be condescending. It was seen as negative when it was controlling, unnecessary, or overly intimate.

reflect & relate

The next time you are out among people, look around. Can you tell whether other people are enjoying being with one another, or whether they are finding the experience annoying? How can you tell?

Gazing and Staring: The Eyes Have It   We usually feel that we can learn much from eye contact. When other people "look us squarely in the eye," we may assume that they are being assertive or open with us. Avoidance of eye contact may suggest deception or depression. Gazing is interpreted as a sign of liking or friendliness (Kleinke, 1986). In one study, men and women were asked to gaze into each other's eyes for two minutes (Kellerman et al., 1989). After doing so, they reported having passionate feelings toward one another. (Watch out!)

Of course, a gaze is not the same thing as a persistent hard stare. A hard stare is interpreted as a provocation or a sign of anger. Adolescent males sometimes engage in staring contests as an assertion of dominance. The male who looks away first loses the contest. In a classic series of field experiments, Phoebe Ellsworth and her colleagues (1972) subjected drivers stopped at red lights to hard stares by riders of motor scooters (see Figure 14.4). When the light changed, people who were stared at crossed the intersection more rapidly than people who were not. People who are stared at exhibit higher levels of physiological arousal than people who are not (Strom & Buck, 1979).

■ **Gazing Versus Staring**
Gazing into an attractive person's eyes can give rise to feelings of passion, but people interpret a hard stare as an aversive challenge.

Figure 14.4

Diagram of an Experiment in Hard Staring and Avoidance

A 1978 study by Greenbaum and Rosenfeld found that the confederate of the experimenter stared at some drivers and not at others. Recipients of the stares drove across the inter-section more rapidly once the light turned green. Why?

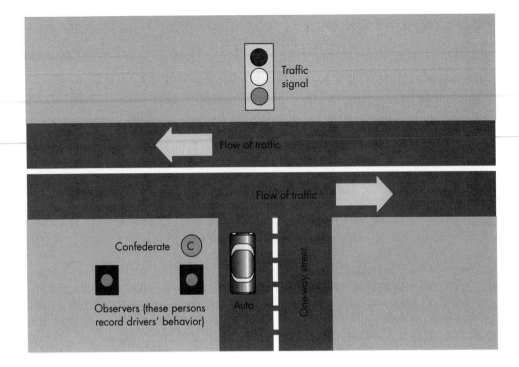

Traffic signal

Flow of traffic

Flow of traffic

Confederate (C)

Observers (these persons record drivers' behavior)

Auto

One-way street

() Learning Connections

◄◄   *Social Perception—Looking Out, Looking Within*   ►►

REVIEW:

6 Research shows that first impressions
  (a) never change,
  (b) are an example of the recency effect,
  (c) are believed only when they are consistent with stereotypes,
  (d) tend to endure.

7 Which of the following statements demonstrates a dispositional attribution?
  (a) "Something got the best of him,"
  (b) "He did what he thought was right,"
  (c) "He did it that way because of the weather,"
  (d) "He couldn't refuse the money."

8 Attributing too much of other people's behavior to dispositional factors is called
  (a) the fundamental attribution error,
  (b) the actor–observer effect,

  (c) internalization,
  (d) evaluation apprehension.

9 We tend to make an external attribution for behavior when that behavior is low in
  (a) distinctiveness,
  (b) dissonance,
  (c) consensus,
  (d) consistency.

10 Research into touching shows that
  (a) touching is always welcome,
  (b) touching is a sign of a deepening relationship,
  (c) women use touching more than men do,
  (d) touching is an invitation to sex.

CRITICAL THINKING:
Why is it that we tend to hold others accountable for their misdeeds but excuse ourselves for the bad things we do? How can you use this information to enhance your social relationships?

Go to WWW

http://academic.cengage.com/psychology/rathus
for an interactive version of this review.

SOCIAL INFLUENCE: ARE YOU AN INDIVIDUAL OR ONE OF THE CROWD?

Most people would be reluctant to wear blue jeans to a funeral, walk naked on city streets, or, for that matter, wear clothes at a nudist colony. This is because other people and groups can exert enormous pressure on us to behave according to their norms. **Social influence** is the area of social psychology that studies the ways in which people alter the thoughts, feelings, and behavior of others (Baron et al., 2006; Cialdini & Goldstein, 2004). We already learned how attitudes can be changed through persuasion. In this section we describe a couple of classic experiments that demonstrate how people influence others to engage in destructive obedience or conform to social norms.

Obedience to Authority: Does Might Make Right?

Throughout history soldiers have followed orders—even when it comes to slaughtering innocent civilians. The Turkish slaughter of Armenians, the Nazi slaughter of Jews, the mutual slaughter of Hutus and Tutsis in Rwanda—these are all examples of the tragedies that can arise from simply following orders. We may say we are horrified by such crimes, and we cannot imagine why people engage in them. But how many of us would refuse to follow orders issued by authority figures? *Why will so many people commit crimes against humanity if they are ordered to do so? (Why don't they refuse?)*

The Milgram Studies: Shocking Stuff at Yale   Yale University psychologist Stanley Milgram also wondered how many people would resist immoral requests made by authority figures. To find out, he undertook a series of classic experiments at the university that have become known as the Milgram studies on obedience.

In an early phase of his work, Milgram (1963) placed ads in New Haven (Connecticut) newspapers for people who would be willing to participate in studies on learning and memory. He enlisted 40 people ranging in age from 20 to 50—teachers, engineers, laborers, salespeople, people who had not completed elementary school, people with graduate degrees.

Let's suppose that you have answered the ad. You show up at the university in exchange for a reasonable fee ($4.50, which in the early 1960s might easily fill your gas tank) and to satisfy your own curiosity. You may be impressed. After all, Yale is a venerable institution that dominates the city. You are no less impressed by the elegant labs, where you meet a distinguished behavioral scientist dressed in a white coat and another person who has responded to the ad. The scientist explains that the purpose of the experiment is to study the *effects of punishment on learning.* The experiment requires a "teacher" and a "learner." By chance, you are appointed the teacher and the other recruit the learner.

You, the scientist, and the learner enter a laboratory room containing a threatening chair with dangling straps. The scientist straps the learner in. The learner expresses some concern, but this is, after all, for the sake of science. And this is Yale University, isn't it? What could happen to a person at Yale?

You follow the scientist to an adjacent room, from which you are to do your "teaching." This teaching promises to have an impact. You are to punish the learner's errors by pressing levers marked from 15 to 450 volts on a fearsome-looking console. Labels describe 28 of the 30 levers as running the gamut from "Slight Shock" to "Danger: Severe Shock." The last two levers are simply labeled "XXX." Just in case you have no idea what electric shock feels like, the scientist gives you a sample 45-volt shock. It stings. You pity the person who might receive more.

Your learner is expected to learn pairs of words, which are to be read from a list. After hearing the list once, the learner is to produce the word that pairs with the stimulus word from a list of four alternatives. This is done by pressing a switch that lights one of four panels in your room. If it is the correct panel, you proceed to the next stimulus word. If not, you

Social influence The area of social psychology that studies the ways in which people influence the thoughts, feelings, and behavior of others.

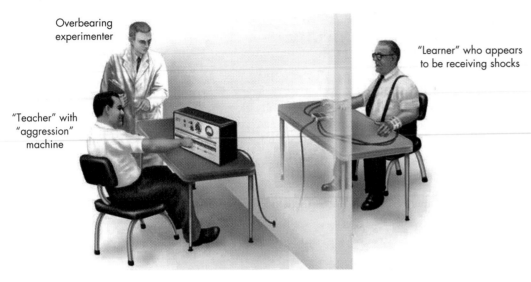

Overbearing experimenter

"Learner" who appears to be receiving shocks

"Teacher" with "aggression" machine

Figure 14.5
The Experimental Setup in the Milgram Studies
When the "learner" makes an error, the experimenter prods the "teacher" to deliver a painful electric shock.

are to deliver an electric shock. With each error, you are to increase the voltage of the shock (see Figure 14.5).

You probably have some misgivings. Electrodes have been strapped to the learner's wrists, and the scientist has applied electrode paste "to avoid blisters and burns." You have also been told that the shocks will cause "no permanent tissue damage," although they might be extremely painful. Still, the learner is going along. And after all, this is Yale.

The learner answers some items correctly and then makes some errors. With mild concern you press the levers up through 45 volts. You've tolerated that much yourself. Then a few more mistakes are made. You press the 60-volt lever, then 75. The learner makes another mistake. You pause and look at the scientist, who is reassuring: "Although the shocks may be painful, there is no permanent tissue damage, so please go on." The learner makes more errors, and soon you are up to a shock of 300 volts. But now the learner is pounding on the other side of the wall! Your chest tightens, and you begin to perspire. "Damn science and the $4.50!" you think. You hesitate and the scientist says, "The experiment requires that you continue." After the delivery of the next stimulus word, the learner chooses no answer at all. What are you to do? "Wait for 5 to 10 seconds," the scientist instructs, "and then treat no answer as a wrong answer." But after the next shock the pounding on the wall resumes! Now your heart is racing, and you are convinced you are causing extreme pain and discomfort. Is it possible that no lasting damage is being done? Is the experiment that important, after all? What to do? You hesitate again, and the scientist says, "It is absolutely essential that you continue." His voice is very convincing. "You have no other choice," he says, "you *must* go on." You can barely think straight, and for some unaccountable reason you feel laughter rising in your throat. Your finger shakes above the lever. *What are you to do?*

Milgram had foreseen that some "teachers" in his experiment would hesitate. He had therefore conceived standardized statements that his assistants would use when subjects balked—for example: "Although the shocks may be painful, there is no permanent tissue damage, so please go on." "The experiment requires that you continue." "It is absolutely essential that you continue." "You have no other choice, you *must* go on."

To repeat: If you are a teacher in the Milgram study, what do you do? Milgram (1963, 1974) found out what most people in his sample would do. The sample was a cross-section of the male population of New Haven. Of the 40 men in this phase of his research, only 5 refused to go beyond the 300-volt level, the level at which the learner first pounded the wall. Nine other "teachers" defied the scientist within the 300-volt range. But 65% of the subjects complied with the scientist throughout the series, believing they were delivering 450-volt, XXX-rated shocks. ◄► **Truth or Fiction Revisited:** Therefore, it appears to be true that most people will torture an innocent person, just because they are ordered to do so.

Were these subjects unfeeling? Not at all. Milgram was impressed by their signs of stress. They trembled, they stuttered, they bit their lips. They groaned, they sweated, they dug their fingernails into their flesh. Some had fits of laughter, although laughter was inappropriate. One salesperson's laughter was so convulsive that he could not continue with the experiment.

Milgram's initial research on obedience was limited to a sample of New Haven men. Could he generalize his findings to other men or to women? Would college students, who are considered to be independent thinkers, show more defiance? A replication of Milgram's study with a sample of Yale men yielded similar results. What about women, who are supposedly less aggressive than men? In subsequent research, women, too, administered shocks to the learners. All this took place in a nation that values independence and free will.

In various phases of Milgram's research, nearly half or the majority of the subjects complied throughout the series, believing that they were delivering 450-volt, XXX-rated shocks. These findings held for men from the New Haven community and for male students at Yale, and for women.

On Deception and Truth at Yale   I have said that the "teachers" in the Milgram studies *believed* that they were shocking other people when they pressed the levers on the console. They weren't. The only real shock in this experiment was the 45-volt sample given to the teachers. Its purpose was to make the procedure believable.

The learners in the experiment were actually confederates of the experimenter. They had not answered the newspaper ads but were in on the truth from the start. The "teachers" were the only real subjects. They were led to believe they had been chosen at random for the teacher role, but the choosing was rigged so that newspaper recruits would always become teachers.

Milgram debriefed his subjects after the experiment was complete. He explained the purpose and methods of his research in detail. He emphasized the fact that they had not actually harmed anyone. But of course the subjects did believe that they were hurting other people as the experiment was being carried out. As you can imagine, the ethics of the Milgram studies have been debated by psychologists for four decades (Slife & Rubenstein, 1992). College and university review committees might not allow these experiments to be conducted today.

Why Did People in the Milgram Studies Obey the Experimenters?   In any event, many people obey the commands of others even when they are required to perform immoral tasks. But *why?* Why did Germans "just follow orders" during the Holocaust? Why did "teachers" obey the experimenter in Milgram's study? We do not have all the answers, but we can offer a number of hypotheses:

1. *Socialization.* Despite the expressed American ideal of independence, we are socialized from early childhood to obey authority figures such as parents and teachers. Obedience to immoral demands may be the ugly sibling of socially desirable respect for authority figures (Blass, 1999).
2. *Lack of social comparison.* In Milgram's experimental settings, experimenters displayed command of the situation. Teachers (subjects), however, were on the experimenter's ground and very much on their own so they did not have the opportunity to compare their ideas and feelings with those of other people in the same situation. They therefore were less likely to have a clear impression of what to do.
3. *Perception of legitimate authority.* One phase of Milgram's research took place within the hallowed halls of Yale University. Subjects might have been overpowered by the reputation and authority of the setting. An experimenter at Yale might have appeared to be a highly legitimate authority figure—as might a government official or a high-ranking officer in the military (Blass & Schmitt, 2001). Yet further research showed that the university setting contributed to compliance but was not fully responsible for it. The percentage of individuals who complied with the experimenter's demands dropped from 65% to 48% when Milgram (1974) replicated the study in a dingy storefront in a nearby town. At first glance, this finding might seem encouraging. But the main point of the Milgram studies is that most people are willing to engage in morally reprehensible acts at the behest of a legitimate-looking authority figure. Hitler and his henchmen were authority figures in Nazi Germany. "Science" and Yale University legitimized the authority of the experimenters in the Milgram studies.
4. *Foot-in-the-door.* The **foot-in-the-door technique** might have contributed to the obedience of the teachers. Once they had begun to deliver shocks to learners, they might have conceptualized themselves as people who help researchers and found it progressively more difficult to extricate themselves from the situation (Burger & Guadagno, 2003; Rodafinos et al., 2005). Soldiers, similarly, are first taught to obey

Foot-in-the-door technique A method for inducing compliance in which a small request is followed by a larger request.

orders unquestioningly in unimportant matters such as dress and drill. By the time they are ordered to risk their lives, they have been saluting smartly and following commands without question for quite some time.

5. *Inaccessibility of values.* People are more likely to act in accordance with their attitudes when their attitudes are readily available, or accessible. Most people believe that it is wrong to harm innocent people. But strong emotions interfere with clear thinking. As the teachers in the Milgram experiments became more aroused, their attitudes might thus have become less "accessible." As a result, it might have become progressively more difficult for them to behave according to these attitudes.

6. *Buffers.* Several buffers decreased the effect of the learners' pain on the teachers. For example, the "learners" (actually confederates of the experimenter) were in another room. When they were in the same room with the teachers, the teachers' compliance rate dropped from 65% to 40%. Moreover, when the teacher held the learner's hand on the shock plate, the compliance rate dropped to 30%. In modern warfare, opposing military forces may be separated by great distances. They may be little more than a blip on a radar screen. It is one thing to press a button to launch a missile or aim a piece of artillery at a distant troop carrier or a faraway mountain ridge. It is another to hold a weapon to a victim's throat.

■ Conformity: Do Many Make Right?

We are said to **conform** when we change our behavior to adhere to social norms. **Social norms** are widely accepted expectations concerning social behavior. Explicit social norms are often made into rules and laws such as those that require us to whisper in libraries and to slow down when driving past a school. There are also unspoken or implicit social norms, such as those that cause us to face the front in an elevator or to be "fashionably late" for social gatherings. Can you think of some instances in which you have conformed to social pressure? (Would you wear blue jeans if everyone else wore slacks or skirts?)

Richard Douglas Rose

The tendency to conform to social norms is often good. Many norms have evolved because they promote comfort and survival. Group pressure can also promote maladaptive behavior, as when people engage in risky behavior because "everyone is doing it." *Why do so many people tend to follow the crowd?*

To answer this question, let us look at a classic experiment on conformity conducted by Solomon Asch in the early 1950s. We then examine factors that promote conformity.

■ **Conformity**
What factors influence the ways in which adolescents dress?

Conform To change one's attitudes or overt behavior to adhere to social norms.

Social norms Explicit and implicit rules that reflect social expectations and influence the ways people behave in social situations.

Seven Line Judges Can't Be Wrong: The Asch Study   Can you believe what you see with your own eyes? Seeing is believing, isn't it? Not if you were a subject in Asch's (1952) study.

Let's say you entered a laboratory room with seven other subjects, supposedly taking part in an experiment on visual discrimination. At the front of the room stood a man holding cards with lines drawn on them.

The eight of you were seated in a series. You were given the seventh seat, a minor fact at the time. The man explained the task. There was a single line on the card on the left. Three lines were drawn on the card at the right (see Figure 14.6). One line on the right card was the same length as the line on the left card. You and the other subjects were to call out, one at a time, which of the three lines—1, 2, or 3—was the same length as the one on the card on the left. Simple.

A. Standard line

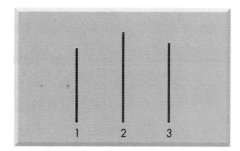

B. Comparison lines

Figure 14.6
Cards Used in the Asch Study on Conformity
Which line on card B—1, 2, or 3—is the same length as the line on card A? Line 2, right? But would you say "2" if you were a member of a group and six people answering ahead of you all said "3"? Are you sure?

The subjects to your right spoke out in order: "3," "3," "3," "3," "3," "3." Now it was your turn. Line 3 was clearly the same length as the line on the first card, so you said "3." The fellow after you then chimed in: "3." That's all there was to it. Then two other cards were set up at the front of the room. This time line 2 was clearly the same length as the line on the first card. The answers were "2," "2," "2," "2," "2," "2." Again it was your turn. You said "2," and perhaps your mind began to wander. Your stomach was gurgling a bit. The fellow after you said "2."

Another pair of cards was held up. Line 3 was clearly the correct answer. The six people on your right spoke in turn: "1," "1 . . ." Wait a second! ". . . 1," "1." You forgot about dinner and studied the lines briefly. No, line 1 was too short by a good half inch. But the next two subjects said "1" and suddenly it was your turn. Your hands had become sweaty, and there was a lump in your throat. You wanted to say "3," but was it right? There was really no time, and you had already paused noticeably. You said "1," and so did the last fellow.

Now your attention was riveted on the task. Much of the time you agreed with the other seven judges, but sometimes you did not. And for some reason beyond your understanding, they were in perfect agreement even when they were wrong—assuming you could trust your eyes. The experiment was becoming an uncomfortable experience, and you began to doubt your judgment. ◆ **Truth or Fiction Revisited:** Therefore, seeing is not always believing—especially when the group sees things differently.

The discomfort in the Asch study was caused by the pressure to conform. Actually, the other seven recruits were confederates of the experimenter. They prearranged a number of incorrect responses. The sole purpose of the study was to see whether you would conform to the erroneous group judgments.

How many people in Asch's study caved in? How many went along with the crowd rather than give what they thought to be the right answer? Seventy-five percent. *Three out of four agreed with the majority's wrong answer at least once.*

Factors That Influence Conformity   Several factors increase the tendency to conform. They include the following:

- belonging to a collectivist rather than an individualistic society (Phalet & Schoenpflug, 2001),
- the desire to be liked by other members of the group (but valuing being right over being liked *decreases* the tendency to conform),
- low self-esteem,
- social shyness (Santee & Maslach, 1982), and
- lack of familiarity with the task.

Other factors in conformity include group size and social support. The likelihood of conformity, even to incorrect group judgments, increases rapidly as group size grows to five members, then rises more slowly as the group grows to about eight members. At about that point the maximum chance of conformity is reached. Yet finding one other person who supports your minority opinion is apparently enough to encourage you to stick to your guns (Morris et al., 1977).

( ) Learning Connections

◀◀ Social Influence—Are You an Individual or One of the Crowd? ▶▶

REVIEW:

11 Milgram found that "teachers" who were willing to shock the "learners"
   (a) were ordinary people,
   (b) had not completed college,
   (c) were males only,
   (d) had to be told that the shock was not real.

12 Milgram's studies on obedience have been criticized on ground that
   (a) they were not ethical,
   (b) they were all carried out at Yale University,

(c) the statistics used to analyze results were faulty,
(d) participants were never informed of the true purposes of the study.

13 Conformity is defined as
   (a) obedience to authority,
   (b) deindividuation,
   (c) behavior in accordance with social norms,
   (d) diffusion of responsibility.

CRITICAL THINKING:
Critical thinkers do not overgeneralize. Most people would probably agree that it is good for children to be obedient. But is it always good for children—and for adults—to be obedient? As an individual, how can you determine whether or not it is good for *you* to be obedient? How do we define the limits?

Go www
to
http://academic.cengage.com/psychology/rathus
for an interactive version of this review.

GROUP BEHAVIOR

To be human is to belong to groups. Groups have much to offer us. They help us satisfy our needs for affection, attention, and belonging. They empower us to do things we could not manage by ourselves. But groups can also pressure us into doing things we might not do if we were acting alone, such as taking great risks or attacking other people.

This section considers ways in which people behave differently as group members than they would as individuals. We begin with social facilitation.

■ Social Facilitation: Monkey See, Monkey Do Faster?

When you are given a group assignment, do you work harder or less hard than you would alone? Why?

One effect of groups on individual behavior is **social facilitation,** or the effects on performance that result from the presence of others. *Do we run faster when we are in a group?* Apparently so. Runners and bicycle riders tend to move faster when they are members of a group. This effect is not limited to people. Dogs and cats eat more rapidly around others. Even roaches—yes, roaches—run more rapidly when other roaches are present (Zajonc, 1980).

Research suggests that the presence of other people increases our levels of arousal, or motivation (Platania & Moran, 2001; Thomas et al., 2002). At high levels of arousal, our

Social facilitation The process by which a person's performance is increased when other members of a group engage in similar behavior.

performance of simple tasks is facilitated. Our performance of complex responses may be impaired, however. For this reason, a well-rehearsed speech may be delivered more masterfully before a larger audience. An offhand speech or a question-and-answer session may be hampered by a large audience.

Social facilitation may be influenced by **evaluation apprehension** as well as arousal (Platania & Moran, 2001; Thomas et al., 2002). Our performance before a group is affected not only by the presence of others but also by concern that they are evaluating us. When giving a speech, we may "lose our thread" if we are distracted by the audience and focus too much on its apparent reaction. If we believe that we have begun to flounder, evaluation apprehension may skyrocket. As a result, our performance may falter even more.

The presence of others can also impair performance—not when we are acting *before* a

■ **Social Facilitation**
Runners tend to move faster when they are members of a group. Does the presence of other people raise our levels of arousal or produce "evaluation apprehension"?

group but when we are anonymous members *of* a group (Guerin, 1999). Workers, for example, may "goof off" or engage in *social loafing* on humdrum jobs when they believe they will not be found out and held accountable. Under these conditions there is no evaluation apprehension. There may also be **diffusion of responsibility** in groups. Each person may feel less obligation to help because others are present, especially if the others are perceived as being capable of doing the job (Hart et al., 2001). Group members may also reduce their efforts if an apparently capable member makes no contribution but "rides free" on the efforts of others.

How would you perform in a tug of war? Would the presence of other people pulling motivate you to pull harder? (If so, we might attribute the result to social facilitation, unless you personally enjoy tugging [Smith et al., 2001].) Or would the fact that no one can tell how hard you are pulling encourage you to "loaf"? (If so, should we attribute the result to diffusion of responsibility?)

reflect & relate

Families, classes, religious groups, political parties, nations, circles of friends, bowling teams, sailing clubs, conversation groups, therapy groups— how many groups do you belong to? How does belonging to these groups influence your behavior? Do these groups sometimes push or pull you in different directions?

Group Decision Making: Is a Camel a Horse Made by a Committee?

Organizations use groups such as committees or juries to make decisions in the belief that group decisions are more accurate than individual decisions (Gigone & Hastie, 1997). *How do groups make decisions?* Social psychologists have discovered a number of "rules," or **social decision schemes,** that govern much of group decision making (Stasser, 1999). Here are some examples:

1. *The majority-wins scheme.* In this commonly used scheme, the group arrives at the decision that was initially supported by the majority. This scheme appears to guide decision making most often when there is no single objectively correct decision. An example is a decision about which car models to build when their popularity has not been tested in the court of public opinion.
2. *The truth-wins scheme.* In this scheme, as more information is provided and opinions are discussed, the group comes to recognize that one approach is objectively correct. For example, a group deciding whether to use SAT scores in admitting students to college would profit from information about whether the scores do predict college success.

Evaluation apprehension Concern that others are evaluating our behavior.

Diffusion of responsibility The spreading or sharing of responsibility for a decision or behavior within a group.

Social decision schemes Rules for predicting the final outcome of group decision making on the basis of the members' initial positions.

How Will They Make Their Decision?
Will the majority prevail? Will someone point to a significant piece of evidence that sways the vote? Will the group follow the lead of the first person to change his or her mind? What other possibilities are there?

3. *The two-thirds majority scheme.* Juries tend to convict defendants when two-thirds of the jury initially favors conviction.
4. *The first-shift rule.* In this scheme, the group tends to adopt the decision that reflects the first shift in opinion expressed by any group member. If a car-manufacturing group is divided on whether to produce a convertible, it may opt to do so after one member of the group who initially was opposed to the idea changes her mind. Similarly, if a jury is deadlocked, the members may eventually follow the lead of the first juror to switch his position.

Polarization and the "Risky Shift"

We might think that a group decision would be more conservative than an individual decision. After all, shouldn't there be an effort to compromise, to "split the difference"? We might also expect that a few mature individuals would be able to balance the opinions of daredevils. *Are group decisions more risky or more conservative than those of the individual members of the group? Why?*

Groups do not always appear to work as we might expect, however. Consider the **polarization** effect. As an individual, you might recommend that your company risk an investment of $500,000 to develop or market a new product. Other company executives, polled individually, might risk similar amounts. If you were gathered together to make a group decision, however, you would probably recommend either an amount well above this figure or nothing at all (Kamalanabhan et al., 2000; Mordock, 1997). This group effect is called *polarization,* or the taking of an extreme position. If you had to gamble on which way the decision would go, however, you would do better to place your money on movement toward the higher sum—that is, to bet on a **risky shift.** Why?

One possibility is that one member of the group may reveal information of which the others were not aware. This information may clearly point in one direction or the other. With doubts removed, the group becomes polarized. It moves decisively in the appropriate direction. It is also possible that social facilitation occurs in the group setting and that the resulting greater motivation prompts more extreme decisions.

Why, however, do groups tend to take *greater* risks than those their members would take as individuals? One answer is diffusion of responsibility (Kamalanabhan et al., 2000; Mordock, 1997). If the venture flops, the blame will not be placed on you alone. Remember the self-serving bias: You can always say (and think) that the failure was the result of a group decision. You thus protect your self-esteem (Larrick, 1993). If the venture pays off, however, you can attribute the outcome to your cool analysis and boast of your influence on the group. Note that all this behavior fits right in with what is known about the self-serving bias.

Groupthink: When Smart People Think as One, Dumb Decisions May Follow

Smart people working collectively can be dumber than the sum of their brains.
—SCHWARTZ & WALD, 2003

Groupthink, a concept originated by Irving Janis (1982), is a problem that sometimes arises in group decision making. ***What is groupthink?*** In **groupthink,** group members tend to be more influenced by group cohesiveness and a dynamic leader than by the realities of the situation (Eaton, 2001; Postmes et al., 2001). Group problem solving may degenerate into groupthink when a group senses an external threat (Rempel & Fisher, 1998). Groupthink is usually fueled by a dynamic group leader. The threat heightens the cohesiveness of the

Polarization In social psychology, taking an extreme position or attitude on an issue.

Risky shift The tendency to make riskier decisions as a member of a group than as an individual acting independently.

Groupthink A process in which group members are influenced by cohesiveness and a dynamic leader to ignore external realities as they make decisions.

group and is a source of stress. Under stress, group members tend not to consider all their options carefully. Flawed decisions are frequently made as a result.

Groupthink has been connected with fiascos such as the Bay of Pigs invasion of Cuba, the escalation of the Vietnam War, the Watergate scandal, and NASA's decision to launch the *Challenger* and *Columbia* space shuttles despite engineers' warnings about the dangers created by cold weather and falling foam (Bartholomew et al., 2000; Brownstein, 2003; Schwartz & Wald, 2003). Janis (1982) and other researchers (Brownstein, 2003; Postmes et al., 2001; Turner & Pratkanis, 1998) note several characteristics of groupthink that contribute to flawed group decisions:

1. *Feelings of invulnerability.* Each decision-making group might have believed that it was beyond the reach of critics or the law—in some cases, because the groups consisted of powerful people who were close to the president of the United States.
2. *The group's belief in its rightness.* These groups apparently believed in the rightness of what they were doing. In some cases, they were carrying out the president's wishes. In the case of the *Challenger* launch, NASA had a track record of successful launches.
3. *Discrediting of information contrary to the group's decision.* The government group involved in the Iran-Contra affair knowingly broke the law. Its members apparently discredited the law by (a) deciding that it was inconsistent with the best interests of the United States, and (b) enlisting private citizens to do the dirty work so that the government was not directly involved.
4. *Pressures on group members to conform.* Group cohesiveness and a dynamic leader pressure group members to conform. Striving for unanimity overrides the quest for realism, and authority can trump expertise.
5. *Stereotyping of members of the out-group.* Members of the group that broke the law in the Iran-Contra affair reportedly stereotyped people who would oppose them as "communist sympathizers" and "knee-jerk liberals."

Groupthink can be averted if group leaders encourage members to remain skeptical about options and to feel free to ask probing questions and disagree with one another.

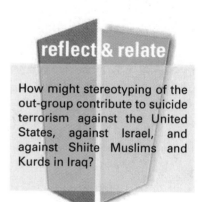

How might stereotyping of the out-group contribute to suicide terrorism against the United States, against Israel, and against Shiite Muslims and Kurds in Iraq?

▬▬ Mob Behavior and Deindividuation: The "Beast with Many Heads"

Have you ever done something as a member of a group that you would not have done as an individual? What was it? What motivated you? How do you feel about it?

The Frenchman Gustave Le Bon (1895/1960) branded mobs and crowds as irrational, resembling a "beast with many heads." Mob actions such as race riots and lynchings sometimes seem to operate on a psychology of their own. *Do mobs bring out the beast in us? How is it that mild-mannered people commit mayhem when they are part of a mob?*

Deindividuation When people act as individuals, fear of consequences and self-evaluation tend to prevent them from engaging in antisocial behavior. But in a mob, they may experience **deindividuation,** a state of reduced self-awareness and lowered concern for social evaluation. Many factors lead to deindividuation. These include anonymity, diffusion of responsibility, arousal due to noise and crowding, and a focus on emerging group norms rather than on one's own values (Baron et al., 2006). Under these circumstances crowd members behave more aggressively than they would as individuals.

Police know that mob actions are best averted early by dispersing small groups that could gather into a crowd. On an individual level, perhaps we can resist deindividuation by instructing ourselves to stop and think whenever we begin to feel highly aroused in a group. If we dissociate ourselves from such groups when they are forming, we are more likely to remain critical and avoid behavior that we might later regret.

What role might deindividuation play in terrorist acts?

Deindividuation The process by which group members may discontinue self-evaluation and adopt group norms and attitudes.

■ Protesters Are Contained by Police

The French social thinker Gustave Le Bon branded mobs as irrational, like a "beast with many heads." Police are taught that it's useful to confront groups as early as possible, to prevent them from becoming so highly emotionally aroused that they forget their values as individuals and focus on the emerging group norms.

—■— Altruism and the Bystander Effect: Some Watch While Others Die

Altruism—selfless concern for the welfare of others—is connected with some heroic and some very strange behavior throughout the animal kingdom (Zahavi, 2003). Humans have sacrificed themselves to ensure the survival of their children or of comrades in battle. Primates sometimes suicidally attack an approaching leopard to give others the opportunity to escape.

These behaviors are heroic. But consider the red spider's strange ways (Begley & Check, 2000). After depositing its sperm into a female red spider, the male of the species will do a flip into her mouth and become her dinner! Clearly, the red spider is not bothered by the spark of consciousness, and it certainly is blind to the light of reason. But evolutionary psychologists might argue that the self-sacrificing behavior of the male red spider is actually selfish from an evolutionary point of view. How, you might wonder, can individuals sacrifice themselves and at the same time be acting in their own self-interests? To answer the question, you should also know that female red spiders are promiscuous; they will mate with multiple suitors. Eating a "lover" slows them down, however, increasing the probability that *his* sperm will fertilize her eggs and that his genes will survive and be transmitted to the next generation. We could thus say that the male red spider is altruistic in that he puts the welfare of future generations ahead of his own. Fatherhood ain't easy.

Red spiders, of course, do not think—at least, not in any humanly understandable sense of the concept of thinking. But people do. So how, one might ask, could the murder of 28-year-old Kitty Genovese have happened? It took place in New York City more than 40 years ago (Rasenberger, 2004). Murder was not unheard of in the Big Apple, but Kitty had screamed for help as her killer stalked her for more than half an hour and stabbed her in three separate attacks. Thirty-eight neighbors heard the commotion. Twice the assault was interrupted by their voices and bedroom lights. Each time the attacker returned. Yet nobody came to the victim's aid. No one even called the police. ◆▶ **Truth or Fiction Revisited:** Therefore, it is true that nearly 40 people stood by and did nothing while a woman was being stabbed to death.

Why? Some witnesses said matter-of-factly that they did not want to get involved. One said that he was tired. Still others said, "I don't know." As a nation, are we a callous bunch who would rather watch than help when others are in trouble?

Why do people sometimes sacrifice themselves for others and, at other times, ignore people who are in trouble? Why did 38 bystanders allow Kitty Genovese to die? When do we decide to come to the aid of someone who is in trouble?

The Helper: Who Helps?   It turns out that many factors are involved in helping behavior. The following are among them:

1. Observers are more likely to help when they are in a good mood (Baron et al., 2006). Perhaps good moods impart a sense of personal power—the feeling that we can handle the situation (Cunningham et al., 1990; Dulin & Hill, 2003).
2. People who are empathic are more likely to help people in need (Darley, 1993). Empathic people feel the distress of others, feel concern for them, and can imagine what it must be like to be in need. Women are more likely than men to be empathic and thus more likely to help people in need (Trobst et al., 1994).
3. Bystanders may not help unless they believe that an emergency exists (Baron et al., 2006). Perhaps some people who heard Kitty Genovese's calls for help were not certain of what was happening. (But remember that others admitted they did not want to get involved.)

Altruism   Unselfish concern for the welfare of others.

4. Observers must assume the responsibility to act (Baron et al., 2006). It may seem logical that a group of people would be more likely to have come to the aid of Kitty Genovese than a lone person. After all, a group could more effectively have overpowered her attacker. Yet research by Darley and Latané (1968) suggests that a lone person may have been more likely to try to help her.

  In their classic experiment, male subjects were performing meaningless tasks in cubicles when they heard a (convincing) recording of a person apparently having an epileptic seizure. When the men thought that four other persons were immediately available, only 31% tried to help the victim. When they thought that no one else was available, however, 85% of them tried to help. As in other areas of group behavior, it seems that *diffusion of responsibility* inhibits helping behavior in groups or crowds. When we are in a group, we are often willing to let George (or Georgette) do it. When George isn't around, we are more willing to help others ourselves. (Perhaps some who heard Kitty Genovese thought, "Why should I get involved? Other people can hear her too.")

5. Observers must know what to do (Baron et al., 2006). We hear of cases in which people impulsively jump into the water to save a drowning child and then drown themselves. Most of the time, however, people do not try to help unless they know what to do. For example, nurses are more likely than people without medical training to try to help accident victims (Cramer et al., 1988). Observers who are not sure that they can take charge of the situation may stay on the sidelines for fear of making a social blunder and being ridiculed. Or they may fear getting hurt themselves. (Perhaps some who heard Kitty Genovese thought, "If I try to intervene, I may get killed or make an idiot of myself.")

6. Observers are more likely to help people they know (Rutkowski et al., 1983). Aren't we also more likely to give to charity when asked directly by a coworker or supervisor in the socially exposed situation of the office as compared with a letter received in the privacy of our own homes?

  Evolutionary psychologists suggest that altruism is a natural aspect of human nature—even if not in the same way as in the case of the red spider! Self-sacrifice sometimes helps close relatives or others who are similar to us to survive. Self-sacrifice is "selfish" from a genetic or evolutionary point of view (Bruene & Ribbert, 2002). It helps us perpetuate a genetic code similar to our own. This view suggests that we are more likely to be altruistic with our relatives rather than strangers, however. The Kitty Genoveses of the world may remain out of luck unless they are surrounded by kinfolk or friends.

7. Observers are more likely to help people who are similar to themselves. Being able to identify with the person in need appears to promote helping behavior (Cialdini et al., 1997). Poorly dressed people are more likely to succeed in requests for a dime with poorly dressed strangers. Well-dressed people are more likely to get money from well-dressed strangers (Hensley, 1981).

reflect & relate

Research concerning altruism and the bystander effect highlight the fact that we are members of a vast, interdependent social fabric. The next time you see a stranger in need, what will you do? Are you sure?

Ordinary People in Extraordinary Times   Now that we have come this far, we are ready to reconsider who the suicide terrorists are likely to be. Check out the nearby "A Closer Look" feature: "Who Are the Suicide Terrorists? A Case of a Fundamental Attribution Error?"

But let us not end this chapter and this book on a negative note. Let us think, instead, about the altruism of the firefighters, police officers, and ordinary people who came to the aid of the victims of the suicide terrorism of September 11, 2001. Following the attacks, thousands evacuated lower Manhattan by ferry to New Jersey. Residents of New Jersey drove up and down the streets near the ferry, asking if they could give evacuees rides or help in any other way. And people heading away from the devastation in Manhattan were happy to share their taxi cabs, even with strangers. If you know a little about New York, you know that's rather special—but also something done by ordinary people in extraordinary times.

A Closer Look

Who Are the Suicide Terrorists? A Case of a Fundamental Attribution Error?

A Closer Look

Following the attacks of September 11, 2001, President George W. Bush labeled the suicide terrorists "evil cowards." Senator John Warner declared, "Those who would commit suicide in their assaults on the free world are not rational and are not deterred by rational concepts." Attempting to fend off anti-Islamic rage, some Islamic leaders advised their followers to say that "terrorists are extremist maniacs who don't represent Islam at all" (cited by Altran, 2005).

Evil. Cowardly. Irrational. Maniacal. Do such concepts begin to paint a psychological portrait of suicide terrorists? Information about them comes from people who knew them before they committed their acts, and from studies of would-be suicide terrorists who were prevented from carrying out their missions.

So, what have we learned? We could say "not much" and we could say "a great deal." How do we resolve this contradiction? Perhaps with the help of social psychology. Those who have studied the nature of evil, such as Stanley Milgram,

■ **Why Did They Fly into the World Trade Center and the Pentagon?**
Was it a matter of personality and personal choice? Was it a web of situational factors? What does social psychology have to teach us about the nature of evil?

find that many, perhaps most, perpetrators of evil are "ordinary people" (Baumeister, 1996; Berkowitz, 2004b). The Consortium of Social Science Associations (COSSA) (2003) testified to Congress that they had to conclude there was no clear profile of the suicide terrorist. Suicide terrorists averaged 21 or 22 years of age, but some were younger and many were older. Some were devout Muslims but most seemed to be no more devout than their communities. Most had at least some high school education, and some had attended college.

The U.S. Council of Foreign Relations (2002) reported a study of Palestinian suicide terrorists recruited by Hamas. Whereas suicidal people in general tend to be depressed, even desperate, the Council noted that many suicide bombers held paying jobs, even in poverty-stricken communities. They harbored strong hatred of Israel, just as the suicide bombers of 9/11 harbored strong hatred of the United States. After a bombing, Hamas gave the families of bombers several thousand dollars and assured them that their sons had died as martyrs in a holy struggle (a *jihad*). COSSA and the Council speculate that some of the suicide terrorists might have had "masculine self-image problems" and been seeking recognition—but not all of them.

So, in seeking a profile, are we making a fundamental attribution error? According to attribution theory, we tend to attribute too much of other people's behavior to internal factors such as attitudes and choice (Gilovich & Eibach, 2001; Reeder, 2001). Moreover, victims of crime and terrorism tend to make the fundamental attribution error in explaining what they have suffered and may overlook the situational influences that contribute to provoke the act (Baumeister, 1996; Berkowitz, 2004b; Zimbardo, 2004).

People tend to explain behavior in terms of personal traits and personal choice, even when significant factors are at work in the person's society. As noted by Scott Altran (2005), who has studied suicide terrorism:

> U.S. government and media characterizations of Middle East suicide bombers as craven homicidal lunatics may suffer from a fundamental attribution error: No instances of religious or political suicide terrorism stem from lone actions of cowering or unstable bombers. Psychologist Stanley Milgram found that ordinary Americans also readily obey destructive orders under the right circumstances.

If suicide terrorists are responding to group pressure and magnetic leaders, do we absolve them of guilt for their crimes? Not at all. But perhaps we need to recognize that there is little if anything that is special or extraordinary about them. ■

FBI/Getty Images

❝❞ Learning Connections

 Group Behavior

REVIEW:

14 According to Zajonc's view of social facilitation, the presence of others influences us by
  (a) decreasing evaluation apprehension,
  (b) increasing our levels of arousal,
  (c) making us anonymous,
  (d) creating diffusion of responsibility.

15 When we are members of a group, we are most likely to engage in social loafing when
  (a) we experience evaluation apprehension,
  (b) our level of arousal increases,
  (c) we are anonymous,
  (d) the leader is an authority figure.

16 When juries are deadlocked, they are most likely to arrive at a verdict by means of the
  (a) two-thirds rule,
  (b) majority-wins scheme,
  (c) first-shift rule,
  (d) truth-wins scheme.

17 The "risky shift" refers to the finding that
  (a) attitudes become polarized during a group process,
  (b) people undergo deindividuation when they are members of a mob,
  (c) people behave recklessly when ordered about by an authority figure,
  (d) group decisions are often riskier than individual decisions.

18 Mob behavior appears to be characterized by all of the following, with the exception of
  (a) reduced self-awareness,
  (b) focusing of individual attention on the group process,
  (c) arousal due to noise and crowding,
  (d) assumption of personal responsibility.

CRITICAL THINKING:
According to evolutionary theory, self-sacrifice can be "selfish." How does evolutionary theory explain this view? Do you agree or disagree? Explain.

Go to www
http://academic.cengage.com/psychology/rathus for an interactive version of this review.

RECITE—*An Active Summary*™

Recite to Go! *Don't have time to study right now? You can study on the go!*
Go to your companion website and download an audio version of this review section to your media player. You can
also access an interactive flash-card version of this review from your website.

1. What is social psychology?	Social psychology studies the factors that influence people's thoughts, feelings, and behaviors in social situations.
2. What are attitudes?	Attitudes are behavioral and cognitive tendencies to evaluate particular people, places, or things with favor or disfavor.
3. Do people do as they think? (For example, do people really vote their consciences?)	When we are free to act as we wish, our behavior is often consistent with our beliefs and feelings. But as indicated by the term *A–B problem,* the links between attitudes (A) and behaviors (B) are often weak to moderate.
4. Where do attitudes come from?	Attitudes can be learned by means of conditioning or learning by observation. However, people also appraise and evaluate situations and often form their own judgments.
5. Can you really change people's attitudes and behavior?	People attempt to change other people's attitudes and behavior by means of persuasion. According to the elaboration likelihood model, persuasion occurs through central and peripheral routes. Repeated messages generally "sell" better than messages delivered once. People tend to respond more to fear appeals than to purely factual presentations. Persuasive communicators tend to show expertise, trustworthiness, attractiveness, or similarity to the audience.
6. What is cognitive-dissonance theory?	Cognitive-dissonance theory hypothesizes that people dislike situations in which their attitudes and behavior are inconsistent. Such situations apparently induce cognitive dissonance, which people can reduce by changing their attitudes.
7. What factors contribute to attraction in our culture?	Men seem to find large eyes and narrows jaws to be attractive in women. In our culture, slenderness is considered attractive in both men and women, and tallness is valued in men. We are more attracted to good-looking people. Similarity in attitudes and sociocultural factors also enhance attraction. According to the matching hypothesis, we tend to seek dates and mates at our own level of attractiveness.
8. What is love?	Sternberg's theory suggests that love has three components: intimacy, passion, and commitment. Romantic love is the combination of passion and intimacy. Consummate love has all three factors.
9. Do first impressions really matter?	First impressions can last because we tend to label or describe people in terms of the behavior we see initially.
10. What are the primacy and recency effects?	The primacy effect refers to the fact that we often judge people in terms of our first impressions. The recency effects appears to be based on the fact that recently learned information is easier to remember.
11. What is attribution theory? Why do we assume that other people intend the mischief that they do?	The attribution process is the tendency to infer the motives and traits of others through observation of their behavior. In dispositional attributions, we attribute people's behavior to internal factors. In situational attributions, we attribute people's behavior to external forces. According to the actor–observer effect, we tend to attribute the behavior of others to internal, dispositional factors, but we tend to attribute our own behavior to external, situational factors. The fundamental attribution error is the tendency to attribute too much of other people's behavior to dispositional factors.

12. What is body language?	Body language refers to communicating by means of posture and gesture. People who feel positively toward one another position themselves closer together and are more likely to touch. Gazing into another's eyes can be a sign of love, but a hard stare is an aversive challenge.
13. Why will so many people commit crimes against humanity if they are ordered to do so? (Why don't they refuse?)	The majority of subjects in the Milgram studies complied with the demands of authority figures, even when the demands required that they hurt innocent people by means of electric shock. Factors contributing to obedience include socialization, lack of social comparison, perception of legitimate authority figures, the foot-in-the-door technique, inaccessibility of values, and buffers between perpetrator and victim.
14. Why do so many people tend to follow the crowd?	Asch's research in which subjects judged the lengths of lines suggests that most people will follow the crowd, even when the crowd is wrong. Personal factors such as desire to be liked by group members, low self-esteem, high self-consciousness, and shyness contribute to conformity. Group size also contributes.
15. Do we run faster when we are in a group?	The concept of social facilitation refers to the effects on performance that result from the presence of other people. The presence of others may facilitate performance for reasons such as increased arousal and evaluation apprehension. Anonymous group members, however, may experience diffusion of responsibility and performance may fall off, as in social loafing.
16. How do groups make decisions?	Social psychologists have identified several decision-making schemes, including the majority-wins scheme, the truth-wins scheme, the two-thirds majority scheme, and the first-shift rule.
17. Are group decisions more risky or more conservative than those of the individual members of the group? Why?	Group decisions tend to be more polarized and riskier than individual decisions, largely because groups diffuse responsibility. Group decisions may be highly productive when group members are knowledgeable, there is an explicit procedure for arriving at decisions, and there is a process of give and take.
18. What is groupthink?	Groupthink is unrealistic decision making that is fueled by the perception of threats to the group. It is facilitated by a dynamic group leader, feelings of invulnerability, the group's belief in its rightness, the discrediting of contradictory information, conformity, and stereotyping of out-group people.
19. Do mobs bring out the beast in us? How is it that mild-mannered people commit mayhem when they are part of a mob?	Highly emotional crowds may induce attitude-discrepant behavior through the process of deindividuation, which is a state of reduced self-awareness and lowered concern for social evaluation. The high emotions are connected with arousal which makes it more difficult to access one's own values.
20. Why do people sometimes sacrifice themselves for others and, at other times, ignore people who are in trouble?	A number of factors contribute to altruism (the tendency to help others). These include empathy, a good mood, feelings of responsibility, knowledge of how to help, and acquaintance with—and similarity to—the person in trouble. According to the bystander effect, we are unlikely to aid people in distress when we are members of crowds because crowds diffuse responsibility.

Key Terms

Situationist perspective 506
Social psychology 506
Attitude 507
A–B problem 507
Elaboration likelihood model 508
Fear appeal 509
Selective avoidance 510
Selective exposure 510
Cognitive-dissonance theory 510
Attitude-discrepant behavior 510
Effort justification 511
Stereotype 511
Attraction 514
Matching hypothesis 516
Reciprocity 516
Triangular model of love 517

Intimacy 517
Passion 517
Commitment 517
Consummate love 517
Romantic love 517
Oxytocin 517
Social perception 519
Primacy effect 520
Recency effect 520
Attribution 520
Attribution process 521
Dispositional attribution 521
Situational attribution 521
Fundamental attribution error 521
Actor–observer effect 521
Self-serving bias 522

Consensus 522
Consistency 522
Distinctiveness 522
Social influence 525
Foot-in-the-door technique 527
Conform 528
Social norms 528
Social facilitation 530
Evaluation apprehension 531
Diffusion of responsibility 531
Social decision schemes 531
Polarization 532
Risky shift 532
Groupthink 532
Deindividuation 533
Altruism 534

Active Learning Resources

Visit Your Companion Website
for This Book

http://academic.cengage.com/psychology/rathus

Check out this companion website where you will find online resources directly linked to your book. This is where you'll access the videos highlighted in your Video Connections feature. You can answer the questions online and email them to your professor. In addition you'll find downloadable audio review material, interactive versions of the study aids, Power Visuals for mastering and reviewing key concepts, as well as quizzing, and much more!

CENGAGENOW™

http://academic.cengage.com

Need help studying? This site is your one-stop study shop. Take a Pre-Test and Cengage NOW will generate a Personalized Study Plan based on your test results. The Study Plan will identify the topics you need to review and direct you to online resources to help you master those topics. You can then take a Post-Test to help you determine the concepts you have mastered and what you still need to work on. In addition you can access interactive media including the videos highlighted in your Video Connections box.

Author Blog

What does your author Spence Rathus have to say about the state of psychology? Visit your companion website every Tuesday and click on "Author Blog." This is where he'll talk about the most recent controversies and hot topics in psychology. This will keep you up to date with what your author is thinking and give you great insight into modern psychology.

APPENDIX A
Statistics

truth or fiction?

T	F	Basketball players could be said to be abnormal.
T	F	Being a "10" is not always a good thing.
T	F	You should not assume that you can walk across a river with an average depth of 4 feet.
T	F	Adding people's incomes and then dividing them by the number of people can be an awful way of showing the average income.
T	F	Psychologists express your IQ score in terms of how deviant you are.
T	F	An IQ score of 130 is more impressive than an SAT score of 500.

Go to www

*http://academic.cengage.com/pstchology/rathus
for an interactive version of this Truth or Fiction feature.*

STATISTICS

Imagine that some visitors from outer space arrive outside Madison Square Garden in New York City. Their goal this dark and numbing winter evening is to learn all they can about planet Earth. They are drawn inside the Garden by lights, shouts, and warmth. The spotlighting inside rivets their attention to a wood-floored arena where the New York Big Apples are hosting the California Quakes in a briskly contested basketball game.

Our visitors use their sophisticated instruments to take some measurements of the players. Some interesting statistics are sent back to their planet of origin: It appears that (1) 100% of Earthlings are male and (2) the height of Earthlings ranges from 6 feet 1 inch to 7 feet 2 inches.

These measurements are called **statistics**. *What is statistics?* Statistics is the name given the science concerned with obtaining and organizing numerical information or measurements. Our imagined visitors have sent home statistics about the gender and size of human beings that are at once accurate and misleading. Although they accurately measured the basketball players (we have translated their units of measurement into feet and inches for readers' convenience), their small **sample** of Earth's **population** was, shall we say, distorted.

What are samples and populations? A population is a complete group of people, other animals, or measures from which a sample is drawn. For example, all people on Earth could be defined as the population of interest. So could all women, or all women in the United States. A sample is a group of measures drawn from a population. Fortunately for us Earthlings, about half of the world's population is female. And the **range** of heights observed by the aliens, of 6 feet 1 inch to 7 feet 2 inches, is both restricted and too high—much too high. People vary in height by more than 1 foot and 1 inch. And our **average** height is not between 6 feet 1 inch and 7 feet 2 inches; rather, it is a number of inches below.

Psychologists, like our imagined visitors, are vitally concerned with measuring human as well as animal characteristics and traits—not just physical characteristics as height, but also psychological traits such as intelligence, sociability, aggressiveness, neatness, anxiety, and depression. By observing the central tendencies (averages) and variations in measurement from person to person, psychologists can say that one person is average or above average in intelligence, or that someone else is less anxious than, say, 60% of the population.

But psychologists, unlike our aliens, attempt to select a sample that accurately represents the entire population. Professional basketball players do not represent the entire human species. ◆ **Truth or Fiction Revisited:** Basketball players are taller, stronger, and more agile than the rest of us. They also make more sneaker commercials. Their "abnormalities" are assets to them, of course, not deficits.

In this appendix we survey some of the statistical methods used by psychologists to draw conclusions about the measurements they take in research. First we discuss *descriptive statistics* and learn what types of statements we can make about height and other human traits. Then we discuss the *normal curve* and learn why basketball players are abnormal—at least in terms of height. We explain *correlation coefficients* and provide you with some less-than-shocking news: As a group, students who study obtain higher grades than students who do not study. Finally, we have a look at *inferential statistics,* and we see why we can be bold enough to say that the difference in height between basketball players and other people is not a chance fluctuation or fluke. Basketball players are in fact *statistically significantly* taller than the general population.

---

reflect & relate

Look around at the various people in your family, your neighborhood, your classes. To what degree do you believe they represent the population of the United States? Explain.

Statistics Numerical facts assembled in such a manner that they provide useful information about measures or scores. (From the Latin *status,* meaning "standing" or "position.")

Sample Part of a population.

Population A complete group from which a sample is selected.

Range A measure of variability defined as the high score in a distribution minus the low score.

Average The central tendency of a group of measures, expressed either as the mean, median, or mode of a distribution.

Learning Connections

DESCRIPTIVE STATISTICS

Being told that someone is a "10" may sound great at first. However, it is not very descriptive unless you know something about how the scores on the scale are distributed and how frequently one finds a 10. Fortunately—for 10s, if not for the rest of us—one usually means that the person is a 10 on a scale of from 1 to 10, and that 10 is the highest possible score on the scale. If this is not sufficient, one will also be told that 10s are few and far between—rather unusual statistical events. ◆ **Truth or Fiction Revisited**: But note that the scale could also vary from 0 to 100, in which case a score of 10 would place one nearer to the bottom of the scale and make a score of 50 the center point of the scale. With such a scale, being a 10 would be much less impressive.

The idea of the scale from 1 to 10 may not be very scientific, but it does suggest something about **descriptive statistics**. *What is descriptive statistics?* (Why isn't it always good to be a "10"?) Descriptive statistics is the branch of statistics that provides information about distributions of scores. We can use descriptive statistics to clarify our understanding of a distribution of scores such as heights, test grades, IQs, or even increases or decreases in measures of aggressive behavior following the drinking of alcohol. For example, descriptive statistics can help us determine measures of central tendency (averages) and to determine how much fluctuation or variability there is in the scores. Being a 10 loses much of its charm if the average score is an 11. Being a 10 is more remarkable in a distribution whose scores range from 1 to 10 than it is in a distribution whose scores range from 9 to 11.

Let us now consider some of the concerns of descriptive statistics: the frequency distribution, measures of central tendency (types of averages), and measures of variability.

■ The Frequency Distribution

What is a frequency distribution? A **frequency distribution** takes scores or items of raw data, puts them into order as from the lowest to the highest, and indicates how often a score appears. A frequency distribution groups data according to class intervals, although the class may be a single unit (one), as in Table A.2. Table A.1 shows the rosters for a recent

Descriptive statistics The branch of statistics that is concerned with providing descriptive information about a distribution of scores.

Frequency distribution An ordered set of data that indicates the frequency (how often) with which scores appear.

TABLE A.1 ■ Rosters of Quakes Versus Big Apples at New York

A glance at the rosters for a recent basketball game in which the New York Big Apples "entertained" the California Quakes shows that the heights of the team members, combined, ranged from 6 feet 1 inch to 7 feet 2 inches. Do the heights of the team members represent those of the general male population? What do you think?

CALIFORNIA QUAKES		NEW YORK BIG APPLES	
2 Callahan	6'7"	3 Roosevelt	6'1"
5 Daly	6'11"	12 Chaffee	6'5"
6 Chico	6'2"	13 Baldwin	6'9"
12 Capistrano	6'3"	25 Delmar	6'6"
21 Brentwood	6'5"	27 Merrick	6'8"
25 Van Nuys	6'3"	28 Hewlett	6'6"
31 Clemente	6'9"	33 Hollis	6'9"
32 Whittier	6'8"	42 Bedford	6'5"
41 Fernando	7'2"	43 Coram	6'2"
43 Watts	6'9"	45 Hampton	6'10"
53 Huntington	6'6"	53 Ardsley	6'10"

TABLE A.2 ■ Frequency Distribution of Basketball Players (Quakes and Big Apples Combined), with a One-Inch Class Interval

CLASS INTERVAL	NUMBER OF PLAYERS IN CLASS
6'1"–6'1.9"	1
6'2"–6'2.9"	2
6'3"–6'3.9"	2
6'4"–6'4.9"	0
6'5"–6.5.9"	3
6'6"–6'6.9"	3
6'7"–6'7.9"	1
6'8"–6'8.9"	2
6'9"–6'9.9"	4
6'10"–6'10.9"	2
6'11"–6'11.9"	1
7'0"–7'0.9"	0
7'1"–7'1.9"	0
7.2"–7'2.9"	1

TABLE A.3 ■ **Frequency Distribution of Heights of Basketball Players, Using a Three-Inch Class Interval**

CLASS INTERVAL	NUMBER OF PLAYERS IN CLASS
6'1"–6'3.9"	5
6'4"–6'6.9"	6
6'7"–6'9.9"	7
6'10"–7'0.9"	3
7'1"–7'3.9"	1

basketball game between the California Quakes and the New York Big Apples. The players are listed according to the numbers on their uniforms. Table A.2 shows a frequency distribution of the heights of the players, with the two teams combined. The class interval in Table A.2 is 1 inch.

It would also be possible to use other class intervals, such as 3 inches, as shown in Table A.3. In determining the size of a class interval, the researcher tries to collapse the data into a small enough number of classes to ensure that they will be meaningful at a glance. But the researcher also tries to keep a large enough number of categories (classes) to ensure that important differences are not obscured.

Table A.3 obscures the fact that no players are 6 feet 4 inches tall. If the researcher believes that this information is extremely important, a class interval of 1 inch may be maintained.

Figure A.1 shows two methods of graphing the information in Table A.3: the **frequency histogram** and the **frequency polygon.** Students sometimes have difficulty interpreting graphs, but the purpose of graphs is to reveal key information about frequency distributions at a glance. Note that in both kinds of graph, the frequency histogram and the frequency polygon, the class intervals are usually drawn along the horizontal line. The horizontal line is also known as the X-axis. The numbers of cases (scores, persons, or events) in each class interval are shown along the vertical line, which is also known as the Y-axis. In the histogram, the number of scores in each class interval is represented by a bar—a rectangular solid—so that the graph looks like a series of steps. In the polygon, the number of scores in

Frequency histogram A graphic representation of a frequency distribution that uses rectangular solids (bars) to represent the frequency with which scores appear.

Frequency polygon A graphic representation of a frequency distribution that connects the points that show the frequencies with which scores appear, thereby creating a multisided geometric figure.

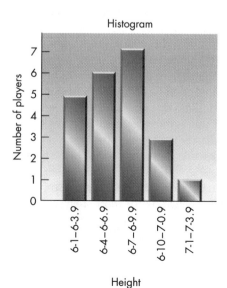

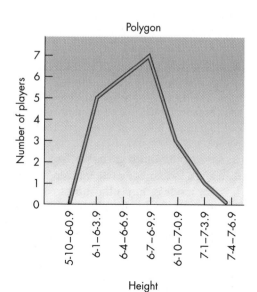

Figure A.1

Two Graphical Representations of the Data in Table A.3

The graph on the left is called a frequency histogram, or bar graph. The graph on the right is called a frequency polygon.

each class interval is plotted as a point. The points are connected to form a many-sided geometric figure (polygon). Note that empty class intervals were added at each end of the frequency polygon so that the sides of the figure could be brought down to the X-axis to close the geometric figure.

━━■━ Measures of Central Tendency

Never try to walk across a river just because it has an average depth of four feet.
—MARTIN FRIEDMAN

◆▶ **Truth or Fiction Revisited:** A river with an average depth of 4 feet could be over your head in many places, so, as suggested in the quip by Martin Friedman, a measure of central tendency can sometimes be misleading. ***What are measures of central tendency?*** Measures of central tendency are "averages" that show the center or balancing points of a frequency distribution. There are three commonly used types of measures of central tendency: the *mean, median,* and *mode.* Each attempts to describe something about the scores in a frequency distribution through the use of a typical or representative number.

The **mean** is what most people think of as "the average." We obtain the mean of a distribution by adding up the scores and then dividing the sum by the number of scores. In the case of the basketball players, it would be advisable to first convert the heights into a single unit, such as inches (6′1″ becomes 73″, and so on). If we add all the heights in inches and then divide by the number of players (22), we obtain a mean height of 78.73″. If we convert that number back into units of feet and inches, we obtain 6′6.73″.

The **median** is the score of the middle case in a distribution. It is the score beneath which 50% of the cases fall. In a distribution with an even number of cases, such as the distribution of the heights of the 22 basketball players as shown in Table A.2, we obtain the median by finding the mean of the two middle cases. When we list the 22 cases in ascending order (moving from lowest to highest), the 11th case is 6′6″ and the 12th case is 6′7″. Therefore, the median of the distribution is (6′6″ + 6′7″)/2, or 6′6½″.

When we analyze the heights of the basketball players, we find that the mean and median are similar. Either one serves as a useful indicator of the central tendency of the data. But suppose we are trying to find the average savings of 30 families living on a suburban block. Let us assume that 29 of the 30 families have savings between $8,000 and $12,000, adding up to $294,000. But the 30th family has savings of $1,400,000! The mean savings for a family on this block would thus be $56,467. The mean can be greatly distorted by one or two extreme scores. An IQ score of 145 would similarly distort the mean of the IQ scores of a class of 20 students, among whom the other 19 IQ scores ranged from 93 to 112. Then, too, if a few basketball players signed up for one of your classes, the mean of the students' heights would be distorted in an upward direction. ◆▶ **Truth or Fiction Revisited:** Therefore, adding people's incomes and then dividing them by the number of people can be an awful way of showing the average income. A few extremely high incomes, or IQ scores, or heights can distort the average of a group in an upward direction.

When there are a few extreme scores in a distribution, the median is a better indicator of central tendency. The median savings on our hypothetical block would lie between $8,000 and $12,000. Thus it would be more representative of the central tendency of savings. Studies of the incomes of families in the United States usually report median rather than mean incomes just to avoid the distortion of findings that would occur if the incomes of a handful of billionaires were treated in the same way as more common incomes. On the other hand, one could argue that choosing the median as the average obscures or hides the extreme scores, which are just as "real" as the other scores. Perhaps it is best to use the median and a footnote—a rather big footnote.

The **mode** is simply the most frequently occurring score or measure in a distribution. The mode of the data in Table A.1 is 6′9″ because this height occurs most often among the players on the two teams. The median class interval for the data shown in Table A.3 is 6′6½″ to 6′9½″. With this particular distribution, the mode is somewhat higher than the mean or median.

In some cases the mode is a more appropriate description of the central tendency of a distribution than the mean or the median. Figure A.2 shows a **bimodal** distribution—that

Mean A type of average that is calculated by adding all the scores and then dividing by the number of scores.

Median The central score in a frequency distribution; the score beneath which 50% of the cases fall.

Mode The most frequently occurring number or score in a distribution.

Bimodal Having two modes.

is, a distribution with two modes. This is a hypothetical distribution of test scores obtained by a class. The mode at the left indicates the most common class interval (45 to 49) for students who did not study, and the mode to the right shows the most common class interval (65 to 69) for students who did study. (Don't be alarmed. I'm sure that the professor, who is extremely fair, will be delighted to curve the grades so that the interval of 75 to 79 is an A+ and the interval of 65 to 69 is at least a B.) The mean and median test scores would probably lie within the 55 to 59 class interval, yet use of that interval as the measure of central tendency could obscure rather than reveal the important aspects of this distribution of test scores. It might suggest that the test was too hard, not that a number of students chose not to study. Similarly, one of the distribution's modes might be a bit larger than the other, so one could follow the exact rule for finding the mode and report just one of them. But this approach would also hide the meaning of this particular distribution of scores. All in all, it is clearly best to visualize this distribution of scores as bimodal. Even when the modes are not exactly equal, it is often most accurate to report distributions as bimodal, or, when there are three or more modes, as multimodal. One chooses one's measure or measures of central tendency to describe the essential features of a frequency distribution, not to hide them.

▬■▬ Measures of Variability

Our hypothetical class obtained test scores ranging from call intervals of 35 to 39 to call intervals of 75 to 79. That is, the scores *varied* from the lower class interval to the higher class interval. Now, if all the students had obtained scores from 55 to 59 or from 65 to 69, the scores would not have varied as much; that is, they would have clustered closer to one another and would have had lower variability.

What are measures of variability? The measures of the variability of a distribution inform us about the spread of scores—that is, about the typical distances of scores from the average score. Two commonly used measures of variability are the *range* of scores and the *standard deviation* of scores.

The range of scores in a distribution is defined as the difference between the highest score and the lowest score. The range is obtained by subtracting the lowest score from the highest score. The range of heights in Table A.2 is obtained by subtracting 6′1″ from 7′2″, or 1′1″. It is useful to know the range of temperatures when we move to an area with a different climate so that we may anticipate the weather and dress for it appropriately. A teacher must have some understanding of the range of abilities or skills in a class in order to teach effectively. An understanding of the range of human heights can be used to design doorways, beds, and headroom in automobiles. Even so, the typical doorway is 6′8″ high; and, as we saw with the California Quakes and New York Big Apples, some people will have to duck to get through.

The range is an imperfect measure of variability because of the manner in which it is influenced by extreme scores. The range of savings of the 30 families on our suburban block is $1,400,000 minus $8,000, or $1,392,000. This is a large number, and it is certainly true. However, it tells us little about the *typical* variation of savings accounts, which lie within a more restricted range of $8,000 to $12,000.

The **standard deviation** is a statistic that does a better job of showing how the scores in a distribution are distributed (spread) about the mean. It is usually better than the range because it considers every score in the distribution, not just the extreme (highest and lowest) scores. Consider Figure A.3. Each distribution in the figure has the same number of scores, the same mean, and the same range of scores. However, the scores in the distribution on the right side cluster more closely about the mean. Therefore, the standard deviation of the distribution on the right is smaller. That is, the typical score deviates less from the mean score.

The standard deviation is usually abbreviated as S.D. It is calculated by the formula

$$\text{S.D.} = \sqrt{\frac{\text{Sum of } d^2}{N}}$$

where *d* equals the deviation of each score from the mean of the distribution and *N* equals the number of scores in the distribution.

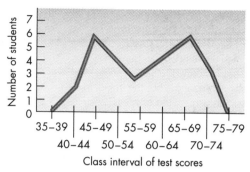

Figure A.2
A Bimodal Distribution.
This hypothetical distribution represents students' scores on a test. The mode at the left represents the central tendency of the test scores of students who did not study. The mode at the right represents the mode of the test scores of students who did study. (I'm allowed to be moralistic about studying; I wrote the book.)

reflect & relate

Would it take a 3.00, 4.00, or 5.00 grade point average for you to be a perfect student? Would yet another number be required? Explain?

Standard deviation A measure of the variability of a distribution, obtained by the formula

Figure A.3
Hypothetical Distributions of Student Test Scores
Each distribution has the same number of scores, the same mean, even the same range, but the standard deviation (a measure of variability) is greater for the distribution on the left because the scores tend to be farther from the mean.

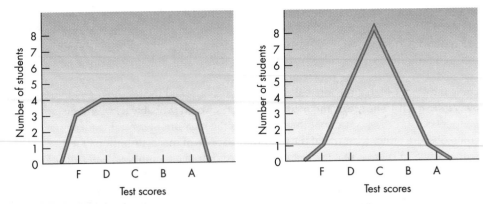

Let us find the mean and standard deviation of the IQ scores listed in column 1 of Table A.4. To obtain the mean we add all the scores, attain 1,500, and then divide by the number of scores (15) to obtain a mean of 100. We obtain the deviation score (d) for each IQ score by subtracting the score from 100. The d for an IQ score of 85 equals 100 minus 85, or 15, and so on. Then we square each d and add the squares. The S.D. equals the square root of the sum of squares (1,426) divided by the number of scores (15), or 9.75.

TABLE A.4 ■ Hypothetical Scores Obtained from an IQ Testing

IQ SCORE	D (DEVIATION SCORE)	D² (DEVIATION SCORE SQUARED)
85	15	225
87	13	169
89	11	121
90	10	100
93	7	49
97	3	9
97	3	9
100	0	0
101	−1	1
104	−4	16
105	−5	25
110	−10	100
112	−12	144
113	−13	169
117	−17	289
Sum of IQ scores = 1,500		Sum of d^2 scores = 1,426

$$\text{Mean} = \frac{\text{Sum of scores}}{\text{Number of scores}} = \frac{1,500}{15} = 100$$

$$\text{Standard Deviation (S.D.)} = \sqrt{\frac{\text{Sum of } d^2}{N}} = \sqrt{\frac{1,426}{15}} = \sqrt{95.07} = 9.75$$

TABLE A.5 ■ Computation of Standard Deviations for Test-Score Distributions in Figure A.3

DISTRIBUTION AT LEFT			DISTRIBUTION TO THE RIGHT		
GRADE	D	D²	GRADE	D	D²
A (4)	2	4	A (4)	2	4
A (4)	2	4	B (3)	1	1
A (4)	2	4	B (3)	1	1
B (3)	1	1	B (3)	1	1
B (3)	1	1	B (3)	1	1
B (3)	1	1	C (2)	0	0
B (3)	1	1	C (2)	0	0
C (2)	0	0	C (2)	0	0
C (2)	0	0	C (2)	0	0
C (2)	0	0	C (2)	0	0
C (2)	0	0	C (2)	0	0
D (1)	−1	1	C (2)	0	0
D (1)	−1	1	C (2)	0	0
D (1)	−1	1	D (1)	−1	1
D (1)	−1	1	D (1)	−1	1
F (0)	−2	4	D (1)	−1	1
F (0)	−2	4	D (1)	−1	1
F (0)	−2	4	F (0)	−2	4

Sum of grades = 36
Mean grade = 36/18 = 2
Sum of d^2 = 32
Sum of grades = 36
Mean grade = 36/18 = 2
Sum of d^2 = 32
S.D. = $\sqrt{32/18}$ = 1.33

Sum of grades = 36
Mean grade = 36/18 = 2
Sum of d^2 = 16
Sum of grades = 36
Mean grade = 36/18 = 2
Sum of d^2 = 16
S.D. = $\sqrt{16/18}$ = 0.94

As an additional exercise, we can show that the S.D. of the test scores on the left (in Figure A.3) is greater than that for the scores on the right. First we assign the grades a number according to a 4.0 system. Let A = 4, B = 3, C = 2, D = 1, and F = 0. The S.D. for each distribution is computed in Table A.5. The larger S.D. for the distribution on the left indicates that the scores in that distribution are more variable, or tend to be farther from the mean.

Learning Connections

◄◄ *Descriptive Statistics* ▶▶

REVIEW:

3 A(n) _____ distribution takes items of data, puts them into order, and indicates how often a score appears.
   (a) number,
   (b) average,
   (c) deviation,
   (d) frequency.

4 We obtain the _____ of a distribution by adding the scores and then dividing the sum by the number of scores.
   (a) mean,
   (b) median,
   (c) mode,
   (d) deviation.

5 The _____ of a distribution is the most frequently appearing number.
   (a) mean,
   (b) median,
   (c) mode,
   (d) average.

6 The standard deviation is calculated by the formula:

$$\text{S.D.} = \sqrt{\frac{\text{Sum of } \_\_{}^{2}}{N}}$$

   (a) r,
   (b) d,
   (c) x,
   (d) m.

CRITICAL THINKING:
Provide examples of distributions in which the median and mode are better measures of central tendency than the mean. Why is being a "10" more remarkable in a distribution whose scores range from 1 to 10 than in a distribution whose scores range from 9 to 11?

Go www
to
http://academic.cengage.com/psychology/rathus
for an interactive version of this review.

THE NORMAL CURVE

Many human traits and characteristics including height and intelligence seem to be distributed in a pattern known as a normal distribution. *What is a normal distribution?* In a **normal distribution,** the mean, median, and mode all fall at the same data point or score. Scores cluster most heavily about the mean, fall off rapidly in either direction at first (as shown in Figure A.4), and then taper off more gradually.

The curve in Figure A.4 is bell-shaped. This type of distribution is also called a **normal curve** or bell-shaped curve. This curve is hypothesized the distribution of variables in which different scores are determined by chance variation. Height is thought to be largely determined by chance combinations of genetic material. A distribution of the heights of a random sample of the population approximates normal distributions for men and women, with the mean of the distribution for men a few inches higher than the mean for women.

Test developers traditionally assumed that intelligence was also randomly or normally distributed among the population. For that reason, they constructed intelligence tests so that scores would be distributed as close to "normal" as possible. In actuality, IQ scores are also influenced by environmental factors and chromosomal abnormalities, so that the resultant curves are not perfectly normal. The means of most IQ tests are defined as scores of 100 points. The Wechsler scales are constructed to have standard deviations of 15 points, as shown in Figure A.4. A standard deviation of 15 points causes 50% of the Wechsler scores to fall between 90 and 110, which is called the "broad average" range. About 68% of scores (two out of three) fall between 85 and 115 (within a standard deviation of the mean), and

Normal distribution A symmetrical distribution that is assumed to reflect chance fluctuations; approximately 68% of cases lie within a standard deviation of the mean.

Normal curve Graphic presentation of a normal distribution, which shows a characteristic bell shape.

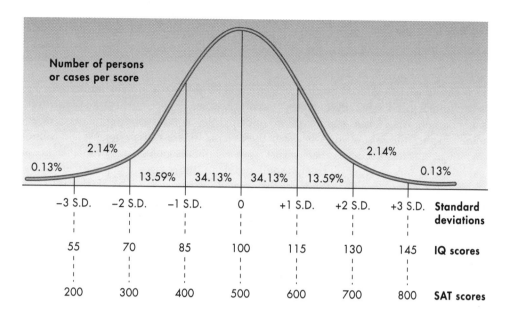

A Bell-Shaped or Normal Curve
In a normal curve, approximately two out of three cases (68%) lie within a standard deviation (S.D.) from the mean. The mean, median, and mode all lie at the same score. IQ tests and the Scholastic Assessment Tests (SATs) are constructed so that their distributions approximate the normal curve.

more than 95% fall between 70 and 130 — that is, within two standard deviations of the mean. ◈ **Truth or Fiction Revisited:** Psychologists, therefore, may express your IQ score in terms of how deviant you are. The more extreme high (and low) IQ scores deviate more from the mean score.

The Scholastic Assessment Tests (SATs) were constructed so that the mean scores would be 500 points and the S.D. would be 100 points. Thus a score of 600 would equal or excel that of some 84% to 85% of the test takers. Because of the complex interaction of variables that determine SAT scores, their distribution is not exactly normal either. Moreover, the actual mean scores and standard deviations tend to vary from year to year, and, in the case of the SAT IIs, from test to test. The normal curve is an idealized curve.

◈ **Truth or Fiction Revisited:** An IQ score of 130 may therefore be more impressive than an SAT score of 500. The IQ score of 130 is two standard deviations above the mean and exceeds that of more than 97% of the population. An SAT score of 500 is the mean SAT score and thus equals or excels that of about 50% of the population.

reflect & relate

Do you tend to place yourself on the normal curve according to traits such as extraversion, conscientiousness, and openness to new experience? Explain. Which of the following scores would you rather receive: a Wechsler IQ score of 130 or an SAT score of 500? Which score is more "normal"? Explain.

⟲ Learning Connections

◀◀   *The Normal Curve*   ▶▶

REVIEW:

7 A normal distribution yields a graph with the shape of a(n) _____.
   (a) straight line,
   (b) polygon,
   (c) standard deviation,
   (d) bell.

8 The means of most IQ tests are defined as scores of _____ points.
   (a) 16,
   (b) 67,
   (c) 100,
   (d) 500.

CRITICAL THINKING:
Do you feel that people should be informed of their IQ scores? Explain.

Go to
http://academic.cengage.com/psychology/rathus
for an interactive version of this review.

THE CORRELATION COEFFICIENT

What is the relationship between intelligence and educational achievement? Between cigarette smoking and lung cancer among humans? Between the personality trait of introversion and numbers of dates among college students? We cannot run experiments to determine whether the relationships between these variables are causal, because we cannot manipulate the independent variable. That is, we cannot assign high or low intelligence at random. Nor can we (ethically) assign some people to smoke cigarettes and others not to smoke. People must be allowed to make their own decisions, so it is possible that the same factors that lead some people to smoke—or to continue to smoke after they have experimented with cigarettes—also lead to lung cancer. (Even if we were to assign a group of people to a nonsmoking condition, could we monitor them continuously to make sure that they weren't sneaking puffs?) Nor can we designate who will be introverted and who will be extraverted. True, we could encourage people to act as if they are introverted or extraverted, but behavior is not the same thing as a personality trait. We cannot run true experiments to answer any of these questions, but the **correlation coefficient** can be used to reveal whether there is a relationship between intelligence and achievement, a relationship between smoking and cancer, or a relationship between personality and dating. Correlational research shows that smoking and cancer are related but does not reveal cause and effect. However, experimental research with animals does strongly suggest that smoking will cause cancer in humans.

What is the correlation coefficient? The correlation coefficient is a statistic that describes the relationship between two variables. A correlation coefficient can vary from +1.00 to −1.00. A correlation coefficient of +1.00 is called a perfect positive correlation, and it describes the relationship between temperatures as measured by the Fahrenheit and Centigrade scales. A correlation coefficient of −1.00 is a perfect negative correlation, and a correlation of 0 (zero) reveals no relationship between variables.

As suggested by Figures A.5 and A.6, most correlation coefficients in psychological research are less than perfect. The left-hand graph in Figure A.5 reveals a positive relationship between time spent studying and grade point averages. Because there is a positive correlation between the variables but the relationship is not perfect, the correlation coefficient will lie between 0.00 and +1.00. Perhaps it is about +0.60 or +0.70. However, we cannot absolutely predict what a person's GPA will be if we know the hours per week that he or she spends studying (nor can we predict exactly how much time the person spends studying on the basis of his or her GPA). Nevertheless, it would seem advisable to place oneself among those who spend a good deal of time studying if one wishes to achieve a good GPA.

reflect & relate

In you own experience, how would you explain the correlation between students' test scores and the amount of time they put into studying? Is studying the only factor involved in their grades? Explain.

Correlation coefficient A number between −1.00 and +1.00 that indicates the direction (negative or positive) and extent (from none to perfect) of the relationship between two variables.

Figure A.5
Positive and Negative Correlations
When there is a positive correlation between variables, as there is between intelligence and achievement, one increases as the other increases. By and large, the more time students spend studying, the better their grades are likely to be, as suggested in the diagram to the left. (Each dot represents the amount of time a student spends studying each week and his or her grade point average.) But there is a negative correlation between grades and juvenile delinquency. As the number of delinquent acts per year increases, one's grade point average tends to decline. Correlational research may suggest but does not demonstrate cause and effect.

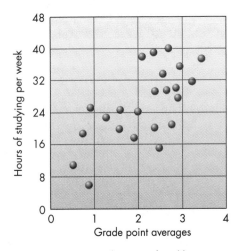

Positive correlation, as found between intelligence and academic achievment

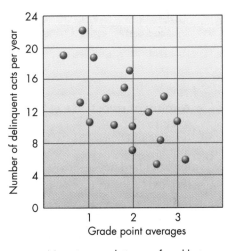

Negative correlation, as found between delinquency and academic achievment

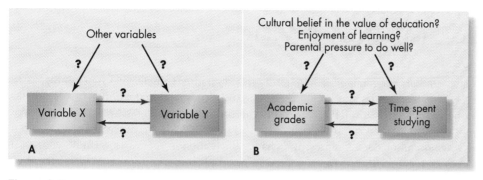

Figure A.6
Correlational Relationships, Cause and Effect
Correlational relationships may suggest but do not demonstrate cause and effect. In part A, there is a correlation between variables X and Y. Does this mean that either variable X causes variable Y or that variable Y causes variable X? Not necessarily. Other factors could affect both variables X and Y. Consider the examples of academic grades (variable X) and time spent studying (variable Y) in part B. There is a positive correlation between the two. Does this mean that studying contributes to good grades? Perhaps. Does it mean that good grades encourage studying? Again, perhaps. But there could also be other variables—such as cultural belief in the value of education, enjoyment of learning, even parental pressure to do well—that contribute both to time spent studying and good grades.

The right-hand drawing in Figure A.5 reveals a negative relationship between number of delinquent acts committed per year and GPA. The causal connection is less than perfectly clear. Does delinquency interfere with studying and academic achievement? Does poor achievement weaken a student's commitment to trying to get ahead through work? Do feelings of distance from "the system" contribute both to delinquent behavior and a low GPA? The answers are not to be found in Figure A.5, but the negative correlation between delinquent behavior and GPA does suggest that it is worthwhile to study the issues involves and—for a student—to distance himself or herself from delinquent behavior if he or she wishes to achieve in the academic world.

⟨⟩ Learning Connections

◀◀   *The Correlation Coefficient*   ▶▶

REVIEW:

9 For a large sample of students, the correlation between IQ test scores and academic grades _____ is most likely to be somewhere near
   (a) −1.00,
   (b) 0.0
   (c) +0.65,
   (d) +1.00.

10 The most accurate statement about the relationship between correlational research and cause and effect is that
   (a) correlational research may suggest but does not reveal cause and effect,
   (b) there is no relationship between correlation and cause and effect,
   (c) cause and effect can only be determined by statistical analysis,
   (d) demonstrated cause and effect does not suggest a correlational relationship.

CRITICAL THINKING:
Why is the correlation between grades at your college and the price of eggs in the local supermarket likely to be close to zero?

Go to www ▶▶
http://academic.cengage.com/psychology/rathus
for an interactive version of this review.

INFERENTIAL STATISTICS

Head Start programs have apparently raised children's intellectual functioning, as reflected in their grades and IQ scores. In one such study, children enrolled in a Head Start program obtained a mean IQ score of 99, whereas children similar in background who were not enrolled in Head Start obtained a mean IQ score of 93. Is this difference of six points in IQ *significant,* or does it represent a chance fluctuation in scores? In a study reported in Chapter 1, college students were provoked by people in league with the researchers. Some of the students believed they had drunk alcohol (in a cocktail with tonic water); others believed they had drunk tonic water only. The students were then given the opportunity to shock the individuals who had provoked them. Students who believed they had drunk alcohol chose higher levels of shock than students who believed they had drunk tonic water only. Did the mean difference in shock level chosen by the two groups of students represent actual differences between the groups, or might it have been a chance fluctuation? The individuals in the Head Start study were a sample of young children. The individuals in the alcohol study were a sample of college students. Inferential statistics help us determine whether we can conclude that the differences between such samples reflect real differences that are found in the populations that they represent.

Descriptive statistics enables us to provide descriptive information about samples of scores. *What are inferential statistics?* **Inferential statistics** assist us in determining whether we can generalize differences among samples to the populations that they represent.

Figure A.7 shows the distribution of heights of 1,000 men and 1,000 women who were selected at random from the general U.S. population. The mean height for men is greater than the mean height for women. Can we conclude, or **infer,** that this difference in height is not just a chance fluctuation but represents an actual difference between the general populations of men and women? Or must we avoid such an inference and summarize our results by stating only that the mean height of the sample of men in the study was greater than the mean height of the sample of women in the study?

If we could not draw inferences about populations from studies of samples, our research findings would be limited indeed. We could only speak about the specific individuals studied. There would be no point to learning about any study in which you did not participate because it would not apply to you! Fortunately, that is not the case. Inferential statistics permits us to extend findings with samples to the populations from which they were drawn.

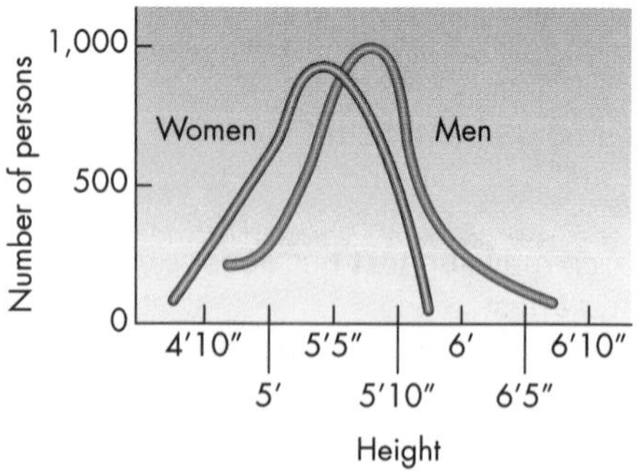

Inferential statistics The branch of statistics that is concerned with confidence with which conclusions drawn about samples can be extended to the populations from which the samples were drawn.

Infer To go from the particular to the general; to draw a conclusion.

◾ Statistically Significant Differences

We asked whether the differences in height between our samples of men and women were simply a chance fluctuation or whether they represented actual differences between the heights of men and women. Researchers tend not to talk about "real differences" or "actual differences" between groups, however. Instead, they speak of statistically significant differences. Similarly, researchers asked whether differences in IQ scores between children in Head Start programs and other children from similar backgrounds were chance fluctuations or statistically significant differences. *What are "statistically significant" differences?* Statistically significant differences are differences that are unlikely to be due to chance fluctuation. Psychologists usually do not accept a difference as being statistically significant unless the probability (p) that it is due to chance fluctuation is less than 1 in 20 (i.e., $p < .05$). They are more comfortable labeling a difference as statistically significant when the probability (p) that it is due to chance fluctuation is less than 1 in 100 (i.e., $p < .01$).

Psychologists use formulas involving the means (e.g., mean IQ scores of 93 versus 99) and the standard deviations of sample groups to determine whether differences in means are statistically significant. As you can see in Figure A.8, the farther apart group means are, the more likely it is that they are statistically significant. In other words, if the men are on the average 5 inches taller than the women, it is more likely that the difference is statistically significant than if them men are only one-quarter of an inch taller on average. Principle 1:

Figure A.7
Distribution of Heights for Random Samples of Men and Women
Note that the mean height of the men is greater than that of the women. Is the group mean difference in height statistically significant? Researchers use a tool called inferential statistics to determine the answer.

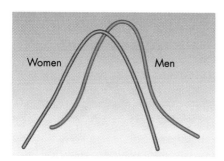 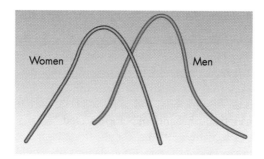

Figure A.8
Decreasing and Increasing the Mean Group Difference in Heights
Everything else being equal, the greater the difference in group means, the greater the probability that the difference is statistically significant. The distribution on the right shows a greater difference in group means; therefore, there is a greater probability that the difference is statistically significant.

Everything else being equal, the greater the difference between means, the greater the probability that the difference is statistically significant. This makes common sense. After all, if you were told that your neighbor's car had gotten one-tenth of a mile more per gallon of gas than your car in the past year, you would probably attribute the difference to chance fluctuation. But if the difference were greater, say 14 miles per gallon, you would probably assume that the difference reflected an actual difference in driving habits or the efficiency of the automobile.

As you can see in Figure A.9, the smaller the standard deviations (a measure of variability) of the groups, the more likely it is that the difference between means is statistically significant. Consider the extreme example in which there is *no* variability within each group. That is, imagine that every woman in the randomly selected sample of 1,000 women is exactly 5′5″ tall. Similarly, imagine that every man in the randomly selected sample of 1,000 men is exactly 5′10″ tall. In such a case the heights of the men and women would not overlap at all, and it would appear that the differences were statistically significant. Consider the other extreme—one with unnaturally large variability. Imagine that the heights of the women vary from 2′ to 14′ and that the heights of the men vary from 2′1″ to 14′3″. In such a case we might be more likely to assume that the difference in group means of 5″ was a chance fluctuation. Principle 2: Everything else being equal, the smaller the variability of the distributions of scores, the greater the probability that the difference in group means is statistically significant.

Therefore, we cannot conclude that men are taller than women unless we know the average heights of men and women and how much the heights within each group vary. We must know both the central tendencies (means) and variability of the two distributions of heights in order to infer that the mean heights are statistically significantly different.

We have been "eyeballing" the data and making assumptions. We have been relying on what one professor of mine called the "Wow!" effect. As noted, psychologists and other researchers actually use mathematical techniques that take group means and standard deviations into account to determine whether group differences are statistically significant. It is often the case that eyeballing real data does not yield clear results or even good guesses.

reflect & relate

Suppose that some aliens "borrowed" you for a while and studied you to learn about the human species. What could they correctly infer about all people from studying you? What errors would they make if they assumed that other people were just like you?

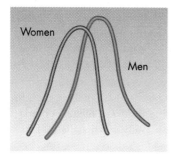 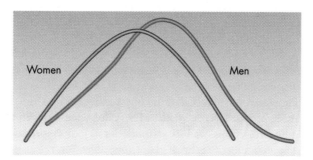

Figure A.9

Decreasing and Increasing the Variability of the Distributions of Scores
Everything else being equal, the smaller the variability in group scores, the greater the probability that the difference in groups means is statistically significant. The distribution on the right shows a greater difference in the variability of the groups; therefore, there is a *lower* probability that the difference in group means is statistically significant.

Samples and Populations

Inferential statistics are mathematical tools that psychologists apply to samples of scores to determine whether they can generalize or extend their findings to populations of scores. They must therefore be quite certain that the samples involved actually represent the populations from which they were drawn. Sampling techniques are crucial. Random sampling is the best method, and sampling is random only if every member of the target population has an equal chance of being selected.

It matters little how sophisticated our statistical methods are if the samples studied do not represent the target populations. We could use a variety of sophisticated statistical techniques to analyze the heights of the New York Big Apples and the California Quakes, but none of these methods would tell us much about the height of the general population. Or about the height of women. (Or about the height of people who can't pass the ball, shoot, or play defense.)

Life Connections
Thinking Critically About "Junk Statistics"

When you read popular magazines or go online, you are frequently asked to participate in polls on political matters, sports, and who is the hottest new pop star. Perhaps you complete a questionnaire and mail it in, or, more likely, you click on a few answers and then send them in electronically—getting instant feedback on the results of the poll.

Statistics is an exact science, yet very often we wind up with useless or misleading results. Critical thinkers have an attitude of skepticism, and skepticism may best be directed toward the results of magazine and online surveys of sexual behavior. These surveys sound impressive because they often obtain completed questionnaires from many thousands of readers. We can also grant that their answers are probably computed and analyzed flawlessly. Why, then, should we be skeptical of the published results? The answer, in a nutshell, is volunteer bias. That is, the respondents did not represent the American population. In fact, they might have represented no one other than themselves. In the case of research on sexual behavior, volunteers may represent subgroups of the population—or of readers of the magazines in question—who are willing to disclose intimate information and be more liberal in their sexual practices.

For example, Playboy magazine commissioned a survey of sexual practices in the 1970s, as reported in Morton Hunt's *Sexual Behavior in the 1970's*. The survey sample was drawn randomly from phone book listings in 24 American cities. People were asked to participate in small group discussions focusing on trends in sexual practices in the United States. Hunt argued that his final sample of 2,026 subjects was stratified properly as to the ages and races of urban residents across a diverse sample of American cities, but 80% of the people contacted refused to participate. It is logical to assume that the 20% who did participate were more open and frank about sexual issues than the population at large.

Social scientist Edward Laumann and his colleagues (1994), who labored to obtain a nationally representative example for the NHSLS study, are particularly harsh in their judgment of surveys like the one conducted by Hunt. They write that "such studies, in sum, produce junk statistics of no value whatsoever in making valid and reliable population projections" (p. 45). Numbers can look impressive, especially when statistics from large samples are generated by computers. But the critical reader will ask *who* completed the questionnaire and whom they represented. ■

( ) Learning Connections

◀◀ *Inferential Statistics* ▶▶

REVIEW:

11 Psychologists usually do not accept a difference as being statistically significant unless the probability that it is due to chance fluctuation is less than one in _____.
(a) 10,
(b) 20,
(c) 50,
(d) 100.

12 Psychologists use formulas involving the means and _____ deviations of sample groups to determine whether differences in means are statistically significant.
(a) range,
(b) correlational,
(c) normal,
(d) standard.

CRITICAL THINKING:
What does it mean to say that the difference in heights between men and women is *statistically significant*? After all, many women are taller than many men.

Go to
http://academic.cengage.com/psychology/rathus
for an interactive version of this review.

RECITE—*An Active Summary*™

Recite to Go! *Don't have time to study right now? You can study on the go!*
Go to your companion website and download an audio version of this review section to your media player. You can also access an interactive flash-card version of this review from your website.

1. What is statistics?	Statistics is the science that assembles data in such a way that they provide useful information about measures or scores. Such measures or scores include people's height, weight, and scores on psychological tests such as IQ tests.
2. What are samples and populations?	A sample is part of a population. A population is a complete group from which a sample is drawn. The example with basketball players shows that a sample must represent its population if it is to provide accurate information about the population.
3. What is descriptive statistics?	Descriptive statistics is the branch of statistics that provides information about the central tendencies and variabilities of distributions of scores.
4. What is a frequency distribution?	A frequency distribution organizes a set of data, usually from low scores to high scores, and indicates how frequently a score appears. Class intervals may be used on large sets of data to provide a quick impression of how the data tend to cluster. The histogram and frequency polygon are two ways of graphing data to help people visualize the way in which the data are distributed.

5. What are measures of central tendency?	Measures of central tendency are "averages" that show the center or balancing points of a frequency distribution. The mean—which is what most people consider the average—is obtained by adding the scores in a distribution and dividing by the number of scores. The median is the score of the middle or central case in a distribution. The mode is the most common score in a distribution. Distributions can be bimodal (having two modes) or multimodal.
6. What are measures of variability?	Measures of variability provide information about the spread of scores in a distribution. The range is defined as the difference between the highest and lowest scores. The standard deviation is a statistic that shows how scores cluster around the mean. Distributions with higher standard deviations are more spread out.
7. What is a normal distribution?	The normal or bell-shaped curve is hypothesized to occur when the scores in a distribution occur by chance. The normal curve has one mode, and approximately two of three scores (68%) are found within one standard deviation of the mean. Fewer than 5% of cases are found beyond two standard deviations from the mean.
8. What is the correlation coefficient?	The correlation coefficient is a statistic that describes how variables such as IQ and grade point averages are related. It varies from $+1.00$ to -1.00. When correlations between two variables are positive, it means that one (such as school grades) tends to rise as the other (such as IQ) rises.
9. What are inferential statistics?	Inferential statistics is the branch of statistics that indicates whether researchers can extend their findings with samples to the populations from which they were drawn.
10. What are "statistically significant" differences?	Statistically significant differences are believed to represent real differences between groups, and not chance fluctuation.

Key Terms

Active Learning Resources

Visit Your Companion Website for This Book

http://academic.cengage.com/psychology/rathus

Check out this companion website where you will find online resources directly linked to your book. This is where you'll access the videos highlighted in your Video Connections feature. You can answer the questions online and email them to your professor. In addition you'll find downloadable audio review material, interactive versions of the study aids, Power Visuals for mastering and reviewing key concepts, as well as quizzing, and much more!

CENGAGENOW™   **http://academic.cengage.com**

Need help studying? This site is your one-stop study shop. Take a Pre-Test and Cengage NOW will generate a Personalized Study Plan based on your test results. The Study Plan will identify the topics you need to review and direct you to online resources to help you master those topics. You can then take a Post-Test to help you determine the concepts you have mastered and what you still need to work on. In addition you can access interactive media including the videos highlighted in your Video Connections box.

Author Blog

What does your author Spence Rathus have to say about the state of psychology? Visit your companion website every Tuesday and click on "Author Blog." This is where he'll talk about the most recent controversies and hot topics in psychology. This will keep you up to date with what your author is thinking and give you great insight into modern psychology.

APPENDIX B
Answers

SELF-ASSESSMENTS

Scoring Key for the "Dare You Say What You Think? The Social-Desirability Scale"
(Chapter 1, p. 26)

Place a check mark on the appropriate line of the scoring key each time your answer agrees with the one listed in the scoring key. Add the check marks and record the total number of check marks below.

1. T ✓	10. F ____	19. F ____	28. F ____
2. T ____	11. F ____	20. T ____	29. T ____
3. F ____	12. F ____	21. T ____	30. F ____
4. T ____	13. T ____	22. F ____	31. T ____
5. F ____	14. F ____	23. F ____	32. F ____
6. F ____	15. F ____	24. T ____	33. T ____
7. T ____	16. T ____	25. T ____	
8. T ____	17. T ____	26. T ____	
9. F ____	18. T ____	27. T ____	

Interpreting Your Score

LOW SCORERS (0–8)
About one respondent in six earns a score between 0 and 8. Such respondents answered in a socially *undesirable* direction much of the time. It may be that they are more willing than most people to respond to tests truthfully, even when their answers might meet with social disapproval.

AVERAGE SCORERS (9–19)
About two respondents in three earn a score from 9 through 19. They tend to show an average degree of concern for the social desirability of their responses, and it may be that their general behavior represents an average degree of conformity to social rules and conventions.

HIGH SCORERS (20–33)
About one respondent in six earns a score between 20 and 33. These respondents may be highly concerned about social approval and respond to test items in such as way as to avoid the disapproval of people who may read their responses. Their general behavior may show high conformity to social rules and conventions.

Answer Key for "Symptoms of PMS"
(Chapter 2, p. 68)

There are no numerical answers to this Self-Assessment. Ask yourself, rather, whether you are experiencing any moderate to disabling psychological or physical symptoms of PMS. We advise you to discuss any symptoms that are moderate or more severe with your physician, preferably a gynecologist. It is important for your health that you discuss any "disabling" symptoms with your gynecologist. Even if you have some mild symptoms, you may want to check them off and bring them to the attention of your gynecologist. Nothing is to be gained by suffering in silence.

Scoring Key for the "Sleep Quiz—Are You Getting Your Z's?"
(Chapter 5, p. 184)

Psychologist James Maas, the author of *Power Sleep* (Harper-Collins, 1999), writes that an answer of "true" to two or more of the statements in the questionnaire may be a sign of a sleep problem.

Scoring Key for "Are You 'Addicted' to the Internet?"
(Chapter 5, p. 192)

"Yes" answers are in the direction of being "addicted" to the Internet. The term *addiction* implies habitual behavior that is difficult to control and tends to be reserved by the American Psychiatric Association for abuse of substances, including alcohol, cigarettes, heroin, and cocaine. However, the term is often used more loosely to refer to any habitual self-destructive behavior that involves cravings.

There are no norms for this self-assessment. Instead, be honest with yourself as you review the items. Is you use of the Internet interfering with your academic or social life? Does it seem to be out of control? Do you find yourself "in a fever" to get online? If any of these are true, you may find it helpful to follow some of the suggestions in the chapter for "breaking the habit."

Answer Key for "Puzzles, Problems, and Just Plain Fun"
(Chapter 8, p. 284) and to the Duncker Candle Problem

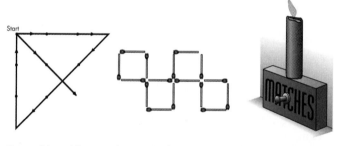

For problem 1C, note that each of the letters is the first letter of the numbers one through eight. Therefore, the two missing letters are *NT*, for *n*ine and *t*en. The solutions to problems 2 and 3 and to the Duncker candle problem are shown in this illustration. To solve the Duncker candle problem, use the thumbtack to pin the matchbox to the wall. Then set the candle on top of the box. Functional fixedness prevents many people from conceptualizing the matchbox as anything more than a device to hold matches. Commonly given *wrong* answers include trying to affix the bottom of the candle to the wall with melted wax or trying to tack the candle to the wall. And what of the coined stamped with the date 544 BCE? BCE stands for "before the common era," that is, before the birth of Jesus. Prior to the birth of Jesus, people did not know He was going to be born.

Scoring Key for the "Remote Associates Test"
(Chapter 8, p. 305)

1. Dog
2. Cold
3. Glasses
4. Club
5. Boat
6. Defense
7. Black
8. Pit
9. Writer

Scoring Key for "The Sensation-Seeking Scale"
(Chapter 9, p. 326)

Because this is a shortened version of a questionnaire, no norms are available. However, answers in agreement with the following key point in the direction of sensation seeking:

1. A
2. A
3. A
4. B
5. A
6. B
7. A
8. A
9. B
10. A
11. A
12. A
13. B

Answer Key for the "Are You Type A or B?" Questionnaire
(Chapter 10, p. 372)

Type A people are ambitious, hard driving, and chronically discontent with their current achievements. Type Bs, by contrast, are more relaxed, more involved with the quality of life.

"Yes" answers suggest the Type A behavior pattern, which is marked by a sense of time urgency and constant struggle. In appraising your "type," you need not be overly concerned with the precise number of "yes" answers; we have no normative data for you. But as Freidman and Rosenman (1974, p. 85) note, you should have little trouble spotting yourself as "hard core" or "moderately afflicted"—that is, if you are honest with yourself.

Answer Key for the "Locus of Control Scale"
(Chapter 10, p. 375)

Place a check mark in the blank space in the scoring key, below, each time your answer agrees with the answer in the key. The number of checkmarks is your total score.

Scoring Key:

1. Yes ____	11. Yes ____	21. Yes ____	31. Yes ____
2. No ____	12. Yes ____	22. No ____	32. No ____
3. Yes ____	13. No ____	23. Yes ____	33. Yes ____
4. No ____	14. Yes ____	24. Yes ____	34. No ____
5. Yes ____	15. No ____	25. No ____	35. Yes ____
6. No ____	16. Yes ____	26. No ____	36. Yes ____
7. Yes ____	17. Yes ____	27. Yes ____	37. Yes ____
8. Yes ____	18. Yes ____	28. No ____	38. No ____
9. No ____	19. Yes ____	29. Yes ____	39. Yes ____
10. Yes ____	20. No ____	30. No ____	40. No ____

TOTAL SCORE ____

Interpreting Your Score

LOW SCORERS (0–8)
About one respondent in three earns a score of from 0 to 8. Such respondents tend to have an internal locus of control. They see themselves as responsible for the reinforcements they attain (and fail to attain) in life.

AVERAGE SCORERS (9–16)
Most respondents earn from 9 to 16 points. Average scorers may see themselves as partially in control of their lives. Perhaps they see themselves as in control at work, but not in their social lives—or vice versa.

HIGH SCORERS (17–40)
About 15 percent of respondents attain scores of 17 or above. High scorers tend largely to see life as a game of chance, and success as a matter of luck or the generosity of others.

Scoring Key for "Do You Demand Your Rights or Do You Wimp Out? The Assertiveness Schedule"
(Chapter 13, p. 485)

Tabulate your score as follows: For those items followed by an asterisk (*), change the signs (plus to minus; minus to plus). For example, if the response to an asterisked item was 2, place a minus sign (−) before the two. If the response to an asterisked item was −3, change the minus sign to a plus sign (+) by adding a vertical stroke. Then add up the scores of the 30 items.

Scores on the assertiveness schedule can vary from +90 to −90. Table B.1 will show you how your score compares to those of 764 college women and 637 men from 35 campuses across the United States. For example, if you are a woman and your score was 26, it exceeded that of 80 percent of the women in the sample. A score of 15 for a male exceeds that of 55–60 percent of the men in the sample.

Key for "The Love Scale"
(Chapter 14, p. 518)

First add your scores for the items on each of the three components—Intimacy, Passion, and Decision/Commitment—and divide each total by 15. This procedure will yield an average rating for each subscale. An average rating of 5 on a particular subscale indicates a moderate level of the component represented by the subscale. A higher rating indicates a greater level. A lower rating indicates a lower level. Examining your ratings on these components will give you an idea of the degree to which you perceive your love relationship to be characterized by these three components of love. For example, you might find that passion is stronger than decision/commitment, a pattern that is common in the early stages of an intense romantic relationship. You might find it interesting to complete the questionnaire a few months or perhaps a year or so from now to see how your feelings about your relationship change over time. You might also ask your partner to complete the scale so that the two of you can compare your respective scores. Comparing your ratings for each component with those of your partner will give you an idea of the degree to which you and your partner see your relationship in a similar way.

TABLE B.1 ■ Percentiles for Scores on the RAS

WOMEN'S SCORES	PERCENTILE	MEN'S SCORES
55	99	65
48	97	54
45	95	48
37	90	40
31	85	33
26	80	30
23	75	26
19	70	24
17	65	19
14	60	17
11	55	15
8	50	11
6	45	8
2	40	6
−1	35	3
−4	30	1
−8	25	−3
−13	20	−7
−17	15	−11
−24	10	−15
−34	5	−24
−39	3	−30
−48	1	−41

SOURCE: J. S. Nevid & S. A. Rathus (1978). Multivariate and normative data pertaining to the RAS with the college population. *Behavior Therapy, 9,* 675.

LEARNING CONNECTIONS

Chapter 1   What Is Psychology?

1. C	5. C	9. B	13. C
2. B	6. B	10. A	14. D
3. B	7. A	11. A	15. A
4. C	8. D	12. B	16. D

Chapter 2   Biology and Psychology

1. D	5. B	9. C	13. C
2. B	6. D	10. A	14. A
3. C	7. A	11. A	
4. B	8. B	12. D	

Chapter 3   The Voyage Through the Life Span

1. B	5. B	9. B	13. B
2. A	6. A	10. D	14. A
3. D	7. D	11. A	15. A
4. C	8. B	12. D	16. C

Chapter 4   Sensation and Perception

1. D	7. C	13. C	19. B
2. A	8. A	14. A	20. C
3. D	9. A	15. A	21. A
4. B	10. C	16. B	22. D
5. A	11. B	17. D	23. C
6. D	12. C	18. D	24. B

Chapter 5   Consciousness

1. A	4. A	7. D	10. B
2. D	5. A	8. C	11. D
3. C	6. D	9. C	12. C

Chapter 6   Learning

1. C	5. A	9. D	13. A
2. A	6. B	10. C	
3. C	7. B	11. D	
4. D	8. A	12. C	

Chapter 7   Memory: Remembrance of Things Past—and Future

1. B	6. A	11. D	16. A
2. C	7. B	12. B	17. D
3. D	8. A	13. D	18. A
4. C	9. C	14. A	
5. D	10. D	15. C	

Chapter 8   Thinking, Language, and Intelligence

1. D	6. B	11. D	16. D
2. C	7. A	12. A	17. B
3. A	8. C	13. B	18. B
4. B	9. A	14. A	
5. D	10. C	15. A	

Chapter 9   Motivation and Emotion

1. C	6. D	11. A	16. A
2. B	7. A	12. B	17. A
3. D	8. B	13. C	18. C
4. B	9. D	14. A	19. A
5. B	10. B	15. D	20. B

Chapter 10   Stress, Health, and Adjustment

1. C	5. A	9. A	13. C
2. B	6. C	10. C	14. D
3. D	7. A	11. A	15. D
4. A	8. B	12. B	

Chapter 11   Personality: Theory and Measurement

1. C	6. A	11. C	16. A
2. D	7. D	12. A	17. C
3. A	8. A	13. D	18. B
4. C	9. B	14. B	19. A
5. C	10. D	15. D	20. D

Chapter 12   Psychological Disorders

1. A	6. A	11. B	16. A	21. A
2. A	7. A	12. A	17. B	
3. A	8. C	13. C	18. D	
4. B	9. B	14. C	19. C	
5. C	10. D	15. B	20. D	

Chapter 13   Methods of Therapy

1. D	6. B	11. D	16. D
2. A	7. C	12. C	17. B
3. B	8. D	13. D	18. D
4. C	9. C	14. C	19. C
5. A	10. A	15. A	20. A

Chapter 14   Social Psychology

1. D	6. D	11. A	16. C
2. A	7. B	12. A	17. D
3. D	8. A	13. C	18. D
4. D	9. D	14. B	
5. C	10. C	15. C	

Appendix A   Statistics

1. A	4. A	7. D	10. A
2. C	5. C	8. C	11. B
3. D	6. B	9. C	12. D

references

ABBEY, A. (1987). Misperceptions of friendly behavior as sexual interest. *Psychology of Women Quarterly, 11,*173–194.

ABBEY, A., ET AL. (2001). Alcohol and sexual assault. *Alcohol Research & Health, 25*(1), 43–51.

ABRAHAM, H. D., & DUFFY, F. H. (2001). EEG coherence in post-LSD visual hallucinations. *Psychiatry Research: Neuroimaging, 107*(3), 151–163.

ACKARD, D. M., NEUMARK-SZTAINER, D., HANNAN, P. J., FRENCH, S., & STORY, M. (2001). Binge and purge behavior among adolescents: Associations with sexual and physical abuse in a nationally representative sample: The Commonwealth Fund survey. *Child Abuse & Neglect, 25*(6), 771–785.

AGRAS, W. S., WALSH, T., FAIRBURN, C. G., WILSON, G. T., & KRAEMER, H. C. (2000). A multicenter comparison of cognitive-behavioral therapy and interpersonal psychotherapy for bulimia nervosa. *Archives of General Psychiatry, 57*(5), 459–466.

AIKINS, D. E., & CRASKE, M. G. (2001). Cognitive theories of generalized anxiety disorder. *Psychiatric Clinics of North America, 24*(1), 57–74.

AINSWORTH, M. D. S., BLEHAR, M. C., WATERS, E., & WALL, S. (1978). *Patterns of attachment: A psychological study of the strange situation.* Hillsdale, NJ: Erlbaum.

AINSWORTH, M. D. S., & BOWLBY, J. (1991). An ethological approach to personality development. *American Psychologist, 46,* 333–341.

ALBARRACÍN, D., & WYER, R. S., JR. (2000).The cognitive impact of past behavior: Influences on beliefs, attitudes, and future behavioral decisions. *Journal of Personality and Social Psychology, 79*(1), 5–22.

ALEXANDER, C. N., ET AL. (1996). Trial of stress reduction for hypertension in older African Americans: II. Sex and risk subgroup analysis. *Hypertension, 28,* 228–237.

ALLPORT, G. W., & ODDBERT, H. S. (1936). Trait names: A psycholexical study. *Psychological Monographs, 47,* 1–36.

ALTMAN, L. K. (2005, May 16). Studies find disparity in U.S. cancer care. *The New York Times online.*

ALTRAN, S. (Accessed 2005, May). Genesis and future of suicide terrorism. http://www.interdisciplines.org/terrorism/papers/1.

AMERICAN CANCER SOCIETY. (2005a). Cancer facts & figures 2005. http://www.cancer.org.

AMERICAN CANCER SOCIETY. (2005b). Cancer facts & figures for African Americans 2005–2006. http://www.cancer.org.

AMERICAN CANCER SOCIETY. (2005c; accessed 2005, September 23). Alcohol increases breast cancer risk. http://www.cancer.org/docroot/NWS/content/NWS_1_1x_Alcohol_Increases_Breast_Cancer_Risk.asp.

AMERICAN HEART ASSOCIATION. (2005a). Heart disease and stroke statistics—2005 update. http://www.americanheart.org.

AMERICAN HEART ASSOCIATION. (2005b). Leading causes of death—Statistics. http://www.americanheart.org/presenter.jhtml?identifier=3000963.

AMERICAN LUNG ASSOCIATION (2005). http://www.lungusa.org.

AMERICAN PSYCHIATRIC ASSOCIATION (2000). *Diagnostic and statistical manual of mental disorders* (4th ed., text revision). *DSM–IV–TR.* Washington, DC: Author.

AMERICAN PSYCHOLOGICAL ASSOCIATION (1998, March 16). Sexual harassment: Myths and realities. APA Public Information Home Page; http://www.apa.org.

AMERICAN PSYCHOLOGICAL ASSOCIATION (2002). Ethical principles of psychologists and code of conduct. *American Psychologist, 57*(12), 1060–1073.

AMERICAN PSYCHOLOGICAL ASSOCIATION RESEARCH OFFICE (2000). First-year (full-time) students in doctoral-level departments of psychology by race/ethnicity: 1999–2000. *Graduate Study in Psychology 2000.* Washington, DC: American Psychological Association.

ANDERSEN, B. (2005). Cited in Kolata, G. (2005, November 29). Preventing cancer: Does stress cause cancer? Probably not, research finds. *The New York Times online.*

ANDERSEN, B., & BAUM, A. (2001). *Psychosocial interventions for cancer.* Washington, DC: American Psychological Association.

ANDERSEN, B. L. (2002). Biobehavioral outcomes following psychological interventions for cancer patients. *Journal of Consulting & Clinical Psychology, 70*(3), 590–610.

ANDERSEN, B. L., KIECOLT-GLASER, J. K., & GLASER, R. (1994). A biobehavioral model of cancer stress and disease course. *American Psychologist, 49,* 389–404.

ANDERSON, C., & HORNE, J. A. (2004). Presleep relaxed 7–8 Hz EEG from left frontal region: Marker of localised neuropsychological performance? *Physiology & Behavior, 81*(4), 657–664.

ANDERSON, C. A. (2001). Heat and violence. *Current Directions in Psychological Science, 10*(1), 33–38.

ANDERSON, C. A. (2003). Violent video games: Myths, facts, and unanswered questions. *Psychological Science Agenda: Science Briefs, 16*(5), 1–3.

ANDERSON, C. A. (2004). An update on the effects of violent video games. *Journal of Adolescence, 27,* 113–122.

ANDERSON, C. A., BERKOWITZ, L., DONNERSTEIN, E., HUESMANN, R. L., JOHNSON, J., LINZ, D., MALAMUTH, N., & WARTELLA, E. (2003). The influence of media violence on youth. *Psychological Science in the Public Interest, 4,* 81–110.

ANDERSON, C. A., ET AL. (2004). Violent video games: Specific effects of violent content on aggressive thoughts and behavior. *Advances in Experimental Social Psychology, 36,* 199–249.

ANDERSON, C. A., & DENEVE, K. M. (1992). Temperature, aggression, and the negative affect escape model. *Psychological Bulletin, 111,* 347–351.

ANDERSON, C. A., & DILL, K. E. (2000). Video games and aggressive thoughts, feelings, and behavior in the laboratory and in life. *Journal of Personality and Social Psychology, 78*(4), 772–790.

ANDERSON, E. S., WINETT, R. A., & WOJCIK, J. R. (2000). Social-cognitive determinants of nutrition behavior among supermarket food shoppers: A structural equation analysis. *Health Psychology, 19*(5), 479–486.

ANDERSON, E. S., WINETT, R. A., WOJCIK, J. R., WINETT, S. G., & BOWDEN, T. (2001). A computerized social cognitive intervention for nutrition behavior: Direct and mediated effects on fat, fiber, fruits and vegetables, self-efficacy and outcome expectations among food shoppers. *Annals of Behavioral Medicine, 23*(2), 88–100.

ANDERSON, J. R. (1991). Is human cognition adaptive? *Behavioral and Brain Sciences, 14,* 471–517.

ANDERSON, K. G., SANKIS, L. M., & WIDIGER, T. A. (2001). Pathology versus statistical infrequency: Potential sources of gender bias in personality disorder criteria. *Journal of Nervous & Mental Disease, 189*(10), 661–668.

ANDERSON, K. P., LAPORTE, D. J., & CRAWFORD, S. (2000). Child abuse and bulimic symptomology: Review of specific abuse variables. *Child Abuse and Neglect 24*(11), 1495–1502.

ANDREASEN, N. C. (2003). From molecule to mind: Genetics, genomics, and psychiatry. *American Journal of Psychiatry, 160,* 613.

ANDREOU, G., ET AL. (2002). Handedness, asthma, and allergic disorders: Is there an association? *Psychology, Health & Medicine, 7*(1), 53–60.

ANGER-DÍAZ, B., SCHLANGER, K., RINCON, C., &

MENDOZA, A. B. (2004). Problem-solving across cultures: Our Latino experience. *Journal of Systemic Therapies, 23*(4), 11–27.

ANNAS, G. J. (2005, April 4). "Culture of life" politics at the bedside—The case of Terri Schiavo. *New England Journal of Medicine,* http://www.nejm.org.

ANTON, R. F. (2001). Pharmacologic approaches to the management of alcoholism. *Journal of Clinical Psychiatry, 62*(Suppl. 20), 11–17.

ANTONI, M. H. (2003). Psychoneuroendocrinology and psychoneuroimmunology of cancer: Plausible mechanisms worth pursuing? *Brain, Behavior & Immunity, 17*(Suppl. 1), S84–S91.

ANTONI, M. H., & PITTS, M. (2003). Editorial: Journal of Psychosomatic Research: Special issue. *Journal of Psychosomatic Research, 54*(3), 179–183.

ANTONI, M. H., ET AL. (2005). Increases in a marker of immune system reconstitution are predated by decreases in 24-h urinary cortisol output and depressed mood during a 10-week stress management intervention in symptomatic HIV-infected men. *Journal of Psychosomatic Research, 58*(1), 3–13.

APPERLOO, M. J. A., VAN DER STEGE, J. G., HOEK, A., & WEIJMAR SCHULTZ, W. C. M. (2003). In the mood for sex: The value of androgens. *Journal of Sex & Marital Therapy, 29*(2), 87–102.

ARCHER, J. (2000). Sex differences in aggression between heterosexual partners: A meta-analytic review. *Psychological Bulletin, 126*(5), 651–680.

ARCHER, J. (2001). Method and theory in cross-cultural studies of aggression. In J. M. Ramirez & D. S. Richardson (Eds.), *Cross-cultural approaches to research on aggression and reconciliation* (pp. 214–228). Hauppauge, NY: Nova Science Publishers.

ARENDT, J. (2000). Melatonin, circadian rhythms, and sleep. *The New England Journal of Medicine online, 343*(15).

ARNETT, J. J. (1999). Adolescent storm and stress, reconsidered. *American Psychologist, 54*(5), 317–326.

ARNETT, J. J. (2000). Emerging adulthood. *American Psychologist, 55*(5), 469–480.

ARNOLD, H. M., NELSON, C. L., SARTER, M., & BRUNO, J. P. (2003). Sensitization of cortical acetylcholine release by repeated administration of nicotine in rats. *Psychopharmacology, 165*(4), 346–358.

ARONOFF, J., & LITEVIN, G. H. (1971). Achievement motivation training and executive advancement. *Journal of Applied Behavioral Science, 7*(2), 215–229.

ARTHRITIS FOUNDATION. (2000, April 6). Pain in America: Highlights from a Gallup survey. http://www.arthritis.org/answers/sop_factsheet.asp.

ASCH, S. E. (1952). *Social psychology.* Englewood Cliffs, NJ: Prentice-Hall.

ASHTON, C. H. (2001). Pharmacology and effects of cannabis: a brief review. *The British Journal of Psychiatry, 178,* 101–106.

ASPINWALL, L. G., & STAUDINGER, U. M. (2003). *A psychology of human strengths: Fundamental questions and future directions for a positive psychology.* Washington, DC: American Psychological Association.

ASTIN, J. A. (2004). Mind-body therapies for the management of pain. *Clinical Journal of Pain, 20*(1), 27–32.

ATKINS, M. S., ET AL. (2002). Suspensions and detention in an urban, low-income school: Punishment or reward? *Journal of Abnormal Child Psychology, 30*(4), 361–371.

ATKINSON, R. C. (1975). Mnemotechnics in second-language learning. *American Psychologist, 30,* 821–828.

ATKINSON, R. C., & SHIFFRIN, R. M. (1968). Human memory: A proposed system and its control processes. In K. Spence (Ed.), *The psychology of learning and motivation* (Vol. 2). New York: Academic Press.

AYLLON, T., & HAUGHTON, E. (1962). Control of the behavior of schizophrenic patients by food. *Journal of the Experimental Analysis of Behavior, 5,* 343–352.

AZAR, B. (1995). Several genetic traits linked to alcoholism. *APA Monitor, 26*(5), 21–22.

AZAR, B. (1996a). Musical studies provide clues to brain functions. *APA Monitor, 27*(4), 1, 24.

AZAR, B. (1996b). Scientists examine cancer patients' fears. *APA Monitor, 27*(8), 32.

AZAR, B. (1996c). Training is enhanced by virtual reality. *APA Monitor, 26*(3), 24.

AZAR, B. (1997a). Poor recall mars research and treatment. *APA Monitor, 28*(1), 1, 29.

AZAR, B. (1997b). Environment is key to serotonin levels. *APA Monitor, 28*(4), 26, 29.

AZAR, B. (1997c). Nature, nurture: Not mutually exclusive. *APA Monitor, 28*(5), 1, 28.

AZAR, B. (2002). At the frontier of science. *Monitor on Psychology online, 33*(1).

BACALTCHUK, J., HAY, P., & MARI, J. J. (2000). Antidepressants versus placebo for the treatment of bulimia nervosa: A systematic review. *Australian & New Zealand Journal of Psychiatry, 34*(2), 310–317.

BADDELEY, A. (1982). *Your memory: A user's guide.* New York: Macmillan.

BAHRICK, H. P., BAHRICK, P. O., & WITTLINGER, R. P. (1975). Fifty years of memory for names and faces. *Journal of Experimental Psychology: General, 104,* 54–75.

BAILEY, J. M. (2003a). Personal communication.

BAILEY, J. M. (2003b). *The man who would be queen: The science of gender-bending and transsexualism.* Washington, DC: Joseph Henry Press.

BAILEY, J. M., & PILLARD, R. C. (1991). A genetic study of male sexual orientation. *Archives of General Psychiatry, 48,* 1089–1096.

BAJOR, J. K., & BALTES, P. B. (2003). The relationship between selection optimization with compensation, conscientiousness, motivation, and performance. *Journal of Vocational Behavior, 63*(3), 347–367.

BAKER, C. W., WHISMAN, M. A., & BROWNELL, K. D. (2000). Studying intergenerational transmission of eating attitudes and behaviors: Methodological and conceptual questions. *Health Psychology, 19*(4), 376–381.

BAKER, L. A., DeFRIES, J. C., & FULKER, D. W. (1983). Longitudinal stability of cognitive ability in the Colorado adoption project. *Child Development, 54,* 290–297.

BAKER, M. C. (2001). *The atoms of language: The mind's hidden rules of grammar.* New York: Basic Books.

BALABAN, E. (2004). Neurobiology: Why voles stick together. *Nature, 429,* 711–712.

BALDO, J. V., DELIS, D. C., WILKINS, D. P., & SHIMAMURA, A. P. (2004). Is it bigger than a breadbox? Performance of patients with prefrontal lesions on a new executive function test. *Archives of Clinical Neuropsychology, 19*(3), 407–419.

BALTES, P. B., & STAUDINGER, U. M. (2000). Wisdom: A metaheuristic (pragmatic) to orchestrate mind and virtue toward excellence. *American Psychologist, 55,* 122–136.

BANDELOW, B., ET AL. (2000). Salivary cortisol in panic attacks. *American Journal of Psychiatry, 157,* 454–456.

BANDURA, A. (1986). *Social foundations of thought and action: A social-cognitive theory.* Englewood Cliffs, NJ: Prentice-Hall.

BANDURA, A. (1997). *Self efficacy: The exercise of control.* New York: Freeman.

BANDURA, A. (1999). Social cognitive theory: An agentic perspective. *Asian Journal of Social Psychology, 2*(1), 21–41.

BANDURA, A. (2002). Social cognitive theory in cultural context. *Applied Psychology: An International Review, 51*(2), 269–290.

BANDURA, A., BARBARANELLI, C., VITTORIO CAPRARA, G., & PASTORELLI, C. (2001). Self-efficacy beliefs as shapers of children's aspirations and career trajectories. *Child Development, 72*(1), 187–206.

BANDURA, A., BLANCHARD, E. B., & RITTER, B. (1969). The relative efficacy of desensitization and modeling approaches for inducing behavioral, affective, and cognitive changes. *Journal of Personality and Social Psychology, 13,* 173–199.

BANDURA, A., & LOCKE, E. A. (2003). Negative self-efficacy and goal effects revisited. *Journal of Applied Psychology, 88*(1), 87–99.

BANDURA, A., & McDONALD, F. J. (1963). Influence of social reinforcement and the behavior of models in shaping children's moral judgments. *Journal of Abnormal and Social Psychology, 67,* 274–281.

BANDURA, A., PASTORELLI, C., BARBARANELLI, C., & CAPRARA, G. V. (1999). Self-efficacy pathways to childhood depression. *Journal of Personality & Social Psychology, 76*(2), 258–269.

BANDURA, A., ROSS, S. A., & ROSS, D. (1963). Imitation of film-mediated aggressive models. *Journal of Abnormal and Social Psychology, 66,* 3–11.

BANDURA, A., TAYLOR, C. B., WILLIAMS, S. L., MEDFORD, I. N., & BARCHAS, J. D. (1985). Catecholamine secretion as a function of perceived coping self-efficacy. *Journal of Consulting and Clinical Psychology, 53,* 406–414.

BANK, B. J., & HANSFORD, S. L. (2000). Gender and friendship: Why are men's best same-sex friendships less intimate and supportive? *Personal Relationships, 7*(1), 63–78.

BANKS, M. S., & SHANNON, E. (1993). Spatial and chromatic visual efficiency in human neonates. In C. E. Granrud (Ed.), *Visual perception and cognition in infancy.* Hillsdale, NJ: Erlbaum.

BANYARD, V. L., WILLIAMS, L. M., SIEGEL, J. A., & WEST, C. M. (2003). Childhood sexual abuse in the lives of Black women: Risk and resilience in a longitudinal study. *Women & Therapy, 25*(3–4), 45–58.

BARBER, J. G. (2001). Relative misery and youth suicide. *Australian & New Zealand Journal of Psychiatry, 35*(1), 49–57.

BARBER, T. X. (2000). A deeper understanding of hypnosis: Its secrets, its nature, its essence. *American Journal of Clinical Hypnosis, 42*(3–4), 208–272.

BARD, P. (1934). The neurohumoral basis of emotional reactions. In C. A. Murchison (Ed.), *Handbook of general experimental psychology.* Worcester, MA: Clark University Press.

BARLOW, D. H., GORMAN, J. M., SHEAR, M. K., & WOODS, S. W. (2000). Cognitive-behavioral therapy, imipramine, or their combination for panic disorder: A randomized controlled trial. *Journal of the American Medical Association, 283,* 2529–2536.

BARNARD, C. J., COLLINS, S. A., DAISLEY, J. N., & BEHNKE, J. M. (2005). Maze performance and immunity costs in mice. *Behaviour, 142*(2), 241–263.

BARNETT, W. S. (1998). Long-term cognitive and academic effects of early childhood education of children in poverty. *Preventive Medicine: An International Journal Devoted to Practice & Theory, 27*(2), 204–207.

BARON, R. A., BYRNE, D., & BRANSCOMBE, N. R. (2006). *Social psychology* (11th ed.). Boston: Allyn & Bacon.

BARRINGER, F. (1993, April 1). Some traps of surveys. *The New York Times,* pp. A1, B9.

BARRIOS, A. A. (2001). A theory of hypnosis based on principles of conditioning and inhibition. *Contemporary Hypnosis, 18*(4), 163–203.

BARTELS, M., RIETVELD, M. J. H., VAN BAAL, G. C. M., & BOOMSMA, D. I. (2002). Genetic and environmental influences on the development of intelligence. *Behavior Genetics, 32*(4), 237–249.

BARTHOLOMEW, R., ET AL. (2000). Unit 9: Group processes. In Davis, M. H. (Ed.) *Annual editions: Social psychology 2000/2001* (4th ed., pp. 192–224). New York: Dushkin/Mcgraw-Hill.

BARTHOLOW, B. D., & ANDERSON, C. A. (2002). Effects of violent video games on aggressive behavior: Potential sex differences. *Journal of Experimental Social Psychology, 38,* 283–290.

BARTOSHUK, L. M. (2000). Psychophysical advances aid the study of genetic variation in taste. *Appetite, 34*(1), 105.

BASCH, M. F. (1980). *Doing psychotherapy.* New York: Basic Books.

BASIC BEHAVIORAL SCIENCE TASK FORCE OF THE NATIONAL ADVISORY MENTAL HEALTH COUNCIL. (1996a). Basic behavioral science research for mental health: Vulnerability and resilience. *American Psychologist, 51,* 22–28.

BASIC BEHAVIORAL SCIENCE TASK FORCE OF THE NATIONAL ADVISORY MENTAL HEALTH COUNCIL. (1996b). Basic behavioral science research for mental health: Perception, attention, learning, and memory. *American Psychologist, 51,* 133–142.

BASIC BEHAVIORAL SCIENCE TASK FORCE OF THE NATIONAL ADVISORY MENTAL HEALTH COUNCIL. (1996c). Basic behavioral science research for mental health: Sociocultural and environmental practices. *American Psychologist, 51,* 722–731.

BASSETTI, C., VELLA, S., DONATI, F., WIELEPP, P., & WEDER, B. (2000). SPECT during sleepwalking. *Lancet, 356,* 484–485.

BATTAGLIA, F. P., SUTHERLAND, G. R., & MCNAUGHTON, B. L. (2004). Local sensory cues and place cell directionality: Additional evidence of prospective coding in the hippocampus. *Journal of Neuroscience, 24*(19), 4541–4550.

BAUCOM, D. H., SHOHAM, V., MUESER, K. T., DAIUTO, A. D., & STICKLE, T. R. (1998). Empirically supported couple and family interventions for marital distress and adult mental health problems. *Journal of Consulting and Clinical Psychology, 66,* 53–88.

BAUER, M. E., ET AL. (2003). Altered glucocorticoid immunoregulation in treatment resistant depression. *Psychoneuroendocrinology, 28*(1), 49–65.

BAUMGARTNER, F. (2002). The effect of hardiness in the choice of coping strategies in stressful situations. *Studia Psychologica, 44*(1), 69–75.

BAUMEISTER, R. F. (1996). *Evil: Inside human cruelty and violence.* New York: W. H. Freeman/Times Books/Henry Holt & Co.

BAUMEISTER, R. F., CATANESE, K. R., & VOHS, K. D. (2001). Is there a gender difference in strength of sex drive? Theoretical views, conceptual distinc-

tions, and a review of relevant evidence. *Personality & Social Psychology Review, 5*(3), 242–273.

BAUMRIND, D. (1973). The development of instrumental competence through socialization. In A. D. Pick (Ed.), *Minnesota Symposia on Child Development* (Vol. 7). Minneapolis: University of Minnesota Press.

BAUMRIND, D. (1991a). The influence of parenting style on adolescent competence and substance abuse. *Journal of Early Adolescence, 11,* 56–95.

BAUMRIND, D. (1991b). Parenting styles and adolescent development. In J. Brooks-Gunn, R. Lerner, & A. C. Petersen (Eds.), *Encyclopedia of Adolescence, II.* New York: Garland.

BAUMRIND, D. (1993). The average expectable environment is not good enough. *Child Development, 64,* 1299–1317.

BAUMRIND, D., LARZELERE, R. E., & COWAN, P. A. (2002). Ordinary physical punishment: Is it harmful? Comment on Gershoff (2002). *Psychological Bulletin, 128*(4), 580–589.

BEAUTRAIS, A. L. (2003). Suicide and serious suicide attempts in youth: A multiple-group comparison study. *American Journal of Psychiatry, 160,* 1093–1099.

BECK, A. T. (2000). Cited in Chamberlin, J. (2000). An historic meeting of the minds. *Monitor on Psychology, 31*(9), 27.

BECK, A. T., BROWN, G., BERCHICK, R. J., STEWART, B. L., & STEER, R. A. (1990). Relationship between hopelessness and ultimate suicide. *American Journal of Psychiatry, 147,* 190–195.

BECK, A. T., ET AL. (2001). Dysfunctional beliefs discriminate personality disorders. *Behaviour Research & Therapy, 39*(10), 1213–1225.

BECKHAM, J. C., ET AL. (2000). Ambulatory cardiovascular activity in Vietnam combat veterans with and without posttraumatic stress disorder. *Journal of Consulting and Clinical Psychology, 68,* 269–276.

BEGLEY, S., & CHECK, E. (2000, August 5). Sex and the single fly. *Newsweek,* pp. 44–45.

BEITCHMAN, J. H., ET AL. (2001). Comorbidity of psychiatric and substance use disorders in late adolescence: A cluster analytic approach. *American Journal of Drug & Alcohol Abuse, 27*(3), 421–440.

BEKOFF, M. (2002). *Minding animals: Awareness, emotions, and heart.* New York: Oxford University Press.

BELLER, M., & GAFNI, N. (2000). Can item format (multiple choice vs. open-ended) account for gender differences in mathematics achievement? *Sex Roles, 42*(1–2), 1–21.

BELSKY, J., WEINRAUB, M., OWEN, M., & KELLY, J. (2001, April). Quantity of child care and problem behavior. In J. Belsky (Chair), *Early childcare and children's development prior to school entry.* Symposium conducted at the 2001 Biennial Meetings of the Society for Research in Child Development, Minneapolis, MN.

BEM, D. J., & HONORTON, C. (1994). Does Psi exist? Replicable evidence for an anomalous process of information transfer. *Psychological Bulletin, 115,* 4–18.

BEM, D. J., PALMER, J., & BROUGHTON, R. S. (2001). Updating the ganzfeld database: A victim of its own success? *Journal of Parapsychology, 65*(3), 207–218.

BENDA, B. B., & CORWYN, R. F. (2002).The effect of abuse in childhood and in adolescence on violence among adolescents. *Youth & Society, 33*(3), 339–365.

BENSON, H. (1975). *The relaxation response.* New York: Morrow.

BEN-ZUR, H. (2002). Associations of type A behavior with the emotional traits of anger and curiosity. *Anxiety, Stress & Coping: An International Journal, 15*(1), 95–104.

BERGEN, A. W., ET AL. (2003). Candidate genes for anorexia nervosa in the 1p33–36 linkage region: Serotonin 1D and delta opioid receptor loci exhibit significant association to anorexia nervosa. *Molecular Psychiatry, 8*(4), 397–406.

BERK, M. S., HENRIQUES, G. R., WARMAN, D. M., BROWN, G. K., & BECK, A. T. (2004). A cognitive therapy intervention for suicide attempters: An overview. *Cognitive and Behavioral Practice. 11*(3), 265–277.

BERKOWITZ, L. (1988). Frustrations, appraisals, and aversively stimulated aggression. *Aggressive Behavior, 14,* 3–11.

BERKOWITZ, L. (2004a). On the nature and operation of impulsive affective aggression. *Revue Internationale de Psychologie Sociale, 17*(2), 63–106.

BERKOWITZ, L. (2004b). Two views of evil: Evil is not only banal. *PsycCRITIQUES.*

BERNAL, M. E., ET AL. (1999). Relevance of multicultural training to students' applications to clinical psychology programs. *Cultural Diversity & Ethnic Minority Psychology, 5*(1), 43–55.

BERNARDIN, H. J., COOKE, D. K., & VILLANOVA, P. (2000). Conscientiousness and agreeableness as predictors of rating leniency. *Journal of Applied Psychology, 85*(2), 232–236.

BERNHARDT, P. C., DABBS, J. M., JR., FIELDEN, J. A., & LUTTER, C. D. (1998). Testosterone changes during vicarious experiences of winning and losing among fans at sporting events. *Physiology & Behavior, 65*(1), 59–62.

BERNSTEIN, W. M., STEPHENSON, B. O., SNYDER, M. L., & WICKLUND, R. A. (1983). Causal ambiguity and heterosexual affiliation. *Journal of Experimental Social Psychology, 19,* 78–92.

BERNTSON, G. G. (2004). Truth or lie: The science and politics of polygraphy. *PsycCRITIQUES.*

BEXTON, W. H., HERON, W., & SCOTT, T. H. (1954). Effects of decreased variation in the sensory environment. *Canadian Journal of Psychology, 8,* 70–76.

BIDELL, M. P., TURNER, J. A., & CASAS, J. M. (2002). First impressions count: Ethnic/racial and lesbian/gay/bisexual content of professional psychology application materials. *Professional Psychology: Research & Practice, 33*(1), 97–103.

BIENVENU, O. J., ET AL. (2005). Anxiety and depressive disorders and the five-factor model of personality: A higher- and lower-order personality trait investigation in a community sample. *Depression & Anxiety, 20*(2), 92–97.

BIGELOW, B. J. (2001). Relational scaffolding of school motivation: Developmental continuities in students' and parents' ratings of the importance of school goals. *Journal of Genetic Psychology, 162*(1), 75–92.

BILKEY, D. K. (2004). Neuroscience: In the place space. *Science, 305,* 1245–1246.

BIONDI, M., & PICARDI, A. (2005). Increased maintenance of obsessive-compulsive disorder remission after integrated serotonergic treatment and cognitive psychotherapy compared with medication alone. *Psychotherapy & Psychosomatics, 74*(2), 123–128.

BIRKS, Y., & ROGER, D. (2000). Identifying components of type-A behaviour: "Toxic" and "nontoxic" achieving. *Personality & Individual Differences, 28*(6), 1093–1105.

BISHOP, E. G., ET AL. (2003). Development genetic analysis of general cognitive ability from 1 to 12 years in a sample of adoptees, biological siblings, and twins. *Intelligence, 31*(1), 31–49.

BISHOP, G. D., ET AL. (2003). Job demands, decisional control, and cardiovascular responses. *Journal of Occupational Health Psychology, 8*(2), 146–156.

BIZER, G. Y., ET AL. (2004). The impact of personality on cognitive, behavioral, and affective political processes: The effects of need to evaluate. *Journal of Personality, 72*(5), 995–1027.

BJORKLUND, D. F. (2000). *Children's thinking* (3rd ed). Pacific Grove, CA: Brooks/Cole.

BLAGROVE, M., FARMER, L., & WILLIAMS, E. (2004). The relationship of nightmare frequency and nightmare distress to well-being. *Journal of Sleep Research, 13*(2), 129–136.

BLAIR, R., & JAMES, R. (2001). Neurocognitive models of aggression, the antisocial personality disorders, and psychopathy. *Journal of Neurology, Neurosurgery & Psychiatry, 71*(6), 727–731.

BLAIR, R. , & JAMES, R. (2003). Neurobiological basis of psychopathy. *British Journal of Psychiatry, 182,* 5–7.

BLAKE, P., FRY, R., & PESJACK, M. (1984). *Self-assessment and behavior change manual* (pp. 43–47). New York: Random House.

BLANCHARD, E. B. (1992). Psychological treatment of benign headache disorders. *Journal of Consulting and Clinical Psychology, 60,* 537–551.

BLANCHARD, E. B., ET AL. (1990). Placebo-controlled evaluation of abbreviated progressive muscle relaxation and of relaxation combined with cognitive therapy in the treatment of tension headache. *Journal of Consulting and Clinical Psychology, 58,* 210–215.

BLANCHARD, E. B., ET AL. (2003). A controlled evaluation of cognitive behavioral therapy for posttraumatic stress in motor vehicle accident survivors. *Behaviour Research & Therapy, 41*(1), 79–96.

BLANCO-COLIO, L. M., ET AL. (2000). Red wine intake prevents nuclear factor-B activation in peripheral blood mononuclear cells of healthy volunteers during postprandial lipemia. *Circulation, 102,* 1020–1026.

BLASCOVICH, J., SPENCER, S. J., QUINN, D., & STEELE, C. (2001). African Americans and high blood pressure: The role of stereotype threat. *Psychological Science, 12*(3), 225–229.

BLASS, T. (1999). The Milgram paradigm after 35 years: Some things we now know about obedience to authority. *Journal of Applied Social Psychology, 29*(5), 955–978.

BLASS, T., & SCHMITT, C. (2001). The nature of perceived authority in the Milgram paradigm: Two replications. *Current Psychology: Developmental, Learning, Personality, Social, 20*(2), 115–121.

BLUM, R. W., HARMON, B., HARRIS, L., & BERGEISEN, L (1992). American Indian–Alaska Native youth health. Journal of the American Medical Association, *268*(7), 874.

BLUMENTHAL, J. A., SHERWOOD, A., GULLETTE, E. C. D., GEORGIADES, A., & TWEEDY, D. (2002). Biobehavioral approaches to the treatment of essential hypertension. *Journal of Consulting and Clinical Psychology, 70*(3), 569–589.

BLUMENTHAL, J. A., ET AL. (2005). Effects of exercise and stress management training on markers of cardiovascular risk in patients with ischemic heart disease: A randomized controlled trial. *Journal of the American Medical Association, 293*(13), 1626–1634.

BODAMAR, M. D., & GARDNER, R. A. (2002). How cross-fostered chimpanzees (Pan troglodytes) initiate and maintain conversations. *Journal of Comparative Psychology, 116*(1), 12–26.

BOGEN, J. E. (1969). The other side of the brain II: An appositional mind. *Bulletin of the Los Angeles Neurological Society, 34,* 135–162.

BOGEN, J. E. (1998). My developing understanding of Roger Wolcott Sperry's philosophy. *Neuropsychologia, 36*(10), 1089–1096.

BOGEN, J. E. (2000). Split-brain basics: Relevance for the concept of one's other mind. *Journal of the American Academy of Psychoanalysis, 28*(2), 341–369.

BOHLIN, G., HAGEKULL, B., & RYDELL, A. (2000). Attachment and social functioning: A longitudinal study from infancy to middle childhood. *Social Development, 9*(1), 24–39.

BONGAR, B. (2002). *The suicidal patient: Clinical and legal standards of care* (2nd ed.). Washington, DC: American Psychological Association.

BONIN, M. F., MCCREARY, D. R., & SADAVA, S. W. (2000). Problem drinking behavior in two community-based samples of adults: Influence of gender, coping, loneliness, and depression. *Psychology of Addictive Behaviors, 14*(2), 151–161.

BOOTH, C. L., KELLY, J. F., SPIEKER, S. J., & ZUCKERMAN, T. G. (2003). Toddlers' attachment security to child-care providers: The Safe and Secure Scale. *Early Education & Development, 14*(1), 83–100.

BOSKIND-WHITE, M., & WHITE, W. C. (1983). *Bulimarexia: The binge/purge cycle.* New York: W. W. Norton.

BOTH, L., NEEDHAM, D., & WOOD, E. (2004). Examining tasks that facilitate the experience of incubation while problem-solving. *Alberta Journal of Educational Research, 50*(1), 57–67.

BOUCHARD, T. J., JR., & LOEHLIN, J. C. (2001). Genes, evolution, and personality. *Behavior Genetics, 31*(3), 243–273.

BOUCHARD, T. J., JR., LYKKEN, D. T., MCGUE, M., SEGAL, N. L., & TELLEGEN, A. (1990). Sources of human psychological differences: The Minnesota study of twins reared apart. *Science, 250,* 223–228.

BOWER, G. H. (1981). Mood and memory. *American Psychologist, 36,* 129–148.

BOWLBY, J. (1988). *A secure base.* New York: Basic Books.

BOYATZIS, R. E. (1974). The effect of alcohol consumption on the aggressive behavior of men. *Quarterly Journal for the Study of Alcohol, 35,* 959–972.

BOYD-FRANKLIN, N. (2001). Using the multisystems model with an African American family: Cross-racial therapy and supervision. In S. H. McDaniel, et al. (Eds.), *Casebook for integrating family therapy: An ecosystemic approach* (pp. 395–400). Washington, DC: American Psychological Association.

BRADLEY, R. H., ET AL. (1989). Home environment and cognitive development in the first 3 years of life. *Developmental Psychology, 25,* 217–235.

Brain-link camera gives blind a limited view. (2000, January 18). *The New York Times online.*

BRAKKE, K. E., & SAVAGE-RUMBAUGH, E. S. (1996).The development of language skills in pan: II. Production. *Language & Communication, 16*(4), 361–380.

BRANAMAN, T. F., & GALLAGHER, S. N. (2005). Polygraph testing in sex offender treatment: A review of limitations. *American Journal of Forensic Psychology, 23*(1), 45–64.

BRAND, J. (2000). Cited in McFarling, U. L. (2000, August 27). Sniffing out genes' role in our senses of taste and smell. *The Los Angeles Times online.*

BRANSFORD, J. D., NITSCH, K. E., & FRANKS, J. J. (1977). Schooling and the facilitation of knowing. In R. C. Anderson, R. J. Spiro, & W. E. Montague (Eds.), *Schooling and the acquisition of knowledge.* Hillsdale, NJ: Erlbaum.

BRAUN, B. G. (1988). *Treatment of multiple personality disorder.* Washington, DC: American Psychiatric Press.

BRAY, F., & ATKIN, W. (2004). International cancer patterns in men: Geographical and temporal variations in cancer risk and the role of gender. *Journal of Men's Health & Gender, 1*(1), 38–46.

BRIGMAN, S., & CHERRY, K. E. (2002). Age and skilled performance: Contributions of working memory and processing speed. *Brain & Cognition, 50*(2), 242–256.

BRISSETTE, I., SCHEIER, M. F., & CARVER, C. S. (2002). The role of optimism in social network development, coping, and psychological adjustment during a life transition. *Journal of Personality & Social Psychology, 82*(1), 102–111.

BRODY, J. E. (1997, March 26). Race and weight. *The New York Times,* p. C8.

BRODY, J. E. (2000, April 25). Memories of things that never were. *The New York Times,* p. F8.

BRODY, J. E. (2005, March 22). What's good for the heart is good for the head. *The New York Times online.*

BROOK, J. S., ZHENG, L., WHITEMAN, M., & BROOK, D. W. (2001). Aggression in toddlers: Associations with parenting and marital relations. *Journal of Genetic Psychology, 162*(2), 228–241.

BROOM, A. (2005). The eMale: Prostate cancer, masculinity and online support as a challenge to medical expertise. *Journal of Sociology, 41*(1), 87–104.

BROWN, A. S. (2003). A review of the déjà vu experience. *Psychological Bulletin, 129*(3), 394–413.

BROWN, A. S., & SUSSER, E. S. (2002). In utero infection and adult schizophrenia. *Mental Retardation & Developmental Disabilities Research Reviews, 8*(1), 51–57.

BROWN, G. K., NEWMAN, C. F., CHARLESWORTH, S. E., CRITS-CHRISTOPH, P., & BECK, A. T. (2004). An open clinical trial of cognitive therapy for borderline personality disorder. *Journal of Personality Disorders, 18*(3), 257–271.

BROWN, R., & MCNEILL, D. (1966). The tip-of-the-tongue phenomenon. *Journal of Verbal Learning and Verbal Behavior, 5,* 325–337.

BROWNELL, K. D., & HORGEN, K. B. (2003). *Food fight: The inside story of the food industry, America's obesity crisis, and what we can do about it.* New York: Mc-Graw-Hill.

BROWNSTEIN, A. L. (2003). Biased predecision processing. *Psychological Bulletin, 129*(4), 545–568.

BRUCE, N. W., & SANDERS, K. A. (2001). Incidence and duration of romantic attraction in students progressing from secondary to tertiary education. *Journal of Biosocial Science, 33*(2), 173–184.

BRUENE, M., & RIBBERT, H. (2002). Grundsaetzliches zur Konzeption einer evolutionaeren Psychiatrie. *Schweizer Archiv für Neurologie und Psychiatrie, 153*(1), 4–11.

BUCHANAN, R. W., PEARLSON, G., & TAMMINGA, C. A. (2004). Prefrontal cortex, structural analysis: Segmenting the prefrontal cortex. *American Journal of Psychiatry, 161*(11), 1978.

BUCKLEY, P. F., BUCHANAN, R. W., TAMMINGA, C. A., & SCHULZ, S. C. (2000). Schizophrenia research. *Schizophrenia Bulletin, 26*(2), 411–419.

BUCKNER, R. L., WHEELER, M. E., & SHERIDAN, M. A. (2001). Encoding processes during retrieval tasks. *Journal of Cognitive Neuroscience, 13*(3), 406–415.

BULL, N. J., HUNTER, M., & FINLAY, D. C. (2003). Cue gradient and cue density interact in the detection and recognition of objects defined by motion, contrast, or texture. *Perception, 32*(1), 29–39.

BURGESS, R. L., & DRAIS, A. A. (2001). Explaining child maltreatment: From behavior analysis to behavioral biology. *Revista Mexicana de Analisis de la Conducta, 27*(2), 201–224.

BUSHMAN, B. J. (1998). Priming effects of media violence on the accessibility of aggressive constructs in memory. *Personality & Social Psychology Bulletin, 24*(5), 537–545.

BUSHMAN, B. J., & ANDERSON, C. A. (2001). Media violence and the American public. *American Psychologist, 56*(6/7), 477–489.

BUSHMAN, B. J., & ANDERSON, C. A. (2002). Violent video games and hostile expectations: A test of the general aggression model. *Personality and Social Psychology Bulletin, 28*, 1679–1686.

BUSHMAN, B. J., WANG, M., & ANDERSON, C. A. (2005). Is the curve relating temperature to aggression linear or curvilinear? Assaults and temperature in Minneapolis reexamined. *Journal of Personality and Social Psychology, 89*(1), 62–66.

BUSS, D. M. (1992). Is there a universal human nature? *Contemporary Psychology, 37*, 1262–1263.

BUSS, D. M. (1994). *The evolution of desire.* New York: Basic Books.

BUSS, D. M. (1995). Psychological sex differences. *American Psychologist, 50*, 164–168.

BUSS, D. M. (1999). Adaptive individual differences revisited. *Journal of Personality, 67*(2), 259–264.

BUSS, D. M. (2000). The evolution of happiness. *American Psychologist, 55*, 15–23.

BUSS, D. M. (2003). Sexual strategies: A journey into controversy. *Psychological Inquiry, 14*(3–4), 219–226.

BUTCHER, J. (2000). Dopamine hypothesis gains further support. *The Lancet, 356*, 139–146.

BUTLER, A. C., & BECK, J. S. (2001). Cognitive therapy outcomes. A review of meta-analyses. *Tidsskrift for Norsk Psykologforening, 38*(8), 698–706.

BUTLER, J. C. (2000). Personality and emotional correlates of right-wing authoritarianism. *Social Behavior & Personality, 28*(1), 1–14.

CACIOPPO, J. T., HAWKLEY, L. C., & BERNSTON, G. G. (2003). The anatomy of loneliness. *Current Directions in Psychological Science, 12*(3), 71–74.

CACIOPPO, J. T., MARTZKE, J. S., PETTY, R. E., & TASSINARY, L. G. (1988). Specific forms of facial EMG response index emotions during an interview. *Journal of Personality and Social Psychology, 54*, 552–604.

CAFFRAY, C. M., & SCHNEIDER, S. L. (2000). Why do they do it? Affective motivators in adolescents' decisions to participate in risk behaviours. *Cogntiion & Emotion, 14*(4), 543–576.

CAIRNEY, J., & WADE, T. J. (2002). Single parent mothers and mental health care service use. *Social Psychiatry & Psychiatric Epidemiology, 37*(5), 236–242.

Californians losing fight against flab. (2000, June 14). Reuters News Agency online.

CAMPBELL, W. K., SEDIKIDES, C., REEDER, G. D., & ELLIOTT, A. J. (2000). Among friends? An examination of friendship and the self-serving bias. *British Journal of Social Psychology, 39*(2), 229–239.

CAMPOS, J. J. (2000). Cited in Azar, B. (2000). What's in a face? *Monitor on Psychology, 31*(1), 44–45.

CAMPOS, J. J., HIATT, S., RAMSEY, D., HENDERSON, C., & SVEJDA, M. (1978). The emergence of fear on the visual cliff. In M. Lewis & L. Rosenblum (Eds.), *The origins of affect.* New York: Plenum.

CAMRAS, L. (2000). Cited in Azar, B. (2000). What's in a face? *Monitor on Psychology, 31*(1), 44–45.

CANALIS, R. F., & LAMBERT, P. R. (2000). *The ear: Comprehensive otology.* Philadelphia: Lippincott Williams & Wilkins.

CANETTI, L., BACHAR, E., & BERRY, E. M. (2002). Food and emotion. *Behavioural Processes, 60*(2), 157–164.

CANNON, W. B. (1927). The James-Lange theory of emotions: A critical examination and an alternative theory. *American Journal of Psychology, 39*, 106–124.

CANNON, W. B. (1932). *The wisdom of the body.* New York: Norton.

CANNON, W. B., & WASHBURN, A. (1912). An explanation of hunger. *American Journal of Physiology, 29*, 441–454.

CANTALUPO, C., & HOPKINS, W. D. (2001). Asymmetric Broca's area in great apes: A region of the ape brain is uncannily similar to one linked with speech in humans. *Nature, 414*(6863), 505.

CAREY, B. (2005, January 4). After food and shelter, help in coping with unbearable loss. *The New York Times online.*

CARLSON, J. G., & HATFIELD, E. (1992). *Psychology of emotion.* Fort Worth: Harcourt Brace Jovanovich.

CARLSSON, K., ET AL. (2000). Tickling expectations: Neural processing in anticipation of a sensory stimulus. *Journal of Cognitive Neuroscience, 12*, 691–703.

CARMICHAEL, L. L., HOGAN, H. P., & WALTER, A. A. (1932). An experimental study of the effect of language on the reproduction of visually perceived form. *Journal of Experimental Psychology, 15*, 73–86.

CARROLL, D. (2004). *Psychology of language* (4th ed.). Belmont, CA: Wadsworth Publishing Company.

CARROLL, M. E., & OVERMIER, J. B. (2001). *Animal research and human health.* Washington, DC: American Psychological Association.

CASSADAY, H. J., ET AL. (2003). Intraventricular 5,7-dihydroxytryptamine lesions disrupt acquisition of working memory task rules but not performance once learned. *Progress in Neuro-Psychopharmacology & Biological Psychiatry, 27*(1), 147–156.

CASTILLO-RICHMOND, A., ET AL. (2000). Effects of stress reduction on carotid atherosclerosis in hypertensive African Americans. *Stroke, 31*, 568.

CATHER, C., ET AL. (2005). A pilot study of functional cognitive behavioral therapy (fCBT) for schizophrenia. *Schizophrenia Research, 74*(2–3), 201–209.

CATTELL, R. B. (1949). *The culture-free intelligence test.* Champaign, IL: Institute for Personality and Ability Testing.

CDC (See Centers for Disease Control and Prevention.)

CECI, S. J., & BRUCK, M. (1993). Suggestibility of the child witness. *Psychological Bulletin, 113*, 403–439.

CELLAR, D. F., NELSON, Z. C., & YORKE, C. M. (2000). The five-factor model and driving behavior: Personality and involvement in vehicular accidents. *Psychological Reports, 86*(2), 454–456.

CENTERS FOR DISEASE CONTROL AND PREVENTION (1995). *Suicide surveillance: 1980–1990.* Washington, DC: USDHHS.

CENTERS FOR DISEASE CONTROL AND PREVENTION. (2000a, June 9). Youth risk behavior surveillance—United States, 1999. *Morbidity and Mortality Weekly Report, 49*(SS05), 1–96.

CENTERS FOR DISEASE CONTROL AND PREVENTION. (2000b). Suicide in the United States. Page updated January 28, 2000. http://www.cdc.gov/ncipc/factsheets/suifacts.htm.

CENTERS FOR DISEASE CONTROL AND PREVENTION. (2000c). National and state-specific pregnancy rates among adolescents—United States, 1995–1997. *Morbidity and Mortality Weekly Report, 49*(27).

CENTERS FOR DISEASE CONTROL AND PREVENTION. (2000d). *National Vital Statistics Reports, 48*(3).

CENTERS FOR DISEASE CONTROL AND PREVENTION. (2001, December 3). Sexually transmitted disease surveillance 2000. Atlanta, GA: Division of STD Prevention, National Center for HIV, STD and TB Prevention.

CENTERS FOR DISEASE CONTROL AND PREVENTION. (2003). *HIV/AIDS surveillance report: U.S. HIV and AIDS cases reported through December 2002, 14*(2).

CENTERS FOR DISEASE CONTROL AND PREVENTION. (2005a, April 21). Overweight and obesity: Health consequences. http://www.cdc.gov/nccd php/dnpa/obesity/consequences.htm.

CENTERS FOR DISEASE CONTROL AND PREVENTION. (2005b, April 14). Physical activity for everyone. http://www.cdc.gov/nccdphp/dnpa/physical/index.htm.

CERVANTES, J. M., & PARHAM, T. A. (2005). Toward a meaningful spirituality for people of color: Lessons for the counseling practitioner. *Cultural Diversity & Ethnic Minority Psychology, 11*(1), 69–81.

CERVILLA, J. A., ET AL. (2000). Long-term predictors of cognitive outcome in a cohort of older people with hypertension. *British Journal of Psychiatry, 177*, 66–71.

CHAFEE, M. V., & GOLDMAN-RAKIC, P. S. (2000). Inactivation of parietal and prefrontal cortex reveals interdependence of neural activity during memory-guided saccades. *Journal of Neurophysiology, 83*(3), 1550–1566.

CHAK, K., & LEUNG, L. (2004). Shyness and locus of control as predictors of Internet addiction and Internet use. *CyberPsychology & Behavior, 7*(5), 559–570.

CHANCE, S. E., BROWN, R. T., DABBS, J. M., JR., & CASEY, R. (2000). Testosterone, intelligence and behavior disorders in young boys. *Personality & Individual Differences, 28*(3), 437–445.

CHANG, D. F., & SUE, S. (2003). The effects of race and problem type on teachers' assessments of student behavior. *Journal of Consulting & Clinical Psychology, 71*(2), 235–242.

CHANG, T., TRACEY, T. J. G., & MOORE, T. L. (2005). The dimensional structure of Asian American acculturation: An examination of prototypes. *Self & Identity, 4*(1), 25–43.

CHAPLIN, W. F., PHILLIPS, J. B., BROWN, J. D., CLANTON, N. R., & STEIN, J. L. (2000). Handshaking, gender, personality, and first impressions. *Journal of Personality and Social Psychology, 79*(1), 110–117.

CHASSIN, L., PRESSON, C. C., ROSE, J. S., & SHERMAN, S. J. (2001). From adolescence to adulthood: Age-related changes in beliefs about cigarette smoking in a Midwestern community sample. *Health Psychology, 20*(5), 377–386.

CHEN, C., ET AL. (2004). Association analysis of dopamine D2-like receptor genes and methamphetamine abuse. *Psychiatric Genetics, 14*(4), 223–226.

CHEN, S. W., & DAVENPORT, D. S. (2005). Cognitive-behavioral therapy with Chinese American clients: Cautions and modifications. *Psychotherapy: Theory, Research, Practice, Training, 42*(1), 101–110.

CHENG, H., & FURNHAM, A. (2001). Attributional style and personality as predictors of happiness and mental health. *Journal of Happiness Studies, 2*(3), 307–327.

Chioqueta, A. P., & Stiles, T. C. (2005). Personality traits and the development of depression, hopelessness, and suicide ideation. *Personality & Individual Differences, 38*(6), 1283–1291.

Chomsky, N. (1980). Rules and representations. *Behavioral and Brain Sciences, 3,* 1–16.

Chomsky, N. (1991). Linguistics and cognitive science. In A. Kasher (Ed.), *The Chomskyan turn.* Cambridge, MA: Blackwell.

Chu, L., Ma, E. S. K., Lam, K. K. Y., Chan, M. F., & Lee, D. H. S. (2005). Increased alpha 7 nicotinic acetylcholine receptor protein levels in Alzheimer's disease patients. *Dementia & Geriatric Cognitive Disorders, 19*(2–3), 106–112.

Chua, S. C., Jr. (2004). Molecular and cellular correlates of the developmental acquisition of mechanisms modulating ingestive behavior. *Physiology & Behavior, 82*(1), 145–147.

Chuang, Y. (2002). Sex differences in mate selection preference and sexual strategy: Tests for evolutionary hypotheses. *Chinese Journal of Psychology, 44*(1), 75–93.

Cialdini, R. B. (2000). Cited in McKinley, J. C., Jr. (2000, August 11). It isn't just a game: Clues to avid rooting. *The New York Times online.*

Cialdini, R. B., & Goldstein, N. J. (2004). Social influence: Compliance and conformity. *Annual Review of Psychology, 55,* 591–621.

Cialdini, R. B., et al. (1976). Basking in reflected glory: Three (football) field studies. *Journal of Personality & Social Psychology, 34*(3), 366–375.

Cialdini, R. B., et al. (1997). Reinterpreting the empathy-altruism relationship: When one into one equals oneness. *Journal of Personality & Social Psychology, 73*(3), 481–494.

Ciarrochi, J. (2004). Relationships between dysfunctional beliefs and positive and negative indices of well-being: A critical evaluation of the common beliefs survey–III. *Journal of Rational-Emotive & Cognitive Behavior Therapy, 22*(3), 171–188.

Clark, S. E., & Loftus, E. F. (1996). The construction of space alien abduction memories. *Psychological Inquiry, 7*(2), 140–143.

Clark, S. E., & Loftus, E. F. (2004). The psychological pay dirt of space alien abduction memories. *PsycCRITIQUES.*

Clarke-Stewart, K. A. (1990). The "effects" of infant day care reconsidered. In N. Fox & G. G. Fein (Eds.), *Infant day care* (pp. 61–86). Norwood, NJ: Ablex.

Clarke-Stewart, K. A. (1991). A home is not a school: The effects of child care on children's development. *Journal of Social Issues, 47,* 105–123.

Clarke-Stewart, K. A., & Beck, R. J. (1999). Maternal scaffolding and children's narrative retelling of a movie story. *Early Childhood Research Quarterly, 14*(3), 409–434.

Clayton, E. C., & Williams, C. L. (2000). Adrenergic activation of the nucleus tractus solitarius potentiates amygdala norepinephrine release and enhances retention performance in emotionally arousing and spatial memory tasks. *Behavioural Brain Research. 112*(1–2), 151–158.

Clènet, F., Hascoët, M., Fillion, G., Galons, H., & Bourin, M. (2005). Role of GABA-ergic and serotonergic systems in the anxiolytic-like mechanism of action of a 5-HT-moduline antagonist in the mouse elevated plus maze. *Behavioural Brain Research, 158*(2), 339–348.

CNS Spectrums. (2005). Cognitive-behavioral therapy. *CNS Spectrums, 10*(2), 119–122.

Cohen, L. L. (2002). Reducing infant immunization distress through distraction. *Health Psychology, 21*(2), 207–211.

Cohen, S., Doyle, W. J., Turner, R., Alper, C. M., & Skoner, D. P. (2003). Sociability and susceptibility to the common cold. *Psychological Science, 14*(5), 389–395.

Cohen, S., Gottlieb, B. H., & Underwood, L. G. (2001a). Social relationships and health: Challenges for measurement and intervention. *Advances in Mind-Body Medicine, 17*(2), 129–141.

Cohen, S., Miller, G. E., & Rabin, B. S. (2001b). Psychological stress and antibody response to immunization: A critical review of the human literature. *Psychosomatic Medicine, 63*(1), 7–18.

Cohn, E. G., & Rotton, J. (2000). Weather, seasonal trends, and property crimes in Minneapolis, 1987–1988. A moderator-variable time-series analysis of routine activities. *Journal of Environmental Psychology, 20*(3), 257–272.

Cohn, E. G., & Rotton, J. (2005). The curve is still out there: A reply to Bushman, Wang, and Anderson's (2005) "Is the curve relating temperature to aggression linear or curvilinear?" *Journal of Personality and Social Psychology, 89*(1), 67–70.

Cohn, L. D., Macfarlane, S., Yanez, C., & Imai, W. K. (1995). Risk-perception: Differences between adolescents and adults. *Health Psychology, 14,* 217–222.

Collaer, M. L., & Hines, M. (1995). Human behavioral sex differences: A role for gonadal hormones during early development? *Psychological Bulletin, 118,* 55–107.

Collaer, M. L., & Nelson, J. D. (2002). Large visuospatial sex difference in line judgment: Possible role of attentional factors. *Brain & Cognition, 49*(1), 1–12.

Colom, R., Flores-Mendoza, C., & Rebollo, I. (2003). Working memory and intelligence. *Personality & Individual Differences, 34*(1), 33–39.

Coltraine, S., & Messineo, M. (2000). The perpetuation of subtle prejudice: Race and gender imagery in 1990s television advertising. *Sex Roles, 42*(5–6), 363–389.

Colvin, M. K., Funnell, M. G., & Gazzaniga, M. S. (2005). Numerical processing in the two hemispheres: Studies of a split-brain patient. *Brain & Cognition, 57*(1), 43–52.

Comas-Díaz, L. (2003). The Black Madonna: The psychospiritual feminism of Guadeloupe, Kali, and Monserrat. In L. B. Silverstein & T. J. Goodrich (Eds.), *Feminist family therapy: Empowerment in social context* (pp. 147–160). Washington, DC: American Psychological Association.

Comaty, J. E., Stasio, M., & Advokat, C. (2001). Analysis of outcome variables of a token economy system in a state psychiatric hospital: A program evaluation. *Research in Developmental Disabilities, 22*(3), 233–253.

Compas, B. E., Haaga, D. A. F., Keefe, F. J., Leitenberg, H., & Williams, D. A. (1998). Sampling of empirically supported psychological treatments from health psychology: Smoking, chronic pain, cancer, and bulimia nervosa. *Journal of Consulting and Clinical Psychology, 66,* 89–112.

Concar, D. (2002, April 20). Ecstasy on the brain. http://www.NewScientist.com.

Conklin, H. M., & Iacono, W. G. (2002). Schizophrenia: A neurodevelopmental perspective. *Current Directions in Psychological Science, 11*(1), 33–37.

Conrad, P. J., Peterson, J. B., & Pihl, R. O. (2001). Reliability and validity of alcohol-induced heart rate increase as a measure of sensitivity to the stimulant properties of alcohol. *Psychopharmacology, 157*(1), 20–30.

Consortium of Social Science Associations. (2003, May 23). McQueary testifies to Homeland Security Science Subcommittee. *Washington Update, 22*(10), 1–7.

Constantinidis, C., Franowicz, M. N., & Goldman-Rakic, P. S. (2001). Coding specificity in cortical microcircuits: A multiple-electrode analysis of primate prefontal cortex. *Journal of Neuroscience, 21*(10), 3646–3655.

Conte, J., M., Schwenneker, H. H., Dew, A. F., & Romano, D. M. (2001). Incremental validity of time urgency and other Type A subcomponents in predicting behavioral and health criteria. *Journal of Applied Social Psychology, 31*(8), 1727–1748.

Cooper, M., Galbraith, M., & Drinkwater, J. (2001). Assumptions and beliefs in adolescents with anorexia nervosa and their mothers. *Eating Disorders: The Journal of Treatment & Prevention, 9*(3), 217–223.

Cooper, M. L. (2002). Alcohol use and risky sexual behavior among college students and youth: Evaluating the evidence. *Journal of Studies on Alcohol* (Suppl. 14), 101–117.

Cooper, Z., & Fairburn, C. G. (2001). A new cognitive behavioural approach to the treatment of obesity. *Behaviour Research & Therapy, 39*(5), 499–511.

Corballis, P. M., Funnell, M. G., & Gazzaniga, M. S. (2002). Hemispheric asymmetries for simple visual judgments in the split brain. *Neuropsychologia, 40*(4), 401–410.

Corwin, R. L. (2000). Biological and behavioral consequences of food restriction. *Appetite, 34*(1), 112.

Cory, G. A. (2002). MacLean's evolutionary neuroscience, the CSN model and Hamilton's rule: Some developmental, clinical, and social policy implications. *Brain & Mind, 3*(1), 151–181.

COSSA. See Consortium of Social Science Associations.

Council on Foreign Relations. (2002). Terrorism. http://www.cfrterrorism.org/groups/hamas_print.html.

Courtenay, W. H. (2000). Engendering health: A social constructionist examination of men's health beliefs and behaviors. *Psychology of Men & Masculinity, 1*(1), 4–15.

Cowen, P. J. (2002). Cortisol, serotonin and depression: All stressed out? *British Journal of Psychiatry, 180*(2), 99–100.

Cox, B. J., Borger, S. C., Asmundson, G. J. G., & Taylor, S. (2000). Hypochondriasis: Dimensions of hypochondriasis and the five-factor model of personality. *Personality & Individual Differences, 29*(1), 99–108.

Cox, W. M., & Alm, R. (2005, February 25). Scientists are made, not born. *The New York Times online.*

Craik, F. I. M., & Lockhart, R. S. (1972). Levels of processing. *Journal of Verbal Learning and Verbal Behavior, 11,* 671–684.

Cramer, P. (2000). Defense mechanisms in psychology today. *American Psychologist, 55*(6), 637–646.

Cramer, R. E., McMaster, M. R., Bartell, P. A., & Dragna, M. (1988). Subject competence and minimization of the bystander effect. *Journal of Applied Social Psychology, 18,* 1133–1148.

Crano, W. D. (2000) Milestones in the psychological analysis of social influence. *Group Dynamics, 4*(1), 68–80.

Craske, M. G., & Zucker, B. G. (2001). Consideration of the APA practice guideline for the treatment of patients with panic disorder: Strengths and limitations for behavior therapy. *Behavior Therapy, 32*(2), 259–281.

CREWS, D. (1994). Animal sexuality. *Scientific American, 270*(1), 108–114.

CRICK, N. R., & DODGE, K. A. (1994). A review and reformulation of social information-processing mechanisms in children's social adjustment. *Psychological Bulletin, 115*, 74–101.

CRISP, R. J., & NICEL, J. K. (2004). Disconfirming intergroup evaluations: Asymmetric effects for ingroups and out-groups. *Journal of Social Psychology, 144*(3), 247–271.

CROWE, R. A. (1990). Astrology and the scientific method. *Psychological Reports, 67*, 163–191.

CRUSCO, A. H., & WETZEL, C. G. (1984). The Midas touch: The effects of interpersonal touch on restaurant tipping. *Personality and Social Psychology Bulletin, 10*, 512–517.

CUIJPERS, P., VAN STRATEN, A., & DONKER, M. (2005). Personality traits of patients with mood and anxiety disorders. *Psychiatry Research, 133*(2–3), 229–237.

Culture gaps could inhibit counseling of Katrina victims. (2005, September 13). *USA Today*.

CUMMINS, R. A. (2000). Personal income and subjective well-being: A review. *Journal of Happiness Studies, 1*(2), 133–158.

CUMMINS, R. A., & NISTICO, H. (2002). Maintaining life satisfaction: The role of positive cognitive bias. *Journal of Happiness Studies, 3*(1), 37–69.

CUMSILLE, P. E., SAYER, A. G., & GRAHAM, J. W. (2000). Perceived exposure to peer and adult drinking as predictors of growth in positive alcohol expectancies during adolescence. *Journal of Consulting and Clinical Psychology, 68*(3), 531–536.

CUNNINGHAM, M. R., SHAFFER, D. R., BARBEE, A. P., WOLFF, P. L., & KELLEY, D. J. (1990). Separate processes in the relation of elation and depression to helping. *Journal of Experimental Social Psychology, 26*, 13–33.

CURTIS, R. C., & MILLER, K. (1986). Believing another likes or dislikes you: Behavior making the beliefs come true. *Journal of Personality and Social Psychology, 51*, 284–290.

CYRANOWSKI, J. M., FRANK, E., YOUNG, E., & SHEAR, M. M. (2000). Adolescent onset of the gender difference in lifetime rates of major depression: A theoretical model. *Archives of General Psychiatry, 57*(1), 21–27.

DABBS, J. M., JR., CHANG, E-L., STRONG, R. A., & MILUN, R. (1998). Spatial ability, navigation strategy, and geographic knowledge among men and women. *Evolution & Human Behavior, 19*(2), 89–98.

DABBS, J. M., JR., HARGROVE, M. F., & HEUSEL, C. (1996). Testosterone differences among college fraternities: Well-behaved vs. rambunctious. *Personality & Individual Differences, 20*(2), 157–161.

DALKVIST, J. (2001). The ganzfeld method: Its current status. *European Journal of Parapsychology, 16*, 19–22.

DAMASIO, A. R. (2000). A neural basis for sociopathy. *Archives of General Psychiatry online, 57*(2).

DANNER, M. (2005, September 11). Taking stock of the forever war. *The New York Times Magazine*, pp. 44–53, 68, 86–87.

DARLEY, J. M. (1993). Research on morality. *Psychological Science, 4*, 353–357.

DARLEY, J. M., & LATANÉ, B. (1968). Bystander intervention in emergencies: Diffusion of responsibility. *Journal of Personality and Social Psychology, 8*, 377–383.

DARWIN, C. A. (1872). *The expression of the emotions in man and animals*. London: J. Murray.

DASGUPTA, N., & GREENWALD, A. G. (2001). On the malleability of automatic attitudes: Combating automatic prejudice with images of admired and disliked individuals. *Journal of Personality and Social Psychology, 81*(5), 800–814.

DAVIS, C., STRACHAN, S., & BERKSON, M. (2004). Sensitivity to reward: Implications for overeating and overweight. *Appetite, 42*(2), 131–138.

DAVIS, S. (2000). Testosterone and sexual desire in women. *Journal of Sex Education & Therapy, 25*(1), 25–32.

DAVIS, T. L., & LIDDELL, D. L. (2002). Getting inside the house: The effectiveness of a rape prevention program for college fraternity men. *Journal of College Student Development, 43*(1), 35–50.

DAWOOD, K., PILLARD, R. C., HORVATH, C., REVELLE, W., & BAILEY, J. M. (2000). Familial aspects of male homosexuality. *Archives of Sexual Behavior, 29*(2), 155–163.

DAWSON, T. L. (2002). New tools, new insights: Kohlberg's moral judgement stages revisited. *International Journal of Behavioral Development, 26*(2), 154–166.

DEANGELIS, T. (1994a). Educators reveal keys to success in classroom. *APA Monitor, 25*(1), 39–40.

DEANGELIS, T. (1994b). Experts see little impact from insanity plea ruling. *APA Monitor, 25*(6), 28.

DEANGELIS, T. (1996). Women's contributions large; recognition isn't. *APA Monitor, 27*(4), 12–13.

DEANGELIS, T. (2000). Is Internet addiction real? *APA Monitor, 31*(4), 24–26.

DEANGELIS, T. (2002). A genetic link to anorexia. *APA Monitor, 33*(3), 34–36.

DECASPER, A. J., & PRESCOTT, P. A. (1984). Human newborns' perception of male voices. *Developmental Psychobiology, 17*, 481–491.

DEEP, A. L., ET AL. (1999). Sexual abuse in eating disorder subtypes and control women: The role of comorbid substance dependence in bulimia nervosa. *International Journal of Eating Disorders, 25*(1), 1–10.

DE GUERRERO, M. C. M., & VILLAMIL, O. S. (2000). Activating the ZPD: Mutual scaffolding in L2 peer revision. *Modern Language Journal, 84*(1), 51–68.

DEHGHANI, M., SHARPE, L., & NICHOLAS, M. K. (2004). Modification of attentional biases in chronic pain patients: A preliminary study. *European Journal of Pain, 8*(6), 585–594.

DE HOUWER, J., THOMAS, S., & BAEYENS, F. (2001). Associative learning of likes and dislikes: A review of 25 years of research on human evaluative conditioning. *Psychological Bulletin, 127*(6), 853–869.

DE JONG, P. F., & DAS-SMAAL, E. A. (1995). Attention and intelligence. *Journal of Educational Psychology, 87*, 80–92.

DELGADO, J. M. R. (1969). *Physical control of the mind*. New York: Harper & Row.

DELVES, P. J., & ROITT, I. M. (2000). Advances in immunology: The immune system. *The New England Journal of Medicine online, 343*(1).

DE MELLO, M. F., ET AL. (2005). A systematic review of research findings on the efficacy of interpersonal therapy for depressive disorders. *European Archives of Psychiatry & Clinical Neuroscience, 255*(2), 75–82.

DE MICHELE, P. E., GANSNEDER, B., & SOLOMON, G. B. (1998). Success and failure attributions of wrestlers: Further evidence of the self-serving bias. *Journal of Sport Behavior, 21*(3), 242–255.

DENNERSTEIN, L. L. (2003). The sexual impact of

menopause. In S. B. Levine, et al. (Eds.), *Handbook of clinical sexuality for mental health professionals* (pp. 187–198). New York: Brunner-Routledge.

DENNIS, H. (2000). Cited in Stewart, J. Y., & Armet, E. (2000, April 3). Aging in America: Retirees reinvent the concept. *Los Angeles Times online*.

Depression Research at the National Institute of Mental Health. (2000). NIH Publication No. 00–4501. http://www.nimh.nih.gov/publicat/depresfact.cfm.

DERUBEIS, R. J., & CRITS-CHRISTOPH, P. (1998). Empirically supported individual and group psychological treatments for adult mental disorders. *Journal of Consulting and Clinical Psychology, 66*, 37–52.

DERUBEIS, R. J., ET AL. (2005). Cognitive therapy vs. medications in the treatment of moderate to severe depression. *Archives of General Psychiatry, 62*(4), 409–416.

DESTENO, D., PETTY, R. E., RUCKER, D. D., WEGENER, D. T., & BRAVERMAN, J. (2004). Discrete emotions and persuasion: The role of emotion-induced expectancies. *Journal of Personality & Social Psychology, 86*(1), 43–56.

DEVILLY, G. J. (2002). Eye movement desensitization and reprocessing: A chronology of its development and scientific standing. *Scientific Review of Mental Health Practice, 1*(2), 113–138.

DEVRIES, R. (2000). Vygotsky, Piaget, and education: A reciprocal assimilation of theories and educational practices. *New Ideas in Psychology, 18*(2–3), 187–213.

DEWIT, D. J., ET AL. (2000). Age at first alcohol use: A risk factor for the development of alcohol disorders. *American Journal of Psychiatry, 157*, 745–750.

DE WIT, H., CREAN, J., & RICHARDS, J. B. (2000). Effects of d-amphetamine and ethanol on a measure of behavioral inhibition in humans. *Behavioral Neuroscience, 114*(4), 830–837.

DIAMOND, L. M. (2004). Emerging perspectives on distinctions between romantic love and sexual desire. *Current Directions in Psychological Science, 13*(3), 116–119.

DICKSON, N., PAUL, C., HERBISON, P., & SILVA, P. (1998). First sexual intercourse: age, coercion, and later regrets reported by a birth cohort. *British Medical Journal, 316*, 29–33.

DIENER, E., NAPA SCOLLON, C. K., OISHI, S., DZOKOTO, V., SUH, E. M. (2000). Positivity and the construction of life satisfaction judgments: Global happiness is not the sum of its parts. *Journal of Happiness Studies, 1*(2), 159–176.

DIERKER, L. C., ET AL. (2001). Association between psychiatric disorders and the progression of tobacco use behaviors. *Journal of the American Academy of Child & Adolescent Psychiatry, 40*(10), 1159–1167.

DIETRICH, A. (2004). Neurocognitive mechanisms underlying the experience of flow. *Consciousness & Cognition: An International Journal, 13*(4), 746–761.

DIFEDE, J. (2005). In Lake, M. (2005, May 2). Virtual reality heals 9/11 wounds. http://www.cnn.com/2005/TECH/04/29/spark.virtual/index.html.

DIFEDE, J., & HOFFMAN, H. G. (2002). Virtual reality exposure therapy for World Trade Center posttraumatic stress disorder: A case report. *CyberPsychology & Behavior, 5*(6), 529–535.

DILALLA, D. L., CAREY, G., GOTTESMAN, I. I., & BOUCHARD, T. J., JR. (1996). Heritability of MMPI personality indicators of psychopathology in twins reared apart. *Journal of Abnormal Psychology, 105*, 491–499.

DILALLA, D. L., GOTTESMAN, I. I., CAREY, G., &

BOUCHARD, T. J., JR. (1999). Heritability of MMPI Harris-Lingoes and Subtle-Obvious subscales in twins reared apart. *Assessment, 6*(4), 353–366.

DILALLA, L. F. (Ed.). (2004). *Behavior genetics principles: Perspectives in development, personality, and psychopathology.* Washington, DC: American Psychological Association.

DISETH, T. H. (2005). Dissociation in children and adolescents as reaction to trauma—An overview of conceptual issues and neurobiological factors. *Nordic Journal of Psychiatry, 59*(2), 79–91.

DOBBINS, I. G., SIMONS, J. S., & SCHACTER, D. L. (2004). fMRI evidence for separable and lateralized prefrontal memory monitoring processes. *Journal of Cognitive Neuroscience, 16*(6), 908–920.

DOBLIN, R. (2002). A clinical plan for MDMA (ecstasy) in the treatment of posttraumatic stress disorder (PTSD): Partnering with the FDA. *Journal of Psychoactive Drugs, 34*(2), 185–194.

DOCHERTY, N. M. (2005). Cognitive impairments and disordered speech in schizophrenia: Thought disorder, disorganization, and communication failure perspectives. *Journal of Abnormal Psychology, 114*(2), 269–278.

DODGE, K. A., LAIRD, R., LOCHMAN, J. E., ZELLI, A., & CONDUCT PROBLEMS PREVENTION RESEARCH GROUP U.S. (2002). Multidimensional latent-construct analysis of children's social information processing patterns: Correlations with aggressive behavior problems. *Psychological Assessment, 14*(1), 60–73.

DODSON, C. S., & SCHACTER, D. L. (2001). "If I had said it I would have remembered it": Reducing false memories with a distinctiveness heuristic. *Psychonomic Bulletin & Review, 8*(1), 155–161.

DOGIL, G., ET AL. (2002). The speaking brain: A tutorial introduction to fMRI experiments in the production of speech, prosody and syntax. *Journal of Neurolinguistics, 15*(1), 59–90.

DOHERTY, K., MILITELLO, F. S., KINNUNEN, T., & GARVEY, A. J. (1996). Nicotine gum dose and weight gain after smoking cessation. *Journal of Consulting and Clinical Psychology, 64*, 799–807.

DOLLARD, J., DOOB, L. W., MILLER, N. E., MOWRER, O. H., & SEARS, R. R. (1939). *Frustration and aggression.* New Haven, CT: Yale University Press.

DOMHOFF, G. W. (2001). A new neurocognitive theory of dreams. *Dreaming: Journal of the Association for the Study of Dreams, 11*(1), 13–33.

DOMHOFF, G. W. (2003). *The scientific study of dreams: Neural networks, cognitive development, and content analysis.* Washington, DC: American Psychological Association.

DONNERSTEIN, E. I., & WILSON, D. W. (1976). Effects of noise and perceived control on ongoing and subsequent aggressive behavior. *Journal of Personality and Social Psychology, 34*, 774–781.

DOVIDIO, J. F., ET AL. (2004). Perspective and prejudice: Antecedents and mediating mechanisms. *Personality & Social Psychology Bulletin, 30*(12), 1537–1549.

DRURY, L. J. (2003). Community care for people who are homeless and mentally ill. *Journal of Health Care for the Poor & Underserved, 14*(2), 194–207.

DUBBERT, P. M. (2002). Physical activity and exercise: Recent advances and current challenges. *Journal of Consulting and Clinical Psychology, 70*(3), 526–536.

DUCKITT, J., & FISHER, K. (2003). The impact of social threat on world view and ideological attitudes. *Political Psychology, 24*(1), 199–222.

DUCKITT, J., WAGNER, C., DU PLESSIS, I., & BIRUM, I. (2002). The psychological bases of ideology and prejudice: Testing a dual process model. *Journal of Personality & Social Psychology, 83*(1), 75–93.

DUENWALD, M. (2002, January 22). Body's defender goes on the attack. *The New York Times,* pp. F1, F9.

DUFFY, V. B., PETERSON, J. M., & BARTOSHUK, L. M. (2004). Associations between taste genetics, oral sensation and alcohol intake. *Physiology & Behavior, 82*(2–3), 435–445.

DUKA, T., TASKER, R., & MCGOWAN, J. F. (2000). The effects of 3-week estrogen hormone replacement on cognition in elderly healthy females. *Psychopharmacology, 149*(2), 129–139.

DULIN, P. L., & HILL, R. D. (2003). Relationships between altruistic activity and positive and negative affect among low-income older adult service providers. *Aging & Mental Health, 7*(4), 294–299.

DUNKLEY, D. M., ZUROFF, D. C., & BLANKSTEIN, K. R. (2003). Self-critical perfectionism and daily affect: Dispositional and situational influences on stress and coping. *Journal of Personality & Social Psychology, 84*(1), 234–252.

DURBIN, D. L., DARLING, N., STEINBERG, L., & BROWN, B. B. (1993). Parenting style and peer group membership among European American adolescents. *Journal of Research on Adolescence, 3*(1), 87–100.

DUVAL, T. S., & SILVIA, P. J. (2002). Self-awareness, probability of improvement, and the self-serving bias. *Journal of Personality & Social Psychology, 82*(1), 49–61.

DWECK, C. S. (2002a). Messages that motivate: How praise molds students' beliefs, motivation, and performance (in surprising ways). In J. Aronson, (Ed.), *Improving academic achievement: Impact of psychological factors on education* (pp. 37–60). San Diego: Academic Press.

DWECK, C. S. (2002b). The development of ability conceptions. In A. Wigfield & J. S. Eccles (Eds.), *Development of achievement motivation* (pp. 57–88). San Diego: Academic Press.

D'YDEWALLE, G., LUWEL, K., & BRUNFAUT, E. (1999). The importance of on-going concurrent activities as a function of age in time- and event-based prospective memory. *European Journal of Cognitive Psychology, 11*(2), 219–237.

EAGLE, M. (2000). Repression, part I of II. *Psychoanalytic Review, 87*(1), 1–38.

EAGLY, A. H. (2000). Cited in Goode, E. (2000, May 19). Response to stress found that's particularly female. *The New York Times,* p. A20.

EAGLY, A. H., ASHMORE, R. D., MAKHIJANI, M. G., & LONGO, L. C. (1991). What is beautiful is good, but . . . *Psychological Bulletin, 110*, 109–128.

EASTERLIN, R. A. (2001). Life cycle welfare: Trends and differences. *Journal of Happiness Studies, 2*(1), 1–12.

EASTERLIN, R. A. (2002). Is reported happiness five years ago comparable to present happiness? A cautionary note. *Journal of Happiness Studies, 3*(2), 193–198.

EATON, J. (2001). Management communication: The threat of groupthink. *Corporate Communications, 6*(4), 183–192.

EAVES, L., ET AL. (2000). Genetic and environmental causes of covariation in interview assessments of disruptive behavior in child and adolescent twins. *Behavior Genetics, 30*(4), 321–334.

EBERLY, M. B., & MONTEMAYOR, R. (1999). Adolescent affection and helpfulness toward parents: A 2-year follow-up. *Journal of Early Adolescence, 19*(2), 226–248.

EBBINGHAUS, H. (1913). *Memory: A contribution to experimental psychology.* (H. A. Roger & C. E. Bussenius, Trans.). New York: Columbia University Press. (Original work published 1885).

EDWARDS, S. (2005). Constructivism does not only happen in the individual: Sociocultural theory and early childhood education. *Early Child Development & Care, 175*(1), 37–47.

EGAWA, T., ET AL. (2002). Impairment of spatial memory in kaolin-induced hydrocephalic rats is associated with changes in the hippocampal cholinergic and noradrenergic contents. *Behavioural Brain Research, 129*(1–2), 31–39.

EHRLICH, P. R. (2000). Cited in Angier, N. (2000, October 10). A conversation with Dr. Paul R. Ehrlich—On human nature, genetics and the evolution of culture. *The New York Times online.*

EICH, E. (1995). Searching for mood dependent memory. *Psychological Science, 6*, 67–75.

EICHENBAUM, H., & FORTIN, N. (2003). Episodic memory and the hippocampus: It's about time. *Current Directions in Psychological Science, 12*(2), 53–57.

EKMAN, P. (1980). *The face of man.* New York: Garland.

EKMAN, P. (1993). Facial expression and emotion. *American Psychologist, 48*, 384–392.

EKMAN, P. (1999). Facial expressions. In T. Dalgleish & M. J. Power (Eds.), *Handbook of cognition and emotion* (pp. 301–320). New York: John Wiley & Sons.

EKMAN, P. (2003). Cited in Foreman, J. (2003, August 5). A conversation with: Paul Ekman: The 43 facial muscles that reveal even the most fleeting emotions. *The New York Times online.*

EKMAN, P., & ROSENBERG, E. (1997). *What the face reveals.* New York: Oxford University Press.

EKMAN, P., ET AL. (1987). Universals and cultural differences in the judgments of facial expressions of emotion. *Journal of Personality and Social Psychology, 53*, 712–717.

ELKIND, D. (1967). Egocentrism in adolescence. *Child Development, 38*, 1025–1034.

ELKIND, D. (1985). Egocentrism redux. *Developmental Review, 5*, 218–226.

ELKIND, D., & BOWEN, R. (1979). Imaginary audience behavior in children and adolescents. *Developmental Psychology, 15*(1), 38–44.

ELLICKSON, P. L., TUCKER, J. S., KLEIN, D. J., & MCGUIGAN, K. A. (2001). Prospective risk factors for alcohol misuse in late adolescence. *Journal of Studies on Alcohol, 62*(6), 773–782.

ELLIOTT, A. K., & MIRSKY, A. F. (2002). Cognitive antecedents of violence and aggression. In J. Glicksohn (Ed.), *The neurobiology of criminal behavior* (pp. 111–136). Dordrecht, Netherlands: Kluwer Academic Publishers.

ELLIS, A. (2000). Cited in Chamberlin, J. (2000). An historic meeting of the minds. *Monitor on Psychology, 31*(9), 27.

ELLIS, A. (2002). The role of irrational beliefs in perfectionism. In G. L. Flett & P. L. Hewitt (Eds.), *Perfectionism: Theory, research, and treatment.* Washington, DC: American Psychological Association.

ELLIS, A. (2004a). How my theory and practice of psychotherapy has influenced and changed other psychotherapies. *Journal of Rational-Emotive & Cognitive Behavior Therapy, 22*(2), 79–83.

ELLIS, A. (2004b). Why rational emotive behavior therapy is the most comprehensive and effective form of behavior therapy. *Journal of Rational-Emotive & Cognitive Behavior Therapy, 22*(2), 85–92.

ELLSWORTH, P. C., CARLSMITH, J. M., & HENSON, A. (1972). The stare as a stimulus to flight in human subjects. *Journal of Personality and Social Psychology, 21*, 302–311.

EMMONS, R. A., & KING, L. A. (1988). Conflict among personal strivings: Immediate and long-term implications for psychological and physical well-being. *Journal of Personality & Social Psychology, 54*(6), 1040–1048.

ENARD, W., ET AL. (2002). Molecular evolution of FOXP2, a gene involved in speech and language. *Nature, 418*(6900), 869–872.

ENGELS, G. I., GARNEFSKI, N., & DIEKSTRA, R. F. W. (1993). Efficacy of rational-emotive therapy. *Journal of Consulting and Clinical Psychology, 61,* 1083–1090.

ERANTI, S. V., & MCLOUGHLIN, D. M. (2003). Electroconvulsive therapy—State of the art. *British Journal of Psychiatry, 182,* 8–9.

ERIKSON, E. H. (1963). *Childhood and society.* New York: W. W. Norton.

ERIKSON, E. H. (1968). *Identity: Youth and crisis.* New York: W. W. Norton.

ERON, L. D. (1982). Parent–child interaction, television violence, and aggression of children. *American Psychologist, 37,* 197–211.

ERON, L. D. (2000). A psychological perspective. In V. B. Van Hasselt & M. Hersen, (Eds.), *Aggression and violence: An introductory text* (pp. 23–39). Needham Heights, MA: Allyn & Bacon.

ERSKINE, A., MARKHAM, R., & HOWIE, P. (2001). Children's script-based inferences: Implications for eyewitness testimony. *Cognitive Development, 16*(4), 871–887.

ESLINGER, P. J., FLAHERTY-CRAIG, C. V., & BENTON, A. L. (2004). Developmental outcomes after early prefrontal cortex damage. *Brain & Cognition, 55*(1), 84–403.

EVANS, L., ET AL. (2005). Familiality of temperament in bipolar disorder: Support for a genetic spectrum. *Journal of Affective Disorders, 85*(1–2), 153–168.

EVANS, S. W., ET AL. (2001). Dose-response effects of methylphenidate on ecologically valid measures of academic performance and classroom behavior in adolescents with ADHD. *Experimental & Clinical Psychopharmacology, 9*(2), 163–175.

EYSENCK, H. J., & EYSENCK, M. W. (1985). *Personality and individual differences.* New York: Plenum.

FALLER, H., BUELZEBRUCK, H., DRINGS, P., & LANG, H. (1999). Coping, distress, and survival among patients with lung cancer. *Archives of General Psychiatry, 56*(8), 756–762.

FANTZ, R. L. (1961). The origin of form perception. *Scientific American, 204*(5), 66–72.

FARAONE, S. V., SU, J., & TSUANG, M. T. (2004). A genome-wide scan of symptom dimensions in bipolar disorder pedigrees of adult probands. *Journal of Affective Disorders, 82*(Suppl. 1), S71–S78.

FARBER, B. A., BRINK, D. C., & RASKIN, P. M. (1996). *The psychotherapy of Carl Rogers: Cases and commentary* (pp. 74–75). New York: Guilford Press.

FARMER, A., ELEY, T. C., & MCGUFFIN, P. (2005). Current strategies for investigating the genetic and environmental risk factors for affective disorders. *British Journal of Psychiatry, 186*(3), 179–181.

FAROOQI, I. S., ET AL. (2003). Clinical spectrum of obesity and mutations in the melanocortin 4 receptor gene. *New England Journal of Medicine, 348*(12), 1085–1095.

FARR, S. A., FLOOD, J. F., & MORLEY, J. E. (2000a). The effect of cholinergic, GABAergic, serotonergic, and glutamatergic receptor modulation on posttrial memory processing in the hippocampus. *Neurobiology of Learning & Memory, 73*(2), 150–167.

FARR, S. A., UEZU, K. CREONTE, T. A., FLOOD, J. F., &

MORLEY, J. E. (2000b). Modulation of memory processing in the cingulate cortex of mice. *Pharmacology, Biochemistry & Behavior, 65*(3), 363–368.

FAVARO, A. (2005). The relationship between temperament and impulsive behaviors in eating disordered subjects. *Eating Disorders: The Journal of Treatment & Prevention, 13*(1), 61–70.

FEENEY, B. C. (2004). A secure base: Responsive support of goal strivings and exploration in adult intimate relationships. *Journal of Personality & Social Psychology, 87*(5), 631–648.

FEINGOLD, A. (1992a). Gender differences in mate selection preferences. *Psychological Bulletin, 112,* 125–139.

FEINGOLD, A. (1992b). Good-looking people are not what we think. *Psychological Bulletin, 111,* 304–341.

FEINGOLD, A. (1994). Gender differences in personality: A meta-analysis. *Psychological Bulletin, 116,* 429–456.

FEINGOLD, A. (1998). Gender stereotyping for sociability, dominance, character, and mental health: A meta-analysis of findings from the bogus stranger paradigm. *Genetic, Social & General Psychology Monographs, 124*(3), 253–270.

FELSON, R. B. (2002). *Violence and gender reexamined.* Washington, DC: American Psychological Association.

FEOLA, T. W., DE WIT, H., & RICHARDS, J. B. (2000). Effects of *d*-amphetamine and alcohol on a measure of behavioral inhibition in rats. *Behavioral Neuroscience, 114*(4), 838–848.

FESTINGER, L. (1957). *A theory of cognitive dissonance.* Evanston, IL: Row, Peterson.

FESTINGER, L., & CARLSMITH, J. M. (1959). Cognitive consequences of forced compliance. *Journal of Abnormal and Social Psychology, 58,* 203–210.

FIEDLER, K., SCHMID, J., & STAHL, T. (2002). What is the current truth about polygraph lie detection? *Basic & Applied Social Psychology, 24*(4), 313–324.

FIELD, T. M. (1991). Young children's adaptations to repeated separations from their mothers. *Child Development, 62,* 539–547.

FIELD, T. M. (1991). Quality infant day-care and grade school behavior and performance. *Child Development, 62,* 863–870.

FIELDS, R. D. (2005, February). Making memories stick. *Scientific American,* 75–81.

FIELLIN, D. A., ET AL. (2001). Methadone maintenance in primary care: A randomized controlled trial. *Journal of the American Medical Association, 286*(14), 1724–1731.

FIFER, W. P., & MOON, C. (2003). Prenatal development. In A. Slater & G. Bremner (Eds.), *An introduction to developmental psychology* (pp. 95–114). Malden, MA: Blackwell Publishers.

FILLEY, C. M., ET AL. (2001). Toward an understanding of violence: Neurobehavioral aspects of unwarranted physical aggression: Aspen Neurobehavioral Conference Consensus Statement. *Neuropsychiatry, Neuropsychology & Behavioral Neurology, 14*(1), 1–14.

FINKENAUER, C., ET AL. (1998). Flashbulb memories and the underlying mechanisms of their formation: Toward an emotional-integrative model. *Memory & Cognition, 26*(3), 516–531.

FIRST, M. B., ET AL. (2004). Clinical utility as a criterion for revising psychiatric diagnoses. *American Journal of Psychiatry, 161*(6), 946–954.

FISCHER, M., HAND, I., & ANGENENDT, J. (1998). Langzeiteffekte von Kurzzeit-Verhaltenstherapien bei Agoraphobie. *Zeitschrift für Klinische Psychologie. Forschung und Praxis, 17*(3), 225–243.

FISHER, H. E. (2000). Brains do it: Lust, attraction and attachment. *Cerebrum, 2,* 23–42.

FLAVELL, J. H. (2000). Development of children's knowledge about the mental world. *International Journal of Behavioral Development, 24*(1), 15–23.

FLAVELL, J. H., MILLER, P. H., & MILLER, S. A. (2002). *Cognitive development* (4th ed.). Upper Saddle River, NJ: Prentice Hall.

FLEGAL, K. M., CARROLL, M. D., OGDEN, C. L., & JOHNSON, C. L. (2002). Prevalence and trends in obesity among U.S. adults, 1999–2000. *Journal of the American Medical Association, 288*(14), 1723–1727.

FLETT, G. L., & HEWITT, P. L. (2002). *Perfectionism.* Washington, DC: American Psychological Association.

FLETT, G. L., MADORSKY, D., HEWITT, P. L., & HEISEL, M. J. (2002). Perfectionism cognitions, rumination, and psychological distress. *Journal of Rational-Emotive & Cognitive Behavior Therapy, 20*(1), 33–47.

FLORES, E., CICCHETTI, D., & ROGOSCH, F. A. (2005). Predictors of resilience in maltreated and non-maltreated Latino children. *Developmental Psychology, 41*(2), 338–351.

FLOURI, E., & BUCHANAN, A. (2003). The role of father involvement and mother involvement in adolescents' psychological well-being. *British Journal of Social Work, 33*(3), 399–406.

FOERSTER, J., HIGGINS, E. T., & STRACK, F. (2000). When stereotype disconfirmation is a personal threat: How prejudice and prevention focus moderate incongruency effects. *Social Cognition, 18*(2), 178–197.

FOLKMAN, S., & MOSKOWITZ, T. (2000a). Positive affect and the other side of coping. *American Psychologist, 55*(6), 647–654.

FOLKMAN, S., & MOSKOWITZ, J. T. (2000b). The context matters. *Personality & Social Psychology Bulletin, 26*(2), 150–151.

FOLLINGSTAD, D., & MCCORMICK, M. (2002). *Law and mental health professionals.* Washington, DC: American Psychological Association.

FOLTIN, R. W., WARD, A. S., HANEY, M., HART, C. L., & COLLINS, E. D. (2003). The effects of escalating doses of smoked cocaine in humans. *Drug & Alcohol Dependence, 70*(2), 149–157.

FONTAINE, K. R., REDDEN, D. T., WANG, C., WESTFALL, A. O., & ALLISON, D. B. (2003). Years of life lost due to obesity. *Journal of the American Medical Association, 289*(2), 187–193.

FÖRSTER, J., HIGGINS, E. T., & WERTH, L. (2004). How threat from stereotype disconfirmation triggers self-defense. *Social Cognition, 22*(1), 54–74.

FORTIN, S., GODBOUT, L., & BRAUN, C. M. J. (2002). Strategic sequence planning and prospective memory impairments in frontally lesioned head trauma patients performing activities of daily living. *Brain & Cognition, 48*(2–3), 361–365.

FOURNIER, A. K., EHRHART, I. J., GLINDEMANN, K. E., & GELLER, E. S. (2004). Intervening to decrease alcohol abuse at university parties: Differential reinforcement of intoxication level. *Behavior Modification, 28*(2), 167–181.

FOUTS, R. S. (1997). *Next of kin: What chimpanzees have taught me about who we are.* New York: Morrow.

FOX, E., RUSSO, R., BOWLES, R., & DUTTON, K. (2001). Do threatening stimuli draw or hold visual attention in subclinical anxiety? *Journal of Experimental Psychology: General, 130*(4), 681–700.

FRANCIS, L. J., KATZ, Y. J., YABLON, Y., & ROBBINS, M. (2004). Religiosity, personality, and happiness: A study among Israeli male undergraduates. *Journal of Happiness Studies, 5*(4), 315–333.

FRANK, E., & KUPFER, D. J. (2003). Progress in the therapy of mood disorders: Scientific support. *American Journal of Psychiatry, 160,* 1207–1208.

FRANKLIN, A. J., & BOYD-FRANKLIN, N. (2000). Invisibility syndrome: A clinical model of the effects of racism on African-American males. *American Journal of Orthopsychiatry, 70*(1), 33–41.

FREEMAN, H. P., & PAYNE, R. (2000). Racial injustice in health care. *The New England Journal of Medicine, 342,* 1045–1047.

FREEMAN, M. S., SPENCE, M. J., & OLIPHANT, C. M. (1993, June). *Newborns prefer their mothers' low-pass filtered voices over other female filtered voices.* Paper presented at the annual convention of the American Psychological Society, Chicago.

FREESE, T. E., MIOTTO, K., & REBACK, C. J. (2002). The effects and consequences of selected club drugs. *Journal of Substance Abuse Treatment, 23*(2), 151–156.

FREUD, S. (1927). A religious experience. In *Standard edition of the complete psychological works of Sigmund Freud* (Vol. 21). London: Hogarth Press, 1964.

FREUND, A. M., & BALTES, P. B. (2002). The adaptiveness of selection, optimization, and compensation as strategies of life management: Evidence from a preference study on proverbs. *Journals of Gerontology: Series B: Psychological Sciences & Social Sciences, 57B*(5), P426–P434.

FREUND, C. S. (1990). Maternal regulation of children's problem-solving behavior and its impact on children's performance. *Child Development, 61,* 113–126.

FREY, B. S., & STUTZER, A. (2000). Happiness prospers in democracy. *Journal of Happiness Studies, 1*(3), 79–102.

FRIAS-ARMENTA, M. (2002). Long-term effects of child punishment on Mexican women: A structural model. *Child Abuse & Neglect, 26*(4), 371–386.

FRIEDMAN, M., & ULMER, D. (1984). *Treating Type A behavior and your heart.* New York: Fawcett Crest.

FRISCH, R. (1997). Cited in Angier, N. (1997). Chemical tied to fat control could help trigger puberty. *The New York Times,* pp. C1, C3.

FRITSCH, G., & HITZIG, E. (1960). On the electrical excitability of the cerebrum. In G. von Bonin (Ed.), *Some papers on the cerebral cortex.* Springfield, IL: Charles C. Thomas. (Original work published 1870)

FRODI, A. M., MACAULEY, J., & THOME, P. R. (1977). Are women always less aggressive than men? A review of the experimental literature. *Psychological Bulletin, 84,* 634–660.

FROMME, K., ET AL. (2004). Biological and behavioral markers of alcohol sensitivity. *Alcoholism: Clinical & Experimental Research, 28*(2), 247–256.

FUERTES, A., ET AL. (2002). Factores asociados a las conductas sexuales de reigso en la adolencia. *Infancia y Aprendizaje, 25*(3), 347–361.

FUJI, K. (2002). Field experiments on operant conditioning of wild pigeons (Columbia livia). *Japanese Journal of Animal Psychology, 52*(1), 9–14.

FULIGNI, A. J., & WITKOW, M. (2004). The postsecondary educational progress of youth from immigrant families. *Journal of Research on Adolescence, 14*(2), 159–183.

FULLER, R. L., LUCK, S. J., McMAHON, R. P., & GOLD, J. M. (2005). Working memory consolidation is abnormally slow in schizophrenia. *Journal of Abnormal Psychology, 114*(2), 279–290.

FURNHAM, A., BADMIN, N., & SNEADE, I. (2002). Body image dissatisfaction: Gender differences in eating attitudes, self-esteem, and reasons for exercise. *Journal of Psychology, 136*(6), 581–596.

FURNHAM, A., & CHENG, H. (2000). Perceived parental behaviour, self-esteem and happiness. *Social Psychiatry & Psychiatric Epidemiology, 35*(10), 463–470.

FURNHAM, A., PETRIDES, K. V., SISTERSON, G., & BALUCH, B. (2003). Repressive coping style and positive self-presentation. *British Journal of Health Psychology, 8*(2), 223–249.

FUSTER, J. M. (2000). The prefrontal cortex of the primate: A synopsis. *Psychobiology, 28*(2), 125–131.

GAAB, J., ROHLEDER, N., NATER, U. M., & EHLERT, U. (2005). Psychological determinants of the cortisol stress response: The role of anticipatory cognitive appraisal. *Psychoneuroendocrinology, 30*(6), 599–610.

GAIS, S., & BORN, J. (2004). Declarative memory consolidation: Mechanisms acting during human sleep. *Learning & Memory, 11*(6), 679–685.

GALAMBOS, N. L., BARKER, E. T., & ALMEIDA, D. M. (2003). Parents do matter: Trajectories of change in externalizing and internalizing problems in early adolescence. *Child Development, 74*(2), 578–594.

GALLAGHER, A. M., ET AL. (2000). Gender differences in advanced mathematical problem solving. *Journal of Experimental Child Psychology, 75*(3), 165–190.

GARB, H. N., WOOD, J. M., LILIENFELD, S. O., & NEZWORSKI, M. T. (2005). Roots of the Rorschach controversy. *Clinical Psychology Review, 25*(1), 97–118.

GARCIA, J., BRETT, L. P., & RUSINIAK, K. W. (1989). Limits of Darwinian conditioning. In S. B. Klein & R. R. Mowrer (Eds.), *Contemporary learning theories: Instrumental conditioning theory and the impact of biological constraints on learning.* Hillsdale, NJ: Erlbaum.

GARCIA, J., & KOELLING, R. A. (1966). Relation of cue to consequences in avoidance learning. *Psychonomic Science 4,* 123–124.

GARCIA-PALACIOS, A., HOFFMAN, H., CARLIN, A., FURNESS, T. A., & BOTELLA, C. (2002). Virtual reality in the treatment of spider phobia: A controlled study. *Behaviour Research & Therapy, 40*(9), 983–993.

GARDNER, H. (1983/1993). *Frames of mind.* New York: Basic Books.

GARDNER, H. (2001, April 5). Multiple intelligence. *The New York Times,* p. A20.

GARNETS, L. D. (2002). Sexual orientations in perspective. *Cultural Diversity and Ethnic Minority Psychology, 8*(2), 115–129.

GATCHEL, R. J., & OORDT, M. S. (2003). Insomnia. In R. J. Gatchel & M. S. Oordt (Eds.), *Clinical health psychology and primary care: Practical advice and clinical guidance for successful collaboration* (pp. 135–148). Washington, DC: American Psychological Association.

GAY, M., PHILIPPOT, P., & LUMINET, O. (2002). Differential effectiveness of psychological interventions for reducing osteoarthritis pain: A comparison of Erickson hypnosis and Jacobson relaxation. *European Journal of Pain, 6*(1), 1–16.

GEERS, A., SPEHAR, B., & SEDEY, A. (2002). Use of speech by children from total communication programs who wear cochlear implants. *American Journal of Speech-Language Pathology, 11*(1), 50–58.

GEGENFURTNER, K. R., & KIPER, D. C. (2003). Color vision. *Annual Review of Neuroscience, 26,* 181–206.

GENDALL, K. A., BULIK, C. M., JOYCE, P. R., McINTOSH, V. V., & CARTER, F. A. (2000). Menstrual cycle irregularity in bulimia nervosa: Associated factors and changes with treatment. *Journal of Psychosomatic Research, 49*(6), 409–415.

GENTRY, M. V., ET AL. (2000). Nicotine patches improve mood and response speed in a lexical decision task. *Addictive Behaviors, 25*(4), 549–557.

GERNSBACHER, M. A., & KASCHAK, M. P. (2003). Neuroimaging studies of language production and comprehension. *Annual Review of Psychology, 54,* 91–114.

GERSHOFF, E. T. (2002). Corporal punishment by parents and associated child behaviors and experiences: A meta-analytic and theoretical review. *Psychological Bulletin, 128*(4), 539–579.

GERSHON, J., ZIMAND, E., PICKERING, M., ROTHBAUM, B. O., & HODGES, L. (2004). A pilot and feasibility study of virtual reality as a distraction for children with cancer. *Journal of the American Academy of Child & Adolescent Psychiatry, 43*(10), 1243–1249.

GESCHWIND, N., & GALABURDA, A. M. (1987). *Cerebral lateralization: Biological mechanisms, associations, and pathology.* Cambridge, MA: Harvard University Press.

GETZELS, J. W., & JACKSON, P. W. (1962). *Creativity and intelligence.* New York: Wiley.

GIBSON, K. R. (2002). Evolution of human intelligence: The roles of brain size and mental construction. *Brain, Behavior & Evolution, 59*(1–2), 10–20.

GIGNAC, G., & VERNON, P. A. (2003). Digit symbol rotation: A more g-loaded version of the traditional digit symbol subtest. *Intelligence, 31*(1), 1–8.

GIGONE, D., & HASTIE, R. (1997). Proper analysis of the accuracy of group judgments. *Psychological Bulletin, 121,* 149–167.

GIJSMAN, H. J., ET AL. (2002). A dose-finding study on the effects of branch chain amino acids on surrogate markers of brain dopamine function. *Psychopharmacology, 160*(2), 192–197.

GILI-PLANAS, M., ROCA-BENNASAR, M., FERRER-PEREZ, V., & BERNARDO-ARROYO, M. (2001). Suicidal ideation, psychiatric disorder, and medical illness in a community epidemiological study. *Suicide & Life-Threatening Behavior, 31*(2), 207–213.

GILL, T. M., DiPIETRO, L., & KRUMHOLZ, H. M. (2000). Role of exercise stress testing and safety monitoring for older persons starting an exercise person. *Journal of the American Medical Association, 284,* 342–349.

GILLIGAN, C. (1982). *In a different voice.* Cambridge, MA: Harvard University Press.

GILLIGAN, C., LYONS, P., & HANMER, T. J. (Eds.). (1990). *Making connections.* Cambridge, MA: Harvard University Press.

GILLIGAN, C., ROGERS, A. G., & TOLMAN, D. L. (Eds.). (1991). *Women, girls, and psychotherapy.* New York: Haworth.

GILLIGAN, C., WARD, J. V., & TAYLOR, J. M. (1989). *Mapping the moral domain: A contribution of women's thinking to psychological theory and education.* Cambridge, MA: Harvard University Press.

GILOVICH, T., & EIBACH, R. (2001). The fundamental attribution error where it really counts. *Psychological Inquiry, 12*(1), 23–26.

GILOVICH, T., ET AL. (Eds.). (2002). *Heuristics and biases: The psychology of intuitive judgment* (pp. 348–366). New York: Cambridge University Press.

GLANTZ, L. A., & LEWIS, D. A. (2000). Decreased dendritic spine density on prefrontal cortical pyramidal neurons in schizophrenia. *Archives of General Psychiatry, 57*(1), 65–73.

GLASER, R., ET AL. (1993). Stress and the memory T-cell response to the Epstein-Barr virus. *Health Psychology, 12,* 435–442.

GOADSBY, P. J., LIPTON, R. B., & FERRARI, M. D. (2002). Drug therapy: Migraine—Current understanding and treatment. *New England Journal of Medicine, 346,* 257–270.

GODDEN, D. R., & BADDELEY, A. D. (1975). Context-dependent memory in two natural environments: On land and underwater. *British Journal of Psychology, 66,* 325–331.

GODFREY, J. R. (2004). Toward optimal health: The experts discuss therapeutic humor. *Journal of Women's Health, 13*(5), 474–479.

GOLDEN, N. H. (2002). A review of the female athlete triad (amenorrhea, osteoporosis and disordered eating). *International Journal of Adolescent Medicine & Health, 14*(1), 9–17.

GOLDMAN-RAKIC, P. S. (1995). Cited in Goleman, D. (1995, May 2). Biologists find site of working memory. *The New York Times,* pp. C1, C9.

GOLDMAN-RAKIC, P. S., CASTNER, S. A., SVENSSON, T. H., SIEVER, L. J., & WILLIAMS, G. V. (2004). Targeting the dopamine D-sub-1 receptor in schizophrenia: insights for cognitive dysfunction. *Psychopharmacology, 174*(1), 3–16.

GOLDMAN-RAKIC, P. S., MULY, E. C., III, & WILLIAMS, G. V. (2000a). D-sub-1 receptors in prefrontal cells and circuits. *Brain Research Reviews, 31*(2–3), 295–301.

GOLDMAN-RAKIC, P. S., ET AL. (2000b). Memory. In M. S. Gazzaniga (Ed.), *The new cognitive neurosciences* (2nd ed., pp. 733–840). Cambridge, MA: MIT Press.

GOLDSMITH, H. (1993). Cited in Adler, T. (1993). Shy, bold temperament? It's mostly in the genes. *APA Monitor, 24*(1), 7, 8.

GOLDSMITH, H., ET AL. (2003). Research psychologists' roles in the genetic revolution. *American Psychologist, 58*(4), 318–319.

GOLDSTEIN, E. B. (2004). *Sensation and perception, media edition.* (6th ed.). Belmont, CA: Wadsworth Publishing Company.

GOLEMAN, D. J. (1995). *Emotional intelligence.* New York: Bantam Books.

GOMEZ, P., ZIMMERMANN, P., GUTTORMSEN-SCHÄR, S., & DANUSER, B. (2005). Respiratory responses associated with affective processing of film stimuli. *Biological Psychology, 68*(3), 223–235.

GONZALEZ, C., DANA, J., KOSHINO, H., & JUST, M. (2005). The framing effect and risky decisions: Examining cognitive functions with fMRI. *Journal of Economic Psychology, 26*(1), 1–20.

GOODALL, J. (2000). *My life with the chimpanzees.* New York: Pocket Books.

GOODE, E. (2000, June 25). Thinner: The male battle with anorexia. *The New York Times,* p. MH8.

GOODE, E. (2002, June 12). Anorexia strategy: Family as doctor. *The New York Times,* pp. F1, F7.

GOODENOUGH, F. L., & HARRIS, D. B. (1950). Studies in the psychology of children's drawings: II 1928–1949. *Psychological Bulletin, 47,* 369–433.

GOODWIN, P. J., ET AL. (2001). The effect of group psychosocial support on survival in metastatic breast cancer. *New England Journal of Medicine, 345*(24), 1719–1726.

GORDON, B. N., BAKER-WARD, L., & ORNSTEIN, P. A. (2001). Children's testimony: A review of research on memory for past experiences. *Clinical Child & Family Psychology Review, 4*(2), 157–181.

GORMAN, J. M. (2001). A call to action: Overcoming anxiety through active coping. *American Journal of Psychiatry, 158*(12), 1953–1955.

GORODETSKY, M., & KLAVIR, R. (2003). What can we learn from how gifted/average pupils describe their processes of problem solving? *Learning & Instruction, 13*(3), 305–325.

GOTTESMAN, I. I. (1991). *Schizophrenia genesis.* New York: Freeman.

GOULD, S. J. (2002). *The structure of evolutionary theory.* Cambridge, MA: Belknap Press/Harvard University Press.

GRADY, C. L., MCINTOSH, A. R., RAJAH, M. N., BEIG, S., & CRAIK, F. I. M. (1999). The effects of age on the neural correlates of episodic encoding. *Cerebral Cortex, 9*(8), 805–814.

GRAHAM, C., & PETTINATO, S. (2001). Happiness, markets, and democracy: Latin America in comparative perspective. *Journal of Happiness Studies, 2*(3), 237–268.

GRANOT, D., & MAYSELESS, O. (2001). Attachment security and adjustment to school in middle childhood. *International Journal of Behavioral Development, 25*(6), 530–541.

GRANT, H. M., ET AL. (1998). Context-dependent memory for meaningful material: Information for students. *Applied Cognitive Psychology, 12*(6), 617–623.

GREEN J. P., & LYNN, S. J. (2000). Hypnosis and suggestion-based approaches to smoking cessation: An examination of the evidence. *International Journal of Clinical & Experimental Hypnosis, 48*(2), 195–224.

GREENBERGER, E., CHEN, C., TALLY, S. R., & DONG, Q. (2000). Family, peer, and individual correlates of depressive symptomology among U.S. and Chinese adolescents. *Journal of Consulting and Clinical Psychology, 68,* 209–219.

GREENLEES, I., ET AL. (2005). Impact of opponents' clothing and body language on impression formation and outcome expectations. *Journal of Sport & Exercise Psychology, 27*(1), 39–52.

GREGORY, N. (2004). Crime and the family: Like grandfather, like father, like son? *British Journal of Forensic Practice, 6*(4), 32–36.

GRIFFIN, K. W., BOTVIN, G. J., NICHOLS, T. R., & SCHEIER, L. M. (2004). Low perceived chances for success in life and binge drinking among inner-city minority youth. *Journal of Adolescent Health, 34*(6), 501–507.

GRÖN, G., WUNDERLICH, A. P., SPITZER, M., TOMCZAK, R., & RIEPE, M. W. (2000). Brain activation during human navigation: gender-different neural networks as substrate of performance. *Nature Neuroscience, 3*(4), 404–408.

GRUSEC, J. E. (2002). Parenting socialization and children's acquisition of values. In M. H. Bornstein (Ed.), *Handbook of parenting: Vol. 5: Practical issues in parenting* (2nd ed., pp. 143–167). Mahwah, NJ: Lawrence Erlbaum Associates, Publishers.

GUERIN, B. (1999). Social behaviors as determined by different arrangements of social consequences: Social loafing, social facilitation, deindividuation, and a modified social loafing. *Psychological Record, 49*(4), 565–578.

GULCUR, L., STEFANCIC, A., SHINN, M., TSEMBERIS, S., & FISCHER, S. N. (2003). Housing, hospitalization and cost outcomes for homeless individuals with psychiatric disabilities participating in continuum of care and housing first programmes. *Journal of Community & Applied Social Psychology, 13*(2), 171–186.

GUMP, B. B., & MATTHEWS, K. A. (2000). Are vacations good for your health? The 9-year mortality experience after the Multiple Risk Factor Intervention Trial. *Psychosomatic Medicine, 62*(5), 608–612.

GUNTER, C., & DHAND, R. (2002). Human biology by proxy. Introductory article to an entire issue on the mouse genome. *Nature, 420,* 509.

GUPTA, V. B., NWOSA, N. M., NADEL, T. A., & INAMDAR, S. (2001). Externalizing behaviors and television viewing in children of low-income minority parents. *Clinical Pediatrics, 40*(6), 337–341.

GURRERA, R. J., NESTOR, P. G., & O'DONNELL, B. F. (2000). Personality traits in schizophrenia: Comparison with a community sample. *Journal of Nervous & Mental Disease, 188*(1), 31–35.

HAAGA, D. A. F., & DAVISON, G. C. (1993). An appraisal of rational-emotive therapy. *Journal of Consulting and Clinical Psychology, 61,* 215–220.

HABIB, M., & ROBICHON, F. (2003). Structural correlates of brain asymmetry: Studies in left-handed and dyslexic individuals. In K. Hugdahl & R. J. Davidson (Eds.), *The asymmetrical brain* (pp. 681–716). Cambridge, MA: MIT Press.

HADEN, C. A., ORNSTEIN, P. A., ECKERMAN, C. O., & DIDOW, S. M. (2001). Mother-child conversational interactions as events unfold: Linkages to subsequent remembering. *Child Development, 72*(4), 1016–1031.

HAENEN, J. (2001). Outlining the teaching–learning process: Piotr Gal'perin's contribution. *Learning & Instruction, 11*(2), 157–170.

HAKIM, A. A., ET AL. (1998). Effects of walking on mortality among nonsmoking retired men. *New England Journal of Medicine, 338,* 94–99.

HALFDAHL, A. R., & GRAY-LITTLE, B. (2002). Explicating methods in reviews of race and self-esteem. *Psychological Bulletin, 128*(3), 409–416.

HALPERN, D. F. (1989). *Thought and knowledge.* (2nd ed.). Hillsdale, NJ: Erlbaum.

HALPERN, D. F. (1997). Sex differences in intelligence: Implications for education. *American Psychologist, 52,* 1091–1102.

HALPERN, D. F. (2003). Sex differences in cognitive abilities. *Applied Cognitive Psychology, 17*(3), 375–376.

HALPERN, D. F., HANSEN, C., & RIEFER, D. (1990). Analogies as an aid to understanding and memory. *Journal of Educational Psychology, 82,* 298–305.

HALPERN, D. F., & LAMAY, M. L. (2000). The smarter sex: A critical review of sex differences in intelligence. *Educational Psychology Review, 12*(2), 229–246.

HAMILTON, M. (2001). Who believes in astrology? Effect of favorableness of astrologically derived personality descriptions on acceptance of astrology. *Personality & Individual Differences, 31*(6), 895–902.

HAMILTON, N. A., KAROLY, P., & KITZMAN, H. (2004). Self-regulation and chronic pain: The role of emotion. *Cognitive Therapy & Research, 28*(5), 559–576.

HAN, W., LEVENTHAL, T., & LINVER, M. R. (2004). The Home Observation for Measurement of the Environment (HOME) in middle childhood: A study of three large-scale data sets. *Parenting: Science & Practice, 4*(2–3), 189–210.

HANKIN, B. L., & ABRAMSON, L. Y. (2001). Development of gender differences in depression: An elaborated cognitive vulnerability-transactional stress theory. *Psychological Bulletin, 127*(6), 773–796.

HANKIN, B. L., FRALEY, R. C., & ABELA, J. R. Z. (2005). Daily depression and cognitions about stress: Evidence for a traitlike depressogenic cognitive style and the prediction of depressive symptoms in a prospective daily diary study. *Journal of Personality and Social Psychology, 88*(4), 673–685.

HANSELL, N. K., ET AL. (2001). Genetic influence on ERP slow wave measures of working memory. *Behavior Genetics, 31*(6), 603–614.

HARIDAKIS, P. M. (2002). Viewer characteristics, exposure to television violence, and aggression. *Media Psychology, 4*(4), 323–352.

HARKER, L., & KELTNER, D. (2001). Expressions of positive emotion in women's college yearbook pictures and their relationship to personality and life outcomes across adulthood. *Journal of Personality and Social Psychology, 80*(1), 112–124.

HARKNESS, K. L., & LUTHER, J. (2001). Clinical risk factors for the generation of life events in major depression. *Journal of Abnormal Psychology, 110*(4), 564–572.

HARLEY, K., & REESE, E. (1999). Origins of autobiographical memory. *Developmental Psychology, 35*(5), 1338–1348.

HARLOW, H. F. (1959). Love in infant monkeys. *Scientific American, 200,* 68–86.

HARLOW, H. F., & ZIMMERMANN, R. R. (1959). Affectional responses in the infant monkey. *Science, 130,* 421–432.

HARLOW, J. M. (1868). Recovery from the passage of an iron bar through the head. *Publication of the Massachusetts Medical Society, 2,* 327.

HARRIS, S. R., KEMMERLING, R. L., & NORTH, M. M. (2002). Brief virtual reality therapy for public speaking anxiety. *CyberPsychology & Behavior, 5*(6), 543–550.

HART, A. J., ET AL. (2000). Differential response in the human amygdala to racial outgroup vs. ingroup face stimuli. *NeuroReport, 11*(11), 2351–2355.

HART, J. W., BRIDGETT, D. J., & KARAU, S. J. (2001). Coworker ability and effort as determinants of individual effort on a collective task. *Group Dynamics, 5*(3), 181–190.

HARTON, H. C., & BOEDEKER, E. C., JR. (2005). On the many advantages of cybersex. *PsycCRITIQUES, 50*(4).

HASSINGER, H. J., SEMENCHUK, E. M., & O'BRIEN, W. H. (1999). Appraisal and coping responses to pain and stress in migraine headache sufferers. *Journal of Behavioral Medicine, 22*(4), 327–340.

HAWKLEY, L. C., & CACIOPPO, J. T. (2004). Stress and the aging immune system. *Brain, Behavior & Immunity, 18*(2), 114–119.

Health, United States (2002). http:/www.cdc.gov/nchs (National Center for Health Statistics).

HEIMPEL, S. A., WOOD, J. V., MARSHALL, M. A., & BROWN, J. D. (2002). Do people with low self-esteem really want to feel better? Self-esteem differences in motivation to repair negative moods. *Journal of Personality & Social Psychology, 82*(1), 128–147.

HEINRICHS, R. W. (2005). The primacy of cognition in schizophrenia. *American Psychologist, 60*(3), 229–242.

HEINZ, A. (2004). Reward and dependence—A psychological and neurobiological analysis of reward mechanisms and of their role in dependence (European University Studies, Vol. 685). *Addiction, 99*(11), 1482.

HEINZ, A., ET AL. (2003). Effects of acute psychological stress on adhesion molecules interleukins and sex hormones: Implications for coronary heart disease. *Psychopharmacology, 165*(2), 111–117.

HELMS, J. E. (1992). Why is there no study of cultural equivalence in standardized cognitive abil-

ity testing? *American Psychologist, 47,* 1083–1101.

HENDIN, H., MALTSBERGER, J. T., LIPSCHITZ, A., POLLINGER, H., & KYLE, J. (2001). Recognizing and responding to a suicide crisis. *Suicide & Life-Threatening Behavior, 31*(2), 115–128.

HENDRICK, S., & HENDRICK, C. (2002). Love. In C. R. Snyder & S. J. Lopez (Eds.), *Handbook of positive psychology* (pp. 472–484). London: Oxford University Press.

HENG, M. A. (2000). Scrutinizing common sense: The role of practical intelligence in intellectual giftedness. *Gifted Child Quarterly, 44*(3), 171–182.

HENKER, B., WHELEN, C. K., JAMMER, L. D., & DELFINO, R. J. (2002). Anxiety, affect, and activity in teenagers: Monitoring daily life with electronic diaries. *Journal of the American Academy of Child and Adolescent Psychiatry, 41*(6), 660–670.

HENRY, D., ET AL. (2000). Normative influences on aggression in urban elementary school classrooms. *American Journal of Community Psychology, 28*(1), 59–81.

HENSLEY, W. E. (1981). The effects of attire, location, and sex on aiding behavior. *Journal of Nonverbal Behavior, 6,* 3–11.

HENSLEY, W. E. (1994). Height as a basis for interpersonal attraction. *Adolescence, 29*(114), 469–474.

HERBERT, B. (2005, September 26). A waking nightmare. *The New York Times online.*

HERGENHAHN, B. R. (2005). *History of psychology* (5th ed.). Belmont, CA: Wadsworth Publishing Company.

HERRMANN, D. J. (1991). *Super memory.* Emmaus, PA: Rodale.

HERTZ-PANNIER, L., ET AL. (2002). Late plasticity for language in a child's non-dominant hemisphere: A pre- and post-surgery fMRI study. *Brain, 125*(2), 361–372.

HEWSTONE, M., & HAMBERGER, J. (2000). Perceived variability and stereotype change. *Journal of Experimental Social Psychology, 36*(2), 103–124.

HICKMAN, G. P., BARTHOLOMAE, S., & MCKENRY, P. C. (2000). Influence of parenting style on the adjustment and academic achievement of traditional college freshmen. *Journal of College Student Development, 41*(1), 41–54.

HICKS, A. R., OGDEN, B. A., & VARNER, K. J. (2003). Cardiovascular responses elicited during binge administration of cocaine. *Physiology & Behavior, 80*(1), 115–122.

HILDEBRANDT, T., LANGENBUCHER, J., & SCHLUND, D. G. (2004). Muscularity concerns among men: Development of attitudinal and perceptual measures. *Body Image, 1*(2), 169–181.

HILL, W. L., BALLARD, S., COYER, M. J., & ROWLEY, T. (2005). The interaction of testosterone and breeding phase on the reproductive behavior and use of space of male zebra finches. *Hormones & Behavior, 47*(4), 452–458.

HILSENROTH, M. J., BAITY, M. R., MOONEY, M. A., & MEYER, G. J. (2004). DSM-IV major depressive episode criteria: An evaluation of reliability and validity across three different rating methods. *International Journal of Psychiatry in Clinical Practice, 8*(1), 3–10.

HINES, D. A., & SAUDINO, K. J. (2003). Gender differences in psychological, physical, and sexual aggression among college students using the Revised Conflict Tactics Scales. *Violence & Victims, 18*(2), 197–217.

HINGSON, R., ET AL. (2002). A call to action: Changing the culture of drinking at U.S. colleges. Na-

tional Institutes of Health: National Institute of Alcohol Abuse and Alcoholism. Washington, DC.

HIXON, M. D. (1998). Ape language research: A review and behavioral perspective. *Analysis of Verbal Behavior, 15,* 17–39.

HJERL, K., ET AL. (2003). Depression as a prognostic for breast cancer mortality. *Psychosomatics: Journal of Consultation Liaison Psychiatry, 44*(1), 24–30.

HOBSON, J. A. (2003). *Dreaming: An introduction to the science of sleep.* New York: Oxford University Press.

HOFF, E. (2005). *Language development* (3rd ed.). Belmont, CA: Wadsworth Publishing Company.

HOFFMAN, H. G. (2004). Virtual-reality therapy. *Scientific American, 291*(2), 58–65, 58–65.

HOFFMAN, P. (2003, February 8). Who's best at chess? For now, it's neither man nor machine. *The New York Times online.*

HOGE, C. W., ET AL. (2004). Combat duty in Iraq and Afghanistan, mental health problems, and barriers to care. *New England Journal of Medicine, 351*(1), 13–22.

HOHWY, J., & FRITH, C. (2004). Can neuroscience explain consciousness? *Journal of Consciousness Studies, 11*(7–8), 180–198.

HOLDEN, E. W., DEICHMANN, M. M., & LEVY, J. D. (1999). Empirically supported treatments in pediatric psychology: Recurrent pediatric headache. *Journal of Pediatric Psychology, 24*(2), 91–109.

HOLLAND, J. L. (1996). Exploring careers with a typology. *American Psychologist, 51,* 397–406.

HOLLINGER, L. M., & BUSCHMANN, M. B. (1993). Factors influencing the perception of touch by elderly nursing home residents and their health caregivers. *International Journal of Nursing Studies, 30,* 445–461.

HOLLINGSHEAD, A. B., & REDLICH, F. C. (1958). *Social class and mental illness.* New York: Wiley.

HOLLMANN, F. W., & MULDER, T. J. (2000, January 13). Census Bureau projects doubling of nation's population by 2100. U.S. Census Bureau: Public Information Office.

HOLLON, S. D., ET AL. (2005). Prevention of relapse following cognitive therapy vs. medications in moderate to severe depression. *Archives of General Psychiatry, 62*(4), 417–422.

HOLMES, M. M., PUTZ, O., CREWS, D., & WADE, J. (2005). Normally occurring intersexuality and testosterone induced plasticity in the copulatory system of adult leopard geckos. *Hormones & Behavior, 47*(4), 439–445.

HOLMES, T. H., & RAHE, R. H. (1967). The social readjustment rating scale. *Journal of Psychosomatic Research, 11,* 213–218.

HOLROYD, K. A. (2002). Assessment and psychological management of recurrent headache disorders. *Journal of Consulting & Clinical Psychology, 70*(3), 656–677.

HONG, Y., MORRIS, M. W., CHIU, C., & BENET-MARTINEZ, V. (2000). A dynamic constructivist approach to culture and cognition. *American Psychologist, 55*(7), 709–720.

HONORTON, C. (1985). Meta-analysis of psi Ganzfeld research. *Journal of Parapsychology, 49,* 51–91.

HONORTON, C., ET AL. (1990). Psi communication in the Ganzfeld. *Journal of Parapsychology, 54,* 99–139.

HONTS, C. R., HODES, R. L., & RASKIN, D. C. (1985). Effects of physical countermeasures on the physiological detection of deception. *Journal of Applied Psychology, 70*(1), 177–187.

HOOVER, R. N. (2000). Cancer: Nature, nurture, or

both. *New England Journal of Medicine, 343,* 135–136.

HORGAN, O., & MACLACHLAN, M. (2004). Psychosocial adjustment to lower-limb amputation: A review. *Disability & Rehabilitation: An International Multidisciplinary Journal, 26*(14–15), 837–850.

HORN, J. M. (1983). The Texas adoption project. *Child Development, 54,* 268–275.

HORNEY, K. (1967). *Feminine psychology.* New York: W. W. Norton.

HORNSTEIN, E. P., VERWEIJ, J., & SCHNAPF, J. L. (2004). Electrical coupling between red and green cones in primate retina. *Nature Neuroscience, 7*(7), 745–750.

HOROWITZ, T. S., CADE, B. E., WOLFE, J. M., & CZEISLER, C. A. (2003). Searching night and day: A dissociation of effects of circadian phase and time awake on visual selective attention and vigilance. *Psychological Science, 14*(6), 549–557.

HOVEY, J. D. (2000). Acculturative stress, depression, and suicidal ideation in Mexican immigrants. *Cultural Diversity and Ethnic Minority Psychology, 6*(2), 134–151.

HOYBYE, M. T., JOHANSEN, C., & TJORNHOJ-THOMSEN, T. (2005). Online interaction. Effects of storytelling in an Internet breast cancer support group. *Psycho-Oncology, 14*(3), 211–220.

HUBEL, D. H., & WIESEL, T. N. (1979). Brain mechanisms of vision. *Scientific American, 241,* 150–162.

HUBER, D., & HENRICH, G. (2003). Personality traits and stress sensitivity in migraine patients. *Behavioral Medicine, 29*(1), 4–13.

HUESMANN, L. R., MOISE-TITUS, J., PODOLSKI, C., & ERON, L. D. (2003). Longitudinal relations between children's exposure to TV violence and their aggressive and violent behavior in young adulthood: 1977–1992. *Developmental Psychology, 39*(2), 201–221.

HULSHOFF, P., ET AL. (2000). Prenatal exposure to famine and brain morphology in schizophrenia. *American Journal of Psychiatry, 157*(7), 1170–1172.

HUMAN GENOME SEQUENCING CONSORTIUM. (2004, October 29). Cited in "Number of genes in human genome lower than previously estimated." News Office, Massachusetts Institute of Technology. http://web.mit.edu/newsoffice/2004/humangenome.html.

HUNTJENS, R. J. C., ET AL. (2003). Interidentity amnesia for neutral, episodic information in dissociative identity disorder. *Journal of Abnormal Psychology, 112*(2), 290–297.

HUSKINSON, T. L. H., & HADDOCK, G. (2004). Individual differences in attitude structure: Variance in the chronic reliance on affective and cognitive information. *Journal of Experimental Social Psychology, 40*(1), 82–90.

HVAS, L., REVENTLOW, S., & MALTERUD, K. (2004). Women's needs and wants when seeing the GP in relation to menopausal issues. *Scandinavian Journal of Primary Health Care, 22*(2), 118–121.

HWU, H., LIU, C., FANN, C. S., OU-YANG, W., & LEE, S. F. (2003). Linkage of schizophrenia with chromosome 1q loci in Taiwanese families. *Molecular Psychiatry, 8*(4), 445–452.

HYDE, J. S., & PLANT, E. A. (1995). Magnitude of psychological gender differences. *American Psychologist, 50,* 159–161.

IACONO, W. G., & LYKKEN, D. T. (1997). The validity of the lie detector: Two surveys of scientific opinion. *Journal of Applied Psychology, 82*(3), 426–433.

IIDAKA, T., ANDERSON, N. D., KAPUR, S., CABEZA, R., & CRAIK, F. I. M. (2000). The effect of divided attention on encoding and retrieval in episodic memory revealed by positron emission tomography. *Journal of Cognitive Neuroscience, 12*(2), 267–280.

INHELDER, B., & PIAGET, J. (1958). *The growth of logical thinking from childhood to adolescence.* Chicago: University of Chicago Press.

INSEL, T. R. (2000). Toward a neurobiology of attachment. *Review of General Psychology, 4*(2), 176–185.

IRIBARREN, C., ET AL. (2000). Association of hostility with coronary artery calcification in young adults: The CARDIA study. *Journal of the American Medical Association, 283,* 2546–2551.

ISABELLA, R. A. (1998). Origins of attachment: The role of context, duration, frequency of observation, and infant age in measuring maternal behavior. *Journal of Social & Personal Relationships, 15*(4), 538–554.

ISARIDA, T., & ISARIDA, T. (1999). Effects of contextual changes between class and intermission on episodic memory. *Japanese Journal of Psychology, 69*(6), 478–485.

IVERSON, P., ET AL. (2003). A perceptual interference account of acquisition difficulties for non-native phonemes. *Cognition, 87*(1), B47–B57.

IVEY, A. E., & BROOKS-HARRIS, J. E. (2005). Integrative psychotherapy with culturally diverse clients. In J. C. Norcross & M. R. Goldfried (Eds.), *Handbook of psychotherapy integration* (2nd ed., pp. 321–339). London: Oxford University Press.

IZARD, C. E. (1984). Emotion-cognition relationships and human development. In C. E. Izard, J. Kagan, & R. B. Zajonc (Eds.), *Emotions, cognition, and behavior.* New York: Cambridge University Press.

IZARD, C. E. (1990). Facial expression and the regulation of emotions. *Journal of Personality and Social Psychology, 58,* 487–498.

IZARD, C. E. (1994). Basic emotions, relations among emotions, and emotion-cognition relations. *Psychological Bulletin, 115,* 561–565.

JABLENSKY, A. V., & KALAYDJIEVA, L. V. (2003). Genetic epidemiology of schizophrenia: Phenotypes, risk factors, and reproductive behavior. *American Journal of Psychiatry, 160,* 425–429.

JACKS, J. Z., & DEVINE, P. G. (2000). Attitude importance, forewarning of message content, and resistance to persuasion. *Basic & Applied Social Psychology, 22*(1), 19–29.

JACKSON, H., & NUTTALL, R. L. (2001). Risk for preadolescent suicidal behavior: An ecological model. *Child & Adolescent Social Work Journal, 18*(3), 189–203.

JACOANGELI, F., ET AL. (2002). Osteoporosis and anorexia nervosa: Relative role of endocrine alterations and malnutrition. *Eating & Weight Disorders, 7*(3), 190–195.

JACOB, S., MCCLINTOCK, M. K., ZELANO, B., & OBER, C. (2002, January 22). Paternally inherited HLA alleles are associated with women's choice of male odor. *Nature Genetics online.*

JACOB, S., ET AL. (2002). Body odour preferences in men and women: Do they aim for specific MHC combinations or simply heterozygosity? *Nature Genetics, 30,* 175–179.

JACOBI, C., DAHME, B., & DITTMANN, R. (2002). Cognitive–behavioural, fluoxetine and combined treatment for bulimia nervosa: Short- and long-term results. *European Eating Disorders Review, 10*(3), 179–198.

JAFFEE, S., & HYDE, J. S. (2000). Gender differences in moral orientation. *Psychological Bulletin, 126*(5), 703–726.

JAMES, L. E., & BURKE, D. M. (2000). Phonological priming effects on word retrieval and tip-of-the-tongue experiences in young and older adults. *Journal of Experimental Psychology—Learning, Memory, and Cognition, 26*(6), 1378–1391.

JAMES, W. (1890). *The principles of psychology.* New York: Henry Holt.

JAMES, W. (1904). Does "consciousness" exist? *Journal of Philosophy, Psychology, and Scientific Methods, 1,* 477–491.

JAMISON, K. R. (1997). Manic-depressive illness and creativity. *Scientific American Mysteries of the Mind, 7*(1), 44–49.

JAMISON, K. R. (2000). Suicide and bipolar disorder. *Journal of Clinical Psychiatry, 61*(Suppl. 9), 47–51.

JANIS, I. L. (1982). *Groupthink* (2nd ed.). Boston: Houghton Mifflin.

JANKE, E. A., HOLROYD, K. A., & ROMANEK, K. (2004). Depression increases onset of tension-type headache following laboratory stress. *Pain, 111*(3), 230–238.

JANOWITZ, H. D., & GROSSMAN, M. I. (1949). Effects of variations in nutritive density on intake of food in dogs and cats. *American Journal of Physiology, 158,* 184–193.

JANOWSKY, J. S., CHAVEZ, B., & ORWOLL, E. (2000). Sex steroids modify working memory. *Journal of Cognitive Neuroscience, 12,* 407–414.

JANUS, C., ET AL. (2000). A peptide immunization reduces behavioural impairment and plaques in a model of Alzheimer's disease. *Nature, 408*(6815), 979–981.

JEFFERY, R. W., HENNRIKUS, D. J., LANDO, H. A., MURRAY, D. M., & LIU, J. W. (2000). Reconciling conflicting findings regarding postcessation weight concerns and success in smoking cessation. *Health Psychology, 19,* 242–246.

JEMMOTT, J. B., ET AL. (1983). Academic stress, power motivation, and decrease in secretion rate of salivary secretory immunoglobin A. *Lancet, 1,* 1400–1402.

JENKINS, A. M., ET AL. (2003). Ethnic minorities. In D. K. Freedheim (Ed.), *Handbook of psychology: History of psychology* (Vol. 1, pp. 483–508). New York: John Wiley & Sons.

JENSEN, M. P., TURNER, J. A., & ROMANO, J. M. (1994). Correlates of improvement in multidisciplinary treatment of chronic pain. *Journal of Consulting and Clinical Psychology, 62,* 172–179.

JENSEN, M. P., ET AL. (2005). Hypnotic analgesia for chronic pain in persons with disabilities: A case series. *International Journal of Clinical & Experimental Hypnosis, 53*(2), 198–228.

JOHANSEN, M., KARTERUD, S., PEDERSEN, G., GUDE, T., & FALKUM, E. (2004). An investigation of the prototype validity of the borderline DSM–IV construct. *Acta Psychiatrica Scandinavica, 109*(4), 289–298.

JOHNS, A. (2001). Psychiatric effects of cannabis. *The British Journal of Psychiatry, 178,* 116–122.

JOHNSTON, L. D., O'MALLEY, P. M., & BACHMAN, J. G. (2001). *Monitoring the Future national survey results on drug use, 1975–2000. Volume I: Secondary school students* (NIH Publication No. 01-4924). Bethesda, MD: National Institute on Drug Abuse.

JOHNSTON, L. D., O'MALLEY, P. M., & BACHMAN, J. G. (2003). *Monitoring the Future national results on adolescent drug use: Overview of key findings 2002.* Bethesda, MD: National Institute on Drug Abuse.

JOINER, T. E., JR. (2002). The trajectory of suicidal behavior over time. *Suicide & Life-Threatening Behavior, 32*(1), 33–41.

JOINER, T. E., JR., HEATHERTON, T. F., RUDD, M. D., & SCHMIDT, N. B. (1997). Perfectionism, perceived weight status, and bulimic symptoms. *Journal of Abnormal Psychology, 106,* 145–153.

JONES, C. J., & MEREDITH, W. (2000). Developmental paths of psychological health from early adolescence to later adulthood. *Psychology and Aging, 15*(2), 351–360.

JONES, J. L., & LEARY, M. R. (1994). Effects of appearance-based admonitions against sun exposure on tanning intentions in young adults. *Health Psychology, 13,* 86–90.

JONES, M. C. (1924). Elimination of children's fears. *Journal of Experimental Psychology, 7,* 381–390.

JONES, S., ET AL. (2002, September 15). The Internet goes to college: How students are living in the future with today's technology. Pew Internet & American Life Project, Lee Rainee, Director. http://www.pewinternet.org.

JONSDOTTIR, I. H., HELLSTRAND, K., THOREN, P., & HOFFMAN, P. (2000). Enhancement of natural immunity seen after voluntary exercise in rats. Role of central opioid receptors. *Life Sciences, 66*(13), 1231–1239.

JORGENSEN, R. S., JOHNSON, B. T., KOLODZIEJ, M. E., & SCHREER, G. E. (1996). Elevated blood pressure and personality. *Psychological Bulletin, 120,* 293–320.

KADDOUR, J. (2003). Psychological endurance (hardiness): Definitional, nomological, and critical aspects. *European Review of Applied Psychology, 53*(3–4), 227–237.

KAHNEMAN, D., & FREDERICK, S. (2002). Representativeness revisited: Attribute substitution in intuitive judgment. In T. Gilovich, et al. (Eds.), *Heuristics and biases: The psychology of intuitive judgment* (pp. 49–81). New York: Cambridge University Press.

KAINZ, K. (2002). A behavioral conditioning program for treatment of nocturnal enuresis. *Behavior Therapist, 25*(10), 185–187.

KAISER FAMILY FOUNDATION, HOLT, T., GREENE, L., & DAVIS, J. (2003). *National Survey of Adolescents and Young Adults: Sexual health knowledge, attitudes and experiences.* Menlo Park, CA: Henry J. Kaiser Family Foundation.

KALIN, N. H. (2003). Nonhuman primate studies of fear, anxiety, and temperament and the role of benzodiazepine receptors and GABA systems. *Journal of Clinical Psychiatry, 64*(Suppl. 3), 41–44.

KALIVAS, P. W. (2003). Predisposition to addiction: Pharmacokinetics, pharmacodynamics, and brain circuitry. *American Journal of Psychiatry, 160,* 1–2.

KALLGREN, C. A., RENO, R. R., & CIALDINI, R. B. (2000). A focus theory of normative conduct: When norms do and do not affect behavior. *Personality & Social Psychology Bulletin, 26*(8), 1002–1012.

KAMALANABHAN, T. J., SUNDER, D. L., & VASANTHI, M. (2000). An evaluation of the Choice Dilemma Questionnaire as a measure of risk-taking propensity. *Social Behavior & Personality, 28*(2), 149–156.

KAMPHAUS, R. W., PETOSKEY, M. D., & ROWE, E. W. (2000). Current trends in psychological testing of children. *Professional Psychology: Research and Practice, 31*(2), 155–164.

KANDEL, E. R. (2001). The molecular biology of memory storage: A dialogue between genes and synapses. *Science, 294,* 1030–1038.

KAPUR, S. (2003). Psychosis as a state of aberrant salience: A framework linking biology, phenomenology, and pharmacology in schizophrenia. *American Journal of Psychiatry, 160*(1), 13–23.

KARLBERG, L., ET AL. (1998). Is there a connection between car accidents, near accidents, and Type A drivers? *Behavioral Medicine, 24*(3), 99–106.

KARON, B. P., & WIDENER, A. (1998). Repressed memories: The real story. *Professional Psychology: Research & Practice, 29*(5), 482–487.

KARWAUTZ, A., ET AL. (2001). Individual-specific risk factors for anorexia nervosa: A pilot study using a discordant sister-pair design. *Psychological Medicine, 31*(2), 317–329.

KASAI, K., ET AL. (2003). Progressive decrease of left Heschl gyrus and planum temporale gray matter volume in first-episode schizophrenia: A longitudinal magnetic resonance imaging study. *Archives of General Psychiatry, 60*(8), 766–775.

KASEN, S., COHEN, P., BERENSON, K., CHEN, H., & DUFUR, S. (2005). Dual work and family roles and depressive symptoms in two birth cohorts of women. *Social Psychiatry & Psychiatric Epidemiology, 40*(4), 301–307.

KASHIMA, Y. (2000). Maintaining cultural stereotypes in the serial reproduction of narratives. *Personality & Social Psychology Bulletin, 26*(5), 594–604.

KASLOW, N. J., ET AL., (2002). Risk and protective factors for suicidal behavior in abused African American women. *Journal of Consulting & Clinical Psychology, 70*(2), 311–319.

KATARIA, S. (2004). A clinical guide to pediatric sleep: Diagnosis and management of sleep problems. *Journal of Developmental & Behavioral Pediatrics, 25*(2), 132–133.

KATERNDAHL, D., BURGE, S., & KELLOGG, N. (2005). Predictors of development of adult psychopathology in female victims of childhood sexual abuse. *Journal of Nervous & Mental Disease, 193*(4), 258–264.

KATIGBAK, M. S., CHURCH, A. T., GUANZON-LAPENA, M. A., CARLOTA, A. J., & DEL PILAR, G. H. (2002). Are indigenous personality dimensions culture specific? Philippine inventories and the five-factor model. *Journal of Personality & Social Psychology, 82*(1), 89–101.

KAYE, W. H., ET AL. (2004). Genetic analysis of bulimia nervosa: Methods and sample description. *International Journal of Eating Disorders, 35*(4), 556–570.

KAZUOMI KARIO, J. E., ET AL. (2001). Gender differences in associations of diurnal blood pressure variation, awake physical activity, and sleep quality with negative affect: The Work Site Blood Pressure Study. *Hypertension, 38,* 997–1002.

KELLER, A., ET AL. (2003). Progressive loss of cerebellar volume in childhood-onset schizophrenia. *American Journal of Psychiatry, 160,* 128–133.

KELLER, M. B., ET AL. (2000). A comparison of nefazodone, the cognitive behavioral-analysis system of psychotherapy, and their combination for the treatment of chronic depression. *The New England Journal of Medicine, 342*(20), 1462–1470.

KELLERMAN, J., LEWIS, J., & LAIRD, J. D. (1989). Looking and loving: The effects of mutual gaze on feelings of romantic love. *Journal of Research in Personality, 23,* 145–161.

KELLEY, H. H., & MICHELA, J. L. (1980). Attribution theory and research. *Annual Review of Psychology, 31,* 457–501.

KELLMAN, P. J., & VON HOFSTEN, C. (1992). The world of the moving infant. In C. Rovee-Collier & L. P. Lipsitt (Eds.), *Advances in Infancy Research* (Vol. 7). Norwood, NJ: Ablex.

KELLY, A. (2000). Helping construct desirable identities: A self-presentational view of psychotherapy. *Psychological Bulletin, 126*(4), 475–494.

KENDLER, H. H. (2005). Psychology and phenomenology: A clarification. *American Psychologist, 60*(4), 318–324.

KENDLER, K.S., ET AL. (1997). Resemblance of psychotic symptoms and syndromes in affected sibling pairs from the Irish study of high-density schizophrenia families: Evidence for possible etiologic heterogeneity. *American Journal of Psychiatry, 154,* 191–198.

KENDLER, K. S., ET AL. (2000a). Illicit psychoactive substance use, heavy use, abuse, and dependence in a U.S. population-based sample of male twins. *Archives of General Psychiatry, 57,* 261–269.

KENDLER, K. S., MYERS, J. M., & NEALE, M. C. (2000b). A multidimensional twin study of mental health in women. *American Journal of Psychiatry, 157,* 506–513.

KENDLER, K. S., THORNTON, L. M., GILMAN, S. E., & KESSLER, R. C. (2000c). Sexual orientation in a U.S. national sample of twin and nontwin sibling pairs. *American Journal of Psychiatry, 157,* 1843–1846.

KENDLER, K. S., THORNTON, L. M., & PEDERSEN, N. L. (2000d). Tobacco consumption in Swedish twins reared apart and reared together. *Archives of General Psychiatry, 57,* 886–892.

KENDLER, K. S., MYERS, J., PRESCOTT, C. A., & NEALE, M. C. (2001). The genetic epidemiology of irrational fears and phobias in men. *Archives of General Psychiatry, 58*(3), 257–265.

KENNEDY, C. H. (2002). Effects of REM sleep deprivation on a multiple schedule of appetitive reinforcement. *Behavioural Brain Research, 128*(2), 205–214.

KENRICK, D. T., & MACFARLANE, S. W. (1986). Ambient temperature and horn honking. *Environment and Behavior, 18,* 179–191.

KÉRI, S. (2003). Genetics, psychology, and determinism. *American Psychologist, 58*(4), 319.

KERNS, J. G., & BERENBAUM, H. (2002). Cognitive impairments associated with formal thought disorder in people with schizophrenia. *Journal of Abnormal Psychology, 111*(2), 211–224.

KESSLER, R. C. (2003). Epidemiology of women and depression. *Journal of Affective Disorders, 74*(1), 5–13.

KESSLER, R. C., ET AL. (2003). The epidemiology of major depressive disorder: Results from the National Comorbidity Survey Replication (NCS-R). *Journal of the American Medical Association, 289*(23), 3095–3105.

KESSLER, R. C., ET AL. (2005a) Lifetime prevalence and age-of-onset distributions of DSM-IV disorders in the National Comorbidity Survey Replication. *Archives of General Psychiatry, 62*(6), 593–602.

KESSLER, R. C., BERGLUND, P., BORGES, G., NOCK, M., & WANG, P. S. (2005b). Trends in suicide ideation, plans, gestures, and attempts in the United States, 1990–1992 to 2001–2003. *Journal of the American Medical Association, 293,* 2487–2495.

KESSLER, R. C., CHIU, W. T., DEMLER, O., & WALTERS, E. E. (2005c). Prevalence, severity, and comorbidity of 12-month *DSM–IV* disorders in the National Comorbidity Survey Replication. *Archives of General Psychiatry, 62*(6), 617–627.

KEYES, C. L. M., & HAIDT, J. (2003). *Flourishing: Positive psychology and the life well-lived.* Washington, DC: American Psychological Association.

KEYES, D. (1995). *The minds of Billy Milligan.* New York: Bantam Books.

KHAN, A. A., JACOBSON, K. C., GARDNER, C. O., PRESCOTT, C. A., & KENDLER, K. S. (2005). Personality and comorbidity of common psychiatric disorders. *British Journal of Psychiatry, 186*(3), 190–196.

KIECOLT-GLASER, J. K., MARUCHA, P. T., ATKINSON, C., & GLASER, R. (2001). Hypnosis as a modulator of cellular immune dysregulation during acute stress. *Journal of Consulting & Clinical Psychology, 69*(4), 674–682.

KIECOLT-GLASER, J. K., McGUIRE, L., ROBLES, T. F., & GLASER, R. (2002a). Psychoneuroimmunology and psychosomatic medicine: Back to the future. *Psychosomatic Medicine, 64*(1), 15–28.

KIECOLT-GLASER, J. K., McGUIRE, L., ROBLES, T. F., & GLASER, R. (2002b). Emotions, morbidity, and mortality: New perspectives from psychoneuroimmunology. *Annual Review of Psychology, 53*(1), 83–107.

KIHLSTROM, J. F. (2002). No need for repression. *Trends in Cognitive Sciences, 6*(12), 502.

KILSHAW, D., & ANNETT, M. (1983). Right- and left-hand skill: Effects of age, sex, and hand preferences showing superior in left-handers. *British Journal of Psychology, 74,* 253–268.

KIM, B. S. K., BRENNER, B. R., LIANG, C. T. H., & ASAY, P. A. (2003). A qualitative study of adaptation experiences of 1.5-generation Asian Americans. *Cultural Diversity & Ethnic Minority Psychology, 9*(2), 156–170.

KIM, B. S. K., & OMIZO, M. M. (2003). Asian cultural values, attitudes toward seeking professional psychological help, and willingness to see a counselor. *Counseling Psychologist, 31*(3), 343–361.

KIM, H., ET AL. (2002). Oxidative damage causes formation of lipofuscin-like substances in the hippocampus of the senescence-accelerated mouse after kainate treatment. *Behavioural Brain Research, 131*(1–2), 211–220.

KIM, K., & ROHNER, R. P. (2002). Parental warmth, control, and involvement in schooling: Predicting academic achievement among Korean American adolescents. *Journal of Cross-Cultural Psychology, 33*(2), 127–140.

KIMURA, D. (2002, May). Sex differences in the brain. *Scientific American Mind, 12*(1), 32–37.

KING, S. (2005). In Lake, M. (2005, May 2). Virtual reality heals 9/11 wounds. http://www.cnn.com/2005/TECH/04/29/spark.virtual/index.html.

KINSEY, A. C., POMEROY, W. B., & MARTIN, C. E. (1948). *Sexual behavior in the human male.* Philadelphia: W. B. Saunders.

KINSEY, A. C., POMEROY, W. B., MARTIN, C. E., & GEBHARD, P. H. (1953). *Sexual behavior in the human female.* Philadelphia: W. B. Saunders.

KIRSCH, I. (2000). The response set theory of hypnosis. *American Journal of Clinical Hypnosis, 42*(3–4), 274–292.

KIRSCH, I., LYNN, S. J., VIGORITO, M., & MILLER, R. R. (2004). The role of cognition in classical and operant conditioning. *Journal of Clinical Psychology, 60*(4), 369–392.

KIRSCHENBAUM, H., & JOURDAN, A. (2005). The current status of Carl Rogers and the person-centered approach. *Psychotherapy: Theory, Research, Practice, Training, 42*(1), 37–51.

KLACZYNSKI, P. A. (2001). Framing effects on adolescent task representations, analytic and heuristic processing and decision making. Implications for the normative/descriptive gap. *Journal of Applied Developmental Psychology, 22*(3), 289–309.

KLEIN, D. N., ET AL. (2003). Therapeutic alliance in depression treatment: Controlling for prior change and patient characteristics. *Journal of Consulting and Clinical Psychology, 71,* 997–1006.

KLEINDIENST, N., & GREIL, W. (2003). Lithium in the long-term treatment of bipolar disorders. *European Archives of Psychiatry & Clinical Neuroscience, 253*(3), 120–125.

KLEINKE, C. L. (1977). Compliance to requests made by gazing and touching experimenters in field settings. *Journal of Experimental Social Psychology, 13,* 218–223.

KLEINKE, C. L. (1986). Gaze and eye contact. *Psychological Review, 100,* 78–100.

KLEINMUNTZ, B., & SZUCKO, J. J. (1984). Lie detection in ancient and modern times. *American Psychologist, 39,* 766–776.

KLÜVER, H., & BUCY, P. C. (1939). Preliminary analysis of functions of the temporal lobe in monkeys. *Archives of Neurology and Psychiatry, 42,* 979–1000.

KNAFO, A., IERVOLINO, A. C., & PLOMIN, R. (2005). Masculine girls and feminine boys: Genetic and environmental contributions to atypical gender development in early childhood. *Journal of Personality & Social Psychology, 88*(2), 400–412.

KOBASA, S. C. O. (1990). Stress-resistant personality. In R. E. Ornstein & C. Swencionis (Eds.), *The healing brain* (pp. 219–230). New York: Guilford Press.

KOBASA, S. C. O., MADDI, S. R., PUCCETTI, M. C., & ZOLA, M. A. (1994). Effectiveness of hardiness, exercise, and social support as resources against illness. In A. Steptoe & J. Wardle (Eds.), *Psychosocial processes and health* (pp. 247–260). Cambridge, England: Cambridge University Press.

KOHLBERG, L. (1969). *Stages in the development of moral thought and action.* New York: Holt, Rinehart and Winston.

KOHLBERG, L. (1981). *The philosophy of moral development.* San Francisco: Harper & Row.

KÖHLER, W. (1925). *The mentality of apes.* New York: Harcourt Brace World.

KOLLINS, S. H., & RUSH, C. R. (2002). Sensitization to the cardiovascular but not subject-rated effects of oral cocaine in humans. *Biological Psychiatry, 51*(2), 143–150.

KOOIJMAN, C. M., ET AL. (2000). Phantom pain and phantom sensations in upper limb amputees: An epidemiological study. *Pain, 87*(1), 33–41.

KOPELMAN, M. D. (2002). Disorders of memory. *Brain, 125*(10), 2152–2190.

KOSS, M. P. (1993). Rape. *American Psychologist, 48,* 1062–1069.

KOSS, M. P. (2003). Evolutionary models of why men rape: Acknowledging the complexities. In C. B. Travis (Ed.), *Evolution, gender, and rape* (pp. 191–205). Cambridge, MA: MIT Press.

KOSS, M. P., BAILEY, J. A., YUAN, N. P., HERRERA, V. M., & LICHTER, E. L. (2003). Depression and PTSD in survivors of male violence: Research and training initiatives to facilitate recovery. *Psychology of Women Quarterly, 27*(2), 130–142.

KOSS, M. P., FIGUEREDO, A. J., & PRINCE, R. J. (2002). Cognitive mediation of rape's mental, physical and social health impact: Tests of four models in cross-sectional data. *Journal of Consulting & Clinical Psychology, 70*(4), 926–941.

KRAMER, P. D. (2003, June 22). Your Zoloft might prevent a heart attack. *The New York Times,* p. WK3.

KRANTZ, D. S., CONTRADA, R. J., HILL, D. R., & FRIEDLER, E. (1988). Environmental stress and biobehavioral antecedents of coronary heart disease. *Journal of Consulting and Clinical Psychology, 56,* 333–341.

KRCMAR, M., & COOKE, M. C. (2001). Children's moral reasoning and their perceptions of television violence. *Journal of Communication, 51*(2), 300–316.

KROES, G., VEERMAN, J. W., & DE BRUYN, E. E. J. (2005). The impact of the Big Five personality traits on reports of child behavior problems by different informants. *Journal of Abnormal Child Psychology, 33*(2), 231–240.

KROGER, J. K., ET AL. (2002). Recruitment of anterior dorsolateral prefrontal cortex in human reasoning: A parametric study of relational complexity. *Cerebral Cortex, 12*(5), 477–485.

KUCZMARSKI, R. J., ET AL. (2000, December 4). CDC Growth charts: United States. Advance data from vital and health statistics, no. 314. Hyattsville, MD: National Center for Health Statistics.

KURZWEIL, R. C. (2000, June 19). Will my PC be smarter than I am? *Time,* pp. 82–83.

KURZWEIL, R. C. (2004, January 22). Generating visual art. U.S. patent application #20040012590.

KURZWEIL, R. C., & KEKLAK, J. A. (2003, February 20). Basic poetry generation. U.S. patent application #20030036040.

KWATE, N. O. A. (2001). Intelligence or misorientation? Eurocentrism in the WICS-III. *Journal of Black Psychology, 27*(2), 221–238.

KYLE, T. M., & WILLIAMS, S. (2000, May). Results of the 1998–1999 APA survey of graduate departments of psychology. APA Research Office. Washington, DC: American Psychological Association.

LABIANO, L. M., & BRUSASCA, C. (2002). Psychological treatments in arterial hypertension. *Interdisciplinaria, 19*(1), 85–97.

LACKNER, J. M., CAROSELLA, A. M., & FEUERSTEIN, M. (1996). Pain expectancies, pain, and functional self-efficacy expectancies as determinants of disability in patients with chronic low back disorders. *Journal of Consulting and Clinical Psychology, 64,* 212–220.

LAHTI, A. C., ET AL. (2001). Abnormal patterns of regional cerebral blood flow in schizophrenia with primary negative symptoms during an effortful auditory recognition task. *American Journal of Psychiatry, 158,* 1797–1808.

LALUMIÈRE, M. L., BLANCHARD, R., & ZUCKER, K. J. (2000). Sexual orientation and handedness in men and women: A meta-analysis. *Psychological Bulletin, 126*(4), 575–592.

LAM, A. G., & SUE, S. (2001). Client diversity. *Psychotherapy: Theory, Research, Practice, Training, 38*(4), 479–486.

LANCASTER, T., STEAD, L., SILAGY, C., & SOWDEN, A. (2000). Regular review: Effectiveness of interventions to help people stop smoking: Findings from the Cochrane Library. *British Medical Journal, 321,* 355–358.

LANG, A. R., GOECKNER, D. J., ADESSO, V. J., & MARLATT, G. A. (1975). Effects of alcohol on aggression in male social drinkers. *Journal of Abnormal Psychology, 84,* 508–518.

LANG, E. V., ET AL. (2000). Adjunctive non-pharmacological analgesia for invasive medical procedures: a randomised trial. *The Lancet, 355,* 1486–1490.

LANG, F. R., & HECKHAUSEN, J. (2001). Perceived control over development and subjective well-being: Differential benefits across adulthood. *Journal of Personality & Social Psychology, 81*(3), 509–523.

LANGER, E. J., RODIN, J., BECK, P., WEINAN, C., &

Spitzer, L. (1979). Environmental determinants of memory improvement in late adulthood. *Journal of Personality and Social Psychology, 37,* 2003–2013.

Langlois, J. H., et al. (2000). Maxims or myths of beauty? A meta-analytic and theoretical review. *Psychological Bulletin, 126*(3), 390–423.

Lanier, S. A., Hayes, J. E., & Duffy, V. B. (2005). Sweet and bitter tastes of alcoholic beverages mediate alcohol intake in of-age undergraduates. *Physiology & Behavior, 83*(5), 821–831.

Larkin, M. (2000). Can lost hearing be restored? *The Lancet, 356,* 741–748.

Larrick, R. P. (1993). Motivational factors in decision theories. *Psychological Bulletin, 113,* 440–450.

Lashley, K. S. (1950). In search of the engram. In *Symposium of the Society for Experimental Biology* (Vol. 4). New York: Cambridge University Press.

Laumann, E. O., Gagnon, J. H., Michael, R. T., & Michaels, S. (1994). *The social organization of sexuality.* Chicago: University of Chicago Press.

Laumann, E. O., Paik, A., & Rosen, R. C. (1999). Sexual dysfunction in the United States. Prevalence and predictors. *Journal of the American Medical Association, 281*(6), 537–544.

Laungani, P. (2002). The counselling interview: First impressions. *Counselling Psychology Quarterly, 15*(1), 107–113.

Lavee, Y., & Ben-Ari, A. (2003). Daily stress and uplifts during times of political tension: Jews and Arabs in Israel. *American Journal of Orthopsychiatry, 73*(1), 65–73.

Lavie, P. (2001). Current concepts: Sleep disturbances in the wake of traumatic events. *New England Journal of Medicine, 345,* 1825–1832.

Lavie, P., & Herer, P., & Hoffstein, H. (2000). Obstructive sleep apnoea syndrome as a risk factor for hypertension: population study. *British Medical Journal, 320,* 479–482.

Lavine, H., Lodge, M., & Freitas, K. (2005). Threat, authoritarianism, and selective exposure to information. *Political Psychology, 26*(2), 219–244.

Lawson, W. B., & Strickland, T. L. (2004). Racial and ethnic issues affect treatment for bipolar disorder. *Psychiatric Annals, 34*(1), 17–20.

Lazar, S. W., et al. (2000). Functional brain mapping of the relaxation response and meditation. *Neuroreport: For Rapid Communication of Neuroscience Research, 11*(7), 1581–1585.

Lazarus, R. S., DeLongis, A., Folkman, S., & Gruen, R. (1985). Stress and adaptational outcomes. *American Psychologist, 40,* 770–779.

Leahey, E., & Guo, G. (2001). Gender differences in mathematical trajectories. *Social Forces, 80*(2), 713–732.

Le Bon, G. (1960). *The crowd.* New York: Viking. (Original work published 1895)

Lecci, L., & Cohen, D. J. (2002). Perceptual consequences of an illness-concern induction and its relation to hypochondriacal tendencies. *Health Psychology, 21*(2), 147–156.

LeDoux, J. E. (1998). Fear and the brain: Where have we been, and where are we going? *Biological Psychiatry, 44*(12), 1229–1238.

Lee, O., & Shin, M. (2004). Addictive consumption of avatars in cyberspace. *CyberPsychology & Behavior, 7*(4), 417–420.

Lefcourt, H. M. (1997). Cited in Clay, R. A. (1997). Researchers harness the power of humor. *APA Monitor, 28*(9), 1, 18.

Lefcourt, H. M., & Martin, R. A. (1986). *Humor and life stress.* New York: Springer-Verlag.

Lefcourt, H. M., Miller, R. S., Ware, E. E., &

Sherk, D. (1981). Locus of control as a modifier of the relationship between stressors and moods. *Journal of Personality and Social Psychology, 41,* 357–369.

Lehman, B. J., & Crano, W. D. (2002). The pervasive effects of vested interest on attitude-criterion consistency in political judgment. *Journal of Experimental Social Psychology, 38*(2), 101–112.

Leichsenring, F., & Leibing, E. (2003). The effectiveness of psychodynamic therapy and cognitive behavior therapy in the treatment of personality disorders: A meta-analysis. *American Journal of Psychiatry, 160,* 1223–1232.

Leitch, M. L. (2005, May 31). Just like bodies, psyches can drown in disasters. *The New York Times online.*

Leland, J. (2005, March 27). The Schiavo case: Final moments. *The New York Times online.*

Le Melledo, J., et al. (2001). The influence of Type A behavior pattern on the response to the panicogenic agent CCK-4. *Journal of Psychosomatic Research, 51*(3), 513–520.

Lensvelt-Mulders, G., & Hettema, J. (2001). Genetic analysis of autonomic reactivity to psychologically stressful situations. *Biological Psychology, 58*(1), 25–40.

Leonard, B. E. (2005). Mind over matter: Regulation of peripheral inflammation by the CNS. *Human Psychopharmacology: Clinical & Experimental, 20*(1), 71–72.

Leonard, S., Steiger, H., & Kao, A. (2003). Childhood and adulthood abuse in bulimic and non-bulimic women: Prevalences and psychological correlates. *International Journal of Eating Disorders, 33*(4), 397–405.

Leor, J., Poole, K., & Kloner, R. A. (1996). Sudden cardiac death triggered by an earthquake. *New England Journal of Medicine, 334,* 413–419.

Leppel, K. (2002). Similarities and differences in the college persistence of men and women. *Review of Higher Education: Journal of the Association for the Study of Higher Education, 25*(4), 433–450.

Leslie, M. B., Stein, J. A., & Rotheram-Borus, M. J. (2002). Sex-specific predictors of suicidality among runaway youth. *Journal of Community Psychology, 31*(1), 27–40.

Less sex, more protection, fewer pregnancies. (2004, March 7). *The New York Times,* p. 36N.

Lester, D., Yang, B., & Lindsay, M. (2004). Suicide bombers: Are psychological profiles possible? *Studies in Conflict & Terrorism, 27*(4), 283–295.

Letourneau, E. J., Schoenwald, S. K., & Sheidow, A. J. (2004). Children and adolescents with sexual behavior problems. *Child Maltreatment: Journal of the American Professional Society on the Abuse of Children, 9*(1), 49–61.

Leuthardt, E. C., Schalk, G., Wolpaw, J. R., Ojemann, J. G., & Moran, D. W. (2004). A brain-computer interface using electrocorticographic signals in humans. *Journal of Neural Engineering, 1,* 63–71.

Levenston, G. K., Patrick, C. J., Bradley, M. M., & Lang, P. J. (2000). The psychopath as observer: Emotion and attention in picture processing. *Journal of Abnormal Psychology, 109*(3), 373–385.

Lever, J. P. (2004). Poverty and subjective well-being in Mexico. *Social Indicators Research, 68*(1), 1–33.

Levin, R., & Fireman, G. (2002). Nightmare prevalence, nightmare distress, and self-reported psychological disturbance. *Sleep: Journal of Sleep & Sleep Disorders Research, 25*(2), 205–212.

Levine, D. (2000). Virtual attraction: What rocks

your boat. *CyberPsychology & Behavior, 3*(4), 565–573.

Levinson, D. J., Darrow, C. N., Klein, E. B., Levinson, M. H., & McKee, B. (1978). *The seasons of a man's life.* New York: Knopf.

Levinson, D. J. (1996). *The seasons of a woman's life.* New York: Knopf.

Levy, D., et al. (2000). Evidence for a gene influencing blood pressure on chromosome 17: Genome scan linkage results for longitudinal blood pressure phenotypes in subjects from the Framingham Heart Study. *Hypertension, 36,* 477–483.

Lewinsohn, P. M., Brown, R. A., Seeley, J. R., & Ramsey, S. E. (2000a). Psychological correlates of cigarette smoking abstinence, experimentation, persistence, and frequency during adolescence. *Nicotine & Tobacco Research, 2*(2), 121–131.

Lewinsohn, P. M., Rohde, P., Seeley, J. R., Klein, D. N., & Gotlib, I. H. (2000b). Natural course of adolescent major depressive disorder in a community sample: Predictors of recurrence in young adults. *American Journal of Psychiatry, 157,* 1584–1591.

Leyton, M., et al. (2000). Acute tyrosine depletion and alcohol ingestion in healthy women. *Alcoholism: Clinical & Experimental Research, 24*(4), 459–464.

Li, G., Baker, S. P., Smialek, J. E., & Soderstrom, C. A. (2001). Use of alcohol as a risk factor for bicycling injury. *Journal of the American Medical Association, 284,* 893–896.

Li, W., & DeVries, S. H. (2004). Separate blue and green cone networks in the mammalian retina. *Nature Neuroscience, 7*(7), 751–756.

Lidow, M. S., et al. (2001). Antipsychotic treatment induces alterations in dendrite- and spine-associated proteins in dopamine-rich areas of the primate cerebral cortex. *Biological Psychiatry, 49*(1), 1–12.

Lieber, C. S. (1990). Cited in Barroom biology: How alcohol goes to a woman's head (January 14). *The New York Times,* p. E24.

Liederman, J., Kantrowitz, L., & Flannery, K. (2005). Male vulnerability to reading disability is not likely to be a myth: A call for new data. *Journal of Learning Disabilities, 38*(2), 109–129.

Lim, M. M., et al. (2004). Enhanced partner preference in a promiscuous species by manipulating the expression of a single gene. *Nature, 429,* 754–757.

Linde, J. A., Jeffery, R. W., Finch, E. A., Ng, D. M., & Rothman, A. J. (2004). Are unrealistic weight loss goals associated with outcomes for overweight women? *Obesity Research, 12*(3), 569–576.

Linden, W., Chambers, L., Maurice, J., & Lenz, J. W. (1993). Sex differences in social support, self-deception, hostility, and ambulatory cardiovascular activity. *Health Psychology, 12,* 376–380.

Lisanby, S. H., et al. (2000). The effects of electroconvulsive therapy on memory of autobiographical and public events. *Archives of General Psychiatry, 57*(6), 581–590.

Little, A. C., & Perrett, D. I. (2002). Putting beauty back in the eye of the beholder. *Psychologist, 15*(1), 28–32.

Liu, Y., Curtis, J. T., & Wang, Z. (2001). Vasopressin in the lateral septum regulates pair bond formation in male prairie voles (*Microtus ochrogaster*). *Behavioral Neuroscience, 115*(4), 910–919.

Lochman, J. E., & Dodge, K. A. (1994). Social-cognitive processes of severely violent, moderately aggressive, and nonaggressive boys. *Journal of Consulting and Clinical Psychology, 62*, 366–374.

Lochman, J. E., & Wells, K. C. (2002). Contextual social-cognitive mediators and child outcome: A test of the theoretical model in the Coping Power program. *Development & Psychopathology, 14*(4), 945–967.

Löckenhoff, C. E., & Carstensen, L. L. (2004). Socioemotional selectivity theory, aging, and health: The increasingly delicate balance between regulating emotions and making tough choices. *Journal of Personality, 72*(6), 1395–1424.

Loftus, E. F. (1979). The malleability of human memory. *American Scientist, 67*(3), 312–320.

Loftus, E. F. (1983). Silence is not golden. *American Psychologist, 38*, 564–572.

Loftus, E. F. (1993). Psychologists in the eyewitness world. *American Psychologist, 48*, 550–552.

Loftus, E. F. (1994). Conference on memory, Harvard Medical School. Cited in D. Goleman (1994, May 31). Miscoding is seen as the root of false memories. *The New York Times*, pp. C1, C8.

Loftus, E. F. (1997). Cited in Loftus consulting in Oklahoma City bombing trial. *APA Monitor, 28*(4), 8–9.

Loftus, E. F. (2001). Imagining the past. *Psychologist, 14*(11), 584–587.

Loftus, E. F. (2004). Memories of things unseen. *Current Directions in Psychological Science, 13*(4), 145–147.

Loftus, E. F., & Bernstein, D. M. (2005). Rich false memories: The royal road to success. In A. F. Healy (Ed.), *Experimental cognitive psychology and its applications* (pp. 101–113). Washington, DC: American Psychological Association.

Loftus, E. F., & Loftus, G. R. (1980). On the permanence of stored information in the brain. *American Psychologist, 35*, 409–420.

Loftus, E. F., & Palmer, J. C. (1974). Reconstruction of automobile destruction. *Journal of Verbal Learning and Verbal Behavior, 13*, 585–589.

Loftus, G. R. (1983). The continuing persistence of the icon. *Behavioral and Brain Sciences, 6*, 28.

Loftus, G. R., & Loftus, E. F. (1976). *Human memory*. Hillsdale, NJ: Erlbaum.

Longer, healthier, better. (1997, March 9). *The New York Times Magazine*, pp. 44–45.

Loop, M. S., Shows, J. F., Mangel, S. C., & Kuyk, T. K. (2003). Colour thresholds in dichromats and normals. *Vision Research, 43*(9), 983–992.

Lopez, S. R., & Guarnaccia, P. J. J. (2000). Cultural psychopathology: Uncovering the social world of mental illness. *Annual Review of Psychology, 51*, 571–598.

Lorenz, K. Z. (1981). *The foundations of ethology*. New York: Springer-Verlag.

Los Angeles Unified School District. (2000). Youth Suicide Prevention Information. http://www.sanpedro.com/spyc/suicide.htm.

Lotufo, Z., Jr., & Martins, J. C. (2004). Revenge and religion. In J. H. Ellens (Ed.), *The destructive power of religion: Violence in Judaism, Christianity, and Islam, Vol. 2: Religion, psychology, and violence* (pp. 131–153). Westport, CT: Praeger Publishers/Greenwood Publishing Group.

Louie, K., & Wilson, M. A. (2001). Temporally structured replay of awake hippocampal ensemble activity during rapid eye movement sleep. *Neuron, 29*(1), 145–156.

Loving, T. J., & Agnew, C. R. (2001). Socially desirable responding in close relationships: A dual-component approach and measure. *Journal of Social & Personal Relationships, 18*(4), 551–573.

Lu, L. (1999). Personal or environmental causes of happiness: A longitudinal analysis. *Journal of Social Psychology, 139*(1), 79–90.

Lu, L. (2001). Understanding happiness: A look into the Chinese folk psychology. *Journal of Happiness Studies, 2*(4), 407–432.

Luborsky, L., et al. (2002). The dodo bird verdict is alive and well—mostly. *Clinical Psychology: Science & Practice, 9*(1), 2–12.

Lucas, T. W., et al. (2004). Marital satisfaction in four cultures as a function of homogamy, male dominance and female attractiveness. *Sexualities, Evolution & Gender, 6*(2–3), 97–130.

Luchins, A. S. (1957). Primacy-recency in impression formation. In C. I. Hovland (Ed.), *The order of presentation in persuasion*. New Haven, CT: Yale University Press.

Luczak, S. E., Elvine-Kreis, B., Shea, S. H., Carr, L. G., & Wall, T. L. (2002). Genetic risk for alcoholism relates to level of response to alcohol in Asian-American men and women. *Journal of Studies on Alcohol, 63*(1), 74–82.

Ludwick-Rosenthal, R., & Neufeld, R. W. J. (1993). Preparation for undergoing an invasive medical procedure. *Journal of Consulting and Clinical Psychology, 61*, 156–164.

Lydiard, R. B. (2003). The role of GABA in anxiety disorders. *Journal of Clinical Psychiatry, 64*(Suppl. 3), 21–27.

Lydiard, R. B., Brawman, A., Mintzer, O., & Ballenger, J. C. (1996). Recent developments in the psychopharmacology of anxiety disorders. *Journal of Consulting and Clinical Psychology, 64*, 660–668.

Lykken, D. T., & Csikszentmihalyi, M. (2001). Happiness—stuck with what you've got? *Psychologist, 14*(9), 470–472.

Lykken, D. T., McGue, M., Tellegen, A., & Bouchard, T. J., Jr. (1992). Emergenesis: Genetic traits that may not run in families. *American Psychologist, 47*, 1565–1577.

Lynn, S. J., & Kirsch, I. I. (1996). Alleged alien abductions: False memories, hypnosis, and fantasy proneness. *Psychological Inquiry, 7*(2), 151–155.

Lynn, S. J., Shindler, K., & Meyer, E. (2003). Hypnotic suggestibility, psychopathology, and treatment outcome. *Sleep & Hypnosis, 5*(1), 2–10.

Maas, J. B. (1998). *Power sleep: Revolutionary strategies that prepare your mind and body for peak performance*. New York: Villard.

Maccoby, E. E. (1990). Gender and relationships. *American Psychologist, 45*, 513–520.

Maccoby, E. E. (1992). The role of parents in the socialization of children: An historical overview. *Developmental Psychology, 28*, 1006–1017.

Maccoby, E. E. (2000). Perspectives on gender development. *International Journal of Behavioral Development, 24*(4), 398–406.

MacDonald, D. J., & Standing, L. G. (2002). Does self-serving bias cancel the Barnum effect? *Social Behavior & Personality, 30*(6), 625–630.

MacDonald, M. G. (1999). Suicide-intervention trainees' perceptions of awareness for warning signs of suicide. *Psychological Reports, 85*(3, Pt. 2 [Special Issue]), 1195–1198.

MacDonald, T. K., MacDonald, G., Zanna, M. P., & Fong, G. T. (2000). Alcohol, sexual arousal, and intentions to use condoms in young men: Applying alcohol myopia theory to risky sexual behavior. *Health Psychology, 19*, 290–298.

Macfarlane, J. A. (1975). Olfaction in the development of social preferences in the human neonate. In M. A. Hofer (Ed.), *Parent-infant interaction*. Amsterdam: Elsevier.

MacGregor, J. (2005). *Sunday money*. New York: HarperCollins.

Maciejewski, P. K., Prigerson, H. G., & Mazure, C. M. (2000). Self-efficacy as a mediator between stressful life events and depressive symptoms: Differences based on history of prior depression. *British Journal of Psychiatry, 176*, 373–378.

Mackert, B., et al. (2003). The eloquence of silent cortex: Analysis of afferent input to deafferented cortex in arm amputees. *Neuroreport: For Rapid Communication of Neuroscience Research, 14*(3), 409–412.

Macrae, C. N., Mitchell, J. P., & Pendry, L. F. (2002). What's in a forename? Cue familiarity and stereotypical thinking. *Journal of Experimental Social Psychology, 38*(2), 186–193.

Magnavita, N., et al. (1997). Type A behaviour pattern and traffic accidents. *British Journal of Medical Psychology, 70*(1), 103–107.

Maher, B. A., & Maher, W. B. (1994). Personality and psychopathology. *Journal of Abnormal Psychology, 103*, 72–77.

Mahmud, A., & Feely, F. (2003). Effect of smoking on arterial stiffness and pulse pressure amplification. *Hypertension, 41*, 183–187.

Maier, N. R. F., & Schneirla, T. C. (1935). *Principles of animal psychology*. New York: McGraw-Hill.

Male PMT behind men behaving badly. (2002, March 6). http://iafrica.com/highlife/hislife/features/903658.htm.

Malgady, R. G., Rogler, L. H., & Costantino, G. (1990). Hero/heroine modeling for Puerto Rican adolescents. *Journal of Consulting and Clinical Psychology, 58*, 469–474.

Malkin, E. (2004, November 11). In health care, gap between rich and poor persists, W.H.O. says. *The New York Times online.*

Maltby, N., Kirsch, I., Mayers, M., & Allen, G. J. (2002). Virtual reality exposure therapy for the treatment of fear of flying: A controlled investigation. *Journal of Consulting & Clinical Psychology, 70*(5), 1112–1118.

Mamtani, R., & Cimino, A. (2002). A primer of complementary and alternative medicine and its relevance in the treatment of mental health problems. *Psychiatric Quarterly, 73*(4), 367–381.

Marian, V., & Neisser, U. (2000). Language-dependent recall of autobiographical memories. *Journal of Experimental Psychology: General, 129*(3), 361–368.

Markon, K. E., Krueger, R. F., Bouchard, T. J., Jr., & Gottesman, I. I. (2002). Normal and abnormal personality traits: Evidence for genetic and environmental relationships in the Minnesota Study of Twins Reared Apart. *Journal of Personality, 70*(5), 661–693.

Marks, I. M. (2002). The maturing of therapy: Some brief psychotherapies help anxiety/depressive disorders but mechanisms of action are unclear. *British Journal of Psychiatry, 180*(3), 200–204.

Marks, I. M., & Dar, R. (2000). Fear reduction by psychotherapies: Recent findings, future directions. *The British Journal of Psychiatry, 176*, 507–511.

Markus, H., & Kitayama, S. (1991). Culture and the self. *Psychological Review, 98*(2), 224–253.

Marsh, R. L., Hicks, J. L., & Cook, G. I. (2005). On the relationship between effort toward an ongoing task and cue detection in event-based prospective memory. *Journal of Experimental Psychology: Learning, Memory & Cognition, 31*(1), 68–75.

Marshall, M. A., & Brown, J. D. (2004). Expectations and realizations: The role of expectancies in achievement settings. *Motivation & Emotion, 28*(4), 347–361.

MARTIN, C. L., & RUBLE, D. (2004). Children's search for gender cues: Cognitive perspectives on gender development. *Current Directions in Psychological Science, 13*(2), 67–70.

MARTIN, C. L., RUBLE, D. N., & SZKRYBALO, J. (2002). Cognitive theories of early gender development. *Psychological Bulletin, 128*(6), 903–933.

MARTIN, R. A., & LEFCOURT, H. M. (1983). Sense of humor as a moderator of the relation between stressors and moods. *Journal of Personality and Social Psychology, 45,* 1313–1324.

MARTIN, S. (2002). Easing migraine pain. *Monitor on Psychology, 33*(4), 71.

MARTINEZ-TABOAS, A., & BERNAL, G. (2000). Dissociation, psychopathology, and abusive experiences in a nonclinical Latino university student group. *Cultural Diversity & Ethnic Minority Psychology, 6*(1), 32–41.

MARTTUNEN, M. J., ET AL. (1998). Completed suicide among adolescents with no diagnosable psychiatric disorder. *Adolescence, 33*(131), 669–681.

MASLOW, A. H. (1970). *Motivation and personality* (2nd ed.). New York: Harper & Row.

MASTERS, K. S., LACAILLE, R. A., & SHEARER, D. S. (2003). The acute affective response of Type A Behaviour Pattern individuals to competitive and noncompetitive exercise. *Canadian Journal of Behavioural Science, 35*(1), 25–34.

MASTERS, W. H., & JOHNSON, V. E. (1966). *Human sexual response.* Boston: Little, Brown.

MASTERS, W. H., & JOHNSON, V. E. (1970). *Human sexual inadequacy.* Boston: Little, Brown.

MATCHEN, J., & DESOUZA, E. (2000). The sexual harassment of faculty members by students. *Sex Roles, 42*(3–4), 295–306.

MATT, G. E., VASQUEZ, C., & CAMPBELL, W. K. (1992). Mood-congruent recall of affectively toned stimuli: A meta-analytic review. *Clinical Psychology Review, 12,* 227–255.

MAY, R. (2005). How do we know what works? *Journal of College Student Psychotherapy, 19*(3), 69–73.

MAZUR, A. (2002). Take a chimp, add language, melt the glaciers. . . . *Journal for the Theory of Social Behaviour, 32*(1), 29–39.

MAZURE, C. M., ET AL. (2000). Adverse life events and cognitive-personality characteristics in the prediction of major depression and antidepressant response. *American Journal of Psychiatry, 157,* 896–903.

MAZZELLA, R., & FEINGOLD, A. (1994). The effects of physical attractiveness, race, socioeconomic status, and gender of defendants and victims on judgments of mock jurors. *Journal of Applied Social Psychology, 24*(15), 1315–1344.

MCANDREW, F. T. (2002). New evolutionary perspectives on altruism: Multilevel-selection and costly-signaling theories. *Current Directions in Psychological Science, 11*(2), 79–82.

MCANDREW, S. (2000). Sexual health through leadership and "sanuk" in Thailand. *British Medical Journal, 321*(7253), 114.

MCCLAVE, E. Z. (2000). Linguistic functions of head movements in the context of speech. *Journal of Pragmatics, 32*(7), 855–878.

MCCLELLAND, D. C. (1958). Methods of measuring human motivation. In J. W. Atkinson (Ed.), *Motives in fantasy, action, and society.* Princeton, NJ: Van Nostrand.

MCCLELLAND, D. C. (1965). Achievement and entrepreneurship. *Journal of Personality and Social Psychology, 1,* 389–392.

MCCOURT, K., ET AL. (1999). Authoritarianism revisited: Genetic and environmental influences examined in twins reared apart and together. *Personality & Individual Differences, 27*(5), 985–1014.

MCCRAE, R. R., & COSTA, P. T., JR. (1997). Personality trait structure as a human universal. *American Psychologist, 52,* 509–516.

MCCRAE, R. R., & COSTA, P. T., JR. (2002). Cited in Azar, B. (2002). Searching for genes that explain our personalities. *Monitor on Psychology, 33*(8), 44–46.

MCCRAE, R. R., ET AL. (2000). Nature over nurture: Temperament, personality, and life span development. *Journal of Personality & Social Psychology, 78*(1), 173–186.

MCDANIEL, M. A., GLISKY, E. L., GUYNN, M. J., & ROUTHIEAUX, B. C. (1999). Prospective memory: A neuropsychological study. *Neuropsychology, 13*(1), 103–110.

MCDOUGALL, W. (1904). The sensations excited by a single momentary stimulation of the eye. *British Journal of Psychology, 1,* 78–113.

MCDOUGALL, W. (1908). *An introduction to social psychology.* London: Methuen.

MCELROY, S. L., ET AL. (2000). Placebo-controlled trial of sertraline in the treatment of binge eating disorder. *American Journal of Psychiatry, 157,* 1004–1006.

MCGAUGH, J. L. (Accessed 2005, May 5). How emotions strengthen memory. http://www.loc.gov/loc/brain/emotion/Mcgaugh.html.

MCGAUGH, J. L., MCINTYRE, C. K., & POWER, A. E. (2002). Amygdala modulation of memory consolidation: Interaction with other brain systems. *Neurobiology of Learning & Memory. 78*(3), 539–552.

MCGRATH, E., KEITA, G. P., STRICKLAND, B. R., & RUSSO, N. F. (1990). *Women and depression.* Washington, DC: American Psychological Association.

MCGRATH, P. (2004). Psychological methods of pain control: Basic science and clinical perspectives. *Pain Research & Management, 9*(4), 217–217.

MCGRAW, A. P., MELLERS, B. A., & RITOV, I. (2004). The affective costs of overconfidence. *Journal of Behavioral Decision Making, 17*(4), 281–295.

MCGUE, M., PICKENS, R. W., & SVIKIS, D. S. (1992). Sex and age effects on the inheritance of alcohol problems: A twin study. *Journal of Abnormal Psychology, 101,* 3–17.

MCGUIRE, L., KIECOLT-GLASER, J. K., & GLASER, R. (2002). Depressive symptoms and lymphocyte proliferation in older adults. *Journal of Abnormal Psychology, 111*(1), 192–197.

MCKEE, P., & BARBER, C. E. (2001). Plato's theory of aging. *Journal of Aging & Identity, 6*(2), 93–104.

MCKENZIE, C. R. M., LEE, S. M., & CHEN, K. K. (2002). When negative evidence increases confidence: Changes in belief after hearing two sides of a dispute. *Journal of Behavioral Decision Making, 15*(1), 1–18.

MCLAREN, L. (2002). Cited in Wealthy women most troubled by poor body image. (2002, February 11). Reuters online.

MCMURRAN, M., BLAIR, M., & EGAN, V. (2002). An investigation of the correlations between aggression, impulsiveness, social problem-solving, and alcohol use. *Aggressive Behavior, 28,* 439–445.

MCNALLY, R. J., & CLANCY, S. A. (2005). Sleep paralysis, sexual abuse, and space alien abduction. *Transcultural Psychiatry, 42*(1), 113–122.

MCNEIL, T. F., CANTOR-GRAAE, E., & WEINBERGER, D. R. (2000). Relationship of obstetric complications and differences in size of brain structures in monozygotic twin pairs discordant for schizophrenia. *American Journal of Psychiatry, 157,* 203–212.

MCSHERRY, B. (2005). Men behaving badly: Current issues in provocation, automatism, mental impairment and criminal responsibility. *Psychiatry, Psychology and Law, 12*(1), 15–22.

MEIJER, J., & ELSHOUT, J. J. (2001). The predictive and discriminant validity of the zone of proximal development. *British Journal of Educational Psychology, 71*(1), 93–113.

MELLON, M. W., & MCGRATH, M. L. (2000). Empirically supported treatments in pediatric psychology: Nocturnal enuresis. *Journal of Pediatric Psychology, 25*(4), 193–214.

MELMED, R. N. (2003). Mind, body, and medicine: An integrative text. *American Journal of Psychiatry, 160*(3), 605–606.

MELTZOFF, A. N., & GOPNIK, A. (1997). *Words, thoughts, and theories.* Cambridge, MA: MIT Press.

MELZACK, R. (1999, August). From the gate to the neuromatrix. *Pain* (Suppl. 6), S121–S126.

METCALFE, J. (1986). Premonitions of insight predict impending error. *Journal of Experimental Psychology: Learning, Memory, and Cognition, 12,* 623–634.

METZ, R. (2005, March 10). Think of a number . . . Come on, think! *The New York Times online.*

MEYER, B., ET AL. (2002). Treatment expectancies, patient alliance, and outcome: Further analysys from the National Institute of Mental Health treatment of depression collaborative research program. *Journal of Consulting and Clinical Psychology, 70,* 1051–1055.

MEYER-LINDENBERG, A., ET AL. (2001). Evidence for abnormal cortical functional connectivity during working memory in schizophrenia. *American Journal of Psychiatry, 158,* 1809–1817.

MICHAEL, R. T., GAGNON, J. H., LAUMANN, E. O., & KOLATA, G. (1994). *Sex in America: A definitive survey.* Boston: Little, Brown.

MICHELS, K. B., ET AL. (2000). Prospective study of fruit and vegetable consumption and incidence of colon and rectal cancers. *Journal of the National Cancer Institute, 92*(21), 1740–1752.

MICHELSON, D., ET AL. (2000). Female sexual dysfunction associated with antidepressant administration: A randomized, placebo-controlled study of pharmacologic intervention. *American Journal of Psychiatry, 157,* 239–243.

MICHINOV, E., & MICHINOV, N. (2001). The similarity hypothesis: A test of the moderating role of social comparison orientation. *European Journal of Social Psychology, 31*(5), 549–555.

MIGDOW, J. (2003). The problem with pleasure. *Journal of Trauma & Dissociation, 4*(1), 5–25.

MILAR, K. S. (2000). The first generation of women psychologists and the psychology of women. *American Psychologist, 55*(6), 616–619.

MILES, J. (2005, May 22). Nascar nation. *The New York Times Book Review,* pp. 1, 10–11.

MILGRAM, S. (1963). Behavioral study of obedience. *Journal of Abnormal and Social Psychology, 67,* 371–378.

MILGRAM, S. (1974). *Obedience to authority.* New York: Harper & Row.

MILGRAM, S. (1977). *The individual in a social world.* Reading, MA: Addison-Wesley.

MILIUS, S. (2002). Rescue Rat: Could wired rodents save the day? *Science News Online.* http://www.phschool.com/science/science_news/articles/rescue_rat.html.

MILLER, A. L., WYMAN, S. E., HUPPERT, J. D., GLASSMAN, S. L., & RATHUS, J. H. (2000). Analysis of behavioral skills utilized by suicidal adolescents receiving dialectical behavior therapy. *Cognitive & Behavioral Practice, 7*(2), 183–187.

MILLER, A. R., ROSENFELD, P. J., SOSKINS, M., & JHEE, M. (2002). P300 amplitude and topography in an autobiographical paradigm involving simulated amnesia. *Journal of Psychophysiology, 16*(1), 1–11.

MILLER, D. A., SMITH, E. R., & MACKIE, D. M. (2004). Effects of intergroup contact and political predispositions on prejudice: Role of intergroup emotions. *Group Processes & Intergroup Relations, 7*(3), 221–237.

MILLER, G. A. (1956). The magical number seven, plus or minus two: Some limits on our capacity for processing information. *Psychological Review, 63,* 81–97.

MILLER, G. E., & COHEN, S. (2001). Psychological interventions and the immune system: A meta-analytic review and critique. *Health Psychology, 20*(1), 47–63.

MILLER, N. E. (1944). Experimental studies of conflict. In J. McVicker Hunt (Ed.), *Personality and the behavior disorders* (Vol. I, pp. 431–465). Oxford, England: Ronald Press.

MILLER, N. E. (1969). Learning of visceral and glandular responses. *Science, 163,* 434–445.

MILLER, N. E. (1995). Clinical-experimental interactions in the development of neuroscience. *American Psychologist, 50,* 901–911.

MILLER, S. M., SHODA, Y., & HURLEY, K. (1996). Applying cognitive-social theory to health- protective behavior: Breast self-examination in cancer screening. *Psychological Bulletin, 199,* 70–94.

MILNE, R. D., SYNGENIOTIS, A., JACKSON, G., & CORBALLIS, M. C. (2002). Mixed lateralization of phonological assembly in developmental dyslexia. *Neurocase, 8*(3), 205–209.

MILNER, B. R. (1966). Amnesia following operation on temporal lobes. In C. W. M. Whitty & O. L. Zangwill (Eds.), *Amnesia.* London: Butterworth.

MILSTEAD, M., LAPSLEY, D., & HALE, C. (1993, March). *A new look at imaginary audience and personal fable.* Paper presented at the meeting of the Society for Research in Child Development, New Orleans, LA.

MILTON, J., & WISEMAN, R. (1999). Does psi exist? Lack of replication of an anomalous process of information transfer. *Psychological Bulletin, 125*(4), 387–391.

MINTON, H. L. (2000). Psychology and gender at the turn of the century. *American Psychologist, 55*(6), 613–615.

MISCHEL, W., & SHODA, Y. (1995). A cognitive-affective system theory of personality. *Psychological Review, 102,* 246–268.

MITTAL, M., & WIELING, E. (2004). The influence of therapists' ethnicity on the practice of feminist family therapy: A pilot study. *Journal of Feminist Family Therapy, 16*(2), 25–42.

MOLDEN, D. C., & DWECK, C. S. (2000). Meaning and motivation. In C. Sansone & J. M. Harackiewicz (Eds.), *Intrinsic and extrinsic motivation: The search for optimal motivation and performance,* (pp. 131–159). San Diego: Academic Press.

MOLFESE, V. J., DILALLA, L. F., & BUNCE, D. (1997). Prediction of the intelligence test scores of 3– to 8–year-old children by home environment, socioeconomic status, and biomedical risks. *Merrill-Palmer Quarterly, 43*(2), 219–234.

MOLFESE, V. J., MODGLIN, A., & MOLFESE, D. L. (2003). The role of environment in the development of reading skills: A longitudinal study of preschool and school-age measures. *Journal of Learning Disabilities, 36*(1), 59–67.

MONTGOMERY, G. H., DUHAMEL, K. N., & REDD, W. H. (2000). A meta-analysis of hypnotically induced analgesia: How effective is hypnosis? *International Journal of Clinical & Experimental Hypnosis, 48*(2), 138–153.

MOORE, C. C., ROMNEY, A. K., & HSIA, T. (2002). Cultural, gender, and individual differences in perceptual and semantic structures of basic colors in Chinese and English. *Journal of Cognition & Culture, 2*(1), 1–28.

MORAHAN-MARTIN, J., & SCHUMACHER, P. (2003). Loneliness and social uses of the Internet. *Computers in Human Behavior, 19*(6), 659–671.

MORDOCK, B. (1997). Skepticism, data, risky shift, polarization, and attitude change: Their role in implementing innovations. *Psychologist-Manager Journal, 1*(1), 41–46.

MORGAN, D., ET AL. (2000). A peptide vaccination prevents memory loss in an animal model of Alzheimer's disease. *Nature, 408*(6815), 982–984.

MORO, C., & RODRIGUEZ, C. (2000). La creation des representations chez l'enfant au travers des processus de semiosis. *Enfance, 52*(3), 287–294.

MORRIS, W. N., MILLER, R. S., & SPANGENBERG, S. (1977). The effects of dissenter position and task difficulty on conformity and response conflict. *Journal of Personality, 45,* 251–256.

MORRISON, E. S., ET AL. (1980). *Growing up sexual.* New York: Van Nostrand Reinhold Co.

MORUZZI, G., & MAGOUN, H. W. (1949). Brain stem reticular formation and activation of the EEG. *Electroencephalography & Clinical Neurophysiology, 1,* 455–473.

MOSS, D. P. (2002). Cited in Clay, R. A. (2002). A renaissance for humanistic psychology. *Monitor on Psychology, 33*(8), 42–43.

MOSS, E., & ST-LAURENT, D. (2001). Attachment at school age and academic performance. *Developmental Psychology, 37*(6), 863–874.

MOTT, M. (2005). Did animals sense tsunami was coming? *National Geographic News.*

MOYÀ-SOLÀ, S., KÖHLER, M., ALBA, D. M., CASANOVAS-VILAR, I., & GALINDO, J. (2004). Pierolapithecus catalaunicus, a new middle Miocene great ape from Spain. *Science, 19,* 1339–1344.

MOZAFFARIAN, D., ET AL. (2003). Cereal, fruit, and vegetable fiber intake and the risk of cardiovascular disease in elderly individuals. *Journal of the American Medical Association, 289,* 1659–1666.

MUEHLBERGER, A., HERRMANN, M. J., WIEDEMANN, G., ELLGRING, H., & PAULI, P. (2001). Repeated exposure of flight phobics to flights in virtual reality. *Behaviour Research & Therapy, 39*(9), 1033–1050.

MUESER, K. T., & MCGURK, S. R. (2004). Schizophrenia. *Lancet, 363*(9426), 2063–2072.

MUIR, G. D. (2000). Early ontogeny of locomotor behaviour: A comparison between altricial and precocial animals. *Brain Research Bulletin, 53*(5), 719–726.

MUKAMAL, K. J., MACLURE, M., MULLER, J. E., SHERWOOD, J. B., & MITTLEMAN, M. A. (2001). Prior alcohol consumption and mortality following acute myocardial infarction. *Journal of the American Medical Association, 285*(15), 1965–1970.

MULLEN, B., ET AL. (1987). Newscasters' facial expressions and voting behavior of viewers. *Journal of Personality and Social Psychology, 51*(2), 291–295.

MULVIHILL, K. (2000, March 14). Many miss out on migraine remedies. *The New York Times online.*

MUNRO, G. D., & MUNRO, J. E. (2000). Using daily horoscopes to demonstrate expectancy confirmation. *Teaching of Psychology, 27*(2), 114–116.

MURRAY, H. A. (1938). *Explorations in personality.* New York: Oxford University Press.

MUSALLAM, S., CORNEIL, B. D., GREGER, B., SCHERBERGER, H., & ANDERSEN, R. (2004). Cognitive control signals for neural prosthetics. *Science, 305,* 258–262.

MUSSWEILER, T., & BODENHAUSEN, G. V. (2002). I know you are, but what am I? Self-evaluative consequences of judging in-group and out-group members. *Journal of Personality & Social Psychology, 82*(1), 19–32.

MUSTANSKI, B. S. (2004). Sex & the Internet: A guidebook for clinicians. *Archives of Sexual Behavior, 33*(5), 516–518.

MYERS, L. B., & BREWIN, C. R. (1994). Recall of early experience and the repressive coping style. *Journal of Abnormal Psychology, 103,* 288–292.

NABEL, E. G. (2003). Cardiovascular disease. *New England Journal of Medicine, 349*(1), 60–72.

NADER, K., SCHAFE, G. E., & LE DOUX, J. E. (2000). Fear memories require protein synthesis in the amygdala for reconsolidation after retrieval. *Nature, 406*(6797), 722–726.

NAGOURNEY, E. (2001, November 27). Mind and body: In heart disease, head can be an ally. *The New York Times,* p. F9.

NAGOURNEY, E. (2002, April 2). Neal E. Miller is dead at 92; studied brain and behavior. *The New York Times,* p. A21.

NAGTEGAAL, J. E., ET AL. (2000). Effects of melatonin on the quality of life in patients with delayed sleep phase syndrome. *Journal of Psychosomatic Research, 48*(1), 45–50.

NAGTEGAAL, M. (2004). The dilemma of free will in forensic psychology. *Psycholoog, 39*(1), 2004, 3–9.

NAIMI, T. S., ET AL. (2003a). Binge drinking among U.S. adults. *Journal of the American Medical Association, 289*(1), 70–75.

NAIMI, T. S., ET AL. (2003b). Definitions of binge drinking. *Journal of the American Medical Association, 289*(13), 1636.

NATIONAL CENTER FOR HEALTH STATISTICS. (2005, June 19). Self-inflicted injury/suicide. Atlanta: Centers for Disease Control and Prevention. http://www.cdc.gov/nchs/fastats/suicide.htm.

NATIONAL CENTER FOR INJURY PREVENTION AND CONTROL. (2005, June 19). Suicide: Fact sheet. http://www.cdc.gov/ncipc/factsheets/suifacts.htm.

NATIONAL SCIENCE FOUNDATION (2002). Science and technology: Public attitudes and public understanding. http://www.nsf.gov/sbe/srs/seind02/c7/c7h.htm.

NATIONAL SLEEP FOUNDATION (2001, November 19). Events of 9–11 took their toll on Americans' sleep, particularly for women, according to new National Sleep Foundation poll. http://www.sleepfoundation.org/whatsnew/crisis_poll.html.

NATIONAL SLEEP FOUNDATION (2005a). Helping yourself to a good night's sleep.http://www.sleepfoundation.org/publications/goodnights.html.

NATIONAL SLEEP FOUNDATION (2005b). *2005 Sleep in America Poll.* Washington, DC: National Sleep Foundation. http://www.sleepfoundation.org.

Nature editorial. (2004). *True lies. Nature, 428*(6984), 679.

NAVARRO, J. F., & MALDONADO, E. (2002). Acute and subchronic effects of MDMA ("ecstasy") on anxiety in male mice tested in the elevated plus-maze. *Progress in Neuro-Psychopharmacology & Biological Psychiatry, 26*(6), 1151–1154.

NEISSER, U. (1991). A case of misplaced nostalgia. *American Psychologist, 46*(1), 34–36.

NEISSER, U. (1993). Cited in Goleman, D. J. (1993, April 6). Studying the secrets of childhood memory. *The New York Times,* pp. C1, C11.

NEISSER, U. (1997a). Never a dull moment. *American Psychologist, 52,* 79–81.

NEISSER, U. (1997b). Cited in Sleek, S. (1997). Can "emotional intelligence" be taught in today's schools? *APA Monitor, 28*(6), 25.

NEISSER, U., ET AL. (1996). Intelligence: Knowns and unknowns. *American Psychologist, 51,* 77–101.

NELSON, K., HAMPSON, J., & SHAW, L. K. (1993). Nouns in early lexicons: Evidence, explanations, and implications. *Journal of Child Language, 20,* 228.

NESTADT, G., ET AL. (2000). A family study of obsessive-compulsive disorder. *Archives of General Psychiatry, 57*(4), 358–363.

NEUMARK-SZTAINER, D., ET AL. (2002a). Ethnic/racial differences in weight-related concerns and behaviors among adolescent girls and boys: Findings from Project EAT. *Journal of Psychosomatic Research, 53*(5), 963–974.

NEUMARK-SZTAINER, D., STORY, M., HANNAN, P. J., & CROLL, J. (2002b). Overweight status and eating patterns among adolescents: Where do youths stand in comparison with the Healthy People 2010 objectives? *American Journal of Public Health., 92*(5), 844–851.

NEVEUS, T., CNATTINGIUS, S., OLSSON, U., & HETTA, J. (2002). Sleep habits and sleep problems among a community sample of schoolchildren. *Journal of the American Academy of Child & Adolescent Psychiatry, 41*(7), 828.

NEWCOMB, M. D., & LOCKE, T. F. (2001). Intergenerational cycle of maltreatment: A popular concept obscured by methodological limitations. *Child Abuse & Neglect, 25*(9), 1219–1240.

NEWCOMB, P. (2005). Cited in Kolata, G. (2005, November 29). Preventing cancer: Does stress cause cancer? Probably not, research finds. *The New York Times online.*

NEWMAN, L. S., & BAUMEISTER, R. F. (1998). Abducted by aliens: Spurious memories of interplanetary masochism. In S. J. Lynn & K. M. McConkey (Eds), *Truth in memory* (pp. 284–303). New York: Guilford Press.

NEWPORT, E. L. (1998). Cited in Azar, B. (1998). Acquiring sign language may be more innate than learned. *APA Monitor, 29*(4), 12.

NEWPORT, F., & STRAUSBERG, M. (2001). Americans' belief in psychic and paranormal phenomena is up over last decade. Gallup News Service. Poll analyses. June 8. http://www.gallup.com/poll/releases.

NEZLEK, J. B., HAMPTON, C. P., & SHEAN, G. D. (2000). Clinical depression and day-to-day social interaction in a community sample. *Journal of Abnormal Psychology, 109*(1), 11–19.

NICHOLS, L. A., & NICKI, R. (2004). Development of a psychometrically sound Internet addiction scale: A preliminary step. *Psychology of Addictive Behaviors, 18*(4), 381–384.

NIMH. See National Institute of Mental Health.

Ninety-six percent of cosmos puzzles astronomers. (2003, June 20). Associated Press.

No, S. (2004). From prejudice to intergroup emotions: Differentiated reactions to social groups. *Asian Journal of Social Psychology, 7*(1), 119–122.

NOCK, M. K., & KAZDIN, A. E. (2002). Examination of affective, cognitive, and behavioral factors and suicide-related outcomes in children and young adolescents. *Journal of Community Psychology, 31*(1), 48–58.

NOLEN-HOEKSEMA, S. (2000). The role of rumination in depressive disorders and mixed anxiety/depressive symptoms. *Journal of Abnormal Psychology, 109*(3), 504–511.

NOLEN-HOEKSEMA, S. (2001). Gender differences in depression. *Current Directions in Psychological Science, 10*(5), 173–176.

NOLEN-HOEKSEMA, S., & KEITA, G. W. (2003). Women and depression: Introduction. *Psychology of Women Quarterly, 27*(2), 89–90.

NORTON, A. (2000, July 21). A drink a day keeps brain in tip-top shape. Reuters News Agency online.

NOVICK, L. R., & COTÉ, N. (1992). The nature of expertise in anagram solution. In *Proceedings of the Fourteenth Annual Conference of the Cognitive Science Society.* Hillsdale, NJ: Erlbaum.

NOWAKOWSKA, C., STRONG, C. M., SANTOSA, C. M., WANG, P. W., & KETTER, T. A. (2005). Temperamental commonalities and differences in euthymic mood disorder patients, creative controls, and healthy controls. *Journal of Affective Disorders, 85*(1–2), 207–215.

NOWICKI, S., & STRICKLAND, B. R. (1973). A locus of control scale for children. *Journal of Consulting and Clinical Psychology, 40*(1), 148–154.

NUGENT, A. (2004a, August 19). Application of Hebbian and anti-Hebbian learning to nanotechnology-based physical neural networks. U.S. Patent application #20040162796.

NUGENT, A. (2004b, September 30). Adaptive neural network utilizing nanotechnology-based components. U.S. Patent application #20040193558.

NULAND, S. (2005, February). Do you want to live forever? *MIT Technology Review, 108*(2), 36–45.

NURNBERGER, J. I., JR., ET AL. (2001). Evidence for a locus on chromosome 1 that influences vulnerability to alcoholism and affective disorder. *American Journal of Psychiatry, 158,* 718–724.

NURNBERGER, J. I., JR., ET AL. (2004). A family study of alcohol dependence: Coaggregation of multiple disorders in relatives of alcohol-dependent probands. *Archives of General Psychiatry, 61*(12), 1246–1256.

NYBERG, L., ET AL. (2000). Large scale neurocognitive networks underlying episodic memory. *Journal of Cognitive Neuroscience, 12*(1), 163–173.

Obesity is linked to birth defects. (1996, April 10). *The New York Times,* p. C10.

O'BRIEN, C. P. (1996). Recent developments in the pharmacotherapy of substance abuse. *Journal of Consulting and Clinical Psychology, 64,* 677–686.

O'DELL, C. D., & HOYERT, M. D. (2002). Active and passive touch: A research methodology project. *Teaching of Psychology, 29*(4), 292–294.

OEHMAN, A., & MINEKA, S. (2001). Fears, phobias, and preparedness: Toward an evolved module of fear and fear learning. *Psychological Review, 108*(3), 483–522.

OGAWA, K., NITTONO, H., & HORI, T. (2002). Brain potential associated with the onset and offset of rapid eye movement (REM) during REM sleep. *Psychiatry & Clinical Neurosciences, 56*(3), 259–260.

OHAYON, M. M., GUILLEMINAULT, C., & PRIEST, R. G. (1999). Night terrors, sleepwalking, and confusional arousals in the general population: Their frequency and relationship to other sleep and mental disorders. *Journal of Clinical Psychiatry, 60*(4), 268–276.

OHNO, H., URUSHIHARA, R., SEI, H., & MORITA, Y. (2002). REM sleep deprivation suppresses acquisition of classical eyeblink conditioning. *Sleep: Journal of Sleep Research & Sleep Medicine, 25*(8), 877–881.

OKAZAKI, S. (1997). Sources of ethnic differences between Asian American and White American college students on measures of depression and social anxiety. *Journal of Abnormal Psychology, 106*(1), 52–60.

OKTEDALEN, O., SOLBERG, E. E., HAUGEN, A. H., & OPSTAD, P. K. (2001). The influence of physical and mental training on plasma beta-endorphin level and pain perception after intensive physical exercise. *Stress & Health: Journal of the International Society for the Investigation of Stress, 17*(2), 121–127.

OLANOW, W. M. (2000, July). Clinical and pathological perspective on Parkinsonism. Paper presented to the World Alzheimer Congress 2000, Washington, DC.

OLDENBURG, D. (2005, January 9). A sense of doom: Animal instinct for disaster. *Washington Post.*

OLDS, J. (1969). The central nervous system and the reinforcement of behavior. *American Psychologist, 24,* 114–132.

OLDS, J., & MILNER, P. (1954). Positive reinforcement produced by electrical stimulation of the septal area and other regions of the rat brain. *Journal of Comparative and Physiological Psychology, 47,* 419–427.

OLTHOF, A., & ROBERTS, W. A. (2000). Summation of symbols by pigeons (*Columba livia*): The importance of number and mass of reward items. *Journal of Comparative Psychology, 114*(2), 158–166.

OMER, H., & ELITZUR, A. C. (2001). What would you say to the person on the roof? A suicide prevention text. *Suicide & Life-Threatening Behavior, 31*(2), 129–139.

ORPEN, C. (1995). The Multifactorial Achievement Scale as a predictor of salary growth and motivation among middle-managers. *Social Behavior & Personality, 23*(2), 159–162.

OSTATNÍKOVÁ, D., ET AL. (2002). Biological aspects of intellectual giftedness. *Studia Psychologica, 44*(1), 3–13.

OTANI, H., ET AL. (2005). Remembering a nuclear accident in Japan: Did it trigger flashbulb memories? *Memory, 13*(1), 6–20.

PABAN, V., SOUMIREU-MOURAT, B., & ALESCIO-LAUTIER, B. (2003). Behavioral effects of arginine-sup-8–vasopressin in the Hebb-Williams maze. *Behavioural Brain Research, 141*(1), 1–9.

PACE, S. (2004). A grounded theory of the flow experiences of Web users. International Journal of Human-Computer Studies, 60(3), 327–363.

PAPPAS, G., QUEEN, S., HADDEN, W., & FISHER, G. (1993). The increasing disparity of mortality between socioeconomic groups in the United States, 1960 and 1986. *New England Journal of Medicine, 329,* 103–109.

PARK, J., & BANAJI, M. R. (2000). Mood and heuristics: The influence of happy and sad states on sensitivity and bias in stereotyping. *Journal of Personality & Social Psychology, 78*(6), 1005–1023.

PARK, N., PETERSON, C., & SELIGMAN, M. E. P. (2005). *Character strengths in forty nations and fifty states.* Unpublished manuscript, University of Rhode Island.

PARKER, A. (2001). The ganzfeld: Suggested improvements of an apparently successful method for psi research. *European Journal of Parapsychology, 16,* 23–29.

PARR, L. A., WINSLOW, J. T., HOPKINS, W. D., & DE WAAL, F. B. M. (2000). Recognizing facial cues: Individual discrimination by chimpanzees (*Pan troglodytes*) and Rhesus monkeys (Macaca mulatta). *Journal of Comparative Psychology, 114*(1), 47–60.

PARROTT, A. (Ed.) (2003). Cognitive deficits and cognitive normality in recreational cannabis and ecstasy/MDMA users. *Human Psychopharmacology: Clinical & Experimental, 18*(2), 89–90.

PASIC, J., LEVY, W. C., & SULLIVAN, M. D. (2003). Cytokines in depression and heart failure. *Psychosomatic Medicine, 65*(2), 181–193.

PASTOR, L. H. (2004). Countering the psychological consequences of suicide terrorism. *Psychiatric Annals, 34*(9), 701–707.

PATRY, A. L., & PELLETIER, L. G. (2001). Extraterrestrial beliefs and experiences: An application of the theory of reasoned action. *Journal of Social Psychology, 141*(2), 199–217.

PATTERSON, D. R. (2004). Treating pain with hypnosis. *Current Directions in Psychological Science, 13*(6), 252–255.

PATTERSON, G. R., DISHION, T. J., & YOERGER, K. (2000). Adolescent growth in new forms of problem behavior: Macro- and micro-peer dynamics. *Prevention Science, 1*(1), 3–13.

PATTERSON, J. L. (2000). Observed and reported expressive vocabulary and word combinations in bilingual toddlers. *Journal of Speech, Language & Hearing Research, 43*(1), 121–128.

PAVLOV, I. (1927). *Conditioned reflexes.* London: Oxford University Press.

PEARS, K. C., & CAPALDI, D. M. (2001). Intergenerational transmission of abuse: A two-generational prospective study of an at-risk sample. *Child Abuse & Neglect, 25*(11), 1439–1461.

PELHAM, W. E., ET AL. (2002). Effects of methylphenidate and expectancy on children with ADHD: Behavior, academic performance, and attributions in a summer treatment program and regular classroom settings. *Journal of Consulting & Clinical Psychology, 70*(2), 320–335.

PENFIELD, W. (1969). Consciousness, memory, and man's conditioned reflexes. In K. H. Pribram (Ed.), *On the biology of learning.* New York: Harcourt Brace Jovanovich.

PENTNEY, A. R. (2001). An exploration of the history and controversies surrounding MDMA and MDA. *Journal of Psychoactive Drugs, 33*(3), 213–221.

PENTON-VOAK, I. S., & PERRETT, D. I. (2000). Female preference for male faces changes cyclically: Further evidence. *Evolution & Human Behavior, 21*(1), 39–48.

PEPLAU, L. A. (2003). Human sexuality: How do men and women differ? *Current Directions in Psychological Science, 12*(2), 37–40.

PERLS, F. S. (1971). *Gestalt therapy verbatim.* New York: Bantam.

PERNA, F. M., ANTONI, M. H., BAUM, A., GORDON, P., & SCHNEIDERMAN, N. (2003). Cognitive behavioral stress management effects on injury and illness among competitive athletes: A randomized clinical trial. *Annals of Behavioral Medicine, 25*(1), 66–73.

PERRAS, B., ET AL. (1997). Verbal memory after three months of intranasal vasopressin in healthy old humans. *Psychoneuroendocrinology, 22*(6), 387–396.

PERRETT, D. I. (1994). *Nature.* Cited in Brody, J. E. (1994, March 21). Notions of beauty transcend culture, new study suggests. *The New York Times,* p. A14.

PETERS, M., ET AL. (2004). Migraine and chronic daily headache management: A qualitative study of patients' perceptions. *Scandinavian Journal of Caring Sciences, 18*(3), 294–303.

PETERSON, C. (2002). Children's long-term memory for autobiographical events. *Developmental Review, 22*(3), 370–402.

PETERSON, C., PARK, N., & SELIGMAN, M. E. P. (2005). Orientations to happiness and life satisfaction: The full life versus the empty life. *Journal of Happiness Studies, 6*(1), 25–41.

PETERSON, C., & SELIGMAN, M. E. P. (2004). *Character strengths and virtues: A handbook and classification.* Washington, DC: American Psychological Association.

PETERSON, L. R., & PETERSON, M. J. (1959). Short-term retention of individual verbal items. *Journal of Experimental Psychology, 58,* 193–198.

PETRILL, S. A., & DEATER-DECKARD, K. (2004). The heritability of general cognitive ability: A within-family adoption design. *Intelligence, 32*(4), 403–409.

PETRILL, S. A., PIKE, A., PRICE, T., & PLOMIN, R. (2004). Chaos in the home and socioeconomic status are associated with cognitive development in early childhood: Environmental mediators identified in a genetic design. *Intelligence, 32*(5), 445–460.

PETROV, E. S., VARLINSKAYA, E. I., & SPEAR, N. E. (2001). Self-administration of ethanol and saccharin in newborn rats: Effects on suckling plasticity. *Behavioral Neuroscience, 115*(6), 1318–1331.

PETRY, N. M., MARTIN, B., COONEY, J. L., & KRANZLER, H. R. (2000). Give them prizes and they will come: Contingency management for treatment of alcohol dependence. *Journal of Consulting and Clinical Psychology, 68,* 250–257.

PETTY, R. E., FLEMING, M. A., & WHITE, P. H. (1999). Stigmatized sources and persuasion: Prejudice as a determinant of argument scrutiny. *Journal of Personality & Social Psychology, 76*(1), 19–34.

PETTY, R. E., WEGENER, D. T., & FABRIGAR, L. R. (1997). Attitudes and attitude change. *Annual Review of Psychology, 48,* 609–647.

PHALET, K., & SCHOENPFLUG, U. (2001). Intergenerational transmission of collectivism and achievement values in two acculturation contexts: The case of Turkish families in Germany and Turkish and Moroccan families in the Netherlands. *Journal of Cross-Cultural Psychology, 32*(2), 186–201.

PHINNEY, J. S. (1996). When we talk about American ethnic groups, what do we mean? *American Psychologist, 51,* 918–927.

PHINNEY, J. S. (2000). Identity formation across cultures: The interaction of personal, societal, and historical change. *Human Development, 43*(1), 27–31.

PHINNEY, J. S. (2003). Ethic identity and acculturation. In K. M. Chun, et al. (Eds.), *Acculturation: Advances in theory, measurement, and applied research* (pp. 63–81). Washington, DC: American Psychological Association.

PHINNEY, J. S. (2005). Ethnic identity in late modern times. *Identity, 5*(2), 187–194.

PHINNEY, J. S., CANTU, C. L., & KURTZ, D. A. (1997). Ethnic and American identity as predictors of self-esteem among African American, Latino, and White adolescents. *Journal of Youth & Adolescence, 26*(2), 165–185.

PHINNEY, J. S., & DEVICH-NAVARRO, M. (1997). Variations in bicultural identification among African American and Mexican American adolescents. *Journal of Research on Adolescence, 7*(1), 3–32.

PIAGET, J. (1932). *The moral judgment of the child.* London: Kegan Paul.

PIAGET, J. (1963). *The origins of intelligence in children.* New York: W. W. Norton.

PIAGET, J., & SMITH, L. (Trans.). (2000). Commentary on Vygotsky's criticisms of language and thought of the child and judgment and reasoning in the child. *New Ideas in Psychology, 18*(2–3), 241–259.

PICKENS, C. L., & HOLLAND, P. C. (2004). Conditioning and cognition. *Neuroscience & Biobehavioral Reviews, 28*(7), 651–661.

PIERCE, C. A. (1996). Body height and romantic attraction: A meta-analytic test of the male-taller norm. *Social Behavior & Personality, 24*(2), 143–149.

PIHL, R. O., PETERSON, J. B., & FINN, P. (1990). Inherited predisposition to alcoholism. *Journal of Abnormal Psychology, 99,* 291–301.

PILLARD, R. C., & WEINRICH, J. D. (1986). Evidence of familial nature of male homosexuality. *Archives of General Psychiatry, 43*(8), 808–812.

PIND, J., GUNNARSDOTTIR, E. K., & JOHANNESSON, H. S. (2003). Raven's Standard Progressive Matrices: New school age norms and a study of the test's validity. *Personality and Individual Differences, 34*(3), 375–386.

PINEL, J. P. J., ASSANAND, S., & LEHMAN, D. R. (2000). Hunger, eating, and ill health. *American Psychologist, 55*(10), 1105–1116.

PINKER, S. (1990). Language acquisition. In D. N. Osherson & H. Lasnik (Eds.), *An invitation to cognitive science: Language* (Vol. 1). Cambridge, MA: MIT Press, a Bradford Book.

PINKER, S. (1994a). *The language instinct.* New York: William Morrow.

PINKER, S. (1994b, June 19). Building a better brain. *The New York Times Book Review,* pp. 13–14.

PINKER, S. (1997). Words and rules in the human brain. *Nature, 387*(6633), 547–548.

PINKER, S. (1999). Out of the minds of babes. *Science, 283*(5398), 40–41.

PINKHAM, A. E., GLOEGE, A. T., FLANAGAN, S., & PENN, D. L. (2004). Group cognitive-behavioral therapy for auditory hallucinations: A pilot study. *Cognitive & Behavioral Practice, 11*(1), 93–98.

PINNELL, C. M., & COVINO, N. A. (2000). Empirical findings on the use of hypnosis in medicine: A critical review. *International Journal of Clinical & Experimental Hypnosis, 48*(2), 170–194.

PINQUART, M., & SÖRENSEN, S. (2000). Influences of socioeconomic status, social network, and competence on subjective well-being in later life: A meta-analysis. *Psychology and Aging, 15*(2), 187–224.

PLATANIA, J., & MORAN, G. P. (2001). Social facilitation as a function of mere presence of others. *Journal of Social Psychology, 141*(2), 190–197.

PLOMIN, R. (2000). Behavioural genetics in the 21st century. *International Journal of Behavioral Development, 24*(1), 30–34.

PLOMIN, R. (2001). Genetics and behaviour. *Psychologist, 14*(3), 134–139.

PLOMIN, R. (Ed.). (2002). *Behavioral genetics in the postgenomic era.* Washington, DC: American Psychological Association.

PLOMIN, R., & CRABBE, J. (2000). DNA. *Psychological Bulletin, 126*(6), 806–828.

PLOMIN, R., DEFRIES, J. C., MCCLEARN, G. E., & RUTTER, M. (1997). *Behavioral genetics.* New York: Freeman.

PLOMIN, R., EMDE, R., BRAUNGART, J. M., & CAMPOS, J. (1993). Genetic change and continuity from fourteen to twenty months: The MacArthur Longitudinal Twin Study. *Child Development, 64*(5), 1354–1376.

PLOMIN, R., & MCGUFFIN, P. (2003). Psychopathology in the postgenomic era. *Annual Review of Psychology, 54,* 205–228.

PLOMIN, R., OWEN, M. J., & McGUFFIN, P. (1994). The genetic basis of complex human behaviors. *Science, 264,* 1733–1739.

POINTER, S. C., & BOND, N. W. (1998). Context-dependent memory: Colour versus odor. *Chemical Senses, 23*(3), 359–362.

POL, H. E. H., ET AL. (2000). Prenatal exposure to famine and brain morphology in schizophrenia. *American Journal of Psychiatry, 157,* 1170–1172.

POPE, H. G., KOURI, E. M., & HUDSON, J. I. (2000). Effects of supraphysiologic doses of testosterone on mood and aggression in normal men: A randomized controlled trial. *Archives of General Psychiatry, 57,* 133–140.

POPE, J. H., ET AL. (2000). Missed diagnoses of acute cardiac ischemia in the emergency department. *The New England Journal of Medicine, 342,* 1163–1170.

PORTER, R. H., MAKIN, J. W., DAVIS, L. B., & CHRISTENSEN, K. M. (1992). Breast-fed infants respond to olfactory cues from their own mother and unfamiliar lactating females. *Infant Behavior and Development, 15,* 85–93.

POSADA, G., ET AL. (2002). Maternal caregiving and infant security in two cultures. *Developmental Psychology, 38*(1), 67–78.

POSTMES, T., SPEARS, R., & CIHANGIR, S. (2001). Quality of decision making and group norms. *Journal of Personality & Social Psychology, 80*(6), 918–930.

POWER, T. G., STEWART, C. D., HUGHES, S. O., & ARBONA, C. (2005). Predicting patterns of adolescent alcohol use: A longitudinal study. *Journal of Studies on Alcohol, 66*(1), 74–81.

POWERS, R. (2000, May 7). American dreaming. *The New York Times Magazine,* pp. 66–67.

POWERS, S. W., ET AL. (2001). A pilot study of one-session biofeedback training in pediatric headache. *Neurology, 56*(1), 133.

PRIOR, S. M., & WELLING, K. A. (2001). "Read in your head": A Vygotskian analysis of the transition from oral to silent reading. *Reading Psychology, 22*(1), 1–15.

PROCHASKA, J. O., & NORCROSS, J. C. (2003). *Systems of psychotherapy* (5th ed.). Belmont, CA: Wadsworth.

PRYCE, C. R., BETTSCHEN, D., BAHR, N. I., & FELDON, J. (2001). Comparison of the effects of infant handling, isolation, and nonhandling on acoustic startle, prepulse inhibition, locomotion, and HPA activity in the adult rat. *Behavioral Neuroscience, 115*(1), 71–83.

PULIDO, R., & MARCO, A. (2000) El efecto Barnum en estudiantes universitarios y profesionales de la psicologia en Mexico./The Barnum effect in university students and psychology professionals in Mexico. *Revista Intercontinental de Psicologia y Educacion. 2*(2), 59–66.

PULLEY, B. (1998, June 16). Those seductive snake eyes: Tales of growing up gambling. *The New York Times,* A1, A28.

PYRYT, M. C. (2000). Finding "g": Easy viewing through higher order factor analysis. *Gifted Child Quarterly, 44*(3), 190–192.

QIN, P., AGERBO, E., & MORTENSEN, P. B. (2003). Suicide risk in relation to socioeconomic, demographic, psychiatric, and familial factors: A national register-based study of all suicides in Denmark, 1981–1997. *American Journal of Psychiatry, 160,* 765–772.

QUALLS, S. H., & ABELES, N. (Eds.). (2000). *Psychology and the aging revolution: How we adapt to longer life* (pp. 3–9). Washington, DC: American Psychological Association.

QUILL, T. E. (2005, April 4). Terri Schiavo—A tragedy compounded. *New England Journal of Medicine,* http://www.nejm.org.

RACHMAN, S. (2000). Joseph Wolpe (1915–1997): Obituary. *American Psychologist, 55*(4), 431–432.

RADEL, M., ET AL. (2005). Haplotype-based localization of an alcohol dependence gene to the 5q34 y-aminobutyric acid type A gene cluster. *Archives of General Psychiatry, 62*(1), 47–55.

RAHMAN, Q., & WILSON, G. D. (2003). Born gay? The psychobiology of human sexual orientation. *Personality & Individual Differences, 34*(8), 1337–1382.

RAHMAN, Q., WILSON, G. D., & ABRAHAMS, S. (2004). Biosocial factors, sexual orientation and neurocognitive functioning. *Psychoneuroendocrinology, 29*(7), 867–881.

RAINE, A., ET AL. (2000). Reduced prefrontal gray matter volume and reduced autonomic activity in antisocial personality disorder. *Archives of General Psychiatry, 57*(2), 119–127.

RAINVILLE, P., ET AL. (2002). Hypnosis modulates activity in brain structures involved in the regulation of consciousness. *Journal of Cognitive Neuroscience, 14*(6), 887–901.

RAKOWSKI, W. (1995). Cited in Margoshes, P. (1995). For many, old age is the prime of life. *APA Monitor, 26*(5), 36–37.

RAMEL, W., GOLDIN, P. R. CARMONA, P. E., & McQUAID, J. R. (2004). The effects of mindfulness meditation on cognitive processes and affect in patients with past depression. *Cognitive Therapy & Research, 28*(4), 433–455.

RAMSEY, J. L., & LANGLOIS, J. H. (2002). Effects of the "beauty is good" stereotype on children's information processing. *Journal of Experimental Child Psychology, 81*(3), 320–340.

RAMSEY, J. L., ET AL. (2004). Origins of a stereotype: Categorization of facial attractiveness by 6-month-old infants. *Developmental Science, 7*(2), 201–211.

RANDEL, B., STEVENSON, H. W., & WITRUK, E. (2000). Attitudes, beliefs, and mathematics achievement of German and Japanese high school students. *International Journal of Behavioral Development, 24*(2), 190–198.

RAPPAPORT, N. B., McANULTY, D. P., & BRANTLEY, P. J. (1988). Exploration of the Type A behavior pattern in chronic headache sufferers. *Journal of Consulting and Clinical Psychology, 56,* 621–623.

RASENBERGER, J. (2004, February 8). Kitty, 40 years later. *The New York Times online.*

RATH, N. (2002). The power to feel fear and the one to feel happiness are the same. *Journal of Happiness Studies, 3*(1), 1–21.

RATHORE, S. S., ET AL. (2000). Race, sex, poverty, and the medical treatment of acute myocardial infarction in the elderly. *Circulation, 102,* 642–648.

RATHUS, J. H., & SANDERSON, W. C. (1999). *Marital distress: Cognitive behavioral interventions for couples.* Northvale, NJ: Jason Aronson.

RATHUS, S. A. (1973). A 30-item schedule for assessing assertive behavior. *Behavior Therapy, 4,* 398–406.

RATHUS, S. A., NEVID, J. S., & FICHNER-RATHUS, L. (2005). *Human sexuality in a world of diversity* (6th ed.). Boston: Allyn & Bacon.

RAUCHS, G., ET AL. (2004). Consolidation of strictly episodic memories mainly requires rapid eye movement sleep. *Sleep: Journal of Sleep & Sleep Disorders Research, 27*(3), 395–401.

RAYNOR, H., A., & EPSTEIN, L. H. (2001). Dietary variety, energy regulation, and obesity. *Psychological Bulletin, 127*(3), 325–341.

READY, T. (2000, June 7). Meditation apparently good for the heart as well as the mind. Healtheon/WebMD.

RECTOR, N. A., RICHTER, M. A., & BAGBY, R. M. (2005). The impact of personality on symptom expression in obsessive-compulsive disorder. *Journal of Nervous & Mental Disease, 193*(4), 231–236.

REED, J. M., & SQUIRE, L. R. (1997). Impaired recognition memory in patients with lesions limited to the hippocampal formation. *Behavioral Neuroscience, 111*(4), 667–675.

REEDER, G. D. (2001). On perceiving multiple causes and inferring multiple internal attributes. *Psychological Inquiry, 12*(1), 34–36.

REESE, C. M., & CHERRY, K. E. (2002). The effects of age, ability, and memory monitoring on prospective memory task performance. *Aging, Neuropsychology & Cognition, 9*(2), 98–113.

REGIER, T., KAY, P., & COOK, R. S. (2005). Focal colors are universal after all. *Proceedings of the National Academy of Sciences, 102*(23), 8386–8391.

REINECKE, M. A., DuBOIS, D. L., & SCHULTZ, T. M. (2001). Social problem solving, mood, and suicidality among inpatient adolescents. *Cognitive Therapy & Research, 25*(6), 743–756.

REIS, H. T., ET AL. (1990). What is smiling is beautiful and good. *European Journal of Social Psychology, 20,* 259–267.

REMPEL, M. W., & FISHER, R. J. (1998). Perceived threat, cohesion, and group problem solving in intergroup conflict. *International Journal of Conflict Management, 8*(3), 216–234.

RENNINGER, K. A., & WOZNIAK, R. H. (1985). Effect of interest on attentional shift, recognition, and recall in young children. *Developmental Psychology, 21,* 624–632.

RESCORLA, R. A. (1967). Inhibition of delay in Pavlovian fear conditioning. *Journal of Comparative & Physiological Psychology, 64*(1), 114–120.

RESCORLA, R. A. (1988). Pavlovian conditioning: It's not what you think it is. *American Psychologist, 43,* 151–160.

RESCORLA, R. A. (1999). Partial reinforcement reduces the associative change produced by nonreinforcement. *Journal of Experimental Psychology: Animal Behavior Processes, 25*(4), 403–414.

RESNICK, M., ET AL. (1992, March 24). *Journal of the American Medical Association.* Cited in Young Indians prone to suicide, study finds. *The New York Times,* March 25, 1992, p. D24.

REST, J. R. (1983). Morality. In P. H. Mussen, J. Flavell, & E. Markman (Eds.), *Handbook of child psychology: Vol. 3. Cognitive development.* New York: Wiley.

REZVANI, A. H., & LEVIN, E. D. (2001). Cognitive effects of nicotine. *Biological Psychiatry, 49*(3), 258–267.

RHEE, S. H., & WALDMAN, I. D. (2002). Genetic and environmental influences on antisocial behavior: A meta-analysis of twin and adoption studies. *Psychological Bulletin, 128*(3), 490–529.

RIBEIRO, S., & NICOLELIS, M. A. L. (2004). Reverberation, storage, and postsynaptic propagation of memories during sleep. *Learning & Memory, 11*(6), 686–696.

RICE, K. G., & DELLWO, J. P. (2001). Within-semester stability and adjustment correlates of the Multidimensional Perfectionism Scale. *Measurement & Evaluation in Counseling & Development, 34*(3), 146–156.

RICHARDS, J. C., HOF, A., & ALVARENGA, M. (2000). Serum lipids and their relationships with hostility and angry affect and behaviors in men. *Health Psychology, 19*(4), 393–398.

RICHARDSON, G. E. (2002). The metatheory of resilence and resiliency. *Journal of Clinical Psychology, 58*(3), 307–321.

RICKARD, T. C., ET AL. (2000). The calculating brain: An fMRI study. *Neuropsychologia, 38*(3), 325–335.

RILLING, J. K., WINSLOW, J. T., & KILTS, C. D. (2004). The neural correlates of mate competition in dominant male rhesus macaques. *Biological Psychiatry, 56*(5), 364–375.

RIQUE, J. (2004). Dissenting equals moral cultures in cyberspace: Sanctuaries of sexuality, conflict, and subversion. *PsycCRITIQUES, 49*(Suppl. 7).

RISO, L. P., ET AL. (2003). Cognitive aspects of chronic depression. *Journal of Abnormal Psychology, 112*(1), 72–80.

RIZZO, A. A., & SCHULTHEIS, M. T. (2002). Expanding the boundaries of psychology: The application of virtual reality. *Psychological Inquiry, 13*(2), 134–140.

ROBBINS, J. (2000, July 4). Virtual reality finds a real place as a medical aid. *The New York Times online.*

ROBBINS, S. B., LE, H., & LAUVER, K. (2005). Promoting successful college outcomes for all students. *Psychological Bulletin, 131*(3), 410–411.

ROBERSON, D., DAVIDOFF, J., & SHAPIRO, L. (2002). Squaring the circle: The cultural relativity of good shape. *Journal of Cognition & Culture, 2*(1), 29–51.

ROBINS, R. W., GOSLING, S. D., & CRAIK, K. H. (1999). An empirical analysis of trends in psychology. *American Psychologist, 54*(2), 117–128.

RODAFINOS, A., VUCEVIC, A., & SIDERIDIS, G. D. (2005). The effectiveness of compliance techniques: Foot in the door versus door in the face. *Journal of Social Psychology, 145*(2), 237–239.

ROELOFS, K., ET AL. (2002). Hypnotic susceptibility in patients with conversion disorder. *Journal of Abnormal Psychology, 111*(2), 390–395.

ROGERS, C. R. (1951). *Client-centered therapy.* Boston: Houghton Mifflin.

ROMERO, E., LUENGO, M. A., & SOBRAL, J. (2001). Personality and antisocial behaviour: Study of temperamental dimensions. *Personality & Individual Differences, 31*(3), 329–348.

RONCESVALLES, M. N. C., WOOLLACOTT, M. H., & JENSEN, J. L. (2001). Development of lower extremity kinetics for balance control in infants and young children. *Journal of Motor Behavior, 33*(2), 180–192.

ROSALES, G. A., NAVARRO, M. D., & CARDOSA, D. (2001). Variation in attitudes toward immigrants measured among Latino, African American, Asian, and Euro-American students. In M. López-Garza & D. R. Diaz (Eds.), *Asian and Latino immi-grants in a restructuring economy: The metamorphosis of Southern California* (pp. 353–366). Stanford, CA: Stanford University Press.

ROSENBAUM, D. E. (2000, May 16). On left-handedness, its causes and costs. *The New York Times,* pp. F1, F6.

ROSENBAUM, M. (2002). Ecstasy: America's new "reefer madness." *Journal of Psychoactive Drugs, 34*(2), 137–142.

ROSENSTEIN, D., & OSTER, H. (1988). Differential facial responses to four basic tastes. *Child Development, 59,* 1555–1568.

ROSENTHAL, E. (1993, July 20). Listening to the emotional needs of cancer patients. *The New York Times,* pp. C1, C7.

ROSER, M., & GAZZANIGA, M. S. (2004). Automatic brains—Interpretive minds. *Current Directions in Psychological Science, 13*(2), 56–59.

ROSS, J. L., ROELTGEN, D., FEUILLAN, P., KUSHNER, H., & CUTLER, W. B. (2000). Use of estrogen in young girls with Turner syndrome: Effects on memory. *Neurology, 54*(1), 164–170.

ROSS, S. R., LUTZ, C. J., & BAILLEY, S. E. (2002). Positive and negative symptoms of schizotypy and the Five-Factor Model: A domain and facet level analysis. *Journal of Personality Assessment, 79*(1), 53–72.

ROTH, B. L., HANIZAVAREH, S. M., & BLUM, A. E. (2004). Serotonin receptors represent highly favorable molecular targets for cognitive enhancement in schizophrenia and other disorders. *Psychopharmacology, 174*(1), 17–24.

ROTH, G. (2000). The evolution and ontogeny of consciousness. *Neural correlates of consciousness: Empirical and conceptual questions.* Cambridge, MA: MIT Press.

ROTHBAUM, B. O., & HODGES, L. F. (1999). The use of virtual reality exposure in the treatment of anxiety disorders. *Behavior Modification, 23*(4), 507–525.

ROTTER, J. B. (1990). Internal versus external control of reinforcement. *American Psychologist, 45,* 489–493.

ROTTON, J., & COHN, E. G. (2000). Violence is a curvilinear function of temperature in Dallas: A replication. *Journal of Personality and Social Psychology, 78*(6), 1074–1081.

ROTTON, J., & COHN, E. G. (2004). Outdoor temperature, climate control and criminal assault: The spatial and temporal ecology of violence. *Environment & Behavior, 36*(2), 276–306.

ROVEE-COLLIER, C. (1999). The development of infant memory. *Current Directions in Psychological Science, 8*(3), 80–85.

ROWE, J. B., OWEN, A. M., JOHNSRUDE, I. S., & PASSINGHAM, R. E. (2001). Imaging the mental components of a planning task. *Neuropsychologia, 39*(3), 315–327.

RUBINSTEIN, S., & CABALLERO, B. (2000). Is Miss America an undernourished role model? *Journal of the American Medical Association online, 283*(12).

RUDE, S. S., HERTEL, P. T., JARROLD, W., COVICH, J., & HEDLUND, S. (1999). Depression-related impairments in prospective memory. *Cognition & Emotion, 13*(3), 267–276.

RUDY, D., & GRUSEC, J. E. (2001). Correlates of authoritarian parenting in individualist and collectivist cultures and implications for understanding the transmission of values. *Journal of Cross-Cultural Psychology, 32*(2), 202–212.

RUFF, S., ET AL. (2003). Neural substrates of impaired categorical perception of phonemes in adult dyslexics: An fMRI study. *Brain & Cognition, 53*(2) 331–334.

RUITER, R. A. C., ABRAHAM, C., & KOK, G. (2001). Scary warnings and rational precautions: A review of the psychology of fear appeals. *Psychology & Health, 16*(6), 613–630.

RUSH, A. J., KHATAMI, M., & BECK, A. T. (1975). Cognitive and behavior therapy in chronic depression. *Behavior Therapy, 6,* 398–404.

RUSHTON, J. P., SKUY, M., & FRIDJHON, P. (2003). Performance on Raven's Advanced Progressive Matrices by African, East Indian, and White engineering students in South Africa. *Intelligence, 31*(2), 123–137.

RUTKOWSKI, G. K., GRUDER, C. L., & ROMER, D. (1983). Group cohesiveness, social norms, and bystander intervention. *Journal of Personality and Social Psychology, 44,* 545–552.

RUTKOWSKI, K. (2001). Anxiety, depression and nightmares in PTSD. *Archives of Psychiatry & Psychotherapy, 3*(2), 41–50.

RUTTER, M., & SILBERG, J. (2002). Gene-environment interplay in relation to emotional and behavioral disturbance. *Annual Review of Psychology, 53*(1), 463–490.

RYDER, A. G., ALDEN, L. E., & PAULHUS, D. L. (2000). Is acculturation unidimensional or bidimensional? A head-to-head comparison in the prediction of personality, self-identity, and adjustment. *Journal of Personality and Social Psychology, 79*(1), 49–65.

RYMER, R. (1993). *Genie: An abused child's flight from silence.* New York: HarperCollins.

SABBAGH, C. (2005). An integrative Etic-Emic approach to portraying the Halutziut system of societal equity: Comparing Israeli Jew and Israeli Arab perceptions of justice. *Journal of Cross-Cultural Psychology, 36*(1), 147–166.

SACHSSE, U., VON DER HEYDE, S., & HUETHER, G. (2002). Stress regulation and self-mutilation. *American Journal of Psychiatry, 159*(4), 672.

SACKS, F. M., ET AL. (2001). Effects on blood pressure of reduced dietary sodium and the Dietary Approaches to Stop Hypertension (DASH) Diet. *The New England Journal of Medicine, 344*(1), 3–10.

SAGI, A., KOREN-KARIE, N., GINI, M., ZIV, Y., & JOELS, T. (2002). Shedding further light on the effects of various types and quality of early child care on infant-mother attachment relationship: The Haifa Study of Early Child Care. *Child Development, 73*(4), 1166–1186.

SAGRESTANO, L. M., MCCORMICK, S. H., PAIKOFF, R. L., & HOLMBECK, G. N. (1999). Pubertal development and parent-child conflict in low-income, urban, African American adolescents. *Journal of Research on Adolescence, 9*(1), 85–107.

SALMON, P., ET AL. (2004). Mindfulness meditation in clinical practice. *Cognitive & Behavioral Practice, 11*(4), 434–446.

SALOVEY, P., ROTHMAN, A. J., DETWEILER, J. B., & STEWARD, W. T. (2000). Emotional states and physical health. *American Psychologist, 55,* 110–121.

SALOVEY, P., STROUD, L. R., WOOLERY, A., & EPEL, E. S. (2002). Perceived emotional intelligence, stress reactivity, and symptom reports: Further explorations using the trait meta-mood scale. *Psychology & Health, 17*(5), 611–627.

SALOVEY, P., & WEGENER, D. T. (2003). Communicating about health: Message framing, persuasion and health behavior. In J. Suls & K. A. Wallston (Eds.), *Social psychological foundations of health and illness* (pp. 54–81). Malden, MA: Blackwell Publishers.

SAMPAIO, D., ET AL. (2000). Representacoes sociais do suicidio em estudantes do ensino secundario. *Analise Psicologica, 18*(2), 139–155.

SANDERS, G. S. (1984). Effects of context cues on eyewitness identification responses. *Journal of Applied Social Psychology, 14,* 386–397.

SANDMAN, C., & CRINELLA, F. (1995) Cited in Margoshes, P. (1995). For many, old age is the prime of life. *APA Monitor, 26*(5), 36–37.

SANGRADOR, J. L., & YELA, C. (2000). "What is beautiful is loved": Physical attractiveness in love relationships in a representative sample. *Social Behavior & Personality, 28*(3), 207–218.

SANNA, L. J., & MEIER, S. (2000). Looking for clouds in a silver lining: Self-esteem, mental simulations, and temporal confidence changes. *Journal of Research in Personality, 34*(2), 236–251.

SANSONE, R. A., & LEVITT, J. L. (2005). Borderline personality and eating disorders. *Eating Disorders: The Journal of Treatment & Prevention, 13*(1), 71–83.

SANTEE, R. T., & MASLACH, C. (1982). To agree or not to agree: Personal dissent amid social pressure to conform. *Journal of Personality and Social Psychology, 42*(4), 690–700.

SANTONASTASO, P., FRIEDERICI, S., & FAVARO, A. (2001). Sertraline in the treatment of restricting anorexia nervosa: An open controlled trial. *Journal of Child & Adolescent Psychopharmacology, 11*(2), 143–150.

SARBIN, T. R., & COE, W. C. (1972). *Hypnosis*. New York: Holt, Rinehart and Winston.

SARTOR, J. J., BALTHAZART, J., & BALL, G. F. (2005). Coordinated and dissociated effects of testosterone on singing behavior and song control nuclei in canaries (Serinus canaria). *Hormones & Behavior, 47*(4), 467–476.

SARWER, D. B., & CRERAND, C. E. (2004). Body image and cosmetic medical treatments. *Body Image, 1*(1), 99–111.

SAUNDERS, K. W. (2003). Regulating youth access to violent video games: Three responses to First Amendment concerns. http://www.law.msu.edu/lawrev/2003-1/2-Saunders.pdf.

SAVAGE, C. R., ET AL. (2001). Prefrontal regions supporting spontaneous and directed application of verbal learning strategies. Evidence from PET. *Brain, 124*(1), 219–231.

SAVAGE-RUMBAUGH, E. S., ET AL. (1993). *Monographs of the Society for Research in Child Development, 58*(3–4), v-221.

SAVAGE-RUMBAUGH, E. S., & FIELDS, W. M. (2000). Linguistic, cultural and cognitive capacities of bonobos (Pan paniscus). *Culture & Psychology, 6*(2), 131–153.

SAVE THE CHILDREN. (2004). *State of the World's Mothers 2004*. http://www.savethechildren.org/mothers/report_2004/index.asp.

SAVIC, I., BERGLUND, H., & LINDSTRÖM, P. (2005). Brain response to putative pheromones in homosexual men. *Proceedings of the National Association of Sciences, 102*, 7356–7361.

SAWA, A., & SNYDER, S. H. (2002, April 26). Schizophrenia: Diverse approaches to a complex disease. *Science*, pp. 692–695.

SAXE, L., & BEN-SHAKHAR, G. (1999). Admissibility of polygraph tests: The application of scientific standards post-Daubert. *Psychology, Public Policy & Law, 5*(1), 203–223.

SCARR, S., & KIDD, K. K. (1983). Developmental behavior genetics. In M. Haith & J. J. Campos (Eds.), *Handbook of child psychology*. New York: Wiley.

SCARR, S., & WEINBERG, R. A. (1976). IQ test performance of Black children adopted by White families. *American Psychologist, 31*, 726–739.

SCARR, S., & WEINBERG, R. A. (1977). Intellectual similarities within families of both adopted and biological children. *Intelligence, 1*, 170–191.

SCARR, S., & WEINBERG, R. A. (1983). The Minnesota adoption studies: Genetic differences and malleability. *Child Development, 54*, 260–267.

SCHACHTER, S. (1959). *The psychology of affiliation*. Stanford, CA: Stanford University Press.

SCHACHTER, S., & SINGER, J. E. (1962). Cognitive, social, and physiological determinants of emotional state. *Psychological Review, 69*, 379–399.

SCHACTER, D. L. (1992). Understanding implicit memory: A cognitive neuroscience approach. *American Psychologist, 47*(4), 559–569.

SCHACTER, D. L. (1999). The seven sins of memory: Insights from psychology and cognitive neuroscience. *American Psychologist, 54*(3), 182–203.

SCHACTER, D. L. (2000). Memory: Memory systems. In A. E. Kazdin (Ed.), *Encyclopedia of psychology* (Vol. 5, pp. 169–172). Washington, DC: American Psychological Association.

SCHACTER, D. L., & BADGAIYAN, R. D. (2001). Neuroimaging of priming: New perspectives on implicit and explicit memory. *Current Directions in Psychological Science, 10*(1), 1–4.

SCHACTER, D. L., BADGAIYAN, R. D., & ALPERT, N. M. (1999). Visual word stem completion priming within and across modalities: A PET study. *Neuroreport: For Rapid Communication of Neuroscience Research, 10*(10), 2061–2065.

SCHACTER, D. L., COOPER, L. A., & TREADWELL, J. (1993). Preserved priming of novel objects across size transformation in amnesic patients. *Psychological Science, 4*(5), 331–335.

SCHACTER, D. L., DOBBINS, I. G., & SCHNYER, D. M. (2004). Specificity of priming: A cognitive neuroscience perspective. *Nature Reviews Neuroscience, 5*(11), 853–862.

SCHAIE, K. W., WILLIS, S. L., & CASKIE, G. I. L. (2004). The Seattle longitudinal study: Relationship between personality and cognition. *Aging, Neuropsychology & Cognition, 11*(2–3), 304–324.

SCHARFF, L., MARCUS, D. A., & MASEK, B. J. (2002). A controlled study of minimal-contact thermal biofeedback treatment in children with migraine. *Journal of Pediatric Psychology, 27*(2), 109–119.

SCHATZKIN, A., ET AL. (2005). Lack of effect of a low-fat, high-fiber, diet on the recurrence of colorectal adenomas. Polyp Prevention Trial Study Group. *New England Journal of Medicine, 342*, 1149–1155.

SCHIFFMAN, S. S. (2000). Taste quality and neural coding: Implications from psychophysics and neurophysiology. *Physiology and Behavior, 69*(1–2), 147–159.

SCHIFFMAN, S. S., ET AL. (2003). Effect of repeated presentation on sweetness intensity of binary and ternary mixtures of sweeteners. *Chemical Senses, 28*(3), 219–229.

SCHMIDT, N. B., ET AL. (2000). Evaluating gene × psychological risk factor effects in the pathogenesis of anxiety: A new model approach. *Journal of Abnormal Psychology, 109*(2), 308–320.

SCHMITT, D. P. (2003). Universal sex differences in the desire for sexual variety: Tests from 52 nations, 6 continents, and 13 islands. *Journal of Personality and Social Psychology, 85*(1), 85–104.

SCHMITT, D. P., SHACKELFORD, T. K., DUNTLEY, J., TOOKE, W., & BUSS, D. M. (2001). The desire for sexual variety as a key to understanding basic human mating strategies. *Personal Relationships, 8*(4), 425–455.

SCHNEIDER, K. J., BUGENTAL, J. F. T., & PIERSON, J. F. (Eds.). (2003). The handbook of humanistic psychology: Leading edges in theory, research, and practice. *Psychotherapy Research, 13*(1), 119–121.

SCHNEIDER, L. S., ET AL. (2003). An 8-week multicenter, parallel-group, double-blind, placebo-controlled study of sertraline in elderly outpatients with major depression. *American Journal of Psychiatry, 160*, 1277–1285.

SCHNEIDER, R. H., ET AL. (1995). A randomized controlled trial of stress reduction for hypertension in older African Americans. *Hypertension, 26*, 820.

SCHNEIDER, T. R., ET AL. (2001). Visual and auditory message framing effects on tobacco smoking. *Journal of Applied Social Psychology, 31*(4), 667–682.

SCHNEIDERMAN, N., IRONSON, G., & SIEGEL, S. D. (2005). Stress and health: Psychological, behavioral, and biological determinants. *Annual Review of Clinical Psychology, 1*(1), 607–628.

SCHREDL, M., CIRIC, P., GÖTZ, S., & WITTMANN, L. (2004). Typical dreams: Stability and gender differences. *Journal of Psychology: Interdisciplinary & Applied, 138*(6), 485–494.

SCHUCKIT, M. A. (1996). Recent developments in the pharmacotherapy of alcohol dependence. *Journal of Consulting and Clinical Psychology, 64*, 669–676.

SCHUCKIT, M. A., ET AL. (2001) A genome-wide search for genes that relate to a low level of response to alcohol. *Alcoholism: Clinical & Experimental Research, 25*(3), 323–329.

SCHUPF, N. (2000, July). Epidemiology of dementia in Down syndrome. Paper presented to the World Alzheimer Congress 2000, Washington, DC.

SCHUSTER, M. A., ET AL. (2001). A national survey of stress reactions after the September 11, 2001, terrorist attacks. *New England Journal of Medicine, 345*(20), 1507–1512.

SCHWARTZ, J., & WALD, M. L. (2003, March 9). NASA's curse? "Groupthink" is 30 years old, and still going strong. *The New York Times online*.

SCHWARTZ, J. R. L. (2004). Pharmacologic management of daytime sleepiness. *Journal of Clinical Psychiatry, 65*(Suppl. 16), 46–49.

SCHWARTZ, R. M., & GOTTMAN, J. M. (1976). Toward a task analysis of assertive behavior. *Journal of Consulting and Clinical Psychology, 44*, 910–920.

SCHWARTZER, R., & RENNER, B. (2000). Social-cognitive predictors of health behavior: Action self-efficacy and coping self-efficacy. *Health Psychology, 19*(5), 487–495.

SCHYNS, P. (2001). Income and satisfaction in Russia. *Journal of Happiness Studies, 2*(2), 173–204.

SCOTT, T. R. (2001). The role of taste in feeding. *Appetite, 37*(2), 111–113.

SCRUGGS, T. E., & MASTROPIERI, M. A. (1992). Remembering the forgotten art of memory. *American Educator, 16*(4), 31–37.

SEGAL, E. (2004). Incubation in insight problem solving. *Creativity Research Journal, 16*(1), 141–148.

SEGAL, N. L., & ROY, A. (2001). Suicidal attempts and ideation in twins whose co-twins' deaths were non-suicides: Replication and elaboration. *Personality & Individual Differences, 31*(3), 445–452.

SEGAN, C. J., BORLAND, R., & GREENWOOD, K. M. (2002). Do transtheoretical model measures predict the transition from preparation to action in smoking cessation? *Psychology & Health, 17*(4), 417–435.

SEIDMAN, S. M. (2003). The aging male: Androgens, erectile dysfunction, and depression. *Journal of Clinical Psychiatry, 64*(Suppl. 10), 31–37.

SELEMON, L. D., KLEINMAN, J. E., HERMAN, M. M., & GOLDMAN-RAKIC, P. S. (2002). Smaller frontal gray matter volume in postmortem schizophrenic brains. *American Journal of Psychiatry, 159*(12), 1983–1991.

SELEMON, L. D., MRZLJAK, J., KLEINMAN, J. E., HERMAN, M. M., & GOLDMAN-RAKIC, P. S. (2003). Regional specificity in the neuropathologic substrates of schizophrenia: A morphometric analysis of Broca's area 44 and area 9. *Archives of General Psychiatry, 60*(1), 69–77.

SELIGMAN, M. E. P. (1995). The effectiveness of psychotherapy: The *Consumer Reports* study. *American Psychologist, 50*, 965–974.

SELIGMAN, M. E. P. (1996, August). Predicting and preventing depression. Master lecture presented to the meeting of the American Psychological Association, Toronto.

SELIGMAN, M. E. P., STEEN, T. A., PARK, N., & PETERSON, C. (2005). Positive psychology progress: Empirical validation of interventions. *American Psychologist, 60*(5), 410–421.

SELYE, H. (1976). *The stress of life* (Rev. ed.). New York: McGraw-Hill.

SELYE, H. (1980). The stress concept today. In I. L. Kutash, et al. (Eds.), *Handbook on stress and anxiety*. San Francisco: Jossey-Bass.

SERRUYA, M. D., HATSOPOULOS, N. G., PANINSKI, L., FELLOWS, M. R., & DONOGHUE, J. P. (2002). Instant neural control of a movement signal. *Nature, 416*, 141–142.

SHADISH, W. R. (2002). Revisiting field experiments: Field notes for the future. *Psychological Methods, 7*(1), 3–18.

SHADISH, W. R., MATT, G. E., NAVARRO, A. M., & PHILLIPS, G. (2000). The effects of psychological therapies under clinically representative conditions: A meta-analysis. *Psychological Bulletin, 126*(4), 512–529.

SHAFRAN, R., COOPER, Z., & FAIRBURN, C. (2002). Clinical perfectionism: A cognitive–behavioural analysis. *Behaviour Research and Therapy, 40*(7), 773–791.

SHANKER, S. G., SAVAGE-RUMBAUGH, E. S., & TAYLOR, T. J. (1999). Kanzi: A new beginning. *Animal Learning & Behavior, 27*(1), 24–25.

SHAPIRO, F. (1989). Efficacy of the eye movement desensitization procedure in the treatment of traumatic memories. *Journal of Traumatic Stress, 2*, 199–223.

SHAPLEY, R., & HAWKEN, M. (2002). Neural mechanisms for color perception in the primary visual cortex. *Current Opinion in Neurobiology, 12*(4), 426–432.

SHAYLEY, A. Y., ET AL. (2000). Auditory startle response in trauma survivors with posttraumatic stress disorder: A prospective study. *American Journal of Psychiatry, 157*, 255–261.

SHAYWITZ, B. A., ET AL. (1995). Sex differences in the functional organization of the brain for language. *Nature, 373*, 607–609.

SHENAL, B. V., & HARRISON, D. W. (2003). Investigation of the laterality of hostility, cardiovascular regulation, and auditory recognition. *International Journal of Neuroscience, 113*(2), 205–222.

SHENEFELT, P. D. (2003). Hypnosis-facilitated relaxation using self-guided imagery during dermatologic procedures. *American Journal of Clinical Hypnosis, 45*(3), 225–232.

SHEPPERD, J. A., & KOCH, E. J. (2005). Pitfalls in teaching judgment heuristics. *Teaching of Psychology, 32*(1), 43–46.

SHERMAN, J. W., & FROST, L. A. (2000). On the encoding of stereotype-relevant information under cognitive load. *Personality & Social Psychology Bulletin, 26*(1), 26–34.

SHERRINGTON, J. M., HAWTON, K. E., FAGG, J., ANDREWS, B., & SMITH, D. (2001). Outcome of women admitted to hospital for depressive illness: Factors in the prognosis of severe depression. *Psychological Medicine, 31*(1), 115–125.

SHIFFMAN, S., ET AL. (2000). Dynamic effects of self-efficacy on smoking lapse and relapse. *Health Psychology, 19*(4), 315–323.

SHIMAMURA, A. P. (2002). Memory retrieval and executive control processes. In D. T. Stuss & R. T. Knight (Eds.), *Principles of frontal lobe function* (pp. 210–220). London: Oxford University Press.

SHNEIDMAN, E. S. (1998). Perspectives on suicidology: Further reflections on suicide and psychache. *Suicide & Life-Threatening Behavior, 28*(3), 245–250.

SHNEIDMAN, E. S. (2001). *Comprehending suicide*. Washington, DC: American Psychological Association.

SIEBER, J. E. (2004). Using our best judgment in conducting human research. *Ethics & Behavior, 14*(4), 297–304.

SIEGEL, J. M. (2002). The REM sleep–memory consolidation hypothesis. *Science, 294*(5544), 1058–1063.

SIKES, V., & SIKES, C. (2005). A response to May's commentary on "A look at EMDR: Technique, research and use with college students." *Journal of College Student Psychotherapy, 19*(3), 75–79.

SILVER, E. (1994). Cited in DeAngelis, T. (1994). Experts see little impact from insanity plea ruling. *APA Monitor, 25*(6), 28.

SILVER, J. M., YUDOFSKY, S. C., & ANDERSON, K. E. (2005). Aggressive disorders. In J. M. Silver, et al. (Eds.), *Textbook of traumatic brain injury* (pp. 259–277). Washington, DC: American Psychiatric Publishing.

SILVER, S. M., ROGERS, S., KNIPE, J., & COLELLI, G. (2005). EMDR therapy following the 9/11 terrorist attacks: A community-based intervention project in New York City. *International Journal of Stress Management, 12*(1), 29–42.

SIMISTER, J., & COOPER, C. (2005). Thermal stress in the U.S.A.: Effects on violence and on employee behaviour. *Stress & Health: Journal of the International Society for the Investigation of Stress, 21*(1), 3–15.

SIMONTON, D. K. (2000). Creativity: Cognitive, personal, developmental, and social aspects. *American Psychologist, 55*, 151–158.

SIMPSON, M., & PERRY, J. D. (1990). Crime and climate. *Environment and Behavior, 22*, 295–300.

SIMPSON, M. L., OLEJNIK, S., TAM, A. Y., & SUPATTATHUM, S. (1994). Elaborative verbal rehearsals and college students' cognitive performance. *Journal of Educational Psychology, 86*, 267–278.

SINGAREDDY, R. K., & BALON, R. (2002). Sleep in posttraumatic stress disorder. *Annals of Clinical Psychiatry, 14*(3), 183–190.

SINGH, R., & HO, S. Y. (2000). Attitudes and attraction: A new test of the attraction, repulsion and similarity-dissimilarity asymmetry hypotheses. *British Journal of Social Psychology, 39*(2), 197–211.

SINGLETARY, K. W., & GAPSTUR, S. M. (2001). Alcohol and breast cancer: Review of epidemiologic and experimental evidence and potential mechanisms. *Journal of the American Medical Association, 286*(17), 2143–2151.

SKELTON, C. (2005). Boys and schooling in the early years. *International Journal of Early Years Education, 13*(1), 83–84.

SKINNER, B. F. (1938). *The behavior of organisms: An experimental analysis*. New York: Appleton.

SKINNER, B. F. (1948). *Walden Two*. New York: Macmillan.

SKINNER, B. F. (1957). *Verbal behavior*. New York: Appleton.

SKINNER, B. F. (1972). *Beyond freedom and dignity*. New York: Knopf.

SKINNER, B. F. (1983). Intellectual self-management in old age. *American Psychologist, 38*, 239–244.

Sleepers suffer WTC nightmares. (2001, November 22). The Associated Press.

SLIFE, B., & RUBINSTEIN, J. (Eds.). (1992). *Taking sides: Clashing views on controversial psychological issues* (7th ed., pp. 2–21). Guilford, CT: Dushkin Publishing Group.

SLOBIN, D. I. (1983). Crosslinguistic evidence for basic child grammar. Paper presented at the biennial meeting of the Society for Research in Child Development, Detroit.

SLOMAN, S. A. (1996). The empirical case for two systems of reasoning. *Psychological Bulletin, 119*, 3–22.

SLOMAN, S. A., HARRISON, M. C., & MALT, B. C. (2002). Recent exposure affects artifact naming. *Memory & Cognition, 30*(5), 687–695.

SMETANA, J. G., DADDIS, C., & CHUANG, S. S. (2003). "Clean your room!" A longitudinal investigation of adolescent–parent conflict and conflict resolution in middle-class African American families. *Journal of Adolescent Research, 18*(6), 631–650.

SMILEY, J. (2000, May 7). The good life. *The New York Times magazine*, pp. 58–59.

SMITH, B. N., KERR, N. A., MARKUS, M. J., & STASSON, M. F. (2001). Individual differences in social loafing: Need for cognition as a motivator in collective performance. *Group Dynamics, 5*(2), 150–158.

SMITH, D. (2003a). Ten ways practitioners can avoid frequent ethical pitfalls. *Monitor on Psychology, 34*(1), 50–55.

SMITH, D. (2003b). Five principles for research ethics. *Monitor on Psychology, 34*(1), 56–60.

SMITH, D. (2003c). What you need to know about the new code: The chair of APA's Ethics Code Task Force highlights changes to the 2002 Ethics Code. *Monitor on Psychology online, 34*(1).

SMITH, G. F., & DORFMAN, D. (1975). The effect of stimulus uncertainty on the relationship between frequency of exposure and liking. *Journal of Personality and Social Psychology, 31*, 150–155.

SMITH, M. L., & GLASS, G. V. (1977). Meta-analysis of psychotherapy outcome studies. *American Psychologist, 32*, 752–760.

SMITH, R. A., & WEBER, A. L. (2005). Applying social psychology in everyday life. In F. W. Schneider, et al. (Eds.), *Applied social psychology: Understanding and addressing social and practical problems* (pp. 75–99). Thousand Oaks, CA: Sage Publications.

SMITH, T. W., & RUIZ, J. M. (2002). Course of coronary heart disease: Current status and implications for research and practice. *Journal of Consulting and Clinical Psychology, 70*(3), 548–568.

SMITH, V. (2000, February 16). Female heart, geography link shown. The Associated Press.

SMITS, T., STORMS, G., ROSSEEL, Y., & DE BOECK, P. (2002). Fruits and vegetables categorized: An application of the generalized context model. *Psychonomic Bulletin & Review, 9*(4), 836–844.

SOLL, J. B., & KLAYMAN, J. (2004). Overconfidence in interval estimates. *Journal of Experimental Psychology: Learning, Memory & Cognition, 30*(2), 299–314.

SOMERFIELD, M. R., & MCCRAE, R. R. (2000). Stress and coping research: Methodological challenges, theoretical advances, and clinical applications. *American Psychologist, 55*(6), 620–625.

SONG, I., LAROSE, R., EASTIN, M. S., & LIN, C. A. (2004). Internet gratifications and Internet addiction: On the uses and abuses of new media. *CyberPsychology & Behavior, 7*(4), 384–394.

SOOKMAN, D., PINARD, G., & BECK, A. T. (2001). Vulnerability schemas in obsessive-compulsive disorder. *Journal of Cognitive Psychotherapy, 15*(2), 109–130.

SORENSON, S. B., & RUTTER, C. M. (1991). Transgenerational patterns of suicide attempt. *Journal of Consulting and Clinical Psychology, 59*, 861–866.

SOSKINS, M., ROSENFELD, J. P., & NIENDAM, T. (2001). Peak to peak measurement of P300 recorded at 0.3 Hz high pass filter settings in intraindividual diagnosis. *International Journal of Psychophysiology, 40*(2), 173–180.

SOUSSIGNAN, R. (2002). Duchenne smile, emotional experience, and autonomic reactivity: A test of the facial feedback hypotheses. *Emotion, 2*(1), 52–74.

SPASOJEVIC, J., & ALLOY, L. B. (2001). Rumination as a common mechanism relating depressive risk factors to depression. *Emotion, 1*(1), 25–37.

SPENCER, M. B., NOLL, E., & CASSIDY, E. (2005). Monetary incentives in support of academic achievement: Results of a randomized field trial involving high-achieving, low-resource, ethnically diverse urban adolescents. *Evaluation Review, 29*(3), 199–222.

SPERLING, G. (1960). The information available in brief visual presentations. *Psychological Monographs, 74*, 1–29.

SPERANZA, M., ET AL. (2001). Obsessive compulsive disorders in eating disorders. *Eating Behaviors, 2*(3), 193–207.

SPERRY, R. W. (1982). Some effects of disconnecting the cerebral hemispheres. *Science, 217*(4566), 1223–1226.

SPERRY, R. W. (1998). A powerful paradigm made stronger. *Neuropsychologia, 36*(10), 1063–1068.

SPIERS, H. J., MAGUIRE, E. A., & BURGESS, N. (2001). Hippocampal amnesia. *Neurocase, 7*(5), 357–382.

SPRECHER, S. (1998). Insiders' perspectives on reasons for attraction to a close other. *Social Psychology Quarterly, 61*(4), 287–300.

SPRECHER, S., SULLIVAN, Q., & HATFIELD, E. (1994). Mate selection preferences. *Journal of Personality and Social Psychology, 66*(6), 1074–1080.

SQUIRE, L. R. (2004). Memory systems of the brain: A brief history and current perspective. *Neurobiology of Learning & Memory, 82*(3), 171–177.

STACY, A. W., BENTLER, P. M., & FLAY, B. R. (1994). Attitudes and health behavior in diverse populations. *Health Psychology, 13*, 73–85.

STAMLER, J., ET AL. (2000). Relationship of baseline serum cholesterol levels in 3 large cohorts of younger men to long-term coronary, cardiovascular, and all-cause mortality and to longevity. *Journal of the American Medical Association, 284*, 311–318.

STAMPFER, M. J., HU, F. B., MANSON, J. E., RIMM, E. B., & WILLETT, W. C. (2000). Primary prevention of coronary heart disease in women through diet and lifestyle. *New England Journal of Medicine, 343*(1), 16–22.

STAMPFER, M. J., KANG, J. H., CHEN, J., CHERRY, R., & GRODSTEIN, F. (2005). Effects of moderate alcohol consumption on cognitive function in women. *New England Journal of Medicine, 352*(3), 245–253.

STANGOR, C., SWIM, J. K., VAN ALLEN, K. L., & SECHRIST, G. B. (2002). Reporting discrimination in public and private contexts. *Journal of Personality & Social Psychology, 82*(1), 69–74.

STAPLEY, J. C. (2005). Situating sadness: Women's depression in social context. *Sex Roles, 52*(3–4), 261–262.

STASSER, G. (1999). A primer of social decision scheme theory: Models of group influence, competitive model-testing, and prospective modeling. *Organizational Behavior & Human Decision Processes, 80*(1), 3–20.

STEELE, C. M. (1994, October 31). Bizarre black IQ claims abetted by media. *San Francisco Chronicle.*

STEELE, C. M. (1996, August). The role of stereotypes in shaping intellectual identity. Master lecture presented to the meeting of the American Psychological Association, Toronto.

STEELE, C. M. (1997). A threat in the air: How stereotypes shape intellectual identity and performance. *American Psychologist, 52*, 613–629.

STEELE, C. M., & JOSEPHS, R. A. (1990). Alcohol myopia. *American Psychologist, 45*, 921–933.

STEIN, M. B., & KEAN, Y. M. (2000). Disability and quality of life in social phobia: Epidemiologic findings. *American Journal of Psychiatry, 157*, 1606–1613.

STEINBERG, L. (1996). *Beyond the classroom.* New York: Simon & Schuster.

STEINBERG, L. (2001). We know some things: Parent–adolescent relationships in retrospect and prospect. *Journal of Research on Adolescence, 11*(1), 1–19.

STEINBERG, L., BROWN, B. B., & DORNBUSCH, S. M. (1996). Ethnicity and adolescent achievement. *American Educator, 20*(2), 28–35.

STEINBERG, L., LAMBORN, S. D., DORNBUSCH, S. M., & DARLING, N. (1992). Impact of parenting practices on adolescent achievement: Authoritative parenting, school involvement, and encouragement to succeed. *Child Development, 63*, 1266–1281.

STERNBERG, R. J. (1988). Triangulating love. In R. J. Sternberg & M. J. Barnes (Eds.), *The psychology of love.* New Haven, CT: Yale University Press.

STERNBERG, R. J. (1997a). What does it mean to be smart? *Educational Leadership, 54*, 20–24.

STERNBERG, R. J. (1997b). The concept of intelligence and its role in lifelong learning and success. *American Psychologist, 52*, 1030–1037.

STERNBERG, R. J. (2000). Wisdom as a form of giftedness. *Gifted Child Quarterly, 44*(4), 252–260.

STERNBERG, R. J. (2001). What is the common thread of creativity? *American Psychologist, 56*(4), 360–362.

STERNBERG, R. J., LAUTREY, J., & LUBART, T. I. (2003). *Models of intelligence: International perspectives.* Washington, DC: American Psychological Association.

STERNBERG, R. J., & LUBART, T. I. (1995). *Defying the crowd: Cultivating creativity in a culture of conformity.* New York: Free Press.

STERNBERG, R. J., & LUBART, T. I. (1996). Investing in creativity. *American Psychologist, 51*, 677–688.

STERNBERG, R. J., & WILLIAMS, W. M. (1997). Does the Graduate Record Examination predict meaningful success in the graduate training of psychologists? *American Psychologist, 52*, 630–641.

STEVENS, S. E., HYNAN, M. T., & ALLEN, M. (2000). A meta-analysis of common factor and specific treatment effects across the outcome domains of the phase model of psychotherapy. *Clinical Psychology: Science and Practice, 7*, 273–290.

STEVENSON, H. W., LEE, S. Y., & STIGLER, J. W. (1986). Mathematics achievement of Chinese, Japanese, and American children. *Science, 231*, 693–699.

STEWART, A. E. (2005). Attributions of responsibility for motor vehicle crashes. *Accident Analysis & Prevention. 37*(4), 681–688.

STEWART, J. Y., & ARMET, E. (2000, April 3). Aging in America: Retirees reinvent the concept. *Los Angeles Times online.*

STICE, E., AKUTAGAWA, D., GAGGAR, A., & AGRAS, W. S. (2000a). Negative affect moderates the relation between dieting and binge eating. *International Journal of Eating Disorders, 27*(2), 218–229.

STICKGOLD, R., HOBSON, J. A., FOSSE, R., & FOSSE, M. (2001). Sleep, learning, and dreams: Off-line memory reprocessing. *Science, 294*(5544), 1052–1057.

STIER, D. S., & HALL, J. A. (1984). Gender differences in touch. *Journal of Personality and Social Psychology, 47*, 440–459.

STORM, L., & ERTEL, S. (2001). Does psi exist? Comments on Milton and Wiseman's (1999) meta-analysis of Ganzfeld research. *Psychological Bulletin, 127*(3), 424–433.

STORM, L., & ERTLE, S. (2002). The Ganzfeld debate continued: A response to Milton & Wiseman (2001). *Journal of Parapsychology, 66*(1), 73–82.

STRAUBE, E. R., & OADES, R. D. (1992). *Schizophrenia.* San Diego: Academic Press.

STRAUS, M. (1995). Cited in Collins, C. (1995, May 11). Spanking is becoming the new don't. *The New York Times*, p. C8.

STREET, A. E., KING, L. A., KING, D. W., & RIGGS, D. S. (2003). The associations among male-perpetrated partner violence, wives' psychological distress and children's behavior problems: A structural equation modeling analysis. *Journal of Comparative Family Studies, 34*(1), 23–40.

STRICKLAND, T. L., & GRAY, G. (2000). Neurobehavioral disorders and pharmacologic intervention: The significance of ethnobiological variation in drug responsivity. In E. Fletcher-Janzen, et al. (Eds.), Handbook of cross-cultural neuropsychology (pp. 361–369). Dordrecht, Netherlands: Kluwer Academic Publishers.

STRIEGEL-MOORE, R. H., & CACHELIN, F. M. (2001). Etiology of eating disorders in women. *Counseling Psychologist, 29*(5), 635–661.

STRIEGEL-MOORE, R. H., ET AL. (2003). Eating disorders in White and Black women. *American Journal of Psychiatry, 160*, 1326–1331.

STRIEGEL-MOORE, R. H., ET AL. (2004). Changes in weight and body image over time in women with eating disorders. *International Journal of Eating Disorders, 36*(3), 315–327.

STROELE, A., ET AL. (2002). GABA-sub(A) receptor-modulating neuroactive steroid composition in patients with panic disorder before and during paroxetine treatment. *American Journal of Psychiatry, 159*(1), 145–147.

STROM, J. C., & BUCK, R. W. (1979). Staring and participants' sex. *Personality and Social Psychology Bulletin, 5*, 114–117.

STROTE, J., LEE, J. E., & WECHSLER, H. (2002). Increasing MDMA use among college students: Results of a national survey. *Journal of the American Academy of Child & Adolescent Psychiatry, 41*(10), 1215.

STROUD, M. W., THORN, B. E., JENSEN, M. P., & BOOTHBY, J. L. (2000). The relation between pain beliefs, negative thoughts, and psychosocial functioning in chronic pain patients. *Pain, 84*(2–3), 347–352.

STUNKARD, A. J., HARRIS, J. R., PEDERSEN, N. L., & McLEARN, G. E. (1990). A separated twin study of the body mass index. *New England Journal of Medicine, 322*, 1483–1487.

STUTTS, J. C., WILKINS, J. W., OSBERG, J. S., & VAUGHN, B. V. (2003). Driver risk factors for sleep-related crashes. *Accident Analysis & Prevention, 35*(3), 321–331.

STUTZER, A. (2004). The role of income aspirations in individual happiness. *Journal of Economic Behavior & Organization, 54*(1), 89–109.

SUE, S. (1999). Science, ethnicity, and bias: Where have we gone wrong? *American Psychologist, 54*, 1070–1077.

SUFKA, K. J., & PRICE, D. D. (2002). Gate control theory reconsidered. *Brain & Mind, 3*(2), 277–290.

SULER, J. (2004). Computer and cyberspace "addiction." *International Journal of Applied Psychoanalytic Studies, 1*(4), 359–362.

SULER, J. (2005, March 29). Psychological qualities of cyberspace. http://www.rider.edu/~suler/psycyber/netself.html.

SULLIVAN, A. (2000, April 2). The He hormone. *The New York Times Magazine*, pp. 46–51ff.

SULLIVAN, E. V., ET AL. (2000). Contribution of alcohol abuse to cerebellar volume deficits in men with schizophrenia. *Archives of General Psychiatry, 57*, 894–902.

SULLIVAN, J. M. (2000). Cellular and molecular mechanisms underlying learning and memory impairments produced by cannabinoids. *Learning & Memory, 7*(3), 132–139.

SUTTLE, C. M., BANKS, M. S., & GRAF, E. W. (2002). FPL and sweep VEP to tritan stimuli in young human infants. *Vision Research, 42*(26), 2879–2891.

SUVISAARI, J., MAUTEMPS, N., HAUKKA, J., HOVI, T., & LÖÖNNQVIST, J. (2003). Childhood central nervous system viral infections and adult schizophrenia. *American Journal of Psychiatry, 160*, 1183–1185.

SUVISAARI, J. M., HAUKKA, J. K., & LOENNQVIST, J. K. (2002). "Seasonal fluctuation in schizophrenia": Dr. Suvisaari and colleagues reply. *American Journal of Psychiatry, 159*(3), 500.

SWENDSEN, J. D., ET AL. (2000). Mood and alcohol consumption: An experience sampling test of the self-medication hypothesis. *Journal of Abnormal Psychology, 109*(2), 198–204.

SWERDLOW, N. R., ET AL. (2003). Prestimulus modification of the startle reflex: Relationship to personality and psychological markers of dopamine function. *Biological Psychology, 62*(1), 17–26.

SWINYARD, W. R., KAU, A., & PHUA, H. (2001). Happiness, materialism, and religious experience in the U.S. and Singapore. *Journal of Happiness Studies, 2*(1), 13–32.

SZALA, M. (2002). Two-level pattern recognition in a class of knowledge-based systems. *Knowledge-Based Systems, 15*(1–2), 95–101.

TACON, A. M., MCCOMB, J., CALDERA, Y., & RANDOLPH, P. (2003). Mindfulness meditation, anxiety reduction, and heart disease: A pilot study. *Family & Community Health, 26*(1), 25–33.

TAFFE, M. A., ET AL. (2002). Cognitive performance of MDMA-treated rhesus monkeys: Sensitivity to serotonergic challenge. *Neuropsychopharmacology, 27*(6), 993–1005.

TAIT, R. C. (2005). Mind matters: Psychological interventions for chronic pain. *Clinical Journal of Pain, 21*(1), 106–107.

TAKAHASHI, T., ET AL. (2002). Melatonin alleviates jet lag symptoms caused by an 11-hour eastward flight. *Psychiatry & Clinical Neurosciences, 56*(3), 301–302.

TALWAR, S. K., ET AL. (2002). Behavioral Neuroscience. Rat navigation guided by remote control. *Nature, 417*(May 2), 37–38.

TANASESCU, M., ET AL. (2002). Exercise type and intensity in relation to coronary heart disease in men. *Journal of the American Medical Association, 288*, 1994–2000.

Tapes raise new doubts about "Sybil" personalities. (1998, August 19). *The New York Times online*.

TAYLOR, D. M., TILLERY, S. I., & SCHWARTZ, A. B. (2002). Direct cortical control of 3D neuroprosthetic devices. *Science, 296*, 1829–1832.

TAYLOR, D. J., & MCFATTER, R. M. (2003). Cognitive performance after sleep deprivation: Does personality make a difference? *Personality & Individual Differences, 34*(7), 1179–1193.

TAYLOR, M. A., & FINK, M. (2003). Catatonia in psychiatric classification: A home of its own. *American Journal of Psychiatry, 160*, 1233–124.

TAYLOR, S., ET AL. (2003). Comparative efficacy, speed, and adverse effects of three PTSD treatments: Exposure therapy, EMDR, and relaxation training. *Journal of Consulting and Clinical Psychology, 71*, 330–338.

TAYLOR, S. E. (2000). Cited in Goode, E. (2000, May 19). Response to stress found that's particularly female. *The New York Times*, p. A20.

TAYLOR, S. E., KEMENY, M. E., REED, G. M., BOWER, J. E., & GRUENEWALD, T. L. (2000a). Psychological resources, positive illusions, and health. *American Psychologist, 55*(1), 99–109.

TAYLOR, S. E., ET AL. (2000b). Biobehavioral responses to stress in females: Tend-and-befriend, not fight-or-flight. *Psychological Review, 107*(3), 411–429.

TEACHOUT, T. (2000, April 2). For more artists, a fine old age. *The New York Times online*.

TELLER, D. Y. (1998). Spatial and temporal aspects of infant color vision. *Vision Research, 38*(21), 3275–3282.

TENENBAUM, H. R., & LEAPER, C. (2002). Are parents' gender schemas related to their children's gender-related cognitions? A meta-analysis. *Developmental Psychology, 38*(4), 615–630.

TENNEN, H., & AFFLECK, G. (2000). The perception of personal control: Sufficiently important to warrant careful scrutiny. *Personality & Social Psychology Bulletin, 26*(2), 152–156.

TERRACE, H. S. (1979, November). How Nim Chimpsky changed my mind. *Psychology Today*, pp. 65–76.

TETLOCK, P. E., & MCGRAW, A. P. (2005). Theoretically framing relational framing. *Journal of Consumer Psychology, 15*(1), 35–37.

THASE, M. E. (2004). Therapeutic alternatives for difficult-to-treat depression: A narrative review of the state of the evidence. *CNS Spectrums, 9*(11, Suppl. 12), 808–821.

THOM, A., SARTORY, G., & JÖHREN, P. (2000). Comparison between one-session psychological treatment and benzodiazepine in dental phobia. *Journal of Consulting and Clinical Psychology, 68*(3), 378–387.

THOMAS, A. K., & LOFTUS, E. F. (2002). Creating bizarre false memories through imagination. *Memory & Cognition, 30*(3), 423–431.

THOMAS, S. L., SKITKA, L. J., CHRISTEN, S., & JURGENA, M. (2002). Social facilitation and impression formation. *Basic & Applied Social Psychology, 24*(1), 67–70.

THOMPSON, C. P., ANDERSON, L. P., & BAKEMAN, R. A. (2000). Effects of racial socialization and racial identity on acculturative stress in African American college students. *Cultural Diversity and Ethnic Minority Psychology, 6*(2), 196–210.

THOMPSON, P. M., ET AL. (2001). Mapping adolescent brain change reveals dynamic wave of accelerated gray matter loss in very early-onset schizophrenia. *Proceedings of the National Academy of Sciences, 98*(20), 11650–11655.

THURSTONE, L. L. (1938). Primary mental abilities. *Psychometric Monographs, 1*.

THURSTONE, L. L., & THURSTONE, T. G. (1963). *SRA primary abilities*. Chicago: SRA.

TIGNER, R. B., & TIGNER, S. S. (2000). Triarchic theories of intelligence: Aristotle and Sternberg. *History of Psychology, 3*(2), 168–176.

TKACHUK, G. A., & MARTIN, G. L. (1999). Exercise therapy for patients with psychiatric disorders: Research and clinical implications. *Professional Psychology: Research and Practice, 30*(3), 275–282.

TOLMAN, E. C., & HONZIK, C. H. (1930). Introduction and removal of reward, and maze performance in rats. *University of California Publications in Psychology, 4*, 257–275.

TONG, H. (2001). Loneliness, depression, anxiety, and the locus of control. *Chinese Journal of Clinical Psychology, 9*(3), 196–197.

TORMALA, Z. L., & PETTY, R. E. (2004). Source credibility and attitude certainty: A metacognitive analysis of resistance to persuasion. *Journal of Consumer Psychology, 14*(4), 427–442.

TOWNSEND, E., ET AL. (2001). The efficacy of problem-solving treatments after deliberate self-harm: Meta-analysis of randomized controlled trials with respect to depression, hopelessness and improvement in problems. *Psychological Medicine, 31*(6), 979–988.

TRAFTON, J. G., ALTMANN, E. M., BROCK, D. P., & MINTZ, F. E. (2003). Preparing to resume an interrupted task: Effects of prospective goal encoding and retrospective rehearsal. *International Journal of Human-Computer Studies, 58*(5), 583–603.

TRIANDIS, H. C. (2001). Individualism–collectivism and personality. *Journal of Personality, 69*(6), 907–924.

TRIANDIS, H. C., & SUH, E. M. (2002). Cultural influences on personality. *Annual Review of Psychology, 53*(1), 133–160.

TRINH, N., ET AL. (2003). Efficacy of cholinesterase inhibitors in the treatment of neuropsychiatric symptoms and functional impairment in Alzheimer disease. *Journal of the American Medical Association, 289*, 210–216.

TROBST, K. K., COLLINS, R. L., & EMBREE, J. M. (1994). The role of emotion in social support provision. *Journal of Social and Personal Relationships, 11*, 45–62.

TRULL, T. J., STEPP, S. D., & DURRETT, C. A. (2003). Research on borderline personality disorder: An update. *Current Opinion in Psychiatry, 16*(1), 77–82.

TRYON, R. C. (1940). Genetic differences in maze learning in rats. *Yearbook of the National Society for Studies in Education, 39*, 111–119.

TSAI, G., & COYLE, J. T. (2002). Glutamatergic mechanisms in schizophrenia. *Annual Review of Pharmacology & Toxicology, 42*, 165–179.

TSANG, Y. C. (1938). Hunger motivation in gastrectomized rats. *Journal of Comparative Psychology, 26*, 1–17.

TSOU, M., & LIU, J. (2001). Happiness and domain satisfaction in Taiwan. *Journal of Happiness Studies, 2*(3), 269–288.

TULVING, E. (1985). How many memory systems are there? *American Psychologist, 40*, 385–398.

TULVING, E., & MARKOWITSCH, H. J. (1998). Episodic and declarative memory: Role of the hippocampus. *Hippocampus, 8*(3), 198–204.

TURK, D. C., & OKIFUJI, A. (2002). Psychological factors in chronic pain: Evolution and revolution. *Journal of Consulting and Clinical Psychology, 70*(3), 678–690.

TURKINGTON, D., DUDLEY, R., WARMAN, D. M., & BECK, A. T. (2004). Cognitive-behavioral therapy for schizophrenia: A review. *Journal of Psychiatric Practice, 10*(1), 5–16.

TURNBULL, C. M. (1961). Some observations regarding the experiences and behavior of the BaMbuti Pygmies. *American Journal of Psychology, 74*, 304–308.

TURNER, A. M., & GREENOUGH, W. T. (1985). Differential rearing effects on rat visual cortex synapses: I. Synaptic and neuronal density and synapses per neuron. *Brain Research, 329*, 195–203.

TURNER, M. E., & PRATKANIS, A. R. (1998). A social identity maintenance model of groupthink. *Organizational Behavior & Human Decision Processes, 73*(2–3), 210–235.

TVERSKY, A., & KAHNEMAN, D. (1982). Judgment

under uncertainty. In D. Kahneman, P. Slovic, & A. Tversky (Eds.), *Judgment under uncertainty: Heuristics and biases.* New York: Cambridge University Press.

Tyrka, A. R., Waldron, I., Graber, J. A., & Brooks-Gunn, J. (2002). Prospective predictors of the onset of anorexic and bulimic syndromes. *International Journal of the Eating Disorders, 32*(3), 282–290.

Ukestad, L. K., & Wittrock, D. A. (1996). Pain perception and coping in female tension headache sufferers and headache-free controls. *Health Psychology, 15,* 65–68.

Ulett, G. A., & Wedding, D. (2003). Electrical stimulation, endorphins, and the practice of clinical psychology. *Journal of Clinical Psychology in Medical Settings, 10*(2), 129–131.

Updegraff, J. A., Taylor, S. E., Kemeny, M. E., & Wyatt, G. E. (2002). Positive and negative effects of HIV infection in women with low socioeconomic resources. *Personality & Social Psychology Bulletin, 28*(3), 382–394.

USBC (U.S. Bureau of the Census). (2000). *Statistical abstract of the United States* (120th ed.). Washington, DC: U.S. Government Printing Office.

USBC (U.S. Bureau of the Census). (2002). *Statistical abstract of the United States* (122nd ed.). Washington, DC: U.S. Government Printing Office.

USBC (U.S. Bureau of the Census). (2003). *Statistical abstract of the United States* (123rd ed.). Washington, DC: U.S. Government Printing Office.

U.S. Department of Education, NCES. (2004). *Digest of Education Statistics 2003* (NCES 2004–024).

USDHHS (U.S. Department of Health and Human Services). (2004). Child Abuse and Neglect Fatalities: Statistics and Interventions *Child Maltreatment 2002* (U.S. Department of Health and Human Services, 2004). http://nccanch.acf.hhs.gov/pubs/factsheets/fatality.cfm.

Utter, J., Neumark-Sztainer, D., Wall, M., & Story, M. (2003). Reading magazine articles about dieting and associated weight control behaviors among adolescents. *Journal of Adolescent Health, 32*(1), 78–82.

Uzakov, S., Frey, J. U., & Korz, V. (2005). Reinforcement of rat hippocampal LTP by holeboard training. *Learning & Memory, 12,* 165–171.

Valmaggia, L. R., Van Der Gaag, M., Tarrier, N., Pijnenborg, M., & Sloof, C. J. (2005). Cognitive-behavioural therapy for refractory psychotic symptoms of schizophrenia resistant to atypical antipsychotic medication: Randomised controlled trial. *British Journal of Psychiatry, 186*(4), 324–330.

Van Anders, S. M., & Hampson, E. (2005). Testing the prenatal androgen hypothesis: Measuring digit ratios, sexual orientation, and spatial abilities in adults. *Hormones & Behavior, 47*(1), 92–98.

Van Anders, S. M., Chernick, A. B., Chernick, B. A., Hampson, E., & Fisher, W. A. (2005). Preliminary clinical experience with androgen administration for pre- and postmenopausal women with hypoactive sexual desire. *Journal of Sex & Marital Therapy, 31*(3), 173–185.

Vandenbergh, J. G. (1993). Cited in Angier, N. (1993, August 24). Female gerbil born with males is found to be begetter of sons. *The New York Times,* p. C4.

van de Wetering, S., Bernstein, D. M., & Loftus, E. F. (2002). Public education against false memories: A modest proposal. *International Journal of Cognitive Technology, 7*(2), 4–7.

van Hiel, A., Kossowska, M., & Mervielde, I. (2000). The relationship between Openness to Experience and political ideology. *Personality & Individual Differences, 28*(4), 741–751.

Vasterling, J. J., et al. (2002). Attention, learning, and memory performances and intellectual resources in Vietnam veterans: PTSD and no disorder comparisons. *Neuropsychology, 16*(1), 5–14.

Veale, D. (2004). Advances in a cognitive behavioural model of body dysmorphic disorder. *Body Image, 1*(1), 113–125.

Veenstra-Vanderweele, J., & Cook, E. H. (2003). Genetics of childhood disorders: XLVI. Autism, part 5: Genetics of autism. *Journal of the American Academy of Child and Adolescent Psychiatry, 42*(1), 116–118.

Velting, D. M., Rathus, J. H., & Miller, A. L. (2000). MACI personality scale profiles of depressed adolescent suicide attempters: A pilot study. *Journal of Clinical Psychology, 56*(10), 1381–1385.

Vernberg, E. M., La Greca, A. M., Silverman, W. K., & Prinstein, M. J. (1996). Prediction of posttraumatic stress symptoms in children after Hurricane Andrew. *Journal of Abnormal Psychology, 105,* 237–248.

Vernon, D., et al. (2003). The effect of training distinct neurofeedback protocols on aspects of cognitive performance. *International Journal of Psychophysiology, 47*(1), 75–85.

Video games calm kids before surgery. (2004, December 10). Associated Press.

Vik, P. W., Carrello, P., Tate, S. R., & Field, C. (2000). Progression of consequences among heavy-drinking college students. *Psychology of Addictive Behaviors, 14*(2), 91–101.

Villa, K. K., & Abeles, N. (2000). Broad spectrum intervention and the remediation of prospective memory declines in the able elderly. *Aging & Mental Health, 4*(1), 21–29.

Volkow, N. D., et al. (2001a). Association of dopamine transporter reduction with psychomotor impairment in methamphetamine abusers. *American Journal of Psychiatry, 158,* 377–382.

Volkow, N. D., et al. (2001b). Higher cortical and lower subcortical metabolism in detoxified methamphetamine abusers. *American Journal of Psychiatry, 158,* 383–389.

Volz, J. (2000). Successful aging: The second 50. *Monitor on Psychology, 30*(1), 24–28.

Von Békésy, G. (1957). The ear. *Scientific American, 197*(2), 66–78.

Vorobyev, V. A., et al. (2004). Linguistic processing in visual and modality-nonspecific brain areas: PET recordings during selective attention. *Cognitive Brain Research, 20*(2), 309–322.

Vygotsky, L. (1978). *Mind in society: The development of higher psychological processes.* Cambridge, MA: Harvard University Press.

Vygotsky, L. S. (1962). *Thought and language.* Cambridge, MA: MIT Press.

Wadden, T. A., Brownell, K. D., & Foster, G. D. (2002). Obesity: Responding to the global epidemic. *Journal of Consulting and Clinical Psychology, 70*(3), 510–525.

Wade, N. (2005, May 10). For gay men, an attraction to a different kind of sweat. *The New York Times online.*

Wade, T. D., Bulik, C. M., Neale, M., & Kendler, K. S. (2000). Anorexia nervosa and major depression: Shared genetic and environmental risk factors. *American Journal of Psychiatry, 157*(3), 469–471.

Wagar, B. M., & Thagard, P. (2004). Spiking Phineas Gage: A neurocomputational theory of cognitive-affective integration in decision making. *Psychological Review, 111*(1), 67–79.

Wagner, R. K. (1997). Intelligence, training, and employment. *American Psychologist, 52*(10), 1059–1069.

Walk, R. D., & Gibson, E. J. (1961). A comparative and analytical study of visual depth perception. *Psychological Monographs, 75*(15).

Walker, E., Kestler, L., Bollini, A., & Hochman, K. M. (2004). Schizophrenia: Etiology and course. *Annual Review of Psychology, 55,* 401–430.

Wall, T. L., Carr, L. G., & Ehlers, C. L. (2003). Protective association of genetic variation in alcohol dehydrogenase with alcohol dependence in Native American Mission Indians. *American Journal of Psychiatry, 160,* 41–46.

Walle, A. H. (2004). Native Americans and alcoholism therapy: The example of Handsome Lake as a tool of recovery. *Journal of Ethnicity in Substance Abuse, 3*(2), 55–79.

Walsh, B. T., et al. (2000). Fluoxetine for bulimia nervosa following poor response to psychotherapy. *American Journal of Psychiatry, 157,* 1332–1334.

Walther, E., Nagengast, B., & Trasselli, C. (2005). Evaluative conditioning in social psychology: Facts and speculations. *Cognition & Emotion, 19*(2), 175–196.

Wang, C. (2002). Emotional intelligence, general self-efficacy, and coping style of juvenile delinquents. *Chinese Mental Health Journal, 16*(8), 565–567.

Wang, J., Lin, W., & Chen, Z. (2002). The effects of psychological intervention on chemotherapy of cancer patients. *Psychological Science* (China), *25*(5), 517–519.

Wang, Q. (2003). Infantile amnesia reconsidered: A cross-cultural analysis. *Memory, 11*(1), 65–80.

Wang, X., et al. (2000). Longitudinal study of earthquake-related PTSD in a randomly selected community sample in North China. *American Journal of Psychiatry, 157,* 1260–1266.

Wann, D. L., Royalty, J., & Roberts, A. (2000). The self-presentation of sports fans: Investigating the importance of team identification and self-esteem. *Journal of Sport Behavior, 23*(2), 198–206.

Wann, D. L., & Schrader, M. P. (2000). Controllability and stability in the self-serving attributions of sport spectators. *Journal of Social Psychology, 140*(2), 160–168.

Ward, A., Lyubomirsky, S., Sousa, L., & Nolen-Hoeksema, S. (2003). Can't quite commit: Rumination and uncertainty. *Personality & Social Psychology Bulletin, 29*(1), 96–107.

Warman, D. M., & Beck, A. T. (2003). Cognitive behavioral therapy for schizophrenia: An overview of treatment. *Cognitive & Behavioral Practice, 10*(3), 248–254.

Warman, D. M., & Cohen, R. (2000). Stability of aggressive behaviors and children's peer relationships. *Aggressive Behavior, 26*(4), 277–290.

Warman, D. M., Grant, P., Sullivan, K., Caroff, S., & Beck, A. T. (2005). Individual and group cognitive-behavioral therapy for psychotic disorders: A pilot investigation. *Journal of Psychiatric Practice, 11*(1), 27–34.

Wartik, N. (2000, June 25). Depression comes out of hiding. *The New York Times,* pp. MH1, MH4.

Watanabe, A., Nakao, K., Tokuyama, M., &

TAKEDA, M. (2005). Prediction of first episode of panic attack among white-collar workers. *Psychiatry & Clinical Neurosciences, 59*(2), 119–126.

WATERMAN, A. S., ET AL. (2003). Predicting the subjective experience of intrinsic motivation: The roles of self-determination, the balance of challenges and skills, and self-realization values. *Personality & Social Psychology Bulletin, 29*(11), 1447–1458.

WATERS, M. (2000). Psychologists spotlight growing concern of higher suicide rates among adolescents. *Monitor on Psychology, 31*(6), 41.

WATSON, D., HUBBARD, B., & WIESE, D. (2000). Self-other agreement in personality and affectivity: The role of acquaintanceship, trait visibility, and assumed similarity. *Journal of Personality & Social Psychology, 78*(3), 546–558.

WATSON, J. B. (1913). Psychology as the behaviorist views it. *Psychological Review, 20*, 158–177.

WATSON, J. B. (1924). *Behaviorism.* New York: W. W. Norton.

WATSON, J. B., & RAYNER, R. (1920). Conditioned emotional reactions. *Journal of Experimental Psychology, 3*, 1–14.

WATSON, M., HAVILAND, J. S., GREER, S., DAVIDSON, J., & BLISS, J. M. (1999). Influence of psychological response on survival in breast cancer: A population-based cohort study. *The Lancet, 354*(9187), 1331–1336.

WEAVER, C. A., III, & KRUG, K. S. (2004). Consolidation-like effects in flashbulb memories: Evidence from September 11, 2001. *American Journal of Psychology, 117*(4), 517–530.

WEBSTER, J. D. (2003). An exploratory analysis of a self-assessed wisdom scale. *Journal of Adult Development, 10*(1), 13–22.

WECHSLER, D. (1975). Intelligence defined and undefined. *American Psychologist, 30*, 135–139.

WEGENER, D. T., PETTY, R. E., DETWEILER-BEDELL, B. T., & JARVIS, W. B. G. (2001). Implications of attitude change theories for numerical anchoring: Anchor plausibility and the limits of anchor effectiveness. *Journal of Experimental Social Psychology, 37*(1), 62–69.

WEINER, R. D. (2000). Retrograde amnesia with electroconvulsive therapy. *Archives of General Psychiatry online, 57*(6).

WEINMANN, M., BADER, J., ENDRASS, J., & HELL, D. (2001). Sind Kompetenz- und Kontrollueberzeugungen depressionsabhaengig? Eine Verlaufsuntersuchung. *Zeitschrift fuer Klinische Psychologie und Psychotherapie, 30*(3), 153–158.

WEISS, A., ET AL. (2005). Cross-sectional age differences in personality among Medicare patients aged 65 to 100. *Psychology and Aging, 20*(1), 182–185.

WELLS, G. L., & OLSEN, E. A. (2003). Eyewitness testimony. *Annual Review of Psychology, 54*, 277–295.

WERNER, P., OLCHOVSKY, D., SHEMI, G., & VERED, I. (2003). Osteoporosis health-related behaviors in secular and orthodox Israeli Jewish women. *Maturitas, 46*(4), 283–294.

WEST, R., & CRAIK, F. I. M. (1999). Age-related decline in prospective memory: The roles of cue accessibility and cue sensitivity. *Psychology & Aging, 14*(2), 264–272.

WETZLER, S. E., & SWEENEY, J. A. (1986). Childhood amnesia. In D. C. Rubin (Ed.), *Autobiographical memory.* New York: Cambridge University Press.

WHANG, L. S., & CHANG, G. (2004). Lifestyles of virtual world residents: Living in the on-line game "Lineage." *CyberPsychology & Behavior, 7*(5), 592–600.

WHEELER, M. A., & McMILLAN, C. T. (2001). Focal retrograde amnesia and the episodic-semantic distinction. *Cognitive, Affective & Behavioral Neuroscience, 1*(1), 22–36.

WHEELER, M. E., & TREISMAN, A. M. (2002). Binding in short-term visual memory. *Journal of Experimental Psychology: General, 131*(1), 48–64.

WHITE, C. L., KASHIMA, K., BRAY, G. A., & YORK, D. A. (2000b). Effect of a serotonin 1–A agonist on food intake of Osborne-Mendel and S5B/PI rats. *Physiology & Behavior, 68*(5), 715–722.

WHITFIELD, K. E., WEIDNER, G., CLARK, R., & ANDERSON, N. B. (2002). Sociodemographic diversity and behavioral medicine. *Journal of Consulting and Clinical Psychology, 70*(3), 463–481.

WHORF, B. (1956). *Language, thought, and reality.* New York: Wiley.

WIDIGER, T. A., & COSTA, P. T., JR. (1994). Personality and personality disorders. *Journal of Abnormal Psychology, 103*, 78–91.

WIDYANTO, L., & McMURRAN, M. (2004). The psychometric properties of the Internet Addiction Test. *CyberPsychology & Behavior, 7*(4), 443–450.

WIEBE, R. E., & McCABE, S. B. (2002). Relationship perfectionism, dysphoria, and hostile interpersonal behaviors. *Journal of Social & Clinical Psychology, 21*(1), 67–91.

WIENS, A. N., & MENUSTIK, C. E. (1983). Treatment outcome and patient characteristics in an aversion therapy program for alcoholism. *American Psychologist, 38*, 1089–1096.

WILCOX, D. T., RICHARDS, F., & O'KEEFFE, Z. C. (2004). Resilience and risk factors associated with experiencing childhood sexual abuse. *Child Abuse Review, 13*(5), 338–352.

WILFORD, J. N. (2005, February 15). For Neanderthals and Homo Sapiens, was it de-lovely? *The New York Times online.*

WILGOREN, J. (2000, March 15). Effort to curb binge drinking in college falls short. *The New York Times,* p. A16.

WILHELM, F. H., GEVIRTZ, R., & ROTH, W. T. (2001). Respiratory dysregulation in anxiety, functional cardiac, and pain disorders: Assessment, phenomenology, and treatment. *Behavior Modification, 25*(4), 513–545.

WILKINSON, D., & ABRAHAM, C. (2004). Constructing an integrated model of the antecedents of adolescent smoking. *British Journal of Health Psychology, 9*(3), 315–333.

WILLETT, W. C. (2002). Balancing lifestyle and genomics research for disease prevention. *Science, 296*(5568), 695–698.

WILLETT, W. C. (2005). Diet and cancer: An evolving picture. *Journal of the American Medical Association, 293*(2), 233–234.

WILLIAMS, J. E., ET AL. (2000). Anger proneness predicts coronary heart disease risk : Prospective analysis from the Atherosclerosis Risk In Communities (ARIC) study. *Circulation, 101*(17), 2034–2039.

WILLIAMS, M. S., THOMSEN, S. R., & McCOY, J. K. (2003). Looking for an accurate mirror: A model for the relationship between media use and anorexia. *Eating Behaviors, 4*(2), 127–134.

WILLIAMS, R. B., BAREFOOT, J. C., & SCHNEIDERMAN, N. (2003). Psychosocial risk factors for cardiovascular disease: More than one culprit at work. *Journal of the American Medical Association, 290*(16), 2190–2192.

WILLIAMS, S. M., ET AL. (2000). Combinations of variations in multiple genes are associated with hypertension. *Hypertension, 36*, 2–6.

WILLOUGHBY, T., WOOD, E., & KHAN, M. (1994). Isolating variables that impact on or detract from the effectiveness of elaboration strategies. *Journal of Educational Research, 86*, 279–289.

WILLS, T. A., SANDY, J. M., & YAEGER, A. M. (2002). Moderators of the relation between substance use level and problems: Test of a self-regulation model in middle adolescence. *Journal of Abnormal Psychology, 111*(1), 3–21.

WILSON, G. T., FAIRBURN, C. C., AGRAS, W. S., WALSH, B. T., & KRAEMER, H. (2002). Cognitive-behavioral therapy for bulimia nervosa: Time course and mechanisms of change. *Journal of Consulting & Clinical Psychology, 70*(2), 267–274.

WILSON, K. D., & FARAH, M. J. (2003). When does the visual system use viewpoint-invariant representations during recognition? *Cognitive Brain Research, 16*(3), 399–415.

WILSON, R. S. (1983). The Louisville twin study: Developmental synchronies in behavior. *Child Development, 54*, 298–316.

WILSON, W., ET AL. (2000). Brain morphological changes and early marijuana use: A magnetic resonance and positron emission tomography study. *Journal of Addictive Diseases, 19*(1), 1–22.

WINERMAN, L. (2005). A virtual cure. *Monitor on Psychology, 36*(7), 87–89.

WINOCUR, G., ET AL. (2000). Cognitive rehabilitation in clinical neuropsychology. *Brain & Cognition, 42*(1), 120–123.

WINZELBERG, A. J., ET AL. (2000). Effectiveness of an Internet-based program for reducing risk factors for eating disorders. *Journal of Consulting and Clinical Psychology, 68*, 346–350.

WISEMAN, R., & SMITH, M. D. (2002). Assessing the role of cognitive and motivational biases in belief in the paranormal. *Journal of the Society for Psychical Research, 66*(868), 157–166.

WOLKIN, A., ET AL. (2003). Inferior frontal white matter anisotropy and negative symptoms of schizophrenia: A diffusion tensor imaging study. *American Journal of Psychiatry, 160*, 572–574.

WOLOSHYN, V. E., PAIVIO, A., & PRESSLEY, M. (1994). Use of elaborative interrogation to help students acquire information consistent with prior knowledge and information inconsistent with prior knowledge. *Journal of Educational Psychology, 86*, 79–89.

WOLPAW, J. R., BIRBAUMER, N., McFARLAND, D. J., PFURTSCHELLER, G., & VAUGHAN, T. M (2002). Brain-computer interfaces for communication and control. *Clinical Neurophysiology, 113*, 767–791.

WOOD, W. (2000). Attitude change: Persuasion and social influence. *Annual Review of Psychology, 51*, 539–570.

WOODY, E., & SZECHTMAN, H. (2000). Hypnotic hallucinations: Towards a biology of epistemology. *Contemporary Hypnosis, 17*(1), 4–14.

WRITING COMMITTEE FOR THE ENRICHD INVESTIGATORS. (2003). Effects of treating depression and low perceived social support on clinical events after myocardial infarction: The Enhancing Recovery in Coronary Heart Disease Patients (ENRICHD) Randomized Trial. *Journal of the American Medical Association, 289*(23), 3106–3116.

WU, P., ET AL. (2001). Factors associated with use of mental health services for depression by children and adolescents. *Psychiatric Services, 52*(2), 189–195.

WUNDAR, E. (2003). Self-attribution, sun-sign traits, and the alleged role of favourableness as a moderator variable: Long-term effect or artefact? *Personality & Individual Differences, 35*(8), 1783–1789.

XIE, Y., & GOYETTE, K. (2003). Social mobility and the educational choices of Asian Americans. *Social Science Research, 32*(3), 467–498.

XIN, X. ET AL. (2001). Effects of alcohol reduction on blood pressure. *Hypertension, 38,* 1112.

YACOUBIAN, G. S. (2003). Correlates of ecstasy use among high school seniors surveyed through Monitoring the Future. *Drugs: Education, Prevention & Policy, 10*(1), 65–72.

YAFFE, K., ET AL. (2000). Cognitive decline in women in relation to non-protein-bound oestradiol concentrations. *The Lancet, 356,* 708–712.

YANG, O. S. (2000). Guiding children's verbal plan and evaluation during free play: An application of Vygotsky's genetic epistemology to the early childhood classroom. *Early Childhood Education Journal, 28*(1), 3–10.

YANG, Y., ET AL. (2005). Volume reduction in prefrontal gray matter in unsuccessful criminal psychopaths. *Biological Psychiatry, 57*(10), 1103–1108.

YANOVSKI, S. Z., & YANOVSKI, J. A. (2002). Drug therapy: Obesity. *New England Journal of Medicine, 346,* 591–602.

YARBROUGH, M. M., WILLIAMS, D. P., & ALLEN, M. M. (2004). Risk factors associated with osteoporosis in Hispanic women. *Journal of Women & Aging, 16*(3–4), 91–104.

YATHAM, L. N., ET AL. (2000). Brain serotonin$_2$ receptors in major depression: A positron emission tomography study. *Archives of General Psychiatry, 57,* 850–858.

YBARRA, G. J., PASSMAN, R. H., & EISENBERG, C. S. L. (2000). The presence of security blankets or mothers (or both) affects distress during pediatric examinations. *Journal of Consulting and Clinical Psychology, 68,* 322–330.

YEH, C., & CHANG, T. (2004). Understanding the multidimensionality and heterogeneity of the Asian American experience. *PsycCRITIQUES.*

YEHUDA, R. (2002). Post-traumatic stress disorder. *New England Journal of Medicine, 346*(2), 108–114.

YEHUDA, R. (2003). Hypothalamic-pituitary-adrenal alterations in PTSD: Are they relevant to understanding cortisol alterations in cancer? *Brain, Behavior & Immunity, 17*(Suppl. 1), S73–S83.

YEN, S., ZLOTNICK, C., & COSTELLO, E. (2002). Affect regulation in women with borderline personality disorder traits. *Journal of Nervous & Mental Disease, 190*(10), 693–696.

YESAVAGE, J. A., ET AL. (2002). Modeling the prevalence and incidence of Alzheimer's disease and mild cognitive impairment. *Journal of Psychiatric Research, 36*(5), 281–286.

YIP, T., & CROSS, W. E., JR. (2004). A daily diary study of mental health and community involvement outcomes for three Chinese American social identities. *Cultural Diversity & Ethnic Minority Psychology, 10*(4), 394–408.

YOKOTA, F., & THOMPSON, K. M. (2000). Violence in G-rated animated films. *Journal of the American Medical Association, 283,* 2716–2720.

YOUNG, E. A., ET AL. (2003). Mineralocorticoid receptor function in major depression. *Archives of General Psychiatry, 60,* 24–28.

ZAGAR, K., & RUBENSTEIN, A. (2002). *The inside story on teen girls.* Washington, DC: American Psychological Association.

ZAHAVI, A. (2003). Anniversary essay: Indirect selection and individual selection in sociobiology: My personal views on theories of social behavior. *Animal Behaviour, 65*(5), 859–863.

ZAJONC, R. B. (1968). Attitudinal effects of mere exposure. *Journal of Personality and Social Psychology, Monograph Supplement 2*(9), 1–27.

ZAJONC, R. B. (1980). Compresence. In P. Paulus (Ed.), *The psychology of group influence.* Hillsdale, NJ: Erlbaum.

ZAJONC, R. B. (2001). Mere exposure: A gateway to the subliminal. *Current Directions in Psychological Science, 10*(6), 224–228.

ZALA, S. M., & PENN, D. J. (2004). Abnormal behaviours induced by chemical pollution: A review of the evidence and new challenges. *Animal Behaviour, 68*(4), 649–664.

ZAND, D. H., ET AL. (2004) The recruitment process: Factors that predict African American adolescents initial engagement into an alcohol, tobacco, and other drug prevention study. *Journal of Ethnicity in Substance Abuse, 3*(2), 43–54.

ZEICHNER, A., PARROTT, D. J., & FREY, F. C. (2003). Gender differences in laboratory aggression under response choice conditions. *Aggressive Behavior, 29*(2), 95–106.

ZIEGLER, D. J., & HAWLEY, J. L. (2001). Relation of irrational thinking and the Pessimistic Explanatory Style. *Psychological Reports, 88*(2), 483–488.

ZIGLER, E. (1999). Head Start is not child care. *American Psychologist, 54*(2), 142.

ZIMBARDO, P. G. (2004). A situationist perspective on the psychology of evil: Understanding how good people are transformed into perpetrators. In A. G. Miller (Ed.), *The social psychology of good and evil* (pp. 21–50). New York: Guilford Press.

ZIMBARDO, P. G., LABERGE, S., & BUTLER, L. D. (1993). Psychophysiological consequences of unexplained arousal. *Journal of Abnormal Psychology, 102,* 466–473.

ZIMMER, C. (2002–2003). Searching for your inner chimp. *Natural History, 112*(December, 2002–January, 2003).

ZIMPRICH, D., & MARTIN, M. (2002). Can longitudinal changes in processing speed explain longitudinal age changes in fluid intelligence? *Psychology & Aging, 17*(4), 690–695.

ZIZAK, D. M., & REBER, A. S. (2004). Implicit preferences: The role(s) of familiarity in the structural mere exposure effect. *Consciousness & Cognition: An International Journal, 13*(2), 336–362.

ZOLA, S., SQUIRE, L. R., & LOMBROSO, P. J. (2003). Genetics of childhood disorders: XLIX. Learning and memory, part 2: Multiple memory systems. *Journal of the American Academy of Child & Adolescent Psychiatry, 42*(4), 504–506.

ZUCKER, A. N., OSTROVE, J. M., & STEWART, A. J. (2002). College-educated women's personality development in adulthood: Perceptions and age differences. *Psychology & Aging, 17*(2), 236–244.

ZUCKERMAN, M. (1971). Dimensions of sensation seeking. *Journal of Consulting and Clinical Psychology, 36*(1), 45–52.

glossary

A–B problem The issue of how well we can predict behavior on the basis of attitudes.

Absolute threshold The minimal amount of energy that can produce a sensation.

Accommodation According to Piaget, the modification of schemas so that information inconsistent with existing schemas can be integrated or understood.

Acculturation The process of adaptation in which immigrants and native groups identify with a new, dominant culture by learning about that culture and making behavioral and attitudinal changes.

Acetylcholine (ACh) A neurotransmitter involved in muscle contractions and memory formation.

Acoustic code Mental representation of information as a sequence of sounds.

Acquired drives Drives that are acquired through experience, or learned.

Acrophobia Fear of high places.

Action potential The electrical impulse that provides the basis for the conduction of a neural impulse along an axon of a neuron.

Activating effect The arousal-producing effects of sex hormones that increase the likelihood of sexual behavior.

Activation–synthesis model The view that dreams reflect activation of cognitive activity by the reticular activating system and synthesis of this activity into a pattern by the cerebral cortex.

Actor–observer effect The tendency to attribute our own behavior to situational factors but to attribute the behavior of others to dispositional factors.

Acute stress disorder A disorder, like PTSD, that is characterized by feelings of anxiety and helplessness and caused by a traumatic event. Acute stress disorder occurs within a month of the event and lasts from 2 days to 4 weeks.

Adolescence The period of life bounded by puberty and the assumption of adult responsibilities.

Affect (AFF-ekt) Feeling or emotional response, particularly as suggested by facial expression and body language.

Afferent neurons Neurons that transmit messages from sensory receptors to the spinal cord and brain. Also called *sensory neurons.*

Afterimage The lingering visual impression made by a stimulus that has been removed.

Agoraphobia Fear of open, crowded places.

Alarm reaction The first stage of the general adaptation syndrome (GAS), which is triggered by the impact of a stressor and characterized by sympathetic activity.

Algorithm A systematic procedure for solving a problem that works invariably when it is correctly applied.

All-or-none principle The fact that a neuron fires an impulse of the same strength whenever its action potential is triggered.

Alpha waves Rapid low-amplitude brain waves that have been linked to feelings of relaxation.

Altruism Unselfish concern for the welfare of others.

Alzheimer's disease A progressive form of mental deterioration characterized by loss of memory, language, problem solving, and other cognitive functions.

Amniotic sac A sac within the uterus that contains the embryo or fetus.

Amphetamines Stimulants derived from *alpha-methyl-beta-phenyl-ethyl-amine,* a colorless liquid consisting of carbon, hydrogen, and nitrogen.

Amygdala A part of the limbic system that apparently facilitates stereotypical aggressive responses.

Anal stage In psychoanalytic theory, the second stage of psychosexual development, when gratification is attained through anal activities.

Analytical psychology Jung's psychoanalytic theory, which emphasizes the collective unconscious and archetypes.

Anchoring and adjustment heuristic A decision-making heuristic in which a presumption or first estimate serves as a cognitive anchor. As we receive additional information, we make adjustments but tend to remain in the proximity of the anchor.

Androgens Male sex hormones.

Animism The belief that inanimate objects move because of will or spirit.

Anorexia nervosa A life-threatening eating disorder characterized by dramatic weight loss and a distorted body image.

Anterograde amnesia Failure to remember events that occur after physical trauma because of the biological effects of the traumatic experience.

Antibodies Substances formed by white blood cells that recognize and destroy antigens.

Antidepressant Acting to relieve depression; a drug that acts to relieve depression.

Antigen A substance that stimulates the body to mount an immune system response to it. (The contraction for *anti*body *gen*erator.)

Antisocial personality disorder The diagnosis given a person who is in frequent conflict with society, yet who is undeterred by punishment and experiences little or no guilt and anxiety.

Aphagic Characterized by undereating.

Aphasia A disruption in the ability to understand or produce language.

Apnea Temporary absence or cessation of breathing. (From Greek and Latin roots meaning "without" and "breathing.")

Applied research Research conducted in an effort to find solutions to particular problems.

Approach–approach conflict A type of conflict in which the goals that produce opposing motives are positive and within reach.

Approach–avoidance conflict A type of conflict in which the same goal produces approach and avoidance motives.

Aptitude A natural ability or talent.

Archetypes Basic, primitive images or concepts hypothesized by Jung to reside in the collective unconscious.

Artificialism The belief that natural objects have been created by human beings.

Assimilation According to Piaget, the inclusion of a new event into an existing schema.

Asylum An institution for the care of people with psychological disorders.

Attachment The enduring affectional tie that binds one person or animal to another.

Attitude An enduring mental representation of a person, place, or thing that evokes an emotional response and related behavior.

Attitude-discrepant behavior Behavior inconsistent with an attitude; in cognitive dissonance theory, attitude-discrepant behavior may modify an attitude.

Attraction In social psychology, an attitude of liking or disliking (negative attraction).

Attribution A belief as to why people behave in a certain way.

Attribution process The process by which people draw inferences about the motives and traits of others.

Attributional style One's tendency to attribute one's behavior to internal or external factors, stable or unstable factors, and so on.

Auditory nerve The axon bundle that transmits neural impulses from the organ of Corti to the brain.

Authoritarian parents Parents who are rigid in their rules and who demand obedience for the sake of obedience.

Authoritative parents Parents who are strict but warm. Authoritative parents demand mature behavior but use reason rather than force in discipline.

Autonomic nervous system (ANS) The division of the peripheral nervous system that regulates glands and activities such as heartbeat, respiration, digestion, and dilation of the pupils.

Autonomy Self-direction.

Availability heuristic A decision-making heuristic in which our estimates of frequency or probability of events are based on how easy it is to find examples.

Avatar An image representing a user in a multi-user virtual reality space.

Average The central tendency of a group of measures, expressed either as the mean, median, or mode of a distribution.

Aversive conditioning A behavior-therapy technique in which undesired responses are inhibited by pairing repugnant or offensive stimuli with them.

Avoidance–avoidance conflict A type of conflict in which the goals are negative, but avoidance of one requires approaching the other.

Avoidant personality disorder A personality disorder in which the person is unwilling to enter relationships without assurance of acceptance because of fears of rejection and criticism.

Axon A long, thin part of a neuron that transmits impulses to other neurons from branching structures called *terminal buttons*.

Barbiturate An addictive depressant used to reduce pain, relieve anxiety, or induce sleep.

Basilar membrane A membrane that lies coiled within the cochlea.

Behavior rehearsal Practice.

Behavior therapy Systematic application of the principles of learning to the direct modification of a client's problem behaviors.

Behaviorism The school of psychology that defines psychology as the study of observable behavior and studies relationships between stimuli and responses.

Behavior-rating scale A systematic means for recording the frequency with which target behaviors occur.

Bimodal Having two modes.

Binocular cues Stimuli suggestive of depth that involve simultaneous perception by both eyes.

Biofeedback training (BFT) The systematic feeding back to an organism information about a bodily function so that the organism can gain control of that function.

Biopsychosocial Having to do with the interactions of biological, psychological, and social or sociocultural factors.

Biopsychosocial perspective Description or explanation of psychological disorders in terms of the interactions of biological, psychological, and social or sociocultural factors.

Bipolar cells Neurons that conduct neural impulses from rods and cones to ganglion cells.

Bipolar disorder A disorder in which the mood alternates between two extreme poles (elation and depression). Previously referred to as *manic depression*.

Blind In experimental terminology, unaware of whether or not one has received a treatment.

Blind spot The area of the retina where axons from ganglion cells meet to form the optic nerve.

Body dysmorphic disorder A somatoform disorder characterized by preoccupation with an imagined or exaggerated physical defect in one's appearance.

Borderline personality disorder A personality disorder characterized by instability in relationships, self-image, mood, and lack of impulse control.

Bottom-up processing The organization of the parts of a pattern to recognize, or form an image of, the pattern they compose.

Brightness constancy The tendency to perceive an object as being just as bright even though lighting conditions change its intensity.

Broca's aphasia A language disorder characterized by slow, laborious speech.

Bulimia nervosa An eating disorder characterized by repeated cycles of binge eating and purging.

Case study A carefully drawn biography that may be obtained through interviews, questionnaires, and psychological tests.

Catastrophize To interpret negative events as being disastrous; to "blow out of proportion."

Catatonic schizophrenia A type of schizophrenia characterized by striking motor impairment.

Catharsis Release of emotional tension, as after a traumatic experience, that has the effect of contributing to the restoration of one's psychological well-being.

Center According to Piaget, to focus one's attention.

Central nervous system The brain and spinal cord.

Cerebellum A part of the brain involved in muscle coordination and balance.

Cerebral cortex The wrinkled surface area (gray matter) of the cerebrum.

Cerebrum The large mass of the forebrain, which consists of two hemispheres.

Chromosome A microscopic rod-shaped body in the cell nucleus carrying genes that transmit hereditary traits from generation to generation. Humans normally have 46 chromosomes.

Chunk A stimulus or group of stimuli that are perceived as a discrete piece of information.

Circadian rhythm A cycle that is connected with the 24-hour period of the earth's rotation. (From the Latin *circa*, meaning "about," and *dia*, meaning "day.")

Classical conditioning A simple form of learning in which a neutral stimulus comes to evoke the response usually evoked by another stimulus by being paired repeatedly with the other stimulus. As a result, an organism comes to associate or anticipate events. Also referred to as *respondent conditioning* or *Pavlovian conditioning*.

Claustrophobia Fear of tight, small places.

Client-centered therapy Carl Rogers's method of psychotherapy, which emphasizes the creation of a warm, therapeutic atmosphere that frees clients to engage in self-exploration and self-expression. Also referred to as *person-centered therapy*.

Clinical scales Groups of test items that measure the presence of various abnormal behavior patterns.

Clitoris The female sex organ that is most sensitive to sexual sensation; a smooth, round knob of tissue that is situated above the urethral opening.

Closure The tendency to perceive a broken figure as being complete or whole.

Cochlea The inner ear; the bony tube that contains the basilar membrane and the organ of Corti.

Cognitive Having to do with mental processes such as sensation and perception, memory, intelligence, language, thought, and problem solving.

Cognitive therapy A form of therapy that focuses on how clients' cognitions (e.g., expectations, attitudes, beliefs, and so forth) lead to distress and may be modified to relieve distress and promote adaptive behavior.

Cognitive-behavioral therapy (CBT) An approach to therapy that uses cognitive and behavioral techniques that have been validated by research.

Cognitive-dissonance theory The view that we are motivated to make our cognitions or beliefs consistent.

Collective unconscious Jung's hypothesized store of vague memories that represent the history of humankind.

Collectivist A person who defines herself or himself in terms of relationships to other people and groups and gives priority to group goals.

Color constancy The tendency to perceive an object as being the same color even though lighting conditions change its appearance.

Commitment The decision to maintain a relationship.

Common fate The tendency to perceive elements that move together as belonging together.

Complementary Descriptive of colors of the spectrum that when combined produce white or nearly white light.

Compulsion An irresistible urge to repeat an act or engage in ritualistic behavior such as hand washing.

Computerized axial tomography (CAT Scan) A method of brain imaging that passes a narrow X-ray beam through the head and measures structures that reflect the rays from various angles, enabling a computer to generate a three-dimensional image.

Concept A mental category that is used to class together objects, relations, events, abstractions, or qualities that have common properties.

Concrete-operational stage Piaget's third stage, characterized by logical thought concerning tangible objects, conservation, and subjective morality.

Conditional positive regard Judgment of another person's value on the basis of the acceptability of that person's behaviors.

Conditioned reinforcer A secondary reinforcer.

Conditioned response (CR) In classical conditioning, a learned response to a conditioned stimulus.

Conditioned stimulus (CS) A previously neutral stimulus that elicits a conditioned response because it has been paired repeatedly with a stimulus that already elicited that response.

Conditions of worth Standards by which the value of a person is judged.

Cones Cone-shaped photoreceptors that transmit sensations of color.

Conflict Being torn in different directions by opposing motives. Feelings produced by being in conflict.

Conform To change one's attitudes or overt behavior to adhere to social norms.

Conscious Self-aware.

Consensus General agreement.

Conservation According to Piaget, recognition that basic properties of substances such as weight and mass remain the same when superficial features change.

Consistency In attribution theory, the degree to which the same person acts in the same way on different occasions.

Consummate love The combination of passion, intimacy, and commitment; the ideal form of love in Sternberg's model.

Contact comfort A hypothesized primary drive to seek physical comfort through contact with another; a theoretical source of attachment.

Context-dependent memory Information that is better retrieved in the context in which it was encoded and stored, or learned.

Contingency theory The view that learning occurs when stimuli provide information about the likelihood of the occurrence of other stimuli.

Continuity   The tendency to perceive a series of points or lines as having unity.

Continuous reinforcement   A schedule of reinforcement in which every correct response is reinforced.

Control groups   In experiments, groups whose members do not obtain the treatment, while other conditions are held constant.

Conventional level   According to Kohlberg, a period during which moral judgments largely reflect social conventions. A "law and order" approach to morality.

Convergence   In sensation and perception, a binocular cue for depth based on the inward movement of the eyes as they attempt to focus on an object that is drawing nearer.

Convergent thinking   A thought process that narrows in on the single best solution to a problem.

Conversion disorder   A somatoform disorder in which anxiety or unconscious conflicts are "converted" into physical symptoms that often have the effect of helping the person cope with anxiety or conflict.

Cornea   Transparent tissue forming the outer surface of the eyeball.

Corpus callosum   A thick fiber bundle that connects the hemispheres of the cortex.

Correlation   An association or relationship among variables, as we might find between height and weight or between study habits and school grades.

Correlation coefficient   A number between +1.00 and −1.00 that expresses the strength and direction (positive or negative) of the relationship between two variables.

Correlational method   A mathematical method of determining whether one variable increases or decreases as another variable increases or decreases. For example, there is a correlation between intelligence test scores and grades in school.

Counterconditioning   A fear-reduction technique in which pleasant stimuli are associated with fear-evoking stimuli so that the fear-evoking stimuli lose their aversive qualities.

Creative self   According to Adler, the self-aware aspect of personality that strives to achieve its full potential.

Creativity   The ability to generate novel and useful solutions to problems.

Critical period   A period of time when an instinctive response can be elicited by a particular stimulus.

Crystallized intelligence   One's lifetime of intellectual achievement, as shown largely through vocabulary and knowledge of world affairs.

Daily hassles   Notable daily conditions and experiences that are threatening or harmful to a person's well-being.

Dark adaptation   The process of adjusting to conditions of lower lighting by increasing the sensitivity of rods and cones.

Debrief   To explain the purposes and methods of a completed procedure to a participant.

Decentration   Simultaneous focusing on more than one dimension of a problem, so that flexible, reversible thought becomes possible.

Decibel (dB)   A unit expressing the loudness of a sound.

Defense mechanism   In psychoanalytic theory, an unconscious function of the ego that protects it from anxiety-evoking material by preventing accurate recognition of this material.

Deindividuation   The process by which group members may discontinue self-evaluation and adopt group norms and attitudes.

Delta waves   Strong, slow brain waves usually emitted during stage 4 sleep.

Delusions   False, persistent beliefs that are unsubstantiated by sensory or objective evidence.

Dendrites   Rootlike structures, attached to the cell body of a neuron, that receive impulses from other neurons.

Dependent variable   A measure of an assumed effect of an independent variable.

Depolarize   To reduce the resting potential of a cell membrane from about −70 millivolts toward zero.

Depressant   A drug that lowers the rate of activity of the nervous system.

Descriptive statistics   The branch of statistics that is concerned with providing descriptive information about a distribution of scores.

Desensitization   The type of sensory adaptation in which we become less sensitive to constant stimuli. Also called *negative adaptation*.

Dichromat   A person who is sensitive to black–white and either red–green or blue–yellow and hence partially color-blind.

Difference threshold   The minimal difference in intensity required between two sources of energy so that they will be perceived as being different.

Diffusion of responsibility   The spreading or sharing of responsibility for a decision or behavior within a group.

Direct inner awareness   Knowledge of one's own thoughts, feelings, and memories.

Discrimination   In conditioning, the tendency for an organism to distinguish between a conditioned stimulus and similar stimuli that do not forecast an unconditioned stimulus.

Discriminative stimulus   In operant conditioning, a stimulus that indicates that reinforcement is available.

Disorganized schizophrenia   A type of schizophrenia characterized by disorganized delusions, vivid hallucinations, and inappropriate affect.

Displace   In memory theory, to cause information to be lost from short-term memory by adding new information.

Displaced   Transferred.

Displacement   The quality of language that permits one to communicate information about objects and events in another time and place.

Dispositional attribution   An assumption that a person's behavior is determined by internal causes such as personal attitudes or goals.

Dissociative amnesia   A dissociative disorder marked by loss of memory or self-identity; skills and general knowledge are usually retained.

Dissociative disorders   Disorders in which there are sudden, temporary changes in consciousness or self-identity.

Dissociative fugue   A dissociative disorder in which one experiences amnesia and then flees to a new location.

Dissociative identity disorder   A disorder in which a person appears to have two or more distinct identities or personalities that may alternately emerge.

Distinctiveness   In attribution theory, the extent to which the person responds differently in different situations.

Divergent thinking   A thought process that attempts to generate multiple solutions to problems.

Dizygotic (DZ) twins   Twins that develop from two fertilized ova and who are thus as closely related as brothers and sisters in general. Also called *fraternal twins*.

DNA   Abbreviation for deoxyribonucleic acid, the substance that forms the basic material of chromosomes. It takes the form of a double helix and contains the genetic code.

Dopamine   A neurotransmitter that is involved in Parkinson's disease and that appears to play a role in schizophrenia.

Double-blind study   A study in which neither the subjects nor the observers know who has received the treatment.

Down syndrome   A condition caused by an extra chromosome on the 21st pair and characterized by mental deficiency, a broad face, and slanting eyes.

Dream   In this usage, Levinson's term for the overriding drive of youth to become someone important, to leave one's mark on history.

Drive   A condition of arousal in an organism that is associated with a need.

Drive for superiority   Adler's term for the desire to compensate for feelings of inferiority.

Drive-reduction theory   The view that organisms learn to engage in behaviors that have the effect of reducing drives.

Eating disorders   A group of disorders marked by persistent, gross disturbances in eating patterns.

Echo   A mental representation of an auditory stimulus (sound) that is held briefly in sensory memory.

Echoic memory   The sensory register that briefly holds mental representations of auditory stimuli.

Efferent neurons   Neurons that transmit messages from the brain or spinal cord to muscles and glands. Also called *motor neurons*.

Effort justification   In cognitive-dissonance theory, the tendency to seek justification (acceptable reasons) for strenuous efforts.

Ego   The second psychic structure to develop, characterized by self-awareness, planning, and delay of gratification.

Ego analyst   A psychoanalyst therapist who focuses on the conscious, coping behavior of the ego instead of the hypothesized, unconscious functioning of the id.

Ego identity   Erikson's term for a firm sense of who one is and what one stands for.

Ego integrity versus despair   Erikson's term for the crisis of late adulthood, characterized by the task of maintaining one's sense of identity despite physical deterioration.

Egocentrism   According to Piaget, the assumption that others view the world as one does oneself.

Eidetic imagery   The maintenance of detailed visual memories over several minutes.

Ejaculation   Propulsion of seminal fluid (semen) from the penis by contraction of muscles at the base of the penis.

Elaboration likelihood model   The view that persuasive messages are evaluated (elaborated) on the basis of central and peripheral cues.

Elaborative rehearsal   A method for increasing retention of new information by relating it to information that is well known.

Electra complex   A conflict of the phallic stage in which the girl longs for her father and resents her mother.

Electroconvulsive therapy (ECT)   Treatment of disorders like major depression by passing an electric current (that causes a convulsion) through the head.

Electroencephalograph (EEG)   A method of detecting brain waves by means of measuring the current between electrodes placed on the scalp.

Electromyograph (EMG)   An instrument that measures muscle tension.

Embryonic stage The baby from the third through the eighth weeks following conception, during which time the major organ systems undergo rapid differentiation.

Emotion A feeling state with cognitive, physiological, and behavioral components.

Empathy Ability to perceive a client's feelings from the client's frame of reference. A quality of a good client-centered therapist.

Encoding Modifying information so that it can be placed in memory. The first stage of information processing.

Endocrine system The body's system of ductless glands that secrete hormones and release them directly into the bloodstream.

Endorphins Neurotransmitters that are composed of amino acids and that are functionally similar to morphine.

Engram (1) An assumed electrical circuit in the brain that corresponds to a memory trace. (2) An assumed chemical change in the brain that accompanies learning. (From the Greek *en-*, meaning "in," and *gramma*, meaning "something that is written or recorded.")

Epilepsy Temporary disturbances of brain functions that involve sudden neural discharges.

Episodic memory Memories of events experienced by a person or that take place in the person's presence.

Erogenous zone An area of the body that is sensitive to sexual sensations.

Estrus The periodic sexual excitement of many mammals, as governed by levels of sex hormones.

Ethical Moral; referring to one's system of deriving standards for determining what is moral.

Ethnic group A group characterized by common features such as cultural heritage, history, race, and language.

Ethologist A scientist who studies the characteristic behavior patterns of species of animals.

Eustress (YOU-stress) Stress that is healthful.

Evaluation apprehension Concern that others are evaluating our behavior.

Evolutionary psychology The perspective on psychology that studies the ways in which adaptation and natural selection are connected with mental processes and behavior.

Excitement phase The first phase of the sexual response cycle, which is characterized by muscle tension, increases in the heart rate, and erection in the male and vaginal lubrication in the female.

Exemplar A specific example.

Exhaustion stage The third stage of the GAS, characterized by weakened resistance and possible deterioration.

Existentialism The view that people are free and responsible for their own behavior.

Expectancies Personal predictions about the outcomes of potential behaviors.

Experiment A scientific method that seeks to confirm cause-and-effect relationships by introducing independent variables and observing their effects on dependent variables.

Experimental groups In experiments, groups whose members obtain the treatment.

Explicit memory Memory that clearly and distinctly expresses (explicates) specific information.

Externals People who perceive the ability to attain reinforcements as being largely outside themselves.

Extinction An experimental procedure in which stimuli lose their ability to evoke learned responses because the events that had followed the stimuli no longer occur. (The learned responses are said to be *extinguished.*)

Extraversion A trait characterized by tendencies to be socially outgoing and to express feelings and impulses freely.

Eye-movement desensitization and reprocessing (EMDR) A method of treating stress disorders by having clients visually follow a rapidly oscillating finger while they think of the traumatic events connected with the disorders.

Facial-feedback hypothesis The view that stereotypical facial expressions can contribute to stereotypical emotions.

Factor analysis A statistical technique that allows researchers to determine the relationships among large number of items such as test items.

Fear appeal A type of persuasive communication that influences behavior on the basis of arousing fear instead of rational analysis of the issues.

Feature detectors Neurons in the sensory cortex that fire in response to specific features of sensory information such as lines or edges of objects.

Feedback In assertiveness training, information about the effectiveness of a response.

Feeling-of-knowing experience Same as *tip-of-the-tongue phenomenon.*

Fetal stage The baby from the third month following conception through childbirth, during which time there is maturation of organ systems and dramatic gains in length and weight.

Fight-or-flight reaction An innate adaptive response to the perception of danger.

Fixation In psychoanalytic theory, arrested development. Attachment to objects of an earlier stage.

Fixation time The amount of time spent looking at a visual stimulus.

Fixed-interval schedule A schedule in which a fixed amount of time must elapse between the previous and subsequent times that reinforcement is available.

Fixed-ratio schedule A schedule in which reinforcement is provided after a fixed number of correct responses.

Flashbacks Distorted perceptions or hallucinations that occur days or weeks after LSD usage but mimic the LSD experience.

Flat affect A severe reduction in emotional expressiveness, found among many people with schizophrenia or serious depression.

Flavor A complex quality of food and other substances that is based on their odor, texture, and temperature as well as their taste.

Flooding A behavioral fear-reduction technique based on principles of classical conditioning. Fear-evoking stimuli (CSs) are presented continuously in the absence of actual harm so that fear responses (CRs) are extinguished.

Flow An altered state of consciousness that people may experience when deeply involved in an enjoyable activity.

Fluid intelligence Mental flexibility as shown in learning rapidly to solve new kinds of problems.

Foot-in-the-door technique A method for inducing compliance in which a small request is followed by a larger request.

Forced-choice format A method of presenting test questions that requires a respondent to select one of a number of possible answers.

Formal-operational stage Piaget's fourth stage, characterized by abstract logical thought and deduction from principles.

Fovea An area near the center of the retina that is dense with cones and where vision is consequently most acute.

Frame of reference One's unique pattern of perceptions and attitudes which influences the ways in which one evaluates events.

Framing effect The influence of wording, or the context in which information is presented, on decision making.

Free association In psychoanalysis, the uncensored uttering of all thoughts that come to mind.

Frequency theory The theory that the pitch of a sound is reflected in the frequency of the neural impulses that are generated in response to the sound.

Frequency distribution An ordered set of data that indicates the frequency (how often) with which scores appear.

Frequency histogram A graphic representation of a frequency distribution that uses rectangular solids (bars) to represent the frequency with which scores appear.

Frequency polygon A graphic representation of a frequency distribution that connects the points that show the frequencies with which scores appear, thereby creating a multisided geometric figure.

Functional fixedness The tendency to view an object in terms of its name or familiar usage.

Functional MRI (fMRI) A form of MRI that enables researchers to observe the brain "while it works" by taking repeated scans.

Functionalism The school of psychology that emphasizes the uses or functions of the mind rather than the elements of experience.

Fundamental attribution error The assumption that others act predominantly on the basis of their dispositions, even when there is evidence suggesting the importance of their situations.

g Spearman's symbol for general intelligence, which he believed underlay more specific abilities.

Gamma-aminobutyric acid (GABA) An inhibitory neurotransmitter that apparently helps calm anxiety.

Ganglion cells Neurons whose axons form the optic nerve.

Gender The culturally defined concepts of *masculinity* and *femininity.*

Gender role A cluster of behaviors that characterizes traditional "feminine" or "masculine" behaviors within a cultural setting.

Gender-schema theory A cognitive view of gender-typing that proposes that once girls and boys become aware of their anatomic sex, they begin to blend their self-expectations and self-esteem with the ways in which they fit the gender roles prescribed in a given culture.

Gender-typing The process by which people acquire the traits considered appropriate for people of their sex in a given cultural setting.

Gene A basic unit of heredity, which is found at a specific point on a chromosome.

General adaptation syndrome (GAS) Selye's term for a hypothesized three-stage response to stress.

Generalization In conditioning, the tendency for a conditioned response to be evoked by stimuli that are similar to the stimulus to which the response was conditioned.

Generalize To extend from the particular to the general; to apply observations based on a sample to a population.

Generalized anxiety disorder Feelings of dread and foreboding and sympathetic arousal of at least 6 months' duration.

Generativity versus stagnation Erikson's term for the crisis of middle adulthood, characterized by the task of being productive and contributing to younger generations.

Genetics The area of biology that focuses on heredity.

Genital stage The mature stage of psychosexual development, characterized by preferred expression of libido through intercourse with an adult of the other gender.

Genotype One's genetic makeup, based on the sequencing of the nucleotides we term A, C, G, and T.

Genuineness Recognition and open expression of the therapist's own feelings.

Germinal stage The first stage of prenatal development, during which the dividing mass of cells has not become implanted in the uterine wall. Also called the *period of the ovum*.

Gestalt psychology The school of psychology that emphasizes the tendency to organize perceptions into wholes and to integrate separate stimuli into meaningful patterns.

Gestalt therapy Fritz Perls' form of psychotherapy, which attempts to integrate conflicting parts of the personality through directive methods designed to help clients perceive their whole selves.

Gland An organ that secretes one or more chemical substances such as hormones, saliva, or milk.

Glial cells Cells that nourish and insulate neurons, direct their growth, and remove waste products from the nervous system.

Gray matter In the spinal cord, the grayish neurons and neural segments that are involved in spinal reflexes.

Groupthink A process in which group members are influenced by cohesiveness and a dynamic leader to ignore external realities as they make decisions.

Hallucination A perception in the absence of sensory stimulation that is confused with reality.

Hallucinogen A substance that causes hallucinations.

Health psychology The field of psychology that studies the relationships between psychological factors (e.g., attitudes, beliefs, situational influences, and behavior patterns) and the prevention and treatment of physical illness.

Heredity The transmission of traits from parent to offspring by means of genes.

Heritability The degree to which the variations in a trait from one person to another can be attributed to, or explained by, genetic factors.

Hertz (Hz) A unit expressing the frequency of sound waves. One hertz equals one cycle per second.

Heterosexual Referring to people who are sexually aroused by, and interested in forming romantic relationships with, people of the other sex.

Heuristics Rules of thumb that help us simplify and solve problems.

Hierarchy An ordered arrangement; a *fear-stimulus hierarchy* refers to the ordering of stimuli according to the amount of fear they evoke.

Higher-order conditioning (1) According to behaviorists, a classical conditioning procedure in which a previously neutral stimulus comes to elicit the response brought forth by a *conditioned* stimulus by being paired repeatedly with that conditioned stimulus. (2) According to cognitive psychologists, the learning of relationships among events, none of which evokes an unlearned response.

Hippocampus A structure in the limbic system that is involved in the formation of memories.

Holophrase A single word used to express complex meanings.

Homeostasis The tendency of the body to maintain a steady state.

Homosexual Referring to people who are sexually aroused by, and interested in forming romantic relationships with, people of the same sex. (Derived from the Greek *homos*, meaning "same," not from the Latin *homo*, meaning "man.")

Hormone A substance secreted by an endocrine gland that regulates various body functions.

Hue The color of light, as determined by its wavelength.

Humanism The philosophy and school of psychology that asserts that people are conscious, self-aware, and capable of free choice, self-fulfillment, and ethical behavior.

Hydrocarbons Chemical compounds consisting of hydrogen and carbon.

Hyperphagic Characterized by excessive eating.

Hypertension High blood pressure.

Hypnosis A condition in which people are highly suggestible and behave as though they are in a trance.

Hypochondriasis A somatoform disorder characterized by persistent belief that one is ill despite lack of medical findings.

Hypothalamus A bundle of nuclei below the thalamus involved in key bodily and psychological functions including body temperature, motivation, and emotion.

Hypothesis In psychology, a specific statement about behavior or mental processes that is tested through research.

Icon A mental representation of a visual stimulus that is held briefly in sensory memory.

Iconic memory The sensory register that briefly holds mental representations of visual stimuli.

Id The psychic structure, present at birth, that represents physiological drives and is fully unconscious.

Ideas of persecution Erroneous beliefs or delusions that one is being victimized or persecuted.

Identification In psychoanalytic theory, the unconscious effort to become like another person.

Illusions Sensations that give rise to misperceptions.

Imaginary audience An aspect of adolescent egocentrism; the belief that other people are as concerned with our thoughts and behaviors as we are.

Immune system The system of the body that recognizes and destroys disease organisms that invade the body.

Implicit memory Memory that is suggested (implied) but not plainly expressed, as illustrated in the things that people *do* but do not state clearly.

Imprinting A process occurring during a critical period in the development of an organism, in which that organism forms an attachment in a manner that will afterward be difficult to modify.

Incentive An object, person, or situation perceived as being capable of satisfying a need.

Incest taboo The cultural prohibition against marrying or having sexual relations with a close blood relative.

Incubation In problem solving, a hypothetical process that sometimes occurs when we stand back from a frustrating problem for a while and the solution "suddenly" appears.

Independent variable A condition in a scientific study that is manipulated so that its effects may be observed.

Individual psychology Adler's psychoanalytic theory, which emphasizes feelings of inferiority and the creative self.

Individualist A person who defines herself or himself in terms of personal traits and gives priority to her or his own goals rather than those of the group to which she or he belongs.

Infantile amnesia Inability to recall events that occur prior to the age of 2 or 3. Also termed *childhood amnesia*.

Infer To go from the particular to the general; to draw a conclusion.

Inferential statistics The branch of statistics that is concerned with confidence with which conclusions drawn about samples can be extended to the populations from which the samples were drawn.

Inferiority complex Feelings of inferiority hypothesized by Adler to serve as a central motivating force.

Infinite creativity The capacity to combine words into original sentences.

Inflammation Increased blood flow to an injured area of the body, resulting in redness, warmth, and an increased supply of white blood cells.

Informed consent A subject's agreement to participate in research after receiving information about the purposes of the study and the nature of the treatments.

Insight In Gestalt psychology, the sudden reorganization of the relationships among the elements of a problem, allowing its solution.

Instinct A stereotyped pattern of behavior that is triggered by a particular stimulus and nearly identical among members of a species, even when they are reared in isolation. Also termed a *fixed action pattern*.

Instinctive An inborn pattern of behavior that is triggered by a particular stimulus.

Instrumental competence Ability to manipulate one's environment to achieve one's goals.

Intelligence A complex and controversial concept. According to David Wechsler, the "capacity . . . to understand the world [and the] resourcefulness to cope with its challenges."

Intelligence quotient (IQ) (1) Originally, a ratio obtained by dividing a child's score (or mental age) on an intelligence test by chronological age. (2) Generally, a score on an intelligence test.

Interference theory The view that we may forget stored material because other learning interferes with it.

Internals People who perceive the ability to attain reinforcements as being largely within themselves.

Internet addiction A self-defeating behavior pattern in which one is preoccupied with online activity to the extent that it disrupts one's functioning in the real world.

Interpersonal psychotherapy (ITP) A short-term dynamic therapy that focuses on clients' relationships and the direct alleviation of negative emotions such as anxiety and depression.

Intimacy Close acquaintance and familiarity; a characteristic of a relationship in which partners share their inmost feelings.

Intimacy versus isolation Erikson's life crisis of young adulthood, which is characterized by the task of developing abiding intimate relationships.

Introspection Deliberate looking into one's own cognitive processes to examine one's thoughts and feelings.

Introversion A trait characterized by intense imagination, the tendency to inhibit impulses, and, a frequent preference for solitude over social interaction.

Iris   A muscular membrane whose dilation regulates the amount of light that enters the eye.

Just noticeable difference (jnd)   The minimal amount by which a source of energy must be increased or decreased so that a difference in intensity will be perceived.

Kinesthesis   The sense that informs us about the positions and motion of parts of our bodies.

La belle indifférence   A French term descriptive of the lack of concern for their (imagined) medical problem sometimes shown by people with conversion disorders.

Language   The communication of information by means of symbols arranged according to rules of grammar.

Language acquisition device (LAD)   In psycholinguistic theory, neural "prewiring" that facilitates the child's learning of grammar.

Latency   In psychoanalytic theory, a phase of psychosexual development characterized by repression of sexual impulses.

Latent   Hidden or concealed.

Lateral hypothalamus   An area at the side of the hypothalamus that appears to function as a start-eating center.

Learned helplessness   A model for the acquisition of depressive behavior, based on findings that organisms in aversive situations learn to show inactivity when their operants go unreinforced.

Learning   (1) According to behaviorists, a relatively permanent change in behavior that results from experience. (2) According to cognitive theorists, the process by which organisms make relatively permanent changes in the way they represent the environment because of experience. These changes influence the organism's behavior but do not fully determine it.

Lens   A transparent body behind the iris that focuses an image on the retina.

Leukocytes   White blood cells.

Libido   Sexual interest or drive.

Limbic system   A group of structures involved in memory, motivation, and emotion that forms a fringe along the inner edge of the cerebrum.

Linguistic-relativity hypothesis   The view that language structures the way in which we view the world.

Locus of control   The place (locus) to which an individual attributes control over the receiving of reinforcers—either inside or outside the self.

Long-term memory   The type or stage of memory capable of relatively permanent storage.

Long-term potentiation (LTP)   Enhanced efficiency in synaptic transmission that follows brief, rapid stimulation.

LSD   Lysergic acid diethylamide; a hallucinogen.

Magnetic resonance imaging (MRI)   A method of brain imaging that places a person in a magnetic field and uses radio waves to cause the brain to emit signals which reveal shifts in the flow of blood which, in turn, indicate brain activity.

Maintenance rehearsal   Mental repetition of information to keep it in memory.

Major depressive disorder   A serious to severe depressive disorder in which the person may show loss of appetite, psychomotor retardation, and impaired reality testing.

Manic   Elated, showing excessive excitement.

Marijuana   The dried vegetable matter of the *Cannabis sativa* plant.

Matching hypothesis   The view that people tend to choose persons similar to themselves in attractiveness and attitudes in the formation of interpersonal relationships.

Maturation   The process of development as guided by the unfolding of the genetic code.

Mean   A type of average that is calculated by adding all the scores and then dividing by the number of scores.

Means–end analysis   A heuristic device in which we try to solve a problem by evaluating the difference between the current situation and the goal.

Median   The central score in a frequency distribution; the score beneath which 50% of the cases fall.

Medulla   An oblong area of the hindbrain involved in regulation of heartbeat and respiration.

Memory   The processes by which information is encoded, stored, and retrieved.

Memory trace   An assumed change in the nervous system that reflects the impression made by a stimulus. Memory traces are said to be "held" in sensory registers.

Menarche   The beginning of menstruation.

Menopause   The cessation of menstruation.

Mental age (MA)   The accumulated months of credit that a person earns on the Stanford–Binet Intelligence Scale.

Mental set   The tendency to respond to a new problem with an approach that was successfully used with similar problems.

Mescaline   A hallucinogen derived from the mescal (peyote) cactus.

Meta-analysis   A statistical method for combining and averaging the results of individual research studies.

Metamemory   Self-awareness of the ways in which memory functions, allowing the person to encode, store, and retrieve information effectively.

Method of savings   A measure of retention in which the difference between the number of repetitions originally required to learn a list and the number of repetitions required to relearn the list after a certain amount of time has elapsed is calculated.

Midlife crisis   A crisis experienced by many people during the midlife transition when they realize that life may be more than halfway over and they reassess their achievements in terms of their dreams.

Midlife transition   Levinson's term for the ages from 40 to 45, which are characterized by a shift in psychological perspective from viewing ourselves in terms of years lived to viewing ourselves in terms of the years we have left.

Migraine headaches   Throbbing headaches that are connected with changes in the supply of blood to the head.

Mindfulness meditation (MM)   A form of meditation that provides clients with techniques they can use to focus on the present moment rather than ruminate about problems.

Mode   The most frequently occurring number or score in a distribution.

Model   In social cognitive theory, an organism that exhibits behaviors that others will imitate or acquire through observational learning.

Modeling   A behavior-therapy technique in which a client observes and imitates a person who approaches and copes with various objects or situations.

Monochromat   A person who is sensitive to black and white only and hence color-blind.

Monocular cues   Stimuli suggestive of depth that can be perceived by one eye.

Monozygotic (MZ) twins   Twins that develop from a single fertilized ovum that divides in two early in prenatal development. MZ twins thus share the same genetic code. Also called *identical twins.*

Motion parallax   A monocular cue for depth based on the perception that nearby objects appear to move more rapidly in relation to our own motion.

Motive   A hypothetical state within an organism that propels the organism toward a goal. (From the Latin *movere,* meaning "to move.")

Motor cortex   The section of cortex that lies in the frontal lobe, just across the central fissure from the sensory cortex. Neural impulses in the motor cortex are linked to muscular responses throughout the body.

Multiple approach–avoidance conflict   A type of conflict in which each of a number of goals produces approach and avoidance motives.

Multiple personality disorder   The previous term for *dissociative identity disorder.*

Mutation   A sudden change in the genetic code that results in variation in an inheritable characteristic.

Mutism   Refusal to talk.

Myelin   A fatty substance that encases and insulates axons, facilitating transmission of neural impulses.

Myotonia   Muscle tension.

Narcolepsy   A "sleep attack" in which a person falls asleep suddenly and irresistibly.

Narcotics   A group of addictive drugs used to relieve pain and induce sleep. The term is usually reserved for opiates.

Natural selection   A core concept of the theory of evolution that holds that adaptive genetic variations among members of a species enable individuals with those variations to survive and reproduce. As a result, such variations tend to be preserved, whereas nonadaptive variations tend to drop out.

Naturalistic observation   A scientific method in which organisms are observed in their natural environments.

Nature   The inborn, innate character of an organism.

Need   A state of deprivation.

Negative correlation   A relationship between two variables in which one variable increases as the other decreases.

Negative reinforcer   A reinforcer that when *removed* increases the frequency of operant behavior.

Negative symptoms   The deficiencies among people with schizophrenia, such as flat affect, lack of motivation, loss of pleasure, and social withdrawal.

Nerve   A bundle of axons from many neurons.

Neural impulse   The electrochemical discharge of a nerve cell, or neuron.

Neuron   A nerve cell.

Neuroticism   A personality trait characterized largely by persistent anxiety; Eysenck's term for emotional instability, as contrasted with emotional stability.

Neurotransmitters   Chemical substances involved in the transmission of neural impulses from one neuron to another.

Nonconscious   Descriptive of bodily processes such as the growing of hair, of which we cannot become conscious. We may "recognize" that our hair is growing but cannot directly experience the biological process.

Non-rapid-eye-movement (NREM) sleep Stages of sleep 1 through 4.

Nonsense syllables Meaningless sets of two consonants, with a vowel sandwiched in between, that are used to study memory.

Nonspecific factors Those factors in psychotherapy that are common to many approaches, such as the "therapeutic alliance" with the client.

Norepinephrine A neurotransmitter whose action is similar to that of the hormone epinephrine and that may play a role in mood disorders.

Normal curve Graphic presentation of a normal distribution, which shows a characteristic bell shape.

Normal distribution A symmetrical distribution that is assumed to reflect chance fluctuations; approximately 68% of cases lie within a standard deviation of the mean.

Nurture The sum total of the environmental factors that affect an organism from conception onward; contrasted with *nature*. (In another usage, *nurture* refers to the act of nourishing and otherwise promoting the development of youngsters.)

Object permanence Recognition that objects removed from sight still exist, as demonstrated in young children by continued pursuit of an object that has been covered or hidden.

Objective responsibility According to Piaget, the assignment of blame according to the amount of damage done rather than the motives of the actor.

Objective tests Tests whose items must be answered in a specified, limited manner. Tests whose items have concrete answers that are considered correct.

Observational learning The acquisition of knowledge and skills through the observation of others (who are called *models*) rather than by means of direct experience.

Obsession A recurring thought or image that seems beyond control.

Oedipus complex A conflict of the phallic stage in which the boy wishes to possess his mother sexually and perceives his father as a rival in love.

Olfactory nerve The nerve that transmits information concerning odors from olfactory receptors to the brain.

Operant behavior Voluntary responses that are reinforced.

Operant conditioning A simple form of learning in which an organism learns to engage in behavior because it is reinforced.

Opiates A group of narcotics derived from the opium poppy that provide a euphoric rush and depress the nervous system.

Opioids Chemicals that act on opiate receptors but are not derived from the opium poppy.

Opponent-process theory The theory that color vision is made possible by three types of cones, some of which respond to red or green light, some to blue or yellow, and some to the intensity of light.

Optic nerve The nerve that transmits sensory information from the eye to the brain.

Oral stage In psychoanalytic theory, the first stage of psychosexual development, during which gratification is hypothesized to be attained primarily through oral activities.

Organ of Corti The receptor for hearing that lies on the basilar membrane in the cochlea.

Organizing effect The directional effect of sex hormones—for example, along stereotypically masculine or feminine lines.

Orgasm The height or climax of sexual excitement, involving involuntary muscle contractions, release of sexual tensions, and, usually, subjective feelings of pleasure.

Orienting reflex An unlearned response in which an organism attends to a stimulus.

Overregularization The application of regular grammatical rules for forming inflections such as the past tense and plurals to irregular verbs and nouns, as in referring to more than one sheep as *sheeps*.

Oxytocin A pituitary hormone that stimulates labor in pregnant women and is connected with maternal behaviors such as cuddling and caring for young.

Paired associates Nonsense syllables presented in pairs in experiments that measure recall.

Panic disorder The recurrent experiencing of attacks of extreme anxiety in the absence of external stimuli that usually elicit anxiety.

Paranoid personality disorder A personality disorder characterized by persistent suspiciousness, but not involving the disorganization of paranoid schizophrenia.

Paranoid schizophrenia A type of schizophrenia characterized primarily by delusions—commonly of persecution—and vivid hallucinations.

Parasympathetic The branch of the ANS that is most active during processes (such as digestion) that restore the body's reserves of energy.

Parasympathetic nervous system The branch of the autonomic nervous system that is most active during processes that restore reserves of energy to the body, such as relaxing and eating. When people relax, the parasympathetic nervous system decelerates the heart rate, normalizes the blood pressure, and relaxes muscles.

Partial reinforcement One of a variety of reinforcement schedules in which not every correct response is reinforced.

Passion Strong romantic and sexual feelings.

Pathogen A microscopic organism (e.g., bacterium or virus) that can cause disease.

Perception The process by which sensations are organized into an inner representation of the world.

Peripheral nervous system The part of the nervous system consisting of the somatic nervous system and the autonomic nervous system.

Permissive parents Parents who impose few, if any, rules and who do not supervise their children closely.

Personal fable An aspect of adolescent egocentrism; beliefs that our feelings and ideas are special and that we are invulnerable.

Personality The distinct patterns of behavior, thoughts, and feelings that characterize a person's adaptation to the demands of life.

Personality disorders Enduring patterns of maladaptive behavior that are sources of distress to the individual or others.

Perspective A monocular cue for depth based on the convergence (coming together) of receding parallel lines.

Phallic stage In psychoanalytic theory, the third stage of psychosexual development, characterized by a shift of libido to the phallic region. (From the Greek *phallos*, referring to an image of the penis. However, Freud used the term *phallic* to refer both to boys and girls.)

Phencyclidine (PCP) A hallucinogen whose name is an acronym for its chemical structure.

Phenotype One's actual development and appearance, as based on one's *genotype* and environmental influences (i.e., both nature and nurture).

Pheromone A chemical secretion detected by other members of the species that stimulates stereotypical behaviors.

Photoreceptors Cells that respond to light.

Physiological drives Unlearned drives with a biological basis, such as hunger, thirst, and avoidance of pain.

Pitch The highness or lowness of a sound, as determined by the frequency of the sound waves.

Pituitary gland The gland that secretes growth hormone, prolactin, antidiuretic hormone, and other hormones; sometimes referred to as the *master gland*.

Place theory The theory that the pitch of a sound is determined by the section of the basilar membrane that vibrates in response to the sound.

Placebo A bogus treatment that has the appearance of being genuine; a "sugar pill."

Placenta A membrane that permits the exchange of nutrients and waste products between the mother and fetus but does not allow the maternal and fetal bloodstreams to mix.

Plateau phase The second phase of the sexual response cycle, which is characterized by increases in vasocongestion, muscle tension, heart rate, and blood pressure in preparation for orgasm.

Polarization In social psychology, taking an extreme position or attitude on an issue.

Polarize In biological psychology, to prepare a neuron for firing by creating an internal negative charge in relation to the fluid outside the cell membrane.

Polygenic Referring to traits that are influenced by combinations of genes.

Pons A structure of the hindbrain involved in respiration, attention, and sleep and dreaming.

Population A complete group of organisms or events; a complete group from which a sample is selected.

Positive correlation A relationship between variables in which one variable increases as the other increases.

Positive psychology The field of psychology that is about personal well-being and satisfaction; joy, sensual pleasure, and happiness; and optimism and hope for the future.

Positive reinforcer A reinforcer that increases the frequency of operant behavior when it is presented.

Positive symptoms The excessive and sometimes bizarre symptoms of schizophrenia, including hallucinations, delusions, and loose associations.

Positron emission tomography (PET scan) A method of brain imaging that injects a radioactive tracer into the bloodstream and assesses activity of parts of the brain according to the amount of glucose they metabolize.

Postconventional level According to Kohlberg, a period during which moral judgments are derived from moral principles and people look to themselves to set moral standards.

Posttraumatic stress disorder (PTSD) A disorder that follows a distressing event outside the range of normal human experience and that is characterized by features such as intense fear, avoidance of stimuli associated with the event, and reliving of the event.

Preconscious In psychodynamic theory, descriptive of material that is not in awareness but can be brought into awareness by focusing one's attention.

Preconventional level According to Kohlberg, a

period during which moral judgments are based largely on expectation of rewards or punishments.

Predictive validity   The extent to which an observation permits one to make a prediction; for example, the extent to which a diagnosis permits one to predict the course of a psychological disorder and the type of treatment that may be of help.

Prefrontal lobotomy   The severing or destruction of a section of the frontal lobe of the brain.

Preoperational stage   The second of Piaget's stages, characterized by illogical use of words and symbols, spotty logic, and egocentrism.

Presbyopia   A condition characterized by brittleness of the lens.

Primacy effect   In social psychology, the tendency to evaluate others in terms of first impressions.

Primary drives   Unlearned, or physiological, drives.

Primary mental abilities   According to Thurstone, the basic abilities that make up intelligence.

Primary reinforcer   An unlearned reinforcer.

Priming   The activation of specific associations in memory, often as a result of repetition and without making a conscious effort to access the memory.

Proactive interference   The interference by old learning with the ability to retrieve material learned recently.

Projective test   A psychological test that presents ambiguous stimuli onto which the test taker projects his or her own personality in making a response.

Prospective memory   Memory to perform an act in the future, as at a certain time or when a certain event occurs.

Prototype   A concept of a category of objects or events that serves as a good example of the category.

Proximity   Nearness; the perceptual tendency to group together objects that are near one another.

Psychic structure   In psychoanalytic theory, a hypothesized mental structure that is intended to help explain behavior.

Psychoanalysis   Freud's method of psychotherapy, which emphasizes the importance of unconscious motives and conflicts as determinants of human behavior. (Also the name of Freud's theory of personality.)

Psychoanalytic theory   Sigmund Freud's perspective, which emphasizes the importance of unconscious motives and conflicts as forces that determine behavior.

Psychodynamic   Referring to Freud's theory, which proposes that the motion of underlying forces of personality determines our thoughts, feelings, and behavior.

Psycholinguistic theory   The view that language learning involves an interaction between environmental factors and an inborn tendency to acquire language.

Psychological disorders   Patterns of behavior or mental processes that are connected with emotional distress or significant impairment in functioning.

Psychological hardiness   A cluster of traits that buffer stress and are characterized by commitment, challenge, and control.

Psychology   The science that studies behavior and mental processes.

Psychomotor retardation   Slowness in motor activity and (apparently) in thought.

Psychoneuroimmunology   The field that studies the relationships between psychological factors (e.g., attitudes and behavior) and the functioning of the immune system.

Psychosexual development   In psychoanalytic theory, the process by which libidinal energy is expressed through different erogenous zones during different stages of development.

Psychosocial development   Erikson's theory of personality and development, which emphasizes social relationships and eight stages of growth.

Psychosurgery   Surgery intended to promote psychological changes or to relieve disordered behavior.

Psychotherapy   A systematic interaction between a therapist and a client that brings psychological principles to bear on influencing the client's thoughts, feelings, or behavior to help the client overcome abnormal behavior or adjust to problems in living.

Puberty   The period of physical development during which sexual reproduction becomes possible.

Punishment   An unpleasant stimulus that suppresses the behavior it follows.

Pupil   The black-looking opening in the center of the iris, through which light enters the eye.

Pure research   Research conducted without concern for immediate applications.

Random sample   A sample drawn so that each member of a population has an equal chance of being selected to participate.

Range   A measure of variability defined as the high score in a distribution minus the low score.

Rapid flight of ideas   Rapid speech and topic changes, characteristic of manicky behavior.

Rapid smoking   An aversive conditioning method for quitting smoking in which the smoker inhales rapidly, thus rendering once-desirable cigarette smoke aversive.

Rapid-eye-movement (REM) sleep   A stage of sleep characterized by rapid eye movements, which have been linked to dreaming.

Rational emotive behavior therapy (REBT)   Albert Ellis's form of therapy that encourages clients to challenge and correct irrational expectations and maladaptive behaviors.

Reality testing   The capacity to perceive one's environment and oneself according to accurate sensory impressions.

Rebound anxiety   Anxiety that can occur when one discontinues use of a tranquilizer.

Recall   Retrieval or reconstruction of learned material.

Recency effect   In social psychology, the tendency to evaluate others in terms of the most recent impression.

Receptor site   A location on a dendrite of a receiving neuron tailored to receive a neurotransmitter.

Reciprocity   In interpersonal attraction, the tendency to return feelings and attitudes that are expressed about us.

Recognition   In information processing, the easiest memory task, involving identification of objects or events encountered before.

Reflex   A simple unlearned response to a stimulus.

Refractory period   In neuroscience, a phase following firing during which a neuron is less sensitive to messages from other neurons and will not fire. In the sexual response cycle, a period of time following orgasm during which an individual is not responsive to sexual stimulation.

Reinforce   To follow a response with a stimulus that increases the frequency of the response.

Reinforcement   A stimulus that follows a response and increases the frequency of the response.

Relearning   A measure of retention. Material is

usually relearned more quickly than it is learned initially.

Reliability   The consistency of a method of assessment, such as a psychological test or a manual describing the symptoms of psychological disorders.

Replicate   Repeat, reproduce, copy.

Representativeness heuristic   A decision-making heuristic in which people make judgments about samples according to the populations they appear to represent.

Repression   In Freud's psychodynamic theory, a defense mechanism that protects the person from anxiety by automatically ejecting anxiety-evoking ideas and impulses from awareness.

Resistance   The tendency to block the free expression of impulses and primitive ideas—a reflection of the defense mechanism of repression.

Resistance stage   The second stage of the GAS, characterized by prolonged sympathetic activity in an effort to restore lost energy and repair damage. Also called the *adaptation stage.*

Resolution phase   The fourth phase of the sexual response cycle, during which the body returns to its prearoused state.

Response set   A tendency to answer test items according to a bias—for example, to make oneself seem perfect or bizarre.

Response set theory   The view that response expectancies play a key role in the production of the experiences suggested by the hypnotist.

Resting potential   The electrical potential across the neural membrane when it is not responding to other neurons.

Reticular activating system (RAS)   A part of the brain involved in attention, sleep, and arousal.

Retina   The area of the inner surface of the eye that contains rods and cones.

Retinal disparity   A binocular cue for depth based on the difference in the image cast by an object on the retinas of the eyes as the object moves closer or farther away.

Retrieval   The location of stored information and its return to consciousness. The third stage of information processing.

Retroactive interference   The interference of new learning with the ability to retrieve material learned previously.

Retrograde amnesia   Failure to remember events that occur prior to a physical trauma because of the biological effects of the traumatic experience.

Retrospective memory   Memory for past events, activities, and learning experiences, as shown by explicit (episodic and semantic) and implicit memories.

Reversibility   According to Piaget, recognition that processes can be undone, that things can be made as they were.

Reward   A pleasant stimulus that increases the frequency of the behavior it follows.

Risky shift   The tendency to make riskier decisions as a member of a group than as an individual acting independently.

Rods   Rod-shaped photoreceptors that are sensitive only to the intensity of light.

Role diffusion   Erikson's term for lack of clarity in one's life roles (due to failure to develop ego identity).

Role theory   A theory that explains hypnotic events in terms of the person's ability to act *as though* he or she were hypnotized.

Romantic love   An intense, positive emotion that involves sexual attraction, feelings of caring, and the belief that one is in love.

Rooting   The turning of an infant's head toward a touch, such as by the mother's nipple.

Rote Mechanical associative learning that is based on repetition.

s Spearman's symbol for *specific* factors, or *s factors*, which he believed accounted for individual abilities.

Saccadic eye movement The rapid jumps made by a person's eyes as they fixate on different points.

Sample Part of a population.

Satiety The state of being satisfied; fullness.

Savings The difference between the number of repetitions originally required to learn a list and the number of repetitions required to re-learn the list after a certain amount of time has elapsed.

Scaffolding Vygotsky's term for temporary cognitive structures or methods of solving problems that help the child as he or she learns to function independently.

Schema According to Piaget, a hypothetical mental structure that permits the classification and organization of new information and can influence perception of persons, objects, and situations.

Schizoid personality disorder A personality disorder characterized by social withdrawal.

Schizophrenia A psychotic disorder characterized by loss of control of thought processes and inappropriate emotional responses.

Schizotypal personality disorder A personality disorder characterized by oddities of thought and behavior, but not involving bizarre psychotic behaviors.

Secondary reinforcer A stimulus that gains reinforcement value through association with established reinforcers.

Secondary sex characteristics Characteristics that distinguish the sexes, such as distribution of body hair and depth of voice, but that are not directly involved in reproduction.

Second-hand smoke Smoke from tobacco products being used by other people.

Sedative A drug that relieves nervousness or agitation or puts one to sleep.

Selection factor A source of bias that may occur in research findings when subjects are allowed to choose for themselves a certain treatment in a scientific study, as opposed to being randomly assigned to that treatment.

Selective attention The focus of consciousness on a particular stimulus.

Selective avoidance Diverting one's attention from information that is inconsistent with one's attitudes.

Selective exposure Deliberately seeking and attending to information that is consistent with one's attitudes.

Selective serotonin-reuptake inhibitors (SSRIs) Drugs that work by blocking the reuptake of serotonin by presynaptic neurons; mainly used as antidepressants, but also for other disorders such as panic disorder and anorexia nervosa.

Self-actualization According to Maslow and other humanistic psychologists, self-initiated striving to become what one is capable of being. The motive for reaching one's full potential and for expressing one's unique capabilities.

Self-efficacy expectations Our beliefs that we can bring about desired changes through our own efforts.

Self-ideal A mental image of what we believe we ought to be.

Self-monitoring Keeping a record of one's own behavior to identify problems and record successes.

Self-serving bias The tendency to view one's successes as stemming from internal factors and one's failures as stemming from external factors.

Semantic code Mental representation of information according to its meaning.

Semantic memory General knowledge, as opposed to episodic memory.

Semanticity Meaning. The quality of language in which words are used as symbols for objects, events, or ideas.

Sensation The stimulation of sensory receptors and the transmission of sensory information to the central nervous system.

Sensitization The type of sensory adaptation in which we become more sensitive to stimuli that are low in magnitude. Also called *positive adaptation.*

Sensorimotor stage The first of Piaget's stages of cognitive development, characterized by coordination of sensory information and motor activity, early exploration of the environment, and lack of language.

Sensory adaptation The processes by which organisms become more sensitive to stimuli that are low in magnitude and less sensitive to stimuli that are constant or ongoing in magnitude.

Sensory memory The type or stage of memory first encountered by a stimulus. Sensory memory holds impressions briefly, but long enough so that series of perceptions are psychologically continuous.

Sensory register A system of memory that holds information briefly, but long enough so that it can be processed further. There may be a sensory register for every sense.

Serial-position effect The tendency to recall more accurately the first and last items in a series.

Serotonin A neurotransmitter, deficiencies of which have been linked to affective disorders, anxiety, and insomnia.

Serum cholesterol Cholesterol in the blood.

Sex chromosomes The 23rd pair of chromosomes, whose genetic material determines the sex of the individual.

Sexual orientation The directionality of one's sexual and romantic interests; that is, whether one is sexually attracted to, and desires to form a romantic relationship with, members of the other sex or of one's own sex.

Sexual response cycle Masters' and Johnson's model of sexual response, which consists of four stages or phases.

Shape constancy The tendency to perceive an object as being the same shape although the retinal image varies in shape as it rotates.

Shaping A procedure for teaching complex behaviors that at first reinforces approximations of the target behavior.

Short-term memory The type or stage of memory that can hold information for up to a minute or so after the trace of the stimulus decays. Also called *working memory.*

Signal-detection theory The view that the perception of sensory stimuli involves the interaction of physical, biological, and psychological factors.

Similarity The perceptual tendency to group together objects that are similar in appearance.

Situational attribution An assumption that a person's behavior is determined by external circumstances such as social pressure.

Situationist perspective The view that social influence can goad people into doing things that are inconsistent with their usual behavior.

Size constancy The tendency to perceive an object as being the same size even as the size of its retinal image changes according to the object's distance.

Sleep terrors Frightening dreamlike experiences that occur during the deepest stage of NREM sleep. Nightmares, in contrast, occur during REM sleep.

Social cognitive theory A cognitively oriented learning theory in which observational learning and person variables such as values and expectancies play major roles in individual differences. Previously termed *social learning theory.*

Social decision schemes Rules for predicting the final outcome of group decision making on the basis of the members' initial positions.

Social facilitation The process by which a person's performance is increased when other members of a group engage in similar behavior.

Social influence The area of social psychology that studies the ways in which people influence the thoughts, feelings, and behavior of others.

Social norms Explicit and implicit rules that reflect social expectations and influence the ways people behave in social situations.

Social perception A subfield of social psychology that studies the ways in which we form and modify impressions of others.

Social phobia An irrational, excessive fear of public scrutiny.

Social psychology The field of psychology that studies the nature and causes of people's thoughts and behavior in social situations.

Social-cognitive theory A school of psychology in the behaviorist tradition that includes cognitive factors in the explanation and prediction of behavior. Formerly termed *social-learning theory.*

Sociocultural perspective The view that focuses on the roles of ethnicity, gender, culture, and socioeconomic status in personality formation, behavior, and mental processes.

Somatic nervous system The division of the peripheral nervous system that connects the central nervous system with sensory receptors, skeletal muscles, and the surface of the body.

Somatoform disorders Disorders in which people complain of physical (somatic) problems even though no physical abnormality can be found.

Somatosensory cortex The section of cortex in which sensory stimulation is projected. It lies just behind the central fissure in the parietal lobe.

Species A category of biological classification consisting of related organisms who are capable of interbreeding.

Specific factors Those factors in psychotherapy that are specific to a given approach, such as free association in psychoanalysis or systematic desensitization in behavior therapy.

Specific phobia Persistent fear of a specific object or situation.

Spinal cord A column of nerves within the spine that transmits messages from sensory receptors to the brain and from the brain to muscles and glands throughout the body.

Spinal reflex A simple, unlearned response to a stimulus that may involve as few as two neurons.

Spontaneous recovery The recurrence of an extinguished response as a function of the passage of time.

Standard deviation A measure of the variability of a distribution, obtained by the formula

$$S.D. = \sqrt{\frac{\text{Sum of } d^2}{N}}$$

Standardization In psychological testing, the process by which one obtains and organizes test scores from various population groups, so that the results of a person completing a test can be compared to those of others of his or her sex, in his or her age group, and so on.

State-dependent memory Information that is better retrieved in the physiological or emotional state in which it was encoded and stored, or learned.

Statistics Numerical facts assembled in such a manner that they provide useful information about measures or scores. (From the Latin *status*, meaning "standing" or "position.")

Stereotype A fixed, conventional idea about a group.

Stimulant A drug that increases activity of the nervous system.

Stimulus An environmental condition that elicits a response.

Storage The maintenance of information over time.

Stratified sample A sample drawn so that identified subgroups in the population are represented proportionally in the sample.

Stress The demand that is made on an organism to adapt.

Stroboscopic motion A visual illusion in which the perception of motion is generated by a series of stationary images that are presented in rapid succession.

Structuralism The historic school of psychology that argued that the mind consists of three basic elements—sensations, feelings, and images—that combine to form experience.

Stupor A condition in which the senses, thought, and movement are dulled.

Subjective moral judgment According to Piaget, moral judgment that is based on the motives of the perpetrator.

Subjective value The desirability of an object or event.

Substance abuse Persistent use of a substance even though it is causing or compounding problems in meeting the demands of life.

Substance dependence Loss of control over use of a substance. Biologically speaking, dependence is typified by tolerance, withdrawal symptoms, or both.

Successive approximations In operant conditioning, a series of behaviors that gradually become more similar to a target behavior.

Superego In psychoanalytic theory, the third psychic structure, which functions as a moral guardian and sets forth standards for behavior.

Suppression The deliberate, or conscious, placing of certain ideas, impulses, or images out of awareness.

Survey A method of scientific investigation in which a large sample of people answer questions about their attitudes or behavior.

Sympathetic nervous system The branch of the autonomic nervous system that is most active during processes that spend body energy from stored reserves, such as in a fight-or-flight reaction to a predator or when you are anxious about a big test. When people experience fear, the sympathetic nervous system accelerates the heart rate, raises the blood pressure, tenses muscles, and so on.

Synapse A junction between the axon terminals of one neuron and the dendrites or cell body of another neuron.

Systematic desensitization A behavioral fear-reduction technique in which a hierarchy of fear-evoking stimuli is presented while the person remains relaxed.

Systematic random search An algorithm for solving problems in which each possible solution is tested according to a particular set of rules.

Taste buds The sensory organs for taste. They contain taste cells and are mostly located on the tongue.

Taste cells Receptor cells that are sensitive to taste.

Texture gradient A monocular cue for depth based on the perception that closer objects appear to have rougher (more detailed) surfaces.

Thalamus An area near the center of the brain involved in the relay of sensory information to the cortex and in the functions of sleep and attention.

Theory A formulation of relationships underlying observed events.

Theta waves Slow brain waves produced during the hypnagogic state.

Thinking Paying attention to information, mentally representing it, reasoning about it, and making decisions about it.

Time out Removal of an organism from a situation in which reinforcement is available when unwanted behavior is shown.

Tip-of-the-tongue (TOT) phenomenon The feeling that information is stored in memory although it cannot be readily retrieved. Also called the *feeling-of-knowing experience*.

Token economy A controlled environment in which people are reinforced for desired behaviors with tokens (such as poker chips) that may be exchanged for privileges.

Tolerance Habituation to a drug, with the result that increasingly higher doses of the drug are needed to achieve similar effects.

Top-down processing The use of contextual information or knowledge of a pattern in order to organize parts of the pattern, as in using a picture of a completed puzzle to help fit the pieces together.

Trait A relatively stable aspect of personality that is inferred from behavior and assumed to give rise to consistent behavior.

Transcendental meditation (TM) The simplified form of meditation brought to the United States by the Maharishi Mahesh Yogi and used as a method for coping with stress.

Transference In psychoanalytic theory, responding to one person (such as a spouse or the psychoanalyst) in a way that is similar to the way one responded to another person (such as a parent) in childhood.

Treatment In experiments, a condition received by subjects so that its effects may be observed.

Triangular model of love Sternberg's view that love involves combinations of three components: intimacy, passion, and commitment.

Trichromat A person with normal color vision.

Trichromatic theory The theory that color vision is made possible by three types of cones, some of which respond to red light, some to green, and some to blue.

Trust versus mistrust Erikson's first stage of psychosocial development, during which children do—or do not—come to trust that primary caregivers and the environment will meet their needs.

Type A behavior Behavior characterized by a sense of time urgency, competitiveness, and hostility.

Umbilical cord A tube between the mother and her developing child through which nutrients and waste products are conducted.

Unconditional positive regard A persistent expression of esteem for the value of a person, but not necessarily an unqualified acceptance of all of the person's behaviors.

Unconditioned response (UCR) An unlearned response to an unconditioned stimulus.

Unconditioned stimulus (UCS) A stimulus that elicits a response from an organism prior to conditioning.

Unconscious In psychodynamic theory, descriptive of ideas and feelings that are not available to awareness by simple focusing of attention. Also: without consciousness.

Uninvolved parents Parents who generally leave their children to themselves.

Uplifts Pleasant conditions and experiences.

Validity The extent to which a method of assessment, such as a psychological test or a manual describing the symptoms of psychological disorders measures the traits or behavior patterns it is supposed to assess.

Validity scales Groups of test items that indicate whether a person's responses accurately reflect that individual's traits.

Variable-interval schedule A schedule in which a variable amount of time must elapse between the previous and subsequent times that reinforcement is available.

Variable-ratio schedule A schedule in which reinforcement is provided after a variable number of correct responses.

Vasocongestion In the sexual response cycle, engorgement of blood vessels with blood, which swells the genitals and breasts as one is sexually aroused.

Ventromedial nucleus (VMN) A central area on the underside of the hypothalamus that appears to function as a stop-eating center.

Vestibular sense The sense of equilibrium that informs us about our bodies' positions relative to gravity.

Virtual therapy The use of a virtual environment to assist people overcome fears and phobias. (Also: the use of telecommunications and computer links to carry out a psychologist–patient therapy session.)

Visual acuity Sharpness of vision.

Visual code Mental representation of information as a picture.

Volunteer bias A source of bias or error in research reflecting the prospect that people who offer to participate in research studies differ systematically from people who do not.

Waxy flexibility A feature of catatonic schizophrenia in which people can be molded into postures that they maintain for quite some time.

Weber's constant The fraction of the intensity by which a source of physical energy must be increased or decreased so that a difference in intensity will be perceived.

Wernicke's aphasia A language disorder characterized by difficulty comprehending the meaning of spoken language.

White matter In the spinal cord, axon bundles that carry messages from and to the brain.

Wish fulfillment A primitive method used by the id to attempt to gratify basic instincts.

Withdrawal symptoms A characteristic cluster of symptoms that results from sudden decrease in an addictive drug's level of usage.

Working memory The memory system that holds the information necessary for solving problems and meeting other goals; the system that keeps information "in mind."

Zone of proximal development (ZPD) Vygotsky's term for the situation in which a child carries out tasks with the help of someone who is more skilled, frequently an adult who represents the culture in which the child develops.

Zygote A fertilized ovum (egg cell).

name index

subject index